GABRIEL MANTZ

EUROPEAN FOOTBALL

INTERNATIONAL LINE-UPS & STATISTICS 1902-2016

VOLUME 4

British Library Cataloguing in Publication Data
A catalogue record for this book is available from the British Library

ISBN 978-1-86223-348-5

72 St. Peter's Avenue, Cleethorpes, N.E. Lincolnshire, DN35 8HU, England

Web site www.soccer-books.co.uk
e-mail info@soccer-books.co.uk

Printed in the UK by 4edge Ltd.

Dear Readers,

The fourth book in our series containing statistics for all matches played by European national teams, this volume contains statistics for the national teams of Finland, France, Georgia, Germany and Gibraltar from their very first games through to the present day.

The Finnish national team played its first international match relatively early but has never managed to qualify for a finals tournament of either the FIFA World Cup or the European Championships. Despite this, they made very good progress during the 2000s, under the experienced coach Roy Hodgson, and achieved notable results against much more established European teams during this period. It is worth mentioning that Finland have won the Nordic Championship on two occasions. Undoubtedly, the best Finnish player of all time, Jari Litmanen, played for a number of great European clubs including Ajax Amsterdam, Liverpool FC and FC Barcelona.

France is just one of three national teams to have won all three of most important trophies recognized by FIFA: the FIFA World Cup (1998), the FIFA Confederations Cup (2001, 2003), and the Olympic Tournament (1984). In addition they were also winners of the UEFA European Championship in 1984 and 2000. Throughout their history, they have had a number of great players including Just Fontaine (all-time top scorer of the FIFA World Cup with 13 goals in 1958, a record to this day) and Raymond Kopa. Later, Michel Platini (three times winner of the Ballon d'Or) and Zinedine Zidane (three times FIFA World Player of the Year) stand out from the crowd. In addition to their on-field contribution to the game, France produced such great football pioneers as Jules Rimet, FIFA president from 1921 to 1954 (who was involved in the founding of the Fédération Internationale de Football Association, the organisation of Olympic amateur football tournaments and, later, the FIFA World Cup!). Also, Henri Delaunay, the first general secretary of UEFA who was largely responsible for the creation of the European Football Championship and Gabriel Hanot who was one of the principal founders of other European Club competitions.

Georgia, who gained independence from the Soviet Union in 1991, was a late arrival on the international football stage and did not become a member of UEFA and FIFA until 1992. Since then, Georgia have not managed to qualify for finals tournaments of either the FIFA World Cup or the UEFA Euro Championship and their best results are a 5-0 win over Wales in 1994 and a remarkable 1-0 win against Spain in June 2016.

Germany have one of the most successful national teams in international competitions, having won a total of four FIFA World Cups (1954, 1974 and 1990 as West Germany and again in 2014 after reunification) together with three European Championships (1972 and 1980 as West Germany and in 1996 after reunification). In addition, they have also been runners-up three times in the European Championships, four times in the FIFA World Cup and remain the only nation to have won both the men's and women's FIFA World Cups. Germany is also the only European nation to have won a FIFA World Cup in the Americas. The list of great German players and personalities is huge: Fritz Walter, Franz Beckenbauer (Ballon d'Or winner 1972 and 1976), Karl-Heinz Rummenigge (Ballon d'Or winner in 1980 and 1981), Gerhard Müller (Ballon d'Or winner in 1970, top European goalscorer in 1970 and 1972, top goalscorer of the 1970 World Cup), Lothar Matthäus (Ballon d'Or winner in 1990), Matthias Sammer (Ballon d'Or winner in 1996), Oliver Kahn (Best Player of the 2002 World Cup), Miroslav Klose (top goalscorer of the 2002 World Cup), Toni Kroos, Manuel Neuer and many others. Their great coaches – Sepp Herberger, Helmut Schön, Franz Beckenbauer and Joachim Löw – have all excelled on the world stage. This book contains statistics for the Germany teams before the Second World War and after 1990 and also for the West Germany teams from post-war to reunification. Statistics for East Germany can be found in Volume 3 of this series of books.

Gibraltar became a member of UEFA in May 2013 and the qualification competition of the 2016 UEFA European Championship tournament marked their first entrance in one of the major competitions. As Gibraltar is the smallest UEFA member with a population of just 30,000, it is perhaps not too surprising that they duly lost all of their qualification matches and ended with the poorest goal difference of any country in the competition!

As for the other books of this series, this fourth volume contains statistics for all the matches played by the "A" national team of each country from their first match until the end of 2016. For each match played, besides the names of the players who appeared, you will find the number of caps won and goals scored for each player up to and including that game. There is also information about the stadium, referee and attendance for each game and, of course, the name of the coach of the national team. In addition to the individual match information, a second section lists all the players to make an international appearance for each country showing total numbers of caps won and goals scored, the period when the player made his international appearances and the club (or clubs) he was playing for at the time. A third section presents information for all the national coaches/managers and a fourth section presents head-to-head statistics for each country versus all opponents faced in international matches.

I hope you will find all the information you require about the national teams covered in this book and that you will enjoy the read!

The Author

SUMMARY

ABBREVIATIONS

FG/Nr Number of first match played for the national team / Player counter
DOB Date of birth

FIFA COUNTRY CODES – EUROPE

ALB	Albania
AND	Andorra
ARM	Armenia
AUT	Austria
AZE	Azerbaijan
BLR	Belarus
BEL	Belgium
BIH	Bosnia-Herzegovina
BUL	Bulgaria
CRO	Croatia
CYP	Cyprus
CZE	Czech Republic
DEN	Denmark
ENG	England
EST	Estonia
FRO	Faroe Islands
FIN	Finland
FRA	France
GEO	Georgia
GER	Germany
GRE	Greece
HUN	Hungary
ISL	Iceland
ISR	Israel
ITA	Italy
KAZ	Kazakhstan
LVA	Latvia
LIE	Liechtenstein
LTU	Lithuania
LUX	Luxembourg
MKD	Macedonia
MLT	Malta
MDA	Moldova
MNE	Montenegro
NED	Netherlands
NIR	Northern Ireland
NOR	Norway
POL	Poland
POR	Portugal
IRL	Republic of Ireland
ROU	Romania
RUS	Russia
SMR	San Marino
SCO	Scotland
SRB	Serbia
SVK	Slovakia
SVN	Slovenia
ESP	Spain
SWE	Sweden
SUI	Switzerland
TUR	Turkey
UKR	Ukraine
WAL	Wales

FIFA COUNTRY CODES – DEFUNCT EUROPEAN COUNTRIES

TCH	Czechoslovakia
GDR	East Germany
SAA	Saar
URS	Soviet Union
GER	West Germany
YUG	Yugoslavia

FINLAND

The Country:
Suomen tasavalta (Republic of Finland) Capital: Helsinki Surface: 338,424 km^2 Inhabitants: 5,488,543 Time: UTC+2

The FA:
Suomen Palloliitto Urheilukatu 1 PO Box 191, 00251 Helsinki Foundation date: 1907 Member of FIFA since: 1908 Member of UEFA since: 1954

NATIONAL TEAM RECORDS

EUROPEAN CHAMPIONSHIP	
1960	Did not enter
1964	Did not enter
1968	Qualifiers
1972	Qualifiers
1976	Qualifiers
1980	Qualifiers
1984	Qualifiers
1988	Qualifiers
1992	Qualifiers
1996	Qualifiers
2000	Qualifiers
2004	Qualifiers
2008	Qualifiers
2012	Qualifiers
2016	Qualifiers

FIFA WORLD CUP	
1930	Did not enter
1934	Did not enter
1938	Qualifiers
1950	*Withdrew*
1954	Qualifiers
1958	Qualifiers
1962	Qualifiers
1966	Qualifiers
1970	Qualifiers
1974	Qualifiers
1978	Qualifiers
1982	Qualifiers
1986	Qualifiers
1990	Qualifiers
1994	Qualifiers
1998	Qualifiers
2002	Qualifiers
2006	Qualifiers
2010	Qualifiers
2014	Qualifiers

OLYMPIC FOOTBALL TOURNAMENTS 1908-2016							
1908	-	**1948**	-	**1972**	*Withdrew*	**1996**	Qualifiers
1912	-	**1952**	Round 1	**1976**	Qualifiers	**2000**	Qualifiers
1920	-	**1956**	-	**1980**	Group Stage	**2004**	Qualifiers
1924	-	**1960**	Qualifiers	**1984**	Qualifiers	**2008**	Qualifiers
1928	-	**1964**	Qualifiers	**1988**	Qualifiers	**2012**	Qualifiers
1936	Qualifiers	**1968**	Qualifiers	**1992**	Qualifiers	**2016**	Qualifiers

FIFA CONFEDERATIONS CUP 1992-2013
None

PLAYER WITH MOST INTERNATIONAL CAPS – Top 5				
1.	Jari Olavi LITMANEN	-	137 caps	(1989-2010)
2.	Sami Hyypiä	-	105 caps	(1992-2010)
	Jonatan Lillebror Johansson	-	105 caps	(1996-2010)
4.	Ari-Juhani Hjelm	-	100 caps	(1983-1996)
5.	Joonas Einari Kolkka	-	98 caps	(1994-2010)

PLAYER WITH MOST INTERNATIONAL GOALS – Top 5				
1.	Jari Olavi LITMANEN	-	32 goals	/ 137 caps ()
2.	Mikael Kaj Forssell	-	29 goals	/ 87 caps ()
3.	Jonatan Lillebror Jojansson	-	22 goals	/ 105 caps ()
4.	Ari-Juhani Hjelm	-	20 goals	/ 100 caps ()
5.	Mika-Matti Paatelainen	-	18 goals	/ 70 caps ()

FULL INTERNATIONALS (1911-2016)

1. 22.10.1911 **FINLAND – SWEDEN** **2-5(2-1)**
Eläintarha Stadion, Helsinki; Referee: Arvo Eerikäinen (Finland); Attendance: 2,000
FIN: Gustaf Holmström (1/0), Jalmari Holopainen (1/0), Gösta Löfgren (1/0), Kaarlo Soinio (Cap) (1/0), Uno Lindebäck (1/0), Viljo Lietola (1/0), Lauri Tanner (1/0), Paul Jerima (1/0), Jarl Öhman (1/0), Ernst Schybergson (1/0), Algoth Niska (1/0).
Goals: Uno Lindebäck (3), Paul Jerima (5).

2. 27.06.1912 **SWEDEN - FINLAND** **7-1(1-1)**
Råsunda Idrottsplats, Stockholm; Referee: Hugo Meisl (Austria); Attendance: 3,000
FIN: August Syrjäläinen (1/0), Jalmari Holopainen (2/0), Eino Soinio (Cap) (1/0), Gösta Löfgren (2/0), Kaarlo Soinio (2/0), Viljo Lietola (2/0), Ragnar Wickström (1/0), Bror Wiberg (1/1), Artturi Nyyssönen (1/0), Jarl Öhman (2/0), Algoth Niska (2/0).
Goal: Bror Wiberg (38).

3. 29.06.1912 **FINLAND - ITALY** **3-2(2-2,2-2)** 5th OG. 1st Round.
Tranebergs Idrottsplats, Stockholm (Sweden); Referee: Hugo Meisl (Austria); Attendance: 600
FIN: August Syrjäläinen (2/0), Jalmari Holopainen (3/0), Eino Soinio (2/1), Gösta Löfgren (3/0), Knut Lund (1/0), Kaarlo Soinio (Cap) (3/0), Ragnar Wickström (2/0), Bror Wiberg (2/2), Artturi Nyyssönen (2/0), Jarl Öhman (3/1), Algoth Niska (3/0).
Goal: Jarl Öhman (2), Eino Soinio (40), Bror Wiberg (105).

4. 30.06.1912 **FINLAND - RUSSIA** **2-1(1-0)** 5th OG. 2nd Round.
Tranebergs Idrottsplats, Stockholm; Referee: Per Sjöblom (Sweden); Attendance: 200
FIN: August Syrjäläinen (3/0), Jalmari Holopainen (4/0), Eino Soinio (3/1), Gösta Löfgren (Cap) (4/0), Knut Lund (2/0), Viljo Lietola (3/0), Ragnar Wickström (3/0), Bror Wiberg (3/3), Artturi Nyyssönen (3/0), Jarl Öhman (4/2), Algoth Niska (4/0).
Goal: Bror Wiberg (34), Jarl Öhman (81).

5. 02.07.1912 **ENGLAND Olympic - FINLAND** **4-0(2-0)** 5th OG. Semi-Finals.
Olympiastadion, Stockholm (Sweden); Referee: Ruben Gelbord (Sweden); Attendance: 4,000
FIN: August Syrjäläinen (4/0), Jalmari Holopainen (5/0), Eino Soinio (4/1), Gösta Löfgren (Cap) (5/0), Knut Lund (3/0), Viljo Lietola (4/0), Ragnar Wickström (4/0), Bror Wiberg (4/3), Artturi Nyyssönen (4/0), Jarl Öhman (5/2), Algoth Niska (5/0).

6. 04.07.1912 **NETHERLANDS – FINLAND** **9-0(4-0)** 5th OG. Third Place Play-off.
Olympiastadion, Stockholm (Sweden); Referee: Per Sjöblom (Sweden); Attendance: 1,000
FIN: August Syrjäläinen (5/0), Jalmari Holopainen (6/0), Eino Soinio (5/1), Gösta Löfgren (Cap) (6/0), Knut Lund (4/0), Viljo Lietola (5/0), Lauri Tanner (2/0), Bror Wiberg (5/3), Artturi Nyyssönen (5/0), Jarl Öhman (6/2), Algoth Niska (6/0).

7. 24.05.1914 **SWEDEN – FINLAND** **4-3(1-1)**
Råsunda Idrottsplats, Stockholm; Referee: August Heiberg-Kahrs (Norway); Attendance: 2,000
FIN: Gunnar Helin (1/0), Fjalar Bergroth (1/0), Ilmari Saxell (1/0), Alexander Holmström (1/0), Hugo Mantila (1/0), Rudolf Lundqvist (1/0), Arthur Johansson (1/0), Knut Johansson (1/1), Ragnar Wickström (Cap) (5/0), Lars Schybergson (1/2), Richard Schybergson (1/0).
Goals: Lars Schybergson (35), Knut Johansson (48), Lars Schybergson (62).

8. 29.05.1919 **SWEDEN – FINLAND** **1-0(0-0)**
Olympiastadion, Stockholm: Hagbard Vestergaard (Denmark); Attendance: 8,000
FIN: Niilo Tammisalo (1/0), Arthur Englund (1/0), Ilmari Saxell (2/0), Eino Soinio (6/1), Charles Stormbom (1/0), Verner Eklöf (1/0), Holger Thorn (1/0), Gunnar Öhman (1/0), Jarl Öhman (Cap) (7/2), Lars Schybergson (2/2), Paavo Jaale (1/0).

9. 28.09.1919 **FINLAND - SWEDEN** **3-3(2-0)**
Töölön Pallokenttä, Helsinki; Referee: Hagbard Vestergaard (Denmark); Attendance: 5,000
FIN: Niilo Tammisalo (2/0), Arthur Englund (2/0), Ilmari Saxell (3/0), Eino Soinio (7/1), Charles Stormbom (2/0), Hugo Mantila (2/0), Holger Thorn (Cap) (2/1), Gunnar Öhman (2/0), Ragnar Wickström (6/2), Verner Eklöf (2/0), Aarne Linna (1/0).
Goals: Ragnar Wickström (22, 37), Holger Thorn (75).

10. 30.05.1920 **SWEDEN – FINLAND** **4-0(1-0)**
Olympiastadion, Stockholm; Referee: Paul Putz (Belgium); Attendance: 10,000
FIN: Niilo Tammisalo (3/0), Arthur Englund (3/0), Ilmari Saxell (4/0), Eino Soinio (8/1) [67.Lauri Sandström (1/0)], Charles Stormbom (Cap) (3/0), Hugo Mantila (3/0), Jarl Österholm (1/0), Gunnar Öhman (3/0), Jarl Öhman (8/2), Verner Eklöf (3/0), Hjalmar Kelin (1/0).

11. 19.09.1920 **FINLAND - SWEDEN** **1-0(1-0)**
Töölön Pallokenttä, Helsinki; Referee: Thorvald Johnson (Norway); Attendance: 6,000
FIN: Niilo Tammisalo (4/0), Arthur Englund (4/0), Ilmari Saxell (5/0), Eino Soinio (9/1), Charles Stormbom (4/0), Aarne Vihavainen (1/0), Jarl Österholm (2/0), Bruno Mantila (1/0), Jarl Öhman (Cap) (9/3), Verner Eklöf (4/0), Hjalmar Kelin (2/0).
Goal: Jarl Öhman (36).

12. 17.10.1920 **FINLAND - ESTONIA** **6-0(4-0)**
Töölön Pallokenttä, Helsinki; Referee: Kaarlo Soinio (Finland); Attendance: 2,500
FIN: Niilo Tammisalo (5/0), Arthur Englund (Cap) (5/0), Ilmari Saxell (6/0), Eino Soinio (10/1), Charles Stormbom (5/0), Aarne Vihavainen (2/0), Jarl Österholm (3/1), Gunnar Öhman (4/1), Lauri Tanner (3/2), Verner Eklöf (5/2), Hjalmar Kelin (3/0).
Goals: Gunnar Öhman (5), Verner Eklöf (7), Jarl Österholm (9), Lauri Tanner (22), Verner Eklöf (57), Lauri Tanner (75).

13. 25.05.1921 **NORWAY – FINLAND** **3-2(2-2)**
Gressbanen ved Holmen i Aker, Kristiania; Referee: Ernst Albihn (Sweden); Attendance: 14,000
FIN: Niilo Tammisalo (6/0), Arthur Englund (Cap) (6/0), Ragnar Wickström (7/2), Eino Soinio (11/1), Charles Stormbom (6/0), Hugo Mantila (4/0), Yrjö Tornivuori (1/0), Gunnar Öhman (5/1), Bruno Mantila (2/1), Verner Eklöf (6/3), Hjalmar Kelin (4/0).
Goals: Verner Eklöf (15), Bruno Mantila (30).

14. 29.05.1921 **SWEDEN– FINLAND** **0-3(0-2)**
Stockholms Stadion, Stockholm; Referee: Lauritz Andersen (Denmark); Attendance: 17,000
FIN: Niilo Tammisalo (7/0), Arthur Englund (Cap) (7/0), Ragnar Wickström (8/2), Eino Soinio (12/1), Charles Stormbom (7/0), Hugo Mantila (5/0), Yrjö Tornivuori (2/0), Gunnar Öhman (6/2), Bruno Mantila (3/1), Verner Eklöf (7/3), Hjalmar Kelin (5/2).
Goals: Gunnar Öhman (10), Hjalmar Kelin (28, 88).

15. 31.07.1921 **FINLAND - AUSTRIA** **2-3(1-0)**
Töölön Pallokenttä, Helsinki; Referee: Wolf Simon Boas (Netherlands); Attendance: 6,000
FIN: Niilo Tammisalo (8/0), Arthur Englund (Cap) (8/0), Ragnar Wickström (9/2), Eino Soinio (13/1), Charles Stormbom (8/0), Hugo Mantila (6/0), Yrjö Tornivuori (3/0), Gunnar Öhman (7/2), Bruno Mantila (4/2), Verner Eklöf (8/3), Hjalmar Kelin (6/2).
Goals: Bruno Mantila (20), Josef Blum (65 own goal).

16. 28.08.1921 **ESTONIA - FINLAND** **0-3(0-2)**
Tiigiveski Spordiplats, Tallinn; Referee: Bengt Sjöström (Finland); Attendance: 3,000
FIN: Harald Eleuvuo (1/0), Niilo Koskinen (1/0), Sven Lydman (1/0), Aarre Åkerberg (1/0), Charles Stormbom (9/0), Martin Jansson (1/0), Adolf Höglander (1/0), Vilho Hirvonen (1/1), Verner Eklöf (Cap) (9/4), Einar Grannas (1/1), Aarne Linna (2/0).
Goals: Einar Grannas (3), Vilho Hirvonen (9), Verner Eklöf (78 penalty).

17. 18.09.1921 **FINLAND - GERMANY** **3-3(1-2)**
Töölön Pallokenttä, Helsinki; Referee: Ernst Albihn (Sweden); Attendance: 8,000
FIN: Niilo Tammisalo (9/0), Arthur Englund (Cap) (9/0), Ragnar Wickström (10/2), Aarne Vihavainen (3/0), Eino Soinio (14/1), Hugo Mantila (7/0), Holger Thorn (3/2), Gunnar Öhman (8/3), Bruno Mantila (5/2), Verner Eklöf (10/5), Hjalmar Kelin (7/2).
Goals: Verner Eklöf (12), Holger Thorn (54), Gunnar Öhman (88).

18. 05.06.1922 **FINLAND - SWEDEN** **1-4(1-2)**
Töölön Pallokenttä, Helsinki; Referee: Hugo Meisl (Austria); Attendance: 5,000
FIN: Niilo Tammisalo (10/0), Ragnar Wickström (11/2), Sven Lydman (2/0), Eino Soinio (15/1), Hugo Mantila (Cap) (8/0), Aarne Vihavainen (4/0), William Kanerva (1/0), Arvi Katajavuori (1/1), Bruno Mantila (6/2), Verner Eklöf (11/5), Hjalmar Kelin (8/2). Trainer: Jarl Öhman (1).
Goal: Arvi Katajavuori (24).

19. 13.07.1922 **FINLAND - HUNGARY** **1-5(0-1)**
Töölön Pallokenttä, Helsinki; Referee: Arthur Björklund (Sweden); Attendance: 5,000
FIN: Niilo Tammisalo (11/0), Ragnar Wickström (12/2), Sven Lydman (3/0), Aarne Vihavainen (5/0), Eino Soinio (16/1), Hugo Mantila (Cap) (9/0), William Kanerva (2/0), Arvi Katajavuori (2/1), Jarl Öhman (10/3), Verner Eklöf (12/5) [66.Leo Leivo (1/0)], Hjalmar Kelin (9/3). Trainer: Jarl Öhman (2).
Goal: Hjalmar Kelin (57).

20. 11.08.1922 **FINLAND - ESTONIA** **10-2(4-2)**
Töölön Pallokenttä, Helsinki; Referee: Gösta Löfgren (Finland); Attendance: 2,000
FIN: Niilo Tammisalo (12/0), Arthur Englund (Cap) (10/0), Ragnar Wickström (13/2), Aarre Åkerberg (2/0), Eino Soinio (17/1), Lauri Virta (1/0), Jarl Österholm (4/1), Jarl Öhman (11/9), Bruno Mantila (7/4), Verner Eklöf (13/7), Hjalmar Kelin (10/3). Trainer: Jarl Öhman (3).
Goals: Bruno Mantila (4), Jarl Öhman (10, 14 penalty, 37, 46), Verner Eklöf (52), Jarl Öhman (55), Verner Eklöf (58), Jarl Öhman (69), Bruno Mantila (85).

21. 26.08.1922 **FINLAND - NORWAY** **1-3(0-2)**
Töölön Pallokenttä, Helsinki; Referee: Eric Gustavsson (Sweden); Attendance: 5,000
FIN: Niilo Tammisalo (13/0), Arthur Englund (Cap) (11/0), Ragnar Wickström (14/2), Eino Soinio (18/1), Charles Stormbom (10/0), Hugo Mantila (10/0), Yrjö Tornivuori (4/0), Jarl Öhman (12/9), Bruno Mantila (8/4), Verner Eklöf (14/8), Hjalmar Kelin (11/3). Trainer: Jarl Öhman (4).
Goal: Verner Eklöf (70).

22. 17.06.1923 **NORWAY - FINLAND** **3-0(1-0)**
Gressbanen ved Holmen i Aker, Kristiania; Referee: John Fowler (England); Attendance: 12,000
FIN: Niilo Tammisalo (14/0), Ragnar Wickström (Cap) (15/2) (Cap) [62.Martin Jansson (2/0)], Sven Lydman (4/0), Charles Stormbom (11/0), Eino Soinio (19/1), Hugo Mantila (11/0), Gunnar Åström (1/0), Bertel Silve (1/0), Verner Eklöf (15/8), Aarne Linna (3/0), Hjalmar Kelin (12/3).

23. 20.06.1923 **SWEDEN - FINLAND** **5-4(3-2)**
Strömvallen, Gävle; Referee: Dr. Peco J. Bauwens (Germany); Attendance: 4,055
FIN: Niilo Tammisalo (15/0), Ragnar Wickström (Cap) (16/2), Sven Lydman (5/0), Eino Soinio (20/1) [46.Martin Jansson (3/0)], Charles Stormbom (12/0), Hugo Mantila (12/0), Gunnar Åström (2/0), Bertel Silve (2/0), Verner Eklöf (16/9), Aarne Linna (4/2), Hjalmar Kelin (13/4).
Goals: Hjalmar Kelin (2), Aarne Linna (20, 54), Verner Eklöf (55).

24. 12.08.1923 **GERMANY - FINLAND** **1-2(1-2)**
Dresdner Kampfbahn, Dresden; Referee: Johannes Mutters (Netherlands); Attendance: 25,000
FIN: Niilo Tammisalo (16/0), Arthur Englund (Cap) (12/0), Sven Lydman (6/0), Ilmari Laine (1/0), Eino Soinio (21/1), Hugo Mantila (13/0), Väinö Moisio (1/0), Kalle Korma (1/0), Verner Eklöf (17/9), Aarne Linna (5/3), Hjalmar Kelin (14/4).
Goals: Henry Müller (10 own goal), Aarne Linna (27).

25. 15.08.1923 **AUSTRIA - FINLAND** **2-1(1-1)**
Hohe Warte, Wien; Referee: František Cejnar (Czechoslovakia); Attendance: 45,000
FIN: Niilo Tammisalo (17/0), Arthur Englund (Cap) (13/0), Sven Lydman (7/0), Tuovi Koskinen (1/0), Eino Soinio (22/1), Hugo Mantila (14/0), Kalle Korma (2/0), Verner Eklöf (18/10), Arvi Katajavuori (3/1), Aarne Linna (6/3), Hjalmar Kelin (15/4).
Goal: Verner Eklöf (42).

26. 19.08.1923 **HUNGARY - FINLAND** **3-1(0-1)**
Üllöi út, Budapest; Referee: Max Seemann (Austria); Attendance: 16,000
FIN: Niilo Tammisalo (18/0), Hjalmar Kelin (16/4), Sven Lydman (8/0), Tuovi Koskinen (2/0), Eino Soinio (23/1), Hugo Mantila (15/0), Paul Kulves (1/0), Kalle Korma (3/0), Verner Eklöf (Cap) (19/10), Aarne Linna (7/4), Vilho Kettunen (1/0).
Goal: Aarne Linna (40).

27. 23.09.1923 **FINLAND - POLAND** **5-3(3-1)**
Töölön Pallokenttä, Helsinki; Referee: August Silber (Estonia); Attendance: 3,000
FIN: Niilo Tammisalo (19/0), Ragnar Wickström (17/2), Sven Lydman (9/0), Charles Stormbom (13/0), Eino Soinio (24/1), Hugo Mantila (16/0), Hjalmar Kelin (17/4), Kalle Korma (4/2), Verner Eklöf (Cap) (20/12), Aarne Linna (8/5), Gunnar Åström (3/0).
Goals: Verner Eklöf (19), Aarne Linna (29), Verner Eklöf (43), Kalle Korma (50, 60)

28. 30.09.1923 **ESTONIA - FINLAND** **2-1(1-0)**
Spordi Staadion, Tallinn; Referee: Gunnar Sund (Finland); Attendance: 4,000
FIN: Harald Elevuo (2/0), Ivar Grannas (1/0), Sven Lydman (10/0), Tuovi Koskinen (3/0), Charles Stormbom (14/0), Lauri Virta (2/0), Gunnar Åström (Cap) (4/0), Aarne Linna (9/5), Torsten Österlund (1/1), Vilho Kettunen (2/0), William Kanerva (3/0).
Goal: Torsten Österlund (80).

29. 17.06.1924 **FINLAND - TURKEY** **2-4(1-3)**
Töölön Pallokenttä, Helsinki; Referee: Gösta Löfgren (Finland); Attendance: 6,000
FIN: Niilo Tammisalo (20/0), Niilo Koskinen (2/0), Sven Lydman (Cap) (11/0), Alexander Karjagin (1/0), Charles Stormbom (15/0), Hugo Mantila (17/0), Bertel Silve (3/0), Aulis Koponen (1/0), Kalle Korma (5/3), Aarne Linna (10/5), Hjalmar Kelin (18/5).
Goals: Hjalmar Kelin (28), Kalle Korma (85 penalty).

30. 28.07.1924 **FINLAND - SWEDEN** **5-7(5-2)**
Töölön Pallokenttä, Helsinki; Referee: Julius Reinans (Estonia); Attendance: 3,500
FIN: Niilo Tammisalo (21/0), Niilo Koskinen (3/0), Sven Lydman (12/0), Alexander Karjagin (2/1), Eino Soinio (25/1), Lauri Virta (3/0), Niilo Yrjölä (1/0), Aulis Koponen (2/1), Verner Eklöf (Cap) (21/13), Kalle Korma (6/5), Hjalmar Kelin (19/5).
Goals: Kalle Korma (9, 12), Verner Eklöf (25), Aulis Koponen (29), Alexander Karjagin (42).

31. 10.08.1924 **POLAND - FINLAND** **1-0(0-0)**
Stadion Agrykola, Warszawa; Referee: Štepán Zeníšek (Czechoslovakia); Attendance: 4,000
FIN: Niilo Tammisalo (22/0), Rafael Sjöman (1/0), Sven Lydman (13/0), Alexander Karjagin (3/1), Eino Soinio (26/1), Lauri Virta (4/0), Bertel Silve (4/0), Aulis Koponen (3/1), Verner Eklöf (Cap) (22/13), Kalle Korma (7/5), Hjalmar Kelin (20/5).

32. 14.08.1924 **LATVIA - FINLAND** **0-2(0-2)**
LSB Stadions, Riga; Referee: Heinrich Plhak (Austria); Attendance: 4,000
FIN: Niilo Tammisalo (23/0), Rafael Sjöman (2/0), Sven Lydman (14/0), Arvo Närvänen (1/0), Alexander Karjagin (4/1), Lauri Virta (5/0), William Kanerva (4/0), Aulis Koponen (4/2), Verner Eklöf (Cap) (23/13), Kalle Korma (8/6), Bertel Silve (5/0).
Goals: Kalle Korma (13), Aulis Koponen (30).

33. 23.08.1924 **FINLAND - NORWAY** **2-0(2-0)**
Töölön Pallokenttä, Helsinki; Referee: Ruben Gelbord (Sweden); Attendance: 3,000
FIN: Niilo Tammisalo (24/0), Niilo Koskinen (4/0), Sven Lydman (15/0), Arvo Närvänen (2/0), Eino Soinio (27/1), Lauri Virta (6/0), Adolf Höglander (2/0), Aulis Koponen (5/2), Verner Eklöf (Cap) (24/13), Kalle Korma (9/7), William Kanerva (5/1).
Goals: William Kanerva (34), Kalle Korma (42).

34. 14.09.1924 **FINLAND - ESTONIA** **4-0(1-0)**
Töölön Pallokenttä, Helsinki; Referee: Axel Bergqvist (Sweden); Attendance: 4,000
FIN: Niilo Tammisalo (25/0), Niilo Koskinen (5/0), Sven Lydman (16/0), Alexander Karjagin (5/1), Eino Soinio (28/2), Lauri Virta (7/0), Holger Thorn (4/2), Aulis Koponen (6/4), Verner Eklöf (Cap) (25/13), Kalle Korma (10/7), William Kanerva (6/2).
Goals: William Kanerva (10), Eino Soinio (70), Aulis Koponen (80, 85).

35. 07.06.1925 **NORWAY - FINLAND** **1-0(0-0)**
Gressbanen ved Holmen i Aker, Oslo; Referee: Axel Bergqvist (Sweden); Attendance: 12,000
FIN: Harald Elevuo (3/0), Niilo Koskinen (6/0), Sven Lydman (17/0), Arvo Närvänen (3/0), Eino Soinio (29/2), Aarne Linna (11/5), William Kanerva (7/2), Aulis Koponen (7/4), Verner Eklöf (Cap) (26/13), Kalle Korma (11/7), Hjalmar Kelin (21/5).

36. 09.06.1925 **SWEDEN - FINLAND** **4-0(2-0)**
Slottsskogsvallen, Göteborg; Referee: Ragnvald Smedvik (Norway); Attendance: 7,500
FIN: Harald Elevuo (4/0), Niilo Koskinen (7/0) [46.Albin Lönnberg (1/0)], Sven Lydman (18/0), Arvo Närvänen (4/0) [67.Tuovi Koskinen (4/0)], Eino Soinio (30/2), Aarne Linna (12/5), William Kanerva (8/2), Aulis Koponen (8/4), Verner Eklöf (Cap) (27/13), Kalle Korma (12/7), Hjalmar Kelin (22/5).

37. 26.06.1925 **FINLAND - GERMANY** **3-5(0-1)**
Töölön Pallokenttä, Helsinki; Referee: Simon Benzer (Sweden); Attendance: 3,500
FIN: Harald Elevuo (5/0), Niilo Koskinen (8/0), Sven Lydman (Cap) (19/0), Alexander Karjagin (6/1), Eino Soinio (31/2), Aarne Linna (13/5), William Kanerva (9/2), Aulis Koponen (9/6), Arvi Katajavuori (4/1), Albin Lönnberg (2/0), Hjalmar Kelin (23/6).
Goals: Hjalmar Kelin (28), Aulis Koponen (50 penalty,83).

38. 05.07.1925 **ESTONIA - FINLAND** **2-0(2-0)**
Kalev Staadion, Tallinn; Referee: Imre Josza (Hungary); Attendance: 3,000
FIN: Harald Elevuo (6/0), Niilo Koskinen (9/0), Sven Lydman (Cap) (20/0), Arvo Närvänen (5/0), Alexander Karjagin (7/1), Aarne Linna (14/5), Aarne Tolonen (1/0), Aulis Koponen (10/6), Arvi Katajavuori (5/1), Kalle Korma (13/7), Hjalmar Kelin (24/6).

39. 10.07.1925 **FINLAND - AUSTRIA** **1-2(1-1)**
Töölön Pallokenttä, Helsinki; Referee: Axel Bergqvist (Sweden); Attendance: 4,000
FIN: Harald Elevuo (7/0), Niilo Koskinen (10/0), Sven Lydman (21/0), Arvo Närvänen (6/0), Alexander Karjagin (8/1), Aarne Linna (15/5), Aarne Tolonen (2/0), Aulis Koponen (11/6) [65.William Kanerva (10/2)], Verner Eklöf (Cap) (28/14), Albin Lönnberg (3/0), Hjalmar Kelin (25/6).
Goal: Verner Eklöf (3 penalty).

40. 09.08.1925 **FINLAND - LATVIA** **3-1(0-0)**
Töölön Pallokenttä, Helsinki; Referee: Theodor Malm (Sweden); Attendance: 2,000
FIN: Arthur Lindroos (1/0) [46.Yrjö Kanerva (1/0)], Niilo Koskinen (11/0), Sven Lydman (22/0), Arvo Närvänen (7/0), Eino Soinio (32/2), Vieno Nikander (1/0), Untamo Kulmala (1/0), Jarl Lesch (1/0), Verner Eklöf (Cap) (29/15), Kalle Korma (14/9), Hjalmar Kelin (26/6).
Goals: Kalle Korma (74), Verner Eklöf (79), Kalle Korma (85).

41. 30.08.1925 **FINLAND - POLAND** **2-2(1-0)**
Töölön Pallokenttä, Helsinki; Referee: Trygve Högberg (Norway); Attendance: 2,500
FIN: Harald Elevuo (8/0), Niilo Koskinen (12/0), Sven Lydman (23/0), Arvo Närvänen (8/0), Eino Soinio (33/2), Aarne Linna (16/6), Untamo Kulmala (2/1), Kalle Korma (15/9), Verner Eklöf (Cap) (30/15), Joshua Nadbornik (1/0), Hjalmar Kelin (27/6).
Goals: Aarne Linna (40), Untamo Kulmala (85).

42. 27.09.1925 **DENMARK - FINLAND** **3-3(1-3)**
Aarhus Stadion, Aarhus; Referee: Johan Mutters (Netherlands); Attendance: 6,500
FIN: Harald Elevuo (9/0), Hjalmar Kelin (28/6), Sven Lydman (24/0), Arvo Närvänen (9/0), Eino Soinio (34/2), Aarne Linna (17/6), Karl Alakari (1/0), Aulis Koponen (12/7), Verner Eklöf (Cap) (31/17), Kalle Korma (16/9), Aarne Tolonen (3/0).
Goals: Verner Eklöf (24, 35), Aulis Koponen (42).

43. 06.06.1926 **FINLAND - NORWAY** **2-5(0-1)**
Töölön Pallokenttä, Helsinki; Referee: Knut Lundstedt (Sweden); Attendance: 4,000
FIN: Niilo Tammisalo (26/0), Hjalmar Kelin (29/6), Sven Lydman (25/0), Max Viinioksa (1/0), Arvo Närvänen (10/0), Aarne Linna (18/6), Gunnar Åström (5/0), Bertel Silve (6/0), Verner Eklöf (Cap) (32/17), Kalle Korma (17/9), William Kanerva (11/4).
Goals: William Kanerva (70, 85).

44. 20.06.1926 **FINLAND - DENMARK** **3-2(2-2)**
Töölön Pallokenttä, Helsinki; Referee: Gustaf Elberg (Sweden); Attendance: 5,000
FIN: Niilo Tammisalo (27/0), Tuovi Koskinen (5/0), Sven Lydman (Cap) (26/0), Max Viinioksa (2/0), Kurt Nylund (1/0), Toivo Ovaska (1/0), Gunnar Åström (6/0), Albin Lönnberg (4/2), Leo Laaksonen (1/0), William Kanerva (12/4), Hjalmar Kelin (30/7).
Goals: Albin Lönnberg (6, 61), Hjalmar Kelin (23).

45. 26.07.1926 **FINLAND - SWEDEN** **2-3(2-0)**
Töölön Pallokenttä, Helsinki; Referee: Dr. Peco J. Bauwens (Germany); Attendance: 4,000
FIN: Niilo Tammisalo (28/0), Niilo Koskinen (13/0), Sven Lydman (Cap) (27/0), Max Viinioksa (3/0), Eino Soinio (35/2), Arvo Närvänen (11/0), Gunnar Åström (7/0), Albin Lönnberg (5/2), Sulo Saario (1/1), William Kanerva (13/5), Hjalmar Kelin (31/7).
Goals: William Kanerva (5), Sulo Saario (29).

46. 08.08.1926 **POLAND - FINLAND** **7-1(3-1)**
Stadion Warta, Poznań; Referee: František Cejnar (Czechoslovakia); Attendance: 9,000
FIN: Harald Elevuo (10/0), Niilo Koskinen (14/0), Sven Lydman (Cap) (28/0), Max Viinioksa (4/0), Eino Soinio (36/2), Arvo Närvänen (12/0), Untamo Kulmala (3/1), Aulis Koponen (13/7), Leo Laaksonen (2/1), Albin Lönnberg (6/2) [46.Hugo Kuhlberg (1/0)], Hjalmar Kelin (32/7).
Goal: Leo Laaksonen (40).

47. 12.08.1926 **LATVIA - FINLAND** **1-4(0-3)**
ASK Stadions, Riga; Referee: August Silber (Estonia); Attendance: 4,000
FIN: Harald Elevuo (11/0), Niilo Koskinen (15/0), Sven Lydman (Cap) (29/0), Max Viinioksa (5/0), Eino Soinio (37/2), Arvo Närvänen (13/0), Bertel Silve (7/1), Aulis Koponen (14/9) [64.Hugo Kuhlberg (2/0)], Leo Laaksonen (3/1), Albin Lönnberg (7/3), Hjalmar Kelin (33/7).
Goals: Aulis Koponen (13, 19), Bertel Silve (25), Albin Lönnberg (75).

48. 05.09.1926 **FINLAND - ESTONIA** **1-1(0-1)**
Töölön Pallokenttä, Helsinki; Referee: Elias Englund (Sweden); Attendance: 3,000
FIN: Niilo Tammisalo (29/0), Niilo Koskinen (16/0), Tuovi Koskinen (6/0), Max Viinioksa (6/0), Kurt Nylund (2/0) [64.Eino Soinio (38/2)], Arvo Närvänen (14/0), Gunnar Åström (8/0), Bertel Silve (8/1), Sulo Saario (2/2), Albin Lönnberg (Cap) (8/3), Hjalmar Kelin (34/7).
Goal: Sulo Saario (70).

49. 12.06.1927 **SWEDEN - FINLAND** **6-2(2-0)**
Stockholms Stadion, Stockholm; Referee: Ragnvald Smedvik (Norway); Attendance: 17,000
FIN: Yrjö Kanerva (2/0), Tuovi Koskinen (7/0), Hjalmar Kelin (Cap) (35/7), Max Viinioksa (7/0), Arvo Närvänen (15/0), Toivo Ovaska (2/0), Gunnar Åström (9/2), Aulis Koponen (15/9), Sulo Saario (3/2), Albin Lönnberg (9/3), Ragnar Lindbäck (1/0).
Goals: Gunnar Åström (77, 86).

50. 15.06.1927 **NORWAY - FINLAND** **3-1(1-0)**
Ullevaal Stadion, Oslo; Referee: Arthur Björklund (Sweden); Attendance: 16,000
FIN: Yrjö Kanerva (3/0), Tuovi Koskinen (8/0), Hjalmar Kelin (Cap) (36/7), Max Viinioksa (8/0), Arvo Närvänen (16/0), Toivo Ovaska (3/0), Gunnar Åström (10/3), Aulis Koponen (16/9), Sulo Saario (4/2), Albin Lönnberg (10/3), Ragnar Lindbäck (2/0).
Goal: Gunnar Åström (54).

51. 10.08.1927 **ESTONIA - FINLAND** **2-1(1-0)**
Kadriorg Staadion, Tallinn; Referee: Axel Bergqvist (Sweden); Attendance: 5,000
FIN: Yrjö Kanerva (4/0), Niilo Koskinen (17/0), Hjalmar Kelin (Cap) (37/7), Max Viinioksa (9/0), Arvo Närvänen (17/0), Toivo Ovaska (4/0) [57.Eino Soinio (39/2)], Gunnar Åström (11/3), Aulis Koponen (17/9), Untamo Kulmala (4/2), Albin Lönnberg (11/3) [27.William Kanerva (14/5)], Yrjö Suontausta (1/0).
Goal: Untamo Kulmala (52).

52. 11.09.1927 **FINLAND - LATVIA** **3-1(2-0)**
Töölön Pallokenttä, Helsinki; Referee: Heinrich Paal (Estonia); Attendance: 1,500
FIN: Yrjö Kanerva (5/0), Niilo Koskinen (18/0), Heimo Saarilahti (1/0), Max Viinioksa (10/0), Eino Soinio (40/2), Arvo Närvänen (18/0), Karl Alakari (2/0), Aulis Koponen (18/10), Kalle Korma (18/10), William Kanerva (15/5), Hjalmar Kelin (Cap) (38/7).
Goals: Aulis Koponen (40), Lauks (41 own goal), Kalle Korma (75).

53. 03.06.1928 **FINLAND - NORWAY** **0-6(0-3)**
Töölön Pallokenttä, Helsinki; Referee: Ragnar Bäckström (Sweden); Attendance: 6,000
FIN: Yrjö Kanerva (6/0), Niilo Koskinen (19/0), Heimo Saarilahti (2/0), Max Viinioksa (11/0), Arvo Närvänen (19/0), Reino Hintsa (1/0), Gunnar Åström (Cap) (12/3), Aulis Koponen (19/10), Leo Laaksonen (4/1), Kalle Korma (19/10) [42.William Kanerva (16/5)], Hjalmar Kelin (39/7).

54. 12.08.1928 **FINLAND - ESTONIA** **2-2(1-1)**
Töölön Pallokenttä, Helsinki; Referee: Alf Hillerström (Sweden); Attendance: 3,000
FIN: Charles Holmberg (1/0), Niilo Koskinen (20/0) [46.Hjalmar Kelin (40/7)], Heimo Saarilahti (3/0), Max Viinioksa (12/0), Sakari Laesmaa (1/0), Arvo Närvänen (20/0), Gunnar Åström (Cap) (13/4), Edvard Hollmen (1/0), Albin Lönnberg (12/3), William Kanerva (17/6), Yrjö Suontausta (2/0).
Goals: Gunnar Åström (30), William Kanerva (65).

55. 19.08.1928 **LATVIA - FINLAND** **2-1(0-0)**
LSB Stadions, Riga; Referee: Heinrich Paal (Estonia); Attendance: 1,000
FIN: Charles Holmberg (2/0) [46.Armas Karlsson (1/0)], Hjalmar Kelin (41/7) [46.Tuovi Koskinen (9/0)], Heimo Saarilahti (4/0), Max Viinioksa (13/0), Sakari Laesmaa (2/0), Arvo Närvänen (21/0), Gunnar Åström (Cap) (14/4), Edvard Hollmen (2/0), Albin Lönnberg (13/4), William Kanerva (18/6), Yrjö Suontausta (3/0).
Goal: Albin Lönnberg (90 penalty).

56. 02.09.1928 **FINLAND - SWEDEN** **2-3(0-2)**
Töölön Pallokenttä, Helsinki; Referee: Karl Andersen (Norway); Attendance: 5,000
FIN: Charles Holmberg (3/0), Niilo Koskinen (Cap) (21/0), Heimo Saarilahti (5/0), Max Viinioksa (14/0), Sakari Laesmaa (3/0), Arvo Närvänen (22/0), Gunnar Åström (15/4), Jarl Malmgren (1/1), Albin Lönnberg (14/4), William Kanerva (19/7), Hjalmar Kelin (42/7).
Goals: Jarl Malmgren (55), William Kanerva (75).

57. 14.06.1929 **SWEDEN – FINLAND** **3-1(2-0)** Nordic Championship
Stockholms Stadion, Stockholm; Referee: Frederik Schielderop (Norway); Attendance: 16,982
FIN: Charles Holmberg (4/0), Niilo Koskinen (Cap) (22/0), Frans Karjagin (1/0), Max Viinioksa (15/0), Arvo Närvänen (23/0), Axel Lindbäck (1/0), Gunnar Åström (16/4), Aulis Koponen (20/11), Lauri Lehtinen (1/0), Albin Lönnberg (15/4), William Kanerva (20/7).
Goal: Aulis Koponen (73).

58. 18.06.1929 **NORWAY - FINLAND** **4-0(3-0)** Nordic Championship
Ullevaal Stadion, Oslo; Referee: Carl Ohlsson (Sweden); Attendance: 12,000
FIN: Charles Holmberg (5/0), Heimo Saarilahti (6/0), Frans Karjagin (2/0), Max Viinioksa (16/0), Arvo Närvänen (24/0), Viljo Lindroos (1/0), Gunnar Åström (Cap) (17/4), Aulis Koponen (21/11), Lauri Lehtinen (2/0), Albin Lönnberg (16/4) [46.Holger Sarnola (1/0)], William Kanerva (21/7).

59. 25.07.1929 **ESTONIA - FINLAND** **1-1(1-1)**
Kadriorg Staadion, Tallinn; Referee: Gustaf Ekberg (Sweden); Attendance: 3,000
FIN: Charles Holmberg (6/0), Niilo Koskinen (Cap) (23/0), Frans Karjagin (3/0), Max Viinioksa (17/0), Pentti Larvo (1/0), Axel Lindbäck (2/0), Arvo Kanerva (1/0), Aulis Koponen (22/12), Albin Lönnberg (17/4), Joshua Nadbornik (2/0), Ragnar Lindbäck (3/0).
Goal: Aulis Koponen (3).

60. 27.08.1929 **FINLAND - ESTONIA** **2-1(1-0)**
Töölön Pallokenttä, Helsinki; Referee: Osborn Wenzel (Sweden); Attendance: 3,000
FIN: Charles Holmberg (7/0), Niilo Koskinen (Cap) (24/0), Frans Karjagin (4/0), Max Viinioksa (18/0), Pentti Larvo (2/0), Axel Lindbäck (3/0), Gunnar Åström (18/4), Aulis Koponen (23/13), Albin Lönnberg (18/5), Arvo Närvänen (25/0), Ragnar Lindbäck (4/0).
Goals: Albin Lönnberg (15 penalty), Aulis Koponen (53).

61. 15.09.1929 **FINLAND – LATVIA** **3-1(3-1)**
Töölön Pallokenttä, Helsinki; Referee: Axel Bergqvist (Sweden); Attendance: 4,000
FIN: Charles Holmberg (8/0), Niilo Koskinen (Cap) (25/0), Frans Karjagin (5/0), Max Viinioksa (19/0), Pentti Larvo (3/0), Arvo Närvänen (26/1), Gunnar Åström (19/4), Torsten Svanström (1/1), Albin Lönnberg (19/5), Jarl Malmgren (2/1), Yrjö Suontausta (4/1).
Goals: Torsten Svanström (10), Arvo Närvänen (13), Yrjö Suontausta (17).

62. 13.10.1929 **DENMARK - FINLAND** **8-0(4-0)** Nordic Championship
Idrætsparken, København; Referee: Moritz Fuchs (Germany); Attendance: 20,000
FIN: Charles Holmberg (9/0), Niilo Koskinen (Cap) (26/0), Frans Karjagin (6/0), Max Viinioksa (20/0), Pentti Larvo (4/0), Axel Lindbäck (4/0), Gunnar Åström (20/4), William Kanerva (22/7), Sulo Saario (5/2), Viljo Kuhlberg (1/0), Olof Strömsten (1/0).

63. 20.10.1929 **GERMANY - FINLAND** **4-0(0-0)**
Altonaer Stadion, Hamburg; Referee: Bjarne Beck (Norway); Attendance: 20,000
FIN: Charles Holmberg (10/0), Niilo Koskinen (Cap) (27/0), Frans Karjagin (7/0), Max Viinioksa (21/0), Pentti Larvo (5/0), Kaarlo Oksanen (1/0) [22.Alfons Nylund (1/0)], Gunnar Åström (21/4), William Kanerva (23/7), Sulo Saario (6/2), Viljo Kuhlberg (2/0), Yrjö Suontausta (5/1).

64. 01.06.1930 **NORWAY - FINLAND** **6-2(4-0)** Nordic Championship
Ullevaal Stadion, Oslo; Referee: Dr. Otto Remke (Denmark); Attendance: 13,000
FIN: Armas Karlsson (2/0), Frans Karjagin (8/0), Kaarlo Oksanen (2/0), Max Viinioksa (Cap) (22/0), Pentti Larvo (6/0), Arvo Närvänen (27/1), Gunnar Åström (22/5), Aulis Koponen (24/13), Sulo Saario (7/3), Viljo Kuhlberg (3/0), William Kanerva (24/7).
Goals: Sulo Saario (66), Gunnar Åström (77).

65. 16.06.1930 **FINLAND - DENMARK** **1-6(0-3)** Nordic Championship
Töölön Pallokenttä, Helsinki; Referee: Carl Ohlsson (Sweden); Attendance: 6,500
FIN: Gunnar Närhinen (1/0) [48.Charles Holmberg (11/0)], Niilo Koskinen (Cap) (28/0), Kaarlo Oksanen (3/0), Max Viinioksa (23/0), Pentti Larvo (7/0), Arvo Närvänen (28/1), Gunnar Åström (23/5), Aulis Koponen (25/13), Sulo Saario (8/3), Joshua Nadbornik (3/0), William Kanerva (25/8).
Goal: William Kanerva (88)

66. 04.08.1930 **LATVIA - FINLAND** **3-0(1-0)**
JKS Stadions, Riga; Referee: Georg Muntau (Germany); Attendance: 3,000
FIN: Oiva Laine (1/0), Eino Turunen (1/0), Kaarlo Oksanen (4/0), Max Viinioksa (Cap) (24/0), Arthur Hestenaes (1/0), Lauri Sinikari (1/0), Ilmari Mantila (1/0), Aulis Koponen (26/13), Eero Kettunen (1/0), Viljo Kuhlberg (4/0), Nuutti Lintamo (1/0).

67. 06.08.1930 **ESTONIA - FINLAND** **4-0(2-0)**
Kadriorg Staadion, Tallinn; Referee: Gustavs Kruminš (Latvia); Attendance: 3,000
FIN: Oiva Laine (2/0), Eino Turunen (2/0) [14.Emil Nordberg (1/0)], Kaarlo Oksanen (5/0), Max Viinioksa (Cap) (25/0), Pentti Larvo (8/0), Lauri Sinikari (2/0), Gunnar Åström (24/5), Aulis Koponen (27/13), Sulo Saario (9/3), Viljo Kuhlberg (5/0), Nuutti Lintamo (2/0) [46.Ilmari Mantila (2/0)].

68. 28.09.1930 **FINLAND - SWEDEN** **4-4(4-1)** Nordic Championship
Töölön Pallokenttä, Helsinki; Referee: Dr. Otto Remke (Denmark); Attendance: 7,152
FIN: Charles Holmberg (12/0), Frans Karjagin (9/0), Kaarlo Oksanen (6/0), Alfons Nylund (2/0), Arvo Närvänen (Cap) (29/1), Axel Lindbäck (5/0), Gunnar Åström (25/5), Aulis Koponen (28/14), Lauri Lehtinen (3/3), Jarl Malmgren (3/1), Nuutti Lintamo (3/0).
Goals: Lauri Lehtinen (9, 40, 41), Aulis Koponen (15).

69. 17.06.1931 **FINLAND - ESTONIA** **3-1(3-0)**
Töölön Pallokenttä, Helsinki; Referee: Ivar Gustafsson (Sweden); Attendance: 3,851
FIN: Oiva Laine (3/0), Frans Karjagin (10/0), Kaarlo Oksanen (7/0), Alfons Nylund (3/0), Pentti Larvo (9/0), Max Viinioksa (26/0), Gunnar Åström (Cap) (26/7), Ernst Grönlund (1/0), Lauri Lehtinen (4/3), Olof Strömsten (2/1), Nuutti Lintamo (4/0).
Goals: Olof Strömsten (1), Gunnar Åström (36, 44).

70. 03.07.1931 **SWEDEN – FINLAND** **8-2(5-0)** Nordic Championship
Stockholms Stadion, Stockholm; Referee: Dr. Otto Remke (Denmark); Attendance: 20,000
FIN: Oiva Laine (4/0), Frans Karjagin (11/0), Kaarlo Oksanen (8/0), Arthur Hestenaes (2/0), Pentti Larvo (10/0), Lauri Sinikari (3/0), Max Viinioksa (Cap) (27/0), Ernst Grönlund (2/1), Lauri Lehtinen (5/3) [46.Olof Strömsten (3/1)], Holger Salin (1/0), Nuutti Lintamo (5/1).
Goals: Nuutti Lintamo (76), Ernst Grönlund (87 penalty).

71. 19.08.1931 **FINLAND - LATVIA** **4-0(3-0)**
Töölön Pallokenttä, Helsinki; Referee: Heinrich Paal (Estonia); Attendance: 3,500
FIN: Armas Karlsson (3/0) [40.Gunnar Närhinen (2/0)], Frans Karjagin (12/0), Kaarlo Oksanen (9/0), Alfons Nylund (4/0), Pentti Larvo (11/0), Lauri Sinikari (4/0), Gunnar Åström (Cap) (27/8), Ernst Grönlund (3/3), Jarl Malmgren (4/2), Holger Salin (2/0), Nuutti Lintamo (6/1).
Goals: Ernst Grönlund (12), Jarl Malmgren (15), Ernst Grönlund (23), Gunnar Åström (63).

72. 06.09.1931 **FINLAND - NORWAY** **4-4(2-3)** Nordic Championship
Töölön Pallokenttä, Helsinki; Referee: Knut Lensing (Sweden); Attendance: 700
FIN: Armas Karlsson (4/0), Frans Karjagin (13/0), Kaarlo Oksanen (10/0), Alfons Nylund (5/0), Pentti Larvo (12/0), Arvo Närvänen (30/1), Gunnar Åström (Cap) (28/10), Ernst Grönlund (4/3), Jarl Malmgren (5/2), Holger Salin (3/1), William Kanerva (26/9).
Goals: William Kanerva (3), Holger Salin (5), Gunnar Åström (56, 75).

73. 11.10.1931 **DENMARK - FINLAND** **2-3(2-1)** Nordic Championship
Idrætsparken, København; Referee: Ivan Eklind (Sweden); Attendance: 22,000
FIN: Armas Karlsson (5/0), Frans Karjagin (14/0), Kaarlo Oksanen (11/0), Max Viinioksa (28/0), Jarl Malmgren (6/2), Arvo Närvänen (31/1), Gunnar Åström (Cap) (29/11), Kurt Weckström (1/0), Ernst Grönlund (5/3), Olof Strömsten (4/3), William Kanerva (27/9).
Goals: Gunnar Åström (41), Olof Strömsten (76, 85).

74. 16.05.1932 **SWEDEN – FINLAND** **7-1(4-1)**
Stockholms Stadion, Stockholm; Referee: Peder Christian Andersen (Norway); Attendance: 20,500
FIN: Gunnar Närhinen (3/0) [37.Viljo Halme (1/0)], Frans Karjagin (15/0), Kaarlo Oksanen (12/0), Max Viinioksa (29/0), Pentti Larvo (13/0), Leo Karjagin (1/0), Gunnar Åström (Cap) (30/11), Kurt Weckström (2/0), Ernst Grönlund (6/3), Holger Salin (4/1), William Kanerva (28/10).
Goal: William Kanerva (10).

75. 10.06.1932 **FINLAND - SWEDEN** **1-3(1-1)** Nordic Championship
Töölön Pallokenttä, Helsinki; Referee: Thoralf Kristiansen (Norway); Attendance: 7,000
FIN: Viljo Halme (2/0), Frans Karjagin (16/0), Kaarlo Oksanen (13/0), Max Viinioksa (30/0), Pentti Larvo (14/0), Arvo Närvänen (32/1), Gunnar Åström (Cap) (31/11), Aulis Koponen (29/14), Ernst Grönlund (7/4), Holger Salin (5/1), Nuutti Lintamo (7/1).
Goal: Ernst Grönlund (6).

76. 17.06.1932 **NORWAY - FINLAND** **2-1(1-1)** Nordic Championship
Ullevaal Stadion, Oslo; Referee: Carl Ohlsson (Sweden); Attendance: 18,000
FIN: Viljo Halme (3/0), Veli Leskinen (1/0), Kaarlo Oksanen (14/0), Max Viinioksa (Cap) (31/0), Pentti Larvo (15/0), Arvo Närvänen (33/1), Eero Ronkanen (1/0), Aulis Koponen (30/14), Ernst Grönlund (8/5), William Kanerva (29/10), Nuutti Lintamo (8/1).
Goal: Ernst Grönlund (35).

77. 01.07.1932 **FINLAND - GERMANY** **1-4(1-1)**
Töölön Pallokenttä, Helsinki; Referee: John Erik Andersson (Sweden); Attendance: 3,917
FIN: Viljo Halme (4/0), Veli Leskinen (2/0), Kaarlo Oksanen (15/0), Max Viinioksa (32/0), Pentti Larvo (16/0), Arvo Närvänen (34/1), Gunnar Åström (Cap) (32/12), Aulis Koponen (31/14), Ernst Grönlund (9/5), Olof Strömsten (5/3), Nuutti Lintamo (9/1).
Goal: Gunnar Åström (14).

78. 17.08.1932 **ESTONIA - FINLAND** **0-3(0-3)**
Kadriorg Staadion, Tallinn; Referee: Alfreds Latsiviuš (Latvia); Attendance: 5,000
FIN: Viljo Halme (5/0), Frans Karjagin (17/0), Kaarlo Oksanen (16/0), Max Viinioksa (33/0), Pentti Larvo (17/0), Arvo Närvänen (35/1), Gunnar Åström (Cap) (33/12), Ernst Grönlund (10/5), Jarl Malmgren (7/3), Holger Salin (6/2), Nuutti Lintamo (10/2).
Goals: Holger Salin (9), Jarl Malmgren (25), Nuutti Lintamo (37).

79. 30.08.1932 **FINLAND - DENMARK** **4-2(2-1)** Nordic Championship
Töölön Pallokenttä, Helsinki; Referee: Elias Englund (Sweden); Attendance: 7,500
FIN: Viljo Halme (6/0), Frans Karjagin (18/0), Kaarlo Oksanen (17/0), Max Viinioksa (34/0), Pentti Larvo (18/0), Arvo Närvänen (36/1), Gunnar Åström (Cap) (34/12), Ernst Grönlund (11/5), Jarl Malmgren (8/5), Holger Salin (7/2), Nuutti Lintamo (11/4).
Goals: Jarl Malmgren (27), Nuutti Lintamo (36), Jarl Malmgren (53), Nuutti Lintamo (70).

80. 14.07.1933 **SWEDEN – FINLAND** **2-0(0-0)** Nordic Championship
Stockholms Stadion, Stockholm; Referee: Poul Yssing (Denmark); Attendance: 15,246
FIN: Viljo Halme (7/0), Frans Karjagin (19/0), Kaarlo Oksanen (18/0), Max Viinioksa (35/0), Jarl Malmgren (9/5), Arvo Närvänen (37/1), Gunnar Åström (Cap) (35/12), Ernst Grönlund (12/5), Albin Lönnberg (20/5), Holger Salin (8/2), Nuutti Lintamo (12/4).

81. 09.08.1933 **FINLAND - LITHUANIA** **9-2(5-1)**
Töölön Pallokenttä, Helsinki; Referee: Voldemar Röks (Estonia); Attendance: 3,196
FIN: Viljo Halme (8/0), Frans Karjagin (20/0), Kaarlo Oksanen (19/0), Max Viinioksa (36/1), Jarl Malmgren (10/5), Arvo Närvänen (38/1), Gunnar Åström (Cap) (36/14), Kurt Weckström (3/0), Leo Karjagin (2/2), Ernst Grönlund (13/7), Eero Ronkanen (2/2).
Goals: Gunnar Åström (2), Max Viinioksa (7), Ernst Grönlund (19), Eero Ronkanen (32), Leo Karjagin (41), Eero Ronkanen (67), Ernst Grönlund (68), Gunnar Åström (70), Leo Karjagin (83).

82. 16.08.1933 **FINLAND - ESTONIA** **2-1(0-1)**
Töölön Pallokenttä, Helsinki; Referee: Ragnar Bäckström (Sweden); Attendance: 3,950
FIN: Viljo Halme (9/0), Frans Karjagin (21/0), Kaarlo Oksanen (20/0), Max Viinioksa (37/1), Jarl Malmgren (11/5), Arvo Närvänen (39/1), Gunnar Åström (Cap) (37/14), Kurt Weckström (4/1), Leo Karjagin (3/2), Ernst Grönlund (14/7), Eero Ronkanen (3/2).
Goals: Kurt Weckström (48), Eugen Einman (65 own goal).

83. 03.09.1933 **FINLAND - NORWAY** **1-5(1-2)** Nordic Championship
Töölön Pallokenttä, Helsinki; Referee: Gustaf Ekberg (Sweden); Attendance: 6,271
FIN: Viljo Halme (10/0), Frans Karjagin (22/0), Ragnar Lindbäck (5/0), Max Viinioksa (38/1), Jarl Malmgren (12/5), Arvo Närvänen (40/1), Gunnar Åström (Cap) (38/15), Kurt Weckström (5/1), Ernst Grönlund (15/7), Holger Salin (9/2), Nuutti Lintamo (13/4).
Goal: Gunnar Åström (32).

84. 08.10.1933 **DENMARK - FINLAND** **2-0(1-0)** Nordic Championship
Idrætsparken, København; Referee: Thoralf Kristiansen (Norway); Attendance: 24,000
FIN: Viljo Halme (11/0), Frans Karjagin (23/0), Kaarlo Oksanen (21/0), Max Viinioksa (39/1), Pentti Larvo (19/0), Arvo Närvänen (41/1), Gunnar Åström (Cap) (39/15), Ernst Grönlund (16/7), Jarl Malmgren (13/5), Leo Karjagin (4/2), Nuutti Lintamo (14/4).

85. 03.07.1934 **FINLAND - DENMARK** **2-1(1-1)** Nordic Championship
Töölön Pallokenttä, Helsinki; Referee: Georg Wittboldt (Sweden); Attendance: 5,722
FIN: Viljo Halme (12/0), Frans Karjagin (24/0), Veli Leskinen (3/0) [43.Kaarlo Oksanen (22/0)], Max Viinioksa (40/1), William Kanerva (30/10), Leo Karjagin (5/2), Lauri Taipale (1/1), Aulis Koponen (32/14), Jarl Malmgren (Cap) (14/5), Ernst Grönlund (17/7), Holger Salin (10/3).
Goals: Lauri Taipale (19), Holger Salin (64).

86. 08.08.1934 **ESTONIA - FINLAND** **1-1(0-1)**
Kadriorg Staadion, Tallinn; Referee: Ragnar Bäckström (Sweden); Attendance: 5,000
FIN: Viljo Halme (13/0), Frans Karjagin (25/0), Kaarlo Oksanen (23/0), Max Viinioksa (41/1), William Kanerva (31/10), Leo Karjagin (6/2), Lauri Taipale (2/2), Aulis Koponen (33/14), Jarl Malmgren (Cap) (15/5), Ernst Grönlund (18/7), Yrjö Kylmälä (1/0).
Goal: Lauri Taipale (20).

87. 09.08.1934 **HUNGARY Amateurs - NETHERLANDS** **3-4(2-2)**
Kadriorg Staadion, Tallinn; Referee: Ragnar Bäckström (Sweden); Attendance: 3,000
FIN: Viljo Halme (14/0), Frans Karjagin (26/0), Kaarlo Oksanen (24/0), Max Viinioksa (42/1), William Kanerva (32/10), Leo Karjagin (7/2), Lauri Taipale (3/3), Aulis Koponen (34/14), Jarl Malmgren (Cap) (16/7), Ernst Grönlund (19/7), Yrjö Kylmälä (2/1).
Goals: Lauri Taipale (13), Yrjö Kylmälä (36), Jarl Malmgren (71, 73).

88. 14.08.1934 **LATVIA - FINLAND** **1-1(0-0)**
JKS Stadions, Riga; Referee: Valerijonas Balciúnas (Lithuania); Attendance: 5,000
FIN: Viljo Halme (15/0), Frans Karjagin (27/0), Kaarlo Oksanen (25/0), Max Viinioksa (Cap) (43/1), William Kanerva (33/10), Leevi Kekkonen (1/0), Lauri Taipale (4/3), Ernst Grönlund (20/7), Leo Karjagin (8/2), Holger Salin (11/3), Yrjö Kylmälä (3/2).
Goal: Yrjö Kylmälä (78).

89. 16.08.1934 **LITHUANIA - FINLAND** **1-0(0-0)**
Kariuomenės Stadionas, Kaunas; Referee: Janis Redlichs (Latvia); Attendance: 5,000
FIN: Viljo Halme (16/0), Frans Karjagin (28/0), Kaarlo Oksanen (26/0), Max Viinioksa (Cap) (44/1), William Kanerva (34/10), Leevi Kekkonen (2/0), Lauri Taipale (5/3), Ernst Grönlund (21/7), Leo Karjagin (9/2) [46.Olof Strömsten (6/3)], Holger Salin (12/3), Yrjö Kylmälä (4/2).

90. 02.09.1934 **NORWAY - FINLAND** **4-2(4-1)** Nordic Championship
Ullevaal Stadion, Oslo; Referee: Ejner Ullrich (Denmark); Attendance: 15,000
FIN: Viljo Halme (17/0), Frans Karjagin (29/0), Kaarlo Oksanen (27/0), Max Viinioksa (45/1), William Kanerva (35/10), Leo Karjagin (10/2), Eero Ronkanen (4/2), Jarl Malmgren (Cap) (17/7), Albin Lönnberg (21/7), Ernst Grönlund (22/7), Olof Strömsten (7/3).
Goals: Albin Lönnberg (27, 67).

91. 23.09.1934 **FINLAND - SWEDEN** **5-4(3-2)** Nordic Championship
Töölön Pallokenttä, Helsinki; Referee: Dr. Otto Remke (Denmark); Attendance: 10,442
FIN: Viljo Halme (18/0), Frans Karjagin (30/0), Kaarlo Oksanen (28/0), Max Viinioksa (46/1), William Kanerva (Cap) (36/10), Leo Karjagin (11/2), Lauri Taipale (6/3) [46.Gunnar Åström (40/16)], Aulis Koponen (35/16), Pentti Larvo (20/0), Ernst Grönlund (23/7), Nuutti Lintamo (15/6).
Goals: Aulis Koponen (2, 21), Nuutti Lintamo (38), Gunnar Åström (49), Nuutti Lintamo (51).

92. 06.06.1935 **FINLAND - LATVIA** **4-1(0-1)**
Töölön Pallokenttä, Helsinki; Referee: Ivan Eklind (Sweden); Attendance: 4,000
FIN: Viljo Halme (19/0), Frans Karjagin (31/0), Kaarlo Oksanen (29/0), Leevi Kekkonen (3/0), William Kanerva (Cap) (37/11), Antero Rinne (1/0), Pentti Eronen (1/0), Aulis Koponen (36/16) [55.Kurt Weckström (6/3)], Jarl Malmgren (18/7), Ernst Grönlund (24/7), Nuutti Lintamo (16/7).
Goals: William Kanerva (50 penalty), Kurt Weckström (60, 65), Nuutti Lintamo (85).

93. 12.06.1935 **SWEDEN – FINLAND** **2-2(0-1)** Nordic Championship
Stockholms Stadion, Stockholm; Referee: Thoralf Kristiansen (Norway); Attendance: 14,500
FIN: Viljo Halme (20/0), Frans Karjagin (32/0), Kaarlo Oksanen (30/0), William Kanerva (Cap) (38/11), Jarl Malmgren (19/7), Leo Karjagin (12/2), Gunnar Åström (41/16), Kurt Weckström (7/5), Pentti Larvo (21/0), Ernst Grönlund (25/7), Nuutti Lintamo (17/7).
Goals: Kurt Weckström (11, 76).

94. 07.08.1935 **FINLAND - ESTONIA** **2-2(1-1)**
Töölön Pallokenttä, Helsinki; Referee: Otto Ohlsen (Sweden); Attendance: 4,359
FIN: Viljo Halme (21/0), Frans Karjagin (33/0), Kaarlo Oksanen (31/0), Max Viinioksa (47/1), William Kanerva (Cap) (39/11), Leo Karjagin (13/2), Aulis Koponen (37/16), Kurt Weckström (8/5), Pentti Larvo (22/2), Ernst Grönlund (26/7), Nuutti Lintamo (18/7).
Goals: Pentti Larvo (38, 85).

95. 18.08.1935 **GERMANY - FINLAND** **6-0(3-0)**
„Heinrich Zisch" Stadion, München; Referee: Bruno Pfützner (Czechoslovakia); Attendance: 35,000
FIN: Risto Rinne (1/0), Frans Karjagin (34/0), Kaarlo Oksanen (32/0), Max Viinioksa (48/1), Jarl Malmgren (Cap) (20/7), Leo Karjagin (14/2), Aulis Koponen (38/16), Kurt Weckström (9/5), Pentti Larvo (23/2) [42.Tauno Kekkonen (1/0)], Ernst Grönlund (27/7), Holger Salin (13/3).

96. 08.09.1935 **FINLAND - NORWAY** **1-5(1-1)** Nordic Championship
Töölön Pallokenttä, Helsinki; Referee: Ivar Gustafsson (Sweden); Attendance: 6,557
FIN: Risto Rinne (2/0), Frans Karjagin (35/0), Kaarlo Oksanen (33/0), Max Viinioksa (49/1), Jarl Malmgren (Cap) (21/7), William Kanerva (40/11), Pentti Eronen (2/0), Kurt Weckström (10/5), Pentti Larvo (24/3), Tauno Kekkonen (2/0), Nuutti Lintamo (19/7).
Goal: Pentti Larvo (28).

97. 06.10.1935 **DENMARK - FINLAND** **5-1(3-0)** Nordic Championship
Idrætsparken, København; Referee: John Johansson (Sweden); Attendance: 27,000
FIN: Viljo Halme (22/0), Frans Karjagin (36/0), Kaarlo Oksanen (34/0), Max Viinioksa (50/1) [32.Vilho Lehto (1/0)], Jarl Malmgren (Cap) (22/7), Lauri Sinikari (5/0), Paavo Virtanen (1/0), Ernst Grönlund (28/8), Pentti Larvo (25/3), Yrjö Sotiola (1/0), Holger Salin (14/3).
Goal: Ernst Grönlund (47).

98. 30.06.1936 **FINLAND - DENMARK** **1-4(0-1)** Nordic Championship
Töölön Pallokenttä, Helsinki; Referee: Sölve Flisberg (Sweden); Attendance: 8,357
FIN: Viljo Halme (23/0), Frans Karjagin (37/0), Ragnar Lindbäck (6/0), Eino Virtanen (1/0), Jarl Malmgren (Cap) (23/7), William Kanerva (41/11) [46.Antero Rinne (2/0)], Kurt Weckström (11/5), Ernst Grönlund (29/8), Pentti Larvo (26/3), Yrjö Sotiola (2/0), Holger Salin (15/4). Trainer: Ferdinand Fabra (Germany, 1).
Goal: Holger Salin (18).

99. 06.08.1936 **PERU - FINLAND** **7-3(3-1)** 12th OG. 1st Round.
Stadion am Gesundbrunnen, Berlin (Germany); Referee: Rinaldo Barlassina (Italy); Attendance: 2,500
FIN: Paavo Salminen (1/0), Frans Karjagin (38/0), Arvo Närvänen (42/1), William Kanerva (42/12), Jarl Malmgren (Cap) (24/7), Eino Lahti (1/0), Kurt Weckström (12/5), Erkki Gustafsson (1/0), Pentti Larvo (27/4), Ernst Grönlund (30/9), Aatos Lehtonen (1/0). Trainer: Ferdinand Fabra (Germany, 2).
Goals: William Kanerva (42 penalty), Ernst Grönlund (75), Pentti Larvo (80).

100. 20.08.1936 **ESTONIA - FINLAND** **2-2(0-1)**
Kadriorg Staadion, Tallinn; Referee: Ragnar Bäckström (Sweden); Attendance: 4,500
FIN: Paavo Salminen (2/0), Veli Leskinen (4/0), Ragnar Lindbäck (7/0), William Kanerva (43/12), Jarl Malmgren (Cap) (25/7), Antero Rinne (3/0) [46.Eino Lahti (2/0)], Pentti Eronen (3/0), Kurt Weckström (13/6), Aatos Lehtonen (2/0), Ernst Grönlund (31/10), Holger Salin (16/4). Trainer: Ferdinand Fabra (Germany, 3).
Goals: Ernst Grönlund (36), Kurt Weckström (63).

101. 06.09.1936 **NORWAY - FINLAND** **0-2(0-1)** Nordic Championship
Ullevaal Stadion, Oslo; Referee: Dr. Otto Remke (Denmark); Attendance: 17,000
FIN: Paavo Salminen (3/0), Veli Leskinen (5/0), Kaarlo Oksanen (35/0), William Kanerva (44/12), Jarl Malmgren (Cap) (26/7), Antero Rinne (4/0), Lauri Taipale (7/3), Kurt Weckström (14/7), Pentti Larvo (28/4), Aatos Lehtonen (3/1), Holger Salin (17/4). Trainer: Ferdinand Fabra (Germany, 4).
Goals: Kurt Weckström (23), Aatos Lehtonen (48).

102. 27.09.1936 **FINLAND - SWEDEN** **1-2(0-1)** Nordic Championship
Töölön Pallokenttä, Helsinki; Referee: Kolbjørn Daehlen (Norway); Attendance: 11,922
FIN: Paavo Salminen (4/0), Veli Leskinen (6/0), Kaarlo Oksanen (36/0), William Kanerva (45/13), Jarl Malmgren (Cap) (27/7), Antero Rinne (5/0), Kurt Weckström (15/7), Ernst Grönlund (32/10), Aatos Lehtonen (4/1), Pentti Larvo (29/4), Lauri Lehtinen (6/3). Trainer: Ferdinand Fabra (Germany, 5).
Goal: William Kanerva (85 penalty).

103. 20.05.1937 **FINLAND - ENGLAND** **0-8(0-4)**
Töölön Pallokenttä, Helsinki; Referee: Rudolf Eklöw (Sweden); Attendance: 9,533
FIN: Paavo Salminen (5/0), Frans Karjagin (39/0), Kaarlo Oksanen (Cap) (37/0), Eino Lahti (3/0), Armas Pyy (1/0), Antero Rinne (6/0), Paavo Virtanen (2/0), Kurt Weckström (16/7), Aatos Lehtonen (5/1), Pentti Larvo (30/4), Yrjö Kylmälä (5/2). Trainer: Ferdinand Fabra (Germany, 6).

104. 16.06.1937 **SWEDEN – FINLAND** **4-0(0-0)** 3rd FIFA WC. Qualifiers, Nordic Championship
Råsundastadion, Stockholm; Referee: Kolbjørn Daehlen (Norway); Attendance: 19,544
FIN: Paavo Salminen (6/0), Frans Karjagin (40/0), Ragnar Lindbäck (8/0), Eino Lahti (4/0), Kaarlo Oksanen (Cap) (38/0), Eino Kilpi (1/0), Lauri Taipale (8/3), Kurt Weckström (17/7), Aatos Lehtonen (6/1), Sulo Salo (1/0), Yrjö Kylmälä (6/2). Trainer: Ferdinand Fabra (Germany, 7).

105. 29.06.1937 **FINLAND - GERMANY** **0-2(0-1)** 3rd FIFA WC. Qualifiers
Töölön Pallokenttä, Helsinki; Referee: Dr. Otto Remke (Denmark); Attendance: 6,619
FIN: Viljo Halme (24/0), Frans Karjagin (41/0), Ragnar Lindbäck (9/0), Eino Lahti (5/0), Kaarlo Oksanen (Cap) (39/0), Eino Kilpi (2/0), Lauri Taipale (9/3), Kurt Weckström (18/7), Pentti Larvo (31/4), Ernst Grönlund (33/10), Nuutti Lintamo (20/7). Trainer: Ferdinand Fabra (Germany, 8).

106. 19.08.1937 **FINLAND - ESTONIA** **0-1(0-0)** 3rd FIFA WC. Qualifiers
Urheilupuisto, Turku; Referee: Ivan Eklind (Sweden); Attendance: 4,797
FIN: Viljo Halme (25/0), Frans Karjagin (42/0), Ilmari Oksanen (1/0), William Kanerva (46/13), Jarl Malmgren (Cap) (28/7), Eino Lahti (6/0), Paavo Virtanen (3/0), Kurt Weckström (19/7), Aatos Lehtonen (7/1), Sulo Salo (2/0), Holger Salin (18/4).

107. 05.09.1937 **FINLAND - NORWAY** **0-2(0-1)** Nordic Championship
Töölön Pallokenttä, Helsinki; Referee: Sölve Flisberg (Sweden); Attendance: 7,881
FIN: Viljo Halme (26/0), Frans Karjagin (43/0), Ragnar Lindbäck (10/0), William Kanerva (47/13), Armas Pyy (2/0), Eino Lahti (7/0), Gunnar Åström (42/16), Kurt Weckström (20/7), Jarl Malmgren (Cap) (29/7), Tauno Kekkonen (3/0), Holger Salin (19/4).

108. 17.10.1937 **DENMARK - FINLAND** **2-1(0-1)** Nordic Championship
Idrætsparken, København; Referee: Alfred Birlem (Germany); Attendance: 27,000
FIN: Viljo Halme (27/0), Frans Karjagin (44/0), Veli Leskinen (7/0), William Kanerva (48/13), Jarl Malmgren (Cap) (30/7), Antero Rinne (7/0), Gunnar Åström (43/16), Ernst Grönlund (34/10), Karl-Erik Roslund (1/0), Kurt Weckström (21/7), Eino Mäkelä (1/1).
Goal: Eino Mäkelä (24).

109. 15.06.1938 **SWEDEN – FINLAND** **2-0(1-0)**
Råsundastadion, Stockholm; Referee: Oscar Arvid Carlson (Norway); Attendance: 11,044
FIN: Paavo Salminen (7/0), Frans Karjagin (45/0), Olavi Laakso (1/0), Heikki Kultti (1/0), Armas Pyy (3/0), Leo Karjagin (15/2), Pentti Eronen (4/0), Erkki Gustafsson (2/0), Aatos Lehtonen (8/1), Veikko Asikainen (1/0), Lauri Lehtinen (Cap) (7/3).

110. 17.06.1938 **NORWAY - FINLAND** **9-0(6-0)** Nordic Championship
Ullevaal Stadion, Oslo; Referee: Valdemar Laursen (Denmark); Attendance: 28,000
FIN: Viljo Halme (28/0), Frans Karjagin (46/0), Jarl Malmgren (Cap) (31/7), Eino Virtanen (2/0), Armas Pyy (4/0), Eino Lahti (8/0), Pentti Eronen (5/0), Kurt Weckström (22/7), Ernst Grönlund (35/10), Veikko Asikainen (2/0), Eino Mäkelä (2/1).

111. 04.07.1938 **FINLAND - SWEDEN** **2-4(2-1)** Nordic Championship
Olympiastadion, Helsinki; Referee: Dr. Peco J. Bauwens (Germany); Attendance: 15,301
FIN: Paavo Salminen (8/0), Veli Leskinen (Cap) (8/0), Olavi Laakso (2/0), Veikko Asikainen (3/0), Armas Pyy (5/0), Antero Rinne (8/0), Pentti Eronen (6/0), Holger Granström (1/1), Aatos Lehtonen (9/1), Ernst Grönlund (36/10), Nuutti Lintamo (21/8).
Goals: Nuutti Lintamo (2), Holger Granström (36).

112. 17.08.1938 **ESTONIA - FINLAND** **1-3(1-1)**
Kadriorg Staadion, Tallinn; Referee: Karl Brust (Germany); Attendance: 6,000
FIN: Paavo Salminen (9/0), Veli Leskinen (Cap) (9/0), Frans Karjagin (47/0), Veikko Asikainen (4/0), Armas Pyy (6/0), William Kanerva (49/13), Pentti Eronen (7/1), Holger Granström (2/1), Aatos Lehtonen (10/2), Kurt Weckström (23/8), Eino Mäkelä (3/1).
Goals: Kurt Weckström (27), Pentti Eronen (85), Aatos Lehtonen (87).

113. 31.08.1938 **FINLAND - DENMARK** **2-1(1-0)** Nordic Championship
Olympiastadion, Helsinki; Referee: Rudolf Eklöw (Sweden); Attendance: 11,368
FIN: Paavo Salminen (10/0), Veli Leskinen (Cap) (10/0), Frans Karjagin (48/0), Veikko Asikainen (5/0), Eino Lahti (9/0), Antero Rinne (9/0), Pentti Eronen (8/1), Holger Granström (3/1), Aatos Lehtonen (11/3), Kurt Weckström (24/8), Nuutti Lintamo (22/9).
Goals: Nuutti Lintamo (12), Aatos Lehtonen (47).

114. 18.09.1938 **FINLAND - LITHUANIA** **3-1(1-1)**
Olympiastadion, Helsinki; Referee: Eduard Eelma (Estonia); Attendance: 6,457
FIN: Paavo Salminen (11/0), Veli Leskinen (Cap) (11/0), Frans Karjagin (49/0), Veikko Asikainen (6/0), Eino Lahti (10/0), William Kanerva (50/13), Pentti Eronen (9/1), Holger Granström (4/1), Aatos Lehtonen (12/6), Urho Teräs (1/0), Eino Mäkelä (4/1) [46.Holger Salin (20/4)].
Goals: Aatos Lehtonen (30, 57, 77).

115. 09.06.1939 **SWEDEN – FINLAND** **5-1(3-1)** Nordic Championship
Råsundastadion, Stockholm; Referee: Reidar Randers-Johansen (Norway); Attendance: 16,989
FIN: Viljo Halme (29/0), Veli Leskinen (Cap) (12/0), Frans Karjagin (50/0), Veikko Asikainen (7/0), Armas Pyy (7/0), Eino Lahti (11/0), Pentti Eronen (10/1), Erkki Gustafsson (3/0), Aatos Lehtonen (13/6), Urho Teräs (2/1), Anton Honka (1/0). Trainer: Gábor Obitz (Hungary, 1).
Goal: Urho Teräs (10).

116. 15.06.1939 **DENMARK - FINLAND** **5-0(3-0)**
Idrætsparken, København; Referee: Wilhelm Peters (Germany); Attendance: 34,000
FIN: Thure Sarnola (1/0), Veli Leskinen (Cap) (13/0), Frans Karjagin (51/0), Veikko Asikainen (8/0), Eino Lahti (12/0), Heikki Kultti (2/0), Pentti Eronen (11/1), Holger Granström (5/1), Erik Åberg (1/0), Urho Teräs (3/1), Anton Honka (2/0). Trainer: Gábor Obitz (Hungary, 2).

117. 20.07.1939 **FINLAND - ITALY** **2-3(1-2)**
Olympiastadion, Helsinki; Referee: Ivan Eklind (Sweden); Attendance: 15,547
FIN: Thure Sarnola (2/0), Veli Leskinen (Cap) (14/0), Frans Karjagin (52/0), Eino Lahti (13/0), Armas Pyy (8/0), Antero Rinne (10/0), Pentti Eronen (12/1), Holger Granström (6/1), Aatos Lehtonen (14/7), Kurt Weckström (25/9), Nuutti Lintamo (23/9). Trainer: Gábor Obitz (Hungary, 3).
Goals: Aatos Lehtonen (22), Kurt Weckström (87)

118. 04.08.1939 **FINLAND - ESTONIA** **4-2(0-1)**
Olympiastadion, Helsinki; Referee: Arvíds Jurgens (Latvia); Attendance: 6,154
FIN: Thure Sarnola (3/0), Veli Leskinen (Cap) (15/0), Frans Karjagin (53/0), Eino Lahti (14/0), Armas Pyy (9/0) [50.Leo Karjagin (16/2)], Antero Rinne (11/0), Pentti Eronen (13/2), Holger Granström (7/1), Aatos Lehtonen (15/7), Kurt Weckström (26/9), Yrjö Kylmälä (7/5). Trainer: Gábor Obitz (Hungary, 4).
Goals: Yrjö Kylmälä (49, 65, 78), Pentti Eronen (88 penalty).

119. 03.09.1939 **FINLAND - NORWAY** **1-2(0-1)** Nordic Championship
Olympiastadion, Helsinki; Referee: Rudolf Eklöw (Sweden); Attendance: 8,729
FIN: Thure Sarnola (4/0), Veli Leskinen (Cap) (16/0), Ilmari Oksanen (2/0), Eino Lahti (15/0), Armas Pyy (10/0), Antero Rinne (12/0), Pentti Eronen (14/3), Holger Granström (8/1), Aatos Lehtonen (16/7), Kurt Weckström (27/9), Urho Teräs (4/1). Trainer: Gábor Obitz (Hungary, 5).
Goal: Pentti Eronen (66).

120. 17.09.1939 **DENMARK - FINLAND** **8-1(2-0)** Nordic Championship
Idrætsparken, København; Referee: Ivan Eklind (Sweden); Attendance: 20,000
FIN: Viljo Halme (30/0), Veli Leskinen (Cap) (17/0) [40.Ragnar Lindbäck (11/0)], Ilmari Oksanen (3/0), Eino Lahti (16/0), Armas Pyy (11/0), Antero Rinne (13/0), Pentti Eronen (15/3), Holger Granström (9/2), Aatos Lehtonen (17/7), Yrjö Sotiola (3/0), Kurt Weckström (28/9). Trainer: Gábor Obitz (Hungary, 6).
Goal: Holger Granström (69).

121. 24.09.1939 **FINLAND - LATVIA** **0-3(0-1)**
Olympiastadion, Helsinki; Referee: Dr. Otto Remke (Denmark); Attendance: 4,097
FIN: Thure Sarnola (5/0) [46.Paavo Salminen (12/0)], Eino Lahti (17/0), Ilmari Oksanen (4/0), Veikko Asikainen (9/0), Armas Pyy (Cap) (12/0) [30.Veli Leskinen (18/0)], Antero Rinne (14/0), Kurt Weckström (29/9), Oleg Bogomoloff (1/0), Aatos Lehtonen (18/7), Yrjö Sotiola (4/0), Erik Beijar (1/0).

122. 29.08.1940 **FINLAND - SWEDEN** **2-3(1-2)**
Olympiastadion, Helsinki; Referee: Dr. Peco J. Bauwens (Germany); Attendance: 15,578
FIN: Thure Sarnola (6/0), Toivo Asikainen (1/0), Frans Karjagin (54/0), Viljo Heinonen (1/0), Eino Lahti (Cap) (18/0), Veikko Asikainen (10/0), Kurt Weckström (30/10), Holger Granström (10/2), Leo Turunen (1/0), Urho Teräs (5/1), Erik Beijar (2/1).
Goals: Kurt Weckström (29 penalty), Erik Beijar (58).

123. 01.09.1940 **GERMANY - FINLAND** **13-0(7-0)**
VfB Stadion, Leipzig; Referee: Dr. Otto Remke (Denmark); Attendance: 40,000
FIN: Thure Sarnola (7/0), Toivo Asikainen (2/0), Frans Karjagin (55/0), Viljo Heinonen (2/0), Eino Lahti (Cap) (19/0), Veikko Asikainen (11/0), Kurt Weckström (31/10), Holger Granström (11/2), Eino Karhu (1/0), Urho Teräs (6/1), Lauri Lehtinen (8/3).

124. 22.09.1940 **SWEDEN – FINLAND** **5-0(1-0)**
Råsundadastadion, Stockholm; Referee: Valdemar Laursen (Denmark); Attendance: 22,000
FIN: Thure Sarnola (8/0), Veli Leskinen (Cap) (19/0), Frans Karjagin (56/0), Veikko Asikainen (12/0), Eino Lahti (20/0), Leo Karjagin (17/2), Kurt Weckström (32/10), Holger Granström (12/2), Leo Turunen (2/0), Ernst Grönlund (37/10), Erik Beijar (3/1).

125. 05.10.1941 **FINLAND - GERMANY** **0-6(0-2)**
Olympiastadion, Helsinki; Referee: Ragnar Ericsson (Sweden); Attendance: 7,138
FIN: Thure Sarnola (9/0), Frans Karjagin (Cap) (57/0), Ilmari Oksanen (5/0), Eino Virtanen (3/0), Armas Pyy (13/0), Veikko Asikainen (13/0), Lasse Salo (1/0), Kurt Weckström (33/10), Aatos Lehtonen (19/7), Verner Peltonen (1/0) [Sulo Salo (3/0)], Holger Salin (21/4).

126. 15.09.1943 **FINLAND - HUNGARY** **0-3(0-2)**
Olympiastadion, Helsinki; Referee: Ivan Eklind (Sweden); Attendance: 9,662
FIN: Thure Sarnola (10/0), Gunnar Westerholm (1/0), Erik Åberg (Cap) (2/0), Veikko Asikainen (14/0), Tauno Aitio (1/0), Yrjö Sotiola (5/0), Väinö Kultti (1/0), Kurt Weckström (34/10), Urho Teräs (7/1), Oleg Bogomoloff (2/0), Erik Beijar (4/1).

127. 03.10.1943 **FINLAND - SWEDEN** **1-1(0-0)**
Olympiastadion, Helsinki; Referee: Bertil Ahlfors (Finland); Attendance: 10,644
FIN: Thure Sarnola (11/0), Veli Leskinen (20/0), Erik Åberg (Cap) (3/0), Veikko Asikainen (15/0), Armas Pyy (14/0), Yrjö Sotiola (6/0), Kaarlo Niilonen (1/0), Anatol Hasso (1/0), Urho Teräs (8/2), Kurt Weckström (35/10), Holger Salin (22/4).
Goal: Urho Teräs (86)

128. 26.08.1945 **SWEDEN – FINLAND** **7-2(2-2)**
Ullevi Stadion, Göteborg; Referee: Reidar Randers Johansen (Norway); Attendance: 18,532
FIN: Thure Sarnola (12/0), Kurt Martin (1/0), Eino Lahti (Cap) (21/0), Veikko Asikainen (16/0), Tauno Koistinen (1/0), Toivo Paananen (1/0), Helge Svahn (1/0), Anton Honka (3/0), Sven Veijola (1/0), Urho Teräs (9/2) [65.Yrjö Sotiola (7/0)], Erik Beijar (5/3). Trainer: Axel Mårtensson (Sweden, 1).
Goals: Erik Beijar (27, 29).

129. 30.09.1945 **FINLAND - SWEDEN** **1-6(1-1)**
Olympiastadion, Helsinki; Referee: Ludwig Jörkow (Denmark); Attendance: 15,981
FIN: Thure Sarnola (13/0), Kurt Martin (2/0), Stig-Göran Myntti (1/0), Veikko Asikainen (Cap) (17/0), Tauno Koistinen (2/0), Eino Lahti (22/0), Anton Honka (4/0), John Sjöberg (1/0) [46.Leo Turunen (3/0)], Yrjö Sotiola (8/1), Kaarlo Niilonen (2/0), Erik Beijar (6/3). Trainer: Axel Mårtensson (Sweden, 2).
Goal: Yrjö Sotiola (25).

130. 28.06.1946 **NORWAY - FINLAND** **12-0(6-0)**
Brann Stadion, Bergen; Referee: Gunnar Dahlner (Sweden); Attendance: 22,000
FIN: Mauno Rintanen (1/0), Kurt Martin (3/0), Stig-Göran Myntti (2/0), Veikko Asikainen (18/0), Erik Åberg (Cap) (4/0), Viljo Heinonen (3/0), Helge Svahn (2/0), Keijo Kihlman (1/0), Börje Herrman (1/0), Yrjö Sotiola (9/1), Erik Beijar (7/3). Trainer: Niilo Tammisalo (1).

131. 01.09.1946 **FINLAND - DENMARK** **2-5(1-1)**
Olympiastadion, Helsinki; Referee: Ivan Eklind (Sweden); Attendance: 17,778
FIN: Olavi Laaksonen (1/0) [78.Thure Sarnola (14/0)], Kurt Martin (4/0), Erik Åberg (Cap) (5/0), Veikko Asikainen (19/0), Tauno Koistinen (3/0), Veikko Forsblom (1/0), Helge Svahn (3/1), Kaarlo Niilonen (3/0), Sven Veijola (2/0) [46.Yrjö Sotiola (10/1)], Asser Salo (1/0), Erik Beijar (8/4). Trainer: Niilo Tammisalo (2).
Goals: Helge Svahn (8), Erik Beijar (90).

132. 15.09.1946 **FINLAND - SWEDEN** **0-7(0-2)**
Olympiastadion, Helsinki; Referee: Reidar Randers-Johansen (Norway); Attendance: 18,521
FIN: Olavi Laaksonen (2/0), Kurt Martin (5/0), Eero Saarnio (1/0), Veikko Asikainen (Cap) (20/0), Tauno Koistinen (4/0), Veikko Forsblom (2/0), Helge Svahn (4/1), Asser Salo (2/0), Leo Turunen (4/0), Urho Teräs (10/2), Erik Beijar (9/4). Trainer: Niilo Tammisalo (3).

133. 26.06.1947 **FINLAND - NORWAY** **1-2(1-1)**
Olympiastadion, Helsinki; Referee: Tore Sjöberg (Sweden); Attendance: 14,806
FIN: Kurt Sand (1/0), Kurt Martin (6/0), Leo Turunen (5/0), Veikko Asikainen (21/0), Tauno Koistinen (5/0), Veikko Forsblom (3/0), Helge Svahn (5/1), Anatol Hasso (2/1), Stig-Göran Myntti (3/0), Erik Åberg (Cap) (6/0), Erik Beijar (10/4). Trainer: Aatos Lehtonen (1).
Goal: Anatol Hasso (29).

134. 24.08.1947 **SWEDEN – FINLAND** **7-0(5-0)** Nordic Championship
Ryavallen, Borås; Referee: A. Rasmussen (Denmark); Attendance: 24,000
FIN: Kurt Sand (2/0), Armas Niemi (1/0), Leo Turunen (6/0), Veikko Asikainen (Cap) (22/0), Tauno Koistinen (6/0) [12.Kalevi Lehtovirta (1/0)], Veikko Forsblom (4/0), Helge Svahn (6/1), Stig-Göran Myntti (4/0), Sven Veijola (3/0) [55.Mauritz Schick (1/0)], Jorma Vaihela (1/0), Erik Beijar (11/4). Trainer: Aatos Lehtonen (2).

135. 07.09.1947 **FINLAND - NORWAY** **3-3(3-2)** Nordic Championship
Olympiastadion, Helsinki; Referee: Valdemar Laursen (Denmark); Attendance: 13,533
FIN: Kurt Sand (3/0), Åke Lindman (1/0), Veikko Forsblom (5/0), Veikko Asikainen (Cap) (23/0), Leo Turunen (7/0), Mauritz Schick (2/0), Harry Reunanen (1/1), Åke Forsman (1/0), Jorma Vaihela (2/0), Stig-Göran Myntti (5/2), Erik Beijar (12/4). Trainer: Aatos Lehtonen (3).
Goals: Herry Reunanen (14), Stig-Göran Myntti (20, 23).

136. 17.09.1947 **FINLAND - POLAND** **1-4(1-1)**
Olympiastadion, Helsinki; Referee: Thorlav Kristiansen (Norway); Attendance: 12,315
FIN: Kurt Sand (4/0), Åke Lindman (2/0), Veikko Forsblom (6/0), Veikko Asikainen (Cap) (24/0), Leo Turunen (8/0), Mauritz Schick (3/0), Åke Pettersson (1/0), Åke Forsman (2/1), Jorma Vaihela (3/0), Stig-Göran Myntti (6/2), Erik Beijar (13/4). Trainer: Aatos Lehtonen (4)
Goal: Åke Forsman (18)

137. 05.10.1947 **DENMARK - FINLAND** **4-1(3-0)** Nordic Championship
Aarhus Stadion, Aarhus; Referee: John Erik Andersson (Sweden); Attendance: 22,500
FIN: Kurt Sand (5/0), Helge Johansson (1/0), Eero Saarnio (2/0) [50.Åke Pettersson (2/0)], John Sjöberg (2/0), Leo Turunen (Cap) (9/0), Mauritz Schick (4/0), Jorma Vaihela (4/0), Åke Forsman (3/1), Stig-Göran Myntti (7/2), Olof Stolpe (1/1), Allan Möller (1/0). Trainer: Aatos Lehtonen (5).
Goal: Olof Stolpe (83).

138. 15.06.1948 **FINLAND - DENMARK** **0-3(0-1)** Nordic Championship
Olympiastadion, Helsinki; Referee: Ivan Eklind (Sweden); Attendance: 29,464
FIN: Olavi Laaksonen (3/0), Kurt Martin (7/0), Stig-Göran Myntti (8/2), Veikko Asikainen (25/0), Leo Turunen (Cap) (10/0), Veikko Forsblom (7/0), Åke Forsman (4/1), Aulis Rytkönen (1/0), Anatol Hasso (3/1), Gunnar Myrttinen (1/0), Kalevi Lehtovirta (2/0). Trainer: Aatos Lehtonen (6).

139. 02.07.1948 **ICELAND - FINLAND** **2-0(0-0)**
Melavöllur, Reykjavík; Referee: John Nilsson (Sweden); Attendance: 8,000
FIN: Olavi Laaksonen (4/0), Kurt Martin (8/0), Stig-Göran Myntti (9/2), Veikko Asikainen (26/0), Leo Turunen (Cap) (11/0), Veikko Forsblom (8/0), Matti Paananen (1/0), Aulis Rytkönen (2/0), Gunnar Myrttinen (2/0), Yrjö Sotiola (11/1), Erik Beijar (14/4). Trainer: Aatos Lehtonen (7).

140. 05.09.1948 **NORWAY - FINLAND** **2-0(1-0)** Nordic Championship
Ullevaal Stadion, Oslo; Referee: Ivan Eklind (Sweden); Attendance: 25,000
FIN: Thure Sarnola (15/0), Kurt Martin (9/0), Stig-Göran Myntti (10/2), Veikko Asikainen (Cap) (27/0), Tapio Pylkkönen (1/0), Mauritz Schick (5/0), Per-Erik Hägg (1/0), Aulis Rytkönen (3/0), Harry Reunanen (2/1), Jorma Vaihela (5/0), Kalevi Lehtovirta (3/0). Trainer: Aatos Lehtonen (8).

141. 19.09.1948 **FINLAND - SWEDEN** **2-2(2-1)** Nordic Championship
Olympiastadion, Helsinki; Referee: Ludwig Jørkow (Denmark); Attendance: 15,407
FIN: Thure Sarnola (16/0), Kurt Martin (10/0), Stig-Göran Myntti (11/2), Veikko Asikainen (Cap) (28/0), Tapio Pylkkönen (2/0), Mauritz Schick (6/0), Per-Erik Hägg (2/0), Aulis Rytkönen (4/1), Harry Reunanen (3/1), Oleg Bogomoloff (3/0), Kalevi Lehtovirta (4/1). Trainer: Aatos Lehtonen (9).
Goals: Kalevi Lehtovirta (41), Aulis Rytkönen (43).

142. 17.10.1948 **POLAND - FINLAND** **1-0(0-0)**
Stadion Wojska Polskiego, Warszawa; Referee: Béla Barna (Hungary); Attendance: 40,000
FIN: Thure Sarnola (17/0), Kurt Martin (11/0), Stig-Göran Myntti (12/2), Veikko Asikainen (Cap) (29/0), Tapio Pylkkönen (3/0), Mauritz Schick (7/0), Helge Svahn (7/1), Aulis Rytkönen (5/1), Jorma Saarinen (1/0), Jorma Vaihela (6/0), Kalevi Lehtovirta (5/1). Trainer: Aatos Lehtonen (10).

143. 15.05.1949 **FINLAND - ENGLAND** **0-4(0-1)**
Olympiastadion, Helsinki; Referee: Ivan Eklind (Sweden); Attendance: 22,116
FIN: Thure Sarnola (18/0), Kurt Martin (12/0), Stig-Göran Myntti (13/2), Veikko Asikainen (Cap) (30/0), Tapio Pylkkönen (4/0), Sven Wentjärv (1/0), Per-Erik Hägg (3/0), Aulis Rytkönen (6/1), Olavi Lilja (1/0), Jorma Vaihela (7/0), Kalevi Lehtovirta (6/1). Trainer: Aatos Lehtonen (11).

144. 16.06.1949 **FINLAND - NETHERLANDS** **1-4(1-0)**
Olympiastadion, Helsinki; Referee: Thøger Nordbø (Norway); Attendance: 7,782
FIN: Thure Sarnola (19/0), Kurt Martin (13/0), Stig-Göran Myntti (14/2), Veikko Asikainen (Cap) (31/0), Tapio Pylkkönen (5/0), Sven Wentjärv (2/0), Olavi Lilja (2/0), Aulis Rytkönen (7/1), Harry Reunanen (4/2), Jorma Vaihela (8/0), Kalevi Lehtovirta (7/1). Trainer: Aatos Lehtonen (12).
Goal: Harry Reunanen (87).

145. 08.07.1949 **FINLAND - NORWAY** **1-1(0-0)** Nordic Championship
Olympiastadion, Helsinki; Referee: Aksel Asmussen (Denmark); Attendance: 11,264
FIN: Olavi Laaksonen (5/0), Kurt Martin (14/0), Eero Saarnio (3/0), Veikko Asikainen (Cap) (32/0), Tapio Pylkkönen (6/0), Erik Beijar (15/4), Aulis Rytkönen (8/1), Stig-Göran Myntti (15/2), Karl Kallio (1/0), Jorma Vaihela (9/1), Kalevi Lehtovirta (8/1). Trainer: Aatos Lehtonen (13).
Goal: Jorma Vaihela (75).

146. 08.09.1949 **REPUBLIC OF IRELAND - FINLAND** **3-0(2-0)** 4th FIFA WC. Qualifiers
Dalymount Park, Dublin; Referee: William H. Evans (England); Attendance: 22,479
FIN: Thure Sarnola (20/0), Kurt Martin (15/0), Eero Saarnio (4/0), Veikko Asikainen (Cap) (33/0), Tapio Pylkkönen (7/0), Erik Beijar (16/4), Helge Svahn (8/1), Stig-Göran Myntti (16/2), Aulis Rytkönen (9/1), Jorma Vaihela (10/1), Kalevi Lehtovirta (9/1). Trainer: Aatos Lehtonen (14).

147. 11.09.1949 **DENMARK - FINLAND** **0-2(0-2)** Nordic Championship
Idrætsparken, København; Referee: Gunnar Dahlner (Sweden); Attendance: 25,700
FIN: Thure Sarnola (21/0), Kurt Martin (16/0), Eero Saarnio (5/0), Veikko Asikainen (Cap) (34/0), Tapio Pylkkönen (8/0), Erik Beijar (17/4), Aulis Rytkönen (10/2), Stig-Göran Myntti (17/2), Yrjö Asikainen (1/1), Jorma Vaihela (11/1), Kalevi Lehtovirta (10/1). Trainer: Aatos Lehtonen (15).
Goals: Yrjö Asikainen (18), Aulis Rytkönen (25).

148. 02.10.1949 **SWEDEN – FINLAND** **8-1(5-1)** 4th FIFA WC. Qualifiers, Nordic Championship
Malmö Stadion, Malmö; Referee: Ludwig Jørkow (Denmark); Attendance: 19,000
FIN: Thure Sarnola (22/0) [46.Olavi Laaksonen (6/0)], Kurt Martin (17/0), Eero Saarnio (6/0), Veikko Asikainen (35/0), Tapio Pylkkönen (9/0), Erik Beijar (18/4), Aulis Rytkönen (11/2), Stig-Göran Myntti (18/2), Yrjö Asikainen (Cap) (2/1), Jorma Vaihela (12/2), Kalevi Lehtovirta (11/1). Trainer: Aatos Lehtonen (16).
Goal: Jorma Vaihela (4).

149. 09.10.1949 **FINLAND – REPUBLIC OF IRELAND** **1-1(0-1)** 4th FIFA WC. Qualifiers
Olympiastadion, Helsinki; Referee: Just Bronkhorst (Netherlands); Attendance: 13,437
FIN: Olavi Laaksonen (7/0), Kurt Martin (18/0), Eero Saarnio (7/0), Veikko Asikainen (Cap) (36/0), Tapio Pylkkönen (10/0), Erik Beijar (19/4), Jorma Vaihela (13/3), Stig-Göran Myntti (19/2), Yrjö Asikainen (3/1), Urho Teräs (11/2), Helge Saarinen (1/0). Trainer: Aatos Lehtonen (17).
Goal: Jorma Vaihela (89).

150. 11.06.1950 **FINLAND - NETHERLANDS** **4-1(3-0)**
Olympiastadion, Helsinki; Referee: Ivan Eklind (Sweden); Attendance: 16,564
FIN: Olavi Laaksonen (8/0), Kurt Martin (19/0), Stig-Göran Myntti (20/3), Veikko Asikainen (Cap) (37/0), Tapio Pylkkönen (11/0), Erik Beijar (20/4), Jorma Vaihela (14/4), Aulis Rytkönen (12/3), Yrjö Asikainen (4/2), Olof Stolpe (2/1), Kalevi Lehtovirta (12/1). Trainer: Aatos Lehtonen (18).
Goals: Stig-Göran Myntti (13 penalty), Yrjö Asikainen (30), Aulis Rytkönen (44), Jorma Vaihela (89).

151. 27.08.1950 **FINLAND - DENMARK** **1-2(0-1)** Nordic Championship
Olympiastadion, Helsinki; Referee: Johan Narvestad (Norway); Attendance: 20,062
FIN: Thure Sarnola (23/0), Åke Lindman (3/0), Stig-Göran Myntti (21/3), Veikko Asikainen (Cap) (38/0), Tapio Pylkkönen (12/0), Erik Beijar (21/4), Jorma Vaihela (15/4), Aulis Rytkönen (13/3), Yrjö Asikainen (5/3), Olavi Lilja (3/0), Kalevi Lehtovirta (13/1). Trainer: Aatos Lehtonen (19).
Goal: Yrjö Asikainen (69).

152. 07.09.1950 **FINLAND - YUGOSLAVIA** **3-2(1-2)**
Olympiastadion, Helsinki; Referee: John Erik Andersson (Sweden); Attendance: 16,297
FIN: Thure Sarnola (24/0), Åke Lindman (4/0), Stig-Göran Myntti (22/3), Veikko Asikainen (Cap) (39/0), Tapio Pylkkönen (13/0), Erik Beijar (22/4), Jorma Vaihela (16/5), Aulis Rytkönen (14/3), Yrjö Asikainen (6/4), Olavi Lilja (4/0), Kalevi Lehtovirta (14/2). Trainer: Aatos Lehtonen (20).
Goals: Jorma Vaihela (29), Yrjö Asikainen (50), Kalevi Lehtovirta (65).

153. 10.09.1950 **NORWAY - FINLAND** **4-1(1-0)** Nordic Championship
Ullevaal Stadion, Oslo; Referee: Ludwig Jørkow (Denmark); Attendance: 25,780
FIN: Thure Sarnola (25/0), Åke Lindman (5/0), Stig-Göran Myntti (23/3), Veikko Asikainen (40/0), Tapio Pylkkönen (14/0), Erik Beijar (23/4), Jorma Vaihela (17/5), Aulis Rytkönen (15/3), Yrjö Asikainen (Cap) (7/4), Olavi Lilja (5/1), Kalevi Lehtovirta (15/2). Trainer: Aatos Lehtonen (21).
Goal: Olavi Lilja (88).

154. 24.09.1950 **FINLAND - SWEDEN** **0-1(0-0)** Nordic Championship
Olympiastadion, Helsinki; Referee: Axel Asmussen (Denmark); Attendance: 25,784
FIN: Olavi Laaksonen (9/0), Åke Lindman (6/0), Stig-Göran Myntti (24/3), Veikko Asikainen (Cap) (41/0), Tapio Pylkkönen (15/0), Erik Beijar (24/4), Jorma Vaihela (18/5), Aulis Rytkönen (16/3), Yrjö Asikainen (8/4), Kalevi Lehtovirta (16/2), Kalle Lahti (1/0). Trainer: Aatos Lehtonen (22).

155. 10.05.1951 **ENGLAND Amateur - FINLAND** **3-2(2-1)**
County Ground, Swindon; Referee: Benjamin Mervyn Griffiths (Wales); Attendance: 14,499
FIN: Olavi Laaksonen (10/0), Kurt Martin (20/0), Stig-Göran Myntti (25/3), Veikko Asikainen (Cap) (42/0), Tapio Pylkkönen (16/0), Erik Beijar (25/4), Kauko Korpela (1/0), Aulis Rytkönen (17/3), Jorma Vaihela (19/6), Kalevi Lehtovirta (17/2), Kalle Lahti (2/1). Trainer: Aatos Lehtonen (23).
Goals: Jorma Vaihela (17), Kalle Lahti (81).

156. 16.08.1951 **FINLAND - NORWAY** **1-1(1-0)** Nordic Championship
Olympiastadion, Helsinki; Referee: John Nilsson (Sweden); Attendance: 22,415
FIN: Olavi Laaksonen (11/0), Kurt Martin (21/0), Stig-Göran Myntti (26/3), Reino Suojanen (1/0), Tapio Pylkkönen (17/0), Erik Beijar (26/4), Jorma Vaihela (20/7), Veikko Asikainen (Cap) (43/0), Aulis Rytkönen (18/3), Kalevi Lehtovirta (18/2), Rainer Forss (1/0). Trainer: Aatos Lehtonen (24).
Goal: Jorma Vaihela (39).

157. 02.09.1951 **SWEDEN – FINLAND** **3-2(1-2)** Nordic Championship
Råsundastadion, Stockholm; Referee: Johan Narvestad (Norway); Attendance: 19,202
FIN: Olavi Laaksonen (12/0), Kurt Martin (22/0), Åke Lindman (7/0), Veikko Asikainen (Cap) (44/0), Tapio Pylkkönen (18/0), Erik Beijar (27/4), Jorma Vaihela (21/8), Aulis Rytkönen (19/3), Stig-Göran Myntti (27/3), Kalevi Lehtovirta (19/3), Olof Stolpe (3/1). Trainer: Aatos Lehtonen (25).
Goals: Jorma Vaihela (10), Kalevi Lehtovirta (18).

158. 30.09.1951 **DENMARK - FINLAND** **1-0(1-0)** Nordic Championship
Idrætsparken, København; Referee: Ivan Eklind (Sweden); Attendance: 31,700
FIN: Olavi Laaksonen (13/0), Kurt Martin (23/0), Åke Lindman (8/0), Veikko Asikainen (Cap) (45/0), Tapio Pylkkönen (19/0), Erik Beijar (28/4), Jorma Vaihela (22/8), Aulis Rytkönen (20/3), Stig-Göran Myntti (28/3), Kalevi Lehtovirta (20/3), Olof Stolpe (4/1). Trainer: Aatos Lehtonen (26).

159. 27.10.1951 **NETHERLANDS - FINLAND** **4-4(2-2)**
Stadion Feijenoord, Rotterdam; Referee: George Mitchell (Scotland); Attendance: 65,000
FIN: Olavi Laaksonen (14/0), Kurt Martin (24/0), Stig-Göran Myntti (29/3), Veikko Asikainen (Cap) (46/0), Tapio Pylkkönen (20/0), Erik Beijar (29/4), Jorma Vaihela (23/9), Aulis Rytkönen (21/4), Seppo Pelkonen (1/0), Kalevi Lehtovirta (21/5), Olof Stolpe (5/1). Trainer: Aatos Lehtonen (27).
Goals: Kalevi Lehtovirta (24, 44), Aulis Rytkönen (57), Jorma Vaihela (69).

160. 04.11.1951 **LUXEMBOURG - FINLAND** **3-0(2-0)**
Stade Municipal, Luxembourg; Referee: Klas Schipper (Netherlands); Attendance: 10,000
FIN: Olavi Laaksonen (15/0), Kurt Martin (25/0), Stig-Göran Myntti (30/3), Veikko Asikainen (Cap) (47/0), Tapio Pylkkönen (21/0), Erik Beijar (30/4), Jorma Vaihela (24/9), Aulis Rytkönen (22/4), Seppo Pelkonen (2/0), Kalevi Lehtovirta (22/5), Olof Stolpe (6/1). Trainer: Aatos Lehtonen (28).

161. 18.11.1951 **HUNGARY - FINLAND** **8-0(4-0)**
Megyeri út, Budapest; Referee: Jaroslav Vlček (Czechoslovakia); Attendance: 45,000
FIN: Olavi Laaksonen (16/0), Kurt Martin (26/0), Stig-Göran Myntti (31/3), Veikko Asikainen (Cap) (48/0), Tapio Pylkkönen (22/0), Erik Beijar (31/4), Jorma Vaihela (25/9), Aulis Rytkönen (23/4), Seppo Pelkonen (3/0), Kalevi Lehtovirta (23/5), Kalle Lahti (3/1). Trainer: Aatos Lehtonen (29).

162. 10.06.1952 **NORWAY - FINLAND** **1-2(1-1)**
Ullevaal Stadion, Oslo; Referee: John Erik Andersson (Sweden); Attendance: 21,732
FIN: Olavi Laaksonen (17/0), Åke Lindman (9/0), Stig-Göran Myntti (32/3), Veikko Asikainen (Cap) (49/0), Esko Valkama (1/0), Erik Beijar (32/4), Rainer Forss (2/0), Aulis Rytkönen (24/4), Nils Rikberg (1/2), Kalevi Lehtovirta (24/5), Seppo Pelkonen (4/0). Trainer: Aatos Lehtonen (30).
Goals: Nils Rikberg (45, 49).

163. 13.06.1952 **FINLAND - SWEDEN** **3-1(0-1,1-1)**
Ullevaal Stadion, Oslo; Referee: Helge Andersen (Denmark); Attendance: 19,766
FIN: Mauno Rintanen (2/0), Åke Lindman (10/0), Stig-Göran Myntti (33/3), Veikko Asikainen (Cap) (50/0), Tapio Pylkkönen (23/0), Erik Beijar (33/4), Jorma Vaihela (26/10), Aulis Rytkönen (25/4), Nils Rikberg (2/4), Kalevi Lehtovirta (25/5), Olof Stolpe (7/1). Trainer: Aatos Lehtonen (31)
Goals: Nils Rikberg (50), Jorma Vaihela (104), Nils Rikberg (120).

164. 22.06.1952 **FINLAND - HUNGARY** **1-6(0-3)**
Olympiastadion, Helsinki; Referee: John Erik Andersson (Sweden); Attendance: 17,634
FIN: Mauno Rintanen (3/0), Åke Lindman (11/0), Stig-Göran Myntti (34/3), Veikko Asikainen (Cap) (51/0), Tapio Pylkkönen (24/0), Erik Beijar (34/4), Jorma Vaihela (27/10), Aulis Rytkönen (26/4), Nils Rikberg (3/4), Kalevi Lehtovirta (26/6), Olof Stolpe (8/1). Trainer: Aatos Lehtonen (32).
Goal: Kalevi Lehtovirta (61).

165. 19.07.1952 **FINLAND – AUSTRIA Olympic** **3-4(3-2)** 14th OG.1st Round.
Olympiastadion, Helsinki; Referee: William Ling (England); Attendance: 33,053
FIN: Olavi Laaksonen (18/0), Åke Lindman (12/0), Stig-Göran Myntti (35/3), Veikko Asikainen (Cap) (52/0), Esko Valkama (2/0), Erik Beijar (35/4), Jorma Vaihela (28/10), Aulis Rytkönen (27/5), Nils Rikberg (4/4), Kalevi Lehtovirta (27/6), Olof Stolpe (9/3). Trainer: Aatos Lehtonen (33).
Goals: Olof Stolpe (18, 34), Aulis Rytkönen (35).

166. 04.08.1952 **FINLAND – CHINA P.R.** **4-0(3-0)**
Töölön Pallokenttä, Helsinki; Referee: Sten Ahlner (Sweden); Attendance: 4,821
FIN: Olavi Laaksonen (19/0), Kurt Martin (27/0), Stig-Göran Myntti (36/3), Veikko Asikainen (Cap) (53/0), Esko Valkama (3/0), Erik Beijar (36/4), Jorma Vaihela (29/12), Aulis Rytkönen (28/5) [60.Nils Rikberg (5/4)], Seppo Pelkonen (5/1), Kalevi Lehtovirta (28/6), Olof Stolpe (10/4). Trainer: Aatos Lehtonen (34).
Goals: Jorma Vaihela (8), Olof Stolpe (10), Seppo Pelkonen (12), Jorma Vaihela (55).

167. 31.08.1952 **NORWAY - FINLAND** **7-2(2-1)** Nordic Championship
Ullevaal Stadion, Oslo; Referee: John Nilsson (Sweden); Attendance: 24,025
FIN: Olavi Laaksonen (20/0), Kurt Martin (28/0), Stig-Göran Myntti (37/3), Veikko Asikainen (Cap) (54/0), Tapio Pylkkönen (25/0), Seppo Pelkonen (6/1), Jorma Vaihela (30/12), Aulis Rytkönen (29/5), Nils Rikberg (6/5), Kalevi Lehtovirta (29/7), Olof Stolpe (11/4). Trainer: Aatos Lehtonen (35).
Goals: Kalevi Lehtovirta (15), Nils Rikberg (80).

168. 21.09.1952 **FINLAND - SWEDEN** **1-8(0-3)** Nordic Championship
Olympiastadion, Helsinki; Referee: Edvin Pedersen (Norway); Attendance: 20,832
FIN: Mauno Rintanen (4/0), Åke Lindman (13/0), Kalevi Lilja (1/0), Veikko Asikainen (Cap) (55/0), Stig-Göran Myntti (38/3), Erik Beijar (37/4), Åke Forsberg (1/0), Aulis Rytkönen (30/5), Nils Rikberg (7/5), Seppo Pelkonen (7/2), Olof Stolpe (12/4) [46.Olli Forsgren (1/0)]. Trainer: Aatos Lehtonen (36).
Goal: Seppo Pelkonen (51).

169. 05.10.1952 **FINLAND - DENMARK** **2-1(1-0)** Nordic Championship
Olympiastadion, Helsinki; Referee: Erik Westman (Sweden); Attendance: 9,022
FIN: Olavi Laaksonen (Cap) (21/0), Gunnar Myrttinen (3/0), Stig-Göran Myntti (39/3), Martti Laitinen (1/0), Lauri Lehtinen (1/0), Aimo Sommarberg (1/0), Olli Forsgren (2/0), Aulis Rytkönen (31/6), Nils Rikberg (8/6), Aulis Vahtonen (1/0), Kalevi Lehtovirta (30/7). Trainer: Aatos Lehtonen (37).
Goals: Nils Rikberg (18), Aulis Rytkönen (71).

170. 25.05.1953 **FINLAND - BELGIUM** **2-4(0-3)** 5th FIFA WC. Qualifiers
Olympiastadion, Helsinki; Referee: Leo Helge (Denmark); Attendance: 22,051
FIN: Matti Jokinen (1/0), Kurt Martin (Cap) (29/0), Stig-Göran Myntti (40/3), Sulo Parkkinen (1/0), Lauri Lehtinen (2/0), Martti Laitinen (2/0), Rainer Forss (3/0), Maati Hiltunen (1/0), Seppo Pelkonen (8/2), Olavi Lahtinen (1/0), Kalevi Lehtovirta (31/9). Trainer: Aatos Lehtonen (38).
Goals: Kalevi Lehtovirta (50, 75).

171. 05.08.1953 **FINLAND - SWEDEN** **3-3(0-2)** 5th FIFA WC. Qualifiers
Olympiastadion, Helsinki; Referee: Folke Bålstad (Norway); Attendance: 13,849
FIN: Aarre Klinga (1/0), Kurt Martin (30/0), Åke Lindman (14/0), Aimo Pulkkinen (1/0), Lauri Lehtinen (3/0), Seppo Pelkonen (9/2), Rainer Forss (4/0), Stig-Göran Myntti (Cap) (41/3), Nils Rikberg (9/7), Olavi Lahtinen (2/1), Kalevi Lehtovirta (32/10). Trainer: Aatos Lehtonen (39).
Goals: Kalevi Lehtovirta (63), Olavi Lahtinen (67), Nils Rikberg (70).

172. 16.08.1953 **SWEDEN - FINLAND** **4-0(2-0)** 5th FIFA WC. Qualifiers, Nordic Championship
Råsundastadion, Stockholm; Referee: Aksel Asmussen (Denmark); Attendance: 27,132
FIN: Aarre Klinga (2/0), Kurt Martin (31/0), Åke Lindman (15/0), Aimo Pulkkinen (2/0), Lauri Lehtinen (4/0), Seppo Pelkonen (10/2), Rainer Forss (5/0), Stig-Göran Myntti (Cap) (42/3), Nils Rikberg (10/7), Olavi Lahtinen (3/1), Kalevi Lehtovirta (33/10). Trainer: Aatos Lehtonen (40).

173. 30.08.1953 **FINLAND - NORWAY** **1-4(1-3)** Nordic Championship
Olympiastadion, Helsinki; Referee: Helge Andersen (Denmark); Attendance: 20,819
FIN: Aarre Klinga (3/0), Kurt Martin (32/0), Stig-Göran Myntti (Cap) (43/3), Aimo Pulkkinen (3/0), Lauri Lehtinen (5/0), Seppo Pelkonen (11/2), Olli Forsgren (3/0), Matti Hiltunen (2/0), Nils Rikberg (11/7), Olavi Lahtinen (4/2), Kalevi Lehtovirta (34/10). Trainer: Aatos Lehtonen (41).
Goal: Olavi Lahtinen (37).

174. 23.09.1953 **BELGIUM - FINLAND** **2-2(1-0)** 5th FIFA WC. Qualifiers
Stade Heysel, Brussel; Referee: René Baumberger (Switzerland); Attendance: 13,804
FIN: Mauno Rintanen (Cap) (5/0), Kurt Martin (33/0), Åke Lindman (16/0), Seppo Pelkonen (12/2), Pekka Kupiainen (1/0), Reino Suojanen (2/0), Jorma Vaihela (31/13), Aulis Rytkönen (32/6), Nils Rikberg (12/7), Olavi Lahtinen (5/3), Kalevi Lehtovirta (35/10). Trainer: Aatos Lehtonen (42).
Goals: Olavi Lahtinen (83), Jorma Vaihela (90).

175. 04.10.1953 **DENMARK - FINLAND** **6-1(4-1)** Nordic Championship
Idrætsparken, København; Referee: Edvin Pedersen (Norway); Attendance: 32,200
FIN: Mauno Rintanen (Cap) (6/0), Kurt Martin (34/0), Åke Lindman (17/0), Aimo Kasurinen (1/0), Pekka Kupiainen (2/0), Reino Suojanen (3/0), Olof Stolpe (13/4), Stig-Göran Myntti (44/3), Seppo Pelkonen (13/2), Olavi Lahtinen (6/3), Jorma Vaihela (32/13). Trainer: Aatos Lehtonen (43).
Goal: Erik Køppen (40 own goal).

176. 25.05.1954 **FINLAND - SCOTLAND** **1-2(0-1)**
Olympiastadion, Helsinki; Referee: Sten Ahlner (Sweden); Attendance: 21,685
FIN: Mauno Rintanen (Cap) (7/0) [48.Aarre Klinga (4/0)], Åke Lindman (18/0), Ibert Henriksson (1/0), Turkka Sundbäck (1/0), Lauri Lehtinen (6/0), Aimo Sommarberg (2/0), Pertti Vanhanen (1/0), Matti Hiltunen (3/0), Rainer Forss (6/0), Olavi Lahtinen (7/4), Börje Nygård (1/0). Trainer: Aatos Lehtonen (44).
Goal: Olavi Lahtinen (85).

177. 04.06.1954 **SWEDEN – FINLAND** **6-0(4-0)** Swedish jubilee
Ullevi Stadion, Göteborg; Referee: Petter Gundersen (Norway); Attendance: 24,809
FIN: Aarre Klinga (5/0), Åke Lindman (19/0), Ibert Henriksson (2/0), Turkka Sundbäck (2/0), Lauri Lehtinen (7/0), Stig-Göran Myntti (Cap) (45/3), Jorma Vaihela (33/13), Hannu Kankkonen (1/0), Rainer Forss (7/0), Matti Hiltunen (4/0), Olli Forsgren (4/0). Trainer: Aatos Lehtonen (45).

178. 13.06.1954 **FINLAND - DENMARK** **2-2(1-0)** Nordic Championship
Olympiastadion, Helsinki; Referee: Erik Westman (Sweden); Attendance: 17,539
FIN: Aarre Klinga (6/0), Kurt Martin (35/0), Ibert Henriksson (3/0), Turkka Sundbäck (3/0), Lauri Lehtinen (8/0), Stig-Göran Myntti (Cap) (46/4), Hannu Kankkonen (2/0), Matti Hiltunen (5/1), Rainer Forss (8/0), Seppo Pelkonen (14/2), Olavi Lahtinen (8/4). Trainer: Aatos Lehtonen (46).
Goals: Stig-Göran Myntti (45), Matti Hiltunen (58).

179. 15.08.1954 **FINLAND - SWEDEN** **1-10(1-6)** Nordic Championship
Olympiastadion, Helsinki; Referee: Øivind Helgesen (Norway); Attendance: 15,049
FIN: Aarre Klinga (7/0), Kurt Martin (36/0), Åke Lindman (20/0), Turkka Sundbäck (4/0), Lauri Lehtinen (9/0), Stig-Göran Myntti (Cap) (47/4), Aarno Niinimäki (1/0), Matti Hiltunen (6/1), Rainer Forss (9/0), Olavi Lahtinen (9/5), Paavo Lyytikäinen (1/0). Trainer: Aatos Lehtonen (47).
Goal: Olavi Lahtinen (40).

180. 29.08.1954 **NORWAY - FINLAND** **3-1(0-1)** Nordic Championship
Ullevaal Stadion, Oslo; Referee: Helge Andersen (Denmark); Attendance: 21,048
FIN: Matti Jokinen (2/0), Pertti Koivisto (1/0), Åke Lindman (21/0), Pertti Vanhanen (2/0), Pekka Kupiainen (3/0), Stig-Göran Myntti (Cap) (48/4), Hannu Kankkonen (3/0), Kai Pahlman (1/0), Matti Hiltunen (7/2), Olavi Lahtinen (10/5), Rainer Forss (10/0). Trainer: Aatos Lehtonen (48).
Goal: Matti Hiltunen (8).

181. 19.05.1955 **FINLAND - HUNGARY** **1-9(0-4)**
Olympiastadion, Helsinki; Referee: John Erik Andersson (Sweden); Attendance: 29,233
FIN: Pentti Tähtinen (1/0), Åke Lindman (22/0), Antti Nieminen (1/0) [46.Pertti Koivisto (2/0)], Seppo Pelkonen (15/2), Pekka Kupiainen (Cap) (4/0), Pertti Vanhanen (3/0), Pentti Mustonen (1/0) [46.Juhani Peltonen (1/0)], Matti Hiltunen (8/3), Martti Järvinen (1/0), Kai Pahlman (2/0), Olavi Lahtinen (11/5). Trainer: Aatos Lehtonen (49).
Goal: Matti Hiltunen (64).

182. 19.06.1955 **DENMARK - FINLAND** **2-1(1-0)** Nordic Championship
Idrætsparken, København; Referee: John Nilsson (Sweden); Attendance: 22,000
FIN: Pentti Tähtinen (2/0), Åke Lindman (23/0), Stig-Göran Myntti (Cap) (49/4), Seppo Pelkonen (16/2), Pekka Kupiainen (5/0), Pertti Vanhanen (4/0), Aarno Niinimäki (2/0), Simo Lehmusvirta (1/1), Pentti Jokela (1/0), Olavi Lahtinen (12/5) [Sulo Parkkinen (2/0)], Juhani Peltonen (2/0). Trainer: Aatos Lehtonen (50).
Goal: Simo Lehmusvirta (59).

183. 14.08.1955 **FINLAND - NORWAY** **1-3(1-1)** Nordic Championship
Olympiastadion, Helsinki; Referee: Ludwig Jørkow (Denmark); Attendance: 16,916
FIN: Pentti Tähtinen (3/0), Åke Lindman (24/0), Stig-Göran Myntti (50/4), Alpo Lintamo (1/0), Pekka Kupiainen (6/0), Pertti Vanhanen (5/0), Rainer Forss (11/0), Olavi Lahtinen (13/5), Matti Hiltunen (9/4), Veikko Asikainen (Cap) (56/0), Juhani Peltonen (3/0). Trainer: Aatos Lehtonen (51).
Goal: Matti Hiltunen (10).

184. 28.08.1955 **SWEDEN – FINLAND** **3-0(1-0)** Nordic Championship
Olympiastadion, Helsingborg; Referee: Josef Larsen (Norway); Attendance: 19,539
FIN: Matti Jokinen (3/0), Åke Lindman (25/0), Stig-Göran Myntti (Cap) (51/4), Alpo Lintamo (2/0), Bjarne Lindgren (1/0), Pertti Vanhanen (6/0), Rainer Forss (12/0), Seppo Pelkonen (17/2), Matti Hiltunen (10/4), Olavi Lahtinen (14/5), Juhani Peltonen (4/0). Trainer: Kurt Weinreich (West Germany, 1).

185. 11.09.1955 **FINLAND - POLAND** **1-3(0-0)**
Olympiastadion, Helsinki; Referee: Sergei Archipov (Soviet Union); Attendance: 12,961
FIN: Matti Jokinen (4/0), Åke Lindman (26/0), Stig-Göran Myntti (Cap) (52/4) [46.Väinö Pajunen (1/0)], Aimo Pulkkinen (4/0), Erik Sjöberg (1/0), Pertti Vanhanen (7/0), Simo Lehmusvirta (2/1), Helles Kontkanen (1/0) [46.Turkka Tamminen (1/0)], Yrjö Asikainen (9/5), Matti Hiltunen (11/4), Juhani Peltonen (5/0). Trainer: Kurt Weinreich (West Germany, 2).
Goal: Yrjö Asikainen (84).

186. 13.11.1955 **YUGOSLAVIA - FINLAND** **8-0(4-0)**
Stadion Igralište, Split, Split; Referee: Yiannis Ioannidis (Cyprus); Attendance: 10,000
FIN: Matti Jokinen (Cap) (5/0), Väinö Pajunen (2/0), Antti Nieminen (2/0), Alpo Lintamo (3/0), Lauri Lehtinen (10/0), Reijo Jalava (1/0), Simo Lehmusvirta (3/1) [46.Matti Salmelainen (1/0)], Olavi Lahtinen (15/5), Matti Hiltunen (12/4) [46.Olli Forsgren (5/0)], Kai Pahlman (3/0), Juhani Peltonen (6/0). Trainer: Kurt Weinreich (West Germany, 3).

187. 20.05.1956 **FINLAND - ENGLAND** **1-5(1-3)**
Olympiastadion, Helsinki; Referee: Carl Frederik Jørgensen (Denmark); Attendance: 20,177
FIN: Keijo Hurri (1/0) [40.Aarre Klinga (8/0)], Väinö Pajunen (3/0), Aimo Sommarberg (3/0), Alpo Lintamo (4/0), Lauri Lehtinen (Cap) (11/0), Reijo Jalava (2/0), Juhani Peltonen (7/0), Matti Hiltunen (13/4), Kai Pahlman (4/0), Olavi Lahtinen (16/5), Olli Forsgren (6/1). Trainer: Kurt Weinreich (West Germany, 4).
Goal: Olli Forsgren (42).

188. 10.06.1956 **FINLAND - SWEDEN** **1-3(1-3)** Nordic Championship
Olympiastadion, Helsinki; Referee: Helge Andersen (Denmark); Attendance: 15,465
FIN: Keijo Hurri (2/0), Raimo Hagström (1/0), Aimo Sommarberg (4/0), Aimo Pulkkinen (5/0), Lauri Lehtinen (Cap) (12/0), Kauko Hakkarainen (1/0), Keijo Voutilainen (1/0), Kai Pahlman (5/0), Olli Forsgren (7/1), Olavi Lahtinen (17/6), Juhani Peltonen (8/0). Trainer: Kurt Weinreich (West Germany, 5).
Goal: Olavi Lahtinen (20).

189. 29.06.1956 **FINLAND - ICELAND** **2-1(1-1)**
Olympiastadion, Helsinki; Referee: Sven Rydberg (Sweden); Attendance: 12,108
FIN: Keijo Hurri (3/0), Raimo Hagström (2/0), Aimo Sommarberg (5/0), Aimo Pulkkinen (6/0), Lauri Lehtinen (Cap) (13/0), Kauko Hakkarainen (2/0), Keijo Voutilainen (2/0), Kai Pahlman (6/0), Olli Forsgren (8/3), Olavi Lahtinen (18/6), Juhani Peltonen (9/0). Trainer: Kurt Weinreich (West Germany, 6).
Goals: Olli Forsgren (40, 73).

190. 26.08.1956 **NORWAY - FINLAND** **1-1(0-1)** Nordic Championship
Ullevaal Stadion, Oslo; Referee: Gösta Lindberg (Sweden); Attendance: 22,000
FIN: Keijo Hurri (4/0), Raimo Hagström (3/0), Aimo Sommarberg (6/0), Alpo Lintamo (5/0), Lauri Lehtinen (Cap) (14/0), Asko Laiho (1/0), Keijo Voutilainen (3/0), Kai Pahlman (7/0), Olli Forsgren (9/4) [31.Pentti Mustonen (2/0)], Olavi Lahtinen (19/6), Åke Pettersson (3/0). Trainer: Kurt Weinreich (West Germany, 7).
Goal: Olli Forsgren (8).

191. 16.09.1956 **FINLAND - DENMARK** **0-4(0-3)** Nordic Championship
Olympiastadion, Helsinki; Referee: Øyvind Helgesen (Norway); Attendance: 14,914
FIN: Keijo Hurri (5/0), Raimo Hagström (4/0) [6.Kalevi Lilja (2/0)], Aimo Sommarberg (7/0), Alpo Lintamo (6/0), Lauri Lehtinen (Cap) (15/0), Kauko Hakkarainen (3/0), Keijo Voutilainen (4/0), Kai Pahlman (8/0), Matti Sundelin (1/0), Olavi Lahtinen (20/6), Olli Forsgren (10/4). Trainer: Kurt Weinreich (West Germany, 8).

192. 04.11.1956 **POLAND - FINLAND** **5-0(2-0)**
Stadion Wisła, Kraków; Referee: Alfred Grill (Austria); Attendance: 40,000
FIN: Matti Kannas (1/0), Ralf Sjöberg (1/0), Aimo Sommarberg (8/0), Alpo Lintamo (7/0), Bjarne Lindgren (2/0) [46.Pentti Styck (1/0)], Reijo Jalava (3/0), Hannu Kankkonen (4/0), Timo Iivarinen (1/0), Kai Pahlman (9/0), Stig-Göran Myntti (Cap) (53/4), Juhani Peltonen (10/0). Trainer: Kurt Weinreich (West Germany, 9).

193. 18.06.1957 **FINLAND - DENMARK** **2-0(2-0)**
Olympiastadion, Helsinki; Referee: Øyvind Helgesen (Norway); Attendance: 11,870
FIN: Matti Kannas (2/0), Alpo Lintamo (8/0), Unto Nevalainen (1/0), Kauko Hakkarainen (4/0), Aimo Sommarberg (9/0), Stig-Göran Myntti (Cap) (54/4), Rainer Forss (13/0), Olavi Lahtinen (21/6), Mauri Vanhanen (1/1), Kai Pahlman (10/1), Juhani Peltonen (11/0). Trainer: Kurt Weinreich (West Germany, 10).
Goals: Kai Pahlman (4), Mauri Vanhanen (44).

194. 19.06.1957 **FINLAND - SWEDEN** **1-5(1-1,1-1)**
Olympiastadion, Helsinki; Referee: Aage Poulsen (Denmark); Attendance: 13,956
FIN: Matti Kannas (3/0), Alpo Lintamo (9/0), Unto Nevalainen (2/0), Kauko Hakkarainen (5/0), Lauri Lehtinen (16/0), Stig-Göran Myntti (Cap) (55/5), Rainer Forss (14/0), Helles Kontkanen (2/0) [Aimo Sommarberg (10/0)], Mauri Vanhanen (2/1), Kai Pahlman (11/1), Juhani Peltonen (12/0). Trainer: Kurt Weinreich (West Germany, 11).
Goal: Stig-Göran Myntti (60 penalty).

195. 05.07.1957 **FINLAND - POLAND** **1-3(0-1)** 6th FIFA WC. Qualifiers
Olympiastadion, Helsinki; Referee: Birger Nielsen (Norway); Attendance: 9,137
FIN: Matti Kannas (4/0), Erkki Harell (1/0), Alpo Lintamo (10/0), Stig-Göran Myntti (Cap) (56/5), Aimo Sommarberg (11/0), Kauko Hakkarainen (6/0), Hannu Kankkonen (5/0), Olavi Lahtinen (22/6), Mauri Vanhanen (3/2), Kai Pahlman (12/1), Juhani Peltonen (13/0). Trainer: Kurt Weinreich (West Germany, 12)
Goal: Mauri Vanhanen (78).

196. 27.07.1957 **SOVIET UNION - FINLAND** **2-1(1-1)** 6th FIFA WC. Qualifiers
Dinamo Stadium, Moskva; Referee: Friedrich Mayer (Austria); Attendance: 60,000
FIN: Matti Kannas (5/0), Erkki Harell (2/0), Alpo Lintamo (11/0), Stig-Göran Myntti (Cap) (57/5), Aimo Sommarberg (12/0), Kauko Hakkarainen (7/0), Pertti Vanhanen (8/0), Unto Nevalainen (3/0), Kai Pahlman (13/1), Olavi Lahtinen (23/7), Juhani Peltonen (14/0). Trainer: Kurt Weinreich (West Germany, 13).
Goal: Olavi Lahtinen (42).

197. 15.08.1957 **FINLAND - SOVIET UNION** **0-10(0-7)** 6th FIFA WC. Qualifiers
Olympiastadion, Helsinki; Referee: Aksel Asmunssen (Denmark); Attendance: 18,154
FIN: Matti Kannas (6/0), Erkki Harell (3/0), Alpo Lintamo (12/0), Stig-Göran Myntti (Cap) (58/5), Aimo Sommarberg (13/0), Kauko Hakkarainen (8/0), Sven-Erik Sundberg (1/0), Hannu Kankkonen (6/0), Kai Pahlman (14/1), Unto Nevalainen (4/0), Juhani Peltonen (15/0). Trainer: Kurt Weinreich (West Germany, 14).

198. 01.09.1957 **FINLAND - NORWAY** **0-4(0-3)** Nordic Championship
Olympiastadion, Helsinki; Referee: Sten Ahlner (Sweden); Attendance: 15,723
FIN: Matti Kannas (7/0), Erkki Harell (4/0), Ralf Sjöberg (2/0) [69.Alpo Lintamo (13/0)], Stig-Göran Myntti (Cap) (59/5), Lauri Lehtinen (17/0), Kauko Hakkarainen (9/0), Kai Pahlman (15/1), Hannu Kankkonen (7/0), Nils Rikberg (13/7), Kalevi Lehtovirta (36/10), Juhani Peltonen (16/0). Trainer: Kurt Weinreich (West Germany, 15).

199. 15.09.1957 **FINLAND – ENGLAND Amateur** **4-3(2-2)**
Olympiastadion, Helsinki; Referee: Nikolai Latyshev (Soviet Union); Attendance: 7,975
FIN: Juhani Ollila (1/0), Erkki Harell (5/0), Matti Haahti (1/0), Stig-Göran Myntti (Cap) (60/5), Alpo Lintamo (14/0), Olli Heinonen (1/0), Juhani Peltonen (17/0), Kai Pahlman (16/1), Matti Sundelin (2/1), Olli Rajala (1/1), Kalevi Lehtovirta (37/12). Trainer: Kurt Weinreich (West Germany, 16).
Goals: Olli Rajala (31), Kalevi Lehtovirta (32, 47), Matti Sundelin (80).

200. 22.09.1957 **SWEDEN – FINLAND** **5-1(1-0)** Nordic Championship
Råsundastadion, Stockholm; Referee: Karl Jørgensen (Denmark); Attendance: 22,192
FIN: Matti Kannas (8/0), Erkki Harell (6/0), Matti Haahti (2/0), Reijo Jalava (4/0), Aimo Sommarberg (14/0), Olli Heinonen (2/0), Juhani Peltonen (18/0), Hannu Kankkonen (8/0), Matti Sundelin (3/2), Kai Pahlman (Cap) (17/1), Kalevi Lehtovirta (38/12). Trainer: Kurt Weinreich (West Germany, 17).
Goal: Matti Sundelin (72).

201. 13.10.1957 **DENMARK - FINLAND** **3-0(0-0)** Nordic Championship
Idrætsparken, København; Referee: Robert Holley Davidson (Scotland); Attendance: 33,200
FIN: Matti Jokinen (6/0), Erkki Harell (7/0), Matti Haahti (3/0), Reijo Jalava (5/0), Aimo Sommarberg (Cap) (15/0), Olli Heinonen (3/0), Juhani Peltonen (19/0), Hannu Kankkonen (9/0), Nils Rikberg (14/7), Olavi Lahtinen (24/7), Kalevi Lehtovirta (39/12). Trainer: Kurt Weinreich (West Germany, 18).

202. 03.11.1957 **POLAND - FINLAND** **4-0(2-0)** 6th FIFA WC. Qualifiers
Stadion Dziesięciolecia, Warszawa; Referee: Albert Dusch (Germany); Attendance: 90,000
FIN: Matti Jokinen (7/0), Erkki Harell (8/0), Aimo Sommarberg (Cap) (16/0), Matti Haahti (4/0), Aimo Pulkkinen (7/0), Olli Heinonen (4/0), Ossi Vilppunen (1/0), Hannu Kankkonen (10/0), Martti Järvinen (2/0), Juhani Peltonen (20/0), Markku Kumpulampi (1/0). Trainer: Kurt Weinreich (West Germany, 19).

203. 15.06.1958 **NORWAY - FINLAND** **2-0(1-0)** Nordic Championship
Ullevaal Stadion, Oslo; Referee: Gottfried Dienst (Switzerland); Attendance: 19,000
FIN: Voitto Vilermo (1/0), Unto Nevalainen (5/0), Matti Haahti (5/0), Turkka Tamminen (2/0), Lauri Lehtinen (Cap) (18/0), Olli Heinonen (5/0), Hannu Kankkonen (11/0), Olavi Lahtinen (25/7), Kai Pahlman (18/1), Kalevi Lehtovirta (40/12), Juhani Peltonen (21/0). Trainer: Kurt Weinreich (West Germany, 20).

204. 20.08.1958 **FINLAND - SWEDEN** **1-7(0-3)** Nordic Championship
Olympiastadion, Helsinki; Referee: Harald Heltberg (Norway); Attendance: 13,418
FIN: Voitto Vilermo (2/0), Unto Nevalainen (6/0), Matti Haahti (6/0), Aimo Pulkkinen (8/0), Lauri Lehtinen (Cap) (19/0), Reijo Jalava (6/0), Juhani Peltonen (22/0), Olavi Lahtinen (26/7), Kai Pahlman (19/1), Olli Heinonen (6/0) [46.Kauko Korpela (2/1)], Kalevi Lehtovirta (41/12). Trainer: Kurt Weinreich (West Germany, 21).
Goal: Kauko Korpela (54).

205. 14.09.1958 **FINLAND - DENMARK** **1-4(0-3)** Nordic Championship
Olympiastadion, Helsinki; Referee: Piotr Belov (Soviet Union); Attendance: 9,272
FIN: Voitto Vilermo (3/0), Matti Haahti (7/0), Alpo Lintamo (15/0), Stig-Göran Myntti (Cap) (61/5), Lauri Lehtinen (20/0), Reijo Jalava (7/0), Matti Hiltunen (14/4), Olavi Lahtinen (27/7), Kai Pahlman (20/2), Teppo Rastio (1/0), Kalevi Lehtovirta (42/12). Trainer: Kurt Weinreich (West Germany, 22)
Goal: Kai Pahlman (82)

206. 11.10.1958 **ENGLAND Amateur - FINLAND** **3-2(0-0)**
Champion Hill Stadium, Dulwich, London; Referee: Peter Fitzsimmons (Scotland); Attendance: 7,500
FIN: Aarre Klinga (9/0), Taisto Ruippo (1/0), Matti Haahti (8/0), Unto Nevalainen (7/0), Ralf Sjöberg (3/0), Kalevi Lehtovirta (Cap) (43/12), Matti Hiltunen (15/4), Lauri Häyhä (1/0), Carl-Magnus Ekman (1/1), Kai Pahlman (21/2), Markku Kumpulampi (2/1). Trainer: Kurt Weinreich (West Germany, 23).
Goals: Carl-Magnus Ekman (65), Markku Kumpulampi (85).

207. 28.06.1959 **FINLAND - NORWAY** **2-4(0-3)** Nordic Championship
Olympiastadion, Helsinki; Referee: Aage Poulsen (Denmark); Attendance: 11,915
FIN: Anders Westerholm (1/0), Reijo Jalava (8/0), Matti Haahti (9/0), Unto Nevalainen (Cap) (8/0), Ralf Sjöberg (4/0) [30.Lauri Lehtinen (21/0)], Kauko Hakkarainen (10/0), Carl-Magnus Ekman (2/1), Hannu Kankkonen (12/2), Keijo Airola (1/0), Mauno Nurmi (1/0), Matti Hiltunen (16/4). Trainer: Aatos Lehtonen (52).
Goals: Hannu Kankkonen (75, 90).

208. 02.08.1959 **SWEDEN – FINLAND** **3-1(2-1)** Nordic Championship
Malmö Stadion, Malmö; Referee: Karl Jørgensen (Denmark); Attendance: 19,555
FIN: Matti Kannas (9/0), Reijo Jalava (9/0), Matti Haahti (10/0), Unto Nevalainen (Cap) (9/1), Lauri Lehtinen (22/0), Stig Holmqvist (1/0), Carl-Magnus Ekman (3/1), Kai Pahlman (22/2), Rolf Rosqvist (1/0), Matti Hiltunen (17/4), Markku Kumpulampi (3/1). Trainer: Aatos Lehtonen (53).
Goal: Unto Nevalainen (13).

209. 06.09.1959 **FINLAND – EAST GERMANY** **3-2(2-2)**
Olympiastadion, Helsinki; Referee: Jarl Hansen (Denmark); Attendance: 7,055
FIN: Anders Westerholm (2/0) [51.Jouni Gröndahl (1/0)], Reijo Jalava (10/0), Matti Haahti (11/0), Unto Nevalainen (Cap) (10/1), Lauri Lehtinen (23/0), Stig Holmqvist (2/0), Markku Kumpulampi (4/1) [46.Carl-Magnus Ekman (4/1)], Matti Hiltunen (18/5), Rolf Rosqvist (2/1), Kai Pahlman (23/3), Keijo Voutilainen (5/0). Trainer: Aatos Lehtonen (54).
Goals: Kai Pahlman (31), Matti Hiltunen (45), Rolf Rosqvist (47).

210. 04.10.1959 **DENMARK - FINLAND** **4-0(2-0)** Nordic Championship
Idrætsparken, København; Referee: Leif Gulliksen (Norway); Attendance: 35,000
FIN: Anders Westerholm (3/0), Reijo Jalava (11/0), Matti Haahti (12/0), Unto Nevalainen (11/1), Lauri Lehtinen (24/0), Stig Holmqvist (3/0), Matti Hiltunen (19/5), Kai Pahlman (24/3), Matti Sundelin (4/2), Hannu Kankkonen (13/2), Kalevi Lehtovirta (Cap) (44/12). Trainer: Aatos Lehtonen (55)

211. 18.10.1959 **FINLAND - POLAND** **1-3(0-1)** 17th OG. Qualifiers
Olympiastadion, Helsinki; Referee: Bertil Wilhelm Lööw (Sweden); Attendance: 10,818
FIN: Aarre Klinga (10/0), Reijo Jalava (12/0), Martti Hyvärinen (1/0), Aulis Järvinen (1/0), Rainer Forss (15/0), Unto Nevalainen (Cap) (12/1), Matti Hiltunen (20/5), Hannu Kankkonen (14/3), Tor Österlund (1/0), Kai Pahlman (25/3), Juhani Peltonen (23/0). Trainer: Aatos Lehtonen (56).
Goal: Hannu Kankkonen (48).

212. 08.11.1959 **POLAND - FINLAND** **6-2(4-2)** 17th OG. Qualifiers
Stadion Śląski, Chorzów; Referee: Werner Bergmann (East Germany); Attendance: 22,000
FIN: Anders Westerholm (4/0), Reijo Jalava (13/0), Matti Haahti (13/0), Unto Nevalainen (Cap) (13/1), Rainer Forss (16/0), Stig Holmqvist (4/0), Carl-Magnus Ekman (5/1), Hannu Kankkonen (15/3), Tor Österlund (2/1), Kai Pahlman (26/3), Juhani Peltonen (24/1). Selection: Aatos Lehtonen (57). Trainer: Aatos Lehtonen (57).
Goals: Tor Österlund (7), Juhani Peltonen (20).

213. 11.11.1959 **WEST GERMANY Olympic - FINLAND** **2-1(1-0)** 17th OG. Qualifiers
Leimbach Stadion, Siegen; Referee: Antonin Vrbovec (Czechoslovakia); Attendance: 25,000
FIN: Jouni Gröndahl (2/0), Reijo Jalava (14/0), Matti Haahti (14/0), Unto Nevalainen (14/1), Lauri Lehtinen (25/0), Rainer Forss (17/0), Hannu Kankkonen (16/4), Kai Pahlman (27/3), Tor Österlund (3/1), Stig Holmqvist (5/0), Juhani Peltonen (25/1). Trainer: Aatos Lehtonen (58).
Goal: Hannu Kankkonen (86).

214. 18.05.1960 **FINLAND – WEST GERMANY Olympic** **3-2(1-1)** 17th OG. Qualifiers
Olympiastadion, Helsinki; Referee: Eric Johansson (Sweden); Attendance: 7,578
FIN: Anders Westerholm (5/0), Reijo Jalava (15/0), Rainer Forss (18/0), Unto Nevalainen (15/2), Lauri Lehtinen (26/0), Holger Strömberg (1/0), Pentti Helin (1/0), Hannu Kankkonen (17/4), Tor Österlund (4/1), Kai Pahlman (28/4), Juhani Peltonen (26/2). Trainer: Aatos Lehtonen (59).
Goals: Kai Pahlman (1), Unto Nevalainen (52), Juhani Peltonen (71).

215. 22.06.1960 **FINLAND - SWEDEN** **0-3(0-1)** Nordic Championship
Olympiastadion, Helsinki; Referee: Kurt Tschenscher (West Germany); Attendance: 16,156
FIN: Urho Örn (1/0), Reijo Jalava (16/0), Martti Hyvärinen (2/0), Holger Strömberg (2/0), Lauri Lehtinen (27/0), Olli Heinonen (7/0), Hannu Kankkonen (18/4), Unto Nevalainen (Cap) (16/2), Tor Österlund (5/1), Kai Pahlman (29/4), Juhani Peltonen (27/2). Trainer: Aatos Lehtonen (60).

216. 10.08.1960 **DENMARK - FINLAND** **2-1(1-1)** Nordic Championship
Idrætsparken, København; Referee: Bengt Lundell (Sweden); Attendance: 40,000
FIN: Urho Örn (2/0), Reijo Jalava (17/0), Matti Haahti (15/0), Unto Nevalainen (Cap) (17/2), Lauri Lehtinen (28/0), Olli Heinonen (8/0), Hannu Kankkonen (19/4), Martti Hyvärinen (3/0), Tor Österlund (6/1), Kai Pahlman (30/4), Juhani Peltonen (28/2). Trainer: Aatos Lehtonen (61).
Goals: Poul Jensen (4 own goal).

217. 28.08.1960 **NORWAY - FINLAND** **6-3(2-1)** Nordic Championship
Ullevaal Stadion, Oslo; Referee: Valdemar Hansen (Denmark); Attendance: 17,703
FIN: Urho Örn (3/0), Reijo Jalava (18/0), Matti Haahti (16/0), Unto Nevalainen (Cap) (18/2), Lauri Lehtinen (29/0), Olli Heinonen (9/0), Hannu Kankkonen (20/6), Aulis Rytkönen (33/6), Keijo Airola (2/0), Kai Pahlman (31/5), Juhani Peltonen (29/2). Trainer: Aatos Lehtonen (62).
Goals: Kai Pahlman (20 penalty), Hannu Kankkonen (52, 59).

218. 25.09.1960 **FINLAND - FRANCE** **1-2(1-0)** 7th FIFA WC. Qualifiers
Olympiastadion, Helsinki; Referee: Johannes Malka (West Germany); Attendance: 15,572
FIN: Carl-Gustaf Nabb (1/0), Reijo Jalava (19/0), Antti Nieminen (3/0), Olli Heinonen (10/0), Veijo Valtonen (1/0), Stig Holmqvist (6/0), Aulis Rytkönen (34/6), Unto Nevalainen (Cap) (19/2), Nils Rikberg (15/7), Kai Pahlman (32/6), Juhani Peltonen (30/2). Trainer: Aatos Lehtonen (63).
Goal: Kai Pahlman (30 penalty).

219. 30.10.1960 **EAST GERMANY - FINLAND** **5-1(3-0)**
Ostseestadion, Rostock; Referee: Tage Sørensen (Denmark); Attendance: 30,000
FIN: Carl-Gustaf Nabb (2/0), Olli Mäkinen (1/0), Reijo Jalava (20/0), Olli Heinonen (11/0), Veijo Valtonen (2/0), Stig Holmqvist (7/0), Martti Hyvärinen (4/0), Aulis Rytkönen (Cap) (35/7), Matti Sundelin (5/2), Kai Pahlman (33/6), Juhani Peltonen (31/2). Trainer: Aatos Lehtonen (64).
Goal: Aulis Rytkönen (86).

220. 16.06.1961 **FINLAND - BULGARIA** **0-2(0-1)** 7th FIFA WC. Qualifiers
Olympiastadion, Helsinki; Referee: Nikolai Latyshev (Soviet Union); Attendance: 11,977
FIN: Anders Westerholm (6/0), Martti Hyvärinen (5/0), Matti Haahti (17/0), Unto Nevalainen (20/2), Olli Heinonen (Cap) (12/0), Stig Holmqvist (8/0), Sauli Pietiläinen (1/0), Hannu Kankkonen (21/6), Semi Nuoranen (1/0), Kai Pahlman (34/6), Juhani Peltonen (32/2). Trainer: Aatos Lehtonen (65).

221. 27.06.1961 **FINLAND - NORWAY** **4-1(3-1)** Nordic Championship
Olympiastadion, Helsinki; Referee: Einar Boström (Sweden); Attendance: 8,712
FIN: Anders Westerholm (7/0), Martti Hyvärinen (6/0), Matti Haahti (18/0) [49.Olli Mäkinen (2/0)], Unto Nevalainen (21/2), Olli Heinonen (Cap) (13/0), Stig Holmqvist (9/1), Sauli Pietiläinen (2/0), Kai Pahlman (35/7), Semi Nuoranen (2/1), Matti Mäkelä (1/1), Juhani Peltonen (33/2). Trainer: Aatos Lehtonen (66).
Goals: Kai Pahlman (19), Matti Mäkelä (30), Stig Holmqvist (41), Semi Nuoranen (57).

222. 09.08.1961 **SWEDEN – FINLAND** **4-0(2-0)** Nordic Championship
Idrottspark, Norrköping; Referee: Jarl Hansen (Denmark); Attendance: 19,868
FIN: Anders Westerholm (8/0), Martti Hyvärinen (7/0), Matti Haahti (19/0), Unto Nevalainen (22/2), Olli Heinonen (Cap) (14/0), Stig Holmqvist (10/1), Sauli Pietiläinen (3/0), Kai Pahlman (36/7), Hannu Kankkonen (22/6), Matti Mäkelä (2/1), Markku Kumpulampi (5/1). Trainer: Aatos Lehtonen (67).

223. 28.09.1961 **FRANCE - FINLAND** **5-1(3-1)** 7th FIFA WC. Qualifiers
Stade Parc des Princes, Paris; Referee: Gottfried Dienst (Switzerland); Attendance: 17,013
FIN: Anders Westerholm (9/0), Martti Hyvärinen (8/0), Matti Haahti (20/0), Unto Nevalainen (23/2), Olli Heinonen (Cap) (15/0), Yrjö Pärnänen (1/0), Sauli Pietiläinen (4/0), Kai Pahlman (37/8), Stig Holmqvist (11/1), Aulis Rytkönen (36/7), Arno Nordlund (1/0). Trainer: Aatos Lehtonen (68).
Goal: Kai Pahlman (44).

224. 15.10.1961 **DENMARK - FINLAND** **9-1(3-0)** Nordic Championship
Idrætsparken, København; Referee: Alfred Haberfellner (Austria); Attendance: 35,600
FIN: Anders Westerholm (10/0), Martti Hyvärinen (9/0), Matti Haahti (21/0), Unto Nevalainen (24/2), Olli Heinonen (Cap) (16/0), Yrjö Pärnänen (2/0), Sauli Pietiläinen (5/0), Hannu Kankkonen (23/6), Tor Österlund (7/2), Kai Pahlman (38/8), Arno Nordlund (2/0). Trainer: Aatos Lehtonen (69).
Goal: Tor Österlund (81).

225. 29.10.1961 **BULGARIA - FINLAND** **3-1(2-1)** 7th FIFA WC. Qualifiers
Nationalen stadion "Vasil Levski", Sofia; Referee: Cezmi Basar (Turkey); Attendance: 45,000
FIN: Carl-Gustaf Nabb (3/0), Reijo Jalava (21/0), Matti Haahti (22/0), Raimo Lukander (1/0), Olli Heinonen (Cap) (17/0), Yrjö Pärnänen (3/0), Sauli Pietiläinen (6/1), Kalevi Nupponen (1/0), Mauno Nurmi (2/0), Semi Nuoranen (3/1), Paavo Lyytikäinen (2/0). Trainer: Aatos Lehtonen (70).
Goal: Sauli Pietiläinen (9).

226. 19.06.1962 **FINLAND - SWEDEN** **0-3(0-1)** Nordic Championship
Olympiastadion, Helsinki; Referee: Erling Rolf Olsen (Norway); Attendance: 17,555
FIN: Markku Talsi (1/0), Esko Kemi (1/0), Matti Haahti (23/0), Pertti Vanhanen (9/0), Pertti Mäkipää (1/0), Olli Heinonen (Cap) (18/0), Markku Kumpulampi (6/1), Juhani Peltonen (34/2), Tor Österlund (8/2), Rauno Ruotsalainen (1/0), Semi Nuoranen (4/1). Trainer: Kaarlo Olavi Laaksonen (1).

227. 26.08.1962 **NORWAY - FINLAND** **2-1(1-1)** Nordic Championship
Brann Stadion, Bergen; Referee: Werner Treichel (West Germany); Attendance: 20,500
FIN: Jouni Gröndahl (3/0) [46.Matti Korhonen (1/0)], Pertti Mäkipää (2/0), Matti Haahti (Cap) (24/0), Pertti Vanhanen (10/0), Ralf Sjöberg (5/0), Stig Holmqvist (12/1), Markku Kumpulampi (7/1), Mauno Nurmi (3/0), Rauli Virtanen (1/0) [60.Keijo Voutilainen (6/0)], Juhani Peltonen (35/2), Matti Mäkelä (3/2). Trainer: Kaarlo Olavi Laaksonen (2).
Goal: Matti Mäkelä (18).

228. 16.09.1962 **FINLAND - DENMARK** **1-6(1-4)** Nordic Championship
Olympiastadion, Helsinki; Referee: Sergei Alimov (Soviet Union); Attendance: 9,276
FIN: Matti Korhonen (2/0), Pertti Mäkipää (3/0), Matti Haahti (25/0), Pertti Vanhanen (Cap) (11/0), Ralf Sjöberg (6/0), Olli Rajala (2/1), Markku Kumpulampi (8/1), Matti Mäkelä (4/2), Rauli Virtanen (2/1), Juhani Peltonen (36/2), Kai Pahlman (39/8). Trainer: Kaarlo Olavi Laaksonen (3).
Goal: Rauli Virtanen (13).

229. 03.06.1963 **DENMARK - FINLAND** **1-1(0-1)** Nordic Championship
Idrætsparken, København; Referee: Birger Nielsen (Norway); Attendance: 21,600
FIN: Jouni Gröndahl (4/0), Olli Mäkinen (3/0), Esko Kemi (2/0), Pertti Vanhanen (12/0), Ralf Sjöberg (7/0), Olli Heinonen (19/0), Olli Rajala (3/1), Rauno Ruotsalainen (2/0) [Matti Hiltunen (21/5)], Mauno Nurmi (4/0), Kai Pahlman (Cap) (40/9), Juhani Peltonen (37/2). Trainer: Kaarlo Olavi Laaksonen (4).
Goal: Kai Pahlman (62).

230. 27.06.1963 **FINLAND - NORWAY** **2-0(0-0)** Nordic Championship
Olympiastadion, Helsinki; Referee: Bramming Sørensen (Denmark); Attendance: 11,603
FIN: Jouni Gröndahl (5/0), Olli Mäkinen (4/0), Esko Kemi (3/0), Pertti Vanhanen (13/0), Ralf Sjöberg (8/0), Olli Heinonen (Cap) (20/0), Mauri Paavilainen (1/0), Stig Holmqvist (13/1), Juha Lyytikäinen (1/1), Kai Pahlman (41/10), Matti Mäkelä (5/2). Trainer: Kaarlo Olavi Laaksonen (5).
Goals: Kai Pahlman (53 penalty), Juha Lyytikäinen (68).

231. 22.07.1963 **SOVIET UNION - FINLAND** **7-0(4-0)** 18th OG. Qualifiers
Centralniy Stadium, Kyiv; Referee: Milan Fencl (Czechoslovakia); Attendance: 48,000
FIN: Jouni Gröndahl (6/0), Olli Mäkinen (5/0), Esko Kemi (4/0), Pertti Vanhanen (Cap) (14/0), Thor-Björn Lundqvist (1/0), Esko Heltola (1/0), Aulis Laine (1/0), Rauno Ruotsalainen (3/0), Pertti Utriainen (1/0), Esko Malm (1/0), Matti Mäkelä (6/2). Trainer: Kaarlo Olavi Laaksonen (6).

232. 01.08.1963 **FINLAND - SOVIET UNION** **0-4(0-2)** 18th OG. Qualifiers
Olympiastadion, Helsinki; Referee: Bertil Wilhelm Lööw (Sweden); Attendance: 6,485
FIN: Jouni Gröndahl (7/0), Raimo Elo (1/0), Esko Kemi (5/0), Pertti Vanhanen (Cap) (15/0), Thor-Björn Lundqvist (2/0), Ralf Sjöberg (9/0), Matti Mäkelä (7/2), Rauno Ruotsalainen (4/0), Pertti Utriainen (2/0), Esko Heltola (2/0), Timo Rantala (1/0). Trainer: Kaarlo Olavi Laaksonen (7).

233. 14.08.1963 **SWEDEN – FINLAND** **0-0** Nordic Championship
Råsundastadion, Stockholm; Referee: Hannes Sigurdson (Iceland); Attendance: 7,778
FIN: Jouni Gröndahl (8/0), Raimo Elo (2/0), Esko Kemi (6/0), Pertti Vanhanen (16/0), Thor-Björn Lundqvist (3/0), Ralf Sjöberg (10/0), Rauno Ruotsalainen (5/0), Kalevi Nupponen (2/0), Hannu Kankkonen (24/6), Olli Heinonen (Cap) (21/0), Juhani Peltonen (38/2). Trainer: Kaarlo Olavi Laaksonen (8).

234. 07.06.1964 **FINLAND – WEST GERMANY** **1-4(1-3)**
Olympiastadion, Helsinki; Referee: Curt Liedberg (Sweden); Attendance: 11,056
FIN: Jouni Gröndahl (9/0), Pertti Mäkipää (4/0), Reijo Kanerva (1/0), Simo Syrjävaara (1/0), Stig Holmqvist (14/1), Olli Heinonen (Cap) (22/0), Matti Mäkelä (8/2) [Martti Hyvärinen (10/0)], Aulis Rytkönen (37/7), Hannu Kankkonen (25/6), Rauno Ruotsalainen (6/0), Juhani Peltonen (39/3). Trainer: Kaarlo Olavi Laaksonen (9).
Goal: Juhani Peltonen (24).

235. 02.08.1964 **FINLAND - SWEDEN** **1-0(0-0)** Nordic Championship
Olympiastadion, Helsinki; Referee: Helmut Köhler (East Germany); Attendance: 15,551
FIN: Martti Halme (1/0), Pertti Mäkipää (5/0), Timo Kautonen (1/0), Simo Syrjävaara (2/0), Aarno Rinne (1/0), Olli Heinonen (Cap) (23/0) [46.Kaj Österberg (1/0)], Semi Nuoranen (5/1), Juhani Peltonen (40/3), Arto Tolsa (1/0), Stig Holmqvist (15/1), Harri Järvi (1/1). Trainer: Kaarlo Olavi Laaksonen (10).
Goal: Harri Järvi (59).

236. 20.08.1964 **NORWAY - FINLAND** **2-0(2-0)** Nordic Championship
Lerkendal Stadion, Trondheim; Referee: Einar Poulsen (Denmark); Attendance: 17,056
FIN: Martti Halme (2/0), Pertti Mäkipää (6/0), Timo Kautonen (2/0), Simo Syrjävaara (3/0), Aarno Rinne (2/0), Olli Heinonen (Cap) (24/0), Semi Nuoranen (6/1), Juhani Peltonen (41/3), Arto Tolsa (2/0), Stig Holmqvist (16/1), Harri Järvi (2/1). Trainer: Kaarlo Olavi Laaksonen (11).

237. 23.08.1964 **ICELAND - FINLAND** **0-2(0-1)**
Laugardalsvöllur, Reykjavík; Referee: P. J. Graham (Republic of Ireland); Attendance: 6,000
FIN: Martti Halme (3/0), Timo Kautonen (3/0), Reima Nummila (1/0), Stig Holmqvist (17/1), Aarno Rinne (3/0), Olli Heinonen (Cap) (25/0), Semi Nuoranen (7/1), Juhani Peltonen (42/3), Harri Järvi (3/2), Kaj Österberg (2/0), Rauno Kestilä (1/1). Trainer: Kaarlo Olavi Laaksonen (12).
Goals: Harri Järvi (34), Rauno Kestilä (75).

238. 06.09.1964 **FINLAND - DENMARK** **2-1(1-0)** Nordic Championship
Olympiastadion, Helsinki; Referee: Bertil Wilhelm Lööw (Sweden); Attendance: 16,319
FIN: Martti Halme (4/0), Pertti Mäkipää (7/0), Timo Kautonen (4/0), Stig Holmqvist (18/1), Aarno Rinne (4/0), Olli Heinonen (Cap) (26/0), Semi Nuoranen (8/1), Juhani Peltonen (43/4), Arto Tolsa (3/0) [30.Martti Hyvärinen (11/0)], Kaj Österberg (3/0), Harri Järvi (4/3). Trainer: Kaarlo Olavi Laaksonen (13).
Goals: Harri Järvi (24), Juhani Peltonen (76).

239. 21.10.1964 **SCOTLAND - FINLAND** **3-1(3-0)** 8th FIFA WC. Qualifiers
Hampden Park, Glasgow; Referee: Joseph Hannet (Belgium); Attendance: 54,442
FIN: Martti Halme (5/0), Pertti Mäkipää (8/0), Tirno Kautonen (5/0), Stig Holmqvist (Cap) (19/1), Aarno Rinne (5/0), Veijo Valtonen (3/0), Harri Järvi (5/3), Juhani Peltonen (44/5), Arto Tolsa (4/0), Simo Syrjävaara (4/0), Martti Hyvärinen (12/0). Trainer: Kaarlo Olavi Laaksonen (14).
Goal: Juhani Peltonen (70).

240. 04.11.1964 **ITALY - FINLAND** **6-1(3-0)** 8th FIFA WC. Qualifiers
Stadio "Luigi Ferraris", Genova; Referee: Manuel Lousada Rodrigues (Portugal); Attendance: 22,778
FIN: Martti Halme (6/0), Pertti Mäkipää (9/0), Timo Kautonen (6/0), Stig Holmqvist (20/1), Aarno Rinne (6/0), Veijo Valtonen (4/0), Markku Lahti (1/0), Juhani Peltonen (45/6), Kaj Österberg (4/0), Simo Syrjävaara (5/0), Martti Hyvärinen (13/0). Trainer: Kaarlo Olavi Laaksonen (15).
Goal: Juhani Peltonen (88).

241. 27.05.1965 **FINLAND - SCOTLAND** **1-2(1-1)** 8th FIFA WC. Qualifiers
Olympiastadion, Helsinki; Referee: Erwin Vetter (East Germany); Attendance: 20,162
FIN: Lars Näsman (1/0), Pertti Mäkipää (10/0), Timo Kautonen (7/0), Stig Holmqvist (21/1), Aarno Rinne (7/0), Olli Heinonen (Cap) (27/0), Markku Kumpulampi (9/1), Juhani Peltonen (46/6), Martti Hyvärinen (14/1), Rauno Ruotsalainen (7/0), Semi Nuoranen (9/1). Trainer: Kaarlo Olavi Laaksonen (16).
Goal: Martti Hyvärinen (5).

242. 09.06.1965 **DENMARK - FINLAND** **3-1(0-1)** Nordic Championship
Idrætsparken, København; Referee: Gerhard Schulenburg (West Germany); Attendance: 33,400
FIN: Lars Näsman (2/0), Pertti Mäkipää (11/0), Timo Kautonen (8/0), Kalervo Paananen (1/0), Aarno Rinne (8/0), Olli Heinonen (Cap) (28/0), Markku Kumpulampi (10/1), Rauno Ruotsalainen (8/0), Arto Tolsa (5/1), Martti Hyvärinen (15/1), Semi Nuoranen (10/1). Trainer: Kaarlo Olavi Laaksonen (17).
Goal: Arto Tolsa (7).

243. 23.06.1965 **FINLAND - ITALY** **0-2(0-1)** 8th FIFA WC. Qualifiers
Olympiastadion, Helsinki; Referee: Tofik Bakhramov (Soviet Union); Attendance: 19,995
FIN: Lars Näsman (3/0), Pertti Mäkipää (12/0), Reima Nummila (2/0), Timo Kautonen (9/0), Reijo Kanerva (2/0), Olli Heinonen (Cap) (29/0), Markku Kumpulampi (11/1), Juhani Peltonen (47/6), Arto Tolsa (6/1), Kai Pahlman (42/10), Semi Nuoranen (11/1). Trainer: Kaarlo Olavi Laaksonen (18).

244. 08.08.1965 **FINLAND - NORWAY** **4-0(1-0)** Nordic Championship
Olympiastadion, Helsinki; Referee: Einar Boström (Sweden); Attendance: 16,525
FIN: Lars Näsman (4/0), Pertti Mäkipää (13/0), Reima Nummila (3/0), Timo Kautonen (10/0), Reijo Kanerva (3/0), Simo Syrjävaara (6/0), Markku Kumpulampi (12/2), Matti Mäkelä (9/2), Asko Mäkilä (1/1), Kai Pahlman (Cap) (43/11), Tommy Lindholm (1/1). Trainer: Kaarlo Olavi Laaksonen (19).
Goals: Kai Pahlman, Asko Mäkilä, Markku Kumpulampi, Tommy Lindholm.

245. 22.08.1965 **SWEDEN – FINLAND** **2-2(1-1)** Nordic Championship
Skogsvallen, Lulea; Referee: Carl V. Hansen (Denmark); Attendance: 13,970
FIN: Lars Näsman (5/0), Pertti Mäkipää (14/0), Reima Nummila (4/0), Timo Kautonen (11/0), Reijo Kanerva (4/0), Simo Syrjävaara (7/0), Markku Kumpulampi (13/2), Matti Mäkelä (10/2), Asko Mäkilä (2/2), Kai Pahlman (Cap) (44/12), Tommy Lindholm (2/1). Trainer: Kaarlo Olavi Laaksonen (20).
Goals: Kai Pahlman (35), Asko Mäkilä (56).

246. 26.09.1965 **FINLAND - POLAND** **2-0(2-0)** 8th FIFA WC. Qualifiers
Olympiastadion, Helsinki; Referee: Hans Granlund (Norway); Attendance: 7,859
FIN: Lars Näsman (6/0), Pertti Mäkipää (15/0), Reima Nummila (5/0), Timo Kautonen (12/0), Reijo Kanerva (5/0), Juhani Peltonen (48/7), Semi Nuoranen (12/2), Matti Mäkelä (11/2), Asko Mäkilä (3/2), Kai Pahlman (Cap) (45/12), Tommy Lindholm (3/1). Trainer: Kaarlo Olavi Laaksonen (21).
Goals: Juhani Peltonen (1), Semi Nuoranen (27).

247. 24.10.1965 **POLAND - FINLAND** **7-0(6-0)** 8th FIFA WC. Qualifiers
Stadion Pogoń, Szczecin; Referee: Alois Obtulovič (Czechoslovakia); Attendance: 31,000
FIN: Lars Näsman (7/0), Pertti Mäkipää (16/0), Reima Nummila (6/0), Timo Kautonen (13/0), Reijo Kanerva (6/0), Simo Syrjävaara (8/0), Markku Kumpulampi (14/2), Markku Lahti (2/0), Arvo Lamberg (1/0), Kai Pahlman (46/12), Tommy Lindholm (4/1). Trainer: Kaarlo Olavi Laaksonen (22).

248. 27.10.1965 **WEST GERMANY Amateur - FINLAND** **6-2(4-2)**
Stadion an der Berliner Strasse, Wiesbaden; Referee: Norman Mootz (Luxembourg); Attendance: 7,000
FIN: Lars Näsman (8/0) [46.Martti Halme (7/0)], Pertti Mäkipää (17/0), Reima Nummila (7/0), Timo Kautonen (14/0), Reijo Kanerva (7/0), Simo Syrjävaara (9/0), Markku Kumpulampi (15/2), Matti Mäkelä (12/2), Asko Mäkilä (4/3) [46.Arvo Lamberg (2/0)], Kai Pahlman (Cap) (47/13), Tommy Lindholm (5/1). Trainer: Kaarlo Olavi Laaksonen (23).
Goals: Asko Mäkilä (4), Kai Pahlman (10 penalty).

249. 08.05.1966 **FINLAND - ISRAEL** **0-3(0-0)**
Olympiastadion, Helsinki; Referee: Arvo Jokinen (Finland); Attendance: 14,788
FIN: Martti Halme (8/0), Pertti Mäkipää (18/0), Reima Nummila (8/0), Timo Kautonen (15/0), Reijo Kanerva (8/0), Juhani Peltonen (49/7) [30.Raimo Kauppinen (1/0)], Semi Nuoranen (13/2), Matti Mäkelä (13/2), Asko Mäkilä (5/3) [10.Mauri Paavilainen (2/0)], Mauri Tuuri (1/0), Kai Pahlman (Cap) (48/13). Trainer: Kaarlo Olavi Laaksonen (24).

250. 04.06.1966 **FINLAND - SWEDEN** **1-0(1-0)** Nordic Championship
Olympiastadion, Helsinki; Referee: Birger Nielsen (Norway); Attendance: 29,622
FIN: Martti Halme (9/0), Pertti Mäkipää (19/0), Reima Nummila (9/0), Timo Kautonen (16/0), Reijo Kanerva (9/0), Simo Syrjävaara (10/0), Markku Kumpulampi (16/2), Matti Mäkelä (14/2), Tommy Lindholm (6/2), Kai Pahlman (Cap) (49/13) [15.Mauno Nurmi (5/0)], Aulis Laine (2/0). Trainer: Kaarlo Olavi Laaksonen (25).
Goal: Tommy Lindholm (20).

251. 26.06.1966 **FINLAND - ENGLAND** **0-3(0-2)**
Olympiastadion, Helsinki; Referee: Frede Hansen (Denmark); Attendance: 12,899
FIN: Martti Halme (10/0), Pertti Mäkipää (20/0), Rainer Aho (1/0), Timo Kautonen (17/0), Reijo Kanerva (10/0), Seppo Kilponen (1/0), Markku Kumpulampi (17/2), Matti Mäkelä (Cap) (15/2), Markku Hyvärinen (1/0), Aulis Laine (3/0), Antero Hyttinen (1/0). Trainer: Kaarlo Olavi Laaksonen (26).

252. 14.08.1966 **NORWAY - FINLAND** **1-1(1-0)** Nordic Championship
Stavanger Stadion, Stavanger; Referee: Gerhard Schulenburg (West Germany); Attendance: 11,500
FIN: Lars Näsman (9/0), Pertti Mäkipää (21/0), Reima Nummila (10/0), Timo Kautonen (18/0), Reijo Kanerva (11/0), Simo Syrjävaara (11/0), Markku Kumpulampi (18/2), Matti Mäkelä (16/2), Tommy Lindholm (7/3), Kai Pahlman (Cap) (50/13), Aulis Laine (4/0). Trainer: Kaarlo Olavi Laaksonen (27).
Goal: Tommy Lindholm (68).

253. 18.09.1966 **FINLAND - DENMARK** **2-1(1-1)** Nordic Championship
Olympiastadion, Helsinki; Referee: Kurt Tschenscher (West Germany); Attendance: 19,222
FIN: Lars Näsman (10/0), Pertti Mäkipää (22/1), Reima Nummila (11/0) [Rainer Aho (2/0)], Timo Kautonen (19/0), Reijo Kanerva (12/0), Simo Syrjävaara (12/0), Juhani Peltonen (50/7), Matti Mäkelä (17/2), Tommy Lindholm (8/3), Kai Pahlman (Cap) (51/13), Aulis Laine (5/1). Trainer: Kaarlo Olavi Laaksonen (28).
Goals: Pertti Mäkipää (37), Aulis Laine (62).

254. 02.10.1966 **FINLAND - AUSTRIA** **0-0** 3rd EC. Qualifiers
Olympiastadion, Helsinki; Referee: Peter Coates (Republic of Ireland); Attendance: 10,700
FIN: Lars Näsman (11/0), Pertti Mäkipää (23/1), Reima Nummila (12/0), Timo Kautonen (20/0), Reijo Kanerva (13/0), Simo Syrjävaara (13/0), Juhani Peltonen (51/7), Matti Mäkelä (Cap) (18/2), Tommy Lindholm (9/3), Markku Hyvärinen (2/0), Aulis Laine (6/1). Trainer: Kaarlo Olavi Laaksonen (29).

255. 16.10.1966 **GREECE - FINLAND** **2-1(1-0)** 3rd EC. Qualifiers
Stádio Kautatzógleio, Thessaloníki; Referee: Zdeněk Valeš (Czechoslovakia); Attendance: 30,000
FIN: Lars Näsman (12/0), Pertti Mäkipää (24/2), Reima Nummila (13/0), Timo Kautonen (21/0), Reijo Kanerva (14/0), Simo Syrjävaara (14/0), Juhani Peltonen (52/7), Matti Mäkelä (Cap) (19/2), Arto Tolsa (7/1), Markku Hyvärinen (3/0), Aulis Laine (7/1). Trainer: Kaarlo Olavi Laaksonen (30).
Goal: Pertti Mäkipää (57).

256. 10.05.1967 **FINLAND - GREECE** **1-1(1-1)** 3rd EC. Qualifiers
Olympiastadion, Helsinki; Referee: Pieter Paulus Roomer (Netherlands); Attendance: 14,056
FIN: Martti Halme (11/0), Rainer Aho (3/0), Timo Kautonen (22/0), Reijo Kanerva (15/0), Reima Nummila (14/0), Matti Mäkelä (Cap) (20/2), Pertti Mäkipää (25/2), Semi Nuoranen (14/2), Arto Tolsa (8/1), Tommy Lindholm (10/3), Juhani Peltonen (53/8). Trainer: Kaarlo Olavi Laaksonen (31).
Goal: Juhani Peltonen (18).

257. 24.05.1967 **FINLAND – NETHERLANDS Olympic** **0-0** 19th OG. Qualifiers
Olympiastadion, Helsinki; Referee: Anvar Zverev (Soviet Union); Attendance: 19,181
FIN: Martti Halme (12/0), Pertti Mäkipää (26/2), Timo Kautonen (23/0), Reijo Kanerva (16/0), Pentti Kokko (1/0), Matti Mäkelä (Cap) (21/2), Aulis Laine (8/1), Semi Nuoranen (15/2), Markku Hyvärinen (4/0), Tommy Lindholm (11/3), Kai Pahlman (52/13). Trainer: Kaarlo Olavi Laaksonen (32).

258. 01.06.1967 **FINLAND - NORWAY** **0-2(0-1)** Nordic Championship
Olympiastadion, Helsinki; Referee: Arnth Jensen (Denmark); Attendance: 6,672
FIN: Martti Halme (13/0), Pertti Mäkipää (27/2) [86.Seppo Kilponen (2/0)], Timo Kautonen (24/0), Reijo Kanerva (17/0), Rainer Aho (4/0), Markku Hyvärinen (5/0), Martti Hyvärinen (16/1), Juhani Peltonen (54/8), Tommy Lindholm (12/3), Kai Pahlman (Cap) (53/13), Aulis Laine (9/1). Trainer: Kaarlo Olavi Laaksonen (33).

259. 14.06.1967 **NETHERLANDS Olympic - FINLAND** **0-1(0-0)** 19th OG. Qualifiers
Stadion Nieuw Monnikenhuize, Arnhem; Referee: Hubert Burguet (Belgium); Attendance: 5,000
FIN: Lars Näsman (13/0), Pertti Mäkipää (Cap) (28/2), Seppo Kilponen (3/0), Timo Kautonen (25/0), Rainer Aho (5/0), Markku Hyvärinen (6/0), Simo Syrjävaara (15/0), Markku Kumpulampi (19/2), Tommy Lindholm (13/3), Martti Hyvärinen (17/1) [46.Semi Nuoranen (16/2)], Aulis Laine (10/2). Trainer: Kaarlo Olavi Laaksonen (34).
Goal: Aulis Laine (61).

20.06.1967 **SCANDINAVIA - SOVIET UNION** **2-2(1-1)**
Olympiastadion, Helsinki; Referee: Magnus Petursson (Iceland); Attendance: 16,254
SCANDINAVIA: Lars Näsman (14/0), Pertti Mäkipää (29/2) [46.Reima Nummila (15/0)], Timo Kautonen (26/0), Nils Arne Eggen (Norway), Hans Selander (Sweden), Juhani Peltonen (55/8), Olav Nielsen (Norway) [65.Simo Syrjävaara (16/0)], Bengt Schmidt-Hansen (Denmark), Finn Laudrup (Denmark), Inge Danielsson (Sweden), Tommy Lindholm (14/4).
Goals: Tommy Lindholm (40), Olav Nielsen (48).
The Finnish players received a cap!

260. 10.08.1967 **SWEDEN – FINLAND** **2-0(1-0)** Nordic Championship
Råsundastadion, Stockholm; Referee: Stanislaw Eksztajn (Poland); Attendance: 11,000
FIN: Lars Näsman (15/0), Pertti Mäkipää (Cap) (30/2), Timo Nummelin (1/0), Timo Kautonen (27/0), Reima Nummila (16/0), Juhani Peltonen (56/8), Simo Syrjävaara (17/0), Kai Pahlman (54/13), Tommy Lindholm (15/4), Arto Tolsa (9/1), Aulis Laine (11/2). Trainer: Kaarlo Olavi Laaksonen (35).

261. 30.08.1967 **SOVIET UNION - FINLAND** **2-0(1-0)** 3rd EC. Qualifiers
Lenin Stadium, Moskva; Referee: Muzaffer Sarvan (Turkey); Attendance: 80,000
FIN: Lars Näsman (16/0), Pertti Mäkipää (Cap) (31/2), Seppo Kilponen (4/0), Timo Kautonen (28/0), Reima Nummila (17/0), Juhani Peltonen (57/8), Simo Syrjävaara (18/0), Kai Pahlman (55/13), Matti Mäkelä (22/2), Arto Tolsa (10/1), Aulis Laine (12/2). Trainer: Kaarlo Olavi Laaksonen (36).

262. 06.09.1967 **FINLAND - SOVIET UNION** **2-5(2-3)** 3rd EC. Qualifiers
Kupittaan Jalkapallostadion, Turku; Referee: Pavel Spotak (Czechoslovakia); Attendance: 7,793
FIN: Lars Näsman (17/0), Matti Pitko (1/0), Seppo Kilponen (5/0), Pertti Mäkipää (Cap) (32/2), Reima Nummila (18/0), Matti Mäkelä (23/2), Simo Syrjävaara (19/1), Aulis Laine (13/2), Arto Tolsa (11/1), Juhani Peltonen (58/9), Semi Nuoranen (17/2). Trainer: Kaarlo Olavi Laaksonen (37).
Goals: Juhani Peltonen (18 penalty), Simo Syrjävaara (25).

263. 24.09.1967 **AUSTRIA - FINLAND** **2-1(1-0)** 3rd EC. Qualifiers
Praterstadion, Wien; Referee: Milivoje Gugulović (Yugoslavia); Attendance: 28,000
FIN: Lars Näsman (18/0), Matti Pitko (2/0), Seppo Kilponen (6/0), Timo Kautonen (29/0) [*sent off 80*], Reima Nummila (19/0), Matti Mäkelä (24/2), Simo Syrjävaara (20/1), Semi Nuoranen (18/2), Tommy Lindholm (16/4), Arto Tolsa (12/1), Juhani Peltonen (59/10). Trainer: Kaarlo Olavi Laaksonen (38).
Goal: Juhani Peltonen (57).

264. 15.10.1967 **FINLAND – FRANCE Olympic** **1-1(1-1)** 19th OG. Qualifiers
Olympiastadion, Helsinki; Referee: Alexandru Pîrvu (Romania); Attendance: 7,691
FIN: Lars Näsman (19/0), Pertti Mäkipää (Cap) (33/2), Seppo Kilponen (7/0), Timo Kautonen (30/0), Reima Nummila (20/0), Urho Partanen (1/0), Simo Syrjävaara (21/1), Arto Tolsa (13/2), Tommy Lindholm (17/4), Markku Hyvärinen (7/0), Aulis Laine (14/2). Trainer: Kaarlo Olavi Laaksonen (39).
Goal: Arto Tolsa (22).

265. 22.10.1967 **DENMARK - FINLAND** **3-0(1-0)** Nordic Championship
Idrætsparken, København; Referee: Ivar Hornslien (Norway); Attendance: 35,000
FIN: Lars Näsman (20/0), Pertti Mäkipää (Cap) (34/2), Seppo Kilponen (8/0), Timo Kautonen (31/0), Reima Nummila (21/0), Matti Mäkelä (25/2) [*sent off 68*], Urho Partanen (2/0), Juhani Peltonen (60/10), Tommy Lindholm (18/4), Arto Tolsa (14/2), Aulis Laine (15/2). Trainer: Kaarlo Olavi Laaksonen (40).

266. 29.10.1967 **FRANCE Olympic - FINLAND** **3-1(1-1)** 19th OG. Qualifiers
Stade Parc des Princes, Paris; Referee: Joaquim Fernandes de Campos (Portugal); Attendance: 5,702
FIN: Lars Näsman (21/0), Pertti Mäkipää (Cap) (35/2), Seppo Kilponen (9/0), Timo Kautonen (32/0), Rainer Aho (6/0), Markku Hyvärinen (8/0), Simo Syrjävaara (22/1), Semi Nuoranen (19/2), Tommy Lindholm (19/5), Arto Tolsa (15/2), Aulis Laine (16/2). Trainer: Kaarlo Olavi Laaksonen (41).
Goal: Tommy Lindholm (30).

267. 04.06.1968 **FINLAND - DENMARK** **1-3(0-2)** Nordic Championship
Olympiastadion, Helsinki; Referee: Sven Jonsson (Sweden); Attendance: 16,082
FIN: Lars Näsman (22/0), Ismo Niskakoski (1/0), Pertti Mäkipää (36/2), Seppo Kilponen (10/0), Reima Nummila (22/0), Matti Mäkelä (26/2), Simo Syrjävaara (Cap) (23/1), Semi Nuoranen (20/2), Arto Tolsa (16/3), Tommy Lindholm (20/5), Juhani Peltonen (61/10). Trainer: Kaarlo Olavi Laaksonen (42).
Goal: Arto Tolsa (60).

268. 19.06.1968 **FINLAND - BELGIUM** **1-2(1-0)** 9th FIFA WC. Qualifiers
Olympiastadion, Helsinki; Referee: Anvar Zverev (Soviet Union); Attendance: 10,578
FIN: Paavo Heinonen (1/0), Pertti Mäkipää (37/2), Jouni Jalonen (1/0), Simo Syrjävaara (Cap) (24/1), Seppo Kilponen (11/0), Timo Nummelin (2/0), Turo Flink (1/1), Semi Nuoranen (21/2), Arto Tolsa (17/3), Raimo Toivanen (1/0), Tommy Lindholm (21/5). Trainer: Kaarlo Olavi Laaksonen (43).
Goal: Turo Flink (16).

269. 18.08.1968 **NORWAY - FINLAND** **4-1(1-0)** Nordic Championship
Ullevaal Stadion, Oslo; Referee: Carl V. Hansen (Denmark); Attendance: 18,276
FIN: Paavo Heinonen (2/0), Ismo Niskakoski (2/0) [46.Juhani Haavisto (1/0)], Jouni Jalonen (2/0), Simo Syrjävaara (Cap) (25/1), Pertti Haikonen (1/0), Timo Nummelin (3/0), Raimo Toivanen (2/0), Aulis Laine (17/2), Arvo Lamberg (3/0) [63.Arto Tolsa (18/4)], Kai Pahlman (56/13), Tommy Lindholm (22/5). Trainer: Kaarlo Olavi Laaksonen (44).
Goal: Arto Tolsa (75).

270. 11.09.1968 **FINLAND - SWEDEN** **0-3(0-1)** Nordic Championship
Olympiastadion, Helsinki; Referee: Karl Riegg (West Germany); Attendance: 18,100
FIN: Paavo Heinonen (3/0), Pertti Mäkipää (38/2), Seppo Kilponen (12/0), Jouni Jalonen (3/0), Rainer Aho (7/0), Raimo Saviomaa (1/0), Simo Syrjävaara (Cap) (26/1), Aulis Laine (18/2), Arto Tolsa (19/4), Arvo Lamberg (4/0), Tommy Lindholm (23/5). Trainer: Kaarlo Olavi Laaksonen (45).

271. 25.09.1968 **YUGOSLAVIA - FINLAND** **9-1(2-0)** 9th FIFA WC. Qualifiers
Stadion JNA, Beograd; Referee: Mitko Zhukov (Bulgaria); Attendance: 12,000
FIN: Lars Näsman (23/0), Pertti Mäkipää (Cap) (39/2), Jouni Jalonen (4/0), Seppo Kilponen (13/0), Pertti Haikonen (2/0), Timo Nummelin (4/0), Pekka Heikkilä (1/0), Semi Nuoranen (22/2), Arto Tolsa (20/5), Raimo Toivanen (3/0), Tommy Lindholm (24/5). Trainer: Kaarlo Olavi Laaksonen (46).
Goal: Arto Tolsa (88).

272. 09.10.1968 **BELGIUM - FINLAND** **6-1(3-0)** 9th FIFA WC. Qualifiers
Regenboogstadion, Waregem; Referee: János Biróczky (Hungary); Attendance: 17,000
FIN: Paavo Heinonen (4/0), Pertti Mäkipää (Cap) (40/2), Jouni Jalonen (5/0), Seppo Kilponen (14/0), Jarmo Flink (1/0), Timo Nummelin (5/0), Pekka Heikkilä (2/0) [84.Raimo Toivanen (4/0)], Semi Nuoranen (23/2), Arto Tolsa (21/5), Antero Nikkanen (1/0) [46.Miikka Toivola (1/0)], Tommy Lindholm (25/6). Trainer: Kaarlo Olavi Laaksonen (47).
Goal: Tommy Lindholm (88 penalty).

273. 02.04.1969 **NETHERLANDS Amateur - FINLAND** **2-0(0-0)**
Stadion Zwart Wit '28, Rotterdam; Referee: Arie van Gemert (Netherlands); Attendance: 3,800
FIN: Paavo Heinonen (5/0), Pertti Mäkipää (Cap) (41/2), Seppo Kilponen (15/0), Jouni Jalonen (6/0), Timo Kautonen (33/0), Pekka Heikkilä (3/0), Markku Hyvärinen (9/0) [Miikka Toivola (2/0)], Semi Nuoranen (24/2), Arto Tolsa (22/5), Raimo Toivanen (5/0), Tommy Lindholm (26/6). Trainer: Kaarlo Olavi Laaksonen (48).

274. 15.05.1969 **FINLAND – NETHERLANDS Amateur** **3-1(0-1)**
Olympiastadion, Helsinki; Referee: Reino Koskinen (Finland); Attendance: 6,717
FIN: Lars Näsman (24/0), Pertti Mäkipää (Cap) (42/2), Seppo Kilponen (16/0), Raimo Saviomaa (2/0), Timo Kautonen (34/0), Markku Hyvärinen (10/0), Timo Nummelin (6/1), Semi Nuoranen (25/2) [Juhani Peltonen (62/10)], Arto Tolsa (23/5), Kari Lehtolainen (1/2), Tommy Lindholm (27/6). Trainer: Kaarlo Olavi Laaksonen (49).
Goals: Kari Lehtolainen (49, 83), Timo Nummelin (70).

275. 22.05.1969 **SWEDEN – FINLAND** **4-0(1-0)** Nordic Championship
Varendsvallen, Växjö; Referee: Frede Hansen (Denmark); Attendance: 15,678
FIN: Lars Näsman (25/0), Pertti Mäkipää (Cap) (43/2), Seppo Kilponen (17/0), Raimo Saviomaa (3/0), Timo Kautonen (35/0), Markku Hyvärinen (11/0) [Raimo Toivanen (6/0)], Timo Nummelin (7/1), Juhani Peltonen (63/10), Arto Tolsa (24/5), Kari Lehtolainen (2/2), Tommy Lindholm (28/6). Trainer: Kaarlo Olavi Laaksonen (50).

276. 04.06.1969 **FINLAND - YUGOSLAVIA** **1-5(1-3)** 9th FIFA WC. Qualifiers
Olympiastadion, Helsinki; Referee: Stanislaw Eksztajn (Poland); Attendance: 8,740
FIN: Lars Näsman (26/0) [46.Seppo Patrikainen (1/0)], Pertti Mäkipää (Cap) (44/2), Seppo Kilponen (18/0), Timo Kautonen (36/0), Pertti Haikonen (3/0), Raimo Toivanen (7/0), Matti Mäkelä (27/2), Teuvo Andelmin (1/0), Arto Tolsa (25/6) [75.Pekka Talaslahti (1/0)], Juhani Peltonen (64/10), Tommy Lindholm (29/6). Trainer: Kaarlo Olavi Laaksonen (51).
Goal: Arto Tolsa (20).

277. 25.06.1969 **FINLAND - SPAIN** **2-0(2-0)** 9th FIFA WC. Qualifiers
Olympiastadion, Helsinki; Referee: Günter Männig (Austria); Attendance: 11,838
FIN: Lars Näsman (27/0), Pertti Mäkipää (Cap) (45/2), Seppo Kilponen (19/0), Raimo Saviomaa (4/0), Timo Kautonen (37/0), Timo Nummelin (8/1), Matti Mäkelä (28/2), Teuvo Andelmin (2/0), Arto Tolsa (26/7), Kalevi Nupponen (3/0), Tommy Lindholm (30/7). Trainer: Kaarlo Olavi Laaksonen (52).
Goals: Tommy Lindholm (7), Arto Tolsa (20).

278. 24.07.1969 **FINLAND - ICELAND** **3-1(3-1)**
Olympiastadion, Helsinki; Referee: Curt Nystrand (Sweden); Attendance: 8,380
FIN: Seppo Patrikainen (2/0), Pertti Mäkipää (Cap) (46/2), Seppo Kilponen (20/0), Raimo Saviomaa (5/0), Timo Kautonen (38/0), Matti Mäkelä (29/2), Timo Nummelin (9/1), Semi Nuoranen (26/2) [70.Mauri Paavilainen (3/0)], Arvo Lamberg (5/0), Olavi Rissanen (1/1), Tommy Lindholm (31/8). Trainer: Kaarlo Olavi Laaksonen (53).
Goals: Schram (3 owngoal), Olavi Rissanen (6), Tommy Lindholm (42).

279. 24.08.1969 **FINLAND - NORWAY** **2-2(2-2)** Nordic Championship

Olympiastadion, Helsinki; Referee: Einar Boström (Sweden); Attendance: 10,727

FIN: Martti Halme (14/0) [46.Seppo Patrikainen (3/0)], Pertti Mäkipää (Cap) (47/2), Seppo Kilponen (21/0), Raimo Saviomaa (6/0), Timo Kautonen (39/0), Jarmo Flink (2/0), Timo Nummelin (10/1), Pentti Toivola (1/0), Arto Tolsa (27/8), Matti Mäkelä (30/2), Tommy Lindholm (32/9). Trainer: Kaarlo Olavi Laaksonen (54).

Goals: Arto Tolsa (5), Tommy Lindholm (13).

280. 10.09.1969 **DENMARK - FINLAND** **5-2(4-1)** Nordic Championship

Idrætsparken, København; Referee: Theodorus Boosten (Netherlands); Attendance: 23,000

FIN: Seppo Patrikainen (4/0), Pertti Mäkipää (Cap) (48/2), Seppo Kilponen (22/0), Henry Forssell (1/0), Timo Kautonen (40/0), Jarmo Flink (3/0), Raimo Saviomaa (7/0), Pentti Toivola (2/0), Arto Tolsa (28/9), Matti Mäkelä (31/2), Tommy Lindholm (33/10). Trainer: Kaarlo Olavi Laaksonen (55).

Goals: Tommy Lindholm (3), Arto Tolsa (90).

281. 15.10.1969 **SPAIN - FINLAND** **6-0(5-0)** 9th FIFA WC. Qualifiers

Estadio Municipal "José Antonio Primo de Rivera", La Línea; Referee: Robert Héliès (France); Attendance: 20,904

FIN: Lars Näsman (28/0) [15.Timo Nevanperä (1/0)], Pertti Mäkipää (Cap) (49/2), Seppo Kilponen (23/0), Henry Forssell (2/0), Esko Ranta (1/0), Arvo Lamberg (6/0), Raimo Saviomaa (8/0), Juhani Peltonen (65/10), Arto Tolsa (29/9), Raimo Toivanen (8/0), Tommy Lindholm (34/10) [46.Seppo Mäkelä (1/0)]. Trainer: Kaarlo Olavi Laaksonen (56).

282. 21.05.1970 **FINLAND – WEST GERMANY Amateur** **0-0**

Olympiastadion, Helsinki; Referee: Hans Carlsson (Sweden); Attendance: 5,843

FIN: Lars Näsman (29/0), Pertti Mäkipää (50/2), Seppo Kilponen (24/0) [70.Henry Forssell (3/0)], Raimo Saviomaa (9/0), Timo Kautonen (41/0), Timo Nummelin (11/1), Pekka Heikkilä (4/0), Semi Nuoranen (27/2) [46.Veikko Hovivuori (1/0)], Arto Tolsa (30/9), Matti Mäkelä (Cap) (32/2), Tommy Lindholm (35/10). Trainer: Kaarlo Olavi Laaksonen (57).

283. 03.06.1970 **FINLAND - DENMARK** **1-1(0-0)** Nordic Championship

Olympiastadion, Helsinki; Referee: Norman C. Burtenshaw (England); Attendance: 8,044

FIN: Lars Näsman (30/0), Pertti Mäkipää (51/2), Henry Forssell (4/0), Seppo Kilponen (25/0), Timo Kautonen (42/0), Raimo Saviomaa (10/0), Pekka Heikkilä (5/0), Juhani Peltonen (66/10), Arto Tolsa (31/10), Matti Mäkelä (Cap) (33/2), Tommy Lindholm (36/10). Trainer: Kaarlo Olavi Laaksonen (58).

Goal: Arto Tolsa (58).

284. 17.06.1970 **NORWAY - FINLAND** **2-0(0-0)** Nordic Championship

Brann Stadion, Bergen; Referee: Gerhard Kunze (East Germany); Attendance: 13,000

FIN: Lars Näsman (31/0), Pertti Mäkipää (52/2), Seppo Kilponen (26/0), Raimo Saviomaa (11/0), Timo Kautonen (43/0), Raimo Toivanen (9/0), Pekka Heikkilä (6/0), Juhani Peltonen (67/10) [Kalevi Nupponen (4/0)], Arto Tolsa (32/10), Matti Mäkelä (Cap) (34/2), Tommy Lindholm (37/10). Trainer: Kaarlo Olavi Laaksonen (59).

285. 26.08.1970 **FINLAND - SWEDEN** **1-2(0-0)** Nordic Championship

Olympiastadion, Helsinki; Referee: Henry Öberg (Norway); Attendance: 17,070

FIN: Paavo Heinonen (6/0), Pertti Mäkipää (Cap) (53/2), Seppo Kilponen (27/0), Henry Forssell (5/0), Timo Kautonen (44/0), Raimo Saviomaa (12/0), Pekka Heikkilä (7/0), Juhani Peltonen (68/10), Pentti Toivola (3/0), Raimo Toivanen (10/0) [Kari Lehtolainen (3/2)], Tommy Lindholm (38/11). Trainer: Kaarlo Olavi Laaksonen (60).

Goal: Tommy Lindholm (90 penalty).

286. 23.09.1970 **FINLAND – ENGLAND Amateur** **1-3(1-1)**

Olympiastadion, Helsinki; Referee: Ove Dahlberg (Sweden); Attendance: 2,343

FIN: Paavo Heinonen (7/0), Pertti Mäkipää (Cap) (54/2), Seppo Kilponen (28/0), Henry Forssell (6/0), Jouko Suomalainen (1/0) [Esa Korhonen (1/0)], Raimo Saviomaa (13/0), Raimo Toivanen (11/0), Matti Vanhanen (1/0) [Matti Paatelainen (1/0)], Pentti Toivola (4/0), Timo Rahja (1/0), Tommy Lindholm (39/12). Trainer: Kaarlo Olavi Laaksonen (61).

Goal: Tommy Lindholm (22).

287. 07.10.1970 **CZECHOSLOVAKIA – FINLAND** **1-1(1-1)** 4th EC. Qualifiers

Stadion Letná, Praha; Referee: William O'Neill (Republic of Ireland); Attendance: 7,857

FIN: Paavo Heinonen (8/0), Pertti Mäkipää (Cap) (55/2), Seppo Kilponen (29/0), Vilho Rajantie (1/0), Timo Kautonen (45/0), Jouko Suomalainen (2/0), Pekka Heikkilä (8/0), Raimo Toivanen (12/0), Pentti Toivola (5/0), Olavi Litmanen (1/0), Matti Paatelainen (2/1) [73.Seppo Mäkelä (2/0)]. Trainer: Kaarlo Olavi Laaksonen (62).

Goal: Matti Paatelainen (41).

288. 11.10.1970 **ROMANIA – FINLAND** **3-0(2-0)** 4th EC. Qualifiers

Stadion 23 August, Bucureşti; Referee: Leonidas Vamvakopoulos (Greece); Attendance: 50,000

FIN: Paavo Heinonen (9/0), Pertti Mäkipää (Cap) (56/2), Seppo Kilponen (30/0), Vilho Rajantie (2/0), Timo Kautonen (46/0), Jouko Suomalainen (3/0) [55.Seppo Mäkelä (3/0)], Pekka Heikkilä (9/0) [67.Olavi Litmanen (2/0)], Raimo Saviomaa (14/0), Pentti Toivola (6/0), Raimo Toivanen (13/0), Matti Paatelainen (3/1). Trainer: Kaarlo Olavi Laaksonen (63).

289. 20.05.1971 **SWEDEN – FINLAND** **4-1(0-1)** Nordic Championship

Ryavallen, Borås; Referee: Hans Joachim (West Germany); Attendance: 13,020

FIN: Lars Näsman (32/0), Erkki Vihtilä (1/0) [74.Tapani Rainio (1/0)], Timo Kautonen (47/0), Vilho Rajantie (3/0), Jouko Suomalainen (4/0), Seppo Kilponen (Cap) (31/0), Pekka Heikkilä (10/0) [Pentti Toivola (7/0)], Raimo Toivanen (14/0), Matti Paatelainen (4/2), Arto Tolsa (33/10), Tommy Lindholm (40/12). Trainer: Kaarlo Olavi Laaksonen (64).

Goal: Matti Paatelainen (16).

290. 26.05.1971 **FINLAND - WALES** **0-1(0-0)** 4th EC. Qualifiers

Olympiastadion, Helsinki; Referee: Günter Männig (East Germany); Attendance: 5,410

FIN: Lars Näsman (33/0), Timo Kautonen (Cap) (48/0), Raimo Saviomaa (15/0), Vilho Rajantie (4/0), Jouko Suomalainen (5/0), Timo Nummelin (12/1), Pekka Heikkilä (11/0), Raimo Toivanen (15/0) [Jarmo Flink (4/0)], Matti Paatelainen (5/2), Arto Tolsa (34/10), Tommy Lindholm (41/12). Trainer: Kaarlo Olavi Laaksonen (65).

291. 16.06.1971 **FINLAND - CZECHOSLOVAKIA** **0-4(0-2)** 4th EC. Qualifiers
Olympiastadion, Helsinki; Referee: Marian Srodecki (Poland); Attendance: 4,658
FIN: Lars Näsman (34/0), Timo Kautonen (49/0), Vilho Rajantie (5/0), Seppo Kilponen (Cap) (32/0), Jouko Suomalainen (6/0), Timo Nummelin (13/1), Pekka Heikkilä (12/0) [Matti Paatelainen (6/2)], Raimo Toivanen (16/0) [Tommy Lindholm (42/12)], Arto Tolsa (35/10), Jarmo Flink (5/0), Olavi Rissanen (2/1). Trainer: Kaarlo Olavi Laaksonen (66).

292. 25.08.1971 **FINLAND - NORWAY** **1-1(0-1)** Nordic Championship
Olympiastadion, Helsinki; Referee: Kaj Sørensen (Denmark); Attendance: 6,225
FIN: Timo Nevanperä (2/0), Jouko Suomalainen (7/0) [46.Seppo Kilponen (33/0)], Raimo Saviomaa (16/0), Vilho Rajantie (6/0), Esko Ranta (2/0), Raimo Toivanen (Cap) (17/0), Tapio Raatikainen (1/0) [*sent off 47*], Miikka Toivola (3/0), Heikki Suhonen (1/1), Jarmo Flink (6/0), Tommy Lindholm (43/12). Trainer: Kaarlo Olavi Laaksonen (67).
Goal: Heikki Suhonen (71).

293. 08.09.1971 **DENMARK - FINLAND** **0-0** Nordic Championship
Idrætsparken, København; Referee: Rolf Hennum Andersen (Norway); Attendance: 14,000
FIN: Lars Näsman (35/0), Jouko Suomalainen (8/0), Ari Mäkynen (1/0), Vilho Rajantie (7/0) [4 Raimo Saviomaa (17/0)], Esko Ranta (3/0), Raimo Toivanen (Cap) (18/0), Pekka Heikkilä (13/0), Miikka Toivola (4/0) [Pentti Toivola (8/0)], Heikki Suhonen (2/1), Jarmo Flink (7/0), Tommy Lindholm (44/12). Trainer: Kaarlo Olavi Laaksonen (68).

294. 22.09.1971 **FINLAND - ROMANIA** **0-4(0-2)** 4th EC. Qualifiers
Olympiastadion, Helsinki; Referee: Pius Kamber (Switzerland); Attendance: 2,084
FIN: Lars Näsman (36/0) [46.Paavo Heinonen (10/0)], Jouko Suomalainen (9/0), Raimo Saviomaa (18/0), Ari Mäkynen (2/0), Esko Ranta (4/0), Raimo Toivanen (Cap) (19/0) [58.Timo Nummelin (14/1)], Pekka Heikkilä (14/0), Miikka Toivola (5/0), Timo Rahja (2/0), Antero Nikkanen (2/0), Tommy Lindholm (45/12). Trainer: Kaarlo Olavi Laaksonen (69).

295. 13.10.1971 **WALES - FINLAND** **3-0(1-0)** 4th EC. Qualifiers
Vetch Field, Swansea; Referee: Kaj Rasmussen (Denmark); Attendance: 10,301
FIN: Lars Näsman (37/0), Seppo Kilponen (Cap) (34/0), Raimo Saviomaa (19/0), Ari Mäkynen (3/0), Pekka Kosonen (1/0), Raimo Elo (3/0), Jarmo Flink (8/0), Miikka Toivola (6/0), Heikki Suhonen (3/1) [30.Henry Bergström (1/0)], Pekka Heikkilä (15/0), Tommy Lindholm (46/12). Trainer: Kaarlo Olavi Laaksonen (70).

296. 07.03.1972 **NETHERLANDS Amateur - FINLAND** **2-1(1-0)**
Zuiderpark Stadion, Den Haag; Referee: Theo Booij (Netherlands); Attendance: 1,500
FIN: Paavo Heinonen (11/0), Jouko Suomalainen (10/0), Vilho Rajantie (8/0), Ari Mäkynen (4/0), Esko Ranta (5/0), Pekka Heikkilä (16/0), Matti Mäkelä (Cap) (35/2), Miikka Toivola (7/0), Juhani Tapola (1/1), Henry Bergström (2/0), Jarmo Flink (9/0). Trainer: Kaarlo Olavi Laaksonen (71).
Goal: Juhani Tapola (63).

297. 28.05.1972 **FINLAND - NORWAY** **0-0** Nordic Championship
Kupittaan Jalkapallostadion, Turku; Referee: Curt Nystrand (Sweden); Attendance: 4,828
FIN: Paavo Heinonen (12/0), Pekka Kosonen (2/0), Henry Forssell (7/0) [46.Vesa Kallio (1/0)], Vilho Rajantie (9/0), Esko Ranta (6/0), Jouko Suomalainen (Cap) (11/0), Jarmo Flink (10/0), Miikka Toivola (8/0), Arto Tolsa (36/10) [76.Pekka Heikkilä (17/0)], Matti Paatelainen (7/2), Juhani Tapola (2/1). Trainer: Kaarlo Olavi Laaksonen (72).

298. 07.06.1972 **DENMARK - FINLAND** **3-0(0-0)** Nordic Championship
Idrætsparken, København; Referee: Henry Öberg (Norway); Attendance: 23,301
FIN: Paavo Heinonen (13/0), Pekka Kosonen (3/0), Vilho Rajantie (10/0), Jouko Suomalainen (Cap) (12/0), Esko Ranta (7/0), Jarmo Flink (11/0), Hannu Asikainen (1/0) [Pekka Heikkilä (18/0)], Olavi Litmanen (3/0) [65.Heikki Suhonen (4/1)], Miikka Toivola (9/0), Matti Paatelainen (8/2), Semi Nuoranen (28/2). Trainer: Kaarlo Olavi Laaksonen (73).

299. 21.06.1972 **FINLAND - ALBANIA** **1-0(0-0)** 10th FIFA WC. Qualifiers
Olympiastadion, Helsinki; Referee: Bertil Wilhelm Lööw (Sweden); Attendance: 1,431
FIN: Timo Nevanperä (3/0), Pekka Kosonen (4/0), Vilho Rajantie (11/0), Ari Mäkynen (5/0), Esko Ranta (8/0), Jouko Suomalainen (Cap) (13/0), Pekka Heikkilä (19/0), Olavi Litmanen (4/0), Miikka Toivola (10/1), Heikki Suhonen (5/1), Semi Nuoranen (29/2). Trainer: Kaarlo Olavi Laaksonen (74).
Goal: Miikka Toivola (13).

300. 16.07.1972 **FINLAND - SOVIET UNION** **1-1(0-1)**
Hietalahden Jalkapallostadion, Vaasa; Referee: Rolf Nyhus (Norway); Attendance: 6,040
FIN: Timo Nevanperä (4/0), Pekka Kosonen (5/0), Vilho Rajantie (12/0), Raimo Saviomaa (20/0), Esko Ranta (9/0), Jouko Suomalainen (Cap) (14/0), Pekka Heikkilä (20/0), Olavi Litmanen (5/0) [16.Olavi Rissanen (3/2)], Miikka Toivola (11/1), Matti Paatelainen (9/2), Semi Nuoranen (30/2). Trainer: Kaarlo Olavi Laaksonen (75).
Goal: Olavi Rissanen (76).

301. 30.07.1972 **WEST GERMANY Amateur - FINLAND** **1-2(0-1)**
Lohmühle Stadion, Lübeck; Referee: Kaj Sørensen (Denmark); Attendance: 5,643
FIN: Timo Nevanperä (5/0), Pekka Kosonen (6/0), Vilho Rajantie (13/0), Raimo Saviomaa (21/0), Esko Ranta (10/0), Jouko Suomalainen (Cap) (15/1) [54.Martti Kuusela (1/0)], Pekka Heikkilä (21/0), Miikka Toivola (12/1), Olavi Rissanen (4/3), Matti Paatelainen (10/2), Semi Nuoranen (31/2). Trainer: Kaarlo Olavi Laaksonen (76).
Goals: Jouko Suomalainen (14), Olavi Rissanen (90).

302. 20.09.1972 **FINLAND - ROMANIA** **1-1(0-0)** 10th FIFA WC. Qualifiers
Olympiastadion, Helsinki; Referee: Stanislaw Eksztajn (Poland); Attendance: 5,519
FIN: Timo Nevanperä (6/0), Pekka Kosonen (7/0), Vilho Rajantie (14/0), Raimo Saviomaa (22/0), Esko Ranta (11/0), Pekka Heikkilä (22/0), Henry Forssell (8/0) [77.Heikki Suhonen (6/1)], Miikka Toivola (13/1), Olavi Rissanen (5/4), Matti Paatelainen (11/2), Semi Nuoranen (Cap) (32/2) [75.Jarmo Flink (12/0)]. Trainer: Kaarlo Olavi Laaksonen (77).
Goal: Olavi Rissanen (86).

303. 07.10.1972 **EAST GERMANY - FINLAND** **5-0(0-0)** 10th FIFA WC. Qualifiers
Dynamo Stadion, Dresden; Referee: Liuben Radunchev (Bulgaria); Attendance: 16,000
FIN: Timo Nevanperä (7/0), Pekka Kosonen (8/0), Vilho Rajantie (15/0), Raimo Saviomaa (Cap) (23/0), Esko Ranta (12/0), Henry Forssell (9/0), Pekka Heikkilä (23/0), Miikka Toivola (14/1), Olavi Rissanen (6/4), Heikki Suhonen (7/1) [70.Matti Paatelainen (12/2)], Jarmo Flink (13/0) [50.Semi Nuoranen (33/2)]. Trainer: Kaarlo Olavi Laaksonen (78).

304. 04.04.1973 **ENGLAND Amateur - FINLAND** **3-0(1-0)**
Home Park, Plymouth; Referee: Charles H. Nicholls (England); Attendance: 1,472
FIN: Timo Nevanperä (8/0), Pekka Kosonen (9/0), Vilho Rajantie (16/0), Raimo Saviomaa (24/0) [Ari Mäkynen (6/0)], Esko Ranta (13/0), Jouko Suomalainen (Cap) (16/1), Henry Forssell (10/0) [Heikki Suhonen (8/1)], Pekka Heikkilä (24/0), Olavi Rissanen (7/4), Matti Paatelainen (13/2), Miikka Toivola (15/1). Trainer: Kaarlo Olavi Laaksonen (79).

305. 24.05.1973 **FINLAND – NETHERLANDS Amateur** **1-0(0-0)**
Olympiastadion, Helsinki; Referee: Anders Mattsson (Finland); Attendance: 6,416
FIN: Göran Enckelman (1/0), Henry Forssell (11/0), Vilho Rajantie (17/0), Raimo Saviomaa (25/0), Esko Ranta (14/0), Jouko Suomalainen (Cap) (17/1), Antero Nikkanen (3/0), Eero Virkkunen (1/0), Olavi Köykkä (1/0) [27.Matti Paatelainen (14/3)], Heikki Suhonen (9/1), Miikka Toivola (16/1). Trainer: Kaarlo Olavi Laaksonen (80).
Goal: Matti Paatelainen (58)

306. 06.06.1973 **FINLAND – EAST GERMANY** **1-5(0-3)** 10th FIFA WC. Qualifiers
Ratinan Stadion, Tampere; Referee: Pavel Kazakov (Soviet Union); Attendance: 6,104
FIN: Göran Enckelman (2/0), Henry Forssell (12/0), Vilho Rajantie (18/0), Raimo Saviomaa (26/0), Esko Ranta (15/0), Jouko Suomalainen (Cap) (18/1), Antero Nikkanen (4/0), Eero Virkkunen (2/0) [46.Heikki Suhonen (10/1)], Jarmo Manninen (1/1), Matti Paatelainen (15/3), Miikka Toivola (17/1). Trainer: Kaarlo Olavi Laaksonen (81).
Goal: Jarmo Manninen (89).

307. 08.07.1973 **SWEDEN – FINLAND** **1-1(1-0)** Nordic Championship
Örjans Vall, Halmstad; Referee: Harry Öberg (Norway); Attendance: 16,547
FIN: Pertti Alaja (1/0), Eero Virkkunen (3/0), Arto Tolsa (37/10), Raimo Saviomaa (27/0), Esko Ranta (16/0), Jouko Suomalainen (Cap) (19/2), Antero Nikkanen (5/0) [34.Martti Kuusela (2/0)], Timo Rahja (3/0), Miikka Toivola (18/1), Matti Paatelainen (16/3), Heikki Suhonen (11/1). Trainer: Kaarlo Olavi Laaksonen (82).
Goal: Jouko Suomalainen (46).

308. 29.08.1973 **FINLAND - SWEDEN** **1-2(1-0)** Nordic Championship
Olympiastadion, Helsinki; Referee: Edgar Petersen (Denmark); Attendance: 18,552
FIN: Pertti Alaja (2/0), Eero Virkkunen (4/0), Raimo Saviomaa (28/0), Vilho Rajantie (19/0), Esko Ranta (17/0), Jouko Suomalainen (Cap) (20/2), Antero Nikkanen (6/0), Miikka Toivola (19/1), Heikki Suhonen (12/2), Tuomo Haapa (1/0), Hannu Lamberg (1/0). Trainer: Kaarlo Olavi Laaksonen (83).
Goal: Heikki Suhonen (34).

309. 10.10.1973 **ALBANIA - FINLAND** **1-0(1-0)** 10th FIFA WC. Qualifiers
Stadiumi „Kombëtar Qemal Stafa“, Tiranë; Referee: Aurelio Angonese (Italy); Attendance: 16,581
FIN: Pertti Alaja (3/0), Eero Virkkunen (5/0), Raimo Saviomaa (29/0), Ari Mäkynen (7/0) [66.Vesa Kallio (2/0)], Esko Ranta (18/0), Jouko Suomalainen (Cap) (21/2), Miikka Toivola (20/1), Olavi Paavolainen (1/0), Jarmo Manninen (2/1), Henry Bergström (3/0), Heikki Suhonen (13/2) [76.Matti Paatelainen (17/3)]. Trainer: Kaarlo Olavi Laaksonen (84).

310. 14.10.1973 **ROMANIA - FINLAND** **9-0(5-0)** 10th FIFA WC. Qualifiers
Stadionul 23 August, Bucureşti; Referee: Gyula Emsberger (Hungary); Attendance: 13,525
FIN: Pertti Alaja (4/0), Eero Virkkunen (6/0), Raimo Saviomaa (30/0), Vilho Rajantie (20/0) [75.Henry Forssell (13/0)], Esko Ranta (19/0), Jouko Suomalainen (Cap) (22/2), Vesa Kallio (3/0), Olavi Paavolainen (2/0), Jarmo Manninen (3/1), Matti Paatelainen (18/3) [65.Henry Bergström (4/0)], Miikka Toivola (21/1). Trainer: Kaarlo Olavi Laaksonen (85).

311. 06.06.1974 **FINLAND - DENMARK** **1-1(0-1)** Nordic Championship
Raatti Stadion, Oulu; Referee: Svein Inge Thime (Norway); Attendance: 9,210
FIN: Pertti Alaja (5/0), Eero Virkkunen (7/0), Artol Tolsa (38/10), Erkki Vihtilä (2/0), Esko Ranta (20/0), Jouko Suomalainen (Cap) (23/2), Antero Nikkanen (7/0), Raimo Hukka (1/0) [46.Miikka Toivola (22/1)], Jarmo Manninen (4/1) [Pentti Toivola (9/0)], Olavi Rissanen (8/4), Matti Paatelainen (19/4). Trainer: Kaarlo Olavi Laaksonen (86).
Goal: Matti Paatelainen (71).

312. 15.08.1974 **NORWAY - FINLAND** **1-2(0-2)** Nordic Championship
Ullevaal Stadion, Oslo; Referee: Erik Fredriksson (Sweden); Attendance: 11,000
FIN: Pertti Alaja (6/0), Eero Virkkunen (8/0), Raimo Saviomaa (31/0), Erkki Vihtilä (3/0), Esko Ranta (21/0), Jouko Suomalainen (Cap) (24/2), Antero Nikkanen (8/0) [Miikka Toivola (23/1)], Aki Heiskanen (1/1), Olavi Rissanen (9/4) [Tommy Lindholm (47/12)], Matti Paatelainen (20/5), Juha-Pekka Laine (1/0). Trainer: Kaarlo Olavi Laaksonen (87).
Goals: Aki Heiskanen (29), Matti Paatelainen (37).

313. 19.08.1974 **ICELAND - FINLAND** **2-2(2-1)**
Laugardalsvöllur, Reykjavík; Referee: Kyle Rollo (Scotland); Attendance: 3,500
FIN: Pertti Alaja (7/0), Eero Virkkunen (9/0), Raimo Saviomaa (32/0), Erkki Vihtilä (4/0), Esko Ranta (22/0), Jouko Suomalainen (Cap) (25/2), Antero Nikkanen (9/0) [46.Timo Rahja (4/0)], Aki Heiskanen (2/1), Miikka Toivola (24/1), Matti Paatelainen (21/6), Juha-Pekka Laine (2/1). Trainer: Kaarlo Olavi Laaksonen (88).
Goal: Matti Paatelainen (43), Juha-Pekka Laine (60).

314. 01.09.1974 **FINLAND - POLAND** **1-2(1-1)** 5th EC. Qualifiers
Olympiastadion, Helsinki; Referee: John Wright Paterson (Scotland); Attendance: 18,795
FIN: Pertti Alaja (8/0), Henry Forssell (14/0), Arto Tolsa (39/10), Erkki Vihtilä (5/0), Esko Ranta (23/0), Jouko Suomalainen (Cap) (26/2), Timo Rahja (5/1) [81.Antero Nikkanen (10/0)], Aki Heiskanen (3/1), Miikka Toivola (25/1), Matti Paatelainen (22/6) [64.Jarmo Manninen (5/1)], Juha-Pekka Laine (3/1). Trainer: Kaarlo Olavi Laaksonen (89).
Goal: Timo Rahja (3).

315. 25.09.1974 **FINLAND - NETHERLANDS** **1-3(1-2)** 5th EC. Qualifiers
Olympiastadion, Helsinki; Referee: Wolfgang Riedel (East Germany); Attendance: 20,449
FIN: Harri Holli (1/0), Raimo Saari (1/0), Arto Tolsa (40/10), Erkki Vihtilä (6/0), Esko Ranta (24/0), Jouko Suomalainen (Cap) (27/2), Aki Heiskanen (4/1) [60.Olavi Rissanen (10/4)], Raimo Hukka (2/0) [54.Miikka Toivola (26/1)], Timo Rahja (6/2), Rutger Pettersson (1/0), Juha-Pekka Laine (4/1). Trainer: Kaarlo Olavi Laaksonen (90).
Goal: Timo Rahja (16).

316. 09.10.1974 **POLAND - FINLAND** **3-0(2-0)** 5th EC. Qualifiers
Stadion Warta, Poznań; Referee: Dušan Maksimović (Yugoslavia); Attendance: 30,000
FIN: Harri Holli (2/0), Raimo Saari (2/0), Arto Tolsa (41/10), Erkki Vihtilä (7/0), Esko Ranta (25/0), Jouko Suomalainen (Cap) (28/2), Aki Heiskanen (5/1) [46.Rutger Pettersson (2/0)], Timo Rahja (7/2), Miikka Toivola (27/1), Matti Paatelainen (23/6) [46.Juha-Pekka Laine (5/1)], Olavi Rissanen (11/4). Trainer: Kaarlo Olavi Laaksonen (91).

317. 16.04.1975 **NETHERLANDS Amateur - FINLAND** **1-1(1-1)**
Zuiderpark Stadion, Den Haag; Referee: Johannes F. Beck (Netherlands); Attendance: 1,000
FIN: Göran Enckelman (3/0), Erkki Vihtilä (8/0), Erkki Lehtinen (1/0), Matti Paatelainen (Cap) (24/6), Esko Ranta (26/0), Jouko Suomalainen (29/2), Hannu Hämäläinen (1/0), Jukka Pirinen (1/0), Olavi Rissanen (12/5), Aki Heiskanen (6/1) [46.Raimo Kuuluvainen (1/0)], Miikka Toivola (28/1). Trainer: Martti Kosma (1).
Goal: Olavi Rissanen (33).

318. 15.05.1975 **FINLAND - NORWAY** **3-5(1-1)** 21st OG. Qualifiers, Nordic Championship
Olympiastadion, Helsinki; Referee: Erik Fredriksson (Sweden); Attendance: 12,301
FIN: Göran Enckelman (4/0), Erkki Vihtilä (9/0), Erkki Lehtinen (2/0), Matti Paatelainen (Cap) (25/6), Esko Ranta (27/0), Jouko Suomalainen (30/2), Hannu Hämäläinen (2/0), Jukka Pirinen (2/0), Olavi Rissanen (13/5), Olavi Köykkä (2/0) [55.Aki Heiskanen (7/2)], Miikka Toivola (29/3). Trainer: Martti Kosma (2).
Goals: Miikka Toivola (3), Aki Heiskanen (65), Miikka Toivola (67).

319. 05.06.1975 **FINLAND - ITALY** **0-1(0-1)** 5th EC. Qualifiers
Olympiastadion, Helsinki; Referee: Walter Eschweiler (West Germany); Attendance: 17,732
FIN: Göran Enckelman (5/0), Erkki Vihtilä (10/0), Arto Tolsa (42/10), Matti Paatelainen (Cap) (26/6), Esko Ranta (28/0), Jouko Suomalainen (31/2), Pauno Kymäläinen (1/0) [46.Olavi Rissanen (14/5)], Aki Heiskanen (8/2), Jarmo Manninen (6/1), Juha-Pekka Laine (6/1) [77.Kalle Nieminen (1/0)], Miikka Toivola (30/3). Trainer: Aulis Rytkönen (1).

320. 18.06.1975 **NORWAY - FINLAND** **1-1(1-1)** 21st OG. Qualifiers
Stavanger Stadion, Stavanger; Referee: Bernt Nielsen (Denmark); Attendance: 12,800
FIN: Göran Enckelman (6/0), Pauno Kymäläinen (2/0) [34.Kalle Nieminen (2/0)], Erkki Vihtilä (11/0), Matti Paatelainen (Cap) (27/6), Esko Ranta (29/0), Jouko Suomalainen (32/2), Aki Heiskanen (9/2), Miikka Toivola (31/3), Olavi Rissanen (15/5), Jarmo Manninen (7/2), Heikki Suhonen (14/2). Trainer: Aulis Rytkönen (2).
Goal: Jarmo Manninen (61).

321. 25.06.1975 **DENMARK - FINLAND** **2-0(1-0)** Nordic Championship
Idrætsparken, København; Referee: Erik Axelryd (Sweden); Attendance: 13,600
FIN: Göran Enckelman (7/0), Arto Tolsa (43/10), Erkki Vihtilä (12/0), Matti Paatelainen (Cap) (28/6), Esko Ranta (30/0), Jouko Suomalainen (33/2), Aki Heiskanen (10/2), Miikka Toivola (32/3), Olavi Rissanen (16/5), Heikki Suhonen (15/2), Jarmo Manninen (8/2) [55.Juha-Pekka Laine (7/1)]. Trainer: Aulis Rytkönen (3).

322. 03.09.1975 **NETHERLANDS - FINLAND** **4-1(2-1)** 5th EC. Qualifiers
Goffertstadion, Nijmegen; Referee: Eric Smyton (Northern Ireland); Attendance: 19,000
FIN: Göran Enckelman (8/0), Erkki Vihtilä (13/0), Matti Paatelainen (Cap) (29/7), Henry Forssell (15/0), Esko Ranta (31/0), Jouko Suomalainen (34/2), Aki Heiskanen (11/2), Hannu Hämäläinen (3/0) [Pertti Jantunen (1/0)], Olavi Rissanen (17/5) [Jukka-Pekka Laine (8/1)], Ari Mäkynen (8/0), Eero Rissanen (1/0). Trainer: Aulis Rytkönen (4).
Goal: Matti Paatelainen (9).

323. 27.09.1975 **ITALY - FINLAND** **0-0** 5th EC. Qualifiers
Stadio Olimpico, Roma; Referee: Kostas Xanthoulis (Greece); Attendance: 29,203
FIN: Göran Enckelman (9/0), Erkki Vihtilä (14/0), Matti Paatelainen (Cap) (30/7), Arto Tolsa (44/10), Esko Ranta (32/0), Jouko Suomalainen (35/2), Aki Heiskanen (12/2), Pertti Jantunen (2/0), Olavi Rissanen (18/5) [1 Hannu Hämäläinen (4/0)], Ari Mäkynen (9/0) [28.Timo Kautonen (50/0)], Miikka Toivola (33/3). Trainer: Aulis Rytkönen (5).

324. 19.05.1976 **FINLAND - SWITZERLAND** **1-0(0-0)**
Väinölänniemi Stadion, Kuopio; Referee: Erik Fredriksson (Sweden); Attendance: 7,007
FIN: Göran Enckelman (10/0), Timo Kautonen (51/0), Arto Tolsa (45/10), Erkki Vihtilä (15/0), Esko Ranta (33/0), Pertti Jantunen (3/1), Jouko Suomalainen (36/2), Hannu Hämäläinen (5/0) [57.Juha-Pekka Laine (9/1); 86.Esa Heiskanen (1/0)], Olavi Rissanen (19/5), Aki Heiskanen (13/2), Matti Paatelainen (Cap) (31/7). Trainer: Aulis Rytkönen (6).
Goal: Pertti Jantunen (87).

325. 01.06.1976 **FINLAND - SWEDEN** **0-2(0-0)** Nordic Championship
Olympiastadion, Helsinki; Referee: Ivar Fredriksen (Norway); Attendance: 16,116
FIN: Göran Enckelman (11/0), Erkki Vihtilä (16/0), Arto Tolsa (46/10), Ari Mäkynen (10/0), Esko Ranta (34/0), Pertti Jantunen (4/1), Jouko Suomalainen (37/2), Esa Heiskanen (2/0) [62.Juha-Pekka Laine (10/1)], Olavi Rissanen (20/5), Aki Heiskanen (14/2), Matti Paatelainen (32/7). Trainer: Aulis Rytkönen (7).

326. 13.06.1976 **FINLAND - ENGLAND** **1-4(1-2)** 11th FIFA WC. Qualifiers
Olympiastadion, Helsinki; Referee: Alfred Delcourt (Belgium); Attendance: 24,336
FIN: Göran Enckelman (12/0), Erkki Vihtilä (17/0), Arto Tolsa (47/10), Ari Mäkynen (11/0), Esko Ranta (35/0), Pertti Jantunen (5/1), Jouko Suomalainen (38/2) [65.Seppo Pyykkö (1/0)], Esa Heiskanen (3/0), Olavi Rissanen (21/5), Aki Heiskanen (15/2), Matti Paatelainen (Cap) (33/8). Trainer: Aulis Rytkönen (8).
Goal: Matti Paatelainen (28).

327. 14.07.1976 **FINLAND - ICELAND** **1-0(1-0)**
Olympiastadion, Helsinki; Referee: John Bartley Homewood (England); Attendance: 6,769
FIN: Göran Enckelman (13/0), Erkki Vihtilä (18/0), Arto Tolsa (48/10), Ari Mäkynen (12/0), Esko Ranta (36/0), Pertti Jantunen (6/1), Seppo Pyykkö (2/0) [67.Jyrki Nieminen (1/0)], Esa Heiskanen (4/1) [89.Raimo Vierikko (1/0)], Olavi Rissanen (22/5), Aki Heiskanen (16/2) [80.Jouko Suomalainen (39/2)], Matti Paatelainen (Cap) (34/8). Trainer: Aulis Rytkönen (9).
Goal: Esa Heiskanen (12).

328. 11.08.1976 **SWEDEN – FINLAND** **6-0(2-0)** Nordic Championship
Malmö Stadion, Malmö; Referee: Torben Månsson (Denmark); Attendance: 11,737
FIN: Göran Enckelman (14/0), Erkki Vihtilä (19/0), Jouko Suomalainen (40/2), Ari Mäkynen (13/0), Esko Ranta (37/0), Pertti Jantunen (7/1), Jyrki Nieminen (2/0), Esa Heiskanen (5/1) [70.Juha Helin (1/0)], Olavi Rissanen (23/5), Aki Heiskanen (17/2) [46.Miikka Toivola (34/3)], Matti Paatelainen (Cap) (35/8). Trainer: Aulis Rytkönen (10).

329. 25.08.1976 **FINLAND - TURKEY** **2-1(1-0)**
Olympiastadion, Helsinki; Referee: Sven Jonsson (Sweden); Attendance: 5,240
FIN: Pertti Alaja (9/0), Teppo Heikkinen (1/0), Erkki Vihtilä (20/0), Ari Mäkynen (14/0), Esko Ranta (38/0), Pertti Jantunen (8/1), Jouko Suomalainen (41/2) [70.Esa Heiskanen (6/1)], Miikka Toivola (35/3), Olavi Rissanen (24/5) [64.Jyrki Nieminen (3/0)], Aki Heiskanen (18/3), Matti Paatelainen (Cap) (36/9). Trainer: Aulis Rytkönen (11).
Goals: Aki Heiskanen (37), Matti Paatelainen (81).

330. 08.09.1976 **SCOTLAND - FINLAND** **6-0(4-0)**
Hampden Park, Glasgow; Referee: Gordon Kew (England); Attendance: 16,338
FIN: Pertti Alaja (10/0) [46.Göran Enckelman (15/0)], Teppo Heikkinen (2/0) [75.Matti Ahonen (1/0)], Erkki Vihtilä (21/0), Ari Mäkynen (15/0), Esko Ranta (39/0), Pertti Jantunen (9/1), Jouko Suomalainen (42/2), Miikka Toivola (36/3), Olavi Rissanen (25/5), Juha Dahllund (1/0), Matti Paatelainen (Cap) (37/9) [37.Jyrki Nieminen (4/0)]. Trainer: Aulis Rytkönen (12).

331. 22.09.1976 **FINLAND - LUXEMBOURG** **7-1(3-0)** 11th FIFA WC. Qualifiers
Olympiastadion, Helsinki; Referee: Svein Inge Thime (Norway); Attendance: 4,555
FIN: Göran Enckelman (16/0),Teppo Heikkinen (3/1), Erkki Vihtilä (22/0), Ari Mäkynen (16/1), Esko Ranta (40/0), Pertti Jantunen (10/1), Esa Heiskanen (7/3) [53.Jyrki Nieminen (5/0)], Miikka Toivola (37/3), Olavi Rissanen (26/7), Aki Heiskanen (19/4), Matti Paatelainen (Cap) (38/9) [75.Seppo Pyykkö (3/0)]. Trainer: Aulis Rytkönen (13).
Goals: Aki Heiskanen (15), Esa Heiskanen (22, 27), Olavi Rissanen (51), Teppo Heikkinen (54), Olavi Rissanen (61), Ari Mäkynen (82 penalty).

332. 13.10.1976 **ENGLAND - FINLAND** **2-1(1-0)** 11th FIFA WC. Qualifiers
Wembley Stadium, London; Referee: Ulf Helmer Johan Eriksson (Sweden); Attendance: 92,000
FIN: Göran Enckelman (17/0), Teppo Heikkinen (4/1), Erkki Vihtilä (23/0), Ari Mäkynen (17/1), Esko Ranta (41/0), Pertti Jantunen (11/1) [61.Esa Heiskanen (8/3)], Jouko Suomalainen (43/2) [67.Seppo Pyykkö (4/0)], Miikka Toivola (38/3), Jyrki Nieminen (6/1), Aki Heiskanen (20/4), Matti Paatelainen (Cap) (39/9). Trainer: Aulis Rytkönen (14).
Goal: Jyrki Nieminen (48).

333. 06.04.1977 **TURKEY - FINLAND** **1-2(1-0)**
Stadı 19 Mayis, Ankara; Referee: Otto Anderco (Romania); Attendance: 45,000
FIN: Pertti Alaja (11/0), Teppo Heikkinen (5/1) [Jarmo Ilola (1/0)], Erkki Vihtilä (24/0), Ari Mäkynen (18/1) [86.Raimo Vierikko (2/0)], Esko Ranta (42/0), Pertti Jantunen (12/1), Jouko Suomalainen (44/2), Miikka Toivola (39/3), Jyrki Nieminen (7/2), Aki Heiskanen (21/4) [Olavi Rissanen (27/7)], Matti Paatelainen (Cap) (40/10). Trainer: Aulis Rytkönen (15).
Goals: Matti Paatelainen (64), Jyrki Nieminen (76).

334. 26.05.1977 **LUXEMBOURG - FINLAND** **0-1(0-0)** 11th FIFA WC. Qualifiers
Stade Municipal, Luxembourg; Referee: Ole Amundsen (Denmark); Attendance: 1,700
FIN: Göran Enckelman (18/0), Teppo Heikkinen (6/1), Erkki Vihtilä (25/0), Arto Tolsa (49/10), Esko Ranta (43/0), Pertti Jantunen (13/1), Jouko Suomalainen (45/2), Miikka Toivola (40/3) [62.Jyrki Nieminen (8/2)], Olavi Rissanen (28/7), Aki Heiskanen (22/5) [78.Kai Haaskivi (1/0)], Matti Paatelainen (Cap) (41/10). Trainer: Aulis Rytkönen (16).
Goal : Aki Heiskanen (58).

335. 08.06.1977 **FINLAND - ITALY** **0-3(0-1)** 11th FIFA WC. Qualifiers
Olympiastadion, Helsinki; Referee: Robert Héliès (Fra); Attendance: 17,539
FIN: Göran Enckelman (19/0), Teppo Heikkinen (7/1), Erkki Vihtilä (26/0), Arto Tolsa (50/10), Esko Ranta (44/0), Pertti Jantunen (14/1), Jouko Suomalainen (46/2), Miikka Toivola (41/3) [51.Jyrki Nieminen (9/2)], Olavi Rissanen (29/7), Aki Heiskanen (23/5) [69.Markku Närvä (1/0)], Matti Paatelainen (Cap) (42/10). Trainer: Aulis Rytkönen (17).

336. 22.06.1977 **FINLAND - DENMARK** **1-2(0-0)** Nordic Championship
Olympiastadion, Helsinki; Referee: Lars-Åke Björck (Sweden); Attendance: 9,783
FIN: Pertti Alaja (12/0), Teppo Heikkinen (8/1), Erkki Vihtilä (27/0), Arto Tolsa (Cap) (51/10), Esko Ranta (45/0), Pertti Jantunen (15/1), Jouko Suomalainen (47/2) [66.Kai Haaskivi (2/0)], Miikka Toivola (42/3), Olavi Rissanen (30/7), Aki Heiskanen (24/5) [72.Matti Paatelainen (43/10)], Jyrki Nieminen (10/3). Trainer: Aulis Rytkönen (18).
Goal: Jyrki Nieminen (83).

337. 18.08.1977 **NORWAY - FINLAND** **1-1(1-0)** Nordic Championship
Ullevaal Stadion, Oslo; Referee: Paul Jensen (Denmark); Attendance: 10,263
FIN: Pekka Hieta (1/0), Teppo Heikkinen (9/1) [67.Markku Närvä (2/0)], Erkki Vihtilä (28/0), Arto Tolsa (52/10), Esko Ranta (46/0), Pertti Jantunen (16/1), Kai Haaskivi (3/0), Miikka Toivola (43/3) [Juha Dahllund (2/0)], Olavi Rissanen (31/7), Aki Heiskanen (25/5) [57.Reima Kokko (1/0)], Matti Paatelainen (Cap) (44/11). Trainer: Aulis Rytkönen (19).
Goal: Matti Paatelainen (85).

338. 07.09.1977 **FINLAND – WEST GERMANY** **0-1(0-1)**
Olympiastadion, Helsinki; Referee: Viktor Dzarkov (Soviet Union); Attendance: 14,324
FIN: Göran Enckelman (20/0), Teppo Heikkinen (10/1), Erkki Vihtilä (29/0), Arto Tolsa (53/10), Esko Ranta (47/0), Pertti Jantunen (17/1), Kai Haaskivi (4/0), Miikka Toivola (44/3), Olavi Rissanen (32/7), Aki Heiskanen (26/5) [77.Jouko Suomalainen (48/2)], Matti Paatelainen (Cap) (45/11). Trainer: Aulis Rytkönen (20).

339. 05.10.1977 **SWITZERLAND - FINLAND** **2-0(1-0)**
Hardturm Stadion, Zürich; Referee: Alain Delmer (France); Attendance: 7,800
FIN: Pertti Alaja (13/0), Teppo Heikkinen (11/1) [30.Teuvo Vilen (1/0)], Erkki Vihtilä (30/0), Juha Helin (2/0), Esko Ranta (48/0), Kai Haaskivi (5/0), Jouko Suomalainen (49/2), Miikka Toivola (45/3), Olavi Rissanen (33/7) [55.Jukka Pirinen (3/0); 60.Markku Närvä (3/0)], Heikki Suhonen (16/2), Matti Paatelainen (Cap) (46/11). Trainer: Aulis Rytkönen (21).

340. 15.10.1977 **ITALY - FINLAND** **6-1(3-0)** 11th FIFA WC. Qualifiers
Stadio Comunale, Torino; Referee: Nikolai Dudin (Bulgaria); Attendance: 62,888
FIN: Göran Enckelman (21/0), Jouko Suomalainen (50/2) [7.Reijo Vaittinen (1/0)], Erkki Vihtilä (31/0), Ari Mäkynen (19/1), Esko Ranta (49/0), Pertti Jantunen (18/1), Kai Haaskivi (6/1), Miikka Toivola (46/3), Heikki Suhonen (17/2), Aki Heiskanen (27/5) [61.Teppo Heikkinen (12/1)], Matti Paatelainen (Cap) (47/11). Trainer: Aulis Rytkönen (22).
Goal: Kai Haaskivi (67).

341. 05.04.1978 **SOVIET UNION - FINLAND** **10-2(4-0)**
Hrazdan Stadium, Erevan; Referee: Jerzy Kacprzak (Poland); Attendance: 11,700
FIN: Göran Enckelman (22/0), Erkki Vihtilä (Cap) (32/0), Arto Tolsa (54/10), Ari Mäkynen (20/1), Esko Ranta (50/0), Seppo Pyykkö (5/0), Leo Houtsonen (1/0) [46.Pertti Jantunen (19/1)], Miikka Toivola (47/3), Arto Uimonen (1/0) [46.Olavi Rissanen (34/7)], Aki Heiskanen (28/6), Jyrki Nieminen (11/4). Trainer: Aulis Rytkönen (23).
Goals: Aki Heiskanen (66), Jyrki Nieminen (89).

342. 03.05.1978 **FINLAND - MEXICO** **0-1(0-0)**
Olympiastadion, Helsinki; Referee: Kjell Johansson (Finland); Attendance: 6,054
FIN: Pertti Alaja (14/0), Erkki Vihtilä (33/0), Arto Tolsa (55/10), Ari Mäkynen (21/1), Esko Ranta (51/0), Pertti Jantunen (20/1), Arto Uimonen (2/0), Miikka Toivola (48/3), Olavi Rissanen (35/7) [46.Seppo Pyykkö (6/0)], Aki Heiskanen (29/6) [75.Leo Houtsonen (2/0)], Jyrki Nieminen (12/4). Trainer: Aulis Rytkönen (24).

343. 24.05.1978 **FINLAND - GREECE** **3-0(1-0)** 6th EC. Qualifiers
Olympiastadion, Helsinki; Referee: Heinz Einbeck (East Germany); Attendance: 7,740
FIN: Pertti Alaja (15/0), Erkki Vihtilä (34/0), Arto Tolsa (56/10), Ari Mäkynen (22/1), Esko Ranta (52/0), Pertti Jantunen (21/1), Aki Heiskanen (30/6), Miikka Toivola (49/3), Leo Houtsonen (3/0) [61.Olavi Rissanen (36/7)], Atik Ismail (1/2), Jyrki Nieminen (13/5). Trainer: Aulis Rytkönen (25).
Goals: Atik Ismail (36, 82), Jyrki Nieminen (82).

344. 28.06.1978 **SWEDEN – FINLAND** **2-1(1-0)** Nordic Championship
Ryavallen, Borås; Referee: Torben Månsson (Denmark); Attendance: 6,600
FIN: Pertti Alaja (16/0), Erkki Vihtilä (35/0), Arto Tolsa (57/10), Juha Helin (3/0), Teuvo Vilen (2/0), Pertti Jantunen (22/1), Aki Heiskanen (31/6) [60.Kalle Nieminen (3/0)], Miikka Toivola (50/3), Seppo Pyykkö (7/0) [60.Olavi Rissanen (37/7)], Atik Ismail (2/3), Jyrki Nieminen (14/5). Trainer: Aulis Rytkönen (26).
Goal: Atik Ismail (84).

345. 09.08.1978 **FINLAND - NORWAY** **1-1(0-0)** Nordic Championship
Olympiastadion, Helsinki; Referee: Marian Kuston (Poland); Attendance: 7,481
FIN: Pertti Alaja (17/0), Erkki Vihtilä (36/0), Teuvo Vilen (3/0), Juha Helin (4/0), Esko Ranta (53/0), Pertti Jantunen (23/1) [72.Antti Ronkainen (1/0)], Jouko Suomalainen (51/2) [30.Seppo Pyykkö (8/0)], Miikka Toivola (51/3), Arto Uimonen (3/0) [Olavi Rissanen (38/7)], Atik Ismail (3/4), Jyrki Nieminen (15/5). Trainer: Aulis Rytkönen (27).
Goal: Atik Ismail (79).

346. 30.08.1978 **FINLAND - POLAND** **0-1(0-0)**
Olympiastadion, Helsinki; Referee: Henry Öberg (Norway); Attendance: 4,242
FIN: Pertti Alaja (18/0), Erkki Vihtilä (37/0), Risto Salonen (1/0), Juha Helin (5/0), Esko Ranta (54/0), Antti Ronkainen (2/0) [46.Pertti Jantunen (24/1)], Jouko Suomalainen (Cap) (52/2) [78.Kalle Nieminen (4/0)], Miikka Toivola (52/3), Seppo Pyykkö (9/0) [71.Arto Uimonen (4/0)], Atik Ismail (4/4), Jyrki Nieminen (16/5). Trainer: Aulis Rytkönen (28).

347. 20.09.1978 **FINLAND - HUNGARY** **2-1(1-0)** 6th EC. Qualifiers
Olympiastadion, Helsinki; Referee: Erik Fredriksson (Sweden); Attendance: 4,797
FIN: Pertti Alaja (19/0), Erkki Vihtilä (38/0), Arto Tolsa (58/10), Risto Salonen (2/0), Esko Ranta (55/0), Pertti Jantunen (25/1), Jouko Suomalainen (53/2) [60.Juha Helin (6/0)], Miikka Toivola (53/3), Seppo Pyykkö (10/1) [76.Arto Uimonen (5/0)], Atik Ismail (5/5), Jyrki Nieminen (17/5). Trainer: Aulis Rytkönen (29).
Goals: Atik Ismail (30), Seppo Pyykkö (53).

348. 11.10.1978 **GREECE - FINLAND** **8-1(5-0)** 6th EC. Qualifiers
Stádio "Leoforos Alexandras", Athína; Referee: Marcel van Langehove (Belgium); Attendance: 9,000
FIN: Göran Enckelman (23/0), Erkki Vihtilä (39/0), Arto Tolsa (59/10), Risto Salonen (3/0), Esko Ranta (56/0), Pertti Jantunen (26/1), Jouko Suomalainen (54/2) [74.Kalle Nieminen (5/0)], Aki Heiskanen (32/7), Seppo Pyykkö (11/1) [29.Arto Uimonen (6/0)], Atik Ismail (6/5), Jyrki Nieminen (18/5). Trainer: Aulis Rytkönen (30).
Goal: Aki Heiskanen (61).

349. 05.02.1979 **IRAQ - FINLAND** **1-0(0-0)**
Al-Shaab Stadium, Baghdad; Referee : n/a; Attendance: 12,000
FIN: Pertti Alaja (20/0) [60.Stefan Lindström (1/0)], Mikko Lampi (1/0), Juha Helin (7/0), Kari Virtanen (1/0) [Risto Salonen (4/0)], Esko Ranta (57/0), Pasi Rautiainen (1/0), Seppo Pyykkö (12/1), Miikka Toivola (54/3), Reima Kokko (2/0) [Anders Backman (1/0)], Atik Ismail (7/5) [Harri Lindholm (1/0)], Jyrki Nieminen (19/5). Trainer : Esko Malm (1).

350. 07.02.1979 **IRAQ - FINLAND** **2-0(2-0)**
Al-Shaab Stadium, Baghdad; Referee : n/a; Attendance: 8,000
FIN: Pertti Alaja (21/0), Miikka Toivola (55/3), Juha Helin (8/0), Seppo Pyykkö (13/1), Risto Salonen (5/0), Jyrki Nieminen (20/5) [46.Olavi Rissanen (39/7)], Esko Ranta (58/0), Reima Kokko (3/0), Mikko Lampi (2/0) [46.Teuvo Vilen (4/0)], Atik Ismail (8/5), Pasi Rautiainen (2/0). Trainer : Esko Malm (2).

351. 09.02.1979 **BAHRAIN - FINLAND** **0-1(0-0)**

Isa Town Stadium, Manama; Referee : n/a; Attendance: 5,000

FIN: Stefan Lindström (2/0), Teuvo Vilen (5/0), Mikko Lampi (3/0), Juha Helin (9/0), Kari Virtanen (2/0) [Risto Salonen (6/0)], Hannu Turunen (1/0), Seppo Pyykkö (14/1) [Miikka Toivola (56/3)], Reima Kokko (4/0), Anders Backman (2/1), Olavi Rissanen (40/7), Harri Lindholm (2/0). Trainer : Esko Malm (3).

Goal: Anders Backman (55).

352. 10.05.1979 **DENMARK Olympic - FINLAND** **1-1(0-0)** 22nd OG. Qualifiers

Aalborg Stadion, Aalborg; Referee: Francis Rion (Belgium); Attendance: 2,700

FIN: Olli Isoaho (1/0), Teuvo Vilen (6/0) [*sent off 86*], Risto Salonen (7/0), Kari Virtanen (3/0), Mikko Lampi (4/0), Juha Dahllund (3/0), Arto Uimonen (7/0), Kalle Nieminen (6/0), Harri Lindholm (3/1), Pasi Rautiainen (3/0), Hannu Rajaniemi (1/0). Trainer: Jiří Pešek (Czechoslovakia, 1).

Goal: Harri Lindholm (50).

353. 07.06.1979 **FINLAND – DENMARK Olympic** **4-1(2-0)** 22nd OG. Qualifiers

Urheilukeskus, Kotka; Referee: Anatoliy Milchenko (Soviet Union); Attendance: 3,581

FIN: Stefan Lindström (3/0), Mikko Lampi (5/0), Juha Dahllund (4/0), Juha Helin (10/1), Juha Rissanen (1/0), Risto Rosenberg (1/1) [Pasi Rautiainen (4/0)], Harri Lindholm (4/1), Kalle Nieminen (7/1), Arto Uimonen (8/0), Petteri Kupiainen (1/0), Hannu Rajaniemi (2/1). Trainer: Jiří Pešek (Czechoslovakia, 2)

Goals: Juha Helin (12), Risto Rosenberg (21), Hannu Rajaniemi (61), Kalle Nieminen (70).

354. 04.07.1979 **FINLAND - SOVIET UNION** **1-1(0-1)** 6th EC. Qualifiers

Olympiastadion, Helsinki; Referee: Ole Amundsen (Denmark); Attendance: 13,119

FIN: Pertti Alaja (22/0), Mikko Lampi (6/0), Leo Houtsonen (4/0), Arto Tolsa (60/10), Esko Ranta (59/0), Seppo Pyykkö (15/1) [77.Risto Salonen (8/0)], Miikka Toivola (57/3) [28.Reima Kokko (5/0)], Petteri Kupiainen (2/0), Jyrki Nieminen (21/5), Atik Ismail (9/6), Pasi Rautiainen (5/0). Trainer: Esko Malm (4).

Goal: Atik Ismail (55).

355. 09.08.1979 **FINLAND – NORWAY Olympic** **0-1(0-0)** 22nd OG. Qualifiers

Väinölänniemi Stadion, Kuopio; Referee: Ole Amundsen (Denmark); Attendance: 6,129

FIN: Olli Isoaho (2/0), Mikko Lampi (7/0), Leo Houtsonen (5/0), Juha Helin (11/1), Juha Rissanen (2/0), Kari Virtanen (4/0), Harri Lindholm (5/1) [62.Arto Uimonen (9/0)], Kalle Nieminen (8/1) [46.Hannu Turunen (2/0)], Heikki Lampi (1/0), Petteri Kupiainen (3/0), Hannu Rajaniemi (3/1). Trainer: Jiří Pešek (Czechoslovakia, 3).

356. 29.08.1979 **FINLAND - DENMARK** **0-0** Nordic Championship

Urheilupuisto, Mikkeli; Referee: Ingemar Johansson (Sweden); Attendance: 4,433

FIN: Pertti Alaja (23/0), Mikko Lampi (8/0), Arto Tolsa (61/10), Leo Houtsonen (6/0), Esko Ranta (60/0), Pasi Rautiainen (6/0), Seppo Pyykkö (16/1), Miikka Toivola (58/3), Petteri Kupiainen (4/0) [78.Reima Kokko (6/0)], Atik Ismail (10/6) [61.Heikki Suhonen (18/2)], Jyrki Nieminen (22/5). Trainer: Esko Malm (5).

357. 13.09.1979 **WEST GERMANY Olympic - FINLAND** **2-0(1-0)** 22nd OG. Qualifiers

Niederrhein Stadion, Oberhausen; Referee: Luigi Agnolin (Italy)

FIN: Olli Isoaho (3/0), Mikko Lampi (9/0), Kari Virtanen (5/0), Juha Helin (12/1), Juha Rissanen (3/0), Risto Rosenberg (2/1) [85.Jarmo Kaivonurmi (1/0)], Tuomo Hakala (1/0) [70.Harri Lindholm (6/1)], Matti Ahonen (2/0), Juhani Himanka (1/0), Petteri Kupiainen (5/0), Hannu Rajaniemi (4/1). Trainer: Jiří Pešek (Czechoslovakia, 4).

358. 26.09.1979 **DENMARK - FINLAND** **1-0(0-0)** Nordic Championship

Idrætsparken, København; Referee: Kaare Lindboe (Norway); Attendance: 24,400

FIN: Stefan Lindström (4/0) [47.Seppo Sairanen (1/0)], Mikko Lampi (10/0), Arto Tolsa (62/10) [52.Juha Helin (13/1)], Teuvo Vilen (7/0), Esko Ranta (61/0), Pasi Rautiainen (7/0), Seppo Pyykkö (17/1), Miikka Toivola (59/3), Olavi Rissanen (41/7) [75.Heikki Suhonen (19/2)], Ossi Loikkanen (1/0), Jyrki Nieminen (23/5). Trainer: Esko Malm (6).

359. 10.10.1979 **FINLAND – WEST GERMANY Olympic** **0-0** 22nd OG. Qualifiers

Olympiastadion, Helsinki; Referee: Roger Schoeters (Belgium); Attendance: 2,602

FIN: Seppo Sairanen (2/0), Mikko Lampi (11/0) [79.Aki Lahtinen (1/0)], Kari Virtanen (6/0), Juha Helin (14/1), Juha Rissanen (4/0), Leo Houtsonen (7/0), Tuomo Hakala (2/0), Pasi Rautiainen (8/0), Juhani Himanka (2/0), Petteri Kupiainen (6/0), Jarmo Kaivonurmi (2/0) [66.Harri Lindholm (7/1)]. Trainer: Jiří Pešek (Czechoslovakia, 5).

360. 17.10.1979 **HUNGARY - FINLAND** **3-1(2-0)** 6th EC. Qualifiers

Nagyerdei stadion, Debrecen; Referee: Charles George Rainier Corver (Netherlands); Attendance: 18,000

FIN: Seppo Sairanen (3/0), Mikko Lampi (12/0), Arto Tolsa (63/10), Leo Houtsonen (8/0), Esko Ranta (62/0), Seppo Pyykkö (18/1), Miikka Toivola (60/4), Pasi Rautiainen (9/0), Kai Haaskivi (7/1), Atik Ismail (11/6) [68.Petteri Kupiainen (7/0)], Heikki Suhonen (20/2) [60.Juhani Himanka (3/0)]. Trainer: Esko Malm (7).

Goal: Miikka Toivola (47).

361. 26.10.1979 **NORWAY Olympic - FINLAND** **1-1(1-1)** 22nd OG. Qualifiers

Stavanger Stadion, Stavanger; Referee: Erik Fredriksson (Sweden); Attendance: 9,400

FIN: Pekka Hieta (2/0), Aki Lahtinen (2/0), Kari Virtanen (7/0) [53.Ari Heikkinen (1/0)], Juha Helin (15/1), Juha Rissanen (5/0), Antti Ronkainen (3/0), Juhani Himanka (4/0), Hannu Turunen (3/0), Raimo Kuuluvainen (2/0), Pasi Rautiainen (10/1), Harri Lindholm (8/1). Trainer: Jiří Pešek (Czechoslovakia, 6).

Goal: Pasi Rautiainen (44).

362. 31.10.1979 **SOVIET UNION - FINLAND** **2-2(0-0)** 6th EC. Qualifiers

Lenin Stadium, Moskva; Referee: Aleksandar Nikić (Yugoslavia); Attendance: 1,500

FIN: Seppo Sairanen (4/0), Mikko Lampi (13/0), Arto Tolsa (64/10), Erkki Vihtilä (40/0), Esko Ranta (63/0), Leo Houtsonen (9/0), Seppo Pyykkö (19/1) [46.Hannu Turunen (4/0)], Kai Haaskivi (8/2), Juhani Himanka (5/0) [72.Tuomo Hakala (3/1)], Atik Ismail (12/6), Jyrki Nieminen (24/5). Trainer: Esko Malm (8).

Goals: Kai Haaskivi (76), Tuomo Hakala (82).

363. 20.11.1979 **MEXICO - FINLAND** **1-1(1-0)**

Estadio Azteca, Ciudad de México; Referee: Domingo de la Mora (Mexico); Attendance: 30,000

FIN: Seppo Sairanen (5/0), Erkki Vihtilä (41/0), Arto Tolsa (65/10), Kari Virtanen (8/0), Esko Ranta (64/0), Leo Houtsonen (10/0), Juhani Himanka (6/0) [77.Heikki Suhonen (21/2)], Antti Ronkainen (4/0) [46.Hannu Turunen (5/0)], Kai Haaskivi (9/2) [*sent off 88*], Tuomo Hakala (4/1) [80.Juha Helin (16/1)], Jyrki Nieminen (25/6). Trainer: Esko Malm (9).

Goal: Jyrki Nieminen (52).

364. 25.11.1979 **BERMUDA - FINLAND** **0-2(0-1)**
National Stadium, Devonshire, Hamilton; Referee: n/a; Attendance: 3,000
FIN: Pekka Hieta (3/0), Erkki Vihtilä (42/0) [Aki Lahtinen (3/0)], Arto Tolsa (66/10), Juha Helin (17/1), Esko Ranta (65/0), Hannu Turunen (6/0), Kari Virtanen (9/0), Leo Houtsonen (11/0) [Ari Heikkinen (2/0)], Juhani Himanka (7/1) [Antti Ronkainen (5/0)], Tuomo Hakala (5/1), Jyrki Nieminen (26/7). Trainer: Esko Malm (10).
Goals: Jyrki Nieminen (45), Juhani Himanka (52).

365. 22.05.1980 **FINLAND - SWEDEN** **0-2(0-2)** Nordic Championship
Olympiastadion, Helsinki; Referee: Ib Nielsen (Denmark); Attendance: 9,196
FIN: Seppo Sairanen (6/0), Mikko Lampi (14/0) [46.Aki Lahtinen (4/0)], Arto Tolsa (67/10), Leo Houtsonen (12/0), Esko Ranta (66/0), Petteri Kupiainen (8/0) [46.Miikka Toivola (61/4)], Kari Virtanen (10/0), Pasi Rautiainen (11/1), Seppo Pyykkö (20/1), Atik Ismail (13/6) [72.Tuomo Hakala (6/1)], Jyrki Nieminen (27/7). Trainer: Esko Malm (11).

366. 04.06.1980 **FINLAND - BULGARIA** **0-2(0-1)** 12th FIFA WC. Qualifiers
Olympiastadion, Helsinki; Referee: Brian Robert McGinlay (Scotland); Attendance: 7,805
FIN: Seppo Sairanen (7/0) [8.Pekka Nurmio (1/0)], Mikko Lampi (15/0), Arto Tolsa (68/10), Leo Houtsonen (13/0), Esko Ranta (67/0), Antti Ronkainen (6/0) [65.Atik Ismail (14/6)], Seppo Pyykkö (21/1), Miikka Toivola (62/4), Pasi Rautiainen (12/1), Tuomo Hakala (7/1), Jyrki Nieminen (28/7). Trainer: Esko Malm (12).

367. 25.06.1980 **ICELAND - FINLAND** **1-1(0-0)**
Laugardalsvöllur, Reykjavík; Referee: Søren Hansen (Denmark); Attendance: 6,000
FIN: Olli Isoaho (4/0), Aki Lahtinen (5/0), Juha Helin (18/1), Kari Virtanen (11/0), Ari Heikkinen (3/0) [Teuvo Vilen (8/0)], Hannu Turunen (7/0) [56.Tomi Jalo (1/0)], Juha Dahllund (5/0), Vesa Pulliainen (1/0), Juhani Himanka (8/1), Ari Tissari (1/1), Jouko Alila (1/0) [24.Jouko Soini (1/0)]. Trainer: Esko Malm (13).
Goal: Ari Tissari (46).

368. 21.07.1980 **YUGOSLAVIA Olympic - FINLAND** **2-0(0-0)** 22nd OG. 1st Round.
Dinamo Stadium, Minsk (Soviet Union); Referee: Mario Vásquez Rubio (Mexico); Attendance: 50,000
FIN: Olli Isoaho (5/0), Aki Lahtinen (6/0), Juha Helin (19/1), Kari Virtanen (12/0), Ari Heikkinen (4/0) [63.Teuvo Vilen (9/0)], Hannu Turunen (8/0), Juha Dahllund (6/0) [63.Raimo Kuuluvainen (3/0)], Vesa Pulliainen (2/0), Juhani Himanka (9/1), Ari Tissari (2/1), Jouko Alila (2/0). Trainer: Esko Malm (14).

369. 23.07.1980 **IRAQ Olympic - FINLAND** **0-0** 22nd OG. 1st Round.
Centralniy Stadium, Kiev (Soviet Union); Referee: Ramón Castro Calderón (Cuba); Attendance: 40,000
FIN: Olli Isoaho (6/0), Aki Lahtinen (7/0), Juha Helin (20/1), Kari Virtanen (13/0), Teuvo Vilen (10/0), Hannu Turunen (9/0), Juha Dahllund (7/0), Vesa Pulliainen (3/0), Juhani Himanka (10/1), Ari Tissari (3/1) [24.Jouko Soini (2/0)], Jouko Alila (3/0) [74.Tomi Jalo (2/0)]. Trainer: Esko Malm (15).

370. 25.07.1980 **FINLAND – COSTA RICA Olympic** **3-0(2-0)** 22nd OG. 1st Round.
Centralniy Stadium, Kiev (Soviet Union); Referee: Albanni Abdul Wahab (Zambia); Attendance: 50,000
FIN: Olli Isoaho (7/0), Aki Lahtinen (8/0), Juha Helin (21/1), Kari Virtanen (14/0), Teuvo Vilen (11/0), Hannu Turunen (10/0), Juha Dahllund (8/0), Vesa Pulliainen (4/0), Juhani Himanka (11/1) [61.Jouko Soini (3/1)], Ari Tissari (4/2) [78.Juha Rissanen (6/0)], Jouko Alila (4/1). Trainer: Esko Malm (16).
Goals: Ari Tissari (17), Jouko Alila (57), Jouko Soini (87).

371. 21.08.1980 **NORWAY - FINLAND** **6-1(2-1)** Nordic Championship
Ullevaal Stadion, Oslo; Referee: Kjell Johansson (Sweden); Attendance: 10,640
FIN: Stefan Lindström (5/0), Aki Lahtinen (9/0), Arto Tolsa (69/10), Leo Houtsonen (14/0) [60.Vesa Pulliainen], Mikko Lampi (16/0) [58.Matti Ahonen (3/0)], Pasi Rautiainen (13/1) [46.Kari Virtanen (15/0)], Juha Dahllund (9/0), Seppo Pyykkö (22/1), Tuomo Hakala (8/1), Ari Tissari (5/2), Juhani Himanka (12/2). Trainer: Esko Malm (17).
Goal: Juhani Himanka (43).

372. 03.09.1980 **ALBANIA - FINLAND** **2-0(2-0)** 12th FIFA WC. Qualifiers
Stadiumi „Kombëtar Qemal Stafa", Tiranë; Referee: Emmanuel Platopoulos (Greece); Attendance: 25,000
FIN: Olli Isoaho (8/0), Aki Lahtinen (10/0), Arto Tolsa (70/10), Juha Helin (22/1) [46.Hannu Turunen (11/0)], Matti Ahonen (4/0), Vesa Pulliainen (6/0) [46.Hannu Rajaniemi (5/1)], Juha Dahllund (10/0), Seppo Pyykkö (23/1), Tuomo Hakala (9/1), Kari Virtanen (16/0), Juhani Himanka (13/2). Trainer: Esko Malm (18).

373. 24.09.1980 **FINLAND - AUSTRIA** **0-2(0-1)** 12th FIFA WC. Qualifiers
Olympiastadion, Helsinki; Referee: Clive Thomas (Wales); Attendance: 8,099
FIN: Olli Isoaho (9/0), Aki Lahtinen (11/0), Arto Tolsa (71/10), Leo Houtsonen (15/0), Esko Ranta (68/0), Kari Virtanen (17/0), Seppo Pyykkö (24/1), Juha Dahllund (11/0), Antti Ronkainen (7/0) [60.Hannu Turunen (12/0)], Ari Tissari (6/2), Hannu Rajaniemi (6/1) [75.Ari Jalasvaara (1/0)]. Trainer: Esko Malm (19).

374. 30.11.1980 **BOLIVIA - FINLAND** **3-0(1-0)**
Estadio "Hernando Siles Zuazo", La Paz; Referee: Jorge Antequera (Bolivia); Attendance: 8,000
FIN: Olavi Huttunen (1/0), Aki Lahtinen (12/0), Arto Tolsa (72/10), Juha Rissanen (7/0), Kari Bergqvist (1/0), Hannu Turunen (13/0) [Juha Annunen (1/0)], Hannu Rajaniemi (7/1), Jukka Ikäläinen (1/0) [Juha Äijälä (1/0)], Antti Ronkainen (8/0), Pasi Jaakonsaari (1/0), Ari Valvee (1/0) [Raimo Kuuluvainen (4/0)]. Trainer: Esko Malm (20).

375. 04.12.1980 **BOLIVIA - FINLAND** **2-2(1-1)**
Estadio "Ramón 'Tahuichi' Aguilera", Santa Cruz de la Sierra; Referee: Luis Barrancos Álvarez (Bolivia); Attendance: 11,238
FIN: Olavi Huttunen (2/0), Aki Lahtinen (13/0), Arto Tolsa (73/10), Reijo Vaittinen (2/0), Kari Bergqvist (2/0), Hannu Turunen (14/0), Raimo Kuuluvainen (5/0) [Juha Annunen (2/0)], Jukka Ikäläinen (2/0), Antti Ronkainen (9/0), Pasi Jaakonsaari (2/1) [Ari Jalasvaara (2/0)], Ari Valvee (2/1). Trainer: Esko Malm (21).
Goal: Pasi Jaakonsaari (12), Ari Valvee (90).

376. 08.12.1980 **URUGUAY - FINLAND** **6-0(0-0)**
Estadio Centenario, Montevideo; Referee: José Luis Martínez Bazán (Uruguay); Attendance: 10,000
FIN: Olavi Huttunen (3/0) [Pekka Nurmio (2/0)], Aki Lahtinen (14/0) [Juha Rissanen (8/0)], Arto Tolsa (74/10), Reijo Vaittinen (3/0), Kari Bergqvist (3/0), Hannu Turunen (15/0), Raimo Kuuluvainen (6/0) [Juha Annunen (3/0)], Jukka Ikäläinen (3/0) [Juha Äijälä (2/0)], Antti Ronkainen (10/0), Pasi Jaakonsaari (3/1), Ari Valvee (3/1). Trainer: Esko Malm (22).

377. 01.03.1981 **FINLAND - SWEDEN** **2-1(2-1)**
Suurhalli, Lahti (indoor); Referee: Mauri Laakso (Finland); Attendance: 4,000
FIN: Olli Isoaho (10/0), Arto Tolsa (75/10), Aki Lahtinen (15/0), Reijo Vaittinen (4/0), Esa Pekonen (1/0) [74.Kari Bergqvist (4/0)], Jukka Ikäläinen (4/1), Juha Dahllund (12/0) [74.Simo Kokko (1/0)], Kari Virtanen (18/0) [65.Leo Houtsonen (16/0)], Pasi Jaakonsaari (4/1) [46.Antti Ronkainen (11/0)], Hannu Rajaniemi (8/2), Jyrki Nieminen (29/7). Trainer: Esko Malm (23).
Goals: Hannu Rajaniemi (4), Jukka Ikäläinen (8).

378. 13.05.1981 **BULGARIA - FINLAND** **4-0(1-0)** 12th FIFA WC. Qualifiers
Nationalen stadion "Vasil Levski", Sofia; Referee: Eduard Sostarić (Yugoslavia); Attendance: 10,000
FIN: Olli Isoaho (11/0), Aki Lahtinen (16/0), Arto Tolsa (76/10), Reijo Vaittinen (5/0), Esa Pekonen (2/0) [80.Kari Bergqvist (5/0)], Jukka Ikäläinen (5/1), Juha Dahllund (13/0) [63.Pasi Jaakonsaari (5/1)], Seppo Pyykkö (25/1), Leo Houtsonen (17/0), Atik Ismail (15/6), Ari Valvee (4/1). Trainer: Esko Malm (24).

379. 24.05.1981 **FINLAND – WEST GERMANY** **0-4(0-3)** 12th FIFA WC. Qualifiers
Keskusurheilukenttä, Lahti; Referee: John Carpenter (Republic of Ireland); Attendance: 10,030
FIN: Olli Isoaho (12/0), Aki Lahtinen (17/0), Arto Tolsa (77/10) [46.Juha Helin (23/1)], Reijo Vaittinen (6/0), Leo Houtsonen (18/0), Jukka Ikäläinen (6/1), Kari Virtanen (19/0), Seppo Pyykkö (26/1), Petteri Kupiainen (9/0), Keijo Kousa (1/0), Ari Valvee (5/1) [63.Atik Ismail (16/6)]. Trainer: Esko Malm (25).

380. 17.06.1981 **AUSTRIA - FINLAND** **5-1(2-0)** 12th FIFA WC. Qualifiers
Linzer Stadion, Linz; Referee: Alojzy Jarguz (Poland); Attendance: 27,000
FIN: Olavi Huttunen (4/0), Aki Lahtinen (18/0), Juha Helin (24/1), Leo Houtsonen (19/0), Reijo Vaittinen (7/0), Kari Virtanen (20/0), Juha Dahllund (14/0), Jukka Ikäläinen (7/1), Hannu Turunen (16/0), Ari Valvee (6/2), Keijo Kousa (2/0) [60.Hannu Rajaniemi (9/2)]. Trainer: Esko Malm (26).
Goal: Ari Valvee (71).

381. 02.07.1981 **FINLAND - NORWAY** **3-1(1-0)** Nordic Championship
Olympiastadion, Helsinki; Referee: Peer Frickmann (Denmark); Attendance: 9,941
FIN: Olavi Huttunen (5/0), Esa Pekonen (3/0) [81.Kari Bergqvist (6/0)], Aki Lahtinen (19/0), Reijo Vaittinen (8/0), Jyrki Nieminen (30/7), Hannu Turunen (17/1), Juha Dahllund (15/0) [72.Kari Virtanen (21/0)], Jukka Ikäläinen (8/1), Peter Utriainen (1/0), Keijo Kousa (3/1), Hannu Rajaniemi (10/3). Trainer: Esko Malm (27).
Goals: Keijo Kousa (31), Hannu Rajaniemi (60), Hannu Turunen (61).

382. 29.07.1981 **SWEDEN – FINLAND** **1-0(1-0)** Nordic Championship
Örjans Vall, Halmstad; Referee: Ole Amundsen (Denmark); Attendance: 9,595
FIN: Olavi Huttunen (6/0), Leo Houtsonen (20/0), Juha Dahllund (16/0), Reijo Vaittinen (9/0), Aki Lahtinen (20/0), Hannu Turunen (18/1), Jukka Ikäläinen (9/1), Seppo Pyykkö (27/1), Peter Utriainen (2/0), Keijo Kousa (4/1), Hannu Rajaniemi (11/3) [46.Ari Valvee (7/2)]. Trainer: Esko Malm (28).

383. 12.08.1981 **FINLAND - DENMARK** **1-2(1-1)** Nordic Championship
Ratinan Stadion, Tampere; Referee: Ulf Eriksson (Sweden); Attendance: 4,444
FIN: Olavi Huttunen (7/0), Aki Lahtinen (21/0), Juha Dahllund (17/0), Reijo Vaittinen (10/0), Jyrki Nieminen (31/7), Leo Houtsonen (21/0), Jukka Ikäläinen (10/1), Seppo Pyykkö (28/1) [46.Hannu Turunen (19/1)], Peter Utriainen (3/0) [63.Kari Virtanen (22/0)], Keijo Kousa (5/1), Ari Valvee (8/3) [68.Pasi Jaakonsaari (6/1)]. Trainer: Esko Malm (29).
Goal: Ari Valvee (17).

384. 02.09.1981 **FINLAND - ALBANIA** **2-1(0-0)** 12th FIFA WC. Qualifiers
Urheilukeskus, Kotka; Referee: Ib Nielsen (Denmark); Attendance: 6,830
FIN: Olli Isoaho (13/0), Aki Lahtinen (22/0), Juha Dahllund (18/0), Reijo Vaittinen (11/0), Esa Pekonen (4/0), Hannu Turunen (20/1), Leo Houtsonen (22/1), Seppo Pyykkö (29/1) [79.Antti Ronkainen (12/0)], Peter Utriainen (4/0), Keijo Kousa (6/2), Pasi Jaakonsaari (7/1). Trainer: Esko Malm (30).
Goals: Leo Houtsonen (61), Keijo Kousa (85).

385. 23.09.1981 **WEST GERMANY - FINLAND** **7-1(2-1)** 12th FIFA WC. Qualifiers
Ruhrstadion, Bochum; Referee: Norbert Rolles (Luxembourg); Attendance: 46,000
FIN: Olli Isoaho (14/0), Esa Pekonen (5/0), Juha Dahllund (19/0), Leo Houtsonen (23/1), Aki Lahtinen (23/0), Hannu Turunen (21/2), Jukka Ikäläinen (11/1) [71.Jyrki Nieminen (32/7)], Seppo Pyykkö (30/1), Peter Utriainen (5/0), Keijo Kousa (7/2), Pasi Jaakonsaari (8/1) [71.Antti Ronkainen (13/0)]. Trainer: Esko Malm (31).
Goal: Hannu Turunen (41).

386. 20.02.1982 **FINLAND - SWEDEN** **2-2(1-2)**
Suurhalli, Lahti (indoor); Referee: Reidar Björnestad (Norway); Attendance: 1,000
FIN: Olavi Huttunen (8/0) [46.Olli Isoaho (15/0)], Ilkka Remes (1/0), Risto Salonen (9/0), Reijo Vaittinen (12/0) [71.Mikael Granskog (1/0)], Esa Pekonen (6/0), Juha Dahllund (20/0), Jukka Ikäläinen (12/1) [46.Juha Annunen (4/0)], Peter Utriainen (6/0) [65.Anders Backman (3/1)], Pasi Jaakonsaari (9/3), Juhani Himanka (14/2) [65.Ari Valvee (9/3)], Jari Parikka (1/0). Trainer: Martti Kuusela (1).
Goals: Pasi Jaakonsaari (30, 74).

387. 21.02.1982 **FINLAND - SWEDEN** **2-1(2-0)**
Suurhalli, Lahti (indoor); Referee: Reidar Björnestad (Norway); Attendance: 1,000
FIN: Pertti Alaja (24/0), Ilkka Remes (2/0), Jukka Ikäläinen (13/2) [63.Risto Salonen (10/0)], Mikael Granskog (2/0), Esa Pekonen (7/0) [*sent off 51*], Juha Dahllund (21/0), Peter Utriainen (7/0) [62.Juha Annunen (5/0)], Hannu Turunen (22/2), Pasi Jaakonsaari (10/4), Juhani Himanka (15/2) [46.Ari Valvee (10/3), Anders Backman (4/1)], Jari Parikka (2/0). Trainer: Martti Kuusela (2).
Goals: Pasi Jaakonsaari (17), Jukka Ikäläinen (31).

388. 28.04.1982 **NORWAY - FINLAND** **1-1(0-1)** Nordic Championship
Stavanger Stadion, Stavanger; Referee: Peer Frickmann (Denmark); Attendance: 5,700
FIN: Pertti Alaja (25/0), Aki Lahtinen (24/0), Jukka Ikäläinen (14/2), Mikael Granskog (3/0), Esa Pekonen (8/0), Hannu Turunen (23/2), Kai Haaskivi (10/2), Pasi Rautiainen (14/1), Juhani Himanka (16/2) [61.Ilkka Remes (3/0)], Atik Ismail (17/6) [46.Jari Parikka (3/0)], Jyrki Nieminen (33/8). Trainer: Martti Kuusela (3).
Goal: Jyrki Nieminen (16).

389. 03.06.1982 **FINLAND - ENGLAND** **1-4(0-2)**
Olympiastadion, Helsinki; Referee: Romualdas Yushka (Soviet Union); Attendance: 21,521
FIN: Pertti Alaja (26/0) [68.Olavi Huttunen (9/0)], Aki Lahtinen (25/0), Jukka Ikäläinen (15/2), Mikael Granskog (4/0), Esa Pekonen (9/0), Hannu Turunen (24/2) [64.Pauno Kymäläinen (3/0)], Kai Haaskivi (11/3), Pasi Rautiainen (15/1), Juhani Himanka (17/2), Atik Ismail (18/6), Jyrki Nieminen (34/8) [55.Ari Valvee (11/3)]. Trainer: Martti Kuusela (4).
Goal: Kai Haaskivi (83 penalty).

390. 11.07.1982 **FINLAND - ICELAND** **3-2(2-0)**
Olympiastadion, Helsinki; Referee: Bo Helen (Sweden); Attendance: 7,491
FIN: Olavi Huttunen (10/0), Peter Utriainen (8/0) [72.Vesa Mars (1/0)], Pauno Kymäläinen (4/0), Mikael Granskog (5/0), Esa Pekonen (10/0), Hannu Turunen (25/2), Jukka Ikäläinen (16/2), Juhani Himanka (18/3), Atik Ismail (19/7), Pasi Jaakonsaari (11/4) [77.Keijo Kousa (8/3)], Jari Parikka (4/0). Trainer: Martti Kuusela (5).
Goals: Atik Ismail (1), Juhani Himanka (34), Keijo Kousa (86).

391. 11.08.1982 **DENMARK - FINLAND** **3-2(1-2)** Nordic Championship
Idrætsparken, København; Referee: Ulf Eriksson (Sweden); Attendance: 5,700
FIN: Olavi Huttunen (11/0), Ilkka Remes (4/0), Pauno Kymäläinen (5/0), Aki Lahtinen (26/0), Esa Pekonen (11/0), Hannu Turunen (26/3), Jukka Ikäläinen (17/2), Jari Parikka (5/0), Juhani Himanka (19/3), Atik Ismail (20/7), Ari Valvee (12/4) [77.Keijo Kousa (9/3)]. Trainer: Martti Kuusela (6).
Goal: Ari Valvee (8), Hannu Turunen (37).

392. 08.09.1982 **FINLAND - POLAND** **2-3(0-2)** 7th EC. Qualifiers
Väinölänniemi Stadion, Kuopio; Referee: Marcel Van Langenhove (Belgium); Attendance: 2,845
FIN: Olavi Huttunen (12/0), Aki Lahtinen (27/0), Pauno Kymäläinen (Cap) (6/0), Mikael Granskog (6/0), Esa Pekonen (12/0), Hannu Turunen (27/3), Jukka Ikäläinen (18/2), Pasi Rautiainen (16/1), Juhani Himanka (20/3) [71.Keijo Kousa (10/4)], Atik Ismail (21/7) [66.Ari Valvee (13/5)], Ilkka Remes (5/0). Trainer: Martti Kuusela (7).
Goals: Ari Valvee (82), Keijo Kousa (84).

393. 22.09.1982 **FINLAND - PORTUGAL** **0-2(0-1)** 7th EC. Qualifiers
Olympiastadion, Helsinki; Referee: Klaus Scheurell (East Germany); Attendance: 3,132
FIN: Olli Isoaho (16/0), Aki Lahtinen (Cap) (28/0), Pauno Kymäläinen (7/0), Reijo Vaittinen (13/0), Esa Pekonen (13/0), Hannu Turunen (28/3), Ilkka Remes (6/0), Pasi Rautiainen (17/1) [46.Ari Valvee (14/5)], Juhani Himanka (21/3) [79.Keijo Kousa (11/4)], Atik Ismail (22/7), Jari Parikka (6/0). Trainer: Martti Kuusela (8).

394. 13.10.1982 **SOVIET UNION - FINLAND** **2-0(1-0)** 7th EC. Qualifiers
Lenin Stadium, Moskva; Referee: Jakob Baumann (Switzerland); Attendance: 18,000
FIN: Olavi Huttunen (13/0), Aki Lahtinen (29/0) [55.Atik Ismail (23/7)], Pauno Kymäläinen (8/0), Mikael Granskog (7/0), Ilkka Remes (7/0), Hannu Turunen (29/3), Esa Pekonen (14/0), Vesa Mars (2/0), Juhani Himanka (22/3) [74.Keijo Kousa (12/4)], Peter Utriainen (9/0), Ari Valvee (15/5). Trainer: Martti Kuusela (9).

395. 16.03.1983 **EAST GERMANY - FINLAND** **3-1(3-0)**
„Ernst Grube“ Stadion, Magdeburg; Referee: Alexandru Mustăţea (Romania); Attendance: 12,000
FIN: Olavi Huttunen (14/0), Esa Pekonen (15/0), Pauno Kymäläinen (9/0), Mikael Granskog (8/0), Ilkka Remes (8/0), Hannu Turunen (30/3), Atik Ismail (24/7) [66.Ari Hjelm (1/1)], Jukka Ikäläinen (19/2), Leo Houtsonen (24/1), Ilpo Talvio (1/0) [46.Pasi Rasimus (1/0)], Keijo Kousa (13/4) [62.Juha Annunen (6/0)]. Trainer: Martti Kuusela (10).
Goal: Ari Hjelm (82).

396. 17.04.1983 **POLAND - FINLAND** **1-1(1-1)** 7th EC. Qualifiers
Stadion Dziesięciolecia, Warszawa; Referee: Reidar Bjørnstad (Norway); Attendance: 70,000
FIN: Olli Isoaho (17/0), Esa Pekonen (16/0), Pauno Kymäläinen (Cap) (10/0), Mikael Granskog (9/0), Ilkka Remes (9/0) [41.Aki Lahtinen (30/0)], Hannu Turunen (31/3), Atik Ismail (25/7), Kari Ukkonen (1/0), Leo Houtsonen (25/1), Tuomo Hakala (10/1), Mika Lipponen (1/0) [66.Ari Hjelm (2/1). Trainer: Martti Kuusela (11).
Goal: Pawel Janas (5 own goal).

397. 04.05.1983 **FINLAND – POLAND Olympic** **0-4(0-2)** 23rd OG. Qualifiers
Olympiastadion, Helsinki; Referee: Erik Fredriksson (Sweden); Attendance: 3,130
FIN: Ismo Korhonen (1/0), Ilkka Remes (10/0), Pauno Kymäläinen (11/0), Mikael Granskog (10/0), Erkka Petäjä (1/0), Pasi Rasimus (2/0), Jari Rantanen (1/0), Kari Ukkonen (2/0), Juha Annunen (7/0) [65.Ilpo Talvio (2/0)], Ari Hjelm (3/1), Jari Parikka (7/0) [46.Mika Lipponen (2/0)]. Trainer: Martti Kuusela (12).

398. 18.05.1983 **FINLAND – EAST GERMANY Olympic** **0-1(0-1)** 23rd OG. Qualifiers
Keskusurheilukenttä, Kokkola; Referee: Ulf Eriksson (Sweden); Attendance: 4,500
FIN: Peter Lindholm (1/0) [46.Ismo Korhonen (2/0)], Erkka Petäjä (2/0), Pauno Kymäläinen (12/0) [51.Jari Rantanen (2/0)], Mikael Granskog (11/0), Ari Lyytikkä (1/0), Pasi Rasimus (3/0), Ilkka Remes (11/0), Kari Ukkonen (3/0), Jari Parikka (8/0), Ari Hjelm (4/1), Mika Lipponen (3/0). Trainer: Martti Kuusela (13).

399. 25.05.1983 **POLAND Olympic - FINLAND** **3-2(2-1)** 23rd OG. Qualifiers
Stadion Gwardia, Bialystok; Referee: Jan Redelfs (West Germany); Attendance: 35,000
FIN: Ismo Korhonen (3/0), Ari Lyytikkä (2/0), Pauno Kymäläinen (13/0), Mikael Granskog (12/0), Erkka Petäjä (3/0), Pasi Rasimus (4/0), Ilkka Remes (12/0), Kari Ukkonen (4/0), Jari Parikka (9/0) [15.Juha Annunen (8/0)], Jari Rantanen (3/0) [75.Vesa Mars (3/0)], Ari Hjelm (5/3). Trainer: Martti Kuusela (14).
Goals: Ari Hjelm (37, 52).

400. 01.06.1983 **FINLAND - SOVIET UNION** **0-1(0-0)**
Olympiastadion, Helsinki; Referee: Dušan Krchnak (Czechoslovakia); Attendance: 16,966
FIN: Olavi Huttunen (15/0), Aki Lahtinen (31/0), Pauno Kymäläinen (14/0), Mikael Granskog (13/0), Esa Pekonen (17/0), Hannu Turunen (32/3), Leo Houtsonen (26/1), Kari Ukkonen (5/0), Pasi Rautiainen (18/1), Atik Ismail (26/7) [65.Tuomo Hakala (11/1)], Ari Valvee (16/5). Trainer: Martti Kuusela (15).

401. 15.06.1983 **FINLAND – NORWAY Olympic** **1-1(1-1)** 23rd OG. Qualifiers
Urheilukeskus, Kuopio; Referee: Anatoliy Milchenko (Soviet Union); Attendance: 2,153
FIN: Ismo Korhonen (4/0), Ilkka Remes (13/0), Pauno Kymäläinen (15/0), Mikael Granskog (14/0), Erkka Petäjä (4/0), Pasi Rasimus (5/0), Simo Kokko (2/0), Kari Ukkonen (6/0) [77.Kimmo Lipponen (1/0)], Juha Annunen (9/1), Mika Lipponen (4/0), Ari Hjelm (6/3) [77.Jari Rantanen (4/0)]. Trainer: Martti Kuusela (16).
Goal: Juha Annunen (39).

402. 22.06.1983 **DENMARK Olympic - FINLAND** **3-0(1-0)** 23rd OG. Qualifiers
Aarhus Stadion, Aahus; Referee: Joël Quiniou (France); Attendance: 2,150
FIN: Peter Lindholm (2/0), Ari Lyytikkä (3/0) [46.Simo Kokko (3/0)], Pauno Kymäläinen (16/0), Mikael Granskog (15/0), Erkka Petäjä (5/0), Pasi Rasimus (6/0), Ilkka Remes (14/0), Kari Ukkonen (7/0), Juha Annunen (10/1) [78.Kimmo Lipponen (2/0)], Mika Lipponen (5/0), Jari Rantanen (5/0). Trainer: Martti Kuusela (17).

403. 24.08.1983 **FINLAND – DENMARK Olympic** **0-0** 23rd OG. Qualifiers
Keskuskenttä, Rovaniemi; Referee: Bo Helen (Sweden); Attendance: 2,677
FIN: Peter Lindholm (3/0), Ari Lyytikkä (4/0), Pauno Kymäläinen (17/0), Mikael Granskog (16/0), Erkka Petäjä (6/0), Pasi Rasimus (7/0), Ilkka Remes (15/0), Juha Annunen (11/1), Mika Lipponen (6/0), Ari Hjelm (7/3), Arto Uimonen (10/0) [74.Vesa Mars (4/0)]. Trainer: Martti Kuusela (18).

404. 07.09.1983 **FINLAND - SWEDEN** **0-3(0-3)**
Olympiastadion, Helsinki; Referee: Erik Steen (Denmark); Attendance: 8,513
FIN: Olavi Huttunen (16/0) [46.Pertti Alaja (27/0)], Aki Lahtinen (32/0), Kari Virtanen (23/0), Mikael Granskog (17/0), Esa Pekonen (18/0) [46.Jukka Ikäläinen (20/2)], Hannu Turunen (33/3), Leo Houtsonen (27/1), Kari Ukkonen (8/0), Pasi Rautiainen (19/1) [46.Erkka Petäjä (7/0)], Mika Lipponen (7/0), Ari Valvee (17/5) [77.Ari Hjelm (8/3)]. Trainer: Martti Kuusela (19).

405. 21.09.1983 **PORTUGAL - FINLAND** **5-0(2-0)** 7th EC. Qualifiers
Estádio „José Alvalade", Lisboa; Referee: Karl-Heinz Tritschler (West Germany); Attendance: 15,000
FIN: Pertti Alaja (28/0), Esa Pekonen (19/0), Jukka Ikäläinen (21/2), Mikael Granskog (18/0), Erkka Petäjä (8/0), Hannu Turunen (34/3), Leo Houtsonen (28/1), Kari Ukkonen (9/0), Kari Virtanen (24/0), Mika Lipponen (8/0), Keijo Kousa (14/4). Trainer: Martti Kuusela (20).

406. 05.10.1983 **EAST GERMANY Olympic - FINLAND** **1-0(1-0)** 23rd OG. Qualifiers
Ostseestadion, Rostock; Referee: Josef Pouček (Czechoslovakia); Attendance: 5,000
FIN: Markku Palmroos (1/0), Ilkka Remes (16/0), Pauno Kymäläinen (18/0), Jari Europaeus (1/0), Erkka Petäjä (9/0) [43.Arto Uimonen (11/0)], Pasi Rasimus (8/0) [*sent off 55*], Jari Rantanen (6/0), Kari Ukkonen (10/0), Juha Annunen (12/1) [70.Kimmo Lipponen (3/0)], Mika Lipponen (9/0), Ari Hjelm (9/3). Trainer: Martti Kuusela (21).

407. 26.10.1983 **NORWAY Olympic - FINLAND** **4-2(3-1)** 23rd OG. Qualifiers
Melløs Stadion, Moss; Referee: Walter Eschweiler (Germany); Attendance: 2,067
FIN: Markku Palmroos (2/0), Ilkka Remes (17/0), Pauno Kymäläinen (19/0), Jari Europaeus (2/0), Erkka Petäjä (10/0), Arto Uimonen (12/0), Jari Rantanen (7/0), Juha Annunen (13/2), Sixten Boström (1/1) [67.Kimmo Lipponen (4/0)], Mika Lipponen (10/0) [75.Risto Puustinen (1/0)], Ari Hjelm (10/3). Trainer: Martti Kuusela (22).
Goals: Sixten Boström (9), Juha Annunen (83).

408. 20.02.1984 **FINLAND - UNITED STATES** **0-1(0-1)**
Suurhalli, Lahti (indoor); Referee: Kaj Natri (Finland); Attendance: 500
FIN: Olavi Huttunen (17/0), Esa Pekonen (20/0), Pauno Kymäläinen (20/0), Mikael Granskog (19/0) [70.Juha Annunen (14/2)], Ilkka Remes (18/0), Hannu Turunen (35/3), Leo Houtsonen (29/1), Ari Hjelm (11/3), Ari Valvee (18/5) [46.Jukka Ikäläinen (22/2)], Erkka Petäjä (11/0) [46.Keijo Kousa (15/4)], Risto Puustinen (2/0). Trainer: Martti Kuusela (23).

409. 09.03.1984 **KUWAIT - FINLAND** **1-0(1-0)**
Kuwait City; Referee: Rahdi Moussa Al Haddad (Kuwait); Attendance: 5,200
FIN: Markku Palmroos (3/0), Esa Pekonen (21/0), Pauno Kymäläinen (21/0), Jari Europaeus (3/0), Erkka Petäjä (12/0), Hannu Turunen (36/3) [Ilkka Remes (19/0)], Leo Houtsonen (30/1), Peter Utriainen (10/0) [Juha Annunen (15/2)], Ari Hjelm (12/3) [Keijo Kousa (16/4)], Mika Lipponen (11/0), Sixten Boström (2/1) [Risto Puustinen (3/0)]. Trainer: Martti Kuusela (24).

410. 15.05.1984 **FINLAND - SOVIET UNION** **1-3(0-2)**
Keskuskenttä, Kouvola; Referee: Thorbjörn Aas (Norway); Attendance: 6,700
FIN: Olavi Huttunen (18/0), Esa Pekonen (22/0), Pauno Kymäläinen (22/0), Mikael Granskog (20/0) [71.Markus Törnvall (1/0)], Ilkka Remes (20/0), Hannu Turunen (37/3), Leo Houtsonen (31/1), Erkka Petäjä (13/0), Jari Rantanen (8/1), Mika Lipponen (12/0) [63.Keijo Kousa (17/4)], Ari Valvee (19/5) [79.Arto Uimonen (13/0)]. Trainer: Martti Kuusela (25).
Goal: Jari Rantanen (52).

411. 27.05.1984 **FINLAND – NORTHERN IRELAND** **1-0(0-0)** 13th FIFA WC. Qualifiers
Porin Stadion, Pori; Referee: Karl-Heinz Tritschler (Germany); Attendance: 8,000
FIN: Olavi Huttunen (19/0), Esa Pekonen (23/0), Pauno Kymäläinen (23/0), Jukka Ikäläinen (23/2) [48.Jari Europaeus (4/0)], Erkka Petäjä (14/0), Hannu Turunen (38/3), Leo Houtsonen (32/1), Kari Ukkonen (11/0), Jari Rantanen (9/1), Pasi Rautiainen (20/1), Ari Valvee (20/6). Trainer: Martti Kuusela (26).
Goal: Ari Valvee (55).

412. 16.08.1984 **FINLAND - MEXICO** **0-3(0-1)**
Olympiastadion, Helsinki; Referee: Vladimir Kuznetzov (Soviet Union); Attendance: 5,796
FIN: Olavi Huttunen (20/0) [*sent off 63*], Esa Pekonen (24/0), Pauno Kymäläinen (24/0), Erkka Petäjä (15/0) [75.Risto Puustinen (4/0)], Hannu Turunen (39/3) [63.Markku Palmroos (4/0)], Leo Houtsonen (33/1), Mika Lipponen (13/0), Jari Rantanen (10/1) [46.Ari Hjelm (13/3)], Ari Valvee (21/6), Markus Törnvall (2/0) [46.Jari Europaeus (5/0)], Arto Uimonen (14/0). Trainer: Martti Kuusela (27).

413. 12.09.1984 **FINLAND - POLAND** **0-2(0-1)**
Olympiastadion, Helsinki; Referee: Rolf Haugen (Norway); Attendance: 2,500
FIN: Olavi Huttunen (21/0), Esa Pekonen (25/0), Pauno Kymäläinen (Cap) (25/0), Jari Europaeus (6/0), Erkka Petäjä (16/0), Hannu Turunen (40/3), Leo Houtsonen (34/1), Juha Dahllund (22/0), Mika Lipponen (14/0) [78.Peter Utriainen (11/0)], Ari Hjelm (14/3), Ari Valvee (22/6) [68.Jari Rantanen (11/1)]. Trainer: Martti Kuusela (28).

414. 17.10.1984 **ENGLAND - FINLAND** **5-0(2-0)** 13th FIFA WC. Qualifiers
Wembley Stadium, London; Referee: Andrzej Suchanek (Poland); Attendance: 45,000
FIN: Olavi Huttunen (22/0), Esa Pekonen (26/0), Pauno Kymäläinen (Cap) (26/0), Aki Lahtinen (33/0), Erkka Petäjä (17/0), Kai Haaskivi (12/3) [46.Hannu Turunen (41/3)], Leo Houtsonen (35/1), Kari Ukkonen (12/0), Jukka Ikäläinen (24/2), Pasi Rautiainen (21/1), Ari Valvee (23/6) [70.Ari Hjelm (15/3)]. Trainer: Martti Kuusela (29).

415. 31.10.1984 **TURKEY - FINLAND** **1-2(0-1)** 13th FIFA WC. Qualifiers
Atatürk Stadyumu, Antalya; Referee: Velodi Miminoshvili (Soviet Union); Attendance: 20,000
FIN: Olavi Huttunen (23/0), Aki Lahtinen (34/0), Pauno Kymäläinen (Cap) (27/0), Jukka Ikäläinen (25/2), Esa Pekonen (27/0), Hannu Turunen (42/3), Kari Virtanen (25/0), Kari Ukkonen (13/0), Leo Houtsonen (36/1), Mika Lipponen (15/1), Ari Hjelm (16/4) [86.Ismo Lius (1/0)]. Trainer: Martti Kuusela (30).
Goals: Ari Hjelm (10), Mika Lipponen (68).

416. 14.11.1984 **NORTHERN IRELAND - FINLAND** **2-1(1-1)** 13th FIFA WC. Qualifiers
Windsor Park, Belfast; Referee: Alder Dante da Silva Santos (Portugal); Attendance: 20,000
FIN: Olavi Huttunen (24/0), Aki Lahtinen (35/0), Pauno Kymäläinen (28/0), Jari Europaeus (7/0), Esa Pekonen (28/0), Hannu Turunen (43/3), Leo Houtsonen (37/1), Kari Ukkonen (14/0), Jukka Ikäläinen (26/2), Mika Lipponen (16/2), Ari Hjelm (17/4). Trainer: Martti Kuusela (31).
Goal: Mika Lipponen (22).

417. 20.11.1984 **SAUDI ARABIA - FINLAND** **2-1(0-0)**
Dammam; Referee: Abrahim (Saudi Arabia); Attendance: 6,000
FIN: Olavi Huttunen (25/0), Ilkka Remes (21/0), Risto Salonen (11/0), Jari Europaeus (8/0), Esa Pekonen (29/0), Hannu Turunen (44/3), Kari Virtanen (26/0), Sixten Boström (3/1) [60.Kimmo Lipponen (5/0)], Jukka Ikäläinen (27/2), Ari Hjelm (18/5), Ari Valvee (24/6) [60.Ismo Lius (2/0)]. Trainer: Martti Kuusela (32).
Goal: Ari Hjelm (75 penalty).

418. 22.11.1984 **QATAR - FINLAND** **2-2(1-1)**
Khalifa International Stadium, Doha; Referee: Abdulaziz Mohamed Al Mulla (United Arab Emirates); Attendance: 1,000
FIN: Olavi Huttunen (26/0), Arto Uimonen (15/0) [82.Kimmo Lipponen (6/0)], Pauno Kymäläinen (29/0), Jukka Ikäläinen (28/2), Ilkka Remes (22/1), Hannu Turunen (45/3), Esa Pekonen (30/1), Risto Puustinen (5/0) [75.Sixten Boström (4/1)], Kari Virtanen (27/0), Ari Hjelm (19/5), Ismo Lius (3/0) [46.Ari Valvee (25/6)]. Trainer: Martti Kuusela (33).
Goal: Esa Pekonen (32), Ilka Remes (62).

419. 24.11.1984 **QATAR - FINLAND** **1-1(1-0)**
Khalifa International Stadium, Doha; Referee: Jamaan (Qatar); Attendance: 1,500
FIN: Markku Palmroos (5/0), Arto Uimonen (16/0) [46.Sixten Boström (5/1)], Pauno Kymäläinen (30/0), Jari Europaeus (9/0), Ilkka Remes (23/1), Hannu Turunen (46/3), Esa Pekonen (31/1), Kari Virtanen (28/0), Jukka Ikäläinen (29/2), Risto Puustinen (6/0) [46.Ari Hjelm (20/6)], Ismo Lius (4/0) [46.Ari Valvee (26/6)]. Trainer: Martti Kuusela (34).
Goal: Ari Hjelm (65).

420. 23.01.1985 **SPAIN - FINLAND** **3-1(3-1)**
Estadio "José Rico Pérez", Alicante; Referee: Alphonse Constantin (Belgium); Attendance: 36,000
FIN: Olavi Huttunen (27/0), Aki Lahtinen (36/0), Pauno Kymäläinen (31/0) [59.Markus Törnvall (3/0)], Jari Europaeus (10/0) [46.Kari Virtanen (29/0)], Esa Pekonen (32/1), Hannu Turunen (47/3), Leo Houtsonen (38/1), Kari Ukkonen (15/0), Jukka Ikäläinen (30/2) [54.Ari Valvee (27/6)], Mika Lipponen (17/3), Ari Hjelm (21/6) [79.Jari Parikka (10/0)]. Trainer: Martti Kuusela (35).
Goal: Mika Lipponen (6).

421. 08.02.1985 **CHILE - FINLAND** **2-0(1-0)**
Estadio Sausalito, Viña del Mar; Referee: Guillermo Budge Aguirre (Chile); Attendance: 8,220
FIN: Markku Palmroos (6/0), Esa Pekonen (33/1), Pauno Kymäläinen (32/0), Kari Virtanen (30/0) [63.Markus Törnvall (4/0)], Jyrki Nieminen (35/8) [72.Ilkka Remes (24/1)], Hannu Turunen (48/3), Leo Houtsonen (39/1), Jari Parikka (11/0), Jukka Ikäläinen (31/2), Ari Hjelm (22/6), Ari Valvee (28/6) [72.Risto Puustinen (7/0)]. Trainer: Martti Kuusela (36).

422. 14.02.1985 **URUGUAY - FINLAND** **2-1(2-1)**
Estadio Centenario, Montevideo; Referee: Ramón Ivannoe Barreto Ruíz (Uruguay); Attendance: 29,735
FIN: Olli Isoaho (18/0), Esa Pekonen (34/1), Pauno Kymäläinen (33/0), Kari Virtanen (31/0) [Markus Törnvall (5/0)], Jyrki Nieminen (36/8), Hannu Turunen (49/3), Leo Houtsonen (40/1), Jari Parikka (12/0) [Sixten Boström (6/1)], Jukka Ikäläinen (32/2), Ari Hjelm (23/6), Ari Valvee (29/7) [Risto Puustinen (8/0)]. Trainer: Martti Kuusela (37).
Goal: Ari Valvee (12).

423. 17.02.1985 **ECUADOR - FINLAND** **3-1(2-0)**
Estadio Bellavista, Ambato; Referee: Jorge Enrique Ortíz (Ecuador); Attendance: 12,000
FIN: Kari Laukkanen (1/0), Esa Pekonen (35/1), Jari Europaeus (11/0), Kari Virtanen (32/0) [46.Markus Törnvall (6/0)], Jyrki Nieminen (37/9), Hannu Turunen (50/3) [Ilkka Remes (25/1)], Leo Houtsonen (41/1), Jari Parikka (13/0) [50.Sixten Boström (7/1)], Jukka Ikäläinen (33/2), Ari Hjelm (24/6) [Pauno Kymäläinen (34/0)], Arto Uimonen (17/0) [46.Risto Puustinen (9/0)]. Trainer: Martti Kuusela (38).
Goal: Jyrki Nieminen (89).

424. 26.02.1985 **MEXICO - FINLAND** **2-1(1-0)**
Estadio Unidad Deportiva, Acapulco; Referee: Enrique Mendoza Guillén (Mexico); Attendance: 15,000
FIN: Olli Isoaho (19/0), Esa Pekonen (36/2), Pauno Kymäläinen (35/0) [25.Ilkka Remes (26/1)], Kari Virtanen (33/0), Jyrki Nieminen (38/9), Hannu Turunen (51/3) [82.Arto Uimonen (18/0)], Leo Houtsonen (42/1), Jari Parikka (14/0) [44.Sixten Boström (8/1)], Jukka Ikäläinen (34/2), Ari Hjelm (25/6), Risto Puustinen (10/0). Trainer: Martti Kuusela (39).
Goal: Esa Pekonen (62).

425. 17.04.1985 **POLAND - FINLAND** **2-1(0-0)**
Stadion Odra, Opole; Referee: László Kovács (Hungary); Attendance: 12,500
FIN: Olavi Huttunen (28/0), Erkka Petäjä (18/0), Pauno Kymäläinen (Cap) (36/0), Esa Pekonen (37/2), Jyrki Nieminen (39/9), Hannu Turunen (52/3), Leo Houtsonen (43/1), Kari Ukkonen (16/1) [87.Jari Europaeus (12/0)], Jari Rantanen (12/1), Mika Lipponen (18/3), Ari Hjelm (26/6). Trainer: Martti Kuusela (40).
Goal: Kari Ukkonen (57).

426. 22.05.1985 **FINLAND - ENGLAND** **1-1(1-0)** 13th FIFA WC. Qualifiers

Olympiastadion, Helsinki; Referee: Siegfried Kirschen (East Germany); Attendance: 30,311

FIN: Olavi Huttunen (29/0), Aki Lahtinen (37/0) [84.Erkka Petäjä (19/0)], Pauno Kymäläinen (Cap) (37/0), Jukka Ikäläinen (35/2), Jyrki Nieminen (40/9), Hannu Turunen (53/3), Leo Houtsonen (44/1), Kari Ukkonen (17/1) [78.Ari Hjelm (27/6)], Mika Lipponen (19/3), Pasi Rautiainen (22/1), Jari Rantanen (13/2). Trainer: Martti Kuusela (41).

Goal: Jari Rantanen (5).

427. 06.06.1985 **FINLAND - ROMANIA** **1-1(1-1)** 13th FIFA WC. Qualifiers

Olympiastadion, Helsinki; Referee: Marcel Van Langenhove (Belgium); Attendance: 24,863

FIN: Olavi Huttunen (30/0), Aki Lahtinen (38/0), Pauno Kymäläinen (38/0) [78.Esa Pekonen (38/2)], Leo Houtsonen (45/1), Jyrki Nieminen (41/9) [70.Erkka Petäjä (20/0)], Hannu Turunen (54/3), Pasi Rautiainen (Cap) (23/1), Kari Ukkonen (18/1), Jukka Ikäläinen (36/2), Mika Lipponen (20/4), Jari Rantanen (14/2). Trainer: Marti Kuusela (42).

Goal: Mika Lipponen (26).

428. 28.08.1985 **ROMANIA - FINLAND** **2-0(1-0)** 13th FIFA WC. Qualifiers

Stadionul 1 Mai, Timişoara; Referee: Zoran Petrović (Yugoslavia); Attendance: 35,000

FIN: Olavi Huttunen (31/0), Jari Europaeus (13/0), Hannu Turunen (55/3), Leo Houtsonen (Cap) (46/1), Jyrki Nieminen (42/9), Kari Ukkonen (19/1) [70.Erkka Petäjä (21/0)], Jukka Ikäläinen (37/2), Pasi Rautiainen (24/1), Jari Rantanen (15/2), Ari Hjelm (28/6), Mika Lipponen (21/4). Trainer: Martti Kuusela (43).

429. 25.09.1985 **FINLAND - TURKEY** **1-0(1-0)** 13th FIFA WC. Qualifiers

Ratinan Stadion, Tampere; Referee: Rune Larsson (Sweden); Attendance: 5,616

FIN: Olavi Huttunen (32/0), Aki Lahtinen (39/0), Pauno Kymäläinen (39/0), Jari Rantanen (16/3), Jyrki Nieminen (43/9) [79.Erkka Petäjä (22/0)], Hannu Turunen (56/3), Leo Houtsonen (47/1), Kari Ukkonen (20/1) [57.Mika Lipponen (22/4)], Jukka Ikäläinen (38/2), Pasi Rautiainen (25/1), Ari Hjelm (29/6). Trainer: Martti Kuusela (44).

Goal: Jari Rantanen (38).

430. 22.01.1986 **PORTUGAL - FINLAND** **1-1(0-1)**

Estádio Municipal, Leiria; Referee: José Pez Pérez (Spain); Attendance: 10,000

FIN: Olavi Huttunen (33/0), Erkka Petäjä (23/0) [10.Jari Europaeus (14/0)], Aki Lahtinen (40/0), Jukka Ikäläinen (39/2), Jyrki Nieminen (44/9), Esa Pekonen (39/2), Markus Törnvall (7/0) [74.Ari Valvee (30/7)], Hannu Turunen (57/3), Mika Lipponen (23/4), Ismo Lius (5/0) [83.Keijo Kousa (18/4)], Ari Hjelm (30/7) [70.Ilkka Remes (27/1)]. Trainer: Martti Kuusela (45).

Goal: Ari Hjelm (14).

431. 21.02.1986 **BAHRAIN - FINLAND** **0-0**

Al Ahli Stadium, Manama; Referee: n/a; Attendance: 2,000

FIN: Olavi Huttunen (34/0), Aki Lahtinen (41/0), Jukka Ikäläinen (40/2), Mikael Granskog (21/0), Arto Uimonen (19/0), Ari Valvee (31/7) [Kimmo Tarkkio (1/0)], Markus Törnvall (8/0), Kari Virtanen (34/0), Jari Niinimäki (1/0) [Pasi Rasimus (9/0)], Jari Europaeus (15/0), Ari Hjelm (31/7). Trainer: Martti Kuusela (46).

432. 24.02.1986 **BAHRAIN - FINLAND** **0-4(0-1)**

Al Ahli Stadium, Manama; Referee: n/a; Attendance: 1,500

FIN: Olli Isoaho (20/0), Aki Lahtinen (42/0), Jukka Ikäläinen (41/3), Kimmo Tarkkio (2/0) [Kari Virtanen (35/0)], Arto Uimonen (20/0), Hannu Turunen (58/3), Markus Törnvall (9/1), Jari Europaeus (16/0), Pasi Rasimus (10/1), Ari Valvee (32/8), Ari Hjelm (32/7) [Jari Niinimäki (2/0)]. Trainer: Martti Kuusela (47).

Goals: Ari Valvee (38), Markus Törnvall (59), Jukka Ikäläinen (85), Pasi Rasimus (89)

433. 28.02.1986 **SAUDI ARABIA - FINLAND** **0-1(0-1)**

"Prince Mohamed bin Fahd" Stadium, Dammam; Referee: Abdullah Al Aqeel (Saudi Arabia); Attendance: 16,000

FIN: Olavi Huttunen (35/0), Aki Lahtinen (43/0) [70.Arto Uimonen (21/0)], Jukka Ikäläinen (42/3), Mikael Granskog (22/0), Pasi Rasimus (11/1) [87.Kimmo Tarkkio (3/0)], Hannu Turunen (59/3), Markus Törnvall (10/1), Kari Virtanen (36/1), Jari Europaeus (17/0), Ari Valvee (33/8) [42.Pasi Rautiainen (26/1)], Ari Hjelm (33/7) [66.Jari Niinimäki (3/0)]. Trainer: Martti Kuusela (48).

Goal: Kari Virtanen (38).

434. 17.04.1986 **BRAZIL - FINLAND** **3-0(0-0)**

Estádio "Mané Garrincha", Brasilia; Referee: José de Assis Aragão (Brazil); Attendance: 44,597

FIN: Ismo Korhonen (5/0), Aki Lahtinen (44/0), Jukka Ikäläinen (43/3), Mikael Granskog (23/0), Jyrki Nieminen (45/9) [76.Ismo Lius (6/0)], Hannu Turunen (60/3), Esa Pekonen (40/2), Kari Ukkonen (21/1) [83.Petri Tiainen (1/0)], Jari Rantanen (17/3), Pasi Rautiainen (27/1), Ari Hjelm (34/7) [76.Ari Valvee (34/8)]. Trainer: Martti Kuusela (49).

435. 07.05.1986 **SOVIET UNION - FINLAND** **0-0**

Lenin Stadium, Moskva; Referee: Dan Petrescu (Romania); Attendance: 35,000

FIN: Kari Laukkanen (2/0), Aki Lahtinen (45/0), Kari Ukkonen (22/1), Esa Pekonen (41/2), Jyrki Hännikäinen (1/0), Hannu Turunen (61/3), Jukka Ikäläinen (44/3), Ari Hjelm (35/7), Pasi Rautiainen (28/1), Jari Rantanen (18/3) [78.Ari Valvee (35/8)], Mila Lipponen (24/4). Trainer: Martti Kuusela (50).

436. 05.08.1986 **FINLAND – SWEDEN Olympic** **1-3(1-1)**

Sankariniemi Stadion, Iisalmi; Referee: Tore Hollund (Norway); Attendance: 2,044

FIN: Kari Laukkanen (3/0), Jyrki Hännikäinen (2/0), Reijo Vuorinen (1/0), Petri Sulonen (1/0), Tuomo Pasanen (1/0) [58.Juha Laaksonen (1/0)], Sixten Boström (9/1) [46.Marko Myyry (1/0)], Markus Törnvall (11/1), Petter Setälä (1/0) [46.Jari Rinne (1/0)], Erik Holmgren (1/0), Jari Niinimäki (4/1), Ari Jalasvaara (3/0) [73.Markku Kanerva (1/0)]. Trainer: Jukka Keijo Olavi Vakkila (1).

Goal: Jari Niinimäki (15).

437. 06.08.1986 **FINLAND - SWEDEN** **1-3(0-3)**

Olympiastadion, Helsinki; Referee: Einar Halle (Norway); Attendance: 7,040

FIN: Olavi Huttunen (36/0), Esa Pekonen (42/2), Jyrki Nieminen (46/9), Erkka Petäjä (24/0) [72.Ari Valvee (36/8)], Hannu Turunen (62/3), Jukka Ikäläinen (Cap) (45/3), Mikael Granskog (24/0) [46.Jari Europaeus (18/0)], Ari Hjelm (36/7), Mika Lipponen (25/5), Jari Rantanen (19/3) [46.Leo Houtsonen (48/1)], Pasi Tauriainen (1/0). Trainer: Martti Kuusela (51).

Goal: Mika Lipponen (61).

438. 20.08.1986 **FINLAND – EAST GERMANY** **1-0(0-0)**
Lahden Kisapuisto, Lahti; Referee: Bo Karlsson (Sweden); Attendance: 3,325
FIN: Kari Laukkanen (4/0), Esa Pekonen (43/2), Jukka Ikäläinen (46/3), Jari Europaeus (19/0), Erkka Petäjä (25/0), Hannu Turunen (63/3), Markus Törnvall (12/1) [88.Kari Virtanen (37/1)], Kari Ukkonen (23/1), Pasi Tauriainen (2/0) [83.Ari Valvee (37/8)], Jari Rantanen (20/3), Ari Hjelm (37/8). Trainer: Martti Kuusela (52).
Goal: Ari Hjelm (61).

439. 09.09.1986 **FINLAND – EAST GERMANY Olympic** **1-0(1-0)**
Kimpisen Urheilukeskus, Lappeenranta; Referee: Velodi Miminoshvili (Soviet Union); Attendance: 1,488
FIN: Ismo Korhonen (6/0), Jyrki Hännikäinen (3/0), Reijo Vuorinen (2/0), Erik Holmgren (2/0), Juha Laaksonen (2/0), Jari Rinne (2/0), Miika Juntunen (1/0), Sixten Boström (10/2) [74.Petter Setälä (2/0)], Marko Myyry (2/0), Mika-Matti Paatelainen (1/0) [84.Petri Sulonen (2/0)], Jari Niinimäki (Cap) (5/1) [68.Tommi Paavola (1/0)]. Trainer: Jukka Keijo Olavi Vakkila (2).
Goal: Sixten Boström (30).

440. 10.09.1986 **FINLAND - WALES** **1-1(1-0)** 8th EC. Qualifiers
Olympiastadion, Helsinki; Referee: Gerald Losert (Austria); Attendance: 9,840
FIN: Kari Laukkanen (5/0), Jari Europaeus (20/0), Esa Pekonen (44/2), Jukka Ikäläinen (Cap) (47/3), Erkka Petäjä (26/0), Pasi Tauriainen (3/0), Markus Törnvall (13/1), Kari Ukkonen (24/1), Ari Hjelm (38/9), Mika Lipponen (26/5) [76.Ari Valvee (38/8)], Jari Rantanen (21/3). Trainer: Martti Kuusela (53).
Goal: Ari Hjelm (11).

441. 14.10.1986 **FINLAND – BELGIUM Olympic** **0-2(0-1)** 24th OG. Qualifiers
Ratinan Stadion, Tampere; Referee: Michał Listkiewicz (Poland); Attendance: 878
FIN: Ismo Korhonen (7/0), Jyrki Hännikäinen (4/0) [65.Ismo Lius (7/0)], Erik Holmgren (3/0), Reijo Vuorinen (3/0), Juha Laaksonen (3/0), Jari Rinne (3/0), Miika Juntunen (2/0) [46.Ari Jalasvaara (4/0)], Sixten Boström (11/2), Mika-Matti Paatelainen (2/0), Marko Myyry (3/0), Jari Niinimäki (6/1). Trainer: Jukka Keijo Olavi Vakkila (3).

442. 15.10.1986 **CZECHOSLOVAKIA - FINLAND** **3-0(2-0)** 8th EC. Qualifiers
Stadion Za Luzánkami, Brno; Referee: Gerassimos Germanakos (Greece); Attendance: 25,600
FIN: Kari Laukkanen (6/0), Jari Europaeus (21/0), Esa Pekonen (45/2), Jukka Ikäläinen (Cap) (48/3), Erkka Petäjä (27/0), Markus Törnvall (14/1), Kari Ukkonen (25/1), Pasi Tauriainen (4/0) [29.Ari Valvee (39/8) [*sent off 35*]], Ari Hjelm (39/9) [4.Petri Tiainen (2/0)], Jari Rantanen (22/3), Mika Lipponen (27/5). Trainer: Martti Kuusela (54).

443. 29.10.1986 **DENMARK - FINLAND** **1-0(0-0)** 8th EC. Qualifiers
Idrætsparken, København; Referee: Oliver Donnelly (Northern Ireland); Attendance: 40,300
FIN: Kari Laukkanen (7/0), Jari Europaeus (22/0), Esa Pekonen (46/2), Jukka Ikäläinen (Cap) (49/3), Erkka Petäjä (28/0), Petri Tiainen (3/0), Markus Törnvall (15/1) [70.Pasi Tauriainen (5/0)], Kari Ukkonen (26/1), Ari Hjelm (40/9), Jari Rantanen (23/3), Mika Lipponen (28/5) [77.Ari Jalasvaara (5/0)]. Trainer: Martti Kuusela (55).

444. 18.03.1987 **POLAND - FINLAND** **3-1(2-0)**
Stadion ROW, Rybnik; Referee: Manfred Rossner (East Germany); Attendance: 22,000
FIN: Kari Laukkanen (8/0), Ilkka Remes (28/1), Jari Europaeus (23/0), Jukka Ikäläinen (Cap) (50/4), Erkka Petäjä (29/0), Jouko Vuorela (1/0) [76.Hannu Turunen (64/3)], Markus Törnvall (16/1) [46.Juha Annunen (16/2)], Kari Ukkonen (27/1), Ari Valvee (40/8) [46.Ismo Lius (8/0)], Mika Lipponen (29/5), Ari Hjelm (41/9). Trainer: Martti Kuusela (56).
Goal: Jukka Ikäläinen (46).

445. 01.04.1987 **WALES - FINLAND** **4-0(2-0)** 8th EC. Qualifiers
The Racecourse, Wrexham; Referee: Ignatius van Swieten (Netherlands); Attendance: 7,696
FIN: Kari Laukkanen (9/0), Jari Europaeus (24/0), Esa Pekonen (47/2), Jukka Ikäläinen (Cap) (51/4), Erkka Petäjä (30/0), Hannu Turunen (65/3) [70.Ismo Lius (9/0)], Erik Holmgren (4/0), Pasi Tauriainen (6/0), Petri Tiainen (4/0) [60.Mika Lipponen (30/5)], Ari Hjelm (42/9), Jari Rantanen (24/3). Trainer: Martti Kuusela (57).

446. 29.04.1987 **FINLAND - DENMARK** **0-1(0-0)** 8th EC. Qualifiers
Olympiastadion, Helsinki; Referee: Dimitar Dimitrov (Bulgaria); Attendance: 25,372
FIN: Kari Laukkanen (10/0), Jari Europaeus (25/0), Aki Lahtinen (46/0), Jukka Ikäläinen (Cap) (52/4), Erkka Petäjä (31/0), Esa Pekonen (48/2), Kari Ukkonen (28/1), Petri Tiainen (5/0) [65.Ari Valvee (41/8)], Mika Lipponen (31/5) [65.Ari Hjelm (43/9)], Jari Rantanen (25/3), Ismo Lius (10/0). Trainer: Martti Kuusela (58).

447. 12.05.1987 **FINLAND – AUSTRIA Olympic** **2-1(2-0)** 24th OG. Qualifiers
Porin Stadion, Pori; Referee: Håkan Lundgren (Sweden); Attendance: 3,912
FIN: Kari Laukkanen (11/0), Jyrki Hännikäinen (5/0), Erik Holmgren (5/0), Petri Sulonen (3/0), Juha Laaksonen (4/0), Jari Rinne (4/0), Ilkka Mäkelä (1/0), Sixten Boström (12/2), Ismo Lius (11/0) [76.Markku Kanerva (2/0)], Marko Myyry (4/1), Jari Niinimäki (7/2) [68.Mika-Matti Paatelainen (3/0)]. Trainer: Jukka Keijo Olavi Vakkila (4).
Goals: Merko Myyry (14), Jari Niinimäki (21).

448. 28.05.1987 **FINLAND – BRAZIL** **2-3(1-1)**
Olympiastadion, Helsinki; Referee: Erik Fredriksson (Sweden); Attendance: 37,018
FIN: Kari Laukkanen (12/0), Aki Lahtinen (47/0) [87.Jyrki Hännikäinen (6/0)], Jukka Ikäläinen (Cap) (53/4), Jari Europaeus (26/0), Erkka Petäjä (32/0), Esa Pekonen (49/2) [79.Erik Holmgren (6/0)], Kari Ukkonen (29/1) [64.Pasi Tauriainen (7/0)], Jari Rantanen (26/3), Ismo Lius (12/1), Ari Hjelm (44/10), Petri Tiainen (6/0) [87.Hannu Turunen (66/3)]. Trainer: Martti Kuusela (59).
Goals: Ari Hjelm (15), Ismo Lius (89).

449. 10.06.1987 **FINLAND – CZECHOSLOVAKIA Olympic** **0-2(0-1)** 24th OG. Qualifiers
Äänekoski; Referee: Gudmundur Haraldsson (Iceland); Attendance: 1,511
FIN: Kari Laukkanen (13/0), Jyrki Hännikäinen (7/0), Ilkka Mäkelä (2/0), Petri Sulonen (4/0), Juha Laaksonen (5/0), Jari Rinne (5/0), Pasi Tauriainen (8/0), Sixten Boström (13/2), Ismo Lius (13/1) [60.Markus Törnvall (17/1)], Marko Myyry (5/1), Mika-Matti Paatelainen (4/0) [46.Jari Niinimäki (8/2)]. Trainer: Jukka Keijo Olavi Vakkila (5).

450. 02.09.1987 **YUGOSLAVIA Olympic - FINLAND** **5-0(4-0)** 24th OG. Qualifiers

Stadion Gradski, Banja Luka; Referee: Vadim Zhuk (Soviet Union); Attendance: 26,000

FIN: Kari Laukkanen (14/0), Erkki Putkonen (1/0), Ilkka Mäkelä (3/0), Erik Holmgren (7/0), Juha Laaksonen (6/0), Jari Rinne (6/0), Jarmo Alatensiö (1/0), Sixten Boström (14/2) [65.Tommi Paavola (2/0)], Ismo Lius (14/1), Marko Myyry (6/1), Jari Niinimäki (9/2) [46.Mika-Matti Paatelainen (5/0)]. Trainer: Jukka Keijo Olavi Vakkila (6).

451. 09.09.1987 **FINLAND - CZECHOSLOVAKIA** **3-0(1-0)** 8th EC. Qualifiers

Olympiastadion, Helsinki; Referee: Neil Midgley (England); Attendance: 6,430

FIN: Kari Laukkanen (15/0), Jari Europaeus (27/0), Aki Lahtinen (48/0), Jukka Ikäläinen (Cap) (54/4), Erkka Petäjä (33/0), Erik Holmgren (8/0), Pasi Rautiainen (29/1) [63.Markku Kanerva (3/0)], Petri Tiainen (7/1), Ari Hjelm (45/11), Jari Rantanen (27/3), Ismo Lius (15/2). Trainer: Martti Kuusela (60).

Goals: Ari Hjelm (28), Ismo Lius (72), Petri Tiainen (82).

452. 23.09.1987 **CZECHOSLOVAKIA Olympic - FINLAND** **2-0(1-0)** 24th OG. Qualifiers

Stadion DAC, Dunajská Streda; Referee: Charles Gilson (Luxembourg); Attendance: 4,000

FIN: Kari Laukkanen (16/0), Markku Kanerva (4/0), Ilkka Mäkelä (4/0), Erik Holmgren (9/0), Erkki Putkonen (2/0), Jari Rinne (7/0), Petri Sulonen (5/0), Jarmo Alatensiö (2/0), Petri Tiainen (8/1), Ismo Lius (16/2) [81.Marko Myyry (7/1)], Tommi Paavola (3/0) [65.Kimmo Tarkkio (4/0)]. Trainer: Jukka Keijo Olavi Vakkila (7).

453. 28.10.1987 **BELGIUM Olympic - FINLAND** **1-0(0-0)** 24th OG. Qualifiers

Stade Rocourt, Liège; Referee: Edgar Azzopardi (Malta); Attendance: 3,200

FIN: Kari Laukkanen (17/0), Markku Kanerva (5/0) [75.Jouko Vuorela (2/0)], Mika Ikävalko (1/0), Erik Holmgren (10/0), Kari Rissanen (1/0), Ilkka Mäkelä (5/0), Markus Törnvall (18/1) [60.Jarmo Alatensiö (3/0)], Petri Tiainen (9/1), Ismo Lius (17/2), Marko Myyry (8/1), Pasi Tauriainen (9/0). Trainer: Jukka Keijo Olavi Vakkila (8).

454. 12.01.1988 **FINLAND - CZECHOSLOVAKIA** **2-0(1-0)** Maspalomas Tournament

Estadio Insular, Las Palmas (Spain); Referee: Jiménez Moreno (Spain); Attendance: 1,500

FIN: Kari Laukkanen (18/0), Erkka Petäjä (34/0), Esa Pekonen (50/2), Jari Europaeus (28/0), Erik Holmgren (11/0), Pasi Tauriainen (10/0) [57.Jarmo Alatensiö (4/1)], Markus Törnvall (19/1) [80.Ismo Lius (18/2)], Marko Myyry (9/1), Mika-Matti Paatelainen (6/1), Jari Rantanen (28/3) [27.Ari Valvee (42/8)], Mika Lipponen (32/5). Trainer: Jukka Keijo Olavi Vakkila (9).

Goals: Mika-Matti Paatelainen (11 penalty), Jarmo Alatensiö (88).

455. 15.01.1988 **FINLAND - SWEDEN** **0-1(0-1)** Maspalomas Tournament

Estadio Insular, Las Palmas (Spain); Referee: Jiménez Moreno (Spain); Attendance: 4,129

FIN: Olavi Huttunen (37/0), Jyrki Hännikäinen (8/0), Esa Pekonen (51/2), Jari Europaeus (29/0), Erkka Petäjä (35/0), Petri Sulonen (6/0) [56.Pasi Tauriainen (11/0)], Jari Rinne (8/0) [46.Ari Valvee (43/8)], Markus Törnvall (20/1) [75.Jarmo Alatensiö (5/1)], Marko Myyry (10/1) [46.Ilkka Mäkelä (6/0)], Ismo Lius (19/2), Jari Rantanen (29/3) [*sent off 88*]. Trainer: Jukka Keijo Olavi Vakkila (10).

456. 07.02.1988 **MALTA - FINLAND** **2-0(2-0)** Rothmans Tournament

Ta' Qali National Stadium, Attard; Referee: Edgar Azzopardi (Malta); Attendance: 5,000

FIN: Olavi Huttunen (38/0), Erkka Petäjä (36/0), Esa Pekonen (52/2), Jari Europaeus (30/0), Erik Holmgren (12/0) [65.Marko Myyry (11/1)], Jari Rinne (9/0) [70.Pasi Tauriainen (12/0)], Markus Törnvall (21/1), Kari Rissanen (2/0), Jarmo Alatensiö (6/1), Ari Hjelm (46/11), Ari Valvee (44/8). Trainer: Jukka Keijo Olavi Vakkila (11).

457. 13.02.1988 **FINLAND - TUNISIA** **3-0(2-0)**

Ta' Qali National Stadium, Attard (Malta); Referee: Patrick Fenech (Malta); Attendance: 1,000

FIN: Markku Palmroos (7/0), Erkka Petäjä (37/0), Erik Holmgren (13/0), Jari Europaeus (31/0), Ari Valvee (45/8), Ari Hjelm (47/11), Markus Törnvall (22/1), Mika A. Aaltonen (1/0), Marko Myyry (12/1), Mika Lipponen (33/8), Seppo Nikkilä (1/0). Trainer: Jukka Keijo Olavi Vakkila (12).

Goals: Mika Lipponen (35, 42, 74).

458. 18.05.1988 **FINLAND – YUGOSLAVIA Olympic** **1-2(1-1)** 24th OG. Qualifiers

Urheilupuisto, Mikkeli; Referee: Einar Halle (Norway); Attendance: 1,543

FIN: Markku Palmroos (8/0), Jyrki Hännikäinen (9/0), Mika Ikävalko (2/0), Petri Sulonen (7/0), Erkki Putkonen (3/0), Jari Rinne (10/0), Markku Kallio (1/0) [53.Erkki Valla (1/0)], Jarmo Alatensiö (7/1), Tommi Paavola (4/0), Ismo Lius (20/2), Seppo Nikkilä (2/1) [75.Risto Puustinen (11/0)]. Trainer: Jukka Keijo Olavi Vakkila (13).

Goal: Seppo Nikkilä (12).

459. 19.05.1988 **FINLAND - COLOMBIA** **1-3(1-1)**

Olympiastadion, Helsinki; Referee: Franz Gächter (Switzerland); Attendance: 5,548

FIN: Olavi Huttunen (39/0), Erkka Petäjä (38/0), Esa Pekonen (53/2), Aki Lahtinen (49/0), Erik Holmgren (14/0), Ari Hjelm (48/11), Mika A. Aaltonen (2/0) [66.Kimmo Tarkkio (5/0)], Kari Ukkonen (30/1), Mika Lipponen (34/8) [46.Marko Myyry (13/1)], Mika-Matti Paatelainen (7/1), Jari Rantanen (30/4) [80.Ismo Lius (21/2)]. Trainer: Jukka Keijo Olavi Vakkila (14).

Goal: Jari Rantanen (39).

460. 31.05.1988 **AUSTRIA Olympic - FINLAND** **0-2(0-0)** 24th OG. Qualifiers

Sportzentrum Wolfsberg-Gries, Wolfsberg; Referee: Michel Girard (France); Attendance: 4,100

FIN: Kari Laukkanen (19/0), Jyrki Hännikäinen (10/0), Mika Ikävalko (3/0), Reijo Vuorinen (4/0), Erkki Putkonen (4/0), Erik Holmgren (15/0), Mika A. Aaltonen (3/0), Marko Myyry (14/1), Jarmo Alatensiö (8/1) [68.Jari Rinne (11/0)], Mika-Matti Paatelainen (8/1), Seppo Nikkilä (3/2) [79.Ismo Lius (22/3)]. Trainer: Jukka Keijo Olavi Vakkila (15).

Goals: Seppo Nikkilä (63), Ismo Lius (89).

461. 04.08.1988 **FINLAND - BULGARIA** **1-1(0-0)**

Hietalahden Jalkapallostadion, Vaasa; Referee: Kjell Norby (Norway); Attendance: 5,823

FIN: Kari Laukkanen (20/0), Jyrki Hännikäinen (11/0), Aki Lahtinen (50/0), Jari Europaeus (32/0), Erkka Petäjä (39/0), Jarmo Alatensiö (9/1) [46.Ismo Lius (23/3)], Markus Törnvall (23/1), Erik Holmgren (16/0) [88.Mika Lipponen (35/8)], Marko Myyry (15/2), Mika-Matti Paatelainen (9/1) [52.Jari Rantanen (31/4)], Ari Hjelm (49/11). Trainer: Jukka Keijo Olavi Vakkila (16).

Goal: Marko Myyry (73).

462. 17.08.1988 **FINLAND - SOVIET UNION** **0-0**
Kupittaan Jalkapallostadion, Turku; Referee: Jan Damgaard (Denmark); Attendance: 6,758
FIN: Kari Laukkanen (21/0), Jyrki Hännikäinen (12/0), Erik Holmgren (17/0) [67.Markku Kanerva (6/0)], Erkka Petäjä (40/0), Esa Pekonen (54/2), Jari Europaeus (33/0), Aki Lahtinen (51/0), Marko Myyry (16/2), Jarmo Alatensiö (10/1) [46.Mika A. Aaltonen (4/0)], Jari Rantanen (32/4) [70.Seppo Nikkilä (4/2)], Ismo Lius (24/3) [46.Mika-Matti Paatelainen (10/1)]. Trainer: Jukka Keijo Olavi Vakkila (17).

463. 31.08.1988 **FINLAND – WEST GERMANY** **0-4(0-2)** 14th FIFA WC. Qualifiers
Olympiastadion, Helsinki; Referee: Vadim Zhuk (Soviet Union); Attendance: 31,693
FIN: Kari Laukkanen (22/0), Jyrki Hännikäinen (13/0) [43.Mika Lipponen (36/8)], Aki Lahtinen (52/0), Jari Europaeus (34/0), Erkka Petäjä (41/0), Marko Myyry (17/2), Kari Ukkonen (31/1) [62.Jarmo Alatensiö (11/1)], Esa Pekonen (55/2), Ari Hjelm (50/11), Jari Rantanen (33/4), Mika-Matti Paatelainen (11/1). Trainer: Jukka Keijo Olavi Vakkila (18).

464. 19.10.1988 **WALES - FINLAND** **2-2(2-2)** 14th FIFA WC. Qualifiers
Vetch Field, Swansea; Referee: Gudmundur Haraldsson (Iceland); Attendance: 9,603
FIN: Olavi Huttunen (40/0), Esa Pekonen (56/2), Aki Lahtinen (53/0), Jari Europaeus (35/0), Markku Kanerva (7/0), Marko Myyry (18/2) [86.Mika Lipponen (37/8)], Erik Holmgren (18/0), Kari Ukkonen (32/2), Erkka Petäjä (42/0) [61.Jari Rantanen (34/4)], Mika-Matti Paatelainen (12/2), Ari Hjelm (51/11). Trainer: Jukka Keijo Olavi Vakkila (19).
Goals: Kari Ukkonen (8), Mika-Matti Paatelainen (45).

465. 03.11.1988 **KUWAIT - FINLAND** **0-0**
Sabah Al Salem Stadium, Mansūriya; Referee: Hasan Abdullah Al Hadda (Kuwait); Attendance: 20,000
FIN: Olavi Huttunen (41/0), Ilkka Mäkelä (7/0), Esa Pekonen (57/2), Jari Europaeus (36/0), Markku Kanerva (8/0), Kimmo Tarkkio (6/0) [82.Jyrki Huhtamäki (1/0)], Kari Rissanen (3/0), Jarmo Alatensiö (12/1), Juha Karvinen (1/0) [68.Erkki Valla (2/0)], Ismo Lius (25/3), Jouko Vuorela (3/0) [60.Ari Tegelberg (1/0)]. Trainer: Jukka Keijo Olavi Vakkila (20).

466. 06.11.1988 **KUWAIT - FINLAND** **0-0**
Kuwait City; Referee: Mohammes Shu'Aib (Kuwait); Attendance: 15,000
FIN: Jari Poutiainen (1/0), Ilkka Mäkelä (8/0), Esa Pekonen (58/2), Jari Europaeus (37/0), Markku Kanerva (9/0), Sami Ylä-Jussila (1/0) [46.Kimmo Tarkkio (7/0)], Jarmo Alatensiö (13/1) [60.Erkki Valla (3/0)], Kari Rissanen (4/0), Jyrki Huhtamäki (2/0) [70.Juha Karvinen (2/0)], Ismo Lius (26/3), Ari Tegelberg (2/0) [75.Jouko Vuorela (4/0)]. Trainer: Jukka Keijo Olavi Vakkila (21).

467. 11.01.1989 **EGYPT - FINLAND** **2-1(1-1)**
El Mahalla Stadium, El Mahalla El Kubra; Referee: Ibrahim El Nady (Egypt); Attendance: 40,000
FIN: Kari Laukkanen (23/0), Ilkka Mäkelä (9/0), Esa Pekonen (59/2) [46.Marko Myyry (19/2)], Ari Heikkinen (1/0), Markku Kanerva (10/0), Erkka Petäjä (43/0), Jarmo Alatensiö (14/1) [70.Kimmo Tarkkio (8/0)], Kari Ukkonen (33/2), Ari Hjelm (52/11), Mika-Matti Paatelainen (13/3), Ismo Lius (27/3) [80.Jari Rantanen (35/4)]. Trainer: Jukka Keijo Olavi Vakkila (22).
Goal: Mika-Matti Paatelainen (14).

468. 13.01.1989 **EGYPT - FINLAND** **2-1(1-1)**
International Stadium, Cairo; Referee: Abdel Salas El Hamamsy (Egypt); Attendance: 15,000
FIN: Dan-Ola Eckerman (1/0) [46.Olavi Huttunen (42/0)], Ilkka Mäkelä (10/0), Markku Kanerva (11/0), Erkka Petäjä (44/0) [60.Ari Heikkinen (2/0)], Anders Roth (1/0), Jarmo Alatensiö (15/1) [46.Kari Ukkonen (34/2)], Marko Myyry (20/2), Jari Europaeus (38/0), Ismo Lius (28/3), Kimmo Tarkkio (9/1), Jari Rantanen (36/4) [75.Ari Tegelberg (3/0)]. Trainer: Jukka Keijo Olavi Vakkila (23).
Goal: Kimmo Tarkkio (42).

469. 08.02.1989 **ALGERIA - FINLAND** **2-0(0-0)** Rothmans Tournament
Ta' Qali National Stadium, Attard (Malta); Referee: Victor Mintoff (Malta); Attendance: 1,500
FIN: Dan-Ola Eckerman (2/0), Jyrki Hännikäinen (14/0), Ari Heikkinen (3/0), Jari Europaeus (39/0), Erkka Petäjä (45/0), Marko Myyry (21/2) [60.Anders Roth (2/0)], Erik Holmgren (19/0), Kari Ukkonen (35/2), Markku Kanerva (12/0) [46.Tommi Paavola (5/0)], Kimmo Tarkkio (10/1), Ismo Lius (29/3) [79.Jarmo Alatensiö (16/1)]. Trainer: Jukka Keijo Olavi Vakkila (24).

470. 10.02.1989 **FINLAND - DENMARK** **0-0** Rothmans Tournament
Ta' Qali National Stadium, Attard (Malta); Referee: Charles Agius (Malta); Attendance: 2,500
FIN: Kari Laukkanen (24/0), Jarmo Alatensiö (17/1) [86.Jyrki Hännikäinen (15/0)], Ari Heikkinen (4/0), Jari Europaeus (Cap) (40/0), Erkka Petäjä (46/0), Anders Roth (3/0) [72.Kimmo Tarkkio (11/1)], Erik Holmgren (20/0), Kari Ukkonen (36/2), Markku Kanerva (13/0), Tommi Paavola (6/0) [90.Jyrki Huhtamäki (3/0)], Ismo Lius (30/3). Trainer: Jukka Keijo Olavi Vakkila (25).

471. 12.02.1989 **MALTA - FINLAND** **0-0** Rothmans Tournament
Ta'Qali National Stadium, Attard; Referee: Kurt Sørensen (Denmark); Attendance: 3,000
FIN: Dan-Ola Eckerman (3/0), Jyrki Hännikäinen (16/0), Ari Heikkinen (5/0), Jari Europaeus (41/0), Mika A. Aaltonen (5/0), Jyrki Huhtamäki (4/0) [59.Tommi Paavola (7/0)], Erik Holmgren (21/0), Kari Ukkonen (37/2), Markku Kanerva (14/0), Kimmo Tarkkio (12/1) [67.Marko Myyry (22/2)], Ismo Lius (31/3). Trainer: Jukka Keijo Olavi Vakkila (26).

472. 22.03.1989 **EAST GERMANY - FINLAND** **1-1(0-1)**
Dynamo Stadion, Dresden; Referee: Jozef Marko (Czechoslovakia); Attendance: 14,000
FIN: Kari Laukkanen (25/0), Esa Pekonen (60/2), Ari Heikkinen (6/0), Jari Europaeus (42/0), Markku Kanerva (15/0), Marko Myyry (23/2) [72.Mika A. Aaltonen (6/0)], Erik Holmgren (22/0) [89.Anders Roth (4/0)], Kari Ukkonen (38/2), Ari Hjelm (53/11) [88.Ari Tegelberg (4/0)], Mika Lipponen (38/9), Tommi Paavola (8/0) [80.Erkka Petäjä (47/0)]. Trainer: Jukka Keijo Olavi Vakkila (27).
Goal: Mika Lipponen (29).

473. 31.05.1989 **FINLAND - NETHERLANDS** **0-1(0-0)** 14th FIFA WC. Qualifiers
Olympiastadion, Helsinki; Referee: Piotr Werner (Poland); Attendance: 46,217
FIN: Kari Laukkanen (26/0), Markku Kanerva (16/0), Ari Heikkinen (7/0), Jari Europaeus (43/0), Erik Holmgren (23/0), Marko Myyry (24/2), Kari Ukkonen (39/2) [68.Markus Törnvall (24/1)], Jukka Ikäläinen (55/4), Ari Hjelm (54/11) [83.Erkka Petäjä (48/0)], Mika-Matti Paatelainen (14/3), Mika Lipponen (39/9). Trainer: Jukka Keijo Olavi Vakkila (28).

474. 23.08.1989 **FINLAND - YUGOSLAVIA** **2-2(2-1)**
Väinölänniemi Stadion, Kuopio; Referee: Håkan Lundgren (Sweden); Attendance: 6,386
FIN: Olavi Huttunen (43/0), Erik Holmgren (24/0), Jari Europaeus (44/0), Ari Heikkinen (8/0), Aki Lahtinen (54/0), Jukka Ikäläinen (56/4), Marko Myyry (25/2), Markus Törnvall (25/1), Kimmo Tarkkio (13/2) [84.Ismo Lius (32/3)], Kari Ukkonen (40/3), Mika Lipponen (40/9) [84.Petri Järvinen (1/0)]. Trainer: Jukka Keijo Olavi Vakkila (29).
Goals: Kimmo Tarkkio (1), Kari Ukkonen (27).

475. 06.09.1989 **FINLAND - WALES** **1-0(0-0)** 14th FIFA WC. Qualifiers
Olympiastadion, Helsinki; Referee: Siegfried Kirschen (East Germany); Attendance: 7,480
FIN: Kari Laukkanen (27/0), Aki Lahtinen (55/0), Ari Heikkinen (9/0), Jari Europaeus (45/0), Erik Holmgren (25/0), Kimmo Tarkkio (14/2), Kari Ukkonen (41/3) [82.Pasi Tauriainen (13/0)], Jukka Ikäläinen (57/4), Mika-Matti Paatelainen (15/3) [65.Markus Törnvall (26/1)], Mika Lipponen (41/10), Marko Myyry (26/2). Trainer: Jukka Keijo Olavi Vakkila (30).
Goal: Mika Lipponen (50).

476. 04.10.1989 **WEST GERMANY - FINLAND** **6-1(1-0)** 14th FIFA WC. Qualifiers
Westfalenstadion, Dortmund; Referee: Alan Snoddy (Northern Ireland); Attendance: 40,000
FIN: Kari Laukkanen (28/0), Aki Lahtinen (56/0), Ari Heikkinen (10/0), Jari Europaeus (46/0), Erik Holmgren (26/0), Kimmo Tarkkio (15/2), Kari Ukkonen (42/3), Jukka Ikäläinen (58/4) [71.Ari Hjelm (55/11)], Marko Myyry (27/2), Mika-Matti Paatelainen (16/3) [62.Ismo Lius (33/3)], Mika Lipponen (42/11). Trainer: Jukka Keijo Olavi Vakkila (31).
Goal: Mika Lipponen (75).

477. 22.10.1989 **TRINIDAD AND TOBAGO - FINLAND** **0-1(0-0)**
"Hasely Crawford" Stadium, Port of Spain; Referee: Francis Cezair (Trinidad and Tobago); Attendance: 15,000
FIN: Olavi Huttunen (44/0), Markku Kanerva (17/0), Jouko Vuorela (5/0), Ari Heikkinen (11/0), Erkka Petäjä (49/0), Jari Rinne (12/0) [63.Anders Roth (5/0)], Jarmo Saastamoinen (1/0), Jarmo Alatensiö (18/1), Tommi Paavola (9/0) [79.Jari Olavi Litmanen (1/0)], Ismo Lius (34/4), Ari Valvee (46/8) [55.Jukka Turunen (1/0)]. Trainer: Jukka Keijo Olavi Vakkila (32).
Goal: Ismo Lius (65).

478. 25.10.1989 **TRINIDAD AND TOBAGO - FINLAND** **2-0(0-0)**
"Hasely Crawford" Stadium, Port of Spain; Referee: Gregory Maynard (Trinidad and Tobago); Attendance: 8,000
FIN: Dan-Ola Eckerman (4/0), Markku Kanerva (18/0), Jouko Vuorela (6/0), Ari Heikkinen (12/0), Erkka Petäjä (50/0), Jari Olavi Litmanen (2/0), Jarmo Saastamoinen (2/0) [53.Tommi Paavola (10/0)], Jarmo Alatensiö (19/1) [73.Jari Rinne (13/0)], Anders Roth (6/0), Ismo Lius (35/4), Jukka Turunen (2/0) [53.Ari Valvee (47/8)]. Trainer: Jukka Keijo Olavi Vakkila (33).

479. 15.11.1989 **NETHERLANDS - FINLAND** **3-0(0-0)** 14th FIFA WC. Qualifiers
Stadion Feijenoord, Rotterdam; Referee: Egil Nervik (Norway); Attendance: 50,000
FIN: Kari Laukkanen (29/0), Markku Kanerva (19/0), Ari Heikkinen (13/0), Jari Europaeus (47/0), Erik Holmgren (27/0), Kari Ukkonen (43/3) [56.Pasi Tauriainen (14/0)], Jukka Ikäläinen (59/4), Kimmo Tarkkio (16/2) [75.Erkka Petäjä (51/0)], Mika Lipponen (43/11), Marko Myyry (28/2), Mika-Matti Paatelainen (17/3). Trainer: Jukka Keijo Olavi Vakkila (34).

480. 12.02.1990 **UNITED ARAB EMIRATES - FINLAND** **1-1(0-1)**
"Maktoum bin Rashid" Stadium, Dubai; Referee: Al Amach (United Arab Emirates); Attendance: 3,000
FIN: Olavi Huttunen (45/0), Jouko Vuorela (7/0), Hannu Ollila (1/0), Jari Europaeus (48/0), Erik Holmgren (28/0), Mika J. Aaltonen (1/0), Jarmo Saastamoinen (3/0), Petri Tiainen (10/2) [83.Ilkka Mäkelä (11/0)], Pasi Tauriainen (15/0), Jyrki Huhtamäki (5/0) [63.Niclas Grönholm (1/0)], Jukka Turunen (3/0) [75.Jari Rinne (14/0)]. Trainer: Jukka Keijo Olavi Vakkila (35).
Goal: Petri Tiainen (23).

481. 15.02.1990 **KUWAIT - FINLAND** **0-1(0-0)**
International Stadium, Cairo (Egypt); Referee: Abdel Salas El Hamamsy (Egypt); Attendance: n/a
FIN: Petri Jakonen (1/0), Jouko Vuorela (8/0), Hannu Ollila (2/0) [46.Pasi Tauriainen (16/0); 77.Jukka Turunen (4/0)], Jari Europaeus (49/0), Erik Holmgren (29/0), Mika J. Aaltonen (2/1) [86.Jyrki Huhtamäki (6/0)], Jarmo Saastamoinen (4/0) [12.Jari Rinne (15/0)], Petri Tiainen (11/2) [64.Niclas Grönholm (2/0)], Ilkka Mäkelä (12/0), Mika Lipponen (44/11), Ari Hjelm (56/11). Trainer: Jukka Keijo Olavi Vakkila (36).
Goal: Mika J. Aaltonen (45).

482. 10.03.1990 **UNITED STATES - FINLAND** **2-1(1-0)**
Tampa Stadium, Tampa; Referee: Carlos Arrieta Saras (Costa Rica); Attendance: 22,647
FIN: Petri Jakonen (2/0), Jouko Vuorela (9/0) [89.Niclas Grönholm (3/0)], Ari Heikkinen (14/0), Jari Europaeus (50/0), Erik Holmgren (30/0), Hannu Ollila (3/0) [46.Jyrki Huhtamäki (7/0)], Pasi Tauriainen (17/0) [75.Jukka Turunen (5/0)], Jarmo Saastamoinen (5/0), Jari Olavi Litmanen (3/0), Kimmo Tarkkio (17/3), Ismo Lius (36/4). Trainer: Jukka Keijo Olavi Vakkila (37).
Goal: Kimmo Tarkkio (52).

483. 16.05.1990 **REPUBLIC OF IRELAND - FINLAND** **1-1(0-0)**
Lansdowne Road, Dublin; Referee: Rodger Gifford (Wales); Attendance: 31,556
FIN: Olavi Huttunen (46/0), Jouko Vuorela (10/0), Ari Heikkinen (15/0), Petri Sulonen (8/0), Markku Kanerva (20/0), Hannu Jäntti (1/0) [83.Jukka Turunen (6/0)], Pasi Tauriainen (18/0), Petri Järvinen (2/0), Jari Olavi Litmanen (4/0) [71.Vesa Tauriainen (1/1)], Marko Myyry (29/2) [59.Mika J. Aaltonen (3/1)], Mika-Matti Paatelainen (18/3). Trainer: Jukka Keijo Olavi Vakkila (38).
Goal: Vesa Tauriainen (74).

484. 27.05.1990 **SWEDEN – FINLAND** **6-0(1-0)**
Råsundastadion, Stockholm; Referee: Thorodd Presberg (Norway); Attendance: 12,914
FIN: Kari Laukkanen (30/0), Hannu Jäntti (2/0) [34.Markku Kanerva (21/0)], Ari Heikkinen (16/0), Erik Holmgren (31/0), Jouko Vuorela (11/0) [46.Marko Myyry (30/2); 65.Jari Olavi Litmanen (5/0)], Erkka Petäjä (52/0), Ari Hjelm (57/11), Anders Roth (7/0) [58.Tommi Paavola (11/0)], Pasi Tauriainen (19/0), Kimmo Tarkkio (18/3), Mika-Matti Paatelainen (19/3). Trainer: Jukka Keijo Olavi Vakkila (39).

485. 29.08.1990 **FINLAND - CZECHOSLOVAKIA** **1-1(1-0)**
Urheilupuisto, Kuusankoski; Referee: Peter Mikkelsen (Denmark); Attendance: 1,822
FIN: Olavi Huttunen (47/0), Ilkka Remes (29/1) [75.Tommi Paavola (12/0)], Markku Kanerva (22/0), Jari Europaeus (51/0), Erik Holmgren (32/0), Jari Rinne (16/0), Ari Heikkinen (17/0), Jari Olavi Litmanen (6/0), Petri Järvinen (3/1) [52.Marko Myyry (31/2)], Kimmo Tarkkio (19/3) [80.Mika Lipponen (45/11)], Mika-Matti Paatelainen (20/3). Trainer: Jukka Keijo Olavi Vakkila (40).
Goal: Petri Järvinen (39).

486. 12.09.1990 **FINLAND - PORTUGAL** **0-0** 9th EC. Qualifiers
Olympiastadion, Helsinki; Referee: Jozef Marko (Czechoslovakia); Attendance: 10,240
FIN: Olavi Huttunen (48/0), Jari Rinne (17/0), Erik Holmgren (33/0), Jari Europaeus (52/0), Ari Heikkinen (18/0), Erkka Petäjä (53/0), Kimmo Tarkkio (20/3) [74.Tommi Paavola (13/0)], Jari Olavi Litmanen (7/0), Petri Järvinen (4/1) [84.Marko Myyry (32/2)], Ari Hjelm (58/11), Mika-Matti Paatelainen (21/3). Trainer: Jukka Keijo Olavi Vakkila (41).

487. 11.11.1990 **TUNISIA - FINLAND** **1-2(0-1)**
Stade Olympique “El Menzah”, Tunis; Referee: Mohamed Hansal (Algeria); Attendance: 12,000
FIN: Olavi Huttunen (49/0), Markku Kanerva (23/0) [46.Erkka Petäjä (54/0)], Ari Heikkinen (19/0), Jari Europaeus (53/0), Erik Holmgren (34/0), Jari Rinne (18/0) [65.Ari Tegelberg (5/1)], Ari Hjelm (59/11), Jari Olavi Litmanen (8/0), Pasi Tauriainen (20/0) [65.Tommi Paavola (14/0)], Kimmo Tarkkio (21/3) [84.Jarmo Saastamoinen (6/0)], Mika-Matti Paatelainen (22/4). Trainer: Jukka Keijo Olavi Vakkila (42).
Goals : Mika-Matti Paatelainen (43), Ari Tegelberg (75).

488. 25.11.1990 **MALTA - FINLAND** **1-1(0-0)** 9th EC. Qualifiers
Ta’ Qali National Stadium, Attard; Referee: Sadik Deda (Turkey); Attendance: 6,000
FIN: Olavi Huttunen (50/0), Jari Rinne (19/0) [46.Erkka Petäjä (55/0)], Ari Heikkinen (20/0), Jari Europaeus (54/0), Erik Holmgren (35/1), Marko Myyry (33/2), Jari Olavi Litmanen (9/0), Ari Hjelm (60/11), Pasi Tauriainen (21/0), Kimmo Tarkkio (22/3) [75.Ari Tegelberg (6/1)], Mika-Matti Paatelainen (23/4). Trainer: Jukka Keijo Olavi Vakkila (43).
Goal: Erik Holmgren (87).

489. 13.03.1991 **POLAND - FINLAND** **1-1(1-1)**
Stadion Wojska Polskiego, Warszawa; Referee: Antal Huták (Hungary); Attendance: 4,000
FIN: Olavi Huttunen (51/0), Erkka Petäjä (56/0), Ari Heikkinen (21/0), Jari Europaeus (Cap) (55/0), Erik Holmgren (36/1) [88.Markku Kanerva (24/0)], Ari Hjelm (61/11), Kari Ukkonen (44/3), Jari Olavi Litmanen (10/0), Marko Myyry (34/2) [60.Harri Nyyssönen (1/0)], Kimmo Tarkkio (23/3) [73.Ari Tegelberg (7/1)], Mika-Matti Paatelainen (24/5) [86.Mika Lipponen (46/11)]. Trainer: Jukka Keijo Olavi Vakkila (44).
Goal: Mika-Matti Paatelainen (20).

490. 17.04.1991 **NETHERLANDS - FINLAND** **2-0(1-0)** 9th EC. Qualifiers
Stadion Feijenoord, Rotterdam; Referee: Jan Damgaard (Denmark); Attendance: 27,000
FIN: Olavi Huttunen (52/0), Erik Holmgren (37/1), Ari Heikkinen (22/0), Erkka Petäjä (57/0), Jari Europaeus (56/0), Markku Kanerva (25/0), Kari Ukkonen (45/3), Marko Myyry (35/2), Jari Olavi Litmanen (11/0) [46.Ari Tegelberg (8/1)], Pasi Tauriainen (22/0) [89.Harri Nyyssönen (2/0)], Mika-Matti Paatelainen (25/5). Trainer: Jukka Keijo Olavi Vakkila (45).

491. 16.05.1991 **FINLAND - MALTA** **2-0(0-0)** 9th EC. Qualifiers
Olympiastadion, Helsinki; Referee: Rune Pedersen (Norway); Attendance: 5,150
FIN: Olavi Huttunen (53/0), Erkka Petäjä (58/0), Ari Heikkinen (23/0), Erik Holmgren (38/1), Markku Kanerva (26/0), Marko Myyry (36/2), Jari Olavi Litmanen (12/1), Kari Ukkonen (46/3), Kimmo Tarkkio (24/3) [88.Pasi Tauriainen (23/0)], Mika-Matti Paatelainen (26/5) [74.Tommi Paavola (15/0)], Petri Järvinen (5/2). Trainer: Jukka Keijo Olavi Vakkila (46).
Goals: Petri Järvinen (51), Jari Olavi Litmanen (88).

492. 05.06.1991 **FINLAND - NETHERLANDS** **1-1(0-0)** 9th EC. Qualifiers
Olympiastadion, Helsinki; Referee: Brian McGinlay (Scotland); Attendance: 21,207
FIN: Olavi Huttunen (54/0), Erik Holmgren (39/2), Ari Heikkinen (24/0), Erkka Petäjä (59/0), Tommi Paavola (16/0), Marko Myyry (37/2), Jari Olavi Litmanen (13/1), Kari Ukkonen (47/3) [81.Ari Hjelm (62/11)], Petri Järvinen (6/2), Kimmo Tarkkio (25/3), Mika-Matti Paatelainen (27/5) [66.Ari Tegelberg (9/1)]. Trainer: Jukka Keijo Olavi Vakkila (47).
Goal: Erik Holmgren (77).

493. 11.09.1991 **PORTUGAL - FINLAND** **1-0(1-0)** 9th EC. Qualifiers
Estádio das Antas, Porto; Referee: Arturo Martino (Switzerland); Attendance: 30,000
FIN: Olavi Huttunen (55/0), Pasi Tauriainen (24/0) [59.Jouko Vuorela (12/0)], Erik Holmgren (40/2), Erkka Petäjä (60/0), Ari Heikkinen (25/0), Tommi Paavola (17/0), Kari Ukkonen (48/3) [73.Jari Olavi Litmanen (14/1)], Marko Myyry (38/2), Petri Järvinen (7/2), Kimmo Tarkkio (26/3), Mika-Matti Paatelainen (28/5). Trainer: Jukka Keijo Olavi Vakkila (48).

494. 09.10.1991 **FINLAND - GREECE** **1-1(0-0)** 9th EC. Qualifiers
Olympiastadion, Helsinki; Referee: Sergei Khusainov (Soviet Union); Attendance: 5,225
FIN: Olavi Huttunen (56/0), Ari Heikkinen (26/0), Erik Holmgren (41/2), Erkka Petäjä (61/0), Jouko Vuorela (13/0), Marko Myyry (39/2), Petri Järvinen (8/2) [63.Mika-Matti Paatelainen (29/5)], Kimmo Tarkkio (27/3) [82.Ari Tegelberg (10/1)], Kari Ukkonen (49/4), Ari Hjelm (63/11), Jari Olavi Litmanen (15/1). Trainer: Jukka Keijo Olavi Vakkila (49).
Goal: Kari Ukkonen (50).

495. 30.10.1991 **GREECE - FINLAND** **2-0(0-0)** 9th EC. Qualifiers
Stádio Olympiako „Spiros Louis“, Athína; Referee: Gerhard Kapl (Austria); Attendance: 7,111
FIN: Olavi Huttunen (57/0), Erik Holmgren (42/2), Ari Heikkinen (27/0), Erkka Petäjä (62/0), Jouko Vuorela (14/0) [55.Mika-Matti Paatelainen (30/5)], Jyrki Huhtamäki (8/0) [82.Ari Tegelberg (11/1)], Jari Olavi Litmanen (16/1), Kari Ukkonen (50/4), Petri Järvinen (9/2), Kimmo Tarkkio (28/3), Ari Hjelm (64/11). Trainer: Jukka Keijo Olavi Vakkila (50).

496. 12.02.1992 **TURKEY - FINLAND** **1-1(1-0)**
5th Oçak Stadı, Adana; Referee: Hans-Peter Dellwing (Germany); Attendance: 25,000
FIN: Olavi Huttunen (58/0), Petri Sulonen (9/0), Ari Heikkinen (28/0), Ilkka Remes (30/1), Anders Eriksson (1/0) [80.Ari Tegelberg (12/1)], Juha Karvinen (3/1), Jari Vanhala (1/0) [80.Harri Nyyssönen (3/0)], Petri Helin (1/0), Pasi Tauriainen (25/0), Ari Hjelm (65/11), Antti Sumiala (1/0) [88.Jukka Ruhanen (1/0)]. Trainer: Jukka Keijo Olavi Vakkila (51).
Goal : Juha Karvinen (75).

497. 25.03.1992 **SCOTLAND - FINLAND** **1-1(1-1)**
Hampden Park, Glasgow, Ref : Anders Frisk (Sweden); Attendance: 9,275
FIN: Olavi Huttunen (59/0), Jari Rinne (20/0) [87.Harri Nyyssönen (4/0)], Ari Heikkinen (29/0), Erkka Petäjä (63/0), Anders Eriksson (2/0), Ilkka Remes (31/1), Jari Olavi Litmanen (17/2), Marko Myyry (40/2), Petri Järvinen (10/2), Kimmo Tarkkio (29/3) [69.Jari Vanhala (2/0)], Mika-Matti Paatelainen (31/5). Trainer: Jukka Keijo Olavi Vakkila (52).
Goal: Jari Olavi Litmanen (41).

498. 15.04.1992 **BRAZIL - FINLAND** **3-1(0-1)**
Estádio "José Frageli", Cuiabá; Referee: Joelmes da Costa (Brazil); Attendance: 25,000
FIN: Kari Laukkanen (31/0), Erik Holmgren (43/2), Ari Heikkinen (30/0), Erkka Petäjä (64/0), Anders Eriksson (3/0), Jari Rinne (21/0), Jari Olavi Litmanen (18/2), Marko Myyry (41/2), Jouko Vuorela (15/0) [79.Pasi Tauriainen (26/0)], Ari Tegelberg (13/1) [67.Harri Nyyssönen (5/0)], Jari Vanhala (3/1) [85.Petri Sulonen (10/0)]. Trainer: Jukka Keijo Olavi Vakkila (53).
Goal: Jari Vanhala (39).

499. 14.05.1992 **FINLAND - BULGARIA** **0-3(0-0)** 15th FIFA WC. Qualifiers
Olympiastadion, Helsinki; Referee: Dušan Colić (Yugoslavia); Attendance: 10,000
FIN: Olavi Huttunen (60/0), Erik Holmgren (44/2), Ari Heikkinen (31/0), Erkka Petäjä (65/0), Anders Eriksson (4/0), Jari Rinne (22/0) [76.Jyrki Huhtämaki (9/0)], Jari Olavi Litmanen (19/2), Marko Myyry (42/2), Petri Järvinen (11/2), Kimmo Tarkkio (30/3), Jari Vanhala (4/1) [60.Ari Tegelberg (14/1)]. Trainer: Jukka Keijo Olavi Vakkila (54).

500. 03.06.1992 **FINLAND - ENGLAND** **1-2(1-1)**
Olympiastadion, Helsinki; Referee: Bo Karlsson (Sweden); Attendance: 16,101
FIN: Olavi Huttunen (61/0), Jari Rinne (23/0) [81.Jari Vanhala (5/1)], Petri Järvinen (12/2), Erkka Petäjä (66/0), Erik Holmgren (45/2) [46.Ari Heikkinen (32/0)], Jari Kinnunen (1/0), Jari Olavi Litmanen (20/2) [89.Jouko Vuorela (16/0)], Marko Myyry (43/2), Ari Hjelm (66/12), Kimmo Tarkkio (31/3) [70.Ari Tegelberg (15/1)], Jyrki Huhtamäki (10/0). Trainer: Jukka Keijo Olavi Vakkila (55).
Goal: Ari Hjelm (26).

501. 26.08.1992 **FINLAND - POLAND** **0-0**
Keskuskenttä, Pietarsaari; Referee: Finn Lambeck (Denmark); Attendance: 5,000
FIN: Kari Laukkanen (32/0), Jari Kinnunen (2/0), Markku Kanerva (27/0), Kari Ukkonen (51/4), Ilkka Remes (32/1), Marko Myyry (44/2) [83.Saku Laaksonen (1/0)], Jari Olavi Litmanen (21/2) [89.Jari Vanhala (6/1)], Erik Holmgren (46/2), Ari Hjelm (Cap) (67/12) [80.Jukka Turunen (7/0)], Petri Järvinen (13/2), Mika-Matti Paatelainen (32/5). Trainer: Jukka Keijo Olavi Vakkila (56).

502. 09.09.1992 **FINLAND - SWEDEN** **0-1(0-0)** 15th FIFA WC. Qualifiers
Olympiastadion, Helsinki; Referee: Vadim Zhuk (Belarus); Attendance: 13,617
FIN: Kari Laukkanen (33/0), Erik Holmgren (47/2), Markku Kanerva (28/0), Kari Ukkonen (52/4), Ilkka Remes (33/1), Marko Myyry (45/2) [84.Jari Vanhala (7/1)], Jari Olavi Litmanen (22/2), Petri Järvinen (14/2), Ari Hjelm (68/12), Kimmo Tarkkio (32/3) [78.Pasi Tauriainen (27/0)], Mika-Matti Paatelainen (33/5). Trainer: Jukka Keijo Olavi Vakkila (57).

503. 07.11.1992 **TUNISIA - FINLAND** **1-1(0-1)**
Stade Olympique "El Menzah", Tunis; Referee: Rachid Medjiba (Algeria); Attendance: 8,000
FIN: Antti Niemi (1/0), Jari Kinnunen (3/0), Aki Hyryläinen (1/0), Markku Kanerva (29/0), Ilkka Remes (34/1), Pasi Tauriainen (28/0) [82.Sami Hyypiä (1/0)], Petri Järvinen (15/2), Jari Olavi Litmanen (23/2), Jari Vanhala (8/1) [66.Jari Rinne (24/0)], Ari Hjelm (69/13), Antti Sumiala (2/0) [55.Mika Nurmela (1/0)]. Trainer: Jukka Keijo Olavi Vakkila (58).
Goal: Ari Hjelm (23).

504. 14.11.1992 **FRANCE - FINLAND** **2-1(2-0)** 15th FIFA WC. Qualifiers
Stade Parc des Princes, Paris; Referee: Jozef Marko (Czechoslovakia); Attendance: 30,000
FIN: Kari Laukkanen (34/0), Erik Holmgren (48/2), Markku Kanerva (30/0), Kari Ukkonen (53/4), Erkka Petäjä (67/0) [86.Jari Kinnunen (4/0)], Marko Myyry (46/2), Jari Olavi Litmanen (24/2), Ari Hjelm (70/13), Petri Järvinen (16/3), Kimmo Tarkkio (33/3), Mika-Matti Paatelainen (34/5) [24.Pasi Tauriainen (29/0)]. Trainer: Jukka Keijo Olavi Vakkila (59).
Goal: Petri Järvinen (54).

505. 20.01.1993 **INDIA - FINLAND** **0-0**
„Jawaharlal Nehru" Stadium, Madras; Referee: Sadar Kumar Sen (India)
FIN: Antti Niemi (2/0), Jari Kinnunen (5/0), Aki Hyryläinen (2/0), Markku Kanerva (31/0), Ari Heikkinen (Cap) (33/0), Kim Suominen (1/0), Juha Karvinen (4/1), Marko Rajamäki (1/0), Janne Suokonautio (1/0) [76.Rami Rantanen (1/0)], Jari Vanhala (9/1), Niclas Grönholm (4/0). Trainer: Tommy Lindholm (1).

506. 22.01.1993 **CAMEROON - FINLAND** **0-0** Nehru Cup
„Jawaharlal Nehru" Stadium, Madras (India); Referee: Sirai Ahmed Saudagar (India)
FIN: Petri Jakonen (3/0), Jari Kinnunen (6/0), Aki Hyryläinen (3/0), Markku Kanerva (32/0), Ari Heikkinen (Cap) (34/0), Kim Suominen (2/0), Juha Karvinen (5/1) [61.Pasi Tauriainen (30/0)], Rami Rantanen (2/0), Marko Rajamäki (2/0), Jari Vanhala (10/1) [81.Jukka Ruhanen (2/0)], Niclas Grönholm (5/0). Trainer: Tommy Lindholm (2).

507. 26.01.1993 **INDIA - FINLAND** **0-2(0-0)** Nehru Cup
„Jawaharlal Nehru" Stadium, Madras; Referee: Sk. Badruddin Badhu Badruddin (Bangladesh)
FIN: Petri Jakonen (4/0), Jari Kinnunen (7/0), Aki Hyryläinen (4/0), Markku Kanerva (33/0), Ari Heikkinen (Cap) (35/0), Kim Suominen (3/0), Juha Karvinen (6/1) [52.Niclas Grönholm (6/0)], Rami Rantanen (3/0), Marko Rajamäki (3/1), Pasi Tauriainen (31/1) [73.Jukka Ruhanen (3/0)], Jari Vanhala (11/1). Trainer: Tommy Lindholm (3).
Goals: Pasi Tauriainen (60), Marko Rajamäki (69).

508. 28.01.1993 **CAMEROON - FINLAND** **2-0** Nehru Cup
„Jawaharlal Nehru" Stadium, Madras (India); Referee: Kar Gautam (India)
FIN: Antti Niemi (3/0), Jari Kinnunen (8/0), Aki Hyryläinen (5/0) [68.Rami Nieminen (1/0)], Markku Kanerva (34/0), Ari Heikkinen (Cap) (36/0), Kim Suominen (4/0), Pasi Tauriainen (32/1), Rami Rantanen (4/0), Marko Rajamäki (4/1) [73.Jari Vanhala (12/1)], Niclas Grönholm (7/0), Jukka Ruhanen (4/0). Trainer: Tommy Lindholm (4).

509. 31.01.1993 **KOREA D.P.R. - FINLAND** **3-2(2-0)** Nehru Cup

„Jawaharlal Nehru" Stadium, Madras (India); Referee: Sirai Ahmed Saudagar (India); Attendance: 17,500

FIN: Petri Jakonen (5/0), Jari Kinnunen (9/0), Aki Hyryläinen (6/0), Rami Nieminen (2/0), Ari Heikkinen (Cap) (37/0), Kim Suominen (5/0), Pasi Tauriainen (33/1) [49.Juha Karvinen (7/2)], Marko Rajamäki (5/2), Jari Vanhala (13/1), Jukka Ruhanen (5/0), Niclas Grönholm (8/0). Trainer: Tommy Lindholm (5).

Goals: Juha Karvinen (68), Marko Rajamäki (72).

510. 20.02.1993 **FINLAND - ESTONIA** **0-0; 4-3 on penalties** Baltic Indoor Cup

Myyrmäki halli, Vantaa (indoor); Referee: Juha Hirviniemi (Finland); Attendance: 1,000

FIN: Petri Jakonen (6/0), Jari Kinnunen (10/0), Markku Kanerva (35/0), Erkka Petäjä (68/0), Ari Heikkinen (Cap) (38/0), Marko Rajamäki (6/2), Rami Rantanen (5/0), Pasi Tauriainen (34/1) [32.Jukka Ruhanen (6/0)], Janne Lindberg (1/0), Jari Vanhala (14/1) [78.Aki Hyryläinen (7/0)], Niclas Grönholm (9/0). Trainer: Tommy Lindholm (6).

Penalties: Marko Rajamäki, Niclas Grönholm, Markku Kanerva, Ari Heikkinen, Rami Rantanen (saved).

511. 21.02.1993 **FINLAND - LITHUANIA** **3-0(1-0)** Baltic Indoor Cup

Myyrmäki halli, Vantaa (indoor); Referee: Kaj Natri (Finland); Attendance: 200

FIN: Petri Jakonen (7/0), Jari Kinnunen (11/1), Markku Kanerva (36/0), Erkka Petäjä (69/0) [82.Aki Hyryläinen (8/0)], Ari Heikkinen (Cap) (39/0), Erik Holmgren (49/2), Marko Rajamäki (7/2) [70.Jari Vanhala (15/1)], Rami Rantanen (6/0), Jukka Ruhanen (7/1), Janne Lindberg (2/0), Niclas Grönholm (10/1). Trainer: Tommy Lindholm (7).

Goals: Niclas Grönholm (41), Jukka Ruhanen (49), Jari Kinnunen (54).

512. 13.04.1993 **POLAND - FINLAND** **2-1(1-0)**

Stadion Radomiak, Radom, 13.04.1993; Referee: Bernd Heynemann (Germany); Attendance: 8,000

FIN: Kari Laukkanen (35/0), Jari Kinnunen (12/1), Markku Kanerva (37/0), Anders Eriksson (5/0) [70.Marko Rajamäki (8/2)], Erkka Petäjä (70/0), Ari Heikkinen (40/1), Kim Suominen (6/0) [74.Marko Myyry (47/2)], Janne Lindberg (3/0), Jari Olavi Litmanen (25/2), Ari Hjelm (Cap) (71/13), Mika-Matti Paatelainen (35/5). Trainer: Tommy Lindholm (8).

Goal: Ari Heikkinen (84).

513. 28.04.1993 **BULGARIA - FINLAND** **2-0(2-0)** 15th FIFA WC. Qualifiers

Nationalen stadion "Vasil Levski", Sofia; Referee: Lim Kee Chong (Mauritius); Attendance: 35,000

FIN: Petri Jakonen (8/0), Jari Kinnunen (13/1), Markku Kanerva (38/0), Ari Heikkinen (41/1), Erik Holmgren (50/2), Erkka Petäjä (71/0) [75.Marko Rajamäki (9/2)], Janne Lindberg (4/0), Kim Suominen (7/0), Jari Olavi Litmanen (26/2), Ari Hjelm (Cap) (72/13), Mika-Matti Paatelainen (36/5). Trainer: Tommy Lindholm (9).

514. 13.05.1993 **FINLAND - AUSTRIA** **3-1(2-0)** 15th FIFA WC. Qualifiers

Urheilupuisto, Turku; Referee: John Ferry (Republic of Ireland); Attendance: 13,682

FIN: Petri Jakonen (9/0), Jari Kinnunen (14/1), Markku Kanerva (39/0), Erik Holmgren (51/2) [60.Janne Lindberg (5/0)], Ari Heikkinen (42/1), Erkka Petäjä (72/0), Marko Rajamäki (10/3), Kim Suominen (8/0), Jari Olavi Litmanen (27/2), Ari Hjelm (Cap) (73/14), Mika-Matti Paatelainen (37/6) [76.Niclas Grönholm (11/1)]. Trainer: Tommy Lindholm (10).

Goals: Mika-Matti Paatelainen (17), Marko Rajamäki (20), Ari Hjelm (50).

515. 16.06.1993 **FINLAND - ISRAEL** **0-0** 15th FIFA WC. Qualifiers

Lahden Kisapuisto, Lahti; Referee: Vladimir Pyanikh (Ukraina); Attendance: 4,620

FIN: Petri Jakonen (10/0), Jari Kinnunen (15/1) [85.Janne Lindberg (6/0)], Markku Kanerva (40/0), Erik Holmgren (52/2), Ari Heikkinen (Cap) (43/1), Erkka Petäjä (73/0), Marko Rajamäki (11/3), Kim Suominen (9/0), Jari Olavi Litmanen (28/2), Niclas Grönholm (12/1) [75.Jukka Ruhanen (8/1)], Mika-Matti Paatelainen (38/6). Trainer: Tommy Lindholm (11).

516. 25.08.1993 **AUSTRIA - FINLAND** **3-0(2-0)** 15th FIFA WC. Qualifiers

„Ernst Happel" Stadion, Wien; Referee: Michal Listkiewicz (Poland); Attendance: 21,000

FIN: Petri Jakonen (11/0), Jari Kinnunen (16/1), Markku Kanerva (41/0), Ari Heikkinen (44/1), Erkka Petäjä (74/0), Kim Suominen (10/0), Janne Lindberg (7/0) [68.Jukka Ruhanen (9/1)], Marko Rajamäki (12/3), Jari Olavi Litmanen (29/2) [76.Niclas Grönholm (13/1)], Ari Hjelm (Cap) (74/14), Mika-Matti Paatelainen (39/6). Trainer: Tommy Lindholm (12).

517. 08.09.1993 **FINLAND - FRANCE** **0-2(0-0)** 15th FIFA WC. Qualifiers

Ratinan Stadion, Tampere; Referee: Stephen Lodge (England); Attendance: 7,500

FIN: Petri Jakonen (12/0), Jari Kinnunen (17/1), Markku Kanerva (42/0), Anders Eriksson (6/0), Erkka Petäjä (75/0), Kim Suominen (11/0) [76.Tommi Paavola (18/0)], Janne Lindberg (8/0), Marko Rajamäki (13/3) [78.Jukka Ruhanen (10/1)], Jari Olavi Litmanen (30/2), Ari Hjelm (Cap) (75/14), Mika-Matti Paatelainen (40/6). Trainer: Tommy Lindholm (13).

518. 13.10.1993 **SWEDEN – FINLAND** **3-2(3-1)** 15th FIFA WC. Qualifiers

Råsundastadion, Stockholm; Referee: Ahmet Çakar (Turkey); Attendance: 30,200

FIN: Petri Jakonen (13/0), Jari Kinnunen (18/1), Markku Kanerva (43/0), Ari Heikkinen (45/1), Erkka Petäjä (76/0), Anders Eriksson (7/0) [46.Petri Järvinen (17/3)], Kim Suominen (12/1), Janne Lindberg (9/0), Jari Olavi Litmanen (31/3), Mika A. Aaltonen (7/0), Ari Hjelm (Cap) (76/14). Trainer: Tommy Lindholm (14).

Goals: Kim Suominen (15), Jari Olavi Litmanen (60).

519. 10.11.1993 **ISRAEL - FINLAND** **1-3(0-0)** 15th FIFA WC. Qualifiers

National Stadium, Ramat-Gan, Tel Aviv; Referee: Daniel Roduit (Switzerland); Attendance: 15,000

FIN: Petri Jakonen (14/0), Jari Kinnunen (19/1), Aki Hyryläinen (9/1), Ari Heikkinen (46/1), Erkka Petäjä (77/0), Kim Suominen (13/1), Tommi Paavola (19/1) [72.Mika Nurmela (2/0)], Janne Lindberg (10/0), Jari Olavi Litmanen (32/3), Mika A. Aaltonen (8/0), Ari Hjelm (Cap) (77/15). Trainer: Tommy Lindholm (15).

Goals: Aki Hyryläinen (54), Tommi Paavola (71), Ari Hjelm (84).

520. 25.01.1994 **QATAR - FINLAND** **1-0(1-0)**

"Hamad bin Khalifa" Stadium, Doha; Referee: Hani Saber (Qatar); Attendance: 400

FIN: Petri Jakonen (15/0), Jari Kinnunen (20/1), Erkka Petäjä (78/0), Markku Kanerva (Cap) (44/0), Janne Lindberg (11/0), Kim Suominen (14/1), Jussi Nuorela (1/0), Janne Suokonautio (2/0) [79.Janne Mäkelä (1/0)], Mika Nurmela (3/0), Petri Järvinen (18/3) [74.Jokke Kangaskorpi (1/0)], Niclas Grönholm (14/1) [74.Mika J. Aaltonen (4/1)]. Trainer: Tommy Lindholm (16).

521. 27.01.1994 **QATAR - FINLAND** **0-0**
"Hamad bin Khalifa" Stadium, Doha; Referee: Ali Alhulin (Qatar); Attendance: 200
FIN: Antti Niemi (4/0), Jari Kinnunen (21/1), Erkka Petäjä (79/0) [53.Janne Mäkelä (2/0)], Markku Kanerva (Cap) (45/0), Janne Lindberg (12/0), Kim Suominen (15/1), Jussi Nuorela (2/0), Janne Suokonautio (3/0) [69.Jokke Kangaskorpi (2/0)], Mika Nurmela (4/0), Petri Järvinen (19/3), Niclas Grönholm (15/1) [57.Mika J. Aaltonen (5/1)]. Trainer: Tommy Lindholm (17).

522. 30.01.1994 **OMAN - FINLAND** **0-2(0-1)**
El Shorta Stadium, Muscat; Referee: Sultan Saed Al Mezahmi (Oman); Attendance: 500
FIN: Antti Niemi (5/0), Janne Mäkelä (3/0), Ari Heikkinen (Cap) (47/1), Markku Kanerva (46/1), Janne Lindberg (13/0), Kim Suominen (16/2), Mika J. Aaltonen (6/1), Jokke Kangaskorpi (3/0), Mika Nurmela (5/0), Petri Järvinen (20/3), Jari Kinnunen (22/1) [23.Erkka Petäjä (80/0)]. Trainer: Tommy Lindholm (18).
Goals: Kim Suominen (10), Markku Kanerva (82).

523. 01.02.1994 **OMAN - FINLAND** **1-1(1-0)**
El Shorta Stadium, Muscat; Referee: Ali Al Hosni Ali Bin Mubarak (Oman); Attendance: 500
FIN: Petri Jakonen (16/0), Janne Mäkelä (4/0) [46.Jussi Nuorela (3/0)], Erkka Petäjä (81/0), Markku Kanerva (47/1), Janne Lindberg (14/0), Kim Suominen (17/2), Ari Heikkinen (Cap) (48/1), Mika J. Aaltonen (7/1) [66.Niclas Grönholm (16/2)], Mika Nurmela (6/0), Petri Järvinen (21/3), Jokke Kangaskorpi (4/0) [62.Janne Suokonautio (4/0)]. Trainer: Tommy Lindholm (19).
Goal: Niclas Grönholm (75).

524. 23.02.1994 **MOROCCO - FINLAND** **0-0**
Stade "Mohamed V", Casablanca; Referee: Abdelaziz Bellaftouh (Morocco); Attendance: 20,000
FIN: Petri Jakonen (17/0), Jari Kinnunen (23/1), Erkka Petäjä (82/0), Ari Heikkinen (Cap) (49/1), Markku Kanerva (48/1), Janne Lindberg (15/0) [56.Jokke Kangaskorpi (5/0)], Kim Suominen (18/2), Mika A. Aaltonen (9/0), Antti Sumiala (3/0) [81.Niclas Grönholm (17/2)], Mika Nurmela (7/0), Tommi Paavola (20/1). Trainer: Tommy Lindholm (20).

525. 27.05.1994 **ITALY - FINLAND** **2-0(1-0)**
Stadio "Ennio Tardini", Parma; Referee: László Vágner (Hungary); Attendance: 16,500
FIN: Petri Jakonen (18/0), Jari Kinnunen (24/1), Ari Heikkinen (50/1), Erkka Petäjä (83/0), Markku Kanerva (49/1) [73.Aki Hyryläinen (10/1)], Kim Suominen (19/2), Jari Olavi Litmanen (33/3), Janne Lindberg (16/0) [77.Tommi Paavola (21/1)], Ari Hjelm (Cap) (78/15), Mika A. Aaltonen (10/0) [88.Rami Rantanen (7/0)], Petri Järvinen (22/3). Trainer: Tommy Lindholm (21).

526. 02.06.1994 **FINLAND - SPAIN** **1-2(1-2)**
Ratinan Stadion, Tampere; Referee: Christer Fällström (Sweden); Attendance: 10,250
FIN: Antti Niemi (6/0), Jari Kinnunen (25/1), Janne Mäkelä (5/0), Erkka Petäjä (84/0), Ari Hyryläinen (11/1), Tommi Paavola (22/1) [60.Kim Suominen (20/2)], Mika A. Aaltonen (11/0), Rami Rantanen (8/0) [60.Janne Lindberg (17/0)], Ari Hjelm (Cap) (79/15), Jari Olavi Litmanen (34/3), Petri Järvinen (23/4). Trainer: Tommy Lindholm (22).
Goal: Petri Järvinen (18).

527. 17.08.1994 **DENMARK - FINLAND** **2-1(0-1)**
Parken, København; Referee: Gunter Benkö (Austria); Attendance: 7,692
FIN: Petri Jakonen (19/0), Janne Mäkelä (6/0), Ari Heikkinen (51/1) [31.Erik Holmgren (53/2)], Aki Hyryläinen (12/1), Antti Heinola (1/0), Kim Suominen (21/3), Rami Rantanen (9/0) [72.Tommi Paavola (23/1)], Janne Lindberg (18/0), Ari Hjelm (Cap) (80/15), Mika J. Aaltonen (8/1) [72.Mika Nurmela (8/0)), Mika-Matti Paatelainen (41/6). Trainer: Tommy Lindholm (23).
Goal: Kim Suominen (40).

528. 07.09.1994 **FINLAND - SCOTLAND** **0-2(0-1)** 10th EC. Qualifiers
Olympiastadion, Helsinki; Referee: Ryszard Wójcik (Poland); Attendance: 12,845
FIN: Petri Jakonen (20/0), Janne Mäkelä (7/0), Markku Kanerva (50/1), Aki Hyryläinen (13/1), Antti Heinola (2/0) [30.Erik Holmgren (54/2)], Kim Suominen (22/3), Rami Rantanen (10/0) [41.Petri Järvinen (24/4)], Janne Lindberg (19/0), Ari Hjelm (Cap) (81/15), Jari Olavi Litmanen (35/3), Mika-Matti Paatelainen (42/6). Trainer: Tommy Lindholm (24).

529. 12.10.1994 **GREECE - FINLAND** **4-0(1-0)** 10th EC. Qualifiers
Kautatzogleio, Thessaloníki; Referee: Philippe Leduc (France); Attendance: 30,000
FIN: Petri Jakonen (21/0), Janne Mäkelä (8/0), Markku Kanerva (51/1), Aki Hyryläinen (14/1), Antti Heinola (3/0) [31.Erik Holmgren (55/2)], Kim Suominen (23/3), Petri Järvinen (25/4) [73.Antti Sumiala (4/0)], Janne Lindberg (20/0), Ari Hjelm (Cap) (82/15), Jari Olavi Litmanen (36/3), Mika-Matti Paatelainen (43/6). Trainer: Tommy Lindholm (25).

530. 26.10.1994 **ESTONIA - FINLAND** **0-7(0-6)**
Kadriorg Staadion, Tallinn; Referee: Romans Lajuks (Latvia); Attendance: 500
FIN: Antti Niemi (7/0) [46.Petri Jakonen (22/0)], Janne Mäkelä (9/0) [67.Joonas Einari Kolkka (1/1)], Markku Kanerva (52/1), Aki Hyryläinen (15/1), Anders Eriksson (8/1) [46.Lasse Karjalainen (1/0)], Petri Helin (2/0), Rami Rantanen (11/0), Sami Hyypiä (2/0), Ari Hjelm (Cap) (83/17) [87.Toni Huttunen (1/0)], Jukka Ruhanen (11/3), Antti Sumiala (5/1). Trainer: Jukka Ikäläinen (1).
Goals: Anders Eriksson (5), Jukka Ruhanen (19), Antti Sumiala (29), Ari Hjelm (31, 40), Jukka Ruhanen (41), Joonas Einari Kolkka (85).

531. 16.11.1994 **FINLAND – FAROE ISLANDS** **5-0(1-0)** 10th EC. Qualifiers
Olympiastadion, Helsinki; Referee: Gylfi Thor Orrason (Iceland); Attendance: 5,000
FIN: Kari Laukkanen (36/0), Janne Mäkelä (10/0), Markku Kanerva (53/1), Anders Eriksson (9/1), Petri Helin (3/0), Janne Lindberg (21/0) [78.Marko Rajamäki (14/3)], Antti Sumiala (6/2) [88.Jukka Ruhanen (12/3)], Kari Ukkonen (54/4), Ari Hjelm (Cap) (84/17), Jari Olavi Litmanen (37/5), Mika-Matti Paatelainen (44/8). Trainer: Jukka Ikäläinen (2).
Goals: Antti Sumiala (37), Jari Olavi Litmanen (53 penalty, 72), Mika-Matti Paatelainen (75, 85).

532. 30.11.1994 **SPAIN - FINLAND** **2-0(1-0)**
Estadio La Rosaleda, Málaga; Referee: David Elleray (England); Attendance: 38,000
FIN: Antti Niemi (8/0) [52.Panu Toivonen (1/0)], Janne Mäkelä (11/0), Markku Kanerva (54/1), Anders Eriksson (10/1), Petri Helin (4/0) [76.Toni Huttunen (2/0)], Sami Hyypiä (3/0), Marko Myyry (48/2), Rami Rantanen (12/0) [46.Antti Heinola (4/0)], Ari Hjelm (Cap) (85/17), Jukka Ruhanen (13/3) [46.Joonas Einari Kolkka (2/1)], Antti Sumiala (7/2). Trainer: Jukka Ikäläinen (3).

533. 14.12.1994 **FINLAND – SAN MARINO** **4-1(2-1)** 10th EC. Qualifiers
Olympiastadion, Helsinki; Referee: Hermann Albrecht (Germany); Attendance: 3,140
FIN: Kari Laukkanen (37/0), Janne Mäkelä (12/0), Markku Kanerva (55/1), Anders Eriksson (11/1), Petri Helin (5/0) [74.Marko Myyry (49/2)], Janne Lindberg (22/0), Antti Sumiala (8/2), Kari Ukkonen (55/4), Ari Hjelm (Cap) (86/17), Jari Olavi Litmanen (38/5), Mika-Matti Paatelainen (45/12). Trainer: Jukka Ikäläinen (4).
Goals: Mika-Matti Paatelainen (24, 30, 86, 90).

534. 16.02.1995 **TRINIDAD AND TOBAGO - FINLAND** **2-2**
Queen's Park Oval, Port of Spain; Referee: Austin Eric Harewood (Trinidad and Tobago); Attendance: 1,000
FIN: Antti Niemi (9/0), Rami Nieminen (3/0) [63.Tom Enberg (1/0)], Markku Kanerva (56/1), Anders Eriksson (12/1), Petri Helin (6/1), Sami Hyypiä (4/0), Rami Rantanen (13/0), Antti Heinola (5/0), Ari Hjelm (Cap) (87/17), Petri Tiainen (12/2) [75.Jasse Jalonen (1/0)], Joonas Einari Kolkka (3/2). Trainer: Jukka Ikäläinen (5).
Goals: Petri Helin (52), Joonas Einari Kolkka (88).

535. 08.03.1995 **CZECH REPUBLIC - FINLAND** **4-1(2-0)**
Stadion Za Lužánkami, Brno; Referee: Bohdan Benedik (Slovakia); Attendance: 8,000
FIN: Kari Laukkanen (38/0), Erik Holmgren (56/2), Markku Kanerva (57/1), Anders Eriksson (13/1), Janne Lindberg (23/0), Marko Myyry (50/2), Antti Sumiala (9/2) [79.Jukka Ruhanen (14/3)], Kim Suominen (24/3), Ari Hjelm (Cap) (88/18), Kari Ukkonen (56/4), Marko Rajamäki (15/3) [62.Rami Nieminen (4/0)]. Trainer: Jukka Ikäläinen (6).
Goal: Ari Hjelm (71).

536. 29.03.1995 **SAN MARINO - FINLAND** **0-2(0-1)** 10th EC. Qualifiers
Stadio Olimpico, Serravalle; Referee: David Suheil (Israel); Attendance: 824
FIN: Kari Laukkanen (39/0), Janne Mäkelä (13/0), Kari Ukkonen (57/4), Anders Eriksson (14/1), Petri Helin (7/1), Janne Lindberg (24/0), Antti Sumiala (10/3), Marko Myyry (51/2) [83.Sami Hyypiä (5/0)], Ari Hjelm (Cap) (89/18), Jari Olavi Litmanen (39/6), Petri Järvinen (26/4) [76.Marko Rajamäki (16/3)]. Trainer: Jukka Ikäläinen (7).
Goals: Jari Olavi Litmanen (45), Antti Sumiala (65).

537. 26.04.1995 **FAROE ISLANDS - FINLAND** **0-4(0-0)** 10th EC. Qualifiers
Svangaskarð, Toftir; Referee: Alan Howells (Wales); Attendance: 1,000
FIN: Kari Laukkanen (40/0), Janne Mäkelä (14/0), Kari Ukkonen (58/4), Anders Eriksson (15/1), Petri Helin (8/2), Janne Lindberg (25/1) [82.Kim Suominen (25/3)], Antti Sumiala (11/3) [60.Joonas Einari Kolkka (4/2)], Sami Hyypiä (6/0), Ari Hjelm (Cap) (90/19), Jari Olavi Litmanen (40/6), Mika-Matti Paatelainen (46/13). Trainer: Jukka Ikäläinen (8).
Goals: Ari Hjelm (55), Mika-Matti Paatelainen (75), Janne Lindberg (78), Petri Helin (83).

538. 31.05.1995 **FINLAND - DENMARK** **0-1(0-0)**
Olympiastadion, Helsinki; Referee: Renatus Hendrikus Johannes „René" Temmink (Netherlands); Attendance: 7,112
FIN: Kari Laukkanen (41/0), Janne Mäkelä (15/0), Rami Nieminen (5/0), Marko Tuomela (1/0), Erik Holmgren (57/2), Kim Suominen (26/3), Marko Myyry (52/2) [55.Petri Tiainen (13/2)], Janne Lindberg (26/1), Antti Sumiala (12/3) [63.Tom Enberg (2/0)], Ari Hjelm (Cap) (91/19), Petri Järvinen (27/4) [46.Mika-Matti Paatelainen (47/13)]. Trainer: Jukka Ikäläinen (9).

539. 11.06.1995 **FINLAND - GREECE** **2-1(1-1)** 10th EC. Qualifiers
Olympiastadion, Helsinki; Referee: Hellmut Krug (Germany); Attendance: 10,500
FIN: Kari Laukkanen (42/0), Janne Mäkelä (16/0), Marko Tuomela (2/0), Erik Holmgren (58/2), Petri Helin (9/2), Janne Lindberg (27/1), Antti Sumiala (13/3) [63.Petri Järvinen (28/4)], Marko Myyry (53/2), Ari Hjelm (Cap) (92/20), Jari Olavi Litmanen (41/7), Mika-Matti Paatelainen (48/13) [86.Petri Tiainen (14/2)]. Trainer: Jukka Ikäläinen (10).
Goals: Jari Olavi Litmanen (44 penalty), Ari Hjelm (55).

540. 16.08.1995 **FINLAND - RUSSIA** **0-6(0-3)** 10th EC. Qualifiers
Olympiastadion, Helsinki; Referee: Sándor Puhl (Hungary); Attendance: 14,200
FIN: Kari Laukkanen (43/0), Janne Mäkelä (17/0) [46.Kim Suominen (27/3)], Markku Kanerva (58/1), Erik Holmgren (59/2), Rami Nieminen (6/0), Janne Lindberg (28/1), Antti Sumiala (14/3), Rami Rantanen (14/0) [65.Tommi Grönlund (1/0)], Ari Hjelm (Cap) (93/20), Petri Tiainen (15/2), Mika-Matti Paatelainen (49/13) [46.Petri Järvinen (29/4)]. Trainer: Jukka Ikäläinen (11).

541. 06.09.1995 **SCOTLAND - FINLAND** **1-0(1-0)** 10th EC. Qualifiers
Hampden Park, Glasgow; Referee: Vasiliy Melnichuk (Ukraine); Attendance: 35,505
FIN: Kari Laukkanen (44/0), Kari Rissanen (5/0), Markku Kanerva (59/1), Erik Holmgren (60/2), Kim Suominen (28/3), Janne Lindberg (29/1), Rami Nieminen (7/0) [64.Tommi Grönlund (2/0)], Marko Myyry (54/2), Ari Hjelm (Cap) (94/20), Jari Olavi Litmanen (42/7), Petri Järvinen (30/4). Trainer: Jukka Ikäläinen (12).

542. 04.10.1995 **FINLAND - TURKEY** **0-0**
Olympiastadion, Helsinki; Referee: Tore Hollung (Norway); Attendance: 3,150
FIN: Petri Jakonen (23/0) [46.Antti Niemi (10/0)], Janne Mäkelä (18/0), Jussi Nuorela (4/0), Aki Hyryläinen (16/1), Antti Heinola (6/0) [85.Jari Jäväjä (1/0)], Janne Lindberg (30/1), Tommi Grönlund (3/0), Sami Hyypiä (7/0) [71.Sami Mahlio (1/0)], Ari Hjelm (Cap) (95/20) [85.Kari Rissanen (6/0)], Marko Myyry (55/2), Jokke Kangaskorpi (6/0) [58.Sami Väisänen (1/0)]. Trainer: Jukka Ikäläinen (13).

543. 15.11.1995 **RUSSIA - FINLAND** **3-1(1-1)** 10th EC. Qualifiers
Luzhniki Stadium, Moskva; Referee: Dr. Markus Merk (Germany); Attendance: 3,500
FIN: Antti Niemi (11/0), Kari Rissanen (7/0), Jussi Nuorela (5/0), Aki Hyryläinen (17/1), Rami Nieminen (8/0), Janne Lindberg (31/1), Antti Sumiala (15/3) [76.Jokke Kangaskorpi (7/0)], Kim Suominen (29/4) [88.Harri Ylönen (1/0)], Ari Hjelm (Cap) (96/20), Marko Myyry (56/2), Tommi Grönlund (4/0) [70.Jarkko Koskinen (1/0)]. Trainer: Jukka Ikäläinen (14).
Goal: Kim Suominen (44).

544. 09.02.1996 **THAILAND - FINLAND** **1-0(0-0)** King's Cup
Rajamangala National Stadium, Bangkok; Referee: Selearajen Subramaniam (Malaysia); Attendance: 5,000
FIN: Antti Niemi (12/0), Harri Ylönen (2/0), Lasse Karjalainen (2/0), Kari Rissanen (8/0), Rami Nieminen (9/0) [46.Jarkko Koskinen (2/0)], Kim Suominen (30/4), Tommi Grönlund (5/0) [66.Jasse Jalonen (2/0)], Sami Mahlio (2/0), Ari Hjelm (Cap) (97/20), Petri Järvinen (31/4), Jari Jäväjä (2/0) [46.Jokke Kangaskorpi (8/0)]. Trainer: Jukka Ikäläinen (15).

545. 11.02.1996 **DENMARK - FINLAND** **0-0** King's Cup
Rajamangala National Stadium, Bangkok (Thailand); Referee: Pongsathorn Permpanich (Thailand); Attendance: 10,000
FIN: Kari Laukkanen (45/0), Harri Ylönen (3/0), Lasse Karjalainen (3/0), Kari Rissanen (9/0), Aki Hyryläinen (18/1), Kim Suominen (31/4), Tommi Grönlund (6/0), Jasse Jalonen (3/0) [82.Sami Mahlio (3/0)], Ari Hjelm (Cap) (98/20), Petri Järvinen (32/4), Jarkko Wiss (1/0) [61.Jarkko Koskinen (3/0)]. Trainer: Jukka Ikäläinen (16).

546. 13.02.1996 **ROMANIA - FINLAND** **1-1(1-1)** King's Cup
Rajamangala National Stadium, Bangkok (Thailand); Referee: Pirom Un-Prasert (Thailand); Attendance: 15,000
FIN: Kari Laukkanen (Cap) (46/0), Harri Ylönen (4/0), Lasse Karjalainen (4/0), Kari Rissanen (10/0), Aki Hyryläinen (19/1), Kim Suominen (32/4), Tommi Grönlund (7/0), Jarkko Koskinen (4/1) [20.Jarkko Wiss (2/0)], Tom Enberg (3/0) [56.Sami Mahlio (4/0)], Petri Järvinen (33/4) [20.Jokke Kangaskorpi (9/0)], Jasse Jalonen (4/0). Trainer: Jukka Ikäläinen (17).
Goal: Jarkko Koskinen (15).

547. 16.02.1996 **THAILAND - FINLAND** **5-2(1-1)** King's Cup
Rajamangala National Stadium, Bangkok; Referee: Selearajen Subramaniam (Malaysia); Attendance: 15,000
FIN: Kari Laukkanen (47/0), Harri Ylönen (5/1), Lasse Karjalainen (5/0) [46.Jokke Kangaskorpi (10/0)], Kari Rissanen (11/1), Aki Hyryläinen (20/1), Kim Suominen (33/4), Tommi Grönlund (8/0), Sami Mahlio (5/0) [57.Tom Enberg (4/0)], Ari Hjelm (Cap) (99/20), Petri Järvinen (34/4), Jasse Jalonen (5/0) [46.Jarkko Wiss (3/0)]. Trainer: Jukka Ikäläinen (18).
Goals: Harri Ylönen (30), Kari Rissanen (64).

548. 16.03.1996 **KUWAIT - FINLAND** **0-1(0-0)**
„Al Sadaqua Walsalam" Stadium, Adiliya; Referee: Khaled Abul Sadeq (Kuwait); Attendance: 300
FIN: Petri Jakonen (24/0), Aki Hyryläinen (21/1), Harri Ylönen (6/1), Rami Nieminen (10/0), Aarno Turpeinen (1/0), Kim Suominen (34/4), Kari Ukkonen (59/4), Jokke Kangaskorpi (11/0) [61.Jonatan Lillebror Johansson (1/1)], Ari Hjelm (Cap) (**100**/20) [46.Tom Enberg (5/0)], Tommi Grönlund (9/0), Simo Valakari (1/0) [66.Jasse Jalonen (6/0)]. Trainer: Jukka Ikäläinen (19).
Goal: Jonatan Lillebror Johansson (89).

549. 29.05.1996 **FRANCE - FINLAND** **2-0(2-0)**
Stade de la Meinau, Strasbourg; Referee: Edgar Steinborn (Germany); Attendance: 29,304
FIN: Antti Niemi (13/0), Harri Ylönen (7/1), Aki Hyryläinen (22/1), Lasse Karjalainen (6/0), Antti Heinola (7/0), Sami Hyypiä (8/0), Kim Suominen (35/4), Tommi Grönlund (10/0), Sami Väisänen (2/0), Jari Olavi Litmanen (43/7), Joonas Einari Kolkka (5/2) [81.Jari Jäväjä (3/0)]. Trainer: Jukka Ikäläinen (20).

550. 02.06.1996 **FINLAND - TURKEY** **1-2(1-1)**
Olympiastadion, Helsinki; Referee: Jørn West Larsen (Denmark); Attendance: 8,520
FIN: Antti Niemi (14/0), Harri Ylönen (8/1), Aki Hyryläinen (23/1), Lasse Karjalainen (7/0), Antti Heinola (8/0), Sami Hyypiä (9/0) [77.Rami Nieminen (11/0)], Kim Suominen (36/4), Tommi Grönlund (11/0), Sami Väisänen (3/0) [77.Jari Jäväjä (4/0)], Jari Olavi Litmanen (44/8), Joonas Einari Kolkka (6/2). Trainer: Jukka Ikäläinen (21).
Goal: Jari Olavi Litmanen (25).

551. 14.08.1996 **LATVIA - FINLAND** **0-0**
Daugavas Stadions, Riga; Referee: Oleg Timofeyev (Estonia); Attendance: 5,500
FIN: Antti Niemi (15/0), Kari Rissanen (12/1), Sami Hyypiä (10/0), Rami Nieminen (12/0), Jarkko Koskinen (5/1), Marko Myyry (57/2) [46.Sami Mahlio (6/0)], Janne Lindberg (Cap) (32/1), Antti Sumiala (16/3), Jari Vanhala (16/1) [85.Tommi Grönlund (12/0)], Petri Järvinen (35/4), Joonas Einari Kolkka (7/2) [*sent off 45*]. Trainer: Richard Møller-Nielsen (Denmark, 1).

552. 01.09.1996 **HUNGARY - FINLAND** **1-0(1-0)** 16th FIFA WC. Qualifiers
Népstadion, Budapest; Referee: Hartmut Strampe (Germany); Attendance: 15,000
FIN: Antti Niemi (16/0), Kari Rissanen (13/1), Sami Hyypiä (11/0), Rami Nieminen (13/0) [46.Jyrki Huhtamäki (11/0)], Jarkko Koskinen (6/1), Janne Lindberg (Cap) (33/1), Antti Sumiala (17/3), Sami Mahlio (7/0) [81.Kim Suominen (37/4)], Petri Järvinen (36/4), Kai Nyyssönen (1/0) [65.Joonas Einari Kolkka (8/2)], Jari Vanhala (17/1). Trainer: Richard Møller-Nielsen (Denmark, 2).

553. 06.10.1996 **FINLAND - SWITZERLAND** **2-3(1-2)** 16th FIFA WC. Qualifiers
Olympiastadion, Helsinki; Referee: Gylfi Thor Orrason (Iceland); Attendance: 7,217
FIN: Antti Niemi (17/0), Kari Rissanen (14/1), Aki Hyryläinen (24/1), Jyrki Huhtamäki (12/0), Jarkko Koskinen (7/1), Janne Lindberg (Cap) (34/1) [37.Joonas Einari Kolkka (9/3)], Kim Suominen (38/4), Tommi Grönlund (13/0), Marko Myyry (58/2), Antti Sumiala (18/4) [79.Sami Hyypiä (12/0)], Jari Vanhala (18/1). Trainer: Richard Møller-Nielsen (Denmark, 3).
Goals: Antti Sumiala (41 penalty), Joonas Einari Kolkka (75).

554. 30.10.1996 **FINLAND - ESTONIA** **2-2(0-0)**
Urheilukeskus, Kotka; Referee: Romans Lajuks (Latvia); Attendance: 1,200
FIN: Petri Jakonen (25/0), Kari Rissanen (15/1) [46.Toni Tervonen (1/0)], Jyrki Huhtamäki (Cap) (13/0), Rami Nieminen (14/0), Toni Huttunen (3/0) [46.Kaj Wilhelm Nylund (1/0)], Juha Riippa (1/0), Jarkko Wiss (4/0), Kim Suominen (39/4) [73.Tommi Grönlund (14/1)], Sami Väisänen (4/0), Juha Karvinen (8/2), Jari Vanhala (19/1) [32.Antti Pohja (1/1)]. Trainer: Richard Møller-Nielsen (Denmark, 4).
Goals: Tommi Grönlund (74), Antti Pohja (88).

555. 12.02.1997 **TURKEY - FINLAND** **1-1(1-1)**
Atatürk Stadyumu, Denizli; Referee: Marcel Lică (Romania); Attendance: 15,738
FIN: Kari Laukkanen (48/0) [46.Antti Niemi (18/0)], Aarno Turpeinen (2/0), Kari Rissanen (16/1) [46.Aki Hyryläinen (25/1)], Jussi Nuorela (6/0), Jarkko Koskinen (8/1), Tommi Grönlund (15/1) [61.Mika Nurmela (9/0)], Rami Rantanen (15/0), Jari Olavi Litmanen (Cap) (45/9) [61.Marko Myyry (59/2)], Jari Vanhala (20/1), Antti Sumiala (19/4), Jonatan Lillebror Johansson (2/1) [75.Jarkko Wiss (5/0)]. Trainer: Richard Møller-Nielsen (Denmark, 5).
Goal: Jari Olavi Litmanen (16).

556. 21.02.1997 **MALAYSIA - FINLAND** **2-1(1-0)** Dunhill Cup
Stadium Merdeka, Kuala Lumpur; Referee: Pirom Un-Prasert (Thailand); Attendance: 28,000
FIN: Mikko Kavén (1/0), Jarkko Koskinen (9/1), Toni Tervonen (2/1), Aarno Turpeinen (3/0), Toni Kuivasto (1/0), Sami Mahlio (8/0), Arto Halonen (1/0), Saku Puhakainen (1/0) [72.Mika Motturi (1/0)], Jari Vanhala (Cap) (21/1) [63.Jarkko Wiss (6/0)], Jonatan Lillebror Johansson (3/1), Jari Jäväjä (5/0) [82.Sami Väisänen (5/0)]. Trainer: Richard Møller-Nielsen (Denmark, 6).
Goal: Toni Tervonen (55).

557. 23.02.1997 **CHINA P.R. - FINLAND** **2-1(1-0)** Dunhill Cup
Stadium Merdeka, Kuala Lumpur (Malaysia); Referee: Pirom Un-Prasert (Thailand); Attendance: 12,000
FIN: Tommi Kainulainen (1/0), Jarkko Koskinen (Cap) (10/1), Toni Huttunen (4/0) [75.Sami Väisänen (6/0)], Toni Kuivasto (2/0), Lasse Karjalainen (8/0), Sami Mahlio (9/0), Jarkko Wiss (7/0), Arto Halonen (2/0), Mika Motturi (2/0), Saku Puhakainen (2/1), Jonatan Lillebror Johansson (4/1). Trainer: Richard Møller-Nielsen (Denmark, 7).
Goal: Saku Puhakainen (53).

558. 25.02.1997 **SINGAPORE - FINLAND** **0-1(0-1)** Dunhill Cup
Stadium Merdeka, Kuala Lumpur (Malaysia); Referee: Kim Young-Joo (Korea Republic); Attendance: n/a
FIN: Mikko Kavén (2/0), Toni Tervonen (3/1), Aarno Turpeinen (4/0), Toni Kuivasto (3/0), Mika Motturi (3/0), Lasse Karjalainen (9/0), Sami Mahlio (Cap) (10/0), Jarkko Wiss (8/0), Saku Puhakainen (3/2) [46.Arto Halonen (3/0)], Saku Laaksonen (2/0) [67.Sami Väisänen (7/0)], Jari Jäväjä (6/0). Trainer: Richard Møller-Nielsen (Denmark, 8).
Goal: Saku Puhakainen (6).

559. 02.04.1997 **AZERBAIJAN - FINLAND** **1-2(0-1)** 16th FIFA WC. Qualifiers
„Tofiq Bəhramov“ adına Respublika Stadionu, Bakı; Referee: Graham Poll (England); Attendance: 20,000
FIN: Antti Niemi (19/0), Jussi Nuorela (7/0), Janne Mäkelä (19/0) [73.Kari Rissanen (17/1)], Sami Hyypiä (13/0), Jarkko Koskinen (11/1), Mika Nurmela (10/0), Sami Mahlio (11/0), Jari Olavi Litmanen (Cap) (46/10) [73.Marko Myyry (60/2)], Jarkko Wiss (9/0) [*sent off 79*], Antti Sumiala (20/4), Mika-Matti Paatelainen (50/14). Trainer: Richard Møller-Nielsen (Denmark, 9).
Goals: Jari Olavi Litmanen (25), Mika-Matti Paatelainen (66).

560. 30.04.1997 **NORWAY - FINLAND** **1-1(0-0)** 16th FIFA WC. Qualifiers
Ullevaal Stadion, Oslo; Referee: Dr. Markus Merk (Germany); Attendance: 22,782
FIN: Antti Niemi (20/0), Jussi Nuorela (8/0) [86.Janne Mäkelä (20/0)], Marko Tuomela (3/0), Sami Hyypiä (14/0) [4.Mika Lehkosuo (1/0)], Jarkko Koskinen (12/1), Mika Nurmela (11/0), Jari Olavi Litmanen (Cap) (47/10), Sami Mahlio (12/0), Kari Rissanen (18/1), Jonatan Lillebror Johansson (5/1) [82.Joonas Einari Kolkka (10/3)], Antti Sumiala (21/5). Trainer: Richard Møller-Nielsen (Denmark, 10).
Goal: Antti Sumiala (60).

561. 08.06.1997 **FINLAND - AZERBAIJAN** **3-0(0-0)** 16th FIFA WC. Qualifiers
Olympiastadion, Helsinki; Referee: Alain Hamer (Luxembourg); Attendance: 13,417
FIN: Antti Niemi (21/0), Kari Rissanen (19/1), Sami Hyypiä (15/0), Jussi Nuorela (9/0), Jarkko Koskinen (13/1), Sami Mahlio (13/0), Jari Vanhala (22/2), Mika Nurmela (12/0) [46.Simo Valakari (2/0)], Jari Olavi Litmanen (Cap) (48/11) [83.Kai Nyyssönen (2/0)], Antti Sumiala (22/6), Jonatan Lillebror Johansson (6/1) [61.Joonas Einari Kolkka (11/3)]. Trainer: Richard Møller-Nielsen (Denmark, 11).
Goals: Jari Vanhala (59), Jari Olavi Litmanen (64), Antti Sumiala (81).

562. 20.08.1997 **FINLAND - NORWAY** **0-4(0-2)** 16th FIFA WC. Qualifiers
Olympiastadion, Helsinki; Referee: Vadim Zhuk (Belarus); Attendance: 35,520
FIN: Teuvo Moilanen (1/0), Kari Rissanen (20/1), Jussi Nuorela (10/0), Marko Tuomela (4/0), Jarkko Koskinen (14/1), Sami Mahlio (14/0), Mika Lehkosuo (2/0), Jarkko Wiss (10/0) [46.Jonatan Lillebror Johansson (7/1)], Jari Olavi Litmanen (Cap) (49/11), Antti Sumiala (23/6), Mika-Matti Paatelainen (51/14). Trainer: Richard Møller-Nielsen (Denmark, 12).

563. 06.09.1997 **SWITZERLAND - FINLAND** **1-2(0-1)** 16th FIFA WC. Qualifiers
Olympique de la Pontaise, Lausanne; Referee: Stefano Braschi (Italy); Attendance: 15,000
FIN: Antti Niemi (22/0), Marko Tuomela (5/0), Kari Rissanen (21/1), Juha Reini (1/0), Jarkko Koskinen (15/1), Jari Vanhala (23/2) [46.Mika Lehkosuo (3/0)], Sami Mahlio (15/0), Jari Olavi Litmanen (Cap) (50/12), Simo Valakari (3/0) [36.Toni Kuivasto (4/0)], Antti Sumiala (24/7), Mika-Matti Paatelainen (52/14). Trainer: Richard Møller-Nielsen (Denmark, 13).
Goals: Jari Olavi Litmanen (16), Antti Sumiala (79).

564. 11.10.1997 **FINLAND - HUNGARY** **1-1(0-0)** 16th FIFA WC. Qualifiers
Olympiastadion, Helsinki; Referee: Bernd Heynemann (Germany); Attendance: 31,670
FIN: Teuvo Moilanen (2/0), Harri Ylönen (9/1), Sami Hyypiä (16/0), Jarkko Koskinen (16/1) [82.Kari Rissanen (22/1)], Marko Tuomela (6/0), Sami Mahlio (16/0), Juha Reini (2/0), Simo Valakari (4/0), Jari Olavi Litmanen (Cap) (51/12), Antti Sumiala (25/8) [88.Jonatan Lillebror Johansson (8/1)], Mika-Matti Paatelainen (53/14). Trainer: Richard Møller-Nielsen (Denmark, 14).
Goal: Antti Sumiala (62).

565. 05.02.1998 **CYPRUS - FINLAND** **1-1(0-1)** Cyprus Tournament
Stádio Tsirion, Limassol; Referee: Andreas Georgiou (Cyprus); Attendance: 2,500
FIN: Antti Niemi (23/0), Kari Rissanen (23/1), Aarno Turpeinen (5/0), Marko Tuomela (7/0), Jarkko Wiss (11/0), Aki Riihilahti (1/0), Sami Mahlio (17/0) [46.Toni Kuivasto (5/0)], Teemu Tainio (1/0) [76.Mika Kottila (1/0)], Jonatan Lillebror Johansson (9/2), Harri Ylönen (Cap) (10/1), Janne Oinas (1/0). Trainer: Richard Møller-Nielsen (Denmark, 15).
Goal: Jonatan Lillebror Johansson (30).

566. 09.02.1998 **SLOVAKIA - FINLAND** **2-0(1-0)** Cyprus Tournament
Stádio „Antonis Papadopoulos“, Larnaca (Cyprus); Referee: Kostas Kapitanis (Cyprus); Attendance: 300
FIN: Antti Niemi (24/0), Kari Rissanen (24/1), Aarno Turpeinen (6/0), Harri Ylönen (Cap) (11/1), Janne Oinas (2/0), Toni Kuivasto (6/0), Jarkko Wiss (12/0), Aki Riihilahti (2/0), Teemu Tainio (2/0) [65.Petteri Kaijasilta (1/0)], Jonatan Lillebror Johansson (10/2), Mika Kottila (2/0). Trainer: Richard Møller-Nielsen (Denmark, 16).

567. 25.03.1998 **MALTA - FINLAND** **0-2(0-1)**
Ta' Qali National Stadium, Attard; Referee: Livio Bazzolli (Italy); Attendance: 4,000
FIN: Jussi Jääskeläinen (1/0), Tomi Kinnunen (1/0), Marko Tuomela (8/0), Harri Ylönen (12/1), Aarno Turpeinen (7/0), Simo Valakari (5/0), Sami Mahlio (18/0), Jarkko Wiss (13/1), Aki Riihilahti (3/1), Jonatan Lillebror Johansson (11/2) [71.Teemu Tainio (3/0)], Mika-Matti Paatelainen (Cap) (54/14). Trainer: Richard Møller-Nielsen (Denmark, 17).
Goals: Aki Riihilahti (1), Jarkko Wiss (51).

568. 22.04.1998 **SCOTLAND - FINLAND** **1-1(1-1)**
Easter Road, Edinburgh; Referee: Herman van Dijk (Netherlands); Attendance: 14,315
FIN: Antti Niemi (25/0), Harri Ylönen (13/1), Marko Tuomela (9/0) [65.Tomi Kinnunen (2/0)], Sami Hyypiä (17/0), Jarkko Koskinen (17/1), Sami Mahlio (19/0), Juha Reini (3/0) [46.Aarno Turpeinen (8/0)], Simo Valakari (6/0), Antti Sumiala (26/8) [38.Joonas Einari Kolkka (12/3)], Jari Olavi Litmanen (Cap) (52/12) [46.Aki Riihilahti (4/1)], Jonatan Lillebror Johansson (12/3) [58.Mika-Matti Paatelainen (55/14)]. Trainer: Richard Møller-Nielsen (Denmark, 18).
Goal: Jonatan Lillebror Johansson (10).

569. 27.05.1998 **FINLAND - GERMANY** **0-0**
Olympiastadion, Helsinki; Referee: Claus Bo Larsen (Denmark); Attendance: 18,421
FIN: Antti Niemi (26/0), Marko Tuomela (10/0), Harri Ylönen (14/1), Sami Hyypiä (18/0), Juha Reini (4/0) [81.Aarno Turpeinen (9/0)], Tomi Kinnunen (3/0), Jarkko Wiss (14/1), Jari Olavi Litmanen (Cap) (53/12), Aki Riihilahti (5/1), Jonatan Lillebror Johansson (13/3), Mika-Matti Paatelainen (56/14) [60.Joonas Einari Kolkka (13/3)]. Trainer: Richard Møller-Nielsen (Denmark, 19).

570. 05.06.1998 **FINLAND - FRANCE** **0-1(0-0)**
Olympiastadion, Helsinki; Referee: Konrad Plautz (Austria); Attendance: 21,619
FIN: Antti Niemi (27/0), Harri Ylönen (15/1), Sami Hyypiä (19/0), Tomi Kinnunen (4/0), Aarno Turpeinen (10/0), Aki Riihilahti (6/1), Juha Reini (5/0) [86.Kari Rissanen (25/1)], Joonas Einari Kolkka (14/3), Jarkko Wiss (15/1), Mika-Matti Paatelainen (Cap) (57/14), Jonatan Lillebror Johansson (14/3) [68.Simo Valakari (7/0)]. Trainer: Richard Møller-Nielsen (Denmark, 20).

571. 19.08.1998 **SLOVAKIA - FINLAND** **0-0**
Vsesportovny areal, Košice; Referee: Miroslav Liba (Czech Republic); Attendance: 3,220
FIN: Antti Niemi (28/0) [46.Jussi Jääskeläinen (2/0)], Marko Tuomela (11/0), Harri Ylönen (16/1), Sami Hyypiä (20/0), Aarno Turpeinen (11/0), Sami Mahlio (20/0), Tommi Kautonen (1/0), Jari Olavi Litmanen (Cap) (54/12) [57.Aki Riihilahti (7/1)], Jarkko Wiss (16/1), Antti Sumiala (27/8) [57.Joonas Einari Kolkka (15/3)], Jonatan Lillebror Johansson (15/3) [75.Mika-Matti Paatelainen (58/14)]. Trainer: Richard Møller-Nielsen (Denmark, 21).

572. 05.09.1998 **FINLAND - MOLDOVA** **3-2(2-2)** 11th EC. Qualifiers
Olympiastadion, Helsinki; Referee: Graham Barber (England); Attendance: 18,716
FIN: Antti Niemi (29/0), Harri Ylönen (17/1), Marko Tuomela (12/0), Sami Hyypiä (21/0), Tommi Kautonen (2/0), Aarno Turpeinen (12/0) [46.Juha Reini (6/0)], Jarkko Wiss (17/1), Jonatan Lillebror Johansson (16/4) [80.Antti Sumiala (28/8)], Mika-Matti Paatelainen (59/15), Jari Olavi Litmanen (Cap) (55/12), Joonas Einari Kolkka (16/4) [73.Sami Mahlio (21/0)]. Trainer: Richard Møller-Nielsen (Denmark, 22).
Goals: Joonas Einari Kolkka (8), Jonatan Lillebror Johansson (45), Mika-Matti Paatelainen (63).

573. 10.10.1998 **NORTHERN IRELAND - FINLAND** **1-0(1-0)** 11th EC. Qualifiers
Windsor Park, Belfast; Referee: Zoran Arsić (Yugoslavia); Attendance: 10,200
FIN: Antti Niemi (30/0), Harri Ylönen (18/1), Juha Reini (7/0), Sami Hyypiä (22/0), Tommi Kautonen (3/0), Simo Valakari (8/0), Jari Ilola (1/0), Aki Riihilahti (8/1) [76.Jari Olavi Litmanen (56/12)], Joonas Einari Kolkka (17/4), Mika-Matti Paatelainen (Cap) (60/15), Jonatan Lillebror Johansson (17/4). Trainer: Richard Møller-Nielsen (Denmark, 23).

574. 14.10.1998 **TURKEY - FINLAND** **1-3(0-1)** 11th EC. Qualifiers
"Ali Sami Yen" Stadı, Istanbul; Referee: Dr. Václav Krondl (Czech Republic); Attendance: 20,420
FIN: Antti Niemi (31/0), Harri Ylönen (19/1), Marko Tuomela (13/0), Sami Hyypiä (23/0), Tommi Kautonen (4/0), Juha Reini (8/0), Aki Riihilahti (9/1) [76.Simo Valakari (9/0)], Jari Ilola (2/0), Jari Olavi Litmanen (Cap) (57/13), Mika-Matti Paatelainen (61/16) [46.Joonas Einari Kolkka (18/4)], Jonatan Lillebror Johansson (18/5) [89.Jarmo Saastamoinen (7/0)]. Trainer: Richard Møller-Nielsen (Denmark, 24).
Goals: Mika-Matti Paatelainen (5), Jonatan Lillebror Johansson (51), Jari Olavi Litmanen (90).

575. 03.02.1999 **GREECE - FINLAND** **2-1(0-0)** Cyprus Tournament
Stádio GSZ, Larnaca (Cyprus); Referee: Kostas Kapitanis (Cyprus); Attendance: 2,000
FIN: Jani Viander (1/0), Harri Ylönen (Cap) (20/1), Marko Tuomela (14/0), Jarmo Saastamoinen (8/0), Jouni Räsänen (1/0) [88.Janne Salli (1/0)], Lasse Karjalainen (10/0) [46.Tommi Grönlund (16/1)], Kaj Wilhelm Nylund (2/0), Jari Ilola (3/0), Ville Priha (1/0) [69.Antti Pohja (2/1)], Mika Kottila (3/0), Matti Hiukka (1/0) [46.Petteri Kaijasilta (2/1)]. Trainer: Richard Møller-Nielsen (Denmark, 25).
Goal: Petteri Kaijasilta (63).

576. 05.02.1999 **CYPRUS - FINLAND** **2-1(1-1,1-1)** Cyprus Tournament
Stádio "Tassos Markou", Paralimni; Referee: Andreas Georgiou (Cyprus); Attendance: 1,000
FIN: Jani Viander (2/0), Harri Ylönen (Cap) (21/1), Marko Tuomela (15/0), Jarmo Saastamoinen (9/0), Lasse Karjalainen (11/0) [59.Tommi Grönlund (17/1)], Mika Kottila (4/0) [95.Toni Tervonen (4/1)], Petteri Kaijasilta (3/2) [75.Matti Hiukka (2/0)], Jari Ilola (4/0), Antti Pohja (3/1), Jouni Räsänen (2/0) [73.Ville Priha (2/0)], Kaj Wilhelm Nylund (3/0). Trainer: Richard Møller-Nielsen (Denmark, 26).
Goal: Petteri Kaijasilta (6).

577. 10.02.1999 **POLAND - FINLAND** **1-1(1-1)** International Tournament
Ta' Qali National Stadium, Attard (Malta); Referee: Emmanuel Zammit (Malta); Attendance: 300
FIN: Antti Niemi (32/0) [46.Jussi Jääskeläinen (3/0)], Harri Ylönen (Cap) (22/1), Marko Tuomela (16/0), Sami Hyypiä (24/0), Jari Ilola (5/0), Aki Riihilahti (10/1), Juha Reini (9/0) [52.Mika Lehkosuo (4/0)], Simo Valakari (10/0), Mika Kottila (5/0), Joonas Einari Kolkka (19/4), Jonatan Lillebror Johansson (19/6). Trainer: Richard Møller-Nielsen (Denmark, 27).
Goal: Jonatan Lillebror Johansson (20).

578. 31.03.1999 **GERMANY - FINLAND** **2-0(2-0)** 11th EC. Qualifiers
Frankenstadion, Nürnberg; Referee: Sergei Khusainov (Russia); Attendance: 40,758
FIN: Antti Niemi (33/0), Tomi Kinnunen (5/0), Harri Ylönen (23/1), Sami Hyypiä (25/0), Juha Reini (10/0) [89.Mika Lehkosuo (5/0)], Tommi Kautonen (5/0) [72.Joonas Einari Kolkka (20/4)], Jari Ilola (6/0), Jari Olavi Litmanen (Cap) (58/13), Aki Riihilahti (11/1), Jonatan Lillebror Johansson (20/6), Mika-Matti Paatelainen (62/16) [46.Jarmo Saastamoinen (10/0)]. Trainer: Richard Møller-Nielsen (Denmark, 28).

579. 28.04.1999 **SLOVENIA - FINLAND** **1-1(0-1)**
Stadion Bežigrad, Ljubljana; Referee: Fiorenzo Treossi (Italy); Attendance: 1,500
FIN: Antti Niemi (34/0) [46.Jussi Jääskeläinen (4/0)], Harri Ylönen (24/1), Tomi Kinnunen (6/0) [46.Jarmo Saastamoinen (11/0)], Sami Hyypiä (26/0) [46.Toni Kuivasto (7/0)], Mika Lehkosuo (6/0), Aki Riihilahti (12/1), Tommi Kautonen (6/0), Simo Valakari (11/0), Ville Viljanen (1/0), Mika-Matti Paatelainen (Cap) (63/17), Joonas Einari Kolkka (21/4). Trainer: Richard Møller-Nielsen (Denmark, 29).
Goal: Mika-Matti Paatelainen (22 penalty).

580. 05.06.1999 **FINLAND - TURKEY** **2-4(2-2)** 11th EC. Qualifiers
Olympiastadion, Helsinki; Referee: Dirk Zier Gerardus "Dick" Jol (Netherlands); Attendance: 36,042
FIN: Antti Niemi (35/0), Harri Ylönen (25/1), Toni Kuivasto (8/0), Sami Hyypiä (27/0), Hannu Tihinen (1/1), Aki Riihilahti (13/1), Joonas Einari Kolkka (22/4), Simo Valakari (12/0), Jonatan Lillebror Johansson (21/6), Mika-Matti Paatelainen (64/18), Jari Olavi Litmanen (Cap) (59/13). Trainer: Richard Møller-Nielsen (Denmark, 30).
Goals: Hannu Tihinen (10), Mika-Matti Paatelainen (14).

581. 09.06.1999 **MOLDOVA - FINLAND** **0-0** 11th EC. Qualifiers
Stadionul Republican, Chişinău; Referee: Fiorenzo Treossi (Italy); Attendance: 6,100
FIN: Antti Niemi (36/0), Juha Reini (11/0) [86.Mika Lehkosuo (7/0)], Sami Hyypiä (28/0), Harri Ylönen (26/1), Hannu Tihinen (2/1) [46.Tommi Kautonen (7/0)], Joonas Einari Kolkka (23/4), Aki Riihilahti (14/1), Simo Valakari (13/0), Jari Ilola (7/0), Jonatan Lillebror Johansson (22/6) [61.Mikael Kaj Forssell (1/0)], Mika-Matti Paatelainen (Cap) (65/18). Trainer: Richard Møller-Nielsen (Denmark, 31).

582. 18.08.1999 **BELGIUM - FINLAND** **3-4(1-2)**
„Jan Breydel" stadion, Brügge; Referee: Alain Hamer (Luxembourg); Attendance: 12,000
FIN: Pasi Laaksonen (1/0) [46.Jani Viander (3/0)], Harri Ylönen (27/1), Hannu Tihinen (3/1), Sami Ylä-Jussila (2/0), Toni Kuivasto (9/0), Jarkko Wiss (18/2), Mika Lehkosuo (8/1), Aki Riihilahti (15/1) [40.Vesa Vasara (1/0); 90.Shefki Kuqi (1/0)], Joonas Einari Kolkka (Cap) (24/4) [60.Tommi Kautonen (8/0)], Mika-Matti Paatelainen (66/18) [73.Jarmo Saastamoinen (12/0)], Jonatan Lillebror Johansson (23/8). Trainer: Richard Møller-Nielsen (Denmark, 32).
Goals: Jarkko Wiss (31), Jonatan Lillebror Johansson (45, 53), Mika Lehkosuo (62).

583. 04.09.1999 **FINLAND - GERMANY** **1-2(0-2)** 11th EC. Qualifiers
Olympiastadion, Helsinki; Referee: Antonio López Nieto (Spain); Attendance: 20,184
FIN: Antti Niemi (37/0) [46.Pasi Laaksonen (2/0)], Jarmo Saastamoinen (13/0), Sami Hyypiä (Cap) (29/0), Toni Kuivasto (10/0), Harri Ylönen (28/1) [46.Shefki Kuqi (2/0)], Janne Salli (2/1), Jarkko Wiss (19/2), Aki Riihilahti (16/1), Teemu Tainio (4/0), Jonatan Lillebror Johansson (24/8), Mika Kottila (6/0). Trainer: Richard Møller-Nielsen (Denmark, 33).
Goal: Janne Salli (63).

584. 09.10.1999 **FINLAND - NORTHERN IRELAND** **4-1(1-0)** 11th EC. Qualifiers
Olympiastadion, Helsinki; Referee: Armand Ancion (Belgium); Attendance: 8,217
FIN: Jani Viander (4/0), Mika Lehkosuo (9/1), Toni Kuivasto (11/0), Sami Hyypiä (30/1), Hannu Tihinen (4/1), Jarkko Wiss (20/2) [86.Simo Valakari (14/0)], Joonas Einari Kolkka (25/6), Aki Riihilahti (17/1) [86.Sami Ylä-Jussila (3/0)], Jari Olavi Litmanen (Cap) (60/13), Mika-Matti Paatelainen (67/18), Jonatan Lillebror Johansson (25/9). Trainer: Richard Møller-Nielsen (Denmark, 34).
Goals: Jonatan Lillebror Johansson (9), Sami Hyypiä (63), Joonas Einari Kolkka (73, 83).

585. 31.01.2000 **FINLAND – FAROE ISLANDS** **1-0(0-0)** Nordic Championship
La Manga Club Centro, La Manga (Spain); Referee: Gylfi Thor Orrason (Iceland); Attendance: 2,500
FIN: Jani Viander (5/0), Kaj Wilhelm Nylund (4/0), Janne Salli (3/1), Hannu Tihinen (5/1), Harri Ylönen (29/1), Tommi Grönlund (Cap) (18/1), Mika Lehkosuo (10/1), Jarkko Wiss (21/2) [*sent off 76*], Jari Niemi (1/0) [63.Toni Kallio (1/0)], Vesa Vasara (2/0) [63.Petri Helin (10/2)], Antti Sumiala (29/9) [74.Shefki Kuqi (3/0)]. Trainer: Antti Muurinen (1).
Goal: Antti Sumiala (57).

586. 02.02.2000 **ICELAND - FINLAND** **1-0(1-0)** Nordic Championship
La Manga Club Centro, La Manga (Spain); Referee: Lassin Isaksen (Faroe Islands); Attendance: 2,500
FIN: Pasi Laaksonen (3/0), Kaj Wilhelm Nylund (5/0) [82.Janne Salli (4/1)], Toni Kuivasto (12/0), Jarmo Saastamoinen (14/0) [69.Harri Ylönen (30/1)], Hannu Tihinen (6/1), Tommi Grönlund (Cap) (19/1), Timo Marjamaa (1/0) [59.Antti Sumiala (30/9)], Mika Lehkosuo (11/1), Petri Helin (11/2) [85.Vesa Vasara (3/0)], Shefki Kuqi (4/0), Toni Kallio (2/0) [66.Jari Niemi (2/0)]. Trainer: Antti Muurinen (2).

587. 04.02.2000 **FINLAND - DENMARK** **2-1(1-0)** Nordic Championship
La Manga Club Centro, La Manga (Spain); Referee: Nilsson (Sweden); Attendance: 1,500
FIN: Pasi Laaksonen (4/0), Toni Huttunen (5/0) [80.Shefki Kuqi (5/0)], Janne Salli (5/1) [40.Jarmo Saastamoinen (15/0)], Hannu Tihinen (7/1) [58.Toni Kuivasto (13/0)], Harri Ylönen (31/1), Tommi Grönlund (Cap) (20/1) [46.Mika Lehkosuo (12/1)], Jarkko Wiss (22/2), Timo Marjamaa (2/0), Vesa Vasara (4/2), Antti Sumiala (31/9), Jari Niemi (3/0) [46.Toni Kallio (3/0)]. Trainer: Antti Muurinen (3).
Goals: Vesa Vasara (33, 89).

588. 20.02.2000 **THAILAND - FINLAND** **0-0** King's Cup
Rajamangala National Stadium, Bangkok; Referee: Pongsathorn Permpanich (Thailand)
FIN: Jani Viander (6/0), Harri Ylönen (32/1), Tero Penttilä (1/0), Jarmo Saastamoinen (16/0), Kaj Wilhelm Nylund (6/0), Tommi Grönlund (Cap) (21/1), Jarkko Wiss (23/2), Mika Lehkosuo (13/1), Antti Sumiala (32/9) [81.Mika Kottila (7/0)], Vesa Vasara (5/2) [70.Shefki Kuqi (6/0)], Teemu Tainio (5/0) [61.Petri Helin (12/2)]. Trainer: Antti Muurinen (4).

589. 23.02.2000 **FINLAND - ESTONIA** **4-2(2-0)** King's Cup
Rajamangala National Stadium, Bangkok (Thailand); Referee: Abdul Halim Hamid (Malaysia); Attendance: 20,000
FIN: Magnus Bahne (1/0), Janne Hietanen (1/0), Marko Tuomela (17/2), Toni Kuivasto (14/0), Petri Helin (13/2), Jarkko Wiss (24/2) [71.Mika Lehkosuo (14/1)], Teemu Tainio (6/0), Timo Marjamaa (3/0) [46.Tommi Grönlund (22/1)], Mika Kottila (8/1) [83.Vesa Vasara (6/2)], Shefki Kuqi (7/1), Toni Kallio (4/0). Trainer: Antti Muurinen (5).
Goals: Mika Kottila (12), Marko Tuomela (14, 56), Shefki Kuqi (60).

590. 27.02.2000 **THAILAND - FINLAND** **5-1(3-0)** King's Cup final
Rajamangala National Stadium, Bangkok; Referee: Mohd Nazri Abdullah (Malaysia); Attendance: 15,000
FIN: Magnus Bahne (2/0) [46.Jani Viander (7/0)], Kaj Wilhelm Nylund (7/0), Jarmo Saastamoinen (17/0), Marko Tuomela (18/2), Janne Hietanen (2/0) [46.Harri Ylönen (33/1)], Jarkko Wiss (25/2), Tommi Grönlund (Cap) (23/1), Mika Lehkosuo (15/1), Antti Sumiala (33/9) [46.Toni Kallio (5/1)], Mika Kottila (9/1), Shefki Kuqi (8/1) [62.Vesa Vasara (7/2)]. Trainer: Antti Muurinen (6).
Goal: Toni Kallio (74).

591. 29.03.2000 **WALES - FINLAND** **1-2(0-2)**
Millenium Stadium, Cardiff; Referee: Michael Thomas Ross (Northern Ireland); Attendance: 66,500
FIN: Peter Enckelman (1/0) [46.Teuvo Moilanen (3/0)], Juha Reini (12/0), Sami Hyypiä (31/1), Jarmo Saastamoinen (18/0) [48.Marko Tuomela (19/2)], Hannu Tihinen (8/1), Aki Riihilahti (18/1), Mika Nurmela (13/0), Simo Valakari (15/0) [64.Jarkko Wiss (26/2)], Jari Olavi Litmanen (Cap) (61/14) [69.Mika Lehkosuo (16/1)], Joonas Einari Kolkka (26/6), Mikael Kaj Forssell (2/0) [46.Mika-Matti Paatelainen (68/18)]. Trainer: Antti Muurinen (7).
Goals: Jari Olavi Litmanen (21), Nathan Alexander Blake (42 own goal).

592. 26.04.2000 **POLAND - FINLAND** **0-0**
Stadion Miejski, Poznań; Referee: Attila Juhos (Hungary); Attendance: 17,000
FIN: Antti Niemi (38/0), Harri Ylönen (34/1), Tero Penttilä (2/0), Hannu Tihinen (9/1), Tommi Grönlund (24/1) [46.Aki Riihilahti (19/1)], Mika Lehkosuo (17/1), Mika Nurmela (14/0) [46.Petri Helin (14/2)], Jarkko Wiss (27/2), Jari Olavi Litmanen (Cap) (62/14) [90.Mika Kottila (10/1)], Mikael Kaj Forssell (3/0) [58.Mika-Matti Paatelainen (69/18)], Joonas Einari Kolkka (27/6) [88.Marko Tuomela (20/2)]. Trainer: Antti Muurinen (8).

593. 03.06.2000 **LATVIA - FINLAND** **1-0(0-0)**
Daugavas Stadions, Riga; Referee: Oleg Chykun (Belarus); Attendance: 3,000
FIN: Antti Niemi (39/0), Hannu Tihinen (10/1), Tero Penttilä (3/0) [60.Janne Salli (6/1)], Sami Hyypiä (32/1), Toni Huttunen (6/0) [68.Mika Kottila (11/1)], Jarkko Wiss (28/2), Sami Ylä-Jussila (4/0) [46.Tommi Grönlund (25/1)], Jari Olavi Litmanen (Cap) (63/14), Jonatan Lillebror Johansson (26/9), Mika Nurmela (15/0) [77.Petri Helin (15/2)], Mika-Matti Paatelainen (70/18) [46.Shefki Kuqi (9/1)]. Trainer: Antti Muurinen (9).

594. 16.08.2000 **FINLAND - NORWAY** **3-1(1-0)** Nordic Championship
Finnair Stadion, Helsinki; Referee: Mario van der Ende (Netherlands); Attendance: 10,748
FIN: Jussi Jääskeläinen (5/0), Harri Ylönen (35/1), Aarno Turpeinen (13/0), Sami Hyypiä (33/1), Hannu Tihinen (11/1), Mika Nurmela (16/0) [75.Shefki Kuqi (10/2)], Jarkko Wiss (29/2) [90.Aki Riihilahti (20/1)], Simo Valakari (16/0) [56.Miika Koppinen (1/0)], Jari Olavi Litmanen (Cap) (64/16) [90.Janne Salli (7/1)], Mikael Kaj Forssell (4/0) [81.Mika Kottila (12/1)], Joonas Einari Kolkka (28/6) [66.Janne Saarinen (1/0)]. Trainer: Antti Muurinen (10).
Goals: Jari Olavi Litmanen (24, 61), Shefki Kuqi (90 penalty).

595. 02.09.2000 **FINLAND - ALBANIA** **2-1(1-0)** 17th FIFA WC. Qualifiers
Finnair Stadion, Helsinki; Referee: Renatus Hendrikus Johannes „René" Temmink (Netherlands); Attendance: 10,770
FIN: Jussi Jääskeläinen (6/0), Janne Saarinen (2/0) [*sent off 72*], Sami Hyypiä (34/1), Hannu Tihinen (12/1), Aarno Turpeinen (14/0), Mika Nurmela (17/0) [57.Jonatan Lillebror Johansson (27/9)], Miika Koppinen (2/0) [46.Aki Riihilahti (21/2)], Simo Valakari (17/0), Jari Olavi Litmanen (Cap) (65/17), Mikael Kaj Forssell (5/0) [77.Harri Ylönen (36/1)], Joonas Einari Kolkka (29/6). Trainer: Antti Muurinen (11).
Goals: Jari Olavi Litmanen (45), Aki Riihilahti (67).

596. 07.10.2000 **GREECE - FINLAND** **1-0(0-0)** 17th FIFA WC. Qualifiers
Olympiako "Spiros Louis", Athína; Referee: Dr. Pierluigi Collina (Italy); Attendance: 14,800
FIN: Antti Niemi (40/0), Petri Helin (16/2), Juha Reini (13/0), Sami Hyypiä (35/1), Hannu Tihinen (13/1), Mika Nurmela (18/0), Jarkko Wiss (30/2) [81.Mika Kottila (13/1)], Simo Valakari (18/0), Jari Olavi Litmanen (Cap) (66/17), Jonatan Lillebror Johansson (28/9) [74.Shefki Kuqi (11/2)], Joonas Einari Kolkka (30/6) [46.Mikael Kaj Forssell (6/0)]. Trainer: Antti Muurinen (12).

597. 11.10.2000 **FINLAND - ENGLAND** **0-0** 17th FIFA WC. Qualifiers
Olympiastadion, Helsinki; Referee: Alain Sars (France); Attendance: 36,210
FIN: Antti Niemi (41/0), Petri Helin (17/2) [36.Juha Reini (14/0)], Sami Hyypiä (36/1), Hannu Tihinen (14/1), Janne Saarinen (3/0) [66.Janne Salli (8/1)], Mika Nurmela (19/0), Jarkko Wiss (31/2), Simo Valakari (19/0), Jari Olavi Litmanen (Cap) (67/17), Mikael Kaj Forssell (7/0) [76.Shefki Kuqi (12/2)], Jonatan Lillebror Johansson (29/9). Trainer: Antti Muurinen (13).

598. 15.11.2000 **REPUBLIC OF IRELAND - FINLAND** **3-0(1-0)**
Lansdowne Road, Dublin; Referee: Paul Durkin (England); Attendance: 22,368
FIN: Jussi Jääskeläinen (7/0), Kaj Wilhelm Nylund (8/0), Janne Saarinen (4/0), Petri Pasanen (1/0) [78.Mika Nurmela (20/0)], Hannu Tihinen (15/1), Teemu Tainio (7/0) [66.Toni Kuivasto (15/0)], Jonatan Lillebror Johansson (30/9) [46.Tommi Grönlund (26/1)], Aki Riihilahti (22/2), Jari Olavi Litmanen (Cap) (68/17), Mikael Kaj Forssell (8/0) [46.Shefki Kuqi (13/2)], Joonas Einari Kolkka (31/6) [86.Mika Kottila (14/1)]. Trainer: Antti Muurinen (14).

599. 01.02.2001 **SWEDEN – FINLAND** **0-1(0-1)** Nordic Championship
Tipshallen, Jönköping (indoor); Referee: Roy Helge Olsen (Norway); Attendance: 2,196
FIN: Jani Viander (8/0), Toni Huttunen (7/0) [80.Kaj Wilhelm Nylund (9/0)], Toni Kuivasto (16/0), Jussi Nuorela (11/0), Antti Heinola (9/0) [69.Harri Ylönen (37/1)], Miika Koppinen (3/0) [84.Jarmo Saastamoinen (19/0)], Tommi Grönlund (Cap) (27/1), Timo Marjamaa (4/1) [46.Aki Riihilahti (23/2)], Vesa Vasara (8/2) [65.Antti Pohja (4/1)], Paulus Henrik Roiha (1/0) [46.Mika Kottila (15/1)], Jari Niemi (4/0). Trainer: Antti Muurinen (15).
Goal: Timo Marjamaa (38).

600. 15.02.2001 **KUWAIT – FINLAND** **4-3(2-2)**
„Al Sadaqua Walsalam" Stadium, Adiliya, Kuwait City; Referee: Jumaa Al Ali (Qatar); Attendance: 2,000
FIN: Pasi Laaksonen (5/0), Kaj Wilhelm Nylund (10/0), Marko Tuomela (21/2), Jarmo Saastamoinen (20/0), Antti Heinola (10/0) [64.Toni Huttunen (8/0)], Sami Mahlio (22/0) [71.Miika Koppinen (4/0)], Aki Riihilahti (24/3), Tommi Grönlund (Cap) (28/2), Jari Niemi (5/0) [64.Ville Väisänen (1/0)], Janne Saarinen (5/0), Mika Kottila (16/2). Trainer: Antti Muurinen (16).
Goals: Mika Kottila (2), Tommi Grönlund (33), Aki Riihilahti (90).

601. 18.02.2001 **OMAN – FINLAND** **1-2(1-0)**
"Sultan Qaboos" Sports Complex, Muscat; Referee: Mohamed Muflah (Oman); Attendance: 1,215
FIN: Jani Viander (9/0), Toni Huttunen (9/0), Jussi Nuorela (12/1), Toni Kuivasto (17/0), Miika Koppinen (5/0) [46.Aki Riihilahti (25/4)], Tommi Grönlund (Cap) (29/2), Mika Kottila (17/2) [85.Antti Heinola (11/0)], Jari Niemi (6/0), Vesa Vasara (9/2) [81.Ville Väisänen (2/0)], Harri Ylönen (38/1), Timo Marjamaa (5/1) [46.Sami Mahlio (23/0)]. Trainer: Antti Muurinen (17).
Goals: Jussi Nuorela (58), Aki Riihilahti (78).

602. 20.02.2001 **OMAN – FINLAND** **0-2(0-1)**
"Sultan Qaboos" Sports Complex, Muscat; Referee: Yousef Fadhil (Oman); Attendance: 1,000
FIN: Jani Viander (10/0), Kaj Wilhelm Nylund (11/0) [55.Toni Huttunen (10/0)], Jussi Nuorela (13/1) [55.Jarmo Saastamoinen (21/0)], Toni Kuivasto (18/0), Harri Ylönen (39/1), Aki Riihilahti (26/4), Tommi Grönlund (Cap) (30/2) [46.Timo Marjamaa (6/1)], Sami Mahlio (24/0), Jari Niemi (7/1) [76.Antti Heinola (12/0)], Ville Väisänen (3/1) [77.Marko Tuomela (22/2)], Vesa Vasara (10/2) [71.Mika Kottila (18/2)]. Trainer: Antti Muurinen (18).
Goals: Ville Väisänen (6), Jari Niemi (52).

603. 28.02.2001 **LUXEMBOURG - FINLAND** **0-1(0-0)**
Stade „Josy Barthel", Luxembourg; Referee: Roland Beck (Liechtenstein); Attendance: 1,500
FIN: Peter Enckelman (2/0), Petri Pasanen (2/0), Sami Hyypiä (Cap) (37/1) [46.Toni Kuivasto (19/0)], Hannu Tihinen (16/1), Janne Saarinen (6/0), Jarkko Wiss (32/2), Mika Nurmela (21/0) [64.Shefki Kuqi (14/2)], Tommi Grönlund (31/2) [64.Aki Riihilahti (27/4)], Petri Helin (18/2) [75.Jari Niemi (8/1)], Mikael Kaj Forssell (9/1), Jonatan Lillebror Johansson (31/9) [89.Harri Ylönen (40/1)]. Trainer: Antti Muurinen (19).
Goal: Mikael Kaj Forssell (77).

604. 24.03.2001 **ENGLAND - FINLAND** **2-1(1-1)** 17th FIFA WC. Qualifiers
Anfield Road, Liverpool; Referee: Nikolai Ivanov (Russia); Attendance: 44,262
FIN: Antti Niemi (42/0), Harri Ylönen (41/1) [89.Petri Helin (19/2)], Hannu Tihinen (17/1), Sami Hyypiä (38/1), Petri Pasanen (3/0), Joonas Einari Kolkka (32/6) [63.Shefki Kuqi (15/2)], Mika Nurmela (22/0) [63.Mikael Kaj Forssell (10/1)], Jarkko Wiss (33/2), Aki Riihilahti (28/5), Jari Olavi Litmanen (Cap) (69/17), Jonatan Lillebror Johansson (32/9). Trainer: Antti Muurinen (20).
Goal: Aki Riihilahti (26).

605. 25.04.2001 **HUNGARY - FINLAND** **0-0**
Üllői út, Budapest; Referee: Fiorenzo Treossi (Italy); Attendance: 5,175
FIN: Antti Niemi (43/0), Petri Pasanen (4/0) [59.Harri Ylönen (42/1)], Toni Kuivasto (20/0), Hannu Tihinen (18/1), Kaj Wilhelm Nylund (12/0), Joonas Einari Kolkka (33/6) [81.Jari Niemi (9/1)], Tommi Grönlund (Cap) (32/2), Lasse Karjalainen (12/0) [65.Miika Koppinen (6/0)], Mika Nurmela (23/0) [74.Petri Helin (20/2)], Jonatan Lillebror Johansson (33/9) [87.Jussi Nuorela (14/1)], Mikael Kaj Forssell (11/1) [74.Paulus Henrik Roiha (2/0)]. Trainer: Antti Muurinen (21).

606. 09.05.2001 **ESTONIA - FINLAND** **1-1(0-0)**
Linnastaadionil, Kuressaare; Referee: Andrejs Sipailo (Latvia); Attendance: 2,000
FIN: Antti Niemi (44/0), Kaj Wilhelm Nylund (13/0), Hannu Tihinen (Cap) (19/1), Marko Tuomela (23/2) [46.Jussi Nuorela (15/1)], Janne Saarinen (7/0), Aki Riihilahti (29/5) [46.Lasse Karjalainen (13/0)], Rami Rantanen (16/1) [82.Tommi Kautonen (9/0)], Sami Mahlio (25/0), Mikael Kaj Forssell (12/1) [83.Jari Niemi (10/1)], Shefki Kuqi (16/2), Jonatan Lillebror Johansson (34/9) [83.Vesa Vasara (11/2)]. Trainer: Antti Muurinen (22).
Goal: Rami Rantanen (59).

607. 02.06.2001 **FINLAND - GERMANY** **2-2(2-0)** 17th FIFA WC. Qualifiers
Olympiastadion, Helsinki; Referee: Dirk Zier Gerardus "Dick" Jol (Netherlands); Attendance: 35,774
FIN: Antti Niemi (45/0), Petri Pasanen (5/0), Sami Hyypiä (39/1), Hannu Tihinen (20/1), Kaj Wilhelm Nylund (14/0), Aki Riihilahti (30/5) [79.Tommi Grönlund (33/2)], Mika Nurmela (24/0) [72.Jonatan Lillebror Johansson (35/9)], Rami Rantanen (17/1), Jari Olavi Litmanen (Cap) (70/17), Mikael Kaj Forssell (13/3), Joonas Einari Kolkka (34/6) [84.Shefki Kuqi (17/2)]. Trainer: Antti Muurinen (23).
Goals: Mikael Kaj Forssell (28, 43).

608. 15.08.2001 **FINLAND - BELGIUM** **4-1(3-1)**
Finnair Stadion, Helsinki; Referee: Hartmut Strampe (Germany); Attendance: 10,000
FIN: Antti Niemi (46/0) [61.Peter Enckelman (3/0)], Juha Reini (15/0) [46.Petri Pasanen (6/0)], Sami Hyypiä (40/1) [46.Hannu Tihinen (21/2)], Toni Kuivasto (21/0), Janne Saarinen (8/0), Aki Riihilahti (31/5), Mika Nurmela (25/0) [63.Jonatan Lillebror Johansson (36/9)], Teemu Tainio (8/0), Jari Olavi Litmanen (Cap) (71/18) [76.Jari Niemi (11/1)], Mikael Kaj Forssell (14/4) [81.Mika Kottila (19/2)], Joonas Einari Kolkka (35/7) [72.Rami Rantanen (18/1)]. Trainer: Antti Muurinen (24).
Goals: Mikael Kaj Forssell (2), Joonas Einari Kolkka (14), Jari Olavi Litmanen (30 penalty), Hannu Tihinen (79).

609. 01.09.2001 **ALBANIA - FINLAND** **0-2(0-0)** 17th FIFA WC. Qualifiers
Stadiumi „Kombëtar Qemal Stafa", Tiranë; Referee: Erol Ersoy (Turkey); Attendance: 6,400
FIN: Antti Niemi (47/0), Petri Helin (21/2), Janne Saarinen (9/0), Sami Hyypiä (41/1), Toni Kuivasto (22/0), Mika Nurmela (26/0) [78.Shefki Kuqi (18/3)], Teemu Tainio (9/1), Aki Riihilahti (32/5), Jari Olavi Litmanen (Cap) (72/18) [86.Jari Ilola (8/0)], Mikael Kaj Forssell (15/4) [66.Jonatan Lillebror Johansson (37/9)], Joonas Einari Kolkka (36/7). Trainer: Antti Muurinen (25).
Goals: Teemu Tainio (57), Shefki Kuqi (90).

610. 05.09.2001 **FINLAND - GREECE** **5-1(4-1)** 17th FIFA WC. Qualifiers
Olympiastadion, Helsinki; Referee: Paul Allaerts (Belgium); Attendance: 27,216
FIN: Antti Niemi (48/0), Petri Helin (22/2), Hannu Tihinen (22/2), Sami Hyypiä (42/1), Janne Saarinen (10/0), Mika Nurmela (27/0), Aki Riihilahti (33/6), Teemu Tainio (10/1) [63.Jarkko Wiss (34/2)], Joonas Einari Kolkka (37/8), Jari Olavi Litmanen (Cap) (73/19) [72.Shefki Kuqi (19/3)], Mikael Kaj Forssell (16/6) [80.Jonatan Lillebror Johansson (38/9)]. Trainer: Antti Muurinen (26).
Goals: Mikael Kaj Forssell (14), Aki Riihilahti (21), Joonas Einari Kolkka (38), Mikael Kaj Forssell (45), Jari Olavi Litmanen (56 penalty).

611. 06.10.2001 **GERMANY - FINLAND** **0-0** 17th FIFA WC. Qualifiers
Arena „Auf Schalke", Gelsenkirchen; Referee: Anders Frisk (Sweden); Attendance: 52,000
FIN: Antti Niemi (49/0), Juha Reini (16/0) [79.Petri Helin (23/2)], Sami Hyypiä (43/1), Hannu Tihinen (23/2), Janne Saarinen (11/0), Mika Nurmela (28/0), Aki Riihilahti (34/6), Teemu Tainio (11/1) [82.Tommi Grönlund (34/2)], Jari Olavi Litmanen (Cap) (74/19), Mikael Kaj Forssell (17/6), Jonatan Lillebror Johansson (39/9) [66.Shefki Kuqi (20/3)]. Trainer: Antti Muurinen (27).

612. 04.01.2002 **BAHRAIN - FINLAND** **0-2(0-1)** Bahrain Shoot Soccer Tournament
Bahrain National Stadium, Riffa; Referee: Jassim Al Hail (Qatar); Attendance: 5,000
FIN: Jani Viander (11/0), Harri Ylönen (43/1), Markus Heikkinen (1/0), Jussi Nuorela (16/1), Toni Kuivasto (Cap) (23/0), Miika Koppinen (7/0) [89.Lasse Karjalainen (14/0)], Jarkko Wiss (35/3), Toni Kallio (6/1) [69.Jari Niemi (12/1)], Mika Kottila (20/3), Antti Pohja (5/1) [69.Jari Ilola (9/0)], Petri Helin (24/2) [86.Peter Kopteff (1/0)]. Trainer: Antti Muurinen (28).
Goals: Mika Kottila (43), Jarkko Wiss (79).

613. 07.01.2002 **ALBANIA - FINLAND** **1-1(0-1)** Bahrain Shoot Soccer Tournament
Bahrain National Stadium, Riffa (Bahrain); Referee: Abdul Hussain Habib (Bahrain); Attendance: 4,000
FIN: Mikka Kavén (3/0), Toni Huttunen (11/0), Toni Kuivasto (Cap) (24/0), Jussi Nuorela (17/1), Petri Heinänen (1/0) [11.Aarno Turpeinen (15/0)], Jarkko Wiss (36/3) [78.Antti Pohja (6/1)], Lasse Karjalainen (15/0), Jari Ilola (10/1) [69.Miika Koppinen (8/0)], Peter Kopteff (2/0) [83.Markus Heikkinen (2/0)], Mika Kottila (21/3) [74.Toni Kallio (7/1)], Jari Niemi (13/1) [61.Petri Helin (25/2)]. Trainer: Antti Muurinen (29).
Goal: Jari Ilola (45).

614. 10.01.2002 **FINLAND - MACEDONIA** **3-0(3-0)** Bahrain Shoot Soccer Tournament
Bahrain National Stadium, Riffa (Bahrain); Referee: Suleiman Abou Alo (Syria); Attendance: 1,000
FIN: Jani Viander (12/0), Harri Ylönen (44/1), Jussi Nuorela (18/1), Toni Kuivasto (Cap) (25/0), Aarno Turpeinen (16/0), Petri Helin (26/2) [46.Peter Kopteff (3/0)], Miika Koppinen (9/0) [*sent off 57*], Jarkko Wiss (37/3) [*sent off 74*], Jari Niemi (14/2) [75.Toni Kallio (8/1)], Antti Pohja (7/1) [59.Markus Heikkinen (3/0)], Mika Kottila (22/5) [69.Ville Väisänen (4/1)]. Trainer: Antti Muurinen (30).
Goals: Mika Kottila (17), Jari Niemi (23), Mika Kottila (25).

615. 20.03.2002 **KOREA REPUBLIC - FINLAND** **2-0(0-0)**
Estadio Cartagonova, Cartagena (Spain); Referee: Victor José Esquinas Torres (Spain); Attendance: 500
FIN: Jussi Jääskeläinen (8/0), Janne Saarinen (12/0), Hannu Tihinen (Cap) (24/2), Toni Kuivasto (26/0), Juha Reini (17/0) [46.Harri Ylönen (45/1)], Jonatan Lillebror Johansson (40/9) [82.Markus Heikkinen (4/0)], Simo Valakari (20/0), Mika Väyrynen (1/0) [46.Jarkko Wiss (38/3)], Mika Nurmela (29/0) [46.Antti Pohja (8/1)], Shefki Kuqi (21/3) [89.Jari Niemi (15/2)], Mikael Kaj Forssell (18/6). Trainer: Antti Muurinen (31).

616. 27.03.2002 **PORTUGAL - FINLAND** **1-4(1-3)**
Estádio do Bessa, Porto; Referee: Frank de Bleeckere (Belgium); Attendance: 8,000
FIN: Antti Niemi (50/0), Juha Reini (18/0), Janne Saarinen (13/0) [69.Janne Hietanen (3/0)], Sami Hyypiä (44/1) [46.Toni Kuivasto (27/0)], Hannu Tihinen (25/2), Aki Riihilahti (35/6) [79.Tommi Grönlund (35/2)], Mika Nurmela (30/0) [84.Paulus Henrik Roiha (3/0)], Teemu Tainio (12/1) [86.Simo Valakari (21/0)], Jari Olavi Litmanen (Cap) (75/21), Mikael Kaj Forssell (19/7) [69.Jonatan Lillebror Johansson (41/9)], Joonas Einari Kolkka (38/9). Trainer: Antti Muurinen (32).
Goals: Joonas Einari Kolkka (9), Mikael Kaj Forssell (27), Jari Olavi Litmanen (42, 54).

617. 17.04.2002 **MACEDONIA - FINLAND** **1-0(1-0)**
Stadion "Goce Delčev", Prilep; Referee: Orhan Erdemir (Turkey); Attendance: 5,000
FIN: Antti Niemi (51/0), Petri Pasanen (7/0) [80.Petri Helin (27/2)], Janne Saarinen (14/0) [78.Janne Hietanen (4/0)], Toni Kuivasto (28/0), Hannu Tihinen (26/2), Aki Riihilahti (36/6), Vesa Vasara (12/2) [46.Simo Valakari (22/0)], Teemu Tainio (13/1) [58.Shefki Kuqi (22/3)], Jari Olavi Litmanen (Cap) (76/21), Jonatan Lillebror Johansson (42/9) [69.Paulus Henrik Roiha (4/0)], Joonas Einari Kolkka (39/9). Trainer: Antti Muurinen (33).

618. 22.05.2002 **FINLAND - LATVIA** **2-1(0-1)**
Olympiastadion, Helsinki; Referee: Kristinn Jakobsson (Iceland); Attendance: 8,617
FIN: Antti Niemi (52/0) [46.Jussi Jääskeläinen (9/0)], Petri Pasanen (8/1), Janne Saarinen (15/0), Sami Hyypiä (45/1), Hannu Tihinen (27/2), Aki Riihilahti (37/7) [90.Simo Valakari (23/0)], Mika Nurmela (31/0) [61.Peter Kopteff (4/0)], Tommi Grönlund (36/2) [69.Janne Hietanen (5/0)], Jari Olavi Litmanen (Cap) (77/21) [90.Toni Kuivasto (29/0)], Jonatan Lillebror Johansson (43/9) [46.Shefki Kuqi (23/3)], Joonas Einari Kolkka (40/9) [78.Paulus Henrik Roiha (5/0)]. Trainer: Antti Muurinen (34).
Goals: Aki Riihilahti (70), Petri Pasanen (84).

619. 21.08.2002 **FINLAND – REPUBLIC OF IRELAND** **0-3(0-1)**
Olympiastadion, Helsinki; Referee: Rune Pedersen (Norway); Attendance: 12,225
FIN: Jussi Jääskeläinen (10/0), Petri Pasanen (9/1), Hannu Tihinen (28/2), Sami Hyypiä (46/1) [46.Toni Kuivasto (30/0)], Janne Saarinen (16/0), Mika Nurmela (32/0) [69.Peter Kopteff (5/0)], Teemu Tainio (14/1) [80.Janne Hietanen (6/0)], Jari Ilola (11/1) [59.Aki Riihilahti (38/7)], Joonas Einari Kolkka (41/9) [78.Mika Kottila (23/5)], Jari Olavi Litmanen (Cap) (78/21), Jonatan Lillebror Johansson (44/9) [59.Shefki Kuqi (24/3)]. Trainer: Antti Muurinen (35).

620. 07.09.2002 **FINLAND - WALES** **0-2(0-1)** 12th EC. Qualifiers
Olympiastadion, Helsinki; Referee: Konrad Plautz (Austria); Attendance: 35,883
FIN: Antti Niemi (53/0), Kaj Wilhelm Nylund (15/0) [69.Jonatan Lillebror Johansson (45/9)], Janne Saarinen (17/0) [78.Peter Kopteff (6/0)], Sami Hyypiä (47/1), Hannu Tihinen (29/2), Aki Riihilahti (39/7), Mika Nurmela (33/0) [86.Mika Kottila (24/5)], Teemu Tainio (15/1), Shefki Kuqi (25/3), Jari Olavi Litmanen (Cap) (79/21), Joonas Einari Kolkka (42/9). Trainer: Antti Muurinen (36).

621. 12.10.2002 **FINLAND - AZERBAIJAN** **3-0(1-0)** 12th EC. Qualifiers
Olympiastadion, Helsinki; Referee: Alain Hamer (Luxembourg); Attendance: 11,853
FIN: Antti Niemi (54/0), Petri Pasanen (10/1), Janne Saarinen (18/0), Sami Hyypiä (48/2) [79.Toni Kuivasto (31/0)], Hannu Tihinen (30/3), Aki Riihilahti (40/7), Mika Nurmela (34/0), Teemu Tainio (16/1) [74.Jarkko Wiss (39/3)], Antti Sumiala (34/9) [85.Shefki Kuqi (26/3)], Jari Olavi Litmanen (Cap) (80/21), Joonas Einari Kolkka (43/9). Trainer: Antti Muurinen (37).
Goals: Emin Agayev (14 own goal), Hannu Tihinen (59), Sami Hyypiä (71).

622. 16.10.2002 **YUGOSLAVIA - FINLAND** **2-0(0-0)** 12th EC. Qualifiers
Stadion Crvena zvezda, Beograd; Referee: Dick van Egmond (Netherlands); Attendance: 30,000
FIN: Antti Niemi (55/0), Petri Pasanen (11/1) [63.Juha Reini (19/0) [*sent off 82*]], Janne Saarinen (19/0), Sami Hyypiä (49/2), Toni Kuivasto (32/0), Aki Riihilahti (41/7), Mika Nurmela (35/0), Teemu Tainio (17/1) [82.Shefki Kuqi (27/3)], Antti Sumiala (35/9) [57.Jonatan Lillebror Johansson (46/9)], Jari Olavi Litmanen (Cap) (81/21), Joonas Einari Kolkka (44/9). Trainer: Antti Muurinen (38).

623. 26.01.2003 **BARBADOS - FINLAND** **0-0**
Barbados National Stadium, Bridgetown; Referee: Noel Bynoe (Trinidad and Tobago); Attendance: 5,000
FIN: Mikko Kavén (4/0), Kaj Wilhelm Nylund (16/0), Tero Penttilä (4/0), Toni Kuivasto (33/0), Juuso Kangaskorpi (1/0), Peter Kopteff (7/0), Antti Okkonen (1/0), Simo Valakari (24/0), Miikka Multaharju (1/0) [85.Fredrik Nordback (1/0)], Antti Pohja (9/1) [65.Jari Ilola (12/1)], Mika Kottila (25/5) [60.Jari Niemi (16/2)]. Trainer: Antti Muurinen (39).

624. 29.01.2003 **TRINIDAD AND TOBAGO - FINLAND** **1-2(1-0)**
"Hasely Crawford" Stadium, Port of Spain; Referee: Mark Forde (Barbados); Attendance: 4,000
FIN: Jani Viander (13/0), Rami Hakanpää (1/0), Toni Kuivasto (Cap) (34/0) [65.Miikka Multaharju (2/0)], Marko Tuomela (24/2) [46.Tero Penttilä (5/0)], Juuso Kangaskorpi (2/0), Simo Valakari (25/0), Jari Ilola (13/1) [46.Antti Okkonen (2/0)], Fredrik Nordback (2/0) [46.Antti Pohja (10/1), Peter Kopteff (8/0), Jari Niemi (17/3), Antti Sumiala (36/9) [73.Mika Kottila (26/6)]. Trainer: Antti Muurinen (40).
Goals: Mika Kottila (80), Jari Niemi (83).

625. 12.02.2003 **NORTHERN IRELAND - FINLAND** **0-1(0-0)**
Windsor Park, Belfast; Referee: Douglas McDonald (Scotland); Attendance: 6,137
FIN: Jussi Jääskeläinen (11/0), Toni Kuivasto (35/0), Sami Hyypiä (Cap) (50/3) [70.Markus Heikkinen (5/0)], Hannu Tihinen (31/3), Janne Hietanen (7/0), Mika Nurmela (36/0), Aki Riihilahti (42/7), Simo Valakari (26/0), Joonas Einari Kolkka (45/9) [75.Peter Kopteff (9/0)], Mika Väyrynen (2/0) [60.Jonatan Lillebror Johansson (47/9)], Mikael Kaj Forssell (20/7) [46.Shefki Kuqi (28/3)]. Trainer: Antti Muurinen (41).
Goal: Sami Hyypiä (50).

626. 29.03.2003 **ITALY - FINLAND** **2-0(2-0)** 12th EC. Qualifiers
Stadio "Renzo Barbera", Palermo; Referee: Valentin Ivanov (Russia); Attendance: 34,074
FIN: Antti Niemi (56/0), Petri Pasanen (12/1), Janne Saarinen (20/0), Sami Hyypiä (Cap) (51/3), Hannu Tihinen (32/3), Aki Riihilahti (43/7) [36.Jonatan Lillebror Johansson (48/9)], Mika Nurmela (37/0) [75.Peter Kopteff (10/0)], Jari Ilola (14/1), Mikael Kaj Forssell (21/7), Teemu Tainio (18/1), Joonas Einari Kolkka (46/9) [89.Shefki Kuqi (29/3)]. Trainer: Antti Muurinen (42).

627. 30.04.2003 **FINLAND - ICELAND** **3-0(0-0)**
Pohjola Stadion, Vantaa; Referee: Peter Fröjdfeldt (Sweden); Attendance: 4,005
FIN: Jussi Jääskeläinen (12/0) [46.Peter Enckelman (4/0)], Kaj Wilhelm Nylund (17/0), Janne Saarinen (21/0) [46.Markus Heikkinen (6/0)], Sami Hyypiä (52/3) [63.Jussi Nuorela (19/1)], Toni Kuivasto (36/0), Simo Valakari (27/0), Mika Nurmela (38/0), Jari Ilola (15/1) [57.Peter Kopteff (11/0)], Mikael Kaj Forssell (22/8) [85.Rami Hakanpää (2/0)], Jari Olavi Litmanen (Cap) (82/22) [69.Jonatan Lillebror Johansson (49/10)], Joonas Einari Kolkka (47/9) [72.Paulus Henrik Roiha (6/0)]. Trainer: Antti Muurinen (43).
Goal: Jari Olavi Litmanen (55 penalty), Mikael Kaj Forssell (57), Jonatan Lillebror Johansson (79).

628. 22.05.2003 **NORWAY - FINLAND** **2-0(1-0)**
Ullevaal Stadion, Oslo; Referee: Kenneth Clark (Scotland); Attendance: 13,436
FIN: Peter Enckelman (5/0), Markus Heikkinen (7/0) [72.Fredrik Nordback (3/0)], Toni Kuivasto (37/0), Sami Hyypiä (Cap) (53/3), Janne Saarinen (22/0) [28.Janne Hietanen (8/0); 50.Jussi Nuorela (20/1)], Antti Pohja (11/1) [46.Paulus Henrik Roiha (7/0)], Miika Koppinen (10/0), Simo Valakari (28/0), Peter Kopteff (12/0), Jonatan Lillebror Johansson (50/10) [87.Ville Väisänen (5/1)], Shefki Kuqi (30/3) [82.Daniel Sjölund (1/0)]. Trainer: Antti Muurinen (44).

629. 07.06.2003 **FINLAND – SERBIA & MONTENEGRO** **3-0(2-0)** 12th EC. Qualifiers
Olympiastadion, Helsinki; Referee: Claude Colombo (France); Attendance: 17,343
FIN: Jussi Jääskeläinen (13/0), Petri Pasanen (13/1), Janne Saarinen (23/0), Sami Hyypiä (54/4), Hannu Tihinen (33/3), Simo Valakari (29/0), Mika Nurmela (39/0) [87.Aki Riihilahti (44/7)], Mika Väyrynen (3/0), Mikael Kaj Forssell (23/9) [79.Shefki Kuqi (31/3)], Jari Olavi Litmanen (Cap) (83/22), Joonas Einari Kolkka (48/10) [66.Peter Kopteff (13/0)]. Trainer: Antti Muurinen (45).
Goals: Sami Hyypiä (19), Joonas Einari Kolkka (45), Mikael Kaj Forssell (56).

630. 11.06.2003 **FINLAND - ITALY** **0-2(0-1)** 12th EC. Qualifiers
Olympiastadion, Helsinki; Referee: Željko Sirić (Croatia); Attendance: 36,850
FIN: Jussi Jääskeläinen (14/0), Petri Pasanen (14/1), Janne Saarinen (24/0), Sami Hyypiä (55/4), Hannu Tihinen (34/3), Simo Valakari (30/0) [82.Aki Riihilahti (45/7)], Mika Nurmela (40/0) [69.Peter Kopteff (14/0)], Mika Väyrynen (4/0), Mikael Kaj Forssell (24/9), Jari Olavi Litmanen (Cap) (84/22), Joonas Einari Kolkka (49/10) [78.Jonatan Lillebror Johansson (51/10)]. Trainer: Antti Muurinen (46).

631. 20.08.2003 **DENMARK - FINLAND** **1-1(1-0)**
Parken, København; Referee: Thomas Michael McCurry (Scotland); Attendance: 14,882
FIN: Jussi Jääskeläinen (15/0), Janne Saarinen (25/0), Toni Kuivasto (38/0), Hannu Tihinen (35/3), Juha Reini (20/0) [46.Markus Heikkinen (8/0)], Peter Kopteff (15/0) [46.Joonas Einari Kolkka (50/10)], Simo Valakari (31/0) [46.Aki Riihilahti (46/8)], Mika Väyrynen (5/0) [76.Miika Koppinen (11/0)], Mika Nurmela (Cap) (41/0) [83.Juuso Kangaskorpi (3/0)], Mikael Kaj Forssell (25/9), Jonatan Lillebror Johansson (52/10) [46.Shefki Kuqi (32/3)]. Trainer: Antti Muurinen (47).
Goal: Aki Riihilahti (88).

632. 06.09.2003 **AZERBAIJAN - FINLAND** **1-2(0-0)** 12th EC. Qualifiers
Şafa Stadionu, Bakı; Referee: Vladimír Hriňák (Slovakia); Attendance: 8,000
FIN: Antti Niemi (57/0), Janne Saarinen (26/0), Sami Hyypiä (Cap) (56/4), Petri Pasanen (15/1), Mika Väyrynen (6/0) [69.Aki Riihilahti (47/8)], Mika Nurmela (42/1), Teemu Tainio (19/2) [86.Simo Valakari (32/0)], Mikael Kaj Forssell (26/9), Jonatan Lillebror Johansson (53/10) [46.Peter Kopteff (16/0)], Joonas Einari Kolkka (51/10), Juha Reini (21/0). Trainer: Antti Muurinen (48).
Goals: Teemu Tainio (52), Mika Nurmela (74).

633. 10.09.2003 **WALES - FINLAND** **1-1(1-0)** 12th EC. Qualifiers
Millenium Stadium, Cardiff; Referee: Arturo Daudén Ibañez (Spain); Attendance: 72,500
FIN: Antti Niemi (58/0), Petri Pasanen (16/1) [82.Peter Kopteff (17/0)], Janne Saarinen (27/0) [46.Juha Reini (22/0)], Sami Hyypiä (57/4), Hannu Tihinen (36/3), Aki Riihilahti (48/8), Mika Nurmela (43/1), Teemu Tainio (20/2), Mikael Kaj Forssell (27/10), Mika Väyrynen (7/0) [58.Shefki Kuqi (33/3)], Joonas Einari Kolkka (52/10). Trainer: Antti Muurinen (49).
Goal: Mikael Kaj Forssell (78).

634. 11.10.2003 **FINLAND - CANADA** **3-2(3-0)**
Ratinan Stadion, Tampere; Referee: Charlie Richmond (Scotland); Attendance: 5,350
FIN: Jussi Jääskeläinen (16/0), Janne Saarinen (28/0), Sami Hyypiä (Cap) (58/4) [56.Toni Kuivasto (39/0)], Petri Pasanen (17/1) [78.Mika Kottila (27/6)], Markus Heikkinen (9/0), Joonas Einari Kolkka (53/11) [46.Peter Kopteff (18/0)], Mika Väyrynen (8/0), Teemu Tainio (21/3) [62.Aki Riihilahti (49/8)], Mika Nurmela (44/1), Alexei Eremenko jr. (1/0) [71.Daniel Sjölund (2/0)], Mikael Kaj Forssell (28/11). Trainer: Antti Muurinen (50).
Goals: Mikael Kaj Forssell (14), Joonas Einari Kolkka (16), Teemu Tainio (32).

635. 16.10.2003 **HONDURAS - FINLAND** **1-2(0-0)**
Robertson Stadium, Houston (United States); Referee: Brian Hall (United States); Attendance: 16,000
FIN: Teuvo Moilanen (4/0), Janne Hietanen (9/0), Juha Pasoja (1/0), Toni Kuivasto (40/0), Markus Heikkinen (10/0) [86.Kaj Wilhelm Nylund (18/0)], Peter Kopteff (19/0), Antti Okkonen (3/0) [46.Rami Hakanpää (3/1)], Teemu Tainio (22/4) [76.Miika Koppinen (12/0)], Mika Nurmela (Cap) (45/1) [80.Jari Niemi (18/3)], Alexei Eremenko jr. (2/0) [74.Pekka Lagerblom (1/0)], Paulus Henrik Roiha (8/0) [68.Mika Kottila (28/6)]. Trainer: Antti Muurinen (51).
Goals: Teemu Tainio (60), Rami Hakanpää (68).

636. 19.10.2003 **COSTA RICA - FINLAND** **2-1(1-0)**
Estadio "Alejandro Morera Soto", Alajuela; Referee: Carlos Alberto Batrés González (Guatemala); Attendance: 20,000
FIN: Mikko Kavén (5/0), Markus Heikkinen (11/0) [46.Janne Hietanen (10/0)], Kaj Wilhelm Nylund (19/0), Juha Pasoja (2/0) [64.Paulus Henrik Roiha (9/0)], Toni Kuivasto (41/0), Rami Hakanpää (4/1) [46.Miika Koppinen (13/0)], Mika Nurmela (Cap) (46/2) [*sent off 76*], Teemu Tainio (23/4), Jari Niemi (19/3) [81.Mika Kottila (29/6)], Alexei Eremenko jr. (3/0) [74.Pekka Lagerblom (2/0)], Peter Kopteff (20/0). Trainer: Antti Muurinen (52).
Goal: Mika Nurmela (61 penalty).

637. 03.02.2004 **CHINA P.R. - FINLAND** **2-1(1-0)**
Tianhe Stadium, Guanghzou; Referee: Lee Gi Young (Korea Republic); Attendance: 15,000
FIN: Mikko Kavén (6/0), Kaj Wilhelm Nylund (20/0), Janne Salli (9/1), Toni Kuivasto (Cap) (42/0), Janne Hietanen (11/0) [83.Petri Heinänen (2/0)], Antti Pohja (12/1) [75.Juho Antti Mäkelä (1/0)], Miika Koppinen (14/0), Jari Ilola (16/1) [86.Antti Okkonen (4/0)], Peter Kopteff (21/0), Alexei Eremenko jr. (4/1) [57.Daniel Sjölund (3/0)], Antti Sumiala (37/9) [57.Mika Kottila (30/6)]. Trainer: Antti Muurinen (53).
Goal: Alexei Eremenko jr. (51).

638. 07.02.2004 **CHINA P.R. - FINLAND** **2-1(2-1)**
Shenzen Stadium, Shenzen; Referee: Bae Jae-Yong (Korea Republic); Attendance: 18,000
FIN: Mikko Kavén (7/0), Janne Hietanen (12/0) [72.Daniel Sjölund (4/0) [*sent off 89*]], Janne Salli (10/1), Toni Kuivasto (Cap) (43/0), Petri Heinänen (3/0), Antti Pohja (13/1) [86.Juho Antti Mäkelä (2/0)], Antti Okkonen (5/0), Miika Koppinen (15/0), Peter Kopteff (22/1), Jari Ilola (17/1) [82.Rami Hakanpää (5/1)], Antti Sumiala (38/9) [46.Mika Kottila (31/6)]. Trainer: Antti Muurinen (54).
Goal: Peter Kopteff (37).

639. 31.03.2004 **MALTA - FINLAND** **1-2(0-0)**
Ta' Qali National Stadium, Attard; Referee: Matteo Simone Trefoloni (Italy); Attendance: 1,100
FIN: Antti Niemi (59/0) [46.Jussi Jääskeläinen (17/0)], Petri Pasanen (18/1), Sami Hyypiä (Cap) (59/4) [55.Toni Kuivasto (44/0)], Hannu Tihinen (37/3), Janne Saarinen (29/0) [83.Kaj Wilhelm Nylund (21/0)], Miikka Multaharju (3/0) [46.Mika Nurmela (47/2)], Aki Riihilahti (50/8) [74.Jari Olavi Litmanen (85/23)], Mika Väyrynen (9/0), Peter Kopteff (23/1) [46.Joonas Einari Kolkka (54/11)], Alexei Eremenko jr.. (5/2) [61.Pekka Lagerblom (3/0)], Shefki Kuqi (34/3) [74.Jari Niemi (20/3)]. Trainer: Antti Muurinen (55).
Goals: Alexei Eremenko jr. (51), Jari Olavi Litmanen (84).

640. 28.04.2004 **BOSNIA-HERZEGOVINA - FINLAND** **1-0(0-0)**
Stadion Bilino Polje, Zenica; Referee: Emil Božinovski (Macedonia); Attendance: 17,000
FIN: Antti Niemi (60/0) [47.Mikko Kavén (8/0)], Petri Pasanen (19/1) [49.Janne Salli (11/1)], Sami Hyypiä (60/4) [46.Toni Kuivasto (45/0)], Hannu Tihinen (38/3), Janne Saarinen (30/0) [46.Miikka Koppinen (16/0)], Mika Nurmela (48/2) [81.Miikka Multaharju (4/0)], Mika Väyrynen (10/0) [77.Peter Kopteff (24/1)], Alexei Eremenko jr. (6/2) [46.Aki Riihilahti (51/8)], Joonas Einari Kolkka (55/11), Jari Olavi Litmanen (86/23) [68.Markus Heikkinen (Cap) (12/0)], Jonatan Lillebror Johansson (54/10) [70.Jari Niemi (21/3)]. Trainer: Antti Muurinen (56).

641. 28.05.2004 **FINLAND - SWEDEN** **1-3(1-2)**
Ratinan Stadion, Tampere; Referee: Alberto Undiano Mallenco (Spain); Attendance: 16,500
FIN: Antti Niemi (61/0), Petri Pasanen (20/1), Hannu Tihinen (39/3), Sami Hyypiä (61/4) [64.Toni Kuivasto (46/0)], Juha Reini (23/0), Mika Nurmela (49/2) [86.Jari Ilola (18/1)], Mika Väyrynen (11/0), Alexei Eremenko jr. (7/2) [72.Antti Okkonen (6/0)], Joonas Einari Kolkka (56/11) [81.Jonatan Lillebror Johansson (55/10)], Jari Olavi Litmanen (Cap) (87/24), Mikael Kaj Forssell (29/11). Trainer: Antti Muurinen (57).
Goal: Jari Olavi Litmanen (8 penalty).

642. 18.08.2004 **ROMANIA - FINLAND** **2-1(0-0)** 18th FIFA WC. Qualifiers
Stadionul "Valentin Stănescu", Bucureşti; Referee: Grzegorz Gilewski (Poland); Attendance: 18,000
FIN: Antti Niemi (62/0), Aki Riihilahti (52/8), Janne Saarinen (31/0), Sami Hyypiä (62/4), Petri Pasanen (21/1) [59.Miikka Koppinen (17/0)], Mika Väyrynen (12/0) [*sent off 83*], Mika Nurmela (50/2) [83.Peter Kopteff (25/1)] Toni Kuivasto (47/0), Jonatan Lillebror Johansson (56/10), Jari Olavi Litmanen (Cap) (88/24) [57.Alexei Eremenko jr. (8/3)], Joonas Einari Kolkka (57/11). Trainer: Antti Muurinen (58).
Goal: Alexei Eremenko jr. (90+3 penalty).

643. 04.09.2004 **FINLAND - ANDORRA** **3-0(1-0)** 18th FIFA WC. Qualifiers
Ratinan Stadion, Tampere; Referee: Željko Širić (Croatia); Attendance: 7,437
FIN: Antti Niemi (63/0), Mika Nurmela (51/2), Toni Kuivasto (48/0), Sami Hyypiä (63/4), Petri Pasanen (22/1), Aki Riihilahti (53/9), Antti Pohja (14/1) [59.Peter Kopteff (26/1)], Joonas Einari Kolkka (58/11) [82.Markus Heikkinen (13/0)], Jari Olavi Litmanen (Cap) (89/24) [73.Jonatan Lillebror Johansson (57/10)], Alexei Eremenko jr. (9/5), Mikael Kaj Forssell (30/11). Trainer: Antti Muurinen (59).
Goals: Alexei Eremenko jr. (42), Aki Riihilahti (58), Alexei Eremenko jr. (64).

644. 08.09.2004 **ARMENIA - FINLAND** **0-2(0-1)** 18th FIFA WC. Qualifiers
„Vazgen Sargsyan" Hanrapetakan Stadium, Yerevan; Referee: Paulius Malžinskas (Lithuania); Attendance: 2,864
FIN: Antti Niemi (64/0), Sami Hyypiä (64/4), Aki Riihilahti (54/9), Mika Väyrynen (13/0), Petri Pasanen (23/1), Mika Nurmela (52/2), Toni Kuivasto (49/0), Jari Olavi Litmanen (Cap) (90/24) [46.Pekka Lagerblom (4/0)], Joonas Einari Kolkka (59/11) [85.Antti Pohja (15/1)], Mikael Kaj Forssell (31/12), Alexei Eremenko jr. (10/6) [73.Peter Kopteff (27/1)]. Trainer: Antti Muurinen (60).
Goals: Mikael Kaj Forssell (24), Alexei Eremenko jr. (67).

645. 09.10.2004 **FINLAND - ARMENIA** **3-1(2-1)** 18th FIFA WC. Qualifiers
Ratinan Stadion, Tampere; Referee: Herbert Fandel (Germany); Attendance: 7,894
FIN: Antti Niemi (65/0), Janne Saarinen (32/0) [69.Toni Kallio (9/1)], Aki Riihilahti (55/9), Sami Hyypiä (Cap) (65/4), Petri Pasanen (24/1), Mika Väyrynen (14/0), Mika Nurmela (53/2), Joonas Einari Kolkka (60/11) [83.Jonatan Lillebror Johansson (58/10)], Toni Kuivasto (50/0) [46.Teemu Tainio (24/4)], Shefki Kuqi (35/5), Alexei Eremenko jr. (11/7). Trainer: Antti Muurinen (61).
Goals: Shefki Kuqi (8), Alexei Eremenko jr. (28), Shefki Kuqi (87).

646. 13.10.2004 **NETHERLANDS - FINLAND** **3-1(2-1)** 18th FIFA WC. Qualifiers
Amsterdam ArenA, Amsterdam; Referee: Stephen Graham Bennett (England); Attendance: 49,000
FIN: Antti Niemi (66/0), Petri Pasanen (25/1), Aki Riihilahti (56/9) [59.Jonatan Lillebror Johansson (59/10)], Sami Hyypiä (Cap) (66/4), Mika Väyrynen (15/0) [85.Antti Pohja (16/1)], Mika Nurmela (54/2), Teemu Tainio (25/5), Toni Kuivasto (51/0), Joonas Einari Kolkka (61/11), Shefki Kuqi (36/5), Alexei Eremenko jr. (12/7) [72.Janne Saarinen (33/0)]. Trainer: Antti Muurinen (62).
Goal: Teemu Tainio (14).

647. 17.11.2004 **ITALY - FINLAND** **1-0(1-0)**
Stadio San Filippo, Messina; Referee: Alexandru Dan Tudor (Romania); Attendance: 7,043
FIN: Jussi Jääskeläinen (18/0), Mika Väyrynen (16/0) [68.Antti Okkonen (7/0)], Mika Nurmela (55/2), Toni Kuivasto (52/0), Peter Kopteff (28/1), Toni Kallio (10/1), Jari Olavi Litmanen (Cap) (91/24) [74.Paulus Henrik Roiha (10/0)], Joonas Einari Kolkka (62/11) [62.Miikka Multaharju (5/0)], Alexei Eremenko jr. (13/7) [87.Juuso Kangaskorpi (4/0)], Jonatan Lillebror Johansson (60/10), Shefki Kuqi (37/5). Trainer: Antti Muurinen (63).

648. 01.12.2004 **BAHRAIN - FINLAND** **1-2(1-1)** Bahrain P.M. Cup
Bahrain National Stadium, Riffa; Referee: Talaam Najm (Lebanon); Attendance: 6,000
FIN: Mikko Kavén (9/0), Ari Nyman (1/0), Juha Pasoja (3/0), Toni Kallio (11/1), Janne Hietanen (13/0), Antti Pohja (17/2) [90.Heikki Pulkkinen (1/0)], Jarno Heinikangas (1/0), Antti Okkonen (8/0), Fredrik Svanbäck (1/0) [62.Petri Oravainen (1/0)], Jari Olavi Litmanen (92/24) [76.Toni Pekka Lehtinen (1/0)], Keijo Huusko (1/1) [88.Fredrik Nordback (4/0)]. Trainer: Antti Muurinen (64).
Goals: Antti Pohja (9), Keijo Huusko (67).

649. 03.12.2004 **OMAN - FINLAND** **0-0; 4-3 on penalties** Bahrain P.M. Cup
Bahrain National Stadium, Riffa (Bahrain); Referee: Masoud Moradi (Iran); Attendance: 3,000
FIN: Henri Sillanpää (1/0), Heikki Pulkkinen (2/0) [46.Ari Nyman (2/0)], Janne Räsänen (1/0), Toni Kallio (12/1), Tuomo Könönen (1/0), Antti Pohja (18/2) [75.Petri Oravainen (2/0)], Fredrik Nordback (5/0) [90.Juha Pasoja (4/0)], Jari Olavi Litmanen (93/24), Jussi Kujala (1/0) [46.Antti Okkonen (9/0)], Henri Scheweleff (1/0) [83.Janne Hietanen (14/0)], Toni Pekka Lehtinen (2/0) [77.Keijo Huusko (2/1)]. Trainer: Antti Muurinen (65).
Penalties: Jari Olavi Litmanen, Petri Oravainen, Juha Pasoja (saved), Antti Okkonen, Keijo Huusko (saved).

650. 08.02.2005 **FINLAND - LATVIA** **2-1(1-0)** Cyprus Tournament
Stádio Neo GSP, Nicosia (Cyprus); Referee: Panikos Kailis (Cyprus); Attendance: 50
FIN: Jussi Jääskeläinen (19/0), Hannu Haarala (1/0) [88.Antti Okkonen (10/0)], Toni Kuivasto (53/0), Sami Hyypiä (67/4), Peter Kopteff (29/1), Teemu Tainio (26/5), Aki Riihilahti (57/9), Jari Olavi Litmanen (Cap) (94/24) [67.Keijo Huusko (3/2)], Joonas Einari Kolkka (63/11) [89.Janne Hietanen (15/0)], Jonatan Lillebror Johansson (61/11) [83.Markus Heikkinen (14/0)], Jari Niemi (22/3) [57.Mika Nurmela (56/2)]. Trainer: Antti Muurinen (66).
Goals: Jonatan Lillebror Johansson (31), Keijo Huusko (72).

651. 09.02.2005 **CYPRUS - FINLAND** **1-2(1-0)** Cyprus Tournament
Stádio Neo GSP, Nicosia; Referee: Romāns Lajuks (Latvia); Attendance: 300
FIN: Peter Enckelman (6/0) [46.Mikko Kavén (10/0)], Janne Hietanen (16/0), Hannu Tihinen (Cap) (40/3), Juha Pasoja (5/0) [86.Toni Kuivasto (54/0)], Peter Kopteff (30/1) [60.Hannu Haarala (2/0)], Miikka Multaharju (6/0) [68.Teemu Tainio (27/5)], Markus Heikkinen (15/0), Antti Okkonen (11/0) [60.Jari Niemi (23/3)], Antti Pohja (19/2), Paulus Henrik Roiha (11/2), Keijo Huusko (4/2) [68.Jonatan Lillebror Johansson (62/11)]. Trainer: Antti Muurinen (67).
Goals: Paulus Henrik Roiha (66, 70).

652. 12.03.2005 **KUWAIT - FINLAND** **0-1(0-1)**
Al Kuwait Sports Club Stadium, Kaifan; Referee: Adel Al Shatti (Kuwait); Attendance: 1,500
FIN: Mikko Kavén (11/0), Ari Nyman (3/0) [82.Sampsa Timoska (1/0)], Toni Kuivasto (55/0), Jukka Sauso (1/0), Jani Sarajärvi (1/0) [21.Tuomo Könönen (2/0)], Mika Nurmela (57/2), Jari Ilola (19/1) [89.Fredrik Nordback (6/0)], Jarkko Wiss (40/3), Henri Scheweleff (2/0) [69.Niklas Henrikki Tarvajärvi (1/0)], Mikko Hyyrynen (1/0) [61.Keijo Huusko (5/2)], Njazi Kuqi (1/1) [84.Jarno Heinikangas (2/0)]. Trainer: Antti Muurinen (68).
Goal: Njazi Kuqi (16).

653. 18.03.2005 **SAUDI ARABIA - FINLAND** **1-4(0-1)**
"Prince Mohammad bin Fahd" Stadium, Dammam; Referee: Abdul Rahman Al Amri (Saudi Arabia); Attendance: 8,000
FIN: Henri Sillanpää (2/0), Ari Nyman (4/0) [88.Mikko Hyyrynen (2/0)], Toni Kuivasto (56/1), Sampsa Timoska (2/0) [74.Jukka Sauso (2/0)], Tuomo Könönen (3/0), Fredrik Nordback (7/0) [53.Jarkko Wiss (41/3)], Jari Ilola (20/1), Jarno Heinikangas (3/0), Mika Nurmela (58/3), Niklas Henrikki Tarvajärvi (2/0) [46.Henri Scheweleff (3/0)], Keijo Huusko (6/2) [46.Njazi Kuqi (2/3)]. Trainer: Antti Muurinen (69).
Goals: Toni Kuivasto (4), Njazi Kuqi (71), Mika Nurmela (76), Njazi Kuqi (78).

654. 26.03.2005 **CZECH REPUBLIC - FINLAND** **4-3(2-0)** 18th FIFA WC. Qualifiers
Stadion Na Stínadlech, Teplice; Referee: Claus Bo Larsen (Denmark); Attendance: 16,200
FIN: Jussi Jääskeläinen (20/0), Petri Pasanen (26/1), Aki Riihilahti (58/10), Sami Hyypiä (68/4), Hannu Tihinen (41/3), Peter Kopteff (31/1), Mika Nurmela (59/3), Jari Olavi Litmanen (Cap) (95/25) [78. Jonatan Lillebror Johansson (63/12)], Jari Ilola (21/1), Joonas Einari Kolkka (64/11) [6.Alexei Eremenko jr. (14/7)], Shefki Kuqi (38/5). Trainer: Antti Muurinen (70).
Goals: Jari Olavi Litmanen (46), Aki Riihilahti (73), Jonatan Lillebror Johansson (79).

655. 02.06.2005 **FINLAND - DENMARK** **0-1(0-0)**
Ratinan Stadion, Tampere; Referee: Jan Wegereef (Netherlands); Attendance: 9,238
FIN: Jussi Jääskeläinen (21/0), Mika Nurmela (60/3), Hannu Tihinen (42/3) [58.Toni Kuivasto (57/1)], Sami Hyypiä (69/4), Janne Saarinen (34/0) [68.Toni Kallio (13/1)], Jonatan Lillebror Johansson (64/12) [76.Mika Väyrynen (17/0)], Alexei Eremenko jr. (15/7), Aki Riihilahti (59/10), Peter Kopteff (32/1) [46.Joonas Einari Kolkka (65/11)], Jari Olavi Litmanen (Cap) (96/25) [58.Jarkko Wiss (42/3)], Shefki Kuqi (39/5) [79.Mikael Kaj Forssell (32/12)]. Trainer: Antti Muurinen (71).

656. 08.06.2005 **FINLAND - NETHERLANDS** **0-4(0-1)** 18th FIFA WC. Qualifiers
Olympiastadion, Helsinki; Referee: Alain Hamer (Luxembourg); Attendance: 37,786
FIN: Jussi Jääskeläinen (22/0), Janne Saarinen (35/0), Aki Riihilahti (60/10), Sami Hyypiä (70/4), Mika Väyrynen (18/0), Hannu Tihinen (43/3), Teemu Tainio (28/5) [75.Mikael Kaj Forssell (33/12)], Mika Nurmela (61/3), Jari Olavi Litmanen (Cap) (97/25) [28.Jonatan Lillebror Johansson (65/12)], Alexei Eremenko jr. (16/7) [81.Peter Kopteff (33/1)], Shefki Kuqi (40/5). Trainer: Antti Muurinen (72).

657. 17.08.2005 **MACEDONIA - FINLAND** **0-3(0-2)** 18th FIFA WC. Qualifiers
Stadion Gradski, Skopje; Referee: Matthew David Messias (England); Attendance: 6,800
FIN: Jussi Jääskeläinen (23/0), Petri Pasanen (27/1), Sami Hyypiä (Cap) (71/4), Hannu Tihinen (44/3), Toni Kallio (14/1), Markus Heikkinen (16/0), Pekka Lagerblom (5/0) [79.Jari Olavi Litmanen (98/25)], Teemu Tainio (29/5), Alexei Eremenko jr. (17/9) [84.Janne Saarinen (36/0)], Mikael Kaj Forssell (34/12) [61.Paulus Henrik Roiha (12/3)], Shefki Kuqi (41/5). Trainer: Jyrki Heliskoski (1).
Goal: Alexei Eremenko jr. (8, 45), Paulus Henrik Roiha (87).

658. 03.09.2005 **ANDORRA - FINLAND** **0-0** 18th FIFA WC. Qualifiers
Estadi Comunal de Aixovall, Andorra la Vella; Referee: Johny Ver Eecke (Belgium); Attendance: 860
FIN: Mikko Kavén (12/0), Janne Saarinen (37/0), Sami Hyypiä (Cap) (72/4), Hannu Tihinen (45/3), Toni Kuivasto (58/1), Peter Kopteff (34/1) [46.Pekka Lagerblom (6/0)], Toni Kallio (15/1), Teemu Tainio (30/5), Shefki Kuqi (42/5), Alexei Eremenko jr. (18/9) [64.Aki Riihilahti (61/10)], Mikael Kaj Forssell (35/12) [75.Daniel Sjölund (5/0)]. Trainer: Jyrki Heliskoski (2).

659. 07.09.2005 **FINLAND - MACEDONIA** **5-1(3-0)** 18th FIFA WC. Qualifiers

Ratinan Stadion, Tampere; Referee: Kristinn Jakobsson (Iceland); Attendance: 6,467

FIN: Mikko Kavén (13/0), Petri Pasanen (28/1), Aki Riihilahti (62/10) [72.Peter Kopteff (35/1)], Toni Kuivasto (59/1), Toni Kallio (16/1), Hannu Tihinen (46/4), Janne Saarinen (38/0) [53.Ari Nyman (5/0)], Markus Heikkinen (17/0), Teemu Tainio (Cap) (31/5) [82.Jonatan Lillebror Johansson (66/12)], Alexei Eremenko jr. (19/10), Mikael Kaj Forssell (36/15). Trainer: Jyrki Heliskoski (3).

Goals: Mikael Kaj Forssell (11, 13), Hannu Tihinen (42), Alexei Eremenko jr. (55), Mikael Kaj Forssell (62).

660. 08.10.2005 **FINLAND - ROMANIA** **0-1(0-1)** 18th FIFA WC. Qualifiers

Olympiastadion, Helsinki; Referee: Anton Genov (Bulgaria); Attendance: 11,500

FIN: Jussi Jääskeläinen (24/0), Toni Kallio (17/1), Sami Hyypiä (Cap) (73/4), Toni Kuivasto (60/1), Ari Nyman (6/0) [63.Jonatan Lillebror Johansson (67/12)], Janne Saarinen (39/0) [76.Peter Kopteff (36/1)], Teemu Tainio (32/5), Markus Heikkinen (18/0), Pekka Lagerblom (7/0), Alexei Eremenko jr. (20/10), Mikael Kaj Forssell (37/15) [74.Daniel Sjölund (6/0)]. Trainer: Jyrki Heliskoski (4).

661. 12.10.2005 **FINLAND – CZECH REPUBLIC** **0-3(0-1)** 18th FIFA WC. Qualifiers

Olympiastadion, Helsinki; Referee: Manuel Enrique Mejuto González (Spain); Attendance: 11,234

FIN: Jussi Jääskeläinen (25/0), Janne Saarinen (40/0) [12.Peter Kopteff (37/1)], Sami Hyypiä (Cap) (74/4), Teemu Tainio (33/5), Joonas Einari Kolkka (66/11), Toni Kuivasto (61/1), Daniel Sjölund (7/0) [61.Mikael Kaj Forssell (38/15)], Toni Kallio (18/1), Jonatan Lillebror Johansson (68/12), Markus Heikkinen (19/0), Pekka Lagerblom (8/0) [60.Ari Nyman (7/0)]. Trainer: Jyrki Heliskoski (5).

662. 12.11.2005 **FINLAND - ESTONIA** **2-2(1-0)**

Finnair Stadion, Helsinki; Referee: Grzegorz Gilewski (Poland); Attendance: 1,903

FIN: Mikko Kavén (14/0), Ari Nyman (8/0), Juha Pasoja (6/0), Toni Kuivasto (Cap) (62/1), Tuomo Könönen (4/0), Kari Arkivuo (1/1), Markus Heikkinen (20/0) [59.Tuomas Uusimäki (1/0)], Tuomas Haapala (1/0), Daniel Sjölund (8/1) [86.Ville Taulo (1/0)], Alexei Eremenko jr. (21/10), Paulus Henrik Roiha (13/3) [59.Juho Antti Mäkelä (3/0)]. Trainer: Jyrki Heliskoski (6).

Goals: Daniel Sjölund (7), Kari Arkivuo (59).

663. 21.01.2006 **SAUDI ARABIA - FINLAND** **1-1(0-0)** International Tournament

„Prince Faisal Bin Fahd" Stadium, Riyadh; Referee: Nasser Al Enezi (Kuwait); Attendance: 3,000

FIN: Henri Sillanpää (3/0), Ari Nyman (9/0) [82.Veli Lampi (1/0)], Juha Pasoja (7/0), Toni Kuivasto (63/1), Tuomo Könönen (5/0), Juuso Kangaskorpi (5/0) [82.Ville Taulo (2/0)], Tuomas Uusimäki (2/0), Jari Ilola (22/1) [88.Antti Okkonen (12/0)], Kari Arkivuo (2/1), Jari Olavi Litmanen (Cap) (99/25) [73.Juho Antti Mäkelä (4/0)], Paulus Henrik Roiha (14/4) [90.Jukka Sauso (3/0)]. Trainer: Roy Hodgson (England, 1).

Goal: Paulus Henrik Roiha (87).

664. 25.01.2006 **KOREA REPUBLIC - FINLAND** **1-0(0-0)** International Tournament

„Prince Faisal Bin Fahd" Stadium, Riyadh; Referee: Abdul Rahman Al Amri (Saudi Arabia); Attendance: 200

FIN: Henri Sillanpää (4/0), Ari Nyman (10/0), Juha Pasoja (8/0) [46.Jari Ilola (23/1)], Jukka Sauso (4/0), Tuomo Könönen (6/0), Antti Okkonen (13/0) [69.Juuso Kangaskorpi (6/0)], Tuomas Uusimäki (3/0) [69.Ville Taulo (3/0)], Markus Heikkinen (21/0), Kari Arkivuo (3/1) [83.Jussi Kujala (2/0)], Jari Olavi Litmanen (Cap) (**100**/25) [83.Keijo Huusko (7/2)], Juho Antti Mäkelä (5/0) [60.Paulus Henrik Roiha (15/4)]. Trainer: Roy Hodgson (England, 2).

665. 18.02.2006 **JAPAN - FINLAND** **2-0(0-0)** Kirin Challenge Cup

ECOPA Stadium, Shizuoka; Referee: Lee Gi-Young (Korea Republic); Attendance: 40,702

FIN: Mikko Kavén (15/0), Ari Nyman (11/0), Juha Pasoja (9/0) [87.Jukka Sauso (5/0)], Toni Kuivasto (Cap) (64/1), Toni Kallio (19/1), Tuomas Haapala (2/0), Jari Ilola (24/1) [70.Tuomas Uusimäki (4/0)], Kari Arkivuo (4/1) [80.Juuso Kangaskorpi (7/0)], Pekka Lagerblom (9/0) [80.Veli Lampi (2/0)], Daniel Sjölund (9/1) [75.Jussi Kujala (3/0)], Keijo Huusko (8/2) [87.Tero Taipale (1/0)]. Trainer: Roy Hodgson (England, 3).

666. 28.02.2006 **FINLAND - KAZAKHSTAN** **0-0; 1-3 on penalties** Cyprus Tournament

Stádio GSZ, Lárnaka (Cyprus); Referee: Leontios Trattou (Cyprus); Attendance: 100

FIN: Peter Enckelman (7/0), Ari Nyman (12/0) [64.Veli Lampi (3/0)], Juha Pasoja (10/0), Miika Koppinen (18/0), Toni Kallio (20/1), Pekka Lagerblom (10/0) [83.Mika Väyrynen (19/0)], Tuomas Haapala (3/0) [73.Juho Antti Mäkelä (6/0)], Tuomas Uusimäki (5/0), Kari Arkivuo (5/1), Paulus Henrik Roiha (16/4), Jonatan Lillebror Johansson (Cap) (69/12) [*sent off 78*]. Trainer: Roy Hodgson (England, 4).

Penalties: Paulus Henrik Roiha (miss), Juha Pasoja (miss), Mika Väyrynen, Toni Kallio (miss).

667. 01.03.2006 **FINLAND - BELARUS** **2-2(0-1,2-2); 5-4 on penalties** Cyprus Tournament

Stádio Pafiako, Páphos (Cyprus); Referee: Robert Kranjc (Slovenia); Attendance: 120

FIN: Jussi Jääskeläinen (26/0), Petri Pasanen (29/1), Sami Hyypiä (75/4), Toni Kuivasto (65/1), Hannu Tihinen (47/4), Joonas Einari Kolkka (67/11), Mika Väyrynen (20/0), Aki Riihilahti (63/11), Peter Kopteff (38/1), Jari Olavi Litmanen (Cap) (101/25), Mikael Kaj Forssell (39/16). Trainer: Roy Hodgson (England, 5).

Goals: Aki Riihilahti (82), Mikael Kaj Forssell (90).

Penalties: Jari Olavi Litmanen, Mikael Kaj Forssell, Petri Pasanen, Aki Riihilahti, Mika Väyrynen.

668. 25.05.2006 **SWEDEN - FINLAND** **0-0**

Ullevi Stadion, Göteborg; Referee: Grzegorz Gilewski (Poland); Attendance: 25,754

FIN: Jussi Jääskeläinen (27/0), Petri Pasanen (30/1) [46.Juha Pasoja (11/0)], Toni Kuivasto (66/1), Hannu Tihinen (48/4), Toni Kallio (21/1), Jari Ilola (25/1) [53.Pekka Lagerblom (11/0)], Markus Heikkinen (22/0) [77.Janne Saarinen (41/0)], Joonas Einari Kolkka (68/11) [89.Roni Porokara (1/0)], Jari Olavi Litmanen (Cap) (102/25), Jonatan Lillebror Johansson (70/12) [66.Peter Kopteff (39/1)], Alexei Eremenko jr. (22/10) [77.Mikael Kaj Forssell (40/16)]. Trainer: Roy Hodgson (England, 6).

669. 16.08.2006 **FINLAND – NORTHERN IRELAND** **1-2(0-1)**

Olympiastadion, Helsinki; Referee: Michael Svendsen (Denmark); Attendance: 12,500

FIN: Jussi Jääskeläinen (28/0), Toni Kallio (22/1), Sami Hyypiä (Cap) (76/4) [81.Juha Pasoja (12/0)], Hannu Tihinen (49/4), Petri Pasanen (31/1), Aki Riihilahti (64/11) [46.Mika Väyrynen (21/1)], Jari Ilola (26/1) [46.Jarkko Wiss (43/3)], Joonas Einari Kolkka (69/11) [74.Pekka Lagerblom (12/0)], Mika Nurmela (62/3) [74.Jonatan Lillebror Johansson (71/12)], Alexei Eremenko jr. (23/10), Mikael Kaj Forssell (41/16) [57.Shefki Kuqi (43/5)]. Trainer: Roy Hodgson (England, 7).

Goal: Mika Väyrynen (74).

670. 02.09.2006 **POLAND - FINLAND** **1-3(0-0)** 13th EC. Qualifiers
Stadion Zawisza, Bydgoszcz; Referee: Laurent Duhamel (France); Attendance: 17,000
FIN: Jussi Jääskeläinen (29/0), Petri Pasanen (32/1), Sami Hyypiä (77/4), Hannu Tihinen (50/4), Toni Kallio (23/1), Teemu Tainio (34/5), Markus Heikkinen (23/0), Mika Väyrynen (22/2), Jari Olavi Litmanen (Cap) (103/27) [87.Mikael Kaj Forssell (42/16)], Joonas Einari Kolkka (70/11) [79.Mika Nurmela (63/3)], Jonatan Lillebror Johansson (72/12) [67.Alexei Eremenko jr. (24/10)]. Trainer: Roy Hodgson (England, 8).
Goals: Jari Olavi Litmanen (54, 76 penalty), Mika Väyrynen (85).

671. 06.09.2006 **FINLAND - PORTUGAL** **1-1(1-1)** 13th EC. Qualifiers
Olympiastadion, Helsinki; Referee: Konrad Plautz (Austria); Attendance: 38,015
FIN: Jussi Jääskeläinen (30/0), Petri Pasanen (33/1), Sami Hyypiä (78/4), Hannu Tihinen (51/4), Toni Kallio (24/1), Teemu Tainio (35/5), Mika Väyrynen (23/2), Markus Heikkinen (24/0), Joonas Einari Kolkka (71/11) [82.Alexei Eremenko jr. (25/10)], Jari Olavi Litmanen (Cap) (104/27), Jonatan Lillebror Johansson (73/13) [64.Shefki Kuqi (44/5)]. Trainer: Roy Hodgson (England, 9).
Goal: Jonatan Lillebror Johansson (23).

672. 07.10.2006 **ARMENIA - FINLAND** **0-0** 13th EC. Qualifiers
„Vazgen Sargsyan" Hanrapetakan Stadium, Yerevan; Referee: Damir Skomina (Slovenia); Attendance: 6,000
FIN: Jussi Jääskeläinen (31/0), Petri Pasanen (34/1), Sami Hyypiä (79/4), Hannu Tihinen (52/4), Toni Kallio (25/1), Markus Heikkinen (25/0), Mika Väyrynen (24/2) [74.Mika Nurmela (64/3)], Jari Olavi Litmanen (Cap) (105/27), Joonas Einari Kolkka (72/11), Shefki Kuqi (45/5) [66.Mikael Kaj Forssell (43/16)], Jonatan Lillebror Johansson (74/13) [84.Aki Riihilahti (65/11)]. Trainer: Roy Hodgson (England, 10).

673. 11.10.2006 **KAZAKHSTAN - FINLAND** **0-2(0-1)** 13th EC. Qualifiers
Tsentralny Stadium, Almaty; Referee: Athanasios Briákos (Greece); Attendance: 17,863
FIN: Jussi Jääskeläinen (32/0), Petri Pasanen (35/1), Sami Hyypiä (80/5), Hannu Tihinen (53/4), Toni Kallio (26/1), Jari Ilola (27/1), Mika Väyrynen (25/2) [90+2.Aki Riihilahti (66/11)], Mika Nurmela (65/3), Jari Olavi Litmanen (Cap) (106/28), Joonas Einari Kolkka (73/11), Mikael Kaj Forssell (44/16) [72.Shefki Kuqi (46/5)]. Trainer: Roy Hodgson (England, 11).
Goals: Jari Olavi Litmanen (27), Sami Hyypiä (65).

674. 15.11.2006 **FINLAND - ARMENIA** **1-0(1-0)** 13th EC. Qualifiers
Finnair Stadion, Helsinki; Referee: Craig Thomson (Scotland); Attendance: 10,000
FIN: Jussi Jääskeläinen (33/0), Toni Kallio (27/1), Sami Hyypiä (Cap) (81/5), Hannu Tihinen (54/4), Ari Nyman (13/0), Markus Heikkinen (26/0), Mika Väyrynen (26/2) [46.Jari Ilola (28/1)], Mika Nurmela (66/4), Joonas Einari Kolkka (74/11), Alexei Eremenko jr. (26/10) [88.Shefki Kuqi (47/5)], Jonatan Lillebror Johansson (75/13). Trainer: Roy Hodgson (England, 12).
Goal: Mika Nurmela (8).

675. 28.03.2007 **AZERBAIJAN - FINLAND** **1-0(0-0)** 13th EC. Qualifiers
„Tofiq Bəhramov" adına Respublika Stadionu, Bakı; Referee: Domenico Messina (Italy); Attendance: 14,000
FIN: Jussi Jääskeläinen (34/0), Toni Kallio (28/1), Sami Hyypiä (82/5), Hannu Tihinen (55/4), Petri Pasanen (36/1), Markus Heikkinen (27/0), Mika Väyrynen (27/2), Jari Olavi Litmanen (Cap) (107/28), Joonas Einari Kolkka (75/11) [85.Shefki Kuqi (48/5)], Alexei Eremenko jr. (27/10), Jonatan Lillebror Johansson (76/13) [86.Mikael Kaj Forssell (45/16)]. Trainer: Roy Hodgson (England, 13).

676. 02.06.2007 **FINLAND - SERBIA** **0-2(0-1)** 13th EC. Qualifiers
Olympiastadion, Helsinki; Referee: Manuel Enrique Mejuto González (Spain); Attendance: 33,615
FIN: Jussi Jääskeläinen (35/0), Toni Kallio (29/1), Sami Hyypiä (83/5), Hannu Tihinen (56/4), Petri Pasanen (37/1), Markus Heikkinen (28/0), Mika Väyrynen (28/2), Teemu Tainio (36/5) [28.Joonas Einari Kolkka (76/11)], Jari Ilola (29/1), Shefki Kuqi (49/5) [70.Jari Olavi Litmanen (108/28)], Mikael Kaj Forssell (46/16) [62.Jonatan Lillebror Johansson (77/13)]. Trainer: Roy Hodgson (England, 14).

677. 06.06.2007 **FINLAND - BELGIUM** **2-0(1-0)** 13th EC. Qualifiers
Olympiastadion, Helsinki; Referee: Michael Riley (England); Attendance: 34,188
FIN: Jussi Jääskeläinen (36/0), Toni Kallio (30/1), Petri Pasanen (38/1), Ari Nyman (14/0), Hannu Tihinen (57/4), Markus Heikkinen (29/0), Mika Väyrynen (29/2), Roman Eremenko (1/0), Joonas Einari Kolkka (77/11) [88.Mika Nurmela (67/4)], Alexei Eremenko jr. (28/11) [89.Mikael Kaj Forssell (47/16)], Jonatan Lillebror Johansson (78/14). Trainer: Roy Hodgson (England, 15).
Goals: Jonatan Lillebror Johansson (28), Alexei Eremenko jr. (71).

678. 22.08.2007 **FINLAND - KAZAKHSTAN** **2-1(1-1)** 13th EC. Qualifiers
Ratinan Stadion, Tampere; Referee: Viktor Kassai (Hungary); Attendance: 13,000
FIN: Jussi Jääskeläinen (37/0), Toni Kallio (31/1), Sami Hyypiä (84/5), Hannu Tihinen (58/4), Petri Pasanen (39/1), Roman Eremenko (2/0) [46.Daniel Sjölund (10/1)], Markus Heikkinen (30/0), Joonas Einari Kolkka (78/11) [88.Mika Nurmela (68/4)], Teemu Tainio (37/6) [76.Aki Riihilahti (67/11)], Alexei Eremenko jr. (29/12), Jonatan Lillebror Johansson (79/14). Trainer: Roy Hodgson (England, 16).
Goals: Alexei Eremenko jr. (13), Teemu Tainio (61).

679. 08.09.2007 **SERBIA - FINLAND** **0-0** 13th EC. Qualifiers
Stadion Crvena zvezda, Beograd; Referee: Eric Braamhaar (Netherlands); Attendance: 15,000
FIN: Jussi Jääskeläinen (38/0), Petri Pasanen (40/1), Sami Hyypiä (85/5), Hannu Tihinen (59/4), Toni Kuivasto (67/1), Mika Nurmela (69/4), Teemu Tainio (38/6), Markus Heikkinen (31/0), Alexei Eremenko jr. (30/12) [74.Mikael Kaj Forssell (48/16)], Daniel Sjölund (11/1), Jonatan Lillebror Johansson (80/14) [78.Jarkko Wiss (44/3)]. Trainer: Roy Hodgson (England, 17).

680. 12.09.2007 **FINLAND - POLAND** **0-0** 13th EC. Qualifiers
Olympiastadion, Helsinki; Referee: Herbert Fandel (Germany); Attendance: 34,000
FIN: Jussi Jääskeläinen (39/0), Toni Kuivasto (68/1), Sami Hyypiä (86/5), Hannu Tihinen (60/4), Petri Pasanen (41/1), Daniel Sjölund (12/1), Markus Heikkinen (32/0) [90+1.Jarkko Wiss (45/3)], Teemu Tainio (39/6), Joonas Einari Kolkka (79/11), Alexei Eremenko jr. (31/12), Jonatan Lillebror Johansson (81/14) [72.Mikael Kaj Forssell (49/16)]. Trainer: Roy Hodgson (England, 18).

681. 13.10.2007 **BELGIUM - FINLAND** **0-0** 13th EC. Qualifiers
Stade "Roi Baudoin", Bruxelles; Referee: Costas Kapitanis (Cyprus); Attendance: 4,131
FIN: Jussi Jääskeläinen (40/0), Sami Hyypiä (87/5), Petri Pasanen (42/1), Hannu Tihinen (61/4), Toni Kallio (32/1), Roman Eremenko (3/0), Aki Riihilahti (68/11), Jonatan Lillebror Johansson (82/14) [90.Shefki Kuqi (50/5)], Joonas Einari Kolkka (80/11), Alexei Eremenko jr. (32/12), Daniel Sjölund (13/1) [90+2.Mika Nurmela (70/4)]. Trainer: Roy Hodgson (England, 19).

682. 17.10.2007 **FINLAND - SPAIN** **0-0**

Olympiastadion, Helsinki; Referee: Stéphane Bré (France); Attendance: 8,000

FIN: Antti Niemi (67/0), Petri Pasanen (43/1), Sami Hyypiä (88/5) [47.Hannu Tihinen (62/4)], Mika Väyrynen (30/2) [83.Jari Ilola (30/1)], Toni Kallio (33/1), Toni Kuivasto (69/1), Roman Eremenko (4/0), Aki Riihilahti (69/11) [49.Mika Nurmela (71/4)], Joonas Einari Kolkka (81/11) [75.Veli Lampi (4/0)], Jonatan Lillebror Johansson (83/14), Shefki Kuqi (51/5) [64.Alexei Eremenko jr. (33/12)]. Trainer: Roy Hodgson (England, 20).

683. 17.11.2007 **FINLAND - AZERBAIJAN** **2-1(0-0)** 13th EC. Qualifiers

Olympiastadion, Helsinki; Referee: Alain Hamer (Luxembourg); Attendance: 10,325

FIN: Jussi Jääskeläinen (41/0), Petri Pasanen (44/1), Sami Hyypiä (89/5), Hannu Tihinen (63/4), Toni Kallio (34/1) [66.Mika Väyrynen (31/2)], Joonas Einari Kolkka (82/11), Roman Eremenko (5/0) [80.Shefki Kuqi (52/6)], Teemu Tainio (40/6), Daniel Sjölund (14/1), Mikael Kaj Forssell (50/17), Jonatan Lillebror Johansson (84/14) [59.Jari Olavi Litmanen (109/28)]. Trainer: Roy Hodgson (England, 21).

Goals: Mikael Kaj Forssell (79), Shefki Kuqi (86).

684. 21.11.2007 **PORTUGAL - FINLAND** **0-0** 13th EC. Qualifiers

Estádio do Dragão, Porto; Referee: Luboš Micheľ (Slovakia); Attendance: 50,000

FIN: Jussi Jääskeläinen (42/0), Sami Hyypiä (90/5), Toni Kallio (35/1), Petri Pasanen (45/1), Hannu Tihinen (64/4), Markus Heikkinen (33/0), Joonas Einari Kolkka (83/11) [75.Jonatan Lillebror Johansson (85/14)], Jari Olavi Litmanen (110/28) [67.Mika Väyrynen (32/2)], Daniel Sjölund (15/1), Teemu Tainio (41/6) [69.Roman Eremenko (6/0)], Mikael Kaj Forssell (51/17). Trainer: Roy Hodgson (England, 22).

685. 06.02.2008 **GREECE - FINLAND** **2-1(0-0)**

Stádio Neo GSP, Nicosia (Cyprus); Referee: Panicos Kaillis (Cyprus); Attendance: 500

FIN: Peter Enckelman (8/0), Markus Olof Halsti (1/0), Ari Nyman (15/0) [78.Veli Lampi (5/0)], Toni Kallio (36/1), Juha Pasoja (13/0), Markus Heikkinen (34/0), Mika Väyrynen (33/2), Alexei Eremenko jr. (34/12), Jari Olavi Litmanen (111/29) [70.Roni Porokara (2/0)], Jonatan Lillebror Johansson (86/14) [76.Kari Arkivuo (6/1)], Mikael Kaj Forssell (52/17). Trainer: Stuart William Baxter (Scotland, 1).

Goal: Jari Olavi Litmanen (66).

686. 26.03.2008 **BULGARIA - FINLAND** **2-1(0-1)**

Nationalen stadion "Vasil Levski", Sofia; Referee: Alexandru Dan Tudor (Romania); Attendance: 2,500

FIN: Peter Enckelman (9/0), Veli Lampi (6/0) [79.Ari Nyman (16/0)], Toni Kuivasto (70/1), Juha Pasoja (14/0), Toni Kallio (37/1), Jari Olavi Litmanen (Cap) (112/30) [46.Antti Pohja (20/2)], Teemu Tainio (42/6) [73.Mika Väyrynen (34/2)], Joonas Einari Kolkka (84/11), Roman Eremenko (7/0) [84.Janne Saarinen (42/0)], Jonatan Lillebror Johansson (87/14), Mikael Kaj Forssell (53/17) [61.Fredrik Svanbäck (2/0)]. Trainer: Stuart William Baxter (Scotland, 2).

Goal: Jari Olavi Litmanen (22 penalty).

687. 29.05.2008 **TURKEY - FINLAND** **2-0(1-0)**

MSV-Arena, Duisburg (Germany); Referee: Thorsten Kinhöfer (Germany); Attendance: 15,036

FIN: Peter Enckelman (10/0) [46.Otto Fredrikson (1/0)], Ari Nyman (17/0), Toni Kallio (38/1) [82.Niklas Moisander (1/0)], Juha Pasoja (15/0) [53.Veli Lampi (7/0)], Mika Väyrynen (35/2), Markus Heikkinen (35/0) [61.Jonatan Lillebror Johansson (88/14)], Toni Kuivasto (Cap) (71/1), Roman Eremenko (8/0), Joonas Einari Kolkka (85/11), Alexei Eremenko jr. (35/12) [61.Jari Olavi Litmanen (113/30)], Mikael Kaj Forssell (54/17) [78.Berat Sadik (1/0)]. Trainer: Stuart William Baxter (Scotland, 3).

688. 02.06.2008 **FINLAND - BELARUS** **1-1(0-0)**

Veritas Stadion, Turku; Referee: Damir Skomina (Slovenia); Attendance: 9,000

FIN: Niki Mäenpää (1/0) [69.Peter Enckelman (11/0)], Ari Nyman (18/0), Veli Lampi (8/0), Toni Kallio (39/2), Toni Kuivasto (72/1), Jonatan Lillebror Johansson (89/14), Roman Eremenko (9/0), Teemu Tainio (43/6) [81.Markus Heikkinen (36/0)], Jari Olavi Litmanen (Cap) (114/30) [55.Mika Väyrynen (36/2)], Joonas Einari Kolkka (86/11), Mikael Kaj Forssell (55/17) [81.Berat Sadik (2/0)]. Trainer: Stuart William Baxter (Scotland, 4).

Goal: Toni Kallio (90+4).

689. 20.08.2008 **FINLAND - ISRAEL** **2-0(1-0)**

Ratinan Stadion, Tampere; Referee: Jóhannes Valgeirsson (Iceland); Attendance: 4,929

FIN: Jussi Jääskeläinen (43/0) [46.Niki Mäenpää (2/0)], Veli Lampi (9/0), Sami Hyypiä (91/5) [46.Toni Kuivasto (73/1)], Toni Kallio (Cap) (40/2), Hanu Tihinen (65/4), Mika Väyrynen (37/2) [73.Jari Olavi Litmanen (115/30)], Roman Eremenko (10/0), Jonatan Lillebror Johansson (90/16), Markus Heikkinen (37/0), Joonas Einari Kolkka (87/11), Mikael Kaj Forssell (56/17) [78.Antti Pohja (21/2)]. Trainer: Stuart William Baxter (Scotland, 5).

Goals: Jonatan Lillebror Johansson (42, 88).

690. 06.09.2008 **FINLAND - GERMANY** **3-3(2-2)** 19th FIFA WC. Qualifiers

Olympiastadion, Helsinki; Referee: Viktor Kassai (Hungary); Attendance: 37,150

FIN: Jussi Jääskeläinen (44/0), Veli Lampi (10/0), Petri Pasanen (46/1), Sami Hyypiä (Cap) (92/5), Toni Kallio (41/2), Roman Eremenko (11/0), Markus Heikkinen (38/0), Jonatan Lillebror Johansson (91/17), Mika Väyrynen (38/3) [75.Njazi Kuqi (3/3)], Joonas Einari Kolkka (88/11), Mikael Kaj Forssell (57/17) [41.Daniel Sjölund (16/2)]. Trainer: Stuart William Baxter (Scotland, 6).

Goals: Jonatan Lillebror Johansson (33), Mika Väyrynen (43), Daniel Sjölund (53).

691. 11.10.2008 **FINLAND - AZERBAIJAN** **1-0(0-0)** 19th FIFA WC. Qualifiers

Olympiastadion, Helsinki; Referee: William Collum (Scotland); Attendance: 22,124

FIN: Jussi Jaaskelainen (45/0), Petri Pasanen (47/1), Toni Kallio (42/2), Sami Hyypiä (Cap) (93/5), Hannu Tihinen (66/4), Mika Väyrynen (39/3), Roman Eremenko (12/0) [79.Jari Olavi Litmanen (116/30)], Teemu Tainio (44/6) [90+2.Markus Heikkinen (39/0)], Mikael Kaj Forssell (58/18), Paulus Henrik Roiha (17/4) [62.Antti Pohja (22/2)], Daniel Sjölund (17/2). Trainer: Stuart William Baxter (Scotland, 7).

Goal: Mikael Kaj Forssell (61 penalty).

692. 15.10.2008 **RUSSIA - FINLAND** **3-0(1-0)** 19th FIFA WC. Qualifiers

Lokomotiv Stadium, Moskva; Referee: Kyros Vassaras (Greece); Attendance: 28,000

FIN: Jussi Jääskeläinen (46/0), Petri Pasanen (48/1), Veli Lampi (11/0), Sami Hyypiä (Cap) (94/5), Hannu Tihinen (67/4), Joonas Einari Kolkka (89/11), Markus Heikkinen (40/0), Roman Eremenko (13/0) [66.Teemu Tainio (45/6)], Mika Väyrynen (40/3) [69.Paulus Henrik Roiha (18/4)], Daniel Sjölund (18/2) [85.Jari Olavi Litmanen (117/30)], Mikael Kaj Forssell (59/18). Trainer: Stuart William Baxter (Scotland, 8).

693. 19.11.2008 **SWITZERLAND - FINLAND** **1-0(0-0)**
AFG Arena, St. Gallen; Referee: Alexey Kulbakov (Russia); Attendance: 11,500
FIN: Jussi Jääskeläinen (47/0) [46.Otto Fredrikson (2/0)], Veli Lampi (12/0), Hannu Tihinen (68/4), Sami Hyypia (Cap) (95/5), Niklas Moisander (2/0) [69.Toni Kallio (43/2)], Kasper Woldemar Hämäläinen (1/0) [46.Roman Eremenko (14/0)], Markus Heikkinen (41/0), Teemu Tainio (46/6) [90.Antti Pohja (23/2)], Joonas Einari Kolkka (90/11) [78.Roni Porokara (3/0)], Mika Väyrynen (41/3) [64.Jari Olavi Litmanen (118/30)], Niklas Henrikki Tarvajärvi (3/0). Trainer: Stuart William Baxter (Scotland, 9).

694. 04.02.2009 **JAPAN - FINLAND** **5-1(3-0)**
National Stadium, Tokyo; Referee: Huang Junjie (China P.R.); Attendance: 34,532
FIN: Tomi Maanoja (1/0), Joni Aho (1/0), Toni Kuivasto (74/1), Markus Olof Halsti (2/0), Tuomo Turunen (1/0) [54.Jukka Raitala (1/0)], Kari Arkivuo (7/1) [84.Përparim Hetemaj (1/0)], Jussi Kujala (4/0) [46.Mehmet Hetemaj (1/0)], Tim Sparv (1/0), Roni Porokara (4/1), Jari Olavi Litmanen (119/30) [67.Teemu Pukki (1/0)], Niklas Henrikki Tarvajärvi (4/0) [76.Jarno Parikka (1/0)]. Trainer: Stuart William Baxter (Scotland, 10).
Goal: Roni Porokara (50).

695. 11.02.2009 **PORTUGAL - FINLAND** **1-0(0-0)**
Estádio Algarve, Faro/Loulé; Referee: Carlo Bertolini (Switzerland); Attendance: 19,834
FIN: Jussi Jääskeläinen (48/0) [46.Niki Mäenpää (3/0)], Petri Pasanen (49/1), Sami Hyypiä (Cap) (96/5), Hannu Tihinen (69/4), Toni Kallio (44/2), Roman Eremenko (15/0), Markus Heikkinen (42/0), Jari Olavi Litmanen (120/30) [46.Daniel Sjölund (19/2)], Joonas Einari Kolkka (91/11) [80.Juha Hakola (1/0)], Mikael Kaj Forssell (60/18) [46.Shefki Kuqi (53/6)], Jonatan Lillebror Johansson (92/17). Trainer: Stuart William Baxter (Scotland, 11).

696. 28.03.2009 **WALES - FINLAND** **0-2(0-1)** 19th FIFA WC. Qualifiers
Millennium Stadium, Cardiff; Referee: Eduardo Iturralde González (Spain); Attendance: 22,604
FIN: Jussi Jääskeläinen (49/0), Petri Pasanen (50/1), Sami Hyypiä (Cap) (97/5), Hannu Tihinen (70/4), Toni Kallio (45/2), Alexei Eremenko jr. (36/12) [78.Daniel Sjölund (20/2)], Roman Eremenko (16/0), Jari Olavi Litmanen (121/30) [90.Roni Porokara (5/1)], Markus Heikkinen (43/0), Mikael Kaj Forssell (61/18) [89.Shefki Kuqi (54/7)], Jonatan Lillebror Johansson (93/18). Trainer: Stuart William Baxter (Scotland, 12).
Goals: Jonatan Lillebror Johansson (42), Shefki Kuqi (90+1).

697. 01.04.2009 **NORWAY - FINLAND** **3-2(0-1)**
Ullevaal Stadion, Oslo; Referee: Robert Styles (England); Attendance: 16,239
FIN: Niki Mäenpää (4/0), Petri Pasanen (51/1), Ari Nyman (19/0) [67.Toni Kuivasto (75/1)], Hannu Tihinen (71/4), Toni Kallio (46/2), Roman Eremenko (17/0), Jari Olavi Litmanen (Cap) (122/30) [45.Alexei Eremenko jr. (37/13)], Markus Heikkinen (44/0) [81.Tim Sparv (2/0)], Roni Porokara (6/1) [71.Daniel Sjölund (21/2)], Mikael Kaj Forssell (62/18) [77.Shefki Kuqi (55/7)], Jonatan Lillebror Johansson (94/19). Trainer: Stuart William Baxter (Scotland, 13).
Goal: Jonatan Lillebror Johansson (39), Alexei Eremenko jr. (90+1).

698. 06.06.2009 **FINLAND - LIECHTENSTEIN** **2-1(1-1)** 19th FIFA WC. Qualifiers
Olympiastadion, Helsinki; Referee: Libor Kovarik (Czech Republic); Attendance: 20,319
FIN: Jussi Jääskeläinen (50/0), Petri Pasanen (52/1) [46.Veli Lampi (13/0)], Sami Hyypiä (Cap) (98/5), Hannu Tihinen (72/4), Toni Kallio (47/2), Roman Eremenko (18/0), Teemu Tainio (47/6) [67.Markus Heikkinen (45/0)], Jari Olavi Litmanen (123/30) [72.Shefki Kuqi (56/7)], Alexei Eremenko jr. (38/13), Mikael Kaj Forssell (63/19), Jonatan Lillebror Johansson (95/20). Trainer: Stuart William Baxter (Scotland, 14).
Goal: Mikael Kaj Forssell (33), Jonatan Lillebror Johansson (71).

699. 10.06.2009 **FINLAND - RUSSIA** **0-3(0-1)** 19th FIFA WC. Qualifiers
Olympiastadion, Helsinki; Referee: Konrad Plautz (Austria); Attendance: 37,028
FIN: Jussi Jääskeläinen (51/0), Petri Pasanen (53/1), Sami Hyypiä (Cap) (99/5), Hannu Tihinen (73/4), Toni Kallio (48/2) [54.Niklas Moisander (3/0)], Roman Eremenko (19/0), Jari Olavi Litmanen (124/30) [69.Teemu Tainio (48/6)], Markus Heikkinen (46/0), Alexei Eremenko jr. (39/13) [61.Joonas Einari Kolkka (92/11)], Mikael Kaj Forssell (64/19), Jonatan Lillebror Johansson (96/20). Trainer: Stuart William Baxter (Scotland, 15).

700. 12.08.2009 **SWEDEN - FINLAND** **1-0(1-0)**
Råsundastadion, Stockholm; Referee: Freddy Fautrel (France); Attendance: 15,212
FIN: Otto Fredrikson (3/0), Veli Lampi (14/0), Petri Pasanen (54/1), Sami Hyypiä (Cap) (**100**/5), Niklas Moisander (4/0), Roni Porokara (7/1) [65.Kasper Woldemar Hämäläinen (2/0)], Roman Eremenko (20/0) [83.Markus Heikkinen (47/0)], Jari Olavi Litmanen (125/30) [46.Alexei Eremenko jr. (40/13)], Tim Sparv (3/0) [83.Teemu Tainio (49/6)], Joonas Einari Kolkka (93/11) [46.Përparim Hetemaj (2/0)], Mikael Kaj Forssell (65/19) [77.Berat Sadik (3/0)]. Trainer: Stuart William Baxter (Scotland, 16).

701. 05.09.2009 **AZERBAIJAN - FINLAND** **1-2(0-0)** 19th FIFA WC. Qualifiers
City Stadium, Länkäran; Referee: Stelios Trifonos (Cyprus); Attendance: 12,000
FIN: Jussi Jääskeläinen (52/0), Petri Pasanen (55/1), Hannu Tihinen (Cap) (74/5), Niklas Moisander (5/0), Veli Lampi (15/0), Roman Eremenko (21/0), Teemu Tainio (50/6) [46.Jari Olavi Litmanen (126/30)], Markus Heikkinen (48/0), Jonatan Lillebror Johansson (97/21), Alexei Eremenko jr. (41/13), Shefki Kuqi (57/7) [74.Daniel Sjölund (22/2); 84.Joonas Einari Kolkka (94/11)]. Trainer: Stuart William Baxter (Scotland, 17).
Goals: Hannu Tihinen (74), Jonatan Lillebror Johansson (85).

702. 09.09.2009 **LIECHTENSTEIN - FINLAND** **1-1(0-0)** 19th FIFA WC. Qualifiers
Rheinpark, Vaduz; Referee: Novo Panić (Bosnia-Herzegovina); Attendance: 3,132
FIN: Jussi Jääskeläinen (53/0), Petri Pasanen (56/1), Sami Hyypiä (Cap) (101/5), Hannu Tihinen (75/5), Niklas Moisander (6/0), Roman Eremenko (22/0), Jari Olavi Litmanen (127/31) [82.Shefki Kuqi (58/7)], Markus Heikkinen (49/0), Jonatan Lillebror Johansson (98/21), Alexei Eremenko jr. (42/13), Berat Sadik (4/0) [59.Joonas Einari Kolkka (95/11)]. Trainer: Stuart William Baxter (Scotland, 18).
Goal: Jari Olavi Litmanen (74 penalty).

703. 10.10.2009 **FINLAND - WALES** **2-1(1-1)** 19th FIFA WC. Qualifiers
Olympiastadion, Helsinki; Referee: Milorad Mažić (Serbia); Attendance: 14,000
FIN: Jussi Jääskeläinen (54/0), Petri Pasanen (57/1), Sami Hyypiä (Cap) (102/5), Hannu Tihinen (76/5), Niklas Moisander (7/1), Roman Eremenko (23/0), Jari Olavi Litmanen (128/31) [90+2.Alexei Eremenko jr. (43/13)], Tim Sparv (4/0), Jonatan Lillebror Johansson (99/21) [88.Shefki Kuqi (59/7)], Roni Porokara (8/2), Joonas Einari Kolkka (96/11) [68.Kasper Woldemar Hämäläinen (3/0)]. Trainer: Stuart William Baxter (Scotland, 19).
Goals: Roni Porokara (5), Niklas Moisander (77).

704. 14.10.2009 **GERMANY - FINLAND** **1-1(0-1)** 19th FIFA WC. Qualifiers
HSH Nordbank-Arena, Hamburg; Referee: Howard Melton Webb (England); Attendance: 51,500
FIN: Jussi Jääskeläinen (55/0), Veli Lampi (16/0), Markus Heikkinen (50/0), Sami Hyypiä (Cap) (103/5), Niklas Moisander (8/1), Kasper Woldemar Hämäläinen (4/0) [66.Joonas Einari Kolkka (97/11)], Tim Sparv (5/0), Roman Eremenko (24/0), Roni Porokara (9/2) [72.Shefki Kuqi (60/7)], Jari Olavi Litmanen (129/31) [87.Ari Nyman (20/0)], Jonatan Lillebror Johansson (**100**/22). Trainer: Stuart William Baxter (Scotland, 20).
Goal: Jonatan Lillebror Johansson (11).

705. 18.01.2010 **FINLAND – KOREA REPUBLIC** **0-2(0-1)**
Estadio de Atletismo Ciudad de Málaga, Málaga (Spain); Referee: David Fernández Borbalán (Spain); Attendance: 270
FIN: Otto Fredrikson (4/0), Joni Aho (2/0), Jani Lyyski (1/0), Ari Nyman (21/0), Joel Perovuo (1/0) [85.Paulus Arajuuri (1/0)], Roni Porokara (10/2) [68.Mika Ojala (1/0)], Markus Olof Halsti (3/0), Juska Samuli Savolainen (1/0), Jari Olavi Litmanen (Cap) (130/31) [60.Sebastian Sorsa (1/0)], Jonatan Lillebror Johansson (101/22) [60.Kasper Woldemar Hämäläinen (5/0)], Hermanni Vuorinen (1/0) [74.Timo Furuholm (1/0)]. Trainer: Stuart William Baxter (Scotland, 21).

706. 03.03.2010 **MALTA - FINLAND** **1-2(1-0)**
Ta'Qali National Stadium, Attard; Referee: Mauro Bergonzi (Italy); Attendance: 1,050
FIN: Peter Enckelman (12/0) [46.Otto Fredrikson (5/0)], Jukka Raitala (2/0), Toni Kallio (49/2) [57.Jani Lyyski (2/0)], Veli Lampi (17/0), Niklas Moisander (9/1), Roman Eremenko (25/1), Tim Sparv (6/0) [46.Mika Väyrynen (42/4)], Roni Porokara (11/2), Kasper Woldemar Hämäläinen (6/0) [76.Joonas Einari Kolkka (98/11)], Jari Olavi Litmanen (Cap) (131/31) [46.Teemu Tainio (51/6)], Jonatan Lillebror Johansson (102/22) [83.Teemu Pukki (2/0)]. Trainer: Stuart William Baxter (Scotland, 22).
Goals: Roman Eremenko (67 penalty), Mika Väyrynen (70).

707. 21.05.2010 **ESTONIA - FINLAND** **2-0(1-0)**
A. Le Coq Arena, Tallinn; Referee: István Vad II (Hungary); Attendance: 5,650
FIN: Jukka Lehtovaara (1/0) [46.Lukas Hradecky (1/0)], Ari Nyman (22/0), Veli Lampi (18/0), Niklas Moisander (10/1), Tim Sparv (7/0), Roni Porokara (12/2), Mehmet Hetemaj (2/0) [46.Mika Väyrynen (43/4)], Juska Samuli Savolainen (2/0) [46.Roman Eremenko (26/1)], Juho Antti Mäkelä (7/0) [46.Teemu Pukki (3/0)], Jari Olavi Litmanen (Cap) (132/31) [46.Markus Heikkinen (51/0)], Mika Ääritalo (1/0) [81.Mikael Kaj Forssell (66/19)]. Trainer: Stuart William Baxter (Scotland, 23).

708. 29.05.2010 **POLAND - FINLAND** **0-0**
Stadion Miejski, Kielce; Referee: Marius Ionuţ Avram (Romania); Attendance: 14,000
FIN: Otto Fredrikson (6/0), Kalle Parviainen (1/0), Veli Lampi (19/0) [82.Ville Jalasto (1/0)], Niklas Moisander (11/1), Roman Eremenko (27/1) [90.Tuomo Turunen (2/0)], Tim Sparv (8/0), Roni Porokara (13/2) [66.Mikael Kaj Forssell (67/19)], Kasper Woldemar Hämäläinen (7/0) [81.Joel Perovuo (2/0)], Markus Heikkinen (52/0), Jari Olavi Litmanen (Cap) (133/31) [71.Paulus Henrik Roiha (19/4)], Jonatan Lillebror Johansson (103/22). Trainer: Stuart William Baxter (Scotland, 24).

709. 11.08.2010 **FINLAND - BELGIUM** **1-0(1-0)**
Veritas Stadion, Turku; Referee: Alain Hamer (Luxembourg); Attendance: 7,451
FIN: Otto Fredrikson (7/0), Petri Pasanen (Cap) (58/1), Veli Lampi (20/0), Niklas Moisander (12/1), Roman Eremenko (28/1) [46.Teemu Tainio (52/6)], Tim Sparv (9/0), Alexei Eremenko jr. (44/13) [62.Daniel Sjölund (23/2)], Roni Porokara (14/3) [62.Jari Olavi Litmanen (134/31)], Kasper Woldemar Hämäläinen (8/0) [38.Mika Väyrynen (44/4)], Markus Heikkinen (53/0) [87.Jani Lyyski (3/0)], Mikael Kaj Forssell (68/19) [80.Paulus Henrik Roiha (20/4)]. Trainer: Stuart William Baxter (Scotland, 25).
Goal: Roni Porokara (13).

710. 03.09.2010 **MOLDOVA - FINLAND** **2-0(0-0)** 14th EC. Qualifiers
Stadionul Zimbru, Chişinău; Referee: Robert Małek (Poland); Attendance: 10,300
FIN: Otto Fredrikson (8/0), Petri Pasanen (59/1), Sami Hyypiä (Cap) (104/5) [*sent off 36*], Niklas Moisander (13/1), Roman Eremenko (29/1), Tim Sparv (10/0), Alexei Eremenko jr. (45/13) [81.Mikael Kaj Forssell (69/19)], Roni Porokara (15/3) [75.Mika Väyrynen (45/4)], Markus Heikkinen (54/0), Jari Olavi Litmanen (135/31) [46.Kasper Woldemar Hämäläinen (9/0)], Jonatan Lillebror Johansson (104/22). Trainer: Stuart William Baxter (Scotland, 26).

711. 07.09.2010 **NETHERLANDS - FINLAND** **2-1(1-1)** 14th EC. Qualifiers
Stadion Feijenoord, Rotterdam; Referee: Alexey Nikolaev (Russia); Attendance: 25,000
FIN: Otto Fredrikson (9/0), Petri Pasanen (Cap) (60/1), Veli Lampi (21/0), Niklas Moisander (14/1), Mika Väyrynen (46/4), Roman Eremenko (30/1), Tim Sparv (11/0), Kasper Woldemar Hämäläinen (10/0) [46.Roni Porokara (16/3)], Markus Heikkinen (55/0), Daniel Sjölund (24/2) [68.Jonatan Lillebror Johansson (105/22)], Mikael Kaj Forssell (70/20) [81.Alexei Eremenko jr. (46/13)]. Trainer: Stuart William Baxter (Scotland, 27).
Goal: Mikael Kaj Forssell (18).

712. 12.10.2010 **FINLAND - HUNGARY** **1-2(0-0)** 14th EC. Qualifiers
Olympiastadion, Helsinki; Referee: Alan Kelly (Republic of Ireland); Attendance: 18,532
FIN: Jussi Jääskeläinen (56/0), Petri Pasanen (61/1), Sami Hyypiä (Cap) (105/5), Niklas Moisander (15/1), Mika Väyrynen (47/4), Roman Eremenko (31/1), Tim Sparv (12/0) [72.Jari Olavi Litmanen (136/31)], Roni Porokara (17/3) [71.Alexei Eremenko jr. (47/13)], Markus Heikkinen (56/0), Daniel Sjölund (25/2) [81.Shefki Kuqi (61/7)], Mikael Kaj Forssell (71/21). Trainer: Stuart William Baxter (Scotland, 28).
Goal: Mikael Kaj Forssell (86).

713. 17.11.2010 **FINLAND – SAN MARINO** **8-0(1-0)** 14th EC. Qualifiers
Olympiastadion, Helsinki; Referee: Radek Matejek (Czech Republic); Attendance: 8,192
FIN: Otto Fredrikson (10/0), Petri Pasanen (Cap) (62/1), Veli Lampi (22/0), Niklas Moisander (16/1), Mika Väyrynen (48/5), Roman Eremenko (32/1), Alexei Eremenko jr. (48/13) [80.Shefki Kuqi (62/7)], Kasper Woldemar Hämäläinen (11/2) [70.Roni Porokara (18/4)], Markus Heikkinen (57/0), Daniel Sjölund (26/2) [46.Jari Olavi Litmanen (137/32)], Mikael Kaj Forssell (72/24). Trainer: Olavi Huttunen (1).
Goals: Mika Väyrynen (39), Kasper Woldemar Hämäläinen (49), Mikael Kaj Forssell (51, 59), Kasper Woldemar Hämäläinen (67), Jari Olavi Litmanen (71 penalty), Roni Porokara (73), Mikael Kaj Forssell (78).

714. 09.02.2011 **BELGIUM - FINLAND** **1-1(0-0)**
Stade "Jules Ottenstadion", Gentbrugge; Referee: Cyrille Zimmermann (Switzerland); Attendance: 12,800
FIN: Lukas Hradecky (2/0), Jukka Raitala (3/0), Veli Lampi (Cap) (23/0) [64.Hannu Jarl Johannes Patronen (1/0)], Niklas Moisander (17/1), Joona Toivio (1/0), Roman Eremenko (33/1), Tim Sparv (13/0) [83.Ilja Venäläinen (1/0)], Alexei Eremenko jr. (49/13) [56.Riku Olavi Riski (1/0)], Kasper Woldemar Hämäläinen (12/2) [65.Sebastian Mannström (1/0)], Përparim Hetemaj (3/0) [56.Roni Porokara (19/5)], Mikael Kaj Forssell (73/24) [65.Mika Ääritalo (2/0)]. Trainer: Markku Kanerva (1).
Goal: Roni Porokara (90+3).

715. 29.03.2011 **PORTUGAL - FINLAND** **2-0(1-0)**
Estádio Municipal, Aveiro; Referee: Stephan Studer (Switzerland); Attendance: 13,737
FIN: Otto Fredrikson (11/0), Petri Pasanen (Cap) (63/1), Kari Arkivuo (8/1), Jukka Raitala (4/0), Mika Väyrynen (49/5) [74.Tim Sparv (14/0)], Roman Eremenko (34/1) [87.Joona Toivio (2/0)], Alexei Eremenko jr. (50/13) [87.Riku Olavi Riski (2/0)], Markus Heikkinen (58/0), Përparim Hetemaj (4/0) [63.Sebastian Mannström (2/0)], Daniel Sjölund (27/2) [47.Roni Porokara (20/5)], Berat Sadik (5/0) [74.Mikael Kaj Forssell (74/24)]. Trainer: Markku Kanerva (2).

716. 03.06.2011 **SAN MARINO - FINLAND** **0-1(0-1)** 14th EC. Qualifiers
Stadio Olimpico, Serravalle; Referee: Andrejs Sipailo (Latvia); Attendance: 1,218
FIN: Lukas Hradecky (3/0), Petri Pasanen (Cap) (64/1), Jukka Raitala (5/0), Veli Lampi (24/0), Niklas Moisander (18/1), Mika Väyrynen (50/5), Alexei Eremenko jr. (51/13) [68.Riku Olavi Riski (3/0)], Kasper Woldemar Hämäläinen (13/2), Markus Heikkinen (59/0), Përparim Hetemaj (5/0) [84.Daniel Sjölund (28/2)], Mikael Kaj Forssell (75/25) [90.Berat Sadik (6/0)]. Trainer: Mika-Matti Petteri Paatelainen (1).
Goal: Mikael Kaj Forssell (41).

717. 07.06.2011 **SWEDEN - FINLAND** **5-0(3-0)** 14th EC. Qualifiers
Råsundastadion, Stockholm; Referee: Antony Gautier (France); Attendance: 32,128
FIN: Anssi Jaakkola (1/0), Petri Pasanen (Cap) (65/1), Niklas Moisander (19/1), Joona Toivio (3/0), Mika Väyrynen (51/5), Roman Eremenko (35/1), Alexei Eremenko jr. (52/13) [79.Alexander Michael Ring (1/0)], Kasper Woldemar Hämäläinen (14/2) [46.Mika Ääritalo (3/0)], Markus Heikkinen (60/0) [46.Markus Olof Halsti (4/0)], Përparim Hetemaj (6/0), Mikael Kaj Forssell (76/25). Trainer: Mika-Matti Petteri Paatelainen (2).

718. 10.08.2011 **LATVIA - FINLAND** **0-2(0-0)**
Skonto Stadions, Riga; Referee: Vladislav Bezborodov (Russia); Attendance: 5,314
FIN: Lukas Hradecky (4/0), Kari Arkivuo (9/1) [63.Ville Jalasto (2/0)], Jukka Raitala (6/0), Niklas Moisander (Cap) (20/1), Joona Toivio (4/0), Roman Eremenko (36/1), Kasper Woldemar Hämäläinen (15/3) [76.Mika Väyrynen (52/5)], Përparim Hetemaj (7/0) [51.Tim Sparv (15/0)], Teemu Pukki (4/0) [46.Mika Ojala (2/0)], Riku Olavi Riski (4/0) [70.Markus Heikkinen (61/0)], Mika Ääritalo (4/0) [46.Timo Furuholm (2/1)]. Trainer: Mika-Matti Petteri Paatelainen (3).
Goals: Kasper Woldemar Hämäläinen (58), Timo Furuholm (87).

719. 02.09.2011 **FINLAND - MOLDOVA** **4-1(2-0)** 14th EC. Qualifiers
Olympiastadion, Helsinki; Referee: Anastassios Kakos (Greece); Attendance: 9,056
FIN: Lukas Hradecky (5/0), Kari Arkivuo (10/1), Jukka Raitala (7/0), Niklas Moisander (Cap) (21/1), Joona Toivio (5/0), Roman Eremenko (37/1), Kasper Woldemar Hämäläinen (16/5) [76.Timo Furuholm (3/1)], Përparim Hetemaj (8/0), Daniel Sjölund (29/2) [61.Teemu Pukki (5/0)], Alexander Michael Ring (2/0) [72.Mika Väyrynen (53/5)], Mikael Kaj Forssell (77/26). Trainer: Mika-Matti Petteri Paatelainen (4).
Goals: Kasper Woldemar Hämäläinen (11, 43), Mikael Kaj Forssell (52 penalty), I. Armaş (70 own goal).

720. 06.09.2011 **FINLAND - NETHERLANDS** **0-2(0-1)** 14th EC. Qualifiers
Olympiastadion, Helsinki; Referee: Manuel Gräfe (Germany); Attendance: 21,580
FIN: Lukas Hradecky (6/0), Petri Pasanen (66/1) [78.Jukka Raitala (8/0)], Kari Arkivuo (11/1), Niklas Moisander (Cap) (22/1), Joona Toivio (6/0), Roman Eremenko (38/1), Kasper Woldemar Hämäläinen (17/5), Përparim Hetemaj (9/0) [*sent off 60*], Alexander Michael Ring (3/0), Teemu Pukki (6/0) [61.Mika Väyrynen (54/5)], Mikael Kaj Forssell (78/26) [86.Daniel Sjölund (30/2)]. Trainer: Mika-Matti Petteri Paatelainen (5).

721. 07.10.2011 **FINLAND - SWEDEN** **1-2(0-1)** 14th EC. Qualifiers
Olympiastadion, Helsinki; Referee: Mark Clattenburg (England); Attendance: 23,257
FIN: Lukas Hradecky (7/0), Kari Arkivuo (12/1), Jukka Raitala (9/0), Niklas Moisander (Cap) (23/1), Joona Toivio (7/1), Mika Väyrynen (55/5) [71.Timo Furuholm (4/1)], Roman Eremenko (39/1), Tim Sparv (16/0), Kasper Woldemar Hämäläinen (18/5), Alexander Michael Ring (4/0), Teemu Pukki (7/0) [60.Mikael Kaj Forssell (79/26)]. Trainer: Mika-Matti Petteri Paatelainen (6).
Goal: Joona Toivio (73).

722. 11.10.2011 **HUNGARY - FINLAND** **0-0** 14th EC. Qualifiers
„Puskás Ferenc" Stadion, Budapest; Referee: Alberto Undiano Mallenco (Spain); Attendance: 25,169
FIN: Otto Fredrikson (12/0), Kari Arkivuo (13/1) [55.Veli Lampi (25/0)], Jukka Raitala (10/0), Niklas Moisander (Cap) (24/1), Joona Toivio (8/1), Mika Väyrynen (56/5), Tim Sparv (17/0), Roman Eremenko (40/1), Kasper Woldemar Hämäläinen (19/5) [84.Teemu Pukki (8/0)], Alexander Michael Ring (5/0), Mikael Kaj Forssell (80/26) [67.Timo Furuholm (5/1)]. Trainer: Mika-Matti Petteri Paatelainen (7).

723. 15.11.2011 **DENMARK - FINLAND** **2-1(0-1)**
Blue Water Arena, Esbjerg; Referee: Kristinn Jakobsson (Iceland); Attendance: 15,100
FIN: Otto Fredrikson (13/0) [33.Lukas Hradecky (8/0)], Petri Pasanen (67/1) [76.Juhani Lauri Henrik Ojala (1/0)], Veli Lampi (26/0), Niklas Moisander (Cap) (25/1) [89.Ville Jalasto (3/0)], Roman Eremenko (41/1), Tim Sparv (18/0), Alexei Eremenko jr. (53/14) [25.Daniel Sjölund (31/2)], Markus Olof Halsti (5/0), Kasper Woldemar Hämäläinen (20/5) [90.Mikael Kaj Forssell (81/26)], Alexander Michael Ring (6/0) [68.Përparim Hetemaj (10/0)], Teemu Pukki (9/0). Trainer: Mika-Matti Petteri Paatelainen (8).
Goal: Alexei Eremenko jr. (18).

724. 22.01.2012 **TRINIDAD AND TOBAGO - FINLAND** **2-3(1-1)**
"Hasely Crawford" Stadium, Port of Spain; Referee: Courtney Campbell (Jamaica); Attendance: 400
FIN: Lukas Hradecky (9/0), Mikko Sumusalo (1/0), Joona Toivio (Cap) (9/1), Markus Olof Halsti (6/0), Sebastian Sorsa (2/0) [75.Joni Aho (3/0)], Kasper Woldemar Hämäläinen (21/5) [87.Ilari Äijälä (1/0)], Joni Kauko (1/0) [75.Akseli Pelvas (1/0)], Daniel Sjölund (32/2) [90.Hannu Jarl Johannes Patronen (2/0)], Toni Kolehmainen (1/1), Berat Sadik (7/0) [31.Mika Ääritalo (5/1)], Riku Olavi Riski (5/1) [46.Sebastian Mannström (3/0)]. Trainer: Mika-Matti Petteri Paatelainen (9).
Goals: Riku Olavi Riski (33), Toni Kolehmainen (75), Mika Ääritalo (78).

725. 29.02.2012 **AUSTRIA - FINLAND** **3-1(1-0)**
Wörthersee Stadion, Klagenfurt; Referee: Paolo Valeri (Italy); Attendance: 10,200
FIN: Lukas Hradecky (10/0), Petri Pasanen (68/1), Kari Arkivuo (14/1), Jukka Raitala (11/0) [46.Veli Lampi (27/0)], Niklas Moisander (Cap) (26/1) [77.Joona Toivio (10/1)], Roman Eremenko (42/1), Tim Sparv (19/0), Kasper Woldemar Hämäläinen (22/5) [61.Njazi Kuqi (4/3)], Përparim Hetemaj (11/0) [46.Riku Olavi Riski (6/1)], Alexander Michael Ring (7/0) [78.Mika Ojala (3/0)], Teemu Pukki (10/0) [87.Timo Furuholm (6/2)]. Trainer: Mika-Matti Petteri Paatelainen (10).
Goal: Timo Furuholm (89).

726. 26.05.2012 **FINLAND - TURKEY** **3-2(1-1)**
Red Bull Arena, Wals-Siezenheim; Referee: Manuel Schüttengruber (Switzerland); Attendance: 2,000
FIN: Niki Mäenpää (5/0), Petri Pasanen (Cap) (69/1), Jukka Raitala (12/0), Joona Toivio (11/1) [83.Juhani Lauri Henrik Ojala (2/0)], Jere Juhani Uronen (1/0), Roman Eremenko (43/2), Tim Sparv (20/0) [61.Përparim Hetemaj (12/1)], Roni Porokara (21/5) [61.Kasper Woldemar Hämäläinen (23/5)], Alexander Michael Ring (8/0) [68.Daniel Sjölund (33/2)], Timo Furuholm (7/2) [90.Tuomas Rannankari (1/0)], Teemu Pukki (11/1) [76.Njazi Kuqi (5/3)]. Trainer: Mika-Matti Petteri Paatelainen (11).
Goals: Roman Eremenko (19), Teemu Pukki (73), Përparim Hetemaj (90+1).

727. 01.06.2012 **ESTONIA - FINLAND** **1-2(1-2)** 24th Baltic Championship
Tamme staadion, Tartu; Referee: Vadims Direktorenko (Latvia); Attendance: 2,470
FIN: Niki Mäenpää (6/0), Kari Arkivuo (15/1) [62.Jarkko Erkki Hurme (1/0)], Jukka Raitala (13/0), Joona Toivio (Cap) (12/1), Juhani Lauri Henrik Ojala (3/0), Tim Sparv (21/0), Kasper Woldemar Hämäläinen (24/5) [74.Markus Olof Halsti (7/0)], Përparim Hetemaj (13/1), Alexander Michael Ring (9/0) [*sent off 45+1*], Njazi Kuqi (6/5) [83.Mika Ääritalo (6/1)], Teemu Pukki (12/1) [46.Toni Kolehmainen (2/1)]. Trainer: Mika-Matti Petteri Paatelainen (12).
Goals: Njazi Kuqi (10, 22).

728. 03.06.2012 **FINLAND - LATVIA** **1-1(0-0,1-1,1-1); 5-6 on penalties** 24th Baltic Championship
Linnastaadion, Võru (Estonia); Referee: Gediminas Mažeika (Lithuania); Attendance: 280
FIN: Lukas Hradecky (11/0) [46.Henri Sillanpää (5/0)], Petri Pasanen (Cap) (70/1), Jukka Raitala (14/0) [57.Jarkko Erkki Hurme (2/0)], Paulus Arajuuri (2/0), Tim Sparv (22/0), Roni Porokara (22/5) [57.Njazi Kuqi (7/5)], Markus Olof Halsti (8/0), Daniel Sjölund (34/2), Toni Kolehmainen (3/2), Timo Furuholm (8/2) [73.Mika Ojala (4/0)], Teemu Pukki (13/1). Trainer: Mika-Matti Petteri Paatelainen (13).
Goal: Toni Kolehmainen (52).
Penalties: Teemu Pukki (missed), Daniel Sjölund, Njazi Kuqi, Mika Ojala, Petri Pasanen, Tim Sparv, Jarkko Erkki Hurme (missed), Toni Kolehmainen (missed).

729. 15.08.2012 **NORTHERN IRELAND - FINLAND** **3-3(2-2)**
Windsor Park, Belfast; Referee: Richard Liesveld (Netherlands); Attendance: 9,575
FIN: Niki Mäenpää (7/0), Kari Arkivuo (16/1), Niklas Moisander (Cap) (27/1), Joona Toivio (13/1), Jere Juhani Uronen (2/0), Roman Eremenko (44/2), Tim Sparv (23/1), Alexei Eremenko jr. (54/14) [69.Përparim Hetemaj (14/2)], Kasper Woldemar Hämäläinen (25/5) [69.Toni Kolehmainen (4/2)], Njazi Kuqi (8/5) [84.Daniel Sjölund (35/2)], Teemu Pukki (14/2) [46.Riku Olavi Riski (7/1)]. Trainer: Mika-Matti Petteri Paatelainen (14).
Goals: Tim Sparv (22), Teemu Pukki (24), Përparim Hetemaj (78).

730. 07.09.2012 **FINLAND - FRANCE** **0-1(0-1)** 20th FIFA WC. Qualifiers
Olympiastadion, Helsinki; Referee: Craig Thomson (Scotland); Attendance: 35,111
FIN: Lukas Hradecky (12/0), Kari Arkivuo (17/1), Niklas Moisander (Cap) (28/1), Joona Toivio (14/1), Roman Eremenko (45/2), Tim Sparv (24/1), Markus Olof Halsti (9/0), Kasper Woldemar Hämäläinen (26/5) [78.Njazi Kuqi (9/5)], Përparim Hetemaj (15/2) [65.Alexei Eremenko jr. (55/14)], Alexander Michael Ring (10/0), Teemu Pukki (15/2). Trainer: Mika-Matti Petteri Paatelainen (15).

731. 11.09.2012 **CZECH REPUBLIC - FINLAND** **0-1(0-1)**
Stadion Na Stínadlech, Teplice; Referee: Hubert Siejewicz (Poland); Attendance: 9,053
FIN: Niki Mäenpää (8/0), Kari Arkivuo (18/1), Jukka Raitala (15/0), Niklas Moisander (Cap) (29/1) [60.Paulus Arajuuri (3/0)], Juhani Lauri Henrik Ojala (4/0) [45+1.Joona Toivio (15/1)], Mika Väyrynen (57/5) [46.Daniel Sjölund (36/2); 90+1.Njazi Kuqi (10/5)], Roman Eremenko (46/2), Kasper Woldemar Hämäläinen (27/5) [77.Tim Sparv (25/1)], Përparim Hetemaj (16/2), Alexander Michael Ring (11/0), Teemu Pukki (16/3) [87.Toni Kolehmainen (5/2)]. Trainer: Mika-Matti Petteri Paatelainen (16).
Goal: Teemu Pukki (43).

732. 12.10.2012 **FINLAND - GEORGIA** **1-1(0-0)** 20th FIFA WC. Qualifiers
Olympiastadion, Helsinki; Referee: Yevhen Aranovskiy (Ukraine); Attendance: 12,607
FIN: Niki Mäenpää (9/0), Jukka Raitala (16/0), Niklas Moisander (Cap) (30/1), Juhani Lauri Henrik Ojala (5/0), Jere Juhani Uronen (3/0), Roman Eremenko (47/2), Tim Sparv (26/1), Alexei Eremenko jr. (56/14), Kasper Woldemar Hämäläinen (28/6), Alexander Michael Ring (12/0), Teemu Pukki (17/3) [62.Përparim Hetemaj (17/2)]. Trainer: Mika-Matti Petteri Paatelainen (17).
Goal: Kasper Woldemar Hämäläinen (62).

733. 14.11.2012 **CYPRUS - FINLAND** **0-3(0-2)**
Neo Stádio GSP, Nicosia; Referee: Cristian Pavel Balaj (Romania); Attendance: 300
FIN: Niki Mäenpää (10/0), Kari Arkivuo (19/1) [70.Markus Olof Halsti (10/0)], Joona Toivio (Cap) (16/1), Juhani Lauri Henrik Ojala (6/0), Jere Juhani Uronen (4/0), Tim Sparv (27/1), Kasper Woldemar Hämäläinen (29/6) [83.Njazi Kuqi (11/5)], Përparim Hetemaj (18/3) [62.Toni Kolehmainen (6/3)], Alexander Michael Ring (13/0) [78.Daniel Sjölund (37/2)], Teemu Pukki (18/4) [70.Joel Pohjanpalo (1/0)], Riku Olavi Riski (8/1) [46.Mika Ojala (5/0)]. Trainer: Mika-Matti Petteri Paatelainen (18).
Goals: Teemu Pukki (15), Përparim Hetemaj (29 penalty), Toni Kolehmainen (85).

734. 23.01.2013 **THAILAND - FINLAND** **1-3(0-2)** International Tournament
700th Anniversary Stadium, Chiang Mai; Referee: Võ Minh Trí (Vietnam); Attendance: 23,000
FIN: Jesse Joronen (1/0), Kari Arkivuo (20/1) [75.Jarkko Erkki Hurme (3/0)], Markus Olof Halsti (11/0) [80.Paulus Arajuuri (4/0)], Mikko Sumusalo (2/1), Joona Toivio (Cap) (17/1), Mika Väyrynen (58/5), Teemu Tainio (53/6) [46.Joni Kauko (2/0)], Riku Olavi Riski (9/1) [75.Roni Porokara (23/5)], Kasper Woldemar Hämäläinen (30/6) [65.Sebastian Mannström (4/0)], Rasmus Schüller (1/0) [90+6.Tuomas Rannankari (2/0)], Mikael Kaj Forssell (82/28). Trainer: Mika-Matti Petteri Paatelainen (19).
Goals: Mikko Sumusalo (5), Mikael Kaj Forssell (12, 87).

735. 26.01.2013 **FINLAND - SWEDEN** **0-3(0-1)** International Tournament
700th Anniversary Stadium, Chiang Mai (Thailand); Referee: Chaiya Alee Mahapab (Thailand); Attendance: 5,000
FIN: Lukas Hradecky (13/0), Kari Arkivuo (21/1), Markus Olof Halsti (12/0) [77.Lum Rexhepi (1/0)], Mikko Sumusalo (3/1), Joona Toivio (Cap) (18/1) [46.Paulus Arajuuri (5/0)], Mika Väyrynen (59/5) [32.Sebastian Mannström (5/0)], Teemu Tainio (54/6), Mika Ojala (6/0) [69.Petteri Pennanen (1/0)], Riku Olavi Riski (10/1), Rasmus Schüller (2/0) [58.Joni Kauko (3/0)], Mikael Kaj Forssell (83/28). Trainer: Mika-Matti Petteri Paatelainen (20).

736. 06.02.2013 **ISRAEL - FINLAND** **2-1(1-0)**
Winner Stadium, Netanya; Referee: Padraigh Sutton (Republic of Ireland); Attendance: 2,800
FIN: Niki Mäenpää (11/0), Kari Arkivuo (22/1), Jukka Raitala (17/0) [90+5.Jarkko Erkki Hurme (4/0)], Niklas Moisander (Cap) (31/1), Juhani Lauri Henrik Ojala (7/0), Roman Eremenko (48/2), Tim Sparv (28/1), Mika Ojala (7/0) [46.Alexei Eremenko jr. (57/14)], Toni Kolehmainen (7/3), Teemu Pukki (19/4), Mikael Kaj Forssell (84/28) [73.Petteri Forsell (1/1)]. Trainer: Mika-Matti Petteri Paatelainen (21).
Goal: Petteri Forsell (87).

737. 22.03.2013 **SPAIN - FINLAND** **1-1(0-0)** 20th FIFA WC. Qualifiers
Estadio El Molinón, Gijón; Referee: Ovidiu Haţegan (Romania); Attendance: 27,637
FIN: Niki Mäenpää (12/0), Kari Arkivuo (23/1), Jukka Raitala (18/0), Niklas Moisander (Cap) (32/1), Joona Toivio (19/1), Teemu Tainio (55/6) [69.Tim Sparv (29/1)], Roman Eremenko (49/2), Kasper Woldemar Hämäläinen (31/6), Përparim Hetemaj (19/3), Alexander Michael Ring (14/0), Teemu Pukki (20/5) [90+4.Markus Olof Halsti (13/0)]. Trainer: Mika-Matti Petteri Paatelainen (22).
Goal: Teemu Pukki (79).

738. 26.03.2013 **LUXEMBURG - FINLAND** **0-3(0-1)**
Stade „Josy Barthel", Luxembourg; Referee: Jonathan Lardot (Belgium); Attendance: 856
FIN: Niki Mäenpää (13/0) [47.Lukas Hradecky (14/0)], Kari Arkivuo (24/1) [71.Joona Toivio (20/2)], Jukka Raitala (19/0), Niklas Moisander (Cap) (33/1), Teemu Tainio (56/6) [56.Rasmus Schüller (3/0)], Roman Eremenko (50/2), Tim Sparv (30/1), Markus Olof Halsti (14/0), Kasper Woldemar Hämäläinen (32/6) [76.Riku Olavi Riski (11/1)], Alexander Michael Ring (15/1) [83.Njazi Kuqi (12/5)], Teemu Pukki (21/5) [48.Mikael Kaj Forssell (85/29)]. Trainer: Mika-Matti Petteri Paatelainen (23).
Goals: Alexander Michael Ring (44), Mikael Kaj Forssell (50 penalty), Joona Toivio (90).

739. 07.06.2013 **FINLAND - BELARUS** **1-0(0-0)** 20th FIFA WC. Qualifiers
Olympiastadion, Helsinki; Referee: Eli Hacmon (Israel); Attendance: 24,916
FIN: Niki Mäenpää (14/0), Petri Pasanen (71/1), Kari Arkivuo (25/1) [53.Jarkko Erkki Hurme (5/0)], Jukka Raitala (20/0), Teemu Tainio (Cap) (57/6) [68.Tim Sparv (31/1)], Roman Eremenko (51/2), Markus Olof Halsti (15/0), Kasper Woldemar Hämäläinen (33/6), Përparim Hetemaj (20/3), Alexander Michael Ring (16/1), Teemu Pukki (22/5) [77.Mikael Kaj Forssell (86/29)]. Trainer: Mika-Matti Petteri Paatelainen (24).
Goal: Igor Shitov (57 own goal).

740. 11.06.2013 **BELARUS - FINLAND** **1-1(0-1)** 20th FIFA WC. Qualifiers
Central Stadium, Gomel; Referee: Libor Kovařík (Czech Republic); Attendance: 10,100
FIN: Niki Mäenpää (15/0), Petri Pasanen (72/1), Jukka Raitala (21/0), Niklas Moisander (Cap) (34/1), Jarkko Erkki Hurme (6/0), Roman Eremenko (52/2), Tim Sparv (32/1), Kasper Woldemar Hämäläinen (34/6) [83.Paulus Arajuuri (6/0)], Përparim Hetemaj (21/3), Alexander Michael Ring (17/1), Teemu Pukki (23/6) [76.Timo Furuholm (9/2)]. Trainer: Mika-Matti Petteri Paatelainen (25).
Goal: Teemu Pukki (24).

741. 14.08.2013 **FINLAND - SLOVENIA** **2-0(1-0)**
Veritas Stadion, Turku; Referee: Simon Lee Evans (Wales); Attendance: 5,859
FIN: Niki Mäenpää (16/0), Petri Pasanen (73/1) [79.Juhani Lauri Henrik Ojala (8/0)], Kari Arkivuo (26/1) [69.Markus Olof Halsti (16/0)], Veli Lampi (28/0), Niklas Moisander (Cap) (35/2), Teemu Tainio (58/6), Roman Eremenko (53/2), Rasmus Schüller (4/0) [60.Përparim Hetemaj (22/3)], Alexander Michael Ring (18/1), Teemu Pukki (24/6) [79.Joel Pohjanpalo (2/0); 85.Erfan Zeneli (1/0)], Riku Olavi Riski (12/1) [46.Kasper Woldemar Hämäläinen (35/7)]. Trainer: Mika-Matti Petteri Paatelainen (26).
Goals: Niklas Moisander (35), Kasper Woldemar Hämäläinen (82).

742. 06.09.2013 **FINLAND - SPAIN** **0-2(0-1)** 20th FIFA WC. Qualifiers
Olympiastadion, Helsinki; Referee: Ivan Bebek (Croatia); Attendance: 37,492
FIN: Niki Mäenpää (17/0), Petri Pasanen (74/1), Kari Arkivuo (27/1), Niklas Moisander (Cap) (36/2), Joona Toivio (21/2), Teemu Tainio (59/6) [69.Riku Olavi Riski (13/1)], Roman Eremenko (54/2), Markus Olof Halsti (17/0), Rasmus Schüller (5/0), Alexander Michael Ring (19/1) [69.Kasper Woldemar Hämäläinen (36/7)], Teemu Pukki (25/6) [81.Erfan Zeneli (2/0)]. Trainer: Mika-Matti Petteri Paatelainen (27).

743. 10.09.2013 **GEORGIA - FINLAND** **0-1(0-0)** 20th FIFA WC. Qualifiers
"Mikheil Meskhi" Stadium, Tbilisi; Referee: Leontios Trattou (Cyprus); Attendance: 25,321
FIN: Niki Mäenpää (18/0), Kari Arkivuo (28/1), Veli Lampi (29/0), Niklas Moisander (Cap) (37/2), Juhani Lauri Henrik Ojala (9/0), Teemu Tainio (60/6), Roman Eremenko (55/3), Kasper Woldemar Hämäläinen (37/7) [89.Riku Olavi Riski (14/1)], Përparim Hetemaj (23/3), Alexander Michael Ring (20/1) [71.Tim Sparv (33/1)], Teemu Pukki (26/6) [90+2.Rasmus Schüller (6/0)]. Trainer: Mika-Matti Petteri Paatelainen (28).
Goal: Roman Eremenko (74 penalty).

744. 15.10.2013 **FRANCE - FINLAND** **3-0(1-0)** 20th FIFA WC. Qualifiers
Stade de France, Saint-Denis, Paris; Referee: Michael Koukoulakis (Greece); Attendance: 70,156
FIN: Niki Mäenpää (19/0), Petri Pasanen (75/1), Kari Arkivuo (29/1), Veli Lampi (30/0), Teemu Tainio (Cap) (61/6) [64.Joona Toivio (22/2)], Roman Eremenko (56/3), Markus Olof Halsti (18/0), Kasper Woldemar Hämäläinen (38/7) [79.Riku Olavi Riski (15/1)], Përparim Hetemaj (24/3), Alexander Michael Ring (21/1), Teemu Pukki (27/6) [86.Timo Furuholm (10/2)]. Trainer: Mika-Matti Petteri Paatelainen (29).

745. 16.11.2013 **WALES - FINLAND** **1-1(0-0)**
Cardiff City Stadium, Cardiff: Referee: Sebastièn Delferière (Belgium); Attendance: 11,809
FIN: Lukas Hradecky (15/0), Kari Arkivuo (30/1) [46.Veli Lampi (31/0); 70.Jukka Raitala (22/0)], Niklas Moisander (Cap) (38/2) [62.Petri Pasanen (76/1)], Juhani Lauri Henrik Ojala (10/0) [46.Joona Toivio (23/2)], Jere Juhani Uronen (5/0), Roman Eremenko (57/3), Tim Sparv (34/1), Rasmus Schüller (7/0) [70.Përparim Hetemaj (25/3)], Alexander Michael Ring (22/1), Teemu Pukki (28/6) [63.Kasper Woldemar Hämäläinen (39/7)], Riku Olavi Riski (16/2). Trainer: Mika-Matti Petteri Paatelainen (30).
Goal: Riku Olavi Riski (90+1).

746. 24.01.2014 **OMAN - FINLAND** **0-0**
Nizwa Sports Complex, Nizwa; Referee: Saleh Al Hathlool (Bahrain); Attendance: n/a
FIN: Henri Sillanpää (6/0), Joona Toivio (24/2), Jere Juhani Uronen (6/0), Teemu Tainio (Cap) (62/6), Markus Olof Halsti (19/0), Erfan Zeneli (3/0) [61.Pekka Sihvola (1/0)], Sebastian Sorsa (3/0), Rasmus Schüller (8/0) [77.Sebastian Strandvall (1/0)], Toni Kolehmainen (8/3) [77.Mehmet Hetemaj (3/0)], Mikael Kaj Forssell (87/29) [86.Mika Ojala (8/0)], Nikolai Aleksanteri Alho (1/0). Trainer: Mika-Matti Petteri Paatelainen (31).

747. 05.03.2014 **HUNGARY - FINLAND** **1-2(1-0)**
ETO Park, Győr; Referee: Alexander Harkam (Austria); Attendance: 14,000
FIN: Niki Mäenpää (20/0), Kari Arkivuo (31/1), Niklas Moisander (Cap) (39/2), Juhani Lauri Henrik Ojala (11/0), Roman Eremenko (58/4) [90+4.Sakari Mattila (1/0)], Tim Sparv (35/1), Sebastian Sorsa (4/0) [88.Joona Toivio (25/2)], Përparim Hetemaj (26/3), Toni Kolehmainen (9/3) [70.Alexander Michael Ring (23/1)], Teemu Pukki (29/6) [87.Berat Sadik (8/0)], Riku Olavi Riski (17/2) [64.Joel Pohjanpalo (3/1)]. Trainer: Mika-Matti Petteri Paatelainen (32).
Goals: Joel Pohjanpalo (74), Roman Eremenko (84 penalty).

748. 21.05.2014 **FINLAND – CZECH REPUBLIC** **2-2(2-2)**
Olympiastadion, Helsinki; Referee: Oliver Drachta (Austria); Attendance: 6,547
FIN: Lukas Hradecky (16/0), Jukka Raitala (23/0), Niklas Moisander (Cap) (40/2) [46.Tero Mäntylä (1/0)], Juhani Lauri Henrik Ojala (12/0) [89.Tapio Heikkilä (1/0)], Teemu Tainio (63/6) [46.Rasmus Schüller (9/0)], Tim Sparv (36/1), Sebastian Sorsa (5/0), Përparim Hetemaj (27/3), Alexander Michael Ring (24/1), Teemu Pukki (30/8) [83.Tim Väyrynen (1/0)], Joel Pohjanpalo (4/1) [71.Mika Väyrynen (60/5)]. Trainer: Mika-Matti Petteri Paatelainen (33).
Goals: Teemu Pukki (18, 20).

749. 29.05.2014 **FINLAND - LITHUANIA** **0-1(0-1)** 25th Baltic Championship
Ventspils Olimpiskais Stadions, Ventspils (Latvia); Referee: Vadims Direktorenko (Latvia); Attendance: 631
FIN: Niki Mäenpää (21/0), Jukka Raitala (24/0), Niklas Moisander (Cap) (41/2) [68.Juhani Lauri Henrik Ojala (13/0)], Jarkko Erkki Hurme (7/0), Tero Mäntylä (2/0), Roman Eremenko (59/4) [46.Petteri Forsell (2/1)], Tim Sparv (37/1), Përparim Hetemaj (28/3), Alexander Michael Ring (25/1) [68.Mika Väyrynen (61/5)], Teemu Pukki (31/8) [46.Eero Pekka Sakari Markkanen (1/0)], Riku Olavi Riski (18/2) [73.Joel Pohjanpalo (5/1)]. Trainer: Mika-Matti Petteri Paatelainen (34).

750. 31.05.2014 **ESTONIA - FINLAND** **0-2(0-0)** 25th Baltic Championship
Ventspils Olimpiskais Stadions, Ventspils (Latvia); Referee: Aleksandrs Anufrijevs (Latvia); Attendance: 830
FIN: Lukas Hradecky (17/0), Niklas Moisander (Cap) (42/2), Joona Toivio (26/2) [63.Valtteri Moren (1/1)], Juhani Lauri Henrik Ojala (14/0), Jarkko Erkki Hurme (8/0), Roman Eremenko (60/4), Tim Sparv (38/1), Përparim Hetemaj (29/4) [87.Sakari Mattila (2/0)], Joni Kauko (4/0), Teemu Pukki (32/8) [73.Alexander Michael Ring (26/1)], Joel Pohjanpalo (6/1) [89.Erfan Zeneli (4/0)]. Trainer: Mika-Matti Petteri Paatelainen (35).
Goals: Përparim Hetemaj (49), Valtteri Moren (87).

751. 07.09.2014 **FAROE ISLANDS - FINLAND** **1-3(1-0)** 15th EC. Qualifiers
Tórsvøllur, Tórshavn; Referee: Simon Lee Evans (Wales); Attendance: 3,330
FIN: Niki Mäenpää (22/0), Kari Arkivuo (32/1), Niklas Moisander (Cap) (43/2), Joona Toivio (27/2), Jere Juhani Uronen (7/0) [75.Eero Pekka Sakari Markkanen (2/0)], Roman Eremenko (61/5), Tim Sparv (39/1), Përparim Hetemaj (30/4), Alexander Michael Ring (27/1), Teemu Pukki (33/8) [89.Joel Pohjanpalo (7/1)], Riku Olavi Riski (19/4). Trainer: Mika-Matti Petteri Paatelainen (36).
Goals: Riku Olavi Riski (53, 78), Roman Eremenko (82).

752. 11.10.2014 **FINLAND - GREECE** **1-1(0-1)** 15th EC. Qualifiers
Olympiastadion, Helsinki; Referee: David Fernández Borbalán (Spain); Attendance: 26,548
FIN: Niki Mäenpää (23/0), Kari Arkivuo (33/1), Niklas Moisander (Cap) (44/2), Joona Toivio (28/2), Jarkko Erkki Hurme (9/1), Roman Eremenko (62/5), Tim Sparv (40/1), Përparim Hetemaj (31/4) [46.Kasper Woldemar Hämäläinen (40/7)], Alexander Michael Ring (28/1), Teemu Pukki (34/8) [70.Joel Pohjanpalo (8/1)], Riku Olavi Riski (20/4) [88.Teemu Tainio (64/6)]. Trainer: Mika-Matti Petteri Paatelainen (37).
Goal: Jarkko Erkki Hurme (55).

753. 14.10.2014 **FINLAND - ROMANIA** **0-2(0-0)** 15th EC. Qualifiers
Olympiastadion, Helsinki; Referee: Paolo Tagliavento (Italy); Attendance: 19,408
FIN: Niki Mäenpää (24/0), Kari Arkivuo (34/1), Niklas Moisander (Cap) (45/2), Joona Toivio (29/2), Jarkko Erkki Hurme (10/1), Roman Eremenko (63/5), Tim Sparv (41/1), Kasper Woldemar Hämäläinen (41/7) [74.Eero Pekka Sakari Markkanen (3/0)], Përparim Hetemaj (32/4) [64.Joel Pohjanpalo (9/1)], Alexander Michael Ring (29/1) [*sent off 56*], Teemu Pukki (35/8) [46.Riku Olavi Riski (21/4)]. Trainer: Mika-Matti Petteri Paatelainen (38).

754. 14.11.2014 **HUNGARY - FINLAND** **1-0(0-0)** 15th EC. Qualifiers
Groupama Arena, Budapest; Referee: Clément Turpin (France); Attendance: 19,600
FIN: Lukas Hradecky (18/0), Niklas Moisander (Cap) (46/2), Joona Toivio (30/2), Jarkko Erkki Hurme (11/1), Jere Juhani Uronen (8/0), Roman Eremenko (64/5), Tim Sparv (42/1), Markus Olof Halsti (20/0) [85.Eero Pekka Sakari Markkanen (4/0)], Kasper Woldemar Hämäläinen (42/7) [82.Riku Olavi Riski (22/4)], Përparim Hetemaj (33/4), Teemu Pukki (36/8) [65.Joel Pohjanpalo (10/1)]. Trainer: Mika-Matti Petteri Paatelainen (39).

755. 18.11.2014 **SLOVAKIA - FINLAND** **2-1(2-1)**
Štadión Pod Dubňom, Žilina; Referee: Markus Hameter (Austria); Attendance: 3,998
FIN: Lukas Hradecky (19/0), Kari Arkivuo (35/1) [86.Veli Lampi (32/0)], Niklas Moisander (Cap) (47/2), Jere Juhani Uronen (9/0), Roman Eremenko (65/5), Tim Sparv (43/1), Markus Olof Halsti (21/0), Përparim Hetemaj (34/4) [73.Kasper Woldemar Hämäläinen (43/7)], Joni Kauko (5/0) [73.Sakari Mattila (3/0)], Riku Olavi Riski (23/4), Joel Pohjanpalo (11/1) [46.Teemu Pukki (37/8)]. Trainer: Mika-Matti Petteri Paatelainen (40).
Goal: Tomáš Hubočan (45+2 own goal).

756. 19.01.2015 **SWEDEN - FINLAND** **0-1(0-0)**
Zayed Sports City, Abu Dhabi (United Arab Emirates); Referee: Omar Mohamed Ahmed Hassan Al Ali (United Arab Emirates); Attendance: 100
FIN: Lukas Hradecky (20/0), Kari Arkivuo (36/1), Hannu Jarl Johannes Patronen (3/0), Valtteri Moren (2/1), Jere Juhani Uronen (10/0), Tim Sparv (Cap) (44/1), Erfan Zeneli (5/0) [61.Mika Väyrynen (62/5)], Rasmus Schüller (10/0) [89.Robin Lod (1/0)], Petteri Forsell (3/1) [75.Tim Väyrynen (2/0)], Toni Kolehmainen (10/3) [76.Johannes Laaksonen (1/0)], Teemu Pukki (38/8) [61.Roope Vilhelmi Riski (1/1)]. Trainer: Mika-Matti Petteri Paatelainen (41).
Goal: Roope Vilhelmi Riski (63).

757. 22.01.2015 **YEMEN - FINLAND** **0-0**
The Sevens Stadium, Dubai (United Arab Emirates); Referee: n/a; Attendance: n/a
FIN: Henrik Moisander (1/0), Ville Jalasto (4/0) [59.Kari Arkivuo (37/1)], Hannu Jarl Johannes Patronen (4/0), Veli Lampi (33/0) [46.Jere Juhani Uronen (11/0)], Valtteri Moren (3/1), Mika Väyrynen (63/5) [46.Tim Väyrynen (3/0)], Tim Sparv (Cap) (45/1), Sakari Mattila (4/0), Petteri Forsell (4/1), Robin Lod (2/0) [70.Rasmus Schüller (11/0)], Roope Vilhelmi Riski (2/1) [85.Erfan Zeneli (6/0)]. Trainer: Mika-Matti Petteri Paatelainen (42).

758. 29.03.2015 **NORTHERN IRELAND - FINLAND** **2-1(2-0)** 15th EC. Qualifiers
Windsor Park, Belfast; Referee: Szymon Marciniak (Poland); Attendance: 10,264
FIN: Lukas Hradecky (21/0), Sebastian Sorsa (6/0), Sakari Mattila (5/0), Niklas Moisander (Cap) (48/2), Joona Toivio (31/2) [46.Paulus Arajuuri (7/0)], Jere Juhani Uronen (12/0), Roman Eremenko (66/5), Tim Sparv (46/1), Kasper Woldemar Hämäläinen (44/7) [43.Joel Pohjanpalo (12/1)], Alexander Michael Ring (30/1), Teemu Pukki (39/8) [70.Berat Sadik (9/1)]. Trainer: Mika-Matti Petteri Paatelainen (43).
Goal: Berat Sadik (90+1).

759. 09.06.2015 **FINLAND - ESTONIA** **0-2(0-1)**
Veritas Stadion, Turku; Referee: Jakob Kehlet (Denmark); Attendance: 6,107
FIN: Niki Mäenpää (25/0), Boris Rotenberg (1/0) [46.Mikko Sumusalo (4/1)], Jukka Raitala (25/0), Niklas Moisander (Cap) (49/2) [60.Markus Olof Halsti (22/0)], Joona Toivio (32/2), Thomas Lam (1/0), Roman Eremenko (67/5), Përparim Hetemaj (35/4) [84.Robin Lod (3/0)], Joni Kauko (6/0) [46.Teemu Pukki (40/8)], Riku Olavi Riski (24/4) [72.Eero Pekka Sakari Markkanen (5/0)], Joel Pohjanpalo (13/1) [46.Tim Väyrynen (4/0)]. Trainer: Mika-Matti Petteri Paatelainen (44).

760. 13.06.2015 **FINLAND - HUNGARY** **0-1(0-0)** 15th EC. Qualifiers
Olympiastadion, Helsinki; Referee: Matej Jug (Slovenia); Attendance: 20,434
FIN: Lukas Hradecky (22/0), Kari Arkivuo (38/1), Jukka Raitala (26/0), Markus Olof Halsti (23/0), Sakari Mattila (6/0) [85.Joel Pohjanpalo (14/1)], Niklas Moisander (Cap) (50/2), Roman Eremenko (68/5), Tim Sparv (47/1), Kasper Woldemar Hämäläinen (45/7), Përparim Hetemaj (36/4), Teemu Pukki (41/8) [46.Riku Olavi Riski (25/4)]. Trainer: Mika-Matti Petteri Paatelainen (45).

761. 04.09.2015 **GREECE - FINLAND** **0-1(0-0)** 15th EC. Qualifiers
Stádio „Giórgos Karaïskáki", Peiraiás; Referee: Serhiy Boyko (Ukraine); Attendance: 17,358
FIN: Lukas Hradecky (23/0), Kari Arkivuo (39/1), Markus Olof Halsti (24/0), Paulus Arajuuri (8/0), Joona Toivio (33/2), Jere Juhani Uronen (13/0), Tim Sparv (Cap) (48/1), Kasper Woldemar Hämäläinen (46/7) [46.Berat Sadik (10/1); 81.Sakari Mattila (7/0)], Përparim Hetemaj (37/4), Alexander Michael Ring (31/1), Teemu Pukki (42/8) [67.Joel Pohjanpalo (15/2)]. Trainer: Markku Kanerva (3).
Goal: Joel Pohjanpalo (75).

762. 07.09.2015 **FINLAND - FAROE ISLANDS** **1-0(1-0)** 15th EC. Qualifiers
Olympiastadion, Helsinki; Referee: Marcin Borski (Poland); Attendance: 9,477
FIN: Lukas Hradecky (24/0), Kari Arkivuo (40/1), Markus Olof Halsti (25/0), Paulus Arajuuri (9/0), Jere Juhani Uronen (14/0), Thomas Lam (2/0) [84.Sakari Mattila (8/0)], Tim Sparv (Cap) (49/1), Përparim Hetemaj (38/4), Alexander Michael Ring (32/1), Riku Olavi Riski (26/4) [74.Tim Väyrynen (5/0)], Joel Pohjanpalo (16/3) [90+3.Kasper Woldemar Hämäläinen (47/7)]. Trainer: Markku Kanerva (4).
Goal: Joel Pohjanpalo (23).

763. 08.10.2015 **ROMANIA - FINLAND** **1-1(0-0)** 15th EC. Qualifiers
Arena Naţională, Bucureşti; Referee: Craig Alexander Thomson (Scotland); Attendance: 47,987
FIN: Lukas Hradecky (25/0), Kari Arkivuo (41/1) [64.Ville Jalasto (5/0)], Markus Olof Halsti (26/0), Paulus Arajuuri (10/0) [62.Joona Toivio (34/2)], Niklas Moisander (Cap) (51/2), Jere Juhani Uronen (15/0), Përparim Hetemaj (39/4), Rasmus Schüller (12/0), Alexander Michael Ring (33/1), Teemu Pukki (43/8), Joel Pohjanpalo (17/4) [77.Kasper Woldemar Hämäläinen (48/7)]. Trainer: Markku Kanerva (5).
Goal: Joel Pohjanpalo (66).

764. 11.10.2015 **FINLAND - NORTHERN IRELAND** **1-1(0-1)** 15th EC. Qualifiers
Olympiastadion, Helsinki; Referee: Sergei Karasev (Russia); Attendance: 14,550
FIN: Lukas Hradecky (26/0), Ville Jalasto (6/0), Sakari Mattila (9/0), Paulus Arajuuri (11/1), Juhani Lauri Henrik Ojala (15/0), Jere Juhani Uronen (16/0), Tim Sparv (Cap) (50/1), Rasmus Schüller (13/0) [79.Kasper Woldemar Hämäläinen (49/7)], Alexander Michael Ring (34/1) [44.Robin Lod (4/0)], Berat Sadik (11/1) [66.Teemu Pukki (44/8)], Joel Pohjanpalo (18/4). Trainer: Markku Kanerva (6).
Goal: Paulus Arajuuri (87).

765. 10.01.2016 **SWEDEN - FINLAND** **3-0(1-0)**
"Mohammed Bin Zayed" Stadium, Abu Dhabi (United Arab Emirates); Referee: Abdullah Ali Abdullah Al Jardani (Oman); Attendance: 150
FIN: Mika Hilander (1/0), Ville Jalasto (7/0) [86.Daniel O'Shaughnessy (1/0)], Tapio Heikkilä (2/0), Hannu Jarl Johannes Patronen (5/0) [46.Jarkko Erkki Hurme (12/1)], Jukka Raitala (27/0), Mehmet Hetemaj (4/0) [46.Johannes Laaksonen (2/0)], Rasmus Schüller (14/0) [73.Timo Tahvanainen (1/0)], Petteri Forsell (5/1) [46.Juha Pirinen (1/0)], Teemu Pukki (45/8) [63.Aleksandr Kokko (1/0)], Akseli Pelvas (2/0) [46.Janne Saksela (1/0)], Roope Vilhelmi Riski (3/1) [72.Simon Skrabb (1/0)]. Trainer: Hans Roland Backe (Sweden, 1).

766. 13.01.2016 **FINLAND - ICELAND** **0-1(0-1)**
"Mohammed Bin Zayed" Stadium, Abu Dhabi (United Arab Emirates); Referee: Adel Ali Ahmed Khamis Al Naqbi (United Arab Emirates); Attendance: 50
FIN: Henrik Moisander (2/0), Kari Arkivuo (42/1) [76.Petteri Forsell (6/1)], Tapio Heikkilä (3/0) [61.Hannu Jarl Johannes Patronen (6/0)], Jukka Raitala (28/0) [46.Timo Tahvanainen (2/0)], Juha Pirinen (2/0), Janne Saksela (2/0), Daniel O'Shaughnessy (2/0), Mehmet Hetemaj (5/0) [46.Johannes Laaksonen (3/0)], Rasmus Schüller (15/0) [61.Matej Hradecky (1/0)], Teemu Pukki (46/8), Akseli Pelvas (3/0) [46.Roope Vilhelmi Riski (4/1)]. Trainer: Hans Roland Backe (Sweden, 2).

767. 26.03.2016 **POLAND - FINLAND** **5-0(3-0)**
Stadion Miejski, Wrocław; Referee: Hiroyuki Kimura (Japan); Attendance: 42,068
FIN: Lukas Hradecky (27/0), Kari Arkivuo (43/1), Paulus Arajuuri (12/1), Joona Toivio (35/2), Jere Juhani Uronen (17/0), Roman Eremenko (69/5) [78.Thomas Lam (3/0)], Tim Sparv (Cap) (51/1), Kasper Woldemar Hämäläinen (50/7) [46.Rasmus Schüller (16/0)], Përparim Hetemaj (40/4) [46.Robin Lod (5/0)], Alexander Michael Ring (35/1) [83.Janne Saksela (3/0)], Joel Pohjanpalo (19/4) [62.Teemu Pukki (47/8)]. Trainer: Hans Roland Backe (Sweden, 3).

768. 29.03.2016 **NORWAY - FINLAND** **2-0(0-0)**
Ullevaal Stadion, Oslo; Referee: Neil Louis Kilcoyne Doyle (Republic of Ireland); Attendance: 4,675
FIN: Niki Mäenpää (26/0) [46.Jesse Joronen (2/0)], Kari Arkivuo (44/1) [39.Jukka Raitala (29/0)], Ville Jalasto (8/0) [80.Jere Juhani Uronen (18/0)], Paulus Arajuuri (13/1), Joona Toivio (36/2), Valtteri Moren (4/1) [86.Tim Väyrynen (6/0)], Roman Eremenko (70/5), Tim Sparv (Cap) (52/1), Përparim Hetemaj (41/4), Robin Lod (6/0) [46.Rasmus Schüller (17/0)], Teemu Pukki (48/8) [63.Kasper Woldemar Hämäläinen (51/7)]. Trainer: Hans Roland Backe (Sweden, 4).

769. 01.06.2016 **BELGIUM - FINLAND** **1-1(0-0)**
Stade „Roi Baudouin", Bruxelles; Referee: Hugo Ferreira de Campos Moreira Miguel (Portugal); Attendance: 35,000
FIN: Lukas Hradecky (28/0), Kari Arkivuo (45/1) [71.Janne Saksela (4/0)], Jukka Raitala (30/0), Markus Olof Halsti (27/0), Paulus Arajuuri (14/1), Joona Toivio (37/2), Roman Eremenko (71/5), Tim Sparv (Cap) (53/1), Kasper Woldemar Hämäläinen (52/8) [68.Joel Pohjanpalo (20/4)], Përparim Hetemaj (42/4) [83.Thomas Lam (4/0)], Alexander Michael Ring (36/1) [54.Joni Kauko (7/0)]. Trainer: Hans Roland Backe (Sweden, 5).
Goal: Kasper Woldemar Hämäläinen (53).

770. 06.06.2016 **ITALY - FINLAND** **2-0(1-0)**
Stadio "Marcantonio Bentegodi", Verona; Referee: Hendrikus Sebastiaan Hermanus "Bas" Nijhuis (Netherlands); Attendance: 27,702
FIN: Lukas Hradecky (29/0), Kari Arkivuo (46/1), Markus Olof Halsti (28/0), Paulus Arajuuri (15/1), Joona Toivio (38/2), Jere Juhani Uronen (19/0) [73.Jukka Raitala (31/0)], Roman Eremenko (72/5), Tim Sparv (Cap) (54/1), Përparim Hetemaj (43/4), Alexander Michael Ring (37/1) [73.Thomas Lam (5/0)], Teemu Pukki (49/8) [46.Robin Lod (7/0)]. Trainer: Hans Roland Backe (Sweden, 6).

771. 31.08.2016 **GERMANY - FINLAND** **2-0(0-0)**
Borussia-Park, Mönchengladbach; Referee: Alyaksey Kulbakow (Belarus); Attendance: 30,121
FIN: Lukas Hradecky (30/0), Jukka Raitala (32/0), Markus Olof Halsti (29/0) [72.Sakari Mattila (10/0)], Paulus Arajuuri (16/1) [82.Juhani Lauri Henrik Ojala (16/0)], Niklas Moisander (Cap) (52/2), Jere Juhani Uronen (20/0) [60.Janne Saksela (5/0)], Thomas Lam (6/0), Kasper Woldemar Hämäläinen (53/8) [46.Teemu Pukki (50/8)], Alexander Michael Ring (38/1), Robin Lod (8/0) [60.Rasmus Schüller (18/0)], Joel Pohjanpalo (21/4) [72.Eero Pekka Sakari Markkanen (6/0)]. Trainer: Hans Roland Backe (Sweden, 7).

772. 05.09.2016 **FINLAND - KOSOVO** **1-1(1-0)** 21st FIFA WC. Qualifiers

Veritas Stadion, Turku; Referee: Ivan Kružliak (Slovakia); Attendance: 7,571

FIN: Lukas Hradecky (31/0), Jukka Raitala (33/0), Markus Olof Halsti (30/0), Paulus Arajuuri (17/2), Niklas Moisander (Cap) (53/2), Jere Juhani Uronen (21/0), Thomas Lam (7/0) [65.Alexander Michael Ring (39/1)], Roman Eremenko (73/5), Robin Lod (9/0) [88.Rasmus Schüller (19/0)], Teemu Pukki (51/8) [73.Kasper Woldemar Hämäläinen (54/8)], Joel Pohjanpalo (22/4). Trainer: Hans Roland Backe (Sweden, 8).

Goal: Paulus Arajuuri (18).

773. 06.10.2016 **ICELAND - FINLAND** **3-2(1-2)** 21st FIFA WC. Qualifiers

Laugardalsvöllur, Reykjavík; Referee: Svein Oddvar Moen (Norway); Attendance: 12,000

FIN: Lukas Hradecky (32/0), Paulus Arajuuri (18/2), Niklas Moisander (Cap) (54/2), Sauli Aapo Kasperi Väisänen (1/0), Kari Arkivuo (47/1), Përparim Hetemaj (44/4), Alexander Michael Ring (40/1) [90+4.Rasmus Schüller (20/0)], Markus Olof Halsti (31/0), Robin Lod (10/1), Kasper Woldemar Hämäläinen (55/8) [56.Eero Pekka Sakari Markkanen (7/0); 85.Jukka Raitala (34/0)], Teemu Pukki (52/9). Trainer: Hans Roland Backe (Sweden, 9).

Goals: Teemu Pukki (21), Robin Lod (39).

774. 09.10.2016 **FINLAND - CROATIA** **0-1(0-1)** 21st FIFA WC. Qualifiers

Ratinan Stadium, Tampere; Referee: Ruddy Buquet (France); Attendance: 15,567

FIN: Lukas Hradecky (33/0), Paulus Arajuuri (19/2), Niklas Moisander (Cap) (55/2), Kari Arkivuo (48/1) [46.Rasmus Schüller (21/0)], Jukka Raitala (35/0), Juhani Lauri Henrik Ojala (17/0), Janne Saksela (6/0), Sauli Aapo Kasperi Väisänen (2/0) [87.Roope Vilhelmi Riski (5/1)], Alexander Michael Ring (41/1) [57.Thomas Lam (8/0)], Robin Lod (11/1), Teemu Pukki (53/9). Trainer: Hans Roland Backe (Sweden, 10).

775. 12.11.2016 **UKRAINE - FINLAND** **1-0(1-0)**

Chornomorets Stadion, Odesa; Referee: Manuel Jorge Neves Moreira de Sousa (Portugal); Attendance: 34,000

FIN: Lukas Hradecky (34/0), Kari Arkivuo (49/1), Jukka Raitala (36/0), Markus Olof Halsti (32/0) [63.Thomas Lam (9/0)], Sakari Mattila (11/0), Joona Toivio (39/2), Paulus Arajuuri (Cap) (20/2), Sauli Aapo Kasperi Väisänen (3/0) [83.Janne Saksela (7/0)], Alexander Michael Ring (42/1) [46.Eero Pekka Sakari Markkanen (8/0)], Robin Lod (12/1), Teemu Pukki (54/9). Trainer: Hans Roland Backe (Sweden, 11).

FG/Nr	Name	DOB	Caps	Goals	Period, Clubs
(457/500)	AALTONEN Mika A.	16.11.1965	11	0	1988-1994, AC Bellinzona (3/0), FC Bologna (3/0), Turun Palloseura Turku (2/0), Hapoel Beer Sheva (3/0).
(480/517)	AALTONEN Mika J.	12.03.1967	8	1	1990-1994, Ilves Tampere (3/1), Tampereen Palloveikot (5/0).
(707/673)	ÄÄRITALO Mika	25.07.1985	6	1	2010-2012, Turun Palloseura Turku (6/1).
(116/149)	ÅBERG Erik	30.01.1920	6	0	1939-1947, Helsingin Idrottsföreningen Kamraterna (6/0).
(694/655)	AHO Joni	12.04.1986	3	0	2009-2012, FC International Turku (3/0).
(251/326)	AHO Rainer	19.12.1941	7	0	1966-1968, Turun Palloseura Turku (2/0), FF Jaro JS Pietarsaari (5/0).
(330/404)	AHONEN Matti	10.05.1955	4	0	1976-1980, Vaasan Palloseura (1/0), Oulun Palloseura (3/0).
(724/689)	ÄIJÄLÄ Ilari	30.09.1986	1	0	2012, FK Honka Espoo (1/0).
(374/450)	AIJÄLÄ Juha	02.07.1959	2	0	1980, Oulun Työväen Palloilijat (2/0).
(207/272)	AIROLA Keijo	30.04.1935	2	0	1959-1960, Haka Valkeakoski (2/0).
(126/159)	AITIO Tauno	17.09.1917	1	0	1943, Turun Palloseura Turku (1/0).
(16/045)	ÅKERBERG Aarre	23.02.1897	2	0	1921-1922, HJK Helsinki (2/0).
(307/379)	ALAJA Pertti	18.02.1952	28	0	1973-1983, HJK Helsinki (8/0), Oulun Työväen Palloilijat (5/0), Ikast fS (10/0), Malmö FF (5/0).
(42/077)	ALAKARI Karl	17.11.1904	2	0	1925-1927, Sudet Kouvola (1/0), HJK Helsinki (1/0).
(450/497)	ALATENSIÖ Jarmo	09.11.1963	19	1	1987-1989, Porin Pallotoverit (4/1), IK Brage Borlänge (15/0).
(746/700)	ALHO Nikolai Aleksanteri	12.03.1993	1	0	2014, HJK Helsinki (1/0).
(367/440)	ALILA Juoko	18.11.1950	4	1	1980, KTP Kotka (4/1).
(275/347)	ANDELMIN Teuvo	22.04.1948	2	0	1969, Turun Palloseura Turku (2/0).
(374/449)	ANNUNEN Juha	16.04.1960	16	2	1980-1987, Oulun Työväen Palloilijat (3/0), FC Kuusysi Lahti (13/2).
(705/671)	ARAJUURI Paulus	15.06.1988	20	2	2010-2016, Kalmar FF (6/0), KKS Lech Poznań (14/2).
(662/640)	ARKIVUO Kari	23.06.1983	49	1	2005-2016, FC Lahti (1/1), Sandefjord BK (5/0), Go Ahead Eagles Deventer (1/0), BK Häcken Göteborg (42/0).
(298/373)	ASIKAINEN Hannu	12.01.1948	1	0	1972, Ilves-Kissat Tampere (1/0).
(122/152)	ASIKAINEN Toivo	18.05.1913	2	0	1940, Sudet Kouvola (2/0).
(109/144)	ASIKAINEN Veikko	18.04.1918	56	0	1938-1955, Turun Palloseura Turku (18/0), Haka Valkeakoski (38/0).
(147/198)	ASIKAINEN Yrjö	05.06.1928	9	5	1949-1955, Ilves-Kissat Tampere (8/4), Kronohagens IF (1/1).
(22/054)	ÅSTRÖM Gunnar	15.01.1904	43	16	1922-1937, Helsingin Idrottsföreningen Kamraterna (43/16).
(349/421)	BACKMAN Anders	06.02.1954	4	1	1979-1982, Kokkolan Pallo-Veikot (4/1).
(589/599)	BAHNE Magnus	15.03.1979	2	0	2000, FC International Turku (2/0).
(121/151)	BEIJAR Erik	12.05.1921	37	4	1939-1952, IF Kamraterna Vaasa (37/4).
(374/445)	BERGQVIST Kari	04.04.1957	6	0	1980-1981, KTP Kotka (6/0).
(7/019)	BERGROTH Fjalar	05.01.1892	1	0	1914, IF Kamraterna Åbo (1/0).
(295/370)	BERGSTRÖM Henry	16.02.1950	4	0	1971-1973, Vaasan Palloseura (4/0).
(121/150)	BOGOMOLOFF Oleg	11.09.1920	3	0	1939-1948, Kronohagens IF (3/0).
(407/472)	BOSTRÖM Sixten	15.09.1963	14	2	1983-1987, HJK Helsinki (2/1), BK Häcken Göteborg (6/0), HJK Helsinki (6/1).
(330/403)	DAHLLUND Juha	20.03.1954	22	0	1976-1984, HJK Helsinki (22/0).
(468/510)	ECKERMAN Dan-Ola	26.03.1964	4	0	1988, Turun Palloseura Turku (4/0).
(8/031)	EKLÖF Verner	08.03.1897	32	17	1919-1926, Helsingin Idrottsföreningen Kamraterna (14/8), HJK Helsinki (18/9).
(206/270)	EKMAN Carl Magnus	27.03.1938	5	1	1958-1959, Helsingin Idrottsföreningen Kamraterna (5/1).
(16/042)	ELEVUO Harald (BELEWICZ)	13.10.1901	11	0	1921-1926, Helsingin Palloseura (11/0).
(232/306)	ELO Raimo	10.04.1939	3	0	1963-1971, Helsingin Palloseura (2/0), Helsingin IK (1/0).
(534/548)	ENBERG Tom	26.08.1970	5	0	1995-1996, Turun Palloseura Turku (2/0), Myllykosken Pallo-47 Anjalakoski (3/0).
(305/375)	ENCKELMAN Göran	14.06.1948	23	0	1973-1978, Turun Palloseura Turku (17/0), Haka Valkeakoski (2/0), IFK Nyköping (4/0).
(591/601)	ENCKELMAN Peter	10.03.1977	12	0	2000-2010, Aston Villa FC Birmingham (5/0), Blackburn Rovers FC (2/0), Cardiff City FC (5/0).
(8/029)	ENGLUND Arthur	18.05.1893	13	0	1919-1923, Helsingin Idrottsföreningen Kamraterna (13/0).
(634/617)	EREMENKO jr. Alexei	24.03.1983	57	14	2002-2013, HJK Helsinki (7/2), US Lecce (14/8), FK Saturn Ramenskoe (18/3), FK Metalist Kharkiv (4/0), FF Jaro Pietarsaari (1/0), Kilmarnock FC (8/0), FK Rubin Kazan (5/1).
(677/647)	EREMENKO Roman	19.03.1987	73	5	2007-2016, AC Siena (1/0), Udinese Calcio (8/0), FK Dinamo Kyiv (27/1), FK Rubin Kazan (24/3), FK CSKA Moskva (13/1).
(496/523)	ERIKSSON Anders	19.04.1965	15	1	1992-1995, Rovaniemi Palloseura (4/0), Byrne IL Stavanger (3/0), SFK Lyn Oslo (8/1).
(92/125)	ERONEN Pentti	25.07.1914	15	3	1935-1939, HJK Helsinki (15/3).
(406/471)	EUROPAEUS Jari	29.12.1962	56	0	1983-1991, HJK Helsinki (4/0), Gefle IF (18/0), Öster IF Vaexjö (15/0), RoPS Rovaniemi (10/0), HJK Helsinki (9/0).
(272/343)	FLINK Jarmo	12.09.1948	13	0	1968-1972, Reipas Lahti (1/0), Kuopion Palloseura (7/0), Kuopion Pallo Toverit (5/0).
(268/337)	FLINK Turo	27.04.1943	1	1	1968, Reipas Lahti (1/1).
(168/208)	FORSBERG Åke	08.07.1925	1	0	1952, Kronohagens IF (1/0).
(131/174)	FORSBLOM Veikko	02.09.1922	8	0	1946-1948, Tampereen Palloveikot (2/0), Ilves-Kissat Tampere (6/0).
(736/698)	FORSELL Petteri	16.10.1990	6	1	2013-2016, Bursaspor Kulübü (1/1), IFK Mariehamm (5/0).
(168/209)	FORSGREN Olli	03.11.1929	10	4	1952-1956, Helsingin Palloseura (HPS) (5/0), Kronohagens IF (5/4).
(135/184)	FORSMAN Åke	21.11.1923	4	1	1947-1948, Helsingin Idrottsföreningen Kamraterna (4/1).
(156/203)	FORSS Rainer	20.10.1930	18	0	1951-1960, Pyrkivä Turku (12/0), Turku Toverit (2/0), Turun Weikot (4/0).

(280/352)	FORSSELL Henry	25.12.1947	15	0	1969-1975, HJK Helsinki (15/0).
(581/591)	FORSSELL Mikael Kaj	15.03.1981	87	29	1999-2014, Chelsea FC London (1/0), Crystal Palace FC London (12/3), Chelsea FC London (6/4), VfL Borussia Mönchengladbach (3/1), Chelsea FC London (3/1), Birmingham City FC (6/3), Chelsea FC London (2/0), Birmingham City FC (22/5), Hannover'96 (21/8), Leeds United AFC (5/1), HJK Helsinki (6/3).
(687/649)	FREDRIKSON Otto	30.11.1981	13	0	2008-2011, Lillestrøm SK (3/0), FK Spartak Nalchik (10/0).
(705/670)	FURUHOLM Timo	11.10.1987	10	2	2010-2013, FC International Turku (5/1), TSV Fortuna Düsseldorf (4/1), Hallescher FC (1/0).

(16/049)	GRANNAS Einar	15.12.1898	1	1	1921, IF Kamraterna Åbo (1/1).
(28/062)	GRANNAS Ivar	25.06.1895	1	0	1923, IF Kamraterna Åbo (1/0).
(386/457)	GRANSKOG Mikael	26.03.1961	24	0	1982-1986, IFK Norrköping (24/0).
(111/145)	GRANSTRÖM Holger	25.12.1917	12	2	1938-1940, Kronohagens IF (12/2).
(209/276)	GRONDAHL Jouni	06.02.1938	9	0	1959-1964, Turun Palloseura Turku (9/0).
(480/518)	GRÖNHOLM Niclas	16.06.1968	17	2	1990-1994, Turun Palloseura Turku (3/0), BK Forward (10/1), Myllykosken Pallo-47 Anjalakoski (4/1).
(69/114)	GRÖNLUND Ernst	18.12.1902	37	10	1931-1940, Helsingin Idrottsföreningen Kamraterna (37/10).
(540/551)	GRÖNLUND Tommi	09.12.1969	36	2	1995-2000, HJK Helsinki (14/1), Viborg FF (1/0), Trelleborgs FF (19/1), Heart of Midlothian FC Edinburgh (2/0).
(99/134)	GUSTAFSSON Erkki	31.12.1912	3	0	1936-1939, Helsingin Toverit (3/0).

(199/261)	HAAHTI Matti	08.06.1936	25	0	1957-1962, Ilves-Kissat Tampere (4/0), Helsingin Idrottsföreningen Kamraterna (18/0), Reipas Lahti (3/0).
(308/380)	HAAPA Tuomo	05.05.1946	1	0	1973, Kemin Into (1/0).
(662/641)	HAAPALA Tuomas	20.04.1979	3	0	2005-2006, Myllykosken Pallo-47 Anjalankoski (1/0), Manchester City FC (2/0).
(650/633)	HAARALA Hannu	15.08.1981	2	0	2005, SC Heerenveen (2/0).
(334/406)	HAASKIVI Kai	28.12.1955	12	3	1977-1984, Kronohagens IF (6/1), Houston Hurricane (3/1), Edmonton Drillers (2/1), Cleveland Force (1/0).
(269/340)	HAAVISTO Juhani	20.11.1945	1	0	1968, Kotkan Työväen Palloilijat (1/0).
(140/193)	HAGG Per-Erik	06.09.1926	3	0	1948-1949, Kronohagens IF (3/0).
(188/247)	HAGSTRÖM Raimo	01.11.1934	4	0	1956, Helsingin Palloseura (4/0).
(269/339)	HAIKONEN Pertti	18.04.1948	3	0	1968-1969, Helsingin Ponnistus (3/0).
(357/430)	HAKALA Tuomo	09.10.1957	11	1	1979-1983, Rovaniemi Palloseura (11/1).
(624/615)	HAKANPÄÄ Rami	09.10.1978	5	1	2003-2004, HJK Helsinki (5/1).
(188/248)	HAKKARAINEN Kauko	30.12.1932	10	0	1956-1959, Kuopion Palloseura (10/0).
(695/663)	HAKOLA Juha	27.10.1987	1	0	2009, Heracles Almelo (1/0).
(235/310)	HALME Martti	05.04.1943	14	0	1964-1969, Haka Valkeakoski (14/0).
(74/118)	HALME Viljo	24.01.1907	30	0	1932-1939, HJK Helsinki (22/0), Helsingin Palloseura (8/0).
(556/568)	HALONEN Arto	13.06.1964	3	0	1997, FF Jaro JS Pietarsaari (3/0).
(685/648)	HALSTI Markus Olof	19.03.1984	32	0	2008-2016, GAIS Göteborg (1/0), Malmö FF (20/0), DC United Washington (7/0), FC Midtylland Herning (4/0).
(195/258)	HARELL Erkki	12.03.1930	8	0	1957, Rosenlewin Urheiluliito Pori (8/0).
(127/162)	HASSO Anatol	03.07.1917	3	1	1943-1948, Helsingin Palloseura (3/1).
(317/390)	HÄMÄLÄINEN Hannu	01.01.1948	5	0	1975-1976, Reipas Lahti (5/0).
(693/653)	HÄMÄLÄINEN Kasper Woldemar	08.06.1986	55	8	2008-2016, Turun Palloseura Turku (4/0), Djurgårdens IF Stockholm (26/6), KKS Lech Poznań (19/1), Legia Warszawa (6/1).
(435/480)	HÄNNIKÄINEN Jyrki	30.03.1965	16	0	1986-1989, Kuusysi Lahti (7/0), Turun Palloseura Turku (9/0).
(206/269)	HÄYHÄ Lauri	13.11.1932	1	0	1958, Vaasan Palloseura (1/0).
(271/342)	HEIKKILÄ Pekka	09.12.1946	24	0	1968-1973, Kotkan Työväen Palloilijat (3/0), Helsingin Idrottsföreningen Kamraterna (20/0), Haka Valkeakoski (1/0).
(748/706)	HEIKKILÄ Tapio	08.04.1990	3	0	2014-2016, HJK Helsinki (1/0), SJK Seinäjoki (2/0).
(361/436)	HEIKKINEN Ari	08.04.1957	4	0	1979-1980, Oulun Palloseura (4/0).
(467/509)	HEIKKINEN Ari	08.04.1964	51	1	1988-1994, Turun Palloseura Turku (46/1), Haka Valkeakoski (5/0).
(612/607)	HEIKKINEN Markus	13.10.1978	61	0	2002-2011, HJK Helsinki (4/0), Portsmouth FC (3/0), Aberdeen FC (8/0), Luton Town FC (14/0), SK Rapid Wien (32/0).
(329/402)	HEIKKINEN Teppo	12.11.1950	12	1	1976-1977, Oulun Työväen Palloilijat (12/1).
(613/609)	HEINÄNEN Petri	18.05.1976	3	0	2002-2004, Tampere United (3/0).
(648/622)	HEINIKANGAS Jarno	05.03.1979	3	0	2004-2005, Turun Palloseura Turku (3/0).
(527/543)	HEINOLA Antti	20.03.1973	12	0	1994-2001, HJK Helsinki (6/0), Emmen (2/0), Queen's Park Rangers FC London (4/0).
(199/262)	HEINONEN Olli	07.01.1937	29	0	1957-1965, Ilves-Kissat Tampere (6/0), Reipas Lahti (23/0).
(268/335)	HEINONEN Paavo	30.05.1944	13	0	1968-1972, HJK Helsinki (13/0).
(122/153)	HEINONEN Viljo	13.09.1918	3	0	1940-1946, Sudet Kouvola (3/0).
(312/384)	HEISKANEN Aki	02.02.1952	32	7	1974-1978, Kuopion Pallo Toverit (27/5), Kuopion Palloseura (5/2).
(324/397)	HEISKANEN Esa	23.05.1953	8	3	1976, Kuopion Palloseura (8/3).
(7/018)	HELIN Gunnar		1	0	1914, Kronohagens IF (1/0).
(328/401)	HELIN Juha	04.01.1954	24	1	1976-1981, Haka Valkeakoski (22/1), Rovaniemi Palloseura (2/0).
(214/281)	HELIN Pentti	01.03.1934	1	0	1960, Rauman Pallo (1/0).
(496/525)	HELIN Petri	13.12.1969	27	2	1992-2002, HJK Helsinki (1/0), Ikast fS (8/2), FC Jokerit Helsinki (8/0), Luton Town FC (3/0), Stockport County FC (3/0), Denizlispor Kulübü (4/0).
(231/301)	HELTOLA Esko	27.10.1938	2	0	1963, Kouvolan Urheilijain Palloilijat (1/0), Helsingin Idrottsföreningen Kamraterna (1/0).
(176/222)	HENRIKSSON Ibert	06.05.1928	3	0	1954, Vaasa Idrottsförening Kamraterna (3/0).
(130/172)	HERRMAN Börje	31.10.1921	1	0	1946, Helsingin Idrottsföreningen Kamraterna (1/0).
(66/108)	HESTENAES Arthur	06.08.1908	2	0	1930-1931, IF Kamraterna Åbo (2/0).
(694/658)	HETEMAJ Mehmet	08.12.1987	5	0	2009-2016, AC Thrasivoulos Fylis (1/0), UC AlbinoLeffe (1/0), FC Honka Espoo (1/0), SJK Seinäjoki (2/0).

(694/662)	HETEMAJ Përparim	12.12.1986	**44**	**4**	2009-2016, AEK Athína (2/0), Brescia Calcio (4/0), AC Chievo Verona (38/4).
(337/408)	HIETA Pekka	21.09.1953	**3**	**0**	1977-1979, Kuopion Pallo Toverit (3/0).
(589/600)	HIETANEN Janne	02.06.1978	**16**	**0**	2000-2005, Vaasan Palloseura (2/0), Denizlispor Kulübü (10/0), UD Las Palmas (2/0), Tromsø IL (2/0).
(765/715)	HILANDER Mika	17.08.1983	**1**	**0**	2016, FC Ilves Tampere (1/0).
(170/216)	HILTUNEN Matti	26.01.1933	**21**	**5**	1953-1963, Kuopion Pallo Toverit (12/4), Kronohagens IF (1/0), Kuopion Palloseura (8/1).
(357/431)	HIMANKA Juhani	19.04.1956	**22**	**3**	1979-1982, Oulun Palloseura (13/2), Lillestrøm SK (9/1).
(53/087)	HINTSA Reino	08.07.1907	**1**	**0**	1928, Sudet Kouvola (1/0).
(16/048)	HIRVONEN Vilho	31.12.1894	**1**	**1**	1921, Helsingin Palloseura (1/1).
(574/587)	HIUKKA Matti	05.05.1975	**2**	**0**	1999, FC Jokerit Helsinki (2/0).
(395/461)	HJELM Ari-Juhani	24.02.1962	**100**	**20**	1983-1996, Ilves Tampere (48/11), Stuttgarter Kickers (6/0), Ilves Tampere (16/2), FC St.Pauli Hamburg (9/2), FC Ilves Tampere (7/2), HJK Helsinki (14/3).
(315/386)	HOLLI Harri	19.01.1949	**2**	**0**	1974, Reipas Lahti (2/0).
(54/090)	HOLLMEN Edvard	28.05.1902	**2**	**0**	1928, Kronohagens IF (2/0).
(54/088)	HOLMBERG Charles	28.04.1906	**12**	**0**	1928-1930, Helsingin Idrottsföreningen Kamraterna (12/0).
(436/485)	HOLMGREN Erik	17.12.1964	**60**	**2**	1986-1994, HJK Helsinki (23/0), GAIS Göteborg (29/2), Finnairin Palloilijat Helsinki (8/0).
(208/274)	HOLMQVIST Stig	13.02.1936	**21**	**1**	1959-1965, Helsingin Idrottsföreningen Kamraterna (12/1), HJK Helsinki (8/1), Upon Pallo Lahti (1/0).
(7/022)	HOLMSTRÖM Alexander		**1**	**0**	1914, Kronohagens IF (1/0).
(1/001)	HOLMSTRÖM Gustaf	27.11.1888	**1**	**0**	1911, Helsingin Idrottsföreningen Kamraterna (1/0).
(1/002)	HOLOPAINEN Jalmari	29.06.1892	**6**	**0**	1911-1912, HJK Helsinki (6/0).
(115/147)	HONKA Anton	24.04.1919	**4**	**0**	1938-1945, Turun Palloseura Turku (4/0).
(341/412)	HOUTSONEN Leo	25.10.1958	**48**	**1**	1978-1986, Oulun Palloseura (15/0), Kuopion Palloseura (8/1), Oulun Palloseura (5/0), Kuopion Palloseura (20/0).
(282/356)	HOVIVUORI Veikko	21.06.1948	**1**	**0**	1970, Ilves-Kissat Tampere (1/0).
(16/047)	HÖGLANDER Adolf	06.09.1901	**2**	**0**	1921-1924, IF Kamraterna Åbo (2/0).
(707/674)	HRADECKY Lukas	24.11.1989	**34**	**0**	2010-2016, Esbjerg fB (14/0), Brøndby IF København (8/0), Eintracht Frankfurt (12/0).
(766/722)	HRADECKY Matej	17.04.1995	**1**	**0**	2016, Turun Palloseura Turku (1/0).
(465/505)	HUHTAMÄKI Jyrki	27.08.1967	**13**	**0**	1988-1996, Mikkelin Palloilijat (10/0), Vaasan Palloseura (3/0).
(311/383)	HUKKA Raimo	09.05.1948	**2**	**0**	1974, Reipas Lahti (2/0).
(727/692)	HURME Jarkko Erkki	04.06.1986	**12**	**1**	2012-2016, Turun Palloseura Turku (6/0), Odds BK Skien (5/1), SJK Seinäjoki (1/0).
(187/246)	HURRI Keijo	05.12.1927	**5**	**0**	1956, Kuopion Palloseura (5/0).
(374/444)	HUTTUNEN Ollavi	04.08.1960	**61**	**0**	1980-1992, Haka Valkeakoski (61/0).
(530/546)	HUTTUNEN Toni	12.01.1973	**11**	**0**	1994-2002, Myllykosken Pallo-47 Anjalakoski (11/0).
(648/624)	HUUSKO Keijo	05.08.1980	**8**	**2**	2004-2006, Tornion Pallo-47 (2/1), SFK Lyn Oslo (5/1), Strømsgodset IF (1/0).
(503/531)	HYRYLÄINEN Aki	17.04.1968	**25**	**1**	1992-1997, HJK Helsinki (23/1), FC København (2/0).
(251/329)	HYTTINEN Antero	18.10.1943	**1**	**0**	1966, Mikkelin Palloilijat (1/0).
(251/328)	HYVÄRINEN Markku	11.04.1943	**11**	**0**	1966-1969, Kuopion Palloseura (11/0).
(211/277)	HYVÄRINEN Martti	06.11.1939	**17**	**1**	1959-1967, Kuopion Palloseura (4/0), Reipas Lahti (13/1).
(503/533)	HYYPIÄ Sami	07.10.1973	**105**	**5**	1992-2010, Myllykosken Pallo-47 Anjalakoski (3/0), Willem II Tillburg (23/0), Liverpool FC (73/5), TSV Bayer 04 Leverkusen (6/0).
(652/636)	HYYRYNEN Mikko	01.11.1977	**2**	**0**	2005, Turun Palloseura Turku (2/0).

(192/254)	IIVARINEN Timo	24.09.1936	**1**	**0**	1956, Kuopion Palloseura (1/0).
(374/446)	IKÄLÄINEN Jukka	14.05.1957	**59**	**4**	1980-1989, GIF Sundsvall (3/0), IS Örgryte Göteborg (31/2), Kemin Palloseura (20/2), Kiruna FF (5/0).
(453/498)	IKÄVALKO Mika	28.12.1965	**3**	**0**	1987-1988, HJK Helsinki (3/0).
(573/583)	ILOLA Jari	24.11.1978	**30**	**1**	1998-2007, HJK Helsinki (11/1), IF Elfsborg Borås (19/0).
(333/405)	ILOLA Jarmo	25.08.1956	**1**	**0**	1977, HJK Helsinki (1/0).
(343/414)	ISMAIL Atik	05.01.1957	**26**	**7**	1978-1983, HJK Helsinki (5/5), Beşiktaş JK Istanbul (1/0), HJK Helsinki (6/1), AIK Stockholm (2/0), HJK Helsinki (12/1).
(352/424)	ISOAHO Olli	02.03.1956	**20**	**0**	1979-1986, HJK Helsinki (18/0), DSC Arminia Bielefeld (2/0).

(717/682)	JAAKKOLA Anssi	13.03.1987	**1**	**0**	2011, Kilmarnock FC (1/0).
(374/447)	JAAKONSAARI Pasi	27.03.1959	**11**	**4**	1980-1982, HJK Helsinki (11/4).
(8/034)	JAALE Paavo	21.10.1895	**1**	**0**	1919, HJK Helsinki (1/0).
(481/519)	JAKONEN Petri	09.06.1967	**25**	**0**	1990-1996, HJK Helsinki (2/0), Turun Palloseura Turku (12/0), Myllykosken Pallo-47 Anjalakoski (11/0).
(708/676)	JALASTO Ville	19.04.1986	**8**	**0**	2010-2016, Aalesunds FK (3/0), Stabæk IF Bærum (3/0), HJK Helsinki (2/0).
(373/443)	JALASVAARA Ari	20.07.1959	**5**	**0**	1980-1986, Oulun Palloseura (2/0), Rovaniemi Palloseura (3/0).
(186/244)	JALAVA Reijo	18.02.1932	**21**	**0**	1955-1961, HJK Helsinki (21/0).
(367/441)	JALO Tomi	22.10.1958	**2**	**0**	1980, Turun Palloseura Turku (2/0).
(534/549)	JALONEN Jasse	18.07.1973	**6**	**0**	1995-1996, Turun Palloseura Turku (1/0), Myllykosken Pallo-47 Anjalakoski (5/0).
(268/336)	JALONEN Jouni	15.09.1942	**6**	**0**	1968-1969, Turun Palloseura Turku (6/0).
(16/046)	JANSSON Martin	11.11.1896	**3**	**0**	1921-1922, IF Kamraterna Åbo (3/0).
(322/396)	JANTUNEN Pertti	25.06.1952	**26**	**1**	1975-1978, Reipas Lahti (15/1), CD Málaga (3/0), IFK Eskilstuna (8/0).
(181/234)	JARVINEN Martti	21.09.1933	**2**	**0**	1955-1957, Vaasan Palloseura (1/0), Helsingin Palloseura (1/0).
(567/580)	JÄÄSKELÄINEN Jussi	19.04.1975	**56**	**0**	1998-2010, Bolton Wanderers FC (56/0).
(483/520)	JÄNTTI Hannu	01.03.1963	**2**	**0**	1990, FC Kuusysi Lahti (2/0).
(235/314)	JÄRVI Harri	20.08.1939	**5**	**3**	1964, Hämeenlinnan Tarmo (5/3).
(211/278)	JÄRVINEN Aulis	28.01.1935	**1**	**0**	1959, Rosenlewin Urheiluliito Pori (1/0).

(474/512)	JÄRVINEN Petri	09.05.1966	**36**	**4**	1989-1996, FC Kuusysi Lahti (17/3), Finnairin Palloilijat Helsinki (8/1), SV Waldhoff Mannheim (3/0), Finnairin Palloilijat Helsinki (8/0).
(542/554)	JÄVÄJÄ Jari	16.08.1973	**6**	**0**	1995-1997, Vaasan Palloseura (6/0).
(1/008)	JERIMA Paul	29.12.1892	**1**	**1**	1911, Helsingin Sport (1/1).
(7/024)	JOHANSSON Arthur	19.01.1893	**1**	**0**	1914, Kronohagens IF (1/0).
(137/186)	JOHANSSON Helge	27.02.1926	**1**	**0**	1947, Turun Palloseura Turku (1/0).
(548/560)	JOHANSSON Jonatan Lillebror	16.08.1975	**105**	**22**	1996-2010, Turun Palloseura Turku (1/1), FC Flora Tallinn (5/0), Glasgow Rangers FC (20/8), Charlton Athletic FC London (42/3), Norwich City FC (2/0), Malmö FF (21/5), Hibernian Edinburgh FC (9/5), St. Johnstone FC Perth (1/0), Turun Palloseura Turku (4/0).
(7/025)	JOHANSSON Knut	10.08.1892	**1**	**1**	1914, Kronohagens IF (1/1).
(182/237)	JOKELA Pentti	05.03.1931	**1**	**0**	1955, PP (1/0).
(170/214)	JOKINEN Matti	08.11.1928	**7**	**0**	1953-1957, Vaasa Idrottsförening Kamraterna (5/0), IF Drott Pietarsaari (2/0).
(734/694)	JORONEN Jesse	21.03.1993	**2**	**0**	2013-2016, Maidenhead United FC (1/0), Fulham FC London (1/0).
(439/491)	JUNTUNEN Miika	09.10.1964	**2**	**0**	1986, Oulun Palloseura (1/0), Kemin Palloseura (1/0).
(566/579)	KAIJASILTA Petteri	03.08.1974	**3**	**2**	1998-1999, Turun Palloseura Turku (3/2).
(557/571)	KAINULAINEN Tommi	08.01.1974	**1**	**0**	1997, FF Jaro JS Pietarsaari (1/0).
(357/432)	KAIVONURMI Jarmo	12.11.1957	**2**	**0**	1979, Kuopion Pallo Toverit (2/0).
(144/197)	KALLIO Karl	13.04.1925	**1**	**0**	1949, Kokkolan Pallo-Veikot (1/0).
(458/502)	KALLIO Markku	18.09.1961	**1**	**0**	1988, Rovaniemi Palloseura (1/0).
(585/596)	KALLIO Toni	09.08.1978	**49**	**2**	2000-2010, HJK Helsinki (8/1), Molde FK (19/0), BSC Young Boys Bern (8/0), Fulham FC London (13/1), Sheffield United FC (1/0).
(297/372)	KALLIO Vesa	31.08.1951	**3**	**0**	1972-1973, Kokkolan Pallo-Veikot (3/0).
(59/099)	KANERVA Arvo	27.05.1902	**1**	**0**	1929, Turun Palloseura Turku (1/0).
(436/489)	KANERVA Markku	24.05.1964	**59**	**1**	1986-1995, HJK Helsinki (23/0), IF Elfsborg Borås (7/0), Finnairin Palloilijat Helsinki (13/0), HJK Helsinki (16/1).
(234/308)	KANERVA Reijo	29.01.1944	**17**	**0**	1964-1967, IF Kamraterna Åbo (7/0), Upon Pallo Lahti (10/0).
(18/050)	KANERVA William	26.11.1902	**50**	**13**	1922-1938, HJK Helsinki (10/2), Helsingin Palloseura (40/11).
(40/075)	KANERVA Yrjö	05.02.1901	**6**	**0**	1925-1928, HJK Helsinki (6/0).
(520/541)	KANGASKORPI Jokke	02.03.1972	**11**	**0**	1994-1996, Mikkelin Palloilijat (5/0), FC Haka Valkeakoski (6/0).
(623/611)	KANGASKORPI Juuso	04.09.1975	**7**	**0**	2003-2006, FC Haka Valkeakoski (7/0).
(177/226)	KANKKONEN Hannu	26.01.1934	**25**	**6**	1954-1963, Helsingin Idrottsföreningen Kamraterna (23/6), HJK Helsinki (2/0).
(192/252)	KANNAS Matti	25.09.1928	**9**	**0**	1956-1959, HJK Helsinki (9/0).
(123/155)	KARHU Eino	18.03.1916	**1**	**0**	1940, Sudet Kouvola (1/0).
(29/064)	KARJAGIN Alexander	18.12.1896	**8**	**1**	1924-1925, Helsingin Palloseura (8/1).
(57/093)	KARJAGIN Frans	11.06.1909	**57**	**0**	1929-1941, Helsingin Idrottsföreningen Kamraterna (57/0).
(74/117)	KARJAGIN Leo	31.10.1911	**17**	**2**	1932-1940, Helsingin Idrottsföreningen Kamraterna (17/2).
(530/544)	KARJALAINEN Lasse	22.10.1974	**15**	**0**	1994-2002, FC Jazz Pori (1/0), FC Haka Valkeakoski (14/0).
(55/091)	KARLSSON Armas	13.07.1906	**5**	**0**	1928-1931, IF Kamraterna Åbo (5/0).
(465/504)	KARVINEN Juha	26.09.1966	**8**	**2**	1988-1996, Kuopion Palloseura (2/0), Mikkelin Palloilijat (5/2), Vaasan Palloseura (1/0).
(175/221)	KASURINEN A.	28.01.1928	**1**	**0**	1953, Kuopion Pallo Toverit (1/0).
(18/051)	KATAJAVUORI Arvi	03.01.1898	**5**	**1**	1922-1925, Helsingin Palloseura (5/1).
(724/686)	KAUKO Joni	12.07.1990	**7**	**0**	2012-2016, FC International Turku (1/0), FC Lahti (2/0), FSV Frankfurt (3/0), FC Ebergie Cottbus (1/0).
(249/325)	KAUPINNEN Raimo	17.04.1936	**1**	**0**	1966, HJK Helsinki (1/0).
(235/311)	KAUTONEN Timo	12.03.1945	**51**	**0**	1964-1976, Reipas Lahti (51/0).
(571/582)	KAUTONEN Tommi	24.12.1971	**9**	**0**	1998-2001, Myllykosken Pallo-47 Anjalakoski (4/0), Vaasan Palloseura (5/0).
(556/566)	KAVÉN Mikko	19.02.1975	**15**	**0**	1997-2006, HJK Helsinki (2/0), Tampere United (13/0).
(88/123)	KEKKONEN Leevi	09.09.1908	**3**	**0**	1934-1935, Helsingin Toverit (3/0).
(95/127)	KEKKONEN Tauno	01.05.1910	**3**	**0**	1935-1937, Helsingin Toverit (3/0).
(10/037)	KELIN Hjalmar	28.09.1900	**42**	**7**	1920-1928, HJK Helsinki (42/7).
(226/294)	KEMI Eesko	07.04.1939	**6**	**0**	1962-1963, Oulun Työväen Palloilijat (6/0).
(237/317)	KESTILA Rauno	09.11.1940	**1**	**1**	1964, Upon Pallo Lahti (1/1).
(66/111)	KETTUNEN Eero	16.06.1906	**1**	**0**	1930, Viipurin Palloseura (1/0).
(26/061)	KETTUNEN Vilho	10.08.1899	**2**	**0**	1923, Viipurin Sudet (2/0).
(130/171)	KIHLMAN Keijo	31.05.1920	**1**	**0**	1946, Turun Palloseura Turku (1/0).
(104/137)	KILPI Eino	23.10.1910	**2**	**0**	1937, Helsingin Palloseura (2/0).
(251/327)	KILPONEN Seppo	20.09.1941	**34**	**0**	1966-1971, Oulun Palloseura (30/0), Oulun Työväen Palloilijat (4/0).
(500/528)	KINNUNEN Jari	12.09.1966	**25**	**1**	1992-1994, FC Kuusysi Lahti (19/1), FC Haka Valkeakoski (6/0).
(567/581)	KINNUNEN Tomi	28.03.1969	**6**	**0**	1998-1999, Vaasan Palloseura (4/0), KRC Genk (2/0).
(171/218)	KLINGA Aarre	20.03.1930	**10**	**0**	1953-1959, Kronohagens IF (8/0), Haka Valkeakoski (2/0).
(128/164)	KOISTINEN Tauno	23.12.1918	**6**	**0**	1945-1947, Vaasan Palloseura (6/0).
(180/229)	KOIVISTO Pertti	08.12.1924	**2**	**0**	1954-1955, Kotkan Työväen Palloilijat (2/0).
(765/718)	KOKKO Aleksandr	04.06.1987	**1**	**0**	2016, RoPS Rovaniemi (1/0).
(257/330)	KOKKO Pentti	02.02.1944	**1**	**0**	1967, HJK Helsinki (1/0).
(337/409)	KOKKO Reima	26.03.1952	**6**	**0**	1977-1979, Kronohagens Idrottsförening (1/0), HJK Helsinki (5/0).
(377/452)	KOKKO Simo	21.09.1963	**3**	**0**	1981-1983, HJK Helsinki (3/0).
(724/687)	KOLEHMAINEN Toni	20.07.1988	**10**	**3**	2012-2015, Turun Palloseura Turku (4/2), Hønefoss BK (6/1).
(530/545)	KOLKKA Joonas Einari	28.09.1974	**98**	**11**	1994-2010, Myllykosken Pallo-47 Anjalakoski (4/2), Willem II Tillburg (10/1), PSV Eindhoven (20/3), Panathinaikos AO Athína (15/4), VfL Borussia Mönchengladbach (7/1), Crystal Palace FC London (9/0), ADO Den Haag (3/0), Feyenoord SC Rotterdam (9/0), NAC Breda (21/0).
(185/241)	KONTKANEN Helles	04.11.1932	**2**	**0**	1955-1957, Kronohagens IF (2/0).
(29/065)	KOPONEN Aulis	05.04.1906	**38**	**16**	1924-1935, Helsingin Palloseura (38/16).
(594/602)	KOPPINEN Miika	05.07.1978	**18**	**0**	2000-2006, Tromsø IL (17/0), Rosenborg BK Trondheim (1/0).

(612/608)	KOPTEFF Peter	10.04.1979	**39**	**1**	2002-2006, Viking FK Stavanger (37/1), Stoke City FC (2/0).
(286/360)	KORHONEN Esa	04.01.1944	**1**	**0**	1970, Kokkolan Pallo-Veikot (1/0).
(397/464)	KORHONEN Ismo	10.02.1962	**7**	**0**	1983-1986, FC Kuusysi Lahti (7/0).
(228/298)	KORHONEN Matti	17.05.1938	**2**	**0**	1962, Helsingin Palloseura (2/0).
(24/058)	KORMA Kalle (FALLSTRÖM)	27.12.1900	**19**	**10**	1923-1927, HJK Helsinki (19/10).
(155/201)	KORPELA Kauko	19.05.1931	**2**	**1**	1951-1958, KUV (1/0), HJK Helsinki (1/1).
(543/555)	KOSKINEN Jarkko	29.11.1972	**17**	**1**	1995-1998, Myllykosken Pallo-47 Anjalakoski (13/1), Willem II Tillburg (4/0).
(16/043)	KOSKINEN Niilo	18.07.1898	**28**	**0**	1921-1930, Helsingin Palloseura (28/0).
(25/059)	KOSKINEN Tuovi	09.10.1897	**9**	**0**	1923-1928, Viipurin Sudet (9/0).
(295/369)	KOSONEN Pekka	30.12.1946	**9**	**0**	1971-1973, Reipas Lahti (9/0).
(565/578)	KOTTILA Mika	22.09.1974	**31**	**6**	1998-2004, HJK Helsinki (2/0), SK Brann Bergen (4/0), Trelleborgs FF (16/5), HJK Helsinki (9/1).
(379/453)	KOUSA Keijo	27.07.1959	**18**	**4**	1981-1986, Kuusysi Lahti (18/4).
(649/630)	KÖNÖNEN Tuomo	29.12.1977	**6**	**0**	2004-2006, Myllykosken Pallo-47 Anjalankoski (4/0), Odd Grenland Skien (2/0).
(305/377)	KÖYKKÄ Olavi	21.06.1943	**2**	**0**	1973-1975, Oulun Työväen Palloilijat (2/0).
(46/083)	KUHLBERG Hugo	19.04.1902	**2**	**0**	1926, Helsingin Palloseura (2/0).
(62/101)	KUHLBERG Viljo	01.09.1910	**5**	**0**	1929-1930, Helsingin Palloseura (5/0).
(556/567)	KUIVASTO Toni	31.12.1975	**75**	**1**	1997-2009, Myllykosken Pallo-47 Anjalakoski (6/0), HJK Helsinki (9/0), Viking FK Stavanger (22/0), Djurgårdens IF Stockholm (36/1).
(649/631)	KUJALA Jussi	04.04.1983	**4**	**0**	2004-2009, Tampere United (4/0).
(40/073)	KULMALA Untamo	11.03.1905	**4**	**2**	1925-1928, Turun Palloseura Turku (4/2).
(109/143)	KULTTI Heikki	28.03.1916	**2**	**0**	1938-1939, Vaasan Palloseura (2/0).
(126/160)	KULTTI Väinö	18.12.1917	**1**	**0**	1943, Vaasan Palloseura (1/0).
(26/060)	KULVES Paul	20.03.1899	**1**	**0**	1923, IF Kamraterna Åbo (1/0).
(202/265)	KUMPULAMPI Markku	21.05.1939	**19**	**2**	1957-1967, Haka Valkeakoski (8/1), Upon Pallo Lahti (11/1).
(174/220)	KUPIAINEN Pekka	25.11.1929	**6**	**0**	1953-1955, Kotkan Jäntevä (6/0).
(353/428)	KUPIAINEN Petteri	26.02.1960	**9**	**0**	1979-1981, Kuopion Palloseura (7/0), Club Brugge KV (2/0).
(652/637)	KUQI Njazi	25.03.1983	**12**	**5**	2005-2013, Birmingham City FC (2/3), TuS Koblenz (1/0), Panionios GSS Athína (4/2), PAE Atromitos Athína (5/0).
(582/594)	KUQI Shefki	10.11.1976	**62**	**7**	1999-2010, HJK Helsinki (2/0), FC Jokerit Helsinki (11/2), Stockport County FC (7/1), Sheffield Wednesday FC (13/0), Ipswich Town FC (7/2), Blackburn Rovers FC (3/0), Crystal Palace FC London (6/0), Fulham FC London (3/1), Crystal Palace FC London (4/1), TuS Koblenz (4/0), Derby County FC (2/0).
(317/392)	KUULUVAINEN Raimo	23.04.1955	**6**	**0**	1975-1980, Ilves Tampere (6/0).
(301/374)	KUUSELA Martti	09.10.1945	**2**	**0**	1972-1973, HJK Helsinki (1/0), Haka Valkeakoski (1/0).
(86/122)	KYLMÄLÄ Yrjö	20.09.1911	**7**	**5**	1934-1939, Helsingin Toverit (7/5).
(319/393)	KYMÄLÄINEN Pauno	14.11.1949	**39**	**0**	1975-1985, Turun Palloseura Turku (39/0).

(109/142)	LAAKSO Olavi	23.11.1912	**2**	**0**	1938, Vaasan Palloseura (2/0).
(756/710)	LAAKSONEN Johannes	13.12.1990	**3**	**0**	2015-2016, SJK Seinäjoki (3/0).
(436/488)	LAAKSONEN Juha	24.09.1963	**6**	**0**	1986-1987, Turun Palloseura Turku (6/0).
(44/081)	LAAKSONEN Leo	12.08.1905	**4**	**1**	1926-1928, HJK Helsinki (4/1).
(131/173)	LAAKSONEN Olavi	26.07.1921	**21**	**0**	1946-1952, Turku Toverit (21/0).
(582/592)	LAAKSONEN Pasi	15.08.1972	**5**	**0**	1999-2001, FC Jokerit Helsinki (5/0).
(501/529)	LAAKSONEN Saku	08.08.1970	**2**	**0**	1992-1997, FC Jazz Pori (2/0).
(54/089)	LAESMAA Sakari (LÅNGHOLM)	06.09.1903	**3**	**0**	1928, HJK Helsinki (3/0).
(635/619)	LAGERBLOM Pekka	19.10.1982	**12**	**0**	2003-2006, FC Lahti (2/0), SV Werder Bremen (8/0), 1.FC Köln (2/0).
(99/133)	LAHTI Eino	18.05.1915	**22**	**0**	1936-1945, Vaasan Palloseura (10/0), Helsingin Palloseura (12/0).
(154/200)	LAHTI Kalle	11.04.1928	**3**	**1**	1950-1951, Kotkan Työväen Palloilijat (3/1).
(240/318)	LAHTI Markku	18.04.1945	**2**	**0**	1964-1965, Haka Valkeakoski (2/0).
(359/435)	LAHTINEN Aki	31.10.1958	**56**	**0**	1979-1989, Oulun Palloseura (21/0), Notts County FC (17/0), Kemin Palloseura (10/0), Oulun Työväen Palloilijat (8/0).
(170/217)	LAHTINEN Olavi	05.01.1929	**27**	**7**	1953-1958, HJK Helsinki (27/7).
(190/250)	LAIHO Asko	13.04.1930	**1**	**0**	1956, Kotkan Reipas (1/0).
(231/303)	LAINE Aulis	26.04.1940	**18**	**2**	1963-1968, IF Kamraterna Åbo (18/2).
(24/056)	LAINE Ilmari	14.03.1896	**1**	**0**	1923, Viipurin Sudet (1/0).
(312/385)	LAINE Juha-Pekka	19.08.1948	**10**	**1**	1974-1976, HJK Helsinki (4/1), MVV Maastricht (6/0).
(66/106)	LAINE Oiva	09.06.1908	**4**	**0**	1930-1931, Helsingin Palloseura (4/0).
(169/211)	LAITINEN Martti	09.05.1929	**2**	**0**	1952-1953, Helsingin Ponnistus (2/0).
(759/714)	LAM Thomas	18.12.1993	**9**	**0**	2015-2016, PEC Zwolle (5/0), Nottingham Forest FC (4/0).
(247/323)	LAMBERG Arvo	03.07.1943	**6**	**0**	1965-1969, Gamlakarleby Bollklub (6/0).
(308/381)	LAMBERG Hannu	26.12.1947	**1**	**0**	1973, Kokkolan Palloveikot (1/0).
(355/429)	LAMPI Heikki	30.08.1957	**1**	**0**	1979, Reipas Lahti (1/0).
(349/417)	LAMPI Mikko	03.06.1952	**16**	**0**	1979-1980, Reipas Lahti (16/0).
(663/644)	LAMPI Veli	18.07.1984	**33**	**0**	2006-2015, HJK Helsinki (3/0), FC Zürich (13/0), FC Aarau (3/0), Willem II Tilburg (5/0), FK Arsenal Kyiv (7/0), HJK Helsinki (2/0).
(59/098)	LARVO Pentti	22.12.1908	**31**	**4**	1929-1937, Helsingin Palloseura (31/4).
(423/476)	LAUKKANEN Kari	14.12.1963	**48**	**0**	1985-1997, Kuopion Palloseura (19/0), Stuttgarter Kickers (7/0), KSV Cercle Bruges (4/0), SV Waldhoff Mannheim (12/0), Finnairin Palloilijat Helsinki (6/0).
(560/572)	LEHKOSUO Mika	08.01.1970	**17**	**1**	1997-2000, HJK Helsinki (3/0), AC Perugia (4/0), HJK Helsinki (10/1).
(182/236)	LEHMUSVIRTA Simo	08.03.1931	**3**	**1**	1955, Ilves-Kissat Tampere (3/1).
(317/389)	LEHTINEN Erkki	01.12.1948	**2**	**0**	1975, Haka Valkeakoski (2/0).
(57/095)	LEHTINEN Lauri	11.03.1909	**8**	**3**	1929-1940, Turun Palloseura Turku (8/3).
(169/210)	LEHTINEN Lauri	19.08.1927	**29**	**0**	1952-1960, HJK Helsinki (29/0).
(648/626)	LEHTINEN Toni Pekka	05.05.1984	**2**	**0**	2004, FC Haka Valkeakoski (2/0).

(97/130)	LEHTO Vilho	21.04.1905	**1**	0	1935, Helsingin Palloseura (1/0).
(274/346)	LEHTOLAINEN Kari	08.04.1943	**3**	2	1969-1970, Honka Espoo (2/2), HJK Helsinki (1/0).
(99/135)	LEHTONEN Aatos	15.02.1914	**19**	7	1936-1941, HJK Helsinki (19/7).
(707/672)	LEHTOVAARA Jukka	15.03.1988	**1**	0	2010, Turun Palloseura Turku (1/0).
(134/180)	LEHTOVIRTA Kalevi	20.02.1928	**44**	12	1947-1959, Turun Weikot (16/2), Turun Pyrkivä (19/8), Turun Palloseura Turku (9/2).
(19/052)	LEIVO Leo	28.08.1896	**1**	0	1922, Viipurin Reipas (1/0).
(40/074)	LESCH Jarl	02.06.1904	**1**	0	1925, Kronohagens IF (1/0).
(76/119)	LESKINEN Veli	05.05.1907	**20**	0	1932-1943, Helsingin Toverit (19/0), Haka Valkeakoski (1/0).
(1/006)	LIETOLA Viljo	25.10.1888	**5**	0	1911-1912, HJK Helsinki (5/0).
(168/207)	LILJA Kalevi	10.09.1925	**2**	0	1952-1956, Tampereen Kisatoverit (1/0), Ilves-Kissat Tampere (1/0).
(143/196)	LILJA Olavi	10.08.1928	**5**	1	1949-1950, Tampereen Kisatoverit (5/1).
(57/094)	LINDBÄCK Axel	04.12.1902	**5**	0	1929-1930, Helsingin Idrottsföreningen Kamraterna (5/0).
(49/084)	LINDBÄCK Ragnar	13.11.1906	**11**	0	1927-1939, Helsingin Idrottsföreningen Kamraterna (11/0).
(510/539)	LINDBERG Janne	24.05.1966	**34**	1	1993-1996, Myllykosken Pallo-47 Anjalakoski (22/0), Greenock Morton FC (12/1).
(1/003)	LINDEBÄCK Uno	11.01.1891	**1**	1	1911, Helsingin Idrottsföreningen Kamraterna (1/1).
(184/239)	LINDGREN Bjarne	15.11.1929	**2**	0	1955-1956, Kronohagens IF (2/0).
(349/422)	LINDHOLM Harri	11.02.1958	**8**	1	1979, Reipas Lahti (8/1).
(398/467)	LINDHOLM Peter	08.12.1957	**3**	0	1983, Hudiksvall (3/0).
(244/322)	LINDHOLM Tommy	03.02.1947	**47**	12	1965-1974, Turku Toverit (5/1), Turun Palloseura Turku (20/5), Helsingin Idrottsföreningen Kamraterna (14/6), Reipas Lahti (7/0), Turun Palloseura Turku (1/0).
(135/182)	LINDMAN Åke	11.01.1928	**26**	0	1947-1955, Helsingin Idrottsföreningen Kamraterna (26/0).
(40/071)	LINDROOS Arthur		**1**	0	1925, Kronohagens IF (1/0).
(58/096)	LINDROOS Viljo	20.08.1904	**1**	0	1929, Turun Palloseura Turku (1/0).
(349/420)	LINDSTRÖM Stefan	14.08.1953	**5**	0	1979-1980, Haka Valkeakoski (5/0).
(9/035)	LINNA Aarne	20.08.1896	**18**	6	1919-1926, Helsingin Palloseura (18/6).
(183/238)	LINTAMO Alpo	19.03.1933	**15**	0	1955-1958, Vaasan Palloseura (3/0), Helsingin Palloseura (12/0).
(66/112)	LINTAMO Nuutti	22.12.1909	**23**	9	1930-1939, Vaasan Palloseura (23/9).
(401/469)	LIPPONEN Kimmo	09.12.1962	**6**	0	1983-1984, Turun Palosseura Turku (6/0).
(396/463)	LIPPONEN Mika	09.05.1964	**46**	11	1983-1991, Turun Palloseura Turku (20/4), RCD Mallorca (2/0), FC Twente Enschede (20/7), FC Aarau (4/0).
(477/514)	LITMANEN Jari Olavi	20.02.1971	**137**	32	1989-2010, Reipas Lahti (13/1), HJK Helsinki (7/1), Myllykosken Pallo-47 Anjalakoski (4/0), AFC Ajax Amsterdam (35/11), FC Barcelona (9/4), Liverpool FC (10/4), AFC Ajax Amsterdam (6/1), FC Lahti (9/2), FC Hansa Rostock (4/1), Malmö FF (11/3), *unattached* (2/0), Fulham FC London (3/2), *unattached* (1/0), FC Lahti (3/0), *unattached* (3/0), FC Lahti (17/2).
(287/363)	LITMANEN Olavi	17.04.1945	**5**	0	1970-1972, Reipas Lahti (5/0).
(415/475)	LIUS Ismo	30.11.1965	**36**	4	1984-1990, FC Kuusysi Lahti (36/4).
(756/711)	LOD Robin	17.04.1993	**12**	1	2015-2016, HJK Helsinki (2/0), Panathinaïkos AO Athína (10/1).
(358/433)	LOIKKANEN Ossi	27.04.1951	**1**	0	1979, Kuopion Palloseura (1/0).
(1/004)	LÖFGREN Gösta	10.09.1891	**6**	0	1911-1912, Helsingin Idrottsföreningen Kamraterna (6/0).
(36/069)	LÖNNBERG Albin	15.04.1904	**21**	7	1925-1934, Helsingin Idrottsföreningen Kamraterna (21/7).
(225/291)	LUKANDER Raimo	18.04.1934	**1**	0	1961, Pallo-Pojat Helsinki (1/0).
(3/017)	LUND Knut	17.07.1891	**4**	0	1912, Helsingin Idrottsföreningen Kamraterna (4/0).
(7/023)	LUNDQVIST Rudolf	06.11.1893	**1**	0	1914, Kronohagens IF (1/0).
(231/302)	LUNDQVIST Thor-Björn	27.05.1941	**3**	0	1963, Turun Palloseura Turku (3/0).
(16/044)	LYDMAN Sven	24.10.1900	**29**	0	1921-1926, Helsingin Palloseura (29/0).
(705/664)	LYYSKI Jani	16.03.1983	**3**	0	2010, Djurgårdens IF Stockholm (3/0).
(230/300)	LYYTIKÄINEN Juha	13.05.1938	**1**	1	1963, Helsingin Idrottsföreningen Kamraterna (1/1).
(179/228)	LYYTIKÄINEN Paavo	14.04.1930	**2**	0	1954-1961, HJK Helsinki (1/0), Kronohagens IF (1/0).
(398/468)	LYYTIKKÄ Ari	31.05.1963	**4**	0	1983, Reipas Lahti (4/0).

(694/654)	MAANOJA Tomi	12.09.1986	**1**	0	2009, AIK Stockholm (1/0).
(542/553)	MAHLIO Sami	12.01.1972	**25**	0	1995-2001, Myllykosken Pallo-47 Anjalakoski (21/0), Odd Grenland Skien (4/0).
(231/305)	MALM Esko	23.08.1940	**1**	0	1963, Haka Valkeakoski (1/0).
(56/092)	MALMGREN Jarl	21.09.1908	**31**	7	1928-1938, Helsingin Idrottsföreningen Kamraterna (31/7).
(306/378)	MANNINEN Jarmo	11.03.1951	**8**	2	1973-1975, Porin Ässät (5/1), Turun Palloseura Turku (3/1).
(714/680)	MANNSTRÖM Sebastian	29.10.1988	**5**	0	2011-2013, HJK Helsinki (5/0).
(11/040)	MANTILA Bruno	15.05.1897	**8**	4	1920-1922, Helsingin Palloseura (8/4).
(7/020)	MANTILA Hugo	11.12.1892	**17**	0	1914-1924, Kronohagens IF (9/0), Helsingin Palloseura (8/0).
(66/110)	MANTILA Ilmari	20.02.1896	**2**	0	1930, Helsingin Palloseura (2/0).
(586/597)	MARJAMAA Timo	27.06.1976	**6**	1	2000-2001, FC Jokerit Helsinki (6/1).
(749/707)	MARKKANEN Eero Pekka Sakari	03.07.1991	**8**	0	2014-2016, AIK Stockholm (1/0), Real Madrid CF (4/0), AIK Stockholm (3/0).
(390/458)	MARS Vesa	01.03.1961	**4**	0	1982-1983, Kokkolan Pallo-Veikot (2/0), Turun Palloseura Turku (2/0).
(128/163)	MARTIN Kurt	13.03.1923	**36**	0	1945-1954, Vaasa Idrottsförening Kamraterna (36/0).
(747/703)	MATTILA Sakari	14.07.1989	**11**	0	2014-2016, Aalesunds FK (6/0), Fulham FC London (3/0), Sønderjysk E. Fodbold Haderslev (2/0).
(688/652)	MÄENPÄÄ Niki	23.01.1985	**26**	0	2008-2016, FC Den Bosch (4/0), AZ Alkmaar (2/0), VVV Venlo (19/0), Brighton & Hove Albion FC (1/0).
(108/141)	MÄKELÄ Eino	03.01.1914	**4**	1	1937-1938, HJK Helsinki (4/1).
(447/495)	MÄKELÄ Ilkka	25.06.1963	**12**	0	1987-1990, Haka Valkeakoski (10/0), Mikkelin Palloilijat (2/0).
(520/542)	MÄKELÄ Janne-Pekka	23.07.1971	**20**	0	1994-1997, Myllykosken Pallo-47 Anjalakoski (12/0), Finnairin Palloilijat Helsinki (6/0), Raith Rovers FC (2/0).
(637/620)	MÄKELÄ Juho Antti	23.06.1983	**7**	0	2004-2010, HJK Helsinki (3/0), Heart of Midlothian FC Edinburgh (3/0), HJK Helsinki (1/0).

(221/288)	MÄKELÄ Matti	14.01.1939	**35**	**2**	1961-1972, Tampellan Palloilijat (12/2), Upon Pallo Lahti (13/0), Ilves-Kissat Tampere (6/0), Tampellan Palloilijat (3/0), Ilves-Kissat Tampere (1/0).
(281/355)	MÄKELÄ Seppo	18.01.1945	**3**	**0**	1969-1970, Kokkolan Pallo-Veikot (3/0).
(244/321)	MÄKILA Asko	20.08.1944	**5**	**3**	1965, Haka Valkeakoski (5/3).
(219/285)	MÄKINEN Olli	25.07.1935	**5**	**0**	1960-1963, Haka Valkeakoski (5/0).
(226/295)	MÄKIPÄÄ Pertti	04.08.1941	**56**	**2**	1962-1970, Reipas Lahti (3/0), Tampellan Palloilijat (14/0), Upon Pallo Lahti (18/2), Tampereen Palloveikot (5/0), Tampellan Palloilijat (16/0).
(293/368)	MÄKYNEN Ari	04.07.1949	**22**	**1**	1971-1978, Vaasan Palloseura (19/1), Lappfjärds BK (3/0).
(748/704)	MÄNTYLÄ Tero	18.04.1991	**2**	**0**	2014, PFC Ludogorets Razgrad (2/0).
(562/573)	MOILANEN Teuvo	12.12.1973	**4**	**0**	1997-2003, Preston North End FC (3/0), Heart of Midlothian FC Edinburgh (1/0).
(757/712)	MOISANDER Henrik	29.09.1985	**2**	**0**	2015-2016, FC Lahti (1/0), *unattached* (1/0).
(687/651)	MOISANDER Niklas	29.09.1985	**55**	**2**	2008-2016, FC Zwolle (1/0), AZ'67 Alkmaar (26/1), AFC Ajax Amsterdam (23/1), UC Sampdoria Genova (1/0), SV Werder Bremen (4/0).
(24/057)	MOISIO Väinö		**1**	**0**	1923, Viipurin Sudet (1/0).
(137/188)	MÖLLER Allan	20.12.1923	**1**	**0**	1947, Turku Toverit (1/0).
(750/708)	MOREN Valtteri	15.06.1991	**4**	**1**	2014-2016, HJK Helsinki (3/0), KV RS Waasland-Beveren SK (1/0).
(556/570)	MOTTURI Mika	26.06.1970	**3**	**0**	1997, FC Lahti (3/0).
(623/613)	MULTAHARJU Miika	09.10.1977	**6**	**0**	2003-2005, Myllykosken Pallo-47 Anjalankoski (2/0), Denizlispor Kulübü (4/0).
(181/233)	MUSTONEN Pentti	01.10.1926	**2**	**0**	1955-1956, Kajaanin Palloilijat (2/0).
(129/168)	MYNTTI Stig-Göran	06.08.1925	**61**	**5**	1945-1958, IFK Vaasa (61/5).
(138/190)	MYRTTINEN Gunnar	14.10.1922	**3**	**0**	1948-1952, Porvoon Weikot (2/0), Kronohagens IF (1/0).
(436/486)	MYYRY Marko	15.11.1967	**60**	**2**	1986-1997, Haka Valkeakoski (7/1), SV Meppen (17/1), KSC Lokeren (23/0), SV Meppen (13/0).
(218/283)	NABB Carl-Gustav	09.09.1936	**3**	**0**	1960-1961, Vaasa Idrottsförening Kamraterna (3/0).
(41/076)	NADBORNIK Joshua	05.08.1902	**3**	**0**	1925-1930, HJK Helsinki (1/0), Stjärnan Helsinki (2/0).
(65/105)	NÄRHINEN Gunnar	13.08.1909	**3**	**0**	1930-1932, Helsingin Idrottsföreningen Kamraterna (3/0).
(335/407)	NÄRVÄ Markku	12.11.1952	**3**	**0**	1977, Haka Valkeakoski (3/0).
(32/068)	NÄRVÄNEN Arvo	12.02.1905	**42**	**1**	1924-1936, Viipurin Sudet (42/1).
(241/319)	NÄSMAN Lars	14.07.1943	**37**	**0**	1965-1971, Upon Pallo Lahti (21/0), Vaasa Idrottsförening Kamraterna (6/0), SC Cambuur Leeuwarden (6/0), Helsingin Idrottsföreningen Kamraterna (4/0).
(193/256)	NEVALAINEN Unto	13.06.1935	**24**	**2**	1957-1961, Turun Palloseura Turku (4/0), Helsingin Idrottsföreningen Kamraterna (20/2).
(281/354)	NEVANPERA Timo	01.04.1948	**8**	**0**	1969-1973, Vaasan Palloseura (8/0).
(503/530)	NIEMI Antti	31.05.1972	**67**	**0**	1992-2007, HJK Helsinki (11/0), FC København (10/0), Glasgow Rangers FC (16/0), Heart of Midlothian FC Edinburgh (15/0), Southampton FC (14/0), Fulham FC London (1/0).
(134/178)	NIEMI Armas	05.06.1916	**1**	**0**	1947, Turku Toverit (1/0).
(585/595)	NIEMI Jari	02.02.1977	**23**	**3**	2000-2005, Tampere United (19/3), RAEC Mons (2/0), K St.-Truidense VV (2/0).
(181/232)	NIEMINEN Antti	12.03.1928	**3**	**0**	1955-1960, Haka Valkeakoski (3/0).
(327/400)	NIEMINEN Jyrki	30.03.1951	**46**	**9**	1976-1986, HJK Helsinki (10/3), IFK Eskilstuna (8/2), AIK Stockholm (16/3), HJK Helsinki (12/1).
(319/394)	NIEMINEN Kalle	03.12.1947	**8**	**1**	1975-1979, Mikkeli Pallokissat (8/1).
(508/538)	NIEMINEN Rami	25.02.1966	**14**	**0**	1993-1996, FC Jazz Pori (14/0).
(127/161)	NIILONEN Karlo	03.06.1922	**3**	**0**	1943-1946, Kotkan Työväen Palloilijat (3/0).
(179/227)	NIINIMÄKI Aarno	12.02.1931	**2**	**0**	1954-1955, Ilves-Kissat Tampere (2/0).
(431/477)	NIINIMÄKI Jari	01.12.1957	**9**	**2**	1986-1987, Ilves Tampere (9/2).
(40/072)	NIKANDER Vieno	26.07.1905	**1**	**0**	1925, Turun Palloseura Turku (1/0).
(272/344)	NIKKANEN Antero	01.06.1946	**10**	**0**	1968-1974, Mikkelin Palloilijat (10/0).
(457/501)	NIKKILÄ Seppo	10.01.1962	**4**	**2**	1988, Ilves Tampere (4/2).
(1/011)	NISKA Algoth	05.12.1888	**6**	**0**	1911-1912, Helsingin Idrottsföreningen Kamraterna (6/0).
(267/334)	NISKAKOSI Ismo	02.06.1948	**2**	**0**	1968, Reipas Lahti (2/0).
(623/614)	NORDBACK Fredrik	20.03.1979	**7**	**0**	2003-2005, Örebro SK (7/0).
(67/113)	NORDBERG Emil		**1**	**0**	1930, Kronohagens IF (1/0).
(223/290)	NORDLUND Arno	02.09.1935	**2**	**0**	1961, Hangö Idrottsklub (2/0).
(260/331)	NUMMELIN Timo	07.09.1948	**14**	**1**	1967-1971, Turun Palloseura Turku (14/1).
(237/316)	NUMMILA Reima	16.11.1942	**22**	**0**	1964-1968, Turun Palloseura Turku (22/0).
(220/287)	NUORANEN Semi	14.12.1941	**33**	**2**	1961-1972, Reipas Lahti (13/2), Ilves-Kissat Tampere (14/0), Reipas Lahti (6/0).
(520/540)	NUORELA Jussi	11.08.1974	**20**	**1**	1994-2003, PSV Eindhoven (3/0), FC Haka Valkeakoski (2/0), FC Zwolle (5/0), Myllykosken Pallo-47 Anjalankoski (5/1), Malmö FF (5/0).
(225/292)	NUPPONEN Kalevi	19.01.1942	**4**	**0**	1961-1970, Reipas Lahti (2/0), Ilves-Kissat Tampere (2/0).
(503/532)	NURMELA Mika	26.12.1971	**71**	**4**	1992-2007, FC Haka Valkeakoski (1/0), Malmö FF (7/0), BV Emmen (4/0), SC Heerenveen (28/0), 1.FC Kaiserslautern (21/3), HJK Helsinki (10/1).
(207/273)	NURMI Mauno	23.12.1936	**5**	**0**	1959-1966, Turun Palloseura Turku (5/0).
(366/437)	NURMIO Pekka	14.09.1958	**2**	**0**	1980, Turun Palloseura Turku (2/0).
(176/225)	NYGÅRD Börje	21.04.1930	**1**	**0**	1954, Drott Jakobstad (1/0).
(63/104)	NYLUND Alfons	14.11.1904	**5**	**0**	1929-1931, Helsingin Idrottsföreningen Kamraterna (5/0).
(554/564)	NYLUND Kaj Wilhelm „Ville"	14.02.1972	**21**	**0**	1996-2004, FF Jaro JS Pietarsaari (1/0), HJK Helsinki (20/0).
(44/079)	NYLUND Kurt	24.11.1901	**2**	**0**	1926, Helsingin Idrottsföreningen Kamraterna (2/0).
(648/621)	NYMAN Ari	07.02.1984	**22**	**0**	2004-2010, FC International Turku (13/0), FC Thun (5/0), FC International Turku (4/0).
(2/016)	NYYSSÖNEN Artturi	01.05.1892	**5**	**0**	1912, HJK Helsinki (5/0).
(489/522)	NYYSSÖNEN Harri	15.11.1965	**5**	**0**	1991-1992, Kuopion Palloseura (2/0), FC Haka Valkeakoski (3/0).
(552/561)	NYYSSÖNEN Kai	10.06.1972	**2**	**0**	1996-1997, RWD Molenbeek (2/0).

(565/577)	OINAS Janne	27.11.1973	**2**	**0**	1998, FC Flora Tallinn (2/0).
(723/684)	OJALA Juhani Lauri Henrik	19.06.1989	**17**	**0**	2011-2016, BSC Young Boys Bern (7/0), FK Terek Grozny (7/0), HJK Helsinki (1/0), *unattached* (1/0), SJK Seinäjoki (1/0).
(705/669)	OJALA Mika	21.06.1988	**7**	**0**	2010-2014, FC International Turku (4/0), BK Häcken Göteborg (2/0), *unattached* (1/0).
(623/612)	OKKONEN Antti	06.06.1982	**13**	**0**	2003-2006, Myllykosken Pallo-47 Anjalankoski (3/0), Landskrona BoIS (10/0).
(106/139)	OKSANEN Ilmari	24.12.1906	**5**	**0**	1937-1941, Turun Palloseura Turku (5/0).
(63/103)	OKSANEN Kaarlo	11.01.1909	**39**	**0**	1929-1937, Helsingin Palloseura (39/0).
(480/516)	OLLILA Hannu	19.06.1962	**3**	**0**	1990, Rovaniemi Palloseura (3/0).
(199/260)	OLLILA Juhani	08.07.1936	**1**	**0**	1957, Vaasan Palloseura (1/0).
(648/625)	ORAVAINEN Petri	26.01.1973	**2**	**0**	2004, HJK Helsinki (2/0).
(765/721)	O'SHAUGHNESSY Daniel	10.09.1994	**2**	**0**	2016, Brentford FC (2/0).
(44/080)	OVASKA Toivo	18.12.1899	**4**	**0**	1926-1927, HJK Helsinki (4/0).
(8/033)	ÖHMAN Gunnar	12.01.1896	**8**	**3**	1919-1921, Helsingin Idrottsföreningen Kamraterna (8/3).
(1/009)	ÖHMAN Jarl	14.11.1891	**12**	**9**	1911-1922, Helsingin Idrottsföreningen Kamraterna (12/9).
(215/282)	ÖRN Urho	03.12.1930	**3**	**0**	1960, Kronohagens IF (3/0).
(235/315)	ÖSTERBERG Kaj	08.12.1942	**4**	**0**	1964, Helsingin Palloseura (4/0).
(10/036)	ÖSTERHOLM Jarl	14.06.1896	**4**	**1**	1920-1922, Helsingin Idrottsföreningen Kamraterna (4/1).
(211/279)	ÖSTERLUND Tor	08.07.1935	**8**	**2**	1959-1962, Hangö Idrottsklub (8/2).
(28/063)	ÖSTERLUND Torsten	03.09.1899	**1**	**1**	1923, IF Kamraterna Åbo (1/1).
(242/320)	PAANANEN Kalervo	19.11.1942	**1**	**0**	1965, Kotkan Työväen Palloilijat (1/0).
(139/191)	PAANANEN Matti	25.07.1922	**1**	**0**	1948, Kotkan Työväen Palloilijat (1/0).
(128/165)	PAANANEN Toivo	21.05.1914	**1**	**0**	1945, Kotkan Työväen Palloilijat (1/0).
(286/361)	PAATELAINEN Matti	17.06.1944	**47**	**11**	1970-1977, Helsingin Idrottsföreningen Kamraterna (12/2), Haka Valkeakoski (35/9).
(439/492)	PAATELAINEN Mika-Matti	03.02.1967	**70**	**18**	1986-2000, Haka Valkeakoski (12/2), Dundee United FC (19/3), Aberdeen FC (9/1), Bolton Wanderers FC (13/8), Wolverhampton Wanderers FC (8/2), Hibernian Edinburgh FC (8/2).
(230/299)	PAAVILAINEN Mauri	09.09.1944	**3**	**0**	1963-1969, Haka Valkeakoski (3/0).
(439/493)	PAAVOLA Tommi	09.12.1965	**23**	**1**	1986-1994, Turun Palloseura Turku (3/0), HJK Helsinki (1/0), Haka Valkeakoski (6/0), Hessen Kassell (1/0), KSC Lokeren (5/0), Haka Valkeakoski (1/0), Finnairin Palloilijat Helsinki (2/1), FC 56 Lorient (1/0), Finnairin Palloilijat Helsinki (3/0).
(309/382)	PAAVOLAINEN Olavi	27.12.1950	**2**	**0**	1973, Kokkolan Pallo-Veikot (2/0).
(180/230)	PAHLMAN Kai	08.07.1935	**56**	**13**	1954-1968, Helsingin Palloseura (41/10), HJK Helsinki (15/3).
(185/242)	PAJUNEN Väiniö	01.11.1928	**3**	**0**	1955-1956, Haka Valkeakoski (3/0).
(406/470)	PALMROOS Markku	27.08.1960	**8**	**0**	1983-1988, HJK Helsinki (8/0).
(386/456)	PARIKKA Jari	08.09.1961	**14**	**0**	1982-1985, HJK Helsinki (14/0).
(694/661)	PARIKKA Jarno	21.07.1986	**1**	**0**	2009, HJK Helsinki (1/0).
(170/215)	PARKKINEN Sulo	24.04.1930	**2**	**0**	1953-1955, Kotkan Työväen Palloilijat (2/0).
(223/289)	PÄRNÄNEN Yrjö	05.01.1931	**3**	**0**	1961-1963, Helsingin Idrottsföreningen Kamraterna (3/0).
(264/333)	PARTANEN Uho	08.09.1941	**2**	**0**	1967, Reipas Lahti (2/0).
(708/675)	PARVIAINEN Kalle	03.10.1982	**1**	**0**	2010, FC Haka Valkeakoski (1/0).
(598/604)	PASANEN Petri	24.09.1980	**76**	**1**	2000-2013, AFC Ajax Amsterdam (17/1), Portsmouth FC (3/0), SV Werder Bremen (45/0), FC Red Bull Salzburg (5/0), AGF Aarhus (6/0).
(436/483)	PASANEN Tuomo	03.08.1964	**1**	**0**	1986, Kemin Palloseura (1/0).
(635/618)	PASOJA Juha	16.11.1976	**15**	**0**	2003-2008, FC Haka Valkeakoski (8/0), Ham-Kam Fotball Hamar (7/0).
(275/348)	PATRIKAINEN Seppo	17.07.1945	**4**	**0**	1969, Reipas Lahti (4/0).
(714/679)	PATRONEN Hannu Jarl Johannes	23.05.1984	**6**	**0**	2011-2016, Helsingborgs IF (2/0), Sogndal Fotball (4/0).
(377/451)	PEKONEN Esa	04.11.1961	**60**	**2**	1981-1989, FC Kuusysi Lahti (46/2), AIK Stockholm (14/0).
(159/204)	PELKONEN Seppo	13.03.1930	**17**	**2**	1951-1955, JoPS (7/2), Kuopion Palloseura (10/0).
(181/235)	PELTONEN Juhani	16.06.1936	**68**	**10**	1955-1970, Haka Valkeakoski (43/4), Hamburger SV (6/4), Haka Valkeakoski (19/3).
(125/157)	PELTONEN Verner	12.12.1908	**1**	**0**	1941, Helsinki Toverit (1/0).
(724/688)	PELVAS Akseli	08.02.1989	**3**	**0**	2012-2016, HJK Helsinki (1/0), Falkenbergs FF (2/0).
(735/696)	PENNANEN Petteri	19.09.1990	**1**	**0**	2013, Turun Palloseura Turku (1/0).
(588/598)	PENTTILÄ Tero	09.03.1975	**5**	**0**	2000-2003, Glasgow Rangers FC (3/0), Haka Valkeakoski (2/0).
(705/665)	PEROVUO Joel	11.08.1985	**2**	**0**	2010, Djurgårdens IF Stockholm (2/0).
(397/465)	PETÄJÄ Erkka	13.02.1964	**84**	**0**	1983-1994, Turun Palloseura Turku (17/0), Öster IF Vaexjö (45/0), Malmö FF (4/0), Helsingborgs IF (7/0), Malmö FF (4/0), Yverdon Sports (7/0).
(136/185)	PETTERSSON Åke	20.03.1926	**3**	**0**	1947-1956, Kotkan Jäntevä (3/0).
(315/388)	PETTERSSON Rutger	27.06.1952	**2**	**0**	1974, Pyrkivä Turku (2/0).
(220/286)	PIETILÄINEN Sauli	20.07.1941	**6**	**1**	1961, Kotkan Jäntevä (6/1).
(765/716)	PIRINEN Juha	22.10.1991	**2**	**0**	2016, RoPS Rovaniemi (2/0).
(317/391)	PIRINEN Jukka	09.02.1951	**3**	**0**	1975-1977, Haka Valkeakoski (3/0).
(262/332)	PITKO Matti	18.09.1942	**1**	**0**	1967, Haka Valkeakoski (2/0).
(554/563)	POHJA Antti	11.01.1977	**23**	**2**	1996-2008, Myllykosken Pallo-47 Anjalakoski (1/1), FC Jokerit Helsinki (2/0), Tampere United (1/0), Hammarby IF Stockholm (7/0), Tampere United (7/1), FC Vaduz (1/0), Tampere United (4/0).
(733/693)	POHJANPALO Joel	13.09.1994	**22**	**4**	2012-2016, HJK Helsinki (2/0), VfR Aalen (4/1), TSV Fortuna Düsseldorf (14/3), TSV Bayer 04 Leverkusen (2/0).
(668/646)	POROKARA Roni	12.12.1983	**23**	**5**	2006-2013, FC Honka Espoo (1/0), Örebro SK (17/4), KFC Germinal Beerschot Antwerpen (2/1), K Beerschot AC Antwerpen (2/0), Hapoel Ironi Kiryat Shmona FC (1/0).
(466/507)	POUTIAINEN Jari	29.08.1966	**1**	**0**	1988, Kuopion Palloseura (1/0).
(575/586)	PRIHA Ville	19.09.1975	**2**	**0**	1999, Vaasan Palloseura (2/0).

(556/569)	PUHAKAINEN Saku	14.01.1975	3	2	1997, Turun Palloseura Turku (3/2).
(694/660)	PUKKI Teemu	29.03.1990	54	9	2009-2016, Sevilla FC (1/0), HJK Helsinki (3/0), FC Schalke 04 Gelsenkirchen (20/6), Celtic Glasgow FC (8/2), Brøndby IF København (22/1).
(171/219)	PULKKINEN Aimo	14.06.1928	8	0	1953-1958, Haka Valkeakoski (8/0).
(648/627)	PULKKINEN Heikki	12.08.1982	2	0	2004, AC Allianssi Vantaa (2/0).
(367/438)	PULLIAINEN Vesa	08.05.1957	6	0	1980, Turun Palloseura Turku (6/0).
(450/496)	PUTKONEN Eekki	13.11.1964	4	0	1987-1988, Ilves Tampere (4/0).
(407/473)	PUUSTINEN Risto	28.09.1959	11	0	1983-1988, Porin Pallotoverit (6/0), HJK Helsinki (5/0).
(140/192)	PYLKKONEN Tapio	06.02.1923	25	0	1948-1952, Helsingin Ponnistus (25/0).
(103/136)	PYY Armas	07.05.1913	14	0	1937-1943, HJK Helsinki (14/0).
(326/398)	PYYKKÖ Seppo	24.12.1955	30	1	1976-1981, Oulun Palloseura (21/1), FC Bayer 05 Uerdingen (9/0).
(292/366)	RAATIKAINEN Tapio	24.12.1947	1	0	1971, Tampereen Palloveikot (1/0).
(286/359)	RAHJA Timo	09.10.1948	7	2	1970-1974, HJK Helsinki (7/2).
(289/365)	RAINIO Tapani	11.02.1948	1	0	1971, Turun Palloseura Turku (1/0).
(694/659)	RAITALA Jukka	15.09.1988	36	0	2009-2016, HJK Helsinki (1/0), TSG 1899 Hoffenheim (1/0), SC Paderborn 07 (3/0), CA Osasuna Pamplona (9/0), SC Heerenveen (10/0), FC Vestsjælland Slagelse (2/0), AaB Aalborg (2/0), Songndal Fotball (8/0).
(199/263)	RAJALA Olli	28.11.1937	3	1	1957-1963, Tampereen Palloveikot (1/1), Tampellan Palloilijat (2/0).
(505/535)	RAJAMÄKI Marko	03.10.1968	16	3	1993-1995, Myllykosken Pallo-47 Anjalakoski (14/3), Greenock Morton (2/0).
(352/425)	RAJANIEMI Hannu	15.09.1953	11	3	1979-1981, Sepsi-78 Seinäjoki (11/3).
(287/362)	RAJANTIE Vilho	06.08.1948	20	0	1970-1973, Mikkelin Palloilijat (20/0).
(726/691)	RANNANKARI Tuomas	21.05.1991	2	0	2012-2013, FC Twente Enschede (1/0), SpVgg Greuther Fürth (1/0).
(281/353)	RANTA Esko	14.01.1947	68	0	1969-1980, Ilves-Kissat Tampere (1/0), Tampereen Palloveikot (3/0), Tampellan Palloilijat (8/0), Haka Valkeakoski (56/0).
(232/307)	RANTALA Timo	30.05.1941	1	0	1963, Reipas Lahti (1/0).
(397/466)	RANTANEN Jari	31.12.1961	36	4	1983-1989, HJK Helsinki (16/3), VAV Beerschot Anvers (2/0), IFK Göteborg (8/0), Leicester City FC (10/1).
(505/537)	RANTANEN Rami	25.11.1968	18	1	1993-2001, HJK Helsinki (12/0), Trelleborgs FF (3/0), Atlantis FC Vantaa (3/1).
(395/460)	RASIMUS Pasi	06.03.1962	11	1	1983-1986, HJK Helsinki (11/1).
(205/267)	RASTIO Teppo	15.02.1934	1	0	1958, Ilves-Kissat Tampere (1/0).
(349/419)	RAUTIAINEN Pasi	18.07.1961	29	1	1979-1987, HJK Helsinki (10/1), FC Bayern München (3/0), SV Werder Bremen (2/0), DSC Arminia Bielefeld (13/0), FC Locarno (1/0).
(649/629)	RÄSÄNEN Janne	12.05.1978	1	0	2004, Tampere United (1/0).
(575/585)	RÄSÄNEN Jouni	29.01.1970	2	0	1999, FC Haka Valkeakoski (2/0).
(563/574)	REINI Juha	19.03.1975	22	0	1997-2004, Vaasan Palloseura (5/0), KRC Genk (13/0), AZ'67 Alkmaar (4/0).
(386/455)	REMES Ilkka	29.07.1963	34	1	1982-1992, FC Kuusysi Lahti (34/1).
(135/183)	REUNANEN Harri	14.09.1923	4	2	1947-1949, Rauman Työväen Uheilijat (4/2).
(735/697)	REXHEPI Lum	03.08.1992	1	0	2013, FC Honka Espoo (1/0).
(565/575)	RIIHILAHTI Aki	09.09.1976	69	11	1998-2007, HJK Helsinki (8/1), Vålerenga IF Oslo (13/1), Crystal Palace FC London (42/9), 1.FC Kaiserslautern (3/0), Djurgårdens IF Stockholm (3/0).
(554/562)	RIIPPA Juha	12.09.1968	1	0	1996, FC Jazz Pori (1/0).
(162/206)	RIKBERG Nils	29.03.1928	15	7	1952-1960, Kotkan Jäntevä (12/7), IF Kamraterna Åbo (3/0).
(717/683)	RING Alexander Michael	09.04.1991	42	1	2011-2016, HJK Helsinki (6/0), Borussia VfL Mönchengladbach (11/1), 1.FC Kaiserslautern (25/0).
(235/312)	RINNE Aarno	11.07.1941	8	0	1964-1965, Ilves-Kissat Tampere (8/0).
(92/124)	RINNE Antero	07.08.1913	14	0	1935-1939, HJK Helsinki (14/0).
(436/487)	RINNE Jari	04.05.1964	24	0	1986-1992, FC Kuusysi Lahti (24/0).
(95/126)	RINNE Risto	22.12.1910	2	0	1935, Helsingin Palloseura (2/0).
(130/170)	RINTANEN Mauno	28.11.1925	7	0	1946-1954, Vaasan Palloseura (4/0), HJK Helsinki (3/0).
(714/678)	RISKI Riku Olavi	16.08.1989	26	4	2011-2015, RTS Widzew Łódź (4/0), Hønefoss BK (12/2), Rosenborg BK Trondheim (9/2), IFK Göteborg (1/0).
(756/709)	RISKI Roope Vilhelmi	16.08.1991	4	1	2015-2016, Hønefoss BK (2/1), FK Haugesund (2/0), SJK Seinäjoki (1/0).
(322/395)	RISSANEN Eero	30.11.1948	1	0	1975, Kuopion Palloseura (1/0).
(353/426)	RISSANEN Juha	13.11.1958	8	0	1979-1980, Kuopion Pallo Toverit (8/0).
(453/499)	RISSANEN Kari	29.08.1966	25	1	1987-1998, HJK Helsinki (4/0), Finnairin Palloilijat Helsinki (18/1), Ikast fS (3/0).
(278/350)	RISSANEN Olavi	26.03.1947	41	7	1969-1979, Kuopion Elo (1/1), Kuopion Palloseura (40/6).
(599/605)	ROIHA Paulus Henrik	03.08.1980	20	4	2001-2010, HJK Helsinki (2/0), FC Utrecht (7/0), KSV Cercle Brugge (6/4), ADO Den Haag (1/0), HJK Helsinki (2/0), Åtvidabergs FF (2/0).
(345/415)	RONKAINEN Antti	07.06.1958	13	0	1978-1981, Haka Valkeakoski (5/0), Vasalund (8/0).
(76/120)	RONKANEN Eero	02.11.1908	4	2	1932-1934, Helsingin Palloseura (4/2).
(353/427)	ROSENBERG Risto	14.11.1955	2	1	1979, Turun Palloseura Turku (2/1).
(108/140)	ROSLUND Karl-Erik	23.04.1915	1	0	1937, Helsingin Idrottsföreningen Kamraterna (1/0).
(208/275)	ROSQVIST Rolf	18.04.1932	2	1	1959, Helsingin Idrottsföreningen Kamraterna (2/1).
(759/713)	ROTENBERG Boris	19.05.1986	1	0	2015, FK Dinamo Moskva (1/0).
(468/511)	ROTH Anders	17.03.1967	7	0	1989-1990, Örgryte IS Göteborg (7/0).
(496/527)	RUHANEN Jukka	16.04.1971	14	3	1992-1995, Mikkelin Palloilijat (13/3), FC Jazz Pori (1/0).
(206/268)	RUIPPO Taisto	23.07.1931	1	0	1958, Kuopion Pallo Toverit (1/0).
(226/296)	RUOTSALAINEN Rauno	04.02.1938	8	0	1962-1965, Mikkeli Pallokissat (1/0), Lappeenrannan Pallo (7/0).
(138/189)	RYTKÖNEN Aulis	05.01.1929	37	7	1948-1964, Kuopion Palloseura (31/6), Toulouse FC (1/0), HJK Helsinki (5/1).
(315/387)	SAARI Raimo	23.07.1952	2	0	1974, Turun Palloseura Turku (2/0).
(52/086)	SAARILAHTI Heimo	29.06.1907	6	0	1927-1929, Helsingin Palloseura (6/0).
(147/199)	SAARINEN Helge	28.09.1921	1	0	1949, Turun Palloseura Turku (1/0).

(594/603)	SAARINEN Janne	28.02.1977	42	0	2000-2008, HJK Helsinki (4/0), Rosenborg BK Trondheim (18/0), TSV 1860 München (8/0), FC København (10/0), FC Honka Espoo (1/0), BK Käcken Göteborg (1/0).
(142/194)	SAARINEN Jorma	19.05.1929	1	0	1948, Vaasan Palloseura (1/0).
(45/082)	SAARIO Sulo	19.04.1906	9	3	1926-1930, Helsingin Palloseura (9/3).
(132/176)	SAARNIO Eero	18.04.1926	7	0	1946-1949, Kotkan Työväen Palloilijat (7/0).
(477/513)	SAASTAMOINEN Jarmo	20.09.1967	21	0	1989-2001, FC Kuusysi Lahti (6/0), HJK Helsinki (12/0), Haka Valkeakoski (3/0).
(687/650)	SADIK Berat	14.09.1986	11	1	2008-2015, FC Lahti (2/0), DSC Arminia Bielefeld (2/0), HJK Helsinki (3/0), FC Thun (2/1), FK Krylia Sovetov Samara (2/0).
(358/434)	SAIRANEN Seppo	23.03.1952	7	0	1979-1980, Ilves Tampere (7/0).
(765/717)	SAKSELA Janne	14.03.1993	7	0	2016, RoPS Rovaniemi (7/0).
(70/115)	SALIN Holger	18.09.1911	22	4	1931-1943, Helsingin Idrottsföreningen Kamraterna (22/4).
(575/588)	SALLI Janne	14.12.1977	11	1	1999-2004, FC Haka Valkeakoski (11/1).
(186/245)	SALMELAINEN Matti	19.02.1932	1	0	1955, Kotkan Työväen Palloilijat (1/0).
(99/132)	SALMINEN Paavo	19.11.1911	12	0	1936-1939, Helsingin Toverit (12/0).
(131/175)	SALO Asser	19.06.1921	2	0	1946, Tampereen Palloveikot (2/0).
(125/156)	SALO Lasse	13.03.1917	1	0	1941, Helsinki Toverit (1/0).
(104/138)	SALO Sulo	16.11.1909	3	0	1937-1941, HJK Helsinki (3/0).
(346/416)	SALONEN Risto	11.12.1955	11	0	1978-1984, Turun Palloseura Turku (11/0).
(133/177)	SAND Kurt	03.07.1923	5	0	1947, Vaasa Idrottsförening Kamraterna (5/0).
(10/038)	SANDSTRÖM Lauri	23.12.1898	1	0	1920, Helsingin Idrottsföreningen Kamraterna (1/0).
(652/635)	SARAJÄRVI Jani	09.09.1979	1	0	2005, AC Allianssi Vantaa (1/0).
(58/097)	SARMOLA Holger	25.09.1907	1	0	1929, Helsingin Palloseura (1/0).
(116/148)	SARNOLA Thure	30.04.1917	25	0	1939-1950, Kuopion Pallotoverit (8/0), Helsingin Palloseura (14/0), Ilves-Kissat Tampere (3/0).
(652/634)	SAUSO Jukka	20.06.1982	5	0	2005-2006, Örgryte IS Göteborg (5/0).
(270/341)	SAVIOMAA Raimo	15.04.1946	32	0	1968-1974, Upon Pallo Lahti (1/0), Reipas Lahti (7/0), Lahti-69 (22/0), FC Kuusysi Lahti (2/0).
(705/666)	SAVOLAINEN Juska Samuli	01.09.1983	2	0	2010, FK Haugesund (2/0).
(7/021)	SAXELL Ilmari	06.01.1892	6	0	1914-1920, Kronohagens IF (6/0).
(649/632)	SCHEWELEFF Henri	15.04.1983	3	0	2004-2005, Tampere United (3/0).
(134/181)	SCHICK Mauritz	09.07.1922	7	0	1947-1948, Kronohagens IF (7/0).
(734/695)	SCHÜLLER Rasmus	18.06.1991	21	0	2013-2016, HJK Helsinki (13/0), BK Häcken Göteborg (8/0).
(1/010)	SCHYBERGSON Ernst	29.01.1891	1	0	1911, Kronohagens IF (1/0).
(7/026)	SCHYBERGSON Lars	22.08.1894	2	2	1914-1919, Kronohagens IF (2/2).
(7/027)	SCHYBERGSON Richard	06.04.1893	1	0	1914, Kronohagens IF (1/0).
(436/484)	SETÄLÄ Petter	04.08.1964	1	0	1986, Haka Valkeakoski (1/0).
(746/701)	SIHVOLA Pekka	22.04.1984	1	0	2014, MyPa Kouvola (1/0).
(649/628)	SILLANPÄÄ Henri	04.06.1979	6	0	2004-2014, AC Allianssi Vantaa (4/0), GAIS Göteborg (1/0), Vaasan Palloseura (1/0).
(22/055)	SILVE Bertel	18.03.1905	8	1	1922-1926, HJK Helsinki (8/1).
(66/109)	SINIKARI Lauri (PRÄKTIG)	24.01.1907	5	0	1930-1935, Helsingin Palloseura (5/0).
(185/240)	SJÖBERG Erik	15.07.1928	1	0	1955, Helsingin Idrottsföreningen Kamraterna (1/0).
(129/169)	SJÖBERG John	26.01.1923	2	0	1945-1947, Vaasa Idrottsförening Kamraterna (2/0).
(192/253)	SJÖBERG Ralf	18.01.1936	10	0	1956-1963, Vaasa Idrottsförening Kamraterna (4/0), Tampellan Palloilijat (6/0).
(628/616)	SJÖLUND Daniel	22.04.1983	37	2	2003-2012, Djurgårdens IF Stockholm (37/2).
(31/067)	SJÖMAN Rafael	10.06.1900	2	0	1924, Helsingin Idrottsföreningen Kamraterna (2/0).
(765/719)	SKRABB Simon	19.01.1995	1	0	2016, Gefle IF Gävle (1/0).
(367/442)	SOINI Jouko	02.03.1956	3	1	1980, HJK Helsinki (3/1).
(2/013)	SOINIO Eino	12.11.1894	40	2	1912-1927, HJK Helsinki (34/2), Helsingin Palloseura (6/0).
(1/005)	SOINIO Karlo	28.01.1888	3	0	1911-1912, HJK Helsinki (3/0).
(169/212)	SOMMARBERG Aimo	11.08.1931	16	0	1952-1957, Kokkolan Pallo-Veikot (16/0).
(705/668)	SORSA Sebastian	25.01.1984	6	0	2010, HJK Helsinki (6/0).
(97/129)	SOTIOLA Yrjö	19.05.1913	11	1	1935-1948, Helsingin Palloseura (11/1).
(694/657)	SPARV Tim	20.02.1987	54	1	2009-2016, Halmstads BK (5/0), FC Groningen (27/1), SpVgg Greuther Fürth (6/0), FC Midtjylland Herning (16/0).
(137/187)	STOLPE Olof	18.04.1927	13	4	1947-1953, Vaasa Idrottsförening Kamraterna (13/4).
(8/030)	STORMBOM Charles	26.04.1898	15	0	1919-1924, IF Kamraterna Åbo (15/0).
(746/702)	STRANDVALL Sebastian	16.09.1986	1	0	2014, Vaasan Palloseura (1/0).
(214/280)	STRÖMBERG Holger	28.04.1936	2	0	1960, Helsingin Idrottsföreningen Kamraterna (2/0).
(62/102)	STRÖMSTEN Olof	12.01.1909	7	3	1929-1934, Kronohagens IF (5/3), Helsingin Idrottsföreningen Kamraterna (2/0).
(192/255)	STYCK Pentti	29.10.1930	1	0	1956, HJK Helsinki (1/0).
(292/367)	SUHONEN Heikki	21.06.1951	21	2	1971-1979, Turun Palloseura Turku (7/1), HJK Helsinki (6/1), Turun Palloseura Turku (8/0).
(436/482)	SULONEN Petri	20.06.1963	10	0	1986-1992, Porin Pallotoverit (2/0), Turun Palloseura Turku (8/0).
(496/526)	SUMIALA Antti	20.02.1974	38	9	1992-2004, Ikast fS (2/0), KSC Lokeren (1/0), Ikast fS (5/2), Emmen (5/1), NEC Nijmegen (9/3), FC Twente Enschede (6/2), FC Jokerit Helsinki (5/1), , IFK Norrköping (3/0), Sebatspor Kulübü (2/0).
(724/685)	SUMUSALO Mikko	12.03.1990	4	1	2012-2015, HJK Helsinki (3/1), FC Hansa Rostock (1/0).
(176/223)	SUNDBÄCK Turkka	23.06.1931	4	0	1954, Turku Toverit (4/0).
(197/259)	SUNDBERG Sven Erik	09.11.1934	1	0	1957, Kronohagens IF (1/0).
(191/251)	SUNDELIN Matti	04.12.1934	5	2	1956-1960, Turun Palloseura Turku (5/2).
(156/202)	SUOJANEN Reino	03.09.1925	3	0	1951-1953, Pyrkivä Turku (3/0).
(505/536)	SUOKONAUTIO Janne	20.05.1968	4	0	1993-1994, HJK Helsinki (4/0).
(286/358)	SUOMALAINEN Juoko	08.04.1949	54	2	1970-1978, Kuopion Palloseura (3/0), Kuopion Pallo Toverit (51/2).
(505/534)	SUOMINEN Kim	20.10.1969	39	4	1993-1996, FF Jaro JS Pietarsaari (13/1), Tampere PV (10/2), FC Admira Wacker Wien (6/1), IFK Nörrköping (10/0).

(51/085)	SUONTAUSTA Yrjö	09.12.1901	**5**	**1**	1927-1929, Turun Palloseura Turku (5/1).
(128/166)	SVAHN Helge	27.02.1924	**8**	**1**	1945-1949, Vaasa Idrottsförening Kamraterna (8/1).
(648/623)	SVANBÄCK Fredrik	12.05.1979	**2**	**0**	2004-2008, Helsingborgs IF (1/0), FF Jaro (1/0).
(61/100)	SVANSTRÖM Torsten	31.07.1904	**1**	**1**	1929,Helsingin Idrottsföreningen Kamraterna (1/1).
(2/012)	SYRJÄLÄINEN August	24.04.1891	**5**	**0**	1912, Viipurin Reipas (5/0).
(234/309)	SYRJÄVAARA Simo	14.06.1943	**26**	**1**	1964-1968, IF Kamraterna Åbo (9/0), Upon Pallo Lahti (17/1).
(765/720)	TAHVANAINEN Timo	26.06.1986	**2**	**0**	2016, SJK Seinäjoki (2/0).
(565/576)	TAINIO Teemu	27.11.1979	**64**	**6**	1998-2014, AJ Auxerre (28/5), Tottenham Hotspur FC London (15/1), Sunderland AFC (6/0), Birmingham City FC (2/0), *unattached* (1/0), HJK Helsinki (12/0).
(85/121)	TAIPALE Lauri	11.09.1911	**9**	**3**	1934-1937, Helsingin Toverit (9/3).
(665/645)	TAIPALE Tero	14.12.1972	**1**	**0**	2006, Myllykoskes Pallo-47 Anjalankoski (1/0).
(275/349)	TALASLAHTI Pekka	01.10.1945	**1**	**0**	1969, HJK Helsinki (1/0).
(226/293)	TALSI Markku	20.02.1940	**1**	**0**	1962, Reipas Lahti (1/0).
(395/459)	TALVIO Ilpo	15.09.1961	**2**	**0**	1983, FC Kuusysi Lahti (2/0).
(185/243)	TAMMINEN Turkka	02.01.1931	**2**	**0**	1955-1958, Turku Toverit (2/0).
(8/028)	TAMMISALO Niilo	15.10.1894	**29**	**0**	1919-1926, HJK Helsinki (29/0).
(1/007)	TANNER Lauri	20.11.1890	**3**	**2**	1911-1920, HJK Helsinki (3/2).
(296/371)	TAPOLA Juhani	01.04.1948	**2**	**1**	1972, Haka Valkeakoski (2/1).
(431/478)	TARKKIO Kimmo	15.01.1966	**33**	**3**	1986-1992, HJK Helsinki (7/0), Turun Palloseura Turku (5/1), Hammarby IF Stockholm (4/1), HJK Helsinki (6/1), FC Haka Valkeakoski (6/0), FC Kuusysi Lahti (5/0).
(652/639)	TARVAJÄRVI Niklas	13.03.1983	**4**	**0**	2005-2009, Myllykosken Pallo-47 Anjalankoski (2/0), SBV Vitesse Arnhem (2/0).
(662/643)	TAULO Ville	14.08.1985	**3**	**0**	2005-2006, FC Lahti (3/0).
(437/490)	TAURIAINEN Pasi	04.10.1964	**34**	**1**	1986-1993, Rovaniemi Palloseura (13/0), HJK Helsinki (21/1).
(483/521)	TAURIAINEN Vesa	16.12.1967	**1**	**1**	1990, Rovaniemi Palloseura (1/1).
(181/231)	TÄHTINEN Pentti	11.02.1934	**3**	**0**	1955, Kotkan Työväen Palloilijat (3/0).
(465/506)	TEGELBERG Ari	21.04.1963	**15**	**1**	1988-1992, Rovaniemi Palloseura (15/1).
(114/146)	TERÄS Urho	07.07.1915	**11**	**2**	1938-1949, Turun Palloseura Turku (11/2).
(554/565)	TERVONEN Toni	14.03.1977	**4**	**1**	1996-1999, Kuopion Palloseura (1/0), Finnairin Palloilijat Helsinki (2/1), FK Haugesund (1/0).
(8/032)	THORN Holger	15.10.1895	**4**	**2**	1919-1924, Kronohagens IF (4/2).
(434/479)	TIAINEN Petri	26.09.1966	**15**	**2**	1986-1995, FC Kuusysi Lahti (1/0), AFC Ajax Amsterdam (8/1), HJK Helsinki (2/1), Myllykosken Pallo-47 Anjalakoski (4/0).
(580/590)	TIHINEN Hannu	01.07.1976	**76**	**5**	1999-2009, HJK Helsinki (2/1), Viking FK Stavanger (13/0), West Ham United FC London (1/0), Viking FK Stavanger (11/1), RSC Anderlecht Bruxelles (21/2), FC Zürich (28/1).
(652/638)	TIMOSKA Sampsa	12.02.1979	**2**	**0**	2005, Myllykosken Pallo-47 Anjalankoski (2/0).
(367/439)	TISSARI Ari	24.11.1951	**6**	**2**	1980, Kotkan Työväen Palloilijat (6/2).
(268/338)	TOIVANEN Raimo	03.10.1945	**19**	**0**	1968-1971, Turun Palloseura Turku (19/0).
(714/677)	TOIVIO Joona	10.03.1988	**39**	**2**	2011-2016, Djurgårdens IF Stockholm (18/1), Molde FK (21/1).
(272/345)	TOIVOLA Miika	11.07.1949	**62**	**4**	1968-1980, Pihlavan Työväen Urheilijat (1/0), Turun Palloseura Turku (13/1), HJK Helsinki (48/3).
(279/351)	TOIVOLA Pentti	07.01.1945	**9**	**0**	1969-1974, Mikkelin Palloilijat (8/0), Seinäjoki Palloseura (1/0).
(532/547)	TOIVONEN Panu	26.09.1972	**1**	**0**	1994, Turun Palloseura Turku (1/0).
(38/070)	TOLONEN Aarne	22.08.1899	**3**	**0**	1925, HJK Helsinki (3/0).
(235/313)	TOLSA Arto	09.08.1945	**77**	**10**	1964-1981, KTP Kotka (26/7), VAV Beerschot Anvers (33/3), Kotkan Työväen Palloilijat (18/0).
(13/041)	TORNIVUORI Yrjö	17.12.1895	**4**	**0**	1921-1922, Helsingin Palloseura (4/0).
(410/474)	TÖRNVALL Markus	31.12.1964	**26**	**1**	1984-1989, FC Kuusysi Lahti (6/0), Haka Valkeakoski (9/1), FC Kuusysi Lahti (3/0), Reipas Lahti (5/0), IFK Norrköping (3/0).
(538/550)	TUOMELA Marko	03.03.1972	**24**	**2**	1995-2003, Tampere PV (2/0), FF Jaro JS Pietarsaari (4/0), Tromsø IL (14/2), GIF Sundsvall (4/0).
(548/558)	TURPEINEN Aarno	21.03.1971	**14**	**0**	1996-2002, HJK Helsinki (16/0).
(66/107)	TURUNEN Eino	27.08.1908	**2**	**0**	1930, Viipurin Palloseura (2/0).
(351/423)	TURUNEN Hannu	24.06.1956	**66**	**3**	1979-1987, Kuopion Pallo Toverit (29/3), Kuopion Palloseura (37/0).
(477/515)	TURUNEN Jukka	29.01.1964	**7**	**0**	1989-1992, Kuopion Palloseura (6/0), Myllykosken Pallo-47 Anjalakoski (1/0).
(122/154)	TURUNEN Leo	28.06.1919	**11**	**0**	1940-1948, Viipurin Sudet (11/0).
(694/656)	TURUNEN Tuomo	30.08.1987	**2**	**0**	2009-2010, FC Honka Espoo (1/0), IFK Göteborg (1/0).
(249/324)	TUURI Mauri	25.08.1940	**1**	**0**	1966, Haka Valkeakoski (1/0).
(341/413)	UIMONEN Arto	07.01.1958	**21**	**0**	1978-1986, Haka Valkeakoski (9/0), Ilves Tampere (12/0).
(396/462)	UKKONEN Kari	19.02.1961	**59**	**4**	1983-1994, KSV Cercle Bruges (22/1), KSC Lokeren (7/0), RSC Anderlecht Bruxelles (18/2), FC Antwerpen (6/1), LB Châteauroux (6/0).
(726/690)	URONEN Jere Juhani	13.07.1994	**21**	**0**	2012-2016, Helsingborgs IF (16/0), KRC Genk (5/0).
(231/304)	UTRIAINEN Pertti	23.10.1937	**2**	**0**	1963, IFK Holmsunds (2/0).
(381/454)	UTRIAINEN Peter	20.11.1960	**11**	**0**	1981-1984, Östers IF Växjö (9/0), Gefle IF (2/0).
(662/642)	UUSIMÄKI Tuomas	09.07.1977	**5**	**0**	2005-2006, Örgryte IS Göteborg (5/0).
(169/213)	VAHTONEN Aulis	27.01.1929	**1**	**0**	1952, Turun Palloseura Turku (1/0).
(134/179)	VAIHELA Jorma	30.09.1925	**33**	**13**	1947-1954, Turku Toverit (6/0), Porin Palloilijat (7/3), Rosenlewin Urheiluliito Pori (12/6), Turku Toverit (8/4).
(340/411)	VAITTINEN Reijo	24.01.1956	**13**	**0**	1977-1982, Oulun Palloseura (1/0), Mikkelin Palloilijat (12/0).
(548/559)	VALAKARI Simo	28.04.1973	**32**	**0**	1996-2000, Finnairin Palloilijat Helsinki (1/0), Motherwell FC (14/0), Derby County FC (17/0).
(162/205)	VALKAMA Esko	21.12.1924	**3**	**0**	1952, Ilves-Kissat Tampere (3/0).
(458/503)	VALLA Erkki	08.09.1964	**3**	**0**	1988, HJK Helsinki (3/0).

(218/284)	VALTONEN Veijo	05.01.1936	4	0	1960-1964, Haka Valkeakoski (4/0).
(374/448)	VALVEE Ari	01.12.1960	47	8	1980-1989, Haka Valkeakoski (17/5), Vasalund (9/1), HJK Helsinki (13/2), Haka Valkeakoski (8/0).
(496/524)	VANHALA Jari	29.08.1965	23	2	1992-1997, HJK Helsinki (15/1), FF Jaro JS Pietarsaari (4/0), Finnairin Palloilijat Helsinki (4/1).
(286/357)	VANHANEN Matti	08.03.1944	1	0	1970, Mikkelin Palloilijat (1/0).
(193/257)	VANHANEN Mauri	01.06.1931	3	2	1957, Mikkelin Palloilijat (3/2).
(176/224)	VANHANEN Pertti	09.07.1933	16	0	1954-1963, Kotkan Työväen Palloilijat (2/0), Jakobstads Bollklub (5/0), Kotkan Työväen Palloilijat (9/0).
(582/593)	VASARA Vesa	16.08.1976	12	2	1999-2002, HJK Helsinki (11/2), Kalmar FF (1/0).
(542/552)	VÄISÄNEN Sami	09.05.1973	7	0	1995-1997, FC Haka Valkeakoski (7/0).
(773/723)	VÄISÄNEN Sauli Aapo Kasperi	05.06.1994	3	0	2016, AIK Stockholm (3/0).
(600/606)	VÄISÄNEN Ville	19.04.1977	5	1	2001-2003, FC Haka Valkeakoski (4/1), Bryne FK (1/0).
(615/610)	VÄYRYNEN Mika	28.12.1981	63	5	2002-2015, SC Heerenveen (18/0), PSV Eindhoven (23/3), SC Heerenveen (10/2), *unattached* (3/0), Leeds United AFC (2/0), HJK Helsinki (7/0).
(748/705)	VÄYRYNEN Tim	30.03.1993	6	0	2014-2016, BV Borussia Dortmund (3/0), FC Viktoria Köln (1/0), SG Dynamo Dresden (2/0).
(128/167)	VEIJOLA Sven	30.03.1922	3	0	1945-1947, Vaasa Idrottsförening Kamraterna (3/0).
(714/681)	VENÄLÄINEN Ilja	27.09.1980	1	0	2011, Kuopion Palloseura (1/0).
(143/195)	VENTJÄRVI Sven	08.08.1926	2	0	1949, Vaasan Palloseura (2/0).
(575/584)	VIANDER Jani	18.08.1975	13	0	1999-2003, HJK Helsinki (12/0), Stoke City FC (1/0).
(327/399)	VIERIKKO Raimo	21.01.1950	2	0	1976-1977, Mikkeli Pallokissat (2/0).
(11/039)	VIHAVAINEN Aarne	24.11.1894	5	0	1920-1922, HJK Helsinki (5/0).
(289/364)	VIHTILÄ Erkki	14.05.1951	42	0	1971-1979, Ilves-Kissat Tampere (7/0), Ilves Tampere (16/1), Reipas Lahti (16/0), Ilves Tampere (3/0).
(43/078)	VIINIOKSA Max	27.10.1905	50	1	1926-1935, HJK Helsinki (6/0), Helsingin Palloseura (44/1).
(339/410)	VILEN Teuvo	26.11.1953	11	0	1977-1980, Haka Valkeakoski (11/0).
(203/266)	VILERMO Voitto	09.07.1927	3	0	1958, Helsingin Palloseura (3/0).
(579/589)	VILJANEN Ville	02.02.1971	1	0	1999, Västra Frölunda IF (1/0).
(202/264)	VILPUNEN Ossi	10.03.1936	1	0	1957, Lahden Pallo-Miehet (1/0).
(305/376)	VIRKUNNEN Eero	17.02.1948	9	0	1973-1974, Oulun Työväen Palloilijat (9/0).
(20/053)	VIRTA Lauri	09.04.1897	7	0	1922-1924, Helsingin Palloseura (7/0).
(98/131)	VIRTANEN Eino	01.01.1914	3	0	1936-1941, Helsingin Palloseura (3/0).
(349/418)	VIRTANEN Kari	15.09.1958	37	1	1979-1986, Turun Palloseura Turku (9/0), IFK Eskilstuna (5/0), Turun Palloseura Turku (1/0), IFK Eskilstuna (7/0), AIK Stockholm (14/1), Rovaniemi Palloseura (1/0).
(97/128)	VIRTANEN Paavo	03.11.1915	3	0	1935-1937, Helsingin Palloseura (3/0).
(228/297)	VIRTANEN Rauli	04.01.1939	2	1	1962, Tampellan Palloilijat (2/1).
(188/249)	VOUTILAINEN Keijo	14.09.1936	6	0	1956-1962, Kuopion Palloseura (5/0), Reipas Lahti (1/0).
(444/494)	VUORELA Juoko	26.07.1963	16	0	1987-1992, KontU-71 Helsinki (2/0), HJK Helsinki (14/0).
(705/667)	VUORINEN Hermanni	27.01.1985	1	0	2010, FC Honka Espoo (1/0).
(436/481)	VUORINEN Reijo	18.06.1959	4	0	1986-1988, Haka Valkeakoski (4/0).
(73/116)	WECKSTRÖM Kurt	04.12.1911	35	10	1931-1943, Kronohagens IF (5/1), HJK Helsinki (30/9).
(207/271)	WESTERHOLM Anders	01.09.1937	10	0	1959-1961, Helsingin Idrottsföreningen Kamraterna (10/0).
(126/158)	WESTERHOLM Gunnar	26.06.1917	1	0	1943, Kronohagens IF (1/0).
(2/015)	WIBERG Bror	14.06.1890	5	3	1912, Helsingin Idrottsföreningen Kamraterna (5/3).
(2/014)	WICKSTRÖM Ragnar	12.11.1892	17	2	1912-1923, Kronohagens IF (17/2).
(545/557)	WISS Jarkko	17.04.1972	45	3	1996-2007, FF Jaro JS Pietarsaari (4/0), HJK Helsinki (13/1), Lillestrøm SK (3/1), Moss FK (8/0), Stockport County FC (6/0), Hibernian Edinburgh FC (5/1), Tampere United (6/0).
(466/508)	YLÄ-JUSSILA Sami	07.10.1969	4	0	1988-1999, HJK Helsinki (1/0), FC Jokerit Helsinki (3/0).
(543/556)	YLÖNEN Harri	21.12.1972	45	1	1995-2002, FC Haka Valkeakoski (19/1), SK Brann Bergen (23/0), FC Haka Valkeakoski (3/0).
(30/066)	YRJÖLÄ Niilo	22.10.1900	1	0	1924, Viipurin Sudet (1/0).
(741/699)	ZENELI Erfan	28.12.1986	6	0	2013-2015, HJK Helsinki (2/0), *unattached* (1/0), Maccabi Petah Tikva FC (1/0), HJK Helsinki (2/0).

NATIONAL COACHES

Name	DOB	Period	Matches	P	W	D	L		GF	-	GA	
Jarl ÖHMAN	14.11.1891 †20.01.1936	05.06.1922 – 26.08.1922	[18-21]	4	1	0	3		13	-	14	25.00 %
Ferdinand FABRA (*Germany*)	08.10.1906 †22.12.2007	30.06.1936 – 29.06.1937	[98-105]	8	1	1	6		9	-	29	18.75 %
Gábor OBITZ (*Hungary*)	18.01.1899 †20.03.1953	09.06.1939 – 17.09.1939	[115-120]	6	1	0	5		9	-	25	16.66 %
Axel MÅRTENSSON (*Sweden*)		26.08.1945 – 30.09.1945	[128-129]	2	0	0	2		3	-	13	0.00 %
Niilo TAMMISALO	15.10.1894 †05.02.1982	28.06.1946 – 15.09.1946	[130-132]	3	0	0	3		2	-	24	0.00 %
Aatos LEHTONEN	15.02.1914 †10.04.2005	26.06.1947 – 14.08.1955	[133-183]	51	7	9	35		67	-	152	22.54 %
Kurt WEINREICH (*West Germany*)	12.12.1908 †08.04.1998	28.08.1955 – 11.10.1958	[184-206]	23	3	1	19		20	-	88	15.21 %
Aatos LEHTONEN	15.02.1914 †10.04.2005	28.06.1959 – 29.10.1961	[207-225]	19	3	0	16		22	-	68	15.78 %
Kaarlo Olavi LAAKSONEN	26.07.1921 †27.10.2004	19.06.1962 – 09.10.1974	[226-316]	91	16	21	54		78	-	218	29.12 %
Martti KOSMA	24.06.1927 †29.07.1999	16.04.1975 – 15.05.1975	[317-318]	2	0	1	1		4	-	6	25.00 %
Aulis RYTKÖNEN	05.01.1929	05.06.1975 – 11.10.1978	[319-348]	30	8	4	18		31	-	70	33.33 %
Esko MALM	23.08.1940	05.02.1979 – 23.09.1981	[349-351], [354], [356], [358], [360], [362-385]	31	6	7	18		25	-	65	30.64 %
Jiří PEŠEK (*Czechoslovakia*)	04.06.1927	10.05.1979 – 26.10.1979	[352-353], [355],[357], [359],[361]	6	1	3	2		6	-	6	41.66 %
Martti KUUSELA	09.10.1945	20.02.1982 – 09.09.1987	[386-435], [437-438], [440], [442-446] [448],[451]	60	9	13	38		52	-	114	25.83 %
Jukka Keijo Olavi VAKKILA	02.04.1951	05.08.1986 – 14.11.1992	[436],[439], [441],[447], [449-450], [452-504]	59	10	21	28		43	-	87	34.74 %
Tommy LINDHOLM	03.02.1947	20.01.1993 – 12.10.1994	[505-529]	25	5	7	13		21	-	33	34.00 %
Jukka IKÄLÄINEN	14.05.1957	26.10.1994 – 02.06.1996	[530-550]	21	7	4	10		33	-	32	42.85 %
Richard MØLLER-NIELSEN (*Denmark*)	19.08.1937 †13.02.2014	14.08.1996 – 09.10.1999	[551-584]	34	9	12	13		42	-	46	44.11 %
Antti MUURINEN	04.03.1954	31.01.2000 – 08.06.2005	[585-656]	72	34	12	26		102	-	86	55.55 %
Jyrki HELISKOSKI	28.09.1945	17.08.2005 – 12.11.2005	[657-662]	6	2	2	2		10	-	7	50.00 %
Roy HODGSON (*England*)	09.08.1947	21.01.2006 – 21.11.2007	[663-684]	22	6	11	5		17	-	15	52.27 %
Stuart William BAXTER (Scot*land*)	16.08.1953	06.02.2008 – 12.10.2010	[685-712]	28	8	5	15		27	-	43	37.50 %
Olavi „Olli" HUTTUNEN	04.08.1960		[713]	1	1	0	0		8	-	0	100.00 %
Markku KANERVA	24.05.1964	09.02.2011 – 29.03.2011	[714-715]	2	0	1	1		1	-	3	25.00 %
Mika-Matti Petteri PAATELAINEN	03.02.1967	03.06.2011 – 13.06.2015	[716-760]	45	17	11	17		54	-	56	50.00 %
Markku KANERVA	24.05.1964	04.09.2015 – 11.10.2015	[761-764]	4	2	2	0		4	-	2	75.00 %
Hans Roland BACKE (*Sweden*)	14.02.1952	10.01.2016 – 12.11.2016	[765-775]	11	0	2	9		4	-	22	9.09 %

In the following matches the Finland national football team played without national trainer: [1-17], [22-98], [107-115], [122-128].

National coaches several times in charge:

Name	How often	Matches	M	W	D	L		GF	-	GA	
Aatos LEHTONEN	2x	[134-184], [208-212],[214-226]	69	10	9	50		91	-	226	21.01 %
Markku KANERVA	2x	[714-715], [761-764]	6	2	3	1		5	-	5	58.33 %

HEAD-TO-HEAD STATISTICS

	HOME							AWAY							NEUTRAL							TOTAL						
Albania	3	3	0	0	5	:	2	3	1	0	2	2	:	3	1	0	1	0	1	:	1	7	4	1	2	8	:	6
Algeria															1	0	0	1	0	:	2	1	0	0	1	0	:	2
Andorra	1	1	0	0	3	:	0	1	0	1	0	0	:	0								2	1	1	0	3	:	0
Armenia	2	2	0	0	4	:	1	2	1	1	0	2	:	0								4	3	1	0	6	:	1
Austria	5	1	1	3	6	:	8	5	0	0	5	4	:	15								10	1	1	8	10	:	23
Austria Olympic	2	1	0	1	5	:	5	1	1	0	0	2	:	0								3	2	0	1	7	:	5
Azerbaijan	4	3	1	0	9	:	1	4	3	0	1	6	:	4								8	6	1	1	15	:	5
Bahrain								5	4	1	0	9	:	1								5	4	1	0	9	:	1
Barbados								1	0	1	0	0	:	0								1	0	1	0	0	:	0
Belarus	2	1	1	0	2	:	1	1	0	1	0	1	:	1	1	0	1	0	2	:	2	4	1	3	0	5	:	4
Belgium	5	3	0	2	10	:	7	6	1	4	1	9	:	13								11	4	4	3	19	:	20
Belgium Olym.	1	0	0	1	0	:	2	1	0	0	1	0	:	1								2	0	0	2	0	:	3
Bermuda								1	1	0	0	2	:	0								1	1	0	0	2	:	0
Bolivia								2	0	1	1	2	:	5								2	0	1	1	2	:	5
Bosnia and Herz.								1	0	0	1	0	:	1								1	0	0	1	0	:	1
Brazil	1	0	0	1	2	:	3	2	0	0	2	1	:	6								3	0	0	3	3	:	9
Bulgaria	4	0	1	3	1	:	8	4	0	0	4	2	:	11								8	0	1	7	3	:	19
Cameroon															2	0	1	1	0	:	2	2	0	1	1	0	:	2
Canada	1	1	0	0	3	:	2															1	1	0	0	3	:	2
Chile								1	0	0	1	0	:	2								1	0	0	1	0	:	2
China P.R.	1	1	0	0	4	:	0	2	0	0	2	2	:	4	1	0	0	1	1	:	2	4	1	0	3	7	:	6
Colombia	1	0	0	1	1	:	3															1	0	0	1	1	:	3
Costa Rica															1	0	0	1	1	:	2	1	0	0	1	1	:	2
Costa Rica Oly.															1	1	0	0	3	:	0	1	1	0	0	3	:	0
Croatia	1	0	0	1	0	:	1															1	0	0	1	0	:	1
Cyprus								4	2	1	1	7	:	4								4	2	1	1	7	:	4
Czech Republic	5	1	2	2	6	:	10	5	1	1	3	6	:	12	1	1	0	0	2	:	0	11	3	3	5	14	:	22
Czechoslov Oly.	1	0	0	1	0	:	2	1	0	0	1	0	:	2								2	0	0	2	0	:	4
Denmark	26	8	4	14	33	:	57	30	2	4	24	25	:	93	3	1	2	0	2	:	1	59	11	10	38	60	:	151
Denmark Olym.	2	1	1	0	4	:	1	2	0	1	1	1	:	4								4	1	2	1	5	:	5
East Germany	3	2	0	1	5	:	7	4	0	1	3	3	:	14								7	2	1	4	8	:	21
E. Germany Oly.	2	1	0	1	1	:	1	1	0	0	1	0	:	1								3	1	0	2	1	:	2
Ecuador								1	0	0	1	1	:	3								1	0	0	1	1	:	3
Egypt								2	0	0	2	2	:	4								2	0	0	2	2	:	4
England	9	0	2	7	5	:	31	3	0	0	3	2	:	9								12	0	2	10	7	:	40
England Amateur	2	1	0	1	5	:	6	3	0	0	3	4	:	9								5	1	0	4	9	:	15
England Olympic															1	0	0	1	0	:	4	1	0	0	1	0	:	4
Estonia	15	7	6	2	40	:	19	14	5	4	5	25	:	19	2	2	0	0	6	:	2	31	14	10	7	71	:	40
Faroe Islands	2	2	0	0	6	:	0	2	2	0	0	7	:	1	1	1	0	0	1	:	0	5	5	0	0	14	:	1
France	3	0	0	3	1	:	5	5	0	0	5	2	:	13								8	0	0	8	3	:	18
France Olympic	1	0	1	0	1	:	1	1	0	0	1	1	:	3								2	0	1	1	2	:	4
Georgia	1	0	1	0	1	:	1	1	1	0	0	1	:	0								2	1	1	0	2	:	1
Germany	14	0	4	10	14	:	44	9	1	2	6	5	:	38	1	0	0	1	1	:	2	24	1	6	17	20	:	84
Greece	6	3	3	0	13	:	5	6	1	0	5	3	:	17	1	0	0	1	1	:	2	13	4	3	6	17	:	24
Honduras															1	1	0	0	2	:	1	1	1	0	0	2	:	1
Hungary	8	1	1	6	7	:	28	8	1	2	5	4	:	17	1	1	0	0	4	:	3	17	3	3	11	15	:	48
Iceland	5	5	0	0	12	:	4	5	1	2	2	7	:	8	2	0	0	2	0	:	2	12	6	2	4	19	:	14
India								2	1	1	0	2	:	0								2	1	1	0	2	:	0
Iraq								2	0	0	2	0	:	3								2	0	0	2	0	:	3
Iraq Olympic															1	0	1	0	0	:	0	1	0	1	0	0	:	0
Israel	3	1	1	1	2	:	3	2	1	0	1	4	:	3								5	2	1	2	6	:	6
Italy	5	0	0	5	2	:	11	7	0	1	6	2	:	19	1	1	0	0	3	:	2	13	1	1	11	7	:	32
Japan								2	0	0	2	1	:	7								2	0	0	2	1	:	7
Kazakhstan	1	1	0	0	2	:	1	1	1	0	0	2	:	0	1	0	1	0	0	:	0	3	2	1	0	4	:	1
Korea D.P.R.															1	0	0	1	2	:	3	1	0	0	1	2	:	3
Korea Republic															3	0	0	3	0	:	5	3	0	0	3	0	:	5
Kosovo	1	0	1	0	1	:	1															1	0	1	0	1	:	1
Kuwait								6	2	2	2	5	:	5	1	1	0	0	1	:	0	7	3	2	2	6	:	5
Latvia	7	6	0	1	19	:	8	8	3	2	3	10	:	8	2	1	1	0	3	:	2	17	10	3	4	32	:	18
Liechtenstein	1	1	0	0	2	:	1	1	0	1	0	1	:	1								2	1	1	0	3	:	2
Lithuania	3	3	0	0	15	:	3	1	0	0	1	0	:	1	1	0	0	1	0	:	1	5	3	0	2	15	:	5
Luxembourg	1	1	0	0	7	:	1	4	3	0	1	5	:	3								5	4	0	1	12	:	4
Macedonia	1	1	0	0	5	:	1	2	1	0	1	3	:	1	1	1	0	0	3	:	0	4	3	0	1	11	:	2
Malaysia								1	0	0	1	1	:	2								1	0	0	1	1	:	2
Malta	1	1	0	0	2	:	0	6	3	2	1	7	:	5								7	4	2	1	9	:	5
Mexico	2	0	0	2	0	:	4	2	0	1	1	2	:	3								4	0	1	3	2	:	7
Moldova	2	2	0	0	7	:	3	2	0	1	1	0	:	2								4	2	1	1	7	:	5
Morocco								1	0	1	0	0	:	0								1	0	1	0	0	:	0
Netherlands	7	1	1	5	7	:	16	6	0	1	5	7	:	18	1	0	0	1	0	:	9	14	1	2	11	14	:	43
Netherlands Am.	2	2	0	0	4	:	1	3	0	1	2	2	:	5								5	2	1	2	6	:	6
Netherlands Oly.	1	0	1	0	0	:	0	1	1	0	0	1	:	0								2	1	1	0	1	:	0

Northern Ireland	4	2	1	1	7 : 4	5	1	1	3	6 : 8						9	3	2	4	13 : 12
Norway	29	6	8	15	45 : 72	33	3	6	24	32 : 102						62	9	14	39	77 : 174
Norway Olympic	2	0	1	1	1 : 2	2	0	1	1	3 : 5						4	0	2	2	4 : 7
Oman						5	3	2	0	7 : 2	1	0	1	0	0 : 0	6	3	3	0	7 : 2
Peru											1	0	0	1	3 : 7	1	0	0	1	3 : 7
Poland	13	2	3	8	16 : 26	17	1	4	12	11 : 49	1	0	1	0	1 : 1	31	3	8	20	28 : 76
Poland Olympic	1	0	0	1	0 : 4	1	0	0	1	2 : 3						2	0	0	2	2 : 7
Portugal	3	0	2	1	1 : 3	7	1	2	4	5 : 11						10	1	4	5	6 : 14
Qatar						4	0	3	1	3 : 4						4	0	3	1	3 : 4
Rep. of Ireland	2	0	1	1	1 : 4	3	0	1	2	1 : 7						5	0	2	3	2 : 11
Romania	5	0	2	3	2 : 9	5	0	1	4	2 : 17	1	0	1	0	1 : 1	11	0	4	7	5 : 27
Russia	2	0	0	2	0 : 9	2	0	0	2	1 : 6	1	1	0	0	2 : 1	5	1	0	4	3 : 16
San Marino	2	2	0	0	12 : 1	2	2	0	0	3 : 0						4	4	0	0	15 : 1
Saudi Arabia						4	2	1	1	7 : 4						4	2	1	1	7 : 4
Scotland	3	0	0	3	2 : 6	5	0	2	3	3 : 12						8	0	2	6	5 : 18
Serbia	5	2	1	2	9 : 11	4	0	1	3	1 : 19						9	2	2	5	10 : 30
Singapore											1	1	0	0	1 : 0	1	1	0	0	1 : 0
Slovakia						2	0	1	1	1 : 2	1	0	0	1	0 : 2	3	0	1	2	1 : 4
Slovenia	1	1	0	0	2 : 0	1	0	1	0	1 : 1						2	1	1	0	3 : 1
Soviet Union	8	0	3	5	5 : 25	7	0	2	5	5 : 25						15	0	5	10	10 : 50
Spain	4	1	1	2	3 : 4	4	0	1	3	2 : 12						8	1	2	5	5 : 16
Sweden	41	6	6	29	56 : 131	42	2	5	35	35 : 156	5	2	0	3	4 : 8	88	10	11	67	95 : 295
Sweden Olympic	1	0	0	1	1 : 3											1	0	0	1	1 : 3
Switzerland	2	1	0	1	3 : 3	3	1	0	2	2 : 4						5	2	0	3	5 : 7
Thailand						5	1	1	3	6 : 12						5	1	1	3	6 : 12
Trinidad and Tob						5	3	1	1	8 : 7						5	3	1	1	8 : 7
Tunisia						2	1	1	0	3 : 2	1	1	0	0	3 : 0	3	2	1	0	6 : 2
Turkey	6	2	1	3	8 : 11	5	3	2	0	9 : 5	2	1	0	1	3 : 4	13	6	3	4	20 : 20
Ukraine						1	0	0	1	0 : 1						1	0	0	1	0 : 1
Un. Arab Emirat.						1	0	1	0	1 : 1						1	0	1	0	1 : 1
United States	1	0	0	1	0 : 1	1	0	0	1	1 : 2						2	0	0	2	1 : 3
Uruguay						2	0	0	2	1 : 8						2	0	0	2	1 : 8
Wales	5	2	1	2	4 : 5	7	2	3	2	8 : 12						12	4	4	4	12 : 17
W Germany Am.	1	0	1	0	0 : 0	2	1	0	1	4 : 7						3	1	1	1	4 : 7
W Germany Oly.	2	0	1	1	1 : 2	2	1	0	1	3 : 4						4	1	1	2	4 : 6
Yemen											1	0	1	0	0 : 0	1	0	1	0	0 : 0
Yugoslavia Oly.	1	0	0	1	1 : 2	1	0	0	1	0 : 5	1	0	0	1	0 : 2	3	0	0	3	1 : 9
TOTAL	**321**	**96**	**66**	**159**	**464 : 658**	**402**	**73**	**86**	**243**	**382 : 939**	**52**	**18**	**12**	**22**	**57 : 76**	**775**	**187**	**164**	**424**	**903 : 1673**

FRANCE

The Country:
French Republic (République française)
Capital: Paris
Surface: 643,801 km²
Inhabitants: 66,736,000
Time: UTC+1

The FA:
Fédération Française de Football
87, Boulevard de Grenelle, 75738 Paris Cedex 15
Foundation date: 07.04.1919
Member of FIFA since: 1907
Member of UEFA since: 1954

NATIONAL TEAM RECORDS

EUROPEAN CHAMPIONSHIP	
1960	Final Tournament (4th Place)
1964	Qualifiers
1968	Qualifiers
1972	Qualifiers
1976	Qualifiers
1980	Qualifiers
1984	**Final Tournament (Winners)**
1988	Qualifiers
1992	Final Tournament (Group Stage)
1996	Final Tournament (Semi-Finals)
2000	**Final Tournament (Winners)**
2004	Final Tournament (Quarter-Finals)
2008	Final Tournament (Group Stage)
2012	Final Tournament (Quarter-Finals)
2016	Final Tournament (Runners-up)

FIFA WORLD CUP	
1930	Final Tournament (Group Stage)
1934	Final Tournament (1st Round)
1938	Final Tournament (Quarter-Finals)
1950	*Withdrew*
1954	Final Tournament (Group Stage)
1958	Final Tournament (3rd Place)
1962	Qualifiers
1966	Final Tournament (Group Stage)
1970	Qualifiers
1974	Qualifiers
1978	Final Tournament (Group Stage)
1982	Final Tournament (4th Place)
1986	Final Tournament (3rd Place)
1990	Qualifiers
1994	Qualifiers
1998	**Final Tournament (Winners)**
2002	Final Tournament (Group Stage)
2006	Final Tournament (Runners-up)
2010	Final Tournament (Group Stage)
2014	Final Tournament (Quarter-Finals)

OLYMPIC FOOTBALL TOURNAMENTS 1908-2016							
1908	Final Tournament	**1948**	Quarter-Finals	**1972**	Qualifiers	**1996**	Quarter-Finals
1912	-	**1952**	Qualifiers	**1976**	Quarter-Finals	**2000**	Qualifiers
1920	Semi-Finals	**1956**	-	**1980**	Qualifiers	**2004**	Qualifiers
1924	Quarter-Finals	**1960**	Group Stage	**1984**	**Winners**	**2008**	Qualifiers
1928	1/8-Finals	**1964**	Qualifiers	**1988**	Qualifiers	**2012**	Qualifiers
1936	-	**1968**	Quarter-Finals	**1992**	Qualifiers	**2016**	Qualifiers

FIFA CONFEDERATIONS CUP 1992-2013
2001 (Winners), 2003 (Winners)

PLAYER WITH MOST INTERNATIONAL CAPS – Top 5			
1. Lilian THURAM	-	142 caps	(1994-2008)
2. Thierry Daniel Henry	-	123 caps	(1997-2010)
3. Marcel Desailly	-	116 caps	(1993-2004)
4. Zinedine Zidane	-	108 caps	(1994-2006)
5. Patrick Vieira	-	107 caps	(1997-2009)

PLAYER WITH MOST INTERNATIONAL GOALS – Top 5			
1. Thierry Daniel HENRY	-	51 goals	/ 123 caps (1997-2010)
2. Michel Platini	-	41 goals	/ 72 caps (1976-1987)
3. David Sergio Trézéguet	-	34 goals	/ 71 caps (1998-2008)
4. Zinedine Zidane	-	31 goals	/ 108 caps (1994-2006)
5. Jean-Pierre Papin	-	30 goals	/ 54 caps (1986-1995)

FULL INTERNATIONALS (1904-2016)

1. 01.05.1904 **BELGIUM - FRANCE** **3-3(1-2)**
Stade du Vivier d'Oie, Bruxelles; Referee: John C.Keene (England); Attendance: 1,500
FRA: Maurice Guichard (1/0), Fernand Canelle (Cap) (1/0), Joseph Verlet (1/0), Georges Bilot (1/0), Jacques Davy (1/0), Charles Bilot (1/0), Louis Mesnier (1/1), Marius Royet (1/1), Georges Garnier (1/0), Gaston Cyprès (1/1), Adrien Filez (1/0).
Goals: Louis Mesnier (12), Marius Royet (13), Gaston Cyprès (87).

2. 12.02.1905 **FRANCE - SWITZERLAND** **1-0(0-0)**
Stade Parc des Princes, Paris; Referee: John Lewis (England); Attendance: 500
FRA: Maurice Guichard (2/0), Fernand Canelle (2/0), Joseph Verlet (2/0), Charles Wilkes (1/0), Pierre Allemane (1/0), Eugène Nicolai (1/0), Louis Mesnier (2/1), Marius Royet (2/1), Georges Garnier (Cap) (2/0), Gaston Cyprès (2/2), Adrien Filez (2/0).
Goal: Gaston Cyprès (60).

3. 07.05.1905 **BELGIUM - FRANCE** **7-0(3-0)**
Stade du Vivier d'Oie, Bruxelles; Referee: Rodolf William Seeldrayers (Belgium); after 15 minutes John Lewis (England); Attendance: 300
FRA: Georges Crozier (1/0), Fernand Canelle (3/0), Henri Moigneu (1/0), Eugène Nicolai (2/0), Marius Royet (3/1), Charles Wilkes (2/0), Adrien Filez (3/0), Gaston Cyprès (3/2), Georges Garnier (Cap) (3/0), Louis Mesnier (3/1), R.Gigot (1/0).

4. 22.04.1906 **FRANCE - BELGIUM** **0-5(0-3)**
Stade de La Faisanderie, Saint-Cloud, Paris; Referee: John Wood (England); Attendance: 515
FRA: Georges Crozier (2/0), Joseph Verlet (3/0), Henri Moigneu (2/0), Julien Du Rhéart (1/0), Pierre Allemane (Cap) (2/0), Louis Schubart (1/0), Adrien Filez (4/0), Gaston Cyprès (4/2), Marius Royet (4/1), Louis Mesnier (4/1), Albert Jouve (1/0).

5. 01.11.1906 **FRANCE - ENGLAND Amateurs** **0-15(0-6)**
Stade Parc des Princes, Paris; Referee: Alexandre Guillon (Belgium); Attendance: 1,500
FRA: Zacharie Baton (1/0), Henri Moigneu (3/0), Fernand Canelle (4/0), Charles Wilkes (3/0), Pierre Allemane (Cap) (3/0), Louis Schubart (2/0), Émile Sartorius (1/0), Marius Royet (5/1), André François (1/0), Gaston Cyprès (5/2), J.Verbrugge (1/0).

6. 21.04.1907 **BELGIUM - FRANCE** **1-2(1-1)**
Stade du Vivier d'Oie, Bruxelles; Referee: Herbert James Willing (Netherlands); Attendance: 2,000
FRA: Zacharie Baton (2/0), Fernand Canelle (5/0), Victor Bentall-Sergent (1/0), Henri Moigneu (4/0), Pierre Allemane (Cap) (4/0), Paul Zeiger (1/0), René Camard (1/0), Georges Bon (1/0), André François (2/1), Marius Royet (6/2), André Puget (1/0).
Goals: Marius Royet (41), André François (72).

7. 08.03.1908 **SWITZERLAND - FRANCE** **1-2(1-0)**
Stade Charmilles, Genève; Referee: H.P.Devitte (Switzerland); Attendance: 4,000
FRA: Zacharie Baton (3/0), Joseph Verlet (4/0), Victor Bentall-Sergent (2/0), Maurice Vandendriessche (1/0), Pierre Allemane (Cap) (5/0), Henri Moigneu (5/0), Émile Sartorius (2/1), Albert Jenicot (1/0), André François (3/2), Paul Mathaux (1/0), Gabriel Hanot (1/0).
Goals: Émile Sartorius (??), André François (??).

8. 23.03.1908 **ENGLAND Amateurs - FRANCE** **12-0(6-0)**
Royal Park Stadium, London; Referee: Thomas Kyle (England); Attendance: 6,000
FRA: André Renaux (1/0), Victor Bentall-Sergent (3/0), Henri Moigneu (6/0), Maurice Vandendriessche (2/0), Pierre Allemane (Cap) (6/0), Julien Denis (1/0), Émile Sartorius (3/1), Marius Royet (7/2), André François (4/2), Paul Mathaux (2/0), Gabriel Hanot (2/0).

9. 12.04.1908 **FRANCE - BELGIUM** **1-2(0-2)**
Stade Olympique „Yves du Manoir", Colombes, Paris; Referee: James P.Stark (England); Attendance: 498
FRA: Zacharie Baton (4/0), Joseph Verlet (5/1), Victor Bentall-Sergent (4/0), Charles Wilkes (4/0), Pierre Allemane (Cap) (7/0), Henri Moigneu (7/0), Gabriel Hanot (3/0), Paul Mathaux (3/0), Marius Royet (8/2), Albert Jenicot (2/0), Émile Sartorius (4/1).
Goal: Joseph Verlet (76 penalty).

10. 10.05.1908 **NETHERLANDS - FRANCE** **4-1(2-0)**
Prinsenlaan Stadion, Rotterdam; Referee: Brauburger (Belgium); Attendance: 3,000
FRA: Maurice Tillette (1/0), Fernand Canelle (6/0), Henri Moigneu (8/0), Julien Du Rhéart (2/0), Julien Denis (2/0) [55.Victor Denis (1/0)], Marius Royet (Cap) (9/2), René Eucher (1/0), Louis Mesnier (5/1), André François (5/3), Paul Mathaux (4/0), Gabriel Hanot (4/0).
Goal: André François (75).

11. 19.10.1908 **FRANCE* - DENMARK** **0-9(0-4)** 5th OG. Group Stage.
White City Stadium, London (London); Referee: Thomas Kyle (England); Attendance: 2,000
FRA: Fernand Desrousseaux (1/0), Joseph Verlet (Cap) (6/1), Charles Bilot (2/0), Sadi Dastarac (1/0), Raoul Gressier (1/0), Justin Vialaret (1/0), Pierre Six (1/0), Albert Jenicot (3/0), Henri Holgard (1/0), Paul Mathaux (5/0), Adrien Filez (5/0).
**In this match, France was called „France B".*

12. 22.10.1908 **FRANCE - DENMARK** **1-17(1-6)** 5th OG. Semi-Finals.
White City Stadium, London (London); Referee: Thomas P. Campbell (England); Attendance: 1,000
FRA: Maurice Tillette (2/0), Jean Dubly (1/0), Ursule Wibaut (1/0), Georges Bayrou (1/0), Louis Schubart (3/0), Charles Renaux (1/0), René Fenouillere (1/0), Gaston Cyprès (6/2), André François (Cap) (6/3), Georges Albert (1/0), Émile Sartorius (5/2).
Goal: Émile Sartorius (16).

13. 09.05.1909 **BELGIUM - FRANCE** **5-2(2-0)**
Stade du Vivier d'Oie, Bruxelles; Referee: James R. Schumacher (England); Attendance: 1,500
FRA: Tessier (1/0), Ernest Tossier (1/0), Henri Guerre (1/0), Jean Rigal (1/1), Raymond Gouin (1/0), Jean-Marie Barat (1/0), M.Meunier (1/0), Henri Bellocq (1/0), Henri Mouton (1/1), Félix Julien (1/0), Alfred Compeyrat (1/0).
Goals: Henri Mouton (60), Jean Rigal (89).

14. 22.05.1909 **FRANCE - ENGLAND Amateurs** **0-11(0-6)**
Stade de la FGSPF [Fédération Gymnastique et Sportive des Patronages de France], Gentilly; Referee: Joseph Brauburger (Belgium); Attendance: 390
FRA: Tessier (2/0), André Sollier (1/0), Gilbert Brebion (1/0), Jean Rigal (2/1), Raymond Gouin (2/0), Jean-Marie Barat (2/0), Victor Hitzel (1/0), Henri Bellocq (2/0), Henri Mouton (2/1), Félix Julien (2/0), Jean Pacot (1/0).

15. 03.04.1910 **FRANCE - BELGIUM** **0-4(0-1)**
Stade de la FGSPF, Gentilly; Referee: James B. Stark (Scotland); Attendance: 950
FRA: Tessier (3/0), D.Mercier (1/0), André Sollier (2/0), Jean Rigal (3/1), Jean Ducret (1/0), Eugène Petel (1/0), Maurice Olivier (1/0), Henri Bellocq (3/0), Henri Mouton (3/1), Étienne Jourde (Cap) (1/0), Joseph Delvecchio (1/0).

16. 16.04.1910 **ENGLAND Amateurs - FRANCE** **10-1(6-0)**
Goldstone Ground, Brighton; Referee: Christiaan Jacobus Groothoff (Netherlands); Attendance: 3,500
FRA: Tessier (4/0), D.Mercier (2/0), André Sollier (3/0), Jean Rigal (4/1), Jean Ducret (Cap) (2/0), Henri Vascout (1/0), Henri Bellocq (4/0), Auguste Tousset (1/1), Maurice Olivier (2/0), Henri Mouton (4/1), Étienne Jourde (2/0).
Goal: Auguste Tousset (87).

17. 15.05.1910 **ITALY - FRANCE** **6-2(2-0)**
Arena Civica, Milano; Referee: Henry Goodley (England); Attendance: 4,500
FRA: Tessier (5/0), D.Mercier (3/0), André Sollier (4/0), Jean Rigal (5/1), Jean Ducret (3/1), Henri Vascout (2/0), Henri Mouton (5/1), Henri Sellier (1/0), Henri Bellocq (5/1), Maurice Olivier (3/0), Étienne Jourde (Cap) (3/0).
Goals: Henri Bellocq (50), Jean Ducret (62).

18. 01.01.1911 **FRANCE - HUNGARY** **0-3(0-2)**
Stade du Cercle Athlétique de Paris, Charentonneau; Referee: Charles Barette (Belgium); Attendance: 2,032
FRA: Henri Coulon (1/0), Alfred Gindrat (1/0), André Sollier (5/0), Jean Rigal (6/1), Jean Ducret (Cap) (4/1), Julien Du Rhéart (3/0), Pol Morel (1/0), Henri Bellocq (6/1), Eugène Maës (1/0), Ernest Gravier (1/0), J.Verbrugge (2/0).

19. 23.03.1911 **FRANCE - ENGLAND Amateurs** **0-3(0-1)**
Stade de Paris, Saint-Ouen; Referee: René Wolters (Belgium); Attendance: 1,638
FRA: Henri Coulon (2/0), Alfred Gindrat (2/0), Alfred Compeyrat (2/0), Jean Rigal (7/1), Jean Ducret (5/1), Henri Vascout (3/0), Pol Morel (2/0), Louis Mesnier (Cap) (6/1), Eugène Maës (2/0), Ernest Gravier (2/0), J.Verbrugge (3/0).

20. 09.04.1911 **FRANCE - ITALY** **2-2(2-1)**
Stade de Paris, Saint-Ouen; Referee: Charles Barette (Belgium); Attendance: 1,532
FRA: Henri Coulon (3/0), Charles Bilot (3/0), Joseph Verlet (7/1), Jean Rigal (8/1), Jean Ducret (6/1), Henri Vascout (4/0), Louis Mesnier (Cap) (7/1), Émilien Devic (1/0), Eugène Maës (3/2), Ernest Gravier (3/0), J.Verbrugge (4/0).
Goals: Eugène Maës (14, 40).

21. 23.04.1911 **SWITZERLAND - FRANCE** **5-2(4-0)**
Spitalacker, Genève; Referee: H.P.Devitte (Switzerland); Attendance: 7,000
FRA: Henri Coulon (4/0), Charles Bilot (4/0), Lucien Gamblin (1/0), Henri Vascout (5/0), Jean Ducret (7/1), Jean Rigal (9/1), Marcel Triboulet (1/0), Ernest Gravier (4/0), Eugène Maës (4/3), Louis Mesnier (Cap) (8/2), Georges Geronimi (1/0).
Goals: Louis Mesnier (69), Eugène Maës (70).

22. 30.04.1911 **BELGIUM - FRANCE** **7-1(3-0)**
Rue de Forest, Vorststraat, Bruxelles; Referee: James B. Stark (Scotland); Attendance: 3,000
FRA: Henri Coulon (5/0), Alfred Compeyrat (3/0), Charles Bilot (5/0), Jean Rigal (10/1), Gaston Barreau (Cap) (1/0), Henri Vascout (6/0), Louis Mesnier (9/2), Émilien Devic (2/0), Eugène Maës (5/4), Ernest Gravier (5/0), Étienne Jourde (4/0).
Goal: Eugène Maës (75).

23. 29.10.1911 **LUXEMBOURG - FRANCE** **1-4(1-2)**
Stade Racing Club, Luxembourg; Referee: Raphaël Van Praag (Belgium); Attendance: 4,000
FRA: Pierre Chayrigues (1/0), Maurice Bigué (1/0), Paul Romano (1/0), Gaston Barreau (2/0), Jean Ducret (8/1), Henri Vascout (7/0), Maurice Olivier (4/0), Henri Vialmonteil (1/1), Louis Mesnier (Cap) (10/4), Ernest Gravier (6/1), Francis Vial (1/0).
Goals: Henri Vialmonteil (25), Louis Mesnier (32, 80 penalty), Ernest Gravier (85).

24. 28.01.1912 **FRANCE - BELGIUM** **1-1(0-0)**
Stade de Paris, Saint-Ouen; Referee: James B. Stark (Scotland); Attendance: 2,000
FRA: Pierre Chayrigues (2/0), Alfred Gindrat (3/0), Charles Bilot (6/0), Jean Rigal (11/1), Jean Ducret (Cap) (9/1), Gaston Barreau (3/0), E.Lesmann (1/0), Louis Mesnier (11/4), Eugène Maës (6/5), Henri Vialmonteil (2/1), Marcel Triboulet (2/0).
Goal: Eugène Maës (75).

25. 18.02.1912 **FRANCE - SWITZERLAND** **4-1(0-0)**
Stade de Paris, Saint-Ouen; Referee: Charles Barette (Belgium); Attendance: 2,626
FRA: Pierre Chayrigues (3/0), Alfred Gindrat (4/0), Paul Romano (2/0), Maurice Bigué (2/0), Gaston Barreau (4/0), Jean Ducret (Cap) (10/1), Maurice Olivier (5/0), Louis Mesnier (12/5), Eugène Maës (7/6), Henri Vialmonteil (3/2), Marcel Triboulet (3/1).
Goals: Louis Mesnier (??), Marcel Triboulet (??), Eugène Maës (??), Henri Vialmonteil (83).

26. 17.03.1912 **ITALY - FRANCE** **3-4(1-2)**
Campo di Piazza d'Armi, Torino; Referee: James B. Stark (Scotland); Attendance: 6,000
FRA: Pierre Chayrigues (4/0), A.Fievet (1/0), Paul Romano (3/0), Maurice Bigué (3/0), Gaston Barreau (5/0), Jean Ducret (Cap) (11/1), Fernand Faroux (1/0), Louis Mesnier (13/6), Eugène Maës (8/9), Henri Vialmonteil (4/2), Étienne Jourde (5/0).
Goals: Eugène Maës (10, 38), Louis Mesnier (52), Eugène Maës (66).

27. 12.01.1913 **FRANCE - ITALY** **1-0(1-0)**
Stade de Paris, Saint-Ouen; Referee: Herbert James Willing (Netherlands); Attendance: 3,600
FRA: Pierre Chayrigues (5/0), Lucien Letailleur (1/0), Gabriel Hanot (5/0), Auguste Tousset (2/1), Jean Ducret (Cap) (12/1), Gaston Barreau (6/0), Rochet (1/0), Louis Mesnier (14/6), Eugène Maës (9/10), Henri Vialmonteil (5/2), Abel Lafouge (1/0).
Goal: Eugène Maës (35).

28. 16.02.1913 **BELGIUM - FRANCE** **3-0(2-0)**
Stade du Vivier d'Oie, Bruxelles; Referee: James R. Schumacher (England); Attendance: 6,000
FRA: Pierre Chayrigues (6/0), Gabriel Hanot (6/0), Victor Bentall-Sergent (5/0), Maurice Bigué (4/0), Jean Ducret (Cap) (13/1), Gaston Barreau (7/0), Henri Lesur (1/0), René Jacolliot (1/0), Eugène Maës (10/10), Henri Vialmonteil (6/2), Raymond Dubly (1/0).

29. 27.02.1913 **FRANCE - ENGLAND Amateurs** **1-4(0-2)**
Stade Olympique „Yves du Manoir", Colombes, Paris; Referee: Maurice Goossens (Belgium); Attendance: 2,500
FRA: Pierre Chayrigues (7/0), Fernand Massip (1/0), Lucien Gamblin (2/0), Maurice Bigué (5/0), Jean Ducret (Cap) (14/1), Gaston Barreau (8/0), Henri Lesur (2/0), André Poullain (1/1), Henri Bard (1/0), Ernest Gueguen (1/0), Raymond Dubly (2/0).
Goal: André Poullain (75).

30. 09.03.1913 **SWITZERLAND - FRANCE** **1-4(1-2)**
Stade Charmilles, Genève; Referee: H.P. Devitte (Switzerland); Attendance: 10,000
FRA: Louis Bournonville (1/0), Jean Degouve (1/0), Charles Dujardin (1/0), Charles Montagne (1/1), Jean Ducret (Cap) (15/1), Gaston Barreau (9/0), Henri Lesur (3/0), André Poullain (2/1), Albert Eloy (1/2), Paul Chandelier (1/0), Raymond Dubly (3/1).
Goals: Charles Montagne (13), Albert Eloy (16), Raymond Dubly (67), Albert Eloy (83).

31. 20.04.1913 **FRANCE - LUXEMBOURG** **8-0(2-0)**
Stade de Paris, Saint-Ouen; Referee: Hubert Istace (Belgium); Attendance: 3,000
FRA: Pierre Chayrigues (8/0), Gabriel Hanot (7/0), Lucien Gamblin (3/0), Charles Montagne (2/1), Jean Ducret (Cap) (16/2), Gaston Barreau (10/0), Paul Voyeux (1/0), André Poullain (3/2), Eugène Maës (11/15), Félix Romano (1/1), Raymond Dubly (4/1).
Goals: Eugène Maës (28), André Poullain (30), Eugène Maës (56, 68), Félix Romano (78), Jean Ducret (83), Eugène Maës (86, 88).

32. 25.01.1914 **FRANCE - BELGIUM** **4-3(3-3)**
Stade „Victor Boucquey", Lille; Referee: Herbert Mortimer (England); Attendance: 4,813
FRA: Pierre Chayrigues (9/0), Lucien Gamblin (4/0), Gabriel Hanot (8/1), Émilien Devic (3/0), Jean Ducret (Cap) (17/2), Gaston Barreau (11/0), Henri Lesur (4/0), Henri Bard (2/1), Étienne Jourde (6/1), Paul Chandelier (2/0), Raymond Dubly (5/2).
Goals: Gabriel Hanot (16 penalty), Henri Bard (24), Étienne Jourde (37), Raymond Dubly (65).

33. 08.02.1914 **LUXEMBOURG - FRANCE** **5-4(2-3)**
Stade Racing Club, Luxembourg; Referee: Maurice Goossens (Luxembourg); Attendance: 5,000
FRA: Jean Loubière (1/0), René Bonnet (Cap) (1/0), Jean Degouve (2/0), Émilien Devic (4/0), Jean Ducret (18/3), Maurice Olivier (6/0), Maurice Gastiger (1/0), Henri Bard (3/2), Albert Eloy (2/2), Charles Geronimi (1/1), Marcel Triboulet (4/2).
Goals: Henri Bard (13), Jean Ducret (22 penalty), Charles Geronimi (41), Marcel Triboulet (??).

34. 08.03.1914 **FRANCE - SWITZERLAND** **2-2(0-1)**
Stade de Paris, Saint-Ouen; Referee: John T. Howcroft (England); Attendance: 4,000
FRA: Pierre Chayrigues (10/0), Lucien Gamblin (5/0), Gabriel Hanot (9/1), Maurice Bigué (6/0), Jean Ducret (Cap) (19/3), Albert Jourda (1/0), Maurice Gastiger (2/1), Étienne Jourde (7/1), Émilien Devic (5/1), Albert Schaff (1/0), Raymond Dubly (6/2).
Goals: Émilien Devic (46), Maurice Gastiger (85).

35. 29.03.1914 **ITALY - FRANCE** **2-0(0-0)**
Campo di Piazza d'Armi, Torino; Referee: Charles Barette (Belgium); Attendance: 15,000
FRA: Albert Parsys (1/0), Lucien Gamblin (6/0), Gabriel Hanot (10/1), Maurice Bigué (7/0), Jean Ducret (Cap) (20/3), Albert Jourda (2/0), Henri Lesur (5/0), Jules Dubly (1/0), Jean Picy (1/0), Paul Chandelier (3/0), Raymond Dubly (7/2).

36. 31.05.1914 **HUNGARY - FRANCE** **5-1(1-1)**
Üllői út, Budapest; Referee: Heinrich Retschury (Austria); Attendance: 6,000
FRA: Pierre Chayrigues (11/0), Maurice Mathieu (1/0), Gabriel Hanot (11/1), André Allègre (1/0), Gaston Barreau (Cap) (12/0), Albert Jourda (3/0), Henri Lesur (6/0), Juste Brouzes (1/1), Étienne Jourde (8/1), Émile Dusart (1/0), Marcel Triboulet (5/2).
Goal: Juste Brouzes (1).

37. 09.03.1919 **BELGIUM - FRANCE** **2-2(1-0)**
Stade du Vivier d'Oie, Bruxelles; Referee: Christiaan Jacobus Groothoff (Netherlands); Attendance: 25,000
FRA: Raymond Frémont (1/0), Lucien Gamblin (7/0), Maurice Mathieu (2/0), Albert Mercier (1/0), Émilien Devic (6/1), François Hugues (1/0), Paul Faure (1/0), Gabriel Hanot (Cap) (12/3), Henri Bard (4/2), Louis Darques (1/0), Marcel Triboulet (6/2).
Goals: Gabriel Hanot (80, 89).

38. 18.01.1920 **ITALY - FRANCE** **9-4(4-3)**
Velodromo Sempione, Milano; Referee: John Forster (Switzerland); Attendance: 14,000
FRA: Maurice Cottenet (1/0), Pierre Mony (1/0), Alexis Mony (1/0), Émilien Devic (7/1), Louis Olagnier (1/0), Louis Mistral (1/0), Jules Dewaquez (1/0), Albert Rénier (1/0), Paul Nicolas (1/1), Henri Bard (Cap) (5/4), Raymond Dubly (8/3).
Goals: Paul Nicolas (24), Henri Bard (28, 44), Raymond Dubly (87).

39. 29.02.1920 **SWITZERLAND - FRANCE** **0-2(0-1)**
Stade Charmilles, Genève; Referee: Giovanni Mauro (Italy); Attendance: 20,000
FRA: Albert Parsys (2/0), Alfred Roth (1/0), Édouard Baumann (1/0), Philippe Bonnardel (1/0), François Hugues (2/0), Louis Mistral (2/0), Jules Dewaquez (2/1), Louis Darques (2/0), Paul Nicolas (2/2), Henri Bard (Cap) (6/4), Raymond Dubly (9/3).
Goals: Jules Dewaquez (43), Paul Nicolas (78).

40. 28.03.1920 **FRANCE - BELGIUM** **2-1(1-1)**
Stade Parc des Princes, Paris; Referee: Henry R. Child (England); Attendance: 13,000
FRA: Albert Parsys (3/0), Marcel Vanco (1/0), Lucien Gamblin (8/0), Charles Montagne (3/1), François Hugues (3/0), Maurice Gravelines (1/0), Jules Dewaquez (3/1), Maurice Gastiger (3/1), Paul Nicolas (3/4), Henri Bard (Cap) (7/4), Raymond Dubly (10/3).
Goals: Paul Nicolas (16, 79).

41. 05.04.1920 **FRANCE - ENGLAND Amateurs** **0-5(0-1)**
Stade des Bruyères, Rouen; Referee: Charles Barette (Belgium); Attendance: 14,000
FRA: Maurice Cottenet (2/0), Lucien Gamblin (Cap) (9/0), Marcel Vanco (2/0), Philippe Bonnardel (2/0), François Hugues (4/0), Jean Batmale (1/0), Jules Dewaquez (4/1), Maurice Mercery (1/0), Paul Nicolas (4/4), Émilien Devic (8/1), Raymond Dubly (11/3).

42. 29.08.1920 **FRANCE - ITALY** **3-1(2-1)** 7th OG. 2nd Round.
Kielstadion, Antwerpen (Belgium); Referee: Henri Christophe (Belgium); Attendance: 10,000
FRA: Albert Parsys (4/0), Léon Huot (1/0), Édouard Baumann (2/0), Jean Batmale (2/0), René Petit (1/0), François Hugues (5/0), Jules Dewaquez (5/1), Jean Boyer (1/1), Paul Nicolas (5/5), Henri Bard (Cap) (8/5), Raymond Dubly (12/3).
Goals: Henri Bard (10), Paul Nicolas (14), Jean Boyer (54).

43. 31.08.1920 **FRANCE - CZECHOSLOVAKIA** **1-4(0-1)** 7th OG. Semi-Finals.
Kielstadion, Antwerpen (Belgium); Referee: Johannes Mutters (Netherlands); Attendance: 12,000
FRA: Albert Parsys (5/0), Léon Huot (2/0), Édouard Baumann (3/0), Jean Batmale (3/0), René Petit (2/0), François Hugues (6/0), Jules Dewaquez (6/1), Jean Boyer (2/2), Paul Nicolas (6/5), Henri Bard (Cap) (9/5), Raymond Dubly (13/3).
Goal: Jean Boyer (79).

44. 08.02.1921 **FRANCE - REPUBLIC OF IRELAND Amateurs** **1-2(0-2)**
Stade Parc des Princes, Paris; Referee: Raphaël Van Praag (Belgium); Attendance: 20,000
FRA: Maurice Beaudier (1/0), Lucien Gamblin (Cap) (10/0), Maurice Meyer (1/0), Marcel Vanco (3/0), François Hugues (7/1), Philippe Bonnardel (3/0), Jules Dewaquez (7/1), Louis Darques (3/0), Paul Nicolas (7/5), Paul Bloch (1/0), Raymond Dubly (14/3).
Goal: François Hugues (65).

45. 20.02.1921 **FRANCE - ITALY** **1-2(1-0)**
Stade de l'Huveaune, Marseille; Referee: John Forster (Switzerland); Attendance: 15,000
FRA: Maurice Beaudier (2/0), Eugène Langenove (1/0), Lucien Gamblin (Cap) (11/0), Jean Batmale (4/0), François Hugues (8/1), Philippe Bonnardel (4/0), Jules Dewaquez (8/1), Émilien Devic (9/2), Paul Nicolas (8/5), Henri Bard (10/5), Raymond Dubly (15/3).
Goal: Émilien Devic (22).

46. 06.03.1921 **BELGIUM - FRANCE** **3-1(0-0)**
Parc Duden, Bruxelles; Referee: Johannes Mutters (Netherlands); Attendance: 20,000
FRA: Maurice Beaudier (3/0), Eugène Langenove (2/0), Lucien Gamblin (Cap) (12/0), Albert Jourda (4/0), François Hugues (9/1), Philippe Bonnardel (5/0), Jules Dewaquez (9/2), Antoine Rouches (1/0), Paul Nicolas (9/5), Henri Bard (11/5), Raymond Dubly (16/3).
Goal: Jules Dewaquez (63).

47. 05.05.1921 **FRANCE - ENGLAND Amateurs** **2-1(1-1)**
Stade „Général Jean Joseph Pershing", Paris; Referee: Henri Christophe (Belgium); Attendance: 30,000
FRA: Maurice Cottenet (3/0), Marcel Vanco (4/0), Lucien Gamblin (Cap) (13/0), François Hugues (10/1), Albert Jourda (5/0), Philippe Bonnardel (6/0), Jules Dewaquez (10/3), Jean Boyer (3/3), Paul Nicolas (10/5), Henri Bard (12/5), Raymond Dubly (17/3).
Goals: Jules Dewaquez (6), Jean Boyer (67).

48. 13.11.1921 **FRANCE - NETHERLANDS** **0-5(0-1)**
Stade „Général Jean Joseph Pershing", Paris; Referee: Charles Barette (Belgium); Attendance: 10,000
FRA: Maurice Cottenet (4/0), Marcel Vanco (5/0), Lucien Gamblin (Cap) (14/0), Louis Mistral (3/0), Albert Jourda (6/0), Philippe Bonnardel (7/0), Jules Dewaquez (11/3), Louis Darques (4/0), Édouard Macquart (1/0), Henri Bard (13/5), Raymond Dubly (18/3).

49. 15.01.1922 **FRANCE - BELGIUM** **2-1(0-1)**
Stade Olympique „Yves du Manoir", Colombes, Paris; Referee: William John Edwards (England); Attendance: 20,000
FRA: Émile Friess (1/0), Marcel Vanco (6/0), Édouard Baumann (4/0), François Hugues (11/1), Maurice Gravelines (2/0), Alain Courquin (1/0), Jules Dewaquez (12/4), Robert Accard (1/0), Paul Nicolas (11/5), Louis Darques (5/1), Raymond Dubly (Cap) (19/3).
Goals: Louis Darques (50), Jules Dewaquez (67).

50. 30.04.1922 **FRANCE - SPAIN** **0-4(0-4)**
Stade „Sainte Germaine", Bordeaux; Referee: Raphaël Van Praag (Belgium); Attendance: 10,000
FRA: Émile Friess (2/0), Marcel Vanco (7/0), Grégoire Berg (1/0), Marcel Domergue (1/0), François Hugues (12/1), Philippe Bonnardel (8/0), Jules Dewaquez (13/4), Paul Nicolas (12/5), André Ryssen (1/0), Jean Boyer (4/3), Raymond Dubly (Cap) (20/3).

51. 28.01.1923 **SPAIN - FRANCE** **3-0(2-0)**
Estadio Municipal de Atocha, San Sebastián; Referee: Charles Barette (Belgium); Attendance: 22,000
FRA: Pierre Chayrigues (12/0), Pierre Mony (2/0), Lucien Gamblin (Cap) (15/0), Robert Joyaut (1/0), François Hugues (13/1), Philippe Bonnardel (9/0), Jules Dewaquez (14/4), Juste Brouzes (2/1), Paul Nicolas (13/5), Henri Bard (14/5), Raymond Dubly (21/3).

52. 25.02.1923 **BELGIUM - FRANCE** **4-1(2-0)**
Parc Duden, Bruxelles; Referee: E.A. Newman (England); Attendance: 28,757
FRA: Pierre Chayrigues (13/0), Pierre Mony (3/0), Maurice Depaepe (1/0), Robert Joyaut (2/0), François Hugues (14/1), Philippe Bonnardel (10/0), Gérard Isbecque (1/1), Raymond Wattine (1/0), Jean Boyer (5/3), Louis Darques (6/1), Raymond Dubly (Cap) (22/3).
Goal: Gérard Isbecque (57).

53. 02.04.1923 **NETHERLANDS - FRANCE** **8-1(4-0)**
Sportpark, Amsterdam; Referee: Einer Ulrich (Denmark); Attendance: 30,000
FRA: Charles Berthelot (1/0), Robert Coat (1/0), Pierre Mony (4/0), Robert Joyaut (3/0), François Hugues (Cap) (15/1), Philippe Bonnardel (11/0), Jules Dewaquez (15/4), André Caillet (1/0), Paul Hoenen (1/0), Jean Boyer (6/3), Henri Bard (15/6).
Goal: Henri Bard (82).

54. 22.04.1923 **FRANCE - SWITZERLAND** **2-2(2-1)**
Stade „Général Jean Joseph Pershing", Paris; Referee: Walter Musther (England); Attendance: 20,000
FRA: Pierre Chayrigues (14/0), Paul Baron (1/0), Lucien Gamblin (Cap) (16/0), Robert Joyaut (4/0), François Hugues (16/1), Philippe Bonnardel (12/0), Jules Dewaquez (16/4), Louis Darques (7/1), Paul Nicolas (14/6), Henri Bard (16/6), Raymond Dubly (23/4).
Goals: Raymond Dubly (37), Paul Nicolas (61).

55. 10.05.1923 **FRANCE - ENGLAND** **1-4(0-2)**
Stade „Général Jean Joseph Pershing", Paris; Referee: Charles Barette (Belgium); Attendance: 30,000
FRA: Pierre Chayrigues (15/0), Pierre Mony (5/0), Lucien Gamblin (Cap) (17/0), Louis Mistral (4/0), François Hugues (17/1), Philippe Bonnardel (13/0), Jules Dewaquez (17/5), Louis Darques (8/1), Marcel Dangles (1/0), Henri Bard (17/6), Raymond Dubly (24/4).
Goal: Jules Dewaquez (89).

56. 28.10.1923 **FRANCE - NORWAY** **0-2(0-2)**
Stade Parc des Princes, Paris; Referee: Walton (England); Attendance: 12,000
FRA: Maurice Cottenet (5/0), Marcel Vanco (8/0), Ernest Gravier (7/1), Louis Mistral (5/0), François Hugues (18/1), Marcel Domergue (2/0), Jules Dewaquez (18/5), Louis Darques (9/1), Jean Boyer (7/3), Henri Bard (18/6), Raymond Dubly (Cap) (25/4).

57. 13.01.1924 **FRANCE - BELGIUM** **2-0(1-0)**
Stade Buffalo, Paris; Referee: Ernest Small (England); Attendance: 30,000
FRA: Pierre Chayrigues (16/0), Édouard Baumann (5/0), Bernard Lenoble (1/0), Michel Dupoix (1/0), Marcel Domergue (3/0), Philippe Bonnardel (14/0), Gérard Isbecque (2/1), Jean Boyer (8/3) [25.Robert Accard (2/0)], Albert Rénier (2/1), Ernest Gross (1/1), Raymond Dubly (Cap) (26/4).
Goals: Ernest Gross (43), Albert Rénier (49).

58. 23.03.1924 **SWITZERLAND - FRANCE** **3-0(2-0)**
Stade Charmilles, Genève; Referee: Umberto Meazza (Italy); Attendance: 15,000
FRA: Pierre Chayrigues (17/0), Édouard Baumann (6/0), Bernard Lenoble (2/0), Ernest Cléré (1/0), François Hugues (19/1), Philippe Bonnardel (15/0), Gérard Isbecque (3/1), Robert Accard (3/0), Jean Boyer (9/3), Ernest Gross (2/1), Raymond Dubly (Cap) (27/4).

59. 17.05.1924 **FRANCE - ENGLAND** **1-3(0-2)**
Stade „Général Jean Joseph Pershing", Paris; Referee: Willem Eymers (Netherlands); Attendance: 20,000
FRA: Pierre Chayrigues (18/0), Édouard Baumann (7/0), Ernest Gravier (8/1), Marcel Domergue (4/0), Antoine Parachini (1/0), Philippe Bonnardel (16/0), Jules Dewaquez (19/6), Jean Boyer (10/3), Paul Nicolas (15/6), Ernest Gross (3/1), Raymond Dubly (Cap) (28/4).
Goal: Jules Dewaquez (58).

60. 27.05.1924 **FRANCE - LATVIA** **7-0(3-0)** 8th OG.2nd Round.
Stade de Paris, Saint-Ouen; Referee: Henri Christophe (Belgium); Attendance: 15,000
FRA: Pierre Chayrigues (19/0), Ernest Gravier (9/1), Édouard Baumann (8/0), Antoine Parachini (2/0), Marcel Domergue (5/0), Philippe Bonnardel (17/0), Jules Dewaquez (20/6), Jean Boyer (11/5), Paul Nicolas (16/8), Édouard Crut (1/3), Raymond Dubly (Cap) (29/4).
Goals: Édouard Crut (17), Paul Nicolas (25), Édouard Crut (28), Paul Nicolas (50), Édouard Crut (55), Jean Boyer (71, 87).

61. 01.06.1924 **FRANCE - URUGUAY** **1-5(1-2)** 8th OG. Quarter-Finals.
Stade Olympique „Yves du Manoir", Colombes, Paris; Referee: Lauritz Andersen (Denmark); Attendance: 45,000
FRA: Pierre Chayrigues (20/0), Ernest Gravier (10/1), Marcel Domergue (6/0), Antoine Parachini (3/0), Jean Batmale (5/0), Philippe Bonnardel (18/0), Jules Dewaquez (21/6), Jean Boyer (12/5), Paul Nicolas (17/9), Édouard Crut (2/3), Raymond Dubly (Cap) (30/4).
Goal: Paul Nicolas (12).

62. 04.06.1924 **FRANCE - HUNGARY** **0-1(0-1)**
Stade de la Cavée Verte, Le Havre; Referee: Felix Herren (Switzerland); Attendance: 6,000
FRA: Maurice Cottenet (6/0), Jacques Canthelou (1/0), Léon Huot (3/0), Albert Jourda (Cap) (7/0), Marcel Domergue (7/0), Jean Batmale (6/0), Jules Dewaquez (22/6), Édouard Crut (3/3), Albert Rénier (3/1) [46.Pierre Chesneau (1/0)], Ernest Gross (4/1), Robert Dufour (1/0).

63. 11.11.1924 **BELGIUM - FRANCE** **3-0(1-0)**
Stade à Molenbeek-Saint-Jean, Bruxelles; Referee: Ruben Gelbord (Sweden); Attendance: 27,000
FRA: Maurice Cottenet (7/0), Ernest Gravier (11/1), Jacques Canthelou (2/0), René Dedieu (1/0), François Hugues (Cap) (20/1), Philippe Bonnardel (19/0), Gérard Isbecque (4/1), Georges Denis (1/0), Albert Rénier (4/1), Louis Bloquel (1/0), Raymond Sentubéry (1/0).

64. 22.03.1925 **ITALY - FRANCE** **7-0(1-0)**
Stadio di Corso Marsiglia, Torino; Referee: Heinrich Retschury (Austria); Attendance: 15,000
FRA: Maurice Cottenet (Cap) (8/0), Urbain Wallet (1/0), Marcel Vignoli (1/0), Maurice Thédié (1/0), Paul-Émile Bel (1/0), Philippe Bonnardel (20/0), André Liminana (1/0), Robert Accard (4/0), Charles Bardot (1/0), Louis Bloquel (2/0), Félix Pozo (1/0).

65. 19.04.1925 **FRANCE - AUSTRIA** **0-4(0-3)**
Stade „Général Jean Joseph Pershing", Paris; Referee: Antonio Scamoni (Italy); Attendance: 25,000
FRA: Maurice Cottenet (9/0), Pierre Lienert (1/0), Jacques Canthelou (3/0), Robert Dauphin (1/0), François Hugues (21/1), Philippe Bonnardel (21/0), André Liminana (2/0), Guillaume Lieb (1/0), Paul Nicolas (Cap) (18/9), Ernest Gross (5/1), Julien Buré (1/0).

66. 21.05.1925 **FRANCE - ENGLAND** **2-3(0-1)**
Stade Olympique „Yves du Manoir", Colombes, Paris; Referee: Theodorus van Zwieteren (Netherlands); Attendance: 35,000
FRA: Pierre Chayrigues (21/0), Marcel Vignoli (2/0), Marcel Domergue (8/0), Philippe Bonnardel (22/0), François Hugues (22/1), Robert Dauphin (2/0), Raymond Dubly (31/4), Jean Boyer (13/6), Paul Nicolas (Cap) (19/9), Guillaume Lieb (2/0), Jules Dewaquez (23/7).
Goals: Jean Boyer (62), Jules Dewaquez (75).

67. 11.04.1926 **FRANCE - BELGIUM** **4-3(3-0)**
Stade „Général Jean Joseph Pershing", Paris; Referee: Albert J. Prince-Cox (England); Attendance: 25,000
FRA: Maurice Cottenet (10/0), Urbain Wallet (2/0), Jacques Canthelou (4/0), Georges Moulène (1/0), Marcel Domergue (Cap) (9/0), Alexandre Villaplane (1/0), Jules Dewaquez (24/8), Guillaume Lieb (3/0), Edmond Leveugle (1/1), Édouard Crut (4/5), Maurice Gallay (1/0) [46.Raymond Sentubéry (2/0)].
Goals: Jules Dewaquez (17), Édouard Crut (33), Edmond Leveugle (40), Édouard Crut (59).

68. 18.04.1926 **FRANCE - PORTUGAL** **4-2(2-1)**
Stade des Ponts Jumeaux, Toulouse; Referee: E. Dizerens (Switzerland); Attendance: 16,000
FRA: Maurice Cottenet (11/0), Urbain Wallet (3/0), Jacques Canthelou (5/0), Alexandre Villaplane (2/0), Marcel Domergue (Cap) (10/0), René Dedieu (2/0), Georges Bonello (1/1), Édouard Crut (5/5), Fernand Brunel (1/2), Henri Salvano (1/0), Jules Dewaquez (25/8).
Goals: Henri Salvano (16), Fernand Brunel (40), Georges Bonello (56), Fernand Brunel (65).

69. 25.04.1926 **FRANCE - SWITZERLAND** **1-0(1-0)**
Stade Olympique „Yves du Manoir“, Colombes, Paris; Referee: Bruno Bellini (Italy); Attendance: 15,000
FRA: Maurice Cottenet (12/0), Urbain Wallet (4/0), Jacques Canthelou (6/0), Robert Dauphin (3/0), Marcel Domergue (11/0), Alexandre Villaplane (3/0), Jules Dewaquez (26/8), Guillaume Lieb (4/0), Paul Nicolas (Cap) (20/10), Édouard Crut (6/5), Georges Bonello (2/1).
Goal: Paul Nicolas (12).

70. 30.05.1926 **AUSTRIA - FRANCE** **4-1(1-1)**
Simmeringer Sportplatz, Wien; Referee: František Cejnar (Czechoslovakia); Attendance: 25,000
FRA: Maurice Cottenet (Cap) (13/0), Urbain Wallet (5/0), Jacques Canthelou (7/0), René Dedieu (3/0), Marcel Domergue (12/0), Alexandre Villaplane (4/0), Désiré Gosselin (1/0), Guillaume Lieb (5/0), Raymond Sentubéry (3/0), Édouard Crut (7/6), Maurice Gallay (2/0).
Goal: Édouard Crut (11).

71. 13.06.1926 **FRANCE - YUGOSLAVIA** **4-1(3-1)**
Stade Olympique „Yves du Manoir“, Colombes, Paris; Referee: Paul Putz (Belgium); Attendance: 12,000
FRA: Maurice Cottenet (14/0), Urbain Wallet (6/0), Jacques Canthelou (8/0), René Dedieu (4/0), Marcel Domergue (13/0), Alexandre Villaplane (5/0), Jules Dewaquez (27/8), Guillaume Lieb (6/0), Paul Nicolas (Cap) (21/13), Robert Accard (5/0), Maurice Gallay (3/1).
Goals: Maurice Gallay (16), Paul Nicolas (17, 37, 61).

72. 20.06.1926 **BELGIUM - FRANCE** **2-2(1-1)**
Stade à Molenbeek-Saint-Jean, Bruxelles; Referee: John William Lucas (England); Attendance: 35,000
FRA: Maurice Cottenet (15/0), Jacques Canthelou (9/0), Léon Huot (4/0), René Dedieu (5/0), Marcel Domergue (14/0), Alexandre Villaplane (6/0), Jules Dewaquez (28/9), Guillaume Lieb (7/0), Paul Nicolas (Cap) (22/13) [16.Georges Stuttler (1/0)], Robert Accard (6/1), Maurice Gallay (4/1).
Goals: Robert Accard (3), Jules Dewaquez (89).

73. 16.03.1927 **PORTUGAL - FRANCE** **4-0(2-0)**
Estádio do Lumiar, Lisboa; Referee: Luis Colina Álvarez (Spain); Attendance: 15,000
FRA: Jacques Dhur (1/0), Urbain Wallet (7/0), Jacques Mairesse (1/0), Jacques Wild (1/0), Philippe Bonnardel (Cap) (23/0), Louis Cazal (1/0), André Hurtevent (1/0), Charles Bardot (2/0), Julien Sottiault (1/0), Édouard Crut (8/6), Georges Bonello (3/1).

74. 24.04.1927 **FRANCE - ITALY** **3-3(1-2)**
Stade Olympique „Yves du Manoir“, Colombes, Paris; Referee: Albert J. Prince-Cox (England); Attendance: 35,000
FRA: Maurice Cottenet (16/0), Urbain Wallet (8/0), André Rollet (1/0), Robert Dauphin (4/0), François Hugues (23/1), Jacques Wild (2/0), Jules Dewaquez (Cap) (29/9), Julien Sottiault (2/1), Georges Taisne (1/2), André Maschinot (1/0), Maurice Gallay (5/1).
Goals: Georges Taisne (16, 52), Julien Sottiault (89).

75. 22.05.1927 **FRANCE - SPAIN** **1-4(1-2)**
Stade Olympique „Yves du Manoir“, Colombes, Paris; Referee: Arthur H. Kingscott (England); Attendance: 25,000
FRA: Maurice Cottenet (17/0), Urbain Wallet (9/0), André Rollet (2/0), Louis Cazal (2/0), Robert Dauphin (5/0), Jacques Wild (3/0), Jules Dewaquez (Cap) (30/9), Guillaume Lieb (8/0), Julien Sottiault (3/1), Jean Boyer (14/7), Maurice Gallay (6/1) [46.Marcel Langiller (1/0)].
Goal: Jean Boyer (22).

76. 26.05.1927 **FRANCE - ENGLAND** **0-6(0-2)**
Stade Olympique „Yves du Manoir“, Colombes, Paris; Referee: Henri Maeck (Belgium); Attendance: 25,000
FRA: Alexis Thépot (1/0), Urbain Wallet (10/0), André Rollet (3/0), Robert Dauphin (6/0), François Hugues (Cap) (24/1), Jacques Wild (4/0), Marcel Langiller (2/0), Guillaume Lieb (9/0), Julien Sottiault (4/1), Georges Taisne (2/2), Maurice Gallay (7/1).

77. 12.06.1927 **HUNGARY - FRANCE** **13-1(6-0)**
Üllői út, Budapest; Referee: Heinrich Retschury (Austria); Attendance: 28,000
FRA: Maurice Cottenet (18/0), Urbain Wallet (11/0), André Rollet (4/0) [28.Jean Fidon (1/0)], Aimé Durbec (1/0), René Dedieu (6/0), Jacques Wild (5/0), Jules Dewaquez (Cap) (31/10), Guillaume Lieb (10/0), Julien Sottiault (5/1), Georges Taisne (3/2), Maurice Gallay (8/1).
Goal: Jules Dewaquez (80).

78. 21.02.1928 **FRANCE - REPUBLIC OF IRELAND** **4-0(3-0)**
Stade Buffalo, Paris; Referee: Paul Ruoff (Switzerland); Attendance: 27,000
FRA: Alexis Thépot (2/0), Urbain Wallet (12/0), Marcel Domergue (15/0), Jacques Wild (6/0), Robert Dauphin (7/0), Alexandre Villaplane (7/0), Georges Ouvray (1/1), Guillaume Lieb (11/0), Paul Nicolas (Cap) (23/16), Pierre Seyler (1/0), Victor Farvacques (1/0).
Goals: Paul Nicolas (8, 27, 35), Georges Ouvray (88).

79. 11.03.1928 **SWITZERLAND - FRANCE** **4-3(3-0)**
Stade Olympique de la Pontaise, Lausanne; Referee: Johannes Mutters (Netherlands); Attendance: 18,000
FRA: Alexis Thépot (3/0), Urbain Wallet (13/0), Jacques Wild (7/0), Augustine Chantrel (1/0), Marcel Domergue (16/0), Alexandre Villaplane (8/0), Jules Dewaquez (32/10), Guillaume Lieb (12/1), Paul Nicolas (Cap) (24/17), Pierre Seyler (2/1), Maurice Gallay (9/1).
Goals: Guillaume Lieb (60), Pierre Seyler (80), Paul Nicolas (89).

80. 15.04.1928 **FRANCE - BELGIUM** **2-3(1-2)**
Stade Olympique „Yves du Manoir“, Colombes, Paris; Referee: Albert J. Prince-Cox (England); Attendance: 25,000
FRA: Laurent Henric (1/0), Urbain Wallet (14/0), Marcel Domergue (17/0), Augustine Chantrel (2/0), René Kenner (1/0), Alexandre Villaplane (9/0), Jules Dewaquez (33/10), Charles Bardot (3/2), Paul Nicolas (Cap) (25/17), Marcel Langiller (3/0), Maurice Gallay (10/1).
Goals: Charles Bardot (44, 66).

81. 29.04.1928 **FRANCE - PORTUGAL** **1-1(1-1)**
Stade Parc des Princes, Paris; Referee: Stanley Frederick Rous (England); Attendance: 25,000
FRA: Alexis Thépot (4/0), Urbain Wallet (15/0), Jacques Canthelou (10/0), Augustine Chantrel (3/0), Robert Dauphin (8/0), Alexandre Villaplane (10/0), Jules Dewaquez (34/10), Juste Brouzes (3/1), Paul Nicolas (Cap) (26/18), Henri Pavillard (1/0), Marcel Langiller (4/0).
Goal: Paul Nicolas (44).

82. 13.05.1928 **FRANCE - CZECHOSLOVAKIA** **0-2(0-1)**
Stade Olympique „Yves du Manoir", Colombes, Paris; Referee: Henri Christophe (Belgium); Attendance: 19,000
FRA: Alexis Thépot (5/0), Marcel Domergue (18/0), Urbain Wallet (16/0), Augustine Chantrel (4/0), Robert Dauphin (9/0), Alexandre Villaplane (11/0), Jules Dewaquez (35/10), Juste Brouzes (4/1), Paul Nicolas (Cap) (27/18), Henri Pavillard (2/0), Marcel Langiller (5/0).

83. 17.05.1928 **FRANCE - ENGLAND** **1-5(1-3)**
Stade Olympique „Yves du Manoir", Colombes, Paris; Referee: Dr. Adolf Miesz (Austria); Attendance: 40,000
FRA: Alexis Thépot (6/0), Urbain Wallet (17/0), Jacques Canthelou (11/0), Robert Dauphin (10/0), Marcel Domergue (Cap) (19/0), Alexandre Villaplane (12/0), Jules Monsallier (1/0), Juste Brouzes (5/1), Charles Bardot (4/2), Henri Pavillard (3/0), Marcel Langiller (6/1).
Goal: Marcel Langiller (2).

84. 29.05.1928 **ITALY - FRANCE** **4-3(3-2)** 9th OG. 2nd Round.
Olympisch Stadion, Amsterdam (Netherlands); Referee: Henri Christophe (Belgium); Attendance: 8,000
FRA: Alexis Thépot (7/0), Urbain Wallet (18/0), Marcel Domergue (20/0), Augustine Chantrel (5/0), Robert Dauphin (11/1), Alexandre Villaplane (13/0), Jules Dewaquez (36/10), Juste Brouzes (6/3), Paul Nicolas (Cap) (28/18), Henri Pavillard (4/0), Marcel Langiller (7/1).
Goals: Juste Brouzes (15, 17), Robert Dauphin (61).

85. 24.02.1929 **FRANCE - HUNGARY** **3-0(3-0)**
Stade Olympique „Yves du Manoir", Colombes, Paris; Referee: Paul Ruoff (Switzerland); Attendance: 20,000
FRA: Laurent Henric (2/0), Urbain Wallet (19/0), Marcel Bertrand (1/0), Augustine Chantrel (6/0), Maurice Banide (1/1), Alexandre Villaplane (14/0), Jules Dewaquez (37/10), Guillaume Lieb (13/2), Paul Nicolas (Cap) (29/19), Émile Veinante (1/0), Marcel Galey (1/0).
Goals: Maurice Banide (23), Paul Nicolas (25), Guillaume Lieb (33 penalty).

86. 24.03.1929 **FRANCE - PORTUGAL** **2-0(0-0)**
Stade Olympique „Yves du Manoir", Colombes, Paris; Referee: Raphaël Van Praag (Belgium); Attendance: 25,000
FRA: Laurent Henric (3/0), Urbain Wallet (20/0), Marcel Bertrand (2/0), Manuel Anatol (1/0), Maurice Banide (2/1), Alexandre Villaplane (15/0), Jules Dewaquez (38/10), Guillaume Lieb (14/2), Paul Nicolas (Cap) (30/20), Émile Veinante (2/0), Marcel Galey (2/1).
Goals: Paul Nicolas (49), Marcel Galey (80).

87. 14.04.1929 **SPAIN - FRANCE** **8-1(2-0)**
Estadio Torrero, Zaragoza; Referee: Albert J. Prince-Cox (England); Attendance: 15,000
FRA: Laurent Henric (4/0), Urbain Wallet (21/0), Marcel Bertrand (3/0), Robert Dauphin (12/1), Maurice Banide (3/1), Alexandre Villaplane (16/0), Raoul Dutheil (1/0), Émile Veinante (3/1), Guillaume Lieb (15/2), Paul Nicolas (Cap) (31/20), Marcel Galey (3/1).
Goal: Émile Veinante (86).

88. 09.05.1929 **FRANCE - ENGLAND** **1-4(0-1)**
Stade Olympique „Yves du Manoir", Colombes, Paris; Referee: Louis Baert (Belgium); Attendance: 35,000
FRA: Alexis Thépot (8/0), Manuel Anatol (2/0), Marcel Bertrand (4/0), Yvon Segalen (1/0), Robert Dauphin (13/1), Alexandre Villaplane (17/0), Jules Dewaquez (39/11), André Cheuva (1/0), Paul Nicolas (Cap) (32/20), Edmond Delfour (1/0), Maurice Gallay (11/1).
Goal: Jules Dewaquez (54).

89. 19.05.1929 **FRANCE - YUGOSLAVIA** **1-3(0-2)**
Stade Olympique „Yves du Manoir", Colombes, Paris; Referee: Paul Ruoff (Switzerland); Attendance: 15,000
FRA: Alexis Thépot (9/0), Manuel Anatol (3/0), Marcel Bertrand (5/0), Yvon Segalen (2/0), Robert Dauphin (14/1), Alexandre Villaplane (18/0), Jules Dewaquez (40/11), André Cheuva (2/1), Paul Nicolas (Cap) (33/20), Edmond Delfour (2/0), Maurice Gallay (12/1).
Goal: André Cheuva (63).

90. 26.05.1929 **BELGIUM - FRANCE** **4-1(2-0)**
Stade Vélodrome de Rocourt, Liège; Referee: René Mercet (Switzerland); Attendance: 20,000
FRA: Charles Allé (1/0), Jacques Wild (8/0), Manuel Anatol (4/0), Yvon Segalen (3/0), Robert Dauphin (15/1), Alexandre Villaplane (19/0), Jules Dewaquez (Cap) (41/12), Edmond Delfour (3/0), Jean Boyer (15/7), Henri Pavillard (5/0), Maurice Gallay (13/1).
Goal: Jules Dewaquez (81).

91. 23.02.1930 **PORTUGAL - FRANCE** **2-0(1-0)**
Campo de Ameal, Porto; Referee: John Langenus (Belgium); Attendance: 20,000
FRA: Antonin Lozes (1/0), Manuel Anatol (5/0), André Chardar (1/0), Louis Cazal (3/0), Jean Gautheroux (1/0), Alexandre Villaplane (Cap) (20/0), Ernest Liberati (1/0), Lucien Laurent (1/0), Gustave Dubus (1/0), André Maschinot (2/0), Pierre Korb (1/0).

92. 23.03.1930 **FRANCE - SWITZERLAND** **3-3(2-2)**
Stade Olympique „Yves du Manoir", Colombes, Paris; Referee: Stanley Frederick Rous (England); Attendance: 20,000
FRA: Antonin Lozes (2/0), Manuel Anatol (6/1), André Chardar (2/0), Louis Cazal (4/0), Alexandre Villaplane (21/0), Henri Pavillard (6/0), Ernest Liberati (2/1), André Cheuva (3/2), Paul Nicolas (Cap) (34/20), André Maschinot (3/0), Pierre Korb (2/0).
Goals: André Cheuva (17), Manuel Anatol (34), Ernest Liberati (58).

93. 13.04.1930 **FRANCE - BELGIUM** **1-6(1-5)**
Stade Olympique „Yves du Manoir", Colombes, Paris; Referee: Paul Ruoff (Switzerland); Attendance: 18,000
FRA: Antonin Lozes (3/0), Manuel Anatol (7/1), Marcel Capelle (1/0), Henri Pavillard (7/0), Maurice Banide (4/1), Alexandre Villaplane (Cap) (22/0), Ernest Liberati (3/1), André Cheuva (4/2), Gustave Dubus (2/1), Lucien Laurent (2/0), Pierre Korb (3/0).
Goal: Gustave Dubus (44).

94. 11.05.1930 **FRANCE - CZECHOSLOVAKIA** **2-3(2-2)**
Stade Olympique „Yves du Manoir", Colombes, Paris; Referee: John Langenus (Belgium); Attendance: 28,000
FRA: Alexis Thépot (10/0), Manuel Anatol (8/1), Marcel Capelle (2/0), Jean Laurent (1/0), Maurice Banide (5/1), Louis Cazal (Cap) (5/0) [15.Célestine Delmer (1/0)], Marcel Kauffmann (1/0), Henri Pavillard (8/0), Marcel Pinel (1/0), Edmond Delfour (4/1), Pierre Korb (4/1).
Goals: Pierre Korb (25 penalty), Edmond Delfour (30).

95. 18.05.1930 **FRANCE - SCOTLAND** **0-2(0-1)**
Stade Olympique „Yves du Manoir", Colombes, Paris; Referee: Raphaël Van Praag (Belgium); Attendance: 25,000
FRA: Alexis Thépot (11/0), Manuel Anatol (9/1), Marcel Capelle (3/0), Jean Laurent (2/0), Maurice Banide (6/1), Augustine Chantrel (7/0), Marcel Kauffmann (2/0), Henri Pavillard (Cap) (9/0), Marcel Pinel (2/0), Edmond Delfour (5/1), Pierre Korb (5/1).

96. 25.05.1930 **BELGIUM - FRANCE** **1-2(1-1)**
Stade du Pont d'Ougrée, Liège; Referee: Gustaf Ekberg (Sweden); Attendance: 11,000
FRA: Alexis Thépot (12/0), Étienne Mattler (1/0), Marcel Capelle (4/0), Louis Cazal (6/0) [22.Jean Laurent (3/0)], Célestine Delmer (2/0), Augustine Chantrel (8/0), Marcel Kauffmann (3/0), Henri Pavillard (Cap) (10/0), Marcel Pinel (3/2), Edmond Delfour (6/1), Marcel Langiller (8/1).
Goals: Marcel Pinel (26, 72).

97. 13.07.1930 **MEXICO - FRANCE** **1-4(0-3)** 1st FIFA WC. Group Stage.
Estadio Pocitos, Montevideo (Uruguay); Referee: Domingo Lombardi (Uruguay); Attendance: 4,000
FRA: Alexis Thépot (13/0), Étienne Mattler (2/0), Marcel Capelle (5/0), Alexandre Villaplane (Cap) (23/0), Marcel Pinel (4/2), Augustine Chantrel (9/0), Ernest Liberati (4/1), Edmond Delfour (7/1), André Maschinot (4/2), Lucien Laurent (3/1), Marcel Langiller (9/2).
Goals: Lucien Laurent (19), Marcel Langiller (40), André Maschinot (42, 87).

98. 15.07.1930 **FRANCE - ARGENTINA** **0-1(0-0)** 1st FIFA WC. Group Stage.
Estadio Parque Central, Montevideo (Uruguay); Referee: Gilberto de Almeida Rego (Brazil); Attendance: 38,000
FRA: Alexis Thépot (14/0), Étienne Mattler (3/0), Marcel Capelle (6/0), Alexandre Villaplane (Cap) (24/0), Marcel Pinel (5/2), Augustine Chantrel (10/0), Ernest Liberati (5/1), Edmond Delfour (8/1), André Maschinot (5/2), Lucien Laurent (4/1), Marcel Langiller (10/2).

99. 19.07.1930 **FRANCE - CHILE** **0-1(0-0)** 1st FIFA WC. Group Stage.
Estadio Centenario, Montevideo (Uruguay); Referee: Anibal Tejada (Uruguay); Attendance: 48,000
FRA: Alexis Thépot (15/0), Étienne Mattler (4/0), Marcel Capelle (7/0), Augustine Chantrel (11/0), Célestine Delmer (3/0), Marcel Pinel (6/2), Alexandre Villaplane (Cap) (25/0), Ernest Liberati (6/1), Edmond Delfour (9/1), Émile Veinante (4/1), Marcel Langiller (11/2).

100. 07.12.1930 **FRANCE - BELGIUM** **2-2(1-1)**
Stade Buffalo, Paris; Referee: René Mercet (Switzerland); Attendance: 20,000
FRA: Alexis Thépot (16/0), Étienne Mattler (5/0), André Chardar (3/0), Louis Finot (1/0), Célestine Delmer (4/0), Augustine Chantrel (12/0), Ernest Liberati (7/1), Edmond Delfour (10/1), Marcel Pinel (7/4), Henri Pavillard (Cap) (11/0), Hervé Marc (1/0).
Goals: Marcel Pinel (3, 67).

101. 25.01.1931 **ITALY - FRANCE** **5-0(3-0)**
Stadio Littoriale, Bologna; Referee: Paul Ruoff (Switzerland); Attendance: 48,000
FRA: Alexis Thépot (17/0), Étienne Mattler (6/0), Marcel Capelle (8/0), Louis Finot (2/0), Célestine Delmer (5/0), Augustine Chantrel (13/0), Ernest Liberati (8/1), Edmond Delfour (11/1), Joseph Alcazar (1/0), Henri Pavillard (Cap) (12/0), Pierre Korb (6/1).

102. 15.02.1931 **FRANCE - CZECHOSLOVAKIA** **1-2(1-1)**
Stade Olympique „Yves du Manoir", Colombes, Paris; Referee: John Langenus (Belgium); Attendance: 20,000
FRA: Alexis Thépot (18/0), Étienne Mattler (7/0), Manuel Anatol (10/1), Louis Finot (3/0), Célestine Delmer (6/0), Raoul Diagne (1/0), Raymond Durand (1/0), Edmond Delfour (12/1), Paul Nicolas (Cap) (35/20), Henri Pavillard (13/0), Marcel Langiller (12/3).
Goal: Marcel Langiller (23 penalty).

103. 15.03.1931 **FRANCE - GERMANY** **1-0(1-0)**
Stade Olympique „Yves du Manoir", Colombes, Paris; Referee: Thomas Crewe (England); Attendance: 40,076
FRA: Alexis Thépot (Cap) (19/0), Étienne Mattler (8/0), Manuel Anatol (11/1), Louis Finot (4/0), Joseph Kaucsar (1/0), Pierre Hornus (1/0), Jules Monsallier (2/0), Edmond Delfour (13/1), Roger Rolhion (1/0), Lucien Laurent (5/1) [40.Pierre Korb (7/1)], Marcel Langiller (13/3).
Goal: Reinhold Münzenberg (15 own goal).

104. 14.05.1931 **FRANCE - ENGLAND** **5-2(3-1)**
Stade Olympique „Yves du Manoir", Colombes, Paris; Referee: John Langenus (Belgium); Attendance: 35,000
FRA: Alexis Thépot (Cap) (20/0), Étienne Mattler (9/0), Marcel Capelle (9/0), Louis Finot (5/0), Joseph Kaucsar (2/0), Pierre Hornus (2/0), Ernest Liberati (9/1), Edmond Delfour (14/2), Robert Mercier (1/2), Lucien Laurent (6/2), Marcel Langiller (14/4).
Goals: Lucien Laurent (15), Robert Mercier (18), Marcel Langiller (29), Edmond Delfour (57), Robert Mercier (76).

105. 29.11.1931 **FRANCE - NETHERLANDS** **3-4(1-4)**
Stade Olympique „Yves du Manoir", Colombes, Paris; Referee: Paul Ruoff (Switzerland); Attendance: 25,000
FRA: Alexis Thépot (Cap) (21/0), Étienne Mattler (10/0), André Chardar (4/0), Louis Finot (6/0), Joseph Kaucsar (3/0), Pierre Hornus (3/0), Marcel Kauffmann (4/0), Émile Veinante (5/3), Robert Mercier (2/3), Lucien Laurent (7/2), Marcel Langiller (15/4).
Goals: Robert Mercier (7), Émile Veinante (53, 68).

106. 20.03.1932 **SWITZERLAND - FRANCE** **3-3(2-1)**
Neufeld Stadion, Bern; Referee: Stanley Frederick Rous (England); Attendance: 20,000
FRA: Alexis Thépot (Cap) (22/0), Manuel Anatol (12/1), André Chardar (5/0), Jules Cottenier (1/0), Joseph Kaucsar (4/0), Émile Scharwath (1/0), Ernest Liberati (10/2), Lucien Laurent (8/2), Charles Bardot (5/3), Émile Veinante (6/4), Marcel Langiller (16/4).
Goals: Ernest Liberati (15), Émile Veinante (69), Charles Bardot (71).

107. 10.04.1932 **FRANCE - ITALY** **1-2(1-1)**
Stade Olympique „Yves du Manoir", Colombes, Paris; Referee: René Mercet (Switzerland); Attendance: 45,000
FRA: André Tassin (1/0), Manuel Anatol (13/1), André Chardar (6/0), Émile Scharwath (2/0), Joseph Kaucsar (5/0), Jean Laurent (4/0), Ernest Liberati (11/3), Adolphe Touffait (1/0) [15.Edmond Delfour (15/2)], Charles Bardot (6/3), Lucien Laurent (9/2), Marcel Langiller (Cap) (17/4).
Goal: Ernest Liberati (11).

108. 01.05.1932 **BELGIUM - FRANCE** **5-2(3-0)**
Stade du Jubilé (Centenaire), Bruxelles; Referee: Heinrich Retschury (Austria); Attendance: 28,779
FRA: André Tassin (2/0), Manuel Anatol (14/1), André Chardar (7/0), Émile Scharwath (3/0), Joseph Kaucsar (6/0), Jean Laurent (5/0), Ernest Liberati (12/3), Émile Veinante (7/4), Jean Sécember (1/1), Henri Pavillard (14/1), Marcel Langiller (Cap) (18/4).
Goals: Henri Pavillard (48), Jean Sécember (82).

109. 08.05.1932 **FRANCE - SCOTLAND** **1-3(1-3)**
Stade Olympique „Yves du Manoir", Colombes, Paris; Referee: Albino Carraro (Italy); Attendance: 8,000
FRA: Alexis Thépot (Cap) (23/0), Manuel Anatol (15/1), André Chardar (8/0), Émile Scharwath (4/0), Joseph Kaucsar (7/0), Jean Laurent (6/0), Ernest Liberati (13/3), Joseph Alcazar (2/0), Robert Mercier (3/3), René Gérard (1/0), Marcel Langiller (19/5).
Goal: Marcel Langiller (43 penalty).

110. 05.06.1932 **YUGOSLAVIA - FRANCE** **2-1(1-1)**
Stadion BSK, Beograd; Referee: František Cejnar (Czechoslovakia); Attendance: 12,000
FRA: André Tassin (3/0) [46.Raoul Chaisaz (1/0)], André Chardar (Cap) (9/0), Jacques Mairesse (2/0), Émile Scharwath (5/0), Joseph Kaucsar (8/0), Jean Laurent (7/0), Ernest Liberati (14/3), Jacques Delannoy (1/0), Roger Rolhion (2/0), Joseph Alcazar (3/1), Pierre Korb (8/1).
Goal: Joseph Alcazar (1).

111. 09.06.1932 **BULGARIA - FRANCE** **3-5(0-4)**
Yunak stadion, Sofia; Referee: Ernest Fabriš (Yugoslavia); Attendance: 10,000
FRA: André Tassin (4/0) [62.Raoul Chaisaz (2/0)], André Chardar (10/0), Georges Houyvet (1/0), Émile Scharwath (6/0), Joseph Kaucsar (Cap) (9/0), Jean Laurent (8/0), Ernest Liberati (15/3), Joseph Rodriguez (1/1), Jean Sécember (2/5), Joseph Alcazar (4/1), Pierre Korb (9/1).
Goals: Joseph Rodriguez (1), Jean Sécember (6, 16, 28, 47).

112. 12.06.1932 **ROMANIA - FRANCE** **6-3(3-0)**
Stadionul ONEF, Bucureşti; Referee: Mihály Iváncsics (Hungary); Attendance: 10,000
FRA: André Tassin (5/0), André Chardar (11/1), Jacques Mairesse (Cap) (3/0), Émile Scharwath (7/0), Joseph Kaucsar (10/0), Jean Laurent (9/0), Ernest Liberati (16/3), Jean Sécember (3/5), Joseph Rodriguez (2/1) [42.Roger Rolhion (3/2)], Joseph Alcazar (5/1), Pierre Korb (10/1).
Goals: André Chardar (52 penalty), Roger Rolhion (75, 77).

113. 12.02.1933 **FRANCE - AUSTRIA** **0-4(0-0)** Stade Parc des Princes, Paris,40,000
Stade Parc des Princes, Paris; Referee: John Langenus (Belgium); Attendance: 40,000
FRA: Robert Défossé (1/0), Jules Vandooren (1/0), Jacques Mairesse (4/0), Augustine Chantrel (14/0), Joseph Kaucsar (11/0), Edmond Delfour (16/2), Marcel Kauffmann (5/0), René Gérard (2/0), Jean Nicolas (1/0), Roger Rio (1/0) [26.Robert Mercier (4/3)], Marcel Langiller (Cap) (20/5).

114. 19.03.1933 **GERMANY - FRANCE** **3-3(2-1)**
Grünewaldstadion, Berlin; Referee: Thomas Crewe (England); Attendance: 55,000
FRA: Robert Défossé (2/0), Jules Vandooren (2/0) [9.André Chardar (12/1)], Étienne Mattler (11/0), Augustine Chantrel (15/0), Joseph Kaucsar (12/0), Edmond Delfour (17/2), Ernest Liberati (17/3), René Gérard (3/2), Jean Nicolas (2/0), Roger Rio (2/1), Marcel Langiller (Cap) (21/5).
Goals: Roger Rio (22), René Gérard (81, 83).

115. 26.03.1933 **FRANCE - BELGIUM** **3-0(1-0)**
Stade Olympique „Yves du Manoir", Colombes, Paris; Referee: Stanley Frederick Rous (England); Attendance: 30,000
FRA: Robert Défossé (3/0), Jules Cottenier (2/0), Étienne Mattler (12/0), Paul Poirier (1/0), Joseph Kaucsar (13/0), Edmond Delfour (18/2), Robert Mercier (5/3), René Gérard (4/2), Jean Nicolas (3/1), Roger Rio (3/2), Marcel Langiller (Cap) (22/6).
Goals: Roger Rio (34), Marcel Langiller (74), Jean Nicolas (81).

116. 23.04.1933 **FRANCE - SPAIN** **1-0(1-0)**
Stade Olympique „Yves du Manoir", Colombes, Paris; Referee: William Bangerter (Switzerland); Attendance: 40,000
FRA: Robert Défossé (4/0), Jules Vandooren (3/0) [37.Jules Cottenier (3/0)], Étienne Mattler (13/0), Raoul Diagne (2/0), Joseph Kaucsar (14/0) [37.Georges Verriest (1/0)], Edmond Delfour (19/2), Robert Mercier (6/3), René Gérard (5/2), Jean Nicolas (4/2), Roger Rio (4/2), Marcel Langiller (Cap) (23/6).
Goal: Jean Nicolas (32).

117. 25.05.1933 **FRANCE - WALES** **1-1(0-0)**
Stade Olympique „Yves du Manoir", Colombes, Paris; Referee: Raphaël Van Praag (Belgium); Attendance: 25,000
FRA: Robert Défossé (5/0), Jules Vandooren (4/0), Étienne Mattler (14/0), Célestine Delmer (7/0), Georges Verriest (2/0), Edmond Delfour (20/2), Albert Polge (1/0), Noël Liétaer (1/0), Jean Nicolas (5/3), Roger Rio (5/2), Marcel Langiller (Cap) (24/6).
Goal: Jean Nicolas (78).

118. 10.06.1933 **CZECHOSLOVAKIA - FRANCE** **4-0(1-0)**
Stadion Letná, Praha; Referee: Rutkowski (Poland); Attendance: 18,000
FRA: Robert Défossé (6/0), Roger Rolhion (4/2), Étienne Mattler (15/0), Célestine Delmer (8/0), Georges Verriest (3/0), Edmond Delfour (Cap) (21/2), Albert Polge (2/0), René Gérard (6/2), Émile Veinante (8/4), Roger Rio (6/2), Marceau Lherminé (1/0).

119. 06.12.1933 **ENGLAND - FRANCE** **4-1(3-0)**
White Hart Lane Stadium, London; Referee: John Langenus (Belgium); Attendance: 17,097
FRA: Robert Défossé (7/0), Jules Vandooren (5/0), Étienne Mattler (16/0), Célestine Delmer (9/0), Maurice Banide (7/1), Edmond Delfour (Cap) (22/2), Roger Courtois (1/0), René Gérard (7/2), Jean Nicolas (6/3), Roger Rio (7/2), Émile Veinante (9/5).
Goal: Émile Veinante (78).

120. 21.01.1934 **BELGIUM - FRANCE** **2-3(2-2)**
Stade du Jubilé (Centenaire), Bruxelles; Referee: Walter J. Lewington (England); Attendance: 35,826
FRA: Robert Défossé (8/0), Jules Vandooren (6/0), Étienne Mattler (Cap) (17/0), Louis Finot (7/0), Maurice Banide (8/1), Émile Scharwath (8/0), Ernest Liberati (18/3), Joseph Alcazar (6/1), Jean Nicolas (7/5), Émile Veinante (10/6), Albert Polge (3/0).
Goals: Jean Nicolas (3), Émile Veinante (37), Jean Nicolas (54).

121. 11.03.1934 **FRANCE - SWITZERLAND** **0-1(0-1)**
Stade Parc des Princes, Paris; Referee: Rinaldo Barlassina (Italy); Attendance: 25,000
FRA: Alexis Thépot (Cap) (24/0), Jules Vandooren (7/0), Étienne Mattler (18/0), Max Charbit (1/0), Joseph Kaucsar (15/0), Noël Liétaer (2/0), Alfred Aston (1/0), Joseph Alcazar (7/1), Jean Nicolas (8/5), Roger Rio (8/2), Pierre Korb (11/1).

122. 25.03.1934 **FRANCE - CZECHOSLOVAKIA** **1-2(1-1)**
Stade Olympique „Yves du Manoir", Colombes, Paris; Referee: Walter J. Lewington (England); Attendance: 28,000
FRA: Alexis Thépot (Cap) (25/0), François Vasse (1/0), Étienne Mattler (19/0), Max Charbit (2/0), Célestine Delmer (10/0), Noël Liétaer (3/0), Alfred Aston (2/0), Edmond Delfour (23/2), Jean Nicolas (9/5), Émile Veinante (11/6), Pierre Korb (12/2).
Goal: Pierre Korb (6).

123. 15.04.1934 **LUXEMBOURG - FRANCE** **1-6(0-2)** 2nd FIFA WC. Qualifiers
Stade Municipal, Luxembourg; Referee: Marc Turfkruyer (Belgium); Attendance: 18,000
FRA: Alexis Thépot (Cap) (26/0), Georges Rose (1/0), Étienne Mattler (20/0), Edmond Delfour (24/2), Célestine Delmer (11/0), Noël Liétaer (4/0), Ernest Liberati (19/4), Joseph Alcazar (8/1), Jean Nicolas (10/9), Roger Rio (9/2), Alfred Aston (3/1).
Goals: Alfred Aston (3), Jean Nicolas (26, 67), Ernest Liberati (80), Jean Nicolas (85, 89 penalty).

124. 10.05.1934 **NETHERLANDS - FRANCE** **4-5(4-4)**
Olympisch Stadion, Amsterdam; Referee: R. Wittwer (Switzerland); Attendance: 35,000
FRA: Alexis Thépot (Cap) (27/0), Jacques Mairesse (5/0), Étienne Mattler (21/0), Jules Cottenier (4/0), Georges Verriest (4/0), Noël Liétaer (5/0), Frédéric Keller (1/1), Joseph Alcazar (9/2), Jean Nicolas (11/12), Roger Rio (10/2), Alfred Aston (4/1).
Goals: Frédéric Keller (13), Jean Nicolas (21, 25), Joseph Alcazar (39), Jean Nicolas (76).

125. 27.05.1934 **FRANCE - AUSTRIA** **2-3(1-1,1-1)** 2nd FIFA WC. 1st Round.
Stadio Municipale "Benito Mussolini", Torino (Italy); Referee: Johannes Franciscus van Moorsel (Netherlands); Attendance: 15,000
FRA: Alexis Thépot (Cap) (28/0), Jacques Mairesse (6/0), Étienne Mattler (22/0), Edmond Delfour (25/2), Georges Verriest (5/1), Noël Liétaer (6/0), Frédéric Keller (2/1), Joseph Alcazar (10/2), Jean Nicolas (12/12), Roger Rio (11/2), Alfred Aston (5/1).
Goals: Jean Nicolas (18), Georges Verriest (115 penalty).

126. 16.12.1934 **FRANCE - YUGOSLAVIA** **3-2(1-1)**
Stade Parc des Princes, Paris; Referee: Louis Baert (Belgium); Attendance: 37,000
FRA: Alexis Thépot (Cap) (29/0), Manuel Anatol (16/1), Étienne Mattler (23/0), Louis Gabrillargues (1/0), Georges Verriest (6/1), Noël Liétaer (7/0), Frédéric Keller (3/1), Roger Courtois (2/1), Jean Nicolas (13/15), Roger Rio (12/2), Marcel Langiller (25/6).
Goals: Jean Nicolas (12, 86), Roger Courtois (88).

127. 24.01.1935 **SPAIN - FRANCE** **2-0(1-0)**
Estadio Chamartin, Madrid; Referee: Walter J. Lewington (England); Attendance: 25,000
FRA: Alexis Thépot (Cap) (30/0), Jules Vandooren (8/0), Étienne Mattler (24/0), Louis Gabrillargues (2/0), Georges Verriest (7/1), Maxime Lehmann (1/0), Roger Courtois (3/1), Joseph Alcazar (11/2), Jean Nicolas (14/15), Roger Rio (13/2), Marcel Langiller (26/6).

128. 17.02.1935 **ITALY - FRANCE** **2-1(2-1)**
Stadio Nazionale del P.N.F., Roma; Referee: Louis Baert (Belgium); Attendance: 23,000
FRA: René Llense (1/0), Jules Vandooren (9/0), Étienne Mattler (Cap) (25/0), Louis Gabrillargues (3/0), Georges Verriest (8/1), Edmond Delfour (26/2), Frédéric Keller (4/2), Yvan Beck (1/0), Roger Courtois (4/1), Pierre Duhart (1/0), Alfred Aston (6/1).
Goal: Frédéric Keller (26).

129. 17.03.1935 **FRANCE - GERMANY** **1-3(0-1)**
Stade Parc des Princes, Paris; Referee: Louis Baert (Belgium); Attendance: 39,046
FRA: Alexis Thépot (Cap) (31/0), Jules Vandooren (10/0), Étienne Mattler (26/0), Louis Gabrillargues (4/0), Georges Verriest (9/1), Edmond Delfour (27/2), Alfred Aston (7/1), Yvan Beck (2/0), Jean Nicolas (15/15), Pierre Duhart (2/1), Aimé Nuic (1/0) [37.Jean Sécember (4/5)].
Goal: Pierre Duhart (59).

130. 14.04.1935 **BELGIUM - FRANCE** **1-1(0-1)**
Stade du Jubilé (Centenaire), Bruxelles; Referee: Rudolphe Wittwer (Switzerland); Attendance: 40,500
FRA: René Llense (2/0), Raoul Diagne (3/0), Étienne Mattler (Cap) (27/0), Edmond Delfour (28/2), Georges Verriest (10/1), Max Charbit (3/0), Alfred Aston (8/1), Yvan Beck (3/0), Roger Courtois (5/2), Émile Veinante (12/6), Marcel Langiller (27/6).
Goal: Roger Courtois (20).

131. 19.05.1935 **FRANCE - HUNGARY** **2-0(1-0)**
Stade Olympique „Yves du Manoir", Colombes, Paris; Referee: Walter J. Lewington (England); Attendance: 25,000
FRA: René Llense (3/0), Jules Vandooren (11/0), Étienne Mattler (28/0), Max Charbit (4/0), Georges Verriest (Cap) (11/1), Edmond Delfour (29/2), Alfred Aston (9/1), Yvan Beck (4/0), Roger Courtois (6/4), Lucien Laurent (10/2), Frédéric Keller (5/2).
Goals: Roger Courtois (37, 72).

132. 27.10.1935 **SWITZERLAND - FRANCE** **2-1(1-1)**
Stade Charmilles, Genève; Referee: Walter J. Lewington (England); Attendance: 25,000
FRA: René Llense (4/0), Jules Vandooren (12/0), Étienne Mattler (29/0), Marcel Desrousseaux (1/0), Louis Gabrillargues (5/0), Edmond Delfour (Cap) (30/2), Alfred Aston (10/1), Pierre Duhart (3/1), Roger Courtois (7/4), André Cheuva (5/2), Émile Zermani (1/0).
Goal: Walter Weiler II (4 own goal).

133. 10.11.1935 **FRANCE - SWEDEN** **2-0(1-0)**
Stade Parc des Princes, Paris; Referee: Arthur Barton (England); Attendance: 26,905
FRA: René Llense (5/0), Raoul Diagne (4/0), Étienne Mattler (30/0), Louis Gabrillargues (6/0), Georges Verriest (12/1), Edmond Delfour (Cap) (31/2), Robert Mercier (7/3), André Cheuva (6/2), Roger Courtois (8/5), Kowalczyk Ignace (1/0), Édouard Wawrzeniak (1/0).
Goals: Fritz Berg (33 own goal), Roger Courtois (70).

134. 12.01.1936 **FRANCE - NETHERLANDS** **1-6(0-2)**
Stade Parc des Princes, Paris; Referee: Reginald George Rudd (England); Attendance: 30,000
FRA: René Llense (6/0), Raoul Diagne (5/0), Étienne Mattler (31/0), Louis Gabrillargues (7/0) [26.Maurice Banide (9/1)], Georges Verriest (13/1), Edmond Delfour (Cap) (32/2), Jules Monsallier (3/0), André Cheuva (7/2), Roger Courtois (9/6), Émile Veinante (13/6), Aimé Nuic (2/0) [22.Alfred Aston (11/1)].
Goal: Roger Courtois (64).

135. 09.02.1936 **FRANCE - CZECHOSLOVAKIA** **0-3(0-3)**
Stade Parc des Princes, Paris; Referee: Pedro Escartin (Spain); Attendance: 40,138
FRA: Laurent Di Lorto (1/0), Jules Vandooren (13/0), Étienne Mattler (32/0), Louis Gabrillargues (8/0), Georges Verriest (14/1), Edmond Delfour (Cap) (33/2), Roger Courtois (10/6), Roger Rio (14/2), Jules Bigot (1/0), Kowalczyk Ignace (2/0), Ali Benouna (1/0).

136. 08.03.1936 **FRANCE - BELGIUM** **3-0(1-0)**
Stade Olympique „Yves du Manoir", Colombes, Paris; Referee: Dr. Peco J. Bauwens (Germany); Attendance: 30,000
FRA: Laurent Di Lorto (2/0), Joseph Gonzales (1/0), Charles Zehren (1/0), Maxime Lehmann (2/0), Raymond François (1/0), Edmond Delfour (Cap) (34/2), Edmond Novicki (1/0), Roger Rio (15/3), Roger Courtois (11/8), Pierre Duhart (4/1), Ali Benouna (2/0).
Goals: Roger Courtois (37), Roger Rio (48), Roger Courtois (54).

137. 13.12.1936 **FRANCE - YUGOSLAVIA** **1-0(1-0)**
Stade Parc des Princes, Paris; Referee: Rinaldo Barlassina (Italy); Attendance: 32,903
FRA: Robert Défossé (9/0), Jules Vandooren (Cap) (14/0), Georges Beaucourt (1/0), Mathieu André (1/0), Jean Gautheroux (2/0), ÉmilienMéresse (1/0), Alfred Aston (12/1), Pierre Duhart (5/1), Roger Courtois (12/8), Oscar Heisserer (1/0), Frédéric Keller (6/3).
Goal: Frédéric Keller (19).

138. 24.01.1937 **FRANCE - AUSTRIA** **1-2(1-1)**
Stade Parc des Princes, Paris; Referee: Arthur Barton (England); Attendance: 37,898
FRA: René Llense (7/0), Maurice Dupuis (1/0), Raoul Diagne (6/0), Michel Payen (1/0), Louis Gabrillargues (9/0), Mathieu André (2/0), Edmond Novicki (2/1), Roger Rio (16/3), Jean Nicolas (Cap) (16/15), Georges Janin (1/0), Bernard Antoinette (1/0).
Goal: Edmond Novicki (42).

139. 21.02.1937 **BELGIUM - FRANCE** **3-1(1-1)**
Stade du Jubilé (Centenaire), Bruxelles; Referee: Hans Boekman (Netherlands); Attendance: 37,668
FRA: René Llense (8/0), Maurice Dupuis (2/0), Raoul Diagne (7/0), Michel Payen (2/0), François Bourbotte (1/0), Mathieu André (3/0), Frédéric Keller (7/3), Roger Rio (Cap) (17/4), Roger Courtois (13/8), Pierre Duhart (6/1), Bernard Antoinette (2/0).
Goal: Roger Rio (12).

140. 21.03.1937 **GERMANY - FRANCE** **4-0(2-0)**
„Adolf Hitler" Kampfbahn, Stuttgart; Referee: Rinaldo Barlassina (England); Attendance: 72,000
FRA: Laurent Di Lorto (3/0), Maurice Dupuis (3/0), Raoul Diagne (8/0), Michel Payen (3/0), François Bourbotte (2/0), Edmond Delfour (Cap) (35/2), Jules Bigot (2/0), Roger Rio (18/4), Jean Nicolas (17/15), Kowalczyk Ignace (3/0), Frédéric Keller (8/3).

141. 23.05.1937 **FRANCE - REPUBLIC OF IRELAND** **0-2(0-0)**
Stade Olympique „Yves du Manoir", Colombes, Paris; Referee: Gustav Krist (Czechoslovakia); Attendance: 16,688
FRA: Laurent Di Lorto (4/0), Abdelkader Ben Bouali (1/0), Raoul Diagne (9/0), François Bourbotte (3/0), Georges Meuris (1/0), Edmond Delfour (Cap) (36/2), Michel Lauri (1/0), Kowalczyk Ignace (4/0), Roger Courtois (14/8), Michel Frutuoso (1/0), Alfred Aston (13/1).

142. 10.10.1937 **FRANCE - SWITZERLAND** **2-1(1-0)**
Stade Parc des Princes, Paris; Referee: John Langenus (Belgium); Attendance: 37,000
FRA: Laurent Di Lorto (5/0), Hector Cazenave (1/0), Étienne Mattler (33/0), François Bourbotte (4/0), Marcel Desrousseaux (2/0), Edmond Delfour (Cap) (37/2), Curt Keller (1/0), Yvan Beck (5/0), Roger Courtois (15/8), Émile Veinante (14/8), Marcel Langiller (28/6).
Goals: Émile Veinante (41, 82).

143. 31.10.1937 **NETHERLANDS - FRANCE** **2-3(0-1)**
Olympisch Stadion, Amsterdam; Referee: Wiltshire (England); Attendance: 44,000
FRA: Laurent Di Lorto (6/0), Hector Cazenave (2/0), Étienne Mattler (34/0), François Bourbotte (5/0), Charles Fosset (1/0), Edmond Delfour (Cap) (38/2), Roger Courtois (16/9), Oscar Heisserer (2/0), Jean Nicolas (18/16), Émile Veinante (15/8), Marcel Langiller (29/7).
Goals: Jean Nicolas (12), Marcel Langiller (48), Roger Courtois (73).

144. 05.12.1937 **FRANCE - ITALY** **0-0**
Stade Parc des Princes, Paris; Referee: Hans Wütrich (Switzerland); Attendance: 39,046
FRA: Laurent Di Lorto (7/0), Hector Cazenave (3/0), Étienne Mattler (35/0), François Bourbotte (6/0), Charles Fosset (2/0), Edmond Delfour (Cap) (39/2), Roger Courtois (17/9), Oscar Heisserer (3/0), Jean Nicolas (19/16), Émile Veinante (16/8), Marcel Langiller (30/7).

145. 30.01.1938 **FRANCE - BELGIUM** **5-3(2-2)**
Stade Parc des Princes, Paris; Referee: Arthur James Jewell (England); Attendance: 39,000
FRA: René Llense (9/0), Hector Cazenave (4/0), Étienne Mattler (Cap) (36/0), François Bourbotte (7/0), Auguste Jordan (1/0), Marcel Marchal (1/0), Roger Courtois (18/10), Kowalczyk Ignace (5/1), Jean Nicolas (20/16), Oscar Heisserer (4/1), Émile Veinante (17/10).
Goals: Roger Courtois (8), Émile Veinante (41), Oscar Heisserer (47), Émile Veinante (51), Kowalczyk Ignace (78).

146. 24.03.1938 **FRANCE - BULGARIA** **6-1(2-0)**
Stade Parc des Princes, Paris; Referee: Walter J. Lewington (England); Attendance: 25,000
FRA: Laurent Di Lorto (8/0), Hector Cazenave (5/0), Étienne Mattler (Cap) (37/0), François Bourbotte (8/0), Auguste Jordan (2/0), Raoul Diagne (10/0), Alfred Aston (14/3), Oscar Heisserer (5/1), Jean Nicolas (21/18), Emmanuel Aznar (1/1), Émile Veinante (18/11).
Goals: Jean Nicolas (6), Alfred Aston (29, 62), Emmanuel Aznar (79), Émile Veinante (83), Jean Nicolas (87).

147. 26.05.1938 **FRANCE - ENGLAND** **2-4(2-3)**
Stade Olympique „Yves du Manoir", Colombes, Paris; Referee: Louis Baert (Belgium); Attendance: 46.920
FRA: Laurent Di Lorto (9/0), Hector Cazenave (6/0), Étienne Mattler (Cap) (38/0), François Bourbotte (9/0), Auguste Jordan (3/1), Raoul Diagne (11/0), Roger Courtois (19/10), Michel Brusseaux (1/0), Jean Nicolas (22/19), Oscar Heisserer (6/1), Alfred Aston (15/3).
Goals: Auguste Jordan (32), Jean Nicolas (36).

148. 05.06.1938 **FRANCE - BELGIUM** **3-1(2-1)** 3rd FIFA WC. 1st Round.
Stade Olympique „Yves du Manoir", Colombes, Paris; Referee: Hans Wütrich (Switzerland); Attendance: 30,454
FRA: Laurent Di Lorto (10/0), Hector Cazenave (7/0), Étienne Mattler (Cap) (39/0), Henri Bastien (1/0), Auguste Jordan (4/1), Raoul Diagne (12/0), Alfred Aston (16/3), Oscar Heisserer (7/1), Jean Nicolas (23/21), Edmond Delfour (40/2), Émile Veinante (19/12).
Goals: Jean Nicolas (1), Émile Veinante (11), Jean Nicolas (69).

149. 12.06.1938 **FRANCE - ITALY** **1-3(1-1)** 3rd FIFA WC. Quarter-Finals.
Stade Olympique „Yves du Manoir“, Colombes, Paris; Referee: Louis Baert (Belgium); Attendance: 58,455
FRA: Laurent Di Lorto (11/0), Hector Cazenave (8/0), Étienne Mattler (Cap) (40/0), Henri Bastien (2/0), Auguste Jordan (5/1), Raoul Diagne (13/0), Alfred Aston (17/3), Oscar Heisserer (8/2), Jean Nicolas (24/21), Edmond Delfour (41/2), Émile Veinante (20/12).
Goal: Oscar Heisserer (8).

150. 04.12.1938 **ITALY - FRANCE** **1-0(1-0)**
Stadio „Giorgio Ascarelli“, Napoli; Referee: John Langenus (Belgium); Attendance: 40,000
FRA: René Llense (10/0), Jules Vandooren (15/0), Étienne Mattler (Cap) (41/0), François Bourbotte (10/0), Auguste Jordan (6/1), Raoul Diagne (14/0), Alfred Aston (18/3), Larbi Ben Barek (1/0), Jean Nicolas (25/21), Oscar Heisserer (9/2), Émile Veinante (21/12).

151. 22.01.1939 **FRANCE - POLAND** **4-0(2-0)**
Stade Parc des Princes, Paris; Referee: Albert Jordan (Switzerland); Attendance: 35,000
FRA: René Llense (11/0), Jules Vandooren (16/0), Étienne Mattler (Cap) (42/0), François Bourbotte (11/0), Auguste Jordan (7/1), Roland Schmitt (1/0), Alfred Aston (19/3), Larbi Ben Barek (2/0), Mario Zatelli (1/0), Oscar Heisserer (10/3), Émile Veinante (22/14).
Goals: Émile Veinante (16), Oscar Heisserer (41), Émile Veinante (57), Mario Zatelli (70).

152. 16.03.1939 **FRANCE - HUNGARY** **2-2(1-1)**
Stade Parc des Princes, Paris; Referee: Walter J. Lewington (England); Attendance: 27,367
FRA: Julien Darui (1/0), Jules Vandooren (17/0), Étienne Mattler (Cap) (43/0), François Bourbotte (12/0), Auguste Jordan (8/1), Raoul Diagne (15/0), Alfred Aston (20/3), Larbi Ben Barek (3/1), Roger Courtois (20/10), Oscar Heisserer (11/4), Edmond Weiskopf (1/0).
Goals: Larbi Ben Barek (15), Oscar Heisserer (87).

153. 18.05.1939 **BELGIUM - FRANCE** **1-3(0-1)**
Stade du Jubilé (Centenaire), Bruxelles; Referee: Alexander Donaldson (England); Attendance: 35,793
FRA: Julien Darui (2/0), Jules Vandooren (18/0), Étienne Mattler (Cap) (44/0), François Bourbotte (13/0), Auguste Jordan (9/1), Raoul Diagne (16/0), Jules Bigot (3/0), Larbi Ben Barek (4/1), Désiré Korányi (1/2), Oscar Heisserer (12/4), Jules Mathé (1/1).
Goals: Désiré Korányi (28), Jules Mathé (48), Désiré Korányi (85).

154. 21.05.1939 **FRANCE - WALES** **2-1(2-0)**
Stade Olympique „Yves du Manoir“, Colombes, Paris; Referee: Laurent Franken (Belgium); Attendance: 23,000
FRA: Julien Darui (3/0), Jules Vandooren (19/0), Étienne Mattler (Cap) (45/0), François Bourbotte (14/0), Auguste Jordan (10/1), Raoul Diagne (17/0), Jules Bigot (4/1), Oscar Heisserer (13/4), Désiré Korányi (2/3), Émile Veinante (23/14), Jules Mathé (2/1).
Goals: Jules Bigot (10), Désiré Korányi (13).

155. 28.01.1940 **FRANCE - PORTUGAL** **3-2(2-0)**
Stade Parc des Princes, Paris; Referee: Bainbridge (England); Attendance: 18,083
FRA: Rodolphe Hiden (1/0), Jules Vandooren (20/0), Étienne Mattler (Cap) (46/0), François Bourbotte (15/0), Auguste Jordan (11/1), Raoul Diagne (18/0), Roger Courtois (21/10), Henri Hiltl (1/0), Désiré Korányi (3/5), Oscar Heisserer (14/5), Émile Veinante (24/14).
Goals: Oscar Heisserer (17), Désiré Korányi (23, 75).

156. 08.03.1942 **FRANCE - SWITZERLAND** **0-2(0-2)**
Stade Vélodrome, Marseille; Referee: Pedro Escartin (Spain); Attendance: 39,000
FRA: Julien Darui (4/0), Jules Vandooren (Cap) (21/0), Henri Roessler (1/0), François Bourbotte (16/0), Auguste Jordan (12/1), Roland Schmitt (2/0), Alfred Aston (21/3), André Simonyi (1/0), Désiré Korányi (4/5), Maurice Dupuis (4/0), Henri Arnaudeau (1/0).

157. 15.03.1942 **SPAIN - FRANCE** **4-0(2-0)**
Estadio de Nervión, Sevilla; Referee: António Palhinhas (Portugal); Attendance: 40,000
FRA: Julien Darui (5/0), Jules Vandooren (Cap) (22/0), François Mercier (1/0), François Bourbotte (17/0), Auguste Jordan (13/1), Henri Roessler (2/0), Alfred Aston (22/3), André Simonyi (2/0), Désiré Korányi (5/5), Maurice Dupuis (5/0), Henri Arnaudeau (2/0).

158. 24.12.1944 **FRANCE - BELGIUM** **3-1(2-0)**
Stade Parc des Princes, Paris; Referee: Paul Tréhou (France); Attendance: 24,095
FRA: Alfred Dambach (1/0), André Frey (1/0), Henri Bastien (3/0), Jean Swiatek (1/0), Jules Bigot (5/1), Félix Pironti (1/0), Alfred Aston (Cap) (23/4), Jean Baratte (1/0), Henri Hiltl (2/0), André Simonyi (3/1), Henri Arnaudeau (3/1).
Goals: André Simonyi (38), Henri Arnaudeau (42), Alfred Aston (79).

159. 08.04.1945 **SWITZERLAND - FRANCE** **1-0(0-0)**
Stade Olympique de la Pontaise, Lausanne; Referee: Georges Capdeville (France); Attendance: 25,000
FRA: Julien Darui (6/0), André Frey (2/0), Auguste Jordan (14/1), Maurice Dupuis (6/0), Jules Bigot (6/1), Lucien Jasseron (1/0), Alfred Aston (Cap) (24/4), Ladislas Siklo (1/0), René Bihel (1/0), André Simonyi (4/1), Ernest Vaast (1/0).

160. 26.05.1945 **ENGLAND - FRANCE** **2-2(1-1)**
Wembley Stadium, London; Referee: George Reader (England); Attendance: 65,000
FRA: Julien Darui (7/0), Maurice Dupuis (7/0), Jean Swiatek (2/0), Lucien Jasseron (2/0), Auguste Jordan (15/1), Jean-Claude Samuel (1/0), Alfred Aston (25/4), Oscar Heisserer (Cap) (15/6), René Bihel (2/0), Ladislas Siklo (2/0), Ernest Vaast (2/1).
Goals: Ernest Vaast (44), Oscar Heisserer (90).

161. 06.12.1945 **AUSTRIA - FRANCE** **4-1(2-1)**
Praterstadion, Wien; Referee: Jean Lutz (Switzerland); Attendance: 55,000
FRA: Julien Darui (8/0), Maurice Dupuis (8/0), Auguste Jordan (16/1), Marcel Salva (1/0), Jean-Claude Samuel (2/0), Henri Bastien (4/0), Ladislas Siklo (3/0), Larbi Ben Barek (5/1), Alfred Aston (Cap) (26/4), Émile Bongiorni (1/1), Ernest Vaast (3/1).
Goal: Émile Bongiorni (8).

162. 15.12.1945 **BELGIUM - FRANCE** **2-1(2-0)**
Stade à Molenbeek-Saint-Jean, Bruxelles; Referee: Aad van Welzenes (Netherlands); Attendance: 23,576
FRA: Julien Darui (9/0), Maurice Dupuis (9/0), Gabriel Braun (1/0), Marcel Salva (2/0), Jean-Claude Samuel (3/0), Marcel Ourdouillé (1/0), Ladislas Siklo (4/0), Larbi Ben Barek (6/1), Alfred Aston (Cap) (27/5), Émile Bongiorni (2/1), Ernest Vaast (4/1).
Goal: Alfred Aston (77).

163. 07.04.1946 **FRANCE - CZECHOSLOVAKIA** **3-0(1-0)**
Stade Olympique „Yves du Manoir", Colombes, Paris; Referee: Peter Scherz (Switzerland); Attendance: 52,242
FRA: Julien Darui (10/0), André Grillon (1/0), Antoine Cuissard (1/0), Marcel Salva (3/0), Jean Prouff (1/0), Lucien Leduc (1/0), Oscar Heisserer (16/7), Larbi Ben Barek (7/1), Alfred Aston (Cap) (28/5), René Bihel (3/0), Ernest Vaast (5/3).
Goals: Ernest Vaast (15, 75), Oscar Heisserer (83).

164. 14.04.1946 **PORTUGAL - FRANCE** **2-1(1-0)**
Estádio Nacional, Lisboa; Referee: George Reader (England); Attendance: 62,000
FRA: Julien Darui (11/0), André Grillon (2/0), Antoine Cuissard (2/0), Marcel Salva (4/0), Jean Prouff (2/0), Lucien Leduc (2/0), Oscar Heisserer (17/7), Larbi Ben Barek (8/1), Alfred Aston (Cap) (29/5), René Bihel (4/0), Ernest Vaast (6/4).
Goal: Ernest Vaast (68).

165. 05.05.1946 **FRANCE - AUSTRIA** **3-1(0-1)**
Stade Olympique „Yves du Manoir", Colombes, Paris; Referee: Paul von Wartburg (Switzerland); Attendance: 57,205
FRA: Julien Darui (12/0), André Grillon (3/0), Antoine Cuissard (3/0), Marcel Salva (5/0), Jean Prouff (3/0), Lucien Leduc (3/1), Oscar Heisserer (18/8), Larbi Ben Barek (9/1), Alfred Aston (Cap) (30/5), René Bihel (5/0), Ernest Vaast (7/5).
Goals: Ernest Vaast (66), Oscar Heisserer (83), Lucien Leduc (86).

166. 19.05.1946 **FRANCE - ENGLAND** **2-1(0-0)**
Stade Olympique „Yves du Manoir", Colombes, Paris; Referee: Peter Scherz (Switzerland); Attendance: 58,481
FRA: Julien Darui (13/0), André Grillon (4/0), Marcel Salva (6/0), Jean Prouff (4/1), Antoine Cuissard (4/0), Lucien Leduc (4/1), Alfred Aston (31/5), Oscar Heisserer (Cap) (19/8), Pierre Sinibaldi (1/0), Larbi Ben Barek (10/1), Ernest Vaast (8/6).
Goals: Jean Prouff (54), Ernest Vaast (78).

167. 23.03.1947 **FRANCE - PORTUGAL** **1-0(1-0)**
Stade Olympique „Yves du Manoir", Colombes, Paris; Referee: Cyrill Barrick (England); Attendance: 57,791
FRA: Julien Darui (14/0), André Grillon (5/0), Jean Swiatek (3/0), Roger Marche (1/0), Antoine Cuissard (5/0), Jean Prouff (5/1), Larbi Ben Barek (11/1), Oscar Heisserer (20/8), Roger Courtois (Cap) (22/10), René Bihel (6/1), Michel Jacques (1/0).
Goal: René Bihel (41).

168. 03.05.1947 **ENGLAND - FRANCE** **3-0(0-0)**
Highbury Stadium, London; Referee: Louis Baert (Belgium); Attendance: 54,389
FRA: Julien Darui (15/0), Jean Swiatek (4/0), Jean Grégoire (1/0), Roger Marche (2/0), Antoine Cuissard (6/0), Jean Prouff (6/1), Boleslav Tempowski (1/0), Oscar Heisserer (Cap) (21/8), Ernest Vaast (9/6), Émile Bongiorni (3/1), Jean Lechantre (1/0).

169. 26.05.1947 **FRANCE - NETHERLANDS** **4-0(1-0)**
Stade Olympique „Yves du Manoir", Colombes, Paris; Referee: Stanley Boardman (England); Attendance: 38,215
FRA: Julien Darui (Cap) (16/0), Joseph Jadrejak (1/0), Jean Grégoire (2/0), Sauveur Rodriguez (1/0), Antoine Cuissard (7/0), Jean Prouff (7/1), Jean Baratte (2/2), Roger Carré (1/0), Geoges Dard (1/1), René Alpsteg (1/1), Ernest Vaast (10/6).
Goals: René Alpsteg (17), Jean Baratte (60), Geoges Dard (75), Jean Baratte (86).

170. 01.06.1947 **FRANCE - BELGIUM** **4-2(1-1)**
Stade Olympique „Yves du Manoir", Colombes, Paris; Referee: Jan Beneda (Czechoslovakia); Attendance: 35,176
FRA: Julien Darui (17/0), Joseph Jadrejak (2/0), Jean Grégoire (3/0), André Grillon (6/0), Antoine Cuissard (8/0), Charles Heiné (1/0), Jean Baratte (3/3), Oscar Heisserer (Cap) (22/8), Geoges Dard (2/2), René Alpsteg (2/1), Ernest Vaast (11/8).
Goals: Ernest Vaast (13), Jean Baratte (77), Geoges Dard (83), Ernest Vaast (84).

171. 08.06.1947 **SWITZERLAND - FRANCE** **1-2(1-2)**
Stade Olympique de la Pontaise, Lausanne; Referee: George Reader (England); Attendance: 35,000
FRA: Julien Darui (18/0), Joseph Jadrejak (3/0), Jean Grégoire (4/0), André Grillon (7/0), Antoine Cuissard (9/0), Jean Prouff (8/1), Jean Baratte (4/4), Oscar Heisserer (Cap) (23/8), Charles Heiné (2/0), René Alpsteg (3/2), Ernest Vaast (12/8).
Goals: René Alpsteg (36), Jean Baratte (44).

172. 23.11.1947 **PORTUGAL - FRANCE** **2-4(1-0)**
Estádio Nacional, Lisboa; Referee: Paul von Wartburg (Switzerland); Attendance: 70,000
FRA: Julien Darui (19/0), André Grillon (8/0), Jean Grégoire (5/0), Roger Marche (3/0), Jean Prouff (9/1), Louis Hon (1/0), Oscar Heisserer (Cap) (24/8), Larbi Ben Barek (12/2), René Alpsteg (4/2), Jean Baratte (5/4), Ernest Vaast (13/11).
Goals: Ernest Vaast (47, 51, 77), Larbi Ben Barek (84).

173. 04.04.1948 **FRANCE - ITALY** **1-3(0-3)**
Stade Olympique „Yves du Manoir", Colombes, Paris; Referee: Arthur Edward Ellis (England); Attendance: 60,074
FRA: Marcel Domingo (1/0), André Grillon (9/0), Robert Jonquet (1/0), Roger Marche (4/0), Antoine Cuissard (10/0), Jean Prouff (10/1), Oscar Heisserer (Cap) (25/8), Larbi Ben Barek (13/2), René Alpsteg (5/2), Jean Baratte (6/5), Ernest Vaast (14/11).
Goal: Jean Baratte (71 penalty).

174. 23.05.1948 **FRANCE - SCOTLAND** **3-0(0-0)**
Stade Olympique „Yves du Manoir", Colombes, Paris; Referee: Karel van der Meer (Netherlands); Attendance: 46,032
FRA: Julien Darui (Cap) (20/0), Guy Huguet (1/0), Jean Grégoire (6/0), Roger Marche (5/0), Antoine Cuissard (11/0), Jean Prouff (11/1), Jean Baratte (7/6), Larbi Ben Barek (14/2), Georges Sésia (1/0), Émile Bongiorni (4/2), Pierre Flamion (1/1).
Goals: Émile Bongiorni (55), Pierre Flamion (60), Jean Baratte (79).

175. 06.06.1948 **BELGIUM - FRANCE** **4-2(1-0)**
Stade du Jubilé (Centenaire), Bruxelles; Referee: Dirk Nijs (Netherlands); Attendance: 52,873
FRA: Julien Darui (Cap) (21/0), Guy Huguet (2/0), Jean Grégoire (7/0), Roger Marche (6/0), Antoine Cuissard (12/1), Jean Prouff (12/1), Jean Baratte (8/6), Larbi Ben Barek (15/3), Albert Batteux (1/0), Émile Bongiorni (5/2), Pierre Flamion (2/1).
Goals: Antoine Cuissard (47), Larbi Ben Barek (74).

176. 12.06.1948 **CZECHOSLOVAKIA - FRANCE** **0-4(0-0)**
Stadion Letná, Praha; Referee: Karel van der Meer (Netherlands); Attendance: 50,000
FRA: Julien Darui (Cap) (22/0), Guy Huguet (3/0), Antoine Cuissard (13/1), Roger Marche (7/0), Jean Prouff (13/1), Louis Hon (2/0), Albert Batteux (2/1), Larbi Ben Barek (16/3), Henri Baillot (1/1), Jean Baratte (9/8), Pierre Flamion (3/1).
Goals: Albert Batteux (62), Jean Baratte (66), Henri Baillot (74), Jean Baratte (89).

177. 17.10.1948 **FRANCE - BELGIUM** **3-3(2-1)**
Stade Olympique „Yves du Manoir", Colombes, Paris; Referee: Jean Lutz (Switzerland); Attendance: 55,600
FRA: Julien Darui (Cap) (23/0), Guy Huguet (4/0), Antoine Cuissard (14/1) [41.Henri Guérin (1/0)], Roger Marche (8/0), Jean Prouff (14/1), Louis Hon (3/0), Albert Batteux (3/1), Pierre Sinibaldi (2/0), Henri Baillot (2/1), Jean Baratte (10/9), Pierre Flamion (4/3).
Goals: Pierre Flamion (9), Jean Baratte (22), Pierre Flamion (50).

178. 23.04.1949 **NETHERLANDS - FRANCE** **4-1(3-1)**
Stadion Feijenoord, Rotterdam; Referee: Laurent Franken (Belgium); Attendance: 64,000
FRA: René Vignal (1/0), Marcel Salva (7/0), Robert Jonquet (2/0), Roger Marche (9/0), Antoine Cuissard (15/1), Louis Hon (4/0), Albert Batteux (4/1), Jean Prouff (Cap) (15/1), Roger Gabet (1/0), Jean Baratte (11/10), Pierre Flamion (5/3).
Goal: Jean Baratte (3).

179. 27.04.1949 **SCOTLAND - FRANCE** **2-0(1-0)**
Hampden Park, Glasgow; Referee: William Ling (England); Attendance: 125,631
FRA: René Vignal (2/0), Marcel Salva (8/0), Roger Mindonnet (1/0), Roger Marche (10/0), Robert Jonquet (3/0), Louis Hon (5/0), Antoine Cuissard (16/1), Albert Batteux (Cap) (5/1), Roger Gabet (2/0), Jean Baratte (12/10), Pierre Flamion (6/3).

180. 22.05.1949 **FRANCE - ENGLAND** **1-3(1-2)**
Stade Olympique „Yves du Manoir", Colombes, Paris; Referee: Karel van der Meer (Netherlands); Attendance: 61,308
FRA: René Vignal (3/0), André Grillon (10/0), Roger Mindonnet (2/0), Marcel Salva (9/0), Robert Jonquet (4/0), Louis Hon (6/0), Antoine Cuissard (17/1), Albert Batteux (Cap) (6/1), Roger Gabet (3/0), Roger Quenolle (1/0), Georges Moreel (1/1).
Goal: Georges Moreel (1).

181. 04.06.1949 **FRANCE - SWITZERLAND** **4-2(2-0)**
Stade Olympique „Yves du Manoir", Colombes, Paris; Referee: George Reader (England); Attendance: 33,474
FRA: René Vignal (4/0), André Grillon (11/0), Henri Guérin (2/0), Roger Mindonnet (3/0), Louis Hon (7/0), Jean Grégoire (8/0), Roger Vandooren (1/0), Albert Batteux (Cap) (7/1), Henri Baillot (3/2), Jean Baratte (13/12), Jean Grumellon (1/1).
Goals: Henri Baillot (26), Jean Grumellon (30), Jean Baratte (50, 84).

182. 19.06.1949 **FRANCE - SPAIN** **1-5(0-3)**
Stade Olympique „Yves du Manoir", Colombes, Paris; Referee: Giacomo Bertolio (Italy); Attendance: 52,217
FRA: René Vignal (5/0), André Grillon (12/0), Henri Guérin (3/0), Roger Mindonnet (4/0), Jean Grégoire (9/0), Louis Hon (8/0), Albert Batteux (Cap) (8/1), Ernest Vaast (15/11), Henri Baillot (4/2), Jean Baratte (14/13), Jean Grumellon (2/1).
Goal: Jean Baratte (64 penalty).

183. 09.10.1949 **YUGOSLAVIA - FRANCE** **1-1(1-0)** 4th FIFA WC. Qualifiers
Stadion JNA, Beograd; Referee: Karel van der Meer (Netherlands); Attendance: 50,000
FRA: Abderrahman Ibrir (1/0), André Frey (3/0), Louis Hon (9/0), Roger Marche (11/0), Jean Prouff (Cap) (16/1), Roger Carré (2/0), Pierre Ranzoni (1/0), Roger Vandooren (2/0), Henri Baillot (5/3), Jean Baratte (15/13), Jean Grumellon (3/1).
Goal: Henri Baillot (55).

184. 30.10.1949 **FRANCE - YUGOSLAVIA** **1-1(1-1)** 4th FIFA WC. Qualifiers
Stade Olympique „Yves du Manoir", Colombes, Paris; Referee: Peter Scherz (Switzerland); Attendance: 53,569
FRA: Abderrahman Ibrir (2/0), André Frey (4/0), Louis Hon (10/0), Roger Marche (12/0), Jean Prouff (Cap) (17/1), Jean Luciano (1/0), Roger Vandooren (3/0), André Strappe (1/0), Henri Baillot (6/4), Jean Baratte (16/13), Jean Grumellon (4/1).
Goal: Henri Baillot (8).

185. 13.11.1949 **FRANCE - CZECHOSLOVAKIA** **1-0(1-0)**
Stade Olympique „Yves du Manoir", Colombes, Paris; Referee: William H. Evans (England); Attendance: 38,946
FRA: Abderrahman Ibrir (3/0), Guy Huguet (5/0), Louis Hon (11/0), Roger Marche (13/0), Antoine Cuissard (18/1), Jean Luciano (2/0), Désiré Carré (1/0), André Strappe (2/0), Henri Baillot (7/4), Jean Baratte (Cap) (17/14), Jean Lechantre (2/0).
Goal: Jean Baratte (8 penalty).

186. 11.12.1949 **YUGOSLAVIA - FRANCE** **3-2(1-1,2-2)** 4th FIFA WC. Play-Off
Stadio „Giovani Berta", Firenze (Italy); Referee: Giovanni Galeati (Italy); Attendance: 25,000
FRA: Abderrahman Ibrir (4/0), André Frey (5/0), Louis Hon (12/0), Roger Marche (14/0), Antoine Cuissard (19/1), Jean Luciano (3/1), Marius Walter (1/1), Jean Baratte (Cap) (18/14), Roger Quenolle (2/0), Francis Meano (1/0), Jean Lechantre (3/0).
Goals: Marius Walter (13), Jean Luciano (83).

187. 27.05.1950 **FRANCE - SCOTLAND** **0-1(0-0)**
Stade Olympique „Yves du Manoir", Colombes, Paris; Referee: Julian Arque (Spain); Attendance: 35,568
FRA: Abderrahman Ibrir (5/0), Guy Huguet (6/0), Roger Lamy (1/0), Roger Marche (15/0), Jean Grégoire (10/0), Antoine Cuissard (20/1), André Strappe (3/0), Jean Grumellon (5/1), Henri Baillot (8/4), Jean Baratte (Cap) (19/14), Geoges Dard (3/2).

188. 04.06.1950 **BELGIUM - FRANCE** **4-1(2-1)**
Stade du Heysel, Bruxelles; Referee: Giuseppe Carpani (Italy); Attendance: 45,006
FRA: Paul Sinibaldi (1/0), André Frey (6/0), Jean Swiatek (5/0), Roger Marche (Cap) (16/0), Jean Luciano (4/1), Jean Belver (1/0), André Strappe (4/0), Mustapha Ben M'Barek (1/0), Marius Walter (2/1), Édouard Kargu (1/1), Pierre Flamion (7/3).
Goal: Édouard Kargu (19).

189. 01.11.1950 **FRANCE - BELGIUM** **3-3(1-3)**
Stade Olympique „Yves du Manoir", Colombes, Paris; Referee: Arthur Edward Ellis (England); Attendance: 48,799
FRA: Abderrahman Ibrir (6/0), Manuel Garriga (1/0), Roger Lamy (2/0), Roger Marche (17/0), Henri Arnaudeau (4/1), Roger Scotti (1/0), Édouard Kargu (2/2), Pierre Flamion (8/3), André Strappe (5/0), Jean Baratte (Cap) (20/15), André Doye (1/1).
Goals: André Doye (18), Jean Baratte (69), Édouard Kargu (87).

190. 10.12.1950 **FRANCE - NETHERLANDS** **5-2(3-2)**
Stade Olympique „Yves du Manoir", Colombes, Paris; Referee: Louis Baert (Belgium); Attendance: 37,468
FRA: René Vignal (6/0), Guy Huguet (7/0), Antoine Cuissard (21/1), Roger Marche (18/0), Pierre Ranzoni (2/0), Henri Arnaudeau (5/1), Édouard Kargu (3/2), Pierre Flamion (9/5), André Strappe (6/0), Jean Baratte (Cap) (21/17), André Doye (2/2).
Goals: Pierre Flamion (4), Jean Baratte (29), André Doye (41), Pierre Flamion (47), Jean Baratte (49).

191. 06.02.1951 **FRANCE - YUGOSLAVIA** **2-1(1-1)**
Stade Parc des Princes, Paris; Referee: Laurent Franken (Belgium); Attendance: 33,552
FRA: Julien Darui (24/0), Guy Huguet (8/0), Robert Jonquet (5/0), Roger Marche (Cap) (19/0), Antoine Cuissard (22/1), Henri Arnaudeau (6/1), Roger Vandooren (4/0), Pierre Flamion (10/6), André Strappe (7/1), Édouard Kargu (4/2), André Doye (3/2).
Goals: André Strappe (4), Pierre Flamion (62).

192. 11.05.1951 **NORTHERN IRELAND - FRANCE** **2-2(1-2)**
Windsor Park, Belfast; Referee: Arthur Edward Ellis (England); Attendance: 24,000
FRA: Julien Darui (25/0), Guy Huguet (9/0), Robert Jonquet (6/0), Roger Marche (Cap) (20/0), Antoine Cuissard (23/1), René Gallice (1/0), Antoine Bonifaci (1/1), Édouard Kargu (5/2), André Strappe (8/1), Jean Baratte (22/18), Edmond Haan (1/0).
Goals: Jean Baratte (16), Antoine Bonifaci (28).

193. 16.05.1951 **SCOTLAND - FRANCE** **1-0(0-0)**
Hampden Park, Glasgow; Referee: Herbert Mortimer (England); Attendance: 75,394
FRA: Stéphane Dakoski (1/0), Guy Huguet (10/0), Robert Jonquet (7/0), Roger Marche (Cap) (21/0), Antoine Bonifaci (2/1), Antoine Cuissard (24/1), André Strappe (9/1), Édouard Kargu (6/2), René Alpsteg (6/2), Jean Baratte (23/18), Edmond Haan (2/0).

194. 03.06.1951 **ITALY - FRANCE** **4-1(1-1)**
Stadio „Luigi Ferraris", Genova; Referee: Jean Lutz (Switzerland); Attendance: 52,500
FRA: Stéphane Dakoski (2/0), Guy Huguet (11/0), Robert Jonquet (8/0), Roger Marche (Cap) (22/0), Antoine Cuissard (25/1), Antoine Bonifaci (3/1), André Strappe (10/1), Jean Baratte (24/18) [13.Édouard Kargu (7/2)], René Alpsteg (7/2), Jean Grumellon (6/2), Edmond Haan (3/0).
Goal: Jean Grumellon (34).

195. 03.10.1951 **ENGLAND - FRANCE** **2-2(2-2)**
Highbury Stadium, London; Referee: John Mowatt (Scotland); Attendance: 57,603
FRA: René Vignal (7/0), André Grillon (13/0), Robert Jonquet (9/0), Marcel Salva (10/0), Abdelkader Firoud (1/0), Antoine Bonifaci (4/1), Jean Baratte (Cap) (25/18), Pierre Flamion (11/6), René Alpsteg (8/3), Jean Grumellon (7/2), André Doye (4/3).
Goals: André Doye (18), René Alpsteg (19).

196. 14.10.1951 **SWITZERLAND - FRANCE** **1-2(0-2)**
Stade Charmilles, Genève; Referee: Reginald Leafe (England); Attendance: 33,534
FRA: René Vignal (8/0), André Grillon (14/0), Robert Jonquet (10/0), Marcel Salva (11/0), Abdelkader Firoud (2/0), Antoine Bonifaci (5/1), Jean Baratte (Cap) (26/18), André Doye (5/4), René Alpsteg (9/3), André Strappe (11/1), Jean Grumellon (8/3).
Goals: André Doye (27), Jean Grumellon (34).

197. 01.11.1951 **FRANCE - AUSTRIA** **2-2(2-2)**
Stade Olympique „Yves du Manoir", Colombes, Paris; Referee: William Ling (England); Attendance: 61,687
FRA: René Vignal (9/0), André Grillon (15/0), Robert Jonquet (11/0), Marcel Salva (12/0), Abdelkader Firoud (3/0), Antoine Bonifaci (6/1), Jean Baratte (Cap) (27/18), Thadée Cisowski (1/0) [10.Marceau Stricanne (1/0)], René Alpsteg (10/3), Jean Grumellon (9/5), Pierre Flamion (12/6).
Goals: Jean Grumellon (3, 45).

198. 26.03.1952 **FRANCE - SWEDEN** **0-1(0-0)**
Stade Parc des Princes, Paris; Referee: Henri Bauwens (Belgium); Attendance: 35,779
FRA: René Vignal (10/0), Guy Huguet (12/0), Robert Jonquet (12/0), Marcel Salva (13/0), Abdelkader Firoud (4/0), Albert Dubreucq (1/0), Antoine Bonifaci (7/1), André Doye (6/4), René Alpsteg (11/3), Jean Baratte (Cap) (28/18), Pierre Flamion (13/6).

199. 20.04.1952 **FRANCE - PORTUGAL** **3-0(1-0)**
Stade Olympique „Yves du Manoir", Colombes, Paris; Referee: Alfred Bond (England); Attendance: 35,735
FRA: René Vignal (11/0), André Jacowski (1/0), Robert Jonquet (13/0), Roger Marche (23/0), Abdelkader Firoud (5/0), Antoine Bonifaci (8/1), Jean Baratte (Cap) (29/18), Roger Boury (1/0), André Strappe (12/3), Jean Grumellon (10/5) [4.René Alpsteg (12/4)], Léon Deladerrière (1/0).
Goals: René Alpsteg (15), André Strappe (68, 89).

200. 22.05.1952 **BELGIUM - FRANCE** **1-2(1-2)**
Stade du Heysel, Bruxelles; Referee: Paul von Wartburg (Switzerland); Attendance: 55,485
FRA: René Vignal (12/0), André Jacowski (2/0), Robert Jonquet (14/0), Roger Marche (24/0), Abdelkader Firoud (6/0), Ferenc Koczur „Ferry" (1/0), Jean Baratte (Cap) (30/18), André Doye (7/5), Léon Deladerrière (2/1), André Strappe (13/3), Abdelazziz Ben Tifour (1/0).
Goals: André Doye (22), Léon Deladerrière (24).

201. 05.10.1952 **FRANCE - WEST GERMANY** **3-1(1-1)**
Stade Olympique „Yves du Manoir", Colombes, Paris; Referee: William H. Evans (England); Attendance: 56,021
FRA: Jean Ruminski (1/0), Lazare Gianessi (1/0), Robert Jonquet (15/0), Roger Marche (Cap) (25/0), Armand Penverne (1/0), Antoine Bonifaci (9/1), Thadée Cisowski (2/1), André Strappe (14/4), Joseph Ujlaki (1/1), Raymond Kopa (1/0), Léon Deladerrière (3/1).
Goals: Joseph Ujlaki (4), Thadée Cisowski (81), André Strappe (90).

202. 19.10.1952 **AUSTRIA - FRANCE** **1-2(0-2)**
Praterstadion, Wien; Referee: Arthur Edward Ellis (England); Attendance: 65,000
FRA: Jean Ruminski (2/0), Lazare Gianessi (2/0), Robert Jonquet (16/0), Roger Marche (26/0), Antoine Bonifaci (10/1), Armand Penverne (2/1), Jean Baratte (Cap) (31/19), André Strappe (15/4), Raymond Kopa (2/0), Thadée Cisowski (3/1), Francis Meano (2/0).
Goals: Jean Baratte (10), Armand Penverne (26).

203. 11.11.1952 **FRANCE - NORTHERN IRELAND** **3-1(2-1)**
Stade Olympique „Yves du Manoir", Colombes, Paris; Referee: Klaas Schipper (Netherlands); Attendance: 52,399
FRA: Jean Ruminski (3/0), Lazare Gianessi (3/0), Robert Jonquet (17/0), Roger Marche (Cap) (27/0), Antoine Bonifaci (11/1) [26.Jean Baratte (32/19)], Armand Penverne (3/1), Joseph Ujlaki (2/2), André Strappe (16/4), Raymond Kopa (3/2), Thadée Cisowski (4/1), Stanislas Curyl (1/0).
Goals: Joseph Ujlaki (30), Raymond Kopa (36, 89).

204. 16.11.1952 **REPUBLIC OF IRELAND - FRANCE** **1-1(1-0)**
Dalymount Park, Dublin; Referee: Albert Alsteen (Belgium); Attendance: 40,000
FRA: Jean Ruminski (4/0), Lazare Gianessi (4/0), Robert Jonquet (18/0), Roger Marche (Cap) (28/0), Ferenc Koczur „Ferry" (2/0), Armand Penverne (4/1), Joseph Ujlaki (3/2), Roger Piantoni (1/1), Raymond Kopa (4/2), André Strappe (17/4), Stanislas Curyl (2/0).
Goal: Roger Piantoni (67).

205. 25.12.1952 **FRANCE - BELGIUM** **0-1(0-1)**
Stade Olympique „Yves du Manoir", Colombes, Paris; Referee: William H. Evans (England); Attendance: 38,379
FRA: Jean Ruminski (5/0), Lazare Gianessi (5/0), Robert Jonquet (19/0), Roger Marche (Cap) (29/0), Ferenc Koczur „Ferry" (3/0), Armand Penverne (5/1), Joseph Ujlaki (4/2), Roger Piantoni (2/1), Raymond Kopa (5/2), André Strappe (18/4), Léon Deladerrière (4/1).

206. 14.05.1953 **FRANCE - WALES** **6-1(4-1)**
Stade Olympique „Yves du Manoir", Colombes, Paris; Referee: Abel Da Costa (Portugal); Attendance: 33,020
FRA: Jean Ruminski (6/0), Lazare Gianessi (6/0), Robert Jonquet (20/0), Roger Marche (Cap) (30/0), Antoine Bonifaci (12/2), Jean-Jacques Marcel (1/0), Édouard Kargu (8/2), Roger Piantoni (3/1), Joseph Ujlaki (5/3), Raymond Kopa (6/4), René Gardien (1/2).
Goals: René Gardien (10), Raymond Kopa (14), René Gardien (33), Raymond Kopa (37), Antoine Bonifaci (73), Joseph Ujlaki (88).

207. 11.06.1953 **SWEDEN - FRANCE** **1-0(1-0)**
Råsundastadion, Stockholm; Referee: Edvin Pedersen (Norway); Attendance: 35,571
FRA: François Remetter (1/0), Lazare Gianessi (7/0), Robert Jonquet (21/0), Roger Marche (Cap) (31/0), Jean-Jacques Marcel (2/0), Armand Penverne (6/1), Édouard Kargu (9/2), André Strappe (19/4), Joseph Ujlaki (6/3), Raymond Kopa (7/4), René Gardien (2/2).

208. 20.09.1953 **LUXEMBOURG - FRANCE** **1-6(1-4)** 5th FIFA WC. Qualifiers
Stade Municipal, Luxembourg; Referee: Ernst Dörflinger (Switzerland); Attendance: 10,000
FRA: René Vignal (13/0) [8.François Remetter (2/0)], Lazare Gianessi (8/0), Robert Jonquet (22/0), Roger Marche (Cap) (32/0), Armand Penverne (7/1), Raymond Cicci (1/1), Léon Glovacki (1/1), Pierre Flamion (14/7), Raymond Kopa (8/5), Édouard Kargu (10/3), Roger Piantoni (4/2).
Goals: Roger Piantoni (5), Raymond Kopa (10), Raymond Cicci (41), Léon Glovacki (42), Édouard Kargu (73), Pierre Flamion (88).

209. 04.10.1953 **REPUBLIC OF IRELAND - FRANCE** **3-5(0-2)** 5th FIFA WC. Qualifiers
Dalymount Park, Dublin; Referee: Laurent Franken (Belgium); Attendance: 45,000
FRA: René Vignal (14/0), Lazare Gianessi (9/0), Robert Jonquet (23/0), Roger Marche (Cap) (33/0), Armand Penverne (8/2), Jean-Jacques Marcel (3/0), Léon Glovacki (2/2), Pierre Flamion (15/8), Joseph Ujlaki (7/5), Raymond Kopa (9/5), Roger Piantoni (5/2).
Goals: Léon Glovacki (23), Armand Penverne (40), Joseph Ujlaki (50, 69), Pierre Flamion (72).

210. 18.10.1953 **YUGOSLAVIA - FRANCE** **3-1(0-1)**
Stadion Maksimir, Zagreb; Referee: Erich Steiner (Austria); Attendance: 15,000
FRA: René Vignal (15/0), René Pleimelding (1/0), Robert Jonquet (24/0), Roger Marche (Cap) (34/0), Armand Penverne (9/2), Jean-Jacques Marcel (4/1), Léon Glovacki (3/2), Pierre Flamion (16/8), Joseph Ujlaki (8/5), Raymond Kopa (10/5), Roger Piantoni (6/2).
Goal: Jean-Jacques Marcel (44).

211. 11.11.1953 **FRANCE - SWITZERLAND** **2-4(1-4)**
Stade Olympique „Yves du Manoir", Colombes, Paris; Referee: Arthur Edward Ellis (England); Attendance: 45,986
FRA: René Vignal (16/0) [22.François Remetter (3/0)], Lazare Gianessi (10/0), Roger Marche (Cap) (35/0), Armand Penverne (10/2), Jean-Jacques Marcel (5/1), Robert Jonquet (25/0), Édouard Kargu (11/3), Pierre Flamion (17/8), Joseph Ujlaki (9/7), Raymond Kopa (11/5), Edmond Haan (4/0).
Goals: Joseph Ujlaki (2, 62).

212. 25.11.1953 **FRANCE - REPUBLIC OF IRELAND** **1-0(0-0)** 5th FIFA WC. Qualifiers
Stade Parc des Princes, Paris; Referee: Lucien Van Nuffel (Belgium); Attendance: 32,265
FRA: François Remetter (4/0), Ahmed Mihoubi (1/0), Lazare Gianessi (11/0), Roger Marche (Cap) (36/0), Antoine Cuissard (26/1), Jean-Jacques Marcel (6/1), André Strappe (20/4), Roger Piantoni (7/3), Joseph Ujlaki (10/7), Ben Mohammed Abdesselem (1/0), Léon Deladerrière (5/1).
Goal: Roger Piantoni (73).

213. 17.12.1953 **FRANCE - LUXEMBOURG** **8-0(4-0)** 5th FIFA WC. Qualifiers
Stade Parc des Princes, Paris; Referee: Francis Roeykens (Belgium); Attendance: 20,146
FRA: Jean-Pierre Kress (1/0), Antoine Pazur (1/0), Marius Bruat (1/0), Robert Lemaître (Cap) (1/0), Guilhem Bieganski (1/0), Abderrahman Mahjoub (1/0), Jean Desgranges (1/2), Just Fontaine (1/3), Jacques Foix (1/1), Célestin Oliver (1/0), Jean Vincent (1/2).
Goals: Jean Desgranges (2), Jean Vincent (6, 10), Just Fontaine (21), Jacques Foix (57), Just Fontaine (75, 80), Jean Desgranges (88).

214. 11.04.1954 **FRANCE - ITALY** **1-3(1-2)**
Stade Olympique „Yves du Manoir", Colombes, Paris; Referee: Arthur Edward Ellis (England); Attendance: 61,382
FRA: René Vignal (17/0), Lazare Gianessi (12/0), Robert Jonquet (26/0), Roger Marche (Cap) (37/0), Jean-Jacques Marcel (7/1), Armand Penverne (11/2), Joseph Ujlaki (11/7), Roger Piantoni (8/4), Raymond Kopa (12/5), Thadée Cisowski (5/1), Léon Deladerrière (6/1).
Goal: Roger Piantoni (26).

215. 30.05.1954 **BELGIUM - FRANCE** **3-3(3-2)**
Stade du Heysel, Bruxelles; Referee: Vasa Stefanović (Yugoslavia); Attendance: 54,729
FRA: Jean Ruminski (7/0), Daniel Carpentier (1/0), Antoine Cuissard (Cap) (27/1), Robert Lemaître (2/0), Jean-Jacques Marcel (8/1), Abderrahman Mahjoub (2/0), René Dereuddre (1/0), Raymond Kopa (13/6), André Strappe (21/4), Michel Leblond (1/0), Jean Vincent (2/3).
Goals: Jean Vincent (7), Constant Huysmans (39 own goal), Raymond Kopa (70).

216. 16.06.1954 **YUGOSLAVIA - FRANCE** **1-0(1-0)** 5th FIFA WC. Group Stage.
Stade Olympique de la Pontaise, Lausanne (Switzerland); Referee: Bryan Griffiths (Wales); Attendance: 27,000
FRA: François Remetter (5/0), Lazare Gianessi (13/0), Robert Jonquet (Cap) (27/0), Raymond Kaelbel (1/0), Armand Penverne (12/2), Jean-Jacques Marcel (9/1), Léon Glovacki (4/2), René Dereuddre (2/0), Raymond Kopa (14/6), André Strappe (22/4), Jean Vincent (3/3).

217. 19.06.1954 **FRANCE - MEXICO** **3-2(1-0)** 5th FIFA WC. Group Stage.
Stade Charmilles, Genève (Switzerland); Referee: Martín Manuel Asensi (Spain); Attendance: 19,000
FRA: François Remetter (6/0), Lazare Gianessi (14/0), Raymond Kaelbel (2/0), Roger Marche (Cap) (38/0), Jean-Jacques Marcel (10/1), Abderrahman Mahjoub (3/0), René Dereuddre (3/0), Abdelazziz Ben Tifour (2/0), Raymond Kopa (15/7), André Strappe (23/4), Jean Vincent (4/4).
Goals: Jean Vincent (19), Raúl Cárdenas (46 own goal), Raymond Kopa (88 penalty).

218. 16.10.1954 **WEST GERMANY - FRANCE** **1-3(0-2)**
Niedersachsenstadion, Hannover; Referee: Bryan Griffiths (Wales); Attendance: 85,000
FRA: François Remetter (7/0), Raymond Kaelbel (3/0), Robert Jonquet (28/0), Roger Marche (Cap) (39/0), Abderrahman Mahjoub (4/0), Xercès Louis (1/0), René Dereuddre (4/0), Larbi Ben Barek (17/3) [27.Jacques Foix (2/3)], Pierre Grillet (1/0), Raymond Kopa (16/7), Jean Vincent (5/5).
Goals: Jacques Foix (33), Jean Vincent (35), Jacques Foix (55).

219. 11.11.1954 **FRANCE - BELGIUM** **2-2(0-1)**
Stade Olympique „Yves du Manoir", Colombes, Paris; Referee: Rafael Tamarit Falaguera (Spain); Attendance: 53,674
FRA: François Remetter (8/0), Raymond Kaelbel (4/0), Robert Jonquet (29/0), Roger Marche (Cap) (40/0), Abderrahman Mahjoub (5/0), Xercès Louis (2/0), René Dereuddre (5/0), Jacques Foix (3/3), Pierre Grillet (2/0), Raymond Kopa (17/9), Jean Vincent (6/5).
Goals: Raymond Kopa (75, 87 penalty).

220. 17.03.1955 **SPAIN - FRANCE** **1-2(1-1)**
Estadio Chamartin, Madrid; Referee: Vincenzo Orlandini (Italy); Attendance: 125,000
FRA: François Remetter (9/0), Guilhem Bieganski (2/0), Robert Jonquet (30/0), Roger Marche (Cap) (41/0), Armand Penverne (13/2), Xercès Louis (3/0), Léon Glovacki (5/2), Abderrahman Mahjoub (6/0), Raymond Kopa (18/10), René Bliard (1/0), Jean Vincent (7/6). Trainer: Albert Batteux (1).
Goals: Raymond Kopa (35), Jean Vincent (73).

221. 03.04.1955 **FRANCE - SWEDEN** **2-0(1-0)**
Stade Olympique „Yves du Manoir", Colombes, Paris; Referee: Giorgio Bernardi (Italy); Attendance: 34,738
FRA: François Remetter (10/0), Guilhem Bieganski (3/0), Robert Jonquet (31/0), Roger Marche (Cap) (42/0), Armand Penverne (14/2), Xercès Louis (4/0), Léon Glovacki (6/3), Roger Piantoni (9/4), Maryan Wisnieski (1/0), Célestin Oliver (2/1), Jean Vincent (8/6). Trainer: Albert Batteux (2).
Goals: Célestin Oliver (36), Léon Glovacki (56).

222. 15.05.1955 **FRANCE - ENGLAND** **1-0(1-0)**
Stade Olympique „Yves du Manoir", Colombes, Paris; Referee: Emil Schmetzer (West Germany); Attendance: 54,696
FRA: François Remetter (11/0), Guilhem Bieganski (4/0), Robert Jonquet (32/0), Roger Marche (Cap) (43/0), Armand Penverne (15/2), Xercès Louis (5/0), Léon Glovacki (7/3), René Bliard (2/0), Joseph Ujlaki (12/7), Raymond Kopa (19/11), Jean Vincent (9/6). Trainer: Albert Batteux (3).
Goal: Raymond Kopa (37 penalty).

223. 09.10.1955 **SWITZERLAND - FRANCE** **1-2(0-1)**
„St. Jakob" Stadion, Basel; Referee: Francis Roeykens (Belgium); Attendance: 54,000
FRA: François Remetter (12/0), Simon Zimny (1/0), Robert Jonquet (33/0), Roger Marche (Cap) (44/0), Jean-Jacques Marcel (11/1), Abderrahman Mahjoub (7/0), Joseph Ujlaki (13/7), Léon Glovacki (8/3), Raymond Kopa (20/12), Roger Piantoni (10/5), Jean Vincent (10/6). Trainer: Albert Batteux (4).
Goals: Raymond Kopa (24 penalty), Roger Piantoni (69).

224. 23.10.1955 **SOVIET UNION - FRANCE** **2-2(1-1)**
Dinamo Stadium, Moskva; Referee: Arthur Edward Ellis (England); Attendance: 80,000
FRA: François Remetter (13/0), Xercès Louis (6/0), Robert Jonquet (34/0), Roger Marche (Cap) (45/0), Armand Penverne (16/2), Jean-Jacques Marcel (12/1), Jacques Foix (4/3), Léon Glovacki (9/3), Raymond Kopa (21/13), Roger Piantoni (11/6), Jean Vincent (11/6) [31.René Bliard (3/0)]. Trainer: Albert Batteux (5).
Goals: Raymond Kopa (29), Roger Piantoni (64).

225. 11.11.1955 **FRANCE - YUGOSLAVIA** **1-1(0-1)**
Stade Olympique „Yves du Manoir", Colombes, Paris; Referee: Vincenzo Orlandini (Italy); Attendance: 60,654
FRA: François Remetter (14/0), Xercès Louis (7/0), Robert Jonquet (35/0), Roger Marche (Cap) (46/0), Armand Penverne (17/2), Jean-Jacques Marcel (13/1), Jacques Foix (5/3), Léon Glovacki (10/3), Raymond Kopa (22/13), Roger Piantoni (12/7), Abdelazziz Ben Tifour (3/0). Trainer: Albert Batteux (6).
Goal: Roger Piantoni (88).

226. 25.12.1955 **BELGIUM - FRANCE** **2-1(1-0)**
Stade du Heysel, Bruxelles; Referee: Just Bronkhorst (Netherlands); Attendance: 56,540
FRA: François Remetter (15/0), Xercès Louis (8/0), Robert Jonquet (36/0), Roger Marche (Cap) (47/0), Armand Penverne (18/2), Jean-Jacques Marcel (14/1) [11.Joseph Tellechea (1/0)], Joseph Ujlaki (14/7), Léon Glovacki (11/3), Raymond Kopa (23/13), Roger Piantoni (13/8), René Bliard (4/0). Trainer: Albert Batteux (7).
Goal: Roger Piantoni (63).

227. 15.02.1956 **ITALY - FRANCE** **2-0(0-0)**
Stadio Comunale, Bologna; Referee: Leo Lemešić (Yugoslavia); Attendance: 50,000
FRA: François Remetter (16/0), Xercès Louis (9/0), Robert Jonquet (37/0), Roger Marche (Cap) (48/0), Armand Penverne (19/2), Jean-Jacques Marcel (15/1), Jacques Foix (6/3), Roger Piantoni (14/8), Raymond Kopa (24/13), Michel Leblond (2/0), René Bliard (5/0). Trainer: Albert Batteux (8).

228. 25.03.1956 **FRANCE - AUSTRIA** **3-1(2-0)**
Stade Olympique „Yves du Manoir", Colombes, Paris; Referee: Arthur Edward Ellis (England); Attendance: 42,223
FRA: François Remetter (17/0), Raymond Kaelbel (5/0), Robert Jonquet (38/0), Roger Marche (Cap) (49/0), Xercès Louis (10/0), Jean-Jacques Marcel (16/1), Jean Hédiart (1/0), Roger Piantoni (15/9), Jacques Foix (7/3) [29.Léon Deladerrière (7/1)], Michel Leblond (3/1), Jean Vincent (12/7). Trainer: Albert Batteux (9).
Goals: Michel Leblond (15), Jean Vincent (30), Roger Piantoni (86).

229. 07.10.1956 **FRANCE - HUNGARY** **1-2(0-0)**
Stade Olympique „Yves du Manoir", Colombes, Paris; Referee: Cesare Jonni (Italy); Attendance: 59,457
FRA: François Remetter (18/0), Raymond Kaelbel (6/0), Robert Jonquet (39/0), Roger Marche (Cap) (50/0), Roger Scotti (2/0), Jean-Jacques Marcel (17/1), Pierre Grillet (3/0), Thadée Cisowski (6/2), Just Fontaine (2/3), Roger Piantoni (16/9), Jean Vincent (13/7). Trainer: Albert Batteux (10).
Goal: Thadée Cisowski (51).

230. 21.10.1956 **FRANCE - SOVIET UNION** **2-1(0-0)**
Stade Olympique „Yves du Manoir", Colombes, Paris; Referee: Bryan Griffiths (Wales); Attendance: 62,145
FRA: François Remetter (19/0), Raymond Kaelbel (7/0), Robert Jonquet (40/0), Roger Marche (Cap) (51/0) [32.Joseph Tellechea (2/1)], Xercès Louis (11/0), Jean-Jacques Marcel (18/1), Pierre Grillet (4/0), Rachid Mekhloufi (1/0), Thadée Cisowski (7/2), Roger Piantoni (17/9), Jean Vincent (14/8). Trainer: Albert Batteux (11).
Goals: Joseph Tellechea (46), Jean Vincent (54).

231. 11.11.1956 **FRANCE - BELGIUM** **6-3(4-1)** 6th FIFA WC. Qualifiers
Stade Olympique „Yves du Manoir", Colombes, Paris; Referee: Jack H. Clough (England); Attendance: 46,049
FRA: François Remetter (20/0), Raymond Kaelbel (8/0), Robert Jonquet (41/0), Roger Marche (Cap) (52/0), Xercès Louis (12/0), Jean-Jacques Marcel (19/1), Maryan Wisnieski (2/0), Rachid Mekhloufi (2/0), Thadée Cisowski (8/7), Roger Piantoni (18/9), Jean Vincent (15/9). Trainer: Albert Batteux (12).
Goals: Thadée Cisowski (13, 15), Jean Vincent (18), Thadée Cisowski (44, 72, 88).

232. 24.03.1957 **PORTUGAL - FRANCE** **0-1(0-0)**
Estádio Nacional, Lisboa; Referee: Martín Manuel Asensi (Spain); Attendance: 42,000
FRA: François Remetter (21/0), Raymond Kaelbel (9/0), Robert Jonquet (42/0), Roger Marche (Cap) (53/0), Armand Penverne (20/2), Jean-Jacques Marcel (20/1), Maryan Wisnieski (3/0), Rachid Mekhloufi (3/0), Thadée Cisowski (9/7), Roger Piantoni (19/10), Jean Vincent (16/9). Trainer: Albert Batteux (13).
Goal: Roger Piantoni (55).

233. 02.06.1957 **FRANCE - ICELAND** **8-0(5-0)** 6th FIFA WC. Qualifiers
Stade „Marcel Saupin", Nantes; Referee: Arthur Edward Ellis (England); Attendance: 15,080
FRA: François Remetter (22/0), Raymond Kaelbel (10/0), Robert Jonquet (43/0), Roger Marche (Cap) (54/0), Armand Penverne (21/2), Jean-Jacques Marcel (21/1), Saïd Brahimi (1/1), René Dereuddre (6/1), Célestin Oliver (3/3), Roger Piantoni (20/12), Jean Vincent (17/11). Trainer: Albert Batteux (14).
Goals: Célestin Oliver (6, 11), Jean Vincent (29), René Dereuddre (36), Roger Piantoni (45), Saïd Brahimi (49), Roger Piantoni (81), Jean Vincent (83).

234. 01.09.1957 **ICELAND - FRANCE** **1-5(0-2)** 6th FIFA WC. Qualifiers
Laugardalsvöllur, Reykjavík; Referee: Robert Davidson (Scotland); Attendance: 9,000
FRA: Dominique Colonna (1/0), Raymond Kaelbel (11/0), Robert Jonquet (Cap) (44/0), Richard Boucher (1/0), Armand Penverne (22/2), Jean-Jacques Marcel (22/1), Maryan Wisnieski (4/1), Joseph Ujlaki (15/9), Thadée Cisowski (10/9), Roger Piantoni (21/12), René Bliard (6/0). Trainer: Albert Batteux (15).
Goals: Thadée Cisowski (29, 32), Joseph Ujlaki (48), Maryan Wisnieski (53), Joseph Ujlaki (66).

235. 06.10.1957 **HUNGARY - FRANCE** **2-0(1-0)**
Népstadion, Budapest; Referee: Leopold Sylvain Horn (Netherlands); Attendance: 94,000
FRA: Dominique Colonna (2/0), Raymond Kaelbel (12/0), Mustapha Zitouni (1/0), André Lerond (1/0), Armand Penverne (Cap) (23/2), Pierre Cahuzac (1/0), Maryan Wisnieski (5/1), Joseph Ujlaki (16/9), Just Fontaine (3/3), Roger Piantoni (22/12), Abdelazziz Ben Tifour (4/0). Trainer: Albert Batteux (16).

236. 27.10.1957 **BELGIUM - FRANCE** **0-0** 6th FIFA WC. Qualifiers
Stade du Heysel, Bruxelles; Referee: Leo Helge (Denmark); Attendance: 56,497
FRA: Claude Abbes (1/0), Raymond Kaelbel (13/0), Mustapha Zitouni (2/0), André Lerond (2/0), Armand Penverne (Cap) (24/2), Célestin Oliver (4/3), Saïd Brahimi (2/1), Jean-Jacques Marcel (23/1), Stéphane Bruey (1/0), Michel Leblond (4/1), Jean Vincent (18/11). Trainer: Albert Batteux (17).

237. 27.11.1957 **ENGLAND - FRANCE** **4-0(3-0)**
Wembley Stadium, London; Referee: Nikolai Latyshev (Soviet Union); Attendance: 64,349
FRA: Claude Abbes (2/0), Mustapha Zitouni (3/0), Richard Tylinski (1/0), Raymond Kaelbel (14/0), René Domingo (1/0), Bruno Bollini (1/0), Maryan Wisnieski (6/1), Joseph Ujlaki (17/9), Yvon Douis (1/0), Roger Piantoni (Cap) (23/12), Jean Vincent (19/11). Trainer: Albert Batteux (18).

238. 25.12.1957 **FRANCE - BULGARIA** **2-2(1-0)**
Stade Parc des Princes, Paris; Referee: Günter Ternieden (West Germany); Attendance: 38,086
FRA: Dominique Colonna (3/0), Raymond Kaelbel (15/0), Robert Jonquet (Cap) (45/0), André Lerond (3/0), Armand Penverne (25/2), Pierre Cahuzac (2/0), Maryan Wisnieski (7/2) [36.Rachid Mekhloufi (4/0)], Yvon Douis (2/1), Stéphane Bruey (2/0), Roger Piantoni (24/12), Jean Vincent (20/11). Trainer: Albert Batteux (19).
Goals: Maryan Wisnieski (11), Yvon Douis (56).

239. 13.03.1958 **FRANCE - SPAIN** **2-2(0-1)**
Stade Parc des Princes, Paris; Referee: Jack H. Clough (England); Attendance: 37,983
FRA: Claude Abbes (3/0), Raymond Kaelbel (16/0), Mustapha Zitouni (4/0), André Lerond (4/0), Armand Penverne (Cap) (26/2), Jean-Jacques Marcel (24/1), Maryan Wisnieski (8/2), Yvon Douis (3/1), Just Fontaine (4/4), Roger Piantoni (25/13), Jean Vincent (21/11). Trainer: Albert Batteux (20).
Goals: Just Fontaine (49), Roger Piantoni (65).

240. 16.04.1958 **FRANCE - SWITZERLAND** **0-0**
Stade Parc des Princes, Paris; Referee: Pieter Paulus Roomer (Netherlands); Attendance: 36,019
FRA: François Remetter (23/0), Raymond Kaelbel (17/0), Robert Jonquet (46/0), Roger Marche (Cap) (55/0), Bernard Chiarelli (1/0), Jean-Jacques Marcel (25/1), Maryan Wisnieski (9/2), René Bliard (7/0), Just Fontaine (5/4), Célestin Oliver (5/3), Jean Vincent (22/11). Trainer: Albert Batteux (21).

241. 08.06.1958 **FRANCE - PARAGUAY** **7-3(2-2)** 6th FIFA WC. Group Stage.
Idrottsparken, Norrköping (Sweden); Referee: Juan Garay Gardeazábal (Spain); Attendance: 16,518
FRA: François Remetter (24/0), Raymond Kaelbel (18/0), Robert Jonquet (Cap) (47/0), André Lerond (5/0), Armand Penverne (27/2), Jean-Jacques Marcel (26/1), Maryan Wisnieski (10/3), Just Fontaine (6/7), Raymond Kopa (25/14), Roger Piantoni (26/14), Jean Vincent (23/12). Trainer: Albert Batteux (22).
Goals: Just Fontaine (24, 30), Roger Piantoni (51), Maryan Wisnieski (62), Just Fontaine (68), Raymond Kopa (70), Jean Vincent (84).

242. 11.06.1958 **YUGOSLAVIA - FRANCE** **3-2(1-1)** 6th FIFA WC. Group Stage.
Arosvalen, Västerås (Sweden); Referee: Bryan Griffiths (Wales); Attendance: 12,217
FRA: François Remetter (25/0), Raymond Kaelbel (19/0), Robert Jonquet (48/0), Roger Marche (Cap) (56/0), Armand Penverne (28/2), André Lerond (6/0), Maryan Wisnieski (11/3), Just Fontaine (7/9), Raymond Kopa (26/14), Roger Piantoni (27/14), Jean Vincent (24/12). Trainer: Albert Batteux (23).
Goals: Just Fontaine (4, 85).

243. 15.06.1958 **FRANCE - SCOTLAND** **2-1(2-0)** 6th FIFA WC. Group Stage.
Eyravallen, Örebro (Sweden); Referee: Juan Regis Brozzi (Argentina); Attendance: 13,554
FRA: Claude Abbes (4/0), Raymond Kaelbel (20/0), Robert Jonquet (Cap) (49/0), André Lerond (7/0), Armand Penverne (29/2), Jean-Jacques Marcel (27/1), Maryan Wisnieski (12/3), Just Fontaine (8/10), Raymond Kopa (27/15), Roger Piantoni (28/14), Jean Vincent (25/12). Trainer: Albert Batteux (24).
Goals: Raymond Kopa (4), Just Fontaine (85).

244. 19.06.1958 **FRANCE - NORTHERN IRELAND** **4-0(1-0)** 6th FIFA WC. Quarter-Finals.
Idrottsparken, Norrköping (Sweden); Referee: Juan Garay Gardeazábal (Spain); Attendance: 11,800
FRA: Claude Abbes (5/0), Raymond Kaelbel (21/0), Robert Jonquet (Cap) (50/0), André Lerond (8/0), Armand Penverne (30/2), Jean-Jacques Marcel (28/1), Maryan Wisnieski (13/4), Just Fontaine (9/12), Raymond Kopa (28/15), Roger Piantoni (29/15), Jean Vincent (26/12). Trainer: Albert Batteux (25).
Goals: Maryan Wisnieski (44), Just Fontaine (56, 64), Roger Piantoni (68).

245. 24.06.1958 **BRAZIL - FRANCE** **5-2(2-1)** 6th FIFA WC. Semi-Finals.
Råsundastadion, Stockholm (Sweden); Referee: Bryan Griffiths (Wales); Attendance: 27,100
FRA: Claude Abbes (6/0), Raymond Kaelbel (22/0), Robert Jonquet (Cap) (51/0), André Lerond (9/0), Armand Penverne (31/2), Jean-Jacques Marcel (29/1), Maryan Wisnieski (14/4), Just Fontaine (10/13), Raymond Kopa (29/15), Roger Piantoni (30/16), Jean Vincent (27/12). Trainer: Albert Batteux (26).
Goals: Just Fontaine (9), Roger Piantoni (82).

246. 28.06.1958 **FRANCE - WEST GERMANY** **6-3(3-1)** 6th FIFA WC. Third Place Play-off.
Ullevi Stadion, Göteborg (Sweden); Referee: Juan Regis Brozzi (Argentina); Attendance: 32,483
FRA: Claude Abbes (7/0), Raymond Kaelbel (23/0), Maurice Lafont (1/0), André Lerond (10/0), Armand Penverne (Cap) (32/2), Jean-Jacques Marcel (30/1), Maryan Wisnieski (15/4), Yvon Douis (4/2), Raymond Kopa (30/16), Just Fontaine (11/17), Jean Vincent (28/12). Trainer: Albert Batteux (27).
Goals: Just Fontaine (15), Raymond Kopa (27 penalty), Just Fontaine (36), Yvon Douis (50), Just Fontaine (77, 89).

247. 01.10.1958 **FRANCE - GREECE** **7-1(3-0)** 1st EC. 1st Round.
Stade Parc des Princes, Paris; Referee: Gottfried Dienst (Switzerland); Attendance: 37,590
FRA: Dominique Colonna (4/0), Raymond Kaelbel (24/0), Maurice Lafont (2/0), André Lerond (11/0), Armand Penverne (Cap) (33/2), Jean-Jacques Marcel (31/1), Yvon Douis (5/2), Just Fontaine (12/19), Raymond Kopa (31/17), Thadée Cisowski (11/11), Jean Vincent (29/14). Trainer: Albert Batteux (28).
Goals: Raymond Kopa (23), Just Fontaine (25), Thadée Cisowski (29), Jean Vincent (61), Thadée Cisowski (68), Just Fontaine (85), Jean Vincent (88).

248. 05.10.1958 **AUSTRIA - FRANCE** **1-2(1-0)**
Praterstadion, Wien; Referee: Cesare Jonni (Italy); Attendance: 70,000
FRA: Dominique Colonna (5/0), Raymond Kaelbel (25/0), Maurice Lafont (3/0), André Lerond (12/0), Armand Penverne (Cap) (34/2), Jean-Jacques Marcel (32/1), Léon Deladerrière (8/2), Yvon Douis (6/2), Just Fontaine (13/20), Thadée Cisowski (12/11), Jean Vincent (30/14). Trainer: Albert Batteux (29).
Goals: Léon Deladerrière (54), Just Fontaine (56).

249. 26.10.1958 **FRANCE - WEST GERMANY** **2-2(1-1)**
Stade Olympique „Yves du Manoir", Colombes, Paris; Referee: Arthur Edward Ellis (England); Attendance: 50,992
FRA: Dominique Colonna (6/0) [30.Claude Abbes (8/0)], Raymond Kaelbel (26/0), Maurice Lafont (4/0), André Lerond (13/0), Armand Penverne (Cap) (35/2), Jean-Jacques Marcel (33/1), Léon Deladerrière (9/3), Yvon Douis (7/3), Just Fontaine (14/20), Roger Piantoni (31/16) [42.Thadée Cisowski (13/11)], Jean Vincent (31/14). Trainer: Albert Batteux (30).
Goals: Léon Deladerrière (23), Yvon Douis (69 penalty).

250. 09.11.1958 **FRANCE - ITALY** **2-2(1-0)**
Stade Olympique „Yves du Manoir", Colombes, Paris; Referee: Juan Garay Gardeazábal (Spain); Attendance: 58,122
FRA: Dominique Colonna (7/0), Raymond Kaelbel (27/0), Robert Jonquet (52/0), Roger Marche (Cap) (57/0), Armand Penverne (36/2), André Lerond (14/0), Maryan Wisnieski (16/4), Yvon Douis (8/3), Just Fontaine (15/21), Léon Deladerrière (10/3), Jean Vincent (32/15). Trainer: Albert Batteux (31).
Goals: Jean Vincent (15), Just Fontaine (84).

251. 03.12.1958 **GREECE - FRANCE** **1-1(0-0)** 1st EC. 1st Round.
Stádio „Leoforos Alexandras", Athína; Referee: Vincenzo Orlandini (Italy); Attendance: 26,000
FRA: Claude Abbes (9/0), Raymond Kaelbel (28/0), Bruno Bollini (2/0), Roger Marche (Cap) (58/0), René Ferrier (1/0), André Lerond (15/0), Maryan Wisnieski (17/4), Roland Guillas (1/0), Stéphane Bruey (3/1), Stanislas Dombeck (1/0), Léon Deladerrière (11/3). Trainer: Albert Batteux (32).
Goal: Stéphane Bruey (71).

252. 01.03.1959 **FRANCE - BELGIUM** **2-2(1-1)**
Stade Olympique „Yves du Manoir", Colombes, Paris; Referee: John Kelly (England); Attendance: 42,206
FRA: Dominique Colonna (8/0), Raymond Kaelbel (29/0), Robert Jonquet (53/0), Roger Marche (Cap) (59/0), Jean-Jacques Marcel (34/1), André Lerond (16/0) [23.Joseph Tellechea (3/1)], Maryan Wisnieski (18/4), Roland Guillas (2/0), Henri Skiba (1/0), Édouard Stako (1/0), Jean Vincent (33/17). Trainer: Albert Batteux (33).
Goals: Jean Vincent (2, 68).

253. 11.10.1959 **BULGARIA - FRANCE** **1-0(0-0)**
Nationalen stadion "Vasil Levski", Sofia; Referee: Josef Stoll (Austria); Attendance: 45,000
FRA: Dominique Colonna (9/0), Raymond Kaelbel (30/0), Robert Jonquet (54/0), Roger Marche (Cap) (60/0), Armand Penverne (37/2), André Lerond (17/0), Pierre Grillet (5/0), Just Fontaine (16/21) [*sent off 89*], Raymond Kopa (32/17), Roger Piantoni (32/16) [27.Lucien Muller (1/0)], Jean Vincent (34/17). Trainer: Albert Batteux (34).

254. 11.11.1959 **FRANCE - PORTUGAL** **5-3(3-2)**
Stade Olympique „Yves du Manoir", Colombes, Paris; Referee: Kenneth Aston (England); Attendance: 48,111
FRA: Dominique Colonna (10/0) [62.Georges Lamia (1/0)], Jean Wendling (1/0), Robert Jonquet (55/0), Roger Marche (Cap) (61/0), Armand Penverne (38/2), René Ferrier (2/0), Pierre Grillet (6/1), Lucien Muller (2/1), Raymond Kopa (33/17), Just Fontaine (17/24), Jean Vincent (35/17). Trainer: Albert Batteux (35).
Goals: Just Fontaine (3), Pierre Grillet (11), Lucien Muller (22), Just Fontaine (54, 58).

255. 13.12.1959 **FRANCE - AUSTRIA** **5-2(3-1)** 1st EC. Quarter-Finals.
Stade Olympique „Yves du Manoir", Colombes, Paris; Referee: Martín Manuel Aseni (Spain); Attendance: 43,775
FRA: Georges Lamia (2/0), Jean Wendling (2/0), Robert Jonquet (56/0), Roger Marche (Cap) (62/0), Armand Penverne (39/2), René Ferrier (3/0), François Heutte (1/0), Lucien Muller (3/1), Raymond Kopa (34/17), Just Fontaine (18/27), Jean Vincent (36/19). Trainer: Albert Batteux (36).
Goals: Just Fontaine (6, 18), Jean Vincent (38), Just Fontaine (70), Jean Vincent (80).

256. 17.12.1959 **FRANCE - SPAIN** **4-3(3-1)**
Stade Parc des Princes, Paris; Referee: Reginald A. Leafe (England); Attendance: 38,622
FRA: François Remetter (26/0), Jean Wendling (3/0), Robert Jonquet (Cap) (57/0), Raymond Kaelbel (31/0) [23.Roger Marche (63/1)], Lucien Muller (4/2), René Ferrier (4/0), Roland Guillas (3/0), Yvon Douis (9/3) [52.Bernard Rahis (1/0)], Raymond Kopa (35/17), Just Fontaine (19/28), Jean Vincent (37/20). Trainer: Albert Batteux (37).
Goals: Lucien Muller (27), Just Fontaine (31), Jean Vincent (36), Roger Marche (61).

257. 28.02.1960 **BELGIUM - FRANCE** **1-0(1-0)**
Stade du Heysel, Bruxelles; Referee: Gottfried Dienst (Switzerland); Attendance: 56,257
FRA: Georges Lamia (3/0), Jean Wendling (4/0), Raymond Kaelbel (32/0), André Lerond (18/0), Lucien Muller (5/2), René Ferrier (5/0), Pierre Grillet (7/1), Roland Guillas (4/0), Raymond Kopa (Cap) (36/17), Roger Piantoni (33/16) [40.François Heutte (2/0)], Jean Vincent (38/20). Trainer: Albert Batteux (38).

258. 16.03.1960 **FRANCE - CHILE** **6-0(1-0)**
Stade Parc des Princes, Paris; Referee: Gérard Versyp (Belgium); Attendance: 36,094
FRA: Georges Lamia (4/0), Jean Wendling (5/0), Raymond Kaelbel (33/1), André Chorda (1/0), Georges Peyroche (1/0), René Ferrier (6/0), Pierre Grillet (8/2), Lucien Muller (6/3), François Heutte (3/0), Just Fontaine (20/30), Jean Vincent (Cap) (39/21). Trainer: Albert Batteux (39).
Goals: Raymond Kaelbel (10), Jean Vincent (51), Pierre Grillet (57), Just Fontaine (78, 80), Lucien Muller (82).

259. 27.03.1960 **AUSTRIA - FRANCE** **2-4(1-0)** 1st EC. Quarter-Finals.
Praterstadion, Wien; Referee: Leo Helge (Denmark); Attendance: 39,229
FRA: Georges Lamia (5/0), Jean Wendling (6/0), Raymond Kaelbel (34/1), Bruno Rodzik (1/0), Jean-Jacques Marcel (35/2), René Ferrier (7/0), Pierre Grillet (9/2), Lucien Muller (7/3), Raymond Kopa (Cap) (37/18), François Heutte (4/1), Bernard Rahis (2/1). Trainer: Albert Batteux (40).
Goals: Jean-Jacques Marcel (46), Bernard Rahis (59), François Heutte (77), Raymond Kopa (84 penalty).

260. 06.07.1960 **FRANCE - YUGOSLAVIA** **4-5(2-1)** 1st EC. Semi-Finals.
Stade Parc des Princes, Paris; Referee: Gaston Grandain (Belgium); Attendance: 26,370
FRA: Georges Lamia (6/0), Jean Wendling (7/0), Robert Herbin (1/0), Bruno Rodzik (2/0), Jean-Jacques Marcel (36/2), René Ferrier (8/0), François Heutte (5/3), Lucien Muller (8/3), Maryan Wisnieski (19/5), Michel Stievenard (1/0), Jean Vincent (Cap) (40/22). Trainer: Albert Batteux (41).
Goals: Jean Vincent (12), François Heutte (43), Maryan Wisnieski (52), François Heutte (62).

261. 09.07.1960 **FRANCE - CZECHOSLOVAKIA** **0-2(0-0)** 1st EC.Bronze Medal.
Stade Vélodrome, Marseille; Referee: Cesare Jonni (Italy); Attendance: 9,438
FRA: Jean Taillandier (1/0), Bruno Rodzik (3/0), Robert Jonquet (Cap) (58/0), André Chorda (2/0), Jean-Jacques Marcel (37/2), Robert Siatka (1/0), François Heutte (6/3), Yvon Douis (10/3), Maryan Wisnieski (20/5), Michel Stievenard (2/0), Jean Vincent (41/22). Trainer: Albert Batteux (42).

262. 25.09.1960 **FINLAND - FRANCE** **1-2(1-0)** 7th FIFA WC. Qualifiers
Olympiastadion, Helsinki; Referee: Johannes Malka (West Germany); Attendance: 15,572
FRA: Dominique Colonna (11/0), Jean Wendling (8/0), Bruno Rodzik (4/0), Henri Biancheri (1/0), Raymond Kaelbel (35/1), René Ferrier (9/0), Maryan Wisnieski (21/6), Joseph Ujlaki (18/10), François Heutte (7/3), Roland Guillas (5/0), Jean Vincent (Cap) (42/22). Trainer: Albert Batteux (43).
Goals: Maryan Wisnieski (63), Joseph Ujlaki (83).

263. 28.09.1960 **POLAND - FRANCE** **2-2(1-0)**
Stadion Dziesięciolecia, Warszawa; Referee: Zivota Vlajić (Yugoslavia); Attendance: 50,000
FRA: Jean Taillandier (2/0), Jean Wendling (9/0), Richard Tylinski (2/0), Bruno Rodzik (5/0), Henri Biancheri (2/0), René Ferrier (10/0), Yvon Goujon (1/0), Joseph Ujlaki (19/10), Maryan Wisnieski (22/7), Roland Guillas (6/1), Jean Vincent (Cap) (43/22). Trainer: Albert Batteux (44).
Goals: Roland Guillas (84), Maryan Wisnieski (89).

264. 12.10.1960 **SWITZERLAND - FRANCE** **6-2(2-1)**
„St. Jakob" Stadion, Basel; Referee: Cesare Jonni (Italy); Attendance: 45,000
FRA: Dominique Colonna (12/0), Jean Wendling (10/0), Richard Tylinski (3/0), Georges Peyroche (2/0), Jean-Jacques Marcel (38/2), René Ferrier (11/0), Julien Stopyra (1/0), Joseph Ujlaki (20/10), Maryan Wisnieski (23/7), Yvon Goujon (2/2), Jean Vincent (Cap) (44/22). Trainer: Albert Batteux (45).
Goals: Yvon Goujon (19, 87).

265. 30.10.1960 **SWEDEN - FRANCE** **1-0(1-0)**
Råsundastadion, Stockholm; Referee: Nikolai Latyshev (Soviet Union); Attendance: 34,050
FRA: Jean Taillandier (3/0), Jean Wendling (11/0), Guilhem Bieganski (5/0), Bruno Rodzik (6/0), Lucien Muller (9/3), Jean-Jacques Marcel (39/2), Maryan Wisnieski (24/7), Joseph Ujlaki (21/10), Raymond Kopa (Cap) (38/18), Roger Piantoni (34/16), Jean Vincent (45/22). Trainer: Albert Batteux (46).

266. 11.12.1960 **FRANCE - BULGARIA** **3-0(0-0)** 7th FIFA WC. Qualifiers
Stade Olympique „Yves du Manoir", Colombes, Paris; Referee: Pietro Bonetto (Italy); Attendance: 40,690
FRA: Pierre Bernard (1/0), Jean Wendling (12/0), Guilhem Bieganski (6/0), Jean-Jacques Marcel (Cap) (40/3), Bruno Rodzik (7/0), Yvon Douis (11/3), Guy Sénac (1/0), Roger Piantoni (35/16), Maryan Wisnieski (25/8), Just Fontaine (21/30), Lucien Cossou (1/1). Trainer: Albert Batteux (47).
Goals: Maryan Wisnieski (48), Jean-Jacques Marcel (58), Lucien Cossou (80).

267. 15.03.1961 **FRANCE - BELGIUM** **1-1(1-0)**
Stade Olympique „Yves du Manoir“, Colombes, Paris; Referee: John Kelly (England); Attendance: 36,072
FRA: Pierre Bernard (2/0), Jean Wendling (13/0), Guilhem Bieganski (7/0), Bruno Rodzik (8/0), Guy Sénac (2/0), Bruno Bollini (3/0), Maryan Wisnieski (26/8), Jean-Jacques Marcel (Cap) (41/3), Raymond Kopa (39/18), Roger Piantoni (36/17), Paul Sauvage (1/0). Trainer: Albert Batteux (48).
Goal: Roger Piantoni (3).

268. 02.04.1961 **SPAIN - FRANCE** **2-0(1-0)**
Estadio „Santiago Bernabéu“, Madrid; Referee: Giulio Campanati (Italy); Attendance: 75,000
FRA: Pierre Bernard (3/0) [46.Dominique Colonna (13/0)], Guilhem Bieganski (8/0), François Ludo (1/0), Bruno Rodzik (9/0), Lucien Muller (10/3), Jean-Jacques Marcel (42/3), Raymond Kopa (Cap) (40/18) [31.René Ferrier (12/0)], Roland Guillas (7/1), Serge Roy (1/0), Yvon Douis (12/3), Bernard Rahis (3/1). Trainer: Albert Batteux (49).

269. 28.09.1961 **FRANCE - FINLAND** **5-1(3-1)** 7th FIFA WC. Qualifiers
Stade Parc des Princes, Paris; Referee: Gottfried Dienst (Switzerland); Attendance: 17,013
FRA: Pierre Bernard (4/0), Jean Wendling (14/0), Guilhem Bieganski (9/0), Richard Boucher (2/0), Lucien Muller (11/3), André Lerond (19/0), Maryan Wisnieski (27/9), Jean-Jacques Marcel (Cap) (43/3), Ernest Schultz (1/1), Roger Piantoni (37/18), Jacques Faivre (1/2). Trainer: Albert Batteux (50).
Goals: Jacques Faivre (6), Maryan Wisnieski (12), Jacques Faivre (41), Roger Piantoni (79), Ernest Schultz (86).

270. 18.10.1961 **BELGIUM - FRANCE** **3-0(1-0)**
Stade du Heysel, Bruxelles; Referee: Kevin Howley (England); Attendance: 11,019
FRA: Pierre Bernard (5/0), Jean Wendling (15/0), André Lerond (20/0), Richard Boucher (3/0), Jean-Jacques Marcel (Cap) (44/3), Jean Vincent (46/22), Raymond Kopa (41/18), Khennane Mahi (1/0), Maryan Wisnieski (28/9), Guy Van Sam (1/0), Jacques Faivre (2/2). Trainer: Albert Batteux (51).

271. 12.11.1961 **BULGARIA - FRANCE** **1-0(0-0)** 7th FIFA WC. Qualifiers
Nationalen stadion “Vasil Levski”, Sofia; Referee: Milan Fencl (Czechoslovakia); Attendance: 55,000
FRA: Pierre Bernard (6/0), Jean Wendling (16/0), André Lerond (Cap) (21/0), Bruno Rodzik (10/0), Synakowski Maryan (1/0), René Ferrier (13/0), Roland Guillas (8/1), Lucien Muller (12/3), Khennane Mahi (2/0), Maxime Fulgenzi (1/0), Georges Peyroche (3/0). Trainer: Albert Batteux (52).

272. 10.12.1961 **FRANCE - SPAIN** **1-1(1-0)**
Stade Olympique „Yves du Manoir“, Colombes, Paris; Referee: John Kelly (England); Attendance: 46,496
FRA: Pierre Bernard (7/0), Jean Wendling (17/0), André Lerond (Cap) (22/0), Bruno Rodzik (11/0), Synakowski Maryan (2/0), René Ferrier (14/0), Maryan Wisnieski (29/9), Lucien Muller (13/3), Henri Skiba (2/0), François Heutte (8/4), Guy Van Sam (2/0). Trainer: Albert Batteux (53).
Goal: François Heutte (13).

273. 16.12.1961 **BULGARIA - FRANCE** **1-0(0-0)** 7th FIFA WC. Play-Offs
Stadio San Siro, Milano; Referee: Concetto Lo Bello (Italy); Attendance: 34,740
FRA: Pierre Bernard (8/0), Jean Wendling (18/0), André Lerond (Cap) (23/0), Bruno Rodzik (12/0), Synakowski Maryan (3/0), René Ferrier (15/0), Maryan Wisnieski (30/9), Lucien Muller (14/3), Henri Skiba (3/0), François Heutte (9/4), Guy Van Sam (3/0). Trainer: Albert Batteux (54).

274. 11.04.1962 **FRANCE - POLAND** **1-3(1-2)**
Stade Parc des Princes, Paris; Referee: Pietro Bonetto (Italy); Attendance: 19,698
FRA: Pierre Bernard (9/0), Jean Wendling (19/0), Alain Cornu (1/0), Bruno Rodzik (13/0), Robert Herbin (2/0), René Ferrier (16/0), Hector De Bourgoing (1/1), Casimir Koza (1/0) [35.Roland Guillas (9/1)], Raymond Kopa (Cap) (42/18), Szkudlapski Theo (1/0), Angel Rambert (1/0). Trainer: Albert Batteux (55).
Goal: Hector De Bourgoing (24).

275. 05.05.1962 **ITALY - FRANCE** **2-1(0-1)**
Stadio Comunale, Firenze; Referee: Josef Kandlbinder (West Germany); Attendance: 45,000
FRA: Bruno Ferrero (1/0), Jean Wendling (20/0), André Lerond (24/0), Bruno Rodzik (14/0), Synakowski Maryan (4/0), Jean-Claude Piumi (1/1), Raymond Kopa (Cap) (43/18), Yvon Goujon (3/2), Stéphane Bruey (4/1) [46.Michel Hidalgo (1/0)], Hector De Bourgoing (2/1), Laurent Robuschi (1/0). Trainer: Albert Batteux (56).
Goal: Jean-Claude Piumi (28).

276. 03.10.1962 **ENGLAND - FRANCE** **1-1(0-1)** 2nd EC. Group Stage.
Hillsborough Stadium, Sheffield; Referee: Carl-Waldemar Hansen (Denmark); Attendance: 35,380
FRA: Pierre Bernard (10/0), Jean Wendling (21/0), André Lerond (Cap) (25/0), André Chorda (3/0), Synakowski Maryan (5/0), René Ferrier (17/0), Laurent Robuschi (2/0), Joseph Bonnel (1/0), Raymond Kopa (44/18), Yvon Goujon (4/3), Paul Sauvage (2/0). Trainer: Henri Guérin (1).
Goal: Yvon Goujon (8).

277. 24.10.1962 **WEST GERMANY - FRANCE** **2-2(0-2)**
Neckarstadion, Stuttgart; Referee: Friedrich Seipelt (England); Attendance: 75,000
FRA: Georges Lamia (7/0), Jean Wendling (22/0), André Lerond (Cap) (26/0), Bruno Rodzik (15/0), Synakowski Maryan (6/0), René Ferrier (18/0), Laurent Robuschi (3/0), Joseph Bonnel (2/0), Yvon Goujon (5/4), Édouard Stako (2/1), Paul Sauvage (3/0). Trainer: Henri Guérin (2).
Goals: Édouard Stako (25), Yvon Goujon (32).

278. 11.11.1962 **FRANCE - HUNGARY** **2-3(1-2)**
Stade Olympique „Yves du Manoir“, Colombes, Paris; Referee: Juan Garay Gardeazábal (Spain); Attendance: 35,136
FRA: Pierre Bernard (11/0), Jean Wendling (23/0), André Lerond (Cap) (27/0), Bruno Rodzik (16/0), Synakowski Maryan (7/0), René Ferrier (19/0), Raymond Kopa (45/18), Joseph Bonnel (3/0), Yvon Goujon (6/4), Fleury Di Nallo (1/2), Paul Sauvage (4/0). Trainer: Henri Guérin (3).
Goals: Fleury Di Nallo (18, 75).

279. 09.01.1963 **SPAIN - FRANCE** **0-0**
Estadio Camp Nou, Barcelona; Referee: Jozef Casteleyn (Belgium); Attendance: 72,000
FRA: Pierre Bernard (12/0), Jean Wendling (24/0), André Lerond (Cap) (28/0), André Chorda (4/0), Synakowski Maryan (8/0), René Ferrier (20/0), Yvon Goujon (7/4), Joseph Bonnel (4/0), Yvon Douis (13/3), Serge Masnaghetti (1/0), Paul Sauvage (5/0). Trainer: Henri Guérin (4).

280. 27.02.1963 **FRANCE - ENGLAND** **5-2(3-0)** 2nd EC. Group Stage.
Stade Parc des Princes, Paris; Referee: Josef Kandlbinder (West Germany); Attendance: 23,986
FRA: Pierre Bernard (13/0), Jean Wendling (25/0), André Lerond (Cap) (29/0), Bruno Rodzik (17/0), Synakowski Maryan (9/0), Robert Herbin (3/0), Maryan Wisnieski (31/11), Joseph Bonnel (5/0), Yvon Goujon (8/4), Yvon Douis (14/4), Lucien Cossou (2/3). Trainer: Henri Guérin (5).
Goals: Maryan Wisnieski (3), Yvon Douis (32), Lucien Cossou (43), Maryan Wisnieski (75), Lucien Cossou (82).

281. 17.04.1963 **NETHERLANDS - FRANCE** **1-0(0-0)**
Stadion Feijenoord, Rotterdam; Referee: Johannes Malka (West Germany); Attendance: 41,000
FRA: Pierre Bernard (14/0), Jean Wendling (26/0), André Lerond (Cap) (30/0), Bruno Rodzik (18/0), Synakowski Maryan (10/0), Robert Herbin (4/0), Maryan Wisnieski (32/11), Joseph Bonnel (6/0), Lucien Cossou (3/3), Yvon Douis (15/4), Paul Chillan (1/0). Trainer: Henri Guérin (6).

282. 28.04.1963 **FRANCE - BRAZIL** **2-3(0-1)**
Stade Olympique „Yves du Manoir“, Colombes, Paris; Referee: Concetto Lo Bello (Italy); Attendance: 50,000
FRA: Georges Carnus (1/0), Bruno Rodzik (19/0), André Lerond (Cap) (31/0), André Chorda (5/0), Synakowski Maryan (11/0), Robert Herbin (5/0), Maryan Wisnieski (33/11), Joseph Bonnel (7/0), Yvon Douis (16/4), Fleury Di Nallo (2/3), Lucien Cossou (4/3) [46.Paul Chillan (2/0)]. Trainer: Henri Guérin (7).
Goals: Maryan Wisnieski (70), Fleury Di Nallo (82).

283. 29.09.1963 **BULGARIA - FRANCE** **1-0(1-0)** 2nd EC.2nd Round.
Nationalen stadion "Vasil Levski", Sofia; Referee: Faruk Talu (Turkey); Attendance: 50,000
FRA: Pierre Bernard (15/0), Marcel Adamczyk (1/0), Pierre Michelin (1/0), Marcel Artelesa (1/0), André Chorda (6/0), Joseph Bonnel (8/0), Szkudlapski Theo (2/0), Laurent Robuschi (4/0), Yvon Douis (Cap) (17/4), Lucien Cossou (5/3), Jean-Louis Buron (1/0). Trainer: Henri Guérin (8).

284. 26.10.1963 **FRANCE - BULGARIA** **3-1(1-0)** 2nd EC.2nd Round.
Stade Parc des Princes, Paris; Referee: José María Ortiz de Mendibil Monasterio (Spain); Attendance: 32,223
FRA: Pierre Bernard (16/0), Bruno Rodzik (20/0), Pierre Michelin (2/0), Marcel Artelesa (2/0), André Chorda (7/0), Robert Herbin (6/1), René Ferrier (21/0), Georges Lech (1/0), Yvon Goujon (9/6), Yvon Douis (Cap) (18/4), Jean-Louis Buron (2/0). Trainer: Henri Guérin (9).
Goals: Yvon Goujon (45), Robert Herbin (78), Yvon Goujon (81).

285. 11.11.1963 **FRANCE - SWITZERLAND** **2-2(2-0)**
Stade Parc des Princes, Paris; Referee: Arthur Holland (England); Attendance: 27,350
FRA: Pierre Bernard (17/0), Bruno Rodzik (21/0), Pierre Michelin (3/0), Marcel Artelesa (3/0), André Chorda (8/0), Jean-Claude Piumi (2/1), Robert Herbin (7/1), Georges Lech (2/1), Yvon Goujon (10/6), Yvon Douis (Cap) (19/4), Jean-Louis Buron (3/1). Trainer: Henri Guérin (10).
Goals: Jean-Louis Buron (18), Georges Lech (31).

286. 25.12.1963 **FRANCE - BELGIUM** **1-2(1-2)**
Stade Parc des Princes, Paris; Referee: Josef Stoll (Austria); Attendance: 12,649
FRA: Pierre Bernard (Cap) (18/0), Georges Casolari (1/0), Pierre Michelin (4/0), Marcel Artelesa (4/0), André Chorda (9/0), Robert Herbin (8/1), Lucien Muller (15/3), Georges Lech (3/1), Yvon Goujon (11/6), Serge Masnaghetti (2/1), Jean-Louis Buron (4/1). Trainer: Henri Guérin (11).
Goal: Serge Masnaghetti (33).

287. 25.04.1964 **FRANCE - HUNGARY** **1-3(0-2)** 2nd EC. Quarter-Finals.
Stade Olympique „Yves du Manoir“, Colombes, Paris; Referee: Cesare Jonni (Italy); Attendance: 35,274
FRA: Pierre Bernard (Cap) (19/0), Georges Casolari (2/0), Pierre Michelin (5/0), Marcel Artelesa (5/0), André Chorda (10/0), Joseph Bonnel (9/0), Lucien Muller (16/3), Georges Lech (4/1), Nestor Combin (1/0), Robert Herbin (9/1), Lucien Cossou (6/4). Trainer: Henri Guérin (12).
Goal: Lucien Cossou (73).

288. 23.05.1964 **HUNGARY - FRANCE** **2-1(1-1)** 2nd EC. Quarter-Finals.
Népstadion, Budapest; Referee: Concetto Lo Bello (Italy); Attendance: 70,200
FRA: Pierre Bernard (Cap) (20/0), Georges Casolari (3/0), Daniel Charles-Alfred (1/0), André Chorda (11/0), Marcel Artelesa (6/0), Édouard Stako (3/1), Georges Lech (5/1), Fleury Di Nallo (3/3), Nestor Combin (2/1), Joseph Bonnel (10/0), Angel Rambert (2/0). Trainer: Henri Guérin (13).
Goal: Nestor Combin (2).

289. 04.10.1964 **LUXEMBOURG - FRANCE** **0-2(0-1)** 8th FIFA WC. Qualifiers
Stade Municipal, Luxembourg; Referee: Vital Loraux (Belgium); Attendance: 17,036
FRA: Marcel Aubour (1/0), Jean Djorkaeff (1/0), Marcel Artelesa (7/1), Daniel Charles-Alfred (2/0), André Chorda (12/0), Robert Herbin (10/1), René Ferrier (Cap) (22/0), Georges Lech (6/1), André Guy (1/1), Nestor Combin (3/1), Angel Rambert (3/0). Trainer: Henri Guérin (14).
Goals: André Guy (17), Marcel Artelesa (80).

290. 11.11.1964 **FRANCE - NORWAY** **1-0(0-0)** 8th FIFA WC. Qualifiers
Stade Parc des Princes, Paris; Referee: John Adair (Northern Ireland); Attendance: 33,517
FRA: Marcel Aubour (2/0), Jean Djorkaeff (2/0), Marcel Artelesa (8/1), Daniel Charles-Alfred (3/0), André Chorda (13/0), Joseph Bonnel (11/0), René Ferrier (Cap) (23/0), Georges Lech (7/1), André Guy (2/1), Robert Herbin (11/1), Angel Rambert (4/1). Trainer: Henri Guérin (15).
Goal: Angel Rambert (17).

291. 02.12.1964 **BELGIUM - FRANCE** **3-0(1-0)**
Stade du Heysel, Bruxelles; Referee: Rudolf Kreitlein (West Germany); Attendance: 5,917
FRA: Marcel Aubour (3/0), Bernard Bosquier (1/0), Marcel Artelesa (9/1), Daniel Charles-Alfred (4/0), André Chorda (14/0), Joseph Bonnel (12/0), René Ferrier (Cap) (24/0), Georges Lech (8/1), André Guy (3/1), Edmond Baraffe (1/0), Angel Rambert (5/1). Trainer: Henri Guérin (16).

292. 24.03.1965 **FRANCE - AUSTRIA** **1-2(1-2)**
Stade Parc des Princes, Paris; Referee: Franz Geluck (Belgium); Attendance: 24,206
FRA: Pierre Bernard (Cap) (21/0) [46.Marcel Aubour (4/0)], Jean Djorkaeff (3/0), Denis Devaux (1/0), Robert Péri (1/0), Bernard Bosquier (2/0), Joseph Bonnel (13/0), Marcel Loncle (1/0), Georges Lech (9/1), Jacques Simon (1/0), Daniel Rodighiero (1/0), Gérard Hausser (1/1). Trainer: Henri Guérin (17).
Goal: Gérard Hausser (28).

293. 18.04.1965 **YUGOSLAVIA - FRANCE** **1-0(0-0)** 8th FIFA WC. Qualifiers
Stadion Crvena zvezda, Beograd; Referee: Dimitris Vlahoyannis (Austria); Attendance: 50,000
FRA: Marcel Aubour (5/0), Jean Djorkaeff (4/0), Robert Herbin (Cap) (12/1), Marcel Artelesa (10/1), Bernard Bosquier (3/0), Joseph Bonnel (14/0), Marcel Loncle (2/0), Georges Lech (10/1), Jacques Simon (2/0), Paul Sauvage (6/0), Gérard Hausser (2/1). Trainer: Henri Guérin (18).

294. 03.06.1965 **FRANCE - ARGENTINA** **0-0**
Stade Parc des Princes, Paris; Referee: John Keith Taylor (England); Attendance: 11,931
FRA: Marcel Aubour (6/0), Jean Djorkaeff (5/0), Robert Herbin (Cap) (13/1), Marcel Artelesa (11/1), Louis Cardiet (1/0), Yves Herbet (1/0), Synakowski Maryan (12/0), Georges Lech (11/1), Daniel Rodighiero (2/0), Jacques Simon (3/0), Gérard Hausser (3/1). Trainer: Henri Guérin (19).

295. 15.09.1965 **NORWAY - FRANCE** **0-1(0-1)** 8th FIFA WC. Qualifiers
Ullevaal Stadion, Oslo; Referee: Hugh Phillips (Scotland); Attendance: 31,234
FRA: Marcel Aubour (7/0), Louis Cardiet (2/0), Bernard Bosquier (4/0), Marcel Artelesa (12/1), André Chorda (15/0), Robert Herbin (Cap) (14/1), Synakowski Maryan (13/0), Yves Herbet (2/0), Nestor Combin (4/2), Yvon Douis (20/4), Gérard Hausser (4/1). Trainer: Henri Guérin (20).
Goal: Nestor Combin (22).

296. 09.10.1965 **FRANCE - YUGOSLAVIA** **1-0(0-0)** 8th FIFA WC. Qualifiers
Stade Parc des Princes, Paris; Referee: Frede Hansen (Denmark); Attendance: 36,546
FRA: Marcel Aubour (8/0), Louis Cardiet (3/0), Bernard Bosquier (5/0), Robert Budzinski (1/0), André Chorda (16/0), Joseph Bonnel (15/0), Marcel Artelesa (Cap) (13/1), Yves Herbet (3/0), Nestor Combin (5/2), Philippe Gondet (1/1), Gérard Hausser (5/1). Trainer: Henri Guérin (21).
Goal: Philippe Gondet (77).

297. 06.11.1965 **FRANCE - LUXEMBOURG** **4-1(4-0)** 8th FIFA WC. Qualifiers
Stade Vélodrome, Marseille; Referee: Daniel Zariquiegui (Spain); Attendance: 30,080
FRA: Marcel Aubour (9/0), Louis Cardiet (4/0), Bernard Bosquier (6/0), Robert Budzinski (2/0), André Chorda (17/0), Joseph Bonnel (16/0), Marcel Artelesa (Cap) (14/1), Yves Herbet (4/0), Nestor Combin (6/4), Philippe Gondet (2/3), Gérard Hausser (6/1). Trainer: Henri Guérin (22).
Goals: Philippe Gondet (8), Nestor Combin (11), Philippe Gondet (27), Nestor Combin (38).

298. 19.03.1966 **FRANCE - ITALY** **0-0**
Stade Parc des Princes, Paris; Referee: Joseph Hannet (Belgium); Attendance: 31,795
FRA: Marcel Aubour (10/0), Bernard Bosquier (7/0), Marcel Artelesa (Cap) (15/1), Robert Budzinski (3/0), André Chorda (18/0), Robert Herbin (15/1), Robert Péri (2/0), Edmond Baraffe (2/0), Philippe Gondet (3/3), Jacques Simon (4/0), Gérard Hausser (7/1). Trainer: Henri Guérin (23).

299. 20.04.1966 **FRANCE - BELGIUM** **0-3(0-1)**
Stade Parc des Princes, Paris; Referee: Daniel Zariquiegui (Spain); Attendance: 17,000
FRA: Marcel Aubour (11/0), Jean Djorkaeff (6/0), Bernard Bosquier (8/0), Marcel Artelesa (Cap) (16/1), André Chorda (19/0), Joseph Bonnel (17/0), Robert Herbin (16/1), Edmond Baraffe (3/0), Philippe Gondet (4/3), Jacques Simon (5/0), Gérard Hausser (8/1) [46.Bernard Blanchet (1/0)]. Trainer: Henri Guérin (24).

300. 06.06.1966 **SOVIET UNION - FRANCE** **3-3(2-1)**
Lenin Stadium, Moskva; Referee: Bertil Lööw (Sweden); Attendance: 103,000
FRA: Daniel Éon (1/0), Robert Budzinski (4/0), Jean Djorkaeff (7/0), Marcel Artelesa (Cap) (17/1), Bernard Bosquier (9/0), André Chorda (20/0), Joseph Bonnel (18/1), Robert Herbin (17/1), Bernard Blanchet (2/1), Philippe Gondet (5/4), Gérard Hausser (9/1). Trainer: Henri Guérin (25).
Goals: Bernard Blanchet (19), Philippe Gondet (21), Joseph Bonnel (78).

301. 13.07.1966 **FRANCE - MEXICO** **1-1(0-0)** 8th FIFA WC. Group Stage.
Wembley Stadium, London (England); Referee: Menachem Ashkenazi (Israel); Attendance: 69,237
FRA: Marcel Aubour (12/0), Jean Djorkaeff (8/0), Marcel Artelesa (Cap) (18/1), Robert Budzinski (5/0), Gabriel De Michèle (1/0), Joseph Bonnel (19/1), Bernard Bosquier (10/0), Nestor Combin (7/4), Robert Herbin (18/1), Philippe Gondet (6/4), Gérard Hausser (10/2). Trainer: Henri Guérin (26).
Goal: Gérard Hausser (61).

302. 15.07.1966 **FRANCE - URUGUAY** **1-2(1-2)** 8th FIFA WC. Group Stage.
White City Stadium, London (England); Referee: Dr. Karol Galba (Czechoslovakia); Attendance: 45,662
FRA: Marcel Aubour (13/0), Jean Djorkaeff (9/0), Marcel Artelesa (Cap) (19/1), Robert Budzinski (6/0), Bernard Bosquier (11/0), Joseph Bonnel (20/1), Jacques Simon (6/0), Yves Herbet (5/0), Hector De Bourgoing (3/2), Philippe Gondet (7/4), Gérard Hausser (11/2). Trainer: Henri Guérin (27).
Goal: Hector De Bourgoing (16 penalty).

303. 20.07.1966 **ENGLAND - FRANCE** **2-0(1-0)** 8th FIFA WC. Group Stage.
Wembley Stadium, London; Referee: Arturo Maximo Yamasaki (Peru); Attendance: 98,270
FRA: Marcel Aubour (14/0), Jean Djorkaeff (10/0), Marcel Artelesa (Cap) (20/1), Robert Budzinski (7/0), Bernard Bosquier (12/0), Joseph Bonnel (21/1), Robert Herbin (19/1), Jacques Simon (7/0),Yves Herbet (6/0), Philippe Gondet (8/4), Gérard Hausser (12/2). Trainer: Henri Guérin (28).

304. 28.09.1966 **HUNGARY - FRANCE** **4-2(1-1)**
Népstadion, Budapest; Referee: Dimitris Vlahoyannis (Austria); Attendance: 25,000
FRA: Georges Carnus (2/0), Jean Djorkaeff (11/0), Bernard Bosquier (13/0), Robert Budzinski (Cap) (8/0), André Chorda (21/0), Jean-Claude Suaudeau (1/0), Jacques Simon (8/0) [82.Claude Robin (1/0)], Georges Lech (12/1), Philippe Gondet (9/5), Hervé Revelli (1/1), Gérard Hausser (13/2). Trainer: Jean Arribas – Jean Snella (1).
Goals: Philippe Gondet (26), Hervé Revelli (58).

305. 22.10.1966 **FRANCE - POLAND** **2-1(1-0)** 3rd EC. Qualifiers
Stade Parc des Princes, Paris; Referee: Gerhard Schulenburg (West Germany); Attendance: 23,524
FRA: Georges Carnus (3/0), Jean Djorkaeff (12/0), Claude Robin (2/0), Robert Budzinski (Cap) (9/0), André Chorda (22/0), Jean-Claude Suaudeau (2/0), Jacques Simon (9/0), Yves Herbet (7/0), Georges Lech (13/2), Fleury Di Nallo (4/4), Paul Courtin (1/0). Trainer: Jean Arribas – Jean Snella (2).
Goals: Georges Lech (26), Fleury Di Nallo (85).

306. 11.11.1966 **BELGIUM - FRANCE** **2-1(0-0)** 3rd EC. Qualifiers
Stade du Heysel, Bruxelles; Referee: John Keith Taylor (England); Attendance: 43,404
FRA: Georges Carnus (4/0), Jean Djorkaeff (13/0), Claude Robin (3/0), Robert Budzinski (Cap) (10/0), André Chorda (23/0), Jacques Simon (10/0), Jean-Claude Suaudeau (3/0), Bernard Blanchet (3/1), Hervé Revelli (2/1), Georges Lech (14/3), Gérard Hausser (14/2). Trainer: Jean Arribas – Jean Snella (3).
Goal: Georges Lech (67).

307. 26.11.1966 **LUXEMBOURG - FRANCE** **0-3(0-3)** 3rd EC. Qualifiers
Stade Municipal, Luxembourg; Referee: Laurens van Ravens (Netherlands); Attendance: 3,465
FRA: Georges Carnus (5/0), Jean Djorkaeff (14/0), Marcel Artelesa (Cap) (21/1), Bernard Bosquier (14/0), André Chorda (24/0), Joseph Bonnel (22/1), Michel Watteau (1/0), Yves Herbet (8/1), Hervé Revelli (3/2), Georges Lech (15/4), Laurent Robuschi (5/0). Trainer: Jean Arribas – Jean Snella (4).
Goals: Yves Herbet (8), Hervé Revelli (40), Georges Lech (41).

308. 22.03.1967 **FRANCE - ROMANIA** **1-2(0-1)**
Stade Parc des Princes, Paris; Referee: Günter Baumgärtel (West Germany); Attendance: 23,769
FRA: Daniel Éon (Cap) (2/0) [46.Georges Carnus (6/0)], Jean-Claude Lavaud (1/0), Jean-Claude Piumi (3/1), Louis Provelli (1/0) [20.Robert Budzinski (11/0)], Louis Cardiet (5/0), Jean-Pierre Dogliani (1/1), Jean-Claude Suaudeau (4/0) [65.Joseph Bonnel (23/1)], Bernard Blanchet (4/1), Georges Lech (16/4), Philippe Gondet (10/5), Charly Loubet (1/0). Trainer: Just Fontaine (1).
Goal: Jean-Pierre Dogliani (88).

309. 03.06.1967 **FRANCE - SOVIET UNION** **2-4(2-1)**
Stade Parc des Princes, Paris; Referee: Decio Bentes de Freitas (Portugal); Attendance: 24,778
FRA: Daniel Éon (Cap) (3/0), Gabriel De Michèle (2/0), Gilbert Le Chenadec (1/0), Jean-Claude Piumi (4/1), Louis Cardiet (6/0), Jacques Simon (11/1), Jean Deloffre (1/0), Bernard Blanchet (5/1), André Guy (4/1), Philippe Gondet (11/6) [46.Joseph Bonnel (24/1)], Charly Loubet (2/0). Trainer: Just Fontaine (2).
Goals: Philippe Gondet (11), Jacques Simon (45).

310. 17.09.1967 **POLAND - FRANCE** **1-4(1-2)** 3rd EC. Qualifiers
Stadion Dziesięciolecia, Warszawa; Referee: Ferdinand Marschall (Austria); Attendance: 51,010
FRA: Marcel Aubour (15/0), Jean Djorkaeff (15/0), Roland Mitoraj (1/0), Bernard Bosquier (15/0), Jean Baeza (1/0), Robert Herbin (Cap) (20/2), Henri Michel (1/0), Yves Herbet (9/1), André Guy (5/2), Fleury Di Nallo (5/6), Charly Loubet (3/0). Trainer: Louis Dugauguez (1).
Goals: Robert Herbin (13), Fleury Di Nallo (33), André Guy (63), Fleury Di Nallo (85).

311. 27.09.1967 **WEST GERMANY - FRANCE** **5-1(1-0)**
Olympiastadion, West-Berlin; Referee: Fabio Monti (Italy); Attendance: 85,000
FRA: Marcel Aubour (16/0), Jean Djorkaeff (16/0), Claude Quittet (1/0), Bernard Bosquier (Cap) (16/1), Jean Baeza (2/0), Gilbert Gress (1/0), Robert Péri (3/0) [*sent off 42*], Jacques Simon (12/1) [69.Claude Robin (4/0)], Philippe Gondet (12/6), Fleury Di Nallo (6/6), Charly Loubet (4/0). Trainer: Louis Dugauguez (2).
Goal: Bernard Bosquier (83).

312. 28.10.1967 **FRANCE - BELGIUM** **1-1(0-1)** 3rd EC. Qualifiers
Stade „Marcel Saupin", Nantes; Referee: Francesco Francescon (Italy); Attendance: 14,591
FRA: Marcel Aubour (17/0), Jean Djorkaeff (17/0), Bernard Bosquier (17/1), Claude Quittet (2/0), Jean Baeza (3/0), Yves Herbet (10/1), Henri Michel (2/0), Robert Herbin (Cap) (21/3), Fleury Di Nallo (7/6), Hervé Revelli (4/2), Charly Loubet (5/0). Trainer: Louis Dugauguez (3).
Goal: Robert Herbin (84).

313. 23.12.1967 **FRANCE - LUXEMBOURG** **3-1(1-0)** 3rd EC. Qualifiers
Stade Parc des Princes, Paris; Referee: Anibal Da Silva Oliveira (Portugal); Attendance: 7,320
FRA: Marcel Aubour (18/0), Jean Djorkaeff (18/0), Bernard Bosquier (Cap) (18/1), Claude Quittet (3/0), Jean Baeza (4/0), Richard Krawczyk (1/0), Henri Michel (3/0), Charly Loubet (6/3), Didier Couécou (1/0), Robert Szczepaniak (1/0), Georges Bereta (1/0). Trainer: Louis Dugauguez (4).
Goals: Charly Loubet (42, 47, 53).

314. 06.04.1968 **FRANCE - YUGOSLAVIA** **1-1(0-0)** 3rd EC. Quarter-Finals.
Stade Vélodrome, Marseille; Referee: Erwin Vetter (East Germany); Attendance: 35,423
FRA: Marcel Aubour (19/0), Jean Djorkaeff (19/0), Claude Quittet (4/0), Bernard Bosquier (Cap) (19/1), Jean Baeza (5/0), Robert Herbin (22/3), Jacques Simon (13/1), Charly Loubet (7/3), Nestor Combin (8/4), Fleury Di Nallo (8/7), Georges Bereta (2/0). Trainer: Louis Dugauguez (5).
Goal: Fleury Di Nallo (78).

315. 24.04.1968 **YUGOSLAVIA - FRANCE** **5-1(4-1)** 3rd EC. Quarter-Finals.
Stadion Crvena zvezda, Beograd; Referee: Paul Schiller (Austria); Attendance: 47,747
FRA: Marcel Aubour (20/0), Vincent Estève (1/0), Claude Quittet (5/0), Bernard Bosquier (Cap) (20/1), Jean Baeza (6/0), Yves Herbet (11/1), Jean Djorkaeff (20/0), Robert Szczepaniak (2/0), André Guy (6/2), Fleury Di Nallo (9/8), Charly Loubet (8/3). Trainer: Louis Dugauguez (6).
Goal: Fleury Di Nallo (33).

316. 25.09.1968 **FRANCE - WEST GERMANY** **1-1(0-0)**
Stade Vélodrome, Marseille; Referee: José María Ortiz de Mendibil Monasterio (Spain); Attendance: 22,355
FRA: Georges Carnus (7/0), Jean Djorkaeff (21/0), Roland Mitoraj (2/0), Bernard Bosquier (Cap) (21/2), Jean Baeza (7/0) [67.Roger Lemerre (1/0)], Aimé Jacquet (1/0), André Betta (1/0), Bernard Blanchet (6/1) [34.Charly Loubet (9/3)], Hervé Revelli (5/2), Robert Szczepaniak (3/0), Georges Bereta (3/0). Trainer: Louis Dugauguez (7).
Goal: Bernard Bosquier (72).

317. 17.10.1968 **FRANCE - SPAIN** **1-3(1-0)**
Stade de Gerland, Lyon; Referee: Aurelio Angonese (Italy); Attendance: 35,000
FRA: Georges Carnus (8/0), Jean Djorkaeff (22/0), Roland Mitoraj (3/0), Bernard Bosquier (Cap) (22/2), Jean Baeza (8/0), Aimé Jacquet (2/0), Robert Szczepaniak (4/0) [46.Jacques Simon (14/1)], Robert Herbin (23/3), Bernard Blanchet (7/2), André Guy (7/2), Georges Bereta (4/0). Trainer: Louis Dugauguez (8).
Goal: Bernard Blanchet (22).

318. 06.11.1968 **FRANCE - NORWAY** **0-1(0-0)** 9th FIFA WC. Qualifiers
Stade de la Meinau, Strasbourg; Referee: Francesco Francescon (Italy); Attendance: 18,319
FRA: Georges Carnus (9/0), Roger Lemerre (2/0), Claude Quittet (6/0), Bernard Bosquier (Cap) (23/2), Jean Djorkaeff (23/0), Gilbert Gress (2/0) [73.Charly Loubet (10/3)], Henri Michel (4/0), Robert Szczepaniak (5/0) [46.André Betta (2/0)], Bernard Blanchet (8/2), André Guy (8/2), Georges Bereta (5/0). Trainer: Louis Dugauguez (9).

319. 12.03.1969 **ENGLAND - FRANCE** **5-0(1-0)**
Wembley Stadium, London; Referee: István Zsolt (Hungary); Attendance: 85,000
FRA: Georges Carnus (10/0), Jean Djorkaeff (24/0), Bernard Bosquier (Cap) (24/2), Roger Lemerre (3/0), Jean-Paul Rostagni (1/0), Joseph Bonnel (25/1), Jacques Simon (15/1), Henri Michel (5/0), Yves Herbet (12/1), Charly Loubet (11/3), Georges Bereta (6/0). Trainer: Georges Boulogne (1).

320. 30.04.1969 **FRANCE - ROMANIA** **1-0(0-0)**
Stade Parc des Princes, Paris; Referee: Bruno De Marchi (Italy); Attendance: 18,218
FRA: Yves Chauveau (1/0), Jean Djorkaeff (Cap) (25/0), Jacques Novi (1/0), Roger Lemerre (4/0), Jean-Paul Rostagni (2/0), Henri Michel (6/1), José Broissart (1/0), Charly Loubet (12/3), Hervé Revelli (6/2), Daniel Horlaville (1/0) [46.Georges Bereta (7/0)], Jean-Claude Bras (1/0). Trainer: Georges Boulogne (2).
Goal: Henri Michel (80).

321. 10.09.1969 **NORWAY - FRANCE** **1-3(0-1)** 9th FIFA WC. Qualifiers
Ullevaal Stadion, Oslo; Referee: Laurens van Ravens (Netherlands); Attendance: 22,445
FRA: Georges Carnus (11/0), Jean Djorkaeff (Cap) (26/0), Jacques Novi (2/0), Bernard Bosquier (25/2), Jean-Paul Rostagni (3/0), Henri Michel (7/1), José Broissart (2/0), Charly Loubet (13/3), Hervé Revelli (7/5), Serge Chiesa (1/0) [73.Jean-Michel Larqué (1/0)], Jean-Claude Bras (2/0). Trainer: Georges Boulogne (3).
Goals: Hervé Revelli (9, 48, 77).

322. 15.10.1969 **SWEDEN - FRANCE** **2-0(1-0)** 9th FIFA WC. Qualifiers
Råsundastadion, Stockholm; Referee: Rudolf Glöckner (East Germany); Attendance: 51,954
FRA: Georges Carnus (12/0), Jean Djorkaeff (Cap) (27/0), Jacques Novi (3/0), Bernard Bosquier (26/2), Jean-Paul Rostagni (4/0), José Broissart (3/0), Henri Michel (8/1), Charly Loubet (14/3), Serge Chiesa (2/0), Hervé Revelli (8/5), Georges Bereta (8/0). Trainer: Georges Boulogne (4).

323. 01.11.1969 **FRANCE - SWEDEN** **3-0(3-0)** 9th FIFA WC. Qualifiers
Stade Parc des Princes, Paris; Referee: David Smith (England); Attendance: 17,916
FRA: Georges Carnus (13/0), Jean Djorkaeff (Cap) (28/1), Jacques Novi (4/0), Bernard Bosquier (27/2), Jean-Paul Rostagni (5/0), Henri Michel (9/1), José Broissart (4/0), Jean-Claude Bras (3/2), Charly Loubet (15/3), Georges Lech (17/4), Georges Bereta (9/0). Trainer: Georges Boulogne (5).
Goals: Jean-Claude Bras (39), Jean Djorkaeff (41 penalty), Jean-Claude Bras (43).

324. 08.04.1970 **FRANCE - BULGARIA** **1-1(1-1)**
Stade „Robert Diochon“, Rouen; Referee: Joseph Hannet (Belgium); Attendance: 22,000
FRA: Georges Carnus (14/0), Jean Djorkaeff (Cap) (29/1), Jacques Novi (5/0), Bernard Bosquier (28/2), Jean-Paul Rostagni (6/0), Henri Michel (10/2), José Broissart (5/0) [60.Jean-Noël Huck (1/0)], Jean-Claude Bras (4/2), Hervé Revelli (9/5), Charly Loubet (16/3), Georges Bereta (10/0) [65.Serge Chiesa (3/0)]. Trainer: Georges Boulogne (6).
Goal: Henri Michel (38).

325. 28.04.1970 **FRANCE - ROMANIA** **2-0(2-0)**
Stade „Auguste Delaune“, Reims; Referee: Dittmar Hubert (Switzerland); Attendance: 10,929
FRA: Georges Carnus (15/0), Jean Djorkaeff (Cap) (30/2), Jacques Novi (6/0), Bernard Bosquier (29/2), Jean-Paul Rostagni (7/0), Jean-Claude Bras (5/2), Henri Michel (11/2), Jean-Noël Huck (2/0), Hervé Revelli (10/5), Charly Loubet (17/4), Georges Bereta (11/0). Trainer: Georges Boulogne (7).
Goals: Charly Loubet (10), Jean Djorkaeff (40 penalty).

326. 03.05.1970 **FRANCE - SWITZERLAND** **2-1(1-0)**
„St. Jakob“ Stadion, Basel; Referee: Paul Schiller (Austria); Attendance: 24,500
FRA: Georges Carnus (16/0), Jean Djorkaeff (Cap) (31/2), Jacques Novi (7/0), Bernard Bosquier (30/2), Jean-Paul Rostagni (8/0), Henri Michel (12/2), Michel Mézy (1/0), Jean-Claude Bras (6/2) [48.Georges Lech (18/4)], Hervé Revelli (11/6), Charly Loubet (18/4) [70.Serge Chiesa (4/0); 88.Bernard Blanchet (9/2)], Georges Bereta (12/0). Trainer: Georges Boulogne (8).
Goal: Hervé Revelli (79).

327. 05.09.1970 **FRANCE - CZECHOSLOVAKIA** **3-0(3-0)**
Stade „Léo Lagrange“, Nice; Referee: Rudolf Scheurer (Switzerland); Attendance: 13,418
FRA: Georges Carnus (17/0), Jean Djorkaeff (Cap) (32/2), Jacques Novi (8/0), Bernard Bosquier (31/3), Jean-Paul Rostagni (9/0), Yves Herbet (13/1), Henri Michel (13/2), Michel Mézy (2/0), Philippe Gondet (13/7), Charly Loubet (19/5) [61.Bernard Blanchet (10/2)], Georges Bereta (13/0). Trainer: Georges Boulogne (9).
Goals: Philippe Gondet (8), Charly Loubet (13), Bernard Bosquier (42).

328. 07.10.1970 **AUSTRIA - FRANCE** **1-0(0-0)**
Praterstadion, Wien; Referee: Ferdinand Biwersi (West Germany); Attendance: 25,000
FRA: Georges Carnus (18/0), Jean Djorkaeff (Cap) (33/2), Jacques Novi (9/0), Bernard Bosquier (32/3), Jean-Paul Rostagni (10/0), Yves Herbet (14/1) [78.Jean-Michel Larqué (2/0)], Henri Michel (14/2), Michel Mézy (3/0), Philippe Gondet (14/7) [78.Louis Floch (1/0)], Charly Loubet (20/5) [46.Hervé Revelli (12/6)], Georges Bereta (14/0). Trainer: Georges Boulogne (10).

329. 11.11.1970 **FRANCE - NORWAY** **3-1(1-0)** 4th EC. Qualifiers
Stade de Gerland, Lyon; Referee: Antonio Saldanha Ribeiro (Portugal); Attendance: 10,357
FRA: Georges Carnus (19/0), Jean Djorkaeff (Cap) (34/2), Jacques Novi (10/0), Bernard Bosquier (33/3), Jean-Paul Rostagni (11/0), Henri Michel (15/2), Jean-Noël Huck (3/0), Louis Floch (2/1), Georges Lech (19/5), Charly Loubet (21/5), Michel Mézy (4/1). Trainer: Georges Boulogne (11).
Goals: Louis Floch (30), Georges Lech (55), Michel Mézy (63).

330. 15.11.1970 **BELGIUM - FRANCE** **1-2(0-0)**
Stade du Heysel, Bruxelles; Referee: Kurt Tschenscher (West Germany); Attendance: 19,937
FRA: Georges Carnus (20/0), Roger Lemerre (5/0) [*sent off 79*], Bernard Bosquier (34/3), Jacques Novi (11/0), Jean Djorkaeff (Cap) (35/2), Henri Michel (16/2), Jean-Noël Huck (4/0), Louis Floch (3/1), Marc Molitor (1/2), Georges Lech (20/5), Robert Rico (1/0). Trainer: Georges Boulogne (12).
Goals: Marc Molitor (50, 77).

331. 08.01.1971 **ARGENTINA - FRANCE** **3-4(0-1)**
Estadio „Alberto Jacinto Armando“ [La Bombonera], Buenos Aires; Referee: Barreiro (Argentina); Attendance: 4,500
FRA: Georges Carnus (21/0), Jean Djorkaeff (Cap) (36/3), Jacques Novi (12/0) [*sent off 81*], Bernard Bosquier (35/3), Jean-Paul Rostagni (12/0), Jean-Noël Huck (5/0), Michel Mézy (5/1), Louis Floch (4/1), Charly Loubet (22/6) [46.Hervé Revelli (13/7)], Georges Lech (21/6), Georges Bereta (15/0) [82.Yves Herbet (15/1)]. Trainer: Georges Boulogne (13).
Goals: Charly Loubet (3), Jean Djorkaeff (50 penalty), Georges Lech (64), Hervé Revelli (89).

332. 12.01.1971 **ARGENTINA - FRANCE** **2-0(1-0)**
Estadio Municipal, Mar del Plata; Referee: Arturo Ithurralde (Argentina); Attendance: 18,000
FRA: Georges Carnus (22/0), Jean Djorkaeff (Cap) (37/3), Henri Michel (17/2), Bernard Bosquier (36/3), Jean-Paul Rostagni (13/0), Jean-Noël Huck (6/0), Michel Mézy (6/1), Yves Herbet (16/1), Georges Lech (22/6) [75.Marc Molitor (2/2)], Charly Loubet (23/6), Georges Bereta (16/0) [69.Louis Floch (5/1)]. Trainer: Georges Boulogne (14).

333. 17.03.1971 **SPAIN - FRANCE** **2-2(0-1)**
Estadio „Luis Casanova“, Valencia; Referee: Aurelio Angonese (Italy); Attendance: 41,000
FRA: Georges Carnus (23/0), Jean Djorkaeff (Cap) (38/3), Jacques Novi (13/0), Bernard Bosquier (37/3), Jean-Paul Rostagni (14/0), Henri Michel (18/2), Michel Mézy (7/1), Georges Lech (23/6), Charly Loubet (24/6) [10.Louis Floch (6/1)], Hervé Revelli (14/9), Georges Bereta (17/0). Trainer: Georges Boulogne (15).
Goals: Hervé Revelli (14, 54).

334. 24.04.1971 **HUNGARY - FRANCE** **1-1(0-0)** 4th EC. Qualifiers
Népstadion, Budapest; Referee: Fernandes de Campos (Portugal); Attendance: 45,867
FRA: Georges Carnus (24/0), Roger Lemerre (6/0), Francis Camerini (1/0), Bernard Bosquier (38/3), Jean Djorkaeff (Cap) (39/3), Henri Michel (19/2), Jacques Novi (14/0), Georges Lech (24/6), Hervé Revelli (15/10), Fleury Di Nallo (10/8) [46.Charly Loubet (25/6)], Georges Bereta (18/0). Trainer: Georges Boulogne (16).
Goal: Hervé Revelli (64).

335. 08.09.1971 **NORWAY - FRANCE** **1-3(0-2)** 4th EC. Qualifiers
Ullevaal Stadion, Oslo; Referee: John Wright Paterson (Scotland); Attendance: 16,544
FRA: Georges Carnus (25/0), Jean Djorkaeff (Cap) (40/3), Jacques Novi (15/0), Bernard Bosquier (39/3), Jean-Paul Rostagni (15/0), Henri Michel (20/2), Michel Mézy (8/1), Bernard Blanchet (11/3) [75.Georges Lech (25/6)], Jacques Vergnes (1/1), Charly Loubet (26/7), Georges Bereta (19/0). Trainer: Georges Boulogne (17).
Goals: Jacques Vergnes (33), Charly Loubet (34), Bernard Blanchet (49).

336. 09.10.1971 **FRANCE - HUNGARY** **0-2(0-2)** 4th EC. Qualifiers
Stade Olympique „Yves du Manoir“, Colombes, Paris; Referee: Gaspar Pintado Viu (Spain); Attendance: 21,756
FRA: Georges Carnus (26/0), Jean Djorkaeff (Cap) (41/3), Jacques Novi (16/0), Bernard Bosquier (40/3), Jean-Paul Rostagni (16/0), Henri Michel (21/2), Michel Mézy (9/1), Georges Lech (26/6), Hervé Revelli (16/10), Charly Loubet (27/7) [46.Gilbert Gress (3/0)], Georges Bereta (20/0). Trainer: Georges Boulogne (18).

337. 10.11.1971 **FRANCE - BULGARIA** **2-1(0-0)** 4th EC. Qualifiers
Stade „Marcel Saupin“, Nantes; Referee: John Keith Taylor (England); Attendance: 9,405
FRA: Georges Carnus (27/0), Francis Camerini (2/0), Jacques Novi (17/0), Claude Quittet (7/0), Jean Djorkaeff (Cap) (42/3), Henri Michel (22/2), Michel Mézy (10/1), Bernard Blanchet (12/3), Georges Lech (27/7), Hervé Revelli (17/10) [82.Louis Floch (7/1)], Charly Loubet (28/8). Trainer: Georges Boulogne (19).
Goals: Georges Lech (64), Charly Loubet (87).

338. 04.11.1971 **BULGARIA - FRANCE** **2-1(0-0)** 4th EC. Qualifiers
Nationalen stadion "Vasil Levski", Sofia; Referee: Kurt Tschenscher (West Germany); Attendance: 18,057
FRA: Georges Carnus (28/0), Jean Djorkaeff (Cap) (43/3), Jacques Novi (18/0), Bernard Bosquier (41/3), Marius Trésor (1/0), Henri Michel (23/2), Michel Mézy (11/1), Bernard Blanchet (13/4), Hervé Revelli (18/10) [60.Louis Floch (8/1)], Georges Lech (28/7), Charly Loubet (29/8) [76.Georges Bereta (21/0)]. Trainer: Georges Boulogne (20).
Goal: Bernard Blanchet (84).

339. 08.04.1972 **ROMANIA - FRANCE** **2-0(1-0)**
Stadionul 23 August, Bucureşti; Referee: Josip Strmečki (Yugoslavia); Attendance: 30,000
FRA: Georges Carnus (29/0), Marius Trésor (2/0), Bernard Bosquier (Cap) (42/3), Jacques Novi (19/0), Jean-Paul Rostagni (17/0), Henri Michel (24/2), Michel Mézy (12/1) [46.Claude Quittet (8/0)], Bernard Blanchet (14/4), Georges Lech (29/7), Louis Floch (9/1) [70.Marc Molitor (3/2)], Georges Bereta (22/0) [70.Jean-Michel Larqué (3/0)]. Trainer: Georges Boulogne (21).

340. 11.06.1972 **FRANCE – CENTRAL AMERICA XI** **5-0(1-0)** International Tournament
Estádio Fonte Nova, Salvador de Bahia (Brazil); Referee: Kurt Tschenscher (West Germany); Attendance: 21,422
FRA: Dominique Baratelli (1/0), Jean Djorkaeff (Cap) (44/3), Marius Trésor (3/0), Claude Quittet (9/0), Jean-Paul Rostagni (18/0), Henri Michel (25/2), Michel Mézy (13/1), Bernard Blanchet (15/4) [74.Louis Floch (10/1)], Hervé Revelli (19/13), Jean-Michel Larqué (4/0) [46.Georges Lech (30/7)], Georges Bereta (23/1). Trainer: Georges Boulogne (22).
Goals: Georges Bereta (35), Hervé Revelli (60, 66), J.F.Bulnes (80 own goal), Hervé Revelli (84).

341. 15.06.1972 **FRANCE – AFRICA XI** **2-0(1-0)** International Tournament
Estádio „Rei Pelé“, Maceio (Brazil); Referee: Rudolf Scheurer (Switzerland); Attendance: 10,000
FRA: Dominique Baratelli (2/0), Jean Djorkaeff (Cap) (45/3), Claude Quittet (10/0), Marius Trésor (4/0) [78.Jean-Pierre Adams (1/0)], Jean-Paul Rostagni (19/0), Henri Michel (26/2), Michel Mézy (14/1), Bernard Blanchet (16/5), Hervé Revelli (20/13), Georges Lech (31/7), Georges Bereta (24/1) [46.Louis Floch (11/2)]. Trainer: Georges Boulogne (23).
Goals: Bernard Blanchet (35), Louis Floch (83).

342. 18.06.1972 **FRANCE - COLOMBIA** **3-2(2-1)** International Tournament
Estádio Fonte Nove, Salvador de Bahia (Brazil); Referee: Angel Eduardo Pazos Bianchi (Uruguay); Attendance: 10,000
FRA: Georges Carnus (30/0), Jean Djorkaeff (Cap) (46/3), Claude Quittet (11/0), Marius Trésor (5/0), Jean-François Jodar (1/0), Jean-Pierre Adams (2/0), Henri Michel (27/2), Louis Floch (12/2) [46.Georges Bereta (25/1)], Marc Molitor (4/3) [78.Georges Lech (32/7)], Jean-Michel Larqué (5/0), Charly Loubet (30/10). Trainer: Georges Boulogne (24).
Goals: Charly Loubet (30), Marc Molitor (33 penalty), Charly Loubet (72).

343. 25.06.1972 **ARGENTINA - FRANCE** **0-0** International Tournament
Estádio Fonte Nova, Salvador de Bahia (Brazil); Referee: Armando Marques (Brazil); Attendance: 6,587
FRA: Georges Carnus (31/0), Jean Djorkaeff (Cap) (47/3), Jean-Pierre Adams (3/0), Marius Trésor (6/0), Jean-Paul Rostagni (20/0), Henri Michel (28/2), Georges Lech (33/7), Michel Mézy (15/1), Bernard Blanchet (17/5) [75.Louis Floch (13/2)], Hervé Revelli (21/13) [84.Charly Loubet (31/10)], Georges Bereta (26/1). Trainer: Georges Boulogne (25).

344. 02.09.1972 **GREECE - FRANCE** **1-3(0-0)**
Stádio „Giórgos Karaïskáki", Peiraiás; Referee: Fulvio Pieroni (Italy); Attendance: 10,000
FRA: Georges Carnus (32/0), Jean Djorkaeff (Cap) (48/3) [46.José Broissart (6/0)], Jacques Novi (20/0), Claude Quittet (12/0), Marius Trésor (7/0), Jean-Pierre Adams (4/0), Henri Michel (29/3), Georges Lech (34/7) [46.Charly Loubet (32/10)], Hervé Revelli (22/14), Jean-Michel Larqué (6/1), Georges Bereta (27/1). Trainer: Georges Boulogne (26).
Goals: Henri Michel (67), Hervé Revelli (86), Jean-Michel Larqué (90).

345. 13.10.1972 **FRANCE - SOVIET UNION** **1-0(0-0)** 10th FIFA WC. Qualifiers
Stade Parc des Princes, Paris; Referee: Rudolf Scheurer (Switzerland); Attendance: 29,746
FRA: Georges Carnus (33/0), José Broissart (7/0), Claude Quittet (Cap) (13/0), Marius Trésor (8/0), Jean-Paul Rostagni (21/0), Henri Michel (30/3), Jean-Pierre Adams (5/0), Serge Chiesa (5/0) [85.Charly Loubet (33/10)], Hervé Revelli (23/14), Jean-Michel Larqué (7/1), Georges Bereta (28/2). Trainer: Georges Boulogne (27).
Goal: Georges Bereta (60).

346. 15.11.1972 **REPUBLIC OF IRELAND - FRANCE** **2-1(1-0)** 10th FIFA WC. Qualifiers
Dalymount Park, Dublin; Referee: Kaj Rasmussen (Denmark); Attendance: 26,511
FRA: Georges Carnus (34/0), José Broissart (8/0), Claude Quittet (Cap) (14/0), Marius Trésor (9/0), Jean-Paul Rostagni (22/0), Jean-Noël Huck (7/0), Jean-Pierre Adams (6/0), Charly Loubet (34/10) [63.Marc Molitor (5/3)], Hervé Revelli (24/14), Jean-Michel Larqué (8/2), Georges Bereta (29/2). Trainer: Georges Boulogne (28).
Goal: Jean-Michel Larqué (66).

347. 03.03.1973 **FRANCE - PORTUGAL** **1-2(1-1)**
Stade Parc des Princes, Paris; Referee: Franz Geluck (Belgium); Attendance: 45,267
FRA: Georges Carnus (35/0), José Broissart (9/0), Jean-Pierre Adams (7/0), Marius Trésor (10/0), Jean-Paul Rostagni (23/0), Henri Michel (Cap) (31/3), Michel Mézy (16/1) [85.Jean-Noël Huck (8/0)], Georges Lech (35/7), Marc Molitor (6/4) [75.Louis Floch (14/2)], Hervé Revelli (25/14), Georges Bereta (30/2). Trainer: Georges Boulogne (29).
Goal: Marc Molitor (36).

348. 19.05.1973 **FRANCE - REPUBLIC OF IRELAND** **1-1(0-0)** 10th FIFA WC. Qualifiers
Stade Parc des Princes, Paris; Referee: Nicolae Rainea (Romania); Attendance: 40,405
FRA: Georges Carnus (36/0), Raymond Domenech (1/0), Claude Quittet (Cap) (15/0), Marius Trésor (11/0), Jean-Paul Rostagni (24/0), Henri Michel (32/3), Jean-Pierre Adams (8/0), Louis Floch (15/2), Hervé Revelli (26/14), Jean-Michel Larqué (9/2) [61.Serge Chiesa (6/1)], Georges Bereta (31/2). Trainer: Georges Boulogne (30).
Goal: Serge Chiesa (78).

349. 26.05.1973 **SOVIET UNION - FRANCE** **2-0(0-0)** 10th FIFA WC. Qualifiers
Lenin Stadium, Moskva; Referee: Ferdinand Biwersi (West Germany); Attendance: 75,000
FRA: Dominique Baratelli (3/0), José Broissart (10/0), Bernard Gardon (1/0), Marius Trésor (12/0), Jean-Paul Rostagni (25/0), Henri Michel (33/3), Claude Quittet (Cap) (16/0), Louis Floch (16/2) [46.Michel Mézy (17/1)], Hervé Revelli (27/14), Serge Chiesa (7/1), Georges Bereta (32/2). Trainer: Georges Boulogne (31).

350. 08.09.1973 **FRANCE - GREECE** **3-1(1-0)**
Stade Parc des Princes, Paris; Referee: Paolo Toselli (Italy); Attendance: 30,237
FRA: Dominique Baratelli (4/0), Jean-Claude Osman (1/0), Jean-Pierre Adams (9/0), Marius Trésor (13/0), Pierre Repellini (1/0), Roger Jouve (1/1), Georges Bereta (Cap) (33/2), Marc Molitor (7/4), Serge Chiesa (8/2), Bernard Lacombe (1/0) [57.Marc Berdoll (1/1)], Christian Sarramagna (1/0) [77.Daniel Ravier (1/0)]. Trainer: István Kovács (Romania, 1).
Goals: Roger Jouve (9), Marc Berdoll (59), Serge Chiesa (72).

351. 13.10.1973 **WEST GERMANY - FRANCE** **2-1(0-0)**
Parkstadion, Gelsenkirchen; Referee: Rudolf Scheurer (Switzerland); Attendance: 70,400
FRA: Dominique Baratelli (5/0), Dario Grava (1/0), Jean-Pierre Adams (10/0), Marius Trésor (14/1), Pierre Repellini (2/0), Henri Michel (34/3), Serge Chiesa (9/2), Roger Jouve (2/1), Charly Loubet (35/10), Marc Molitor (8/4) [65.Marc Berdoll (2/1)], Georges Bereta (Cap) (34/2). Trainer: István Kovács (Romania, 2).
Goal: Marius Trésor (82).

352. 21.11.1973 **FRANCE - DENMARK** **3-0(0-0)**
Stade Parc des Princes, Paris; Referee: Heinz Aldinger (West Germany); Attendance: 14,534
FRA: Jean-Paul Bertrand-Demanes (1/0), Pierre Repellini (3/0), Alain Merchadier (1/0), Jean-Pierre Adams (11/0), François Bracci (1/0), Henri Michel (35/3), Georges Bereta (Cap) (35/3), Daniel Ravier (2/0) [80.Claude Papi (1/0)], Serge Chiesa (10/2) [75.Patrick Revelli (1/0)], Hervé Revelli (28/15), Christian Sarramagna (2/0). Trainer: István Kovács (Romania, 3).
Goals: Georges Bereta (57), Søren Larsen (78 own goal), Hervé Revelli (89).

353. 23.03.1974 **FRANCE - ROMANIA** **1-0(0-0)**

Stade Parc des Princes, Paris; Referee: John Bartley Homewood (England); Attendance: 20,224

FRA: Jean-Paul Bertrand-Demanes (2/0), Albert Vanucci (1/0), Jean-Pierre Adams (12/0), Marius Trésor (15/1), François Bracci (2/0), Henri Michel (36/3), Jean-Marc Guillou (1/0), Serge Chiesa (11/2), Christian Dalger (1/0) [57.Patrick Revelli (2/0)], Hervé Revelli (29/15) [82.Marc Berdoll (3/1)], Georges Bereta (Cap) (36/4). Trainer: István Kovács (Romania, 4).

Goal: Georges Bereta (59).

354. 27.04.1974 **CZECHOSLOVAKIA - FRANCE** **3-3(2-2)**

Stadion Letná, Praha; Referee: Günter Männig (East Germany); Attendance: 15,000

FRA: Jean-Paul Bertrand-Demanes (3/0), Albert Vanucci (2/0), Jean-Pierre Adams (13/0) [64.Alain Merchadier (2/0)], Marius Trésor (16/1), François Bracci (3/0), Jean-Noël Huck (9/0), Henri Michel (37/3), Jean-Marc Guillou (2/0), Serge Chiesa (12/3), Bernard Lacombe (2/2), Georges Bereta (Cap) (37/4). Trainer: István Kovács (Romania, 5).

Goals: Serge Chiesa (7), Bernard Lacombe (28, 72).

355. 18.05.1974 **FRANCE - ARGENTINA** **0-1(0-1)**

Stade Parc des Princes, Paris; Referee: Jan Keizer (Netherlands); Attendance: 26,735

FRA: Dominique Baratelli (6/0), Pierre Repellini (4/0), Alain Merchadier (3/0) [46.Jean-François Jodar (2/0)], Jean-Pierre Adams (14/0), François Bracci (4/0), Jean-Noël Huck (10/0), Jean-Marc Guillou (3/0), Georges Bereta (Cap) (38/4), Marc Molitor (9/4), Bernard Lacombe (3/2) [70.Charly Loubet (36/10)], Christian Sarramagna (3/0). Trainer: István Kovács (Romania, 6).

356. 07.09.1974 **POLAND - FRANCE** **0-2(0-2)**

Stadion Olimpijski, Wroclaw; Referee: Erik Fredriksson (Sweden); Attendance: 25,000

FRA: Jean-Paul Bertrand-Demanes (4/0), Jean-François Jodar (3/1), Jean-Pierre Adams (15/0), Marius Trésor (17/1), François Bracci (5/0), Jean-Noël Huck (11/0), Henri Michel (38/3) [87.Alain Merchadier (4/0)], Jean-Marc Guillou (4/0), Alain Giresse (1/0) [72.Patrick Revelli (3/0)], Christian Coste (1/1), Georges Bereta (Cap) (39/4). Trainer: István Kovács (Romania, 7).

Goals: Christian Coste (37), Jean-François Jodar (39).

357. 12.10.1974 **BELGIUM - FRANCE** **2-1(1-1)** 5th EC. Qualifiers

Stade du Heysel, Bruxelles; Referee: Kenneth Burns (England); Attendance: 32,108

FRA: Dominique Baratelli (7/0), Jean-François Jodar (4/1), Jean-Pierre Adams (16/0), Marius Trésor (18/1), François Bracci (6/0), Jean-Noël Huck (12/0), Henri Michel (39/3), Jean-Marc Guillou (5/0), Christian Coste (2/2), Bernard Lacombe (4/2) [83.Jean Gallice (1/0)], Georges Bereta (Cap) (40/4). Trainer: István Kovács (Romania, 8).

Goal: Christian Coste (16).

358. 16.11.1974 **FRANCE - EAST GERMANY** **2-2(0-1)** 5th EC. Qualifiers

Stade Parc des Princes, Paris; Referee: Pablo Augusto Sánchez Ibañez (Spain); Attendance: 45,381

FRA: Jean-Paul Bertrand-Demanes (5/0), Jean-François Jodar (5/1), Jean-Pierre Adams (17/0), Marius Trésor (19/1), François Bracci (7/0), Jean-Noël Huck (13/0), Henri Michel (40/3) [65.Christian Synaeghel (1/0)], Jean-Marc Guillou (6/1), Gérard Soler (1/0), Christian Coste (3/2) [46.Jean Gallice (2/1)], Georges Bereta (Cap) (41/4). Trainer: István Kovács (Romania, 9).

Goals: Jean-Marc Guillou (79), Jean Gallice (89).

359. 26.03.1975 **FRANCE - HUNGARY** **2-0(0-0)**

Stade Parc des Princes, Paris; Referee: Klaus Ohmsen (West Germany); Attendance: 25,000

FRA: René Charrier (1/0), Christian Lopez (1/0) [83.Alain Merchadier (5/0)], Victor Zvunka (1/0), Marius Trésor (20/1), François Bracci (8/0), Jean-Noël Huck (14/0) [70.Claude Papi (2/0)], Henri Michel (41/4), Jean-Marc Guillou (7/1), Yves Triantafilos (1/0), Hervé Revelli (30/15) [60.Patrick Parizon (1/1)], Georges Bereta (Cap) (42/4). Trainer: István Kovács (Romania, 10).

Goals: Henri Michel (56), Patrick Parizon (63).

360. 26.04.1975 **FRANCE - PORTUGAL** **0-2(0-1)**

Stade Olympique „Yves du Manoir", Colombes, Paris; Referee: Hans-Joachim Weyland (West Germany); Attendance: 24,816

FRA: René Charrier (2/0) [46.Dominique Baratelli (8/0)], Jean-François Jodar (6/1) [88.Bernard Boissier (1/0)], Jean-Pierre Adams (18/0), Marius Trésor (21/1), François Bracci (9/0), Jean-Noël Huck (15/0) [46.Jean Gallice (3/1)], Henri Michel (42/4), Jean-Marc Guillou (8/1), Patrick Parizon (2/1), Christian Coste (4/2), Georges Bereta (Cap) (43/4) [72.Yves Mariot (1/0)]. Trainer: István Kovács (Romania, 11).

361. 27.05.1975 **ICELAND - FRANCE** **0-0** 5th EC. Qualifiers

Laugardalsvöllur, Reykjavík; Referee: Malcolm Wright (Northern Ireland); Attendance: 7,613

FRA: Dominique Baratelli (9/0), Christian Lopez (2/0), Jean-Pierre Adams (19/0), Marius Trésor (22/1), François Bracci (10/0), Henri Michel (43/4), Jean-Michel Larqué (10/2), Jean-Marc Guillou (9/1), Jean Gallice (4/1) [75.Patrick Parizon (3/1)], Marc Berdoll (4/1), Georges Bereta (Cap) (44/4). Trainer: István Kovács (Romania, 12).

362. 03.09.1975 **FRANCE - ICELAND** **3-0(1-0)** 5th EC. Qualifiers

Stade „Marcel Saupin", Nantes; Referee: Albert Victor (Luxembourg); Attendance: 14,217

FRA: Dominique Baratelli (10/0), Raymond Domenech (2/0), Jean-Pierre Adams (20/0), Marius Trésor (23/1), François Bracci (11/0), Henri Michel (Cap) (44/4), Jean-Noël Huck (16/0), Jean-Marc Guillou (10/3), Dominique Rocheteau (1/0), Marc Molitor (10/4) [46.Marc Berdoll (5/2)], Albert Emon (1/0). Trainer: István Kovács (Romania, 13).

Goals: Jean-Marc Guillou (20, 74), Marc Berdoll (87).

363. 12.10.1975 **EAST GERMANY - FRANCE** **2-1(0-0)** 5th EC. Qualifiers

Zentralstadion, Leipzig; Referee: Erik Fredriksson (Sweden); Attendance: 28,544

FRA: Dominique Baratelli (11/0), Gérard Janvion (1/0), Jean-Pierre Adams (21/0), Marius Trésor (24/1), François Bracci (12/0), Dominique Bathenay (1/1), Henri Michel (Cap) (45/4), Jean-Marc Guillou (11/3), Dominique Rocheteau (2/0), Jean Gallice (5/1), Albert Emon (2/0). Trainer: István Kovács (Romania, 14).

Goal: Dominique Bathenay (50).

364. 15.11.1975 **FRANCE - BELGIUM** **0-0** 5th EC. Qualifiers

Stade Parc des Princes, Paris; Referee: Robert Holley Davidson (Scotland); Attendance: 35,547

FRA: Dominique Baratelli (12/0), Raymond Domenech (3/0), Charles Orlanducci (1/0), Marius Trésor (25/1), François Bracci (13/0), Jean-Noël Huck (17/0) [46.Jean-Michel Larqué (11/2) [*sent off 67*]], Henri Michel (Cap) (46/4), Jean-Marc Guillou (12/3), Dominique Rocheteau (3/0), Christian Coste (5/2) [78.Jean Gallice (6/1)], Albert Emon (3/0). Trainer: István Kovács (Romania, 15).

365. 27.03.1976 **FRANCE - CZECHOSLOVAKIA** **2-2(1-0)**
Stade Parc des Princes, Paris; Referee: Francis Jean Joseph Elisa Rion (Belgium); Attendance: 19,659
FRA: Jean-Paul Bertrand-Demanes (6/0), Raymond Domenech (4/0), Patrice Rio (1/0), Marius Trésor (26/1), Maxime Bossis (1/0), Michel Platini (1/1), Henri Michel (Cap) (47/4), Gilles Rampillon (1/0) [65.Roger Jouve (3/1)], Gérard Soler (2/1) [51.Didier Six (1/0)], Robert Pintenat (1/0), Albert Emon (4/0). Trainer: Michel Hidalgo (1).
Goals: Gérard Soler (17), Michel Platini (73).

366. 24.04.1976 **FRANCE - POLAND** **2-0(1-0)**
Stade „Félix Bollaert", Lens; Referee: Ferdinand Biwersi (West Germany); Attendance: 14,490
FRA: Dominique Baratelli (13/0), Raymond Domenech (5/0), Patrice Rio (2/0), Carlos Curbelo (1/0), Gérard Farison (1/0), Christian Synaeghel (2/0), Jean-Michel Larqué (Cap) (12/2), Jean-Marc Guillou (13/3) [56.Farès Bousdira (1/0)], Patrick Revelli (4/1), Robert Pintenat (2/1), Didier Six (2/0). Trainer: Michel Hidalgo (2).
Goals: Robert Pintenat (12), Patrick Revelli (63).

367. 22.05.1976 **HUNGARY - FRANCE** **1-0(0-0)**
Népstadion, Budapest; Referee: Franz Wöhrer (Austria); Attendance: 8,726
FRA: Dominique Baratelli (14/0), Gérard Janvion (2/0), Patrice Rio (3/0), Marius Trésor (27/1), Francis Meynieu (1/0), Jean-Michel Larqué (Cap) (13/2), Jean-Marc Guillou (14/3) [50.Carlos Curbelo (2/0)], Michel Platini (2/1), Albert Emon (5/0) [73.Didier Six (3/0)], Robert Pintenat (3/1), Christian Sarramagna (4/0). Trainer: Michel Hidalgo (3).

368. 01.09.1976 **DENMARK - FRANCE** **1-1(0-0)**
Idrætsparken, København; Referee: Lars-Åke Björck (Sweden); Attendance: 23,100
FRA: Dominique Baratelli (15/0), Gérard Janvion (3/0) [46.Raymond Domenech (6/0)], Jean-Pierre Adams (22/0), Marius Trésor (28/1), Maxime Bossis (2/0), Jean-Michel Larqué (Cap) (14/2), Michel Platini (3/2), Dominique Bathenay (2/1), Dominique Rocheteau (4/0), Bernard Lacombe (5/2), Didier Six (4/0). Trainer: Michel Hidalgo (4).
Goal: Michel Platini (89).

369. 09.10.1976 **BULGARIA - FRANCE** **2-2(1-2)** 11th FIFA WC. Qualifiers
Nationalen stadion "Vasil Levski", Sofia; Referee: Ian M.D. Foote (Scotland); Attendance: 45,000
FRA: Dominique Baratelli (16/0), Gérard Janvion (4/0), Christian Lopez (3/0), Marius Trésor (Cap) (29/1), Maxime Bossis (3/0), Dominique Bathenay (3/1), Christian Synaeghel (3/0), Michel Platini (4/3), Jean Gallice (7/1), Bernard Lacombe (6/3), Didier Six (5/0) [61.Olivier Rouyer (1/0)]. Trainer: Michel Hidalgo (5).
Goals: Michel Platini (37), Bernard Lacombe (40).

370. 17.11.1976 **FRANCE - REPUBLIC OF IRELAND** **2-0(0-0)** 11th FIFA WC. Qualifiers
Stade Parc des Princes, Paris; Referee: Dušan Maksimović (Yugoslavia); Attendance: 43,437
FRA: Dominique Baratelli (17/0), Gérard Janvion (5/0), Christian Lopez (4/0), Marius Trésor (Cap) (30/1), Maxime Bossis (4/0), Dominique Bathenay (4/2), Raymond Kéruzoré (1/0), Michel Platini (5/4), Dominique Rocheteau (5/0), Bernard Lacombe (7/3) [71.Olivier Rouyer (2/0)], Didier Six (6/0). Trainer: Michel Hidalgo (6).
Goals: Michel Platini (47), Dominique Bathenay (88).

371. 23.02.1977 **FRANCE - WEST GERMANY** **1-0(0-0)**
Stade Parc des Princes, Paris; Referee: Pablo Augusto Sánchez Ibañez (Spain); Attendance: 45,000
FRA: André Rey (1/0), Patrick Battiston (1/0), Patrice Rio (4/0), Christian Lopez (Cap) (5/0), Gérard Janvion (6/0), Dominique Bathenay (5/2), Christian Synaeghel (4/0) [72.Omar Sahnoun (1/0)], Michel Platini (6/4), Olivier Rouyer (3/1), Bernard Lacombe (8/3) [46.Patrick Revelli (5/1)], Loïc Amisse (1/0) [64.Bruno Zénier (1/0)]. Trainer: Michel Hidalgo (7).
Goal: Olivier Rouyer (52).

372. 30.03.1977 **REPUBLIC OF IRELAND - FRANCE** **1-0(0-0)** 11th FIFA WC. Qualifiers
Lansdowne Road, Dublin; Referee: Erich Linemayr (Austria); Attendance: 48,000
FRA: André Rey (2/0), Gérard Janvion (7/0), Patrice Rio (5/0), Christian Lopez (Cap) (6/0), Thierry Tusseau (1/0), Dominique Bathenay (6/2), Michel Platini (7/4), Christian Synaeghel (5/0), Olivier Rouyer (4/1), Bernard Lacombe (9/3), Dominique Rocheteau (6/0). Trainer: Michel Hidalgo (8).

373. 23.04.1977 **SWITZERLAND - FRANCE** **0-4(0-1)**
Stade Charmilles, Genève; Referee: Alfred Delcourt (Belgium); Attendance: 27,600
FRA: André Rey (3/0), Gérard Janvion (8/0), Patrice Rio (6/0), Christian Lopez (Cap) (7/0), Thierry Tusseau (2/0), Alain Giresse (2/0), Michel Platini (8/5), Omar Sahnoun (2/0), Dominique Rocheteau (7/1), Bruno Baronchelli (1/0) [46.Olivier Rouyer (5/2)], Didier Six (7/1). Trainer: Michel Hidalgo (9).
Goals: Michel Platini (31), Didier Six (73), Dominique Rocheteau (87), Olivier Rouyer (89).

374. 26.06.1977 **ARGENTINA - FRANCE** **0-0**
Estadio „Alberto Jacinto Armando" [La Bombonera], Buenos Aires; Referee: Perez (Peru); Attendance: 55,000
FRA: Dominique Baratelli (18/0), Patrick Battiston (2/0), Marius Trésor (31/1), Patrice Rio (7/0), Maxime Bossis (5/0), Henri Michel (Cap) (48/4) [83.Alain Giresse (3/0)], Omar Sahnoun (3/0), Michel Platini (9/5), Bruno Baronchelli (2/0) [64.Atre Jacques „Zimako" (1/0)], Olivier Rouyer (6/2), Loïc Amisse (2/0) [77.Didier Six (8/1)]. Trainer: Michel Hidalgo (10).

375. 30.06.1977 **BRAZIL - FRANCE** **2-2(1-0)**
Estádio „Jornalista Mário Filho" [Maracanã], Rio de Janeiro; Referee: Romualdo Arppi Filho (Brazil); Attendance: 85,317
FRA: André Rey (4/0), Gérard Janvion (9/0), Marius Trésor (Cap) (32/2), Patrice Rio (8/0), Maxime Bossis (6/0), Omar Sahnoun (4/0), Dominique Bathenay (7/2), Michel Platini (10/5), Atre Jacques „Zimako" (2/0) [59.Olivier Rouyer (7/2)], Bernard Lacombe (10/3), Didier Six (9/2). Trainer: Michel Hidalgo (11).
Goals: Didier Six (52), Marius Trésor (85).

376. 08.10.1977 **FRANCE - SOVIET UNION** **0-0**
Stade Parc des Princes, Paris; Referee: Marcel Van Langenhove (Belgium); Attendance: 40,823
FRA: André Rey (5/0), Gérard Janvion (10/0), Patrice Rio (9/0), Marius Trésor (Cap) (33/2), Thierry Tusseau (3/0), Jean Petit (1/0) [65.Roger Jouve (4/1)], Dominique Bathenay (8/2), Michel Platini (11/5), Christian Dalger (2/0) [65.Dominique Rocheteau (8/1)], Marc Berdoll (6/2), Didier Six (10/2). Trainer: Michel Hidalgo (12).

377. 16.11.1977 **FRANCE - BULGARIA** **3-1(1-0)** 11th FIFA WC. Qualifiers
Stade Parc des Princes, Paris; Referee: Charles George Rainier Corver (Netherlands); Attendance: 44,860
FRA: André Rey (6/0), Gérard Janvion (11/0), Patrice Rio (10/0), Marius Trésor (Cap) (34/2), Maxime Bossis (7/0), Jean-Marc Guillou (15/3), Michel Platini (12/6), Dominique Bathenay (9/2), Dominique Rocheteau (9/2) [70.Christian Dalger (3/1)], Bernard Lacombe (11/3), Didier Six (11/2). Trainer: Michel Hidalgo (13).
Goals: Dominique Rocheteau (38), Michel Platini (63), Christian Dalger (89).

378. 08.02.1978 **ITALY - FRANCE** **2-2(2-0)**
Stadio San Paolo, Napoli; Referee: Angel Franco Martínez (Spain); Attendance: 66,158
FRA: André Rey (7/0), Gérard Janvion (12/0), Patrice Rio (11/0) [74.Christian Lopez (8/0)], Marius Trésor (Cap) (35/2), Maxime Bossis (8/0), Jean-Marc Guillou (16/3) [46.Henri Michel (49/4)], Dominique Bathenay (10/3), Michel Platini (13/7), Christian Dalger (4/1), Bernard Lacombe (12/3), Olivier Rouyer (8/2) [29.Albert Gemmrich (1/0)]. Trainer: Michel Hidalgo (14).
Goals: Dominique Bathenay (50), Michel Platini (81).

379. 08.03.1978 **FRANCE - PORTUGAL** **2-0(2-0)**
Stade Parc des Princes, Paris; Referee: Alexis Ponnet (Belgium); Attendance: 42,241
FRA: André Rey (8/0), Gérard Janvion (13/0), Patrice Rio (12/0), Christian Lopez (9/0) [56.Patrick Battiston (3/0)], Maxime Bossis (9/0), Omar Sahnoun (5/0), Henri Michel (Cap) (50/4), Alain Giresse (4/0), Bruno Baronchelli (3/1), Marc Berdoll (7/3) [75.Loïc Amisse (3/0)], Didier Six (12/2). Trainer: Michel Hidalgo (15).
Goals: Bruno Baronchelli (9), Marc Berdoll (40).

380. 01.04.1978 **FRANCE - BRAZIL** **1-0(0-0)**
Stade Parc des Princes, Paris; Referee: Patrick Partridge (England); Attendance: 46,065
FRA: Jean-Paul Bertrand-Demanes (7/0), Patrick Battiston (4/0) [61.François Bracci (14/0)], Patrice Rio (13/0), Christian Lopez (10/0), Maxime Bossis (10/0), Jean-Marc Guillou (17/3), Henri Michel (Cap) (51/4) [67.Jean Petit (2/0)], Michel Platini (14/8), Bruno Baronchelli (4/1), Marc Berdoll (8/3), Loïc Amisse (4/0) [81.Didier Six (13/2)]. Trainer: Michel Hidalgo (16).
Goal: Michel Platini (86).

381. 11.05.1978 **FRANCE - IRAN** **2-1(1-0)**
Stade Municipal, Toulouse; Referee: Augusto Lamo Castillo (Spain); Attendance: 35,000
FRA: Jean-Paul Bertrand-Demanes (8/0), Gérard Janvion (14/0), Marius Trésor (Cap) (36/2) [58.Christian Lopez (11/0)], Patrice Rio (14/0), Maxime Bossis (11/0), Omar Sahnoun (6/0) [46.Dominique Bathenay (11/3)], Henri Michel (52/4), Raymond Kéruzoré (2/0), Dominique Rocheteau (10/2) [46.Didier Six (14/3)], Bernard Lacombe (13/3) [58.Marc Berdoll (9/3)], Albert Gemmrich (2/1). Trainer: Michel Hidalgo (17).
Goals: Albert Gemmrich (14), Didier Six (70).

382. 19.05.1978 **FRANCE - TUNISIA** **2-0(0-0)**
Stade Du Nord,Villeneuve d'Ascq; Referee: Charles George Rainier Corver (Netherlands); Attendance: 35,000
FRA: Jean-Paul Bertrand-Demanes (9/0), Patrick Battiston (5/0), Patrice Rio (15/0) [86.François Bracci (15/0)], Christian Lopez (12/0), Gérard Janvion (15/0), Jean Petit (3/0), Dominique Bathenay (12/3), Jean-Marc Guillou (Cap) (18/3) [43.Michel Platini (15/9)], Christian Dalger (5/2), Marc Berdoll (10/3) [63.Bernard Lacombe (14/3)], Didier Six (15/3) [46.Olivier Rouyer (9/2)]. Trainer: Michel Hidalgo (18).
Goals: Michel Platini (71), Christian Dalger (74).

383. 02.06.1978 **FRANCE - ITALY** **1-2(1-1)** 11th FIFA WC. Group Stage.
Estadio „José María Minella", Mar del Plata (Argentina); Referee: Nicolae Rainea (Romania); Attendance: 42,373
FRA: Jean-Paul Bertrand-Demanes (10/0), Gérard Janvion (16/0), Patrice Rio (16/0), Marius Trésor (Cap) (37/2), Maxime Bossis (12/0), Henri Michel (53/4), Jean-Marc Guillou (19/3), Michel Platini (16/9), Christian Dalger (6/2), Bernard Lacombe (15/4) [75.Marc Berdoll (11/3)], Didier Six (16/3) [76.Olivier Rouyer (10/2)]. Trainer: Michel Hidalgo (19).
Goal: Bernard Lacombe (1).

384. 06.06.1978 **ARGENTINA - FRANCE** **2-1(1-0)** 11th FIFA WC. Group Stage.
Estadio Monumental „Antonio Vespucio Liberti", Buenos Aires; Referee: Jean Dubach (Switzerland); Attendance: 77,216
FRA: Jean-Paul Bertrand-Demanes (11/0) [55.Dominique Baratelli (19/0)], Patrick Battiston (6/0), Christian Lopez (13/0), Marius Trésor (Cap) (38/2), Maxime Bossis (13/0), Michel Platini (17/10), Henri Michel (54/4), Dominique Bathenay (13/3), Dominique Rocheteau (11/2), Bernard Lacombe (16/4), Didier Six (17/3). Trainer: Michel Hidalgo (20).
Goal: Michel Platini (60).

385. 10.06.1978 **FRANCE - HUNGARY** **3-1(3-1)** 11th FIFA WC. Group Stage.
Estadio „José María Minella", Mar del Plata (Argentina); Referee: Arnaldo David Cesar Coelho (Brazil); Attendance: 28,000
FRA: Dominique Dropsy (1/0), Gérard Janvion (17/0), Christian Lopez (14/1), Marius Trésor (Cap) (39/2), François Bracci (16/0), Jean Petit (4/0), Dominique Bathenay (14/3), Claude Papi (3/0) [46.Michel Platini (18/10)], Dominique Rocheteau (12/3) [75.Didier Six (18/3)], Marc Berdoll (12/4), Olivier Rouyer (11/2). Trainer: Michel Hidalgo (21).
Goals: Christian Lopez (23), Marc Berdoll (38), Dominique Rocheteau (42).

386. 01.09.1978 **FRANCE - SWEDEN** **2-2(0-0)** 6th EC. Qualifiers
Stade Parc des Princes, Paris; Referee: Károly Palotai (Hungary); Attendance: 44,703
FRA: André Rey (9/0), Patrick Battiston (7/0), Patrice Rio (17/0), Christian Lopez (15/1), Maxime Bossis (14/0), Dominique Bathenay (15/3), Henri Michel (Cap) (55/4) [77.Alain Giresse (5/0)], Roger Jouve (5/1), Olivier Rouyer (12/2), Albert Gemmrich (3/1) [65.Marc Berdoll (13/5)], Didier Six (19/4). Trainer: Michel Hidalgo (22).
Goals: Marc Berdoll (72), Didier Six (85).

387. 07.10.1978 **LUXEMBOURG - FRANCE** **1-3(0-1)** 6th EC. Qualifiers
Stade Municipal, Luxembourg; Referee: Hendrik Weerink (Netherlands); Attendance: 12,000
FRA: Dominique Dropsy (2/0), Patrick Battiston (8/0), Christian Lopez (16/1), Marius Trésor (Cap) (40/3), Maxime Bossis (15/0), Jean-François Larios (1/0) [64.Jean Petit (5/0)], Roger Jouve (6/1), Francis Piasecki (1/0), Dominique Rocheteau (13/3) [59.Albert Gemmrich (4/2)], Bernard Lacombe (17/4), Didier Six (20/5). Trainer: Michel Hidalgo (23).
Goals: Didier Six (15), Marius Trésor (63), Albert Gemmrich (80).

388. 08.11.1978 **FRANCE - SPAIN** **1-0(1-0)**
Stade Parc des Princes, Paris; Referee: Walter Eschweiler (West Germany); Attendance: 37,897
FRA: Dominique Dropsy (3/0), Patrick Battiston (9/0), Léonard Specht (1/1), Christian Lopez (17/1), Gérard Janvion (18/0), Henri Michel (Cap) (56/4), Jean Petit (6/0), Francis Piasecki (2/0), Dominique Rocheteau (14/3) [63.Gérard Soler (3/1)], Pierre Pleimelding (1/0) [57.Albert Gemmrich (5/2)], Didier Six (21/5). Trainer: Michel Hidalgo (24).
Goal: Léonard Specht (41).

389. 25.02.1979 **FRANCE - LUXEMBOURG** **3-0(1-0)** 6th EC. Qualifiers
Stade Parc des Princes, Paris; Referee: Ronald Bridges (Wales); Attendance: 46,988
FRA: Dominique Dropsy (4/0), Patrick Battiston (10/0), Léonard Specht (2/1), Marius Trésor (Cap) (41/3), Maxime Bossis (16/0), Henri Michel (57/4), Jean Petit (7/1), Francis Piasecki (3/0) [61.Jean-François Larios (2/1)], Dominique Rocheteau (15/3), Marc Berdoll (14/5) [66.Eric Pécout (1/0)], Albert Emon (6/1). Trainer: Michel Hidalgo (25).
Goals: Jean Petit (38), Albert Emon (60), Jean-François Larios (78).

390. 04.04.1979 **CZECHOSLOVAKIA - FRANCE** **2-0(0-0)** 6th EC. Qualifiers
Štadión Tehelné pole, Bratislava; Referee: Heinz Aldinger (West Germany); Attendance: 48,138
FRA: Dominique Dropsy (5/0), Raymond Domenech (7/0), Léonard Specht (3/1), Christian Lopez (Cap) (18/1), Maxime Bossis (17/0), Jean-François Larios (3/1), Jean Petit (8/1), Michel Platini (19/10), Albert Emon (7/1), Marc Berdoll (15/5), Loïc Amisse (5/0). Trainer: Michel Hidalgo (26).

391. 02.05.1979 **UNITED STATES - FRANCE** **0-6(0-4)**
Giants Stadium, East Rutherford; Referee: Mario Antonio Dorantes García (Mexico); Attendance: 20,951
FRA: Dominique Dropsy (6/0) [46.André Rey (10/0)], Gérard Janvion (19/0), Raymond Domenech (8/0), Marius Trésor (Cap) (42/3), Maxime Bossis (18/0) [80.Patrick Battiston (11/0)], Jean Petit (9/1), Roger Jouve (7/1) [71.Jean-François Larios (4/1)], Michel Platini (20/10), Olivier Rouyer (13/2) [46.Didier Six (22/6)], Bernard Lacombe (18/7) [65.Marc Berdoll (16/5)], Loïc Amisse (6/1). Trainer: Michel Hidalgo (27).
Goals: Bernard Lacombe (8, 14, 37), Donald Droege (42 own goal), Loïc Amisse (61), Didier Six (73).

392. 05.09.1979 **SWEDEN - FRANCE** **1-3(1-1)** 6th EC. Qualifiers
Råsundastadion, Stockholm; Referee: Angel Franco Martínez (Spain); Attendance: 14,395
FRA: Dominique Dropsy (7/0), Patrick Battiston (12/1), Léonard Specht (4/1), Christian Lopez (19/1), Maxime Bossis (19/0), Alain Moizan (1/0), Dominique Bathenay (16/3), Michel Platini (Cap) (21/11), Dominique Rocheteau (16/3) [55.Atre Jacques „Zimako" (3/0)], Bernard Lacombe (19/8), Loïc Amisse (7/1). Trainer: Michel Hidalgo (28).
Goals: Bernard Lacombe (14), Michel Platini (54), Patrick Battiston (71).

393. 10.10.1979 **FRANCE - UNITED STATES** **3-0(3-0)**
Stade Parc des Princes, Paris; Referee: Henrik van Ettekoven (Netherlands); Attendance: 25,000
FRA: Dominique Dropsy (8/0) [46.Ohilippe Bergeroo (1/0)], Gérard Janvion (20/0) [*sent off 88*], Léonard Specht (5/1) [46.Marius Trésor (43/3)], Christian Lopez (20/1), Maxime Bossis (20/0), Dominique Bathenay (17/3), Alain Moizan (2/0), Michel Platini (Cap) (22/12) [42.Jean-François Larios (5/1)], Roland Wagner (1/1) [46.Patrice Lecornu (1/0)], Bernard Lacombe (20/8), Loïc Amisse (8/2). Trainer: Michel Hidalgo (29).
Goals: Michel Platini (5), Roland Wagner (18), Loïc Amisse (23).

394. 17.11.1979 **FRANCE - CZECHOSLOVAKIA** **2-1(0-0)** 6th EC. Qualifiers
Stade Parc des Princes, Paris; Referee: Horst Brummeier (Austria); Attendance: 39,973
FRA: Dominique Dropsy (9/0), Patrick Battiston (13/1), Léonard Specht (6/1), Christian Lopez (Cap) (21/1), Maxime Bossis (21/0), Jean Petit (10/1), Alain Moizan (3/0), Gilles Rampillon (2/1), Atre Jacques „Zimako" (4/0), Bernard Lacombe (21/8) [46.Eric Pécout (2/1)], Loïc Amisse (9/2). Trainer: Michel Hidalgo (30).
Goals: Eric Pécout (67), Gilles Rampillon (76).

395. 27.02.1980 **FRANCE - GREECE** **5-1(2-1)**
Stade Parc des Princes, Paris; Referee: José Luis García Carrion (Spain); Attendance: 29,992
FRA: Dominique Dropsy (10/0) [46.Jean-Luc Ettori (1/0)], Patrick Battiston (14/1), Léonard Specht (7/1), Christian Lopez (22/1), Thierry Tusseau (4/0), Dominique Bathenay (18/4), Didier Christophe (1/1) [70.Bernard Genghini (1/0)], Michel Platini (Cap) (23/14), Patrice Lecornu (2/0) [56.Olivier Rouyer (14/2)], Eric Pécout (3/1) [46.Yannick Stopyra (1/1)], Atre Jacques „Zimako" (5/0). Trainer: Michel Hidalgo (31).
Goals: Dominique Bathenay (7 penalty), Michel Platini (37, 62), Didier Christophe (63), Yannick Stopyra (66).

396. 26.03.1980 **FRANCE - NETHERLANDS** **0-0**
Stade Parc des Princes, Paris; Referee: Paolo Casarin (Italy); Attendance: 41,477
FRA: Dominique Dropsy (11/0), Gérard Janvion (21/0), Léonard Specht (8/1), Marius Trésor (44/3), Maxime Bossis (22/0), Dominique Bathenay (19/4) [64.Gilles Rampillon (3/1)], Didier Christophe (2/1) [78.Thierry Tusseau (5/0)], Michel Platini (Cap) (24/14), Alain Couriol (1/0), Eric Pécout (4/1), Didier Six (23/6) [71.Olivier Rouyer (15/2)]. Trainer: Michel Hidalgo (32).

397. 23.05.1980 **SOVIET UNION - FRANCE** **1-0(1-0)**
Lenin Stadium, Moskva; Referee: Sándor Kuti (Hungary); Attendance: 55,000
FRA: Ohilippe Bergeroo (2/0), Gérard Janvion (22/0), Léonard Specht (9/1), Marius Trésor (45/3), Maxime Bossis (23/0), Jean Amadou Tigana (1/0), Didier Christophe (3/1), Michel Platini (Cap) (25/14), Atre Jacques „Zimako" (6/0), Bernard Lacombe (22/8) [62.Eric Pécout (5/1)], Albert Emon (8/1) [46.Alain Couriol (2/0)]. Trainer: Michel Hidalgo (33).

398. 11.10.1980 **CYPRUS - FRANCE** **0-7(0-4)** 12th FIFA WC. Qualifiers
Stádio Tsirion, Limassol; Referee: Bruno Galler (Switzerland); Attendance: 15,000
FRA: Dominique Dropsy (12/0), Patrick Battiston (15/1), Léonard Specht (10/1), Henri Michel (58/4), Maxime Bossis (24/0), Jean-François Larios (6/3), Jean Amadou Tigana (2/0) [51.Jean Petit (11/1)], Michel Platini (Cap) (26/16), Bruno Baronchelli (5/1) [73.Atre Jacques „Zimako" (7/1)], Bernard Lacombe (23/9), Didier Six (24/7). Trainer: Michel Hidalgo (34).
Goals: Bernard Lacombe (4), Michel Platini (14, 23), Jean-François Larios (40 penalty, 76 penalty), Didier Six (82), Atre Jacques „Zimako" (87).

399. 28.10.1980 **FRANCE - REPUBLIC OF IRELAND** **2-0(1-0)** 12th FIFA WC. Qualifiers
Stade Parc des Princes, Paris; Referee: Augusto Lamo Castillo (Spain); Attendance: 44,800
FRA: Dominique Dropsy (13/0), Patrick Battiston (16/1), Léonard Specht (11/1), Christian Lopez (23/1), Maxime Bossis (25/0), Jean-François Larios (7/3), Jean Amadou Tigana (3/0), Michel Platini (Cap) (27/17) [74.Jean Petit (12/1)], Dominique Rocheteau (17/3), Bernard Lacombe (24/9) [66.Atre Jacques „Zimako" (8/2)], Didier Six (25/7). Trainer: Michel Hidalgo (35).
Goals: Michel Platini (11), Atre Jacques „Zimako" (77).

400. 19.11.1980 **WEST GERMANY - FRANCE** **4-1(2-1)**
Niedersachsenstadion, Hannover; Referee: Rolf Nyhus (Norway); Attendance: 60,400
FRA: Dominique Dropsy (14/0), Gérard Janvion (23/0), Léonard Specht (12/1), Christian Lopez (24/1), Maxime Bossis (26/0), Jean Amadou Tigana (4/0), Jean-François Larios (8/4), Michel Platini (Cap) (28/17), Atre Jacques „Zimako" (9/2), Dominique Rocheteau (18/3) [60.Olivier Rouyer (16/2)], Loïc Amisse (10/2) [79.Didier Six (26/7)]. Trainer: Michel Hidalgo (36).
Goal: Jean-François Larios (39 penalty).

401. 18.02.1981 **SPAIN - FRANCE** **1-0(0-0)**
Estadio „Vicente Calderón", Madrid; Referee: Carol Jurja (Romania); Attendance: 18,000
FRA: Jean Castaneda (1/0), Gérard Janvion (24/0), Léonard Specht (13/1), Christian Lopez (25/1), Maxime Bossis (27/0), Didier Christophe (4/1) [70.Jean Amadou Tigana (5/0)], Alain Moizan (4/0), Jean-François Larios (9/4), Michel Platini (Cap) (29/17), Bruno Baronchelli (6/1) [46.Daniel Xuereb (1/0)], Didier Six (27/7). Trainer: Michel Hidalgo (37).

402. 15.03.1981 **NETHERLANDS - FRANCE** **1-0(0-0)** 12th FIFA WC. Qualifiers
Stadion Feijenoord, Rotterdam; Referee: Luigi Agnolin (Italy); Attendance: 58,000
FRA: Dominique Dropsy (15/0), Gérard Janvion (25/0), Léonard Specht (14/1), Christian Lopez (Cap) (26/1), Maxime Bossis (28/0), Jean-François Larios (10/4), Alain Giresse (6/0), Alain Moizan (5/0) [77.Didier Christophe (5/1)], Dominique Rocheteau (19/3), Bernard Lacombe (25/9) [63.Atre Jacques „Zimako" (10/2)], Didier Six (28/7). Trainer: Michel Hidalgo (38).

403. 29.04.1981 **FRANCE - BELGIUM** **3-2(3-1)** 12th FIFA WC. Qualifiers
Stade Parc des Princes, Paris; Referee: Victoriano Sánchez Arminio (Spain); Attendance: 44,954
FRA: Dominique Dropsy (16/0), Gérard Janvion (26/0), Christian Lopez (Cap) (27/1), Marius Trésor (46/3), Maxime Bossis (29/0), Jean Amadou Tigana (6/0), Alain Giresse (7/0), Bernard Genghini (2/0), Gérard Soler (4/3) [71.Atre Jacques „Zimako" (11/2)], Dominique Rocheteau (20/3), Didier Six (29/8). Trainer: Michel Hidalgo (39).
Goals: Gérard Soler (14), Didier Six (26), Gérard Soler (31).

404. 15.05.1981 **FRANCE - BRAZIL** **1-3(0-2)**
Stade Parc des Princes, Paris; Referee: Gianfranco Menegali (Italy); Attendance: 47,749
FRA: Dominique Dropsy (17/0) [46.Jean Castaneda (2/0)], Gérard Janvion (27/0), Christian Lopez (Cap) (28/1), Marius Trésor (47/3) [23.Léonard Specht (15/1)], Maxime Bossis (30/0), Jean Amadou Tigana (7/0), Alain Moizan (6/0), Bernard Genghini (3/0), Olivier Rouyer (17/2) [78.Patrice Lecornu (3/0)], Philippe Anziani (1/0) [59.Patrick Delamontagne (1/0)], Didier Six (30/9) [*sent off 90*]. Trainer: Michel Hidalgo (40).
Goal: Didier Six.

405. 09.09.1981 **BELGIUM - FRANCE** **2-0(1-0)** 12th FIFA WC. Qualifiers
Stade du Heysel, Bruxelles; Referee: Károly Palotai (Hungary); Attendance: 52,525
FRA: Patrick Hiard (1/0), Gérard Janvion (28/0), Philippe Mahut (1/0), Christian Lopez (29/1), Maxime Bossis (31/0), Alain Moizan (7/0) [60.Yannick Stopyra (2/1)], Jean-François Larios (11/4), Alain Giresse (8/0), Atre Jacques „Zimako" (12/2), Michel Platini (Cap) (30/17), Didier Six (31/9). Trainer: Michel Hidalgo (41).

406. 14.10.1981 **REPUBLIC OF IRELAND - FRANCE** **3-2(3-1)** 12th FIFA WC. Qualifiers
Lansdowne Road, Dublin; Referee: Ulf Eriksson (Sweden); Attendance: 53,000
FRA: Jean Castaneda (3/0), Maxime Bossis (32/0), Philippe Mahut (2/0) [69.François Bracci (17/0)], Christian Lopez (30/1), Gérard Janvion (29/0), René Girard (1/0), Jean-François Larios (12/4), Didier Christophe (6/1), Michel Platini (Cap) (31/18), Alain Couriol (3/0), Bruno Bellone (1/1) [63.Didier Six (32/9)]. Trainer: Michel Hidalgo (42).
Goals: Bruno Bellone (9), Michel Platini (83).

407. 18.11.1981 **FRANCE - NETHERLANDS** **2-0(0-0)** 12th FIFA WC. Qualifiers
Stade Parc des Princes, Paris; Referee: Antonio José da Silva Garrido (Portugal); Attendance: 48,000
FRA: Jean Castaneda (4/0), Gérard Janvion (30/0), Christian Lopez (31/1), Marius Trésor (48/3), Maxime Bossis (33/0), Alain Giresse (9/0), Michel Platini (Cap) (32/19) [75.Jean Amadou Tigana (8/0)], Bernard Genghini (4/0), Dominique Rocheteau (21/3), Bernard Lacombe (26/9) [69.Atre Jacques „Zimako" (13/2)], Didier Six (33/10). Trainer: Michel Hidalgo (43).
Goals: Michel Platini (52), Didier Six (82).

408. 05.12.1981 **FRANCE - CYPRUS** **4-0(2-0)** 12th FIFA WC. Qualifiers
Stade Parc des Princes, Paris; Referee: Edwin Borg (Malta); Attendance: 43,437
FRA: Jean Castaneda (5/0), Gérard Janvion (31/0), Christian Lopez (32/1), Marius Trésor (Cap) (49/3), Maxime Bossis (34/0), Alain Giresse (10/0), Jean Amadou Tigana (9/0), Bernard Genghini (5/1), Dominique Rocheteau (22/4), Bernard Lacombe (27/11), Didier Six (34/10) [63.Bruno Bellone (2/1)]. Trainer: Michel Hidalgo (44).
Goals: Dominique Rocheteau (25), Bernard Lacombe (29, 82), Bernard Genghini (86).

409. 23.02.1982 **FRANCE - ITALY** **2-0(1-0)**
Stade Parc des Princes, Paris; Referee: Walter Eschweiler (West Germany); Attendance: 43,541
FRA: Dominique Baratelli (20/0), Manuel Amoros (1/0), Christian Lopez (33/1), Marius Trésor (50/3), Gérard Janvion (32/0) [46.Patrick Battiston (17/1)], Alain Giresse (11/0), Jean Amadou Tigana (10/0), Michel Platini (Cap) (33/20), Gérard Soler (5/3), Bernard Lacombe (28/11) [64.Dominique Rocheteau (23/4)], Didier Six (35/10) [66.Daniel Bravo (1/1)]. Trainer: Michel Hidalgo (45).
Goals: Michel Platini (19), Daniel Bravo (84).

410. 24.03.1982 **FRANCE - NORTHERN IRELAND** **4-0(2-0)**
Stade Parc des Princes, Paris; Referee: Roger Verhaeghe (Belgium); Attendance: 34,000
FRA: Jean Castaneda (6/0), Manuel Amoros (2/0), Christian Lopez (34/1) [68.Patrick Battiston (18/1)], Marius Trésor (Cap) (51/3), Maxime Bossis (35/0), Jean-François Larios (13/5), Alain Giresse (12/0) [76.René Girard (2/0)], Bernard Genghini (6/2), Alain Couriol (4/1) [75.Gérard Soler (6/3)], Bruno Bellone (3/1), Bruno Zénier (2/1). Trainer: Michel Hidalgo (46).
Goals: Bruno Zénier (31), Alain Couriol (45), Jean-François Larios (57 penalty), Bernard Genghini (80).

411. 28.04.1982 **FRANCE - PERU** **0-1(0-0)**
Stade Parc des Princes, Paris; Referee: André Daina (Switzerland); Attendance: 46,429
FRA: Dominique Baratelli (21/0), Manuel Amoros (3/0), Léonard Specht (16/1), Dominique Bathenay (20/4), Maxime Bossis (36/0), Michel Platini (Cap) (34/20), Jean-François Larios (14/5) [46.Jean Amadou Tigana (11/0)], Bernard Genghini (7/2), Alain Couriol (5/1) [80.Daniel Bravo (2/1)], Dominique Rocheteau (24/4), Bruno Bellone (4/1) [62.Bruno Zénier (3/1)]. Trainer: Michel Hidalgo (47).

412. 14.05.1982 **FRANCE - BULGARIA** **0-0**
Stade de Gerland, Lyon; Referee: Egbert Mulder (Netherlands); Attendance: 45,000
FRA: Jean-Luc Ettori (2/0), Manuel Amoros (4/0), Philippe Mahut (3/0), Marius Trésor (Cap) (52/3), François Bracci (18/0), Jean Amadou Tigana (12/0), Alain Giresse (13/0), Bernard Genghini (8/2) [67.Alain Couriol (6/1)], Daniel Bravo (3/1), Bernard Lacombe (29/11) [77.Yannick Stopyra (3/1)], Bruno Bellone (5/1). Trainer: Michel Hidalgo (48).

413. 02.06.1982 **FRANCE - WALES** **0-1(0-0)**
Stade Municipal, Toulouse; Referee: Viriato Graça Oliva (Portugal); Attendance: 26,671
FRA: Jean Castaneda (7/0), Patrick Battiston (19/1), Marius Trésor (53/3) [46.Philippe Mahut (4/0)], Christian Lopez (35/1), Maxime Bossis (37/0), Jean-François Larios (15/5) [64.Jean Amadou Tigana (13/0)], Alain Giresse (14/0), Michel Platini (Cap) (35/20), Alain Couriol (7/1), Gérard Soler (7/3), Didier Six (36/10) [56.Bruno Bellone (6/1)]. Trainer: Michel Hidalgo (49).

414. 16.06.1982 **ENGLAND - FRANCE** **3-1(1-1)** 12th FIFA WC. Group Stage.
Estadio San Mames, Bilbao (Spain); Referee: Antonio José da Silva Garrido (Portugal); Attendance: 44,172
FRA: Jean-Luc Ettori (3/0), Patrick Battiston (20/1), Christian Lopez (36/1), Marius Trésor (54/3), Maxime Bossis (38/0), René Girard (3/0), Jean-François Larios (16/5) [74.Jean Amadou Tigana (14/0)], Michel Platini (Cap) (36/20), Alain Giresse (15/0), Dominique Rocheteau (25/4) [71.Didier Six (37/10)], Gérard Soler (8/4). Trainer: Michel Hidalgo (50).
Goal: Gérard Soler (24).

415. 11.06.1982 **FRANCE - KUWAIT** **4-1(2-0)** 12th FIFA WC. Group Stage.
Estadio "José Zorilla", Valladolid (Spain); Referee: Miroslav Stupar (Soviet Union); Attendance: 30,043
FRA: Jean-Luc Ettori (4/0), Manuel Amoros (5/0), Gérard Janvion (33/0) [60.Christian Lopez (37/1)], Marius Trésor (55/3), Maxime Bossis (39/1), Alain Giresse (16/0), Michel Platini (Cap) (37/21) [81.René Girard (4/0)], Bernard Genghini (9/3), Gérard Soler (9/4), Bernard Lacombe (30/11), Didier Six (38/11). Trainer: Michel Hidalgo (51).
Goals: Bernard Genghini (31), Michel Platini (43), Didier Six (48), Maxime Bossis (89).

416. 24.06.1982 **CZECHOSLOVAKIA - FRANCE** **1-1(0-0)** 12th FIFA WC. Group Stage.
Estadio "José Zorilla", Valladolid (Spain); Referee: Paolo Casarin (Italy); Attendance: 28,000
FRA: Jean-Luc Ettori (5/0), Manuel Amoros (6/0), Gérard Janvion (34/0), Marius Trésor (56/3), Maxime Bossis (40/1), Alain Giresse (17/0), Michel Platini (Cap) (38/21), Bernard Genghini (10/3), Gérard Soler (10/4) [88.René Girard (5/0)], Bernard Lacombe (31/11) [70.Alain Couriol (8/1)], Didier Six (39/12). Trainer: Michel Hidalgo (52).
Goal: Didier Six (66).

417. 28.06.1982 **AUSTRIA - FRANCE** **0-1(0-1)** 12th FIFA WC. 2nd Round.
Estadio "Vicente Calderón", Madrid; Referee: Károly Palotai (Hungary); Attendance: 37,000
FRA: Jean-Luc Ettori (6/0), Patrick Battiston (21/1), Gérard Janvion (35/0), Marius Trésor (Cap) (57/3), Maxime Bossis (41/1), Alain Giresse (18/0), Bernard Genghini (11/4) [85.René Girard (6/0)], Jean Amadou Tigana (15/0), Gérard Soler (11/4), Bernard Lacombe (32/11) [15.Dominique Rocheteau (26/4)], Didier Six (40/12). Trainer: Michel Hidalgo (53).
Goal: Bernard Genghini (39).

418. 04.07.1982 **FRANCE - NORTHERN IRELAND** **4-1(1-0)** 12th FIFA WC. 2nd Round.
Estadio "Vicente Calderón", Madrid (Spain); Referee: Alojzy Jarguz (Poland); Attendance: 37,000
FRA: Jean-Luc Ettori (7/0), Manuel Amoros (7/0), Gérard Janvion (36/0), Marius Trésor (58/3), Maxime Bossis (42/1), Jean Amadou Tigana (16/0), Alain Giresse (19/2), Bernard Genghini (12/4), Michel Platini (Cap) (39/21), Gérard Soler (12/4) [63.Didier Six (41/12)], Dominique Rocheteau (27/6) [83.Alain Couriol (9/1)]. Trainer: Michel Hidalgo (54).
Goals: Alain Giresse (33), Dominique Rocheteau (46, 68), Alain Giresse (80).

419. 08.07.1982 **WEST GERMANY - FRANCE** **8-7(1-1,1-1,3-3)** 12th FIFA WC. Semi-Finals.
Estadio "ramón Sánchez Pizjuán", Sevilla (Spain); Referee: Charles George Rainier Corver (Netherlands); Attendance: 70,000
FRA: Jean-Luc Ettori (8/0), Manuel Amoros (8/0), Gérard Janvion (37/0), Marius Trésor (59/4), Maxime Bossis (43/1), Jean Amadou Tigana (17/0), Alain Giresse (20/3), Bernard Genghini (13/4) [50.Patrick Battiston (22/1); 60.Christian Lopez (38/1)], Michel Platini (Cap) (40/22), Dominique Rocheteau (28/6), Didier Six (42/12). Trainer: Michel Hidalgo (55).
Goals: Michel Platini (27 penalty), Marius Trésor (93), Alain Giresse (99).

420. 10.07.1982 **POLAND - FRANCE** **3-2(2-1)** 12th FIFA WC. Third Place play-off.
Estadio "José Rico Pérez", Alicante (Spain); Referee: Antonio José da Silva Garrido (Portugal); Attendance: 28,000
FRA: Jean Castaneda (8/0), Manuel Amoros (9/0), Philippe Mahut (5/0), Marius Trésor (Cap) (60/4), Gérard Janvion (38/0) [66.Christian Lopez (39/1)], Jean Amadou Tigana (18/0) [83.Didier Six (43/12)], René Girard (7/1), Jean-François Larios (17/5), Alain Couriol (10/2), Gérard Soler (13/4), Bruno Bellone (7/1). Trainer: Michel Hidalgo (56).
Goals: René Girard (14), Alain Couriol (75).

421. 31.08.1982 **FRANCE - POLAND** **0-4(0-1)**
Stade Parc des Princes, Paris; Referee: Bruno Galler (Switzerland); Attendance: 16,000
FRA: Jean-Luc Ettori (9/0), Manuel Amoros (10/0), Gérard Janvion (39/0), Marius Trésor (Cap) (61/4), Maxime Bossis (44/1) [46.Philippe Mahut (6/0)], Jean Amadou Tigana (19/0), Domonique Bijotat (1/0) [46.Jean-Marc Ferreri (1/0)], Bernard Genghini (14/4), Patrick Delamontagne (2/0), Yannick Stopyra (4/1) [69.Daniel Bravo (4/1)], Gérard Soler (14/4). Trainer: Michel Hidalgo (57).

422. 06.10.1982 **FRANCE - HUNGARY** **1-0(0-0)**
Stade Parc des Princes, Paris; Referee: Roger Verhaeghe (Belgium); Attendance: 15,777
FRA: Jean Castaneda (9/0), Maxime Bossis (45/1), Philippe Mahut (7/0), Marius Trésor (Cap) (62/4), Thierry Tusseau (6/0), Jean Amadou Tigana (20/0) [79.Alain Couriol (11/2)], Bernard Genghini (15/4) [64.Jean-Marc Ferreri (2/0)], Alain Giresse (21/3), Michel Platini (41/22), Laurent Roussey (1/1) [85.Gérard Janvion (40/0)], Didier Six (44/12) [73.Gérard Soler (15/4)]. Trainer: Michel Hidalgo (58).
Goal: Laurent Roussey (65).

423. 10.11.1982 **NETHERLANDS - FRANCE** **1-2(1-1)**
Stadion Feijenoord, Rotterdam; Referee: Roger Schoeters (Belgium); Attendance: 9,693
FRA: Jean-Pierre Tempet (1/0), Patrick Battiston (23/2), Maxime Bossis (46/1), Marius Trésor (63/4), Manuel Amoros (11/0), Jean Amadou Tigana (21/0), Jean-Marc Ferreri (3/0), Michel Platini (Cap) (42/23), Luis Fernandez (1/0), Jean-Marc Ferratge (1/0) [68.François Brisson (1/0)], Laurent Roussey (2/1) [57.Yannick Stopyra (5/1)]. Trainer: Michel Hidalgo (59).
Goals: Patrick Battiston (12), Michel Platini (81).

424. 16.02.1983 **PORTUGAL - FRANCE** **0-3(0-2)**
Estádio Municipal, Guimaraes; Referee: Ulrich Nyffenegger (Switzerland); Attendance: 9,000
FRA: Jean-Pierre Tempet (2/0), Patrick Battiston (24/2), Philippe Mahut (8/0), Maxime Bossis (47/1), Manuel Amoros (12/0), Luis Fernandez (2/0) [75.Thierry Tusseau (7/0)], Alain Giresse (22/3), Michel Platini (Cap) (43/23), Jean-Marc Ferreri (4/1) [63.Jean Amadou Tigana (22/0)], Yannick Stopyra (6/3) [80.Dominique Rocheteau (29/6)], Loïc Amisse (11/2). Trainer: Michel Hidalgo (60).
Goals: Yannick Stopyra (7), Jean-Marc Ferreri (8), Yannick Stopyra (70).

425. 23.03.1983 **FRANCE - SOVIET UNION** **1-1(1-1)**
Stade Parc des Princes, Paris; Referee: George Courtney (England); Attendance: 45,000
FRA: Jean-Pierre Tempet (3/0), Patrick Battiston (25/2), Philippe Mahut (9/0) [78.Thierry Tusseau (8/0)], Maxime Bossis (48/1), Manuel Amoros (13/0), Alain Giresse (23/3), Jean-Marc Ferreri (5/1), Luis Fernandez (3/1), Michel Platini (Cap) (44/23) [46.Jean Amadou Tigana (23/0)], Yannick Stopyra (7/3), Loïc Amisse (12/2) [65.Dominique Rocheteau (30/6)]. Trainer: Michel Hidalgo (61).
Goal: Luis Fernandez (42).

426. 23.04.1983 **FRANCE - YUGOSLAVIA** **4-0(2-0)**
Stade Parc des Princes, Paris; Referee: Aron Schmidhuber (West Germany); Attendance: 40,881
FRA: Jean-Pierre Tempet (4/0), Manuel Amoros (14/0), Yvon Le Roux (1/1), Maxime Bossis (Cap) (49/1), Thierry Tusseau (9/0), Luis Fernandez (4/1), Jean Amadou Tigana (24/0), Jean-Marc Ferreri (6/1) [79.Yannick Stopyra (8/3)], José Touré (1/1) [79.Bernard Genghini (16/4)], Dominique Rocheteau (31/8), Bruno Bellone (8/1) [66.Didier Six (45/12)]. Trainer: Michel Hidalgo (62).
Goals: Yvon Le Roux (22), Dominique Rocheteau (32, 47), José Touré (74).

427. 31.05.1983 **FRANCE - BELGIUM** **1-1(1-1)**
Stade Municipal, Luxembourg; Referee: Norbert Rolles (Luxembourg); Attendance: 5,880
FRA: Jean-Pierre Tempet (5/0), Jean-Christophe Thouvenel (1/0), Yvon Le Roux (2/1), Patrick Battiston (26/2), Manuel Amoros (15/0), Jean-Claude Lemoult (1/0), Luis Fernandez (5/1), Bernard Genghini (17/4) [86.Philippe Vercruysse (1/0)], José Touré (2/1), Gérard Soler (16/4) [64.Yannick Stopyra (9/3)], Didier Six (Cap) (46/13) [64.Bruno Zénier (4/1)]. Trainer: Michel Hidalgo (63).
Goal: Didier Six (11).

428. 07.09.1983 **DENMARK - FRANCE** **3-1(1-1)**
Idrætsparken, København; Referee: Volker Roth (West Germany); Attendance: 17,500
FRA: Joël Bats (1/0), Patrick Battiston (27/2), Yvon Le Roux (3/1), Maxime Bossis (50/1), Manuel Amoros (16/0), Alain Giresse (24/3), Bernard Genghini (18/4), Luis Fernandez (6/1), Michel Platini (Cap) (45/24), Dominique Rocheteau (32/8), Daniel Bravo (5/1). Trainer: Michel Hidalgo (64).
Goal: Michel Platini (26).

429. 05.10.1983 **FRANCE - SPAIN** **1-1(0-0)**
Stade Parc des Princes, Paris; Referee: Rosario Lo Bello (Italy); Attendance: 36,628
FRA: Joël Bats (2/0), William Ayache (1/0), Yvon Le Roux (4/1), Marius Trésor (Cap) (64/4), JEan-Louis Zanon (1/0), Jean-Marc Ferreri (7/1), Jean-Claude Lemoult (2/0), Luis Fernandez (7/1), Michel Platini (46/24) [75.Bernard Genghini (19/4)], Dominique Rocheteau (33/9), Bruno Bellone (9/1) [85.Alain Couriol (12/2)]. Trainer: Michel Hidalgo (65).
Goal: Dominique Rocheteau (60).

430. 12.11.1983 **YUGOSLAVIA - FRANCE** **0-0**
Stadion Maksimir, Zagreb; Referee: Paolo Casarin (Italy); Attendance: 15,000
FRA: Joël Bats (3/0), Maxime Bossis (51/1), Yvon Le Roux (5/1), Marius Trésor (Cap) (65/4), Manuel Amoros (17/0), Luis Fernandez (8/1), Daniel Bravo (6/1), Jean Amadou Tigana (25/0), Alain Giresse (25/3), Dominique Rocheteau (34/9) [46.Jean-Marc Ferreri (8/1)], Bruno Bellone (10/1) [63.Daniel Xuereb (2/0)]. Trainer: Michel Hidalgo (66).

431. 29.02.1984 **FRANCE - ENGLAND** **2-0(0-0)**
Stade Parc des Princes, Paris; Referee: Marcel Van Langenhove (Belgium); Attendance: 45,554
FRA: Joël Bats (4/0), Patrick Battiston (28/2) [72.Thierry Tusseau (10/0)], Yvon Le Roux (6/1), Maxime Bossis (52/1), Manuel Amoros (18/0), Jean Amadou Tigana (26/0), Alain Giresse (26/3), Michel Platini (Cap) (47/26), Luis Fernandez (9/1), José Touré (3/1), Bruno Bellone (11/1) [83.Dominique Rocheteau (35/9)]. Trainer: Michel Hidalgo (67).
Goals: Michel Platini (58, 71).

432. 28.03.1984 **FRANCE - AUSTRIA** **1-0(0-0)**
Stade Parc Lescure, Bordeaux; Referee: Viriato Graça Oliva (Portugal); Attendance: 20,000
FRA: Joël Bats (5/0) [62.Ohilippe Bergeroo (3/0)], Patrick Battiston (29/2), Yvon Le Roux (7/1), Maxime Bossis (53/1), Manuel Amoros (19/0), Luis Fernandez (10/1), Jean Amadou Tigana (27/0), Alain Giresse (Cap) (27/3), Bernard Genghini (20/4), Bernard Lacombe (33/11) [51.Dominique Rocheteau (36/10)], Bruno Bellone (12/1) [65.Didier Six (47/13)]. Trainer: Michel Hidalgo (68).
Goal: Dominique Rocheteau (83).

433. 18.04.1984 **FRANCE - WEST GERMANY** **1-0(0-0)**
Stade de la Meinau, Strasbourg; Referee: Enzo Barbaresco (Italy); Attendance: 39,978
FRA: Joël Bats (6/0), Patrick Battiston (30/2), Yvon Le Roux (8/1), Maxime Bossis (Cap) (54/1) [46.Jean-François Domergue (1/0)], Manuel Amoros (20/0), Luis Fernandez (11/1), Daniel Bravo (7/1), Bernard Genghini (21/5), Didier Six (48/13), Dominique Rocheteau (37/10) [68.Philippe Anziani (2/0)], Bruno Bellone (13/1) [84.Jean-Marc Ferreri (9/1)]. Trainer: Michel Hidalgo (69).
Goal: Bernard Genghini (79).

434. 01.06.1984 **FRANCE - SCOTLAND** **2-0(2-0)**
Stade Vélodrome, Marseille; Referee: Luigi Agnolin (Italy); Attendance: 24,641
FRA: Joël Bats (7/0), Patrick Battiston (31/2), Yvon Le Roux (9/1), Maxime Bossis (55/1), Manuel Amoros (21/0), Jean Amadou Tigana (28/0), Luis Fernandez (12/1) [67.Bernard Genghini (22/5)], Alain Giresse (28/4), Michel Platini (Cap) (48/26), Bernard Lacombe (34/12) [46.Daniel Bravo (8/1)], Bruno Bellone (14/1) [67.Didier Six (49/13)]. Trainer: Michel Hidalgo (70).
Goals: Alain Giresse (14), Bernard Lacombe (29).

435. 12.06.1984 **FRANCE - DENMARK** **1-0(0-0)** 7th EC. Group Stage.
Stade Parc des Princes, Paris; Referee: Volker Roth (West Germany); Attendance: 48,360
FRA: Joël Bats (8/0), Patrick Battiston (32/2), Yvon Le Roux (10/1) [60.Jean-François Domergue (2/0)], Maxime Bossis (56/1), Manuel Amoros (22/0) [*sent off 87*], Jean Amadou Tigana (29/0), Alain Giresse (29/4), Michel Platini (Cap) (49/27), Luis Fernandez (13/1), Bernard Lacombe (35/12), Bruno Bellone (15/1). Trainer: Michel Hidalgo (71).
Goal: Michel Platini (78).

436. 16.06.1984 **FRANCE - BELGIUM** **5-0(3-0)** 7th EC. Group Stage.
Stade de la Beaujoire, Nantes; Referee: Robert Bonar Valentine (Scotland); Attendance: 51,359
FRA: Joël Bats (9/0), Luis Fernandez (14/2), Maxime Bossis (57/1), Patrick Battiston (33/2), Jean-François Domergue (3/0), Jean Amadou Tigana (30/0), Bernard Genghini (23/5) [79.Thierry Tusseau (11/0)], Alain Giresse (30/5), Michel Platini (Cap) (50/30), Bernard Lacombe (36/12) [65.Dominique Rocheteau (38/10)], Didier Six (50/13). Trainer: Michel Hidalgo (72).
Goals: Michel Platini (4), Alain Giresse (31), Luis Fernandez (44), Michel Platini (74 penalty,89).

437. 19.06.1984 **FRANCE - YUGOSLAVIA** **3-2(0-1)** 7th EC. Group Stage.
Stade „Geoffroy Guichard", Saint-Étienne; Referee: André Daina (Switzerland); Attendance: 45,789
FRA: Joël Bats (10/0), Luis Fernandez (15/2), Patrick Battiston (34/2), Maxime Bossis (58/1), Jean-François Domergue (4/0), Jean Amadou Tigana (31/0), Alain Giresse (31/5), Jean-Marc Ferreri (10/1) [77.Daniel Bravo (9/1)], Michel Platini (Cap) (51/33), Dominique Rocheteau (39/10) [46.Thierry Tusseau (12/0)], Didier Six (51/13). Trainer: Michel Hidalgo (73).
Goals: Michel Platini (59, 61, 76).

438. 23.06.1984 **FRANCE - PORTUGAL** **3-2(1-0,1-1)** 7th EC. Semi-Finals.
Stade Vélodrome, Marseille; Referee: Paolo Bergamo (Italy); Attendance: 54,848
FRA: Joël Bats (11/0), Patrick Battiston (35/2), Yvon Le Roux (11/1), Maxime Bossis (59/1), Jean-François Domergue (5/2), Luis Fernandez (16/2), Jean Amadou Tigana (32/0), Alain Giresse (32/5), Michel Platini (Cap) (52/34), Bernard Lacombe (37/12) [66.Jean-Marc Ferreri (11/1)], Didier Six (52/13) [101.Bruno Bellone (16/1)]. Trainer: Michel Hidalgo (74).
Goals: Jean-François Domergue (25, 115), Michel Platini (119).

439. 27.06.1984 **FRANCE - SPAIN** **2-0(0-0)** 7th EC.Final.
Stade Parc des Princes, Paris; Referee: Vojtech Christov (Czechoslovakia); Attendance: 47,368
FRA: Joël Bats (12/0), Patrick Battiston (36/2) [72.Manuel Amoros (23/0)], Yvon Le Roux (12/1) [*sent off 85*], Maxime Bossis (60/1), Jean-François Domergue (6/2), Alain Giresse (33/5), Jean Amadou Tigana (33/0), Luis Fernandez (17/2), Michel Platini (Cap) (53/35), Bernard Lacombe (38/12) [80.Bernard Genghini (24/5)], Bruno Bellone (17/2). Trainer: Michel Hidalgo (75).
Goals: Michel Platini (57), Bruno Bellone (90).

440. 13.10.1984 **LUXEMBOURG - FRANCE** **0-4(0-4)** 13th FIFA WC. Qualifiers
Stade Municipal, Luxembourg; Referee: Henning Lund-Sørensen (Denmark); Attendance: 9,000
FRA: Joël Bats (13/0), Michel Bibard (1/0), Patrick Battiston (37/3), Maxime Bossis (61/1), Manuel Amoros (24/0), Luis Fernandez (18/2), Alain Giresse (34/5), Michel Platini (Cap) (54/36) [57.Jean-Marc Ferreri (12/1)], Thierry Tusseau (13/0), Yannick Stopyra (10/5), François Brisson (2/0) [72.Philippe Anziani (3/0)]. Trainer: Henri Michel (1).
Goals: Patrick Battiston (2), Michel Platini (12), Yannick Stopyra (24, 32).

441. 21.11.1984 **FRANCE - BULGARIA** **1-0(0-0)** 13th FIFA WC. Qualifiers
Stade Parc des Princes, Paris; Referee: Karl-Heinz Tritschler (West Germany); Attendance: 42,084
FRA: Joël Bats (14/0), Michel Bibard (2/0), Didier Sénac (1/0), Maxime Bossis (62/1), Manuel Amoros (25/0), Luis Fernandez (19/2), Bernard Genghini (25/5), Jean Amadou Tigana (34/0), Michel Platini (Cap) (55/37), Yannick Stopyra (11/5) [58.José Touré (4/1); 84.Thierry Tusseau (14/0)], Bruno Bellone (18/2). Trainer: Henri Michel (2).
Goal: Michel Platini (62 penalty).

442. 08.12.1984 **FRANCE - EAST GERMANY** **2-0(1-0)** 13th FIFA WC. Qualifiers
Stade Parc des Princes, Paris; Referee: Paolo Casarin (Italy); Attendance: 43,174
FRA: Joël Bats (15/0), Michel Bibard (3/0), Didier Sénac (2/0), Maxime Bossis (63/1), Manuel Amoros (26/0), Alain Giresse (35/5), Jean Amadou Tigana (35/0), Luis Fernandez (20/2), Michel Platini (Cap) (56/37), Yannick Stopyra (12/6) [84.Philippe Anziani (4/1)], Bruno Bellone (19/2). Trainer: Henri Michel (3).
Goals: Yannick Stopyra (32), Philippe Anziani (89).

443. 03.04.1985 **YUGOSLAVIA - FRANCE** **0-0** 13th FIFA WC. Qualifiers
Stadion Koševo, Sarajevo; Referee: Erik Fredriksson (Sweden); Attendance: 53,500
FRA: Joël Bats (16/0), William Ayache (2/0), Léonard Specht (17/1), Patrick Battiston (38/3), Manuel Amoros (27/0), Jean Amadou Tigana (36/0), Luis Fernandez (21/2) [82.Thierry Tusseau (15/0)], Michel Platini (Cap) (57/37), Alain Giresse (36/5), Yannick Stopyra (13/6) [69.José Touré (5/1)], Bruno Bellone (20/2). Trainer: Henri Michel (4).

444. 02.05.1985 **BULGARIA - FRANCE** **2-0(1-0)** 13th FIFA WC. Qualifiers
Nationalen stadion "Vasil Levski", Sofia; Referee: Brian McGinlay (Scotland); Attendance: 57,000
FRA: Joël Bats (17/0), William Ayache (3/0), Léonard Specht (18/1), Maxime Bossis (64/1), Manuel Amoros (28/0), José Touré (6/1), Jean Amadou Tigana (37/0), Luis Fernandez (22/2) [69.Thierry Tusseau (16/0)], Michel Platini (Cap) (58/37), Yannick Stopyra (14/6), Bruno Bellone (21/2). Trainer: Henri Michel (5).

445. 21.08.1985 **FRANCE - URUGUAY** **2-0(1-0)** Artemio Franchi Cup
Stade Parc des Princes, Paris; Referee: Abel Gnecco (Argentina); Attendance: 20,405
FRA: Joël Bats (18/0), Michel Bibard (4/0), Yvon Le Roux (13/1), Maxime Bossis (65/1), William Ayache (4/0), Luis Fernandez (23/2), Alain Giresse (37/5), Michel Platini (Cap) (59/37), Thierry Tusseau (17/0), Dominique Rocheteau (40/11), José Touré (7/2). Trainer: Henri Michel (6).
Goals: Dominique Rocheteau (5), José Touré (56).

446. 11.09.1985 **EAST GERMANY - FRANCE** **2-0(0-0)** 13th FIFA WC. Qualifiers
Zentralstadion, Leipzig; Referee: Pietro D'Elia (Italy); Attendance: 78,000
FRA: Joël Bats (19/0), Michel Bibard (5/0), Yvon Le Roux (14/1), Maxime Bossis (Cap) (66/1), William Ayache (5/0), Alain Giresse (38/5), Fabrice Poullain (1/0) [75.Bruno Bellone (22/2)], Luis Fernandez (24/2), Michel Platini (60/37), Dominique Rocheteau (41/11), José Touré (8/2). Trainer: Henri Michel (7).

447. 30.10.1985 **FRANCE - LUXEMBOURG** **6-0(4-0)** 13th FIFA WC. Qualifiers
Stade Parc des Princes, Paris; Referee: Michal Listkiewicz (Poland); Attendance: 28,597
FRA: Joël Bats (20/0), William Ayache (6/0), Patrick Battiston (39/3), Maxime Bossis (67/1) [28.Yvon Le Roux (15/1)], Manuel Amoros (29/0), Jean Amadou Tigana (38/0), Alain Giresse (39/6), Michel Platini (Cap) (61/37), Luis Fernandez (25/3), Dominique Rocheteau (42/14) [63.Bruno Bellone (23/2)], José Touré (9/3). Trainer: Henri Michel (8).
Goals: Dominique Rocheteau (4), José Touré (24), Dominique Rocheteau (29), Alain Giresse (36), Luis Fernandez (49 penalty), Dominique Rocheteau (51).

448. 16.11.1985 **FRANCE - YUGOSLAVIA** **2-0(1-0)** 13th FIFA WC. Qualifiers
Stade Parc des Princes, Paris; Referee: Alexis Ponnet (Belgium); Attendance: 45,670
FRA: Joël Bats (21/0), William Ayache (7/0), Yvon Le Roux (16/1) [*sent off 84*], Patrick Battiston (40/3), Manuel Amoros (30/0), Luis Fernandez (26/3), Jean Amadou Tigana (39/0), Alain Giresse (40/6), Michel Platini (Cap) (62/39), Dominique Rocheteau (43/14) [77.Yannick Stopyra (15/6)], José Touré (10/3). Trainer: Henri Michel (9).
Goals: Michel Platini (3, 71).

449. 26.02.1986 **FRANCE - NORTHERN IRELAND** **0-0**
Stade Parc des Princes, Paris; Referee: Alphonse Constantin (Belgium); Attendance: 28,909
FRA: Joël Bats (22/0), William Ayache (8/0) [46.Yvon Le Roux (17/1)], Patrick Battiston (41/3), Maxime Bossis (68/1), Manuel Amoros (31/0), Alain Giresse (41/6), Luis Fernandez (27/3), Thierry Tusseau (18/0) [65.Jean-Marc Ferreri (13/1)], Michel Platini (Cap) (63/39), Dominique Rocheteau (44/14), Jean-Pierre Papin (1/0). Trainer: Henri Michel (10).

450. 26.03.1986 **FRANCE - ARGENTINA** **2-0(1-0)**
Stade Parc des Princes, Paris; Referee: Franz Gächter (Switzerland); Attendance: 40,045
FRA: Joël Bats (23/0), William Ayache (9/0), Patrick Battiston (42/3) [60.Yvon Le Roux (18/1)], Maxime Bossis (Cap) (69/1), Manuel Amoros (32/0), Luis Fernandez (28/3), Jean Amadou Tigana (40/0), Philippe Vercruysse (2/1), Jean-Marc Ferreri (14/2), Daniel Xuereb (3/0) [70.Yannick Stopyra (16/6)], Bruno Bellone (24/2) [24.Dominique Rocheteau (45/14)]. Trainer: Henri Michel (11).
Goals: Jean-Marc Ferreri (15), Philippe Vercruysse (80).

451. 01.06.1986 **FRANCE - CANADA** **1-0(0-0)** 13th FIFA WC. Group Stage.
Estadio Campo Nuevo, León (Belgium); Referee: Hernan Silva (Chile); Attendance: 35,748
FRA: Joël Bats (24/0), Manuel Amoros (33/0), Patrick Battiston (43/3), Maxime Bossis (70/1), Thierry Tusseau (19/0), Alain Giresse (42/6), Jean Amadou Tigana (41/0), Luis Fernandez (29/3), Michel Platini (Cap) (64/39), Jean-Pierre Papin (2/1), Dominique Rocheteau (46/14) [70.Yannick Stopyra (17/6)]. Trainer: Henri Michel (12).
Goal: Jean-Pierre Papin (79).

452. 05.06.1986 **FRANCE - SOVIET UNION** **1-1(0-0)** 13th FIFA WC. Group Stage.
Estadio Campo Nuevo, León (Belgium); Referee: Romualdo Arppi Filho (Brazil); Attendance: 36,540
FRA: Joël Bats (25/0), William Ayache (10/0), Patrick Battiston (44/3), Maxime Bossis (71/1), Manuel Amoros (34/0), Alain Giresse (43/6) [83.Philippe Vercruysse (3/1)], Luis Fernandez (30/4), Michel Platini (Cap) (65/39), Jean Amadou Tigana (42/0), Jean-Pierre Papin (3/1) [76.Bruno Bellone (25/2)], Yannick Stopyra (18/6). Trainer: Henri Michel (13).
Goal: Luis Fernandez (62).

453. 09.06.1986 **FRANCE - HUNGARY** **3-0(1-0)** 13th FIFA WC. Group Stage.
Estadio Campo Nuevo, León (Belgium); Referee: Carlos Alberto Da Silva Valente (Portugal); Attendance: 31,420
FRA: Joël Bats (26/0), William Ayache (11/0), Maxime Bossis (72/1), Patrick Battiston (45/3), Manuel Amoros (35/0), Alain Giresse (44/6), Luis Fernandez (31/4), Jean Amadou Tigana (43/1), Michel Platini (Cap) (66/39), Yannick Stopyra (19/7) [71.Jean-Marc Ferreri (15/2)], Jean-Pierre Papin (4/1) [61.Dominique Rocheteau (47/18)]. Trainer: Henri Michel (14).
Goals: Yannick Stopyra (30), Jean Amadou Tigana (63), Dominique Rocheteau (84).

454. 17.06.1986 **ITALY - FRANCE** **0-2(0-1)** 13th FIFA WC. 2nd Round of 16.
Estadio Olímpico, Ciudad de México (Belgium); Referee: Carlos Esposito (Argentina); Attendance: 71,449
FRA: Joël Bats (27/0), William Ayache (12/0), Maxime Bossis (73/1), Patrick Battiston (46/3), Manuel Amoros (36/0), Alain Giresse (45/6), Luis Fernandez (32/4) [73.Thierry Tusseau (20/0)], Jean Amadou Tigana (44/1), Michel Platini (Cap) (67/40) [71.Jean-Marc Ferreri (16/2)], Dominique Rocheteau (48/18), Yannick Stopyra (20/8). Trainer: Henri Michel (15).
Goals: Michel Platini (15), Yannick Stopyra (57).

455. 21.06.1986 **FRANCE - BRAZIL** **5-4(1-0,1-1,1-1)** 13th FIFA WC. Quarter-Finals.
Estadio Jalisco, Guadalajara (Belgium); Referee: Ioan Igna (Romania); Attendance: 65,777
FRA: Joël Bats (28/0), Manuel Amoros (37/0), Maxime Bossis (74/1), Patrick Battiston (47/3), Thierry Tusseau (21/0), Luis Fernandez (33/4), Alain Giresse (46/6) [84.Jean-Marc Ferreri (17/2)], Michel Platini (Cap) (68/41), Jean Amadou Tigana (45/1), Dominique Rocheteau (49/18) [99.Bruno Bellone (26/2)], Yannick Stopyra (21/8). Trainer: Henri Michel (16).
Goal: Michel Platini (41).

456. 25.06.1986 **FRANCE - WEST GERMANY** **0-2(0-1)** 13th FIFA WC. Semi-Finals.
Estadio Jalisco, Guadalajara (Belgium); Referee: Luigi Agnolin (Italy); Attendance: 47,500
FRA: Joël Bats (29/0), William Ayache (13/0), Maxime Bossis (75/1), Patrick Battiston (48/3), Manuel Amoros (38/0), Luis Fernandez (34/4), Jean Amadou Tigana (46/1), Alain Giresse (47/6) [71.Philippe Vercruysse (4/1)], Michel Platini (Cap) (69/41), Yannick Stopyra (22/8), Bruno Bellone (27/2) [66.Daniel Xuereb (4/0)]. Trainer: Henri Michel (17).

457. 28.06.1986 **FRANCE - BELGIUM** **4-2(2-1,2-2)** 13th FIFA WC. Third Place play-off.
Estadio Cuauhtemoc, Puebla (Belgium); Referee: George Courtney (England); Attendance: 21,500
FRA: Albert Rust (1/0), Michel Bibard (6/0), Yvon Le Roux (19/1) [56.Maxime Bossis (76/1)], Patrick Battiston (Cap) (49/3), Manuel Amoros (39/1), Jean Amadou Tigana (47/1) [84.Thierry Tusseau (22/0)], Bernard Genghini (26/6), Jean-Marc Ferreri (18/3), Philippe Vercruysse (5/1), Jean-Pierre Papin (5/2), Bruno Bellone (28/2). Trainer: Henri Michel (18).
Goals: Jean-Marc Ferreri (27), Jean-Pierre Papin (43), Bernard Genghini (104), Manuel Amoros (111 penalty).

458. 19.08.1986 **SWITZERLAND - FRANCE** **2-0(0-0)**
Stade Olympique de la Pontaise, Lausanne; Referee: Karl-Heinz Tritschler (West Germany); Attendance: 22,000
FRA: Joël Bats (30/0), Jean-Christophe Thouvenel (2/0), Basile Boli (1/0) [80.Jean-Pierre Papin (6/2)], Patrick Battiston (Cap) (50/3), Manuel Amoros (40/1) [68.Jean-François Domergue (7/2)], Jean-Marc Ferreri (19/3), Fabrice Poullain (2/0), Domonique Bijotat (2/0), Philippe Vercruysse (6/1), Yannick Stopyra (23/8), Gérard Buscher (1/0) [68.Bruno Bellone (29/2)]. Trainer: Henri Michel (19).

459. 10.09.1986 **ICELAND - FRANCE** **0-0** 8th EC. Qualifiers
Laugardalsvöllur, Reykjavík; Referee: Alan Ferguson (Scotland); Attendance: 13,700
FRA: Joël Bats (31/0), William Ayache (14/0), Basile Boli (2/0), Patrick Battiston (Cap) (51/3), Manuel Amoros (41/1), Luis Fernandez (35/4), Jean Amadou Tigana (48/1), Philippe Vercruysse (7/1), Bernard Genghini (27/6), Yannick Stopyra (24/8), Stéphane Paille (1/0). Trainer: Henri Michel (20).

460. 11.10.1986 **FRANCE - SOVIET UNION** **0-2(0-0)** 8th EC. Qualifiers
Stade Parc des Princes, Paris; Referee: Paolo Casarin (Italy); Attendance: 40,496
FRA: Joël Bats (32/0), William Ayache (15/0), Basile Boli (3/0) [87.Philippe Vercruysse (8/1)], Philippe Jeannol (1/0), Manuel Amoros (42/1), Jean Amadou Tigana (49/1), Jean-Marc Ferreri (20/3), Luis Fernandez (36/4), Michel Platini (Cap) (70/41), Yannick Stopyra (25/8), Jean-Pierre Papin (7/2) [70.Bruno Bellone (30/2)]. Trainer: Henri Michel (21).

461. 19.11.1986 **EAST GERMANY - FRANCE** **0-0** 8th EC. Qualifiers
Zentralstadion, Leipzig; Referee: George Courtney (England); Attendance: 54,578
FRA: Joël Bats (33/0), William Ayache (16/0), Basile Boli (4/0), Patrick Battiston (52/3), Manuel Amoros (43/1), Jean Amadou Tigana (50/1), Yvon Le Roux (20/1), Fabrice Poullain (3/0), Michel Platini (Cap) (71/41), Yannick Stopyra (26/8), Jean-Pierre Papin (8/2) [70.Bruno Bellone (31/2)]. Trainer: Henri Michel (22).

462. 29.04.1987 **FRANCE - ICELAND** **2-0(1-0)** 8th EC. Qualifiers
Stade Parc des Princes, Paris; Referee: Frederick McKnight (Northern Ireland); Attendance: 27,732
FRA: Joël Bats (34/0), Jean-Christophe Thouvenel (3/0), Basile Boli (5/0), Jean-François Domergue (8/2), Manuel Amoros (44/1), Luis Fernandez (37/4), José Touré (11/3), Michel Platini (Cap) (72/41), Gérald Passi (1/0), Yannick Stopyra (27/9) [67.Jean-Pierre Papin (9/2)], Carmelo Micciche (1/1). Trainer: Henri Michel (23).
Goals: Carmelo Micciche (37), Yannick Stopyra (65).

463. 16.06.1987 **NORWAY - FRANCE** **2-0(0-0)** 8th EC. Qualifiers
Ullevaal Stadion, Oslo; Referee: Werner Föckler (West Germany); Attendance: 8,268
FRA: Joël Bats (35/0), Manuel Amoros (45/1), Jean-Christophe Thouvenel (4/0), Basile Boli (6/0), Jean-François Domergue (9/2), Fabrice Poullain (4/0) [80.Patrick Delamontagne (3/0)], Jean-Marc Ferreri (21/3), Jean Amadou Tigana (Cap) (51/1), Yannick Stopyra (28/9), Gérald Passi (2/0), Carmelo Micciche (2/1) [75.Philippe Fargeon (1/0)]. Trainer: Henri Michel (24).

464. 12.08.1987 **WEST GERMANY - FRANCE** **2-1(2-1)**
Olympiastadion, West-Berlin; Referee: Henning Lund-Sørensen (Denmark); Attendance: 31,000
FRA: Joël Bats (36/0) [85.Bruno Martini (1/0)], William Ayache (17/0), Yvon Le Roux (21/1), Patrick Battiston (Cap) (53/3), Manuel Amoros (46/1), Luis Fernandez (38/4), José Touré (12/3), Fabrice Poullain (5/0), Gérald Passi (3/0), Jean-Pierre Papin (10/2) [55.Gérard Buscher (2/0)], Eric Cantona (1/1). Trainer: Henri Michel (25).
Goal: Eric Cantona (42).

465. 09.09.1987 **SOVIET UNION - FRANCE** **1-1(0-1)** 8th EC. Qualifiers
Lenin Stadium, Moskva; Referee: Gerasimos Germanakos (Greece); Attendance: 86,048
FRA: Joël Bats (37/0), William Ayache (18/0), Rémi Vogel (1/0), Basile Boli (7/0), Manuel Amoros (47/1), Luis Fernandez (Cap) (39/4), Fabrice Poullain (6/0), José Touré (13/4) [74.Jean-Philippe Rohr (1/0)], Gérald Passi (4/0), Philippe Fargeon (2/0) [87.Jean-Pierre Papin (11/2)], Yannick Stopyra (29/9). Trainer: Henri Michel (26).
Goal: José Touré (13).

466. 14.10.1987 **FRANCE - NORWAY** **1-1(0-0)** 8th EC. Qualifiers
Stade Parc des Princes, Paris; Referee: Joaquín Ramón Marcos (Spain); Attendance: 11,308
FRA: Bruno Martini (2/0), Luc Sonor (1/0), Didier Sénac (3/0), Basile Boli (8/0), Manuel Amoros (48/1), Luis Fernandez (Cap) (40/4), Domonique Bijotat (3/0), José Touré (14/4), Philippe Anziani (5/1) [53.Jean-Marc Ferreri (22/3)], Philippe Fargeon (3/1), Eric Cantona (2/1). Trainer: Henri Michel (27).
Goal: Philippe Fargeon (63).

467. 18.11.1987 **FRANCE - EAST GERMANY** **0-1(0-0)** 8th EC. Qualifiers
Stade Parc des Princes, Paris; Referee: Carlos Alberto Da Silva Valente (Portugal); Attendance: 16,581
FRA: Joël Bats (38/0), Basile Boli (9/0), Sylvain Kastendeuch (1/0), Yvon Le Roux (22/1), Manuel Amoros (Cap) (49/1), Bruno Germain (1/0), Domonique Bijotat (4/0) [76.Philippe Fargeon (4/1)], Fabrice Poullain (7/0), Bruno Zénier (5/1), Eric Cantona (3/1), Bruno Bellone (32/2). Trainer: Henri Michel (28).

468. 27.01.1988 **ISRAEL - FRANCE** **1-1(0-0)**
National Stadium, Ramat Gan, Tel Aviv; Referee: Allan Gunn (England); Attendance: 5,000
FRA: Bruno Martini (3/0), William Ayache (19/0), Yvon Le Roux (23/1), Basile Boli (10/0), Manuel Amoros (50/1), José Touré (15/4) [77.Jean-Marc Ferreri (23/3)], Luis Fernandez (Cap) (41/4) [71.Pascal Despeyroux (1/0)], Fabrice Poullain (8/0), Gérald Passi (5/0), Eric Cantona (4/1), Bruno Bellone (33/2) [49.Yannick Stopyra (30/10)]. Trainer: Henri Michel (29).
Goal: Yannick Stopyra (60).

469. 02.02.1988 **FRANCE - SWITZERLAND** **2-1(2-1)** International Tournament
Stade Municipal, Toulouse; Referee: Gérard Biguet (France); Attendance: 10,348
FRA: Bruno Martini (4/0), William Ayache (20/0) [66.Bernard Casoni (1/0)], Basile Boli (11/0), Sylvain Kastendeuch (2/0), Manuel Amoros (Cap) (51/1), Jean-Marc Ferreri (24/3) [80.Domonique Bijotat (5/0)], Fabrice Poullain (9/0), Pascal Despeyroux (2/0), Gérald Passi (6/1), Yannick Stopyra (31/10) [71.Jean-Pierre Papin (12/2)], Philippe Fargeon (5/2). Trainer: Henri Michel (30).
Goals: Gérald Passi (7), Philippe Fargeon (9).

470. 05.02.1988 **FRANCE - MOROCCO** **2-1(1-1)** International Tournament
Stade „Louis II", Monaco; Referee: Michel Vautrot (France); Attendance: 10,000
FRA: Bruno Martini (5/0), Manuel Amoros (Cap) (52/1), Bernard Casoni (2/0), Sylvain Kastendeuch (3/0), Basile Boli (12/0) [75.Yvon Le Roux (24/1)], Domonique Bijotat (6/0), Fabrice Poullain (10/0) [52.Luis Fernandez (42/4)], Yannick Stopyra (32/11) [82.Bruno Bellone (34/2)], Gérald Passi (7/1), Philippe Fargeon (6/2), Jean-Marc Ferreri (25/3). Trainer: Henri Michel (31).
Goals: Abdelmajid Lemriss (9 own goal), Yannick Stopyra (49).

471. 23.03.1988 **FRANCE - SPAIN** **2-1(2-1)**
Stade Parc Lescure, Bordeaux; Referee: Neil Midgley (England); Attendance: 14,441
FRA: Joël Bats (39/0), Luc Sonor (2/0), Yvon Le Roux (25/1), Sylvain Kastendeuch (4/0), Manuel Amoros (53/1) [80.Basile Boli (13/0)], Domonique Bijotat (7/0) [85.Marcel Dib (1/0)], Luis Fernandez (Cap) (43/5), Gérald Passi (8/2), Jean-Philippe Durand (1/0), Jean-Pierre Papin (13/2), Eric Cantona (5/1). Trainer: Henri Michel (32).
Goals: Gérald Passi (8), Luis Fernandez (26).

472. 27.04.1988 **NORTHERN IRELAND - FRANCE** **0-0**
Windsor Park, Belfast; Referee: Keith Cooper (Wales); Attendance: 6,250
FRA: Bruno Martini (6/0), Luc Sonor (3/0), Sylvain Kastendeuch (5/0), Bernard Casoni (3/0), Manuel Amoros (54/1), Domonique Bijotat (8/0), Luis Fernandez (Cap) (44/5), Philippe Vercruysse (9/1) [83.Jean-Marc Ferreri (26/3)], Jean-Philippe Durand (2/0), Yannick Stopyra (33/11), Patrice Garande (1/0) [83.Philippe Fargeon (7/2)]. Trainer: Henri Michel (33).

473. 24.08.1988 **FRANCE - CZECHOSLOVAKIA** **1-1(0-0)**
Stade Parc des Princes, Paris; Referee: Ildefonso Urizar Azpitarte (Spain); Attendance: 15,000
FRA: Joël Bats (40/0), Luc Sonor (4/0), Sylvain Kastendeuch (6/0), Bernard Casoni (4/0), Manuel Amoros (Cap) (55/1), Pascal Despeyroux (3/0), Frank Sauzée (1/0), Gérald Passi (9/2) [64.Philippe Vercruysse (10/1)], Bernard Pardo (1/0), Stéphane Paille (2/1), Jean-Pierre Papin (14/2). Trainer: Henri Michel (34).
Goal: Stéphane Paille (52).

474. 28.09.1988 **FRANCE - NORWAY** **1-0(0-0)** 14th FIFA WC. Qualifiers
Stade Parc des Princes, Paris; Referee: Günther Habermann (East Germany); Attendance: 22,000
FRA: Joël Bats (41/0), Manuel Amoros (Cap) (56/1), Basile Boli (14/0) [63.Sylvain Kastendeuch (7/0)], Bernard Casoni (5/0), Luc Sonor (5/0), Frank Sauzée (2/0), Daniel Bravo (10/1), Marcel Dib (2/0), Gérald Passi (10/2) [76.Stéphane Paille (3/1)], Jean-Pierre Papin (15/3), Daniel Xuereb (5/0). Trainer: Henri Michel (35).
Goal: Jean-Pierre Papin (84 penalty).

475. 22.10.1988 **CYPRUS - FRANCE** **1-1(0-1)** 14th FIFA WC. Qualifiers
Stádio Makareio, Nicosia; Referee: Emilio Soriano Aladren (Spain); Attendance: 2,700
FRA: Joël Bats (42/0), Luc Sonor (6/0), Bernard Casoni (6/0), Basile Boli (15/0), Manuel Amoros (Cap) (57/1), Daniel Bravo (11/1), Marcel Dib (3/0), Frank Sauzée (3/0), Gérald Passi (11/2) [72.Philippe Vercruysse (11/1)], Jean-Pierre Papin (16/3), Daniel Xuereb (6/1) [80.Stéphane Paille (4/1)]. Trainer: Henri Michel (36).
Goal: Daniel Xuereb (44).

476. 19.11.1988 **YUGOSLAVIA - FRANCE** **3-2(1-1)** 14th FIFA WC. Qualifiers
Stadion JNA, Beograd; Referee: Erik Fredriksson (Sweden); Attendance: 7,489
FRA: Joël Bats (43/0), Alain Roche (1/0), Basile Boli (16/0), Sylvain Kastendeuch (8/0), Manuel Amoros (Cap) (58/1), Jean-Marc Ferreri (27/3) [78.Jean-Pierre Papin (17/3)], Marcel Dib (4/0), Frank Sauzée (4/1), Jean Amadou Tigana (52/1), Stéphane Paille (5/1), Christian Perez (1/1) [69.Daniel Bravo (12/1)]. Trainer: Michel Platini (1).
Goals: Christian Perez (3), Frank Sauzée (68).

477. 07.02.1989 **REPUBLIC OF IRELAND - FRANCE** **0-0**
Dalymount Park, Dublin; Referee: John Walter Lloyd (Wales); Attendance: 22,000
FRA: Joël Bats (44/0), Manuel Amoros (Cap) (59/1), Sylvain Kastendeuch (9/0), Luc Sonor (7/0), Patrick Battiston (54/3), Frank Silvestre (1/0) [74.Alain Roche (2/0)], Jean-Philippe Durand (3/0), Frank Sauzée (5/1), Stéphane Paille (6/1) [46.José Touré (16/4)], Jean-Pierre Papin (18/3), Laurent Robert Blanc (1/0) [67.Philippe Vercruysse (12/1)]. Trainer: Michel Platini (2).

478. 08.03.1989 **SCOTLAND - FRANCE** **2-0(1-0)** 14th FIFA WC. Qualifiers
Hampden Park, Glasgow; Referee: Jiří Stiegler (Czechoslovakia); Attendance: 65,204
FRA: Joël Bats (45/0), Manuel Amoros (Cap) (60/1), Frank Silvestre (2/0), Luc Sonor (8/0), Patrick Battiston (55/3), Frank Sauzée (6/1), Jean-Philippe Durand (4/0) [57.Stéphane Paille (7/1)], Thierry Laurey (1/0), Jean-Pierre Papin (19/3), Laurent Robert Blanc (2/0), Daniel Xuereb (7/1) [73.Christian Perez (2/1)]. Trainer: Michel Platini (3).

479. 29.04.1989 **FRANCE - YUGOSLAVIA** **0-0** 14th FIFA WC. Qualifiers
Stade Parc des Princes, Paris; Referee: Tullio Lanese (Italy); Attendance: 39,469
FRA: Joël Bats (46/0), Manuel Amoros (Cap) (61/1), Luc Sonor (9/0), Basile Boli (17/0), Patrick Battiston (56/3), Frank Sauzée (7/1), Daniel Xuereb (8/1) [76.Didier Deschamps (1/0)], Jean-Philippe Durand (5/0) [46.Christophe Cocard (1/0)], Stéphane Paille (8/1), Laurent Robert Blanc (3/0), Christian Perez (3/1). Trainer: Michel Platini (4).

480. 16.08.1989 **SWEDEN - FRANCE** **2-4(1-0)** 14th FIFA WC. Qualifiers
Malmö Stadion, Malmö; Referee: Sharir (Israel); Attendance: 16,619
FRA: Joël Bats (47/0), Manuel Amoros (Cap) (62/1), Yvon Le Roux (26/1), Frank Sauzée (8/1), Eric Di Meco (1/0), Jean-Marc Ferreri (28/3) [70.Laurent Robert Blanc (4/0)], Didier Deschamps (2/0), Bernard Pardo (2/0), Christian Perez (4/1), Jean-Pierre Papin (20/5), Eric Cantona (6/3). Trainer: Michel Platini (5).
Goals: Eric Cantona (57), Jean-Pierre Papin (61, 83), Eric Cantona (87).

481. 05.09.1989 **NORWAY - FRANCE** **1-1(0-1)** 14th FIFA WC. Qualifiers
Ullevaal Stadion, Oslo; Referee: Todor Kolev (Bulgaria); Attendance: 8,564
FRA: Joël Bats (48/0), Manuel Amoros (Cap) (63/1), Frank Sauzée (9/1), Yvon Le Roux (27/1) [56.Frank Silvestre (3/0)], Eric Di Meco (2/0), Christian Perez (5/1), Bernard Pardo (3/0), Didier Deschamps (3/0), Jean-Marc Ferreri (29/3) [75.Laurent Robert Blanc (5/0)], Jean-Pierre Papin (21/6), Eric Cantona (7/3). Trainer: Michel Platini (6).
Goal: Jean-Pierre Papin (40 penalty).

482. 11.10.1989 **FRANCE - SCOTLAND** **3-0(1-0)** 14th FIFA WC. Qualifiers
Stade Parc des Princes, Paris; Referee: Kurt Röthlisberger (Switzerland); Attendance: 25,000
FRA: Joël Bats (Cap) (49/0), Frank Silvestre (4/0), Yvon Le Roux (28/1) [46.Bernard Casoni (7/0)], Frank Sauzée (10/1), Eric Di Meco (3/0) [*sent off 57*], Bernard Pardo (4/0), Didier Deschamps (4/1), Jean-Philippe Durand (6/0), Jean-Marc Ferreri (30/3), Christian Perez (6/1) [81.Daniel Bravo (13/1)], Eric Cantona (8/4). Trainer: Michel Platini (7).
Goals: Didier Deschamps (26), Eric Cantona (63), Stephen Nicol (88 own goal).

483. 18.11.1989 **FRANCE - CYPRUS** **2-0(1-0)** 14th FIFA WC. Qualifiers
Stade Parc des Princes, Paris; Referee: Valeri Butenko (Soviet Union); Attendance: 34,687
FRA: Joël Bats (50/0), Frank Silvestre (5/0), Bernard Casoni (8/0), Frank Sauzée (11/1), Manuel Amoros (Cap) (64/1), Bernard Pardo (5/0), Didier Deschamps (5/2), Jean-Marc Ferreri (31/3), Christian Perez (7/1) [17.Laurent Robert Blanc (6/1)], Jean-Pierre Papin (22/6), Eric Cantona (9/4). Trainer: Michel Platini (8).
Goals: Didier Deschamps (25), Laurent Robert Blanc (75).

484. 21.01.1990 **KUWAIT - FRANCE** **0-1(0-0)**
Al Sadqua Walsalam Stadium, Adiliya; Referee: Ghazi Ali Al Kandi (Kuwait); Attendance: 5,000
FRA: Gilles Rousset (1/0), Frank Silvestre (6/0), Basile Boli (18/0), Frank Sauzée (12/1), Manuel Amoros (Cap) (65/1), Laurent Robert Blanc (7/2), Marcel Dib (5/0), Rémi Garde (1/0), Bernard Pardo (6/0) [46.Didier Deschamps (6/2)], Eric Cantona (10/4) [46.Jean-Pierre Papin (23/6); 77.Eric Di Meco (4/0)], Pascal Vahirua (1/0) [46.Jean-Marc Ferreri (32/3)]. Trainer: Michel Platini (9).
Goal: Laurent Robert Blanc (74).

485. 24.01.1990 **FRANCE - EAST GERMANY** **3-0(2-0)**
Al Sadqua Walsalam Stadium, Adiliya (Kuwait); Referee: Ghazi Ali Al Kandi (Kuwait); Attendance: 1,500
FRA: Bruno Martini (7/0), Manuel Amoros (Cap) (66/1) [81.Basile Boli (19/0)], Bernard Casoni (9/0), Frank Sauzée (13/1) [78.Frank Silvestre (7/0)], Eric Di Meco (5/0), Laurent Robert Blanc (8/2) [84.Marcel Dib (6/0)], Bernard Pardo (7/0), Didier Deschamps (7/3), Jean-Marc Ferreri (33/3) [60.Rémi Garde (2/0)], Eric Cantona (11/6), Pascal Vahirua (2/0). Trainer: Michel Platini (10).
Goals: Eric Cantona (1, 24), Didier Deschamps (73).

486. 28.02.1990 **FRANCE - WEST GERMANY** **2-1(1-1)**
Stade de la Mosson, Montpellier; Referee: Joaquín Ramos Marcos (Spain); Attendance: 22,000
FRA: Bruno Martini (8/0), Manuel Amoros (Cap) (67/1), Bernard Casoni (10/0), Basile Boli (20/0) [49.Laurent Robert Blanc (9/2)], Eric Di Meco (6/0), Jean-Marc Ferreri (34/3) [64.Pascal Vahirua (3/0)], Didier Deschamps (8/3), Bernard Pardo (8/0), Rémi Garde (3/0), Jean-Pierre Papin (24/7), Eric Cantona (12/7). Trainer: Michel Platini (11).
Goals: Eric Cantona (43), Jean-Pierre Papin (82).

487. 28.03.1990 **HUNGARY - FRANCE** **1-3(1-1)**
Népstadion, Budapest; Referee: Tadeusz Diakonowicz (Poland); Attendance: 12,000
FRA: Bruno Martini (9/0), Manuel Amoros (Cap) (68/1) [46.Jean-Philippe Durand (7/0)], Frank Silvestre (8/0), Bernard Casoni (11/0), Frank Sauzée (14/2) [79.Laurent Robert Blanc (10/2)], Bernard Pardo (9/0), Christian Perez (8/1), Luis Fernandez (45/5) [69.Basile Boli (21/0)], Philippe Tibeuf (1/0) [63.Fabrice Divert (1/0)], Jean-Marc Ferreri (35/3), Eric Cantona (13/9). Trainer: Michel Platini (12).
Goals: Eric Cantona (27, 67), Frank Sauzée (70).

488. 15.08.1990 **FRANCE - POLAND** **0-0**
Stade Parc des Princes, Paris; Referee: Neil Midgley (England); Attendance: 15,919
FRA: Bruno Martini (10/0), Manuel Amoros (Cap) (69/1) [76.Jean-Philippe Durand (8/0)], Emmanuel Petit (1/0), Frank Sauzée (15/2), Bernard Casoni (12/0), Luis Fernandez (46/5) [46.Basile Boli (22/0)], Jean-Marc Ferreri (36/3) [59.Pascal Vahirua (4/0)], Bernard Pardo (10/0), Christian Perez (9/1), Eric Cantona (14/9), Jean-Pierre Papin (25/7). Trainer: Michel Platini (13).

489. 05.09.1990 **ICELAND - FRANCE** **1-2(0-1)** 9th EC. Qualifiers
Laugardalsvöllur, Reykjavík; Referee: David F.T. Syme (Scotland); Attendance: 8,000
FRA: Bruno Martini (11/0), Manuel Amoros (Cap) (70/1), Basile Boli (23/0), Frank Sauzée (16/2), Bernard Casoni (13/0), Laurent Robert Blanc (11/2) [75.Jean-Philippe Durand (9/0)], Bernard Pardo (11/0), Didier Deschamps (9/3), Christian Perez (10/1), Jean-Pierre Papin (26/8), Eric Cantona (15/10) [84.Luis Fernandez (47/5)]. Trainer: Michel Platini (14).
Goals: Jean-Pierre Papin (12), Eric Cantona (76).

490. 13.10.1990 **FRANCE - CZECHOSLOVAKIA** **2-1(0-0)** 9th EC. Qualifiers
Stade Parc des Princes, Paris; Referee: George Courtney (England); Attendance: 38,249
FRA: Bruno Martini (12/0), Basile Boli (24/0), Laurent Robert Blanc (12/2), Bernard Casoni (14/0), Jean-Philippe Durand (10/0), Jocelyn Angloma (1/0) [52.Luis Fernandez (48/5)], Didier Deschamps (10/3), Frank Sauzée (Cap) (17/2), Pascal Vahirua (5/0) [84.Frank Silvestre (9/0)], Jean-Pierre Papin (27/10), Eric Cantona (16/10). Trainer: Michel Platini (15).
Goals: Jean-Pierre Papin (59, 82).

491. 17.11.1990 **ALBANIA - FRANCE** **0-1(0-1)** 9th EC. Qualifiers
Stadiumi „Kombëtar Qemal Stafa“, Tiranë; Referee: Bruno Galler (Switzerland); Attendance: 18,000
FRA: Bruno Martini (13/0), Basile Boli (25/1), Frank Sauzée (Cap) (18/2), Laurent Robert Blanc (13/2), Bernard Casoni (15/0), Didier Deschamps (11/3), Bernard Pardo (12/0), Jean-Marc Ferreri (37/3), Christian Perez (11/1), Philippe Tibeuf (2/0) [67.David Ginola (1/0)], Pascal Vahirua (6/0) [82.Jocelyn Angloma (2/0)]. Trainer: Michel Platini (16).
Goal: Basile Boli.

492. 20.02.1991 **FRANCE - SPAIN** **3-1(1-1)** 9th EC. Qualifiers

Stade Parc des Princes, Paris; Referee: Tulio Lanese (Italy); Attendance: 41,174

FRA: Bruno Martini (14/0), Manuel Amoros (Cap) (71/1), Bernard Casoni (16/0), Basile Boli (26/1), Laurent Robert Blanc (14/3), Bernard Pardo (13/0) [51.Luis Fernandez (49/5)], Jean-Philippe Durand (11/0), Frank Sauzée (19/3), Jean-Pierre Papin (28/11), Eric Cantona (17/10), Pascal Vahirua (7/0) [82.Didier Deschamps (12/3)]. Trainer: Michel Platini (17).

Goals: Frank Sauzée (14), Jean-Pierre Papin (58), Laurent Robert Blanc (77).

493. 30.03.1991 **FRANCE - ALBANIA** **5-0(4-0)** 9th EC. Qualifiers

Stade Parc des Princes, Paris; Referee: Einar Halle (Norway); Attendance: 24,181

FRA: Bruno Martini (15/0), Manuel Amoros (Cap) (72/1), Basile Boli (27/1), Laurent Robert Blanc (15/3), Jean-Philippe Durand (12/0), Luis Fernandez (50/5), Frank Sauzée (20/5) [73.Didier Deschamps (13/3)], Christophe Cocard (2/0), Eric Cantona (18/10), Jean-Pierre Papin (29/13), Pascal Vahirua (8/0) [56.Pascal Baills (1/0)]. Trainer: Michel Platini (18).

Goals: Frank Sauzée (1, 19), Jean-Pierre Papin (34 penalty, 42), Blendi Nallbani (81 own goal).

494. 14.08.1991 **POLAND - FRANCE** **1-5(1-2)**

Stadion Lech, Poznań; Referee: Alexei Spirin (Soviet Union); Attendance: 15,000

FRA: Bruno Martini (16/0), Manuel Amoros (Cap) (73/1) [73.Rémi Garde (4/0)], Bernard Casoni (17/0) [77.Frank Silvestre (10/0)], Laurent Robert Blanc (16/4), Basile Boli (28/1), Jocelyn Angloma (3/0), Frank Sauzée (21/6), Luis Fernandez (51/5) [46.Didier Deschamps (14/3)], Jean-Pierre Papin (30/14), Jean-Philippe Durand (13/0) [53.Christian Perez (12/2)], Amara Simba (1/1). Trainer: Michel Platini (19).

Goals: Frank Sauzée, Jean-Pierre Papin, Amara Simba, Laurent Robert Blanc, Christian Perez.

495. 04.09.1991 **CZECHOSLOVAKIA - FRANCE** **1-2(1-0)** 9th EC. Qualifiers

Stade Parc des Princes, Paris; Referee: Erik Mikkelsen (Denmark); Attendance: 50,000

FRA: Bruno Martini (17/0), Laurent Robert Blanc (17/4), Manuel Amoros (Cap) (74/1), Jocelyn Angloma (4/0) [77.Jean-Philippe Durand (14/0)], Basile Boli (29/1), Bernard Casoni (18/0), Didier Deschamps (15/3), Frank Sauzée (22/6), Jean-Pierre Papin (31/16), Christophe Cocard (3/0) [46.Christian Perez (13/2)], Pascal Vahirua (9/0). Trainer: Michel Platini (20).

Goals: Jean-Pierre Papin (53, 89).

496. 12.10.1991 **SPAIN - FRANCE** **1-2(1-2)** 9th EC. Qualifiers

Estadio „Benito Villamarín", Sevilla; Referee: Hubert Förstinger (Austria); Attendance: 27,500

FRA: Bruno Martini (18/0), Manuel Amoros (Cap) (75/1), Laurent Robert Blanc (18/4), Basile Boli (30/1), Bernard Casoni (19/0), Didier Deschamps (16/3), Jocelyn Angloma (5/0), Luis Fernandez (52/6) [82.Jean-Philippe Durand (15/0)], Christian Perez (14/2) [63.Rémi Garde (5/0)], Eric Cantona (19/10), Jean-Pierre Papin (32/17). Trainer: Michel Platini (21).

Goals: Luis Fernandez (13), Jean-Pierre Papin (16).

497. 20.11.1991 **FRANCE - ICELAND** **3-1(1-0)** 9th EC. Qualifiers

Stade Parc des Princes, Paris; Referee: Erik Fredriksson (Sweden); Attendance: 27,381

FRA: Bruno Martini (19/0), Jocelyn Angloma (6/0), Laurent Robert Blanc (19/4), Bernard Casoni (20/0) [46.Basile Boli (31/1)], Manuel Amoros (Cap) (76/1), Didier Deschamps (17/3), Luis Fernandez (53/6) [68.Jean-Philippe Durand (16/0)], Christian Perez (15/2), Eric Cantona (20/12), Amara Simba (2/2), Pascal Vahirua (10/0). Trainer: Michel Platini (22).

Goals: Amara Simba (42), Eric Cantona (59, 68).

498. 19.02.1992 **ENGLAND - FRANCE** **2-0(1-0)**

Wembley Stadium, London; Referee: Aron Schmidhuber (Germany); Attendance: 58,723

FRA: Gilles Rousset (2/0), Manuel Amoros (Cap) (77/1), Jocelyn Angloma (7/0), Basile Boli (32/1), Laurent Robert Blanc (20/4), Bernard Casoni (21/0), Didier Deschamps (18/3), Luis Fernandez (54/6) [71.Jean-Philippe Durand (17/0)], Jean-Pierre Papin (33/17), Christian Perez (16/2) [71.Amara Simba (3/2)], Eric Cantona (21/12). Trainer: Michel Platini (23).

499. 25.03.1992 **FRANCE - BELGIUM** **3-3(2-2)**

Stade Parc des Princes, Paris; Referee: Phillip Don (England); Attendance: 25,000

FRA: Bruno Martini (20/0), Bernard Casoni (22/0), Jocelyn Angloma (8/0), Basile Boli (33/1), Emmanuel Petit (2/0) [46.Jean-Philippe Durand (18/0)], Christian Perez (17/2), Didier Deschamps (19/3), Frank Sauzée (Cap) (23/6) [65.Manuel Amoros (78/1)], Jean-Pierre Papin (34/19), Eric Cantona (22/12), Pascal Vahirua (11/1) [46.Luis Fernandez (55/6)]. Trainer: Michel Platini (24).

Goals: Jean-Pierre Papin (40 penalty), Pascal Vahirua (45), Jean-Pierre Papin (85).

500. 27.05.1992 **SWITZERLAND - FRANCE** **2-1(1-1)**

Stade Olympique de la Pontaise, Lausanne; Referee: Alfred Wieser (Austria); Attendance: 20,000

FRA: Bruno Martini (21/0), Laurent Robert Blanc (21/4), Bernard Casoni (23/0) [46.Emmanuel Petit (3/0)], Didier Deschamps (20/3) [46.Luis Fernandez (56/6)], Frank Sauzée (Cap) (24/6) [71.Rémi Garde (6/0)], Christian Perez (18/2) [46.Christophe Cocard (4/0)], Basile Boli (34/1) [46.Frank Silvestre (11/0)], Jean-Philippe Durand (19/0), Fabrice Divert (2/1), Eric Cantona (23/12) [46.Pascal Vahirua (12/1)], Jocelyn Angloma (9/0). Trainer: Michel Platini (25).

Goal: Fabrice Divert (20).

501. 05.06.1992 **FRANCE - NETHERLANDS** **1-1(1-1)**

Stade „Félix Bollaert", Lens; Referee: Hans-Jürgen Weber (Germany); Attendance: 38,000

FRA: Bruno Martini (22/0), Jocelyn Angloma (10/0) [61.Jean-Philippe Durand (20/0)], Basile Boli (35/1), Laurent Robert Blanc (22/4), Bernard Casoni (24/0), Emmanuel Petit (4/0) [46.Manuel Amoros (79/1)], Frank Sauzée (Cap) (25/6) [61.Luis Fernandez (57/6)], Didier Deschamps (21/3), Jean-Pierre Papin (35/20) [61.Fabrice Divert (3/1)], Eric Cantona (24/12), Pascal Vahirua (13/1) [74.Christian Perez (19/2)]. Trainer: Michel Platini (26).

Goal: Jean-Pierre Papin (12).

502. 10.06.1992 **SWEDEN - FRANCE** **1-1(1-0)** 9th EC. Group Stage.

Råsundastadion, Stockholm; Referee: Alexei Spirin (C.I.S.); Attendance: 29,680

FRA: Bruno Martini (23/0), Jocelyn Angloma (11/0) [66.Luis Fernandez (58/6)], Manuel Amoros (Cap) (80/1), Laurent Robert Blanc (23/4), Bernard Casoni (25/0), Basile Boli (36/1), Didier Deschamps (22/3), Frank Sauzée (26/6), Pascal Vahirua (14/1) [46.Christian Perez (20/2)], Jean-Pierre Papin (36/21), Eric Cantona (25/12). Trainer: Michel Platini (27).

Goal: Jean-Pierre Papin (59).

503. 14.06.1992 **FRANCE - ENGLAND** **0-0** 9th EC. Group Stage.
Malmö Stadion, Malmö (Sweden); Referee: Sándor Puhl (Hungary); Attendance: 26,535
FRA: Bruno Martini (24/0), Manuel Amoros (Cap) (81/1), Laurent Robert Blanc (24/4), Basile Boli (37/1), Bernard Casoni (26/0), Didier Deschamps (23/3), Frank Sauzée (27/6) [46.Jocelyn Angloma (12/0)], Luis Fernandez (59/6) [74.Christian Perez (21/2)], Jean-Philippe Durand (21/0), Eric Cantona (26/12), Jean-Pierre Papin (37/21). Trainer: Michel Platini (28).

504. 17.06.1992 **FRANCE - DENMARK** **1-2(0-1)** 9th EC. Group Stage.
Malmö Stadion, Malmö (Sweden); Referee: Hubert Förstinger (Austria); Attendance: 25,763
FRA: Bruno Martini (25/0), Basile Boli (38/1), Laurent Robert Blanc (25/4), Bernard Casoni (27/0), Manuel Amoros (Cap) (82/1), Didier Deschamps (24/3), Christian Perez (22/2) [81.Christophe Cocard (5/0)], Jean-Philippe Durand (22/0), Jean-Pierre Papin (38/22), Eric Cantona (27/12), Pascal Vahirua (15/1) [46.Luis Fernandez (60/6)]. Trainer: Michel Platini (29).
Goal: Jean-Pierre Papin (61).

505. 26.08.1992 **FRANCE - BRAZIL** **0-2(0-1)**
Stade Parc des Princes, Paris; Referee: Frans Van den Wijngaert (Belgium); Attendance: 34,428
FRA: Bruno Martini (26/0), Emmanuel Petit (5/0) [56.Laurent Fournier (1/0)], William Prunier (1/0), Basile Boli (39/1), Alain Roche (3/0), Jean-Philippe Durand (23/0) [64.Frank Sauzée (28/6)], Didier Deschamps (25/3), Laurent Robert Blanc (26/4) [65.Pascal Vahirua (16/1)], Jean-Pierre Papin (Cap) (39/22), Christophe Cocard (6/0), David Ginola (2/0). Trainer: Gérard Houillier (1).

506. 09.09.1992 **BULGARIA - FRANCE** **2-0(2-0)** 15th FIFA WC. Qualifiers
Nationalen stadion "Vasil Levski", Sofia; Referee: Sándor Puhl (Hungary); Attendance: 45,000
FRA: Bruno Martini (27/0), Laurent Fournier (2/0) [61.Laurent Robert Blanc (27/4)], Emmanuel Petit (6/0), Basile Boli (40/1), Alain Roche (4/0), Bernard Casoni (28/0), Didier Deschamps (26/3), Frank Sauzée (29/6), Jean-Pierre Papin (Cap) (40/22), David Ginola (3/0), Pascal Vahirua (17/1) [61.Jean-Philippe Durand (24/0)]. Trainer: Gérard Houillier (2).

507. 14.10.1992 **FRANCE - AUSTRIA** **2-0(1-0)** 15th FIFA WC. Qualifiers
Stade Parc des Princes, Paris; Referee: Vadim Zhuk (Belarus); Attendance: 39,186
FRA: Bruno Martini (28/0), Frank Sauzée (30/6), Basile Boli (41/1), Bernard Casoni (29/0), Didier Deschamps (27/3), Jean-Luc Sassus (1/0), Laurent Fournier (3/0) [63.Jerôme Gnako (1/0)], Jean-Philippe Durand (25/0), Xavier Gravelaine (1/0) [73.Pascal Vahirua (18/1)], Jean-Pierre Papin (Cap) (41/23), Eric Cantona (28/13). Trainer: Gérard Houillier (3).
Goals: Jean-Pierre Papin (3), Eric Cantona (77).

508. 14.11.1992 **FRANCE - FINLAND** **2-1(2-0)** 15th FIFA WC. Qualifiers
Stade Parc des Princes, Paris; Referee: Jozef Marko (Czechoslovakia); Attendance: 30,000
FRA: Bruno Martini (29/0), Alain Roche (5/0), Basile Boli (42/1), Bernard Casoni (30/0), Jean-Philippe Durand (26/0) [72.Christian Karembeu (1/0)], Frank Sauzée (31/6), Didier Deschamps (28/3), Bixente Lizarazu (1/0), Jean-Pierre Papin (Cap) (42/24), Eric Cantona (29/14), Xavier Gravelaine (2/0) [79.Pascal Vahirua (19/1)]. Trainer: Gérard Houillier (4).
Goals: Jean-Pierre Papin (18), Eric Cantona (31).

509. 17.02.1993 **ISRAEL - FRANCE** **0-4(0-1)** 15th FIFA WC. Qualifiers
National Stadium, Ramat Gan, Tel Aviv; Referee: Ryszard Wójcik (Poland); Attendance: 29,000
FRA: Bernard Lama (1/0), Basile Boli (43/1), Alain Roche (6/1), Laurent Robert Blanc (28/6), Bixente Lizarazu (2/0) [82.Patrice Loko (1/0)], Didier Deschamps (29/3), Frank Sauzée (32/6), Paul Le Guen (1/0), David Ginola (4/0) [63.Emmanuel Petit (7/0)], Jean-Pierre Papin (Cap) (43/24), Eric Cantona (30/15). Trainer: Gérard Houillier (5).
Goals: Eric Cantona (27), Laurent Robert Blanc (62, 84), Alain Roche (89).

510. 27.03.1993 **AUSTRIA - FRANCE** **0-1(0-0)** 15th FIFA WC. Qualifiers
„Ernst Happel" Stadion, Wien; Referee: John Blankenstein (Netherlands); Attendance: 37,500
FRA: Bernard Lama (2/0), Jocelyn Angloma (13/0), Alain Roche (7/1), Laurent Robert Blanc (29/6), Emmanuel Petit (8/0), Bixente Lizarazu (3/0), Didier Deschamps (30/3), Paul Le Guen (2/0), Frank Sauzée (33/6) [88.Corentin Martins (1/0)], Jean-Pierre Papin (Cap) (44/25), Xavier Gravelaine (3/0) [70.Patrice Loko (2/0)]. Trainer: Gérard Houillier (6).
Goal: Jean-Pierre Papin (58).

511. 28.04.1993 **FRANCE - SWEDEN** **2-1(1-1)** 15th FIFA WC. Qualifiers
Stade Parc des Princes, Paris; Referee: Pierluigi Pairetto (Italy); Attendance: 43,134
FRA: Bernard Lama (3/0), Jocelyn Angloma (14/0), Basile Boli (44/1), Laurent Robert Blanc (30/6), Emmanuel Petit (9/0), Frank Sauzée (Cap) (34/6), Paul Le Guen (3/0), Corentin Martins (2/0) [90.Bixente Lizarazu (4/0)], Didier Deschamps (31/3), Eric Cantona (31/17), David Ginola (5/0) [46.Pascal Vahirua (20/1)]. Trainer: Gérard Houillier (7).
Goals: Eric Cantona (43 penalty,82).

512. 28.07.1993 **FRANCE - RUSSIA** **3-1(3-1)**
Stade „Michel d'Ornano", Caen; Referee: Alfredo Trentalange (Italy); Attendance: 19,000
FRA: Bruno Martini (30/0) [46.Bernard Lama (4/0)], Basile Boli (45/1) [61.Jean-Luc Dogon (1/0)], Alain Roche (8/1), Laurent Robert Blanc (31/6), Emmanuel Petit (10/0) [79.Xavier Gravelaine (4/0)], Didier Deschamps (32/3), Paul Le Guen (4/0), Frank Sauzée (35/7) [84.Reynald Pedros (1/0)], Corentin Martins (3/0) [64.Bixente Lizarazu (5/0)], Jean-Pierre Papin (Cap) (45/26), Eric Cantona (32/18). Trainer: Gérard Houillier (8).
Goals: Frank Sauzée (16), Eric Cantona (20), Jean-Pierre Papin (36).

513. 22.08.1993 **SWEDEN - FRANCE** **1-1(0-0)** 15th FIFA WC. Qualifiers
Råsundastadion, Stockholm; Referee: Aron Schmidhuber (Germany); Attendance: 30,530
FRA: Bernard Lama (5/0), Marcel Desailly (1/0), Alain Roche (9/1), Laurent Robert Blanc (32/6), Bixente Lizarazu (6/0), Didier Deschamps (33/3), Paul Le Guen (5/0), Frank Sauzée (36/8), Reynald Pedros (2/0) [80.Pascal Vahirua (21/1)], Jean-Pierre Papin (Cap) (46/26), Eric Cantona (33/18). Trainer: Gérard Houillier (9).
Goal: Frank Sauzée (76).

514. 08.09.1993 **FINLAND - FRANCE** **0-2(0-0)** 15th FIFA WC. Qualifiers
Ratinan Stadion, Tampere; Referee: Stephen Lodge (England); Attendance: 8,000
FRA: Bernard Lama (6/0), Marcel Desailly (2/0), Alain Roche (10/1), Laurent Robert Blanc (33/7), Emmanuel Petit (11/0), Didier Deschamps (34/3) [88.Vincent Guérin (1/0)], Paul Le Guen (6/0), Frank Sauzée (37/8), Corentin Martins (4/0) [72.Reynald Pedros (3/0)], Jean-Pierre Papin (Cap) (47/27), Eric Cantona (34/18). Trainer: Gérard Houillier (10).
Goals: Laurent Robert Blanc (47), Jean-Pierre Papin (55 penalty).

515. 13.10.1993 **FRANCE - ISRAEL** **2-3(2-1)** 15th FIFA WC. Qualifiers
Stade Parc des Princes, Paris; Referee: Alan Snoddy (Northern Ireland); Attendance: 30,000
FRA: Bernard Lama (7/0), Marcel Desailly (3/0), Alain Roche (11/1) [24.Bixente Lizarazu (7/0)], Laurent Robert Blanc (34/7), Emmanuel Petit (12/0), Didier Deschamps (35/3), Paul Le Guen (7/0), Frank Sauzée (38/9), Jean-Pierre Papin (Cap) (48/27), Eric Cantona (35/18), David Ginola (6/1) [86.Youri Djorkaeff (1/0)]. Trainer: Gérard Houillier (11).
Goals: Frank Sauzée (29), David Ginola (39).

516. 17.11.1993 **FRANCE - BULGARIA** **1-2(1-1)** 15th FIFA WC. Qualifiers
Stade Parc des Princes, Paris; Referee: Leslie Mottram (Scotland); Attendance: 48,402
FRA: Bernard Lama (8/0), Marcel Desailly (4/0), Alain Roche (12/1), Laurent Robert Blanc (35/7), Emmanuel Petit (13/0), Didier Deschamps (36/3), Paul Le Guen (8/0), Frank Sauzée (39/9) [81.Vincent Guérin (2/0)], Reynald Pedros (4/0), Jean-Pierre Papin (Cap) (49/27) [69.David Ginola (7/1)], Eric Cantona (36/19). Trainer: Gérard Houillier (12).
Goal: Eric Cantona (32).

517. 16.02.1994 **ITALY - FRANCE** **0-1(0-1)**
Stadio San Paolo, Napoli; Referee: Dr. Markus Merk (Germany); Attendance: 20,000
FRA: Bernard Lama (9/0), Christian Karembeu (2/0) [73.Jean-Pierre Cyprien (1/0)], Alain Roche (13/1), Marcel Desailly (5/0) [90.Corentin Martins (5/0)], Eric Di Meco (7/0), Jerôme Gnako (2/0) [55.Vincent Guérin (3/0)], Didier Deschamps (37/3), Youri Djorkaeff (2/1), Paul Le Guen (9/0), David Ginola (8/1), Eric Cantona (Cap) (37/19). Trainer: Aimé Jacquet (1).
Goal: Youri Djorkaeff (45).

518. 22.03.1994 **FRANCE - CHILE** **3-1(2-1)**
Stade de Gerland, Lyon; Referee: Juan Manuel Brito Arceo (Spain); Attendance: 35,000
FRA: Bernard Lama (10/0), Jocelyn Angloma (15/0), Alain Roche (14/1) [79.Paul Le Guen (10/0)], Marcel Desailly (6/0) [72.Christian Karembeu (3/0)], Bixente Lizarazu (8/0), Didier Deschamps (Cap) (38/3), Youri Djorkaeff (3/2) [46.Corentin Martins (6/1)], Jean-Michel Ferri (1/0), Christophe Cocard (7/0), Jean-Pierre Papin (50/28), David Ginola (9/1) [46.Pascal Vahirua (22/1)]. Trainer: Aimé Jacquet (2).
Goals: Jean-Pierre Papin (7), Youri Djorkaeff (36), Corentin Martins (50).

519. 26.05.1994 **AUSTRALIA - FRANCE** **0-1(0-1)** International Tournament
Universiade Memorial Stadium, Kobe (Japan); Referee: Masayoshi Okada (Japan); Attendance: 16,743
FRA: Fabien Barthez (1/0), Christian Karembeu (4/0), Jocelyn Angloma (16/0), Laurent Robert Blanc (36/7), Eric Di Meco (8/0), Emmanuel Petit (14/0), Jean-Michel Ferri (2/0), Eric Cantona (Cap) (38/20), Christophe Dugarry (1/0) [74.Corentin Martins (7/1)], Jean-Pierre Papin (51/28), David Ginola (10/1) [74.Reynald Pedros (5/0)]. Trainer: Aimé Jacquet (3).
Goal: Eric Cantona (43).

520. 29.05.1994 **JAPAN - FRANCE** **1-4(0-2)** International Tournament
National Stadium, Tokio; Referee: Letchmanasamy Kathirveloo (Malaysia); Attendance: 58,000
FRA: Bernard Lama (11/0), Jocelyn Angloma (17/0) [85.Christian Karembeu (5/0)], Laurent Robert Blanc (37/7), Marcel Desailly (7/0), Eric Di Meco (9/0) [71.Bixente Lizarazu (9/0)], Youri Djorkaeff (4/3), Didier Deschamps (39/3), Paul Le Guen (11/0), Eric Cantona (Cap) (39/20), Jean-Pierre Papin (52/29), David Ginola (11/2) [71.Nicolas Ouédec (1/0)]. Trainer: Aimé Jacquet (4).
Goals: Youri Djorkaeff (16), Jean-Pierre Papin (19), Hisashi Kurosaki (54 own goal), David Ginola (56).

521. 17.08.1994 **FRANCE - CZECH REPUBLIC** **2-2(0-2)**
Stade Parc Lescure, Bordeaux; Referee: Gerd Grabher (Austria); Attendance: 10,000
FRA: Bernard Lama (12/0), Jocelyn Angloma (18/0), Lilian Thuram (1/0), Laurent Robert Blanc (38/7), Bruno Ngotty (1/0), Eric Di Meco (10/0), Marcel Desailly (8/0) [24.Jean-Michel Ferri (3/0)], Eric Cantona (Cap) (40/20), Corentin Martins (8/1) [63.Zinedine Zidane (1/2)], Christophe Dugarry (2/0) [77.Patrice Loko (3/0)], David Ginola (12/2) [46.Bixente Lizarazu (10/0)]. Trainer: Aimé Jacquet (5).
Goals: Zinedine Zidane (85, 87).

522. 07.09.1994 **SLOVAKIA - FRANCE** **0-0** 10th EC. Qualifiers
Štadión Tehelné pole, Bratislava; Referee: Erik Mikkelsen (Denmark); Attendance: 17,000
FRA: Bernard Lama (13/0), Jocelyn Angloma (19/0), Laurent Robert Blanc (39/7), Alain Roche (15/1), Eric Di Meco (11/0), Youri Djorkaeff (5/3) [81.Bixente Lizarazu (11/0)], Didier Deschamps (40/3), Paul Le Guen (12/0), Reynald Pedros (6/0) [64.Christophe Dugarry (3/0)], Eric Cantona (Cap) (41/20), David Ginola (13/2). Trainer: Aimé Jacquet (6).

523. 08.10.1994 **FRANCE - ROMANIA** **0-0** 10th EC. Qualifiers
Stade „Geoffroy Guichard“, Saint-Étienne; Referee: Leif Sundell (Sweden); Attendance: 31,144
FRA: Bernard Lama (14/0), Jocelyn Angloma (20/0), Laurent Robert Blanc (40/7), Alain Roche (16/1), Bixente Lizarazu (12/0), Christian Karembeu (6/0), Eric Cantona (Cap) (42/20), Marcel Desailly (9/0), Reynald Pedros (7/0), Patrice Loko (4/0) [83.Christophe Dugarry (4/0)], Nicolas Ouédec (2/0) [72.Zinedine Zidane (2/2)]. Trainer: Aimé Jacquet (7).

524. 16.11.1994 **POLAND - FRANCE** **0-0** 10th EC. Qualifiers
Stadion Górnik, Zabrze; Referee: Angelo Amendolia (Italy); Attendance: 25,000
FRA: Bernard Lama (15/0), Jocelyn Angloma (21/0), Laurent Robert Blanc (41/7), Alain Roche (17/1), Eric Di Meco (12/0), Christian Karembeu (7/0) [*sent off 52*], Marcel Desailly (10/0), Reynald Pedros (8/0) [27.Youri Djorkaeff (6/3)], Paul Le Guen (13/0), Eric Cantona (Cap) (43/20), Nicolas Ouédec (3/0) [77.Christophe Dugarry (5/0)]. Trainer: Aimé Jacquet (8).

525. 13.12.1994 **AZERBAIJAN - FRANCE** **0-2(0-1)** 10th EC. Qualifiers
"Hüseyin Avni Aker" Stadyumu, Trabzon (Turkey); Referee: Rune Pedersen (Norway); Attendance: 3,000
FRA: Bernard Lama (16/0), Jocelyn Angloma (22/0), Laurent Robert Blanc (42/7), Alain Roche (18/1), Eric Di Meco (13/0), Marcel Desailly (11/0) [71.Jean-Michel Ferri (4/0)], Paul Le Guen (14/0), Reynald Pedros (9/0) [76.Corentin Martins (9/1)], Patrice Loko (5/1), Jean-Pierre Papin (53/30), Eric Cantona (Cap) (44/20). Trainer: Aimé Jacquet (9).
Goals: Jean-Pierre Papin (24), Patrice Loko (55).

526. 18.01.1995 **NETHERLANDS - FRANCE** **0-1(0-1)**
Stadion Nieuw Galgenwaard, Utrecht; Referee: Michel Piraux (Belgium); Attendance: 12,400
FRA: Bernard Lama (17/0), Christian Karembeu (8/0) [88.Lilian Thuram (2/0)], Laurent Robert Blanc (43/7), Marcel Desailly (12/0), Eric Di Meco (14/0), Jean-Michel Ferri (5/0), Paul Le Guen (15/0) [62.Jocelyn Angloma (23/0)], Reynald Pedros (10/0), Eric Cantona (Cap) (45/20), Patrice Loko (6/2), Jean-Pierre Papin (54/30) [68.Nicolas Ouédec (4/0)]. Trainer: Aimé Jacquet (10).
Goal: Patrice Loko (44).

527. 29.03.1995 **ISRAEL - FRANCE** **0-0** 10th EC. Qualifiers
National Stadium, Ramat Gan, Tel Aviv; Referee: James McCluskey (Scotland); Attendance: 45,000
FRA: Bernard Lama (18/0), Jocelyn Angloma (24/0), Laurent Robert Blanc (44/7), Alain Roche (19/1), Eric Di Meco (15/0), Marcel Desailly (13/0), Corentin Martins (10/1) [79.Youri Djorkaeff (7/3)], Paul Le Guen (Cap) (16/0), Reynald Pedros (11/0), Patrice Loko (7/2), Nicolas Ouédec (5/0) [66.David Ginola (14/2)]. Trainer: Aimé Jacquet (11).

528. 26.04.1995 **FRANCE - SLOVAKIA** **4-0(2-0)** 10th EC. Qualifiers
Stade de la Beaujoire, Nantes; Referee: Bernd Heynemann (Germany); Attendance: 26,000
FRA: Bernard Lama (19/0), Jocelyn Angloma (25/0), Laurent Robert Blanc (45/8), Alain Roche (20/1), Eric Di Meco (16/0), Didier Deschamps (Cap) (41/3), Marcel Desailly (14/0), Zinedine Zidane (3/2) [74.Youri Djorkaeff (8/3)], Vincent Guérin (4/1), Patrice Loko (8/2), David Ginola (15/3). Trainer: Aimé Jacquet (12).
Goals: Ondrej Krištofík (27 own goal), David Ginola (42), Laurent Robert Blanc (58), Vincent Guérin (63).

529. 22.07.1995 **NORWAY - FRANCE** **0-0**
Ullevaal Stadion, Oslo; Referee: Hugo Luyten (Netherlands); Attendance: 12,030
FRA: Bernard Lama (20/0), Lilian Thuram (3/0), Laurent Robert Blanc (46/8), Alain Roche (Cap) (21/1), Bixente Lizarazu (13/0), Claude Makélélé (1/0), Zinedine Zidane (4/2) [46.Youri Djorkaeff (9/3)], Paul Le Guen (17/0) [68.Frank Leboeuf (1/0)], Vincent Guérin (5/1), Christophe Cocard (8/0) [73.Corentin Martins (11/1)], Reynald Pedros (12/0). Trainer: Aimé Jacquet (13).

530. 16.08.1995 **FRANCE - POLAND** **1-1(0-1)** 10th EC. Qualifiers
Stade Parc des Princes, Paris; Referee: Manuel Díaz Vega (Spain); Attendance: 40,426
FRA: Bernard Lama (21/0), Jocelyn Angloma (26/0) [66.Christian Karembeu (9/0)], Lilian Thuram (4/0), Frank Leboeuf (2/0) [70.Youri Djorkaeff (10/4)], Bixente Lizarazu (14/0), Didier Deschamps (Cap) (42/3), Marcel Desailly (15/0), Zinedine Zidane (5/2), Vincent Guérin (6/1), Christophe Dugarry (6/0), David Ginola (16/3) [64.Reynald Pedros (13/0)]. Trainer: Aimé Jacquet (14).
Goal: Youri Djorkaeff (86).

531. 06.09.1995 **FRANCE - AZERBAIJAN** **10-0(3-0)** 10th EC. Qualifiers
Stade „Abbé Deschamps", Auxerre; Referee: Alfred Micallef (Malta); Attendance: 15,000
FRA: Bernard Lama (22/0), Jocelyn Angloma (27/0) [57.Lilian Thuram (5/0)], Frank Leboeuf (3/2), Marcel Desailly (Cap) (16/1), Bixente Lizarazu (15/0), Vincent Guérin (7/2), Zinedine Zidane (6/3), Didier Deschamps (43/3), Reynald Pedros (14/1) [67.David Ginola (17/3)], Youri Djorkaeff (11/6), Christophe Dugarry (7/1) [70.Christophe Cocard (9/1)]. Trainer: Aimé Jacquet (15).
Goals: Marcel Desailly (13), Youri Djorkaeff (18), Vincent Guérin (35), Reynald Pedros (49), Frank Leboeuf (53), Christophe Dugarry (66), Zinedine Zidane (72), Frank Leboeuf (74), Youri Djorkaeff (78), Christophe Cocard (90).

532. 11.10.1995 **ROMANIA - FRANCE** **1-3(0-2)** 10th EC. Qualifiers
Stadionul Steaua, Bucureşti; Referee: Pierluigi Pairetto (Italy); Attendance: 25,000
FRA: Fabien Barthez (2/0), Jocelyn Angloma (28/0), Frank Leboeuf (4/2), Marcel Desailly (17/1), Eric Di Meco (Cap) (17/0), Christian Karembeu (10/0), Didier Deschamps (44/3), Zinedine Zidane (7/4) [85.Lilian Thuram (6/0)], Vincent Guérin (8/2), Youri Djorkaeff (12/7) [75.Bixente Lizarazu (16/0)], Christophe Dugarry (8/1) [63.Mickaël Madar (1/0)]. Trainer: Aimé Jacquet (16).
Goals: Christian Karembeu (29), Youri Djorkaeff (41), Zinedine Zidane (73).

533. 15.11.1995 **FRANCE - ISRAEL** **2-0(0-0)** 10th EC. Qualifiers
Stade „Michel d'Ornano", Caen; Referee: Gerd Grabher (Austria); Attendance: 21,500
FRA: Bernard Lama (23/0), Jocelyn Angloma (29/0), Frank Leboeuf (5/2), Marcel Desailly (18/1), Eric Di Meco (18/0) [63.Bixente Lizarazu (17/1)], Christian Karembeu (11/1) [90.Marc Keller (1/0)], Didier Deschamps (45/3), Zinedine Zidane (8/4), Vincent Guérin (Cap) (9/2), Youri Djorkaeff (13/8), Mickaël Madar (2/0) [63.Patrice Loko (9/2)]. Trainer: Aimé Jacquet (17).
Goals: Youri Djorkaeff (69), Bixente Lizarazu (89).

534. 24.01.1996 **FRANCE - PORTUGAL** **3-2(1-2)**
Stade Parc des Princes, Paris; Referee: Dermot Gallagher (England); Attendance: 30,000
FRA: Bernard Lama (24/0), Jocelyn Angloma (30/0) [70.Sabri Lamouchi (1/0)], Frank Leboeuf (6/2), Marcel Desailly (Cap) (19/1), Eric Di Meco (19/0), Christian Karembeu (12/1), Didier Deschamps (46/3), Zinedine Zidane (9/4), Vincent Guérin (10/2) [46.Reynald Pedros (15/2)], Youri Djorkaeff (14/10), Patrice Loko (10/2) [78.Cyrille Pouget (1/0)]. Trainer: Aimé Jacquet (18).
Goals: Youri Djorkaeff (24, 75), Reynald Pedros (77).

535. 21.02.1996 **FRANCE - GREECE** **3-1(1-1)**
Stade des Costières, Nîmes; Referee: Roger Philippi (Luxembourg); Attendance: 23,452
FRA: Bernard Lama (Cap) (25/0), Jocelyn Angloma (31/0) [46.Frank Leboeuf (7/2)], Lilian Thuram (7/0), Marcel Desailly (20/1), Emmanuel Petit (15/0) [77.Cyrille Pouget (2/0)], Didier Deschamps (47/3), Youri Djorkaeff (15/10) [46.Zinedine Zidane (10/5)], Christian Karembeu (13/1), Reynald Pedros (16/2), Sabri Lamouchi (2/0) [70.Pierre Laigle (1/0)], Patrice Loko (11/4). Trainer: Aimé Jacquet (19).
Goals: Patrice Loko (30, 47 penalty), Zinedine Zidane (49).

536. 27.03.1996 **BELGIUM - FRANCE** **0-2(0-0)**
Stade „Roi Baudouin", Bruxelles; Referee: Fritz Stuchlick (Austria); Attendance: 24,417
FRA: Bernard Lama (26/0), Lilian Thuram (8/0) [46.Jocelyn Angloma (32/0)], Laurent Robert Blanc (47/8), Alain Roche (22/1), Eric Di Meco (Cap) (20/0), Christian Karembeu (14/1), Didier Deschamps (48/3), Corentin Martins (12/1), Reynald Pedros (17/2) [73.Pierre Laigle (2/0)], Sabri Lamouchi (3/1), Christophe Dugarry (9/1) [82.Cyrille Pouget (3/0)]. Trainer: Aimé Jacquet (20).
Goals: Phillipe Albert (66 own goal), Sabri Lamouchi (71).

537. 29.05.1996 **FRANCE - FINLAND** **2-0(0-0)**
Stade de la Meinau, Strasbourg; Referee: Edgar Steinborn (Germany); Attendance: 29,304
FRA: Bruno Martini (31/0), Jocelyn Angloma (33/0), Lilian Thuram (9/0), Frank Leboeuf (8/2), Eric Di Meco (21/0) [67.Bixente Lizarazu (18/1)], Marcel Desailly (Cap) (21/1), Corentin Martins (13/1), Vincent Guérin (11/2), Reynald Pedros (18/3), Sabri Lamouchi (4/1) [69.Christian Karembeu (15/1)], Patrice Loko (12/5) [46.Christophe Dugarry (10/1)]. Trainer: Aimé Jacquet (21).
Goals: Patrice Loko (15), Reynald Pedros (18).

538. 01.06.1996 **GERMANY - FRANCE** **0-1(0-1)**
„Gottlieb Daimler" Stadion, Stuttgart; Referee: Ryszard Wójcik (Poland); Attendance: 53,135
FRA: Bernard Lama (27/0), Lilian Thuram (10/0), Laurent Robert Blanc (48/9), Marcel Desailly (22/1), Eric Di Meco (22/0) [66.Bixente Lizarazu (19/1)], Christian Karembeu (16/1) [84.Jocelyn Angloma (34/0)], Didier Deschamps (Cap) (49/3), Zinedine Zidane (11/5) [46.Patrice Loko (13/5)], Vincent Guérin (12/2) [81.Sabri Lamouchi (5/1)], Youri Djorkaeff (16/10), Christophe Dugarry (11/1) [73.Reynald Pedros (19/3)]. Trainer: Aimé Jacquet (22).
Goal: Laurent Robert Blanc (6).

539. 05.06.1996 **FRANCE - ARMENIA** **2-0(1-0)**
Stade Du Nord, Villeneuve D'Ascq (England); Referee: Alain Hamer (Luxembourg); Attendance: 22,000
FRA: Bernard Lama (28/0), Jocelyn Angloma (35/1) [46.Lilian Thuram (11/0)], Laurent Robert Blanc (49/9), Marcel Desailly (23/1), Bixente Lizarazu (20/1), Didier Deschamps (Cap) (50/3), Zinedine Zidane (12/5), Vincent Guérin (13/2) [46.Christian Karembeu (17/1)], Sabri Lamouchi (6/1), Mickaël Madar (3/1), Youri Djorkaeff (17/10) [46.Patrice Loko (14/5)]. Trainer: Aimé Jacquet (23).
Goals: Jocelyn Angloma (16), Mickaël Madar (71).

540. 10.06.1996 **FRANCE - ROMANIA** **1-0(1-0)** 10th EC. Group Stage.
St. James Park, Newcastle (England); Referee: Hellmut Krug (Germany); Attendance: 25,000
FRA: Bernard Lama (29/0), Lilian Thuram (12/0), Laurent Robert Blanc (50/9), Marcel Desailly (24/1), Eric Di Meco (23/0) [68.Bixente Lizarazu (21/1)], Christian Karembeu (18/1), Didier Deschamps (Cap) (51/3), Vincent Guérin (14/2), Zinedine Zidane (13/5) [80.Alain Roche (23/1)], Youri Djorkaeff (18/10), Christophe Dugarry (12/2) [68.Patrice Loko (15/5)]. Trainer: Aimé Jacquet (24).
Goal: Christophe Dugarry (24).

541. 15.06.1996 **FRANCE - SPAIN** **1-1(0-0)** 10th EC. Group Stage.
Elland Road, Leeds (England); Referee: Vadim Zhuk (Belarus); Attendance: 35,626
FRA: Bernard Lama (30/0), Jocelyn Angloma (36/1) [65.Alain Roche (24/1)], Laurent Robert Blanc (51/9), Marcel Desailly (25/1), Bixente Lizarazu (22/1), Didier Deschamps (Cap) (52/3), Vincent Guérin (15/2) [81.Lilian Thuram (13/0)], Christian Karembeu (19/1), Zinedine Zidane (14/5), Youri Djorkaeff (19/11), Patrice Loko (16/5) [74.Christophe Dugarry (13/2)]. Trainer: Aimé Jacquet (25).
Goal: Youri Djorkaeff (48).

542. 18.06.1996 **FRANCE - BULGARIA** **3-1(1-0)** 10th EC. Group Stage.
St. James Park, Newcastle (England); Referee: Dermot Gallagher (England)/Paul Durkin (England); Attendance: 25,000
FRA: Bernard Lama (31/0), Lilian Thuram (14/0), Laurent Robert Blanc (52/10), Marcel Desailly (26/1), Bixente Lizarazu (23/1), Christian Karembeu (20/1), Didier Deschamps (Cap) (53/3), Vincent Guérin (16/2), Zinedine Zidane (15/5) [62.Reynald Pedros (20/3)], Youri Djorkaeff (20/11), Christophe Dugarry (14/2) [70.Patrice Loko (17/6)]. Trainer: Aimé Jacquet (26).
Goals: Laurent Robert Blanc (20), Luboslav Penev (63 own goal), Patrice Loko (90).

543. 22.06.1996 **FRANCE - NETHERLANDS** **0-0; 5-4 on penalties** 10th EC. Quarter-Finals.
Anfield Road, Liverpool (England); Referee: Antonio Jesús López Nieto (Spain); Attendance: 37,465
FRA: Bernard Lama (32/0), Lilian Thuram (15/0), Laurent Robert Blanc (53/10), Marcel Desailly (27/1), Bixente Lizarazu (24/1), Christian Karembeu (21/1), Didier Deschamps (Cap) (54/3), Vincent Guérin (17/2), Zinedine Zidane (16/5), Youri Djorkaeff (21/11), Patrice Loko (18/6) [62.Christophe Dugarry (15/2); 80.Reynald Pedros (21/3)]. Trainer: Aimé Jacquet (27).
Penalties: Zinedine Zidane, Youri Djorkaeff, Bixente Lizarazu, Vincent Guérin, Laurent Robert Blanc.

544. 26.06.1996 **CZECH REPUBLIC - FRANCE** **0-0; 6-5 on penalties** 10th EC. Semi-Finals.
Old Trafford Stadium, Manchester (England); Referee: Leslie Mottram (Scotland); Attendance: 43,877
FRA: Bernard Lama (33/0), Lilian Thuram (16/0) [83.Jocelyn Angloma (37/1)], Alain Roche (25/1), Laurent Robert Blanc (Cap) (54/10), Bixente Lizarazu (25/1), Vincent Guérin (18/2), Sabri Lamouchi (7/1) [62.Reynald Pedros (22/3)], Marcel Desailly (28/1), Zinedine Zidane (17/5), Youri Djorkaeff (22/11), Patrice Loko (19/6). Trainer: Aimé Jacquet (28).
Penalties: Zinedine Zidane, Youri Djorkaeff, Bixente Lizarazu, Vincent Guérin, Laurent Robert Blanc, Reynald Pedros (missed).

545. 31.08.1996 **FRANCE - MEXICO** **2-0(0-0)**
Stade Parc des Princes, Paris; Referee: Joseph Byrne (Republic of Ireland); Attendance: 18,000
FRA: Bernard Lama (34/0), Lilian Thuram (17/0) [88.Sabri Lamouchi (8/1)], Laurent Robert Blanc (55/10), Marcel Desailly (29/1) [46.Frank Leboeuf (9/2) [*sent off 87*]], Bixente Lizarazu (26/1) [79.Vincent Guérin (19/2)], Christian Karembeu (22/1), Youri Djorkaeff (23/12), Didier Deschamps (Cap) (55/3), Reynald Pedros (23/3) [46.Zinedine Zidane (18/5)], Patrice Loko (20/6) [46.Robert Pires (1/0)], Nicolas Ouédec (6/1) [64.Florian Maurice (1/0)]. Trainer: Aimé Jacquet (29).
Goals: Nicolas Ouédec (49), Youri Djorkaeff (53).

546. 09.10.1996 **FRANCE - TURKEY** **4-0(2-0)**
Stade Parc des Princes, Paris; Referee: Jorge Emanuel Monteiro Coroado (Portugal); Attendance: 28,611
FRA: Fabien Barthez (3/0), Christian Karembeu (23/1), Laurent Robert Blanc (56/11), Alain Goma (1/0), Lilian Thuram (18/0) [77.Martin Djétou (1/0)], Sabri Lamouchi (9/1) [23.Vincent Candela (1/0)], Youri Djorkaeff (24/13), Didier Deschamps (Cap) (56/3), Zinedine Zidane (19/5), Reynald Pedros (24/4) [66.Franck Gava (1/0)], Patrice Loko (21/6) [72.Robert Pires (2/1)]. Trainer: Aimé Jacquet (30).
Goals: Laurent Robert Blanc (33), Reynald Pedros (35), Youri Djorkaeff (51), Robert Pires (83).

547. 09.11.1996 **DENMARK - FRANCE** **1-0(1-0)**
Parken, København; Referee: Roy Helge Olsen (Norway); Attendance: 10,645
FRA: Fabien Barthez (4/0), Lilian Thuram (19/0), Bruno Ngotty (2/0), Marcel Desailly (30/1), Vincent Candela (2/0) [74.Pierre Laigle (3/0)], Corentin Martins (14/1) [62.Patrice Loko (22/6)], Christian Karembeu (24/1), Didier Deschamps (Cap) (57/3), Zinedine Zidane (20/5) [80.Marc Keller (2/0)], Youri Djorkaeff (25/13), Reynald Pedros (25/4) [46.Robert Pires (3/1)]. Trainer: Aimé Jacquet (31).

548. 22.01.1997 **PORTUGAL - FRANCE** **0-2(0-1)**
Estádio Primeiro de Maio, Braga; Referee: José Nuñez Manrique (Spain); Attendance: 40,000
FRA: Fabien Barthez (5/0), Lilian Thuram (20/0), Laurent Robert Blanc (57/11), Marcel Desailly (31/1), Pierre Laigle (4/0), Christian Karembeu (25/1), Didier Deschamps (Cap) (58/4) [62.Bruno Ngotty (3/0)], Zinedine Zidane (21/5), Ibrahim Ba (1/1) [62.Youri Djorkaeff (26/13)], Christophe Dugarry (16/2) [78.Patrice Loko (23/6)], Robert Pires (4/1) [78.Patrick Blondeau (1/0)]. Trainer: Aimé Jacquet (32).
Goals: Didier Deschamps (10), Ibrahim Ba (62).

549. 26.02.1997 **FRANCE - NETHERLANDS** **2-1(0-1)**
Stade Parc des Princes, Paris; Referee: Ryszard Wójcik (Poland); Attendance: 35,331
FRA: Bernard Lama (35/0), Lilian Thuram (21/0), Laurent Robert Blanc (Cap) (58/11), Marcel Desailly (32/1), Bixente Lizarazu (27/1) [87.Vincent Candela (3/0)], Christian Karembeu (26/1), Patrick Vieira (1/0) [78.Bruno Ngotty (4/0)], Zinedine Zidane (22/5), Pierre Laigle (5/0) [33.Robert Pires (5/2)], Ibrahim Ba (2/1) [78.Patrice Loko (24/7)], Christophe Dugarry (17/2). Trainer: Aimé Jacquet (33).
Goals: Robert Pires (75), Patrice Loko (83).

550. 02.04.1997 **FRANCE - SWEDEN** **1-0(1-0)**
Stade Parc des Princes, Paris; Referee: Marnix Sandra (Belgium); Attendance: 24,000
FRA: Fabien Barthez (6/0), Lilian Thuram (22/0) [67.Patrick Blondeau (2/0)], Laurent Robert Blanc (Cap) (59/11), Marcel Desailly (33/1), Vincent Candela (4/0), Ibrahim Ba (3/1) [81.Marc Keller (3/0)], Claude Makélélé (2/0), Zinedine Zidane (23/5) [56.Franck Gava (2/0)], Patrick Vieira (2/0) [65.Martin Djétou (2/0)], Youri Djorkaeff (27/14), Christophe Dugarry (18/2) [56.Patrice Loko (25/7)]. Trainer: Aimé Jacquet (34).
Goal: Youri Djorkaeff (45 penalty).

551. 03.06.1997 **FRANCE - BRAZIL** **1-1(0-1)** International Tournament
Stade de Gerland, Lyon; Referee: Kim Milton Nielsen (Denmark); Attendance: 30,000
FRA: Fabien Barthez (7/0), Vincent Candela (5/0), Laurent Robert Blanc (60/11), Marcel Desailly (34/1) [67.Lilian Thuram (23/0)], Bixente Lizarazu (28/1), Christian Karembeu (27/1) [15.Patrick Vieira (3/0)], Zinedine Zidane (24/5), Didier Deschamps (Cap) (59/4), Ibrahim Ba (4/1), Florian Maurice (2/0), Robert Pires (6/2) [46.Marc Keller (4/1)]. Trainer: Aimé Jacquet (35).
Goal: Marc Keller (60).

552. 07.06.1997 **FRANCE - ENGLAND** **0-1(0-0)** International Tournament
Stade de le Mosson, Montpellier; Referee: Said Belqola (Morocco); Attendance: 28,000
FRA: Fabien Barthez (8/0), Lilian Thuram (24/0), Laurent Robert Blanc (61/11), Bruno Ngotty (5/0), Pierre Laigle (6/0) [83.Bixente Lizarazu (29/1)], Youri Djorkaeff (28/14), Patrick Vieira (4/0), Didier Deschamps (Cap) (60/4), Christophe Dugarry (19/2) [76.Zinedine Zidane (25/5)], Nicolas Ouédec (7/1) [63.Patrice Loko (26/7)], Marc Keller (5/1). Trainer: Aimé Jacquet (36).

553. 11.06.1997 **FRANCE - ITALY** **2-2(1-0)** International Tournament
Stade Parc des Princes, Paris; Referee: Antonio Jesús López Nieto (Spain); Attendance: 30,000
FRA: Lionel Charbonnier (1/0), Lilian Thuram (25/0), Frank Leboeuf (10/2), Marcel Desailly (35/1) [85.Bruno Ngotty (6/0)], Bixente Lizarazu (30/1), Ibrahim Ba (5/1), Christian Karembeu (28/1) [66.Patrick Vieira (5/0)], Zinedine Zidane (26/6), Didier Deschamps (Cap) (61/4), Christophe Dugarry (20/2), Florian Maurice (3/0) [64.Youri Djorkaeff (29/15)]. Trainer: Aimé Jacquet (37).
Goals: Zinedine Zidane (12), Youri Djorkaeff (73).

554. 11.10.1997 **FRANCE – SOUTH AFRICA** **2-1(0-1)**
Stade „Félix Bollaert“, Lens; Referee: Roger Philippi (Luxembourg); Attendance: 29,677
FRA: Lionel Letizi (1/0), Lilian Thuram (26/0), Laurent Robert Blanc (62/11), Marcel Desailly (36/1), Vincent Candela (6/0) [73.Pierre Laigle (7/0)], Didier Deschamps (Cap) (62/4), Youri Djorkaeff (30/15) [78.Ibrahim Ba (6/2)], Emmanuel Petit (16/0) [31.Alain Boghossian (1/0)], Robert Pires (7/2) [46.Zinedine Zidane (27/6)], Stéphane Guivarc'h (1/1), Thierry Daniel Henry (1/0). Trainer: Aimé Jacquet (38).
Goals: Stéphane Guivarc'h (53), Ibrahim Ba (83).

555. 12.11.1997 **FRANCE - SCOTLAND** **2-1(1-1)**
Stade „Geoffroy Guichard“, Saint-Étienne; Referee: Antonio Jesús López Nieto (Spain); Attendance: 19,514
FRA: Fabien Barthez (9/0), Lilian Thuram (27/0), Laurent Robert Blanc (63/11), Marcel Desailly (37/1), Pierre Laigle (8/1) [79.Vincent Candela (7/0)], Didier Deschamps (Cap) (63/4), Ibrahim Ba (7/2) [80.Franck Gava (3/0)], Zinedine Zidane (28/6), Emmanuel Petit (17/0) [73.Alain Boghossian (2/0)], Lilian Laslandes (1/0) [71.Youri Djorkaeff (31/16)], Stéphane Guivarc'h (2/1). Trainer: Aimé Jacquet (39).
Goals: Pierre Laigle (35), Youri Djorkaeff (78 penalty).

556. 28.01.1998 **FRANCE - SPAIN** **1-0(1-0)**
Stade de France, Saint-Denis, Paris; Referee: Urs Meier (Switzerland); Attendance: 80,000
FRA: Fabien Barthez (10/0), Lilian Thuram (28/0), Laurent Robert Blanc (64/11), Marcel Desailly (38/1), Alain Boghossian (3/0), Ibrahim Ba (8/2) [82.Robert Pires (8/2)], Didier Deschamps (Cap) (64/4) [62.Vincent Candela (8/0)], Zinedine Zidane (29/7), Youri Djorkaeff (32/16) [90.Frank Leboeuf (11/2)], Bernard Diomède (1/0), Stéphane Guivarc'h (3/1) [75.David Trézéguet (1/0)]. Trainer: Aimé Jacquet (40).
Goal: Zinedine Zidane (20).

557. 25.02.1998 **FRANCE - NORWAY** **3-3(2-1)**
Stade Vélodrome, Marseille; Referee: Jan Wegerheef (Netherlands); Attendance: 55,000
FRA: Fabien Barthez (11/0), Lilian Thuram (29/0), Laurent Robert Blanc (65/12), Marcel Desailly (39/2), Alain Boghossian (4/0), Didier Deschamps (Cap) (65/4), Youri Djorkaeff (33/16), Robert Pires (9/2), Zinedine Zidane (30/8) [62.Claude Makélélé (3/0)], Bernard Diomède (2/0), Stéphane Guivarc'h (4/1) [62.David Trézéguet (2/0)]. Trainer: Aimé Jacquet (41).
Goals: Laurent Robert Blanc (24), Zinedine Zidane (28), Marcel Desailly (90).

558. 25.03.1998 **RUSSIA - FRANCE** **1-0(1-0)**

Luzhniki Stadium, Moskva; Referee: Igor Yaremchuk (Ukraine); Attendance: 25,000

FRA: Lionel Letizi (2/0), Lilian Thuram (30/0), Frank Leboeuf (12/2), Marcel Desailly (40/2), Emmanuel Petit (18/0) [46.Vincent Candela (9/0)], Didier Deschamps (Cap) (66/4) [46.Alain Boghossian (5/0)], Youri Djorkaeff (34/16), Christian Karembeu (29/1) [62.Marc Keller (6/1)], Bernard Diomède (3/0), Sabri Lamouchi (10/1) [73.Robert Pires (10/2)], Stéphane Guivarc'h (5/1). Trainer: Aimé Jacquet (42).

559. 22.04.1998 **SWEDEN - FRANCE** **0-0**

Råsundastadion, Stockholm; Referee: Graham Poll (England); Attendance: 14,018

FRA: Bernard Lama (36/0), Lilian Thuram (31/0), Laurent Robert Blanc (66/12), Martin Djétou (3/0), Bixente Lizarazu (31/1), Didier Deschamps (Cap) (67/4) [68.Patrick Vieira (6/0)], Zinedine Zidane (31/8) [46.Robert Pires (11/2)], Christian Karembeu (30/1), Sabri Lamouchi (11/1), Nicolas Sébastien Anelka (1/0) [68.David Trézéguet (3/0)], Christophe Dugarry (21/2) [46.Youri Djorkaeff (35/16)]. Trainer: Aimé Jacquet (43).

560. 27.05.1998 **FRANCE - BELGIUM** **1-0(0-0)** International Tournament

Stade d'Honneur, Casablanca (Morocco); Referee: Mohammed Guezzaz (Morocco); Attendance: 80,000

FRA: Fabien Barthez (12/0), Lilian Thuram (32/0), Laurent Robert Blanc (67/12), Marcel Desailly (41/2), Bixente Lizarazu (32/1), Didier Deschamps (Cap) (68/4), Youri Djorkaeff (36/16) [46.Christophe Dugarry (22/2)], Robert Pires (12/2) [62.Thierry Daniel Henry (2/0)], Zinedine Zidane (32/9), Emmanuel Petit (19/0), Stéphane Guivarc'h (6/1). Trainer: Aimé Jacquet (44).

Goal: Zinedine Zidane (64).

561. 29.05.1998 **MOROCCO - FRANCE** **2-2(1-1,2-2,2-2); 6-5 on penalties** International Tournament

Stade “Mohamed V”, Casablanca; Referee: Idrissa Seck (Senegal); Attendance: 65,000

FRA: Bernard Lama (37/0), Vincent Candela (10/0), Laurent Robert Blanc (68/13), Frank Leboeuf (13/2), Christian Karembeu (31/1), Didier Deschamps (Cap) (69/4) [46.Patrick Vieira (7/0)], Alain Boghossian (6/0), Zinedine Zidane (33/9) [63.Youri Djorkaeff (37/17)], Bernard Diomède (4/0) [77.Robert Pires (13/2)], Thierry Daniel Henry (3/0), Christophe Dugarry (23/2) [70.David Trézéguet (4/0)]. Trainer: Aimé Jacquet (45).

Goals: Laurent Robert Blanc (24), Youri Djorkaeff (74).

Penalties: Laurent Robert Blanc, Frank Leboeuf, David Trézéguet, Robert Pires, Patrick Vieira, Youri Djorkaeff (missed), Vincent Candela (missed).

562. 05.06.1998 **FINLAND - FRANCE** **0-1(0-0)**

Olympiastadion, Helsinki; Referee: Konrad Plautz (Austria); Attendance: 18,000

FRA: Fabien Barthez (13/0), Lilian Thuram (33/0) [69.Christian Karembeu (32/1)], Laurent Robert Blanc (69/13), Marcel Desailly (42/2), Bixente Lizarazu (33/1), Didier Deschamps (Cap) (70/4), Youri Djorkaeff (38/17), Zinedine Zidane (34/9) [89.Robert Pires (14/2)], Emmanuel Petit (20/0), Christophe Dugarry (24/2) [77.Bernard Diomède (5/0)], Stéphane Guivarc'h (7/1) [75.David Trézéguet (5/1)]. Trainer: Aimé Jacquet (46).

Goal: David Trézéguet (83).

563. 12.06.1998 **FRANCE – SOUTH AFRICA** **3-0(1-0)** 16th FIFA WC. Group Stage.

Stade Vélodrome, Marseille; Referee: Marcio Rezende de Freitas (Brazil); Attendance: 55,077

FRA: Fabien Barthez (14/0), Lilian Thuram (34/0), Marcel Desailly (43/2), Laurent Robert Blanc (70/13), Bixente Lizarazu (34/1), Didier Deschamps (Cap) (71/4), Emmanuel Petit (21/0) [74.Alain Boghossian (7/0)], Zinedine Zidane (35/9), Youri Djorkaeff (39/17) [83.David Trézéguet (6/1)], Thierry Daniel Henry (4/1), Stéphane Guivarc'h (8/1) [27.Christophe Dugarry (25/3)]. Trainer: Aimé Jacquet (47).

Goals: Christophe Dugarry (35), Pierre Issa (78 own goal), Thierry Daniel Henry (90).

564. 18.06.1998 **FRANCE – SAUDI ARABIA** **4-0(1-0)** 16th FIFA WC. Group Stage.

Stade de France, Saint-Denis, Paris; Referee: Arturo P. Brizio Carter (Mexico); Attendance: 80,000

FRA: Fabien Barthez (15/0), Lilian Thuram (35/0), Marcel Desailly (44/2), Laurent Robert Blanc (71/13), Bixente Lizarazu (35/2), Didier Deschamps (Cap) (72/4), Alain Boghossian (8/0), Zinedine Zidane (36/9) [*sent off 70*], Bernard Diomède (6/0) [58.Youri Djorkaeff (40/17)], Thierry Daniel Henry (5/3) [78.Robert Pires (15/2)], Christophe Dugarry (26/3) [29.David Trézéguet (7/2)]. Trainer: Aimé Jacquet (48).

Goals: Thierry Daniel Henry (36), David Trézéguet (68), Thierry Daniel Henry (77), Bixente Lizarazu (84).

565. 24.06.1998 **FRANCE - DENMARK** **2-1(1-1)** 16th FIFA WC. Group Stage.

Stade de Gerland, Lyon; Referee: Pierluigi Collina (Italy); Attendance: 43,300

FRA: Fabien Barthez (16/0), Christian Karembeu (33/1), Marcel Desailly (Cap) (45/2), Frank Leboeuf (14/2), Vincent Candela (11/0), Patrick Vieira (8/0), Emmanuel Petit (22/1) [65.Alain Boghossian (9/0)], Robert Pires (16/2) [72.Thierry Daniel Henry (6/3)], Youri Djorkaeff (41/18), Bernard Diomède (7/0), David Trézéguet (8/2) [86.Stéphane Guivarc'h (9/1)]. Trainer: Aimé Jacquet (49).

Goal: Youri Djorkaeff (13 penalty), Emmanuel Petit (56).

566. 28.06.1998 **FRANCE - PARAGUAY** **1-0(0-0,0-0)** 16th FIFA WC. 2nd Round of 16.

Stade „Félix Bollaert“, Lens; Referee: Ali Mohammed Bujsaim (United Arab Emirates); Attendance: 42,000

FRA: Fabien Barthez (17/0), Lilian Thuram (36/0), Marcel Desailly (46/2), Laurent Robert Blanc (72/14), Bixente Lizarazu (36/2), Didier Deschamps (Cap) (73/4), Youri Djorkaeff (42/18), Emmanuel Petit (23/1) [70.Alain Boghossian (10/0)], Bernard Diomède (8/0) [77.Stéphane Guivarc'h (10/1)], Thierry Daniel Henry (7/3) [65.Robert Pires (17/2)], David Trézéguet (9/2). Trainer: Aimé Jacquet (50).

Goal: Laurent Robert Blanc (114-Golden Goal).

567. 03.07.1998 **FRANCE - ITALY** **0-0; 4-3 on penalties** 16th FIFA WC. Quarter-Finals.

Stade de France, Saint-Denis, Paris; Referee: Hugh Dallas (Scotland); Attendance: 80,000

FRA: Fabien Barthez (18/0), Lilian Thuram (37/0), Marcel Desailly (47/2), Laurent Robert Blanc (73/14), Bixente Lizarazu (37/2), Christian Karembeu (34/1) [65.Thierry Daniel Henry (8/3)], Didier Deschamps (Cap) (74/4), Youri Djorkaeff (43/18), Emmanuel Petit (24/1), Zinedine Zidane (37/9), Stéphane Guivarc'h (11/1) [65.David Trézéguet (10/2)]. Trainer: Aimé Jacquet (51).

Penalties: Zinedine Zidane, Bixente Lizarazu (missed), David Trézéguet, Thierry Daniel Henry, Laurent Robert Blanc.

568. 08.07.1998 **FRANCE - CROATIA** **2-1(0-0)** 16th FIFA WC. Semi-Finals.

Stade de France, Saint-Denis, Paris; Referee: José María Garcia-Aranda Encinar (Spain); Attendance: 80,000

FRA: Fabien Barthez (19/0), Lilian Thuram (38/2), Marcel Desailly (48/2), Laurent Robert Blanc (74/14) [*sent off 74*], Bixente Lizarazu (38/2), Christian Karembeu (35/1) [31.Thierry Daniel Henry (9/3)], Didier Deschamps (Cap) (75/4), Youri Djorkaeff (44/18) [75.Frank Leboeuf (15/2)], Emmanuel Petit (25/1), Zinedine Zidane (38/9), Stéphane Guivarc'h (12/1) [69.David Trézéguet (11/2)]. Trainer: Aimé Jacquet (52).

Goals: Lilian Thuram (47, 70).

569. 12.07.1998 **FRANCE - BRAZIL** **3-0(2-0)** 16th FIFA WC. Final.
Stade de France, Saint-Denis, Paris; Referee: Said Belqola (Morocco); Attendance: 80,000
FRA: Fabien Barthez (20/0), Lilian Thuram (39/2), Marcel Desailly (49/2) [*sent off 68*], Frank Leboeuf (16/2), Bixente Lizarazu (39/2), Christian Karembeu (36/1) [57.Alain Boghossian (11/0)], Didier Deschamps (Cap) (76/4), Youri Djorkaeff (45/18) [76.Patrick Vieira (9/0)], Zinedine Zidane (39/11), Emmanuel Petit (26/2), Stéphane Guivarc'h (13/1) [66.Christophe Dugarry (27/3)]. Trainer: Aimé Jacquet (53).
Goals: Zinedine Zidane (27, 45), Emmanuel Petit (90).

570. 19.08.1998 **AUSTRIA - FRANCE** **2-2(1-1)**
„Ernst Happel“ Stadion, Wien; Referee: Mario van der Ende (Netherlands); Attendance: 44,000
FRA: Bernard Lama (38/0), Christian Karembeu (37/1), Lilian Thuram (40/2), Frank Leboeuf (17/2) [79.Alain Goma (2/0)], Bixente Lizarazu (40/2) [46.Vincent Candela (12/0)], Alain Boghossian (12/1), Didier Deschamps (Cap) (77/4) [46.Frédéric Dehu (1/0)], Zinedine Zidane (40/11) [46.Youri Djorkaeff (46/18)], Tony Vairelles (1/0), Lilian Laslandes (2/1) [82.Florian Maurice (4/0)], Thierry Daniel Henry (10/3) [65.Robert Pires (18/2)]. Trainer: Roger Lemmere (1).
Goals: Lilian Laslandes (16), Alain Boghossian (84).

571. 05.09.1998 **ICELAND - FRANCE** **1-1(1-1)** 11th EC. Qualifiers
Laugardallsvöllur, Reykjavík; Referee: Eric Blareau (Belgium); Attendance: 10,382
FRA: Fabien Barthez (21/0), Christian Karembeu (38/1), Lilian Thuram (41/2), Frank Leboeuf (18/2), Bixente Lizarazu (41/2), Christophe Dugarry (28/4) [67.Thierry Daniel Henry (11/3)], Didier Deschamps (Cap) (78/4), Youri Djorkaeff (47/18), Zinedine Zidane (41/11), Robert Pires (19/2), Lilian Laslandes (3/1). Trainer: Roger Lemmere (2).
Goal: Christophe Dugarry (36).

572. 10.10.1998 **RUSSIA - FRANCE** **2-3(1-2)** 11th EC. Qualifiers
Luzhniki Stadium, Moskva; Referee: Pietro Ceccarini (Italy); Attendance: 20,989
FRA: Bernard Lama (39/0), Lilian Thuram (42/2), Laurent Robert Blanc (75/14), Marcel Desailly (50/2), Bixente Lizarazu (42/2), Didier Deschamps (Cap) (79/4), Emmanuel Petit (27/2) [46.Alain Boghossian (13/2)], Robert Pires (20/3), Zinedine Zidane (42/11), Youri Djorkaeff (48/18) [54.Patrick Vieira (10/0)], Nicolas Sébastien Anelka (2/1) [88.Tony Vairelles (2/0)]. Trainer: Roger Lemmere (3).
Goals: Nicolas Sébastien Anelka (13), Robert Pires (29), Alain Boghossian (81).

573. 14.10.1998 **FRANCE - ANDORRA** **2-0(0-0)** 11th EC. Qualifiers
Stade de France, Saint-Denis, Paris; Referee: Dani Koren (Israel); Attendance: 75,416
FRA: Bernard Lama (40/0), Vincent Candela (13/1), Frank Leboeuf (19/2), Laurent Robert Blanc (76/14), Bixente Lizarazu (43/2), Didier Deschamps (Cap) (80/4), Zinedine Zidane (43/11), Youri Djorkaeff (49/19) [83.Alain Boghossian (14/2)], Christophe Dugarry (29/4) [69.Robert Pires (21/3)], David Trézéguet (12/2) [69.Nicolas Sébastien Anelka (3/1)], Tony Vairelles (3/0). Trainer: Roger Lemmere (4).
Goals: Vincent Candela (53), Youri Djorkaeff (61).

574. 20.01.1999 **FRANCE - MOROCCO** **1-0(0-0)**
Stade Vélodrome, Marseille; Referee: Alain Hamer (Luxembourg); Attendance: 55,000
FRA: Fabien Barthez (22/0), Lilian Thuram (43/2), Laurent Robert Blanc (77/14) [46.Frank Leboeuf (20/2)], Marcel Desailly (51/2), Vincent Candela (14/1), Alain Boghossian (15/2), Didier Deschamps (Cap) (81/4) [46.Emmanuel Petit (28/2)], Zinedine Zidane (44/11) [66.Nicolas Sébastien Anelka (4/1)], Youri Djorkaeff (50/20), Christophe Dugarry (30/4) [46.Robert Pires (22/3)], Florian Maurice (5/0). Trainer: Roger Lemmere (5).
Goal: Youri Djorkaeff (47).

575. 10.02.1999 **ENGLAND - FRANCE** **0-2(0-0)**
Wembley Stadium, London; Referee: Hellmut Krug (Germany); Attendance: 74,111
FRA: Fabien Barthez (23/0), Lilian Thuram (44/2), Laurent Robert Blanc (78/14) [46.Frank Leboeuf (21/2)], Marcel Desailly (52/2), Bixente Lizarazu (44/2), Didier Deschamps (Cap) (82/4) [90.Vincent Candela (15/1)], Zinedine Zidane (45/11), Youri Djorkaeff (51/20) [83.Patrick Vieira (11/0)], Emmanuel Petit (29/2), Robert Pires (23/3) [46.Christophe Dugarry (31/4)], Nicolas Sébastien Anelka (5/3) [83.Sylvain Wiltord (1/0)]. Trainer: Roger Lemmere (6).
Goals: Nicolas Sébastien Anelka (69, 76).

576. 27.03.1999 **FRANCE - UKRAINE** **0-0** 11th EC. Qualifiers
Stade de France, Saint-Denis, Paris; Referee: Günter Benkö (Austria); Attendance: 78,519
FRA: Fabien Barthez (24/0), Lilian Thuram (45/2), Laurent Robert Blanc (79/14), Marcel Desailly (53/2), Bixente Lizarazu (45/2), Didier Deschamps (Cap) (83/4), Robert Pires (24/3) [84.Vikash Dhorasoo (1/0)], Youri Djorkaeff (52/20), Emmanuel Petit (30/2) [78.Alain Boghossian (16/2)], Nicolas Sébastien Anelka (6/3), Christophe Dugarry (32/4) [68.Sylvain Wiltord (2/0)]. Trainer: Roger Lemmere (7).

577. 31.03.1999 **FRANCE - ARMENIA** **2-0(2-0)** 11th EC. Qualifiers
Stade de France, Saint-Denis, Paris; Referee: Yeorgios Bikas (Greece); Attendance: 78,854
FRA: Fabien Barthez (25/0), Lilian Thuram (46/2) [79.Christian Karembeu (39/1)], Laurent Robert Blanc (80/14), Marcel Desailly (54/2), Patrick Vieira (12/0), Youri Djorkaeff (53/20) [69.Robert Pires (25/3)], Didier Deschamps (Cap) (84/4), Alain Boghossian (17/2), Nicolas Sébastien Anelka (7/3), Sylvain Wiltord (3/1), Christophe Dugarry (33/5) [46.David Trézéguet (13/2)]. Trainer: Roger Lemmere (8).
Goals: Sylvain Wiltord (1), Christophe Dugarry (45).

578. 05.06.1999 **FRANCE - RUSSIA** **2-3(0-1)** 11th EC. Qualifiers
Stade de France, Saint-Denis, Paris; Referee: Paul Anthony Durkin (England); Attendance: 78,788
FRA: Fabien Barthez (26/0), Lilian Thuram (47/2), Laurent Robert Blanc (81/14), Marcel Desailly (55/2), Vincent Candela (16/1) [88.Robert Pires (26/3)], Didier Deschamps (Cap) (85/4), Emmanuel Petit (31/3), Youri Djorkaeff (54/20) [90.Alain Boghossian (18/2)], Christophe Dugarry (34/5) [59.Patrick Vieira (13/0)], Nicolas Sébastien Anelka (8/3), Sylvain Wiltord (4/2). Trainer: Roger Lemmere (9).
Goals: Emmanuel Petit (48), Sylvain Wiltord (54).

579. 09.06.1999 **ANDORRA - FRANCE** **0-1(0-0)** 11th EC. Qualifiers
Estadi Olímpic de Montjuïc, Barcelona (Spain); Referee: Michael Ross (Northern Ireland); Attendance: 7,600
FRA: Ulrich Ramé (1/0), Christian Karembeu (40/1), Marcel Desailly (56/2), Frank Leboeuf (22/3), Vincent Candela (17/1), Emmanuel Petit (32/3) [56.Patrick Vieira (14/0)], Alain Boghossian (19/2), Vikash Dhorasoo (2/0) [61.Robert Pires (27/3)], Christophe Dugarry (35/5), Nicolas Sébastien Anelka (9/3), Sylvain Wiltord (5/2). Trainer: Roger Lemmere (10).
Goal: Frank Leboeuf (85 penalty).

580. 18.08.1999 **NORTHERN IRELAND - FRANCE** **0-1(0-0)**
Windsor Park, Belfast; Referee: William Young (Scotland); Attendance: 11,804
FRA: Fabien Barthez (27/0), Lilian Thuram (48/2), Laurent Robert Blanc (82/14), Marcel Desailly (57/2) [65.Frank Leboeuf (23/3)], Bixente Lizarazu (46/2) [56.Vincent Candela (18/1)], Patrick Vieira (15/0) [84.Frédéric Dehu (2/0)], Alain Boghossian (20/2), Robert Pires (28/3), Johan Micoud (1/0), Sylvain Wiltord (6/2) [56.Laurent Robert (1/0)], Lilian Laslandes (4/2) [77.Tony Vairelles (4/0)]. Trainer: Roger Lemmere (11).
Goal: Lilian Laslandes (67).

581. 04.09.1999 **UKRAINE - FRANCE** **0-0** 11th EC. Qualifiers
Olympiyskyi Stadium, Kyiv; Referee: Hugh Dallas (Scotland); Attendance: 70,000
FRA: Fabien Barthez (28/0), Lilian Thuram (49/2), Laurent Robert Blanc (83/14), Marcel Desailly (58/2), Bixente Lizarazu (47/2), Christian Karembeu (41/1), Patrick Vieira (16/0), Didier Deschamps (Cap) (86/4), Zinedine Zidane (46/11), Youri Djorkaeff (55/20) [69.Robert Pires (29/3)], Nicolas Sébastien Anelka (10/3) [59.Lilian Laslandes (5/2)]. Trainer: Roger Lemmere (12).

582. 08.09.1999 **ARMENIA - FRANCE** **2-3(1-1)** 11th EC. Qualifiers
Hrazdan Stadium, Yerevan; Referee: Atanas Uzunov (Bulgaria); Attendance: 14,500
FRA: Fabien Barthez (29/0), Lilian Thuram (50/2), Laurent Robert Blanc (84/14), Marcel Desailly (59/2), Bixente Lizarazu (48/2), Christian Karembeu (42/1), Didier Deschamps (Cap) (87/4), Youri Djorkaeff (56/21), Zinedine Zidane (47/12) [72.Frédéric Dehu (3/0) [*sent off 89*]], Lilian Laslandes (6/3), Sylvain Wiltord (7/2) [66.Laurent Robert (2/0)]. Trainer: Roger Lemmere (13).
Goals: Youri Djorkaeff (45 penalty), Zinedine Zidane (67), Lilian Laslandes (74).

583. 09.10.1999 **FRANCE - ICELAND** **3-2(2-0)** 11th EC. Qualifiers
Stade de France, Saint-Denis, Paris; Referee: Bernd Heynemann (Germany); Attendance: 78,391
FRA: Bernard Lama (41/0), Lilian Thuram (51/2), Laurent Robert Blanc (85/14), Marcel Desailly (60/2), Bixente Lizarazu (49/2), Didier Deschamps (Cap) (88/4), Alain Boghossian (21/2) [90.Patrick Vieira (17/0)], Youri Djorkaeff (57/22), Zinedine Zidane (48/12), Lilian Laslandes (7/3) [63.David Trézéguet (14/3)], Sylvain Wiltord (8/2) [90.Tony Vairelles (5/0)]. Trainer: Roger Lemmere (14).
Goals: Ríkhardur Dadason (18 own goal), Youri Djorkaeff (38), David Trézéguet (71).

584. 13.11.1999 **FRANCE - CROATIA** **3-0(0-0)**
Stade de France, Saint-Denis, Paris; Referee: Luboš Michel (Slovakia); Attendance: 80,000
FRA: Stéphane Porato (1/0), Lilian Thuram (52/2), Frank Leboeuf (24/3), Marcel Desailly (61/2), Vincent Candela (19/1), Patrick Vieira (18/0), Alain Boghossian (22/2) [73.Frédéric Dehu (4/0)], Robert Pires (30/4) [60.Tony Vairelles (6/1)], Johan Micoud (2/0) [85.Didier Deschamps (89/4)], Zinedine Zidane (49/12) [46.Youri Djorkaeff (58/22)], Stéphane Guivarc'h (14/1) [46.Florian Maurice (6/1)]. Trainer: Roger Lemmere (15).
Goals: Robert Pires (46), Florian Maurice (67), Tony Vairelles (73).

585. 23.02.2000 **FRANCE - POLAND** **1-0(0-0)**
Stade de France, Saint-Denis, Paris; Referee: Kyros Vassaras (Greece); Attendance: 74,350
FRA: Fabien Barthez (30/0), Lilian Thuram (53/2), Laurent Robert Blanc (86/14) [46.Frank Leboeuf (25/3)], Marcel Desailly (62/2), Bixente Lizarazu (50/2), Didier Deschamps (Cap) (90/4), Youri Djorkaeff (59/22) [74.Tony Vairelles (7/1)], Zinedine Zidane (50/13), Emmanuel Petit (33/3) [58.Patrick Vieira (19/0)], Sylvain Wiltord (9/2) [58.Robert Pires (31/4)], David Trézéguet (15/3). Trainer: Roger Lemmere (16).
Goal: Zinedine Zidane (88).

586. 29.03.2000 **SCOTLAND - FRANCE** **0-2(0-0)**
Hampden Park, Glasgow; Referee: Rune Pedersen (Norway); Attendance: 48,157
FRA: Ulrich Ramé (2/0), Lilian Thuram (54/2), Laurent Robert Blanc (87/14), Marcel Desailly (63/2), Bixente Lizarazu (51/2), Didier Deschamps (Cap) (91/4) [60.Patrick Vieira (20/0)], Youri Djorkaeff (60/22) [46.Johan Micoud (3/0)], Ludovic Giuly (1/0) [46.Sylvain Wiltord (10/3)], Emmanuel Petit (34/3), Christophe Dugarry (36/5) [71.Robert Pires (32/4)], Thierry Daniel Henry (12/4). Trainer: Roger Lemmere (17).
Goals: Sylvain Wiltord (54), Thierry Daniel Henry (88).

587. 26.04.2000 **FRANCE - SLOVENIA** **3-2(0-2)**
Stade de France, Saint-Denis, Paris; Referee: Abderrahim El Arjoune (Morocco); Attendance: 50,000
FRA: Fabien Barthez (31/0), Lilian Thuram (55/2), Laurent Robert Blanc (88/15), Frank Leboeuf (26/3), Bixente Lizarazu (52/2), Patrick Vieira (21/0), Didier Deschamps (Cap) (92/4) [62.Emmanuel Petit (35/3)], Robert Pires (33/4) [62.Tony Vairelles (8/1)], Zinedine Zidane (51/13), Christophe Dugarry (37/5) [46.Johan Micoud (4/0)], Thierry Daniel Henry (13/4) [46.David Trézéguet (16/5)]. Trainer: Roger Lemmere (18).
Goals: David Trézéguet (62), Laurent Robert Blanc (78), David Trézéguet (90).

588. 28.05.2000 **CROATIA - FRANCE** **0-2(0-1)**
Stadion Maksimir, Zagreb; Referee: Fritz Stuchlik (Austria); Attendance: 10,000
FRA: Fabien Barthez (32/0), Lilian Thuram (56/2), Laurent Robert Blanc (89/15) [75.Frank Leboeuf (27/3)], Marcel Desailly (64/2), Bixente Lizarazu (53/2), Didier Deschamps (Cap) (93/4), Zinedine Zidane (52/13) [82.Vincent Candela (20/1)], Emmanuel Petit (36/3) [46.Patrick Vieira (22/0)], Robert Pires (34/5) [46.David Trézéguet (17/6)], Sylvain Wiltord (11/3), Thierry Daniel Henry (14/4) [60.Johan Micoud (5/0)]. Trainer: Roger Lemmere (19).
Goals: Robert Pires (25), David Trézéguet (70).

589. 04.06.2000 **FRANCE - JAPAN** **2-2(0-1,2-2,2-2); 4-2 on penalties** International Tournament
Stade "Mohamed V", Casablanca; Referee: Abderrahim El-Arjoune (Morocco); Attendance: 40,000
FRA: Fabien Barthez (33/0), Lilian Thuram (57/2), Laurent Robert Blanc (90/15), Marcel Desailly (65/2) [68.Frank Leboeuf (28/3)], Bixente Lizarazu (54/2), Didier Deschamps (Cap) (94/4) [46.Patrick Vieira (23/0)], Zinedine Zidane (53/14) [89.Thierry Daniel Henry (15/4)], Robert Pires (35/5) [46.Youri Djorkaeff (61/23)], Emmanuel Petit (37/3), Sylvain Wiltord (12/3) [46.Christophe Dugarry (38/5)], David Trézéguet (18/6) [76.Nicolas Sébastien Anelka (11/3)]. Trainer: Roger Lemmere (20).
Goals: Zinedine Zidane (61), Youri Djorkaeff (75).
Penalties: Youri Djorkaeff, Thierry Daniel Henry, Frank Leboeuf, Nicolas Sébastien Anelka.

590. 06.06.2000 **MOROCCO - FRANCE** **1-5(0-1)** International Tournament
Stade "Mohamed V", Casablanca; Referee: Ali Mohammed Bujsaim (United Arab Emirates); Attendance: 55,000
FRA: Bernard Lama (42/0), Christian Karembeu (43/1), Marcel Desailly (66/2), Frank Leboeuf (29/3), Vincent Candela (21/1), Patrick Vieira (24/0), Johan Micoud (6/0) [66.Didier Deschamps (95/4)], Youri Djorkaeff (62/24) [61.Zinedine Zidane (54/14)], Christophe Dugarry (39/6) [86.Sylvain Wiltord (13/4)], Nicolas Sébastien Anelka (12/4), Thierry Daniel Henry (16/5) [75.Emmanuel Petit (38/3)]. Trainer: Roger Lemmere (21).
Goals: Thierry Daniel Henry (26), Youri Djorkaeff (55 penalty), Christophe Dugarry (75), Nicolas Sébastien Anelka (84), Sylvain Wiltord (90).

591. 11.06.2000 **FRANCE - DENMARK** **3-0(1-0)** 11th EC. Group Stage.
"Jan Breydel" stadion, Brugge (Belgium); Referee: Günter Benkö (Austria); Attendance: 30,000
FRA: Fabien Barthez (34/0), Lilian Thuram (58/2), Laurent Robert Blanc (91/16), Marcel Desailly (67/2), Bixente Lizarazu (55/2), Youri Djorkaeff (63/24) [58.Patrick Vieira (25/0)], Didier Deschamps (Cap) (96/4), Emmanuel Petit (39/3), Zinedine Zidane (55/14), Nicolas Sébastien Anelka (13/4) [82.Sylvain Wiltord (14/5)], Thierry Daniel Henry (17/6). Trainer: Roger Lemmere (22).
Goals: Laurent Robert Blanc (16), Thierry Daniel Henry (64), Sylvain Wiltord (90).

592. 16.06.2000 **FRANCE - CZECH REPUBLIC** **2-1(1-1)** 11th EC. Group Stage.
"Jan Breydel" stadion, Brugge (Belgium); Referee: Graham Poll (England); Attendance: 30,000
FRA: Fabien Barthez (35/0), Lilian Thuram (59/2), Laurent Robert Blanc (92/16), Marcel Desailly (68/2), Vincent Candela (22/1), Patrick Vieira (26/0), Didier Deschamps (Cap) (97/4), Emmanuel Petit (40/3) [46.Youri Djorkaeff (64/25)], Zinedine Zidane (56/14), Nicolas Sébastien Anelka (14/4) [54.Christophe Dugarry (40/6)], Thierry Daniel Henry (18/7) [90.Sylvain Wiltord (15/5)]. Trainer: Roger Lemmere (23).
Goals: Thierry Daniel Henry (7), Youri Djorkaeff (60).

593. 21.06.2000 **NETHERLANDS - FRANCE** **3-2(1-2)** 11th EC. Group Stage.
Amsterdam ArenA, Amsterdam (Netherlands); Referee: Anders Frisk (Sweden); Attendance: 50,000
FRA: Bernard Lama (43/0), Christian Karembeu (44/1), Frank Leboeuf (30/3), Marcel Desailly (Cap) (69/2), Vincent Candela (23/1), Christophe Dugarry (41/7) [68.Youri Djorkaeff (65/25)], Patrick Vieira (27/0) [90.Didier Deschamps (98/4)], Johan Micoud (7/0), Robert Pires (36/5), David Trézéguet (19/7), Sylvain Wiltord (16/5) [80.Nicolas Sébastien Anelka (15/4)]. Trainer: Roger Lemmere (24).
Goals: Christophe Dugarry (8), David Trézéguet (31).

594. 25.06.2000 **SPAIN - FRANCE** **1-2(2-1)** 11th EC. Quarter-Finals.
"Jan Breydel" stadion, Brugge (Belgium); Referee: Pierluigi Collina (Italy); Attendance: 30,000
FRA: Fabien Barthez (36/0), Lilian Thuram (60/2), Laurent Robert Blanc (93/16), Marcel Desailly (70/2), Bixente Lizarazu (56/2), Youri Djorkaeff (66/26), Didier Deschamps (Cap) (99/4), Patrick Vieira (28/0), Zinedine Zidane (57/15), Christophe Dugarry (42/7), Thierry Daniel Henry (19/7) [81.Nicolas Sébastien Anelka (16/4)]. Trainer: Roger Lemmere (25).
Goals: Zinedine Zidane (33), Youri Djorkaeff (44).

595. 28.06.2000 **FRANCE - PORTUGAL** **2-1(0-1,1-1)** 11th EC. Semi-Finals.
Stade „Roi Baudouin", Bruxelles (Belgium); Referee: Günter Benkö (Austria); Attendance: 47,000
FRA: Fabien Barthez (37/0), Lilian Thuram (61/2), Laurent Robert Blanc (94/16), Marcel Desailly (71/2), Bixente Lizarazu (57/2), Didier Deschamps (Cap) (100/4), Patrick Vieira (29/0), Emmanuel Petit (41/3) [87.Robert Pires (37/5)], Zinedine Zidane (58/16), Nicolas Sébastien Anelka (17/4) [71.Sylvain Wiltord (17/5)], Thierry Daniel Henry (20/8) [105.David Trézéguet (20/7)]. Trainer: Roger Lemmere (26).
Goals: Thierry Daniel Henry (51), Zinedine Zidane (117 penalty, Golden Goal).

596. 02.07.2000 **FRANCE - ITALY** **2-1(0-0,1-1)** 11th EC. Final.
Stadion Feijenoord, Rotterdam (Netherlands); Referee: Anders Frisk (Sweden); Attendance: 48,200
FRA: Fabien Barthez (38/0), Lilian Thuram (62/2), Laurent Robert Blanc (95/16), Marcel Desailly (72/2), Bixente Lizarazu (58/2) [85.Robert Pires (38/5)], Patrick Vieira (30/0), Didier Deschamps (Cap) (101/4), Youri Djorkaeff (67/26) [75.David Trézéguet (21/8)], Zinedine Zidane (59/16), Christophe Dugarry (43/7) [57.Sylvain Wiltord (18/6)], Thierry Daniel Henry (21/8). Trainer: Roger Lemmere (27).
Goals: Sylvain Wiltord (90), David Trézéguet (103, Golden Goal).

597. 16.08.2000 **FRANCE – WORLD XI** **5-1(2-0)**
Stade Vélodrome, Marseille; Referee: Mohammed Guezzaz (Morocco); Attendance: 60,000
FRA: Fabien Barthez (39/0) [46.Ulrich Ramé (3/0)], Vincent Candela (24/1), Laurent Robert Blanc (96/16) [50.Frank Leboeuf (31/3)], Marcel Desailly (73/2), Bixente Lizarazu (59/2) [74.Christian Karembeu (45/1)], Didier Deschamps (Cap) (102/4) [61.Patrick Vieira (31/0)], Zinedine Zidane (60/16), Christophe Dugarry (44/7), Emmanuel Petit (42/3) [46.Youri Djorkaeff (68/26)], David Trézéguet (22/11) [50.Nicolas Sébastien Anelka (18/5)], Thierry Daniel Henry (22/8) [46.Robert Pires (39/6)]. Trainer: Roger Lemmere (28).
Goals: David Trézéguet (12, 28, 47), Robert Pires (55), Nicolas Sébastien Anelka (77).

598. 02.09.2000 **FRANCE - ENGLAND** **1-1(0-0)**
Stade de France, Saint-Denis, Paris; Referee: Juan Ansuategui Roca (Spain); Attendance: 77,000
FRA: Bernard Lama (44/0), Lilian Thuram (63/2) [80.Vincent Candela (25/1)], Laurent Robert Blanc (97/16) [58.Frank Leboeuf (32/3)], Marcel Desailly (74/2), Bixente Lizarazu (60/2), Didier Deschamps (Cap) (103/4) [58.Patrick Vieira (32/0)], Zinedine Zidane (61/16) [65.Robert Pires (40/6)], Youri Djorkaeff (69/26), Emmanuel Petit (43/4), Nicolas Sébastien Anelka (19/5) [46.Sylvain Wiltord (19/6)], Thierry Daniel Henry (23/8) [73.David Trézéguet (23/11)]. Trainer: Roger Lemmere (29).
Goal: Emmanuel Petit (64).

599. 04.10.2000 **FRANCE - CAMEROON** **1-1(1-0)**
Stade de France, Saint-Denis, Paris; Referee: Michel Piraux (Belgium); Attendance: 63,704
FRA: Lionel Letizi (3/0) [59.Richard Dutruel (1/0)], Lilian Thuram (64/2), Frank Leboeuf (33/3), Marcel Desailly (Cap) (75/2), Bixente Lizarazu (61/2) [56.Claude Makélélé (4/0)], Patrick Vieira (33/0), Johan Micoud (8/0) [75.Martin Djétou (4/0)], Emmanuel Petit (44/4), Sylvain Wiltord (20/7) [67.Ludovic Giuly (2/0)], David Trézéguet (24/11) [56.Laurent Robert (3/0)], Thierry Daniel Henry (24/8). Trainer: Roger Lemmere (30).
Goal: Sylvain Wiltord (19).

600. 07.10.2000 **SOUTH AFRICA - FRANCE** **0-0**
Ellis Park Stadium, Johannesburg; Referee: Jelas Masole (Botswana); Attendance: 37,000
FRA: Ulrich Ramé (4/0), Lilian Thuram (65/2) [32.Ludovic Giuly (3/0)], Frank Leboeuf (34/3) [60.Philippe Christanval (1/0)], Marcel Desailly (Cap) (76/2), Christian Karembeu (46/1), Claude Makélélé (5/0), Patrick Vieira (34/0), Laurent Robert (4/0), Martin Djétou (5/0) [75.Emmanuel Petit (45/4)], Nicolas Sébastien Anelka (20/5) [66.David Trézéguet (25/11)], Sylvain Wiltord (21/7) [46.Thierry Daniel Henry (25/8)]. Trainer: Roger Lemmere (31).

601. 15.11.2000 **TURKEY - FRANCE** **0-4(0-3)**
„Ismet Inönü" Stadı, İstanbul; Referee: Yeorgios Borovilos (Greece); Attendance: 9,000
FRA: Fabien Barthez (40/0), Lilian Thuram (66/2) [78.Willy Sagnol (1/0)], Frank Leboeuf (35/3), Marcel Desailly (Cap) (77/2), Vincent Candela (26/1), Patrick Vieira (35/0) [31.Claude Makélélé (6/0)], Johan Micoud (9/1), Zinedine Zidane (62/16) [63.Frédéric Dehu (5/0)], Emmanuel Petit (46/4) [69.Martin Djétou (6/0)], David Trézéguet (26/12) [81.Steve Marlet (1/0)], Sylvain Wiltord (22/8) [57.Laurent Robert (5/1)]. Trainer: Roger Lemmere (32).
Goals: David Trézéguet (15), Sylvain Wiltord (22), Johan Micoud (44), Laurent Robert (74).

602. 27.02.2001 **FRANCE - GERMANY** **1-0(1-0)**
Stade de France, Saint-Denis, Paris; Referee: Alfredo Trentalange (Italy); Attendance: 77,929
FRA: Fabien Barthez (41/0), Willy Sagnol (2/0) [59.Bixente Lizarazu (62/2)], Frank Leboeuf (36/3), Marcel Desailly (Cap) (78/2) [76.Mikaël Silvestre (1/0)], Vincent Candela (27/1), Sylvain Wiltord (23/8) [53.Robert Pires (41/6)], Patrick Vieira (36/0), Emmanuel Petit (47/4), Zinedine Zidane (63/17) [82.Claude Makélélé (7/0)], Christophe Dugarry (45/7), Nicolas Sébastien Anelka (21/5) [59.Thierry Daniel Henry (26/8)]. Trainer: Roger Lemmere (33).
Goal: Zinedine Zidane (17).

603. 24.03.2001 **FRANCE - JAPAN** **5-0(2-0)**
Stade de France, Saint-Denis, Paris; Referee: Dieter Schoch (Switzerland); Attendance: 77,888
FRA: Ulrich Ramé (5/0), Vincent Candela (28/1), Marcel Desailly (Cap) (79/2), Frank Leboeuf (37/3) [35.Mikaël Silvestre (2/0)], Bixente Lizarazu (63/2) [80.Christian Karembeu (47/1)], Emmanuel Petit (48/4) [46.Patrick Vieira (37/0)], Robert Pires (42/6) [60.Johan Micoud (10/1)], Zinedine Zidane (64/18), Sabri Lamouchi (12/1), Christophe Dugarry (46/7) [53.Sylvain Wiltord (24/9)], Thierry Daniel Henry (27/9) [53.David Trézéguet (27/14)]. Trainer: Roger Lemmere (34).
Goals: Zinedine Zidane (9 penalty), Thierry Daniel Henry (13), Sylvain Wiltord (56), David Trézéguet (61, 68).

604. 28.03.2001 **SPAIN - FRANCE** **2-1(1-0)**
Estadio Mestalla, Valencia; Referee: Michael-Lutz Fröhlich (Germany); Attendance: 40,000
FRA: Lionel Letitzi (4/0), Christian Karembeu (48/1), Mikaël Silvestre (3/0), Marcel Desailly (Cap) (80/2), Bixente Lizarazu (64/2), Claude Makélélé (8/0) [58.Robert Pires (43/6)], Patrick Viera (38/0) [77.David Trézéguet (28/15)], Emmanuel Petit (49/4), Zinedine Zidane (65/18) [62.Johan Micoud (11/1)] Christophe Dugarry (47/7) [46.Sylvain Wiltord (25/9)], Thierry Daniel Henry (28/9). Trainer: Roger Lemmere (35).
Goal: David Trézéguet (85).

605. 25.04.2001 **FRANCE - PORTUGAL** **4-0(3-0)**
Stade de France, Saint-Denis, Paris; Referee: Hellmut Krug (Germany); Attendance: 78,832
FRA: Fabien Barthez (42/0), Lilian Thuram (67/2) [70.Vincent Candela (29/1)], Marcel Desailly (Cap) (81/2), Mikaël Silvestre (4/1), Bixente Lizarazu (65/2), Patrick Vieira (39/0) [61.Claude Makélélé (9/0)], Emmanuel Petit (50/4) [86.Willy Sagnol (3/0)], Robert Pires (44/6), Zinedine Zidane (66/18) [46.Youri Djorkaeff (70/27)], Sylvain Wiltord (26/10) [54.David Trézéguet (29/15)], Thierry Daniel Henry (29/10). Trainer: Roger Lemmere (36).
Goals: Sylvain Wiltord (16), Mikaël Silvestre (32), Thierry Daniel Henry (33), Youri Djorkaeff (79).

606. 30.05.2001 **KOREA REPUBLIC - FRANCE** **0-5(0-3)** 5th FIFA Confederations Cup. Group Stage.
World Cup 2002 Stadium, Daegu; Referee: Gamal Mahmoud Ahmed Al Ghandour (Egypt); Attendance: 61,500
FRA: Ulrich Ramé (6/0), Willy Sagnol (4/0), Bixente Lizarazu (66/2), Marcel Desailly (82/2), Mikaël Silvestre (5/1), Patrick Vieira (40/1), Robert Pires (45/6) [83.Olivier Dacourt (1/0)], Eric Carrière (1/0), Steve Marlet (2/1) [67.Sylvain Wiltord (27/11)], Nicolas Sébastien Anelka (22/6), Christophe Dugarry (48/7) [73.Youri Djorkaeff (71/28)]. Trainer: Roger Lemmere (37).
Goals: Steve Marlet (9), Patrick Vieira (19), Nicolas Sébastien Anelka (34), Youri Djorkaeff (80), Sylvain Wiltord (90).

607. 01.06.2001 **AUSTRALIA - FRANCE** **1-0(0-0)** 5th FIFA Confederations Cup. Group Stage.
Suwon World Cup Stadium, Suwon (Korea Republic); Referee: Carlos Alberto Batrés González (Guatemala); Attendance: 44,400
FRA: Grégory Coupet (1/0), Zoumana Camara (1/0), Frank Leboeuf (38/3) [*sent off 78*], Christian Karembeu (49/1), Nicolas Gillet (1/0), Olivier Dacourt (2/0) [74.Robert Pires (46/6)], Youri Djorkaeff (72/28) [88.Patrick Vieira (41/1)], Jérémie Brechet (1/0), Laurent Robert (6/1), Frédéric Née (1/0) [71.Nicolas Sébastien Anelka (23/6)], Sylvian Wiltord (28/11). Trainer: Roger Lemmere (38).

608. 03.06.2001 **FRANCE - MEXICO** **4-0(1-0)** 5th FIFA Confederations Cup. Group Stage.
Ulsan Munsu Football Stadium, Ulsan (Korea Republic); Referee: Ali Mohammed Bujsaim (United Arab Emirates); Attendance: 28,864
FRA: Mikaël Landreau (1/0), Willy Sagnol (5/0), Marcel Desailly (Cap) (83/2), Mikaël Silvestre (6/1), Bixente Lizarazu (67/2), Patrick Vieira (42/1), Robert Pires (47/7) [85.Olivier Dacourt (3/0)], Nicolas Sébastien Anelka (24/6), Eric Carrière (2/2), Steve Marlet (3/1) [65.Laurent Robert (7/1)], Sylvain Wiltord (29/12) [78.Youri Djorkaeff (73/28)]. Trainer: Roger Lemmere (39).
Goals: Sylvain Wiltord (8), Eric Carrière (62), Robert Pires (71), Eric Carrière (83).

609. 07.06.2001 **FRANCE - BRAZIL** **2-1(1-1)** 5th FIFA Confederations Cup. Semi-Finals.
Suwon World Cup Stadium, Suwon (Korea Republic); Referee: Gamal Mahmoud Ahmed Al Ghandour (Egypt); Attendance: 34,527
FRA: Ulrich Ramé (7/0), Willy Sagnol (6/0), Frank Leboeuf (39/3), Marcel Desailly (Cap) (84/3), Bixente Lizarazu (68/2), Christian Karembeu (50/1), Patrick Vieira (43/1), Youri Djorkaeff (74/28) [61.Eric Carrière (3/2)], Robert Pires (48/8), Nicolas Sébastien Anelka (25/6), Sylvain Wiltord (30/12) [65.Laurent Robert (8/1)]. Trainer: Roger Lemmere (40).
Goals: Robert Pires (7), Marcel Desailly (54).

610. 10.06.2001 **JAPAN - FRANCE** **0-1(0-1)** 5th FIFA Confederations Cup. Final.
International Stadium, Yokohama (Japan); Referee: Ali Mohammed Bujsaim (United Arab Emirates); Attendance: 65,335
FRA: Ulrich Ramé (8/0), Christian Karembeu (51/1), Bixente Lizarazu (69/2), Frank Leboeuf (40/3), Marcel Desailly (Cap) (85/3), Patrick Vieira (44/2), Steve Marlet (4/1) [58.Laurent Robert (9/1)], Robert Pires (49/8), Youri Djorkaeff (75/28) [65.Eric Carrière (4/2)], Sylvain Wiltord (31/12), Nicolas Sébastien Anelka (26/6). Trainer: Roger Lemmere (41).
Goal: Patrick Vieira (30).

611. 15.08.2001 **FRANCE - DENMARK** **1-0(1-0)**
Stade de la Beaujoire, Nantes; Referee: Michael MacCurry (Scotland); Attendance: 36,700
FRA: Fabian Barthez (43/0), Lilian Thuram (68/2), Frank Leboeuf (41/3), Marcel Desailly (86/3), Bixente Lizarazu (70/2) [79.Vincent Candela (30/1)], Patrick Vieira (45/2) [71.Willy Sagnol (7/0)], Emmanuel Petit (51/4), Sylvain Wiltord (32/12) [58.Steve Marlet (5/1)], Zinedine Zidane (67/18), Robert Pires (50/9) [65.Johan Micoud (12/1)], Thierry Daniel Henry (30/10) [58.David Trézéguet (30/15)]. Trainer: Roger Lemmere (42).
Goal: Robert Pires (13).

612. 01.09.2001 **CHILE - FRANCE** **2-1(1-0)**
Estadio Nacional, Santiago; Referee: Daniel Orlando Giménez (Argentina); Attendance: 72,728
FRA: Ulrich Ramé (9/0), Lilian Thuram (69/2) [88.Willy Sagnol (8/0)], Marcel Desailly (87/3) [46.Frank Leboeuf (42/3)], Mikaël Silvestre (7/1), Bixente Lizarazu (71/2), Patrick Vieira (46/2) [63.Claude Makélélé (10/0)], Emmanuel Petit (52/4), Sylvain Wiltord (33/12) [46.Thierry Daniel Henry (31/10)], Zinedine Zidane (68/18), Robert Pires (51/9) [69.Steve Marlet (6/1)], David Trézéguet (31/16). Trainer: Roger Lemmere (43).
Goal: David Trézéguet (74).

613. 07.10.2001 **FRANCE - ALGERIA** **4-1(3-1)***
Stade de France, Saint-Denis, Paris; Referee: Paulo Manuel Gomes Costa (Portugal); Attendance: 78,421
FRA: Fabien Barthez (44/0), Lilian Thuram (70/2), Frank Leboeuf (43/3) [46.Mikaël Silvestre (8/1)], Marcel Desailly (88/3) (Cap), Vincent Candela (31/2), Patrick Vieira (47/2), Emmanuel Petit (53/5) [56.Sylvain Wiltord (34/12)], Robert Pires (52/10), Zinedine Zidane (69/18) [46.Youri Djorkaeff (76/28)], Thierry Daniel Henry (32/11) [56.Claude Makélélé (11/0)], David Trézéguet (32/16). Trainer: Roger Lemmere (44).
Goals: Vincent Candela (20), Emmanuel Petit (31), Thierry Daniel Henry (40), Robert Pires (54).
**Match abandoned at mins 75 due to pitch invasion.*

614. 11.11.2001 **AUSTRALIA - FRANCE** **1-1(1-0)**
Cricket Ground, Melbourne; Referee: Simon Micallef (Australia); Attendance: 53,228
FRA: Fabien Barthez (45/0), Christian Karembeu (52/1), Frank Leboeuf (44/3), Marcel Desailly (89/3) (Cap) [83.Mikaël Silvestre (9/1)], Christophe Dugarry (49/7) [58.Sylvain Wiltord (35/12)], Vincent Candela (32/2), Claude Makélélé (12/0) [65.Eric Carrière (5/2)], Robert Pires (53/10), Patrick Vieira (48/2), David Trézéguet (33/17) [65.Nicolas Sébastien Anelka (27/6)], Zinedine Zidane (70/18) [80.Alain Boghossian (23/2)]. Trainer: Roger Lemmere (45).
Goal: David Trézéguet (49).

615. 13.02.2002 **FRANCE - ROMANIA** **2-1(2-0)**
Stade de France, Saint-Denis, Paris; Referee: Dick van Egmond (Netherlands); Attendance: 80,000
FRA: Ulrich Ramé (10/0), Lilian Thuram (71/2), Philippe Christanval (2/0), Marcel Desailly (90/3) (Cap), Vincent Candela (33/2), Patrick Vieira (49/3) [46.Alain Boghossian (24/2)], Emmanuel Petit (54/6) [46.Claude Makélélé (13/0)], Robert Pires (54/10), Zinedine Zidane (71/18) [72.Eric Carrière (6/2)], Christophe Dugarry (50/7) [60.Sylvain Wiltord (36/12)], Thierry Daniel Henry (33/11) [72.David Trézéguet (34/17)]. Trainer: Roger Lemmere (46).
Goals: Patrick Vieira (1), Emmanuel Petit (27).

616. 27.03.2002 **FRANCE - SCOTLAND** **5-0(4-0)**
Stade de France, Saint-Denis, Paris; Referee: Jacek Granat (Poland); Attendance: 80,000
FRA: Fabien Barthez (46/0), Vincent Candela (34/2) [58.Christian Karembeu (53/1)], Frank Leboeuf (45/3) [64.Philippe Christanval (3/0)], Marcel Desailly (91/3) [46.Mikaël Silvestre (10/1)], Bixente Lizarazu (72/2), Patrick Vieira (50/3) [46.Claude Makélélé (14/0)], Emmanuel Petit (55/6), Zinedine Zidane (72/19) [81.Youri Djorkaeff (77/28)], Sylvain Wiltord (37/12) [57.Steve Marlet (7/2)], Thierry Daniel Henry (34/12), David Trézéguet (35/19) [74.Eric Carrière (7/2)]. Trainer: Roger Lemmere (47).
Goals: Zinedine Zidane (12), David Trézéguet (23), Thierry Daniel Henry (32), David Trézéguet (42), Steve Marlet (87).

617. 17.04.2002 **FRANCE - RUSSIA** **0-0**
Stade de France, Saint-Denis, Paris; Referee: Michael Riley (England); Attendance: 78,294
FRA: Fabien Barthez (47/0), Lilian Thuram (72/2), Frank Leboeuf (46/3) [46.Philippe Christanval (4/0)], Marcel Desailly (92/3) (Cap), Bixente Lizarazu (73/2) [79.Vincent Candela (35/2)], Patrick Vieira (51/3), Emmanuel Petit (56/6) [62.Alain Boghossian (25/2)], Zinedine Zidane (73/19), Youri Djorkaeff (78/28) [62.Steve Marlet (8/2)], Thierry Daniel Henry (35/12), Nicolas Sébastien Anelka (28/6) [82.Johan Micoud (13/1)]. Trainer: Roger Lemmere (48).

618. 18.05.2002 **FRANCE - BELGIUM** **1-2(1-1)**
Stade de France, Saint-Denis, Paris; Referee: Valentin Ivanov (Russia); Attendance: 79,959
FRA: Ulrich Ramé (11/0), Lilian Thuram (73/2) [46.Willy Sagnol (9/0)], Frank Leboeuf (47/3), Marcel Desailly (93/3) (Cap), Bixente Lizarazu (74/2) [46.Vincent Candela (36/2)], Patrick Vieira (52/3), Emmanuel Petit (57/6), Sylvain Wiltord (38/12) [80.Alain Boghossian (26/2)], Youri Djorkaeff (79/28) [46.Johan Micoud (14/1)], Christophe Dugarry (51/7), David Trézéguet (36/19) [46.Djibril Cissé (1/0)]. Trainer: Roger Lemmere (49).
Goal: Timmy Simons (40 own goal).

619. 26.05.2002 **KOREA REPUBLIC - FRANCE** **2-3(2-1)**
World Cup 2002 Stadium, Suwon; Referee: Masayoshi Okada (Japan); Attendance: 43,000
FRA: Fabien Barthez (48/0), Marcel Desailly (94/3) (Cap) [72.Mikaël Silvestre (11/1)], Lilian Thuram (74/2) [49.Vincent Candela (37/2)], Frank Leboeuf (48/4), Bixente Lizarazu (75/2) [81.Willy Sagnol (10/0)], Patrick Vieira (53/3) [77.Claude Makélélé (15/0)], Youri Djorkaeff (80/28) [65.Djibril Cissé (2/0)], Zinedine Zidane (74/19) [36.Sylvain Wiltord (39/12)], Emmanuel Petit (58/6), Thierry Daniel Henry (36/12) [48.Christophe Dugarry (52/8)], David Trézéguet (37/20). Trainer: Roger Lemmere (50).
Goals: David Trézéguet (14), Christophe Dugarry (67), Frank Leboeuf (90).

620. 31.05.2002 **FRANCE - SENEGAL** **0-1(0-1)** 17th FIFA WC. Group Stage.
World Cup Stadium, Seoul (Korea Republic); Referee: Ali Mohammed Bujsaim (United Arab Emirates); Attendance: 62,561
FRA: : Fabien Barthez (49/0), Lilian Thuram (75/2), Frank Leboeuf (49/4), Marcel Desailly (95/3) (Cap), Bixente Lizarazu (76/2), Patrick Vieira (54/3), Youri Djorkaeff (81/28) [60.Christophe Dugarry (53/8)], Sylvain Wiltord (40/12) [81.Djibril Cissé (3/0)], Emmanuel Petit (59/6), Thierry Daniel Henry (37/12), David Trézéguet (38/20). Trainer: Roger Lemmere (51).

621. 06.06.2002 **FRANCE - URUGUAY** **0-0** 17th FIFA WC. Group Stage.
Asiad Main Stadium, Busan (Korea Republic); Referee: Felipe Ramos Rizo (Mexico); Attendance: 38,289
FRA: Fabien Barthez (50/0), Lilian Thuram (76/2), Frank Leboeuf (50/4) [16.Vincent Candela (38/2)], Marcel Desailly (96/3) (Cap), Bixente Lizarazu (77/2), Patrick Vieira (55/3), Sylvain Wiltord (41/12) [90.Christophe Dugarry (54/8)], Johan Micoud (15/1), Thierry Daniel Henry (38/12) [*sent off 25*], Emmanuel Petit (60/6), David Trézéguet (39/20) [81.Djibril Cissé (4/0)]. Trainer: Roger Lemmere (52).

622. 11.06.2002 **DENMARK - FRANCE** **2-0(1-0)** 17th FIFA WC. Group Stage.
Munhak Stadium, Incheon (Korea Republic); Referee: Vítor Manuel Melo Pereira (Portugal); Attendance: 48,100
FRA: Fabien Barthez (51/0), Vincent Candela (39/2), Lilian Thuram (77/2), Marcel Desailly (97/3) (Cap), Bixente Lizarazu (78/2), Patrick Vieira (56/3) [71.Johan Micoud (16/1)], Claude Makélélé (16/0), Zinedine Zidane (75/19), Sylvain Wiltord (42/12) [83.Youri Djorkaeff (82/28)], David Trézéguet (40/20), Christophe Dugarry (55/8) [54.Djibril Cissé (5/0)]. Trainer: Roger Lemmere (53).

623. 21.08.2002 **TUNISIA - FRANCE** **1-1(1-1)**
Stade du 7 Novembre, Radès; Referee: Cosimo-Giancarlo Bolognino (Italy); Attendance: 59,223
FRA: Grégory Coupet (2/0), Willy Sagnol (11/0) [46.Emmanuel Petit (61/6)], Lilian Thuram (78/2) [75.Bruno Cheyrou (1/0)], Philippe Christanval (5/0), Vincent Candela (40/2) [64.Jérémie Brechet (2/0)], Mikaël Silvestre (12/2) [46.Marcel Desailly (98/3)], Eric Carrière (8/2) [46.Patrick Vieira (57/3)], Claude Makélélé (17/0), Zinedine Zidane (Cap) (76/19), Thierry Daniel Henry (39/12) [46.Steve Marlet (9/2)], Sidney Rodrigue Noukpo Govou (1/0) [63.Djibril Cissé (6/0)]. Trainer: Jacques Santini (1).
Goal: Mikaël Silvestre (19).

624. 07.09.2002 **CYPRUS - FRANCE** **1-2(1-1)** 12th EC. Qualifiers

Stádio GSP, Nicosia; Referee: Herbert Fandel (Germany); Attendance: 16,000

FRA: Grégory Coupet (3/0), Lilian Thuram (79/2), Philippe Christanval (6/0), Marcel Desailly (99/3), Mikaël Silvestre (13/2), Patrick Vieira (58/3), Claude Makélélé (18/0), Djibril Cissé (7/1), Zinedine Zidane (77/19), Sylvain Wiltord (43/13) [79.Olivier Kapo (1/0)], Steve Marlet (10/2) [70.Sidney Rodrigue Noukpo Govou (2/0)]. Trainer: Jacques Santini (2).

Goals: Djibril Cissé (38), Sylvain Wiltord (52).

625. 12.10.2002 **FRANCE - SLOVENIA** **5-0(2-0)** 12th EC. Qualifiers

Stade de France, Saint-Denis, Paris; Referee: Kim Milton-Nielsen (Denmark); Attendance: 78,600

FRA: Fabien Barthez (52/0), Lilian Thuram (80/2) [84.Willy Sagnol (12/0)], Marcel Desailly (100/3), Mikaël Silvestre (14/2), William Éric Gallas (1/0), Patrick Vieira (59/4), Claude Makélélé (19/0), Zinedine Zidane (78/19), Sylvain Wiltord (44/14) [87.Bruno Cheyrou (2/0)], Thierry Daniel Henry (40/12), Steve Marlet (11/4) [80.Sidney Rodrigue Noukpo Govou (3/1)]. Trainer: Jacques Santini (3).

Goals: Patrick Vieira (10), Steve Marlet (35, 64), Sylvain Wiltord (79), Sidney Rodrigue Noukpo Govou (86).

626. 16.10.2002 **MALTA - FRANCE** **0-4(0-2)** 12th EC. Qualifiers

Ta'Qali National Stadium, Attard; Referee: Alexandru Dan Tudor (Romania); Attendance: 10,000

FRA: Fabien Barthez (53/0), Lilian Thuram (81/2) [84.Philippe Samuel Mexès (1/0)], Marcel Desailly (101/3), Mikaël Silvestre (15/2), William Éric Gallas (2/0), Patrick Vieira (60/4) [70.Olivier Dacourt (4/0)], Claude Makélélé (20/0), Zinedine Zidane (79/19), Sylvain Wiltord (45/15), Thierry Daniel Henry (41/14) [78.Eric Carrière (9/3)], Steve Marlet (12/4). Trainer: Jacques Santini (4).

Goals: Thierry Daniel Henry (25, 36), Silvain Wiltord (59), Eric Carrière (84).

627. 20.11.2002 **FRANCE - YUGOSLAVIA** **3-0(1-0)**

Stade de France, Saint-Denis, Paris; Referee: Eduardo Iturralde González (Spain); Attendance: 60,000

FRA: Fabien Barthez (54/0), Lilian Thuram (82/2) [80.Benoît Pedretti (1/0)], William Éric Gallas (3/0), Marcel Desailly (102/3) [46.Philippe Samuel Mexès (2/0)], Jérémie Brechet (3/0) [14.Mikaël Silvestre (16/2)], Claude Makélélé (21/0) [54.Sylvain Wiltord (46/15)], Emmanuel Petit (62/6), Eric Carrière (10/5) [85.Ludovic Giuly (4/0)], Olivier Kapo (2/1), Steve Marlet (13/4), Thierry Daniel Henry (42/14) [75.Daniel Moreira (1/0)]. Trainer: Jacques Santini (5).

Goals: Eric Carrière (11, 49), Olivier Kapo (69).

628. 12.02.2003 **FRANCE – CZECH REPUBLIC** **0-2(0-1)**

Stade de France, Saint-Denis, Paris; Referee: Wolfgang Stark (Germany); Attendance: 57,354

FRA: Ulrich Ramé (12/0), Lilian Thuram (83/2), William Éric Gallas (4/0), Marcel Desailly (103/3), Bixente Lizarazu (79/2) [75.Mikaël Silvestre (17/2)], Claude Makélélé (22/0) [46.Patrick Vieira (61/4)], Emmanuel Petit (63/6) [75.Benoît Pedretti (2/0)], Sylvain Wiltord (47/15) [46.Robert Pires (55/10)], Zinedine Zidane (80/19), Steve Marlet (14/4) [46.David Trézéguet (41/20)], Thierry Daniel Henry (43/14) [68.Djibril Cissé (8/1)]. Trainer: Jacques Santini (6).

629. 29.03.2002 **FRANCE - MALTA** **6-0(2-0)** 12th EC. Qualifiers

Stade de France, Saint-Denis, Paris; Referee: Emil Božinovski (Macedonia); Attendance: 40,775

FRA: Fabien Barthez (55/0), Lilian Thuram (84/2) [65.Willy Sagnol (13/0)], William Éric Gallas (5/0), Mikaël Silvestre (18/2), Bixente Lizarazu (80/2), Claude Makélélé (23/0), Benoît Pedretti (3/0), Zinedine Zidane (81/21), Sylvain Wiltord (48/16) [73.Sidney Rodrigue Noukpo Govou (4/1)], Thierry Daniel Henry (44/16) [81.Jérôme Rothen (1/0)], David Trézéguet (42/21). Trainer: Jacques Santini (7).

Goals: Sylvain Wiltord (37), Thierry Daniel Henry (38, 54), Zinedine Zidane (57 penalty), David Trézéguet (71), Zinedine Zidane (80)

630. 02.04.2003 **ISRAEL - FRANCE** **1-2(1-2)** 12th EC. Qualifiers

Stadio „Renzo Barbera", Palermo (Italy); Referee: Graham Barber (England); Attendance: 4,000

FRA: Fabien Barthez (56/0), Lilian Thuram (85/2), Mikaël Silvestre (19/2), William Éric Gallas (6/0), Bixente Lizarazu (81/2), Patrick Vieira (62/4), Claude Makélélé (24/0), Sylvain Wiltord (49/16) [66.Sidney Rodrigue Noukpo Govou (5/1)], Zinedine Zidane (82/22), Thierry Daniel Henry (45/16), David Trézéguet (43/22) [74.Djibril Cissé (9/1)]. Trainer: Jacques Santini (8).

Goals: David Trézéguet (23), Zinedine Zidane (45).

631. 30.04.2003 **FRANCE - EGYPT** **5-0(3-0)**

Stade de France, Saint-Denis, Paris; Referee: Massimo Busacca (Switzerland); Attendance: 54,554

FRA: Fabien Barthez (57/0), Willy Sagnol (14/0), William Éric Gallas (7/0), Marcel Desailly (104/3) [75.Philippe Samuel Mexès (3/0)], Bixente Lizarazu (82/2), Sylvain Wiltord (50/16) [71.Daniel Moreira (2/0)], Benoît Pedretti (4/0), Olivier Dacourt (5/0), Robert Pires (56/11) [66.Jérôme Rothen (2/0)], Djibril Cissé (10/2) [83.Mikaël Silvestre (20/2)], Thierry Daniel Henry (46/18) [58.Olivier Kapo (3/2)]. Trainer: Jacques Santini (9).

Goals: Thierry Daniel Henry (26, 34), Robert Pires (45), Djibril Cissé (62), Olivier Kapo (79).

632. 18.06.2003 **FRANCE - COLOMBIA** **1-0(1-0)** 6th FIFA Confederatios Cup. Group Stage.

Stade de Gerlande, Lyon; Referee: Lucilio Batista (Portugal); Attendance: 38,541

FRA: Grégory Coupet (4/0), Lilian Thuram (86/2), Philippe Samuel Mexès (4/0), Marcel Desailly (105/3), Bixente Lizarazu (83/2), Sylvain Wiltord (51/16), Benoît Pedretti (5/0), Olivier Dacourt (6/0), Olivier Kapo (4/2) [61.Robert Pires (57/11)], Djibril Cissé (11/2) [77.Sidney Rodrigue Noukpo Govou (6/1)], Thierry Daniel Henry (47/19) [85.Steve Marlet (15/4)]. Trainer: Jacques Santini (10).

Goal: Thierry Daniel Henry (39 penalty).

633. 20.06.2003 **FRANCE - JAPAN** **2-1(1-0)** 6th FIFA Confederatios Cup. Group Stage.

Stade „Geoffroy Guichard", Saint-Étienne; Referee: Mark Shield (Australia); Attendance: 33,070

FRA: Fabien Barthez (58/0), Willy Sagnol (15/0) [*sent off 90*], William Éric Gallas (8/0), Jean-Alain Boumsong (1/0), Mikaël Silvestre (21/2), Robert Pires (58/12), Ousmane Dabo (1/0), Olivier Dacourt (7/0) [58.Benoît Pedretti (6/0)], Jérôme Rothen (3/0) [67.Sylvain Wiltord (52/16)], Sidney Rodrigue Noukpo Govou (7/2), Steve Marlet (16/4) [80.Thierry Daniel Henry (48/19)]. Trainer: Jacques Santini (11).

Goals: Robert Pires (43 penalty), Sidney Rodrigue Noukpo Govou (66).

634. 22.06.2003 **FRANCE – NEW ZEALAND** **5-0(2-0)** 6th FIFA Confederatios Cup. Group Stage.

Stade de France, Saint-Denis, Paris; Referee: Masoud Moradi (Iran); Attendance: 36,842

FRA: Mickaël Landreau (2/0), Lilian Thuram (87/2), Philippe Samuel Mexès (5/0), Marcel Desailly (106/3), Bixente Lizarazu (84/2), Ludovic Giuly (5/1), Benoît Pedretti (7/0) [69.Ousmane Dabo (2/0)], Olivier Kapo (5/3), Sylvain Wiltord (53/16) [76.Robert Pires (59/13)], Djibril Cissé (12/3), Thierry Daniel Henry (49/20) [74.Steve Marlet (17/4)]. Trainer: Jacques Santini (12).

Goals: Olivier Kapo (17), Thierry Daniel Henry (20), Djibril Cissé (71), Ludovic Giuly (90), Robert Pires (90).

635. 26.06.2003 **FRANCE - TURKEY** **3-2(3-1)** 6th FIFA Confederatios Cup. Semi-Finals.
Stade de France, Saint-Denis, Paris; Referee: Jorge Pietrafiesa Larrionda (Uruguay); Attendance: 41,195
FRA: Grégory Coupet (5/0), Lilian Thuram (88/2), William Éric Gallas (9/0), Marcel Desailly (107/3), Mikaël Silvestre (22/2), Sylvain Wiltord (54/17) [78.Ludovic Giuly (6/1)], Benoît Pedretti (8/0), Olivier Dacourt (8/0), Robert Pires (60/14) [70.Olivier Kapo (6/3)], Sidney Rodrigue Noukpo Govou (8/2) [66.Djibril Cissé (13/3)], Thierry Daniel Henry (50/21). Trainer: Jacques Santini (13).
Goals: Thierry Daniel Henry (11), Robert Pires (26), Sylvain Wiltord (43).

636. 29.06.2003 **FRANCE - CAMEROON** **1-0(0-0,0-0)** 6th FIFA Confederatios Cup. Final.
Stade de France, Saint-Denis, Paris; Referee: Valentin Ivanov (Russia); Attendance: 51,985
FRA: Fabien Barthez (59/0), Willy Sagnol (16/0) [76.Lilian Thuram (89/2)], William Éric Gallas (10/0), Marcel Desailly (108/3), Bixente Lizarazu (85/2), Ludovic Giuly (7/1), Benoît Pedretti (9/0), Olivier Dacourt (9/0) [90.Olivier Kapo (7/3)], Sylvain Wiltord (55/17) [65.Robert Pires (61/14)], Djibril Cissé (14/3), Thierry Daniel Henry (51/22). Trainer: Jacques Santini (14).
Goal: Thierry Daniel Henry (97 Golden Goal).

637. 20.08.2003 **SWITZERLAND - FRANCE** **0-2(0-1)**
Stade Charmilles, Genève; Referee: Paul Allaerts (Belgium); Attendance: 30,000
FRA: Fabien Barthez (60/0), Lilian Thuram (90/2) [61.Willy Sagnol (17/0)], Marcel Desailly (Cap) (109/3) [77.Jean-Alain Boumsong (2/0)], Mikaël Silvestre (23/2), Bixente Lizarazu (86/2), Sylvain Wiltord (56/18) [70.Djibril Cissé (15/3)], Patrick Vieira (63/4) [46.Benoît Pedretti (10/0)], Olivier Dacourt (10/0) [84.Ousmane Dabo (3/0)], Zinedine Zidane (83/22) [70.Ludovic Giuly (8/1)], David Trézéguet (44/22) [61.Robert Pires (62/14)], Thierry Daniel Henry (52/22) [46.Steve Marlet (18/5)]. Trainer: Jacques Santini (15).
Goals: Sylvain Wiltord (12), Steve Marlet (54).

638. 06.09.2003 **FRANCE - CYPRUS** **5-0(3-0)** 12th EC. Qualifiers
Stade de France, Saint-Denis, Paris; Referee: Leslie Irvine (Northern Ireland); Attendance: 50,132
FRA: Fabien Barthez (61/0), Lilian Thuram (91/2) [65.Willy Sagnol (18/0)], Marcel Desailly (Cap) (110/3), Mikaël Silvestre (24/2), Bixente Lizarazu (87/2), Patrick Vieira (64/4) [70.Olivier Dacourt (11/0)], Claude Makélélé (25/0), Robert Pires (63/14), Sylvain Wiltord (57/20), Thierry Daniel Henry (53/23) [75.Steve Marlet (19/5)], David Trézéguet (45/24). Trainer: Jacques Santini (16).
Goals: David Trézéguet (7), Sylvain Wiltord (20, 41), Thierry Daniel Henry (60), David Trézéguet (81).

639. 10.09.2003 **SLOVENIA - FRANCE** **0-2(0-1)** 12th EC. Qualifiers
Stadion Bežigrad, Ljubljana; Referee: Domenico Messina (Italy); Attendance: 8,000
FRA: Fabien Barthez (62/0), Lilian Thuram (92/2), Marcel Desailly (Cap) (111/3), Mikaël Silvestre (25/2), Bixente Lizarazu (88/2), Patrick Vieira (65/4), Claude Makélélé (26/0) [*sent off 67*], Zinedine Zidane (84/22) [78.Robert Pires (64/14)], Sylvain Wiltord (58/20) [75.Willy Sagnol (19/0)], David Trézéguet (46/25) [68.Olivier Dacourt (12/1)], Thierry Daniel Henry (54/23). Trainer: Jacques Santini (17).
Goals: David Trézéguet (9), Olivier Dacourt (71).

640. 11.10.2003 **FRANCE - ISRAEL** **3-0(3-0)** 12th EC. Qualifiers
Stade de France, Saint-Denis, Paris; Referee: Cosimo-Giancarlo Bolognino (Italy); Attendance: 57,009
FRA: Fabien Barthez (63/0), Lilian Thuram (93/2), Jean-Alain Boumsong (3/1), Anthony Réveillère (1/0), Bixente Lizarazu (89/2), Olivier Dacourt (13/1), Benoît Pedretti (11/0), Robert Pires (65/14) [86.Ludovic Giuly (9/1)], Zinedine Zidane (Cap) (85/22), David Trézéguet (47/26) [86.Steve Marlet (20/5)], Thierry Daniel Henry (55/24) [77.Djibril Cissé (16/3)]. Trainer: Jacques Santini (18).
Goals: Thierry Daniel Henry (9), David Trézéguet (24), Jean-Alain Boumsong (42).

641. 15.11.2003 **GERMANY - FRANCE** **0-3(0-1)**
Arena Auf Schalke, Gelsenkirchen; Referee: Stefano Farina (Italy); Attendance: 53,574
FRA: Grégory Coupet (6/0), Willy Sagnol (20/0) [61.William Éric Gallas (11/0)], Lilian Thuram (94/2), Mikaël Silvestre (26/2), Bixente Lizarazu (90/2), Robert Pires (66/14) [73.Sylvain Wiltord (59/20)], Claude Makélélé (27/0), Olivier Dacourt (14/1), Zinedine Zidane (Cap) (86/22), David Trézéguet (48/28) [82.Sidney Rodrigue Noukpo Govou (9/2)], Thierry Daniel Henry (56/25). Trainer: Jacques Santini (19).
Goals: Thierry Daniel Henry (21), David Trézéguet (55, 81).

642. 18.02.2004 **BELGIUM - FRANCE** **0-2(0-1)**
Stade „Roi Baudouin", Bruxelles; Referee: Mark Halsey (England); Attendance: 43,160
FRA: Fabien Barthez (64/0), William Éric Gallas (12/0) [86.Jean-Alain Boumsong (4/1)], Marcel Desailly (Cap) (112/3), Lilian Thuram (95/2), Mikaël Silvestre (27/2) [46.Bixente Lizarazu (91/2)], Patrick Vieira (66/4) [62.Jérôme Rothen (4/0)], Olivier Dacourt (15/1) [18.Claude Makélélé (28/0)], Zinedine Zidane (87/22) [70.Olivier Kapo (8/3)], Sidney Rodrigue Noukpo Govou (10/3) [46.Robert Pires (67/14)], Louis Laurent Saha (1/1) [85.Philippe Samuel Mexès (6/0)], Peguy Luyindula (1/0) [62.Steve Marlet (21/5)]. Trainer: Jacques Santini (20).
Goals: Sidney Rodrigue Noukpo Govou (45), Louis Laurent Saha (75).

643. 31.03.2004 **NETHERLANDS - FRANCE** **0-0**
Stadion Feijenoord, Rotterdam; Referee: Wolfgang Stark (Germany); Attendance: 52,000
FRA: Fabien Barthez (65/0), Willy Sagnol (21/0), Lilian Thuram (96/2) [67.William Éric Gallas (13/0)], Marcel Desailly (Cap) (113/3), Bixente Lizarazu (92/2) [58.Mikaël Silvestre (28/2)], Olivier Dacourt (16/1), Claude Makélélé (29/0) [58.Benoît Pedretti (12/0)], Johan Micoud (17/1), Ludovic Giuly (10/1) [46.Bruno Cheyrou (3/0)], Sidney Rodrigue Noukpo Govou (11/3) [46.Thierry Daniel Henry (57/25)], David Trézéguet (49/28) [67.Peguy Luyindula (2/0)]. Trainer: Jacques Santini (21).

644. 20.05.2004 **FRANCE - BRAZIL** **0-0** FIFA Centennial
Stade de France, Saint-Denis, Paris; Referee: Manuel Enrique Mejuto González (Spain); Attendance: 79,344
FRA: Grégory Coupet (7/0), Lilian Thuram (97/2), Jean-Alain Boumsong (5/1), Marcel Desailly (Cap) (114/3) [46.Bernard Mendy (1/0)], William Éric Gallas (14/0), Robert Pires (68/14) [46.Sylvain Wiltord (60/20)], Claude Makélélé (30/0), Patrick Vieira (67/4), Zinedine Zidane (88/22) [69.Olivier Kapo (9/3)], David Trézéguet (50/28), Thierry Daniel Henry (58/25). Trainer: Jacques Santini (22).

645. 28.05.2004 **FRANCE - ANDORRA** **4-0(1-0)**
Stade de la Mosson, Montpellier; Referee: Mourad Daami (Tunisia); Attendance: 27,753
FRA: Grégory Coupet (8/0), Willy Sagnol (22/0), Marcel Desailly (Cap) (115/3) [69.Lilian Thuram (98/2)], William Éric Gallas (15/0), Mikaël Silvestre (29/2), Patrick Vieira (68/4) [46.Bixente Lizarazu (93/2)], Benoît Pedretti (13/0), Robert Pires (69/14), Sylvain Wiltord (61/22), Louis Laurent Saha (2/2) [69.David Trézéguet (51/28)], Steve Marlet (22/6) [79.Jean-Alain Boumsong (6/1)]. Trainer: Jacques Santini (23).
Goals: Sylvain Wiltord (45; 56), Louis Laurent Saha (68), Steve Marlet (74).

646. 06.06.2004 **FRANCE - UKRAINE** **1-0(1-0)**
Stade de France, Saint-Denis, Paris; Referee: Darko Čeferin (Slovenia); Attendance: 60,446); Attendance: 66,646
FRA: Fabien Barthez (66/0), William Éric Gallas (16/0) [76.Willy Sagnol (23/0)], Lilian Thuram (99/2), Mikaël Silvestre (30/2), Bixente Lizarazu (94/2), Robert Pires (70/14) [83.Sylvain Wiltord (62/22)], Claude Makélélé (31/0) [83.Benoît Pedretti (14/0)], Patrick Vieira (69/4), Zinedine Zidane (Cap) (89/23), Thierry Daniel Henry (59/25), Louis Laurent Saha (3/2) [76.Steve Marlet (23/6)]. Trainer: Jacques Santini (24).
Goal: Zinedine Zidane (89).

647. 13.06.2004 **FRANCE - ENGLAND** **2-1(0-1)** 12th EC. Group Stage.
Estádio da Luz, Lisboa (Portugal); Referee: Dr. Markus Merk (Germany); Attendance: 62,487
FRA: Fabien Barthez (67/0), Lilian Thuram (**100**/2), William Éric Gallas (17/0), Mikaël Silvestre (31/2) [79.Willy Sagnol (24/0)], Bixente Lizarazu (95/2), Robert Pires (71/14) [75.Sylvain Wiltord (63/22)], Patrick Vieira (70/4), Claude Makélélé (32/0) [90.Olivier Dacourt (17/1)], Zinedine Zidane (Cap) (90/25), Thierry Daniel Henry (60/25), David Trézéguet (52/28). Trainer: Jacques Santini (25).
Goals: Zinedine Zidane (90+1,90+3 penalty).

648. 17.06.2004 **CROATIA - FRANCE** **2-2(0-1)** 12th EC. Group Stage.
Estádio „Dr. Magalhães Pessoa“, Leiria (Portugal); Referee: Kim Milton Nielsen (Denmark); Attendance: 29,160
FRA: Fabien Barthez (68/0), William Éric Gallas (18/0) [81.Willy Sagnol (25/0)], Lilian Thuram (101/2), Marcel Desailly (Cap) (116/3), Mikaël Silvestre (32/2), Patrick Vieira (71/4), Olivier Dacourt (18/1) [79.Benoît Pedretti (15/0)], Sylvain Wiltord (64/22) [70.Robert Pires (72/14)], Zinedine Zidane (91/25), Thierry Daniel Henry (61/25), David Trézéguet (53/29). Trainer: Jacques Santini (26).
Goals: Igor Tudor (22 own goal), David Trézéguet (64).

649. 21.06.2004 **FRANCE - SWITZERLAND** **3-1(1-1)** 12th EC. Group Stage.
Estádio Municipal, Coimbra (Portugal); Referee: Luboš Micheľ (Slovakia); Attendance: 28,111
FRA: Fabien Barthez (69/0), Lilian Thuram (102/2), Mikaël Silvestre (33/2), Willy Sagnol (26/0) [46.William Éric Gallas (19/0); 90.Jean-Alain Boumsong (7/1)], Bixente Lizarazu (96/2), Patrick Vieira (72/4), Claude Makélélé (33/0), Robert Pires (73/14), Zinedine Zidane (Cap) (92/26), Thierry Daniel Henry (62/27), David Trézéguet (54/29) [75.Louis Laurent Saha (4/2)]. Trainer: Jacques Santini (27).
Goals: Zinedine Zidane (20), Thierry Daniel Henry (76, 84).

650. 25.06.2004 **GREECE - FRANCE** **1-0(0-0)** 12th EC. Quarter-Finals.
Estádio "José Alvalade", Lisboa (Portugal); Referee: Anders Frisk (Sweden); Attendance: 45,390
FRA: Fabien Barthez (70/0), William Éric Gallas (20/0), Lilian Thuram (103/2), Mikaël Silvestre (34/2), Bixente Lizarazu (97/2), Claude Makélélé (34/0), Olivier Dacourt (19/1) [72.Sylvain Wiltord (65/22)], Zinedine Zidane (Cap) (93/26), Robert Pires (74/14) [79.Jérôme Rothen (5/0)], Thierry Daniel Henry (63/27), David Trézéguet (55/29) [72.Louis Laurent Saha (5/2)]. Trainer: Jacques Santini (28).

651. 18.08.2004 **FRANCE – BOSNIA AND HERZEGOVINA** **1-1(1-1)**
Stade de la Route de Lorient, Rennes; Referee: Douglas McDonald (Scotland); Attendance: 26,527
FRA: Fabien Barthez (Cap) (71/0), William Éric Gallas (21/0), Sébastien Squillaci (1/0) [46.Gaël Givet (1/0)], Éric-Sylvain Bilal Abidal (1/0), Bernard Mendy (2/0), Rio Antonio Zoba Mavuba (1/0) [46.Sidney Rodrigue Noukpo Govou (12/3)], Benoît Pedretti (16/0), Patrice Latyr Evra (1/0) [46.Robert Pires (75/14)], Jérôme Rothen (6/0), Thierry Daniel Henry (64/27) [46.Djibril Cissé (17/3)], Peguy Luyindula (3/1). Trainer: Raymond Domenech (1).
Goal: Peguy Luyindula (7).

652. 04.09.2004 **FRANCE - ISRAEL** **0-0** 18th FIFA WC. Qualifiers
Stade de France, Saint-Denis, Paris; Referee: Renatus Hendrikus Johannes Temmink (Netherlands); Attendance: 43,527
FRA: Grégory Coupet (9/0), William Éric Gallas (22/0), Sébastien Squillaci (2/0), Gaël Givet (2/0), Bernard Mendy (3/0), Patrice Latyr Evra (2/0) [57.Ludovic Giuly (11/1)], Claude Makélélé (35/0), Patrick Vieira (Cap) (73/4), Jérôme Rothen (7/0) [66.Robert Pires (76/14)], Thierry Daniel Henry (65/27), Louis Laurent Saha (6/2). Trainer: Raymond Domenech (2).

653. 08.09.2004 **FAROE ISLANDS - FRANCE** **0-2(0-1)** 18th FIFA WC. Qualifiers
Tórsvøllur, Tórshavn; Referee: Craig Alexander Thomson (Scotland); Attendance: 5,917
FRA: Grégory Coupet (10/0), William Éric Gallas (23/0), Sébastien Squillaci (3/0), Gaël Givet (3/0), Patrice Latyr Evra (3/0), Patrick Vieira (Cap) (74/4) [*sent off 65*], Benoît Pedretti (17/0), Ludovic Giuly (12/2), Robert Pires (77/14), Thierry Daniel Henry (66/27) [64.Vikash Dhorasoo (3/0)], Louis Laurent Saha (7/2) [9.Djibril Cissé (18/4)]. Trainer: Raymond Domenech (3).
Goals: Ludovic Giuly (31), Djibril Cissé (73).

654. 09.10.2004 **FRANCE – REPUBLIC OF IRELAND** **0-0** 18th FIFA WC. Qualifiers
Stade de France, Saint-Denis, Paris; Referee: Arturo Daudén Ibañez (Spain); Attendance: 78,863
FRA: Fabien Barthez (Cap) (72/0), William Éric Gallas (24/0), Gaël Givet (4/0), Sébastien Squillaci (4/0), Mikaël Silvestre (35/2), Olivier Dacourt (20/1) [63.Alou Diarra (1/0)], Rio Antonio Zoba Mavuba (2/0), Robert Pires (78/14), Sylvain Wiltord (66/22), Thierry Daniel Henry (67/27), Djibril Cissé (19/4) [81.Sidney Rodrigue Noukpo Govou (13/3)]. Trainer: Raymond Domenech (4).

655. 13.10.2004 **CYPRUS - FRANCE** **0-2(0-1)** 18th FIFA WC. Qualifiers
Stádio GSP, Nicosia; Referee: Claus Bo Larsen (Denmark); Attendance: 3,319
FRA: Fabien Barthez (73/0), William Éric Gallas (25/0), Gaël Givet (5/0), Sébastien Squillaci (5/0), Mikaël Silvestre (36/2), Patrick Vieira (Cap) (75/4), Olivier Dacourt (21/1) [89.Alou Diarra (2/0)], Robert Pires (79/14) [46.Daniel Moreira (3/0)], Sylvain Wiltord (67/23), Thierry Daniel Henry (68/28), Peguy Luyindula (4/1) [65.Patrice Latyr Evra (4/0)]. Trainer: Raymond Domenech (5).
Goals: Sylvain Wiltord (38), Thierry Daniel Henry (72).

656. 17.11.2004 **FRANCE - POLAND** **0-0**
Stade de France, Saint-Denis, Paris; Referee: Olegário Manuel Bártolo Faustino Benquerença (Portugal); Attendance: 54,480
FRA: Mickaël Landreau (3/0), Willy Sagnol (27/0), Sébastien Squillaci (6/0) [46.Gaël Givet (6/0)], Jean-Alain Boumsong (8/1), William Éric Gallas (26/0), Ludovic Giuly (13/2) [26.Sidney Rodrigue Noukpo Govou (14/3)], Benoît Pedretti (18/0), Patrick Vieira (Cap) (76/4), Florent Yohan Malouda (1/0) [46.Patrice Latyr Evra (5/0)], Louis Laurent Saha (8/2) [65.Camel Meriem (1/0)], Thierry Daniel Henry (69/28). Trainer: Raymond Domenech (6).

657. 09.02.2005 **FRANCE - SWEDEN** **1-1(1-1)**
Stade de France, Saint-Denis, Paris; Referee: Julián Rodríguez Santiago (Spain); Attendance: 56,923
FRA: Grégory Coupet (11/0), Jonathan Zebina (1/0) [68.Éric-Sylvain Bilal Abidal (2/0)], Sébastien Squillaci (7/0), Gaël Givet (7/0), William Éric Gallas (27/0), Ludovic Giuly (14/2) [68.Camel Meriem (2/0)], Patrick Vieira (Cap) (77/4), Benoît Pedretti (19/0), Vikash Dhorasoo (4/0), Thierry Daniel Henry (70/28), David Trézéguet (56/30). Trainer: Raymond Domenech (7).
Goal: David Trézéguet (35).

658. 26.03.2005 **FRANCE - SWITZERLAND** **0-0** 18th FIFA WC. Qualifiers
Stade de France, Saint-Denis, Paris; Referee: Massimo De Santis (Italy); Attendance: 79,373
FRA: Fabien Barthez (74/0), Willy Sagnol (28/0), Jean-Alain Boumsong (9/1), Gaël Givet (8/0), William Éric Gallas (28/0), Ludovic Giuly (15/2), Patrick Vieira (Cap) (78/4), Benoît Pedretti (20/0), Vikash Dhorasoo (5/0) [59.Camel Meriem (3/0)], Sylvain Wiltord (68/23) [81.Sidney Rodrigue Noukpo Govou (15/3)], David Trézéguet (57/30). Trainer: Raymond Domenech (8).

659. 30.03.2005 **ISRAEL - FRANCE** **1-1(0-1)** 18th FIFA WC. Qualifiers
National Stadium, Ramat Gan, Tel-Aviv; Referee: Dr. Markus Merk (Germany); Attendance: 32,150
FRA: Fabien Barthez (75/0), Willy Sagnol (29/0), William Éric Gallas (29/0), Jean-Alain Boumsong (10/1), Gaël Givet (9/0), Alou Diarra (3/0), Patrick Vieira (Cap) (79/4), Benoît Pedretti (21/0), Florent Yohan Malouda (2/0), Sylvain Wiltord (69/23) [90+2.Vikash Dhorasoo (6/0)], David Trézéguet (58/31) [*sent off 55*]. Trainer: Raymond Domenech (9).
Goal: David Trézéguet (50).

660. 31.05.2005 **FRANCE - HUNGARY** **2-1(2-0)**
Stade Municipal Saint-Symphorien, Metz; Referee: Paul Allaerts (Belgium); Attendance: 26,186
FRA: Grégory Coupet (12/0), Éric-Sylvain Bilal Abidal (3/0), William Éric Gallas (30/0) [81.Sébastien Squillaci (8/0)], Jean-Alain Boumsong (11/1), Anthony Réveillère (2/0), Benoît Pedretti (22/0), Vikash Dhorasoo (7/0) [64.Rio Antonio Zoba Mavuba (3/0)], Jérôme Rothen (8/0), Florent Yohan Malouda (3/1), Sylvain Wiltord (Cap) (70/23) [58.Sidney Rodrigue Noukpo Govou (16/3)], Djibril Cissé (20/5) [74.Ludovic Giuly (16/2)]. Trainer: Raymond Domenech (10).
Goals: Djibril Cissé (10), Florent Yohan Malouda (35).

661. 17.08.2005 **FRANCE – IVORY COAST** **3-0(1-0)**
Stade de la Mosson, Montpellier; Referee: Paolo Bertini (Italy); Attendance: 31,457
FRA: Grégory Coupet (13/0), Willy Sagnol (30/0), Lilian Thuram (104/2) [23.Sébastien Squillaci (9/0)], Jean-Alain Boumsong (12/1), William Éric Gallas (31/1), Claude Makélélé (36/0) [89.Alou Diarra (4/0)], Zinedine Zidane (94/27), Vikash Dhorasoo (8/0), Sylvain Wiltord (71/23) [80.David Trézéguet (59/31)], Thierry Daniel Henry (71/29) [71.Djibril Cissé (21/5)], Florent Yohan Malouda (4/1) [71.Jérôme Rothen (9/0)]. Trainer: Raymond Domenech (11).
Goals: William Éric Gallas (28), Zinedine Zidane (62), Thierry Daniel Henry (66).

662. 03.09.2005 **FRANCE – FAROE ISLANDS** **3-0(2-0)** 18th FIFA WC. Qualifiers
Stade „Félix Bollaert", Lens; Referee: Jaroslav Jara (Czech Republic); Attendance: 40,126
FRA: Grégory Coupet (14/0), Willy Sagnol (31/0), Lilian Thuram (105/2) [74.Sébastien Squillaci (10/0)], Jean-Alain Boumsong (13/1), William Éric Gallas (32/1), Patrick Vieira (Cap) (80/4), Claude Makélélé (37/0), Zinedine Zidane (95/27) [58.Vikash Dhorasoo (9/0)], Florent Yohan Malouda (5/1), Djibril Cissé (22/7), Thierry Daniel Henry (72/29) [67.Sylvain Wiltord (72/23)]. Trainer: Raymond Domenech (12).
Goals: Djibril Cissé (17), Súni Olsen (19 own goal), Djibril Cissé (76).

663. 07.09.2005 **REPUBLIC OF IRELAND - FRANCE** **0-1(0-0)** 18th FIFA WC. Qualifiers
Lansdowne Road, Dublin; Referee: Herbert Fandel (Germany); Attendance: 36,000
FRA: Grégory Coupet (15/0), Willy Sagnol (32/0) [90.Gaël Givet (10/0)], Lilian Thuram (106/2), Jean-Alain Boumsong (14/1), William Éric Gallas (33/1), Patrick Vieira (81/4), Claude Makélélé (38/0), Zinedine Zidane (Cap) (96/27) [69.Florent Yohan Malouda (6/1)], Vikash Dhorasoo (10/0), Sylvain Wiltord (73/23), Thierry Daniel Henry (73/30) [76.Djibril Cissé (23/7)]. Trainer: Raymond Domenech (13).
Goal: Thierry Daniel Henry (68).

664. 08.10.2005 **SWITZERLAND - FRANCE** **1-1(0-0)** 18th FIFA WC. Qualifiers
Stade de Suisse, Bern; Referee: Terje Hauge (Norway); Attendance: 31,400
FRA: Grégory Coupet (16/0), Anthony Réveillère (3/0), Lilian Thuram (107/2), Jean-Alain Boumsong (15/1), William Éric Gallas (34/1), Patrick Vieira (82/4), Claude Makélélé (39/0), Zinedine Zidane (Cap) (97/27), Vikash Dhorasoo (11/0) [46.Djibril Cissé (24/8)], Florent Yohan Malouda (7/1) [90.Sidney Rodrigue Noukpo Govou (17/3)], Sylvain Wiltord (74/23). Trainer: Raymond Domenech (14).
Goal: Djibril Cissé (52).

665. 12.10.2005 **FRANCE - CYPRUS** **4-0(3-0)** 18th FIFA WC. Qualifiers
Stade de France, Saint-Denis, Paris; Referee: Wolfgang Stark (Germany); Attendance: 78,864
FRA: Grégory Coupet (17/0), Willy Sagnol (33/0), Lilian Thuram (108/2), Jean-Alain Boumsong (16/1), William Éric Gallas (35/1), Patrick Vieira (83/4) [24.Alou Diarra (5/0)], Sidney Rodrigue Noukpo Govou (18/3) [90+1.Franck Jurietti (1/0)], Vikash Dhorasoo (12/1), Zinedine Zidane (Cap) (98/28), Sylvain Wiltord (75/24) [59.Ludovic Giuly (17/3)], Djibril Cissé (25/8). Trainer: Raymond Domenech (15).
Goals: Zinedine Zidane (29), Sylvain Wiltord (31), Vikash Dhorasoo (43), Ludovic Giuly (84).

666. 09.11.2005 **FRANCE – COSTA RICA** **3-2(0-2)**
Stade de Dillon, Fort-de-France (Martinique); Referee: Gilberto Alcala Piñeda (Mexico); Attendance: 16,216
FRA: Fabien Barthez (76/0), William Éric Gallas (36/1), Lilian Thuram (Cap) (109/2), Gaël Givet (11/0) [72.Jérôme Rothen (10/0)], Éric-Sylvain Bilal Abidal (4/0) [15.Anthony Réveillère (4/0)], Sylvain Wiltord (76/24) [64.Sidney Rodrigue Noukpo Govou (19/3)], Alou Diarra (6/0), Vikash Dhorasoo (13/1), Florent Yohan Malouda (8/1), Nicolas Sébastien Anelka (29/7) [72.Djibril Cissé (26/9)], Thierry Daniel Henry (74/31). Trainer: Raymond Domenech (16).
Goals: Nicolas Sébastien Anelka (49), Djibril Cissé (80), Thierry Daniel Henry (87).

667. 12.11.2005 **FRANCE - GERMANY** **0-0**
Stade de France, Saint-Denis, Paris; Referee: Stephen Bennett (England); Attendance: 58,889
FRA: Grégory Coupet (18/0), Anthony Réveillère (5/0), Lilian Thuram (Cap) (110/2), Jean-Alain Boumsong (17/1), William Éric Gallas (37/1), Willy Sagnol (34/0), Vikash Dhorasoo (14/1) [75.Alou Diarra (7/0)], Claude Makélélé (40/0), Florent Yohan Malouda (9/1) [69.Jérôme Rothen (11/0)], Thierry Daniel Henry (75/31) [46.Nicolas Sébastien Anelka (30/7)], David Trézéguet (60/31) [69.Djibril Cissé (27/9)]. Trainer: Raymond Domenech (17).

668. 01.03.2006 **FRANCE - SLOVAKIA** **1-2(0-0)**
Stade de France, Saint-Denis, Paris; Referee: Craig Thomson (Scotland); Attendance: 56,273
FRA: Fabien Barthez (77/0), Willy Sagnol (35/0), Lilian Thuram (111/2), Jean-Alain Boumsong (18/1), Mikaël Silvestre (37/2) [63.Éric-Sylvain Bilal Abidal (5/0)], Vikash Dhorasoo (15/1), Patrick Vieira (84/4), Alou Diarra (8/0), Zinedine Zidane (Cap) (99/28) [46.Florent Yohan Malouda (10/1)], Nicolas Sébastien Anelka (31/7) [46.Sylvain Wiltord (77/25)], David Trézéguet (61/31) [46.Thierry Daniel Henry (76/31)]. Trainer: Raymond Domenech (18).
Goal: Sylvain Wiltord (75 penalty).

669. 27.05.2006 **FRANCE - MEXICO** **1-0(1-0)**
Stade de France, Saint-Denis, Paris; Referee: Mourad Daami (Tunisia); Attendance: 78,819
FRA: Fabien Barthez (78/0), Willy Sagnol (36/0), Lilian Thuram (112/2) [50.Jean-Alain Boumsong (19/1)], William Éric Gallas (38/1) [46.Mikäel Silvestre (38/2)], Éric-Sylvain Bilal Abidal (6/0), Patrick Vieira (85/4) [46.Sylvain Wiltord (78/25)], Claude Makélélé (41/0) [48.Alou Diarra (9/0)], Florent Yohan Malouda (11/2), Djibril Cissé (28/9), Zinedine Zidane (Cap) (**100**/28) [51.Vikash Dhorasoo (16/1)], David Trézéguet (62/31) [74.Franck Henry Pierre Ribéry (1/0)]. Trainer: Raymond Domenech (19).
Goal: Florent Yohan Malouda (45+1).

670. 31.05.2006 **FRANCE - DENMARK** **2-0(1-0)**
Stade „Félix Bollaert", Lens; Referee: Alan Kelly (Republic of Ireland); Attendance: 39,000
FRA: Fabien Barthez (79/0), Willy Sagnol (37/0) [88.Pascal Chimbonda (1/0)], Lilian Thuram (113/2), William Éric Gallas (39/1), Éric-Sylvain Bilal Abidal (7/0) [82.Mikaël Silvestre (39/2)], Patrick Vieira (86/4), Claude Makélélé (42/0), Florent Yohan Malouda (12/2), Zinedine Zidane (Cap) (101/28) [66.Franck Henry Pierre Ribéry (2/0)], Louis Laurent Saha (9/2) [57.Sylvain Wiltord (79/26)], Thierry Daniel Henry (77/32) [79.Djibril Cissé (29/9)]. Trainer: Raymond Domenech (20).
Goals: Thierry Daniel Henry (13), Sylvain Wiltord (76 penalty).

671. 07.06.2006 **FRANCE – CHINA P.R.** **3-1(1-0)**
Stade „Geoffroy Guichard", Saint-Étienne; Referee: Carlos Megía Dávila (Spain); Attendance: 34,147
FRA: Fabien Barthez (80/0), Willy Sagnol (38/0), Lilian Thuram (114/2), William Éric Gallas (40/1), Éric-Sylvain Bilal Abidal (8/0), Patrick Vieira (87/4) [75.Franck Henry Pierre Ribéry (3/0)], Claude Makélélé (43/0), Florent Yohan Malouda (13/2), Zinedine Zidane (102/28) (Cap), Djibril Cissé (30/9) [13.David Trézéguet (63/32); 84.Sylvain Wiltord (80/26)], Thierry Daniel Henry (78/33). Trainer: Raymond Domenech (21).
Goals: David Trézéguet (30), Wang Yun (89 own goal), Thierry Daniel Henry (90+2).

672. 13.06.2006 **FRANCE - SWITZERLAND** **0-0** 18th FIFA WC. Group Stage.
„Gottlieb-Daimler" Stadion, Stuttgart (Germany); Referee: Valentin Ivanov (Russia); Attendance: 52,000
FRA: Fabien Barthez (81/0), Willy Sagnol (39/0), Lilian Thuram (115/2), William Éric Gallas (41/1), Éric-Sylvain Bilal Abidal (9/0), Patrick Vieira (88/4), Claude Makélélé (44/0), Zinedine Zidane (Cap) (103/28), Sylvain Wiltord (81/26) [84.Vikash Dhorasoo (17/1)], Franck Henry Pierre Ribéry (4/0) [70.Louis Laurent Saha (10/2)], Thierry Daniel Henry (79/33). Trainer: Raymond Domenech (22).

673. 18.06.2006 **FRANCE – KOREA REPUBLIC** **1-1(1-0)** 18th FIFA WC. Group Stage.
Zentralstadion, Leipzig (Germany); Referee: Benito Armando Archundia Téllez (Mexico); Attendance: 43,000
FRA: Fabien Barthez (82/0), Willy Sagnol (40/0), Lilian Thuram (116/2), William Éric Gallas (42/1), Éric-Sylvain Bilal Abidal (10/0), Patrick Vieira (89/4), Claude Makélélé (45/0), Sylvain Wiltord (82/26) [60.Franck Henry Pierre Ribéry (5/0)], Zinedine Zidane (Cap) (104/28) [90+1.David Trézéguet (64/32)], Florent Yohan Malouda (14/2) [88.Vikash Dhorasoo (18/1)], Thierry Daniel Henry (80/34). Trainer: Raymond Domenech (23).
Goal: Thierry Daniel Henry (9).

674. 23.06.2006 **TOGO - FRANCE** **0-2(0-0)** 18th FIFA WC. Group Stage.
FIFA World Cup Stadium (RheinEnergie), Köln (Germany); Referee: Jorge Luis Larrionda Pietrafiesa (Uruguay); Attendance: 45,000
FRA: Fabien Barthez (83/0), Willy Sagnol (41/0), Lilian Thuram (117/2), William Éric Gallas (43/1), Mikaël Silvestre (40/2), Patrick Vieira (Cap) (90/5) [81.Alou Diarra (10/0)], Claude Makélélé (46/0), Franck Henry Pierre Ribéry (6/0) [77.Sidney Rodrigue Noukpo Govou (20/3)], Florent Yohan Malouda (15/2) [74.Sylvain Wiltord (83/26)], David Trézéguet (65/32), Thierry Daniel Henry (81/35). Trainer: Raymond Domenech (24).
Goals: Patrick Vieira (55), Thierry Daniel Henry (61).

675. 27.06.2006 **SPAIN - FRANCE** **1-3(1-1)** 18th FIFA WC. 2nd Round of 16.
FIFA World Cup Stadium (AWD-Arena), Hannover (Germany); Referee: Roberto Rosetti (Italy); Attendance: 43,000
FRA: Fabien Barthez (84/0), Willy Sagnol (42/0), Lilian Thuram (118/2), William Éric Gallas (44/1), Éric-Sylvain Bilal Abidal (11/0), Patrick Vieira (91/6), Claude Makélélé (47/0), Franck Henry Pierre Ribéry (7/1), Zinedine Zidane (Cap) (105/29), Florent Yohan Malouda (16/2) [74.Sidney Rodrigue Noukpo Govou (21/3)], Thierry Daniel Henry (82/35) [88.Sylvain Wiltord (84/26)]. Trainer: Raymond Domenech (25).
Goals: Franck Henry Pierre Ribéry (41), Patrick Vieira (83), Zinedine Zidane (90+2).

676. 01.07.2006 **BRAZIL - FRANCE** **0-1(0-0)** 18th FIFA WC. Quarter-Finals.
FIFA World Cup Stadium (Commerzbank-Arena), Frankfurt (Germany); Referee: Luis Medina Cantalejo (Spain); Attendance: 40,000
FRA: Fabien Barthez (85/0), Willy Sagnol (43/0), Lilian Thuram (119/2), William Éric Gallas (45/1), Éric-Sylvain Bilal Abidal (12/0), Patrick Vieira (92/6), Claude Makélélé (48/0), Franck Henry Pierre Ribéry (8/1) [77.Sidney Rodrigue Noukpo Govou (22/3)], Zinedine Zidane (Cap) (106/29), Florent Yohan Malouda (17/2) [81.Sylvain Wiltord (85/26)], Thierry Daniel Henry (83/36) [86.Louis Laurent Saha (11/2)]. Trainer: Raymond Domenech (26).
Goal: Thierry Daniel Henry (57).

677. 05.07.2006 **PORTUGAL - FRANCE** **0-1(0-1)** 18th FIFA WC. Semi-Finals.
FIFA World Cup Stadium (Allianz-Arena), München (Germany); Referee: Jorge Luis Larrionda Pietrafiesa (Uruguay); Attendance: 66,000
FRA: Fabien Barthez (86/0), Willy Sagnol (44/0), Lilian Thuram (120/2), William Éric Gallas (46/1), Éric-Sylvain Bilal Abidal (13/0), Patrick Vieira (93/6), Claude Makélélé (49/0), Franck Henry Pierre Ribéry (9/1) [72.Sidney Rodrigue Noukpo Govou (23/3)], Zinedine Zidane (Cap) (107/30), Florent Yohan Malouda (18/2) [69.Sylvain Wiltord (86/26)], Thierry Daniel Henry (84/36) [85.Louis Laurent Saha (12/2)]. Trainer: Raymond Domenech (27).
Goal: Zinedine Zidane (33 penalty).

678. 09.07.2006 **ITALY - FRANCE** **1-1(1-1,1-1,1-1); 5-3 on penalties** 18th FIFA WC. Final.
Olympiastadion, Berlin (Germany); Referee: Horacio Marcelo Elizondo (Argentina); Attendance: 69,000
FRA: Fabien Barthez (87/0), Willy Sagnol (45/0), Lilian Thuram (121/2), William Éric Gallas (47/1), Éric-Sylvain Bilal Abidal (14/0), Patrick Vieira (94/6) [56.Alou Diarra (11/0)], Claude Makélélé (50/0), Franck Henry Pierre Ribéry (10/1) [100.David Trézéguet (66/32)], Zinedine Zidane (Cap) (108/31) [*sent off 110*], Florent Yohan Malouda (19/2), Thierry Daniel Henry (85/36) [107.Sylvain Wiltord (87/26)]. Trainer: Raymond Domenech (28).
Goal: Zinedine Zidane (7 penalty).
Penalties: Sylvain Wiltord, David Trézéguet (missed), Éric-Sylvain Bilal Abidal, Willy Sagnol.

679. 16.08.2006 **BOSNIA AND HERZEGOVINA - FRANCE** **1-2(1-1)**
„Asim Ferhatović Hase" Stadion, Sarajevo; Referee: Dr. Franz-Xaver Wack (Germany); Attendance: 35,000
FRA: Grégory Coupet (19/0), Willy Sagnol (46/0), Jean-Alain Boumsong (20/1) [60.Gaël Givet (12/0)], William Éric Gallas (48/2), Éric-Sylvain Bilal Abidal (15/0), Franck Henry Pierre Ribéry (11/1) [69.Julien Faubert (1/1)], Patrick Vieira (Cap) (95/6), Rio Antonio Zoba Mavuba (4/0), Florent Yohan Malouda (20/2) [53.Sylvain Wiltord (88/26)], Louis Laurent Saha (13/2), Thierry Daniel Henry (86/36). Trainer: Raymond Domenech (29).
Goals: William Éric Gallas (41), Julien Faubert (90).

680. 02.09.2006 **GEORGIA - FRANCE** **0-3(0-2)** 13th EC. Qualifiers
„Boris Paichadze" Erovnuli Stadioni, Tbilisi; Referee: Jan Wegereef (Netherlands); Attendance: 57,000
FRA: Grégory Coupet (20/0), Willy Sagnol (47/0), Lilian Thuram (122/2), William Éric Gallas (49/2), Éric-Sylvain Bilal Abidal (16/0), Patrick Vieira (Cap) (96/6), Franck Henry Pierre Ribéry (12/1) [69.Sidney Rodrigue Noukpo Govou (24/3)], Claude Makélélé (51/0) [58.Rio Antonio Zoba Mavuba (5/0)], Florent Yohan Malouda (21/3), Louis Laurent Saha (14/3) [86.Sylvain Wiltord (89/26)], Thierry Daniel Henry (87/36). Trainer: Raymond Domenech (30).
Goals: Florent Yohan Malouda (7), Louis Laurent Saha (16), Malkhaz Asatiani (47 own goal).

681. 06.09.2006 **FRANCE – ITALY** **3-1(2-1)** 13th EC. Qualifiers
Stade de France, Saint-Denis, Paris; Referee: Herbert Fandel (Germany); Attendance: 78,831
FRA: Grégory Coupet (21/0), Willy Sagnol (48/0), Lilian Thuram (123/2), William Éric Gallas (50/2), Éric-Sylvain Bilal Abidal (17/0), Patrick Vieira (Cap) (97/6), Claude Makélélé (52/0), Franck Henry Pierre Ribéry (13/1) [88.Louis Laurent Saha (15/3)], Florent Yohan Malouda (22/3), Sidney Rodrigue Noukpo Govou (25/5) [75.Sylvain Wiltord (90/26)], Thierry Daniel Henry (88/37). Trainer: Raymond Domenech (31).
Goals: Sidney Rodrigue Noukpo Govou (2), Thierry Daniel Henry (17), Sidney Rodrigue Noukpo Govou (55).

682. 07.10.2006 **SCOTLAND - FRANCE** **1-0(0-0)** 13th EC. Qualifiers
Hampden Park, Glasgow; Referee: Massimo Busacca (Switzerland); Attendance: 50,456
FRA: Grégory Coupet (22/0), Willy Sagnol (49/0), Lilian Thuram (124/2), Jean-Alain Boumsong (21/1), Éric-Sylvain Bilal Abidal (18/0), Franck Henry Pierre Ribéry (14/1) [74.Sylvain Wiltord (91/26)], Patrick Vieira (Cap) (98/6), Claude Makélélé (53/0), Florent Yohan Malouda (23/3), David Trézéguet (67/32) [62.Louis Laurent Saha (16/3)], Thierry Daniel Henry (89/37). Trainer: Raymond Domenech (32).

683. 11.10.2006 **FRANCE – FAROE ISLANDS** **5-0(2-0)** 13th EC. Qualifiers
Stade „Auguste-Bonal", Montbéliard; Referee: Sorin Corpodean (Romania); Attendance: 19,314
FRA: Mickaël Landreau (4/0), Willy Sagnol (50/0) [78.François Clerc (1/0)], Lilian Thuram (125/2), William Éric Gallas (51/2), Julien Escudé (1/0), Franck Henry Pierre Ribéry (15/1), Patrick Vieira (Cap) (99/6), Jérémy Toulalan (1/0), Florent Yohan Malouda (24/3), Louis Laurent Saha (17/4) [61.David Trézéguet (68/34)], Thierry Daniel Henry (90/38) [61.Nicolas Sébastien Anelka (32/8)]. Trainer: Raymond Domenech (33).
Goals: Louis Laurent Saha (1), Thierry Daniel Henry (22), Nicolas Sébastien Anelka (76), David Trézéguet (77, 84).

684. 15.11.2006 **FRANCE - GREECE** **1-0(1-0)**
Stade de France, Saint-Denis, Paris; Referee: Dr. Franz-Xaver Wack (Germany); replaced after 46 mins by Volker Wezel (Germany); Attendance: 63,680
FRA: Grégory Coupet (23/0), Willy Sagnol (51/0) [46.François Clerc (2/0)], Lilian Thuram (126/2), William Éric Gallas (52/2), Éric-Sylvain Bilal Abidal (19/0) [46.Patrice Latyr Evra (6/0)], Sylvain Wiltord (92/26), Patrick Vieira (Cap) (**100**/6), Claude Makélélé (54/0) [46.Alou Diarra (12/0)], Florent Yohan Malouda (25/3), Louis Laurent Saha (18/4) [46.Nicolas Sébastien Anelka (33/8)], Thierry Daniel Henry (91/39). Trainer: Raymond Domenech (34).
Goal: Thierry Daniel Henry (26).

685. 07.02.2007 **FRANCE - ARGENTINA** **0-1(0-1)**
Stade de France, Saint-Denis, Paris; Referee: Damir Skomina (Slovenia); Attendance: 79,862
FRA: Grégory Coupet (24/0), Willy Sagnol (52/0) [46.François Clerc (3/0)], Sébastien Squillaci (11/0), Julien Escudé (2/0), Éric-Sylvain Bilal Abidal (20/0), Franck Henry Pierre Ribéry (16/1), Patrick Vieira (Cap) (101/6), Claude Makélélé (55/0) [89.Djibril Cissé (31/9)], Florent Yohan Malouda (26/3) [46.Sidney Rodrigue Noukpo Govou (26/5)], David Trézéguet (69/34) [72.Nicolas Sébastien Anelka (34/8)], Thierry Daniel Henry (92/39). Trainer: Raymond Domenech (35).

686. 24.03.2007 **LITHUANIA - FRANCE** **0-1(0-0)** 13th EC. Qualifiers
„Darius ir Girėnas" Stadionas, Kaunas; Referee: Howard Webb (England); Attendance: 8,000
FRA: Grégory Coupet (25/0), Willy Sagnol (53/0), Lilian Thuram (Cap) (127/2), William Éric Gallas (53/2), Éric-Sylvain Bilal Abidal (21/0), Lassana Diarra (1/0), Claude Makélélé (56/0), Jérémy Toulalan (2/0), Sidney Rodrigue Noukpo Govou (27/5) [62.Djibril Cissé (32/9)], Nicolas Sébastien Anelka (35/9), Florent Yohan Malouda (27/3) [90.Vassiriki Abou Diaby (1/0)]. Trainer: Raymond Domenech (36).
Goal: Nicolas Sébastien Anelka (74).

687. 28.03.2007 **FRANCE - AUSTRIA** **1-0(0-0)**
Stade de France, Saint-Denis, Paris; Referee: Athanassios Briakos (Greece); Attendance: 65,000
FRA: Grégory Coupet (26/0), François Clerc (4/0), Lilian Thuram (Cap) (128/2) [46.William Éric Gallas (54/2)], Philippe Samuel Mexès (7/0) [46.Éric-Sylvain Bilal Abidal (22/0)], Julien Escudé (3/0), Lassana Diarra (2/0), Rio Antonio Zoba Mavuba (6/0), Vassiriki Abou Diaby (2/0) [78.Frédéric Piquionne (1/0)], Samir Nasri (1/0) [70.Florent Yohan Malouda (28/3)], Nicolas Sébastien Anelka (36/9), Djibril Cissé (33/9) [46.Karim Mostafa Benzema (1/1)]. Trainer: Raymond Domenech (37).
Goal: Karim Mostafa Benzema (54).

688. 02.06.2007 **FRANCE - UKRAINE** **2-0(0-0)** 13th EC. Qualifiers
Stade de France, Saint-Denis, Paris; Referee: Luis Medina Cantalejo (Spain); Attendance: 80,051
FRA: Grégory Coupet (27/0), François Clerc (5/0), Lilian Thuram (Cap) (129/2), William Éric Gallas (55/2), Éric-Sylvain Bilal Abidal (23/0), Claude Makélélé (57/0), Jérémy Toulalan (3/0), Franck Henry Pierre Ribéry (17/2), Samir Nasri (2/0) [81.Lassana Diarra (3/0)], Florent Yohan Malouda (29/3), Nicolas Sébastien Anelka (37/10) [76.Djibril Cissé (34/9)]. Trainer: Raymond Domenech (38).
Goals: Franck Henry Pierre Ribéry (57), Nicolas Sébastien Anelka (71).

689. 06.06.2007 **FRANCE - GEORGIA** **1-0(1-0)** 13th EC. Qualifiers
Stade "Abbé-Deschamps", Auxerre; Referee: Lucilio Cardoso Cortez Batista (Portugal); Attendance: 15,000
FRA: Mickaël Landreau (5/0), François Clerc (6/0), Lilian Thuram (Cap) (130/2), William Éric Gallas (56/2), Éric-Sylvain Bilal Abidal (24/0), Claude Makélélé (58/0), Jérémy Toulalan (4/0), Franck Henry Pierre Ribéry (18/2) [90+3.Sidney Rodrigue Noukpo Govou (28/5)], Samir Nasri (3/1), Florent Yohan Malouda (30/3) [65.Djibril Cissé (35/9)], Nicolas Sébastien Anelka (38/10) [90+2.Karim Mostafa Benzema (2/1)]. Trainer: Raymond Domenech (39).
Goal: Samir Nasri (33).

690. 22.08.2007 **SLOVAKIA - FRANCE** **0-1(0-1)**
Štadion „Anton Malatinský", Trnava; Referee: Igor Yegorov (Russia); Attendance: 13,164
FRA: Mickaël Landreau (6/0), François Clerc (7/0) [63.Bacary Sagna (1/0)], Philippe Samuel Mexès (8/0) [88.Jean-Alain Boumsong (22/1)], Éric-Sylvain Bilal Abidal (25/0), Patrice Latyr Evra (7/0), Franck Henry Pierre Ribéry (19/2) [73.Samir Nasri (4/1)], Patrick Vieira (Cap) (102/6) [58.Jérémy Toulalan (5/0)], Claude Makélélé (59/0), Florent Yohan Malouda (31/3), Nicolas Sébastien Anelka (39/10), Thierry Daniel Henry (93/40) [85.Karim Mostafa Benzema (3/1)]. Trainer: Raymond Domenech (40).
Goal: Thierry Daniel Henry (39).

691. 08.09.2007 **ITALY - FRANCE** **0-0** 13th EC. Qualifiers

Stadio „Giuseppe Meazza", Milano; Referee: Luboš Micheľ (Slovakia); Attendance: 80,000

FRA: Mickaël Landreau (7/0), Lassana Diarra (4/0), Lilian Thuram (131/2), Julien Escudé (4/0), Éric-Sylvain Bilal Abidal (26/0), Franck Henry Pierre Ribéry (20/2) [86.Jérémy Toulalan (6/0)], Claude Makélélé (60/0), Patrick Vieira (Cap) (103/6), Florent Yohan Malouda (32/3), Nicolas Sébastien Anelka (40/10), Thierry Daniel Henry (94/40). Trainer: Pierre Mankowski (replacing Raymond Domenech (41)).

692. 12.09.2007 **FRANCE – SCOTLAND** **0-1(0-0)** 13th EC. Qualifiers

Stade de France, Saint-Denis, Paris; Referee: Konrad Plautz (Austria); Attendance: 42,000

FRA: Mickaël Landreau (8/0), Lassana Diarra (5/0), Lilian Thuram (132/2), Julien Escudé (5/0), Éric-Sylvain Bilal Abidal (27/0) [76.Karim Mostafa Benzema (4/1)], Franck Henry Pierre Ribéry (21/2), Patrick Vieira (Cap) (104/6) [69.Samir Nasri (5/1)], Claude Makélélé (61/0), Florent Yohan Malouda (33/3), David Trézéguet (70/34), Nicolas Sébastien Anelka (41/10). Trainer: Raymond Domenech (42).

693. 13.10.2007 **FAROE ISLANDS - FRANCE** **0-6(0-2)** 13th EC. Qualifiers

Tórsvøllur, Tórshavn; Referee: Gabriele Rossi (San Marino); Attendance: 8,076

FRA: Mickaël Landreau (9/0), Bacary Sagna (2/0), Éric-Sylvain Bilal Abidal (28/0), Lilian Thuram (Cap) (133/2), Patrice Latyr Evra (8/0), Franck Henry Pierre Ribéry (22/2) [62.Hatem Ben Arfa (1/1)], Jérémy Toulalan (7/0), Claude Makélélé (62/0) [73.Lassana Diarra (6/0)], Jérôme Rothen (12/1), Nicolas Sébastien Anelka (42/11) [46.Karim Mostafa Benzema (5/3)], Thierry Daniel Henry (95/41). Trainer: Raymond Domenech (43).

Goals: Nicolas Sébastien Anelka (6), Thierry Daniel Henry (8), Karim Mostafa Benzema (50), Jérôme Rothen (66), Karim Mostafa Benzema (81), Hatem Ben Arfa (90+4).

694. 17.10.2007 **FRANCE - LITHUANIA** **2-0(0-0)** 13th EC. Qualifiers

Stade de la Beaujoire, Nantes; Referee: Viktor Kassai (Hungary); Attendance: 34,650

FRA: Mickaël Landreau (10/0), Lassana Diarra (7/0) [70.Hatem Ben Arfa (2/1)], Lilian Thuram (Cap) (134/2), William Éric Gallas (57/2), Éric-Sylvain Bilal Abidal (29/0), Franck Henry Pierre Ribéry (23/2), Claude Makélélé (63/0), Jérémy Toulalan (8/0), Florent Yohan Malouda (34/3), Karim Mostafa Benzema (6/3), Thierry Daniel Henry (96/43). Trainer: Raymond Domenech (44).

Goals: Thierry Daniel Henry (79, 81).

695. 16.11.2007 **FRANCE - MOROCCO** **2-2(1-1)**

Stade de France, Saint-Denis, Paris; Referee: Ruud Bossen (Netherlands); Attendance: 78,000

FRA: Mickaël Landreau (11/0), François Clerc (8/0), William Éric Gallas (58/2) [46.Éric-Sylvain Bilal Abidal (30/0)], Lilian Thuram (Cap) (135/2) [64.Sébastien Squillaci (12/0)], Patrice Latyr Evra (9/0), Claude Makélélé (64/0) [46.Jérémy Toulalan (9/0)], Lassana Diarra (8/0), Sidney Rodrigue Noukpo Govou (29/6) [74.Hatem Ben Arfa (3/1)], Samir Nasri (6/2), Jérôme Rothen (13/1) [81.Mathieu Flamini (1/0)], Karim Mostafa Benzema (7/3) [64.Nicolas Sébastien Anelka (43/11)]. Trainer: Raymond Domenech (45).

Goals: Sidney Rodrigue Noukpo Govou (15), Samir Nasri (75).

696. 21.11.2007 **UKRAINE – FRANCE** **2-2(1-2)** 13th EC. Qualifiers

Olympiyskiy Stadium, Kyiv; Referee: Tom Henning Øvrebø (Norway); Attendance: 15,000

FRA: Sébastien Frey (1/0), François Clerc (9/0), William Éric Gallas (59/2), Lilian Thuram (Cap) (136/2), Éric-Sylvain Bilal Abidal (31/0), Franck Henry Pierre Ribéry (24/2) [89.Hatem Ben Arfa (4/1)], Claude Makélélé (65/0), Lassana Diarra (9/0), Sidney Rodrigue Noukpo Govou (30/7), Thierry Daniel Henry (97/44), Karim Mostafa Benzema (8/3) [46.Samir Nasri (7/2)]. Trainer: Raymond Domenech (46).

Goals: Thierry Daniel Henry (20), Sidney Rodrigue Noukpo Govou (34).

697. 06.02.2008 **SPAIN - FRANCE** **1-0(0-0)**

Estadio La Rosaleda, Málaga; Referee: Tony Asumaa (Finland); Attendance: 38,000

FRA: Grégory Coupet (28/0), Willy Sagnol (54/0), Lilian Thuram (137/2) [46.Julien Escudé (6/0)], William Éric Gallas (60/2), Éric-Sylvain Bilal Abidal (32/0), Lassana Diarra (10/0), Patrick Vieira (Cap) (105/6) [82.Hatem Ben Arfa (5/1)], Jérémy Toulalan (10/0), Florent Yohan Malouda (35/3), Thierry Daniel Henry (98/44), Nicolas Sébastien Anelka (44/11) [60.Karim Mostafa Benzema (9/3)]. Trainer: Raymond Domenech (47).

698. 26.03.2008 **FRANCE - ENGLAND** **1-0(1-0)**

Stade de France, Saint-Denis, Paris; Referee: Florian Meyer (Germany); Attendance: 78,500

FRA: Grégory Coupet (29/0), François Clerc (10/0), Lilian Thuram (Cap) (138/2), William Éric Gallas (61/2), Éric-Sylvain Bilal Abidal (33/0), Claude Makélélé (66/0), Jérémy Toulalan (11/0), Franck Henry Pierre Ribéry (25/3), Florent Yohan Malouda (36/3), David Trézéguet (71/34) [62.Sidney Rodrigue Noukpo Govou (31/7)], Nicolas Sébastien Anelka (45/11) [80.Djibril Cissé (36/9)]. Trainer: Raymond Domenech (48).

Goals: Franck Henry Pierre Ribéry (32 penalty).

699. 27.05.2008 **FRANCE - ECUADOR** **2-0(0-0)**

Stade des Alpes, Grenoble; Referee: Paul Allaerts (Belgium); Attendance: 20,000

FRA: Sébastien Frey (2/0) [46.Stève Mandanda (1/0)], Willy Sagnol (55/0) [74.François Clerc (11/0)], Lilian Thuram (Cap) (139/2), Julien Escudé (7/0) [46.Patrice Latyr Evra (10/0)], Éric-Sylvain Bilal Abidal (34/0), Samir Nasri (8/2), Alou Diarra (13/0) [46.Mathieu Flamini (2/0)], Lassana Diarra (11/0), Hatem Ben Arfa (6/1) [78.Florent Yohan Malouda (37/3)], Nicolas Sébastien Anelka (46/11), Djibril Cissé (37/9) [46.Bafétimbi Fredius Gomis (1/2)]. Trainer: Raymond Domenech (49).

Goals: Bafétimbi Fredius Gomis (59, 86).

700. 31.05.2008 **FRANCE - PARAGUAY** **0-0**

Stade Municipal, Toulouse; Referee: Pedro Proença Oliveira Alves Garcia (Portugal); Attendance: 33,418

FRA: Grégory Coupet (30/0), François Clerc (12/0), Jean-Alain Boumsong (23/1), Sébastien Squillaci (13/0), Patrice Latyr Evra (11/0), Claude Makélélé (67/0) [46.Lassana Diarra (12/0)], Jérémy Toulalan (12/0) [71.Samir Nasri (9/2)], Franck Henry Pierre Ribéry (26/3) [46.Sidney Rodrigue Noukpo Govou (32/7)], Florent Yohan Malouda (38/3), Thierry Daniel Henry (Cap) (99/44) [46.Bafétimbi Fredius Gomis (2/2)], Karim Mostafa Benzema (10/3) [63.Nicolas Sébastien Anelka (47/11)]. Trainer: Raymond Domenech (50).

701. 03.06.2008 **FRANCE - COLOMBIA** **1-0(1-0)**

Stade de France, Saint-Denis, Paris; Referee: Michael Dean (England); Attendance: 79,727

FRA: Grégory Coupet (31/0), Willy Sagnol (56/0), Lilian Thuram (Cap) (140/2), William Éric Gallas (62/2), Éric-Sylvain Bilal Abidal (35/0), Claude Makélélé (68/0), Jérémy Toulalan (13/0), Franck Henry Pierre Ribéry (27/4) [75.Samir Nasri (10/2)], Florent Yohan Malouda (39/3), Karim Mostafa Benzema (11/3) [65.Lassana Diarra (13/0)], Thierry Daniel Henry (**100**/44) [76.Nicolas Sébastien Anelka (48/11)]. Trainer: Raymond Domenech (51).

Goal: Franck Henry Pierre Ribéry (25 penalty).

702. 09.06.2008 **ROMANIA - FRANCE** **0-0** 13th EC. Group Stage.
Letzigrund Stadion, Zürich (Switzerland); Referee: Manuel Enrique Mejuto González (Spain); Attendance: 30,585
FRA: Grégory Coupet (32/0), Willy Sagnol (57/0), Lilian Thuram (Cap) (141/2), William Éric Gallas (63/2), Éric-Sylvain Bilal Abidal (36/0), Franck Henry Pierre Ribéry (28/4), Claude Makélélé (69/0), Jérémy Toulalan (14/0), Florent Yohan Malouda (40/3), Karim Mostafa Benzema (12/3) [78.Samir Nasri (11/2)], Nicolas Sébastien Anelka (49/11) [72.Bafétimbi Fredius Gomis (3/2)]. Trainer: Raymond Domenech (52).

703. 13.06.2008 **NETHERLANDS - FRANCE** **4-1(1-0)** 13th EC. Group Stage.
Stade de Suisse Wankdorf, Bern (Switzerland); Referee: Herbert Fandel (Germany); Attendance: 30,777
FRA: Grégory Coupet (33/0), Willy Sagnol (58/0), Lilian Thuram (Cap) (142/2), William Éric Gallas (64/2), Patrice Latyr Evra (12/0), Claude Makélélé (70/0), Jérémy Toulalan (15/0), Franck Henry Pierre Ribéry (29/4), Florent Yohan Malouda (41/3) [60.Bafétimbi Fredius Gomis (4/2)], Thierry Daniel Henry (101/45), Sidney Rodrigue Noukpo Govou (33/7) [75.Nicolas Sébastien Anelka (50/11)]. Trainer: Raymond Domenech (53).
Goal: Thierry Daniel Henry (71).

704. 17.06.2008 **FRANCE - ITALY** **0-2(0-1)** 13th EC. Group Stage.
Letzigrund Stadion, Zürich (Switzerland); Referee: Ľuboš Micheľ (Slovakia); Attendance: 30,585
FRA: Grégory Coupet (34/0), François Clerc (13/0), William Éric Gallas (65/2), Éric-Sylvain Bilal Abidal (37/0) [*sent off 24*], Patrice Latyr Evra (13/0), Claude Makélélé (71/0), Jérémy Toulalan (16/0), Franck Henry Pierre Ribéry (30/4) [10.Samir Nasri (12/2); 26.Jean-Alain Boumsong (24/1)], Karim Mostafa Benzema (13/3), Sidney Rodrigue Noukpo Govou (34/7) [66.Nicolas Sébastien Anelka (51/11)], Thierry Daniel Henry (Cap) (102/45). Trainer: Raymond Domenech (54).

705. 20.08.2008 **SWEDEN - FRANCE** **2-3(1-1)**
Ullevi Stadion, Göteborg; Referee: Frederikus Johannes „Eric" Braamhaar (Netherlands); Attendance: 30,000
FRA: Stève Mandanda (2/0), Bacary Sagna (3/0), William Éric Gallas (66/2), Philippe Samuel Mexès (9/0), Patrice Latyr Evra (14/0), Jérémy Toulalan (17/0) [90+2.Yoann Miguel Gourcuff (1/0)], Lassana Diarra (14/0), Sidney Rodrigue Noukpo Govou (35/9), Florent Yohan Malouda (42/3) [70.Alou Diarra (14/0)], Karim Mostafa Benzema (14/4), Thierry Daniel Henry (Cap) (103/45). Trainer: Raymond Domenech (55).
Goals: Karim Mostafa Benzema (19), Sidney Rodrigue Noukpo Govou (61, 78).

706. 06.09.2008 **AUSTRIA - FRANCE** **3-1(2-0)** 19th FIFA WC. Qualifiers
„Ernst Happel" Stadion, Wien; Referee: Claus Bo Larsen (Denmark); Attendance: 48,000
FRA: Stève Mandanda (3/0), Bacary Sagna (4/0) [71.Yoann Miguel Gourcuff (2/0)], William Éric Gallas (67/2), Philippe Samuel Mexès (10/0), Patrice Latyr Evra (15/0), Lassana Diarra (15/0), Jérémy Toulalan (18/0), Samir Nasri (13/2) [79.Nicolas Sébastien Anelka (52/11)], Sidney Rodrigue Noukpo Govou (36/10), Karim Mostafa Benzema (15/4), Thierry Daniel Henry (Cap) (104/45). Trainer: Raymond Domenech (56).
Goals: Sidney Rodrigue Noukpo Govou (61).

707. 10.09.2008 **FRANCE - SERBIA** **2-1(0-0)** 19th FIFA WC. Qualifiers
Stade de France, Saint-Denis, Paris; Referee: Olegario Manuel Bartolo Faustino Benquerença (Portugal); Attendance: 53,027
FRA: Stève Mandanda (4/0), Bacary Sagna (5/0), William Éric Gallas (68/2), Éric-Sylvain Bilal Abidal (38/0), Gaël Clichy (1/0), Lassana Diarra (16/0), Jérémy Toulalan (19/0), Sidney Rodrigue Noukpo Govou (37/10) [82.Alou Diarra (15/0)], Yoann Miguel Gourcuff (3/0) [90+2.Mathieu Flamini (3/0)], Karim Mostafa Benzema (16/4) [46.Nicolas Sébastien Anelka (53/12)], Thierry Daniel Henry (Cap) (105/46). Trainer: Raymond Domenech (57).
Goals: Thierry Daniel Henry (53), Nicolas Sébastien Anelka (63).

708. 11.10.2008 **ROMANIA - FRANCE** **2-2(2-1)** 19th FIFA WC. Qualifiers
Stadionul Farul, Constanţa; Referee: Frank De Bleeckere (Belgium); Attendance: 12,800
FRA: Stève Mandanda (5/0), Bacary Sagna (6/0), Jean-Alain Boumsong (25/1), Éric-Sylvain Bilal Abidal (39/0), Patrice Latyr Evra (16/0), Jérémy Toulalan (20/0), Alou Diarra (16/0), Franck Henry Pierre Ribéry (31/5) [90+1.Jimmy Briand (1/0)], Yoann Miguel Gourcuff (4/1), Florent Yohan Malouda (43/3) [37.Karim Mostafa Benzema (17/4)], Thierry Daniel Henry (Cap) (106/46). Trainer: Raymond Domenech (58).
Goals: Franck Henry Pierre Ribéry (36), Yoann Miguel Gourcuff (68).

709. 14.10.2008 **FRANCE - TUNISIA** **3-1(1-1)**
Stade de France, Saint-Denis, Paris; Referee: Anton Genov (Bulgaria); Attendance: 74,564
FRA: Stève Mandanda (6/0), Gaël Clichy (2/0), Jean-Alain Boumsong (26/1), Éric-Sylvain Bilal Abidal (40/0), Rod Fanni (1/0), Alou Diarra (17/0), Jérémy Toulalan (21/0), Yoann Miguel Gourcuff (5/1) [80.Jimmy Briand (2/0)], Franck Henry Pierre Ribéry (32/5) [46.Hatem Ben Arfa (7/1)], Karim Mostafa Benzema (18/5) [68.Florent Sinama-Pongolle (1/0)], Thierry Daniel Henry (Cap) (107/48) [83.Florent Yohan Malouda (44/3)]. Trainer: Raymond Domenech (59).
Goals: Thierry Daniel Henry (40, 49), Karim Mostafa Benzema (58).

710. 19.11.2008 **FRANCE - URUGUAY** **0-0**
Stade de France, Saint-Denis, Paris; Referee: Cyril Zimmermann (Switzerland); Attendance: 79,666
FRA: Hugo Lloris (1/0), Rod Fanni (2/0), William Éric Gallas (69/2), Philippe Samuel Mexès (11/0), Patrice Latyr Evra (17/0), Patrick Vieira (Cap) (106/6) [46.Alou Diarra (18/0)], Yoann Miguel Gourcuff (6/1) [72.Samir Nasri (14/2)], Jérémy Toulalan (22/0), Franck Henry Pierre Ribéry (33/5) [58.Karim Mostafa Benzema (19/5)], Thierry Daniel Henry (108/48) [72.Jimmy Briand (3/0)], Nicolas Sébastien Anelka (54/12) [46.Stève Savidan (1/0)]. Trainer: Raymond Domenech (60).

711. 11.02.2009 **FRANCE - ARGENTINA** **0-2(0-1)**
Stade Vélodrome, Marseille; Referee: Jonas Eriksson (Sweden); Attendance: 60,000
FRA: Stève Mandanda (7/0), Bacary Sagna (7/0), Philippe Samuel Mexès (12/0), William Éric Gallas (70/2), Éric-Sylvain Bilal Abidal (41/0), Franck Henry Pierre Ribéry (34/5), Yoann Miguel Gourcuff (7/1), Lassana Diarra (17/0), Jérémy Toulalan (23/0), Thierry Daniel Henry (Cap) (109/48), Nicolas Sébastien Anelka (55/12) [65.Karim Mostafa Benzema (20/5)]. Trainer: Raymond Domenech (61).

712. 28.03.2009 **LITHUANIA - FRANCE** **0-1(0-0)** 19th FIFA WC. Qualifiers
„Darius ir Girėnas" Stadionas, Kaunas; Referee: Frederikus Johannes „Eric" Braamhaar (Netherlands); Attendance: 8,700
FRA: Stève Mandanda (8/0), Bacary Sagna (8/0), William Éric Gallas (71/2), Sébastien Squillaci (14/0), Patrice Latyr Evra (18/0), Peguy Luyindula (5/1) [64.Karim Mostafa Benzema (21/5)], Lassana Diarra (18/0), Yoann Miguel Gourcuff (8/1) [78.Samir Nasri (15/2)], Jérémy Toulalan (24/0), Franck Henry Pierre Ribéry (35/6), Thierry Daniel Henry (Cap) (110/48). Trainer: Raymond Domenech (62).
Goal: Franck Henry Pierre Ribéry (68).

713. 01.04.2009 **FRANCE - LITHUANIA** **1-0(0-0)** 19th FIFA WC. Qualifiers
Stade de France, Saint-Denis, Paris; Referee: Howard Melton Webb (England); Attendance: 79,543
FRA: Stève Mandanda (9/0), Bacary Sagna (9/0), William Éric Gallas (72/2), Sébastien Squillaci (15/0), Patrice Latyr Evra (19/0), Alou Diarra (19/0), Lassana Diarra (19/0), Yoann Miguel Gourcuff (9/1) [57.Karim Mostafa Benzema (22/5)], Peguy Luyindula (6/1) [51.André-Pierre Gignac (1/0)], Franck Henry Pierre Ribéry (36/7), Thierry Daniel Henry (Cap) (111/48). Trainer: Raymond Domenech (63).
Goal: Franck Henry Pierre Ribéry (75).

714. 02.06.2009 **FRANCE - NIGERIA** **0-1(0-1)**
Stade „Geoffroy Guichard“, Saint-Étienne; Referee: Matthew Dyer (South Africa); Attendance: 25,000
FRA: Stève Mandanda (10/0), Rod Fanni (3/0), Sébastien Squillaci (16/0), Julien Escudé (8/0), Patrice Latyr Evra (20/0), Patrick Vieira (Cap) (107/6), Alou Diarra (20/0) [46.Jérémy Toulalan (25/0)], Loïc Rémy (1/0), Franck Henry Pierre Ribéry (37/7) [70.Sidney Rodrigue Noukpo Govou (38/10)], Karim Mostafa Benzema (23/5) [46.Yoann Miguel Gourcuff (10/1)], Nicolas Sébastien Anelka (56/12) [46.André-Pierre Gignac (2/0)]. Trainer: Raymond Domenech (64).

715. 05.06.2009 **FRANCE - TURKEY** **1-0(1-0)**
Stade de Gerland, Lyon; Referee: Manuel Gräfe (Germany); Attendance: 40,000
FRA: Hugo Lloris (2/0), Bacary Sagna (10/0), Philippe Samuel Mexès (13/0), Jean-Alain Boumsong (27/1), Éric-Sylvain Bilal Abidal (Cap) (42/0), Jérémy Toulalan (26/0), Lassana Diarra (20/0), Yoann Miguel Gourcuff (11/1), Florent Yohan Malouda (45/3) [58.Franck Henry Pierre Ribéry (38/7)], Nicolas Sébastien Anelka (57/12) [58.Sidney Rodrigue Noukpo Govou (39/10)], Karim Mostafa Benzema (24/6) [46.André-Pierre Gignac (3/0)]. Trainer: Raymond Domenech (65).
Goal: Karim Mostafa Benzema (39 penalty).

716. 12.08.2009 **FAROE ISLANDS - FRANCE** **0-1(0-1)** 19th FIFA WC. Qualifiers
Tórsvøllur, Tórshavn; Referee: Mihail Koukoulakis (Greece); Attendance: 2,974
FRA: Hugo Lloris (3/0), Bacary Sagna (11/0), William Éric Gallas (Cap) (73/2), Julien Escudé (9/0), Patrice Latyr Evra (21/0), Lassana Diarra (21/0), Jérémy Toulalan (27/0), Yoann Miguel Gourcuff (12/1), Florent Yohan Malouda (46/3) [65.Franck Henry Pierre Ribéry (39/7)], Nicolas Sébastien Anelka (58/12), André-Pierre Gignac (4/1). Trainer: Raymond Domenech (66).
Goal: André-Pierre Gignac (41).

717. 05.09.2009 **FRANCE - ROMANIA** **1-1(0-0)** 19th FIFA WC. Qualifiers
Stade de France, Saint-Denis, Paris; Referee: Ivna Bebek (Croatia); Attendance: 78,209
FRA: Hugo Lloris (4/0), Bacary Sagna (12/0), William Éric Gallas (74/2), Julien Escudé (10/0), Patrice Latyr Evra (22/0), Lassana Diarra (22/0), Jérémy Toulalan (28/0), Yoann Miguel Gourcuff (13/1) [73.Karim Mostafa Benzema (25/6)], Nicolas Sébastien Anelka (59/12), André-Pierre Gignac (5/1), Thierry Daniel Henry (Cap) (112/49) [57.Franck Henry Pierre Ribéry (40/7)]. Trainer: Raymond Domenech (67).
Goal: Thierry Daniel Henry (48).

718. 09.09.2009 **SERBIA - FRANCE** **1-1(1-1)** 19th FIFA WC. Qualifiers
Stadion Crvena zvezda, Beograd; Referee: Roberto Rosetti (Italy); Attendance: 49,456
FRA: Hugo Lloris (5/0) [*sent off 9*], Bacary Sagna (13/0), William Éric Gallas (75/2), Éric-Sylvain Bilal Abidal (43/0), Patrice Latyr Evra (23/0), Lassana Diarra (23/0), Jérémy Toulalan (29/0), Yoann Miguel Gourcuff (14/1) [85.Alou Diarra (21/0)], Nicolas Sébastien Anelka (60/12), André-Pierre Gignac (6/1) [12.Stève Mandanda (11/0)], Thierry Daniel Henry (Cap) (113/50) [77.Franck Henry Pierre Ribéry (41/7)]. Trainer: Raymond Domenech (68).
Goal: Thierry Daniel Henry (36).

719. 10.10.2009 **FRANCE – FAROE ISLANDS** **5-0(2-0)** 19th FIFA WC. Qualifiers
Stade de Roudourou, Guingamp; Referee: Robert Małek (Poland); Attendance: 16,000
FRA: Stève Mandanda (12/0), Bacary Sagna (14/0), William Éric Gallas (76/3), Éric-Sylvain Bilal Abidal (44/0), Patrice Latyr Evra (24/0), Lassana Diarra (24/0), Jérémy Toulalan (30/0) [62.Moussa Sissoko (1/0)], Sidney Rodrigue Noukpo Govou (40/10) [62.Florent Yohan Malouda (47/3)], Nicolas Sébastien Anelka (61/13), André-Pierre Gignac (7/3) [73.Karim Mostafa Benzema (26/7)], Thierry Daniel Henry (Cap) (114/50). Trainer: Raymond Domenech (69).
Goals: André-Pierre Gignac (34, 38), William Éric Gallas (52), Nicolas Sébastien Anelka (86), Karim Mostafa Benzema (88).

720. 14.10.2009 **FRANCE - AUSTRIA** 19th FIFA WC. Qualifiers
Stade de France, Saint-Denis, Paris; Referee: Pedro Proença Oliveira Alves Garcia (Portugal); Attendance: 78,099
FRA: Hugo Lloris (6/0), Gaël Clichy (3/0), Julien Escudé (11/0), Sébastien Squillaci (17/0), Rod Fanni (4/0), Moussa Sissoko (2/0), Alou Diarra (22/0), Florent Yohan Malouda (48/3), Sidney Rodrigue Noukpo Govou (41/10), Karim Mostafa Benzema (27/8) [79.Bafétimbi Fredius Gomis (5/2)], Thierry Daniel Henry (Cap) (115/51) [51.André-Pierre Gignac (8/4)]. Trainer: Raymond Domenech (70).
Goals: Karim Mostafa Benzema (18), Thierry Daniel Henry (26 penalty), André-Pierre Gignac (66).

721. 14.11.2009 **REPUBLIC OF IRELAND - FRANCE** **0-1(0-0)** 19th FIFA WC. Qualifiers (Play-offs)
Croke Park, Dublin; Referee: Dr. Felix Brych (Germany); Attendance: 74,103
FRA: Hugo Lloris (7/0), Bacary Sagna (15/0), William Éric Gallas (77/3), Éric-Sylvain Bilal Abidal (45/0), Patrice Latyr Evra (25/0), Lassana Diarra (25/0), Yoann Miguel Gourcuff (15/1), Alou Diarra (23/0), Thierry Daniel Henry (Cap) (116/51), Nicolas Sébastien Anelka (62/14), André-Pierre Gignac (9/4) [90+1.Florent Yohan Malouda (49/3)]. Trainer: Raymond Domenech (71).
Goal: Nicolas Sébastien Anelka (72).

722. 18.11.2009 **FRANCE – REPUBLIC OF IRELAND** **1-1(0-1,0-1)** 19th FIFA WC. Qualifiers (Play-offs)
Stade de France, Saint-Denis, Paris; Referee: Martin Hansson (Sweden); Attendance: 79,145
FRA: Hugo Lloris (8/0), Bacary Sagna (16/0), William Éric Gallas (78/4), Julien Escudé (12/0) [9.Sébastien Squillaci (18/0)], Patrice Latyr Evra (26/0), Alou Diarra (24/0), Lassana Diarra (26/0), Yoann Miguel Gourcuff (16/1) [87.Florent Yohan Malouda (50/3)], Nicolas Sébastien Anelka (63/14), Thierry Daniel Henry (Cap) (117/51), André-Pierre Gignac (10/4) [57.Sidney Rodrigue Noukpo Govou (42/10)]. Trainer: Raymond Domenech (72).
Goal: William Éric Gallas (103).

723. 03.03.2010 **FRANCE - SPAIN** **0-2(0-2)**
Stade de France, Saint-Denis, Paris; Referee: Craig Alexander Thomson (Scotland); Attendance: 79,021
FRA: Hugo Lloris (9/0), Michaël Ciani (1/0), Bacary Sagna (17/0), Patrice Latyr Evra (27/0), Julien Escudé (13/0), Franck Henry Pierre Ribéry (42/7) [74.Florent Yohan Malouda (51/3)], Jérémy Toulalan (31/0), Lassana Diarra (27/0), Yoann Miguel Gourcuff (17/1), Thierry Daniel Henry (Cap) (118/51) [65.Sidney Rodrigue Noukpo Govou (43/10)], Nicolas Sébastien Anelka (64/14) [79.Djibril Cissé (38/9)]. Trainer: Raymond Domenech (73).

724. 26.05.2010 **FRANCE – COSTA RICA** **2-1(1-1)**
Stade "Bollaert-Delelis", Lens; Referee: Vladislav Bezborodov (Russia); Attendance: 40,000
FRA: Stève Mandanda (13/0), Bacary Sagna (18/0), Éric-Sylvain Bilal Abidal (46/0), William Éric Gallas (79/4) [47.Sébastien Squillaci (19/0)], Patrice Latyr Evra (Cap) (28/0), Florent Yohan Malouda (52/3) [77.Vassiriki Abou Diaby (3/0)], Franck Henry Pierre Ribéry (43/7) [84.André-Pierre Gignac (11/4)], Jérémy Toulalan (32/0) [46.Thierry Daniel Henry (119/51)], Yoann Miguel Gourcuff (18/1), Sidney Rodrigue Noukpo Govou (44/10) [66.Mathieu Valbuena (1/1)], Nicolas Sébastien Anelka (65/14) [46.Alou Diarra (25/0)]. Trainer: Raymond Domenech (74).
Goals: Douglas Sequeira Solano (22 own goal), Mathieu Valbuena (83).

725. 30.05.2010 **TUNISIA - FRANCE** **1-1(1-0)**
Stade Olympique de Radès, Radès; Referee: Adel El Raay (Lybia); Attendance: 26,000
FRA: Hugo Lloris (10/0), Bacary Sagna (19/0), Éric-Sylvain Bilal Abidal (47/0) [46.Marc Planus (1/0)], William Éric Gallas (80/5) [64.Vassiriki Abou Diaby (4/0)], Patrice Latyr Evra (Cap) (29/0) [64.Sébastien Squillaci (20/0)], Florent Yohan Malouda (53/3), Franck Henry Pierre Ribéry (44/7) [46.Thierry Daniel Henry (120/51)], Jérémy Toulalan (33/0), Yoann Miguel Gourcuff (19/1) [64.Gaël Clichy (4/0)], Sidney Rodrigue Noukpo Govou (45/10) [76.Djibril Cissé (39/9)], Nicolas Sébastien Anelka (66/14) [63.André-Pierre Gignac (12/4)]. Trainer: Raymond Domenech (75).
Goal: William Éric Gallas (62).

726. 04.06.2010 **FRANCE – CHINA P.R.** **0-1(0-0)**
Stade „Michel Volnay", Saint-Pierre (Réunion); Referee: Pedro Proença Oliveira Alves Garcia (Portugal); Attendance: 8,000
FRA: Hugo Lloris (11/0), Bacary Sagna (20/0) [46.Anthony Réveillère (6/0)], Éric-Sylvain Bilal Abidal (48/0), William Éric Gallas (81/5), Patrice Latyr Evra (Cap) (30/0), Florent Yohan Malouda (54/3) [63.Vassiriki Abou Diaby (5/0)], Franck Henry Pierre Ribéry (45/7) [62.André-Pierre Gignac (13/4)], Jérémy Toulalan (34/0), Yoann Miguel Gourcuff (20/1), Sidney Rodrigue Noukpo Govou (46/10) [71.Mathieu Valbuena (2/1)], Nicolas Sébastien Anelka (67/14) [63.Thierry Daniel Henry (121/51)]. Trainer: Raymond Domenech (76).

727. 11.06.2010 **URUGUAY - FRANCE** **0-0** 19th FIFA WC. Group Stage.
Cape Town Stadium, Cape Town (South Africa); Referee: Yuichi Nishimura (Japan); Attendance: 64,100
FRA: Hugo Lloris (12/0), Bacary Sagna (21/0), William Éric Gallas (82/5), Éric-Sylvain Bilal Abidal (49/0), Patrice Latyr Evra (Cap) (31/0), Jérémy Toulalan (35/0), Yoann Miguel Gourcuff (21/1) [75.Florent Yohan Malouda (55/3)], Vassiriki Abou Diaby (6/0), Sidney Rodrigue Noukpo Govou (47/10) [85.André-Pierre Gignac (14/4)], Franck Henry Pierre Ribéry (46/7), Nicolas Sébastien Anelka (68/14) [72.Thierry Daniel Henry (122/51)]. Trainer: Raymond Domenech (77).

728. 17.06.2010 **FRANCE - MEXICO** **0-2(0-0)** 19th FIFA WC. Group Stage.
Peter Mokaba" Stadium, Polokwane (South Africa); Referee: Khalil Ibrahim Al Ghamdi (Saudi Arabia); Attendance: 35,370
FRA: Hugo Lloris (13/0), Bacary Sagna (22/0), William Éric Gallas (83/5), Éric-Sylvain Bilal Abidal (50/0), Patrice Latyr Evra (Cap) (32/0), Jérémy Toulalan (36/0), Vassiriki Abou Diaby (7/0), Sidney Rodrigue Noukpo Govou (48/10) [69.Mathieu Valbuena (3/1)], Franck Henry Pierre Ribéry (47/7), Florent Yohan Malouda (56/3), Nicolas Sébastien Anelka (69/14) [46.André-Pierre Gignac (15/4)]. Trainer: Raymond Domenech (78).

729. 22.06.2010 **FRANCE – SOUTH AFRICA** **1-2(0-2)** 19th FIFA WC. Group Stage.
Free State Stadium, Bloemfontein; Referee: Óscar Julián Ruiz Acosta (Colombia); Attendance: 39,415
FRA: Hugo Lloris (14/0), Bacary Sagna (23/0), William Éric Gallas (84/5), Sébastien Squillaci (21/0), Gaël Clichy (5/0), Alou Diarra (Cap) (26/0) [82.Sidney Rodrigue Noukpo Govou (49/10)], Vassiriki Abou Diaby (8/0), André-Pierre Gignac (16/4) [46.Florent Yohan Malouda (57/4)], Yoann Miguel Gourcuff (22/1) [*sent off 25*], Franck Henry Pierre Ribéry (48/7), Djibril Cissé (40/9) [55.Thierry Daniel Henry (123/51)]. Trainer: Raymond Domenech (79).
Goal: Florent Yohan Malouda (70).

730. 11.08.2010 **NORWAY - FRANCE** **2-1(0-0)**
Ullevaal Stadion, Oslo; Referee: Carlos Velasco Carballo (Spain); Attendance: 15,165
FRA: Stéphane Ruffier (1/0), Rod Fanni (5/0), Philippe Samuel Mexès (Cap) (14/0), Adil Rami (1/0), Aly Cissokho (1/0), Samir Nasri (16/2) [79.Jimmy Briand (4/0)], Charles N'Zogbia (1/0) [46.Lassana Diarra (28/0)], Moussa Sissoko (3/0) [46.Hatem Ben Arfa (8/2)], Yann M'Vila (1/0) [74.Yohan Cabaye (1/0)], Loïc Rémy (2/0) [46.Jérémy Ménez (1/0)], Guillaume Hoarau (1/0) [61.Karim Mostafa Benzema (28/8)]. Trainer: Laurent Robert Blanc (1).
Goal: Hatem Ben Arfa (48).

731. 03.09.2010 **FRANCE - BELARUS** **0-1(0-0)** 14th EC. Qualifiers
Stade de France, Saint-Denis, Paris; Referee: William Collum (Scotland); Attendance: 76,395
FRA: Hugo Lloris (15/0), Bacary Sagna (24/0), Gaël Clichy (6/0), Philippe Samuel Mexès (15/0), Adil Rami (2/0), Florent Yohan Malouda (Cap) (58/4), Jérémy Ménez (2/0) [69.Louis Laurent Saha (19/4); 80.Kévin Gameiro (1/0)], Vassiriki Abou Diaby (9/0), Yann M'Vila (2/0), Loïc Rémy (3/0) [34.Mathieu Valbuena (4/1)], Guillaume Hoarau (2/0). Trainer: Laurent Robert Blanc (2).

732. 07.09.2010 **BOSNIA AND HERZEGOVINA - FRANCE** **0-2(0-0)** 14th EC. Qualifiers
„Asim Ferhatović Hase" Stadion, Sarajevo; Referee: Dr.Felix Brych (Germany); Attendance: 28,000
FRA: Hugo Lloris (16/0), Bacary Sagna (25/0), Gaël Clichy (7/0), Philippe Samuel Mexès (16/0), Adil Rami (3/0), Alou Diarra (Cap) (27/0), Florent Yohan Malouda (59/5) [80.Blaise Matuidi (1/0)], Mathieu Valbuena (5/1), Vassiriki Abou Diaby (10/0), Yann M'Vila (3/0), Karim Mostafa Benzema (29/9). Trainer: Laurent Robert Blanc (3).
Goals: Karim Mostafa Benzema (72), Florent Yohan Malouda (78).

733. 09.10.2010 **FRANCE - ROMANIA** **2-0(0-0)** 14th EC. Qualifiers
Stade de France, Saint-Denis, Paris; Referee: Pedro Proença Oliveira Alves Garcia (Portugal); Attendance: 79,299
FRA: Hugo Lloris (17/0), Anthony Réveillère (7/0), Gaël Clichy (8/0), Philippe Samuel Mexès (17/0), Adil Rami (4/0), Alou Diarra (Cap) (28/0), Florent Yohan Malouda (60/5), Mathieu Valbuena (6/1) [68.Loïc Rémy (4/1)], Samir Nasri (17/2) [74.Yoann Miguel Gourcuff (23/2)], Yann M'Vila (4/0), Karim Mostafa Benzema (30/9) [86.Florent Dimitri Payet (1/0)]. Trainer: Laurent Robert Blanc (4).
Goals: Loïc Rémy (83), Yoann Miguel Gourcuff (90+3).

734. 12.10.2010 **FRANCE - LUXEMBOURG** **2-0(1-0)** 14th EC. Qualifiers
Stade Saint-Symphorien, Metz; Referee: Matej Jug (Slovenia); Attendance: 24,710
FRA: Hugo Lloris (18/0), Anthony Réveillère (8/0), Gaël Clichy (9/0), Philippe Samuel Mexès (18/0), Adil Rami (5/0), Alou Diarra (Cap) (29/0), Florent Yohan Malouda (61/5) [63.Samir Nasri (18/2)], Vassiriki Abou Diaby (11/0), Yoann Miguel Gourcuff (24/3), Karim Mostafa Benzema (31/10) [63.Florent Dimitri Payet (2/0)], Guillaume Hoarau (3/0) [73.Loïc Rémy (5/1)]. Trainer: Laurent Robert Blanc (5).
Goals: Karim Mostafa Benzema (22), Yoann Miguel Gourcuff (76).

735. 17.11.2010 **ENGLAND - FRANCE** **1-2(0-1)**
The National Stadium, Wembley, London; Referee: Claus Bo Larsen (Denmark); Attendance: 85,495
FRA: Hugo Lloris (Cap) (19/0), Bacary Sagna (26/0) [87.Anthony Réveillère (9/0)], Éric-Sylvain Bilal Abidal (51/0), Philippe Samuel Mexès (19/0), Adil Rami (6/0) [46.Mamadou Sakho (1/0)], Florent Yohan Malouda (62/5) [77.Florent Dimitri Payet (3/0)], Mathieu Valbuena (7/2) [68.Alou Diarra (30/0)], Samir Nasri (19/2), Yoann Miguel Gourcuff (25/3) [85.Guillaume Hoarau (4/0)], Yann M'Vila (5/0), Karim Mostafa Benzema (32/11) [67.Loïc Rémy (6/1)]. Trainer: Laurent Robert Blanc (6).
Goals: Karim Mostafa Benzema (16), Mathieu Valbuena (55).

736. 09.02.2011 **FRANCE - BRAZIL** **1-0(0-0)**
Stade de France, Saint-Denis, Paris; Referee: Wolfgang Stark (Germany); Attendance: 79,712
FRA: Hugo Lloris (20/0), Éric-Sylvain Bilal Abidal (52/0), Bacary Sagna (27/0), Philippe Samuel Mexès (20/0), Adil Rami (7/0), Alou Diarra (Cap) (31/0), Florent Yohan Malouda (63/5), Jérémy Ménez (3/0) [69.Loïc Rémy (7/1)], Yoann Miguel Gourcuff (26/3) [86.Yohan Cabaye (2/0)], Yann M'Vila (6/0) [60.Vassiriki Abou Diaby (12/0)], Karim Mostafa Benzema (33/12) [85.Kévin Gameiro (2/0)]. Trainer: Laurent Robert Blanc (7).
Goal: Karim Mostafa Benzema (54).

737. 25.03.2011 **LUXEMBOURG - FRANCE** **0-2(0-1)** 14th EC. Qualifiers
Stade „Josy Barthel", Luxembourg; Referee: Tom Harald Hagen (Norway); Attendance: 8,052
FRA: Hugo Lloris (21/0), Bacary Sagna (28/0), Philippe Samuel Mexès (21/1), Adil Rami (8/0), Patrice Latyr Evra (33/0), Florent Yohan Malouda (64/5), Franck Henry Pierre Ribéry (49/7), Samir Nasri (Cap) (20/2), Yoann Miguel Gourcuff (27/4), Yann M'Vila (7/0), Karim Mostafa Benzema (34/12). Trainer: Laurent Robert Blanc (8).
Goals: Philippe Samuel Mexès (28), Yoann Miguel Gourcuff (72).

738. 29.03.2011 **FRANCE - CROATIA** **0-0**
Stade de France, Saint-Denis, Paris; Referee: Alan Kelly (Republic of Ireland); Attendance: 55,000
FRA: Hugo Lloris (22/0), Anthony Réveillère (10/0), Gaël Clichy (10/0), Philippe Samuel Mexès (22/1), Adil Rami (9/0) [90+4.Mamadou Sakho (2/0)], Alou Diarra (Cap) (32/0), Florent Yohan Malouda (65/5) [59.Franck Henry Pierre Ribéry (50/7)], Blaise Matuidi (2/0) [87.Yann M'Vila (8/0)], Jérémy Ménez (4/0) [60.Loïc Rémy (8/1)], Samir Nasri (21/2) [87.Yoann Miguel Gourcuff (28/4)], Karim Mostafa Benzema (35/12) [75.Kévin Gameiro (3/0)]. Trainer: Laurent Robert Blanc (9).

739. 03.06.2011 **BELARUS - FRANCE** **1-1(1-1)** 14th EC. Qualifiers
Dinamo Stadium, Minsk; Referee: David Fernández Borbalán (Spain); Attendance: 26,500
FRA: Hugo Lloris (23/0), Bacary Sagna (29/0), Éric-Sylvain Bilal Abidal (53/0), Mamadou Sakho (3/0), Adil Rami (10/0), Alou Diarra (Cap) (33/0), Florent Yohan Malouda (66/6), Franck Henry Pierre Ribéry (51/7), Samir Nasri (22/2), Vassiriki Abou Diaby (13/0) [73.Loïc Rémy (9/1)], Karim Mostafa Benzema (36/12). Trainer: Laurent Robert Blanc (10).
Goal: Florent Yohan Malouda (22).

740. 06.06.2011 **UKRAINE - FRANCE** **1-4(0-0)**
Donbass Arena, Donetsk; Referee: Mark Clattenburg (England); Attendance: 15,000
FRA: Stève Mandanda (Cap) (14/0), Anthony Réveillère (11/0), Younès Kaboul (1/1), Mamadou Sakho (4/0) [76.Éric-Sylvain Bilal Abidal (54/0)], Patrice Latyr Evra (34/0), Blaise Matuidi (3/0) [76.Vassiriki Abou Diaby (14/0)], Jérémy Ménez (5/0) [65.Florent Yohan Malouda (67/6)], Yohan Cabaye (3/0) [76.Marvin Martin (1/2)], Yann M'Vila (9/0), Loïc Rémy (10/1) [64.Franck Henry Pierre Ribéry (52/7)], Kévin Gameiro (4/1) [64.Karim Mostafa Benzema (37/12)]. Trainer: Laurent Robert Blanc (11).
Goals: Kévin Gameiro (58), Marvin Martin (87), Younès Kaboul (89), Marvin Martin (90+2).

741. 09.06.2011 **POLAND - FRANCE** **0-1(0-1)**
Pepsi Arena, Warszawa, Paris; Referee: Björn Kuipers (Netherlands); Attendance: 31,000
FRA: Cédric Carrasso (1/0), Bacary Sagna (30/0), Éric-Sylvain Bilal Abidal (Cap) (55/0), Younès Kaboul (2/1) [37.Adil Rami (11/0)], Patrice Latyr Evra (35/0), Alou Diarra (34/0) [46.Vassiriki Abou Diaby (15/0)], Mathieu Valbuena (8/2) [73.Florent Yohan Malouda (68/6)], Yohan Cabaye (4/0) [46.Yann M'Vila (10/0)], Charles N'Zogbia (2/0) [73.Loïc Rémy (11/1)], Marvin Martin (2/2), Guillaume Hoarau (5/0) [78.Kévin Gameiro (5/1)]. Trainer: Laurent Robert Blanc (12).
Goal: Tomasz Jodłowiec (14 own goal).

742. 10.08.2011 **FRANCE - CHILE** **1-1(1-0)**
Stade de la Mosson, Montpellier; Referee: Stuart Steven Attwell (England); Attendance: 30,000
FRA: Hugo Lloris (24/0), Bacary Sagna (31/0) [81.Anthony Réveillère (12/0)], Éric-Sylvain Bilal Abidal (Cap) (56/0), Younès Kaboul (3/1), Gaël Clichy (11/0), Florent Yohan Malouda (69/6) [68.Jérémy Ménez (6/0)], Samir Nasri (23/2) [66.Yohan Cabaye (5/0)], Yann M'Vila (11/0), Marvin Martin (3/2) [77.Blaise Matuidi (4/0)], Karim Mostafa Benzema (38/12) [65.Kévin Gameiro (6/1)], Loïc Rémy (12/2). Trainer: Laurent Robert Blanc (13).
Goal: Loïc Rémy (19).

743. 02.09.2011 **ALBANIA - FRANCE** **1-2(0-2)** 14th EC. Qualifiers
Stadiumi „Kombëtar Qemal Stafa", Tiranë; Referee: Aleksei Nikolaev (Russia); Attendance: 15,600
FRA: Hugo Lloris (25/0), Anthony Réveillère (13/0), Éric-Sylvain Bilal Abidal (57/0), Younès Kaboul (4/1), Patrice Latyr Evra (36/0), Alou Diarra (Cap) (35/0), Florent Yohan Malouda (70/6) [81.Marvin Martin (4/2)], Franck Henry Pierre Ribéry (53/7), Samir Nasri (24/2), Yann M'Vila (12/1), Karim Mostafa Benzema (39/13). Trainer: Laurent Robert Blanc (14).
Goals: Karim Mostafa Benzema (11), Yann M'Vila (18).

744. 06.09.2011 **ROMANIA - FRANCE** **0-0** 14th EC. Qualifiers
Stadionul Naţional, Bucureşti; Referee: Howard Melton Webb (England); Attendance: 49,137
FRA: Hugo Lloris (Cap) (26/0), Bacary Sagna (32/0), Éric-Sylvain Bilal Abidal (58/0), Adil Rami (12/0), Patrice Latyr Evra (37/0), Franck Henry Pierre Ribéry (54/7), Mathieu Valbuena (9/2) [71.Loïc Rémy (13/2)], Yohan Cabaye (6/0) [75.Samir Nasri (25/2)], Yann M'Vila (13/1), Marvin Martin (5/2), Karim Mostafa Benzema (40/13). Trainer: Laurent Robert Blanc (15).

745. 07.10.2011 **FRANCE - ALBANIA** **3-0(2-0)** 14th EC. Qualifiers
Stade de France, Saint-Denis, Paris; Referee: Michael Koukoulakis (Greece); Attendance: 65,239
FRA: Hugo Lloris (Cap) (27/0), Mathieu Debuchy (1/0), Younès Kaboul (5/1), Adil Rami (13/0), Patrice Latyr Evra (38/0) [46.Anthony Réveillère (14/1)], Florent Yohan Malouda (71/7), Samir Nasri (26/2), Yohan Cabaye (7/0) [47.Marvin Martin (6/2)], Yann M'Vila (14/1), Bafétimbi Fredius Gomis (6/2) [80.Djibril Cissé (41/9)], Loïc Rémy (14/3). Trainer: Laurent Robert Blanc (16).
Goals: Florent Yohan Malouda (11), Loïc Rémy (37), Anthony Réveillère (66).

746. 11.10.2011 **FRANCE – BOSNIA AND HERZEGOVINA** **1-1(0-1)** 14th EC. Qualifiers
Stade de France, Saint-Denis, Paris; Referee: Craig Alexander Thomson (Scotland); Attendance: 78,467
FRA: Hugo Lloris (Cap) (28/0), Anthony Réveillère (15/1), Éric-Sylvain Bilal Abidal (59/0), Adil Rami (14/0), Patrice Latyr Evra (39/0), Florent Yohan Malouda (72/7) [61.Marvin Martin (7/2)], Jérémy Ménez (7/0), Samir Nasri (27/3), Yohan Cabaye (8/0) [61.Kévin Gameiro (7/1)], Yann M'Vila (15/1), Loïc Rémy (15/3) [82.Alou Diarra (36/0)]. Trainer: Laurent Robert Blanc (17).
Goal: Samir Nasri (78 penalty).

747. 11.11.2011 **FRANCE – UNITED STATES** **1-0(0-0)**
Stade de France, Saint-Denis, Paris; Referee: Michael Koukoulakis (Greece); Attendance: 70,018
FRA: Hugo Lloris (Cap) (29/0), Mathieu Debuchy (2/0), Jérémy Mathieu (1/0), Adil Rami (15/0), Laurent Koscielny (1/0), Alou Diarra (37/0), Franck Henry Pierre Ribéry (55/7) [64.Loïc Rémy (16/4)], Jérémy Ménez (8/0), Yann M'Vila (16/1) [59.Maxime Gonalons (1/0)], Karim Mostafa Benzema (41/13) [64.Marvin Martin (8/2)], Kévin Gameiro (8/1) [59.Olivier Giroud (1/0)]. Trainer: Laurent Robert Blanc (18).
Goal: Loïc Rémy (74).

748. 15.11.2011 **FRANCE - BELGIUM** **0-0**
Stade de France, Saint-Denis, Paris; Referee: César Muñiz Fernández (Spain); Attendance: 52,825
FRA: Hugo Lloris (Cap) (30/0), Anthony Réveillère (16/1), Éric-Sylvain Bilal Abidal (60/0), Mamadou Sakho (5/0), Adil Rami (16/0), Franck Henry Pierre Ribéry (56/7) [72.Florent Yohan Malouda (73/7)], Yohan Cabaye (9/0), Yann M'Vila (17/1) [42.Maxime Gonalons (2/0)], Marvin Martin (9/2), Karim Mostafa Benzema (42/13) [72.Jérémy Ménez (9/0)], Loïc Rémy (17/4) [72.Olivier Giroud (2/0)]. Trainer: Laurent Robert Blanc (19).

749. 29.02.2012 **GERMANY - FRANCE** **1-2(0-1)**
Weserstadion, Bremen; Referee: Paolo Tagliavento (Italy); Attendance: 37,800
FRA: Hugo Lloris (Cap) (31/0), Mathieu Debuchy (3/0), Éric-Sylvain Bilal Abidal (61/0), Philippe Samuel Mexès (23/1), Adil Rami (17/0), Franck Henry Pierre Ribéry (57/7) [46.Jérémy Ménez (10/0)], Mathieu Valbuena (10/2) [68.Morgan Amalfitano (1/0)], Samir Nasri (28/3), Yohan Cabaye (10/0) [62.Alou Diarra (38/0)], Yann M'Vila (18/1) [62.Florent Yohan Malouda (74/8)], Olivier Giroud (3/1) [76.Louis Laurent Saha (20/4)]. Trainer: Laurent Robert Blanc (20).
Goals: Olivier Giroud (21), Florent Yohan Malouda (69).

750. 27.05.2012 **FRANCE - ICELAND** **3-2(0-2)**
Stade du Hainaut, Valenciennes; Referee: Sébastien Delferière (Belgium); Attendance: 24,000
FRA: Stève Mandanda (15/0), Mathieu Debuchy (4/1), Philippe Samuel Mexès (Cap) (24/1), Adil Rami (18/1), Patrice Latyr Evra (40/0), Jérémy Ménez (11/0) [75.Mathieu Valbuena (11/2)], Samir Nasri (29/3) [60.Marvin Martin (10/2)], Hatem Ben Arfa (9/2) [59.Olivier Giroud (4/1)], Yohan Cabaye (11/0) [59.Alou Diarra (39/0)], Yoann Miguel Gourcuff (29/4) [75.Franck Henry Pierre Ribéry (58/8)], Karim Mostafa Benzema (43/13) [60.Florent Yohan Malouda (75/8)]. Trainer: Laurent Robert Blanc (21).
Goals: Mathieu Debuchy (52), Franck Henry Pierre Ribéry (84), Adil Rami (87).

751. 31.05.2012 **FRANCE - SERBIA** **2-0(2-0)**
Stade "Auguste-Delaune II", Reims; Referee: Knut Kircher (Germany); Attendance: 19,000
FRA: Hugo Lloris (Cap) (32/0), Anthony Réveillère (17/1), Gaël Clichy (12/0), Philippe Samuel Mexès (25/1) [72.Adil Rami (19/1)], Laurent Koscielny (2/0), Florent Yohan Malouda (76/9) [76.Hatem Ben Arfa (10/2)], Franck Henry Pierre Ribéry (59/9) [61.Jérémy Ménez (12/0)], Samir Nasri (30/3), Yohan Cabaye (12/0) [60.Marvin Martin (11/2)], Yann M'Vila (19/1) [7.Alou Diarra (40/0)], Karim Mostafa Benzema (44/13) [61.Olivier Giroud (5/1)]. Trainer: Laurent Robert Blanc (22).
Goals: Franck Henry Pierre Ribéry (11), Florent Yohan Malouda (16).

752. 05.06.2012 **FRANCE - ESTONIA** **4-0(2-0)**
MMArena, Le Mans; Referee: Liran Liany (Israel); Attendance:
FRA: Hugo Lloris (Cap) (33/0), Mathieu Debuchy (5/1), Philippe Samuel Mexès (26/1), Adil Rami (20/1), Patrice Latyr Evra (41/0), Alou Diarra (41/0) [65.Laurent Koscielny (3/0)], Florent Yohan Malouda (77/9) [73.Olivier Giroud (6/1)], Franck Henry Pierre Ribéry (60/10) [65.Marvin Martin (12/2)], Samir Nasri (31/3) [73.Hatem Ben Arfa (11/2)], Yohan Cabaye (13/0) [51.Mathieu Valbuena (12/2)], Karim Mostafa Benzema (45/15) [73.Jérémy Ménez (13/1)]. Trainer: Laurent Robert Blanc (23).
Goals: Franck Henry Pierre Ribéry (26), Karim Mostafa Benzema (36, 47), Jérémy Ménez (90).

753. 11.06.2012 **FRANCE - ENGLAND** **1-1(1-1)** 14th EC. Group Stage.
Donbass Arena, Donetsk (Ukraine); Referee: Nicola Rizzoli (Italy); Attendance: 47,400
FRA: Hugo Lloris (Cap) (34/0), Mathieu Debuchy (6/1), Philippe Samuel Mexès (27/1), Adil Rami (21/1), Patrice Latyr Evra (42/0), Alou Diarra (42/0), Florent Yohan Malouda (78/9) [85.Marvin Martin (13/2)], Franck Henry Pierre Ribéry (61/10), Samir Nasri (32/4), Yohan Cabaye (14/0) [84.Hatem Ben Arfa (12/2)], Karim Mostafa Benzema (46/15). Trainer: Laurent Robert Blanc (24).
Goal: Samir Nasri (39).

754. 15.06.2012 **UKRAINE - FRANCE** **0-2(0-0)** 14th EC. Group Stage.
Donbass Arena, Donetsk; Referee: Björn Kuipers (Netherlands); Attendance: 48,000
FRA: Hugo Lloris (Cap) (35/0), Mathieu Debuchy (7/1), Gaël Clichy (13/0), Philippe Samuel Mexès (28/1), Adil Rami (22/1), Alou Diarra (43/0), Franck Henry Pierre Ribéry (62/10), Jérémy Ménez (14/2) [73.Marvin Martin (14/2)], Samir Nasri (33/4), Yohan Cabaye (15/1) [68.Yann M'Vila (20/1)], Karim Mostafa Benzema (47/15) [76.Olivier Giroud (7/1)]. Trainer: Laurent Robert Blanc (25).
Goals: Jérémy Ménez (53), Yohan Cabaye (56).

755. 19.06.2012 **SWEDEN - FRANCE** **2-0(0-0)** 14th EC. Group Stage.
Olimpiyskiy Stadium, Kyiv (Ukraine); Referee: Pedro Proença Oliveira Alves Garcia (Portugal); Attendance: 63,010
FRA: Hugo Lloris (Cap) (36/0), Mathieu Debuchy (8/1), Gaël Clichy (14/0), Philippe Samuel Mexès (29/1), Adil Rami (23/1), Alou Diarra (44/0), Franck Henry Pierre Ribéry (63/10), Samir Nasri (34/4) [77.Jérémy Ménez (15/2)], Hatem Ben Arfa (13/2) [59.Florent Yohan Malouda (79/9)], Yann M'Vila (21/1) [83.Olivier Giroud (8/1)], Karim Mostafa Benzema (48/15). Trainer: Laurent Robert Blanc (26).

756. 23.06.2012 **SPAIN - FRANCE** **2-0(1-0)** 14th EC. Quarter-Finals.
Donbass Arena, Donetsk (Ukraine); Referee: Nicola Rizzoli (Italy); Attendance: 47,000
FRA: Hugo Lloris (Cap) (37/0), Anthony Réveillère (18/1), Mathieu Debuchy (9/1) [64.Jérémy Ménez (16/2)], Gaël Clichy (15/0), Adil Rami (24/1), Laurent Koscielny (4/0), Florent Yohan Malouda (80/9) [65.Samir Nasri (35/4)], Franck Henry Pierre Ribéry (64/10), Yohan Cabaye (16/1), Yann M'Vila (22/1) [79.Olivier Giroud (9/1)], Karim Mostafa Benzema (49/15). Trainer: Laurent Robert Blanc (27).

757. 15.08.2012 **FRANCE - URUGUAY** **0-0**
Stade Océane, Le Havre; Referee: Daniele Orsato (Italy); Attendance: 25,000
FRA: Hugo Lloris (Cap) (38/0), Mathieu Debuchy (10/1) [28.Christophe Jallet (1/0)], Mamadou Sakho (6/0), Mapou Yanga-Mbiwa (1/0), Patrice Latyr Evra (43/0), Franck Henry Pierre Ribéry (65/10), Rio Antonio Zoba Mavuba (7/0) [46.Étienne Capoue (1/0)], Mathieu Valbuena (13/2) [75.Jimmy Briand (5/0)], Maxime Gonalons (3/0), Karim Mostafa Benzema (50/15) [63.Marvin Martin (15/2)], Olivier Giroud (10/1) [75.Bafétimbi Fredius Gomis (7/2)]. Trainer: Didier Claude Deschamps (1).

758. 07.09.2012 **FINLAND - FRANCE** **0-1(0-1)** 20th FIFA WC. Qualifiers
Olympiastadion, Helsinki; Referee: Craig Alexander Thomson (Scotland); Attendance: 35,111
FRA: Hugo Lloris (Cap) (39/0), Anthony Réveillère (19/1), Mamadou Sakho (7/0), Mapou Yanga-Mbiwa (2/0), Patrice Latyr Evra (44/0), Franck Henry Pierre Ribéry (66/10) [89.Bafétimbi Fredius Gomis (8/2)], Rio Antonio Zoba Mavuba (8/0), Jérémy Ménez (17/2) [62.Mathieu Valbuena (14/2)], Yohan Cabaye (17/1) [72.Blaise Matuidi (5/0)], Vassiriki Abou Diaby (16/1), Karim Mostafa Benzema (51/15). Trainer: Didier Claude Deschamps (2).
Goal: Vassiriki Abou Diaby (20).

759. 11.09.2012 **FRANCE - BELARUS** **3-1(0-0)** 20th FIFA WC. Qualifiers
Stade de France, Saint-Denis, Paris; Referee: Hüseyin Göçek (Turkey); Attendance: 52,552
FRA: Hugo Lloris (Cap) (40/0), Christophe Jallet (2/1), Mamadou Sakho (8/0), Mapou Yanga-Mbiwa (3/0), Patrice Latyr Evra (45/0), Franck Henry Pierre Ribéry (67/11) [90+1.Jérémy Ménez (18/2)], Rio Antonio Zoba Mavuba (9/0), Yohan Cabaye (18/1) [75.Blaise Matuidi (6/0)], Étienne Capoue (2/1), Karim Mostafa Benzema (52/15), Olivier Giroud (11/1) [61.Mathieu Valbuena (15/2)]. Trainer: Didier Claude Deschamps (3).
Goals: Étienne Capoue (49), Christophe Jallet (68), Franck Henry Pierre Ribéry (80).

760. 12.10.2012 **FRANCE - JAPAN** **0-1(0-0)**
Stade de France, Saint-Denis, Paris; Referee: William Collum (Scotland); Attendance: 60,205
FRA: Hugo Lloris (Cap) (41/0), Mathieu Debuchy (11/1) [46.Christophe Jallet (3/1)], Gaël Clichy (16/0), Mamadou Sakho (9/0), Laurent Koscielny (5/0), Blaise Matuidi (7/0) [46.Clément Chantôme (1/0); 75.Bafétimbi Fredius Gomis (9/2)], Jérémy Ménez (19/2) [67.Franck Henry Pierre Ribéry (68/11)], Moussa Sissoko (4/0), Étienne Capoue (3/1) [67.Maxime Gonalons (4/0)], Karim Mostafa Benzema (53/15) [46.Mathieu Valbuena (16/2)], Olivier Giroud (12/1). Trainer: Didier Claude Deschamps (4).

761. 16.10.2012 **SPAIN - FRANCE** **1-1(1-0)** 20th FIFA WC. Qualifiers
Estadio "Vicente Calderón", Madrid; Referee: Dr. Felix Brych (Germany); Attendance: 46,825
FRA: Hugo Lloris (Cap) (42/0), Mathieu Debuchy (12/1), Mamadou Sakho (10/0), Laurent Koscielny (6/0), Patrice Latyr Evra (46/0), Franck Henry Pierre Ribéry (69/11), Blaise Matuidi (8/0), Jérémy Ménez (20/2) [68.Moussa Sissoko (5/0)], Yohan Cabaye (19/1), Maxime Gonalons (5/0) [57.Mathieu Valbuena (17/2)], Karim Mostafa Benzema (54/15) [88.Olivier Giroud (13/2)]. Trainer: Didier Claude Deschamps (5).
Goal: Olivier Giroud (90+4).

762. 14.11.2012 **ITALY - FRANCE** **1-2(1-1)**
Stadio "Ennio Tardini", Parma; Referee: Alberto Undiano Mallenco (Spain); Attendance: 20,000
FRA: Hugo Lloris (Cap) (43/0), Mathieu Debuchy (13/1) [56.Anthony Réveillère (20/1)], Mamadou Sakho (11/0), Laurent Koscielny (7/0), Patrice Latyr Evra (47/0), Franck Henry Pierre Ribéry (70/11) [63.Jérémy Ménez (21/2)], Blaise Matuidi (9/0), Mathieu Valbuena (18/3) [72.Yoann Miguel Gourcuff (30/4)], Moussa Sissoko (6/0) [90+1.Benoît Trémoulinas (1/0)], Étienne Capoue (4/1) [83.Maxime Gonalons (6/0)], Olivier Giroud (14/2) [63.Bafétimbi Fredius Gomis (10/3)]. Trainer: Didier Claude Deschamps (6).
Goals: Mathieu Valbuena (37), Bafétimbi Fredius Gomis (67).

763. 06.02.2013 **FRANCE - GERMANY** **1-2(1-0)**
Stade de France, Saint-Denis, Paris; Referee: Paolo Mazzoleni (Italy); Attendance: 75,000
FRA: Hugo Lloris (Cap) (44/0), Bacary Sagna (33/0), Mamadou Sakho (12/0), Laurent Koscielny (8/0) [46.Adil Rami (25/1)], Patrice Latyr Evra (48/0), Franck Henry Pierre Ribéry (71/11), Blaise Matuidi (10/0) [46.Étienne Capoue (5/1)], Mathieu Valbuena (19/4) [86.Jérémy Ménez (22/2)], Yohan Cabaye (20/1), Moussa Sissoko (7/0) [80.Olivier Giroud (15/2)], Karim Mostafa Benzema (55/15). Trainer: Didier Claude Deschamps (7).
Goal: Mathieu Valbuena (44).

764. 22.03.2013 **FRANCE - GEORGIA** **3-1(1-0)** 20th FIFA WC. Qualifiers
Stade de France, Saint-Denis, Paris; Referee: Ivan Bebek (Croatia); Attendance: 71,147
FRA: Hugo Lloris (Cap) (45/0), Christophe Jallet (4/1), Gaël Clichy (17/0), Mamadou Sakho (13/0), Raphaël Varane (1/0), Franck Henry Pierre Ribéry (72/12) [78.Jérémy Ménez (23/2)], Blaise Matuidi (11/0) [81.Moussa Sissoko (8/0)], Mathieu Valbuena (20/5) [66.Loïc Rémy (18/4)], Paul Labile Pogba (1/0), Karim Mostafa Benzema (56/15), Olivier Giroud (16/3). Trainer: Didier Claude Deschamps (8).
Goals: Olivier Giroud (45+1), Mathieu Valbuena (47), Franck Henry Pierre Ribéry (61).

765. 26.03.2013 **FRANCE - SPAIN** **0-1(0-0)** 20th FIFA WC. Qualifiers
Stade de France, Saint-Denis, Paris; Referee: Viktor Kassai (Hungary); Attendance: 78,329
FRA: Hugo Lloris (Cap) (46/0), Christophe Jallet (5/1) [90+2.Olivier Giroud (17/3)], Laurent Koscielny (9/0), Raphaël Varane (2/0), Patrice Latyr Evra (49/0), Franck Henry Pierre Ribéry (73/12), Blaise Matuidi (12/0), Mathieu Valbuena (21/5), Yohan Cabaye (21/1) [70.Jérémy Ménez (24/2)], Paul Labile Pogba (2/0) [*sent off 78*], Karim Mostafa Benzema (57/15) [82.Moussa Sissoko (9/0)]. Trainer: Didier Claude Deschamps (9).

766. 05.06.2013 **URUGUAY - FRANCE** **1-0(0-0)**
Estadio Centenario, Montevideo; Referee: Julio César Quintana (Paraguay); Attendance: 35,000
FRA: Stève Mandanda (16/0), Bacary Sagna (34/0), Benoît Trémoulinas (2/0), Laurent Koscielny (10/0), Eliaquim Hans Mangala (1/0), Blaise Matuidi (13/0) [76.Yohan Cabaye (22/1)], Mathieu Valbuena (22/5) [67.Clément Grenier (1/0)], Yoann Miguel Gourcuff (31/4) [58.Alexandre Lacazette (1/0)], Étienne Capoue (6/1) [67.Josuha Guilavogui (1/0)], Florent Dimitri Payet (4/0), Olivier Giroud (18/3) [58.Bafétimbi Fredius Gomis (11/3)]. Trainer: Didier Claude Deschamps (10).

767. 09.06.2013 **BRAZIL - FRANCE** **3-0(0-0)**
Arena do Grêmio, Porto Alegre; Referee: Víctor Hugo Carrillo Casanova (Peru); Attendance: 51,919
FRA: Hugo Lloris (Cap) (47/0), Mathieu Debuchy (14/1), Jérémy Mathieu (2/0), Mamadou Sakho (14/0), Adil Rami (26/1), Blaise Matuidi (14/0) [70.Clément Grenier (2/0)], Mathieu Valbuena (23/5) [70.Alexandre Lacazette (2/0)], Yohan Cabaye (23/1) [82.Bafétimbi Fredius Gomis (12/3)], Josuha Guilavogui (2/0), Florent Dimitri Payet (5/0), Karim Mostafa Benzema (58/15) [70.Olivier Giroud (19/3)]. Trainer: Didier Claude Deschamps (11).

768. 14.08.2013 **BELGIUM - FRANCE** **0-0**
Stade „Roi Baudouin", Bruxelles; Referee: Craig Alexander Thomson (Scotland); Attendance: 45,000
FRA: Hugo Lloris (Cap) (48/0), Bacary Sagna (35/0), Éric-Sylvain Bilal Abidal (62/0), Gaël Clichy (18/0), Laurent Koscielny (11/0), Franck Henry Pierre Ribéry (74/12), Mathieu Valbuena (24/5) [74.Clément Grenier (3/0)], Josuha Guilavogui (3/0), Geoffrey Kondogbia (1/0) [63.Étienne Capoue (7/1)], Florent Dimitri Payet (6/0) [63.Samir Nasri (36/4)], Karim Mostafa Benzema (59/15) [74.Olivier Giroud (20/3)]. Trainer: Didier Claude Deschamps (12).

769. 06.09.2013 **GEORGIA - FRANCE** **0-0** 20th FIFA WC. Qualifiers
Dinamo Arena, Tbilisi; Referee: Fırat Aydınus (Turkey); Attendance: 26,360
FRA: Hugo Lloris (Cap) (49/0), Éric-Sylvain Bilal Abidal (63/0), Bacary Sagna (36/0), Laurent Koscielny (12/0), Patrice Latyr Evra (50/0), Franck Henry Pierre Ribéry (75/12), Mathieu Valbuena (25/5), Moussa Sissoko (10/0), Josuha Guilavogui (4/0) [78.Samir Nasri (37/4)], Karim Mostafa Benzema (60/15) [62.André-Pierre Gignac (17/4)], Olivier Giroud (21/3). Trainer: Didier Claude Deschamps (13).

770. 10.09.2013 **BELARUS - FRANCE** **2-4(1-0)** 20th FIFA WC. Qualifiers
Central Stadium, Gomel; Referee: Daniele Orsato (Italy); Attendance: 12,203
FRA: Hugo Lloris (Cap) (50/0), Bacary Sagna (37/0), Éric-Sylvain Bilal Abidal (64/0), Gaël Clichy (19/0), Laurent Koscielny (13/0), Franck Henry Pierre Ribéry (76/14) [80.Moussa Sissoko (11/0)], Blaise Matuidi (15/0), Mathieu Valbuena (26/5) [90+3.Josuha Guilavogui (5/0)], Paul Labile Pogba (3/1), Florent Dimitri Payet (7/0) [61.Samir Nasri (38/5)], Olivier Giroud (22/3). Trainer: Didier Claude Deschamps (14).
Goals: Franck Henry Pierre Ribéry (47 penalty, 64), Samir Nasri (71), Paul Labile Pogba (73).

771. 11.10.2013 **FRANCE - AUSTRALIA** **6-0(4-0)**
Stade "Parc des Princes", Paris; Referee: Artur Manuel Ribeiro Soares Dias (Portugal); Attendance: 38,000
FRA: Hugo Lloris (Cap) (51/0), Mathieu Debuchy (15/2), Éric-Sylvain Bilal Abidal (65/0) [46.Mamadou Sakho (15/0)], Raphaël Varane (3/0), Patrice Latyr Evra (51/0) [64.Gaël Clichy (20/0)], Franck Henry Pierre Ribéry (77/15) [63.Mathieu Valbuena (27/5)], Samir Nasri (39/5), Yohan Cabaye (24/2) [82.Moussa Sissoko (12/0)], Paul Labile Pogba (4/1) [63.Blaise Matuidi (16/0)], Loïc Rémy (19/4), Olivier Giroud (23/5) [46.Karim Mostafa Benzema (61/16)]. Trainer: Didier Claude Deschamps (15).
Goals: Franck Henry Pierre Ribéry (8 penalty), Olivier Giroud (16, 27), Yohan Cabaye (29), Mathieu Debuchy (47), Karim Mostafa Benzema (50).

772. 15.10.2013 **FRANCE - FINLAND** **3-0(1-0)** 20th FIFA WC. Qualifiers
Stade de France, Saint-Denis, Paris; Referee: Michael Koukoulakis (Greece); Attendance: 70,156
FRA: Hugo Lloris (Cap) (52/0), Éric-Sylvain Bilal Abidal (66/0), Mathieu Debuchy (16/2), Laurent Koscielny (14/0), Patrice Latyr Evra (52/0), Blaise Matuidi (17/0) [70.Yohan Cabaye (25/2)], Mathieu Valbuena (28/5), Samir Nasri (40/5) [71.Loïc Rémy (20/4)], Paul Labile Pogba (5/1), Franck Henry Pierre Ribéry (78/16), Olivier Giroud (24/5) [81.Karim Mostafa Benzema (62/17)]. Trainer: Didier Claude Deschamps (16).
Goals: Franck Henry Pierre Ribéry (8), Joona Toivio (75 own goal), Karim Mostafa Benzema (87).

773. 15.11.2013 **UKRAINE - FRANCE** **2-0(0-0)** 20th FIFA WC. Qualifiers (Play-offs)
Olympiyskiy Stadium, Kyiv; Referee: Cüneyt Çakır (Turkey); Attendance: 67,732
FRA: Hugo Lloris (Cap) (53/0), Éric-Sylvain Bilal Abidal (67/0), Mathieu Debuchy (17/2), Laurent Koscielny (15/0) [*sent off 90+1*], Patrice Latyr Evra (53/0), Blaise Matuidi (18/0), Samir Nasri (41/5) [80.Mathieu Valbuena (29/5)], Paul Labile Pogba (6/1), Franck Henry Pierre Ribéry (79/16), Loïc Rémy (21/4) [62.Moussa Sissoko (13/0)], Olivier Giroud (25/5) [70.Karim Mostafa Benzema (63/17)]. Trainer: Didier Claude Deschamps (17).

774. 19.11.2013 **FRANCE - UKRAINE** **3-0(2-0)** 20th FIFA WC. Qualifiers (Play-offs)
Stade de France, Saint-Denis, Paris; Referee: Damir Skomina (Slovenia); Attendance: 77,098
FRA: Hugo Lloris (Cap) (54/0), Mathieu Debuchy (18/2) [78.Bacary Sagna (38/0)], Mamadou Sakho (16/2), Raphaël Varane (4/0), Patrice Latyr Evra (54/0), Blaise Matuidi (19/0), Mathieu Valbuena (30/5), Yohan Cabaye (26/2), Franck Henry Pierre Ribéry (80/16), Paul Labile Pogba (7/1), Karim Mostafa Benzema (64/18) [82.Olivier Giroud (26/5)]. Trainer: Didier Claude Deschamps (18).
Goals: Mamadou Sakho (22), Karim Mostafa Benzema (34), Mamadou Sakho (72).

775. 05.03.2014 **FRANCE - NETHERLANDS** **2-0(2-0)**
Stade de France, Saint-Denis, Paris; Referee: Martin Atkinson (England); Attendance: 80,000
FRA: Hugo Lloris (Cap) (55/0), Mathieu Debuchy (19/2) [81.Bacary Sagna (39/0)], Eliaquim Hans Mangala (2/0), Raphaël Varane (5/0), Patrice Latyr Evra (55/0) [46.Lucas Digne (1/0)], Blaise Matuidi (20/1), Mathieu Valbuena (31/5) [63.Franck Henry Pierre Ribéry (81/16)], Yohan Cabaye (27/2), Paul Labile Pogba (8/1) [81.Moussa Sissoko (14/0)], Karim Mostafa Benzema (65/19) [81.Olivier Giroud (27/5)], Antoine Griezmann (1/0) [68.Loïc Rémy (22/4)]. Trainer: Didier Claude Deschamps (19).
Goals: Karim Mostafa Benzema (32), Blaise Matuidi (41).

776. 27.05.2014 **FRANCE - NORWAY** **4-0(1-0)**
Stade de France, Saint-Denis, Paris; Referee: Padraigh Sutton (Republic of Ireland); Attendance: 70,000
FRA: Stéphane Ruffier (2/0), Mathieu Debuchy (20/2), Mamadou Sakho (Cap) (17/2), Laurent Koscielny (16/0), Patrice Latyr Evra (56/0) [46.Lucas Digne (2/0)], Blaise Matuidi (21/1) [74.Rio Antonio Zoba Mavuba (10/0)], Mathieu Valbuena (32/5) [70.Clément Grenier (4/0)], Yohan Cabaye (28/2) [80.Rémy Cabella (1/0)], Paul Labile Pogba (9/2) [46.Moussa Sissoko (15/0)], Olivier Giroud (28/7), Antoine Griezmann (2/0) [65.Loïc Rémy (23/5)]. Trainer: Didier Claude Deschamps (20).
Goals: Paul Labile Pogba (15), Olivier Giroud (51), Loïc Rémy (67), Olivier Giroud (69).

777. 01.06.2014 **FRANCE - PARAGUAY** **1-1(0-0)**
Stade Allianz Riviera, Nice; Referee: Carlos Clos Gómez (Spain); Attendance: 35,200
FRA: Hugo Lloris (Cap) (56/0), Bacary Sagna (40/0), Mamadou Sakho (18/2) [46.Eliaquim Hans Mangala (3/0)], Laurent Koscielny (17/0), Patrice Latyr Evra (57/0), Blaise Matuidi (22/1) [64.Clément Grenier (5/0)], Mathieu Valbuena (33/5) [72.Moussa Sissoko (16/0)], Yohan Cabaye (29/2) [46.Rio Antonio Zoba Mavuba (11/0)], Paul Labile Pogba (10/2), Loïc Rémy (24/5) [64.Antoine Griezmann (3/1)], Olivier Giroud (29/7). Trainer: Didier Claude Deschamps (21).
Goal: Antoine Griezmann (82).

778. 08.06.2014 **FRANCE - JAMAICA** **8-0(3-0)**
Stade "Pierre Mauroy", Villeneuve-d'Ascq; Referee: Felix Zwayer (Germany); Attendance: 49,600
FRA: Hugo Lloris (Cap) (57/0), Mathieu Debuchy (21/2) [46.Bacary Sagna (41/0)], Mamadou Sakho (19/2), Raphaël Varane (6/0), Patrice Latyr Evra (58/0), Blaise Matuidi (23/3) [72.Paul Labile Pogba (11/2)], Mathieu Valbuena (34/5) [80.Loïc Rémy (25/5)], Yohan Cabaye (30/3) [59.Rio Antonio Zoba Mavuba (12/0)], Moussa Sissoko (17/0), Karim Mostafa Benzema (66/21) [86.Morgan Schneiderlin (1/0)], Olivier Giroud (30/8) [71.Antoine Griezmann (4/3)]. Trainer: Didier Claude Deschamps (22).
Goals: Yohan Cabaye (17), Blaise Matuidi (20), Karim Mostafa Benzema (38), Olivier Giroud (53), Karim Mostafa Benzema (63), Blaise Matuidi (66), Antoine Griezmann (77, 89).

779. 15.06.2014 **FRANCE - HONDURAS** **3-0(1-0)** 20th FIFA WC. Group Stage.
Estádio Beira-Rio, Porto Alegre (Brazil); Referee: Sandro Meira Ricci (Brazil); Attendance: 43,012
FRA: Hugo Lloris (Cap) (58/0), Mathieu Debuchy (22/2), Mamadou Sakho (20/2), Raphaël Varane (7/0), Blaise Matuidi (24/3), Patrice Latyr Evra (59/0), Mathieu Valbuena (35/5) [78.Olivier Giroud (31/8)], Yohan Cabaye (31/3) [65.Rio Antonio Zoba Mavuba (13/0)], Paul Labile Pogba (12/2) [57.Moussa Sissoko (18/0)], Karim Mostafa Benzema (67/23), Antoine Griezmann (5/3). Trainer: Didier Claude Deschamps (23).
Goals: Karim Mostafa Benzema (45 penalty), Noel Eduardo Valladares Bonilla (48 own goal), Karim Mostafa Benzema (72).

780. 20.06.2014 **SWITZERLAND – FRANCE** **2-5(0-3)** 20th FIFA WC. Group Stage.
Arena Fonte Nova, Salvador; Referee: Björn Kuipers (Netherlands); Attendance: 51,003
FRA: Hugo Lloris (Cap) (59/0), Mathieu Debuchy (23/2), Mamadou Sakho (21/2) [66.Laurent Koscielny (18/0)], Raphaël Varane (8/0), Patrice Latyr Evra (60/0), Blaise Matuidi (25/4), Mathieu Valbuena (36/6) [82.Antoine Griezmann (6/3)], Yohan Cabaye (32/3), Moussa Sissoko (19/1), Karim Mostafa Benzema (68/24), Olivier Giroud (32/9) [63.Paul Labile Pogba (13/2)]. Trainer: Didier Claude Deschamps (24).
Goals: Olivier Giroud (17), Blaise Matuidi (18), Mathieu Valbuena (40), Karim Mostafa Benzema (67), Moussa Sissoko (73).

781. 25.06.2014 **ECUADOR - FRANCE** **0-0** 20th FIFA WC. Group Stage.
Estádio „Jornalista Mário Filho“ [Maracanã], Rio de Janeiro; Referee: Noumandiez Doué (Côte d'Ivoire); Attendance: 73,749
FRA: Hugo Lloris (Cap) (60/0), Bacary Sagna (42/0), Mamadou Sakho (22/2) [61.Raphaël Varane (9/0)], Laurent Koscielny (19/0), Lucas Digne (3/0), Blaise Matuidi (26/4) [67.Olivier Giroud (33/9)], Moussa Sissoko (20/1), Morgan Schneiderlin (2/0), Paul Labile Pogba (14/2), Karim Mostafa Benzema (69/24), Antoine Griezmann (7/3) [79.Loïc Rémy (26/5)]. Trainer: Didier Claude Deschamps (25).

782. 30.06.2014 **FRANCE - NIGERIA** **2-0(0-0)** 20th FIFA WC. 2nd Round of 16.
Estádio Nacional „Mané Garrincha“, Brasília; Referee: Mark Geiger (United States); Attendance: 67,882
FRA: Hugo Lloris (Cap) (61/0), Mathieu Debuchy (24/2), Laurent Koscielny (20/0), Raphaël Varane (10/0), Patrice Latyr Evra (61/0), Blaise Matuidi (27/4), Mathieu Valbuena (37/6) [90+4.Moussa Sissoko (21/1)], Yohan Cabaye (33/3), Paul Labile Pogba (15/3), Karim Mostafa Benzema (70/24), Olivier Giroud (34/9) [62.Antoine Griezmann (8/3)]. Trainer: Didier Claude Deschamps (26).
Goals: Paul Labile Pogba (79), Joseph Ikpo Yobo (90+1 own goal).

783. 04.07.2014 **FRANCE - GERMANY** **0-1(0-1)** 20th FIFA WC. Quarter-Finals.
Estádio „Jornalista Mário Filho“ [Maracanã], Rio de Janeiro; Referee: Néstor Fabián Pitana (Argentina); Attendance: 74,240
FRA: Hugo Lloris (Cap) (62/0), Mathieu Debuchy (25/2), Mamadou Sakho (23/2) [72.Laurent Koscielny (21/0)], Raphaël Varane (11/0), Patrice Latyr Evra (62/0), Blaise Matuidi (28/4), Mathieu Valbuena (38/6) [85.Olivier Giroud (35/9)], Yohan Cabaye (34/3) [73.Loïc Rémy (27/5)], Paul Labile Pogba (16/3), Karim Mostafa Benzema (71/24), Antoine Griezmann (9/3). Trainer: Didier Claude Deschamps (27).

784. 04.09.2014 **FRANCE - SPAIN** **1-0(0-0)**
Stade de France, Saint-Denis, Paris; Referee: Alain Bieri (Switzerland); Attendance: 80,000
FRA: Hugo Lloris (Cap) (63/0), Mathieu Debuchy (26/2), Mamadou Sakho (24/2), Raphaël Varane (12/0), Patrice Latyr Evra (63/0) [68.Lucas Digne (4/0)], Blaise Matuidi (29/4) [68.Yohan Cabaye (35/3)], Mathieu Valbuena (39/6) [75.Rémy Cabella (2/0)], Moussa Sissoko (22/1) [78.Morgan Schneiderlin (3/0)], Paul Labile Pogba (17/3), Karim Mostafa Benzema (72/24), Antoine Griezmann (10/3) [58.Loïc Rémy (28/6)]. Trainer: Didier Claude Deschamps (28).
Goal: Loïc Rémy (73).

785. 07.09.2014 **FRANCE - SERBIA** **1-1(0-1)**
Stadion Partizana, Beograd; Referee: Wolfgang Stark (Germany); Attendance: 12,000
FRA: Hugo Lloris (Cap) (64/0), Jérémy Mathieu (3/0), Bacary Sagna (43/0), Lucas Digne (5/0), Raphaël Varane (13/0), Yohan Cabaye (36/3), Moussa Sissoko (23/1) [82.Mathieu Valbuena (40/6)], Morgan Schneiderlin (4/0), Rémy Cabella (3/0) [60.Alexandre Lacazette (3/0)], Paul Labile Pogba (18/4) [74.Blaise Matuidi (30/4)], Loïc Rémy (29/6) [60.Karim Mostafa Benzema (73/24)]. Trainer: Didier Claude Deschamps (29).
Goal: Paul Labile Pogba (13).

786. 11.10.2014 **FRANCE - PORTUGAL** **2-1(1-0)**
Stade de France, Saint-Denis, Paris; Referee: Szymon Marciniak (Poland); Attendance: 79,000
FRA: Stève Mandanda (17/0), Bacary Sagna (44/0), Eliaquim Hans Mangala (4/0), Raphaël Varane (14/0), Patrice Latyr Evra (64/0), Blaise Matuidi (Cap) (31/4), Mathieu Valbuena (41/6) [58.Florent Dimitri Payet (8/0)], Yohan Cabaye (37/3) [71.Moussa Sissoko (24/1)], Paul Labile Pogba (19/5), Karim Mostafa Benzema (74/25) [90.André-Pierre Gignac (18/4)], Antoine Griezmann (11/3) [84.Morgan Schneiderlin (5/0)]. Trainer: Didier Claude Deschamps (30).
Goals: Karim Mostafa Benzema (3), Paul Labile Pogba (69).

787. 14.10.2014 **ARMENIA - FRANCE** **0-3(0-1)**
„Vazgen Sargsyan“ Republican Stadium, Paris; Referee: István Kovács (Romania); Attendance: 10,000
FRA: Stève Mandanda (18/0), Christophe Jallet (6/1), Jérémy Mathieu (4/0), Lucas Digne (6/0), Raphaël Varane (15/0), Blaise Matuidi (Cap) (32/4) [46.Paul Labile Pogba (20/5)], Moussa Sissoko (25/1) [60.Antoine Griezmann (12/4)], Morgan Schneiderlin (6/0), Florent Dimitri Payet (9/0) [60.Rémy Cabella (4/0)], André-Pierre Gignac (19/5) [87.Karim Mostafa Benzema (75/25)], Loïc Rémy (30/7) [73.Mathieu Valbuena (42/6)]. Trainer: Didier Claude Deschamps (31).
Goals: Loïc Rémy (3), André-Pierre Gignac (55 penalty), Antoine Griezmann (83).

788. 14.11.2014 **FRANCE - ALBANIA** **1-1(0-1)**
Stade de la Route de Lorient, Rennes; Referee: Miroslav Zelinka (Czech Republic); Attendance: 25,000
FRA: Hugo Lloris (Cap) (65/0), Christophe Jallet (7/1), Mapou Yanga-Mbiwa (4/0), Lucas Digne (7/0) [70.Layvin Kurzawa (1/0)], Raphaël Varane (16/0), Mathieu Valbuena (43/6) [85.Florent Dimitri Payet (10/0)], Yohan Cabaye (38/3) [59.Antoine Griezmann (13/5)], Moussa Sissoko (26/1) [80.Morgan Schneiderlin (7/0)], Paul Labile Pogba (21/5), Karim Mostafa Benzema (76/25), Alexandre Lacazette (4/0) [70.André-Pierre Gignac (20/5)]. Trainer: Didier Claude Deschamps (32).
Goal: Antoine Griezmann (73).

789. 18.11.2014 **FRANCE - SWEDEN** **1-0(0-0)**
Stade Vélodrome, Marseille; Referee: Jesús Gil Manzano (Spain); Attendance: 55,000
FRA: Stève Mandanda (19/0), Bacary Sagna (45/0), Eliaquim Hans Mangala (5/0), Layvin Kurzawa (2/0) [78.Lucas Digne (8/0)], Raphaël Varane (Cap) (17/1), Mathieu Valbuena (44/6) [68.Alexandre Lacazette (5/0)], Josuha Guilavogui (6/0) [68.Maxime Gonalons (7/0)], Paul Labile Pogba (22/5), Florent Dimitri Payet (11/0) [61.Moussa Sissoko (27/1)], André-Pierre Gignac (21/5) [68.Karim Mostafa Benzema (77/25)], Antoine Griezmann (14/5). Trainer: Didier Claude Deschamps (33).
Goal: Raphaël Varane (84).

790. 26.03.2015 **FRANCE - BRAZIL** **1-3(1-1)**
Stade de France, Saint-Denis, Paris; Referee: Nicola Rizzoli (Italy); Attendance: 80,000
FRA: Stève Mandanda (20/0), Bacary Sagna (46/0), Mamadou Sakho (25/2), Raphaël Varane (18/2), Patrice Latyr Evra (65/0), Blaise Matuidi (33/4) [84.Olivier Giroud (36/9)], Mathieu Valbuena (45/6) [82.Florent Dimitri Payet (12/0)], Moussa Sissoko (28/1) [74.Geoffrey Kondogbia (2/0)], Morgan Schneiderlin (8/0), Karim Mostafa Benzema (78/25), Antoine Griezmann (15/5) [74.Nabil Fekir (1/0)]. Trainer: Didier Claude Deschamps (34).
Goal: Raphaël Varane (21).

791. 29.03.2015 **FRANCE - DENMARK** **2-0(2-0)**
Stade "Geoffroy Guichard", Saint-Étienne; Referee: Ivan Kružliak (Slovakia); Attendance: 38,458
FRA: Stéphane Ruffier (3/0), Christophe Jallet (8/1) [90.Bacary Sagna (47/0)], Benoît Trémoulinas (3/0), Laurent Koscielny (22/0), Raphaël Varane (Cap) (19/2), Morgan Schneiderlin (9/0) [82.Kurt Zouma (1/0)], Geoffrey Kondogbia (3/0) [60.Josuha Guilavogui (7/0)], Florent Dimitri Payet (13/0) [83.Mathieu Valbuena (46/6)], Olivier Giroud (37/10), Alexandre Lacazette (6/1) [71.Blaise Matuidi (34/4)], Antoine Griezmann (16/5) [60.Nabil Fekir (2/0)]. Trainer: Didier Claude Deschamps (35).
Goals: Alexandre Lacazette (14), Olivier Giroud (38).

792. 07.06.2015 **FRANCE - BELGIUM** **3-4(0-2)**
Stade de France, Saint-Denis, Paris; Referee: Marijo Strahonja (Croatia); Attendance: 70,000
FRA: Hugo Lloris (Cap) (66/0), Bacary Sagna (48/0), Benoît Trémoulinas (4/0), Laurent Koscielny (23/0), Raphaël Varane (20/2), Blaise Matuidi (35/4), Mathieu Valbuena (47/7) [73.Nabil Fekir (3/1)], Yohan Cabaye (39/3) [46.Florent Dimitri Payet (14/1)], Moussa Sissoko (29/1), Olivier Giroud (38/10) [80.Paul-Georges Ntep de Madiba (1/0)], Antoine Griezmann (17/5) [46.Alexandre Lacazette (7/1)]. Trainer: Didier Claude Deschamps (36).
Goals: Mathieu Valbuena (53), Nabil Fekir (89), Florent Dimitri Payet (90+1).

793. 13.06.2015 **ALBANIA - FRANCE** **1-0(1-0)**
Elbasan Arena, Elbasan; Referee: Halis Özkahya (Turkey); Attendance: 12,000
FRA: Hugo Lloris (Cap) (67/0), Christophe Jallet (9/1) [72.Bacary Sagna (49/0)], Mamadou Sakho (26/2), Raphaël Varane (21/2), Patrice Latyr Evra (66/0), Florent Dimitri Payet (15/1) [46.Paul Labile Pogba (23/5)], Maxime Gonalons (8/0) [59.Mathieu Valbuena (48/7)], Geoffrey Kondogbia (4/0), Olivier Giroud (39/10) [46.Nabil Fekir (4/1)], Alexandre Lacazette (8/1), Antoine Griezmann (18/5) [59.Paul-Georges Ntep de Madiba (2/0)]. Trainer: Didier Claude Deschamps (37).

794. 04.09.2015 **PORTUGAL - FRANCE** **0-1(0-0)**
Estádio „José Alvalade", Lisboa; Referee: Danny Makkelie (Netherlands); Attendance: 39,853
FRA: Hugo Lloris (Cap) (68/0), Bacary Sagna (50/0), Laurent Koscielny (24/0), Raphaël Varane (22/2), Patrice Latyr Evra (67/0), Blaise Matuidi (36/4), Yohan Cabaye (40/3) [46.Morgan Schneiderlin (10/0)], Moussa Sissoko (30/1) [80.Mathieu Valbuena (49/8)], Paul Labile Pogba (24/5), Karim Mostafa Benzema (79/25) [74.Anthony Joran Martial (1/0)], Nabil Fekir (5/1) [14.Antoine Griezmann (19/5); 88.Olivier Giroud (40/10)]. Trainer: Didier Claude Deschamps (38).
Goal: Mathieu Valbuena (85).

795. 07.09.2015 **FRANCE - SERBIA** **2-1(2-1)**
Nouveau Stade de Bordeaux, Bordeaux; Referee: Artur Ribeiro (Portugal); Attendance: 43,500
FRA: Hugo Lloris (Cap) (69/0), Bacary Sagna (51/0) [46.Mathieu Debuchy (27/2)], Benoît Trémoulinas (5/0), Eliaquim Hans Mangala (6/0), Raphaël Varane (23/2), Blaise Matuidi (37/6) [46.Geoffrey Kondogbia (5/0)], Mathieu Valbuena (50/8) [76.Anthony Joran Martial (2/0)], Morgan Schneiderlin (11/0), Paul Labile Pogba (25/5), Olivier Giroud (41/10) [62.Karim Mostafa Benzema (80/25)], Antoine Griezmann (20/5) [90.Moussa Sissoko (31/1)]. Trainer: Didier Claude Deschamps (39).
Goals: Blaise Matuidi (9, 25).

796. 08.10.2015 **FRANCE - ARMENIA** **4-0(1-0)**
Allianz Riviera, Nice; Referee: Slavko Vinčić (Slovenia); Attendance: 32,136
FRA: Hugo Lloris (Cap) (70/0), Bacary Sagna (52/0), Mamadou Sakho (27/2), Raphaël Varane (24/2), Patrice Latyr Evra (68/0), Blaise Matuidi (38/6) [63.Morgan Schneiderlin (12/0)], Mathieu Valbuena (51/8) [63.Anthony Joran Martial (3/0)], Yohan Cabaye (41/4) [77.Moussa Sissoko (32/1)], Lassana Diarra (29/0), Karim Mostafa Benzema (81/27) [81.Olivier Giroud (42/10)], Antoine Griezmann (21/6) [87.Alexandre Lacazette (9/1)]. Trainer: Didier Claude Deschamps (40).
Goals: Antoine Griezmann (35), Yohan Cabaye (55), Karim Mostafa Benzema (77, 79).

797. 11.10.2015 **DENMARK - FRANCE** **1-2(0-2)**
Telia Parken, København; Referee: Jonas Eriksson (Sweden); Attendance: 18,145
FRA: Stève Mandanda (21/0), Christophe Jallet (10/1), Eliaquim Hans Mangala (7/0), Lucas Digne (9/0), Raphaël Varane (Cap) (25/2) [46.Kurt Zouma (2/0)], Blaise Matuidi (39/6), Moussa Sissoko (33/1), Morgan Schneiderlin (13/0), Olivier Giroud (43/12) [73.Alexandre Lacazette (10/1)], Antoine Griezmann (22/6) [78.Mathieu Valbuena (52/8)], Anthony Joran Martial (4/0) [88.Yohan Cabaye (42/4)]. Trainer: Didier Claude Deschamps (41).
Goals: Olivier Giroud (4, 6).

798. 13.11.2015 **FRANCE - GERMANY** **2-0(1-0)**
Stade de France, Saint-Denis, Paris; Referee: Antonio Mateu Lahoz (Spain); Attendance: 78,000
FRA: Hugo Lloris (Cap) (71/0), Bacary Sagna (53/0), Laurent Koscielny (25/0), Raphaël Varane (26/2), Patrice Latyr Evra (69/0), Blaise Matuidi (40/6) [86.Yohan Cabaye (43/4)], Lassana Diarra (30/0) [80.Morgan Schneiderlin (14/0)], Paul Labile Pogba (26/5), Olivier Giroud (44/13) [68.André-Pierre Gignac (22/6)], Antoine Griezmann (23/6) [80.Hatem Ben Arfa (14/2)], Anthony Joran Martial (5/0) [69.Kingsley Coman (1/0)]. Trainer: Didier Claude Deschamps (42).
Goals: Olivier Giroud (45+1), André-Pierre Gignac (86).

799. 17.11.2015 **ENGLAND - FRANCE** **2-0(1-0)**
The National Stadium, Wembley, London; Referee: Jonas Eriksson (Sweden); Attendance: 71,223
FRA: Hugo Lloris (Cap) (72/0), Bacary Sagna (54/0), Laurent Koscielny (26/0), Lucas Digne (10/0), Raphaël Varane (27/2), Blaise Matuidi (41/6) [46.Paul Labile Pogba (27/5)], Hatem Ben Arfa (15/2) [46.Kingsley Coman (2/0)], Yohan Cabaye (44/4) [57.Lassana Diarra (31/0)], Morgan Schneiderlin (15/0) [82.Moussa Sissoko (34/1)], André-Pierre Gignac (23/6) [57.Olivier Giroud (45/13)], Anthony Joran Martial (6/0) [67.Antoine Griezmann (24/6)]. Trainer: Didier Claude Deschamps (43).

800. 25.03.2016 **NETHERLANDS - FRANCE** **2-3(0-2)**
Amsterdam ArenA, Amsterdam; Referee: Felix Zwayer (Germany); Attendance: 48,000
FRA: Stève Mandanda (22/0), Christophe Jallet (11/1), Laurent Koscielny (27/0), Raphaël Varane (28/2), Patrice Latyr Evra (70/0) [46.Lucas Digne (11/0)], Blaise Matuidi (Cap) (42/7), Florent Dimitri Payet (16/1), Lassana Diarra (32/0) [46.N'Golo Kanté (1/0)], Paul Labile Pogba (28/5) [87.Moussa Sissoko (35/1)], Olivier Giroud (46/14) [73.André-Pierre Gignac (24/6)], Antoine Griezmann (25/7) [46.Anthony Joran Martial (7/0)]. Trainer: Didier Claude Deschamps (44).
Goals: Antoine Griezmann (6), Olivier Giroud (13), Blaise Matuidi (88).

801. 29.03.2016 **FRANCE - RUSSIA** **4-2(2-0)**
Stade de France, Saint-Denis, Paris; Referee: Craig Thomson (Scotland); Attendance: 65,000
FRA: Hugo Lloris (Cap) (73/0), Bacary Sagna (55/0), Mamadou Sakho (28/2), Raphaël Varane (29/2), Patrice Latyr Evra (71/0) [46.Jérémy Mathieu (5/0); 54.Lucas Digne (12/0)], Lassana Diarra (33/0), Paul Labile Pogba (29/5) [69.Moussa Sissoko (36/1)], N'Golo Kanté (2/1), André-Pierre Gignac (25/7) [79.Olivier Giroud (47/14)], Antoine Griezmann (26/7) [63.Florent Dimitri Payet (17/2)], Anthony Joran Martial (8/0) [46.Kingsley Coman (3/1)]. Trainer: Didier Claude Deschamps (45).
Goals: N'Golo Kanté (9), André-Pierre Gignac (38), Florent Dimitri Payet (64), Kingsley Coman (76).

802. 30.05.2016 **FRANCE - CAMEROON** **3-2(2-1)**
Stade de la Beaujoire „Louis Fonteneau", Nantes; Referee: Simon Lee Evans (Wales); Attendance: 37,000
FRA: Hugo Lloris (Cap) (74/0), Bacary Sagna (56/0), Adil Rami (27/1), Laurent Koscielny (28/0), Patrice Latyr Evra (72/0), Blaise Matuidi (43/8), Florent Dimitri Payet (18/3), Lassana Diarra (34/0) [46.N'Golo Kanté (3/1)], Paul Labile Pogba (30/5) [65.Moussa Sissoko (37/1)], Olivier Giroud (48/15) [65.André-Pierre Gignac (26/7)], Kingsley Coman (4/1) [76.Yohan Cabaye (45/4)]. Trainer: Didier Claude Deschamps (46).
Goals: Blaise Matuidi (20), Olivier Giroud (41), Florent Dimitri Payet (90).

803. 04.06.2016 **FRANCE - SCOTLAND** **3-0(3-0)**
Stade Municipal Saint-Symphorien, Metz; Referee: Sébastien Delferière (Belgium); Attendance: 25,057
FRA: Hugo Lloris (Cap) (75/0), Bacary Sagna (57/0), Adil Rami (28/1), Laurent Koscielny (29/1), Patrice Latyr Evra (73/0) [83.Lucas Digne (13/0)], Blaise Matuidi (44/8) [69.Yohan Cabaye (46/4)], Florent Dimitri Payet (19/3) [46.Anthony Joran Martial (9/0)], Paul Labile Pogba (31/5), N'Golo Kanté (4/1) [88.Moussa Sissoko (38/1)], Olivier Giroud (49/17) [63.André-Pierre Gignac (27/7)], Kingsley Coman (5/1) [46.Antoine Griezmann (27/7)]. Trainer: Didier Claude Deschamps (47).
Goals: Olivier Giroud (8, 35), Laurent Koscielny (39).

804. 10.06.2016 **FRANCE - ROMANIA** **2-1(0-0)** 15th EC. Group Stage.
Stade de France, Saint-Denis, Paris; Referee: Viktor Kassai (Hungary); Attendance: 75,113
FRA: Hugo Lloris (Cap) (76/0), Bacary Sagna (58/0), Adil Rami (29/1), Laurent Koscielny (30/1), Patrice Latyr Evra (74/0), Blaise Matuidi (45/8), Florent Dimitri Payet (20/4) [90+2.Moussa Sissoko (39/1)], Paul Labile Pogba (32/5) [77.Anthony Joran Martial (10/0)], N'Golo Kanté (5/1), Olivier Giroud (50/18), Antoine Griezmann (28/7) [66.Kingsley Coman (6/1)]. Trainer: Didier Claude Deschamps (48).
Goals: Olivier Giroud (57), Florent Dimitri Payet (89).

805. 15.06.2016 **FRANCE - ALBANIA** **2-0(0-0)** 15th EC. Group Stage.
Stade Vélodrome, Marseille; Referee: William Collum (Scotland); Attendance: 67,354
FRA: Hugo Lloris (Cap) (77/0), Bacary Sagna (59/0), Adil Rami (30/1), Laurent Koscielny (31/1), Patrice Latyr Evra (75/0), Blaise Matuidi (46/8), Florent Dimitri Payet (21/5), N'Golo Kanté (6/1), Olivier Giroud (51/18) [77.André-Pierre Gignac (28/7)], Anthony Joran Martial (11/0) [46.Paul Labile Pogba (33/5)], Kingsley Coman (7/1) [68.Antoine Griezmann (29/8)]. Trainer: Didier Claude Deschamps (49).
Goals: Antoine Griezmann (90), Florent Dimitri Payet (90+6).

806. 19.06.2016 **SWITZERLAND - FRANCE** **0-0** 15th EC. Group Stage.
Stade "Pierre Mauroy", Lille; Referee: Damir Skomina (Slovenia); Attendance: 45,616
FRA: Hugo Lloris (Cap) (78/0), Bacary Sagna (60/0), Adil Rami (31/1), Laurent Koscielny (32/1), Patrice Latyr Evra (76/0), Yohan Cabaye (47/4), Moussa Sissoko (40/1), Paul Labile Pogba (34/5), André-Pierre Gignac (29/7), Antoine Griezmann (30/8) [77.Blaise Matuidi (47/8)], Kingsley Coman (8/1) [63.Florent Dimitri Payet (22/5)]. Trainer: Didier Claude Deschamps (50).

807. 26.06.2016 **FRANCE - REPUBLIC OF IRELAND** **2-1(0-1)** 15th EC. 2nd Round of 16.
Parc Olympique Lyonnais, Lyon; Referee: Nicola Rizzoli (Italy); Attendance: 56,279
FRA: Hugo Lloris (Cap) (79/0), Bacary Sagna (61/0), Adil Rami (32/1), Laurent Koscielny (33/1), Patrice Latyr Evra (77/0), Blaise Matuidi (48/8), Florent Dimitri Payet (23/5), Paul Labile Pogba (35/5), N'Golo Kanté (7/1) [46.Kingsley Coman (9/1); 90+3.Moussa Sissoko (41/1)], Olivier Giroud (52/18) [73.André-Pierre Gignac (30/7)], Antoine Griezmann (31/10). Trainer: Didier Claude Deschamps (51).
Goals: Antoine Griezmann (57, 61).

808. 03.07.2016 **FRANCE - ICELAND** **5-2(4-0)** 15th EC. Quarter-Finals.
Stade de France, Saint-Denis, Paris; Referee: Björn Kuipers (Netherlands); Attendance: 76,833
FRA: Hugo Lloris (Cap) (80/0), Bacary Sagna (62/0), Laurent Koscielny (34/1) [72.Eliaquim Hans Mangala (8/0)], Samuel Umtiti (1/0), Patrice Latyr Evra (78/0), Blaise Matuidi (49/8), Florent Dimitri Payet (24/6) [80.Kingsley Coman (10/1)], Moussa Sissoko (42/1), Paul Labile Pogba (36/6), Olivier Giroud (53/20) [60.André-Pierre Gignac (31/7)], Antoine Griezmann (32/11). Trainer: Didier Claude Deschamps (52).
Goals: Olivier Giroud (12), Paul Labile Pogba (19), Florent Dimitri Payet (42), Antoine Griezmann (45), Olivier Giroud (59).

809. 07.07.2016 **GERMANY - FRANCE** **0-2(0-1)** 15th EC. Semi-Finals.
Stade Vélodrome, Marseille; Referee: Nicola Rizzoli (Italy); Attendance: 64,078
FRA: Hugo Lloris (Cap) (81/0), Bacary Sagna (63/0), Laurent Koscielny (35/1), Samuel Umtiti (2/0), Patrice Latyr Evra (79/0), Blaise Matuidi (50/8), Florent Dimitri Payet (25/6) [71.N'Golo Kanté (8/1)], Moussa Sissoko (43/1), Paul Labile Pogba (37/6), Olivier Giroud (54/20) [78.André-Pierre Gignac (32/7)], Antoine Griezmann (33/13) [90+2.Yohan Cabaye (48/4)]. Trainer: Didier Claude Deschamps (53).
Goals: Antoine Griezmann (45+2, 72).

810. 10.07.2016 **PORTUGAL - FRANCE** **1-0(0-0,0-0)** 15th EC. Final.
Stade de France, Saint-Denis, Paris; Referee: Mark Clattenburg (England); Attendance: 75,868
FRA: Hugo Lloris (Cap) (82/0), Bacary Sagna (64/0), Laurent Koscielny (36/1), Samuel Umtiti (3/0), Patrice Latyr Evra (80/0), Blaise Matuidi (51/8), Florent Dimitri Payet (26/6) [58.Kingsley Coman (11/1)], Moussa Sissoko (44/1) [110.Anthony Joran Martial (12/0)], Paul Labile Pogba (38/6), Olivier Giroud (55/20) [78.André-Pierre Gignac (33/7)], Antoine Griezmann (34/13). Trainer: Didier Claude Deschamps (54).

811. 01.09.2016 **ITALY - FRANCE** **1-3(1-2)**
Stadio „San Nicola", Bari; Referee: Björn Kuipers (Netherlands); Attendance: 40,000
FRA: Stève Mandanda (23/0), Laurent Koscielny (37/1) [83.Samuel Umtiti (4/0)], Djibril Sidibé (1/0), Layvin Kurzawa (3/1) [90+2.Lucas Digne (14/0)], Raphaël Varane (Cap) (30/2), Blaise Matuidi (52/8) [63.Moussa Sissoko (45/1)], Paul Labile Pogba (39/6), N'Golo Kanté (9/1), Olivier Giroud (56/21) [46.André-Pierre Gignac (34/7)], Antoine Griezmann (35/13) [63.Ousmane Dembélé (1/0)], Anthony Joran Martial (13/1) [46.Florent Dimitri Payet (27/6)]. Trainer: Didier Claude Deschamps (55).
Goals: Anthony Joran Martial (17), Olivier Giroud (28), Layvin Kurzawa (81).

812. 06.09.2016 **BELARUS - FRANCE** **0-0** 21st FIFA WC. Qualifiers
Barysaw Arena, Barysaw; Referee: Ovidiu Haţegan (Romania); Attendance: 12,920
FRA: Stève Mandanda (24/0), Laurent Koscielny (38/1), Djibril Sidibé (2/0), Layvin Kurzawa (4/1), Raphaël Varane (Cap) (31/2), Moussa Sissoko (46/1) [69.Ousmane Dembélé (2/0)], Paul Labile Pogba (40/6), N'Golo Kanté (10/1), Olivier Giroud (57/21) [83.Kévin Gameiro (9/1)], Antoine Griezmann (36/13), Anthony Joran Martial (14/1) [57.Florent Dimitri Payet (28/6)]. Trainer: Didier Claude Deschamps (56).

813. 07.10.2016 **FRANCE - BULGARIA** **4-1(3-1)** 21st FIFA WC. Qualifiers
Stade de France, Saint-Denis, Paris; Referee: Luca Banti (Italy); Attendance: 60,000
FRA: Hugo Lloris (Cap) (83/0), Bacary Sagna (65/0) [27.Djibril Sidibé (3/0)], Laurent Koscielny (39/1), Layvin Kurzawa (5/1), Raphaël Varane (32/2), Blaise Matuidi (53/8), Florent Dimitri Payet (29/7), Moussa Sissoko (47/1), Paul Labile Pogba (41/6), Kévin Gameiro (10/3) [72.André-Pierre Gignac (35/7)], Antoine Griezmann (37/14) [83.Nabil Fekir (6/1)]. Trainer: Didier Claude Deschamps (57).
Goals: Kévin Gameiro (23), Florent Dimitri Payet (26), Antoine Griezmann (38), Kévin Gameiro (59).

814. 10.10.2016 **NETHERLANDS - FRANCE** **0-1(0-1)** 21st FIFA WC. Qualifiers
Amsterdam ArenA, Amsterdam; Referee: Damir Skomina (Slovenia); Attendance: 50,220
FRA: Hugo Lloris (Cap) (84/0), Laurent Koscielny (40/1), Djibril Sidibé (4/0), Layvin Kurzawa (6/1), Raphaël Varane (33/2), Blaise Matuidi (54/8), Florent Dimitri Payet (30/7) [67.Anthony Joran Martial (15/1)], Moussa Sissoko (48/1), Paul Labile Pogba (42/7), Kévin Gameiro (11/3) [80.André-Pierre Gignac (36/7)], Antoine Griezmann (38/14) [90+3.N'Golo Kanté (11/1)]. Trainer: Didier Claude Deschamps (58).
Goal: Paul Labile Pogba (30).

815. 11.11.2016 **FRANCE - SWEDEN** **2-1(0-0)** 21st FIFA WC. Qualifiers
Stade de France, Saint-Denis, Paris; Referee: Milorad Mažić (Serbia); Attendance: 78,000
FRA: Hugo Lloris (Cap) (85/0), Patrice Latyr Evra (81/0), Laurent Koscielny (41/1), Djibril Sidibé (5/0), Raphaël Varane (34/2), Blaise Matuidi (55/8), Florent Dimitri Payet (31/8), Moussa Sissoko (49/1), Paul Labile Pogba (43/8), Olivier Giroud (58/21), Antoine Griezmann (39/14) [88.N'Golo Kanté (12/1)]. Trainer: Didier Claude Deschamps (59).
Goals: Paul Labile Pogba (57), Florent Dimitri Payet (65).

816. 15.11.2016 **FRANCE – IVORY COAST** **0-0**
Stade „Félix Bollaert-Delelis", Lens; Referee: Radu Petrescu (Romania); Attendance: 35,000
FRA: Benoît Costil (1/0), Adil Rami (33/1), Djibril Sidibé (6/0) [69.Sébastien Corchia (1/0)], Lucas Digne (15/0), Raphaël Varane (35/2) [46.Laurent Koscielny (42/1)], Florent Dimitri Payet (32/8), Paul Labile Pogba (44/8) [46.Moussa Sissoko (50/1)], N'Golo Kanté (13/1), Adrien Rabiot (1/0) [78.Thomas Lemar (1/0)], Ousmane Dembélé (3/0) [46.Nabil Fekir (7/1)], Kévin Gameiro (12/3) [63.Olivier Giroud (59/21)]. Trainer: Didier Claude Deschamps (60).

INTERNATIONAL PLAYERS

NTD/Nr	Name	DOB	Caps	Goals	Period, Club
(236/449)	ABBES Claude	24.05.1927	9	0	1957-1958, AS Saint-Étienne (9/0).
(212/419)	ABDESSELEM Ben Mohammed	02.01.1926	1	0	1953, Girondins de Bordeaux (1/0).
(651/802)	ABIDAL Éric-Sylvain Bilal	11.09.1979	67	0	2004-2013, Olympique Lyonnais (24/0), FC Barcelona (37/0), AS Monaco FC (6/0).
(49/155)	ACCARD Robert	26.11.1897	6	1	1922-1926, Havre AC (4/0), Stade Havrais (2/1).
(283/503)	ADAMCZYK Marcel	05.01.1935	1	0	1963, Lille OSC (1/0).
(341/570)	ADAMS Jean-Pierre	10.03.1948	22	0	1972-1976, Olympique Nîmes (8/0), OGC Nice (14/0).
(12/050)	ALBERT Georges	1885	1	0	1908, Cercle Athlétique Paris (1/0).
(101/248)	ALCAZAR Joseph	15.11.1911	11	2	1931-1935, Olympique de Marseille (11/2).
(90/232)	ALLÉ Charles	03.07.1904	1	0	1929, Olympique de Marseille (1/0).
(36/121)	ALLÈGRE André	1890	1	0	1914, UA Intergadzarts (1/0).
(2/013)	ALLEMANE Pierre	19.01.1882	7	0	1905-1908, Racing Club de France (5/0).
(169/359)	ALPSTEG René	03.12.1920	12	4	1947-1952, AS Saint-Étienne (12/4).
(749/861)	AMALFITANO Morgan	20.03.1985	1	0	2012, Olympique de Marseille (1/0).
(371/621)	AMISSE Loïc	09.08.1954	12	2	1977-1983, FC Nantes (12/2).
(409/653)	AMOROS Manuel	01.02.1962	82	1	1982-1992, AS Monaco (61/1), Olympique de Marseille (21/0).
(86/227)	ANATOL Manuel	08.05.1903	16	1	1929-1934, Racing Club de France - Racing Club Paris (16/1).
(137/298)	ANDRÉ Mathieu (Matthäus)	1909	3	0	1936-1937, FC Rouen (3/0).
(559/763)	ANELKA Nicolas Sébastien	14.03.1979	69	14	1998-2010, Arsenal FC London (9/3), Real CF Madrid (8/1), Paris St.Germain FC (10/2), Liverpool FC (1/0), Fenerbahçe SK Istanbul (3/1), Bolton Wanderers FC (12/4), Chelsea FC London (26/3).
(490/711)	ANGLOMA Jocelyn	07.08.1965	37	1	1990-1996, Paris St.Germain FC (2/0), Olympique de Marseille (15/0), Torino Calcio (20/1).
(138/304)	ANTOINETTE Bernard	11.03.1914	2	0	1937, FC Rouen (2/0).
(404/647)	ANZIANI Philippe	29.09.1961	5	1	1981-1987, FC Sochaux-Montbéliard (2/0), AS Monaco (2/1), FC Nantes (1/0).
(156/329)	ARNAUDEAU Henri	23.04.1922	6	1	1942-1951, Girondins-AS du Port Bordeaux (3/1), Stade Français-Red Star Paris (3/0).
(283/505)	ARTELESA Marcel	02.07.1938	21	1	1963-1966, AS Monaco (20/1), Olympique de Marseille (1/0).
(121/276)	ASTON Alfred	16.05.1912	31	5	1934-1946, Red Star Olympique Paris (17/3), Racing Club Paris (3/0), Red Star Olympique Paris (11/2).
(289/511)	AUBOUR Marcel	17.06.1940	20	0	1964-1968, Olympique Lyonnais (14/0), OGC Nice (6/0).
(429/668)	AYACHE William	10.01.1961	20	0	1983-1988, FC Nantes (13/0), Paris St.Germain FC (3/0), Olympique de Marseille (4/0).
(146/315)	AZNAR Emmanuel	23.12.1915	1	1	1938, Olympique de Marseille (1/1).
(547/752)	BA Ibrahim	12.11.1973	8	2	1997-1998, Girondins de Bordeaux (3/1), Milan AC Milano (5/1).
(310/541)	BAEZA Jean	20.08.1942	8	0	1967-1968, AS Monaco (6/0), Red Star FC Paris (2/0).
(176/368)	BAILLOT Henri	13.12.1924	8	4	1948-1950, FC Metz (8/4).
(493/713)	BAILLS Pascal	30.12.1964	1	0	1991, Montpellier Hérault SC (1/0).
(85/224)	BANIDE Maurice	1905	9	1	1929-1936, AS Strasbourg (3/1), FC Mulhouse (3/0), Club Français Paris (2/0), Racing Club Paris (1/0).
(291/515)	BARAFFE Edmond	19.10.1942	3	0	1964-1966, FC Toulouse (3/0).
(13/056)	BARAT Jean-Marie	1885	2	0	1909, AS Bon Conseil (2/0).
(340/569)	BARATELLI Dominique	26.10.1947	21	0	1972-1982, OGC Nice (19/0), Paris St.Germain FC (2/0).
(158/335)	BARATTE Jean	07.06.1923	32	19	1944-1952, Lille OSC (32/19).
(29/101)	BARD Henri	29.04.1892	18	6	1913-1923, Racing Club de France (3/2), Cercle Athlétique Paris (10/3), Racing Club de France (5/1).
(64/187)	BARDOT Charles	07.04.1904	6	3	1925-1932, RC Philippevillois (1/0), AS Cannes (5/3).
(54/167)	BARON Paul	23.05.1895	1	0	1923, Olympique de Paris (1/0).
(373/625)	BARONCHELLI Bruno	13.01.1957	6	1	1977-1981, FC Nantes (6/1).
(22/084)	BARREAU Gaston	07.12.1883	12	0	1911-1914, FEC Levallois (12/0).
(519/733)	BARTHEZ Fabien	28.06.1971	87	0	1994-2006, Olympique de Marseille (1/0), AS Monaco (37/0), Manchester United FC (25/0), Olympique de Marseille (24/0).
(148/317)	BASTIEN Henri "Jean"	21.06.1915	4	0	1938-1945, Olympique de Marseille (4/0).
(363/605)	BATHENAY Dominique	13.02.1954	20	4	1975-1982, AS Saint-Étienne (12/3), Paris St.Germain FC (8/1).
(41/142)	BATMALE Jean	18.09.1895	6	0	1920-1924, Club Français Paris (1/0), US Athlétique Clichy (2/0), Club Français Paris (1/0), Stade Rennais UC (2/0).
(5/021)	BATON Zacharie	1886	4	0	1906-1908, Olympique Lillois (4/0).
(428/667)	BATS Joël	04.01.1957	50	0	1983-1989, AJ Auxerre (17/0), Paris St.Germain FC (33/0).
(175/367)	BATTEUX Albert	02.07.1919	8	1	1948-1949, Stade de Reims (8/1).
(371/620)	BATTISTON Patrick	12.03.1957	56	3	1977-1989, FC Metz (14/1), AS Saint-Étienne (12/1), Girondins de Bordeaux (26/1), AS Monaco (4/0).
(39/138)	BAUMANN Édouard	1895	8	0	1920-1924, Racing Club de France (4/0), CA Sports Généraux (4/0).
(12/047)	BAYROU Georges	21.12.1883	1	0	1908, Gallia Club Paris (1/0).
(137/297)	BEAUCOURT Georges	15.04.1912	1	0	1936, Olympique Lillois (1/0).
(44/147)	BEAUDIER Maurice	1897	3	0	1921, Cercle Athlétique Paris (3/0).
(128/283)	BECK Yvan (BEK)	29.10.1909	5	0	1935-1937, FC Sète (4/0), AS Saint-Étienne (1/0).
(64/185)	BEL Paul-Émile	1900	1	0	1925, CA Vitry (1/0).
(13/058)	BELLOCQ Henri	1884	6	1	1909-1911, Etoile des Deux Lacs (6/1).
(406/652)	BELLONE Bruno	11.03.1962	34	2	1981-1988, AS Monaco (31/2), AS Cannes (3/0).
(188/386)	BELVER Jean	22.05.1921	1	0	1950, OGC Nice (1/0).
(693/823)	BEN ARFA Hatem	07.03.1987	15	2	2007-2015, Olympique Lyonnais (6/1), Olympique de Marseille (1/0), Newcastle United FC (6/1), OGC Nice (2/0).

(150/318)	BEN BAREK Larbi (BEN M'BAREK)	16.06.1917	**17**	**3**	1938-1954, Olympique de Marseille (4/1), Stade Français Paris (12/2), Olympique de Marseille (1/0).
(141/306)	BEN BOUALI Abdelkader	1912	**1**	**0**	1937, Olympique de Marseille (1/0).
(200/404)	BEN TIFOUR Abdelazziz	23.07.1927	**4**	**0**	1952-1957, OGC Nice (1/0), AS Troyes Savinienne (1/0), AS Monaco (2/0).
(135/292)	BENOUNA Ali	23.07.1909	**2**	**0**	1936, FC Sète (2/0).
(6/025)	BENTALL-SERGENT Victor	1887	**5**	**0**	1907-1913, Racing Club de France (4/0), Stade Raphaelois (1/0).
(687/820)	BENZEMA Karim Mostafa	17.12.1987	**81**	**27**	2007-2015, Olympique Lyonnais (24/6), Real Madrid CF (57/21).
(350/579)	BERDOLL Marc	16.04.1953	**16**	**5**	1973-1979, SC Ouest Angers (5/2), Olympique de Marseille (11/3).
(313/548)	BERETA Georges	15.05.1946	**44**	**4**	1967-1975, AS Saint-Étienne (41/4), Olympique de Marseille (3/0).
(50/156)	BERG Grégoire	1899	**1**	**0**	1922, Red Star Strasbourg (1/0).
(393/637)	BERGEROO Philippe	13.01.1954	**3**	**0**	1979-1984, Lille OSC (2/0), FC Toulouse (1/0).
(266/477)	BERNARD Pierre	27.01.1932	**21**	**0**	1960-1965, UA Sedan-Torcy (3/0), Olympique Nîmes (11/0), AS Saint-Étienne (7/0).
(53/163)	BERTHELOT Charles	1901	**1**	**0**	1923, Stade Rennais UC (1/0).
(85/223)	BERTRAND Marcel	1899	**5**	**0**	1929, Club Français Paris (5/0).
(352/582)	BERTRAND-DEMANES Jean-Paul	13.05.1952	**11**	**0**	1973-1978, FC Nantes (11/0).
(316/551)	BETTA André	04.03.1944	**2**	**0**	1968, FC Rouen (2/0).
(262/474)	BIANCHERI Henri	30.07.1932	**2**	**0**	1960, AS Monaco (2/0).
(440/671)	BIBARD Michel	30.11.1958	**6**	**0**	1984-1986, FC Nantes (3/0), Paris St.Germain FC (3/0).
(213/424)	BIEGANSKI Guilhem "Guillaume"	03.11.1932	**9**	**0**	1953-1961, Lille OSC (4/0), Racing Club Lens (5/0).
(135/291)	BIGOT Jules	22.10.1915	**6**	**1**	1936-1945, Olympique Lillois (4/1), Lille OSC (2/0).
(23/086)	BIGUÉ Maurice	1887	**7**	**0**	1911-1914, Cercle Athlétique Paris (7/0).
(159/338)	BIHEL René	02.09.1916	**6**	**1**	1945-1947, Lille OSC (5/0), Havre AC (1/1).
(421/655)	BIJOTAT Dominique	03.01.1961	**8**	**0**	1982-1988, AS Monaco (2/0), Girondins de Bordeaux (6/0).
(1/006)	BILOT Charles	11.03.1883	**6**	**0**	1904-1912, FC Paris (1/0), Cercle Athlétique de Paris (5/0).
(1/004)	BILOT Georges	12.05.1885	**1**	**0**	1904, FC Paris (1/0).
(477/700)	BLANC Laurent Robert	19.11.1965	**97**	**16**	1989-2000, Montpellier Hérault SC (15/3), SSC Napoli (12/1), Olympique Nîmes (3/2), AS Saint Étienne (15/2), AJ Auxerre (9/2), FC Barcelona (7/1), Olympique de Marseille (20/3), Internazionale FC Milano (16/2).
(299/526)	BLANCHET Bernard	01.12.1943	**17**	**5**	1966-1972, FC Nantes (17/5).
(220/437)	BLIARD René	18.10.1932	**7**	**0**	1955-1958, Stade de Reims (7/0).
(44/149)	BLOCH Paul "Poly"	1896	**1**	**0**	1921, FC Mulhouse (1/0).
(548/753)	BLONDEAU Patrick	27.01.1968	**2**	**0**	1997, AS Monaco (2/0).
(63/180)	BLOQUEL Louis	1898	**2**	**0**	1924-1925, US Boulonnaise (2/0).
(554/759)	BOGHOSSIAN Alain	27.10.1970	**26**	**2**	1997-2002, Sampdoria UC Genova (11/0), AC Parma (15/2).
(360/601)	BOISSIER Bernard	03.10.1952	**1**	**0**	1975, Olympique Nîmes (1/0).
(458/676)	BOLI Basile	02.01.1967	**45**	**1**	1986-1993, AJ Auxerre (21/0), Olympique de Marseille (24/0).
(237/453)	BOLLINI Bruno	14.09.1933	**3**	**0**	1957-1961, Racing Club Paris (3/0).
(6/028)	BON Georges	1885	**1**	**0**	1907, US Boulonnaise (1/0).
(68/197)	BONELLO Georges	1901	**3**	**1**	1926-1927, FC Blidéen (3/1).
(161/342)	BONGIORNI Émile	19.03.1921	**5**	**2**	1945-1948, Racing Club Paris (5/2).
(192/393)	BONIFACI Antoine	04.09.1931	**12**	**2**	1951-1953, OGC Nice (12/2).
(39/139)	BONNARDEL Philippe	28.07.1899	**23**	**0**	1920-1927, Gallia Club Paris (2/0), Red Star Club (20/0), US Quervillaise (1/0).
(276/498)	BONNEL Joseph	04.01.1939	**25**	**1**	1962-1969, US Valenciennes-Anzin (24/1), Olympique de Marseille (1/0).
(33/112)	BONNET René	1914	**1**	**0**	1914, AS Française Paris (1/0).
(291/514)	BOSQUIER Bernard	19.06.1942	**42**	**3**	1964-1972, FC Sochaux-Montbéliard (12/0), AS Saint-Étienne (26/3), Olympique de Marseille (4/0).
(365/608)	BOSSIS Maxime	26.06.1955	**76**	**1**	1976-1986, FC Nantes (64/1), Racing Matra Paris (12/0).
(234/445)	BOUCHER Richard	01.03.1932	**3**	**0**	1957-1961, FC Toulouse (3/0).
(633/795)	BOUMSONG SOMKONG Jean-Alain	14.12.1979	**27**	**1**	2003-2009, AJ Auxerre (7/1), Glasgow Rangers FC (1/0), Newcastle United FC (11/0), FC Juventus Torino (3/0), Olympique Lyonnais (5/0).
(139/305)	BOURBOTTE François	24.02.1913	**17**	**0**	1937-1942, SC Fivois (17/0).
(30/103)	BOURNONVILLE Louis		**1**	**0**	1913, RC Arras (1/0).
(199/401)	BOURY Roger	30.12.1925	**1**	**0**	1952, Club Olympique Roubaix-Tourcoing (1/0).
(366/615)	BOUSDIRA Farès	20.09.1953	**1**	**0**	1976, Racing Club Lens (1/0).
(42/146)	BOYER Jean	02.02.1901	**15**	**7**	1920-1929, CA Sports Généraux (2/2), VGA Médoc (1/1), CA Sports Généraux (1/0), SC Choisy-le-Roi (2/0), Olympique de Marseille (9/4).
(352/584)	BRACCI François	31.10.1951	**18**	**0**	1973-1982, Olympique de Marseille (16/0), Girondins de Bordeaux (2/0).
(233/443)	BRAHIMI Saïd	14.03.1931	**2**	**1**	1957, FC Toulouse (2/1).
(320/558)	BRAS Jean-Claude	15.11.1945	**6**	**2**	1969-1970, US Valenciennes-Anzin (1/0), RFC Liègeois (5/2).
(162/343)	BRAUN Gabriel	26.03.1921	**1**	**0**	1945, FC Metz (1/0).
(409/654)	BRAVO Daniel	09.02.1963	**13**	**1**	1982-1989, OGC Nice (4/1), AS Monaco (5/0), OGC Nice (3/0), Paris St.Germain FC (1/0).
(14/063)	BREBION Gilbert	1909	**1**	**0**	1909, Etoile des Deux Lacs (1/0).
(607/783)	BRECHET Jérémie	14.08.1979	**3**	**0**	2001-2002, Olympique Lyonnais (3/0).
(708/830)	BRIAND Jimmy	02.08.1985	**5**	**0**	2008-2012, Stade Rennais FC (3/0), Olympique Lyonnais (2/0).
(423/661)	BRISSON François	09.04.1958	**2**	**0**	1982-1984, Racing Club Lens (2/0).
(320/556)	BROISSART José	20.02.1947	**10**	**0**	1969-1973, Racing Club Paris-Sedan (1/0), AS Saint-Étienne (9/0).
(36/122)	BROUZES Juste	1894	**6**	**3**	1914-1928, Club Athlétique de la Société Générale (1/1), Red Star Club - Red Star Olympique (5/2).
(213/422)	BRUAT Marius	27.06.1930	**1**	**0**	1953, FC Sochaux-Montbéliard (1/0).
(236/450)	BRUEY Stéphane	01.12.1932	**4**	**1**	1957-1962, SCO Angers (4/1).
(68/198)	BRUNEL Fernand	1907	**1**	**2**	1926, Gallia Club Lunel Paris (1/2).
(147/316)	BRUSSEAUX Michel	1913	**1**	**0**	1938, FC Sète (1/0).
(296/524)	BUDZINSKI Robert	21.05.1940	**11**	**0**	1965-1967, FC Nantes (11/0).
(65/192)	BURÉ Julien	10.07.1897	**1**	**0**	1925, Havre AC (1/0).
(283/506)	BURON Jean-Louis	04.03.1934	**4**	**1**	1963, FC Rouen (4/1).

(458/677)	BUSCHER Gérard	05.11.1960	**2**	**0**	1986-1987, Brest Armorique FC (1/0), Racing Matra paris (1/0).
(730/848)	CABAYE Yohan	14.01.1986	**48**	**4**	2010-2016, Lille OSC (4/0), Newcastle United FC (22/2), Paris Saint-Germain FC (13/1), Crystal Palace FC London (9/1).
(776/876)	CABELLA Rémy	08.03.1990	**4**	**0**	2014, Montpellier-Hérault SC (1/0), Newcastle United FC (3/0).
(235/448)	CAHUZAC Pierre	23.07.1927	**2**	**0**	1957, FC Toulouse (2/0).
(53/165)	CAILLET André	1900	**1**	**0**	1923, CA Sports Généraux (1/0).
(607/781)	CAMARA Zoumana	03.04.1979	**1**	**0**	2001, Olympique de Marseille (1/0).
(6/027)	CAMARD René	1886	**1**	**0**	1907, AS Française Paris (1/0).
(334/566)	CAMERINI Francis	25.01.1948	**2**	**0**	1971, AS Saint-Étienne (1/0), OGC Nice (1/0).
(546/749)	CANDELA Vincent	24.10.1973	**40**	**2**	1996-2002, En Avant Guingamp (2/0), AS Roma (38/2).
(1/002)	CANELLE Fernand	02.01.1882	**6**	**0**	1904-1908, Club Français (6/0).
(62/175)	CANTHELOU Jacques	29.03.1904	**11**	**0**	1924-1928, FC Rouen (11/0).
(464/683)	CANTONA Eric	24.05.1966	**45**	**20**	1987-1995, AJ Auxerre (5/1), Montpellier Hérault SC (8/8), Olympique de Marseille (5/1), Olympique Nîmes (2/2), Leeds United FC (9/2), Manchester United FC (16/6).
(93/240)	CAPELLE Marcel	11.12.1904	**9**	**0**	1930-1931, Racing Club de France (9/0).
(757/864)	CAPOUE Étienne	11.07.1988	**7**	**1**	2012-2013, Toulouse FC (7/1).
(294/522)	CARDIET Louis	20.06.1943	**6**	**0**	1965-1967, Stade Rennais UC (6/0).
(282/502)	CARNUS Georges	13.08.1942	**36**	**0**	1963-1973, Stade Français Paris (6/0), AS Saint-Étienne (18/0), Olympique de Marseille (12/0).
(215/431)	CARPENTIER Daniel	19.02.1927	**1**	**0**	1954, UA Sedan-Torcy (1/0).
(741/855)	CARRASSO Cédric	30.12.1981	**1**	**0**	2011, FC Girondins de Bordeaux (1/0).
(185/381)	CARRÉ Désiré	21.05.1923	**1**	**0**	1949, OGC Nice (1/0).
(169/357)	CARRÉ Roger	14.01.1921	**2**	**0**	1947-1949, Lille OSC (2/0).
(606/778)	CARRIÈRE Eric	24.05.1973	**10**	**5**	2001-2002, FC Nantes (4/2), Olympique Lyonnais (6/3).
(286/508)	CASOLARI Georges	05.05.1941	**3**	**0**	1963-1964, AS Monaco (3/0).
(469/691)	CASONI Bernard	04.09.1961	**30**	**0**	1988-1992, SC Toulon et du Var (3/0), Racing Matra Paris (3/0), SC Toulon et du Var (5/0), Olympique de Marseille (19/0).
(401/645)	CASTANEDA Jean	20.03.1957	**9**	**0**	1981-1982, AS Saint-Étienne (9/0).
(73/205)	CAZAL Louis "Pierrot"	1901	**6**	**0**	1927-1930, FC Cette - FC Sète (6/0).
(142/310)	CAZENAVE Hector	1914	**8**	**0**	1937-1938, FC Sochaux-Montbéliard (8/0).
(110/262)	CHAISAZ Raoul	1908	**2**	**0**	1932, Stade Français Paris (2/0).
(30/108)	CHANDELIER Paul	23.01.1892	**3**	**0**	1913-1914, Olympique Lillois (3/0).
(760/865)	CHANTÔME Clément	11.09.1987	**1**	**0**	2012, Paris Saint-Germain FC (1/0).
(79/218)	CHANTREL Augustin	1909	**15**	**0**	1928-1933, Red Star Olympique Paris (6/0), CA Sports Généraux (7/0), Red Star Olympique Paris (2/0).
(121/275)	CHARBIT Max	17.06.1908	**4**	**0**	1934-1935, Olympique de Marseille (4/0).
(553/755)	CHARBONNIER Lionel	25.10.1966	**1**	**0**	1997, AJ Auxerre (1/0).
(91/234)	CHARDAR André	07.10.1906	**12**	**1**	1930-1933, FC Sète (12/1).
(288/510)	CHARLES-ALFRED Daniel	09.05.1934	**4**	**0**	1964, Olympique Nîmes (4/0).
(359/595)	CHARRIER René	01.09.1951	**2**	**0**	1975, Olympique de Marseille (2/0).
(320/554)	CHAUVEAU Yves	14.04.1945	**1**	**0**	1969, Olympique Lyonnais (1/0).
(23/085)	CHAYRIGUES Pierre	01.05.1892	**21**	**0**	1911-1925, Red Star Amical Club - Red Star Club (21/0).
(62/177)	CHESNEAU Pierre	1902	**1**	**0**	1924, FC Blidéen (1/0).
(88/230)	CHEUVA André	30.05.1908	**7**	**2**	1929-1936, Olympique Lillois (4/2), SC Fivois (3/0).
(623/788)	CHEYROU Bruno	10.05.1978	**3**	**0**	2002-2004, Liverpool FC (3/0).
(240/455)	CHIARELLI Bernard	24.02.1934	**1**	**0**	1958, US Valenciennes-Anzin (1/0).
(321/559)	CHIESA Serge	25.12.1950	**12**	**3**	1969-1974, Olympique Lyonnais (12/3).
(281/501)	CHILLAN Paul	17.12.1935	**2**	**0**	1963, Olympique Nîmes (2/0).
(670/812)	CHIMBONDA Pascal	21.02.1979	**1**	**0**	2006, Wigan Athletic FC (1/0).
(258/467)	CHORDA André	20.02.1938	**24**	**0**	1960-1966, OGC Nice (2/0), Girondins de Bordeaux (22/0).
(600/774)	CHRISTANVAL Philippe	31.08.1978	**6**	**0**	2000-2002, AS Monaco (1/0), FC Barcelona (5/0).
(395/639)	CHRISTOPHE Didier	08.12.1956	**6**	**1**	1980-1981, AS Monaco (6/1).
(723/838)	CIANI Michaël	06.04.1984	**1**	**0**	2010, FC Girondins de Bordeaux (1/0).
(208/415)	CICCI Raymond	11.08.1929	**1**	**1**	1953, Stade de Reims (1/1).
(197/397)	CISOWSKI Thadée	16.02.1927	**13**	**11**	1951-1958, FC Metz (1/0), Racing Club Paris (12/11).
(618/786)	CISSÉ Djibril	12.08.1981	**41**	**9**	2002-2011, AJ Auxerre (16/3), Liverpool FC (14/6), Olympique de Marseille (7/0), Panathinaïkos AO Athína (3/0), SS Lazio Roma (1/0).
(730/843)	CISSOKHO Aly	15.09.1987	**1**	**0**	2010, Olympique Lyonnais (1/0).
(683/816)	CLERC François	18.04.1983	**13**	**0**	2006-2008, Olympique Lyonnais (13/0).
(58/172)	CLÉRÉ Ernest	1897	**1**	**0**	1924, Olympique de Paris (1/0).
(707/829)	CLICHY Gaël	26.07.1985	**20**	**0**	2008-2013, Arsenal FC London (10/0), Manchester City FC (10/0).
(53/164)	COAT Robert	1901	**1**	**0**	1923, AS Brestoise (1/0).
(479/702)	COCARD Christophe	23.11.1967	**9**	**1**	1989-1995, AJ Auxerre (9/1).
(234/444)	COLONNA Dominique	04.09.1928	**13**	**0**	1957-1961, Stade de Reims (13/0).
(798/883)	COMAN Kingsley	13.06.1996	**11**	**1**	2015-2016, FC Bayern München (11/1).
(287/509)	COMBIN Nestor	29.12.1940	**8**	**4**	1964-1968, Olympique Lyonnais (2/1), FC Juventus Torino (1/0), AC Varese (3/3), AC Torino (2/0).
(13/061)	COMPEYRAT Alfred	1890	**3**	**0**	1909-1911, Jean d'Arc Levallois (1/0), CA Rosaire (2/0).
(816/890)	CORCHIA Sébastien	01.11.1990	**1**	**0**	2016, Lille OSC (1/0).
(274/489)	CORNU Alain	12.12.1936	**1**	**0**	1962, OGC Nice (1/0).
(266/479)	COSSOU Lucien	29.01.1936	**6**	**4**	1960-1964, AS Monaco (6/4).
(356/591)	COSTE Christian	23.02.1949	**5**	**2**	1974-1975, Lille OSC (5/2).
(816/888)	COSTIL Benoît	03.07.1987	**1**	**0**	2016, Stade Rennais FC (1/0).
(38/129)	COTTENET Maurice	11.02.1895	**18**	**0**	1920-1927, Raincy Sports (2/0), Olympique de Paris (7/0), AS Cannes (9/0).
(106/255)	COTTENIER Jules	1904	**4**	**0**	1932-1934, RC Roubaix (4/0).
(313/546)	COUÉCOU Didier	25.07.1944	**1**	**0**	1967, Girondins de Bordeaux (1/0).
(18/075)	COULON Henri (BEAU)	1881	**5**	**0**	1911, Cercle Athlétique Paris (5/0).
(607/780)	COUPET Grégory	31.12.1972	**34**	**0**	2001-2008, Olympique Lyonnais (34/0).

(396/643)	COURIOL Alain	24.10.1958	**12**	**2**	1980-1983, AS Monaco (11/2), Paris St.Germain FC (1/0).
(49/154)	COURQUIN Albert	1898	**1**	**0**	1922, Olympique Lillois (1/0).
(305/532)	COURTIN Paul	27.03.1942	**1**	**0**	1966, Racing Club Lens (1/0).
(119/274)	COURTOIS Roger	30.05.1912	**22**	**10**	1933-1947, FC Sochaux-Montbéliard (22/10).
(3/015)	CROZIER Georges		**2**	**0**	1905-1906, US Parisienne (2/0).
(60/174)	CRUT Édouard	1901	**8**	**6**	1924-1927, Olympique de Marseille (8/6).
(163/346)	CUISSARD Antoine	19.07.1924	**27**	**1**	1946-1954, AS Saint-Étienne (4/0), FC Lorient (5/0), AS Saint-Étienne (16/1), OGC Nice (2/0).
(366/613)	CURBELO Carlos	28.04.1954	**2**	**0**	1976, AS Nancy-Lorraine (2/0).
(203/410)	CURYL Stanislas	24.04.1929	**2**	**0**	1952, FC Sète (2/0).
(1/010)	CYPRÈS Gaston	19.11.1884	**6**	**2**	1904-1908, FC Paris (2/2), Cercle Athlétique de Paris (4/0).
(517/731)	CYPRIEN Jean-Pierre	12.02.1969	**1**	**0**	1994, AS Saint-Étienne (1/0).

(633/796)	DABO Ousmane	08.02.1977	**3**	**0**	2003, Atalanta Calcio Bergamo (2/0), SS Lazio Roma (1/0).
(606/779)	DACOURT Olivier	25.09.1974	**21**	**1**	2001-2004, Leeds United FC (4/0), AS Roma (17/1).
(193/395)	DAKOSKI Stéphane (DAKOWSKI)	21.06.1921	**2**	**0**	1951, Olympique Nîmes (2/0).
(353/589)	DALGER Christian	18.12.1949	**6**	**2**	1974-1978, AS Monaco (6/2).
(158/331)	DAMBACH Alfred	22.09.1918	**1**	**0**	1944, FC Rouen (1/0).
(55/168)	DANGLES Marcel	1899	**1**	**0**	1923, FC Cette (1/0).
(169/358)	DARD Georges	28.06.1918	**3**	**2**	1947-1950, Olympique de Marseille (3/2).
(37/128)	DARQUES Louis	1896	**9**	**1**	1919-1923, Olympique de Paris (9/1).
(152/321)	DARUI Julien	16.02.1916	**25**	**0**	1939-1951, Olympique Lillois (3/0), Red Star Olympique Paris (2/0), Lille OSC (2/0), C.O. Roubaix-Tourcoing (18/0).
(11/040)	DASTARAC Sadi	1888	**1**	**0**	1908, Gallia Club Paris (1/0).
(65/190)	DAUPHIN Robert	1905	**15**	**1**	1925-1929, Stade Français Paris (15/1).
(1/005)	DAVY Jacques	1882	**1**	**0**	1904, US Parisienne (1/0).
(274/490)	DE BOURGOING Hector	23.07.1934	**3**	**2**	1962-1966, OGC Nice (2/1), Girondins de Bordeaux (1/1).
(301/528)	DE MICHÈLE Gabriel	06.03.1941	**2**	**0**	1966-1967, FC Nantes (2/0).
(745/856)	DEBUCHY Mathieu	28.07.1985	**27**	**2**	2011-2015, Lille OSC (13/1), Newcastle United FC (12/1), Arsenal FC London (2/0).
(63/178)	DEDIEU René	27.08.1899	**6**	**0**	1924-1927, Sporting Club Nîmes (3/0), Stade Olympique Montpellier (3/0).
(113/265)	DÉFOSSÉ Robert	19.06.1909	**9**	**0**	1933-1936, Olympique Lillois (9/0).
(30/104)	DEGOUVE Jean	19.08.1889	**2**	**0**	1913-1914, Olympique Lillois (2/0).
(570/765)	DEHU Frédéric	24.10.1972	**5**	**0**	1998-2000, Racing Club Lens (1/0), FC Barcelona (3/0), Paris St.Germain FC (1/0).
(199/402)	DELADERRIÈRE Léon	26.06.1927	**11**	**3**	1952-1958, FC Nancy (11/3).
(404/648)	DELAMONTAGNE Patrick	18.06.1957	**3**	**0**	1981-1987, AS Nancy-Lorraine (1/0), AS Monaco (1/0), Stade Lavallois (1/0).
(110/261)	DELANNOY Jacques	1912	**1**	**0**	1932, Olympique Lillois (1/0).
(88/231)	DELFOUR Edmond	01.11.1907	**41**	**2**	1929-1938, Stade Français Paris (3/0), Racing Club de France - Racing Club Paris (34/2), RC Roubaix (4/0).
(94/244)	DELMER Célestine	15.02.1907	**11**	**0**	1930-1934, Amiens AC (6/0), Excelsior A.C. Roubaix (5/0).
(309/539)	DELOFFRE Jean	05.10.1939	**1**	**0**	1967, SC Ouest Angers (1/0).
(15/071)	DELVECCHIO Joseph	1885	**1**	**0**	1910, AS Alfortvillaise (1/0).
(811/887)	DEMBÉLÉ Ousmane	15.05.1997	**3**	**0**	2016, BV Borussia Dortmund (3/0).
(63/179)	DENIS Georges	1897	**1**	**0**	1924, AF Garenne-Colombes (1/0).
(8/035)	DENIS Julien	1887	**2**	**0**	1908, RC Calais (2/0).
(10/038)	DENIS Victor	12.01.1889	**1**	**0**	1908, US Tourquennoise (1/0).
(52/160)	DEPAEPE Maurice		**1**	**0**	1923, US Tourquennoise (1/0).
(215/432)	DEREUDDRE René	22.06.1930	**6**	**1**	1954-1957, FC Toulouse (6/1).
(513/728)	DESAILLY Marcel	07.09.1968	**116**	**3**	1993-2004, Olympique de Marseille (3/0), Milan AC Milano (46/2), Chelsea FC London (67/1).
(479/703)	DESCHAMPS Didier	15.10.1968	**103**	**4**	1989-2000, FC Nantes (5/2), Olympique de Marseille (3/1), Girondins de Bordeaux (5/0), Olympique de Marseille (26/0), FC Juventus Torino (46/1), Chelsea FC London (16/0), CF Valencia (2/0).
(213/426)	DESGRANGES Jean	22.04.1929	**1**	**2**	1953, Racing Club Lens (1/2).
(468/690)	DESPEYROUX Pascal	17.11.1965	**3**	**0**	1988, FC Toulouse (3/0).
(11/039)	DESROUSSEAUX Fernand		**1**	**0**	1908, US Tourquennoise (1/0).
(131/286)	DESROUSSEAUX Marcel	13.12.1907	**2**	**0**	1935-1937, Excelsior Roubaix-Tourcoing (2/0).
(292/516)	DEVAUX Denis	09.01.1939	**1**	**0**	1965, RC Strasbourg (1/0).
(20/080)	DEVIC Émilien	1888	**9**	**2**	1911-1921, Cercle Athlétique Paris (2/0), Red Star Amical Club (3/1), CA Sports Généraux (1/0), Racing Club de France (3/1).
(38/134)	DEWAQUEZ Jules	09.03.1899	**41**	**12**	1920-1929, Olympique de Paris (22/6), Olympique de Marseille (19/6).
(576/767)	DHORASOO Vikash	10.10.1973	**18**	**1**	1999-2006, Olympique Lyonnais (2/0), Milan AC Milano (5/0), Paris t. Germain FC (11/1).
(73/202)	DHUR Jacques	1902	**1**	**0**	1927, Stade Français Paris (1/0).
(135/290)	DI LORTO Laurent	01.01.1909	**11**	**0**	1936-1938, Olympique de Marseille (2/0), FC Sochaux-Montbéliard (9/0).
(480/704)	DI MECO Éric	07.09.1963	**23**	**0**	1989-1996, Olympique de Marseille (9/0), AS Monaco (14/0).
(278/499)	DI NALLO Fleury	20.04.1943	**10**	**8**	1962-1971, Olympique Lyonnais (10/8).
(686/818)	DIABY Vassiriki Abou	11.05.1986	**16**	**1**	2007-2012, Arsenal FC London (16/1).
(102/249)	DIAGNE Raoul	10.11.1910	**18**	**0**	1931-1940, Racing Club de France - Racing Club Paris (18/0).
(654/806)	DIARRA Alou	15.07.1981	**44**	**0**	2004-2012, Racing Club Lens (11/0), Olympique Lyonnais (1/0), FC Girondins de Bordeaux (22/0), Olympique de Marseille (10/0).
(686/817)	DIARRA Lassana	13.03.1985	**34**	**0**	2007-2016, Chelsea FC London (3/0), Arsenal FC London (6/0), Portsmouth FC (7/0), Real Madrid CF (12/0), Olympique de Marseille (6/0).
(471/693)	DIB Marcel	10.08.1960	**6**	**0**	1988-1990, AS Monaco (6/0).
(775/875)	DIGNE Lucas	20.07.1993	**15**	**0**	2014-2016, Paris Saint-Germain FC (8/0), AS Roma (5/0), FC Barcelona (2/0).
(556/761)	DIOMÈDE Bernard	23.01.1974	**8**	**0**	1998, AJ Auxerre (8/0).

(487/709)	DIVERT Fabrice	02.09.1967	**3**	**1**	1990-1992, Stade Malherbe Caen (1/0), Montpellier Hérault SC (2/1).
(546/751)	DJÈTOU Martin	15.12.1974	**6**	**0**	1996-2000, AS Monaco (6/0).
(289/512)	DJORKAEFF Jean	27.10.1939	**48**	**3**	1964-1972, Olympique Lyonnais (10/0), Olympique de Marseille (21/2), Paris St.Germain FC (17/1).
(515/730)	DJORKAEFF Youri	09.03.1968	**82**	**28**	1993-2002, AS Monaco (8/3), Paris St.Germain FC (14/8), Internazionale Milano (32/9), 1.FC Kaiserslautern (22/8), Bolton Wanderers FC (6/0).
(308/536)	DOGLIANI Jean-Pierre	17.10.1942	**1**	**1**	1967, SC Ouest Angers (1/1).
(512/726)	DOGON Jean-Luc	13.10.1967	**1**	**0**	1993, Girondins de Bordeaux (1/0).
(251/459)	DOMBECK Stanislas	26.09.1931	**1**	**0**	1958, Stade Rennais UC (1/0).
(348/572)	DOMENECH Raymond	20.01.1952	**8**	**0**	1973-1979, Olympique Lyonnais (6/0), RC Strasbourg (2/0).
(433/670)	DOMERGUE Jean-François	23.06.1957	**9**	**2**	1984-1987, FC Toulouse (6/2), Olympique de Marseille (3/0).
(50/157)	DOMERGUE Marcel	16.11.1901	**20**	**0**	1922-1928, CA Sports Généraux (1/0), FC Cette (2/0), SC Nîmes (11/0), Red Star Olympique Paris (6/0).
(173/362)	DOMINGO Marcel	15.01.1924	**1**	**0**	1948, Stade Français Paris (1/0).
(237/452)	DOMINGO René	28.12.1928	**1**	**0**	1957, AS Saint-Étienne (1/0).
(237/454)	DOUIS Yvon	16.05.1935	**20**	**4**	1957-1965, Lille OSC (8/3), Havre AC (4/0), AS Monaco (8/1).
(189/391)	DOYE André	15.09.1924	**7**	**5**	1950-1952, Girondins de Bordeaux (7/5).
(385/629)	DROPSY Dominique	09.12.1951	**17**	**0**	1978-1981, RC Strasbourg (17/0).
(4/018)	DU RHÉART Julien		**3**	**0**	1906-1911, Société Athlétique de Montrouge (1/0), Club Français Paris (1/0), Red Star Amical Club (1/0).
(12/045)	DUBLY Jean		**1**	**0**	1908, RC Roubaix (1/0).
(35/118)	DUBLY Jules	1887	**1**	**0**	1914, US Tourquennoise (1/0).
(28/098)	DUBLY Raymond	05.11.1893	**31**	**4**	1913-1925, RC Roubaix (31/4).
(198/399)	DUBREUCQ Albert	03.06.1924	**1**	**0**	1952, Lille OSC (1/0).
(91/238)	DUBUS Gustave	26.03.1910	**2**	**1**	1930, FC Sète (2/1).
(15/067)	DUCRET Jean	20.11.1887	**20**	**3**	1910-1914, Etoile des Deux Lacs (16/2), Olympique Lillois (4/1).
(62/176)	DUFOUR Robert		**1**	**0**	1924, Olympique de Paris (1/0).
(519/734)	DUGARRY Christophe	24.03.1972	**55**	**8**	1994-2002, Girondins de Bordeaux (15/2), Milan AC Milano (5/0), Olympique de Marseille (15/3), Girondins de Bordeaux (20/3).
(128/284)	DUHART Pierre (Pedro)	1910	**6**	**1**	1935-1937, FC Sochaux-Montbéliard (6/1).
(30/105)	DUJARDIN Charles	1891	**1**	**0**	1913, US Tourquennoise (1/0).
(57/170)	DUPOIX Michel	1892	**1**	**0**	1924, Racing Club de France (1/0).
(138/301)	DUPUIS Maurice	04.02.1914	**9**	**0**	1937-1945, Racing Club Paris (9/0).
(471/692)	DURAND Jean-Philippe	11.11.1960	**26**	**0**	1988-1992, FC Toulouse (5/0), Girondins de Bordeaux (7/0), Olympique de Marseille (14/0).
(102/250)	DURAND Raymond	29.01.1908	**1**	**0**	1931, Olympique de Marseille (1/0).
(77/213)	DURBEC Aimé	1902	**1**	**0**	1927, Olympique de Marseille (1/0).
(36/123)	DUSART Émile	1892	**1**	**0**	1914, RC Roubaix (1/0).
(87/228)	DUTHEIL Raoul	1905	**1**	**0**	1929, AS Cannes (1/0).
(599/773)	DUTRUEL Richard	24.12.1972	**1**	**0**	2000, FC Barcelona (1/0).

(30/107)	ELOY Albert	1892	**2**	**2**	1913-1914, Olympique Lillois (2/2).
(362/603)	EMON Albert	24.06.1953	**8**	**1**	1975-1980, Olympique de Marseille (5/0), AS Monaco (3/1).
(300/527)	ÉON Daniel	20.12.1939	**3**	**0**	1966-1967, FC Nantes (3/0).
(683/814)	ESCUDÉ Julien	17.08.1979	**13**	**0**	2006-2010, Sevilla FC (13/0).
(315/549)	ESTÉVE Vincent	21.07.1945	**1**	**0**	1968, FC Nantes (1/0).
(395/640)	ETTORI Jean-Luc	29.07.1955	**9**	**0**	1980-1982, AS Monaco (9/0).
(10/037)	EUCHER René		**1**	**0**	1908, AS Française Paris (1/0).
(651/804)	EVRA Patrice Latyr	15.05.1981	**81**	**0**	2004-2016, AS Monaco (5/0), Manchester United FC (57/0), Juventus FC Torino (19/0).

(269/484)	FAIVRE Jacques	25.11.1932	**2**	**2**	1961, AS Saint-Étienne (2/2).
(709/831)	FANNI Rod	06.12.1981	**5**	**0**	2008-2010, Stade Rennais FC (5/0).
(463/682)	FARGEON Philippe	24.04.1964	**7**	**2**	1987-1988, Girondins de Bordeaux (7/2).
(366/614)	FARISON Gérard	15.03.1944	**1**	**0**	1976, AS Saint-Étienne (1/0).
(26/092)	FAROUX Fernand	1891	**1**	**0**	1912, Olympique de Pantin (1/0).
(78/217)	FARVACQUES Victor		**1**	**0**	1928, US Tourquennoise (1/0).
(679/813)	FAUBERT Julien	01.08.1983	**1**	**1**	2006, Girondins de Bordeaux (1/1).
(37/127)	FAURE Paul		**1**	**0**	1919, Racing Club de France (1/0).
(790/879)	FEKIR Nabil	18.07.1993	**7**	**1**	2015-2016, Olympique Lyonnais (7/1).
(12/049)	FENOUILLERE René	1882	**1**	**0**	1908, Red Star Amical Club (1/0).
(423/659)	FERNANDEZ Luis	02.10.1959	**60**	**6**	1982-1992, Paris St.Germain FC (28/3), Racing Club Matra Paris (16/2), AS Cannes (16/1).
(423/660)	FERRATGE Jean-Marc	10.01.1959	**1**	**0**	1982, FC Toulouse (1/0).
(421/656)	FERRERI Jean-Marc	26.12.1962	**37**	**3**	1982-1990, AJ Auxerre (14/2), Girondins de Bordeaux (23/1).
(275/494)	FERRERO Bruno	24.11.1933	**1**	**0**	1962, FC Nancy (1/0).
(518/732)	FERRI Jean-Michel	07.02.1969	**5**	**0**	1994-1995, FC Nantes-Atlantique (5/0).
(251/457)	FERRIER René	07.12.1936	**24**	**0**	1958-1964, AS Saint-Étienne (24/0).
(200/403)	"FERRY" Koczur Ferenc	02.09.1930	**3**	**0**	1952, AS Saint-Étienne (3/0).
(77/214)	FIDON Jean	1906	**1**	**0**	1927, Cercle Athlétique Paris (1/0).
(26/091)	FIEVET A.	1885	**1**	**0**	1912, Olympique de Pantin (1/0).
(1/011)	FILEZ Adrien	27.08.1885	**5**	**0**	1904-1908, US Tourquennoise (5/0).
(100/246)	FINOT Louis	08.07.1909	**7**	**0**	1930-1934, Cercle Athlétique Paris (7/0).
(195/396)	FIROUD Abdelkader	11.10.1919	**6**	**0**	1951-1952, Olympique Nîmes (6/0).
(695/824)	FLAMINI Mathieu	07.03.1984	**3**	**0**	2007-2008, Arsenal FC London (3/0).
(174/366)	FLAMION Pierre	13.03.1924	**17**	**8**	1948-1953, Stade de Reims (7/3), Olympique de Marseille (3/3), Olympique Lyonnais (3/0), AS Troyenne Savinienne (4/2).
(328/563)	FLOCH Louis	28.12.1947	**16**	**2**	1970-1973, AS Monaco (13/2), FC Paris (3/0).
(213/428)	FOIX Jacques	26.11.1930	**7**	**3**	1953-1956, AS Saint-Étienne (7/3).
(213/427)	FONTAINE Just	18.08.1933	**21**	**30**	1953-1960, OGC Nice (1/3), Stade de Reims (20/27).

(143/312)	FOSSET Charles	1910	**2**	**0**	1937, FC Metz (2/0).
(505/716)	FOURNIER Laurent	14.09.1964	**3**	**0**	1992, Paris St.Germain FC (3/0).
(5/023)	FRANÇOIS André	1885	**6**	**3**	1906-1908, RC Roubaix (6/3).
(136/295)	FRANÇOIS Raymond	1910	**1**	**0**	1936, Racing Club Lens (1/0).
(37/124)	FRÉMONT Raymond	07.12.1890	**1**	**0**	1919, Havre AC (1/0).
(158/332)	FREY André	07.11.1919	**6**	**0**	1944-1950, FC Toulouse (6/0).
(696/825)	FREY Sébastien	18.03.1980	**2**	**0**	2007-2008, AC Fiorentina Firenze (2/0).
(49/153)	FRIESS Émile	1901	**2**	**0**	1922, AS Strasbourg (2/0).
(141/309)	FRUTUOSO Michel	21.03.1914	**1**	**0**	1937, RC Roubaix (1/0).
(271/488)	FULGENZI Maxime	26.06.1934	**1**	**0**	1961, UA Sedan-Torcy (1/0).
(178/371)	GABET Roger	12.12.1923	**3**	**0**	1949, Racing Club Paris (3/0).
(126/280)	GABRILLARGUES Louis	01.06.1914	**9**	**0**	1934-1937, FC Sète (9/0).
(85/226)	GALEY Marcel	02.09.1905	**3**	**1**	1929, FC Sète (3/1).
(625/790)	GALLAS William Éric	17.08.1977	**84**	**5**	2002-2010, Chelsea FC London (48/1), Arsenal FC London (36/4).
(67/196)	GALLAY Maurice	1902	**13**	**1**	1926-1929, Olympique de Marseille (13/1).
(357/592)	GALLICE Jean	13.06.1949	**7**	**1**	1974-1976, Girondins de Bordeaux (7/1).
(192/392)	GALLICE René	13.04.1919	**1**	**0**	1951, Girondins de Bordeaux (1/0).
(21/081)	GAMBLIN Lucien	22.07.1890	**17**	**0**	1911-1923, Red Star Amical Club - Red Star Club (17/0).
(731/849)	GAMEIRO Kévin	09.05.1987	**12**	**3**	2010-2016, FC Lorient (5/1), Paris Saint-Germain FC (3/0), Club Atlético de Madrid (4/2).
(472/694)	GARANDE Patrice	27.11.1960	**1**	**0**	1988, AS Saint-Étienne (1/0).
(484/706)	GARDE Rémi	03.04.1966	**6**	**0**	1990-1992, Olympique Lyonnais (6/0).
(206/413)	GARDIEN René	10.02.1928	**2**	**2**	1953, FC Sochaux-Montbéliard (2/2).
(349/573)	GARDON Bernard	02.12.1951	**1**	**0**	1973, FC Nantes (1/0).
(1/009)	GARNIER Georges	1878	**3**	**0**	1904-1905, Club Français Paris (3/0).
(189/389)	GARRIGA Manuel	07.02.1926	**1**	**0**	1950, Girondins de Bordeaux (1/0).
(33/113)	GASTIGER Maurice	03.10.1896	**3**	**1**	1914-1920, FEC Levallois (3/1).
(91/235)	GAUTHEROUX Jean	11.02.1909	**2**	**0**	1930-1936, Racing Club de France (1/0), Excelsior Roubaix-Tourcoing (1/0).
(546/750)	GAVA Franck	03.02.1970	**3**	**0**	1996-1997, Olympique Lyonnais (2/0), Paris St.Germain FC (1/0).
(378/628)	GEMMRICH Albert	13.02.1955	**5**	**2**	1978, RC Strasbourg (5/2).
(395/642)	GENGHINI Bernard	18.01.1958	**27**	**6**	1980-1986, FC Sochaux-Montbéliard (8/2), AS Saint-Étienne (9/2), AS Monaco (9/2), Servette FC Genève (1/0).
(109/260)	GÉRARD René	08.06.1914	**7**	**2**	1932-1933, Sports Olympiques Montpelliérains (7/2).
(467/689)	GERMAIN Bruno	28.04.1960	**1**	**0**	1987, Racing Matra Paris (1/0).
(33/114)	GERONIMI Charles	1895	**1**	**1**	1914, AF Garenne Colobes (1/1).
(21/083)	GERONIMI Georges	1892	**1**	**0**	1911, AF Garenne Colombes (1/0).
(201/406)	GIANESSI Lazare	09.11.1925	**14**	**0**	1952-1954, Club Olympique Roubaix-Tourcoing (7/0), AS Monaco (7/0).
(713/835)	GIGNAC André-Pierre	05.12.1985	**36**	**7**	2009-2016, Toulouse FC (16/4), Olympique de Marseille (5/1), CF Tigres de la Universidad Autónoma de Nuevo León (15/2).
(3/017)	GIGOT R.	1885	**1**	**0**	1905, Club Français Paris (1/0).
(607/782)	GILLET Nicolas	08.11.1976	**1**	**0**	2001, FC Nantes (1/0).
(18/076)	GINDRAT Alfred	1884	**4**	**0**	1911-1912, Red Star Amical Club (4/0).
(491/712)	GINOLA David	25.01.1967	**17**	**3**	1990-1995, Brest Armorique FC (1/0), Paris St.Germain FC (14/3), Newcastle United FC (2/0).
(406/651)	GIRARD René	04.04.1954	**7**	**1**	1981-1982, Girondins de Bordeaux (7/1).
(356/590)	GIRESSE Alain	02.09.1952	**47**	**6**	1974-1986, Girondins de Bordeaux (47/6).
(747/860)	GIROUD Olivier	30.09.1986	**59**	**21**	2011-2016, Montpellier-Hérault SC (9/1), Arsenal FC London (50/20).
(586/772)	GIULY Ludovic	10.07.1976	**17**	**3**	2000-2005, AS Monaco (10/1), FC Barcelona (7/2).
(651/805)	GIVET Gaël	09.10.1981	**12**	**0**	2004-2006, AS Monaco (12/0).
(208/416)	GLOVACKI Léon	19.02.1928	**11**	**3**	1953-1955, Stade de Reims (11/3).
(507/719)	GNAKO Jerôme	17.02.1968	**2**	**0**	1992-1994, AS Monaco (2/0).
(546/748)	GOMA Alain	05.10.1972	**2**	**0**	1996-1998, AJ Auxerre (1/0), Paris St.Germain FC (1/0).
(699/827)	GOMIS Bafétimbi Fredius	06.08.1985	**12**	**3**	2008-2013, AS Saint-Étienne (4/2), Olympique Lyonnais (8/1).
(747/859)	GONALONS MAxime	10.03.1989	**8**	**0**	2011-2015, Olympique Lyonnais (8/0).
(296/525)	GONDET Philippe	17.05.1942	**14**	**7**	1965-1970, FC Nantes (14/7).
(136/293)	GONZALES Joseph	1907	**1**	**0**	1936, SC Fivois (1/0).
(70/200)	GOSSELIN Désiré		**1**	**0**	1926, Stade Olympique de l'Est (1/0).
(13/055)	GOUIN Raymond		**2**	**0**	1909, Jean d'Arc Levallois (2/0).
(263/475)	GOUJON Yvon	21.01.1937	**11**	**6**	1960-1963, FC Sochaux-Montbéliard (2/2), Stade Rennais UC (6/2), FC Rouen (3/2).
(705/828)	GOURCUFF Yoann Miguel	11.07.1986	**31**	**4**	2008-2013, Girondins de Bordeaux (22/1), Olympique Lyonnais (9/3).
(623/787)	GOVOU Sidney Rodrigue Noukpo	24.07.1979	**39**	**10**	2002-2010, Olympique Lyonnais (49/10).
(351/581)	GRAVA Dario	11.02.1948	**1**	**0**	1973, OGC Nice (1/0).
(507/718)	GRAVELAINE Xavier	05.10.1968	**4**	**0**	1992-1993, Stade Malherbe Caen (3/0), Paris St.Germain FC (1/0).
(40/141)	GRAVELINES Maurice	1891	**2**	**0**	1920-1922, Olympique Lillois (2/0).
(18/079)	GRAVIER Ernest	26.08.1892	**11**	**1**	1911-1924, Cercle Athlétique Paris (6/1), FC Cette (5/0).
(168/352)	GRÉGOIRE Jean	20.07.1922	**10**	**0**	1947-1950, Stade Français Paris - Stade Français-Red Star Paris (10/0).
(766/871)	GRENIER Clément	07.01.1991	**5**	**0**	2013-2014, Olympique Lyonnais (5/0).
(311/544)	GRESS Gilbert	17.12.1941	**3**	**0**	1967-1971, VfB Stuttgart (2/0), Olympique de Marseille (1/0).
(11/041)	GRESSIER Raoul		**1**	**0**	1908, RC Calais (1/0).
(775/874)	GRIEZMANN Antoine	21.03.1991	**39**	**14**	2014-2016, Real Sociedad de Fútbol San Sebastián (9/3), Club Atlético de Madrid (30/11).
(218/436)	GRILLET Pierre	21.03.1932	**9**	**2**	1954-1960, Racing Club Paris (9/2).
(163/345)	GRILLON André	01.11.1921	**15**	**0**	1946-1951, Stade Français - Stade Français-Red Star Paris (12/0), Olympique Lyonnais (3/0).
(57/171)	GROSS Ernest	1902	**5**	**1**	1924-1925, Red Star Strasbourg (5/1).
(181/376)	GRUMELLON Jean	01.06.1923	**10**	**5**	1949-1952, Stade Rennais UC (10/5).
(29/102)	GUEGUEN Ernest	1885	**1**	**0**	1913, US Servannaise (1/0).

(177/369)	GUÉRIN Henri	27.08.1921	**3**	**0**	1948-1949, Stade Rennais UC (3/0).
(514/729)	GUÉRIN Vincent	22.11.1965	**19**	**2**	1993-1996, Paris St.Germain FC (19/2).
(13/053)	GUERRE Henri		**1**	**0**	1909, Patronage Olier Paris-Arcueil (1/0).
(1/001)	GUICHARD Maurice		**2**	**0**	1904-1905, US Parisienne (2/0).
(766/872)	GUILAVOGIU Josuha	19.09.1990	**7**	**0**	2013-2015, AS Saint-Étienne (3/0), Club Atlético de Madrid (2/0), VfL Wolfsburg (2/0).
(251/458)	GUILLAS Roland	23.09.1936	**9**	**1**	1958-1962, Girondins de Bordeaux (4/0), AS Saint-Étienne (5/1).
(353/588)	GUILLOU Jean-Marc	20.12.1945	**19**	**3**	1974-1978, SC Ouest Angers (9/1), OGC Nice (10/2).
(554/757)	GUIVARC'H Stéphane	06.09.1970	**14**	**1**	1997-1999, AJ Auxerre (14/1).
(289/513)	GUY André	03.03.1941	**8**	**2**	1964-1968, AS Saint-Étienne (3/1), Lille OSC (1/0), Olympique Lyonnais (4/1).
(192/394)	HAAN Edmond	25.05.1923	**4**	**0**	1951-1953, Racing Strasbourg (4/0).
(7/033)	HANOT Gabriel	06.11.1889	**12**	**3**	1908-1919, US Tourquennoise (11/1), AS Française Paris (1/2).
(292/521)	HAUSSER Gérard	18.03.1939	**14**	**2**	1965-1966, RC Strasbourg (14/2).
(228/441)	HÉDIART Jean	29.01.1931	**1**	**0**	1956, FC Nancy (1/0).
(170/360)	HEINÉ Charles	01.06.1927	**2**	**0**	1947, RC Strasbourg (2/0).
(137/300)	HEISSERER Oscar	18.07.1914	**25**	**8**	1936-1948, RC Strasbourg (8/2), Racing Club Paris (7/4), RC Strasbourg (10/2).
(80/219)	HENRIC Laurent	1905	**4**	**0**	1928-1929, FC Sète (4/0).
(554/758)	HENRY Thierry Daniel	17.08.1977	**123**	**51**	1997-2010, AS Monaco (11/3), Arsenal FC London (81/36), FC Barcelona (31/12).
(294/523)	HERBET Yves	17.08.1945	**16**	**1**	1965-1971, UA Sedan-Torcy - Racing Club Paris-Sedan (11/1), RSC Anderlecht Bruxelles (1/0), Stade de Reims (4/0).
(260/470)	HERBIN Robert	30.03.1939	**23**	**3**	1960-1968, AS Saint-Étienne (23/3).
(255/465)	HEUTTE François	21.02.1938	**9**	**4**	1959-1961, Racing Club Paris (9/4).
(405/649)	HIARD Patrick	27.04.1955	**1**	**0**	1981, Sporting Étoile Club Bastiais (1/0).
(275/497)	HIDALGO Michel	22.03.1933	**1**	**0**	1962, AS Monaco (1/0).
(155/325)	HIDEN Rodolphe (Rudolf)	15.03.1909	**1**	**0**	1940, Racing Club Paris (1/0).
(155/326)	HILTL Henri (Heinrich)	08.11.1910	**2**	**0**	1940-1944, Racing Club Paris (1/0), Excelsior AC Roubaix (1/0).
(14/064)	HITZEL Victor		**1**	**0**	1909, Jean d'Arc Levallois (1/0).
(730/846)	HOARAU Guillaume	05.03.1984	**5**	**0**	2010-2011, Paris Saint-Germain FC (5/0).
(53/166)	HOENEN Paul	1899	**1**	**0**	1923, JA Saint-Ouen (1/0).
(11/044)	HOLGARD Henri		**1**	**0**	1908, Amiens AC (1/0).
(172/361)	HON Louis	11.09.1924	**12**	**0**	1947-1949, Stade Français Paris - Stade Français-Red Star Paris (12/0).
(320/557)	HORLAVILLE Daniel	22.09.1945	**1**	**0**	1969, US Quevillaise (1/0).
(103/252)	HORNUS Pierre	01.02.1908	**3**	**0**	1931, Sports Olympiques Montpelliérains (3/0).
(111/263)	HOUYVET Georges		**1**	**0**	1932, Havre AC (1/0).
(324/561)	HUCK Jean-Noël	20.12.1948	**17**	**0**	1970-1975, RC Strasbourg (6/0), OGC Nice (11/0).
(37/126)	HUGUES François	13.08.1896	**24**	**1**	1919-1927, Red Star Club (10/1), Stade Rennais UC (2/0), Red Star Club (10/0), FC Lyon (2/0).
(174/364)	HUGUET Guy	03.08.1923	**12**	**0**	1948-1952, AS Saint-Étienne (12/0).
(42/144)	HUOT Léon (POISSENOT)	31.12.1898	**4**	**0**	1920-1926, CA Vitry (3/0), Olympique d'Alais (1/0).
(73/206)	HURTEVENT André	1906	**1**	**0**	1927, SC Abbeville (1/0).
(183/377)	IBRIR Abderrahman	10.11.1919	**6**	**0**	1949-1950, FC Toulouse (6/0).
(52/161)	ISBECQUE Gérard	15.03.1897	**4**	**1**	1923-1924, RC Roubaix (4/1).
(28/097)	JACOLLIOT René	1892	**1**	**0**	1913, AS Française Paris (1/0).
(199/400)	JACOWSKI André	05.12.1922	**2**	**0**	1952, Stade de Reims (2/0).
(167/351)	JACQUES Michel	09.01.1924	**1**	**0**	1947, FC Sochaux-Montbéliard (1/0).
(316/550)	JACQUET Aimé	27.11.1941	**2**	**0**	1968, AS Saint-Étienne (2/0).
(169/355)	JADREJAK Joseph (JEDRZEJCZAK)	20.02.1918	**3**	**0**	1947, Lille OSC (3/0).
(757/863)	JALLET Christophe	31.10.1983	**11**	**1**	2012-2016, Paris Saint-Germain FC (5/1), Olympique Lyonnais (6/0).
(138/303)	JANIN Georges	1912	**1**	**0**	1937, Red Star Olympique Paris (1/0).
(363/604)	JANVION Gérard	21.08.1953	**40**	**0**	1975-1982, AS Saint-Étienne (40/0).
(159/336)	JASSERON Lucien	29.12.1913	**2**	**0**	1945, Racing Club Paris (2/0).
(460/679)	JEANNOL Philippe	06.08.1958	**1**	**0**	1986, Paris St.Germain FC (1/0).
(7/031)	JENICOT Albert	1885	**3**	**0**	1908, RC Roubaix (3/0).
(342/571)	JODAR Jean-François	02.12.1949	**6**	**1**	1972-1975, Stade de Reims (6/1).
(173/363)	JONQUET Robert	03.05.1925	**58**	**0**	1948-1960, Stade de Reims (58/0).
(145/313)	JORDAN Auguste "Gusti"	21.02.1909	**16**	**1**	1938-1945, Racing Club Paris (16/1).
(34/115)	JOURDA Albert	1892	**7**	**0**	1914-1924, CA Vitry (3/0), Racing Club de France (2/0), FC Cette (2/0).
(15/070)	JOURDE Étienne	1890	**8**	**1**	1910-1914, CA Vitry (5/0), Club des Sports Athlétiques (3/1).
(4/020)	JOUVE Albert		**1**	**0**	1906, Gallia Club Paris (1/0).
(350/576)	JOUVE Roger	11.03.1949	**7**	**1**	1973-1979, OGC Nice (4/1), RC Strasbourg (3/0).
(51/159)	JOYAUT Robert	1900	**4**	**0**	1923, Red Star Club Paris (4/0).
(13/060)	JULIEN Félix	1884	**2**	**0**	1909, AS Bon Conseil (2/0).
(665/810)	JURIETTI Franck	30.03.1975	**1**	**0**	2005, Girondins de Bordeaux 1/0).
(740/853)	KABUL Younès	04.01.1986	**5**	**1**	2011, Tottenham Hotspur FC London (5/1).
(216/434)	KAELBEL Raymond	31.01.1932	**35**	**1**	1954-1960, RC Strasbourg (5/0), AS Monaco (30/1).
(800/884)	KANTÉ N'Golo	29.03.1991	**13**	**1**	2016, Leicester City FC (8/1), Chelsea FC London (5/0).
(624/789)	KAPO Olivier	27.08.1980	**9**	**3**	2002-2004, AJ Auxerre (9/3).
(508/721)	KAREMBEU Christian	03.12.1970	**53**	**1**	1992-2002, FC Nantes-Atlantique (8/0), Sampdoria UC Genova (20/1), Real CF Madrid (16/0), Middlesbrough FC (7/0), Olympiakos SFP Piraiévs (2/0).
(188/388)	KARGU Édouard (KARGULEWICZ)	16.12.1925	**11**	**3**	1950-1953, Girondins-AS du Port Bordeaux - Girondins de Bordeaux (11/3).
(467/688)	KASTENDEUCH Sylvain	31.07.1963	**9**	**0**	1987-1989, FC Metz (9/0).

(103/251)	KAUCSAR Joseph	20.09.1904	**15**	**0**	1931-1934, Stade Raphaëlois (2/0), Sports Olympiques Montpelliérains (13/0).
(94/242)	KAUFFMANN Marcel	22.05.1910	**5**	**0**	1930-1933, FC Mulhouse (5/0).
(142/311)	KELLER Curt	1918	**1**	**0**	1937, FC Sochaux-Montbéliard (1/0).
(124/279)	KELLER Frédéric "Fritz"	1913	**8**	**3**	1934-1937, Racing Club Strasbourg (8/3).
(533/742)	KELLER Marc	14.01.1968	**6**	**1**	1995-1997, RC Strasbourg (1/0), Karlsruher SC (5/1).
(80/220)	KENNER René	1906	**1**	**0**	1928, CA Vitry (1/0).
(370/618)	KÉRUZORÉ Raymond	17.06.1949	**2**	**0**	1976-1978, Stade Lavallois (2/0).
(768/873)	KONDOGBIA Geoffrey	15.02.1993	**5**	**0**	2013-2015, Sevilla FC (1/0), AS Monaco FC (3/0), FC Internazionale Milano (1/0).
(201/409)	KOPA Raymond (KOPACZEWSKI)	13.10.1931	**45**	**18**	1952-1962, Stade de Reims (24/13), Real Madrid (7/4), Stade de Reims (14/1).
(153/323)	KORÁNYI Désiré (KRONENBERGER Dezső)	28.01.1914	**5**	**5**	1939-1940, FC Sète (5/5).
(91/239)	KORB Pierre	20.04.1908	**12**	**2**	1930-1934, FC Mulhouse (12/2).
(747/858)	KOSCIELNY Laurent	10.09.1985	**42**	**1**	2011-2016, Arsenal FC London (42/1).
(133/288)	Kowalczyk IGNACE	27.12.1913	**5**	**1**	1935-1938, US Valenciennes-Anzin (2/0), Olympique de Marseille (2/0), FC Metz (1/1).
(274/491)	KOZA Casimir (KOZAKIEWICZ)	27.01.1935	**1**	**0**	1962, RC Strasbourg (1/0).
(313/545)	KRAWCZYK Richard	24.05.1947	**1**	**0**	1967, Racing Club Lens (1/0).
(213/420)	KRESS Jean-Pierre	1930	**1**	**0**	1953, RC Strasbourg (1/0).
(788/878)	KURZAWA Layvin	04.09.1992	**6**	**1**	2014-2016, AS Monaco FC (2/0), Paris Saint-Germain FC (4/1).
(766/870)	LACAZETTE Alexandre	28.05.1991	**10**	**1**	2013-2015, Olympique Lyonnais (10/1).
(350/577)	LACOMBE Bernard	15.08.1952	**38**	**12**	1973-1984, Olympique Lyonnais (14/3), AS Saint-Étienne (4/4), Girondins de Bordeaux (20/5).
(246/456)	LAFONT Maurice	13.09.1927	**4**	**0**	1958, Olympique Nîmes (4/0).
(27/095)	LAFOUGE Abel		**1**	**0**	1913, Championnet Sports (1/0).
(535/745)	LAIGLE Pierre	12.09.1970	**8**	**1**	1996-1997, Racing Club Lens (2/0), Sampdoria UC Genova (6/1).
(509/722)	LAMA Bernard	07.04.1963	**44**	**0**	1993-2000, Paris St.Germain FC (35/0), West Ham United FC London (2/0), Paris St.Germain FC (6/0), Stade Rennais FC (1/0).
(254/464)	LAMIA Georges	14.03.1933	**7**	**0**	1959-1962, OGC Nice (7/0).
(534/743)	LAMOUCHI Sabri	09.11.1971	**12**	**1**	1996-2001, AJ Auxerre (11/1), AC Parma (1/0).
(187/384)	LAMY Roger	13.01.1926	**2**	**0**	1950, Racing Club Paris (2/0).
(608/785)	LANDREAU Mikaël	14.05.1979	**11**	**0**	2001-2007, FC Nantes (3/0), Paris Saint-Germain FC (8/0).
(45/150)	LANGENOVE Eugène	1899	**2**	**0**	1921, Olympique de Paris (2/0).
(74/211)	LANGILLER Marcel	02.06.1908	**30**	**7**	1927-1937, Cercle Athlétique Paris (7/1), Excelsior AC Roubaix (17/5), Red Star Olympique Paris (3/0), Cercle Athlétique Paris (3/1).
(387/630)	LARIOS Jean-François	27.08.1956	**17**	**5**	1978-1982, AS Saint-Étienne (17/5).
(321/560)	LARQUÉ Jean-Michel	08.09.1947	**14**	**2**	1969-1976, AS Saint-Étienne (14/2).
(555/760)	LASLANDES Lilian	04.09.1971	**7**	**3**	1997-1999, Girondins de Bordeaux (7/3).
(94/241)	LAURENT Jean	30.12.1906	**9**	**0**	1930-1932, Cercle Athlétique Paris (3/0), FC Sochaux-Montbéliard (6/0).
(91/237)	LAURENT Lucien	10.12.1907	**10**	**2**	1930-1935, Cercle Athlétique Paris (2/0), FC Sochaux (7/2), FC Mulhouse (1/0).
(478/701)	LAUREY Thierry	17.02.1964	**1**	**0**	1989, FC Sochaux-Montbéliard (1/0).
(141/308)	LAURI Michel (Miguel-Angel)	1908	**1**	**0**	1937, FC Sochaux-Montbéliard (1/0).
(308/534)	LAVAUD Jean-Claude	18.05.1938	**1**	**0**	1967, Stade Rennais UC (1/0).
(309/538)	LE CHENADEC Gilbert	13.07.1938	**1**	**0**	1967, FC Nantes (1/0).
(509/723)	LE GUEN Paul	01.03.1964	**17**	**0**	1993-1995, Paris St.Germain FC (17/0).
(426/662)	LE ROUX Yvon	19.04.1960	**28**	**1**	1983-1989, Stade Brestois (2/1), AS Monaco (10/0), FC Nantes (8/0), Olympique de Marseille (5/0), Paris St.Germain FC (3/0).
(215/433)	LEBLOND Michel	10.05.1932	**4**	**1**	1954-1957, Stade de Reims (4/1).
(529/740)	LEBOEUF Frank	23.01.1968	**50**	**4**	1995-2002, RC Strasbourg (8/2), Chelsea FC London (32/1), Olympique de Marseille (10/1).
(284/507)	LECH Georges	02.06.1945	**35**	**7**	1963-1973, Racing Club Lens (16/4), FC Sochaux-Montbéliard (17/3), Stade de Reims (2/0).
(168/354)	LECHANTRE Jean	13.02.1922	**3**	**0**	1947-1949, Lille OSC (3/0).
(393/638)	LECORNU Patrice	24.03.1958	**3**	**0**	1979-1981, SC Ouest Angers (3/0).
(163/348)	LEDUC Lucien	30.12.1918	**4**	**1**	1946, Red Star Olympique Paris (4/1).
(127/281)	LEHMANN Maxime	1906	**2**	**0**	1935-1936, FC Sochaux-Montbéliard (2/0).
(213/423)	LEMAÎTRE Robert	07.03.1929	**2**	**0**	1953-1954, Lille OSC (2/0).
(816/891)	LEMAR Thomas	12.11.1995	**1**	**0**	2016, AS Monaco FC (1/0).
(316/552)	LEMERRE Roger	18.06.1941	**6**	**0**	1968-1971, Racing Club Paris-Sedan (4/0), FC Nantes (1/0), AS Nancy-Lorraine (1/0).
(427/665)	LEMOULT Jean-Claude	28.08.1960	**2**	**0**	1983, Paris St.Germain FC (2/0).
(57/169)	LENOBLE Bernard	16.02.1902	**2**	**0**	1924, Havre AC (2/0).
(235/447)	LEROND André	06.12.1930	**31**	**0**	1957-1963, Olympique Lyonnais (16/0), Stade Français Paris (15/0).
(24/090)	LESMANN E.		**1**	**0**	1912, JA Saint-Ouen (1/0).
(28/096)	LESUR Henri		**6**	**0**	1913-1914, US Tourquennoise (6/0).
(27/093)	LETAILLEUR Lucien	1886	**1**	**0**	1913, FEC Levallois (1/0).
(554/756)	LETIZI Lionel	28.05.1973	**4**	**0**	1997-2001, FC Metz (2/0), Paris St.Germain FC (2/0).
(67/195)	LEVEUGLE Edmond		**1**	**1**	1926, RC Roubaix (1/1).
(118/273)	LHERMINÉ Marceau	1910	**1**	**0**	1933, FC Rouen (1/0).
(91/236)	LIBERATI Ernest	22.03.1908	**19**	**4**	1930-1934, Amiens A.C. (16/3), SC Fivois (3/1).
(65/191)	LIEB Guillaume "Willy"	1904	**15**	**2**	1925-1929, FC Bischwiller (7/0), FC Lyon (3/0), FC Mulhouse (5/2).
(65/189)	LIENERT Pierre		**1**	**0**	1925, CA Sports Généraux (1/0).
(117/272)	LIÉTAER Noël	17.11.1908	**7**	**0**	1933-1934, Excelsior AC Roubaix (7/0).
(64/186)	LIMINANA André		**2**	**0**	1925, SC Bel Abbésien (2/0).

(508/720)	LIZARAZU Bixente (Vincent)	09.12.1969	**97**	**2**	1992-2004, Girondins de Bordeaux (25/1), Athletic Club Bilbao (5/0), FC Bayern München (67/1).
(128/282)	LLENSE René	14.07.1913	**11**	**0**	1935-1939, FC Sète (9/0), AS Saint-Étienne (2/0).
(710/833)	LLORIS Hugo	26.12.1986	**85**	**0**	2008-2016, Olympique Lyonnais (38/0), Tottenham Hotspur FC London (47/0).
(509/724)	LOKO Patrice	06.02.1970	**26**	**7**	1993-1997, FC Nantes-Atlantique (19/6), Paris St.Germain FC (7/1).
(292/518)	LONCLE Marcel	05.01.1936	**2**	**0**	1965, Stade Rennais UC (2/0).
(359/596)	LOPEZ Christian	15.03.1953	**39**	**1**	1975-1982, AS Saint-Étienne (34/1), FC Toulouse (5/0).
(308/537)	LOUBET Charly	26.01.1946	**36**	**10**	1967-1974, OGC Nice (12/3), Olympique de Marseille (13/3), OGC Nice (11/4).
(33/111)	LOUBIÈRE Jean	1892	**1**	**0**	1914, Gallia Club Paris (1/0).
(218/435)	LOUIS Xercès	31.10.1926	**12**	**0**	1954-1956, Racing Club Lens (12/0).
(91/233)	LOZES Antonin	1905	**3**	**0**	1930, FC Sochaux (3/0).
(184/379)	LUCIANO Jean	02.01.1921	**4**	**1**	1949-1950, OGC Nice (4/1).
(268/481)	LUDO François (LUDVIKOVSKI)	04.03.1930	**1**	**0**	1961, AS Monaco (1/0).
(642/799)	LUYINDULA Peguy	27.05.1979	**6**	**1**	2004-2009, Olympique Lyonnais (2/0), Olympique de Marseille (2/1), Paris Saint-Germain FC (2/0).
(730/845)	M'VILA Yann	29.06.1990	**22**	**1**	2010-2012, Stade Rennais FC (22/1).
(48/152)	MACQUART Édouard		**1**	**0**	1921, AS Française Paris (1/0).
(532/741)	MADAR Mickaël	08.05.1968	**3**	**1**	1995-1996, AS Monaco (3/1).
(18/078)	MAËS Eugène	1890	**11**	**15**	1911-1913, Red Star Amical Club (11/15).
(270/485)	Khennane MAHI	21.10.1936	**2**	**0**	1961, Stade Rennais UC (2/0).
(213/425)	MAHJOUB Abderrahman	25.04.1929	**7**	**0**	1953-1955, OGC Nice (3/0), Racing Club Paris (4/0).
(405/650)	MAHUT Philippe	04.03.1956	**9**	**0**	1981-1983, FC Metz (3/0), AS Saint-Étienne (6/0).
(73/203)	MAIRESSE Jacques	1904	**6**	**0**	1927-1934, FC Cette (1/0), Red Star Olympique Paris (5/0).
(529/739)	MAKÉLÉLÉ Claude	18.02.1973	**71**	**0**	1995-2008, FC Nantes-Atlantique (2/0), Olympique de Marseille (1/0), Real CF Madrid (21/0), Chelsea FC London (47/0).
(656/807)	MALOUDA Florent Yohan	13.06.1980	**80**	**9**	2004-2012, Olympique Lyonnais (30/3), Chelsea FC London (50/5).
(699/826)	MANDANDA Stève	28.03.1985	**24**	**0**	2008-2016, Olympique de Marseille (22/0), Crystal Palace FC London (2/0).
(766/869)	MANGALA Eliaquim Hans	13.02.1991	**8**	**0**	2013-2016, FC do Porto (3/0), Manchester City FC (5/0).
(100/247)	MARC Hervé	1903	**1**	**0**	1930, Stade Rennais UC (1/0).
(206/412)	MARCEL Jean-Jacques	13.06.1931	**44**	**3**	1953-1961, FC Sochaux-Montbéliard (10/1), Olympique de Marseille (24/0), SC Toulon (1/1), Racing Club Paris (9/1).
(145/314)	MARCHAL Marcel	1913	**1**	**0**	1938, FC Metz (1/0).
(167/350)	MARCHE Roger	05.03.1924	**63**	**1**	1947-1959, Stade Reims (38/0), Racing Club Paris (25/1).
(360/600)	MARIOT Yves	05.07.1948	**1**	**0**	1975, Olympique Lyonnais (1/0).
(601/776)	MARLET Steve	10.01.1974	**23**	**6**	2000-2004, Olympique Lyonnais (6/1), Fulham FC London (12/4), Olympique de Marseille (5/1).
(793/882)	MARTIAL Anthony Joran	05.12.1995	**15**	**1**	2015-2016, Manchester United FC (15/1).
(740/854)	MARTIN Marvin	10.01.1988	**15**	**2**	2011-2012, FC Sochaux-Montbéliard (14/2), Lille OSC (1/0).
(464/684)	MARTINI Bruno	25.01.1962	**31**	**0**	1987-1996, AJ Auxerre (30/0), Montpellier Hérault SC (1/0).
(510/725)	MARTINS Corentin	11.07.1969	**14**	**1**	1993-1996, AJ Auxerre (17/1).
(74/210)	MASCHINOT André	28.06.1903	**5**	**2**	1927-1930, US Belfort (1/0), FC Sochaux (4/2).
(279/500)	MASNAGHETTI Serge	15.04.1934	**2**	**1**	1963, US Valenciennes-Anzin (2/1).
(29/099)	MASSIP Fernand	1884	**1**	**0**	1913, Red Star Amical Club (1/0).
(7/032)	MATHAUX Paul		**5**	**0**	1908, US Boulonnaise (5/0).
(153/324)	MATHÉ Jules	1915	**2**	**1**	1939, Racing Club Paris (2/1).
(747/857)	MATHIEU Jérémy	29.10.1983	**5**	**0**	2011-2016, Valencia CF (2/0), FC Barcelona (3/0).
(36/120)	MATHIEU Maurice		**2**	**0**	1914-1919, Club Athlétique de la Société Générale (1/0), Red Star Club (1/0).
(96/245)	MATTLER Étienne	25.12.1905	**46**	**0**	1930-1940, FC Sochaux-Montbéliard (46/0).
(732/850)	MATUIDI Blaise	09.04.1987	**55**	**8**	2010-2016, AS Saint-Étienne (3/0), Paris Saint-Germain FC (52/8).
(545/747)	MAURICE Florian	20.01.1974	**6**	**1**	1996-1999, Olympique Lyonnais (3/0), Olympique de Marseille (3/1).
(651/803)	MAVUBA Rio Antonio Zoba	08.03.1984	**13**	**0**	2004-2014, FC Girondins de Bordeaux (6/0), Lille OSC (7/0).
(186/383)	MEANO Francis	22.05.1931	**2**	**0**	1949-1952, Stade de Reims (2/0).
(230/442)	MEKHLOUFI Rachid	12.08.1936	**4**	**0**	1956-1957, AS Saint-Étienne (4/0).
(644/800)	MENDY Bernard	20.08.1981	**3**	**0**	2004, Paris Saint-Germain FC (3/0).
(730/847)	MÉNEZ Jérémy	07.05.1987	**24**	**2**	2010-2013, AS Roma (5/0), Paris Saint-Germain FC (19/2).
(41/143)	MERCERY Maurice	1900	**1**	**0**	1920, AS Française Paris (1/0).
(352/583)	MERCHADIER Alain	13.03.1952	**5**	**0**	1973-1975, AS Saint-Étienne (5/0).
(37/125)	MERCIER Albert		**1**	**0**	1919, Racing Club de France (1/0).
(15/066)	MERCIER D.		**3**	**0**	1910, Etoile des Deux Lacs (3/0).
(157/330)	MERCIER François	1916	**1**	**0**	1942, FC Sète (1/0).
(104/254)	MERCIER Robert (FUROIS)	1909	**7**	**3**	1931-1935, Club Français Paris (6/3), Racing Club Paris (1/0).
(137/299)	MÉRESSE Émilien	1915	**1**	**0**	1936, SC Fivois (1/0).
(656/808)	MERIEM Camel	18.10.1979	**3**	**0**	2004-2005, Girondins de Bordeaux (3/0).
(1/007)	MESNIER Louis	1884	**14**	**6**	1904-1913, FC Paris (2/1), Cercle Athlétique de Paris (12/5).
(13/057)	MEUNIER Maurice	1890	**1**	**0**	1909, Etoile des Deux Lacs (1/0).
(141/307)	MEURIS Georges	14.03.1907	**1**	**0**	1937, Red Star Olympique Paris (1/0).
(626/791)	MEXÈS Philippe Samuel	30.03.1982	**29**	**1**	2002-2012, AJ Auxerre (7/0), AS Roma (15/1), AC Milan (7/0).
(44/148)	MEYER Maurice	1894	**1**	**0**	1921, Red Star Club Paris (1/0).
(367/616)	MEYNIEU Francis	09.01.1953	**1**	**0**	1976, Girondins de Bordeaux (1/0).
(326/562)	MÉZY Michel	15.08.1948	**17**	**1**	1970-1973, Olympique Nîmes (17/1).
(462/681)	MICCICHE Carmelo	16.08.1963	**2**	**1**	1987, FC Metz (2/1).
(310/542)	MICHEL Henri	29.10.1947	**58**	**4**	1967-1980, FC Nantes (58/4).
(283/504)	MICHELIN Pierre	07.01.1937	**5**	**0**	1963-1964, UA Sedan-Torcy (5/0).
(580/769)	MICOUD Johan	24.07.1973	**17**	**1**	1999-2004, Girondins de Bordeaux (7/0), AC Parma (9/1), SV Werder Bremen (1/0).

(212/418)	MIHOUBI Ahmed	02.06.1924	**1**	**0**	1953, FC Toulouse (1/0).
(179/372)	MINDONNET Roger	24.12.1924	**4**	**0**	1949, OGC Nice (4/0).
(38/133)	MISTRAL Louis	04.08.1900	**5**	**0**	1920-1923, Red Star Club (2/0), Olympique de Paris (3/0).
(310/540)	MITORAJ Roland	05.02.1940	**3**	**0**	1967-1968, AS Saint-Étienne (3/0).
(3/016)	MOIGNEU Henri	1887	**8**	**0**	1905-1908, US Tourquennoise (8/0).
(392/635)	MOIZAN Alain	18.11.1953	**7**	**0**	1979-1981, AS Monaco (3/0), Olympique Lyonnais (4/0).
(330/564)	MOLITOR Marc	21.09.1948	**10**	**4**	1970-1975, Racing-Pierrots Strasbourg (6/4), OGC Nice (4/0).
(83/222)	MONSALLIER Jules	23.01.1907	**3**	**0**	1928-1936, Stade Français Paris (1/0), Red Star Olympique Paris (1/0), FC Sète (1/0).
(30/106)	MONTAGNE Charles	1891	**3**	**1**	1913-1920, Olympique Lillois (3/1).
(38/131)	MONY Alexis	09.12.1897	**1**	**0**	1920, US Boulonnaise (1/0).
(38/130)	MONY Pierre	23.03.1896	**5**	**0**	1920-1923, US Boulonnaise (1/0), CA Sports Généraux (4/0).
(180/374)	MOREEL Georges	22.07.1924	**1**	**1**	1949, Racing Club Paris (1/1).
(627/792)	MOREIRA Daniel	08.08.1977	**3**	**0**	2002-2004, Racing Club Lens (2/0), Toulouse FC (1/0).
(18/077)	MOREL Pol	1889	**2**	**0**	1911, Red Star Amical Club (2/0).
(67/193)	MOULÈNE Georges	29.10.1901	**1**	**0**	1926, Cercle Athlétique Paris (1/0).
(13/059)	MOUTON Henri	12.04.1881	**5**	**1**	1909-1910, Etoile des Deux Lacs (5/1).
(252/462)	MULLER Lucien	03.09.1934	**16**	**3**	1959-1964, Stade de Reims (14/3), Real Madrid (2/0).
(188/387)	MUSTAPHA Ben M'Barek	03.05.1926	**1**	**0**	1950, Girondins-AS du Port Bordeaux (1/0).
(730/844)	N'ZOGBIA Charles	28.05.1986	**2**	**0**	2010-2011, Wigan Athletic FC (2/0).
(687/819)	NASRI Samir	26.06.1987	**41**	**5**	2007-2009, Olympique de Marseille (12/2), Arsenal FC London (11/0), Manchester City FC (18/3).
(607/784)	NÉE Frédéric	18.04.1975	**1**	**0**	2001, SEC Bastia (1/0).
(521/737)	NGOTTY Bruno	10.06.1971	**6**	**0**	1994-1997, Olympique Lyonnais (1/0), Paris St.Germain FC (5/0).
(2/014)	NICOLAI Eugène		**2**	**0**	1905, United Sports Club (2/0).
(113/267)	NICOLAS Jean	09.06.1913	**25**	**21**	1933-1938, FC Rouen (25/21).
(38/136)	NICOLAS Paul	04.11.1899	**35**	**20**	1920-1931, Red Star Club - Red Star Olympique (28/18), Amiens SC (7/2).
(320/555)	NOVI Jacques	18.07.1947	**20**	**0**	1969-1972, Olympique de Marseille (20/0).
(136/296)	NOVICKI Edmond	1913	**2**	**1**	1936-1937, Racing Club Lens (2/1).
(792/881)	NTEP DE MATIBA Paul Georges	29.07.1992	**2**	**0**	2015, Stade Rennais FC (2/0).
(129/285)	NUIC Aimé (Ljubomir)	1912	**2**	**0**	1935-1936, CS Metz (2/0).
(38/132)	OLAGNIER Louis	06.11.1889	**1**	**0**	1920, Gallia Club Paris (1/0).
(213/429)	OLIVER Célestin	12.07.1930	**5**	**3**	1953-1958, UA Sedan-Torcy (5/3).
(15/069)	OLIVIER Maurice	10.01.1887	**6**	**0**	1910-1914, Etoile des Deux Lacs (6/0).
(364/606)	ORLANDUCCI Charles	28.10.1951	**1**	**0**	1975, Sporting Étoile Club Bastiais (1/0).
(350/574)	OSMAN Jean-Claude	06.03.1947	**1**	**0**	1973, FC Nantes (1/0).
(520/735)	OUÉDEC Nicolas	28.10.1971	**7**	**1**	1994-1997, FC Nantes-Atlantique (5/0), RCD Espanyol Barcelona (2/1).
(162/344)	OURDOUILLÉ Marcel	18.12.1913	**1**	**0**	1945, Racing Club Lens (1/0).
(78/215)	OUVRAY Georges	11.05.1905	**1**	**1**	1928, Cercle Athlétique Paris (1/1).
(14/065)	PACOT Jean		**1**	**0**	1909, CA Pierrefitte (1/0).
(459/678)	PAILLE Stéphane	27.06.1965	**8**	**1**	1986-1989, FC Sochaux-Montbéliard (8/1).
(352/586)	PAPI Claude	16.04.1949	**3**	**0**	1973-1978, Sporting Étoile Club Bastiais (3/0).
(449/674)	PAPIN Jean-Pierre	05.11.1963	**54**	**30**	1986-1995, Club Brügge KV (1/0), Olympique de Marseille (37/22), Milan AC Milano (14/7), FC Bayern München (2/1).
(59/173)	PARACHINI Antoine	1897	**3**	**0**	1924, FC Cette (3/0).
(473/696)	PARDO Bernard	19.12.1960	**13**	**0**	1988-1991, SC Toulon et du Var (1/0), Girondins de Bordeaux (8/0), Olympique de Marseille (4/0).
(359/599)	PARIZON Patrick	03.06.1950	**3**	**1**	1975, Lille OSC (3/1).
(35/117)	PARSYS Albert	1891	**5**	**0**	1914-1920, US Tourquennoise (5/0).
(462/680)	PASSI Gérald	21.01.1964	**11**	**2**	1987-1988, FC Toulouse (11/2).
(81/221)	PAVILLARD Henri	15.08.1905	**14**	**1**	1928-1931, Stade Français Paris (14/1).
(138/302)	PAYEN Michel	1915	**3**	**0**	1937, FC Rouen (3/0).
(733/851)	PAYET Florent Dimitri	29.03.1987	**32**	**8**	2010-2016, AS Saint-Étienne (3/0), Lille OSC (2/0), Olympique de Marseille (10/1), West Ham United FC London (17/7).
(213/421)	PAZUR Antoine	03.01.1931	**1**	**0**	1953, Lille OSC (1/0).
(389/634)	PÉCOUT Eric	17.02.1956	**5**	**1**	1979-1980, FC Nantes (5/1).
(627/793)	PEDRETTI Benoît	12.11.1980	**22**	**0**	2002-2005, FC Sochaux (15/0), Olympique de Marseille (7/0).
(512/727)	PEDROS Reynald	10.10.1971	**25**	**4**	1993-1996, FC Nantes-Atlantique (22/3), Olympique de Marseille (3/1).
(201/407)	PENVERNE Armand	26.11.1926	**39**	**2**	1952-1959, Stade de Reims (36/2), Red Star Olympique Audonien (3/0).
(476/698)	PEREZ Christian	13.05.1963	**22**	**2**	1988-1992, Paris St.Germain FC (17/2), AS Monaco (5/0).
(292/517)	PÉRI Robert	20.01.1941	**3**	**0**	1965-1967, Stade Français Paris (1/0), Girondins de Bordeaux (2/0).
(15/068)	PETEL Eugène		**1**	**0**	1910, AS Alfortvillaise (1/0).
(488/710)	PETIT Emmanuel	22.09.1970	**63**	**6**	1990-2003, AS Monaco (15/0), Arsenal FC London (26/3), FC Barcelona (9/1), Chelsea FC London (13/2).
(376/627)	PETIT Jean	25.09.1949	**12**	**1**	1977-1980, AS Monaco (12/1).
(42/145)	PETIT René	08.10.1899	**2**	**0**	1920, Stade Bordelais UC (2/0).
(258/468)	PEYROCHE Georges	27.01.1937	**3**	**0**	1960-1961, AS Saint-Étienne (3/0).
(204/411)	PIANTONI Roger	26.12.1931	**37**	**18**	1952-1961, FC Nancy (20/12), Stade de Reims (17/6).
(387/631)	PIASECKI Francis	28.07.1951	**3**	**0**	1978-1979, RC Strasbourg (3/0).
(35/119)	PICY Jean		**1**	**0**	1914, Olympique de Pantin (1/0).
(94/243)	PINEL Marcel	08.07.1908	**7**	**4**	1930, Red Star Olympique Paris (7/4).
(365/611)	PINTENAT Robert	01.05.1948	**3**	**1**	1976, FC Sochaux-Montbéliard (3/1).
(687/821)	PIQUIONNE Frédéric	08.12.1978	**1**	**0**	2007, AS Monaco (1/0).
(545/746)	PIRES Robert	29.01.1973	**79**	**14**	1996-2004, FC Metz (17/2), Olympique de Marseille (21/3), Arsenal FC London (41/9).
(158/334)	PIRONTI Félix	05.04.1921	**1**	**0**	1944, Olympique de Marseille (1/0).

(275/495)	PIUMI Jean-Claude	27.05.1940	**4**	**1**	1962-1967, US Valenciennes-Anzin (4/1).
(725/840)	PLANUS Marc	07.03.1982	**1**	**0**	2010, FC Girondins de Bordeaux (1/0).
(365/609)	PLATINI Michel	21.06.1955	**72**	**41**	1976-1987, AS Nancy-Lorraine (20/10), AS Saint-Étienne (14/10), FC Juventus Torino (38/21).
(388/633)	PLEIMELDING Pierre	19.09.1952	**1**	**0**	1978, Lille OSC (1/0).
(210/417)	PLEIMELDING René	13.02.1925	**1**	**0**	1953, Lille OSC (1/0).
(764/868)	POGBA Paul Labile	15.03.1993	**44**	**8**	2013-2016, Juventus FC Torino (38/6), Manchester City FC (6/2).
(115/269)	POIRIER Paul		**1**	**0**	1933, Red Star Olympique Paris (1/0).
(117/271)	POLGE Albert	1909	**3**	**0**	1933-1934, Sporting Club Nîmes (3/0).
(584/771)	PORATO Stéphane	19.09.1973	**1**	**0**	1999, Olympique de Marseille (1/0).
(534/744)	POUGET Cyrille	06.12.1972	**3**	**0**	1996, FC Metz (3/0).
(29/100)	POULLAIN André	1885	**3**	**2**	1913, Paris St.Germain FC (3/2).
(446/673)	POULLAIN Fabrice	27.08.1962	**10**	**0**	1985-1988, Paris St.Germain FC (10/0).
(64/188)	POZO Félix	1899	**1**	**0**	1925, FC Rouen (1/0).
(163/347)	PROUFF Jean	12.09.1919	**17**	**1**	1946-1949, Stade Rennais UC (13/1), Stade de Reims (4/0).
(308/535)	PROVELLI Louis	21.04.1939	**1**	**0**	1967, US Valenciennes-Anzin (1/0).
(505/715)	PRUNIER William	14.08.1967	**1**	**0**	1992, AJ Auxerre (1/0).
(6/029)	PUGET André	1882	**1**	**0**	1907, Racing Club de France (1/0).
(180/373)	QUENOLLE Roger	19.07.1925	**2**	**0**	1949, Racing Club Paris (2/0).
(311/543)	QUITTET Claude	12.03.1941	**16**	**0**	1967-1973, FC Sochaux-Montbéliard (6/0), OGC Nice (10/0).
(816/889)	RABIOT Adrien	03.04.1995	**1**	**0**	2016, Paris Saint-Germain FC (1/0).
(256/466)	RAHIS Bernard	12.02.1933	**3**	**1**	1959-1961, Olympique Nîmes (3/1).
(274/493)	RAMBERT Angel	12.06.1936	**5**	**1**	1962-1964, Olympique Lyonnais (5/1).
(579/768)	RAMÉ Ulrich	19.09.1972	**12**	**0**	1999-2003, Girondins de Bordeaux (12/0).
(730/842)	RAMI Adil	27.12.1985	**33**	**1**	2010-2016, Lille OSC (11/0), Valencia CF (15/1), Sevilla FC (7/0).
(365/610)	RAMPILLON Gilles	28.07.1953	**3**	**1**	1976-1980, FC Nantes (3/1).
(183/378)	RANZONI Pierre	31.03.1921	**2**	**0**	1949-1950, Stade Français-Red Star Paris (1/0), Havre AC (1/0).
(350/580)	RAVIER Daniel	17.03.1948	**2**	**0**	1973, Olympique Lyonnais (2/0).
(207/414)	REMETTER François	08.08.1928	**26**	**0**	1953-1959, FC Metz (6/0), FC Sochaux-Montbéliard (16/0), Girondins de Bordeaux (3/0), FC Limoges (1/0).
(714/836)	RÉMY Loïc	02.01.1987	**30**	**7**	2009-2014, OGC Nice (2/0), Olympique de Marseille (15/4), Queen's Park Rangers FC London (1/0), Newcastle United FC (9/1), Chelsea FC London (3/2).
(8/034)	RENAUX André	1883	**1**	**0**	1908, RC Roubaix (1/0).
(12/048)	RENAUX Charles	1885	**1**	**0**	1908, RC Roubaix (1/0).
(38/135)	RÉNIER Albert	08.05.1896	**4**	**1**	1920-1924, Havre AC (4/1).
(350/575)	REPELLINI Pierre	27.10.1950	**4**	**0**	1973-1974, AS Saint-Étienne (4/0).
(640/797)	REVEILLÈRE Anthony	10.11.1979	**20**	**1**	2003-2012, Olympique Lyonnais (20/1).
(304/530)	REVELLI Hervé	05.05.1946	**30**	**15**	1966-1975, AS Saint-Étienne (15/10), OGC Nice (12/4), AS Saint-Étienne (3/1).
(352/585)	REVELLI Patrick	22.06.1951	**5**	**1**	1973-1977, AS Saint-Étienne (5/1).
(371/619)	REY André	22.01.1948	**10**	**0**	1977-1979, FC Metz (10/0).
(669/811)	RIBÉRY Franck Henry Pierre	07.04.1983	**81**	**16**	2006-2014, Olympique de Marseille (18/2), FC Bayern München (63/14).
(330/565)	RICO Robert	10.03.1945	**1**	**0**	1970, Stade Rennais UC (1/0).
(13/054)	RIGAL Jean	12.12.1890	**11**	**1**	1909-1912, AF Garenne Colombes (11/1).
(365/607)	RIO Patrice	15.08.1948	**17**	**0**	1976-1978, FC Nantes (17/0).
(113/268)	RIO Roger	13.02.1913	**18**	**4**	1933-1937, FC Rouen (18/4).
(580/770)	ROBERT Laurent	21.05.1975	**9**	**1**	1999-2001, Paris St.Germain FC (9/1).
(304/531)	ROBIN Claude	10.05.1941	**4**	**0**	1966-1967, FC Nantes (4/0).
(275/496)	ROBUSCHI Laurent	05.11.1935	**5**	**0**	1962-1966, Girondins de Bordeaux (5/0).
(476/697)	ROCHE Alain	14.10.1967	**25**	**1**	1988-1996, Girondins de Bordeaux (2/0), Paris St.Germain FC (23/1).
(27/094)	ROCHET	1891	**1**	**0**	1913, CA Boulonnais (1/0).
(362/602)	ROCHETEAU Dominique	14.01.1955	**49**	**15**	1975-1986, AS Saint-Étienne (16/3), Paris St.Germain FC (33/12).
(292/520)	RODIGHIERO Daniel	20.09.1940	**2**	**0**	1965, Stade Rennais UC (2/0).
(111/264)	RODRIGUEZ Joseph	26.05.1908	**2**	**1**	1932, Olympique d'Antibes FC (2/1).
(169/356)	RODRIGUEZ Sauveur	17.10.1920	**1**	**0**	1947, Olympique de Marseille (1/0).
(259/469)	RODZIK Bronislav "Bruno"	29.05.1935	**21**	**0**	1960-1963, Stade de Reims (21/0).
(156/327)	ROESSLER Henri	16.09.1910	**2**	**0**	1942, Red Star Olympique Paris (2/0).
(465/686)	ROHR Jean-Philippe	23.12.1961	**1**	**0**	1987, AS Monaco (1/0).
(103/253)	ROLHION Roger	1909	**4**	**2**	1931-1933, Sports Olympiques Montpelliérains (4/2).
(74/208)	ROLLET André		**4**	**0**	1927, FEC Levallois (4/0).
(31/110)	ROMANO Félix	1895	**1**	**1**	1913, Etoile des Deux Lacs (1/1).
(23/087)	ROMANO Paul	1892	**3**	**0**	1911-1912, Etoile des Deux Lacs (3/0).
(123/278)	ROSE Georges	30.04.1910	**1**	**0**	1934, Stade Rennais UC (1/0).
(319/553)	ROSTAGNI Jean-Paul	14.01.1948	**25**	**0**	1969-1973, AS Monaco (5/0), Girondins de Bordeaux (9/0), Paris St.Germain FC (11).
(39/137)	ROTH Alfred	1891	**1**	**0**	1920, AS Strasbourg (1/0).
(629/794)	ROTHEN Jérôme	31.03.1978	**13**	**1**	2003-2007, AS Monaco (5/0), Paris Saint-Germain FC (8/1).
(46/151)	ROUCHES Antoine	1893	**1**	**0**	1921, Olympique de Paris (1/0).
(484/705)	ROUSSET Gilles	22.08.1963	**2**	**0**	1990-1992, FC Sochaux-Montbéliard (1/0), Olympique Lyonnais (1/0).
(422/657)	ROUSSEY Laurent	27.12.1961	**2**	**1**	1982, AS Saint-Étienne (2/1).
(369/617)	ROUYER Olivier	01.12.1955	**17**	**2**	1976-1981, AS Nancy-Lorraine (17/2).
(268/482)	ROY Serge	09.11.1932	**1**	**0**	1961, AS Monaco (1/0).
(1/008)	ROYET Marius	19.06.1880	**9**	**2**	1904-1908, US Parisienne (9/2).
(730/841)	RUFFIER Stéphane	27.09.1986	**3**	**0**	2010-2015, AS Monaco FC (1/0), AS Saint-Étienne (2/0).
(201/405)	RUMINSKI Jean "César"	13.06.1924	**7**	**0**	1952-1954, Lille OSC (7/0).
(457/675)	RUST Albert	10.10.1953	**1**	**0**	1986, FC Sochaux-Montbéliard (1/0).
(50/158)	RYSSEN André		**1**	**0**	1922, Olympique Lillois (1/0).

(690/822)	SAGNA Bacary	14.02.1983	**65**	**0**	2007-2016, Arsenal FC London (42/0), Manchester City FC (23/0).
(601/775)	SAGNOL Willy	18.03.1977	**58**	**0**	2000-2008, FC Bayern München (58/0).
(642/798)	SAHA Louis Laurent	08.08.1978	**20**	**4**	2004-2012, Manchester United FC (18/4), Everton FC Liverpool (1/0), Tottenham Hotspur FC London (1/0).
(371/623)	SAHNOUN Omar	18.08.1955	**6**	**0**	1977-1978, FC Nantes (6/0).
(735/852)	SAKHO Mamadou	13.02.1990	**28**	**2**	2010-2016, Paris Saint-Germain FC (14/0), Liverpool (14/2).
(161/341)	SALVA Marcel	01.10.1922	**13**	**0**	1945-1952, Racing Club Paris (13/0).
(68/199)	SALVANO Henri		**1**	**1**	1926, FC Blidéen (1/1).
(160/340)	SAMUEL Jean-Claude	11.11.1924	**3**	**0**	1945, Racing Club Paris (3/0).
(350/578)	SARRAMAGNA Christian	29.12.1951	**4**	**0**	1973-1976, AS Saint-Étienne (4/0).
(5/022)	SARTORIUS Émile	1885	**5**	**2**	1906-1907, RC Roubaix (5/2).
(507/717)	SASSUS Jean-Luc	04.10.1962	**1**	**0**	1992, Paris St.Germain FC (1/0).
(267/480)	SAUVAGE Paul	17.09.1939	**6**	**0**	1961-1965, Stade de Reims (5/0), US Valenciennes-Anzin (1/0).
(473/695)	SAUZÉE Frank	28.10.1965	**39**	**9**	1988-1993, Olympique de Marseille (14/2), AS Monaco (6/3), Olympique de Marseille (14/1), Atalanta Bergamo (5/3).
(710/834)	SAVIDAN Stève	29.06.1978	**1**	**0**	2008, Stade Malherbe Caen (1/0).
(34/116)	SCHAFF Albert	08.04.1885	**1**	**0**	1914, Club Athlétique du XIVe Arrondissement de Paris (1/0).
(106/256)	SCHARWATH Émile	20.07.1904	**8**	**0**	1932-1934, AS Strasbourg (7/0), Racing Club Paris (1/0).
(151/319)	SCHMITT Roland	1912	**2**	**0**	1939-1942, FC Sète (1/0), FC Toulouse (1/0).
(778/877)	SCHNEIDERLIN Morgan	08.11.1989	**15**	**0**	2014-2015, Southampton FC (9/0), Manchester United FC (6/0).
(4/019)	SCHUBART Louis	1884	**3**	**0**	1906-1908, Olympique Lillois (3/0).
(269/483)	SCHULTZ Ernest	29.01.1931	**1**	**1**	1961, FC Toulouse (1/1).
(189/390)	SCOTTI Roger	29.07.1925	**2**	**0**	1950-1956, Olympique de Marseille (2/0).
(108/259)	SÉCEMBER Jean	10.04.1911	**4**	**5**	1932-1935, US Tourquennoise (3/5), Excelsior AC Roubaix (1/0).
(88/229)	SEGALEN Yvon	15.04.1906	**3**	**0**	1929, Stade Français Paris (3/0).
(17/074)	SELLIER Henri	1889	**1**	**0**	1910, Etoile des Deux Lacs (1/0).
(441/672)	SÉNAC Didier	02.10.1958	**3**	**0**	1984-1987, Racing Club Lens (2/0), Girondins de Bordeaux (1/0).
(266/478)	SÉNAC Guy	19.03.1932	**2**	**0**	1960-1961, Racing Club Paris (2/0).
(63/181)	SENTUBÉRY Raymond	1900	**3**	**0**	1924-1926, Club Français Paris (3/0).
(174/365)	SÉSIA Georges	08.07.1924	**1**	**0**	1948, FC Nancy (1/0).
(78/216)	SEYLER Pierre		**2**	**1**	1928, AS Strasbourg (2/1).
(261/473)	SIATKA Robert	20.06.1934	**1**	**0**	1960, Stade de Reims (1/0).
(811/886)	SIDIBÉ Djibril	29.07.1992	**6**	**0**	2016, AS Monaco FC (6/0).
(159/337)	SIKLO Ladislas (SMID)	01.05.1915	**4**	**0**	1945, Racing Club Lens (4/0).
(477/699)	SILVESTRE Frank	05.04.1967	**11**	**0**	1989-1992, FC Sochaux-Montbéliard (11/0).
(602/777)	SILVESTRE Mikaël	09.08.1977	**40**	**2**	2001-2006, Manchester United FC (40/2).
(494/714)	SIMBA Amara	23.12.1961	**3**	**2**	1991-1992, Paris St.Germain FC (3/2).
(292/519)	SIMON Jacques "Jacky"	25.03.1941	**15**	**1**	1965-1969, FC Nantes (13/1), Girondins de Bordeaux (2/0).
(156/328)	SIMONYI André (András)	31.03.1914	**4**	**1**	1942-1945, Red Star Olympique Paris (4/1).
(709/832)	SINAMA-PONGOLLE Florent	20.10.1984	**1**	**0**	2008, Club Atlético de Madrid (1/0).
(188/385)	SINIBALDI Paul	03.12.1921	**1**	**0**	1950, Stade de Reims (1/0).
(166/349)	SINIBALDI Pierre	29.02.1924	**2**	**0**	1946-1948, Stade de Reims (2/0).
(719/837)	SISSOKO Moussa	16.08.1989	**50**	**1**	2009-2016, Toulouse FC (6/0), Newcastle United FC (38/1), Tottenham Hotspur FC London (6/0).
(365/612)	SIX Didier	21.08.1954	**52**	**13**	1976-1984, US Valenciennes-Anzin (7/1), Racing Club Lens (11/2), Olympique de Marseille (5/3), KSV Cercle Bruges (3/1), RC Strasbourg (4/2), VfB Stuttgart (16/4), FC Mulhouse (6/0).
(11/043)	SIX Pierre	1888	**1**	**0**	1908, Olympique Lillois (1/0).
(252/460)	SKIBA Henri	14.07.1927	**3**	**0**	1959-1961, Olympique Nîmes (1/0), Stade Français Paris (2/0).
(358/593)	SOLER Gérard	29.03.1954	**16**	**4**	1974-1983, FC Sochaux-Montbéliard (2/1), AS Monaco (1/0), Girondins de Bordeaux (3/2), FC Toulouse (10/1).
(14/062)	SOLLIER André	1890	**5**	**0**	1909-1910, CA Vitry (5/0).
(466/687)	SONOR Luc	15.09.1962	**9**	**0**	1987-1989, AS Monaco (9/0).
(73/207)	SOTTIAULT Julien		**5**	**1**	1927, US Saint Thomas (5/1).
(388/632)	SPECHT Léonard	16.04.1954	**18**	**1**	1978-1985, RC Strasbourg (16/1), Girondins de Bordeaux (2/0).
(651/801)	SQUILLACI Sébastien	11.08.1980	**21**	**0**	2004-2010, AS Monaco (10/0), Olympique Lyonnais (3/0), Sevilla FC (8/0).
(252/461)	STAKO Édouard (STACHOWITZ)	11.01.1934	**3**	**1**	1959-1964, US Valenciennes-Anzin (1/0), Stade Français Paris (2/1).
(260/471)	STIEVENARD Michel	21.09.1937	**2**	**0**	1960, Racing Club Lens (2/0).
(264/476)	STOPYRA Julien	10.01.1933	**1**	**0**	1960, AS Troyenne Savinienne (1/0).
(395/641)	STOPYRA Yannick	09.01.1961	**33**	**11**	1980-1988, FC Sochaux-Montbéliard (9/3), FC Toulouse (24/8).
(184/380)	STRAPPE André	23.02.1928	**23**	**4**	1949-1954, Lille OSC (23/4).
(197/398)	STRICANNE Marceau	01.01.1920	**1**	**0**	1951, Havre AC (1/0).
(72/201)	STUTTLER Georges	1899	**1**	**0**	1926, Red Star Olympique Paris (1/0).
(304/529)	SUAUDEAU Jean-Claude	24.05.1938	**4**	**0**	1966-1967, FC Nantes (4/0).
(158/333)	SWIATEK Jean	11.12.1921	**5**	**0**	1944-1950, Girondins-AS du Port Bordeaux (5/0).
(358/594)	SYNAEGHEL Christian	28.01.1951	**5**	**0**	1974-1977, AS Saint-Étienne (5/0).
(271/487)	Synakowski MARYAN	14.03.1936	**13**	**0**	1961-1965, UA Sedan-Torcy (11/0), Stade Français Paris (1/0), Union Saint-Gilloise (1/0).
(313/547)	SZCZEPANIAK Robert	04.04.1942	**5**	**0**	1967-1968, FC Metz (5/0).

(261/472)	TAILLANDIER Jean	22.01.1938	**3**	**0**	1960, Racing Club Paris (3/0).
(74/209)	TAISNE Georges	13.04.1904	**3**	**2**	1927, Amiens AC (3/2).
(107/257)	TASSIN André	1902	**5**	**0**	1932, Racing Club de France (5/0).
(226/440)	TELLECHEA Joseph	27.11.1926	**3**	**1**	1955-1959, FC Sochaux-Montbéliard (3/1).
(423/658)	TEMPET Jean-Pierre	31.12.1954	**5**	**0**	1982-1983, Stade Lavallois (5/0).
(168/353)	TEMPOWSKI Boleslav	31.05.1921	**1**	**0**	1947, Lille OSC (1/0).
(13/051)	TESSIER		**5**	**0**	1909-1910, AS Bon Conseil (5/0).
(64/184)	THÉDIÉ Maurice	1899	**1**	**0**	1925, Amiens AC (1/0).

(274/492)	Szkudlapski THEO	17.11.1935	**2**	**0**	1962-1963, AS Monaco (2/0).
(76/212)	THÉPOT Alexis	30.07.1906	**31**	**0**	1927-1935, Armoricaine de Brest (1/0), FEC Levallois (6/0), Red Star Olympique Paris 24/0).
(427/664)	THOUVENEL Jean-Christophe	08.10.1958	**4**	**0**	1983-1987, Girondins de Bordeaux (4/0).
(521/736)	THURAM Lilian	01.01.1972	**142**	**2**	1994-2008, AS Monaco (16/0), AC Parma (51/2), FC Juventus Torino (54/0), FC Barcelona (21/0).
(487/708)	TIBEUF Philippe	17.06.1962	**2**	**0**	1990, AS Saint-Étienne (2/0).
(397/644)	TIGANA Jean Amadou	23.06.1955	**52**	**1**	1980-1988, Olympique Lyonnais (7/0), Girondins de Bordeaux (45/1).
(10/036)	TILLETTE Maurice	26.08.1873	**2**	**0**	1908, US Boulonnaise (2/0).
(13/052)	TOSSIER Ernest	1889	**1**	**0**	1909, US Boulonnaise (1/0).
(107/258)	TOUFFAIT Adolphe	29.03.1907	**1**	**0**	1932, Stade Rennais UC (1/0).
(683/815)	TOULALAN Jérémy	10.09.1983	**36**	**0**	2006-2010, Olympique Lyonnais (36/0).
(426/663)	TOURÉ José	24.04.1961	**16**	**4**	1983-1989, FC Nantes (10/3), Girondins de Bordeaux (5/1), AS Monaco (1/0).
(16/073)	TOUSSET Auguste	1888	**2**	**1**	1910-1913, Etoile des Deux Lacs (2/1).
(762/866)	TRÉMOULINAS Benoît	28.12.1985	**5**	**0**	2012-2015, FC Girondins de Bordeaux (2/0), Sevilla FC (3/0).
(338/568)	TRÉSOR Marius	15.01.1950	**65**	**4**	1971-1983, AC Ajaccio (7/0), Olympique de Marseille (38/3), Girondins de Bordeaux (20/1).
(556/762)	TRÉZÉGUET David Sergio	15.10.1977	**71**	**34**	1998-2008, AS Monaco (21/8), FC Juventus Torino (50/26).
(359/598)	TRIANTAFILOS Yves	27.10.1948	**1**	**0**	1975, AS Saint-Étienne (1/0).
(21/082)	TRIBOULET Marcel	1890	**6**	**2**	1911-1914, FEC Levallois (5/2), Racing Club de France (1/0).
(372/624)	TUSSEAU Thierry	19.01.1958	**22**	**0**	1977-1986, FC Nantes (9/0), Girondins de Bordeaux (9/0), Racing Matra Paris (4/0).
(237/451)	TYLINSKI Richard	18.09.1937	**3**	**0**	1957-1960, AS Saint-Étienne (3/0).
(201/408)	UJLAKI Joseph	10.08.1929	**21**	**10**	1952-1958, Olympique Nîmes (6/3), OGC Nice (11/6), Racing Club Paris (4/1).
(808/885)	UMTITI Samuel	14.11.1993	**4**	**0**	2016, Olympique Lyonnais (3/0), FC Barcelona (1/0).
(159/339)	VAAST Ernest	28.10.1922	**15**	**11**	1945-1949, Racing Club Paris (15/11).
(484/707)	VAHIRUA Pascal	09.03.1966	**22**	**1**	1990-1994, AJ Auxerre (22/1).
(570/764)	VAIRELLES Tony	10.04.1973	**8**	**1**	1998-2000, Racing Club Lens (3/0), Olympique Lyonnais (5/1).
(724/839)	VALBUENA Mathieu	28.09.1984	**52**	**8**	2010-2015, Olympique de Marseille (38/6), FK Dinamo Moskva (10/1), Olympique Lyonnais (4/1).
(270/486)	VAN SAM Guy	20.12.1935	**3**	**0**	1961, Racing Club Paris (30).
(40/140)	VANCO Marcel	1887	**8**	**0**	1920-1923, Cercle Athlétique Paris (7/0), RC Roubaix (1/0).
(7/030)	VANDENDRIESSCHE Maurice	1887	**2**	**0**	1908, RC Roubaix (2/0).
(113/266)	VANDOOREN Jules	30.12.1908	**22**	**0**	1933-1942, Olympique Lillois (20/0), Stade de Reims (2/0).
(181/375)	VANDOOREN Roger	27.04.1923	**4**	**0**	1949-1951, Lille OSC (3/0), Club Olympique Roubaix-Tourcoing (1/0).
(353/587)	VANUCCI Albert	09.08.1947	**2**	**0**	1974, FC Sochaux-Montbéliard (1/0).
(764/867)	VARANE Raphaël	25.04.1993	**35**	**2**	2013-2016, Real Madrid CF (35/2).
(16/072)	VASCOUT Henri	1885	**7**	**0**	1910-1911, CA Vitry (7/0).
(122/277)	VASSE François	1907	**1**	**0**	1934, RC Arras (1/0).
(85/225)	VEINANTE Émile	12.06.1907	**24**	**14**	1929-1940, Racing Club de France - Racing Club Paris (24/14).
(5/024)	VERBRUGGE J.		**4**	**0**	1906-1911, AS Française Paris (1/0), Red Star Amical Club (3/0).
(427/666)	VERCRUYSSE Philippe	28.01.1962	**12**	**1**	1983-1989, Racing Club Lens (3/1), Girondins de Bordeaux (5/0), Racing Club Lens (1/0), Olympique de Marseille (3/0).
(335/567)	VERGNES Jacques	21.07.1948	**1**	**1**	1971, Olympique Nîmes (1/1).
(1/003)	VERLET Joseph	16.08.1883	**7**	**1**	1904-1911, FC Paris (2/0), Cercle Athlétique de Paris (5/1).
(116/270)	VERRIEST Georges	15.07.1909	**14**	**1**	1933-1936, RC Roubaix (14/1).
(23/089)	VIAL Francis		**1**	**0**	1911, CA Vitry (1/0).
(11/042)	VIALARET Justin		**1**	**0**	1908, Club Athlétique du XIVe Arrondissement de Paris (1/0).
(23/088)	VIALMONTEIL Henri	1884	**6**	**2**	1911-1913, CA Vitry (6/2).
(549/754)	VIEIRA Patrick	23.06.1976	**107**	**6**	1997-2009, Arsenal FC London (79/4), FC Juventus Torino (15/2), Internazionale FC Milano (12/0).
(178/370)	VIGNAL René	12.08.1926	**17**	**0**	1949-1954, Racing Club Paris (17/0).
(64/183)	VIGNOLI Marcel	1898	**2**	**0**	1925, Olympique de Paris (2/0).
(67/194)	VILLAPLANE Alexandre	12.09.1905	**25**	**0**	1926-1930, FC Cette (6/0), Sporting Club Nîmes (13/0), Racing Club de France (6/0).
(213/430)	VINCENT Jean	29.11.1930	**46**	**22**	1953-1960, Lille OSC (12/7), Stade de Reims (34/15).
(465/685)	VOGEL Rémi	26.11.1960	**1**	**0**	1987, AS Monaco (1/0).
(31/109)	VOYEUX Paul	1884	**1**	**0**	1913, Olympique Lillois (1/0).
(393/636)	WAGNER Roland	22.12.1955	**1**	**1**	1979, RC Strasbourg (1/1).
(64/182)	WALLET Urbain	1901	**21**	**0**	1925-1929, Amiens AC (21/0).
(186/382)	WALTER Marius	05.05.1925	**2**	**1**	1949-1950, Lille OSC (2/1).
(307/533)	WATTEAU Michel	11.10.1945	**1**	**0**	1966, Racing Club Paris-Sedan (1/0).
(52/162)	WATTINE Raymond	1895	**1**	**0**	1923, RC Roubaix (1/0).
(133/289)	WAWRZENIAK Édouard "WAGI"	28.09.1912	**1**	**0**	1935, US Valenciennes-Anzin (1/0).
(152/322)	WEISKOPF Edmond (VIRÁG Ödön)	22.10.1911	**1**	**0**	1939, FC Metz (1/0).
(253/463)	WENDLING Jean	29.04.1934	**26**	**0**	1959-1963, Stade de Reims (26/0).
(12/046)	WIBAUT Ursule	1887	**1**	**0**	1908, Olympique Lillois (1/0).
(73/204)	WILD Jacques	1905	**8**	**0**	1927-1929, Stade Français Paris (8/0).
(2/012)	WILKES Charles	02.06.1879	**4**	**0**	1905-1908, Havre AC (2/0), Havre Sports (2/0).
(575/766)	WILTORD Sylvain	10.05.1974	**92**	**26**	1999-2006, Girondins de Bordeaux (18/6), Arsenal FC London (47/16), Olympique Lyonnais (27/4).
(221/438)	WISNIESKI Maryan	01.02.1937	**33**	**12**	1955-1962, Racing Club Lens (33/12).

(401/646)	XUEREB Daniel	22.05.1959	**8**	**1**	1981-1989, Olympique Lyonnais (1/0), Racing Club Lens (3/0), Paris St.Germain FC (4/1).
(757/862)	YANGA-MBIWA Mapou	15.05.1989	**4**	**0**	2012-2014, Montpellier-Hérault SC (3/0), AS Roma (1/0).
(429/669)	ZANON Jean-Louis	30.11.1960	**1**	**0**	1983, AS St.Étienne (1/0).
(151/320)	ZATELLI Mario	21.12.1912	**1**	**1**	1939, Racing Club Paris (1/1).
(657/809)	ZEBINA Jonathan	19.07.1978	**1**	**0**	2005, FC Juventus Torino (1/0).
(136/294)	ZEHREN Charles	10.10.1910	**1**	**0**	1936, CS Metz (1/0).
(6/026)	ZEIGER Paul		**1**	**0**	1907, US Parisienne (1/0).
(371/622)	ZÉNIER Bernard	21.08.1957	**5**	**1**	1977-1987, FC Metz (1/0), AS Nancy-Lorraine (3/1), FC Metz (1/0).
(131/287)	ZERMANI Émile	1911	**1**	**0**	1935, Olympique de Marseille (1/0).
(521/738)	ZIDANE Zinedine	23.06.1972	**108**	**31**	1994-2006, Girondins de Bordeaux (17/5), FC Juventus Torino (58/14), Real CF Madrid (33/12).
(374/626)	"ZIMAKO" Atre Jacques	28.12.1951	**13**	**2**	1977-1981, AS Saint-Étienne (11/2), FC Sochaux-Montbéliard (2/0).
(223/439)	ZIMNY Simon	18.05.1927	**1**	**0**	1955, Stade de Reims (1/0).
(235/446)	ZITOUNI Mustapha	19.10.1928	**4**	**0**	1957-1958, AS Monaco (4/0).
(791/880)	ZOUMA Kurt	27.10.1994	**2**	**0**	2015, Chelsea FC London (2/0).
(359/597)	ZVUNKA Victor	05.11.1951	**1**	**0**	1975, Olympique de Marseille (1/0).

NATIONAL COACHES

Name	DOB	Period	Matches	P	W	D	L	GF	-	GA	
lbert BATTEUX	02.07.1919 †28.02.2003	17.03.1955 – 05.05.1962	[220-275]	56	24	13	19	126	-	95	54.46 %
lenri GUÉRIN	27.08.1921 †02.04.1995	03.10.1962 – 20.07.1966	[276-303]	28	7	8	13	35	-	41	39.28 %
osé ARRIBAS –	16.01.1921 †28.09.1989	28.09.1966 – 26.11.1966	[304-307]	4	2	0	2	8	-	7	50.00 %
ean SNELLA	09.12.1914 †20.11.1979										
ust FONTAINE	18.08.1933	22.03.1967 – 03.06.1967	[308-309]	2	0	0	2	3	-	6	0.00 %
ouis DUGAUGUEZ	21.02.1918 †22.09.1991	17.09.1967 – 06.11.1968	[310-318]	9	2	3	4	13	-	19	38.88 %
Georges BOULOGNE	01.07.1917 †23.08.1999	12.03.1969 – 26.05.1973	[319-349]	31	15	5	11	49	-	40	56.45 %
stván KOVÁCS (*Romania*)	02.10.1920 †12.05.1995	08.09.1973 – 15.11.1975	[350-364]	15	6	4	5	22	-	15	53.33 %
Aichel HIDALGO	22.03.1933	27.03.1976 – 27.06.1984	[365-439]	75	41	16	18	139	-	72	65.33 %
lenri MICHEL	29.10.1947	13.10.1984 – 22.10.1988	[440-475]	36	16	12	8	46	-	27	55.55 %
Aichel PLATINI	21.06.1955	19.11.1988 – 17.06.1992	[476-504]	29	16	8	5	53	-	28	68.96 %
Gérard HOUILLIER	03.09.1947	26.08.1992 – 17.11.1993	[505-516]	12	7	1	4	20	-	13	62.50 %
Aimé JACQUET	27.11.1941	16.12.1994 – 12.07.1998	[517-569]	53	34	16	3	93	-	27	79.24 %
Roger LEMERRE	18.06.1941	19.08.1998 – 11.06.2002	[570-622]	53	34	11	8	106	-	43	74.52 %
acques SANTINI	25.04.1952	21.08.2002 – 25.06.2004	[623-650]	28	22	4	2	69	-	13	94.06 %
Raymond DOMENECH	24.01.1952	18.08.2004 – 22.06.2010	[651-729]	79	41	24	14	108	-	54	67.08 %
aurent Robert BLANC	19.11.1965	11.08.2010 – 23.06.2012	[730-756]	27	16	7	4	40	-	17	72.22 %
Didier Claude DESCHAMPS	15.10.1968	15.08.2012 – 15.11.2016	[757-816]	60	37	11	12	114	-	49	70.83 %

The C.F.I. (Comitée Français Interfédéral) was responsable for the national squad to 1919. Between 1919 and 1964 responsable was a Selection Comitee. The first "real" national coach was Henri Guérin from July 1964.

HEAD-TO-HEAD STATISTICS

	HOME							AWAY							NEUTRAL							TOTAL						
Africa XI															1	1	0	0	2	:	0	1	1	0	0	2	:	0
Albania	4	3	1	0	11	:	1	3	2	0	1	3	:	2								7	5	1	1	14	:	3
Algeria	1	1	0	0	4	:	1															1	1	0	0	4	:	1
Andorra	2	2	0	0	6	:	0								1	1	0	0	1	:	0	3	3	0	0	7	:	0
Argentina	5	1	1	3	2	:	4	4	1	1	2	5	:	7	2	0	1	1	7	:	9	11	2	3	6	14	:	20
Armenia	3	3	0	0	8	:	0	2	2	0	0	6	:	2								5	5	0	0	14	:	2
Australia	1	1	0	0	6	:	0	1	0	1	0	1	:	1	2	1	0	1	1	:	1	4	2	1	1	8	:	2
Austria	12	7	1	4	22	:	19	9	4	1	4	14	:	18	2	1	0	1	3	:	3	23	12	2	9	39	:	40
Azerbaijan	1	1	0	0	10	:	0								1	1	0	0	2	:	0	2	2	0	0	12	:	0
Belarus	2	1	0	1	3	:	2	3	1	2	0	5	:	3								5	2	2	1	8	:	5
Belgium	35	14	9	12	76	:	70	35	7	7	21	43	:	89	3	2	1	0	6	:	3	73	23	17	33	125	:	162
Bosnia and Herz.	2	0	2	0	2	:	2	2	2	0	0	4	:	1								4	2	2	0	6	:	3
Brazil	9	3	2	4	10	:	12	2	0	1	1	2	:	5	4	2	1	1	6	:	7	15	5	4	6	18	:	24
Bulgaria	11	7	3	1	26	:	10	8	1	1	6	8	:	14	2	1	0	1	3	:	2	21	9	4	8	37	:	26
Cameroon	3	2	1	0	5	:	3															3	2	1	0	5	:	3

Canada											1	1	0	0	1 : 0	1	1	0	0	1 : 0
Cent America XI											1	1	0	0	5 : 0	1	1	0	0	5 : 0
Chile	3	2	1	0	10 : 2	1	0	0	1	1 : 2	1	0	0	1	0 : 1	5	2	1	2	11 : 5
China P.R.	1	1	0	0	3 : 1						1	0	0	1	0 : 1	2	1	0	1	3 : 2
Colombia	2	2	0	0	2 : 0						1	1	0	0	3 : 2	3	3	0	0	5 : 2
Costa Rica	1	1	0	0	2 : 1						1	1	0	0	3 : 2	2	2	0	0	5 : 3
Croatia	3	2	1	0	5 : 1	1	1	0	0	2 : 0	1	0	1	0	2 : 2	5	3	2	0	9 : 3
Cyprus	4	4	0	0	15 : 0	4	3	1	0	12 : 2						8	7	1	0	27 : 2
Czech Republic	15	5	3	7	20 : 23	5	2	1	2	9 : 10	4	1	2	1	4 : 6	24	8	6	10	33 : 39
Denmark	6	6	0	0	11 : 1	4	1	1	2	4 : 6	5	1	0	4	5 : 30	15	8	1	6	20 : 37
East Germany	3	1	1	1	4 : 3	3	0	1	2	1 : 4	1	1	0	0	3 : 0	7	2	2	3	8 : 7
Ecuador	1	1	0	0	2 : 0						1	0	1	0	0 : 0	2	1	1	0	2 : 0
Egypt	1	1	0	0	5 : 0											1	1	0	0	5 : 0
England	15	6	1	8	26 : 38	12	2	3	7	10 : 28	5	1	2	2	4 : 6	32	9	6	17	40 : 72
England Amat.	6	1	0	5	3 : 39	2	0	0	2	1 : 22						8	1	0	7	4 : 61
Estonia	1	1	0	0	4 : 0											1	1	0	0	4 : 0
Faroe Islands	3	3	0	0	13 : 0	3	3	0	0	9 : 0						6	6	0	0	22 : 0
Finland	4	4	0	0	12 : 2	4	4	0	0	6 : 1						8	8	0	0	18 : 3
Georgia	2	2	0	0	4 : 1	2	1	1	0	3 : 0						4	3	1	0	7 : 1
Germany	13	8	3	2	18 : 10	11	3	2	6	17 : 25	4	1	1	2	9 : 9	28	12	6	10	44 : 44
Greece	5	5	0	0	19 : 4	2	1	1	0	4 : 2	1	0	0	1	0 : 1	8	6	1	1	23 : 7
Honduras											1	1	0	0	3 : 0	1	1	0	0	3 : 0
Hungary	12	5	1	6	16 : 17	8	1	1	6	9 : 29	2	2	0	0	6 : 1	22	8	2	12	31 : 47
Iceland	7	7	0	0	27 : 7	5	2	3	0	8 : 3						12	9	3	0	35 : 10
Iran	1	1	0	0	2 : 1											1	1	0	0	2 : 1
Israel	4	2	1	1	7 : 3	4	1	3	0	6 : 2	1	1	0	0	2 : 1	9	4	4	1	15 : 6
Italy	15	3	7	5	20 : 23	16	4	2	10	21 : 47	7	3	1	3	12 : 11	38	10	10	18	53 : 81
Ivory Coast	2	1	1	0	3 : 0											2	1	1	0	3 : 0
Jamaica	1	1	0	0	8 : 0											1	1	0	0	8 : 0
Japan	3	2	0	1	7 : 2	2	2	0	0	5 : 1	1	0	1	0	2 : 2	6	4	1	1	14 : 5
Korea Republic						2	2	0	0	8 : 2	1	0	1	0	1 : 1	3	2	1	0	9 : 3
Kuwait						1	1	0	0	1 : 0	1	1	0	0	4 : 1	2	2	0	0	5 : 1
Latvia	1	1	0	0	7 : 0											1	1	0	0	7 : 0
Lithuania	2	2	0	0	3 : 0	2	2	0	0	2 : 0						4	4	0	0	5 : 0
Luxembourg	7	7	0	0	34 : 2	9	8	0	1	34 : 9						16	15	0	1	68 : 11
Malta	1	1	0	0	6 : 0	1	1	0	0	4 : 0						2	2	0	0	10 : 0
Mexico	2	2	0	0	3 : 0						5	3	1	1	12 : 6	7	5	1	1	15 : 6
Morocco	3	2	1	0	5 : 3	2	1	1	0	7 : 3						5	3	2	0	12 : 6
Netherlands	10	5	2	3	20 : 19	13	6	1	6	20 : 29	2	0	1	1	1 : 4	25	11	4	10	41 : 52
New Zealand	1	1	0	0	5 : 0											1	1	0	0	5 : 0
Nigeria	1	0	0	1	0 : 1						1	1	0	0	2 : 0	2	1	0	1	2 : 1
Northern Ireland	5	3	1	1	12 : 3	3	1	2	0	3 : 2	2	2	0	0	8 : 1	10	6	3	1	23 : 6
Norway	8	4	2	2	13 : 8	7	3	2	2	9 : 7						15	7	4	4	22 : 15
Paraguay	3	1	2	0	2 : 1						1	1	0	0	7 : 3	4	2	2	0	9 : 4
Peru	1	0	0	1	0 : 1											1	0	0	1	0 : 1
Poland	9	4	3	2	11 : 9	6	4	2	0	14 : 4	1	0	0	1	2 : 3	16	8	5	3	27 : 16
Portugal	15	11	1	3	34 : 18	8	5	0	3	12 : 10	2	2	0	0	3 : 1	25	18	1	6	49 : 29
Rep.Ireland Am.	1	0	0	1	1 : 2											1	0	0	1	1 : 2
Rep. of Ireland	7	4	3	0	8 : 3	8	3	2	3	11 : 10						15	7	5	3	19 : 13
Romania	9	6	2	1	12 : 5	5	1	2	2	8 : 11	2	1	1	0	1 : 0	16	8	5	3	21 : 16
Russia	4	2	1	1	9 : 6	2	1	0	1	3 : 3						6	3	1	2	12 : 9
Saudi Arabia	1	1	0	0	4 : 0											1	1	0	0	4 : 0
Scotland	10	6	0	4	19 : 8	5	1	0	4	2 : 6	1	1	0	0	2 : 1	16	8	0	8	23 : 15
Senegal											1	0	0	1	0 : 1	1	0	0	1	0 : 1
Serbia	18	12	4	2	37 : 19	10	0	5	5	8 : 17	3	0	0	3	4 : 7	31	12	9	10	49 : 43
Slovakia	2	1	0	1	5 : 2	2	1	1	0	1 : 0						4	2	1	1	6 : 2
Slovenia	2	2	0	0	8 : 2	1	1	0	0	2 : 0						3	3	0	0	10 : 2
South Africa	2	2	0	0	5 : 1	2	0	1	1	1 : 2						4	2	1	1	6 : 3
Soviet Union	6	2	2	2	6 : 8	5	0	3	2	6 : 9	1	0	1	0	1 : 1	12	2	6	4	13 : 18
Spain	17	8	3	6	22 : 28	13	2	3	8	9 : 28	4	2	1	1	6 : 5	34	12	7	15	37 : 61
Sweden	10	7	2	1	16 : 6	9	3	3	3	12 : 11	1	0	0	1	0 : 2	20	10	5	5	28 : 19
Switzerland	16	6	7	3	25 : 21	19	8	2	9	34 : 36	3	2	1	0	8 : 3	38	16	10	12	67 : 60
Togo											1	1	0	0	2 : 0	1	1	0	0	2 : 0
Tunisia	2	2	0	0	5 : 1	2	0	2	0	2 : 2						4	2	2	0	7 : 3
Turkey	3	3	0	0	8 : 2	1	1	0	0	4 : 0						4	4	0	0	12 : 2
Ukraine	4	3	1	0	6 : 0	5	2	2	1	8 : 5						9	5	3	1	14 : 5
United States	2	2	0	0	4 : 0	1	1	0	0	6 : 0						3	3	0	0	10 : 0
Uruguay	4	1	2	1	3 : 5	1	0	0	1	0 : 1	3	0	2	1	1 : 2	8	1	4	3	4 : 8
Wales	4	2	1	1	9 : 4											4	2	1	1	9 : 4
World XI	1	1	0	0	5 : 1											1	1	0	0	5 : 1
TOTAL	**419**	**241**	**80**	**98**	**831 : 492**	**303**	**110**	**68**	**125**	**450 : 533**	**94**	**43**	**21**	**30**	**160 : 142**	**816**	**394**	**169**	**253**	**1441 : 1167**

GEORGIA

The Country:
Georgia (საქართველო)
Capital: Tbilisi
Surface: 69,700 km²
Inhabitants: 3,720,400
Time: UTC+4

The FA:
Georgian Football Federation
76a Chavchavadze Avenue, 0162 Tbilisi
Foundation date: 1930/1992
Member of FIFA since: 1992
Member of UEFA since: 1992

NATIONAL TEAM RECORDS

EUROPEAN CHAMPIONSHIP	
1960	-
1964	-
1968	-
1972	-
1976	-
1980	-
1984	-
1988	-
1992	-
1996	Qualifiers
2000	Qualifiers
2004	Qualifiers
2008	Qualifiers
2012	Qualifiers
2016	Qualifiers

FIFA WORLD CUP	
1930	-
1934	-
1938	-
1950	-
1954	-
1958	-
1962	-
1966	-
1970	-
1974	-
1978	-
1982	-
1986	-
1990	-
1994	Did not enter
1998	Qualifiers
2002	Qualifiers
2006	Qualifiers
2010	Qualifiers
2014	Qualifiers

OLYMPIC FOOTBALL TOURNAMENTS 1908-2016							
1908	-	**1948**	-	**1972**	-	**1996**	Qualifiers
1912	-	**1952**	-	**1976**	-	**2000**	Qualifiers
1920	-	**1956**	-	**1980**	-	**2004**	Qualifiers
1924	-	**1960**	-	**1984**	-	**2008**	Qualifiers
1928	-	**1964**	-	**1988**	-	**2012**	Qualifiers
1936	-	**1968**	-	**1992**	-	**2016**	Qualifiers

FIFA CONFEDERATIONS CUP 1992-2013
None

PLAYER WITH MOST INTERNATIONAL CAPS – Top 5				
1.	Levan KOBIASHVILI	-	100 caps	(1996-2011)
2.	Zurab Khizanishvili	-	92 caps	(1999-2015)
3.	Kakhaber Kaladze	-	83 caps	(1996-2011)
4.	Giorgi Nemsadze	-	69 caps	(1992-2004)
5.	Aleksandre Iashvili	-	67 caps	(1996-2011)

PLAYER WITH MOST INTERNATIONAL GOALS – Top 5				
1.	Shota ARVELADZE	-	26 goals	/ 61 caps (1992-2007)
2.	Temuri Ketsbaia	-	17 goals	/ 52 caps (1990-2002)
3.	Aleksandre Iashvili	-	15 goals	/ 67 caps (1996-2011)
4.	Levan Kobiashvili	-	12 goals	/ 100 caps (1996-2011)
	Giorgi Demetradze	-	12 goals	/ 56 caps (1996-2003)

FULL INTERNATIONALS (1990-2016)

1. 27.05.1990 **GEORGIA - LITHUANIA** **2-2(0-1)**
Dinamo Stadium, Tbilisi; Referee: Velodi Miminoshvili (Soviet Union); Attendance: 55,000
GEO: Aslan Baladze (1/0), Gela Ketashvili (Cap) (1/0), Kakhaber Tskhadadze (1/0) [70.Kakhaber Kacharava (1/1)], Dmitri Kudinov (1/0), Giorgi Pirtskhalava (1/0), Giorgi Nadiradze (1/0), Temuri Ketsbaia (1/0), Zaza Revishvili (1/0) [46.Rostom Korgashvili (1/0)], Otar Korgalidze (1/0) [46.Melori Bigvava (1/0)], Mamuka Pantsulaya (1/0) [46.Gocha Gogrichiani (1/0)], Gia Guruli (1/1). Trainer: Givi Nodia.
Goals: Gia Guruli (62), Kakhaber Kacharava (81).

2. 02.07.1991 **MOLDOVA - GEORGIA** **2-4(1-2)**
Stadionul Republican, Chişinău; Referee: Aleksandr Gorin (Soviet Union); Attendance: 7,000
GEO: Nikoloz Chkheidze (1/0), Dmitri Kudinov (2/0), Kakhaber Tskhadadze (Cap) (2/0), Murtaz Shelia (1/0), Gia Jishkariani (1/0), David Tsomaia (1/0), Giorgi Kilasonia (1/0), Melori Bigvava (2/0) [59.Mikheil Jishkariani (1/1)], Giorgi Daraselia (1/1), David Kizilashvili (1/0) [65.Mikheil Kavelashvili (1/1)], Temuri Ketsbaia (2/1). Trainer: Anatoli Norakidze.
Goals: Temuri Ketsbaia (5), Giorgi Daraselia (13), Mikheil Jishkariani (79), Mikheil Kavelashvili (88).

3. 02.09.1992 **LITHUANIA – GEORGIA** **1-0(0-0)**
„S. Dariaus ir S. Girėno“ stadionas, Kaunas; Referee: V. Licholajs (Latvia); Attendance: 4,500
GEO: Akaki Devadze (1/0), Kakhaber Gogichaishvili (1/0), Kakhaber Sidamonidze (1/0), Dmitri Kudinov (3/0), Gia Jishkariani (Cap) (2/0), David Tsomaia (2/0), Giorgi Daraselia (2/1), Revaz Arveladze (1/0) [57.Giorgi Nemsadze (1/0)], Gocha Chikovani (1/0), David Kizilashvili (2/0), Shota Arveladze (1/0) [63.David Janashia (1/0)]. Trainer: Anatoli Norakidze (1).

4. 17.09.1992 **GEORGIA – AZERBAIJAN** **6-3(1-1)**
„David Kipiani“ Stadium, Gurjaani; Referee: Guram Sepiashvili (Giorgia); Attendance: 2,000
GEO: Akaki Devadze (2/0) [75.David Janelidze (1/0)], Malkhaz Arziani 1/0), Dmitri Kudinov (4/0), Kakhaber Sidamonidze (2/0) [46.Giorgi Nemsadze (2/0)], Gia Jishkariani (Cap) (3/1), David Tsomaia (3/0), Giorgi Daraselia (3/2) [53.Giorgi Kinkladze (1/0)], Kakhaber Gogichaishvili (2/1) [75.Mikheil Kavelashvili (2/1)], Revaz Arveladze (2/0), David Kizilashvili (3/2), Shota Arveladze (2/1) [75.David Janashia (2/0)]. Trainer: Anatoli Norakidze (2).
Goals: David Kizilashvili (30, 48), Giorgi Daraselia (52), Shota Arveladze (69), Kakhaber Gogichaishvili (71 penalty), Gia Jishkariani (79 penalty).

5. 22.12.1992 **CYPRUS – GEORGIA** **1-0(1-0)**
Stádio Tsirion, Limassol; Referee: A. Onisiforou (Cyprus); Attendance: 2,500
GEO: Akaki Devadze (3/0), Bessarion Chedia (1/0), Kakhaber Tskhadadze (3/0) [46.Temur Kabisashvili (1/0)], Murtaz Shelia (2/0), Gia Jishkariani (Cap) (4/1), David Tsomaia (4/0), Temuri Ketsbaia (3/1), Kakhaber Gogichaishvili (3/1), Kakhaber Kacharava (2/1), David Kizilashvili (4/2) [72.Mikheil Jishkariani (2/1)], Giorgi Daraselia (4/2) [66.Giorgi Nemsadze (3/0)]. Trainer: Anatoli Norakidze (3).

6. 25.05.1993 **AZERBAIJAN – GEORGIA** **1-0(0-0)**
Markazi Stadion, Gəncə; Referee: Rustam Ragimov (Azerbaijan); Attendance: 9,500
GEO: Akaki Devadze (4/0) [46.David Janelidze (2/0)], Giorgi Pirtskhalava (2/0), Kakhaber Sidamonidze (3/0), Nugzar Lobjanidze (1/0), Gia Jishkariani (Cap) (5/1), Kakhaber Gogichaishvili (4/1), Giorgi Nemsadze (4/0), Vasil Sepashvili (1/0) [66.Yuri Gabiskiria (1/0)], Melori Bigvava (3/0) [46.David Janashia (3/0)], Giorgi Daraselia (5/2), David Kizilashvili (5/2).Trainer: Aleksandre Chivadze (1).

7. 08.02.1994 **SLOVENIA – GEORGIA** **1-0(0-0)** International Tournament
Ta'Qali National Stadium, Attard (Malta); Referee: Lawrence Sammut (Malta); Attendance: 1,000
GEO: Akaki Devadze (5/0), Zaza Revishvili (2/0), Kakhaber Tskhadadze (Cap) (4/0), Murtaz Shelia (3/0), Dmitri Kudinov (5/0), Kakhaber Gogichaishvili (5/1), Giorgi Nemsadze (5/0), Gocha Jamarauli (1/0), Temuri Ketsbaia (4/1), Giorgi Kinkladze (2/0) [72.Mikheil Kavelashvili (3/1)], David Kizilashvili (6/2). Trainer: Aleksandre Chivadze (2).

8. 10.02.1994 **MALTA – GEORGIA** **0-1(0-0)** International Tournament
Ta'Qali National Stadium, Attard; Referee: Darko Jamšek (Slovenia); Attendance: 12,000
GEO: Irakli Zoidze (1/0), Zaza Revishvili (3/0), Kakhaber Tskhadadze (Cap) (5/0), Murtaz Shelia (4/0) [75.Besik Beradze (1/0)], Dmitri Kudinov (6/0) [55.Kakhaber Sidamonidze (4/0)], Mikheil Kavelashvili (4/1), Giorgi Nemsadze (6/0), Gocha Jamarauli (2/0), Temuri Ketsbaia (5/2), Giorgi Kinkladze (3/0), David Kizilashvili (7/2). Trainer: Aleksandre Chivadze (3).
Goal: Temuri Ketsbaia (16 penalty).

9. 12.02.1994 **TUNISIA – GEORGIA** **0-2(0-0)** International Tournament
Ta'Qali National Stadium, Attard (Malta); Referee: Charles Agius (Malta); Attendance: 5000
GEO: Akaki Devadze (6/0), Zaza Revishvili (4/0), Kakhaber Sidamonidze (5/0), Murtaz Shelia (Cap) (5/0), Dmitri Kudinov (7/1), Kakhaber Gogichaishvili (6/1), Giorgi Nemsadze (7/0), Gocha Jamarauli (3/0), Besik Beradze (2/0), Giorgi Kinkladze (4/0), Mikheil Kavelashvili (5/2) [80.David Kizilashvili (8/2)]. Trainer: Aleksandre Chivadze (4).
Goals: Mikheil Kavelashvili (48), Dmitri Kudinov (61).

10. 23.02.1994 **ISRAEL – GEORGIA** **2-0(1-0)**
Yud-Alef Stadium, Ashdod; Referee: Haim Lipkovich (Israel); Attendance: 1,500
GEO: Akaki Devadze (7/0), Besik Beradze (3/0) [73.David Janashia (4/0)], Kakhaber Tskhadadze (Cap) (6/0), Nugzar Lobjanidze (2/0), Gia Jishkariani (6/1), Giorgi Nemsadze (8/0) [46.Zaza Oloshvili (1/0)], Gocha Jamarauli (4/0), Zaza Revishvili (5/0), Archil Arveladze (1/0) [46.Mikheil Kavelashvili (6/2)], Temur Tugushi (1/0) [46.Gia Guruli (2/1)], Shota Arveladze (3/1). Trainer: Aleksandre Chivadze (5).

11. 11.06.1994 **NIGERIA – GEORGIA** **5-1(2-1)**
Liberty Stadium, Ibadan; Referee: Oluferni Orimson Olaniyan (Nigeria); Attendance: 9,000
GEO: Irakli Zoidze (2/0) [75.Soso Grishikashvili (1/0)], Besik Beradze (4/0), Kakhaber Tskhadadze (Cap) (7/0), Murtaz Shelia (6/0) [46.Nugzar Lobjanidze (3/0)], Gia Jishkariani (7/1), Dmitri Kudinov (8/1) [65.David Janashia (5/0)], Giorgi Nemsadze (9/0), Gocha Jamarauli (5/0), Revaz Arveladze (3/1), Giorgi Kinkladze (5/0), Archil Arveladze (2/0) [78.Gela Inalishvili (1/0)]. Trainer: Aleksandre Chivadze (6).
Goal: Revaz Arveladze (12).

12. 26.06.1994 **LATVIA - GEORGIA** **1-3(0-1)**
ASK Stadions, Riga; Referee: Algirdas Dubinskas (Lithuania); Attendance: 2,500
GEO: Irakli Zoidze (3/0), Besik Beradze (5/0), Merab Katsitadze (1/0), Giorgi Nemsadze (10/0), Gia Jishkariani (8/1), David Janashia (6/1) [83.Vasil Sepashvili (2/0)], Gela Inalishvili (2/0), Gocha Jamarauli (Cap) (6/1), Temur Tugushi (2/0) [78.Gocha Tkebuchava (1/0)], Giorgi Kinkladze (6/0), Kakhaber Kacharava (3/2). Trainer: Aleksandre Chivadze (7).
Goals: David Janashia (13), Kakhaber Kacharava (74), Gocha Jamarauli (76).

13. 19.07.1994 **GEORGIA - MALTA** **1-1(1-1)**
„Boris Paichadze“ Erovnuli Stadioni, Tbilisi; Referee: Urs Meier (Switzerland); Attendance: 35,200
GEO: Irakli Zoidze (4/0), Zaza Revishvili (6/0), Giorgi Nemsadze (11/0), Murtaz Shelia (7/0), Gia Jishkariani (9/1), Revaz Arveladze (4/1), Gela Inalishvili (3/0) [46.Mikheil Kavelashvili (7/2)], Gocha Jamarauli (Cap) (7/1), Giorgi Kinkladze (7/0), Temur Tugushi (3/0) [46.Archil Arveladze (3/0)], Shota Arveladze (4/2). Trainer: Aleksandre Chivadze (8).
Goal: Shota Arveladze (37 penalty).

14. 07.09.1994 **GEORGIA - MOLDOVA** **0-1(0-1)** 10th EC. Qualifiers
„Boris Paichadze“ Erovnuli Stadioni, Tbilisi; Referee: Ahmet Çakar (Turkey); Attendance: 40,000
GEO: Irakli Zoidze (5/0), Giorgi Nemsadze (12/0), Kakhaber Tskhadadze (Cap) (8/0), Murtaz Shelia (8/0), Mikheil Kavelashvili (8/2), Revaz Arveladze (5/1) [70.Zaza Revishvili (7/0)], Gocha Jamarauli (8/1), Gia Guruli (3/1) [46.Gela Inalishvili (4/0)], Archil Arveladze (4/0), Giorgi Kinkladze (8/0), Shota Arveladze (5/2). Trainer: Aleksandre Chivadze (9).

15. 12.10.1994 **BULGARIA - GEORGIA** **2-0(0-0)** 10th EC. Qualifiers
Nationalen stadion "Vasil Levski", Sofia; Referee: Ladislav Gadoši (Slovakia); Attendance: 50,000
GEO: Akaki Devadze (8/0), Zaza Revishvili (8/0), Kakhaber Tskhadadze (Cap) (9/0), Murtaz Shelia (9/0), Giorgi Chikhradze (1/0), Dmitri Kudinov (9/1), Giorgi Nemsadze (13/0) [72.Gela Inalishvili (5/0)], Kakhaber Gogichaishvili (7/1), Temuri Ketsbaia (6/2), Giorgi Kinkladze (9/0), Shota Arveladze (6/2) [78.Gia Guruli (4/1)]. Trainer: Aleksandre Chivadze (10).

16. 16.11.1994 **GEORGIA - WALES** **5-0(2-0)** 10th EC. Qualifiers
„Boris Paichadze“ Erovnuli Stadioni, Tbilisi; Referee: Alain Sars (France); Attendance: 55,000
GEO: Akaki Devadze (9/0), Zaza Revishvili (9/0), Kakhaber Tskhadadze (Cap) (10/0), Murtaz Shelia (10/0), Giorgi Chikhradze (2/0), Kakhaber Gogichaishvili (8/1), Giorgi Nemsadze (14/0) [42.Gela Inalishvili (6/0)], Gocha Gogrichiani (2/1), Temuri Ketsbaia (7/4) [75.Mikheil Kavelashvili (9/2)], Giorgi Kinkladze (10/1), Shota Arveladze (7/3). Trainer: Aleksandre Chivadze (11).
Goals: Temuri Ketsbaia (31), Giorgi Kinkladze (41), Temuri Ketsbaia (49), Gocha Gogrichiani (59), Shota Arveladze (67).

17. 14.12.1994 **ALBANIA - GEORGIA** **0-1(0-1)** 10th EC. Qualifiers
Stadiumi „Kombëtar Qemal Stafa“, Tiranë; Referee: László Molnár (Hungary); Attendance: 15,000
GEO: Akaki Devadze (10/0), Zaza Revishvili (10/0), Dmitri Kudinov (10/1), Murtaz Shelia (Cap) (11/0), Giorgi Chikhradze (3/0), Kakhaber Gogichaishvili (9/1) [63.Mikheil Jishkariani (3/1)], Gela Inalishvili (7/0), Gocha Gogrichiani (3/1), Temuri Ketsbaia (8/4), Giorgi Kinkladze (11/1), Shota Arveladze (8/4) [75.Gocha Jamarauli (9/1)]. Trainer: Aleksandre Chivadze (12).
Goal: Shota Arveladze (19).

18. 29.03.1995 **GEORGIA - GERMANY** **0-2(0-2)** 10th EC. Qualifiers
„Boris Paichadze“ Erovnuli Stadioni, Tbilisi; Referee: Martin Bodenham (England); Attendance: 75,000
GEO: Akaki Devadze (11/0), Zaza Revishvili (11/0), Kakhaber Tskhadadze (Cap) (11/0), Murtaz Shelia (12/0), Giorgi Chikhradze (4/0), Kakhaber Gogichaishvili (10/1), Dmitri Kudinov (11/1), Gocha Jamarauli (10/1) [64.Gocha Gogrichiani (4/1)], Revaz Arveladze (6/1) [77.Mikheil Kavelashvili (10/2)], Giorgi Kinkladze (12/1), Shota Arveladze (9/4). Trainer: Aleksandre Chivadze (13).

19. 26.04.1995 **GEORGIA - ALBANIA** **2-0(2-0)** 10th EC. Qualifiers
„Boris Paichadze“ Erovnuli Stadioni, Tbilisi; Referee: Roelof Luinge (Netherlands); Attendance: 40,000
GEO: Akaki Devadze (12/0), Giorgi Gudushauri (1/0), Dmitri Kudinov (12/1), Murtaz Shelia (Cap) (13/0) [70.Nugzar Lobjanidze (4/0)], Kakhaber Gogichaishvili (11/1), Gela Inalishvili (8/0), Gocha Jamarauli (11/1), Temuri Ketsbaia (9/5), David Kizilashvili (9/2) [59.Archil Arveladze (5/0)], Giorgi Kinkladze (13/1), Shota Arveladze (10/5). Trainer: Aleksandre Chivadze (14).
Goals: Shota Arveladze (2), Temuri Ketsbaia (42).

20. 07.06.1995 **WALES - GEORGIA** **0-1(0-0)** 10th EC. Qualifiers
Arms Park, Cardiff; Referee: Ilkka Koho (Finland); Attendance: 8,241
GEO: Akaki Devadze (13/0), Besik Beradze (6/0), Kakhaber Tskhadadze (Cap) (12/0), Murtaz Shelia (14/0), Giorgi Chikhradze (5/0), Kakhaber Gogichaishvili (12/1), Gela Inalishvili (9/0), Mikheil Kavelashvili (11/2) [73.Levan Tskitishvili (1/0)], Temuri Ketsbaia (10/5), Giorgi Kinkladze (14/2), Shota Arveladze (11/5) [86.Giorgi Kilasonia (2/0)]. Trainer: Aleksandre Chivadze (15).
Goal: Giorgi Kinkladze (72).

21. 06.09.1995 **GERMANY - GEORGIA** **4-1(1-1)** 10th EC. Qualifiers
Frankenstadion, Nürnberg; Referee: James McCluskey (Scotland); Attendance: 44,500
GEO: Akaki Devadze (14/0), Gocha Gujabidze (1/0), Dmitri Kudinov (13/1), Murtaz Shelia (Cap) (15/0), Giorgi Chikhradze (6/0), Kakhaber Gogichaishvili (13/1) [68.Archil Arveladze (6/0)], Giorgi Nemsadze (15/0), Mikheil Kavelashvili (12/2) [46.Giorgi Kilasonia (3/0)], Temuri Ketsbaia (11/6), Giorgi Kinkladze (15/2), Shota Arveladze (12/5). Trainer: Aleksandre Chivadze (16).
Goal: Temuri Ketsbaia (28).

22. 11.10.1995 **GEORGIA - BULGARIA** **2-1(1-0)** 10th EC. Qualifiers
„Boris Paichadze“ Erovnuli Stadioni, Tbilisi; Referee: Urs Meier (Switzerland); Attendance: 40,000
GEO: Irakli Zoidze (6/0), Giorgi Gudushauri (2/0) [82.Besik Beradze (7/0)], Dmitri Kudinov (14/1), Murtaz Shelia (Cap) (16/0), Giorgi Chikhradze (7/0), Kakhaber Gogichaishvili (14/1), Giorgi Nemsadze (16/0), Gocha Jamarauli (12/1) [74.Giorgi Kilasonia (4/0)], Archil Arveladze (7/0) [46.Mikheil Kavelashvili (13/2)], Giorgi Kinkladze (16/3), Shota Arveladze (13/6). Trainer: Aleksandre Chivadze (17).
Goals: Shota Arveladze (1), Giorgi Kinkladze (47 penalty).

23. 15.11.1995 **MOLDOVA - GEORGIA** **3-2(2-0)** 10th EC. Qualifiers

Stadionul Republican, Chişinău; Referee: Mario van der Ende (Netherlands); Attendance: 7,000

GEO: Irakli Zoidze (7/0), Giorgi Gudushauri (3/0) [58.David Janashia (7/2)], Dmitri Kudinov (15/1), Besik Beradze (8/0), Giorgi Chikhradze (8/0), Kakhaber Gogichaishvili (15/1), Levan Tskitishvili (2/0), Gocha Jamarauli (13/1) [62.Mamuka Machavariani (1/0)], Temuri Ketsbaia (Cap) (12/6), Giorgi Kinkladze (17/3), Shota Arveladze (14/6). Trainer: Aleksandre Chivadze (18).

Goals: David Janashia (68), Vitali Culibaba (81 own goal).

24. 27.03.1996 **CYPRUS - GEORGIA** **0-2(0-0)**

Stádio Tsirion, Limassol; Referee: Andreas Giorgiou (Cyprus); Attendance: 2,000

GEO: Irakli Zoidze (8/0), Giorgi Gudushauri (4/0) [84.Mamuka Machavariani (2/0)], Kakhaber Tskhadadze (Cap) (13/0), Murtaz Shelia (17/0), Dmitri Kudinov (16/1), Kakhaber Gogichaishvili (16/1), Giorgi Nemsadze (17/0), Temuri Ketsbaia (13/7), Gocha Jamarauli (14/2), Mikheil Kavelashvili (14/2) [72.Kakhaber Kaladze (1/0)], Shota Arveladze (15/6). Trainer: Aleksandre Chivadze (19).

Goals: Temuri Ketsbaia (53), Gocha Jamarauli (65).

25. 24.04.1996 **ROMANIA - GEORGIA** **5-0(3-0)**

Stadionul Steaua, Bucureşti; Referee: Athanasios Zahariadis (Greece); Attendance: 11,500

GEO: Akaki Devadze (15/0), Zaza Revishvili (12/0), Kakhaber Tskhadadze (Cap) (14/0) [77.Vasil Sepashvili (3/0)], Dmitri Kudinov (17/1), Giorgi Chikhradze (9/0), Kakhaber Gogichaishvili (17/1) [67.Zurab Ionanidze (1/0)], Giorgi Nemsadze (18/0) [46.Valter Guchua (1/0)], Temuri Ketsbaia (14/7), Giorgi Kinkladze (18/3), Gocha Jamarauli (15/2) [46.Levan Tskitishvili (3/0)], Shota Arveladze (16/6) [46.Gocha Gogrichiani (5/1)]. Trainer: Aleksandre Chivadze (20).

26. 08.05.1996 **GREECE - GEORGIA** **2-1(0-1)**

Stádio Zosimades, Ioannina; Referee: Luan Zilfo (Albania); Attendance: 13,000

GEO: Irakli Zoidze (9/0) [22.Nikoloz Togonidze (1/0)], Giorgi Gudushauri (5/0) [46.Giorgi Demetradze (1/0)], Nugzar Lobjanidze (5/0), Dmitri Kudinov (18/1), Giorgi Chikhradze (10/0), Kakhaber Gogichaishvili (18/1), Giorgi Nemsadze (19/0), Temuri Ketsbaia (Cap) (15/7), Revaz Arveladze (7/1), Gocha Gogrichiani (6/2) [55.Valter Guchua (2/0)], Shota Arveladze (17/6). Trainer: Aleksandre Chivadze (21).

Goal: Gocha Gogrichiani (15).

27. 01.09.1996 **NORWAY - GEORGIA** **1-0(0-0)**

Ullevaal Stadion, Oslo; Referee: Knud Stadsgaard (Denmark); Attendance: 8,910

GEO: Irakli Zoidze (10/0), Dmitri Kudinov (19/1), Kakhaber Tskhadadze (Cap) (15/0), Murtaz Shelia (18/0) [63.Nugzar Lobjanidze (6/0)], Levan Kobiashvili (1/0), Kakhaber Gogichaishvili (19/1), Giorgi Nemsadze (20/0), Revaz Arveladze (8/1) [67.Levan Tskitishvili (4/0)], Giorgi Kinkladze (19/3) [67.Gocha Jamarauli (16/2)], Temuri Ketsbaia (16/7), Shota Arveladze (18/6) [63.Mikheil Kavelashvili (15/2)]. Trainer: Aleksandre Chivadze (22).

28. 09.10.1996 **ITALY - GEORGIA** **1-0(1-0)** 16th WC. Qualifiers

Stadio "Renato Curi", Perugia; Referee: Eric Blareau (Belgium); Attendance: 16,146

GEO: Irakli Zoidze (11/0), Nugzar Lobjanidze (7/0), Kakhaber Tskhadadze (Cap) (16/0), Murtaz Shelia (19/0), Dmitri Kudinov (20/1) [46.Gela Inalishvili (10/0)], Levan Kobiashvili (2/0), Kakhaber Gogichaishvili (20/1), Giorgi Nemsadze (21/0), Gocha Gogrichiani (7/2) [31.Revaz Arveladze (9/1)], Giorgi Kinkladze (20/3), Temuri Ketsbaia (17/7). Trainer: Aleksandre Chivadze (23).

29. 09.11.1996 **GEORGIA - ENGLAND** **0-2(0-2)** 16th WC. Qualifiers

„Boris Paichadze" Erovnuli Stadioni, Tbilisi; Referee: Jorge Emanuel Monteiro Coroado (Portugal); Attendance: 75,000

GEO: Irakli Zoidze (12/0), Nugzar Lobjanidze (8/0), Kakhaber Tskhadadze (Cap) (17/0), Murtaz Shelia (20/0), Levan Kobiashvili (3/0), Kakhaber Gogichaishvili (21/1) [78.Giorgi Gudushauri (6/0)], Giorgi Nemsadze (22/0), Gocha Jamarauli (17/2), Giorgi Kinkladze (21/3), Temuri Ketsbaia (18/7), Shota Arveladze (19/6) [52.Gocha Gogrichiani (8/2)]. Trainer: Aleksandre Chivadze (24).

30. 05.12.1996 **LEBANON - GEORGIA** **4-2(0-0)**

Municipal Stadium, Beirut; Referee: Taleb Ramadan (Lebanon); Attendance: 2,000

GEO: David Aslanadze (1/0), Kakhaber Kaladze (2/0) [*sent off 65*], Shalva Khujadze (1/0) [78.Givi Didava (1/0)], Levan Kobiashvili (4/0), Levan Tskitishvili (5/0), Giorgi Kiknadze (Cap) (1/1), Giorgi Gakhokidze (1/0), Giorgi Daraselia (6/2), Mikheil Potskhveria (1/0) [38.Mikheil Ashvetia (1/0)], Aleksandre Iashvili (1/1) [70.Giorgi Demetradze (2/0)], Zviad Jeladze (1/0). Trainer: Vladimir Gutsaev (1).

Goals: Aleksandre Iashvili (58), Giorgi Kiknadze (67).

31. 08.12.1996 **LEBANON - GEORGIA** **3-2(3-2)**

Municipal Stadium, Beirut; Referee: Ahmad Nabil Ayad (Lebanon); Attendance: 3,500

GEO: David Aslanadze (2/0), Kakhaber Kaladze (3/0), Levan Tskitishvili (6/1) [46.Zviad Jeladze (2/0)], Givi Didava (2/0), Shalva Khujadze (2/0), Levan Kobiashvili (5/0), Giorgi Gakhokidze (2/1), Giorgi Kiknadze (Cap) (2/1), Mikheil Potskhveria (2/0) [65.Giorgi Demetradze (3/0)], Giorgi Daraselia (7/2), Aleksandre Iashvili (2/1). Trainer: Vladimir Gutsaev (2).

Goals: Giorgi Gakhokidze (12 penalty), Levan Tskitishvili (24).

32. 30.03.1997 **GEORGIA - ARMENIA** **7-0(2-0)**

„Boris Paichadze" Erovnuli Stadioni, Tbilisi; Referee: Valentin Ivanov (Russia); Attendance: 30,000

GEO: Irakli Zoidze (13/0) [55.Nikoloz Togonidze (2/0)], Nugzar Lobjanidze (9/0), Kakhaber Tskhadadze (Cap) (18/0), Murtaz Shelia (21/0) [61.Gela Shekiladze (1/0)], Giorgi Chikhradze (11/0) [46.Kakhaber Gogichaishvili (22/1)], Levan Kobiashvili (6/0), Giorgi Nemsadze (23/0), Gocha Jamarauli (18/2) [46.Mikheil Kavelashvili (16/3)], Giorgi Kinkladze (22/4) [61.Giorgi Gakhokidze (3/1)], Temuri Ketsbaia (19/7) [57.Archil Arveladze (8/2)], Shota Arveladze (20/9) [68.Amiran Mujiri (1/0)]. Trainer: David Kipiani (1).

Goals: Shota Arveladze (12), Giorgi Kinkladze (45 penalty), Shota Arveladze (53), Archil Arveladze (58, 60), Shota Arveladze (67), Mikheil Kavelashvili (81).

33. 30.04.1997 **ENGLAND - GEORGIA** **2-0(1-0)** 16th WC. Qualifiers

Wembley Stadium, London; Referee: Rémi Harrel (France); Attendance: 71,208

GEO: Irakli Zoidze (14/0), Gela Shekiladze (2/0), Kakhaber Tskhadadze (Cap) (19/0), Murtaz Shelia (22/0), Giorgi Chikhradze (12/0), Mamuka Machavariani (3/0) [33.Gocha Gogrichiani (9/2); 77.Archil Arveladze (9/2)], Giorgi Nemsadze (24/0), Gocha Jamarauli (19/2), Giorgi Kinkladze (23/4) [62.Giorgi Gakhokidze (4/1)], Temuri Ketsbaia (20/7), Shota Arveladze (21/9). Trainer: David Kipiani (2).

34. 07.06.1997 **GEORGIA - MOLDOVA** **2-0(1-0)** 16th WC. Qualifiers

Dinamo Stadium, Batumi; Referee: Charles Agius (Malta); Attendance: 17,000

GEO: Irakli Zoidze (15/0), Nugzar Lobjanidze (10/0), Kakhaber Tskhadadze (Cap) (20/0), Giorgi Chikhradze (13/0), Levan Kobiashvili (7/0), Kakhaber Gogichaishvili (23/1), Giorgi Nemsadze (25/0) [80.Archil Arveladze (10/2)], Gocha Jamarauli (20/2) [66.Giorgi Kiknadze (3/1)], Giorgi Kinkladze (24/5), Temuri Ketsbaia (21/7) [84.Zaza Janashia (1/0)], Shota Arveladze (22/10). Trainer: David Kipiani (3).

Goals: Shota Arveladze (27), Giorgi Kinkladze (52 penalty).

35. 14.06.1997 **POLAND – GEORGIA** **4-1(2-1)** 16th WC. Qualifiers
Stadion GKS, Katowice; Referee: Günther Benkö (Austria); Attendance: 2,000
GEO: Irakli Zoidze (16/0), Nugzar Lobjanidze (11/0), Kakhaber Tskhadadze (Cap) (21/0) Levan Kobiashvili (8/0) [72.Mikheil Kavelashvili (17/3)], Kakhaber Kaladze (4/0), Kakhaber Gogichaishvili (24/1) [46.Archil Arveladze (11/2)], Giorgi Nemsadze (26/0), Giorgi Kinkladze (25/5), Temuri Ketsbaia (22/7), Gocha Jamarauli (21/2) [46.Giorgi Kiknadze (4/1)], Shota Arveladze (23/11). Trainer: David Kipiani (4).
Goal: Shota Arveladze (25).

36. 10.09.1997 **GEORGIA – ITALY** **0-0** 16th WC. Qualifiers
„Boris Paichadze" Erovnuli Stadioni, Tbilisi; Referee: Rune Pedersen (Norway); Attendance: 51,117
GEO: Nikoloz Togonidze (3/0), Gela Shekiladze (3/0), Kakhaber Tskhadadze (Cap) (22/0) [19.Kakhaber Kaladze (5/0)], Murtaz Shelia (23/0), Giorgi Chikhradze (14/0), Levan Kobiashvili (9/0), Archil Arveladze (12/2) [79.Giorgi Daraselia (8/2)], Mikheil Kavelashvili (18/3), Temuri Ketsbaia (23/7), Giorgi Kinkladze (26/5) [65.Kakhaber Gogichaishvili (25/1)], Shota Arveladze (24/11). Trainer: David Kipiani (5).

37. 24.09.1997 **MOLDOVA – GEORGIA** **0-1(0-1)** 16th WC. Qualifiers
Stadionul Republican, Chişinău; Referee: Dani Koren (Israel); Attendance: 9,000
GEO: Nikoloz Togonidze (4/0), Nugzar Lobjanidze (12/0), Gela Shekiladze (4/0), Kakhaber Kaladze (6/0) [*sent off 63*], Giorgi Chikhradze (15/0), Giorgi Gakhokidze (5/1) [88.Gocha Jamarauli (22/2)], Giorgi Nemsadze (27/0), Mikheil Kavelashvili (19/3) [82.Murtaz Shelia (24/0)], Temuri Ketsbaia (24/8), Giorgi Kinkladze (27/5) [*sent off 71*], Archil Arveladze (13/2) [66.Valter Guchua (3/0)]. Trainer: David Kipiani (6).
Goal: Temuri Ketsbaia (10).

38. 11.10.1997 **GEORGIA – POLAND** **3-0(0-0)** 16th WC. Qualifiers
„Boris Paichadze" Erovnuli Stadioni, Tbilisi; Referee: Luboš Michel' (Slovakia); Attendance: 12,000
GEO: Nikoloz Togonidze (5/0), Nugzar Lobjanidze (13/0), Kakhaber Tskhadadze (Cap) (23/1), Murtaz Shelia (25/0), Giorgi Chikhradze (16/0), Giorgi Gakhokidze (6/1) [63.Gocha Jamarauli (23/2)], Giorgi Nemsadze (28/0), Archil Arveladze (14/3) [82.Kakhaber Gogichaishvili (26/1)], Mikheil Kavelashvili (20/3), Temuri Ketsbaia (25/9) [88.Giorgi Kiknadze (5/1)], Shota Arveladze (25/11). Trainer: David Kipiani (7).
Goals: Archil Arveladze (55), Kakhaber Tskhadadze (66), Temuri Ketsbaia (73).

39. 06.02.1998 **GEORGIA – LATVIA** **2-1(0-0)** International Tournament
Ta'Qali National Stadium, Attard (Malta); Referee: Alfred Micallef (Malta); Attendance: 3,000
GEO: Nikoloz Togonidze (6/0), Gela Shekiladze (5/0), Kakhaber Kaladze (7/0), Murtaz Shelia (26/0), Giorgi Chikhradze (17/0), Giorgi Gakhokidze (7/1), Temuri Ketsbaia (26/9) [82.Levan Tskitishvili (7/1)], Giorgi Nemsadze (Cap) (29/0) [80.Giorgi Kiknadze (6/1)], Gocha Jamarauli (24/4) [74.Levan Silagadze (1/0)], Archil Arveladze (15/3) [46.Mikheil Kavelashvili (21/3)], Shota Arveladze (26/11) [46.Aleksandre Iashvili (3/1)]. Trainer: Vladimir Gutsaev (3).
Goal: Gocha Jamarauli (53, 72).

40. 08.02.1998 **GEORGIA – ALBANIA** **3-0(2-0)** International Tournament
Ta'Qali National Stadium, Attard (Malta); Referee: Charles Agius (Malta); Attendance: 750
GEO: David Gvaramadze (1/0), Levan Silagadze (2/0), Gela Shekiladze (6/0), Murtaz Shelia (27/0), Kakhaber Kaladze (8/0), Giorgi Chikhradze (18/0), Temuri Ketsbaia (27/10), Giorgi Nemsadze (Cap) (30/0), Gocha Jamarauli (25/4) [74.Giorgi Kiknadze (7/1)], Mikheil Kavelashvili (22/4), Aleksandre Iashvili (4/2). Trainer: Vladimir Gutsaev (4).
Goals: Temuri Ketsbaia (20), Mikheil Kavelashvili (29), Aleksandre Iashvili (72).

41. 10.02.1998 **MALTA – GEORGIA** **1-3(0-1)** International Tournament
Ta'Qali National Stadium, Attard; Referee: Bujar Pregja (Albania); Attendance: 2,500
GEO: David Gvaramadze (2/0), Levan Silagadze (3/0) [78.Levan Tskitishvili (8/1)], Kakhaber Kaladze (9/0) [78.Vakhtang Khvadagiani (1/0)], Murtaz Shelia (28/0), Giorgi Chikhradze (19/0) [46.Aleksandre Iashvili (5/2)], Gela Shekiladze (7/0), Temuri Ketsbaia (28/10), Giorgi Kinkladze (28/5), Giorgi Nemsadze (Cap) (31/0), Gocha Jamarauli (26/5) [78.Giorgi Gakhokidze (8/1)], Mikheil Kavelashvili (23/6). Trainer: Vladimir Gutsaev (5).
Goals: Mikheil Kavelashvili (12), Gocha Jamarauli (72), Mikheil Kavelashvili (76).

42. 02.05.1998 **TUNISIA – GEORGIA** **1-1(0-1)**
Stade Olympique, Sousse; Referee: Kamel Berber (Algeria); Attendance: 30,000
GEO: David Gvaramadze (3/0), Gela Shekiladze (8/0), Kakhaber Tskhadadze (24/1), Kakhaber Kaladze (10/0), Levan Silagadze (4/0), Levan Kobiashvili (10/0) [66.Levan Tskitishvili (9/1)], Giorgi Nemsadze (Cap) (32/0), Temuri Ketsbaia (29/10), Giorgi Kinkladze (29/6), Gocha Jamarauli (27/5), Shota Arveladze (27/11). Trainer: Vladimir Gutsaev (6).
Goal: Giorgi Kinkladze (40).

43. 30.05.1998 **RUSSIA – GEORGIA** **1-1(1-1)**
Luzhniki Stadium, Moskva; Referee: Takhir Soulaimanov (Azerbaijan); Attendance: 75,000
GEO: Nikoloz Togonidze (7/0), Gela Shekiladze (9/0), Kakhaber Tskhadadze (25/1), Levan Kobiashvili (11/0), Levan Silagadze (5/0), Giorgi Nemsadze (Cap) (33/0) [15.Givi Didava (3/0)], Giorgi Gakhokidze (9/1) [77.Archil Arveladze (16/3)], Gocha Jamarauli (28/5), Giorgi Kinkladze (30/6) [84.Levan Tskitishvili (10/1)], Shota Arveladze (28/11), Zaza Janashia (2/1) [71.David Chaladze (1/0)]. Trainer: Vladimir Gutsaev (7).
Goal: Zaza Janashia (19).

44. 12.08.1998 **AZERBAIJAN – GEORGIA** **1-0(0-0)**
Markazi Stadion, Gəncə; Referee: Asim Khudiev (Azerbaijan); Attendance: 10,000
GEO: Soso Grishikashvili (2/0), Zurab Popkhadze (1/0), Giorgi Chankotadze (1/0), Giorgi Davidnidze (1/0) [46.Irakli Vashakidze (1/0)], Giorgi Gudushauri (7/0) [70.Kakhaber Kvetenadze (1/0)], Irakli Gemezashvili (1/0) [65.Giorgi Kipiani (1/0)], Gocha Jamarauli (Cap) (29/5), Levan Kobiashvili (12/0), Giorgi Megreladze (1/0) [46.Lasha Monaselidze (1/0)], Kakhaber Chketiani (1/0), Aleksandre Kaidarashvili (1/0). Trainer: Vladimir Gutsaev (8), replaced by Gigla Imnadze.

45. 19.08.1998 **UKRAINE – GEORGIA** **4-0(2-0)**
Olympiyskiy Stadium, Kyiv; Referee: Romans Lajuks (Latvia); Attendance: 12,500
GEO: Nikoloz Togonidze (8/0) [46.David Gvaramadze (4/0)], Givi Didava (4/0) [73.Levan Silagadze (6/0)], Kakhaber Kaladze (11/0), Gela Shekiladze (10/0), Levan Tskitishvili (11/1), Levan Kobiashvili (13/0), Giorgi Nemsadze (Cap) (34/0) [46.Mamuka Tsereteli (1/0)], Gocha Jamarauli (30/5), Temuri Ketsbaia (30/10), Giorgi Kinkladze (31/6), Aleksandre Iashvili (6/2) [61.Giorgi Demetradze (4/0)]. Trainer: Vladimir Gutsaev (9).

46. 05.09.1998 **GEORGIA – ALBANIA** **1-0(0-0)** 11th EC. Qualifiers
„Boris Paichadze" Erovnuli Stadioni, Tbilisi; Referee: Claude Detruche (Switzerland); Attendance: 25,000
GEO: David Gvaramadze (5/0), Kakhaber Kaladze (12/0), Levan Tskitishvili (12/1), Levan Silagadze (7/0) [43.Giorgi Kiknadze (8/1)], Mamuka Tsereteli (2/0), Levan Kobiashvili (14/0), Giorgi Nemsadze (Cap) (35/0), Gocha Jamarauli (31/5), Giorgi Kinkladze (32/6), Temuri Ketsbaia (31/10) [54.Zaza Janashia (3/1) [*sent off 80*]], Aleksandre Iashvili (7/2) [62.Archil Arveladze (17/4)]. Trainer: Vladimir Gutsaev (10).
Goal: Archil Arveladze (65).

47. 10.10.1998 **LATVIA – GEORGIA** **1-0(1-0)** 11th EC. Qualifiers
Daugava Stadions, Riga; Referee: Constantin Zotta (Romania); Attendance: 3,500
GEO: David Gvaramadze (6/0), Kakhaber Kaladze (13/0), Giorgi Gakhokidze (10/1) [60.Giorgi Demetradze (5/0)], Gela Shekiladze (11/0), Mikheil Kavelashvili (24/6), Levan Kobiashvili (15/0), Giorgi Nemsadze (Cap) (36/0), Gocha Jamarauli (32/5), Temuri Ketsbaia (32/10), Giorgi Kinkladze (33/6), Shota Arveladze (29/11). Trainer: Vladimir Gutsaev (11).

48. 14.10.1998 **GREECE – GEORGIA** **3-0(3-0)** 11th EC. Qualifiers
Stádio Olympiako „Spiros Louis", Athína; Referee: Atanas Uzunov (Bulgaria); Attendance: 15,000
GEO: Nikoloz Togonidze (9/0), Gela Shekiladze (12/0), Murtaz Shelia (29/0), Kakhaber Kaladze (14/0), Giorgi Nemsadze (Cap) (37/0), Levan Kobiashvili (16/0), Temuri Ketsbaia (33/10), Gocha Jamarauli (33/5), Giorgi Kinkladze (34/6), Mikheil Kavelashvili (25/6) [59.Giorgi Gakhokidze (11/1)], Shota Arveladze (30/11). Trainer: Vladimir Gutsaev (12).

49. 18.11.1998 **GEORGIA – ESTONIA** **3-1(0-0)**
„Boris Paichadze" Erovnuli Stadioni, Tbilisi; Referee: Merab Malaguradze (Giorgia); Attendance: 28,000
GEO: Soso Grishikashvili (3/0) [76.Giorgi Lomaia (1/0)], Giorgi Balashvili (1/0), Vaja Tarkhnishvili (1/0) [64.Zurab Popkhadze (2/0)], Givi Didava (5/0), Gia Chkaidze (1/0) [72.Zviad Jeladze (3/0)], Giorgi Kiknadze (9/1), Giorgi Revazishvili (1/0) [62.Giorgi Gudushauri (8/0)], Rati Aleksidze (1/0), David Janashia (8/3), Kakhaber Kvetenadze (2/0) [56.David Mujiri (1/0)], Mikheil Ashvetia (2/2). Trainer: Vladimir Gutsaev (13).
Goals: Mikheil Ashvetia (65), David Janashia (72), Mikheil Ashvetia (85).

50. 20.03.1999 **GEORGIA – UKRAINE** **0-1(0-0)**
„Boris Paichadze" Erovnuli Stadioni, Tbilisi; Referee: Slavik Kazaryan (Armenia); Attendance: 40,000
GEO: Soso Grishikashvili (4/0), Giorgi Balashvili (2/0), Vaja Tarkhnishvili (2/0), Mamuka Tsereteli (3/0), Kakhaber Kaladze (15/0), David Janashia (9/3) [30.Rati Aleksidze (2/0)], Gia Chkaidze (2/0), Levan Kobiashvili (17/0), Giorgi Nemsadze (Cap) (38/0) [75.Giorgi Gakhokidze (12/1)], Giorgi Demetradze (6/0), Mikheil Potskhveria (3/0) [57.Mikheil Ashvetia (3/2)]. Trainer: Vladimir Gutsaev (14).

51. 27.03.1999 **GEORGIA – SLOVENIA** **1-1(1-0)** 11th EC. Qualifiers
„Boris Paichadze" Erovnuli Stadioni, Tbilisi; Referee: Alain Hamer (Luxembourg); Attendance: 20,000
GEO: Soso Grishikashvili (5/0), Kakhaber Kaladze (16/0), Giorgi Balashvili (3/0), Gia Chkaidze (3/0), Mamuka Tsereteli (4/0), Rati Aleksidze (3/0) [46.Giorgi Kinkladze (35/6)], Giorgi Nemsadze (Cap) (39/0), Gocha Jamarauli (34/5) [82.Giorgi Daraselia (9/2)], Levan Kobiashvili (18/0), Zaza Janashia (4/2), Giorgi Demetradze (7/0) [74.Mikheil Kavelashvili (26/6)]. Trainer: Vladimir Gutsaev (15).
Goal: Zaza Janashia (42).

52. 28.04.1999 **GEORGIA – NORWAY** **1-4(0-4)** 11th EC. Qualifiers
„Boris Paichadze" Erovnuli Stadioni, Tbilisi; Referee: Sándor Puhl (Hungary); Attendance: 15,000
GEO: Nikoloz Togonidze (10/0), Gela Shekiladze (13/0) [46.Zurab Popkhadze (3/0)], Mamuka Tsereteli (5/0), Kakhaber Kaladze (17/0), Givi Didava (6/0), Giorgi Nemsadze (Cap) (40/0), Aleksandre Rekhviashvili (1/0) [81.Giorgi Kiknadze (10/1)], Gocha Jamarauli (35/5), Levan Kobiashvili (19/0), Zaza Janashia (5/3), Temuri Ketsbaia (34/10) [46.Giorgi Demetradze (8/0)]. Trainer: Vladimir Gutsaev (16).
Goal: Zaza Janashia (58).

53. 30.05.1999 **NORWAY – GEORGIA** **1-0(1-0)** 11th EC. Qualifiers
Ullevaal Stadion, Oslo; Referee: Luc Huyghe (Belgium); Attendance: 18,236
GEO: David Gvaramadze (7/0), Valter Guchua (4/0) [63.David Chichveishvili (1/0)], Kakhaber Kaladze (18/0), Givi Didava (7/0) [46.Zurab Popkhadze (4/0)], Mamuka Tsereteli (6/0), Levan Tskitishvili (13/1), Giorgi Nemsadze (Cap) (41/0), Temuri Ketsbaia (35/10), Gocha Jamarauli (36/5), Mikheil Kavelashvili (27/6), Giorgi Demetradze (9/0) [78.Mikheil Ashvetia (4/2)]. Trainer: Johan Boskamp (Netherlands, 1).

54. 05.06.1999 **GEORGIA – GREECE** **1-2(0-0)** 11th EC. Qualifiers
„Boris Paichadze" Erovnuli Stadioni, Tbilisi; Referee: William Young (Scotland); Attendance: 7,000
GEO: David Gvaramadze (8/0), David Chichveishvili (2/0) [10.Givi Didava (8/0)], Otar Khizaneishvili (1/0), Badri Akhvlediani (1/0) [65.Zurab Khizanishvili (1/0)], Mamuka Tsereteli (7/0), Levan Tskitishvili (14/1) [56.Rati Aleksidze (4/0)], Giorgi Nemsadze (Cap) (42/0), Temuri Ketsbaia (36/11), Gocha Jamarauli (37/5), Mikheil Ashvetia (5/2), Levan Kobiashvili (20/0). Trainer: Johan Boskamp (Netherlands, 2).
Goal: Temuri Ketsbaia (55).

55. 04.09.1999 **SLOVENIA – GEORGIA** **2-1(0-0)** 11th EC. Qualifiers
Central Stadion, Ljubljana; Referee: Jan Wegereef (Netherlands); Attendance: 5,000
GEO: David Gvaramadze (9/0), Badri Akhvlediani (2/0) [46.Gela Shekiladze (14/0)], Givi Didava (9/0), Kakhaber Kaladze (Cap) (19/0), Levan Tskitishvili (15/1), Tengiz Sichinava (1/0), Mikheil Potskhveria (4/0), Levan Kobiashvili (21/0), Mikheil Kavelashvili (28/6), Archil Arveladze (18/4), Shota Arveladze (31/12). Trainer: Johan Boskamp (Netherlands, 3).
Goal: Shota Arveladze (56).

56. 08.09.1999 **GEORGIA – LATVIA** **2-2(1-0)** 11th EC. Qualifiers
„Boris Paichadze" Erovnuli Stadioni, Tbilisi; Referee: Miroslav Radoman (Yugoslavia); Attendance: 4,500
GEO: David Gvaramadze (10/0), Gela Shekiladze (15/0), Givi Didava (10/0), Kakhaber Kaladze (20/0), Mamuka Tsereteli (8/0) [*sent off 80*], Levan Tskitishvili (16/1) [70.Tengiz Sichinava (2/0)], Giorgi Nemsadze (Cap) (43/0), Gocha Jamarauli (38/5), Levan Kobiashvili (22/0), Mikheil Kavelashvili (29/7) [75.Archil Arveladze (19/4)], Shota Arveladze (32/13) [72.Giorgi Demetradze (10/0)]. Trainer: Johan Boskamp (Netherlands, 4).
Goals: Shota Arveladze (30), Mikheil Kavelashvili (52).

57. 09.10.1999 **ALBANIA – GEORGIA** **2-1(2-0)** 11th EC. Qualifiers
Stadiumi „Kombëtar Qemal Stafa", Tiranë; Referee: Alfred Micallef (Malta); Attendance: 650
GEO: Grigol Chanturia (1/0), Gela Shekiladze (16/0), David Chichveishvili (3/0), Givi Didava (11/0), Kakhaber Kaladze (21/0), Levan Kobiashvili (23/0), Giorgi Gakhokidze (13/1), Giorgi Nemsadze (Cap) (44/0), Gocha Jamarauli (39/5), Archil Arveladze (20/4 [83.David Janashia (10/3)], Shota Arveladze (33/14). Trainer: Johan Boskamp (Netherlands, 5).
Goal: Shota Arveladze (52).

58. 02.02.2000 **GEORGIA – SLOVAKIA „Under 21"** **2-0(0-0)** Cyprus Tournament
Stádio „Antonis Papadopoulos", Lárnaca (Cyprus); Referee: Kostas Theodotou (Cyprus); Attendance: 400
GEO: David Gvaramadze (11/0), Gela Shekiladze (17/0) [29.Zurab Khizanishvili (2/0)], Giorgi Nemsadze (Cap) (45/0), Levan Silagadze (8/0), Giorgi Chikhradze (20/0), Gocha Jamarauli (40/5), Temuri Ketsbaia (37/12), Givi Kvaratskhelia (1/0) [38.Tengiz Sichinava (3/0)], Mikheil Kavelashvili (30/8) [89.Revaz Kemoklidze (1/0)], Archil Arveladze (21/4), Zaza Janashia (6/3) [55.Zurab Menteshashvili (1/0)]. Trainers: David Kipiani & Revaz Dzodzuashvili (1).
Goals: Temuri Ketsbaia (83), Mikheil Kavelashvili (86).

59. 04.02.2000 **ROMANIA – GEORGIA** **1-1(0-1,1-1); 4-2 on penalties** Cyprus Tournament
Stádio „Antonis Papadopoulos", Lárnaca (Cyprus); Referee: Kostas Kapitanis (Cyprus).; Attendance: 200
GEO: David Gvaramadze (12/0), Gela Shekiladze (18/0), Zurab Khizanishvili (3/0), Giorgi Nemsadze (Cap) (46/0), Zurab Menteshashvili (2/0) [46.Zaza Janashia (7/3)], Giorgi Chikhradze (21/0), Tengiz Sichinava (4/0), Temuri Ketsbaia (38/13), Gocha Jamarauli (41/5), Archil Arveladze (22/4) [67.Revaz Kemoklidze (2/0)], Mikheil Kavelashvili (31/8) [90+1.Merab Dzodzuashvili (1/0)]. Trainers: David Kipiani & Revaz Dzodzuashvili (2).
Goal: Temuri Ketsbaia (41).
Penalties: Giorgi Nemsadze (missed), Temuri Ketsbaia, Zaza Janashia (miss), Gela Shekiladze.

60. 06.02.2000 **ARMENIA – GEORGIA** **1-2(1-1)** Cyprus Tournament
Stádio Tsirion, Limassol (Cyprus); Referee: Sotiris Konstantinou (Cyprus); Attendance: 6,000
GEO: Soso Grishikashvili (6/0), Levan Silagadze (9/0), Revaz Kemoklidze (3/0), Zurab Menteshashvili (3/1), Giorgi Chikhradze (22/0), Tengiz Sichinava (5/0) [22.Gela Shekiladze (19/0)], Giorgi Nemsadze (Cap) (47/0), Gocha Jamarauli (42/5), Archil Arveladze (23/4), Mikheil Kavelashvili (32/8), Zaza Janashia (8/4) [46.Merab Dzodzuashvili (2/0)]. Trainers: David Kipiani & Revaz Dzodzuashvili (3).
Goals: Zaza Janashia (7), Zurab Menteshashvili (55).

61. 29.03.2000 **ISRAEL – GEORGIA** **1-1(0-1)**
Municipal Stadium, Ashkelon; Referee: Metin Tokat (Turkey); Attendance: 8,500
GEO: Soso Grishikashvili (7/0) [46.David Gvaramadze (13/0)], Levan Silagadze (10/0), Giorgi Nemsadze (Cap) (48/0), Zurab Khizanishvili (4/0), Kakhaber Kaladze (22/0), Gocha Jamarauli (43/5) [73.Zurab Menteshashvili (4/1)], Temuri Ketsbaia (39/13), Giorgi Kinkladze (36/7), Levan Kobiashvili (24/0), Archil Arveladze (24/4) [81.Rati Aleksidze (5/0)], Giorgi Demetradze (11/0) [46.Tengiz Sichinava (6/0)]. Trainers: David Kipiani & Revaz Dzodzuashvili (4).
Goal: Giorgi Kinkladze (27).

62. 26.04.2000 **ARMENIA – GEORGIA** **0-0**
Hrazdan Stadium, Yerevan; Referee: Gennady Yakubovsky (Belarus); Attendance: 15,000
GEO: Soso Grishikashvili (8/0), Levan Mikadze (1/0) [34.Aleksandre Rekhviashvili (2/0)], Levan Silagadze (11/0), Giorgi Nemsadze (Cap) (49/0), Sevasti Todua (1/0), Zurab Khizanishvili (5/0) [72.Givi Didava (12/0)], Rati Aleksidze (6/0) [55.Zurab Menteshashvili (5/1)], Tengiz Sichinava (7/0), Mikheil Kavelashvili (33/8), Giorgi Demetradze (12/0), David Chaladze (2/0) [46.Zurab Ionanidze (2/0)]. Trainers: David Kipiani & Revaz Dzodzuashvili (5).

63. 04.06.2000 **AZERBAIJAN – GEORGIA** **0-0**
„Tofiq Bəhramov" adına Respublika Stadionu, Bakı; Referee: Khagani Mamedov (Azerbaijan); Attendance: 7,000
GEO: David Gvaramadze (14/0), Levan Silagadze (12/0), Sevasti Todua (2/0), Zurab Khizanishvili (6/0), Giorgi Chikhradze (23/0), Tengiz Sichinava (8/0), Levan Kobiashvili (25/0), Temuri Ketsbaia (40/13) [70.Revaz Arveladze (10/1)], Giorgi Kinkladze (37/7) [80.Rati Aleksidze (7/0)], Archil Arveladze (25/4) [70.Aleksandre Iashvili (8/2)], Shota Arveladze (34/14) [86.Kakhaber Gogichaishvili (27/1)]. Trainers: David Kipiani & Revaz Dzodzuashvili (6).

64. 11.06.2000 **ESTONIA – GEORGIA** **1-0(1-0)**
Kadriorg Staadion, Tallinn; Referee: Sten Kaldmaa (Estonia); Attendance: 450
GEO: Soso Grishikashvili (9/0), Levan Silagadze (13/0), Zurab Khizanishvili (7/0), Tengiz Sichinava (9/0) [71.Aleksandre Rekhviashvili (3/0)], Giorgi Nemsadze (Cap) (50/0), Levan Kobiashvili (26/0), Mikheil Kavelashvili (34/8) [56.Giorgi Demetradze (13/0)], Temuri Ketsbaia (41/13) [62.Rati Aleksidze (8/0)], Giorgi Kinkladze (38/7) [71.Revaz Arveladze (11/1)], Archil Arveladze (26/4) [62.David Chaladze (3/0)], Shota Arveladze (35/14). Trainers: David Kipiani & Revaz Dzodzuashvili (7).

65. 16.08.2000 **IRAN – GEORGIA** **2-1(2-0)**
Azadi Stadium, Teheran; Referee: Davoud Abharan (Iran); Attendance: 20,000
GEO: Soso Grishikashvili (10/0) [34.David Gvaramadze (15/0)], Revaz Kemoklidze (4/0) [74.Givi Kvaratskhelia (2/0)], Sevasti Todua (3/0), Mamuka Tsereteli (9/0) [34.Zurab Menteshashvili (6/1)], Tengiz Sichinava (10/0), Levan Kobiashvili (27/0), Giorgi Nemsadze (Cap) (51/0), Gocha Jamarauli (44/5), Temuri Ketsbaia (42/13), Mikheil Kavelashvili (35/9), Shota Arveladze (36/14) [46.Levan Silagadze (14/0)]. Trainers: David Kipiani & Revaz Dzodzuashvili (8).
Goal: Mikheil Kavelashvili (70).

66. 07.10.2000 **LITHUANIA – GEORGIA** **0-4(0-2)** 17th WC. Qualifiers
„S. Dariaus ir S. Girėno" stadionas, Kaunas; Referee: Ryszard Wójcik (Poland); Attendance: 2,317
GEO: David Gvaramadze (16/0), Levan Silagadze (15/0), Aleksandre Rekhviashvili (4/0), Zurab Khizanishvili (8/0), Kakhaber Kaladze (23/0), Levan Kobiashvili (28/0), Giorgi Nemsadze (Cap) (52/0), Temuri Ketsbaia (43/15) [67.Zurab Menteshashvili (7/1)], Mikheil Kavelashvili (36/9), Giorgi Kinkladze (39/8) [71.Gocha Jamarauli (45/5)], Giorgi Demetradze (14/0) [58.Archil Arveladze (27/5)]. Trainers: David Kipiani & Revaz Dzodzuashvili (9).
Goals: Temuri Ketsbaia (19, 34), Giorgi Kinkladze (46), Archil Arveladze (85).

67. 11.10.2000 **ITALY – GEORGIA** **2-0(0-0)** 17th WC. Qualifiers
Stadio Del Conero, Ancona; Referee: Karl Erik Nilsson (Sweden); Attendance: 26,000
GEO: David Gvaramadze (17/0), Levan Silagadze (16/0), Zurab Khizanishvili (9/0), Aleksandre Rekhviashvili (5/0), Kakhaber Kaladze (24/0), Levan Kobiashvili (29/0), Giorgi Nemsadze (Cap) (53/0), Temuri Ketsbaia (44/15) [68.Zurab Menteshashvili (8/1)], Giorgi Kinkladze (40/8) [61.Gocha Jamarauli (46/5)], Mikheil Kavelashvili (37/9), Archil Arveladze (28/5) [61.Giorgi Demetradze (15/0)]. Trainers: David Kipiani & Revaz Dzodzuashvili (10).

68. 14.02.2001 **GEORGIA – UKRAINE** **0-0**
„Boris Paichadze" Erovnuli Stadioni, Tbilisi; Referee: Xaqani Mamedov (Azerbaijan); Attendance: 30,000
GEO: David Gvaramadze (18/0), Levan Silagadze (17/0), Aleksandre Rekhviashvili (6/0), Zurab Khizanishvili (10/0), Kakhaber Kaladze (25/0), Levan Kobiashvili (30/0) [46.Sevasti Todua (4/0)], Revaz Kemoklidze (5/0), Archil Arveladze (29/5) [52.Zurab Menteshashvili (9/1)], Mikheil Kavelashvili (38/9) [66.Levan Tskitishvili (17/1)], Temuri Ketsbaia (Cap) (45/15), Gocha Jamarauli (47/5) [60.Mikheil Ashvetia (6/2)]. Trainers: David Kipiani & Revaz Dzodzuashvili (11).

69. 28.03.2001 **GEORGIA – ROMANIA** **0-2(0-0)** 17th WC. Qualifiers
„Boris Paichadze" Erovnuli Stadioni, Tbilisi; Referee: Rune Pedersen (Norway); Attendance: 27,000
GEO: David Gvaramadze (19/0), Levan Silagadze (18/0) [72.Aleksandre Iashvili (9/2)], Aleksandre Rekhviashvili (7/0), Zurab Khizanishvili (11/0), Kakhaber Kaladze (26/0), Levan Kobiashvili (31/0), Giorgi Nemsadze (Cap) (54/0), Mikheil Kavelashvili (39/9) [52.Zaza Janashia (9/4)], Temuri Ketsbaia (46/15) [60.Revaz Kemoklidze (6/0)], Giorgi Kinkladze (41/8), Shota Arveladze (37/14). Trainers: David Kipiani & Revaz Dzodzuashvili (12).

70. 24.04.2001 **GEORGIA – ISRAEL** **3-2(2-1)**
„Boris Paichadze" Erovnuli Stadioni, Tbilisi; Referee: Sergo Kvaratskhelia (Giorgia); Attendance: 11,000
GEO: Giorgi Lomaia (2/0), Levan Silagadze (19/0), Aleksandre Rekhviashvili (8/0), Zurab Khizanishvili (12/0) [64.Giorgi Chankotadze (2/0)], Valeri Abramidze (1/0), Revaz Kemoklidze (7/0), Giorgi Gakhokidze (14/1) [68.Malkhaz Asatiani (1/0)], Temuri Ketsbaia (Cap) (47/17), Giorgi Kinkladze (42/8) [46.Rati Aleksidze (9/0)], Archil Arveladze (30/6) [89.Levan Melkadze (1/0)], Shota Arveladze (38/14). Trainers: David Kipiani & Revaz Dzodzuashvili (13).
Goals: Temuri Ketsbaia (9, 36), Archil Arveladze (88).

71. 09.05.2001 **GEORGIA – AZERBAIJAN** **1-0(0-0)**
Torpedo Stadium, Kutaisi; Referee: Merab Malaguradze (Giorgia); Attendance: 12,000
GEO: Irakli Zoidze (Cap) (17/0) [46.David Khmelidze (1/0)], Levan Silagadze (20/0), Giorgi Shashiashvili (1/0) [54.Aleksandre Gogoberishvili (1/0)], Valeri Abramidze (2/0) [46.Giorgi Chankotadze (3/0)], Sevasti Todua (5/0), Revaz Kemoklidze (8/0) [46.Valter Guchua (5/0)], Givi Didava (13/0), Edik Sajaia (1/0) [46.Mikheil Makhviladze (1/0)], Zurab Ionanidze (3/1), Mikheil Ashvetia (7/2) [67.Lasha Nozadze (1/0)], Levan Melkadze (2/0) [46.Giorgi Kipiani (2/0)]. Trainers: David Kipiani & Revaz Dzodzuashvili (14).
Goal: Zurab Ionanidze (54).

72. 02.06.2001 **GEORGIA – ITALY** **1-2(0-1)** 17th WC. Qualifiers
„Boris Paichadze" Erovnuli Stadioni, Tbilisi; Referee: Eduardo Iturralde González (Spain); Attendance: 28,000
GEO: Irakli Zoidze (18/0), Levan Silagadze (21/0), Valeri Abramidze (3/0), Aleksandre Rekhviashvili (9/0), Zurab Khizanishvili (13/0) [79.Giorgi Gakhokidze (15/2)], Kakhaber Kaladze (27/0), Giorgi Nemsadze (Cap) (55/0) [35.Shota Arveladze (39/14)], Mikheil Kavelashvili (40/9), Temuri Ketsbaia (48/17), Levan Kobiashvili (32/0), Zurab Menteshashvili (10/1) [61.Archil Arveladze (31/6)]. Trainers: David Kipiani & Revaz Dzodzuashvili (15).
Goal: Giorgi Gakhokidze (80).

73. 06.06.2001 **HUNGARY – GEORGIA** **4-1(2-0)** 17th WC. Qualifiers
Népstadion, Budapest; Referee: Hartmut Strampe (Germany); Attendance: 10,000
GEO: Irakli Zoidze (19/0), Levan Kobiashvili (33/1), Valeri Abramidze (4/0), Aleksandre Rekhviashvili (10/0), Zurab Khizanishvili (14/0), Kakhaber Kaladze (28/0) [67.Sevasti Todua (6/0)], Giorgi Nemsadze (Cap) (56/0) [67.Revaz Kemoklidze (9/0)], Archil Arveladze (32/6), Temuri Ketsbaia (49/17), Mikheil Kavelashvili (41/9) [53.Giorgi Kinkladze (43/8)], Shota Arveladze (40/14). Trainers: David Kipiani & Revaz Dzodzuashvili (16).
Goal: Levan Kobiashvili (77).

74. 15.08.2001 **LUXEMBOURG - GEORGIA** **0-3(0-1)**
Nouveau Stade, Mondercange; Referee: Luc Huyghe (Belgium); Attendance: 1,700
GEO: David Gvaramadze (20/0) [75.Giorgi Lomaia (3/0)], Edik Sajaia (2/0), Zurab Khizanishvili (15/0), Otar Khizaneishvili (2/0), Giorgi Gakhokidze (16/2) [63.Giorgi Shashiashvili (2/0)], Revaz Kemoklidze (10/0), Levan Tskitishvili (18/1), Rati Aleksidze (10/1), Giorgi Demetradze (16/2) [78.Malkhaz Asatiani (2/0)], Gocha Jamarauli (Cap) (48/5), Vladimir Burduli (1/0) [72.Roin Oniani (1/0)]. Trainer: Aleksandre Chivadze (25).
Goals: Giorgi Demetradze (19, 50), Rati Aleksidze (69).

75. 01.09.2001 **GEORGIA – HUNGARY** **3-1(1-1)** 17th WC. Qualifiers
Lokomotivi Stadium, Tbilisi; Referee: Drago Kos (Slovenia); Attendance: 8000
GEO: David Gvaramadze (21/0), Zurab Khizanishvili (16/0), Aleksandre Rekhviashvili (11/0) [*sent off 65*], Kakhaber Kaladze (29/0), Levan Tskitishvili (19/1) [73.Edik Sajaia (3/0)], Levan Kobiashvili (34/1), Giorgi Nemsadze (Cap) (57/0), Mikheil Kavelashvili (42/9) [46.Aleksandre Iashvili (10/3)], Gocha Jamarauli (49/6), Giorgi Kinkladze (44/8), Shota Arveladze (41/15) [62.Giorgi Demetradze (17/2)]. Trainer: Aleksandre Chivadze (26).
Goals: Shota Arveladze (32), Gocha Jamarauli (53), Aleksandre Iashvili (64).

76. 05.09.2001 **GEORGIA – LITHUANIA** **2-0(0-0)** 17th WC. Qualifiers
Lokomotivi Stadium, Tbilisi; Referee: Haim Yakov (Israel); Attendance: 15,000
GEO: David Gvaramadze (22/0), Levan Kobiashvili (35/1), Zurab Khizanishvili (17/0), Edik Sajaia (4/0), Kakhaber Kaladze (30/0), Levan Tskitishvili (20/1), Giorgi Nemsadze (Cap) (58/0), Rati Aleksidze (11/1) [67.Vladimir Burduli (2/0)]), Aleksandre Iashvili (11/5) (1/3) [89.Shota Arveladze (42/15)], Giorgi Kinkladze (45/8), Mikheil Kavelashvili (43/9) [46.Giorgi Demetradze (18/2)]. Trainer: Aleksandre Chivadze (27).
Goals: Aleksandre Iashvili (81, 83).

77. 06.10.2001 **ROMANIA – GEORGIA** **1-1(0-0)**
Stadionul Steaua, Bucureşti; Referee: Ľuboš Micheľ (Slovakia); Attendance: 16,500
GEO: David Gvaramadze (23/0), Levan Kobiashvili (36/1), Zurab Khizanishvili (18/0), Aleksandre Rekhviashvili (12/0), Edik Sajaia (5/0), Kakhaber Kaladze (31/0), Levan Tskitishvili (21/1), Gocha Jamarauli (Cap) (50/6), Aleksandre Iashvili (12/6) [81.Rati Aleksidze (12/1)], Giorgi Kinkladze (46/8) [63.Temuri Ketsbaia (50/17)], Mikheil Kavelashvili (44/9) [75.Vladimir Burduli (3/0)]. Trainer: Aleksandre Chivadze (28).
Goal: Aleksandre Iashvili (55).

78. 27.03.2002 **GEORGIA – SOUTH AFRICA** **4-1(2-0)**
Lokomotivi Stadium, Tbilisi; Referee: Andriy Shandor (Ukraine); Attendance: 15,000
GEO: David Gvaramadze (24/0) [67.Grigol Chanturia (2/0)], Levan Kobiashvili (37/2), Giorgi Shashiashvili (3/0), Aleksandre Rekhviashvili (13/0), Edik Sajaia (6/0) [78.Valeri Abramidze (5/0)], Vladimir Burduli (4/0) [46.Revaz Kemoklidze (11/0)], Aleksandre Amisulashvili (1/0), Gocha Jamarauli (51/6), Temuri Ketsbaia (Cap) (51/17) [46.Vitali Daraselia (1/0)], Giorgi Demetradze (19/4), Aleksandre Iashvili (13/6) [81.Rati Aleksidze (13/2)]. Trainer: Aleksandre Chivadze (29).
Goals: Levan Kobiashvili (14 penalty), Giorgi Demetradze (33), Rati Aleksidze (84), Giorgi Demetradze (86).

79. 17.04.2002 **UKRAINE – GEORGIA** **2-1(1-0)**
Dinamo Stadium, Kyiv; Referee: Ľuboš Micheľ (Slovakia); Attendance: 17,000
GEO: David Gvaramadze (25/0), Levan Kobiashvili (38/2), Giorgi Shashiashvili (4/0), Aleksandre Rekhviashvili (14/0), Edik Sajaia (7/0) [52.Vladimir Burduli (5/1)], Gela Shekiladze (20/0), Aleksandre Amisulashvili (2/0) [84.Vitali Daraselia (2/0)], Gocha Jamarauli (Cap) (52/6) [76.Revaz Kemoklidze (12/0)], Mikheil Kavelashvili (45/9) [46.Givi Didava (14/0)], Giorgi Kinkladze (47/8) [70.Rati Aleksidze (14/2)], Giorgi Demetradze (20/4) [79.Mikheil Ashvetia (8/2)]. Trainer: Aleksandre Chivadze (30).
Goal: Vladimir Burduli (70).

80. 21.08.2002 **TURKEY - GEORGIA** **3-0(1-0)**
„Hüseyin Avni Aker" Stadyumu, Trabzon; Referee: Nikolaos Agelakis (Greece); Attendance: 30,000
GEO: Giorgi Lomaia (4/0), Levan Kobiashvili (39/2), Giorgi Shashiashvili (5/0), Edik Sajaia (8/0) [73.Gela Shekiladze (21/0)], Giorgi Gakhokidze (17/2) [46.Kakhaber Kaladze (32/0)], Levan Tskitishvili (22/1) [46.Vladimir Burduli (6/1)], Giorgi Nemsadze (Cap) (59/0) [71.Givi Didava (15/0)], Gocha Jamarauli (53/6), Giorgi Demetradze (21/4) [80.Aleksandre Amisulashvili (3/0)], Giorgi Kinkladze (48/8) [46.Mamia Jikia (1/0)], Shota Arveladze (43/15). Trainer: Aleksandre Chivadze (31).

81. 08.09.2002 **SWITZERLAND - GEORGIA** **4-1(1-0)** 12th EC. Qualifiers
„St. Jakob" Stadion, Basel; Referee: Vladimír Hriňák (Slovakia); Attendance: 20,000
GEO: David Gvaramadze (26/0), Levan Kobiashvili (40/2), Gela Shekiladze (22/0), Kakhaber Kaladze (33/0), Edik Sajaia (9/0) [46.Aleksandre Rekhviashvili (15/0); 85.Mikheil Kavelashvili (46/9)], Levan Tskitishvili (23/1), Giorgi Nemsadze (Cap) (60/0), Gocha Jamarauli (54/6), Giorgi Demetradze (22/4), Giorgi Kinkladze (49/8) [46.Vladimir Burduli (7/1)], Shota Arveladze (44/16). Trainer: Aleksandre Chivadze (32).
Goal: Shota Arveladze (62).

82. 12.02.2003 **GEORGIA – MOLDOVA** **2-2(0-0)**
Lokomotivi Stadium, Tbilisi; Referee: Gevork Hovhanisyan (Armenia); Attendance: 7,000
GEO: Giorgi Lomaia (5/0) [75.Giorgi Nikuradze (1/0)], Valeri Abramidze (6/0) [64.Revaz Kemoklidze (13/0)], Giorgi Shashiashvili (Cap) (6/0), Givi Didava (16/0) [46.Zurab Menteshashvili (11/1)], Aleksandre Amisulashvili (4/0), Archil Sakhvadze (1/0), Aleksandre Gogoberishvili (2/0), Rati Aleksidze (15/2) [46.Mikheil Ashvetia (9/3)], Mamia Jikia (2/0) [46.Givi Kvaratskhelia (3/0)], David Mujiri (2/0) [46.Vitali Daraselia (3/0)], Shalva Apkhazava (1/0) [46.David Chaladze (4/1)]. Trainer: Aleksandre Chivadze (33).
Goals: David Chaladze (61), Mikheil Ashvetia (83).

83. 29.03.2003 **GEORGIA – REPUBLIC OF IRELAND** **1-2(0-1)** 12th EC. Qualifiers
Lokomotivi Stadium, Tbilisi; Referee: Kyros Vassaras (Greece); Attendance: 15,000
GEO: Giorgi Lomaia (6/0), Otar Khizaneishvili (3/0), Giorgi Shashiashvili (7/0), Aleksandre Amisulashvili (5/0), Levan Kobiashvili (41/3), Levan Tskitishvili (24/1), Giorgi Nemsadze (Cap) (61/0), Gocha Jamarauli (55/6), Temuri Ketsbaia (52/17) [46.Giorgi Demetradze (23/4)], Giorgi Kinkladze (50/8) [72.Givi Didava (17/0)], Aleksandre Iashvili (14/6). Trainer: Aleksandre Chivadze (34).
Goal: Levan Kobiashvili (62).

84. 02.04.2003 **GEORGIA – SWITZERLAND** **0-0** 12th EC. Qualifiers
Lokomotivi Stadium, Tbilisi; Referee: Edo Trivković (Croatia); Attendance: 10,000
GEO: Giorgi Lomaia (7/0), Otar Khizaneishvili (4/0), Zurab Khizanishvili (19/0), Aleksandre Rekhviashvili (16/0), David Kvirkvelia (1/0), Revaz Kemoklidze (14/0), Giorgi Nemsadze (Cap) (62/0) [46.Givi Didava (18/0)], Levan Tskitishvili (25/1), Aleksandre Iashvili (15/6) [46.Shota Arveladze (45/16)], Levan Kobiashvili (42/3), Giorgi Demetradze (24/4) [73.Mikheil Ashvetia (10/3)]. Trainer: Aleksandre Chivadze (35).

85. 30.04.2003 **GEORGIA – RUSSIA** **1-0(1-0)** 12th EC. Qualifiers
Lokomotivi Stadium, Tbilisi; Referee: Dr. Franz-Xaver Wack (Germany); Attendance: 11,500
GEO: Giorgi Lomaia (8/0), Otar Khizaneishvili (5/0), Zurab Khizanishvili (20/0), Kakhaber Kaladze (34/0), David Kvirkvelia (2/0), Levan Tskitishvili (26/1), Giorgi Nemsadze (Cap) (63/0), Vladimir Burduli (8/1) [80.Giorgi Shashiashvili (8/0)], Malkhaz Asatiani (3/1) [75.Givi Didava (19/0)], Giorgi Demetradze (25/4), Mikheil Ashvetia (11/3) [85 Rati Aleksidze (16/2)]. Trainer: Ivan Šušak (Croatia, 1).
Goal: Malkhaz Asatiani (11).

86. 11.06.2003 **REPUBLIC OF IRELAND - GEORGIA** **2-0(1-0)** 12th EC. Qualifiers
Lansdowne Road, Dublin; Referee: Eduardo Iturralde González (Spain); Attendance: 36,000
GEO: Giorgi Lomaia (9/0), Otar Khizaneishvili (6/0), Zurab Khizanishvili (21/0), Kakhaber Kaladze (Cap) (35/0), Aleksandre Amisulashvili (6/0), Givi Didava (20/0) [77.Rati Aleksidze (17/2)], Aleksandre Rekhviashvili (17/0), Vladimir Burduli (9/1), Malkhaz Asatiani (4/1), Giorgi Demetradze (26/4) [61.Vitali Daraselia (4/0)], Shota Arveladze (46/16). Trainer: Ivan Šušak (Croatia, 2).

87. 06.09.2003 **GEORGIA - ALBANIA** **3-0(3-0)** 12th EC. Qualifiers
„Boris Paichadze" Erovnuli Stadioni, Tbilisi; Referee: Nicolai Vollquartz (Denmark); Attendance: 18,000
GEO: Giorgi Lomaia (10/0), Zurab Khizanishvili (22/0), Revaz Kemoklidze (15/0), Vladimir Burduli (10/1) [70.Aleksandre Rekhviashvili (18/0)], David Kvirkvelia (3/0), Levan Kobiashvili (43/3), Giorgi Nemsadze (Cap) (64/0), Mikheil Ashvetia (12/4), Aleksandre Iashvili (16/6), Gocha Jamarauli (56/6) [58.Malkhaz Asatiani (5/1)], Shota Arveladze (47/18) [60.Giorgi Demetradze (27/4)]. Trainer: Merab Jordania (1).
Goals: Shota Arveladze (8), Mikheil Ashvetia (17), Shota Arveladze (43).

88. 10.09.2003 **ALBANIA - GEORGIA** **3-1(0-0)** 12th EC. Qualifiers
Stadiumi „Kombëtar Qemal Stafa", Tiranë; Referee: Marian Salomir (Romania); Attendance: 10,500
GEO: Giorgi Lomaia (11/0), Zurab Khizanishvili (23/0), Revaz Kemoklidze (16/0) [40.Aleksandre Rekhviashvili (19/0)], Givi Didava (21/0) [54.Giorgi Demetradze (28/4)], David Kvirkvelia (4/0), Levan Kobiashvili (44/3), Giorgi Nemsadze (Cap) (65/0), Mikheil Ashvetia (13/4), Aleksandre Iashvili (17/6) [54.Giorgi Kinkladze (51/8)], Gocha Jamarauli (57/6), Shota Arveladze (48/19). Trainer: Merab Jordania (2).
Goal: Shota Arveladze (62).

89. 11.10.2003 **RUSSIA - GEORGIA** **3-1(2-1)** 12th EC. Qualifiers
Lokomotiv Stadium, Moskva; Referee: Konrad Plautz (Austria); Attendance: 30,000
GEO: Giorgi Lomaia (12/0), Zurab Khizanishvili (24/0), Revaz Kemoklidze (17/0), David Kvirkvelia (5/0), Levan Kobiashvili (45/3), Levan Tskitishvili (27/1) [54.Malkhaz Asatiani (6/1)], Giorgi Nemsadze (Cap) (66/0), Mikheil Ashvetia (14/4) [58.Vitali Daraselia (5/0)], Aleksandre Iashvili (18/7), Gocha Jamarauli (58/6) [46.Vladimir Burduli (11/1)], Giorgi Demetradze (29/4). Trainer: Merab Jordania (3).
Goal: Aleksandre Iashvili (3).

90. 18.02.2004 **ROMANIA - GEORGIA** **3-0(1-0)** Cyprus Tournament
Stádio Neo GSZ, Lárnaca (Cyprus); Referee: Romans Lajuks (Latvia); Attendance: 200
GEO: David Gvaramadze (27/0), Revaz Kemoklidze (18/0), Mamuka Tsereteli (10/0), Aleksandre Amisulashvili (7/0), Aleksandre Gogoberishvili (3/0) [68.Levan Korgalidze (1/0)], David Kvirkvelia (6/0) [83.Levan Melkadze (3/0)], Giorgi Nemsadze (Cap) (67/0) [82.Giorgi Gabidauri (1/0)], Lado Akhalaia (1/0) [29.David Siradze (1/0)], Giorgi Kinkladze (52/8) [46.Giorgi Shashiashvili (9/0)], Vitali Daraselia (6/0), Sandro Iashvili (1/0) [83.Levan Magradze (1/0)]. Trainer: Gocha Tkebuchava (1).

91. 19.02.2004 **CYPRUS – GEORGIA** **3-1(1-0)** Cyprus Tournament

Stádio Makareio, Nicosia; Referee: Costas Kapitanis (Cyprus); Attendance: 1,500

GEO: David Gvaramadze (28/0), Revaz Kemoklidze (19/0), Giorgi Shashiashvili (10/0), Mamuka Tsereteli (11/0) [80.Levan Magradze (2/0)], David Kvirkvelia (7/0), Vitali Daraselia (7/0), Giorgi Nemsadze (Cap) (68/0) [80.Levan Korgalidze (2/0)], Aleksandre Gogoberishvili (4/0) [71.Levan Melkadze (4/0)], Giorgi Gabidauri (2/1), Giorgi Kinkladze (53/8), Sandro Iashvili (2/0). Trainer: Gocha Tkebuchava (2).

Goal: Giorgi Gabidauri (56).

92. 21.02.2004 **GEORGIA – ARMENIA** **0-2(0-1)** Cyprus Tournament

Stádio Makareio, Nicosia (Cyprus); Referee: Romans Lajuks (Latvia); Attendance: 300

GEO: Zurab Mamaladze (1/0), Revaz Kemoklidze (20/0) [60.Ilia Kandelaki (1/0)], Giorgi Shashiashvili (11/0), Mamuka Tsereteli (12/0), David Kvirkvelia (8/0), Vitali Daraselia (8/0), Giorgi Nemsadze (Cap) (69/0), Levan Korgalidze (3/0), Giorgi Gabidauri (3/1), Giorgi Kinkladze (54/8), Sandro Iashvili (3/0) [60.Levan Melkadze (5/0)]. Trainer: Gocha Tkebuchava (3).

93. 27.05.2004 **GEORGIA – ISRAEL** **0-1(0-1)**

„Boris Paichadze" Erovnuli Stadioni, Tbilisi; Referee: Oleh Oriekhov (Ukraine); Attendance: 24,000

GEO: Giorgi Lomaia (13/0), Kakhaber Mjavanadze (1/0), Otar Khizaneishvili (7/0), Givi Kvaratskhelia (4/0), Kakhaber Kaladze (Cap) (36/0), Malkhaz Asatiani (7/1) [88.Zurab Menteshashvili (12/1)], Levan Tskitishvili (28/1), David Mujiri (3/0) [65.David Siradze (2/0)], Levan Kobiashvili (46/3) [90.Tornike Aptsiauri (1/0)], Aleksandre Iashvili (19/7), Rati Aleksidze (18/2). Trainer: Alain Giresse (France, 1).

94. 18.08.2004 **MOLDOVA - GEORGIA** **1-0(0-0)**

Stadionul Sheriff, Tiraspol; Referee: Vitaliy Godulyan (Ukraine); Attendance: 8,000

GEO: Giorgi Lomaia (14/0), Kakhaber Mjavanadze (2/0), Zurab Khizanishvili (25/0), Kakhaber Kaladze (Cap) (37/0), Givi Kvaratskhelia (5/0), Levan Kobiashvili (47/3) [80.Tornike Aptsiauri (2/0)], Levan Tskitishvili (29/1) [46.David Mujiri (4/0)], Vladimir Burduli (12/1), Aleksandre Iashvili (20/7) [46.Lasha Jakobia (1/0)], Gocha Jamarauli (59/6), Giorgi Demetradze (30/4) [53.Rati Aleksidze (19/2)]. Trainer: Alain Giresse (France, 2).

95. 04.09.2004 **TURKEY - GEORGIA** **1-1(0-0)** 18th WC. Qualifiers

„Hüseyin Avni Aker" Stadyumu, Trabzon; Referee: Luis Medina Cantalejo (Spain); Attendance: 10,169

GEO: Akaki Devadze (16/0), Kakhaber Mjavanadze (3/0), Otar Khizaneishvili (8/0) [90.Givi Kvaratskhelia (6/0)], Zurab Khizanishvili (26/0), Kakhaber Kaladze (Cap) (38/0), David Kvirkvelia (9/0), Levan Tskitishvili (30/1), Aleksandre Rekhviashvili (20/0) [80.Malkhaz Asatiani (8/2)], Giorgi Demetradze (31/4) [75.Lasha Jakobia (2/0)], Gocha Jamarauli (60/6), Shota Arveladze (49/19). Trainer: Alain Giresse (France, 3).

Goal: Malkhaz Asatiani (84).

96. 08.09.2004 **GEORGIA - ALBANIA** **2-0(1-0)** 18th WC. Qualifiers

„Mikhail Meshki" Stadium, Tbilisi; Referee: Mark Courtney (Northern Ireland); Attendance: 20,000

GEO: Akaki Devadze (17/0), Kakhaber Mjavanadze (4/0), Otar Khizaneishvili (9/0), Lasha Salukvadze (1/0), Kakhaber Kaladze (Cap) (39/0), Levan Tskitishvili (31/1), Gocha Jamarauli (61/6) [78.David Kvirkvelia (10/0)], Malkhaz Asatiani (9/2) [60.Jaba Kankava (1/0)], Levan Kobiashvili (48/3), Aleksandre Iashvili (21/8), Shota Arveladze (50/19) [89.Giorgi Demetradze (32/5)]. Trainer: Alain Giresse (France, 4).

Goals: Aleksandre Iashvili (15), Giorgi Demetradze (90).

97. 13.10.2004 **UKRAINE - GEORGIA** **2-0(1-0)** 18th WC. Qualifiers

Ukrayina Stadium, Lviv; Referee: Wolfgang Stark (Germany); Attendance: 28,000

GEO: Akaki Devadze (18/0), Kakhaber Mjavanadze (5/0) [46.Vladimir Burduli (13/1)], Zurab Khizanishvili (27/0), Otar Khizaneishvili (10/0), Levan Kobiashvili (49/3), Lasha Salukvadze (2/0), Levan Tskitishvili (32/1), Gocha Jamarauli (Cap) (62/6) [85.Giorgi Demetradze (33/5)], Malkhaz Asatiani (10/2), Shota Arveladze (51/19), Aleksandre Iashvili (22/8). Trainer: Alain Giresse (France, 5).

98. 17.11.2004 **GEORGIA - DENMARK** **2-2(1-1)** 18th WC. Qualifiers

„Mikhail Meshki" Stadium, Tbilisi; Referee: Darko Čeferin (Slovenia); Attendance: 20,000

GEO: Akaki Devadze (19/0), Kakhaber Mjavanadze (6/0), Otar Khizaneishvili (11/0), Kakhaber Kaladze (Cap) (40/0), Mamia Jikia (3/0) [72.David Kvirkvelia (11/0)], Levan Kobiashvili (50/3), Levan Tskitishvili (33/1), Malkhaz Asatiani (11/3), Zurab Khizanishvili (28/0), Giorgi Demetradze (34/6), Aleksandre Iashvili (23/8) [72.Shota Arveladze (52/19)]. Trainer: Alain Giresse (France, 6).

Goals: Giorgi Demetradze (33), Malkhaz Asatiani (75).

99. 09.02.2005 **GEORGIA - LITHUANIA** **1-0(0-0)**

„Mikhail Meshki" Stadium, Tbilisi; Referee: Zuhrab Hadıyev (Azerbaijan); Attendance: 2,000

GEO: Giorgi Lomaia (15/0), Kakhaber Mjavanadze (7/0) [46.Giorgi Shashiashvili (12/0)], Aleksandre Amisulashvili (8/0), Lasha Salukvadze (3/0), Zurab Khizanishvili (29/0), David Kvirkvelia (12/0) [46.Givi Kvaratskhelia (7/0)], Gogita Gogua (1/0) [76.David Odikadze (1/0)], Giorgi Kinkladze (Cap) (55/8), Malkhaz Asatiani (12/3) [70.Aleksandre Gogoberishvili (5/0)], Mikheil Ashvetia (15/4), Lasha Jakobia (3/0) [46.Vasil Gigiadze (1/0)]. Trainer: Alain Giresse (France, 7).

Goal: Mikheil Ashvetia (59).

100. 26.03.2005 **GEORGIA - GREECE** **1-3(1-2)** 18th WC. Qualifiers

„Mikhail Meshki" Stadium, Tbilisi; Referee: Roberto Rosetti (Italy); Attendance: 23,000

GEO: Giorgi Lomaia (16/0), Kakhaber Mjavanadze (8/0), David Kvirkvelia (13/0), Otar Khizaneishvili (12/0), Kakhaber Kaladze (Cap) (41/0), Gogita Gogua (2/0) [46.Levan Tskitishvili (34/1)], Levan Kobiashvili (51/3), Malkhaz Asatiani (13/4), Zurab Khizanishvili (30/0), Giorgi Demetradze (35/6), Shota Arveladze (53/19) [62.Aleksandre Iashvili (24/8)]. Trainer: Alain Giresse (France, 8).

Goal: Malkhaz Asatiani (22).

101. 30.03.2005 **GEORGIA - TURKEY** **2-5(2-3)** 18th WC. Qualifiers

„Mikhail Meshki" Stadium, Tbilisi; Referee: Terje Hauge (Norway); Attendance: 10,000

GEO: Akaki Devadze (20/0) [22.Giorgi Lomaia (17/0)], Kakhaber Mjavanadze (9/0), Aleksandre Amisulashvili (9/1), Otar Khizaneishvili (13/0) [17.Lasha Salukvadze (4/0)], Kakhaber Kaladze (Cap) (42/0), Levan Tskitishvili (35/1) [76.Vladimir Burduli (14/1)], Gogita Gogua (3/0) [*sent off 83*], Mikheil Ashvetia (16/4), Malkhaz Asatiani (14/4), Levan Kobiashvili (52/3), Aleksandre Iashvili (25/9). Trainer: Alain Giresse (France, 9).

Goals: Aleksandre Amisulashvili (13), Aleksandre Iashvili (41).

102. 04.06.2005 **ALBANIA - GEORGIA** **3-2(2-0)** 18th WC. Qualifiers
Stadiumi „Kombëtar Qemal Stafa", Tiranë; Referee: Alexandru Dan Tudor (Romania); Attendance: none (*match played behind closed doors*).
GEO: Zviad Sturua (1/0), Levan Magradze (3/0) [64.Vladimir Burduli (15/2)], Lasha Salukvadze (5/0), Zurab Khizanishvili (31/0), Kakhaber Kaladze (Cap) (43/0), Malkhaz Asatiani (15/4) [58.Vitali Daraselia (9/0)], David Kvirkvelia (14/0), Aleksandre Rekhviashvili (21/0), Levan Kobiashvili (53/4), Lasha Jakobia (4/0), Giorgi Demetradze (36/6) [76.Mikhail Bobokhidze (1/0)]. Trainer: Alain Giresse (France, 10).
Goals: Vladimir Burduli (85), Levan Kobiashvili (90+4).

103. 17.08.2005 **KAZAKHSTAN - GEORGIA** **1-2(1-0)** 18th WC. Qualifiers
Tsentralniy Stadium, Almaty; Referee: Richard Havrilla (Slovakia); Attendance: 9,000
GEO: Giorgi Lomaia (18/0), Zurab Menteshashvili (13/1), Kakhaber Aladashvili (1/0) [78.David Odikadze (2/0)], Zurab Khizanishvili (32/0), Kakhaber Kaladze (Cap) (44/0), Jaba Kankava (2/0), Levan Tskitishvili (36/1), Giorgi Gakhokidze (18/2), Aleksandre Iashvili (26/9) [67.David Mujiri (5/0)], Levan Kobiashvili (54/4), Giorgi Demetradze (37/8) [90.Giorgi Ganugrava (1/0)]. Trainer: Gaioz Darsadze (1).
Goals: Giorgi Demetradze (50, 82).

104. 03.09.2005 **GEORGIA - UKRAINE** **1-1(0-1)** 18th WC. Qualifiers
„Mikhail Meshki" Stadium, Tbilisi; Referee: Tom Henning Øvrebø (Norway); Attendance: none (*match played behind closed doors*).
GEO: Giorgi Lomaia (19/0), Zurab Menteshashvili (14/1) [78.Gogita Gogua (4/0)], Zurab Khizanishvili (33/0), Kakhaber Kaladze (Cap) (45/0), Levan Tskitishvili (37/1), Giorgi Gakhokidze (19/3), Jaba Kankava (3/0), Levan Kobiashvili (55/4) [78.David Mujiri (6/0)], Malkhaz Asatiani (16/4) [87.Mikheil Ashvetia (17/4)], David Odikadze (3/0), Giorgi Demetradze (38/8). Trainer: Gaioz Darsadze (2).
Goal: Giorgi Gakhokidze (89).

105. 07.09.2005 **DENMARK - GEORGIA** **6-1(3-1)** 18th WC. Qualifiers
Parken, København; Referee: Emil Božinovski (Macedonia); Attendance: 27,177
GEO: Giorgi Lomaia (20/0), Zurab Menteshashvili (15/1), Levan Tskitishvili (38/1) [82.Lasha Salukvadze (6/0)], Zurab Khizanishvili (34/0) [*sent off 18*], Kakhaber Kaladze (Cap) (46/0), Giorgi Gakhokidze (20/3), Levan Kobiashvili (56/4), Gogita Gogua (5/0), Malkhaz Asatiani (17/4), David Odikadze (4/0) [60.Giorgi Ganugrava (2/0)], Giorgi Demetradze (39/9) [69.David Mujiri (7/0)]. Trainer: Gaioz Darsadze (3).
Goal: Giorgi Demetradze (37 penalty)

106. 08.10.2005 **GEORGIA - KAZAKHSTAN** **0-0** 18th WC. Qualifiers
„Boris Paichadze" Erovnuli Stadioni, Tbilisi; Referee: Jouni Hyytiä (Finland); Attendance: none (*match played behind closed doors*).
GEO: Nukri Revishvili (1/0), Kakhaber Mjavanadze (10/0), Lasha Salukvadze (7/0), Kakhaber Kaladze (Cap) (47/0), Giorgi Ganugrava (3/0), Jaba Kankava (4/0), Mikheil Ashvetia (18/4) [86.Rati Tsinamdzghvrishvili (1/0)], Levan Kobiashvili (57/4), Malkhaz Asatiani (18/4), David Mujiri (8/0), Giorgi Demetradze (40/9). Trainer: Gaioz Darsadze (4).

107. 12.10.2005 **GREECE - GEORGIA** **1-0(1-0)** 18th WC. Qualifiers
Stádio „Giórgos Karaïskáki", Peiraiás; Referee: Matteo Trefoloni (Italy); Attendance: 28,186
GEO: Nukri Revishvili (2/0), Kakhaber Mjavanadze (11/0), Zurab Khizanishvili (35/0), Lasha Salukvadze (8/0) [46.Rati Tsinamdzghvrishvili (2/0)], Kakhaber Kaladze (Cap) (48/0), Giorgi Ganugrava (4/0), Jaba Kankava (5/0), Levan Kobiashvili (58/4), Gogita Gogua (6/0), David Mujiri (9/0), Giorgi Demetradze (41/9) [86.Beka Gotsiridze (1/0)]. Trainer: Gaioz Darsadze (5).

108. 12.11.2005 **BULGARIA - GEORGIA** **6-2(2-0)**
Nationalen stadion "Vasil Levski", Sofia; Referee: Milan Karadžić (Serbia and Montenegro); Attendance: 1,375
GEO: Nukri Revishvili (3/0) [68.Zviad Sturua (2/0)], Kakhaber Mjavanadze (12/0) [46.Gogita Gogua (7/1)], Zurab Khizanishvili (36/0), Lasha Salukvadze (9/0), Kakhaber Kaladze (Cap) (49/0), Giorgi Ganugrava (5/0) [66.Ilia Kandelaki (2/0)], Jaba Kankava (6/0), Levan Kobiashvili (59/4), Giorgi Demetradze (42/9) [54.Mikheil Ashvetia (19/4)], Shota Arveladze (54/19) [68.Lasha Jakobia (5/1)], David Mujiri (10/0) [46.Aleksandre Iashvili (27/9)]. Trainer: Gaioz Darsadze (6).
Goals: Lasha Jakobia (83), Gogita Gogua (90).

109. 16.11.2005 **GEORGIA - JORDAN** **3-2(1-1)**
„Mikhail Meshki" Stadium, Tbilisi; Referee: n/a; Attendance: 8,000
GEO: Nukri Revishvili (4/0), Kakhaber Mjavanadze (13/0), Ilia Kandelaki (3/0), Zurab Khizanishvili (37/0), Kakhaber Kaladze (Cap) (50/0), Giorgi Ganugrava (6/0) [81.Vladimir Burduli (16/2)], Jaba Kankava (7/0), Gogita Gogua (8/1) [74.David Kvirkvelia (15/0)], David Mujiri (11/0) [71.Lasha Jakobia (6/1)], Giorgi Demetradze (43/11) [78.Vitali Daraselia (10/0)], Shota Arveladze (55/20) [54.Mikheil Ashvetia (20/4)]. Trainer: Gaioz Darsadze (7).
Goals: Giorgi Demetradze (4, 64), Shota Arveladze (75).

110. 01.03.2006 **MALTA - GEORGIA** **0-2(0-2)** Malta Tournament
Ta'Qali National Stadium, Attard; Referee: Veaceslav Banari (Moldova); Attendance: 1,100
GEO: Nukri Revishvili (5/0), David Mchedlishvili (1/0) [55.Mirza Bjalava (1/0)], Mate Gvinianidze (1/0), Levan Tskitishvili (39/1), Giorgi Popkhadze (1/0), Giorgi Ganugrava (7/0), Jaba Kankava (8/1) [*sent off 58*], Levan Kobiashvili (Cap) (60/4), David Mujiri (12/0) [61.Kakhaber Makharadze (1/0)], Revaz Gotsiridze (1/0) [82.Giorgi Chelidze (1/0)], Otar Martsvaladze (1/1). Trainer: Klaus Toppmöller (Germany, 1).
Goals: Otar Martsvaladze (8), Jaba Kankava (18).

111. 22.03.2006 **ALBANIA - GEORGIA** **0-0**
Stadiumi „Kombëtar Qemal Stafa", Tiranë; Referee: Paolo Dondarini (Italy); Attendance: 2,000
GEO: Giorgi Lomaia (21/0) [46.Grigol Chanturia (3/0)], Levan Magradze (4/0), Mate Gvinianidze (3/0), Giorgi Shashiashvili (13/0), Zaal Eliava (1/0), Kakhaber Aladashvili (2/0) [88.Giorgi Seturidze (1/0)], Jaba Kankava (9/1) [46.Giorgi Popkhadze (2/0)], Zurab Menteshashvili (16/1) [35.Giorgi Ganugrava (8/0)], Gogita Gogua (9/1) [*sent off 72*], Vasil Gigiadze (2/0), Lasha Jakobia (Cap) (7/1). Trainer: Klaus Toppmöller (Germany, 2).

112. 27.05.2006 **NEW ZEALAND - GEORGIA** **3-1(2-1)**
Sportzentrum, Altenkirchen (Germany); Referee: Wolfgang Stark (Germany); Attendance: 1,000
GEO: Giorgi Lomaia (22/0), Kakhaber Mjavanadze (14/0) [46.Otar Khizaneishvili (14/0)], Zurab Khizanishvili (38/0), Kakhaber Kaladze (Cap) (51/0), David Kvirkvelia (16/0) [66.Ilia Kandelaki (4/0)], Gogita Gogua (10/1) [55.David Mujiri (13/0)], Levan Kobiashvili (61/4), Malkhaz Asatiani (19/4) [66.Zurab Ionanidze (4/1)], Vasil Gigiadze (3/0) [46.Kakhaber Aladashvili (3/0)], Shota Arveladze (56/21), Giorgi Demetradze (44/11) [46.Aleksandre Iashvili (28/9)]. Trainer: Klaus Toppmöller (Germany, 3).
Goal: Shota Arveladze (41).

113. 31.05.2006 **PARAGUAY - GEORGIA** **1-0(1-0)**
Birkenwiese Stadium, Dornbirn (Austria); Referee: Thomas Gangle (Austria); Attendance: 2,000
GEO: Giorgi Lomaia (23/0), Lasha Salukvadze (10/0) [63.Gogita Gogua (11/1)], Kakhaber Kaladze (Cap) (52/0), Zurab Khizanishvili (39/0), Kakhaber Aladashvili (4/0) [63.Giorgi Demetradze (45/11)], Ilia Kandelaki (5/0), Jaba Kankava (10/1), Zurab Menteshashvili (17/1) [78.David Kvirkvelia (17/0)], Otar Martsvaladze (2/1) [71.Aleksandre Iashvili (29/9)], Malkhaz Asatiani (20/4) [74.David Mujiri (14/0)], Shota Arveladze (57/21). Trainer: Klaus Toppmöller (Germany, 4).

114. 16.08.2006 **FAROE ISLANDS - GEORGIA** **0-6(0-3)** 13th EC. Qualifiers
Svangaskarð, Toftir; Referee: Michael Ross (Northern Ireland); Attendance: 2,114
GEO: Grigol Chanturia (4/0), Kakhaber Aladashvili (5/0) [71.Giorgi Gakhokidze (21/3)], Giorgi Shashiashvili (14/0), Malkhaz Asatiani (21/4), Ilia Kandelaki (6/0) [66.David Kvirkvelia (18/0)], Gogita Gogua (12/1) [57.Giorgi Demetradze (46/11)], Jaba Kankava (11/1), Levan Kobiashvili (Cap) (62/5), David Mujiri (15/1), Aleksandre Iashvili (30/10), Shota Arveladze (58/24). Trainer: Klaus Toppmöller (Germany, 5).
Goals: David Mujiri (16), Aleksandre Iashvili (18), Shota Arveladze (37), Levan Kobiashvili (51 penalty), Shota Arveladze (62, 82).

115. 02.09.2006 **GEORGIA - FRANCE** **0-3(0-2)** 13th EC. Qualifiers
„Boris Paichadze" Erovnuli Stadioni, Tbilisi; Referee: Jan Wegereef (Netherlands); Attendance: 53,500
GEO: Grigol Chanturia (5/0), Kakhaber Aladashvili (6/0) [37.Ilia Kandelaki (7/0)], Zurab Khizanishvili (40/0), Malkhaz Asatiani (22/4), Gogita Gogua (13/1), Giorgi Demetradze (47/11), Jaba Kankava (12/1), Levan Kobiashvili (Cap) (63/5), David Mujiri (16/1) [81.Zurab Menteshashvili (18/1)], Shota Arveladze (59/24), Aleksandre Iashvili (31/10) [46.David Kvirkvelia (19/0)]. Trainer: Klaus Toppmöller (Germany, 6).

116. 06.09.2006 **UKRAINE - GEORGIA** **3-2(1-1)** 13th EC. Qualifiers
Olympiyskiy Stadium, Kyiv; Referee: Jaroslav Jara (Czech Republic); Attendance: 30,000
GEO: Grigol Chanturia (6/0), David Imedashvili (1/0) [35.Ilia Kandelaki (8/0)], Zurab Khizanishvili (41/0), Malkhaz Asatiani (23/4), Gogita Gogua (14/1), Jaba Kankava (13/1), Levan Kobiashvili (Cap) (64/5), Zurab Menteshashvili (19/1) [82.Mikheil Ashvetia (21/4)], David Kvirkvelia (20/0) [82.David Mujiri (17/1)], Giorgi Demetradze (48/12), Shota Arveladze (60/25). Trainer: Klaus Toppmöller (Germany, 7).
Goals: Shota Arveladze (37), Giorgi Demetradze (61).

117. 07.10.2006 **GERMANY - GEORGIA** **2-0(1-0)**
Ostseestadion, Rostock; Referee: Gerald Lehner (Austria); Attendance: 28,000
GEO: Giorgi Lomaia (24/0), Mate Gvinianidze (4/0) [73.Otar Khizaneishvili (15/0)], Zurab Khizanishvili (42/0) [*sent off 62*], Kakhaber Kaladze (Cap) (53/0), David Kvirkvelia (21/0) [79.Vasil Gigiadze (4/0)], Zurab Menteshashvili (20/1) [79.Kakhaber Aladashvili (7/0)], Jaba Kankava (14/1), Levan Kobiashvili (65/5), Levan Tskitishvili (40/1) [58.Gogita Gogua (15/1)], Giorgi Demetradze (49/12) [83.Irakli Modebadze (1/0)], Otar Martsvaladze (3/1) [63.Aleksandre Iashvili (32/10)]. Trainer: Klaus Toppmöller (Germany, 8).

118. 11.10.2006 **GEORGIA - ITALY** **1-3(1-1)** 13th EC. Qualifiers
„Boris Paichadze" Erovnuli Stadioni, Tbilisi; Referee: Michael Riley (England); Attendance: 52,000
GEO: Giorgi Lomaia (25/0), Otar Khizaneishvili (16/0), Zurab Khizanishvili (43/0), Kakhaber Kaladze (Cap) (54/0), Giorgi Shashiashvili (15/1), Zurab Menteshashvili (21/1), Jaba Kankava (15/1) [*sent off 60*], Levan Tskitishvili (41/1) [76.Ilia Kandelaki (9/0)], David Kvirkvelia (22/0), Otar Martsvaladze (4/1) [85.Vasil Gigiadze (5/0)], Mikheil Ashvetia (22/4) [70.Aleksandre Iashvili (33/10)]. Trainer: Klaus Toppmöller (Germany, 9).
Goal: Giorgi Shashiashvili (25).

119. 15.11.2006 **GEORGIA - URUGUAY** **2-0(1-0)**
„Boris Paichadze" Erovnuli Stadioni, Tbilisi; Referee: Vitaliy Godulyan (Ukraine); Attendance: 12,000
GEO: Nukri Revishvili (6/0), Gogita Gogua (16/1) [84.Aleksandre Kobakhidze (1/0)], Lasha Salukvadze (11/0), Giorgi Shashiashvili (16/1), Ilia Kandelaki (10/0), Vladimir Burduli (17/2), Zurab Menteshashvili (22/1), Levan Tskitishvili (42/1) [70.Shota Grigalashvili (1/0)], Levan Kobiashvili (66/7), David Siradze (3/0) [74.Rati Tsinamdzghvrishvili (3/0)], Giorgi Demetradze (50/12) [74.Mikheil Ashvetia (23/4)]. Trainer: Klaus Toppmöller (Germany, 10).
Goal: Levan Kobiashvili (38 penalty,61).

120. 07.02.2007 **GEORGIA - TURKEY** **1-0(0-0)**
„Boris Paichadze" Erovnuli Stadioni, Tbilisi; Referee: Romans Lajuks (Latvia); Attendance: 53,000
GEO: Nukri Revishvili (7/0) [46.Giorgi Lomaia (26/0)], Giorgi Shashiashvili (17/1), Lasha Salukvadze (12/0), Zurab Khizanishvili (44/0) [87.Amiran Sanai (1/0)], Zaal Eliava (2/0), Zurab Menteshashvili (23/1), Levan Tskitishvili (43/1), Vladimir Burduli (18/2) [82.Mikheil Ashvetia (24/4)], David Kvirkvelia (23/0) [67.Gogita Gogua (17/1)], Giorgi Demetradze (51/12) [87.Aleksandre Benashvili (2/0)], David Siradze (4/1) [77.David Mujiri (18/1)]. Trainer: Klaus Toppmöller (Germany, 11).
Goal: David Siradze (75).

121. 24.03.2007 **SCOTLAND - GEORGIA** **2-1(1-1)** 13th EC. Qualifiers
Hampden Park, Glasgow; Referee: Nicolai Vollquartz (Denmark); Attendance: 50,850
GEO: Giorgi Lomaia (27/0), Giorgi Shashiashvili (18/1), Lasha Salukvadze (13/0), Zurab Khizanishvili (45/0), Zaal Eliava (3/0), Vladimir Burduli (19/2) [56.David Siradze (5/1)], Zurab Menteshashvili (24/1) [46.Gogita Gogua (18/1)], Levan Tskitishvili (44/1) [90+2.David Mujiri (19/1)], Levan Kobiashvili (67/7), Giorgi Demetradze (52/12), Shota Arveladze (61/26). Trainer: Klaus Toppmöller (Germany, 12).
Goal: Shota Arveladze (41).

122. 28.03.2007 **GEORGIA – FAROE ISLANDS** **3-1(2-0)** 13th EC. Qualifiers
„Boris Paichadze" Erovnuli Stadioni, Tbilisi; Referee: Pavel Saliy (Kazakhstan); Attendance: 15,000
GEO: Giorgi Lomaia (28/0), Giorgi Shashiashvili (19/1), Lasha Salukvadze (14/0), Jaba Kankava (16/1), Levan Kobiashvili (68/7) [61.Zurab Menteshashvili (25/1)], David Kvirkvelia (24/0), David Mujiri (20/1), Levan Tskitishvili (45/1), Aleksandre Iashvili (34/12), David Siradze (6/2), Giorgi Demetradze (53/12). Trainer: Klaus Toppmöller (Germany, 13).
Goals: David Siradze (26), Aleksandre Iashvili (45+1, 90+2 penalty).

123. 02.06.2007 **LITHUANIA - GEORGIA** **1-0(0-0)** 13th EC. Qualifiers
„S. Dariaus ir S. Girėno" stadionas, Kaunas; Referee: Claudio Circhetta (Switzerland); Attendance: 6,000
GEO: Giorgi Lomaia (29/0), Otar Khizaneishvili (17/0), David Kvirkvelia (25/0), Zaal Eliava (4/0), Kakhaber Kaladze (Cap) (55/0), Zurab Khizanishvili (46/0), Levan Tskitishvili (46/1) [79.David Mujiri (21/1)], Zurab Menteshashvili (26/1) [64.Otar Martsvaladze (5/1)], Levan Kobiashvili (69/7), Aleksandre Iashvili (35/12), Giorgi Demetradze (54/12). Trainer: Klaus Toppmöller (Germany, 14).

124. 06.06.2007 **FRANCE - GEORGIA** **1-0(1-0)** 13th EC. Qualifiers
Stade "Abbé-Deschamps", Auxerre; Referee: Lucilio Cardoso Cortez Batista (Portugal); Attendance: 15,000
GEO: Giorgi Lomaia (30/0), David Kvirkvelia (26/0), Otar Khizaneishvili (18/0), Lasha Salukvadze (15/0) [13.David Mujiri (22/1)], Zaal Eliava (5/0) [61.Otar Martsvaladze (6/1)], Mate Gvinianidze (5/0), Kakhaber Kaladze (Cap) (56/0), Zurab Khizanishvili (47/0), Jaba Kankava (17/1) [89.Giorgi Shashiashvili (20/1)], Vladimir Burduli (20/2), Aleksandre Iashvili (36/12). Trainer: Klaus Toppmöller (Germany, 15).

125. 22.08.2007 **LUXEMBOURG - GEORGIA** **0-0**
Stade "Josy Barthel", Luxembourg; Referee: Stephen Weatherall (Northern Ireland); Attendance: 1,123
GEO: Giorgi Lomaia (31/0), David Kvirkvelia (27/0), Otar Khizaneishvili (19/0), Zurab Khizanishvili (48/0), Kakhaber Kaladze (57/0), Levan Tskitishvili (47/1) [78.Zurab Menteshashvili (27/1)], Levan Kobiashvili (70/7) [31.Aleksandre Amisulashvili (10/1)], Vladimir Burduli (21/2) [46.Otar Martsvaladze (7/1)], Malkhaz Asatiani (24/4) [46.David Mujiri (23/1)], Aleksandre Iashvili (37/12), David Siradze (7/2) [46.Vasil Gigiadze (6/0)]. Trainer: Klaus Toppmöller (Germany, 16).

126. 08.09.2007 **GEORGIA - UKRAINE** **1-1(0-1)** 13th EC. Qualifiers
„Boris Paichadze" Erovnuli Stadioni, Tbilisi; Referee: Alain Hamer (Luxembourg); Attendance: 25,000
GEO: Giorgi Lomaia (32/0), Mate Gvinianidze (6/0), Kakhaber Kaladze (58/0), Malkhaz Asatiani (25/4), Lasha Salukvadze (16/0), Levan Tskitishvili (48/1), Zurab Menteshashvili (28/1) [79.Dimitri Tatanashvili (1/0)], Lasha Jakobia (8/1) [62.David Siradze (8/3)], Giorgi Demetradze (55/12), Aleksandre Iashvili (38/12) [62.Levan Kenia (1/0)], Otar Martsvaladze (8/1). Trainer: Klaus Toppmöller (Germany, 17).
Goal: David Siradze (89).

127. 12.09.2007 **AZERBAIJAN - GEORGIA** **1-1(1-0)**
„Tofiq Bəhramov" adına Respublika Stadionu, Bakı; Referee: Kovalenko (Uzbekistan); Attendance: 10,000
GEO: Giorgi Makaridze (1/0), Otar Khizaneishvili (20/0), Malkhaz Asatiani (26/4), Aleksandre Kvakhadze (1/0) [75.David Lomaia (1/0)], Jaba Kankava (18/1), Levan Tskitishvili (49/1) [79.David Bolkvadze (1/0)], Ilia Kandelaki (11/0), Grigol Dolidze (1/0) [76.Lasha Salukvadze (17/0)], Levan Kenia (2/0) [60.Giorgi Dekanosidze (1/0)], Dimitri Tatanashvili (2/1), Lasha Jakobia (9/1) [62.Otar Martsvaladze (9/1)]. Trainer: Klaus Toppmöller (Germany, 18).
Goal: Dimitri Tatanashvili (48).

128. 13.10.2007 **ITALY - GEORGIA** **2-0(1-0)** 13th EC. Qualifiers
Stadio "Luigi Ferraris", Genova; Referee: Carlos Megía Dávila (Spain); Attendance: 23,057
GEO: Giorgi Lomaia (33/0), Giorgi Shashiashvili (21/1) [60.David Siradze (9/3)], Lasha Salukvadze (18/0), Malkhaz Asatiani (27/4), Zurab Khizanishvili (49/0), David Kvirkvelia (28/0), Levan Tskitishvili (Cap) (50/1), Zurab Menteshashvili (29/1), Jaba Kankava (19/1), Levan Mchedlidze (1/0) [60.Levan Kenia (3/0)], Giorgi Demetradze (56/12) [85.Lasha Jakobia (10/1)]. Trainer: Klaus Toppmöller (Germany, 19).

129. 17.10.2007 **GEORGIA - SCOTLAND** **2-0(1-0)** 13th EC. Qualifiers
„Boris Paichadze" Erovnuli Stadioni, Tbilisi; Referee: Knut Kircher (Germany); Attendance: 55,500
GEO: Giorgi Makaridze (2/0), Giorgi Shashiashvili (22/1), Lasha Salukvadze (19/0), Malkhaz Asatiani (28/4), Zurab Khizanishvili (50/0), Jaba Kankava (20/1), Zurab Menteshashvili (30/1), Levan Kenia (4/0) [79.Ilia Kandelaki (12/0)], David Kvirkvelia (29/0), David Siradze (10/4) [89.Lasha Jakobia (11/1)], Levan Mchedlidze (2/1) [85.Aleksandre Kvakhadze (2/0)]. Trainer: Klaus Toppmöller (Germany, 20).
Goals: Levan Mchedlidze (16), David Siradze (64).

130. 16.11.2007 **QATAR - GEORGIA** **1-2(0-0)**
„Thani bin Jassim" Stadium, Al Rayyan; Referee: Jafaar Mahdi Al Khabbaz (Bahrein); Attendance: 300
GEO: Giorgi Makaridze (3/0), Zurab Khizanishvili (51/0) [61.Lasha Salukvadze (20/1)], Malkhaz Asatiani (29/4), Kakhaber Kaladze (Cap) (59/0), Amiran Sanaia (1/0) [61.Giorgi Shashiashvili (23/1)], Shota Grigalashvili (2/0), Jaba Kankava (21/2) [80.Aleksandre Kvakhadze (3/0)], David Kvirkvelia (30/0) [85.Giorgi Dekanosidze (2/0)], Levan Tskitishvili (51/1), Levan Kenia (5/0) [68.Nikoloz Gelashvili (1/0)], Levan Mchedlidze (3/1) [46.Lasha Jakobia (12/1)]. Trainer: Klaus Toppmöller (Germany, 21).
Goals: Jaba Kankava (46), Lasha Salukvadze (64).

131. 21.11.2007 **GEORGIA - LITHUANIA** **0-2(0-0)** 13th EC. Qualifiers
„Boris Paichadze" Erovnuli Stadioni, Tbilisi; Referee: Aleksandar Stavrev (Macedonia); Attendance: 2,000
GEO: Giorgi Makaridze (4/0), Lasha Salukvadze (21/1), Malkhaz Asatiani (30/4), Kakhaber Kaladze (Cap) (60/0), David Kvirkvelia (31/0), Jaba Kankava (22/2), Levan Tskitishvili (52/1), Zurab Menteshashvili (31/1) [31.Otar Martsvaladze (10/1)], Levan Kenia (6/0), Levan Mchedlidze (4/1), David Siradze (11/4) [80.Nikoloz Gelashvili (2/0)]. Trainer: Klaus Toppmöller (Germany, 22).

132. 06.02.2008 **GEORGIA - LATVIA** **1-3(0-3)**
„Boris Paichadze" Erovnuli Stadioni, Tbilisi; Referee: Sergey Shmolik (Belarus); Attendance: 6,000
GEO: Nukri Revishvili (8/0), Lasha Salukvadze (22/1), Malkhaz Asatiani (31/4), Kakhaber Kaladze (Cap) (61/1), Zaal Eliava (6/0), Jaba Kankava (23/2), Giorgi Khidesheli (1/0) [84.Beka Gotsiridze (2/0)], Gogita Gogua (19/1) [75.Shota Grigalashvili (3/0)], Levan Kenia (7/0), Levan Mchedlidze (5/1) [42.Aleksandre Kobakhidze (2/0)], David Siradze (12/4). Trainer: Klaus Toppmöller (Germany, 23).
Goal: Kakhaber Kaladze (46).

133. 26.03.2008 **NORTHERN IRELAND - GEORGIA** **4-1(3-0)**
Windsor Park, Belfast; Referee: Luc Wilmes (Luxembourg); Attendance: 15,000
GEO: Giorgi Makaridze (5/0), Lasha Salukvadze (23/1), Giorgi Shashiashvili (24/1) [81.Lasha Jakobia (13/1)], Kakhaber Kaladze (Cap) (62/1), Aleksandre Kvakhadze (4/0), David Kvirkvelia (32/0), Levan Tskitishvili (53/1) [90.Zaal Eliava (7/0)], Levan Kenia (8/0) [81.Giorgi Khidesheli (2/0)], Jaba Kankava (24/2), Levan Kobiashvili (71/7), Aleksandre Iashvili (39/12). Trainer: Klaus Toppmöller (Germany, 24).
Goal: David Jonathan Healy (55 own goal).

134. 27.05.2008 **ESTONIA - GEORGIA** **1-1(0-0)**
A. Le Coq Arena, Tallinn; Referee: Thomas Vejlgaard (Denmark); Attendance: 2,500
GEO: Giorgi Loria (1/0), Ucha Lobjanidze (1/0), Zurab Khizanishvili (Cap) (52/0), Malkhaz Asatiani (32/4), Giorgi Navalovski (1/0), Levan Kobiashvili (72/7), Levan Tskitishvili (54/1), David Odikadze (5/0) [68.Beka Gotsiridze (3/0)], David Kvirkvelia (33/0) [76.Irakli Klimiashvili (1/0)], Aleksandre Iashvili (40/12) [90.David Mujiri (24/1)], Rati Aleksidze (20/2) [61.Levan Kenia (9/1)]. Trainer: Petar Segrt (Germany, 1).
Goal: Levan Kenia (83).

135. 31.05.2008 **PORTUGAL - GEORGIA** **2-0(2-0)**
Estádio do Fontelo, Viseu; Referee: Meir Levi (Israel); Attendance: 8,500
GEO: Giorgi Loria (2/0), Ucha Lobjanidze (2/0), Zurab Khizanishvili (Cap) (53/0), Malkhaz Asatiani (33/4), Giorgi Navalovski (2/0) [81.Giorgi Merebashvili (1/0)], Zurab Menteshashvili (32/1) [67.Amiran Sanaia (2/0)], Levan Tskitishvili (55/1) [46.Irakli Klimiashvili (2/0)], Levan Kobiashvili (73/7) [46.Beka Gotsiridze (4/0)], Levan Kenia (10/1) [68.Revaz Barabadze (1/0)], Aleksandre Iashvili (41/12) [46.David Devdariani (1/0)], Rati Aleksidze (21/2) [38.David Mujiri (25/1)]. Trainer: Petar Segrt (Germany, 2).

136. 20.08.2008 **WALES - GEORGIA** **1-2(1-0)**
Liberty Stadium, Swansea; Referee: Matej Jug (Slovenia); Attendance: 6,435
GEO: Giorgi Loria (3/0), Ucha Lobjanidze (3/0), Zurab Khizanishvili (Cap) (54/0), Malkhaz Asatiani (34/4), Aleksandre Kvakhadze (5/0), Zurab Menteshashvili (33/1), David Mujiri (26/1) [46.Levan Khmaladze (1/0)], Levan Kenia (11/2) [76.Irakli Klimiashvili (3/0)], David Odikadze (6/0) [86.David Devdariani (2/0)], Aleksandre Iashvili (42/12) [81.Beka Gotsiridze (5/1)], Levan Mchedlidze (6/1) [23.Rati Aleksidze (22/2)]. Trainer: Héctor Raúl Cúper (Argentina, 1).
Goals: Levan Kenia (66), Beka Gotsiridze (90).

137. 06.09.2008 **GEORGIA – REPUBLIC OF IRELAND** **1-2(0-1)** 19th WC. Qualifiers
Stadion am Bruchweg, Mainz (Germany); Referee: Zsolt Szabó (Hungary); Attendance: 4,500
GEO: Giorgi Loria (4/0), Ucha Lobjanidze (4/0), Zurab Khizanishvili (55/0) [83.Malkhaz Asatiani (35/4)], Kakhaber Kaladze (Cap) (63/1), Giorgi Shashiashvili (25/1), Zurab Menteshashvili (34/1), Levan Kenia (12/3), David Odikadze (7/0), Levan Kobiashvili (74/7), Aleksandre Iashvili (43/12) [77.Levan Mchedlidze (7/1)], Rati Aleksidze (23/2) [61.David Siradze (13/4)]. Trainer: Héctor Raúl Cúper (Argentina, 2).
Goal: Levan Kenia (90+2).

138. 10.09.2008 **ITALY - GEORGIA** **2-0(1-0)** 19th WC. Qualifiers
Stadio Friuli, Udine; Referee: Thomas Einwaller (Austria); Attendance: 27,164
GEO: Giorgi Loria (5/0), Ucha Lobjanidze (5/0), Lasha Salukvadze (24/1), Kakhaber Kaladze (Cap) (64/1), Zaal Eliava (8/0) [46.David Kvirkvelia (34/0)], Levan Kenia (13/3), Levan Khmaladze (2/0), Zurab Menteshashvili (35/1) [68.David Odikadze (8/0)], Levan Kobiashvili (75/7), Aleksandre Iashvili (44/12), Levan Mchedlidze (8/1) [55.David Siradze (14/4)]. Trainer: Héctor Raúl Cúper (Argentina, 3).

139. 11.10.2008 **GEORGIA - CYPRUS** **1-1(0-0)** 19th WC. Qualifiers
„Boris Paichadze" Erovnuli Stadioni, Tbilisi; Referee: Radek Matejek (Czech Republic); Attendance: 40,000
GEO: Giorgi Lomaia (34/0), Ucha Lobjanidze (6/0), Lasha Salukvadze (25/1), Zurab Khizanishvili (56/0), Giorgi Shashiashvili (26/1), Zurab Menteshashvili (36/1), Levan Kobiashvili (Cap) (76/8), Luka Razmadze (1/0), Levan Kenia (14/3) [65.Beka Gotsiridze (6/1)], Aleksandre Iashvili (45/12), Levan Mchedlidze (9/1) [76.Rati Aleksidze (24/2)]. Trainer: Héctor Raúl Cúper (Argentina, 4).
Goal: Levan Kobiashvili (73).

140. 15.10.2008 **GEORGIA - BULGARIA** **0-0** 19th WC. Qualifiers
„Boris Paichadze" Erovnuli Stadioni, Tbilisi; Referee: Bjorn Kuipers (Netherlands); Attendance: 35,250
GEO: Giorgi Lomaia (35/0), Ucha Lobjanidze (7/0), Lasha Salukvadze (26/1), Aleksandre Kvakhadze (1/0), Giorgi Shashiashvili (27/1), Zurab Mentesahshvili (37/1), Levan Kobiashvili (Cap) (77/8), Luka Razmadze (2/0), Beka Gotsiridze (7/1) [84.David Odikadze (9/0)], Aleksandre Iashvili (46/12) [71.Giorgi Merebashvili (2/0)], Levan Mchedlidze (10/1) [32.David Siradze (15/4)]. Trainer: Héctor Raúl Cúper (Argentina, 5).

141. 19.11.2008 **ROMANIA - GEORGIA** **2-1(0-1)**
Stadionul Dinamo, Bucureşti; Referee: Kyros Vassaras (Greece); Attendance: 2,000
GEO: Giorgi Lomaia (36/0), Mate Ghvinianidze (6/0) [46.Giorgi Shashiashvili (28/1)], Lasha Salukvadze (27/1), Aleksandr Kvakhadze (7/0), Ilia Kandelaki (13/0), Murtaz Daushvili (1/0), Levan Kobiashvili (Cap) (78/8) [69.Levan Khmaladze (3/0)], Luka Razmadze (3/0), Otar Martsvaladze (11/2) [61.David Odikadze (10/0)], Beka Gotsiridze (8/1) [75.Giorgi Merebashvili (3/0)], Rati Aleksidze (25/2) [57.Levan Mchedlidze (11/1)]. Trainer: Héctor Raúl Cúper (Argentina, 6).
Goal: Otar Martsvaladze (12).

142. 11.02.2009 **REPUBLIC OF IRELAND - GEORGIA** **2-1(0-1)** 19th WC. Qualifiers
Croke Park, Dublin; Referee: Jouni Hyytia (Finland); Attendance: 45,000
GEO: Giorgi Lomaia (37/0), Ucha Lobjanidze (8/0), Zurab Khizanishvili (57/0), Kakhaber Kaladze (Cap) (65/1), David Kvirkvelia (35/0), Levan Kobiashvili (79/8), Zurab Menteshashvili (38/1) [70.Levan Khmaladze (4/0)], Luka Razmadze (4/0), Beka Gotsiridze (9/1) [68.Giorgi Merebashvili (4/0)], David Siradze (16/4) [77.Rati Aleksidze (26/2)], Aleksandre Iashvili (47/13). Trainer: Héctor Raúl Cúper (Argentina, 7).
Goal: Aleksandre Iashvili (1).

143. 28.03.2009 **CYPRUS - GEORGIA** **2-1(1-0)** 19th WC. Qualifiers
Stádio „Andónis Papadópoulos", Lárnaca; Referee: Freddy Fautrel (France); Attendance: 3,000
GEO: Giorgi Lomaia (38/0), Ucha Lobjanidze (9/0), Zurab Khizanishvili (58/0), Aleksandre Kvakhadze (8/0), Giorgi Shashiashvili (29/1), Luka Razmadze (5/0), David Odikadze (11/0), Levan Kobiashvili (Cap) (80/9), Beka Gotsiridze (10/1), Aleksandre Iashvili (48/13), Levan Mchedlidze (12/1) [28.David Siradze (17/4)]. Trainer: Héctor Raúl Cúper (Argentina, 8).
Goal: Levan Kobiashvili (71 penalty).

144. 01.04.2009 **GEORGIA - MONTENEGRO** **0-0** 19th WC. Qualifiers
„Boris Paichadze" Erovnuli Stadioni, Tbilisi; Referee: David Malcolm (Northern Ireland); Attendance: 16,000
GEO: Giorgi Lomaia (39/0), Lasha Salukvadze (28/1), Guram Kashia (1/0), Aleksandre Kvakhadze (9/0), David Kvirkvelia (36/0), David Odikadze (12/0) [65.Irakli Klimiashvili (4/0)], Levan Khmaladze (5/0), Levan Kobiashvili (Cap) (81/9), Aleksandre Iashvili (49/13), Beka Gotsiridze (11/1) [77.David Siradze (18/4)], Giorgi Merebashvili (5/0). Trainer: Héctor Raúl Cúper (Argentina, 9).

145. 06.06.2009 **GEORGIA - MOLDOVA** **1-2(0-1)**
„Mikhail Meshki" Stadium, Tbilisi; Referee: Pavel Saliy (Kazakhstan); Attendance: 7,000
GEO: Giorgi Lomaia (40/0), Giorgi Popkhadze (3/0), Aleksandre Kvakhadze (10/0), Zurab Khizanishvili (59/1), Giorgi Shashiashvili (30/1), David Kvirkvelia (37/0) [60.Giorgi Merebashvili (6/0)], Levan Kobiashvili (Cap) (82/9) [70.Luka Razmadze (6/0)], Murtaz Daushvili (2/0) [77.Levan Kenia (15/3)], Beka Gotsiridze (12/1) [27.Giorgi Seturidze (2/0)], Aleksandre Iashvili (50/13), Rati Aleksidze (27/2) [63.Vladimir Dvalishvili (1/0)]. Trainer: Héctor Raúl Cúper (Argentina, 10).
Goal: Zurab Khizanishvili (85).

146. 10.06.2009 **ALBANIA - GEORGIA** **1-1(0-1)**
Stadiumi „Kombëtar Qemal Stafa“, Tiranë; Referee: Aleksandar Stavrev (Macedonia); Attendance: 2,000
GEO: Grigol Bediashvili (1/0), Ucha Lobjanidze (10/0), Guram Kashia (2/0), Zurab Menteshashvili (60/1), Giorgi Popkhadze (4/0), Luka Razmadze (7/0), Giorgi Seturidze (3/0), Levan Kobiashvili (Cap) (83/9) [80.Irakli Klimiashvili (5/0)], Giorgi Merebashvili (7/0) [59.Otar Martsvaladze (12/2)], Aleksandre Iashvili (51/13) [76.Murtaz Daushvili (3/0)], Vladimir Dvalishvili (2/1) [65.Rati Aleksidze (28/2)]. Trainer: Héctor Raúl Cúper (Argentina, 11).
Goal: Vladimir Dvalishvili (2).

147. 12.08.2009 **MALTA - GEORGIA** **2-0(0-0)**
Ta'Qali National Stadium, Attard; Referee: Panicos Kailis (Cyprus); Attendance: n/a
GEO: Giorgi Lomaia (41/0), Mate Gvinianidze (7/0) [81.Teimuraz Gongadze (1/0)], Guram Kashia (3/0), Giorgi Popkhadze (5/0) [84.Amiran Sanaia (3/0)], Zurab Khizanishvili (61/1), Levan Khmaladze (6/0), Levan Kenia (16/3), Levan Kobiashvili (Cap) (84/9), Giorgi Seturidze (4/0) [68.Giorgi Merebashvili (8/0)], Levan Tskitishvili (56/1) [63.David Devdariani (3/0)], Vladimir Dvalishvili (3/1). Trainer: Héctor Raúl Cúper (Argentina, 12).

148. 05.09.2009 **GEORGIA - ITALY** **0-2(0-0)**
„Boris Paichadze“ Erovnuli Stadioni, Tbilisi; Referee: Marcin Borski (Poland); Attendance: 32,000
GEO: Giorgi Lomaia (42/0), Ucha Lobjanidze (11/0), Zurab Khizanishvili (62/1), Kakhaber Kaladze (Cap) (66/1), Amiran Sanaia (4/0), Levan Kobiashvili (85/9), Luka Razmadze (8/0) [73.Levan Tskitishvili (57/1)], Levan Khmaladze (7/0), Levan Kenia (17/3), Vladimir Dvalishvili (4/1), Jano Ananidze (1/0) [59.Mate Vatsadze (1/0)]. Trainer: Héctor Raúl Cúper (Argentina, 13).

149. 09.09.2009 **ICELAND - GEORGIA** **3-1(2-1)**
Laugardalsvöllur, Reykjavík; Referee: Matteo Trefoloni (Italy); Attendance: 4,726
GEO: Zurab Mamaladze (2/0), Teimuraz Gongadze (2/0) [73.Ucha Lobjanidze (12/0)], Guram Kashia (4/0), Aleksandre Kvakhadze (11/0), Giorgi Popkhadze (6/0), Giorgi Seturidze (5/0), Levan Tskitishvili (Cap) (58/1) [60.Levan Khmaladze (8/0)], Luka Razmadze (9/0), Nikoloz Gelashvili (3/0), David Devdariani (4/0), Vladimir Dvalishvili (5/2). Trainer: Héctor Raúl Cúper (Argentina, 14).
Goal: Vladimir Dvalishvili (33).

150. 10.10.2009 **MONTENEGRO - GEORGIA** **2-1(1-1)**
Gradski Stadium, Podgorica; Referee: Selçuk Dereli (Turkey); Attendance: 5,420
GEO: Giorgi Lomaia (43/0), Ucha Lobjanidze (13/0), Zurab Khizanishvili (63/1), Kakhaber Kaladze (Cap) (67/1), Levan Khmaladze (9/0), Luka Razmadze (10/0), Amiran Sanaia (5/0) [79.Giorgi Popkhadze (7/0)], Giorgi Merebashvili (9/0) [76.David Odikadze (13/0)], Vladimir Dvalishvili (6/3), Nikoloz Gelashvili (4/0) [67.Jaba Lipartia (1/0)], Aleksandre Iashvili (52/13). Trainer: Héctor Raúl Cúper (Argentina, 15).
Goal: Vladimir Dvalishvili (45).

151. 14.10.2009 **BULGARIA - GEORGIA** **6-2(6-1)**
Nationalen stadion "Vasil Levski", Sofia; Referee: Kristinn Jakobsson (Iceland); Attendance: 700
GEO: Giorgi Lomaia (44/0) [29.Zurab Mamaladze (3/0)], Ucha Lobjanidze (14/0), Zurab Khizanishvili (64/1), Kakhaber Kaladze (Cap) (68/1), Levan Khmaladze (10/0) [*sent off 58*], Levan Kobiashvili (86/10), Luka Razmadze (11/0), Amiran Sanaia (6/0) [78.Giorgi Merebashvili (10/0)], Levan Kenia (18/3) [88.David Odikadze (14/0)], Vladimir Dvalishvili (7/4), Aleksandre Iashvili (53/13). Trainer: Héctor Raúl Cúper (Argentina, 16).
Goals: Vladimir Dvalishvili (34), Levan Kobiashvili (51 penalty).

152. 03.03.2010 **GEORGIA - ESTONIA** **2-1(1-0)**
„Boris Paichadze“ Erovnuli Stadioni, Tbilisi; Referee: Veaceslav Banari (Moldova); Attendance: 40,000
GEO: Giorgi Lomaia (45/0), Levan Kobiashvili (87/11), Zurab Khizanishvili (65/1) [57.Zurab Menteshashvili (39/1)], Kakhaber Kaladze (Cap) (69/1), Malkhaz Asatiani (36/4), Lasha Salukvadze (29/1) [67.Giorgi Shashiashvili (31/1)], David Kvirkvelia (38/0), Gogita Gogua (20/1) [83.Guram Kashia (5/0)], Aleksandre Iashvili (54/13) [67.David Siradze (19/5)], Vladimir Dvalishvili (8/4) [46.Mate Vatsadze (2/0)], Otar Martsvaladze (13/2) [46.Giorgi Merebashvili (11/0)]. Trainer: Temuri Ketsbaia (1).
Goals: Levan Kobiashvili (45+4 penalty), David Siradze (90+4).

153. 25.05.2010 **GEORGIA - CAMEROON** **0-0**
Dolomitenstadion, Lienz (Austria); Referee: Bernhard Brugger (Austria); Attendance: 4,000
GEO: Nukri Revishvili (9/0), Levan Kobiashvili (Cap) (88/11), Zurab Khizanishvili (66/1), Aleksandre Amisulashvili (11/1), Malkhaz Asatiani (37/4), Ilia Kandelaki (14/0) [89.Giorgi Shashiashvili (32/1)], Ucha Lobjanidze (15/0), Zurab Menteshashvili (40/1) [58.Tornike Aptsiauri (3/0)], Jano Ananidze (2/0) [58.Nikoloz Gelashvili (5/0)], Aleksandre Iashvili (55/13) [76.Giorgi Merebashvili (12/0)], Vladimir Dvalishvili (9/4) [69.Revaz Barabadze (2/0)]. Trainer: Temuri Ketsbaia (2).

154. 11.08.2010 **MOLDOVA - GEORGIA** **0-0**
Stadionul Zimbru, Chişinău; Referee: Viktor Shvetsov (Ukraine); Attendance: 3,000
GEO: Giorgi Loria (6/0), Levan Kobiashvili (89/11), Zurab Khizanishvili (67/1), Kakhaber Kaladze (Cap) (70/1), Aleksandre Amisulashvili (12/1) [46.David Kvirkvelia (39/0)], Malkhaz Asatiani (38/4) [69.Lasha Salukvadze (30/1)], Ucha Lobjanidze (16/0) [*sent off 74*], Gogita Gogua (21/1) [64.Tornike Aptsiauri (4/0)], Aleksandre Iashvili (56/13) [46.Nikoloz Gelashvili (6/0)], David Siradze (20/5) [56.Giorgi Merebashvili (13/0)], Vladimir Dvalishvili (10/4) [77.Aleksandre Koshkadze (1/0)]. Trainer: Temuri Ketsbaia (3).

155. 03.09.2010 **GREECE - GEORGIA** **1-1(0-1)** 14th EC. Qualifiers
Stádio „Georgios Karaiskakis“, Peiraiás; Referee: Carlos Clos Gómez (Spain); Attendance: 14,794
GEO: Nukri Revishvili (10/0), Levan Kobiashvili (90/11), Zurab Khizanishvili (68/1), Kakhaber Kaladze (Cap) (71/1), Aleksandre Amisulashvili (13/1), Malkhaz Asatiani (39/4), David Kvirkvelia (40/0), Ucha Lobjanidze (17/0), Gogita Gogua (22/1) [87.Giorgi Merebashvili (14/0)], Aleksandre Iashvili (57/14) [54.Jano Ananidze (3/0)], Vladimir Dvalishvili (11/4) [60.Nikoloz Gelashvili (7/0)]. Trainer: Temuri Ketsbaia (4).
Goal: Aleksandre Iashvili (3).

156. 07.09.2010 **GEORGIA - ISRAEL** **0-0** 14th EC. Qualifiers
„Boris Paichadze“ Erovnuli Stadioni, Tbilisi; Referee: Sascha Kever (Switzerland); Attendance: 45,000
GEO: Nukri Revishvili (11/0), Levan Kobiashvili (91/11), Zurab Khizanishvili (69/1), Kakhaber Kaladze (Cap) (72/1), Aleksandre Amisulashvili (14/1), Malkhaz Asatiani (40/4), Ucha Lobjanidze (18/0), Gogita Gogua (23/1) [75.Tornike Aptsiauri (5/0)], Jano Ananidze (4/0), Aleksandre Iashvili (58/14) [46.David Siradze (21/5)], Vladimir Dvalishvili (12/4) [63.Giorgi Merebashvili (15/0)]. Trainer: Temuri Ketsbaia (5).

157. 08.10.2010 **GEORGIA - MALTA** **1-0(0-0)** 14th EC. Qualifiers

„Boris Paichadze" Erovnuli Stadioni, Tbilisi; Referee: Alan Black (Northern Ireland); Attendance: 38,000

GEO: Nukri Revishvili (12/0), Levan Kobiashvili (92/11), Zurab Khizanishvili (70/1), Kakhaber Kaladze (Cap) (73/1), Aleksandre Amisulashvili (15/1), Malkhaz Asatiani (41/4), Lasha Salukvadze (31/1), Gogita Gogua (24/1), Giorgi Merebashvili (16/0) [46.Aleksandre Iashvili (59/14)], Jano Ananidze (5/0) [73.Murtaz Daushvili (4/0)], Vladimir Dvalishvili (13/4) [46.David Siradze (22/6)]. Trainer: Temuri Ketsbaia (6).

Goal: David Siradze (90).

158. 12.10.2010 **LATVIA - GEORGIA** **1-1(0-0)** 14th EC. Qualifiers

Skonto stadions, Riga; Referee: Manuel Jorge Neves Moreira de Sousa (Portugal); Attendance: 4,330

GEO: Nukri Revishvili (13/0), Levan Kobiashvili (93/11), Kakhaber Kaladze (Cap) (74/1), Aleksandre Amisulashvili (16/1), Malkhaz Asatiani (42/4), David Kvirkvelia (41/0) [69.Gogita Gogua (25/1)], Ucha Lobjanidze (19/0), Murtaz Daushvili (5/0), Jano Ananidze (6/0) [79.Lasha Salukvadze (32/1)], Aleksandre Iashvili (60/14) [87.Aleksandre Koshkadze (2/0)], David Siradze (23/7). Trainer: Temuri Ketsbaia (7).

Goal: David Siradze (74).

159. 17.11.2010 **SLOVENIA - GEORGIA** **1-2(0-0)**

Stadion ŠRC Bonifika, Koper; Referee: Mark Whitby (Wales); Attendance: 4,100

GEO: Giorgi Loria (7/0), Zurab Khizanishvili (71/1), Kakhaber Kaladze (Cap) (75/1), David Kvirkvelia (42/0), Akaki Khubutia (1/0), Guram Kashia (6/0), Gocha Khojava (1/0) [46.Aleksandre Guruli (1/1)], Jaba Kankava (25/2) [73.Levan Kakubava (1/0)], Jano Ananidze (7/1) [89.Aleksandre Koshkadze (3/0)], Nikoloz Gelashvili (8/0) [62.Tornike Okriashvili (1/0)], Irakli Modebadze (2/0) [46.Mate Vatsadze (3/0)]. Trainer: Temuri Ketsbaia (8).

Goals: Aleksandre Guruli (67), Jano Ananidze (68).

160. 09.02.2011 **ARMENIA - GEORGIA** **1-2(0-2)**

Tsirion Athlítiko Kentro, Limassol (Cyprus); Referee: Yiannis Anastasiou (Cyprus); Attendance: n/a

GEO: Giorgi Loria (8/0) [46.Nukri Revishvili (14/0)], Levan Kobiashvili (94/11) [46.David Kvirkvelia (43/0)], Zurab Khizanishvili (72/1) [57.Levan Kakubava (2/0)], Kakhaber Kaladze (Cap) (76/1) [46.Aleksandre Amisulashvili (17/1)], Lasha Salukvadze (33/1), Akaki Khubutia (2/0), Gogita Gogua (26/1) [46.Mate Vatsadze (4/0)], Murtaz Daushvili (6/0), Jano Ananidze (8/1), Aleksandre Iashvili (61/15) [50.Giorgi Merebashvili (17/0)], David Siradze (24/8). Trainer: Temuri Ketsbaia (9).

Goals: Aleksandre Iashvili (22), David Siradze (34).

161. 26.03.2011 **GEORGIA - CROATIA** **1-0(0-0)** 14th EC. Qualifiers

„Boris Paichadze" Dinamo Arena, Tbilisi; Referee: Paolo Tagliavento (Italy); Attendance: 54,500

GEO: Nukri Revishvili (15/0), Levan Kobiashvili (95/12), Zurab Khizanishvili (73/1), Kakhaber Kaladze (Cap) (77/1), Aleksandre Amisulashvili (18/1), Lasha Salukvadze (34/1), Akaki Khubutia (3/0), Jaba Kankava (26/2), Murtaz Daushvili (7/0) [73.Gogita Gogua (27/1)], Aleksandre Iashvili (62/15) [62.Otar Martsvaladze (14/2)], Vladimir Dvalishvili (14/4) [46.David Siradze (25/8)]. Trainer: Temuri Ketsbaia (10).

Goal: Levan Kobiashvili (90).

162. 29.03.2011 **ISRAEL - GEORGIA** **1-0(0-0)** 14th EC. Qualifiers

Bloomfield Stadium, Tel Aviv; Referee: Fredy Fautrel (France); Attendance: 13,716

GEO: Nukri Revishvili (16/0), Levan Kobiashvili (96/12), Zurab Khizanishvili (74/1), Kakhaber Kaladze (Cap) (78/1), Aleksandre Amisulashvili (19/1), Lasha Salukvadze (35/1), Akaki Khubutia (4/0), Jaba Kankava (27/2), Murtaz Daushvili (8/0) [46.David Kvirkvelia (44/0)], Aleksandre Iashvili (63/15) [63.Vladimir Dvalishvili (15/4)], Otar Martsvaladze (15/2) [73.David Siradze (26/8)]. Trainer: Temuri Ketsbaia (11).

163. 03.06.2011 **CROATIA - GEORGIA** **2-1(0-1)** 14th EC. Qualifiers

Stadion Poljud, Split; Referee: Stefan Johannesson (Sweden); Attendance: 28,000

GEO: Giorgi Loria (9/0), Zurab Khizanishvili (75/1), Kakhaber Kaladze (Cap) (79/1), Lasha Salukvadze (36/1), David Kvirkvelia (45/0), Gia Grigalava (1/0), Akaki Khubutia (5/0), Guram Kashia (7/0) [80.Jano Ananidze (9/1)], Jaba Kankava (28/3), Aleksandre Iashvili (64/15) [62.Murtaz Daushvili (9/0)], David Siradze (27/8) [56.Vladimir Dvalishvili (16/4)]. Trainer: Temuri Ketsbaia (12).

Goal: Jaba Kankava (16).

164. 10.08.2011 **POLAND - GEORGIA** **1-0(1-0)**

Dialog Arena, Lubin; Referee: Andriy Shandor (Ukraine); Attendance: 12,310

GEO: Giorgi Loria (10/0), Levan Kobiashvili (97/12) [81.David Kvirkvelia (46/0)], Kakhaber Kaladze (Cap) (80/1), Aleksandre Amisulashvili (20/1) [46.Gia Grigalava (2/0)], Akaki Khubutia (6/0), Ucha Lobjanidze (20/0), Jaba Kankava (29/3) [73.Murtaz Daushvili (10/0)], David Targamadze (1/0), Shota Grigalashvili (4/0) [63.Guram Kashia (8/0)], Vladimir Dvalishvili (17/4) [46.Aleksandre Guruli (2/1)], Otar Martsvaladze (16/2) [63.Mate Vatsadze (5/0)]. Trainer: Temuri Ketsbaia (13).

165. 02.09.2011 **GEORGIA - LATVIA** **0-1(0-0)** 14th EC. Qualifiers

„Mikheil Meskhi" Stadioni, Tbilisi; Referee: Leontios Trattou (Cyprus); Attendance: 15,422

GEO: Giorgi Loria (11/0), Levan Kobiashvili (98/12), Zurab Khizanishvili (76/1), Kakhaber Kaladze (Cap) (81/1), Aleksandre Amisulashvili (21/1) [71.Vladimir Dvalishvili (18/4)], Guram Kashia (9/0), Jaba Kankava (30/3), David Targamadze (2/0), Jano Ananidze (10/1) [54.Shota Grigalashvili (5/0)], Aleksandre Iashvili (65/15) [55.David Siradze (28/8)], Otar Martsvaladze (17/2). Trainer: Temuri Ketsbaia (14).

166. 06.09.2011 **MALTA - GEORGIA** **1-1(1-1)** 14th EC. Qualifiers

National Stadium, Ta'Qali; Referee: Paulus Hendrikus Martinus van Boekel (Netherlands); Attendance: 5,000

GEO: Nukri Revishvili (17/0), Levan Kobiashvili (99/12), Zurab Khizanishvili (77/1), Kakhaber Kaladze (Cap) (82/1), Gia Grigalava (3/0), Guram Kashia (10/0), Jaba Kankava (31/4), David Targamadze (3/0), Jano Ananidze (11/1) [77.Aleksandre Kobakhidze (3/0)], Aleksandre Iashvili (66/15) [46.Vladimir Dvalishvili (19/4)], Otar Martsvaladze (18/2) [66.Shota Grigalashvili (6/0)]. Trainer: Temuri Ketsbaia (15).

Goal: Jaba Kankava (15).

167. 11.10.2011 **GEORGIA - GREECE** **1-2(1-0)** 14th EC. Qualifiers

„Mikheil Meskhi" Stadioni, Tbilisi; Referee: Daniele Orsato (Italy); Attendance: 7,824

GEO: Nukri Revishvili (18/0), Levan Kobiashvili (**100**/12), Zurab Khizanishvili (78/1), Kakhaber Kaladze (Cap) (83/1), Aleksandre Amisulashvili (22/1), Guram Kashia (11/0), Jaba Kankava (32/4) [42.Ucha Lobjanidze (21/0)], David Targamadze (4/1), Shota Grigalashvili (7/0) [51.Aleksandre Iashvili (67/15)], Levan Mchedlidze (13/1) [65.Aleksandre Guruli (3/1)], Otar Martsvaladze (19/2). Trainer: Temuri Ketsbaia (16).

Goal: David Targamadze (18).

168. 11.11.2011 **GEORGIA - MOLDOVA** **2-0(2-0)**

„Mikheil Meskhi“ Stadioni, Tbilisi; Referee: Vüsal Äliyev (Azerbaijan); Attendance: 4,000

GEO: Giorgi Loria (12/0), Zurab Khizanishvili (Cap) (79/1) [86.Giorgi Janelidze (1/0)], Aleksandre Amisulashvili (23/1), Gia Grigalava (4/0), Akaki Khubutia (7/0) [86.Shota Grigalashvili (8/0)], Guram Kashia (12/0), Aleksandre Kobakhidze (4/1), Irakli Maisuradze (1/0) [53.Giorgi Ganugrava (9/0)], Jano Ananidze (12/2) [58.Tornike Gorgiashvili (1/0)], Vladimir Dvalishvili (20/4) [56.Irakli Modebadze (3/0)], Nikoloz Gelashvili (9/0) [64.Aleksandre Guruli (4/1)]. Trainer: Temuri Ketsbaia (17).

Goals: Aleksandre Kobakhidze (36), Jano Ananidze (39 penalty).

169. 29.02.2012 **GEORGIA - ALBANIA** **2-1(0-1)**

„Mikheil Meskhi“ Stadioni, Tbilisi; Referee: Ghenadie Sidenco (Moldova); Attendance: 18,000

GEO: Nukri Revishvili (19/0), Zurab Khizanishvili (Cap) (80/1), Aleksandre Amisulashvili (24/2), Gia Grigalava (5/0) [46.David Kvirkvelia (47/0)], Guram Kashia (13/0), Aleksandre Kobakhidze (5/2), Jaba Kankava (33/4) [90+4.Irakli Dzaria (1/0)], Murtaz Daushvili (11/0) [46.Nikoloz Gelashvili (10/0)], David Targamadze (5/1) [90.Shota Grigalashvili (9/0)], Jano Ananidze (13/2) [75.Levan Kenia (19/3)], Vladimir Dvalishvili (21/4) [58.Otar Martsvaladze (20/2)]. Trainer: Temuri Ketsbaia (18).

Goals: Aleksandre Kobakhidze (47), Aleksandre Amisulashvili (88).

170. 24.05.2012 **GEORGIA - TURKEY** **1-3(0-2)**

Red Bull Arena, Wals-Siezenheim (Austria); Referee: Markus Hameter (Austria); Attendance: 700

GEO: Giorgi Loria (13/0), Zurab Khizanishvili (Cap) (81/1), Aleksandre Amisulashvili (25/2), David Kvirkvelia (48/0) [63.Giorgi Popkhadze (8/0)], Guram Kashia (14/0), Ucha Lobjanidze (22/0) [46.Murtaz Daushvili (12/0)], Aleksandre Kobakhidze (6/2), Jaba Kankava (34/4) [72.Jaba Lipartia (2/0)], David Targamadze (6/2) [65.Tornike Okriashvili (2/0)], Vladimir Dvalishvili (22/4) [46.Levan Mchedlidze (14/1)], Nikoloz Gelashvili (11/0) [89.Nika Dzalamidze (1/0)]. Trainer: Temuri Ketsbaia (19).

Goal: David Targamadze (51).

171. 15.08.2012 **LUXEMBOURG - GEORGIA** **1-2(0-2)**

Stade Municipal Obercorn, Differdange; Referee: Clément Turpin (France); Attendance: 1,215

GEO: Giorgi Loria (14/0), Aleksandre Amisulashvili (26/3) [60.Giorgi Popkhadze (9/0)], Gia Grigalava (6/0), Akaki Khubutia (8/0), Guram Kashia (15/0) *sent off 14*], Aleksandre Kobakhidze (7/2) [46.Ucha Lobjanidze (23/0)], Jaba Kankava (Cap) (35/4), David Targamadze (7/2) [46.Murtaz Daushvili (13/0)], Jano Ananidze (14/2) [67.Aleksandre Guruli (5/1)], Tornike Okriashvili (3/0) [90+1.Nikoloz Gelashvili (12/0)], Levan Mchedlidze (15/2) [46.Irakli Sirbiladze (1/0)]. Trainer: Temuri Ketsbaia (20).

Goals: Levan Mchedlidze (2), Aleksandre Amisulashvili (32).

172. 07.09.2012 **GEORGIA - BELARUS** **1-0(0-0)** 20th FIFA WC. Qualifiers

„Boris Paichadze“ Dinamo Arena, Tbilisi; Referee: Stanislav Todorov (Bulgaria); Attendance: 20,000

GEO: Giorgi Loria (15/0), Zurab Khizanishvili (82/1), Aleksandre Amisulashvili (27/3), Gia Grigalava (7/0), Guram Kashia (16/0), Jaba Kankava (Cap) (36/4), Murtaz Daushvili (14/0), David Targamadze (8/2), Jano Ananidze (15/2) [74.Tornike Gorgiashvili (2/0)], Tornike Okriashvili (4/1) [83.Irakli Sirbiladze (2/0)], Levan Mchedlidze (16/2) [56.David Kvirkvelia (49/0)]. Trainer: Temuri Ketsbaia (21).

Goal: Tornike Okriashvili (52).

173. 11.09.2012 **GEORGIA - SPAIN** **0-1(0-0)** 20th FIFA WC. Qualifiers

„Boris Paichadze“ Dinamo Arena, Tbilisi; Referee: Svein Oddvar Moen (Norway); Attendance: 54,598

GEO: Giorgi Loria (16/0) [73.Roin Kvaskhvadze (1/0)], Zurab Khizanishvili (83/1), Aleksandre Amisulashvili (28/3), David Kvirkvelia (50/0), Guram Kashia (17/0), Ucha Lobjanidze (24/0), Jaba Kankava (Cap) (37/4), Murtaz Daushvili (15/0), David Targamadze (9/2) [64.Nika Dzalamidze (2/0)], Tornike Okriashvili (5/1), Levan Mchedlidze (17/2) [79.Irakli Sirbiladze (3/0)]. Trainer: Temuri Ketsbaia (22).

174. 12.10.2012 **FINLAND - GEORGIA** **1-1(0-0)** 20th FIFA WC. Qualifiers

Olympiastadion, Helsinki; Referee: Yevhen Aranovskiy (Ukraine); Attendance: 12,607

GEO: Nukri Revishvili (20/0), Zurab Khizanishvili (84/1), Aleksandre Amisulashvili (29/3), Gia Grigalava (8/0), Guram Kashia (18/1), Aleksandre Kobakhidze (8/2), Jaba Kankava (Cap) (38/4), Murtaz Daushvili (16/0), David Targamadze (10/2) [81.Levan Kenia (20/3)], Tornike Okriashvili (6/1) [67.Jano Ananidze (16/2)], Levan Mchedlidze (18/2) [59.David Devdariani (5/0)]. Trainer: Temuri Ketsbaia (23).

Goal: Guram Kashia (56).

175. 16.10.2012 **BELARUS - GEORGIA** **2-0(2-0)** 20th FIFA WC. Qualifiers

Dynama Stadium, Minsk; Referee: Robert Schörgenhofer (Austria); Attendance: 15,300

GEO: Nukri Revishvili (21/0), Zurab Khizanishvili (85/1), Aleksandre Amisulashvili (30/3), Gia Grigalava (9/0), Guram Kashia (19/1), Aleksandre Kobakhidze (9/2), Jaba Kankava (Cap) (39/4), Murtaz Daushvili (17/0), David Devdariani (6/0) [46.Levan Mchedlidze (19/2)], David Targamadze (11/2) [75.Levan Kenia (21/3)], Tornike Okriashvili (7/1) [49.Jano Ananidze (17/2)]. Trainer: Temuri Ketsbaia (24).

176. 14.11.2012 **GEORGIA - EGYPT** **0-0**

„Mikheil Meskhi“ Stadioni, Tbilisi; Referee: Andris Treimanis (Latvia); Attendance: n/a

GEO: Giorgi Loria (17/0), Aleksandre Amisulashvili (Cap) (31/3), David Kvirkvelia (51/0), Gia Grigalava (10/0), Guram Kashia (20/1), Ucha Lobjanidze (25/0), Aleksandre Kobakhidze (10/2) [56.Aleksandre Guruli (6/1)], Irakli Dzaria (2/0) [76.Tornike Gorgiashvili (3/0)], David Targamadze (12/2) [46.Nika Dzalamidze (3/0)], Shota Grigalashvili (10/0) [69.Irakli Kobalia (1/0)], Jaba Dvali (1/0) [46.Vladimir Dvalishvili (23/4)]. Trainer: Temuri Ketsbaia (25).

177. 06.02.2013 **ALBANIA - GEORGIA** **1-2(1-1)**

Stadiumi „Kombëtar Qemal Stafa“, Tiranë; Referee: Dimitar Meckarovski (Macedonia); Attendance: 3,000

GEO: Roin Kvaskhvadze (2/0) , Zurab Khizanishvili (86/1), Gia Grigalava (11/0) [46.Jaba Kankava (40/4)], Ilia Kandelaki (15/0) [46.David Kvirkvelia (52/0)], Guram Kashia (Cap) (21/1), Ucha Lobjanidze (26/1), Aleksandre Kobakhidze (11/2) [63.Irakli Dzaria (3/0)], Levan Kenia (22/3) [60.Nikoloz Gelashvili (13/0)], David Targamadze (13/2), Nika Dzalamidze (4/0) [46.Tornike Okriashvili (8/1)], Levan Mchedlidze (20/2) [20.Mate Vatsadze (6/1); 77.Gulverd Tomashvili (1/0)]. Trainer: Temuri Ketsbaia (26).

Goals: Mate Vatsadze (41), Ucha Lobjanidze (82).

178. 22.03.2013 **FRANCE - GEORGIA** **3-1(1-0)** 20th FIFA WC. Qualifiers

Stade de France, Saint-Denis, Paris; Referee: Ivan Bebek (Croatia); Attendance: 71,147

GEO: Giorgi Loria (18/0), Zurab Khizanishvili (87/1), Aleksandre Amisulashvili (Cap) (32/3), David Kvirkvelia (53/0), Guram Kashia (22/1), Ucha Lobjanidze (27/1), Aleksandre Kobakhidze (12/3), Murtaz Daushvili (18/0), David Targamadze (14/2) [84.Nikoloz Gelashvili (14/0)], Jano Ananidze (18/2) [46.Levan Kenia (23/3)], Mate Vatsadze (7/1) [73.Vladimir Dvalishvili (24/4)]. Trainer: Temuri Ketsbaia (27).

Goal: Aleksandre Kobakhidze (71).

179. 02.06.2013 **REPUBLIC OF IRELAND - GEORGIA** **4-0(1-0)**
Aviva Stadium, Dublin; Referee: Constantin Sebastian Colțescu (Romania); Attendance: 20,100
GEO: Giorgi Loria (19/0) [*sent off 20*], Zurab Khizanishvili (88/1), David Kvirkvelia (54/0) [69.Giorgi Popkhadze (10/0)], Akaki Khubutia (9/0), Guram Kashia (23/1), Ucha Lobjanidze (28/1) [46.David Targamadze (15/2)], Aleksandre Kobakhidze (13/3) [90.Tornike Gorgiashvili (4/0)], Jaba Kankava (Cap) (41/4), Murtaz Daushvili (19/0) [54.Irakli Dzaria (4/0)], Jano Ananidze (19/2) [22.Omar Migineishvili (1/0)], Nikoloz Gelashvili (15/0) [61.Irakli Maisuradze (2/0)]. Trainer: Temuri Ketsbaia (28).

180. 05.06.2013 **DENMARK - GEORGIA** **2-1(0-0)**
Nordjyske Arena, Aalborg; Referee: Dr. Felix Brych (Germany); Attendance: 6,500
GEO: Giorgi Loria (20/0), Zurab Khizanishvili (89/1), Giorgi Popkhadze (11/0), Akaki Khubutia (10/0), Guram Kashia (24/1), Aleksandre Kobakhidze (14/3) [87.Nikoloz Gelashvili (16/0)], Jaba Kankava (Cap) (42/4), Murtaz Daushvili (20/0) [73.Merab Gigauri (1/0)], Irakli Dzaria (5/1) [63.Ucha Lobjanidze (29/1)], Jano Ananidze (20/2) [63.David Targamadze (16/2)], Vladimir Dvalishvili (25/4) [46.Irakli Sirbiladze (4/0)]. Trainer: Temuri Ketsbaia (29).
Goal: Irakli Dzaria (52).

181. 14.08.2013 **KAZAKHSTAN - GEORGIA** **1-0(1-0)**
Astana Arena, Astana; Referee: Sergey Tsinkevich (Belarus); Attendance: 13,500
GEO: Nukri Revishvili (22/0), Zurab Khizanishvili (90/1), Aleksandre Amisulashvili (33/3), Gia Grigalava (12/0) [64.David Kvirkvelia (55/0)], Guram Kashia (25/1) [82.Shota Grigalashvili (11/0)], Aleksandre Kobakhidze (15/3), Jaba Kankava (Cap) (43/4), David Targamadze (17/2) [68.Nikoloz Gelashvili (17/0)], Jano Ananidze (21/2) [46.Elguja Grigalashvili (1/0)], Tornike Okriashvili (9/1) [46.Vladimir Dvalishvili (26/4)], Irakli Sirbiladze (5/0) [46.Levan Mchedlidze (21/2)]. Trainer: Temuri Ketsbaia (30).

182. 06.09.2013 **GEORGIA - FRANCE** **0-0** 20th FIFA WC. Qualifiers
„Boris Paichadze" Dinamo Arena, Tbilisi; Referee: Fırat Aydınus (Turkey); Attendance: 26,360
GEO: Giorgi Loria (21/0), Aleksandre Amisulashvili (34/3), Gia Grigalava (13/0), Akaki Khubutia (11/0), Guram Kashia (26/1), Ucha Lobjanidze (30/1), Aleksandre Kobakhidze (16/3) [60.Elguja Grigalashvili (2/0)], Jaba Kankava (Cap) (44/4), Jano Ananidze (22/2) [69.David Targamadze (18/2)], Tornike Okriashvili (10/1), Nikoloz Gelashvili (18/0) [79.Vladimir Dvalishvili (27/4)]. Trainer: Temuri Ketsbaia (31).

183. 10.09.2013 **GEORGIA - FINLAND** **0-1(0-0)** 20th FIFA WC. Qualifiers
"Mikheil Meskhi" Stadioni, Tbilisi; Referee: Leontios Trattou (Cyprus); Attendance: 25,321
GEO: Nukri Revishvili (23/0), Aleksandre Amisulashvili (35/3), Gia Grigalava (14/0), Akaki Khubutia (12/0), Guram Kashia (27/1), Ucha Lobjanidze (31/1), Aleksandre Kobakhidze (17/3) [46.David Targamadze (19/2)], Jaba Kankava (Cap) (45/4), Jano Ananidze (23/2) [83.Vladimir Dvalishvili (28/4)], Tornike Okriashvili (11/1), Nikoloz Gelashvili (19/0) [57.Elguja Grigalashvili (3/0)]. Trainer: Temuri Ketsbaia (32).

184. 15.10.2013 **SPAIN - GEORGIA** **2-0(1-0)** 20th FIFA WC. Qualifiers
Estadio "Carlos Belmonte", Albacete; Referee: Florian Meyer (Germany); Attendance: 16,133
GEO: Giorgi Loria (22/0), David Kvirkvelia (56/0), Akaki Khubutia (13/0), Guram Kashia (28/1), Giorgi Khidesheli (3/0), Ucha Lobjanidze (32/1), Aleksandre Kobakhidze (18/3), Irakli Dzaria (6/1), Shota Grigalashvili (12/0) [70.Avtandil Ebralidze (1/0)], Elguja Grigalashvili (4/0) [75.Levan Khmaladze (11/0)], Nikoloz Gelashvili (20/0) [87.Irakli Modebadze (4/0)]. Trainer: Temuri Ketsbaia (33).

185. 05.03.2014 **GEORGIA - LIECHTENSTEIN** **2-0(2-0)**
"Mikheil Meskhi" Stadioni, Tbilisi; Referee: Andris Treimanis (Latvia); Attendance: 6,000
GEO: Giorgi Loria (23/0), Gia Grigalava (15/0) [46.David Kvirkvelia (57/0)], Akaki Khubutia (14/0) [77.Solomon Kvirkvelia (1/0)], Guram Kashia (29/1), Ucha Lobjanidze (33/1), Aleksandre Kobakhidze (19/3) [46.Murtaz Daushvili (21/0)], Jaba Kankava (Cap) (46/4), Jano Ananidze (24/3), Tornike Okriashvili (12/1) [79.Vladimir Dvalishvili (29/4)], Giorgi Chanturia (1/1) [60.Bachana Tskhadadze (1/0)], Avtandil Ebralidze (2/0) [46.Valeri Qazaishvili (1/0)]. Trainer: Temuri Ketsbaia (34).
Goals: Giorgi Chanturia (25), Jano Ananidze (76 penalty).

186. 29.05.2014 **SAUDI ARABIA - GEORGIA** **0-2(0-1)**
Estadio Municipal de Chapín, Jerez de la Frontera (Spain); Referee: Carlos Del Cerro Grande (Spain); Attendance: 100
GEO: Giorgi Loria (24/0), Gia Grigalava (16/0), Akaki Khubutia (15/0), Guram Kashia (30/1) [46.Irakli Dzaria (7/1)], Ucha Lobjanidze (34/1) [77.Lasha Salukvadze (37/1)], Solomon Kvirkvelia (2/0), Aleksandre Kobakhidze (20/3) [69.Giorgi Papava (1/0)], Jaba Kankava (Cap) (47/4), Tornike Okriashvili (13/2) [74.Levan Khmaladze (12/0)], Otar Martsvaladze (21/2) [46.Vladimir Dvalishvili (30/5)], Valeri Qazaishvili (2/0) [58.Levan Kakubava (3/0)]. Trainer: Temuri Ketsbaia (35).
Goals: Tornike Okriashvili (45+2), Vladimir Dvalishvili (71).

187. 03.06.2014 **UNITED ARAB EMIRATES - GEORGIA** **1-0(0-0)**
Stade des Arbères, Meyrin (Switzerland); Referee: Stephan Studer (Switzerland); Attendance: n/a
GEO: Giorgi Loria (25/0), Gia Grigalava (17/0), Akaki Khubutia (16/0) [46.Levan Kakubava (4/0)], Guram Kashia (31/1), Ucha Lobjanidze (35/1), Solomon Kvirkvelia (3/0), Aleksandre Kobakhidze (21/3), Jaba Kankava (Cap) (48/4) [86.Bachana Tskhadadze (2/0)], Irakli Dzaria (8/1) [60.Giorgi Papava (2/0)], Tornike Okriashvili (14/2) [69.Giorgi Papunashvili (1/0)], Valeri Qazaishvili (3/0) [46.Vladimir Dvalishvili (31/5)]. Trainer: Temuri Ketsbaia (36).

188. 07.09.2014 **GEORGIA - REPUBLIC OF IRELAND** **1-2(1-1)** 15th EC. Qualifiers
„Boris Paichadze" Dinamo Arena, Tbilisi; Referee: Bernie Raymond "Kevin" Blom (Netherlands); Attendance: 22,000
GEO: Giorgi Loria (26/0) [46.Roin Kvaskhvadze (3/0)], David Kvirkvelia (58/0), Akaki Khubutia (17/0), Guram Kashia (32/1), Ucha Lobjanidze (36/1), Solomon Kvirkvelia (4/0), Jaba Kankava (Cap) (49/4), Murtaz Daushvili (22/0), Jano Ananidze (25/3) [63.David Targamadze (20/2)], Tornike Okriashvili (15/3) [88.Levan Mchedlidze (22/2)], Nikoloz Gelashvili (21/0). Trainer: Temuri Ketsbaia (37).
Goal: Tornike Okriashvili (38).

189. 11.10.2014 **SCOTLAND - GEORGIA** **1-0(1-0)** 15th EC. Qualifiers
Ibrox Stadium, Glasgow, Scotland; Referee: Miroslav Zelinka (Czech Republic); Attendance: 34,719
GEO: Giorgi Loria (27/0), David Kvirkvelia (59/0) [46.Tornike Okriashvili (16/3)], Gia Grigalava (18/0), Akaki Khubutia (18/0), Ucha Lobjanidze (37/1), Solomon Kvirkvelia (5/0), Jaba Kankava (Cap) (50/4), Murtaz Daushvili (23/0), Giorgi Papava (3/0) [70.Irakli Dzaria (9/1)], Nikoloz Gelashvili (22/0), Valeri Qazaishvili (4/0) [80.Giorgi Chanturia (2/1)]. Trainer: Temuri Ketsbaia (38).

190. 14.10.2014 **GIBRALTAR - GEORGIA** **0-3(0-2)** 15th EC. Qualifiers
Estádio „São João da Venda", Faro (Portugal); Referee: Harald Lechner (Austria); Attendance: 281
GEO: Giorgi Loria (28/0), Gia Grigalava (19/0), Akaki Khubutia (19/0), Ucha Lobjanidze (38/1), Solomon Kvirkvelia (6/0), Jaba Kankava (Cap) (51/5), Irakli Dzaria (10/1), Jano Ananidze (26/3) [80.Avtandil Ebralidze (3/0)], Tornike Okriashvili (17/4), Nikoloz Gelashvili (23/1) [67.Giorgi Papunashvili (2/0)], Giorgi Chanturia (3/1) [76.Vladimir Dvalishvili (32/5)]. Trainer: Temuri Ketsbaia (39).
Goals: Nikoloz Gelashvili (9), Tornike Okriashvili (20), Jaba Kankava (69).

191. 14.11.2014 **GEORGIA - POLAND** **0-4(0-0)** 15th EC. Qualifiers
„Boris Paichadze" Dinamo Arena, Tbilisi; Referee: Paolo Tagliavento (Italy); Attendance: 25,635
GEO: Giorgi Loria (29/0), Gia Grigalava (20/0), Akaki Khubutia (20/0), Guram Kashia (33/1), Ucha Lobjanidze (39/1), Solomon Kvirkvelia (7/0), Aleksandre Kobakhidze (22/3) [88.Nika Dzalamidze (5/0)], Jaba Kankava (Cap) (52/5), Murtaz Daushvili (24/0), Jano Ananidze (27/3) [59.Tornike Okriashvili (18/4)], Levan Mchedlidze (23/2) [68.Giorgi Chanturia (4/1)]. Trainer: Temuri Ketsbaia (40).

192. 25.03.2015 **GEORGIA - MALTA** **2-0(0-0)**
"Mikheil Meskhi" Stadioni, Tbilisi; Referee: Aleksandrs Anufrijevs (Latvia); Attendance: 16,000
GEO: Giorgi Loria (30/0) [46.Nukri Revishvili (24/0)], Aleksandre Amisulashvili (36/3), Giorgi Navalovski (3/0), Guram Kashia (34/1), Solomon Kvirkvelia (8/0) [46.Levan Kenia (24/3)], Aleksandre Kobakhidze (23/3) [84.Nika Dzalamidze (6/0)], Jaba Kankava (Cap) (53/6), Tornike Okriashvili (19/4) [71.Mate Vatsadze (8/1)], Kakhaber Makharadze (2/0), Levan Mchedlidze (24/2) [71.Bachana Tskhadadze (3/0)], Giorgi Chanturia (5/1) [64.Valeri Qazaishvili (5/1)]. Trainer: Kakhaber Tskhadadze (1).
Goals: Jaba Kankava (83), Valeri Qazaishvili (90+1).

193. 29.03.2015 **GEORGIA - GERMANY** **0-2(0-2)** 15th EC. Qualifiers
„Boris Paichadze" Dinamo Arena, Tbilisi; Referee: Clément Turpin (France); Attendance: 52,000
GEO: Giorgi Loria (31/0), Aleksandre Amisulashvili (37/3) [4.Lasha Dvali (1/0)], Giorgi Navalovski (4/0), Guram Kashia (35/1), Ucha Lobjanidze (40/1), Solomon Kvirkvelia (9/0), Aleksandre Kobakhidze (24/3), Jaba Kankava (Cap) (54/6), Tornike Okriashvili (20/4) [46.Giorgi Chanturia (6/1)], Kakhaber Makharadze (3/0) [63.Levan Kenia (25/3)], Levan Mchedlidze (25/2). Trainer: Kakhaber Tskhadadze (2).

194. 09.06.2015 **GEORGIA - UKRAINE** **1-2(0-0)**
Stadion auf der Gugl, Linz (Austria); Referee: Markus Hameter (Austria); Attendance: 700
GEO: Giorgi Loria (32/0), Aleksandre Amisulashvili (Cap) (38/3), Giorgi Navalovski (5/0), Guram Kashia (36/1) [46.Lasha Salukvadze (38/1)], Ucha Lobjanidze (41/1) [71.Kakhaber Aladashvili (8/0)], Lasha Dvali (2/0), Aleksandre Kobakhidze (25/3), Jano Ananidze (28/3), Tornike Okriashvili (21/4) [46.Levan Kenia (26/3)], Valeri Qazaishvili (6/1) [71.Mate Vatsadze (9/2)], Bachana Tskhadadze (4/0) [46.Giorgi Chanturia (7/1)]. Trainer: Kakhaber Tskhadadze (3).
Goal: Mate Vatsadze (81).

195. 13.06.2015 **POLAND - GEORGIA** **4-0(0-0)** 15th EC. Qualifiers
Stadion Narodowy, Warsaw; Referee: Aleksei Kulbakov (Belarus); Attendance: 56,512
GEO: Giorgi Loria (33/0), Aleksandre Amisulashvili (Cap) (39/3), Giorgi Navalovski (6/0), Guram Kashia (37/1), Ucha Lobjanidze (42/1), Lasha Dvali (3/0), Aleksandre Kobakhidze (26/3) [76.Bachana Tskhadadze (5/0)], Jano Ananidze (29/3), Tornike Okriashvili (22/4) [46.Murtaz Daushvili (25/0)], Valeri Qazaishvili (7/1), Mate Vatsadze (10/2) [63.Giorgi Chanturia (8/1)]. Trainer: Kakhaber Tskhadadze (4).

196. 04.09.2015 **GEORGIA - SCOTLAND** **1-0(1-0)** 15th EC. Qualifiers
„Boris Paichadze" Dinamo Arena, Tbilisi; Referee: Ovidiu Alin Haţegan (Romania); Attendance: 23,000
GEO: Nukri Revishvili (25/0), Aleksandre Amisulashvili (40/3), Giorgi Navalovski (7/0), Guram Kashia (38/1), Ucha Lobjanidze (43/1), Solomon Kvirkvelia (10/0), Jaba Kankava (Cap) (55/6), Jano Ananidze (30/3) [82.Murtaz Daushvili (26/0)], Tornike Okriashvili (23/4) [71.Giorgi Merebashvili (18/0)], Valeri Qazaishvili (8/2), Levan Mchedlidze (26/2) [90+3.Mate Vatsadze (11/2)]. Trainer: Kakhaber Tskhadadze (5).
Goal: Valeri Qazaishvili (38).

197. 07.09.2015 **REPUBLIC OF IRELAND - GEORGIA** **1-0(0-0)** 15th EC. Qualifiers
Aviva Stadium, Dublin; Referee: István Vad II (Hungary); Attendance: 27,200
GEO: Nukri Revishvili (26/0), Zurab Khizanishvili (91/1) [81.Levan Kenia (27/3)], Aleksandre Amisulashvili (41/3), Giorgi Navalovski (8/0), Guram Kashia (39/1) [76.Mate Tsintsadze (1/0)], Ucha Lobjanidze (44/1), Solomon Kvirkvelia (11/0), Jaba Kankava (Cap) (56/6), Tornike Okriashvili (24/4), Valeri Qazaishvili (9/2) [64.Giorgi Papunashvili (3/0)], Levan Mchedlidze (27/2). Trainer: Kakhaber Tskhadadze (6).

198. 08.10.2015 **GEORGIA - GIBRALTAR** **4-0(3-0)** 15th EC. Qualifiers
„Boris Paichadze" Dinamo Arena, Tbilisi; Referee: Serhiy Boyko (Ukraine); Attendance: 11,330
GEO: Nukri Revishvili (27/0), Aleksandre Amisulashvili (42/3), Gia Grigalava (21/0), Guram Kashia (40/1), Otar Kakabadze (1/0), Aleksandre Kobakhidze (27/3), Jaba Kankava (Cap) (57/6) [57.Guga Palavandishvili (1/0)], Nika Kvekveskiri (1/0), Tornike Okriashvili (25/5) [58.Nika Dzalamidze (7/0)], Valeri Qazaishvili (10/3), Mate Vatsadze (12/4) [73.Bachana Tskhadadze (6/0)]. Trainer: Kakhaber Tskhadadze (7).
Goals: Mate Vatsadze (30), Tornike Okriashvili (35 penalty), Mate Vatsadze (45), Valeri Qazaishvili (87).

199. 11.10.2015 **GERMANY - GEORGIA** **2-1(0-0)** 15th EC. Qualifiers
Red Bull Arena, Leipzig; Referee: Pavel Královec (Czech Republic); Attendance: 43,630
GEO: Nukri Revishvili (28/0), Aleksandre Amisulashvili (43/3), Giorgi Navalovski (9/0), Guram Kashia (41/1), Ucha Lobjanidze (45/1), Solomon Kvirkvelia (12/0), Jaba Kankava (Cap) (58/7), Nika Kvekveskiri (2/0) [78.Zurab Khizanishvili (92/1)], Tornike Okriashvili (26/5), Valeri Qazaishvili (11/3) [90.Aleksandre Kobakhidze (28/3)], Nikoloz Gelashvili (24/1) [46.Mate Vatsadze (13/4)]. Trainer: Kakhaber Tskhadadze (8).
Goal: Jaba Kankava (53).

200. 11.11.2015 **ESTONIA - GEORGIA** **3-0(0-0)**
A. Le Coq Arena, Tallinn; Referee: Raymond Crangle (Northern Ireland); Attendance: 2,266
GEO: Giorgi Loria (34/0), Aleksandre Amisulashvili (44/3), Giorgi Navalovski (10/0) [68.Giorgi Popkhadze (12/0)], Gia Grigalava (22/0) [68.Lucas Hufnagel (1/0)], Guram Kashia (42/1), Otar Kakabadze (2/0), Aleksandre Kobakhidze (29/3) [46.Giorgi Chanturia (9/1)], Jaba Kankava (Cap) (59/7), Valeri Qazaishvili (12/3) [78.Zakaria Beglarishvili (1/0)], Mate Tsintsadze (2/0) [72.Murtaz Daushvili (27/0)], Mate Vatsadze (14/4) [46.Bachana Tskhadadze (7/0)]. Trainer: Kakhaber Tskhadadze (9).

201. 16.11.2015 **ALBANIA - GEORGIA** **2-2(0-1)**
Stadiumi „Kombëtar Qemal Stafa“, Tiranë; Referee: Davide Massa (Italy); Attendance: 2,000
GEO: Nukri Revishvili (29/0), Aleksandre Amisulashvili (45/4), Giorgi Navalovski (11/0), Gia Grigalava (23/0), Guram Kashia (43/1), Ucha Lobjanidze (46/1), Jaba Kankava (Cap) (60/7), Murtaz Daushvili (28/0), Valeri Qazaishvili (13/3) [82.Aleksandre Kobakhidze (30/3)], Nikoloz Gelashvili (25/1) [77.Bachana Tskhadadze (8/0)], Giorgi Chanturia (10/2) [90.Otar Kakabadze (3/0)]. Trainer: Kakhaber Tskhadadze (10).
Goals: Aleksandre Amisulashvili (2), Giorgi Chanturia (53).

202. 29.03.2016 **GEORGIA - KAZAKHSTAN** **1-1(1-1)**
„Boris Paichadze“ Dinamo Arena, Tbilisi; Referee: Clayton Pisani (Malta); Attendance: 15,000
GEO: Nukri Revishvili (30/0), Aleksandre Amisulashvili (46/4) [46.Solomon Kvirkvelia (13/0)], Giorgi Navalovski (12/0), Guram Kashia (44/1), Ucha Lobjanidze (47/1) [89.Mate Vatsadze (15/4)], Jaba Kankava (Cap) (61/7), Jano Ananidze (31/3) [78.Levan Kenia (28/3)], Tornike Okriashvili (27/6), Valeri Qazaishvili (14/3), Giorgi Aburjania (1/0) [78.Nika Kvekveskiri (3/0)], Giorgi Chanturia (11/2) [46.Nika Katcharava (1/0)]. Trainer: Vladimír Weiss (Slovakia, 1).
Goal: Tornike Okriashvili (38).

203. 27.05.2016 **SLOVAKIA - GEORGIA** **3-1(1-0)**
Renner Arena, Wels (Austria); Referee: Oliver Drachta (Austria); Attendance: 782
GEO: Nukri Revishvili (31/0), Giorgi Navalovski (13/0) [66.Lasha Dvali (4/0)], Guram Kashia (Cap) (45/1), Solomon Kvirkvelia (14/0), Otar Kakabadze (4/0), Aleksandre Kobakhidze (31/3) [46.Aleksandre Amisulashvili (47/4)], Nika Kvekveskiri (4/0), Tornike Okriashvili (28/6), Valeri Qazaishvili (15/3) [78.Jambul Jighauri (1/0)], Vakhtang Tchanturishvili (1/0) [46.Levan Kenia (29/4)], Levan Mchedlidze (28/2) [46.Giorgi Kvilitaia (1/0)]. Trainer: Vladimír Weiss (Slovakia, 2).
Goal: Levan Kenia (71).

204. 03.06.2016 **ROMANIA - GEORGIA** **5-1(2-0)**
Arena Naţională, Bucureşti; Referee: Artur Ribeiro (Portugal); Attendance: 27,934
GEO: Roin Kvaskhvadze (4/0), Aleksandre Amisulashvili (Cap) (48/4), Giorgi Navalovski (14/0) [64.Zurab Tsiskaridze (1/0)], Guram Kashia (46/1), Ucha Lobjanidze (48/1), Solomon Kvirkvelia (15/0), Lasha Dvali (5/0) [34.Levan Mchedlidze (29/2)], Tornike Okriashvili (29/6), Valeri Qazaishvili (16/3), Giorgi Aburjania (2/0) [65.Nika Kvekveskiri (5/0)], Vladimir Dvalishvili (33/5) [78.Giorgi Kvilitaia (2/0)]. Trainer: Vladimír Weiss (Slovakia, 3).
Goal: Cosmin Iosif Moţi (68 own goal).

205. 07.06.2016 **SPAIN - GEORGIA** **0-1(0-1)**
Coliseum „Alfonso Pérez“, Getafe; Referee: Vilhjálmur Alvar Þórarinsson (Iceland); Attendance: 14,650
GEO: Nukri Revishvili (32/0) [55.Roin Kvaskhvadze (5/0)], Aleksandre Amisulashvili (Cap) (49/4), Giorgi Navalovski (15/0) [84.Aleksandre Kobakhidze (32/3)], Guram Kashia (47/1), Ucha Lobjanidze (49/1), Solomon Kvirkvelia (16/0), Tornike Okriashvili (30/7), Valeri Qazaishvili (17/3) [72.Giorgi Kvilitaia (3/0)], Giorgi Aburjania (3/0) [78.Zurab Tsiskaridze (2/0)], Jambul Jighauri (2/0), Vladimir Dvalishvili (34/5) [72.Giorgi Chanturia (12/2)]. Trainer: Vladimír Weiss (Slovakia, 4).
Goal: Tornike Okriashvili (40).

206. 05.09.2016 **GEORGIA - AUSTRIA** **1-2(0-2)** 21st FIFA WC. Qualifiers
„Boris Paichadze“ Dinamo Arena, Tbilisi; Referee: Alyaksey Kulbakow (Belarus); Attendance: 25,000
GEO: Giorgi Loria (35/0), Aleksandre Amisulashvili (Cap) (50/4) [76.Tornike Okriashvili (31/7)], Giorgi Navalovski (16/0), Guram Kashia (48/1), Ucha Lobjanidze (50/1) [84.Giorgi Chanturia (13/2)], Solomon Kvirkvelia (17/0), Murtaz Daushvili (29/0), Jano Ananidze (32/4), Valeri Qazaishvili (18/3), Jambul Jighauri (3/0), Vladimir Dvalishvili (35/5) [63.David Skhirtladze (1/0)]. Trainer: Vladimír Weiss (Slovakia, 5).
Goal: Jano Ananidze (78).

207. 06.10.2016 **REPUBLIC OF IRELAND - GEORGIA** **1-0(0-0)** 21st FIFA WC. Qualifiers
Aviva Stadium, Dublin; Referee: Tony Chapron (France); Attendance: 39,793
GEO: Giorgi Loria (36/0), Giorgi Navalovski (17/0) [89.Aleksandre Kobakhidze (33/3)], Guram Kashia (Cap) (49/1), Solomon Kvirkvelia (18/0), Otar Kakabadze (5/0), Murtaz Daushvili (30/0) [90+3.Nika Katcharava (2/0)], Jano Ananidze (33/4) [74.David Skhirtladze (2/0)], Tornike Okriashvili (32/7), Valeri Qazaishvili (19/3), Valerian Gvilia (1/0), Levan Mchedlidze (30/2). Trainer: Vladimír Weiss (Slovakia, 6).

208. 09.10.2016 **WALES - GEORGIA** **1-1(1-0)** 21st FIFA WC. Qualifiers
Cardiff City Stadium, Cardiff; Referee: Paolo Mazzoleni (Italy); Attendance: 32,652
GEO: Giorgi Loria (37/0), Giorgi Navalovski (18/0), Guram Kashia (Cap) (50/1), Solomon Kvirkvelia (19/0), Otar Kakabadze (6/0), Murtaz Daushvili (31/0), Jano Ananidze (34/4) [90+3.Nika Katcharava (3/0)], Tornike Okriashvili (33/8) [90+1.Jambul Jighauri (4/0)], Valeri Qazaishvili (20/3), Valerian Gvilia (2/0), Levan Mchedlidze (31/2) [75.Vladimir Dvalishvili (36/5)]. Trainer: Vladimír Weiss (Slovakia, 7).
Goal: Tornike Okriashvili (57).

209. 12.11.2016 **GEORGIA - MOLDOVA** **1-1(1-0)**
„Boris Paichadze“ Dinamo Arena, Tbilisi; Referee: Georgi Kabakov (Bulgaria); Attendance: 40,642
GEO: Giorgi Loria (38/0), Giorgi Navalovski (19/0), Guram Kashia (Cap) (51/1), Solomon Kvirkvelia (20/0), Otar Kakabadze (7/0), Murtaz Daushvili (32/0), Tornike Okriashvili (34/8), Valeri Qazaishvili (21/4) [80.David Skhirtladze (3/0)], Giorgi Chanturia (14/2), Valerian Gvilia (3/0) [72.Vladimir Dvalishvili (37/5)], Giorgi Kvilitaia (4/0) [64.Jaba Kankava (62/7)]. Trainer: Vladimír Weiss (Slovakia, 8).
Goal: Valeri Qazaishvili (16).

INTERNATIONAL PLAYERS

FG/Nr	Name	DOB	Caps	Goals	Period, Club
(70/110)	ABRAMIDZE Valeri	17.01.1980	6	0	2001-2003, FC Torpedo Kutaisi (5/0), FK Spartak Moskva (1/0).
(202/230)	ABURJANIA Giorgi	02.01.1995	3	0	2016, Gimnàstic de Tarragona (3/0).
(90/128)	AKHALAIA Lado	26.06.1982	1	0	2004, FC Dinamo Tbilisi (1/0).
(54/100)	AKHVLEDIANI Badri	19.10.1972	2	0	1999, FC Torpedo Kutaisi (2/0).
(103/146)	ALADASHVILI Kakhaber	11.08.1983	8	0	2005-2015, FC Dinamo Tbilisi (1/0), FK Dinamo Kyiv (6/0), FK SCA-Energiya Khabarovsk (1/0).
(49/094)	ALEKSIDZE Rati	03.08.1978	28	2	1998-2009, FC Dinamo Tbilisi (4/0), Chelsea FC London (10/2), FC Dinamo Tbilisi (3/0), FK Rostov (2/0), FC Lokomotivi Tbilisi (6/0), Győri ETO FC (3/0).
(78/121)	AMISULASHVILI Aleksandre	20.08.1982	50	4	2002-2016, FC Dinamo Tbilisi (6/0), FK Dinamo Kyiv (1/0), FK Dnipro Dnipropetrovsk (2/1), FK Spartak Nalchik (2/0), Kayserispor Kulübü (6/0), FK Krasnodar (14/2), FK Krylia Sovetov Samara (4/0), İnter PİK Bakı (4/0), Karşiyaka SK İzmir (6/1), FC Dinamo Tbilisi (5/0).
(148/192)	ANANIDZE Jano	05.09.2009	34	4	2009-2016, FK Spartak Moskva (20/2), FK Rostov-na-Donu (4/1), FK Spartak Moskva (10/1).
(82/125)	APKHAZAVA Shalva	04.08.1980	1	0	2003, Arsenal Kyiv (1/0).
(93/137)	APTSIAURI Tornike	28.11.1979	5	0	2004-2010, FC Tbilisi (2/0), FC Zestafoni (3/0).
(10/044)	ARVELADZE Archil	22.02.1973	32	6	1994-2001, Trabzonspor Kulübü (3/0), FC Dinamo Tbilisi (1/0), Trabzonspor Kulübü (7/2), NAC Breda (15/2), 1.FC Köln (6/2).
(3/028)	ARVELADZE Revaz	15.09.1969	11	1	1992-2000, FC Dinamo Tbilisi (2/0), 1.FC Köln (1/1), FC Dinamo Tbilisi (2/0), Tennis Borussia Berlin (1/0), FC 08 Homburg (1/0), KV Mechelen (2/0), FC Dinamo Tbilisi (2/0).
(3/030)	ARVELADZE Shota	22.02.1973	61	26	1992-2007, FC Dinamo Tbilisi (2/1), Trabzonspor Kulübü (1/0), FC Dinamo Tbilisi (5/3), Trabzonspor Kulübü (15/7), AFC Ajax Amsterdam (17/3), Glasgow Rangers FC (13/5), AZ'67 Alkmaar (8/7).
(4/033)	ARZIANI Malkhaz	15.08.1964	1	0	1992, FC Dinamo Tbilisi (1/0).
(70/111)	ASATIANI Malkhaz	04.08.1981	42	4	2001-2010, FC Torpedo Kutaisi (2/0), FK Lokomotiv Moskva (32/4), FK Dinamo Kyiv (1/0), FK Lokomotiv Moskva (7/0).
(30/069)	ASHVETIA Mikheil	10.11.1977	24	4	1996-2007, FC Dinamo Tbilisi (5/2), FC Torpedo Kutaisi (2/0), FC København (1/0), FK Alania Vladikavkaz (3/1), FK Lokomotiv Moskva (5/1), FK Rostov (4/0), FK Rubin Kazan (3/0), FC Carl Zeiss Jena (1/0).
(30/062)	ASLANADZE David	16.11.1976	2	0	1996, FC Kakheti Telavi (2/0).
(1/001)	BALADZE Aslan	05.06.1960	1	0	1990, FC Batumi (1/0).
(49/090)	BALASHVILI Giorgi	07.08.1973	3	0	1998-1999, FC Lokomotivi Tbilisi (3/0).
(135/183)	BARABADZE Revaz	04.10.1988	2	0	2008-2010, FK Anzhi Makhachkala (2/0).
(146/190)	BEDIASHVILI Grigol	07.02.1980	1	0	2009, FC WIT Georgia Tbilisi (1/0).
(200/229)	BEGLARISHVILI Zakaria	30.04.1990	1	0	2015, FC Flora Tallinn (1/0).
(8/043)	BERADZE Besik	28.02.1968	8	0	1994-1995, FC Dinamo Tbilisi (6/0), FC Samtredia (2/0).
(1/013)	BIGVAVA Melori	17.01.1963	3	0	1990-1993, FC Odishi Zugdidi (2/0), FC Tskhumi Sukhumi (1/0).
(110/156)	BJALAVA Mirza	05.02.1988	1	0	2006, FC Zestafoni (1/0).
(102/145)	BOBOKHIDZE Mikhail	23.11.1981	1	0	2005, FC Lokomotivi Tbilisi (1/0).
(127/173)	BOLKVADZE David	05.06.1980	1	0	2007, FC Ameri Tbilisi (1/0).
(74/119)	BURDULI Vladimir	26.10.1980	21	2	2001-2007, FC Dinamo Tbilisi (13/1), FK Alania Vladikavkaz (3/1), FK Kryvbas Kryviy Rih (4/0), FK Zorja Lugansk (1/0).
(43/077)	CHALADZE David	22.01.1976	4	1	1998-2003, FK Alania Vladikavkaz (1/0), FC Skonto Riga (2/0), FK Rubin Kazan (1/1)
(44/079)	CHANKOTADZE Giorgi	04.10.1977	3	0	1998-2001, FC WIT Georgia Tbilisi (3/0).
(185/217)	CHANTURIA Giorgi	11.04.1993	14	2	2014-2016, CFR 1907 Cluj-Napoca (8/1), MSV Duisburg (4/1), FK Ural Yekaterinburg (2/0).
(57/103)	CHANTURIA Grigol	25.09.1973	6	0	1999-2006, FC Torpedo Kutaisi (1/0), FC Dinamo Batumi (1/0), FC Zestafoni (4/0).
(5/036)	CHEDIA Bessarion „Soso"	09.10.1965	1	0	1992, Olympiakos FC Nicosia (1/0).
(110/158)	CHELIDZE Giorgi	25.10.1986	1	0	2006, FK Lokomotiv Moskva (1/0).
(53/098)	CHICHVEISHVILI David	23.01.1975	3	0	1999, FC Dinamo Batumi (2/0), FK Alania Vladikavkaz (1/0).
(3/029)	CHIKOVANI Gocha	12.10.1962	1	0	1992, FC Dinamo Tbilisi (1/0).
(15/051)	CHIKRADZE Giorgi	01.10.1967	23	0	1994-2000, FK Temp Chepetovka (5/0), FK Shakhtar Donetsk (8/0), FC Dinamo Tbilisi (6/0), FC Lokomotivi Tbilisi (4/0).
(49/092)	CHKAIDZE Gia	27.02.1970	3	0	1998-1999, FC Torpedo Kutaisi (1/0), FK Alania Vladikavkaz (2/0).
(44/083)	CHKETIANI Kakhaber	24.02.1978	1	0	1998, FC Torpedo Kutaisi (1/0).
(2/016)	CHKHEIDZE Nikoloz	29.11.1968	1	0	1991, FC Dinamo Tbilisi (1/0).
(2/021)	DARASELIA Giorgi	17.09.1968	9	2	1991-1999, FC Kutaisi (4/2), FC Torpedo Kutaisi (1/0), FC Kolkheti 1913 Poti (2/0), Hapoel Tel Aviv FC (1/0), Zafririm Holón FC (1/0).
(78/122)	DARASELIA Vitali	27.09.1978	10	0	2002-2005, FC Dinamo Tbilisi (5/0), FK Alania Vladikavkaz (5/0).
(141/187)	DAUSHVILI Murtaz	01.05.1989	32	0	2008-2016, FC Zestafoni (10/0), FK Karpaty Lviv (18/0), Diósgyőri VTK (4/0).
(44/080)	DAVITNIDZE Giorgi	18.08.1978	1	0	1998, FC Merani 91 Tbilisi (1/0).
(127/172)	DEKANOSIDZE Giorgi	02.01.1981	2	0	2007, FC Ameri Tbilisi (2/0).
(26/060)	DEMETRADZE Giorgi	26.09.1976	56	12	1996-2003, FC Dinamo Tbilisi (3/0), FK Alania Vladikavkaz (7/0), FK Dinamo Kyiv (5/0), Real Sociedad de Fútbol San Sebastián (3/2), FK Lokomotiv Moskva (2/2), FK Alania Vladikavkaz (2/0), FK Metalurh Donetsk (14/2), FK Alania Vladikavkaz (7/5), Maccabi Tel Aviv (2/0), FK Metalurh Donetsk (9/1), FK Arsenal Kyiv (2/0).

(3/025)	DEVADZE Akaki	28.11.1971	**20**	**0**	1992-2005, FC Shevardeni-1906 Tbilisi (10/0), FK Rostselmash Rosto (5/0), FC Tbilisi (4/0), FC Spartak Tbilisi (1/0).
(135/182)	DEVDARIANI David	28.10.1987	**6**	**0**	2008-2012, FC Olimpi Rustavi (1/0), AGF Aarhus (5/0).
(30/070)	DIDAVA Givi	21.03.1976	**21**	**0**	1996-2003, FC Dinamo Tbilisi (12/0), FC Torpedo Kutaisi (3/0), Kocaelispo Kulübü (6/0).
(127/171)	DOLIDZE Grigol	25.10.1982	**1**	**0**	2007, FC Ameri Tbilisi (1/0).
(176/210)	DVALI Jaba	08.02.1985	**1**	**0**	2012, FC Dinamo Tbilisi (1/0).
(193/223)	DVALI Lasha	14.05.1995	**5**	**0**	2015- 2016, Kasımpaşa SK İstanbul (3/0), WKS Śląsk Wrocław (2/0).
(145/189)	DVALISHVILI Vladimir	20.04.1986	**37**	**5**	2009-2016, Skonto FC Riga (2/1), Maccabi Haifa FC (18/3), KSP Polonia Warszawa (3/0), Legia Warszawa (8/1), OB Odense (1/0), Pogoń Szczecin (2/0), FC Dinamo Tbilisi (3/0).
(170/207)	DZALAMIDZE Nika	06.01.1992	**7**	**0**	2012-2015, Jagiellonia Białystok (6/0), Çaykur Rizespor Kulübü (1/0).
(169/206)	DZARIA Irakli	01.12.1988	**10**	**1**	2012-2014, FC Dinamo Tbilisi (10/1).
(59/107)	DZODZUASHVILI Merab	04.11.1980	**2**	**0**	2000, FC Lokomotivi Tbilisi (2/0).
(184/216)	EBRALIDZE Avtandil	03.10.1991	**3**	**0**	2013-2014, Gil Vicente FC Barcelos (3/0).
(111/159)	ELIAVA Zaal	02.01.1985	**8**	**0**	2006-2008, FC Skonto Riga (7/0), FC Dinamo Tbilisi (1/0).
(90/132)	GABIDAURI Giorgi	08.12.1979	**3**	**1**	2004, Anorthósis FC Famagusta (3/1).
(6/040)	GABISKIRIA Yuri	01.09.1968	**1**	**0**	1993, FC Tskhumi Sukhumi (1/0).
(30/065)	GAKHOKIDZE Giorgi	05.11.1975	**21**	**3**	1996-2006, FK Alania Vladikavkaz (9/1), PSV Eindhoven (3/0), Maccabi Haifa (1/0), PSV Eindhoven (4/1), FC Twente Enschede (4/1).
(103/147)	GANUGRAVA Giorgi	21.02.1988	**9**	**0**	2005-2006, FC Zestafoni (8/0), Lombard Pápa FC (1/0).
(130/176)	GELASHVILI Nikoloz	05.08.1985	**25**	**1**	2007-2015, FC WIT Georgia Tbilisi (2/0), FC Zestafoni (7/0), VfL Bochum (7/0), Qarabağ FK Ağdam (4/0), KS Flamurtari Vlorë (3/1), Pafos FC (2/0).
(44/081)	GEMEZASHVILI Irakli	06.07.1977	**1**	**0**	1998, FC Arsenali Tbilisi (1/0).
(180/214)	GIGAURI Merab	05.06.1993	**1**	**0**	2013, FC Torpedo Kutaisi (1/0).
(99/142)	GIGIADZE Vasil	03.06.1977	**6**	**0**	2005-2007, FK Tavria Simferopol (1/0), FK Kryvbas Kryviy Rih (4/0), FK Naftovik-Ukrnafta Okkhtyrka (1/0).
(3/026)	GOGICHAISHVILI Kakhaber	31.10.1968	**27**	**1**	1992-2000, FC Shevardeni-1906 Tbilisi (6/1), FC Samtredia (6/0), FC Dinamo Tbilisi (14/0), FC Lokomotivi Tbilisi (1/0).
(71/117)	GOGOBERISHVILI Aleksandre	22.02.1977	**5**	**0**	2001-2005, FC WIT Georgia Tbilisi (1/0), FC Dinamo Tbilisi (3/0), FC Lokomotivi Tbilisi (1/0).
(1/014)	GOGRICHIANI Gocha	12.08.1964	**9**	**2**	1990-1997, FC Tskhumi Sukhumi (1/0), AC Omonia Nicosia (3/1), Evagoras FC Páphos (2/1), FK Zhemchuzhina Sochi (3/0).
(99/141)	GOGUA Gogita	04.10.1983	**27**	**1**	2005-2011, FC Tbilisi (1/0), FK Khimki (7/1), FK Spartak Nalchik (8/0), FK Saturn Ramenskoe (2/0), FK Spartak Nalchik (7/0), FK Volga Nizhny Novgorod (2/0).
(147/191)	GONGADZE Teimuraz	08.09.1985	**2**	**0**	2009, FC Olimpi Rustavi (2/0).
(168/204)	GORGIASHVILI Tornike	27.04.1988	**4**	**0**	2011-2013, FC Zestafoni (4/0).
(107/150)	GOTSIRIDZE Beka	21.02.1982	**12**	**1**	2006-2009, FC Zestafoni (8/1), FK Dnipro Dnipropetrovsk (4/0).
(110/154)	GOTSIRIDZE Revaz	17.01.1981	**1**	**0**	2006, FK KamAZ Neberezhnyye Chelny (1/0).
(181/215)	GRIGALASHVILI Elguja	30.12.1989	**4**	**0**	2013, FC Dinamo Tbilisi (4/0).
(119/163)	GRIGALASHVILI Shota	21.06.1986	**12**	**0**	2006-2013, FC Dinamo Tbilisi (1/0), FC Borjomi (2/0), FC Zestafoni (6/0), FK Alania Vladikavkaz (1/0), Anorthósis FC Famagusta (2/0).
(163/201)	GRIGALAVA Gia	05.08.1989	**23**	**0**	2011-2015, FK Volga Nizhny Novgorod (11/0), FK Krylya Sovetov Samara (1/0), FK Anthi Makhachkala (8/0), Pafos FC (3/0).
(11/047)	GRISHIKASHVILI Soso	25.12.1973	**10**	**0**	1994-2000, FC Kakheti Telavi (1/0), FK Ventspils (2/0), FK Alania Vladikavkaz (2/0), FC Dinamo Tbilisi (5/0).
(25/057)	GUCHUA Valter	06.07.1975	**5**	**0**	1996-2001, FC Samtredia (2/0), FC Dinamo Tbilisi (2/0), FC Torpedo Kutaisi (1/0).
(19/052)	GUDUSHAURI Giorgi	18.02.1973	**8**	**0**	1995-1998, FSV Salmrohr (6/0), FC Lokomotivi Tbilisi (2/0).
(21/054)	GUJABIDZE Gocha	07.07.1971	**1**	**0**	1995, FK Rostselmash Rostov (1/0).
(159/198)	GURULI Aleksandre	09.11.1985	**6**	**1**	2010-2012, FK Karpaty Lviv (4/1), FC Dila Gori (2/0).
(1/011)	GURULI Gia	20.05.1964	**4**	**1**	1990-1994, FC Iberia Tbilisi (1/0), Le Havre AC (1/0), US Dunkerque Littoral (2/0).
(40/075)	GVARAMADZE David	08.11.1975	**28**	**0**	1998-2004, FC Skonto Riga (3/0), FK Kyryla Sovetov Samara (14/0), FC Torpedo Kutaisi (6/0), FC Dinamo Tbilisi (5/0).
(207/237)	GVILIA Valerian	24.05.1994	**3**	**0**	2016, FC BATE Barysaŭ (3/0).
(110/152)	GVINIANIDZE Mate	10.12.1986	**7**	**0**	2006-2009, FK Lokomotiv Moskva (2/0), TSV 1860 München (5/0).
(200/228)	HUFNAGEL Lucas	29.01.1994	**1**	**0**	2015, SC Freiburg (1/0).
(30/067)	IASHVILI Aleksandre	23.10.1977	**67**	**15**	1996-2011, FC Dinamo Tbilisi (2/1), SC Freiburg (34/11), Karlsruher SC (31/3).
(90/129)	IASHVILI Sandro	03.01.1985	**3**	**0**	2004, FC WIT Georgia Tbilisi (3/0).
(116/161)	IMEDASHVILI David	15.12.1984	**1**	**0**	2006, FC WIT Georgia Tbilisi (1/0).
(11/048)	INALISHVILI Gela	03.10.1966	**10**	**0**	1994-1996, FC Dinamo Tbilisi (7/0), Tennis Borussia Berlin (2/0), FC Dinamo Tbilisi (1/0).
(25/058)	IONANIDZE Zurab	02.12.1971	**4**	**1**	1996-2006, FK Zhemchuzhina Sochi (1/0), FC Torpedo Kutaisi (2/1), FC Zestafoni (1/0).
(94/138)	JAKOBIA Lasha	20.08.1980	**13**	**1**	2004-2008, FK Metalist Kharkiv (12/1), FC Vorskla Poltava (1/0).
(7/041)	JAMARAULI Gocha	23.07.1971	**62**	**6**	1993-2004, FC Dinamo Tbilisi (13/1), FK Spartak-Alania Vladikavkaz (2/1), FC Dinamo Tbilisi (2/0), Trabzonspor Kulübü (16/3), FC Zürich (16/1), FC Luzern (3/0), FK Metalurh Donetsk (10/0).
(3/032)	JANASHIA David	07.08.1972	**10**	**3**	1992-1999, FC Torpedo Kutaisi (6/1), FC Samtredia (1/1), FC Torpedo Kutaisi (3/1).
(34/073)	JANASHIA Zaza	10.02.1976	**9**	**4**	1997-2001, FK Lokomotiv Moskva (9/4).
(4/035)	JANELIDZE David	09.02.1973	**2**	**0**	1992-1993, FC Mretebi Tbilisi (2/0).

(168/205)	JANELIDZE Giorgi	25.09.1989	**1**	**0**	2011, FC WIT Georgia Tbilisi (1/0).
(30/068)	JELADZE Zviad	16.12.1973	**3**	**0**	1996-1998, FC Dinamo Tbilisi (3/0).
(203/234)	JIGHAURI Jambul	08.07.1992	**4**	**0**	2016, FC Dinamo Tbilisi (4/0).
(78/123)	JIKIA Mamia	11.12.1975	**3**	**0**	2002-2004, Amica Wronki (2/0), Wisła Płock (1/0).
(2/018)	JISHKARIANI Gia	30.11.1967	**9**	**1**	1991-1994, FC Dinamo Tbilisi (1/0), FC Shevardeni-1906 Tbilisi (8/1).
(2/023)	JISKHARIANI Mikheil	01.10.1969	**3**	**1**	1991-1994, FC Tskhumi Sukhumi (2/1), FK Dinamo Kyiv (1/0).
(5/037)	KABISASHVILI Temur	13.09.1967	**1**	**0**	1992, FC Antsi Tbilisi (1/0).
(1/015)	KACHARAVA Kakhaber	19.11.1966	**3**	**2**	1990-1994, FC Iberia Tbilisi (1/1), Olympiakos FC Nicosia (2/1).
(44/084)	KAIDARASHVILI Aleksandre	02.11.1978	**1**	**0**	1998, FC Dila Gori (1/0).
(198/225)	KAKABADZE Otar	27.06.1995	**7**	**0**	2015-2016, FC Dinamo Tbilisi (4/0), Gimnàstic de Tarragona (3/0).
(159/200)	KAKUBAVA Levan	15.10.1990	**4**	**0**	2010-2014, FC Dinamo Tbilisi (2/0), FC Spartak Tskhinvali Gori (2/0).
(24/056)	KALADZE Kakhaber	27.02.1978	**83**	**1**	1996-2011, FC Dinamo Tbilisi (6/0), FK Dinamo Kyiv (18/0), Milan AC (46/1), Genoa CFC (13/0).
(92/135)	KANDELAKI Ilia	26.12.1981	**15**	**0**	2004-2010, FC Dinamo Tbilisi (1/0), FK Chornomorets Odesa (9/0), FC Carl Zeiss Jena (2/0), SK Sturm Graz (2/0), İnter PİK Bakı (1/0).
(96/140)	KANKAVA Jaba	18.03.1986	**62**	**7**	2004-2016, FC Dinamo Tbilisi (1/0), FK Alania Vladikavkaz (6/0), Arsenal Kyiv (8/1), FK Dnipro Dnipropetrovsk (10/1), FK Kryvbas Krykyi Rih (10/2), FK Dnipro Dnipropetrovsk (19/2), Stade de Reims (8/1).
(144/188)	KASHIA Guram	07.04.1987	**51**	**0**	2009-2016, FC Dinamo Tbilisi (5/0), SBV Vitesse Arnhem (46/1).
(202/231)	KATCHARAVA Nika	13.01.1994	**3**	**0**	2016, FK Rostov-na-Donu (1/0), Ethnikos Achna FC (2/0).
(12/049)	KATSITADZE Merab	25.02.1963	**1**	**0**	1994, FC Kakheti Telavi (1/0).
(2/024)	KAVELASHVILI Mikheil	22.07.1971	**46**	**9**	1991-2002, FC Dinamo Tbilisi (10/2), FK Spartak Vladikavkaz (3/0), Manchester City FC (4/1), Grasshopper-Club Zürich (10/3), FC Zürich (18/3), FC Luzern (1/0).
(58/106)	KEMOKLIDZE Revaz	13.03.1979	**20**	**0**	2000-2003, FC Tbilisi (3/0), FC Dinamo Tbilisi (1/0), FC Torpedo Kutaisi (8/0), Kocaelispor Kulübü (2/0), FC Lokomotivi Tbilisi (6/0).
(126/166)	KENIA Levan	18.10.1990	**29**	**4**	2007-2016, FC Lokomotivi Tbilisi (6/0), FC Schalke 04 Gelsenkirchen (13/3), FK Karpaty Lviv (4/0), SK Slavia Praha (6/1).
(1/002)	KETASHVILI Gela	27.09.1965	**1**	**0**	1990, FC Iberia Tbilisi (1/0).
(1/007)	KETSBAIA Temuri	18.03.1968	**52**	**17**	1990-2002, FC Iberia Tbilisi (1/0), FC Dinamo Tbilisi (1/1), Anorthósis FC Famagusta (3/1), AEK Athína (17/5), Newcastle United FC (19/6), Wolwerhampton Wanderers FC (8/4), Dundee FC (2/0), Anorthósis FC Famagusta (1/0).
(132/177)	KHIDESHELI Giorgi	21.11.1985	**3**	**0**	2008, FC Zestafoni (2/0), FC Torpedo Kutaisi (1/0).
(54/099)	KHIZANEISHVILI Otar	26.09.1981	**20**	**0**	1999-2007, FC Dinamo Tbilisi (1/0), FK Rostselmash Rostov (1/0), FC Dinamo Tbilisi (4/0), FK Dinamo Moskva (5/0), SC Freiburg (9/0).
(54/101)	KHIZANISHVILI Zurab	06.10.1981	**92**	**1**	1999-2015, FC Dinamo Tbilisi (1/0), FC Lokomotivi Tbilisi (9/0), Dundee FC (11/0), Glasgow Rangers FC (11/0), Blackburn Rovers FC (29/1), Newcastle United FC (3/0), Reading FC London (2/0), Blackburn Rovers FC (1/0), Reading FC London (8/0), Kayserispor Kulübü (15/0), İnter PİK Bakı (2/0).
(136/185)	KHMALADZE Levan	06.04.1985	**12**	**0**	2008-2014, FC Dinamo Tbilisi (12/0).
(71/115)	KHMELIDZE David	28.04.1979	**1**	**0**	2001, FK Rostselmash Rostov (1/0).
(159/197)	KHOJAVA Gocha	16.03.1985	**1**	**0**	2010, FK Volga Nizhny Novgorod (1/0).
(159/196)	KHUBUTIA Akaki	17.03.1986	**20**	**0**	2010-2014, CS Gaz Metan Mediaş (5/0), Samsunspor Kulübü (2/0), CS Gaz Metan Mediaş (1/0), FK Mordovia Saransk (8/0), Hapoel Petah Tikva FC (4/0).
(30/063)	KHUJADZE Shalva	10.05.1975	**2**	**0**	1996, FC Kolkheti 1913 Poti (2/0).
(41/076)	KHVADAGIANI Vakhtang	04.04.1972	**1**	**0**	1998, FC Torpedo Kutaisi (1/0).
(30/064)	KIKNADZE Giorgi	26.04.1976	**10**	**1**	1996-1999, FC Dinamo Tbilisi (10/1).
(2/020)	KILASONIA Giorgi	09.09.1968	**4**	**0**	1991-1995, FC Gorda Rustavi (1/0), FC Metalurg Rustavi (3/0).
(4/034)	KINKLADZE Giorgi	06.07.1973	**55**	**8**	1992-2005, FC Dinamo Tbilisi (14/2), Manchester City FC (16/4), AFC Ajax Amsterdam (5/0), Derby County FC (15/2), no club (4/0), Anorthósis FC Famagusta (1/0).
(44/087)	KIPIANI Giorgi	12.08.1978	**2**	**0**	1998-2001, FC Torpedo Kutaisi (2/0).
(2/022)	KIZILASHVILI David	20.01.1971	**9**	**2**	1991-1995, FC Odishi Zugdidi (1/0), FC Shevardeni-1906 Tbilisi (4/2), AC Omonia Nicosia (4/0).
(134/181)	KLIMIASHVILI Irakli	30.05.1988	**5**	**0**	2008-2009, FC WIT Georgia Tbilisi (5/0).
(119/164)	KOBAKHIDZE Aleksandre	11.02.1987	**33**	**3**	2006-2016, FC Dinamo Tbilisi (1/0), FC Dnipro Dnipropetrovsk (1/0), FK Arsenal Kyiv (8/2), FC Dnipro Dnipropetrovsk (11/1), FK Volyn Lutsk (5/0), FC Dnipro Dnipropetrovsk (4/0), FK Volyn Lutsk (2/0), FK Vorskla Poltava (1/0).
(176/211)	KOBALIA Irakli	13.03.1992	**1**	**0**	2012, FC Zugdidi (1/0).
(27/061)	KOBIASHVILI Levan	10.07.1977	**100**	**12**	1996-2011, FC Dinamo Tbilisi (5/0), FK Alania Vladikavkaz (4/0), SC Freiburg (33/3), FC Schalke 04 Gelsenkirchen (44/7), Hertha BSC Berlin (14/2).
(90/131)	KORGALIDZE Levan	21.02.1980	**3**	**0**	2004, FC Skonto Riga (3/0).
(1/009)	KORGALIDZE Otar	02.09.1960	**1**	**0**	1990, FC Guria Lanchkuti (1/0).
(1/012)	KORGASHVILI Rostom	15.12.1964	**1**	**0**	1990, FC Kutaisi (1/0).
(154/195)	KOSHKADZE Aleksandre	04.12.1981	**3**	**0**	2010, FC Dinamo Tbilisi (3/0).
(1/004)	KUDINOV Dmitri	08.02.1963	**20**	**1**	1990-1996, FC Gorda Rustavi (1/0), FC Dinamo Tbilisi (3/0), APOEL FC Nicosia (6/1), Aris Limassol (2/0), FC Dinamo Tbilisi (8/0).
(127/169)	KVAKHADZE Aleksandre	16.08.1981	**11**	**0**	2007-2009, FC WIT Georgia Tbilisi (11/0).
(58/104)	KVARATSKHELIA Givi	11.05.1979	**7**	**0**	2000-2005, FC Lokomotivi Tbilisi (3/0), FC Tbilisi (4/0).
(173/209)	KVASKHVADZE Roin	31.05.1989	**5**	**0**	2012-2016, FC Zestafoni (2/0), AC Othellos Athienou (1/0), FC Torpedo Kutaisi (2/0).
(198/226)	KVEKVESKIRI Nika	29.05.1992	**5**	**0**	2015-2016, İnter PİK Bakı (5/0).
(44/088)	KVETENADZE Kakhaber	03.06.1970	**2**	**0**	1998, FC Torpedo Kutaisi (2/0).
(203/233)	KVILITAIA Giorgi	01.10.1993	**4**	**0**	2016, FC Dinamo Tbilisi (3/0), SK Rapid Wien (1/0).

(84/127)	KVIRKVELIA David	27.06.1980	**59**	**0**	2003-2014, FC Dinamo Tbilisi (12/0), FK Alania Vladikavkaz (3/0), FK Metalurg Zaporizhzhya (16/0), FK Rubin Kazan (6/0), FK Anzhi Makhachkala (1/0), FK Rubin Kazan (4/0), PAE Panionios Athína (4/0), AA Anorthósis Famagusta (2/0), FC Dila Gori (6/0), FC Dinamo Tbilisi (3/0), FC Samtredia (2/0).
(185/220)	KVIRKVELIA Solomon	06.02.1992	**20**	**0**	2014-2016, FK Rubin Kazan (20/0).
(150/194)	LIPARTIA Jaba	16.11.1987	**2**	**0**	2009-2012, FC WIT Georgia Tbilisi (1/0), FK Zorya Luhansk (1/0).
(6/038)	LOBJANIDZE Nugzar	07.09.1971	**13**	**0**	1993-1997, FC Metalurgi Rustavi (1/0), FC Dinamo Tbilisi (7/0), FK CSKA Moskva (3/0), FC Dinamo Tbilisi (2/0).
(134/179)	LOBJANIDZE Ucha	23.02.1987	**50**	**1**	2008-2016, FC Zestafoni (14/0), FC Dnipro Dnipropetrovsk (5/0), FC Kryvbas Kryvyi Rih (10/0), FC Dnipro Dnipropetrovsk (6/0), AC Omonia Nicosia (11/0), FC Dinamo Tbilisi (4/0).
(127/170)	LOMAIA David	18.05.1985	**1**	**0**	2007, FC WIT Georgia Tbilisi (1/0).
(49/096)	LOMAIA Giorgi	08.08.1979	**45**	**0**	1998-2010, FC Merani 91 Tbilisi (1/0), FC Lokomotivi Tbilisi (11/0), FK Spartak Moskva (2/0), FK Khimki (6/0), FK Luch-Energie Vladivostok (5/0), FC Carl Zeiss Jena (5/0), FK Karpati Lviv (1/0), *unattached* (2/0), FC Lokomotivi Tbilisi (7/0), İnter PİK Bakı (5/0).
(134/178)	LORIA Giorgi	27.01.1986	**38**	**0**	2008-2016, FC Dinamo Tbilisi (25/0), OFI Heraklion (8/0), FK Krylia Sovetov Samara (5/0).
(23/055)	MACHAVARIANI Mamuka	27.11.1970	**3**	**0**	1995-1997, FC Dinamo Tbilisi (3/0).
(90/133)	MAGRADZE Levan	15.11.1979	**4**	**0**	2004-2005, AEL FC Limassól (2/0), Skoda Xanthi FC (2/0).
(168/203)	MAISURADZE Irakli	22.08.1988	**2**	**0**	2011-2013, FC Metallurgi Rustavi (1/0), FC Dila Gori (1/0).
(127/168)	MAKARIDZE Giorgi	31.03.1990	**5**	**0**	2007-2008, FC Dinamo Tbilisi (5/0).
(110/157)	MAKHARADZE Kakhaber	20.10.1987	**3**	**0**	2006-2015, FC Dinamo Tbilisi (1/0), FC Pakhtakor Tashkent (2/0).
(71/116)	MAKHVILADZE Mikheil	22.07.1978	**1**	**0**	2001, FC Torpedo Kutaisi (1/0).
(92/134)	MAMALADZE Zurab	10.02.1982	**3**	**0**	2004-2009, FC Lokomotivi Tbilisi (1/0), FC Zestafoni (2/0).
(110/155)	MARTSVALADZE Otar	14.07.1984	**21**	**2**	2006-2014, FK Dinamo Kyiv (6/1), FK Zakarpattya Uzhgorod (4/0), FK Dinamo Kyiv (1/1), FK Anzhi Makhachkala (1/0), FK Volga Nizhny Novgorod (3/0), FK Krasnodar (5/0), FC Dinamo Tbilisi (1/0).
(128/174)	MCHEDLIDZE Levan	23.03.1990	**31**	**2**	2007-2016, Empoli FC (5/1), US Città di Palermo (7/0), Empoli FC (19/1).
(110/151)	MCHEDLISHVILI David	05.04.1988	**1**	**0**	2006, FC Ameri Tbilisi (1/0).
(44/082)	MEGRELADZE Giorgi	21.07.1978	**1**	**0**	1998, FC Torpedo Kutaisi (1/0).
(70/112)	MELKADZE Levan	12.12.1979	**5**	**0**	2001, FC WIT Georgia Tbilisi (2/0), FC Dinamo Tbilisi (3/0).
(58/105)	MENTESHASHVILI Zurab	30.01.1980	**40**	**1**	2000-2010, FC Skonto Riga (10/1), FK Alania Vladikavkaz (1/0), FC Skonto Riga (6/0), FK Shinnik Yaroslavl (5/0), FK Ventspils (16/0), Hapoel Tel Aviv FC (2/0).
(135/184)	MEREBASHVILI Giorgi	15.08.1986	**18**	**0**	2008-2015, FC Dinamo Tbilisi (10/0), FK Vojvodina Novi Sad (7/0), PAE Veroia (1/0).
(179/213)	MIGINEISHVILI Omar	02.06.1984	**1**	**0**	2013, FC Torpedo Kutaisi (1/0).
(62/108)	MIKADZE Levan	13.09.1973	**1**	**0**	2000, FC Lokomotivi Tbilisi (1/0).
(93/136)	MJAVANADZE Kakhaber	02.10.1978	**14**	**0**	2004-2006, FK Anzhi Makhachkala (13/0), FK Chornomorets Odesa (1/0).
(117/162)	MODEBADZE Irakli	04.10.1984	**4**	**0**	2006-2013, FK Metalurg Zaporizhzhya (1/0), FC Olimpi Rustavi (1/0), FC Metallurgi Rustavi (1/0), FC Dila Gori (1/0).
(44/086)	MONASELIDZE Lasha	02.01.1977	**1**	**0**	1998, FK Torpedo Moskva (1/0).
(32/072)	MUJIRI Amiran	20.02.1974	**1**	**0**	1997, FC Dinamo Batumi (1/0).
(49/095)	MUJIRI David	02.01.1978	**26**	**1**	1998-2008, FC Dinamo Tbilisi (1/0), SK Sturm Graz (11/0), FK Krylya Sovetov Samara (13/1), FK Lokomotiv Moskva (1/0).
(1/006)	NADIRADZE Giorgi	12.02.1968	**1**	**0**	1990, FC Kutaisi (1/0).
(134/180)	NAVALOVSKI Giorgi	28.06.1986	**19**	**0**	2008-2016, FK Anzhi Makhachkala (2/0), FK Tosno Tikhvin (4/0), FC Dila Gori (5/0), FK SCA-Energiya Khabarovsk (4/0), PAE Veria (3/0).
(3/031)	NEMSADZE Giorgi	10.05.1972	**69**	**0**	1992-2004, FC Shevardeni-1906 Tbilisi (4/0), FC Dinamo Tbilisi (10/0), FC 08 Homburg (5/0), Trabzonspor Kulübü (7/0), Grasshopper-Club Zürich (11/0), AC Reggiana Reggio nell'Emilia (5/0), FC Lokomotivi Tbilisi (2/0), FC Dinamo Tbilisi (6/0), Dundee FC (19/0).
(82/126)	NIKURADZE Giorgi	01.10.1979	**1**	**0**	2003, KooTeePee (1/0).
(71/118)	NOZADZE Lasha	18.03.1980	**1**	**0**	2001, FC WIT Georgia Tbilisi (1/0).
(99/143)	ODIKADZE David	14.04.1981	**14**	**0**	2005-2009, FC Dinamo Tbilisi (10/0), Győri ETO FC (2/0), İnter PİK Bakı (2/0).
(159/199)	OKRIASHVILI Tornike	12.02.1992	**34**	**8**	2010-2016, FK Shakhtar Donetsk (1/0), FK Illichivets Mariupol (10/1), FK Chornomorets Odessa (3/1), KRC Genk (12/3), Eskişehirspor Kulübü (4/2), *unattached* (1/0), FK Krasnodar (3/1).
(10/046)	OLOSHVILI Zaza		**1**	**0**	1994, (/).
(74/120)	ONIANI Roin	14.01.1975	**1**	**0**	2001, FC Lokomotivi Tbilisi (1/0).
(198/227)	PALAVANDISHVILI Guga	14.08.1993	**1**	**0**	2015, FC Dila Gori (1/0).
(1/010)	PANTSULAYA Mamuka	09.10.1965	**1**	**0**	1990, FC Gorda Rustavi (1/0).
(186/221)	PAPAVA Giorgi	16.02.1993	**3**	**0**	2014, FC Dinamo Tbilisi (3/0).
(187/222)	PAPUNASHVILI Giorgi	02.09.1995	**3**	**0**	2014-2015, FC Dinamo Tbilisi (2/0), SV Werder Bremen (1/0).
(1/005)	PIRTSKHALAVA Giorgi	03.01.1965	**2**	**0**	1990-1993, FC Gorda Rustavi (1/0), FC Metalurgi Rustavi (1/0).
(110/153)	POPKHADZE Giorgi	25.09.1986	**12**	**0**	2006-2015, FC Tbilisi (2/0), Viborg FF (5/0), SK Sturm Graz (1/0), FK Bakı (3/0), KS Flamurtari Vlorë (1/0).
(44/078)	POPKHADZE Zurab	02.06.1972	**4**	**0**	1998-1999, FK Kyryla Sovetov Samara (4/0).
(30/066)	POTSKHVERIA Mikheil	12.08.1975	**4**	**0**	1996-1999, FK Shakhtar Donetsk (2/0), FK Dnipro Dnipropetrovsk (1/0), FK Shakhtar Donetsk (1/0)
(185/218)	QAZAISHVILI Valeri	29.01.1993	**21**	**4**	2014-2016, SBV Vitesse Arnhem (17/3), Legia Warszawa (4/1).

(139/186)	RAZMADZE Luka	30.12.1983	**11**	**0**	2008-2009, FC WIT Georgia Tbilisi (11/0).
(52/097)	REKHVIASHVILI Aleksandre	16.08.1974	**21**	**0**	1999-2005, FC Skonto Riga (15/0), FK Torpedo-Metallurg Moskva (4/0), FK Ventspils (2/0).
(49/093)	REVAZISHVILI Giorgi	31.03.1977	**1**	**0**	1998, FK Kyryla Sovetov Samara (1/0).
(106/148)	REVISHVILI Nukri	02.03.1987	**32**	**0**	2005-2016, FC Torpedo Kutaisi (4/0), FK Rubin Kazan (4/0), FK Anzhi Makhachkala (10/0), FK Krasnodar (3/0), FC Dila Gori (2/0), FC Tosno Tikhvin (1/0), FK Mordovia Saransk (8/0).
(1/008)	REVISHVILI Zaza	23.09.1968	**12**	**0**	1990-1996, FC Iberia Tbilisi (1/0), FC Dinamo Tbilisi (10/0), FK Alania Vladikavkaz (1/0).
(71/114)	SAJAIA Edik	16.02.1981	**9**	**0**	2001-2002, FC WIT Georgia Tbilisi (5/0), FK Torpedo Moskva (4/0).
(82/124)	SAKHVADZE Archil	10.03.1978	**1**	**0**	2003, FC Dinamo Tbilisi (1/0).
(96/139)	SALUKVADZE Lasha	21.12.1981	**38**	**1**	2004-2015, FC Dinamo Tbilisi (2/0), FK Rubin Kazan (30/1), FK Volga Nizhny Novgorod (4/0), İnter PİK Bakı (2/0).
(120/165)	SANAI Amiran	03.09.1989	**2**	**0**	2007, FC Zestafoni (2/0).
(130/175)	SANAIA Amiran	03.09.1989	**6**	**0**	2007-2009, Le Mans FC (6/0).
(6/039)	SEPASHVILI Vasil	17.02.1969	**3**	**0**	1993-1996, FC Alazani Gurjaani (1/0), FC Kakheti Telavi (1/0), FK Lada Togliati (1/0).
(111/160)	SETURIDZE Giorgi	01.04.1985	**5**	**0**	2006-2009, FC Lokomotivi Tbilisi (1/0), FC Olimpi Rustavi (2/0), Standard FK Sumqayit (2/0).
(71/113)	SHASHIASHVILI Giorgi	01.09.1979	**32**	**1**	2001-2008, FC Dinamo Tbilisi (13/0), FK Chornomorets Odesa (7/1), SK Sturm Graz (10/0), PAE Ergotelis Heraklion (2/0).
(32/071)	SHEKILADZE Gela	14.09.1970	**22**	**0**	1997-2002, FC Dinamo Batumi (9/0), K Lierse SK (13/0).
(2/017)	SHELIA Murtaz	25.03.1969	**29**	**0**	1991-1998, FC Dinamo Tbilisi (6/0), 1.FC Saarbrücken (5/0), FC Dinamo Tbilisi (3/0), FK Spartak-Alania Vladikavkaz (11/0), Manchester City FC (4/0).
(55/102)	SICHINAVA Tengiz	15.05.1972	**10**	**0**	1999-2000, FC Dinamo Tbilisi (10/0).
(3/027)	SIDAMONIDZE Kakhaber	17.04.1971	**5**	**0**	1992-1994, FC Mretebi Tbilisi (3/0), FC Samtredia (2/0).
(39/074)	SILAGADZE Levan	04.08.1976	**21**	**0**	1998-2001, FC Skonto Riga (7/0), FK Alania Vladikavkaz (6/0), FC Lokomotivi Tbilisi (3/0), FC Torpedo Kutaisi (5/0).
(90/130)	SIRADZE David	21.10.1981	**28**	**8**	2004-2011, 1.FC Union Berlin (2/0), FC Erzgebirge Aue (4/2), SC Paderborn 07 (5/2), FK Spartak Nalchik (17/4).
(171/208)	SIRBILADZE Irakli	27.09.1982	**5**	**0**	2012-2013, FC Inter Turku (5/0).
(206/236)	SKHIRTLADZE David	16.03.1993	**3**	**0**	2016, Silkeborg IF (3/0).
(102/144)	STURUA Zviad	25.04.1978	**2**	**0**	2005, FC Lokomotivi Tbilisi (1/0), FC Dinamo Tbilisi (1/0).
(164/202)	TARGAMADZE David	22.08.1989	**20**	**2**	2011-2014, FK Oleksandriya (4/1), FK Illichivets Mariupol (16/1).
(49/091)	TARKHNISHVILI Vaja	25.08.1971	**2**	**0**	1998-1999, FC Lokomotivi Tbilisi (1/0), FC Sheriff Tiraspol (1/0).
(126/167)	TATANASHVILI Dimitri	19.10.1983	**2**	**1**	2007, FC Ameri Tbilisi (2/1).
(203/232)	TCHANTURISHVILI Vakhtang	05.08.1993	**1**	**0**	2016, FC Dinamo Tbilisi (1/0).
(12/050)	TKEBUCHAVA Gocha	24.11.1963	**1**	**0**	1994, FC Dinamo Tbilisi (1/0).
(62/109)	TODUA Sevasti	13.05.1976	**6**	**0**	2000-2001, FC WIT Georgia Tbilisi (2/0), FC Lokomotivi Tbilisi (1/0), FC Torpedo Kutaisi (3/0).
(26/059)	TOGONIDZE Nikoloz	24.04.1971	**10**	**0**	1996-1999, FC Dinamo Batumi (10/0).
(177/212)	TOMASHVILI Gulverd	13.10.1988	**1**	**0**	2013, FC Dila Gori (1/0).
(45/089)	TSERETELI Mamuka	17.01.1979	**9**	**0**	1998-2004, FK Alania Vladikavkaz (9/0), FC Dinamo Tbilisi (3/0).
(106/149)	TSINAMDZGHVRISHVILI Rati	22.03.1988	**3**	**0**	2005, FC Ameri Tbilisi (3/0).
(197/224)	TSINTADZE Mate	07.01.1995	**2**	**0**	2015, FC Dinamo Tbilisi (2/0).
(204/235)	TSISKARIDZE Zurab	08.09.1986	**2**	**0**	2016, FK Teplice (2/0).
(185/219)	TSKHADADZE Bachana	23.10.1987	**8**	**0**	2014-2015, İnter PİK Bakı (5/0), KS Flamurtari Vlorë (3/0).
(1/003)	TSKHADADZE Kakhaber	07.09.1968	**25**	**1**	1990-1998, FC Iberia Tbilisi (1/0), FC Dinamo Tbilisi (1/0), FK Dinamo Moskva (1/0), SG Eintracht Frankfurt (14/0), FK Alania Vladikavkaz (6/1), Manchester City FC (2/0).
(20/053)	TSKITISHVILI Levan	10.10.1976	**58**	**1**	1995-2009, FC Dinamo Tbilisi (10/1), SC Freiburg (25/0), FK Metalurh Donetsk (3/0), VfL Wolfsburg (1/0), Paniónios PAE Athína (7/0), FC Lokomotivi Tbilisi (9/0), *unattached* (3/0).
(2/019)	TSOMAIA David	04.09.1967	**4**	**0**	1991-1992, FC Guria Lanchkuti (1/0), FC Alazani Gurjaani (3/0).
(10/045)	TUGUSHI Temur	26.02.1972	**3**	**0**	1994, FC Dinamo Batumi (3/0).
(44/085)	VASHAKIDZE Irakli	13.03.1976	**1**	**0**	1998, FC Torpedo Kutaisi (1/0).
(148/193)	VATSADZE Mate	17.12.1988	**15**	**4**	2009-2016, FC Dinmo Tbilisi (3/0), FK Volga Nizhny Novgorod (2/0), AGF Aarhus (10/4).
(8/042)	ZOIDZE Irakli	21.03.1969	**19**	**0**	1994-2001, FC Dinamo Tbilisi (19/0).

NATIONAL COACHES

Name	DOB	Period	Matches	P	W	D	L		GF	-	GA	
Anatoli „Giga“ NORAKIDZE	30.04.1930 †27.02.1995	02.09.1992 – 22.12.1992	[1-3]	3	1	0	2		6	-	5	33.33 %
Aleksander CHIVADZE	08.04.1955	25.05.1993 – 09.11.1996	[4-27]	24	9	1	14		25	-	35	39.58 %
Vladimir Gavrilovich GUTSAEV	21.12.1952	05.12.1996 – 08.12.1996	[28-29]	2	0	0	2		4	-	7	0.00 %
David KIPIANI	18.11.1951	30.03.1997 – 11.10.1997	[30-36]	7	4	1	2		14	-	6	64.28 %
Vladimir Gavrilovich GUTSAEV	21.12.1952	06.02.1998 – 28.04.1999	[37-50]	14	5	3	6		16	-	20	46.42 %
Johan BOSKAMP (*Netherlands*)	21.10.1948	30.05.1999 – 09.10.1999	[51-55]	5	0	1	4		5	-	9	10.00 %
David KIPIANI & Revaz DZODZUASHVILI	18.11.1951 15.04.1945	02.02.2000 – 06.06.2001	[56-71]	16	5	5	6		17	-	18	46.85 %
Aleksander CHIVADZE	08.04.1955	15.08.2001 – 02.04.2003	[72-82]	11	4	3	4		18	-	16	50.00 %
Ivan ŠUŠAK (*Croatia*)	10.06.1948	30.04.2003 – 11.06.2003	[83-84]	2	1	0	1		1	-	2	50.00 %
Merab JORDANIA	03.09.1965	06.09.2003 – 11.10.2003	[85-87]	3	1	0	2		5	-	6	33.33 %
Gocha TKEBUCHAVA	24.11.1963	18.02.2004 – 21.02.2004	[88-90]	3	0	0	3		1	-	8	0.00 %
Alain GIRESSE (*France*)	02.08.1952	27.05.2004 – 04.06.2005	[91-100]	10	2	2	6		11	-	18	30.00 %
Gaioz DARSADZE	19.06.1964	17.08.2005 – 16.11.2005	[101-107]	7	2	2	3		9	-	17	42.85 %
Klaus TOPPMÖLLER (*Germany*)	12.08.1951	01.03.2006 – 26.03.2008	[108-131]	24	7	4	13		28	-	38	37.50 %
Petar SEGRT (*Germany*)	08.05.1966	27.05.2008 – 31.05.2008	[132-133]	2	0	1	1		1	-	3	25.00 %
Héctor Raúl CÚPER (*Argentina*)	16.11.1955	20.08.2008 – 14.10.2009	[134-149]	16	1	4	11		13	-	30	18.75 %
Temuri KETSBAIA	18.03.1968	03.03.2010 – 14.11.2014	[150-189]	40	13	9	18		34	-	44	43.75 %
Kakhaber TSKHADADZE	07.09.1968	25.03.2015 – 16.11.2015	[190-199]	10	3	1	6		11	-	16	35.00 %
Vladimír WEISS (*Slovakia*)	22.09.1964	29.03.2016 – 09.10.2016	[200-208]	8	1	3	4		7	-	14	31.25 %

National coaches several times in charge:

Name	How often	Matches	M	W	D	L		GF	-	GA	
Aleksander CHIVADZE	2x	[4-27],[72-82]	34	13	4	17		43	-	50	44.11 %
Vladimir Gavrilovich GUTSAEV	2x	[28-29], [37-50]	16	5	3	8		20	-	27	40.62 %

HEAD-TO-HEAD STATISTICS

	HOME					AWAY					NEUTRAL					TOTAL				
Albania	5	5	0	0	10 : 1	8	2	3	3	10 : 12	1	1	0	0	3 : 0	14	8	3	3	23 : 13
Armenia	1	1	0	0	7 : 0	1	0	1	0	0 : 0	3	2	0	1	4 : 4	5	3	1	1	11 : 4
Austria	1	1	0	0	1 : 2											1	1	0	0	1 : 2
Azerbaijan	2	2	0	0	7 : 3	4	0	2	2	1 : 3						6	2	2	2	8 : 6
Belarus	1	1	0	0	1 : 0	1	0	0	1	0 : 2						2	1	0	1	1 : 2
Bulgaria	2	1	1	0	2 : 1	3	0	0	3	4 : 14						5	1	1	3	6 : 15
Cameroon											1	0	1	0	0 : 0	1	0	1	0	0 : 0
Croatia	1	1	0	0	1 : 0	1	0	0	1	1 : 2						2	1	0	1	2 : 2
Cyprus	1	0	1	0	1 : 1	4	1	0	3	4 : 6						5	1	1	3	5 : 7
Denmark	1	0	1	0	2 : 2	2	0	0	2	2 : 8						3	0	1	2	4 : 10
Egypt	1	0	1	0	0 : 0											1	0	1	0	0 : 0
England	1	0	0	1	0 : 2	1	0	0	1	0 : 2						2	0	0	2	0 : 4
Estonia	2	2	0	0	5 : 2	3	0	1	2	1 : 5						5	2	1	2	6 : 7
Faroe Islands	1	1	0	0	3 : 1	1	1	0	0	6 : 0						2	2	0	0	9 : 1
Finland	1	0	0	1	0 : 1	1	0	1	0	1 : 1						2	0	1	1	1 : 2
France	2	0	1	1	0 : 3	2	0	0	2	1 : 4						4	0	1	3	1 : 7
Germany	2	0	0	2	0 : 4	3	0	0	3	2 : 8						5	0	0	5	2 : 12
Gibraltar	1	1	0	0	4 : 0	1	1	0	0	3 : 0						2	2	0	0	7 : 0
Greece	3	0	0	3	3 : 7	4	0	1	3	2 : 7						7	0	1	6	5 : 14
Hungary	1	1	0	0	3 : 1	1	0	0	1	1 : 4						2	1	0	1	4 : 5
Iceland						1	0	0	1	1 : 3						1	0	0	1	1 : 3
Iran						1	0	0	1	1 : 2						1	0	0	1	1 : 2
Israel	3	1	1	1	3 : 3	3	0	1	2	1 : 4						6	1	2	3	4 : 7
Italy	4	0	1	3	2 : 7	4	0	0	4	0 : 7						8	0	1	7	2 : 14
Jordan	1	1	0	0	3 : 2					:					:	1	1	0	0	3 : 2
Kazakhstan	2	0	2	0	1 : 1	2	1	0	1	2 : 2						4	1	2	1	3 : 3
Latvia	3	0	1	2	3 : 6	3	1	1	1	4 : 3	1	1	0	0	2 : 1	7	2	2	3	9 : 10
Lebanon						2	0	0	2	4 : 7						2	0	0	2	4 : 7
Liechtenstein	1	1	0	0	2 : 0											1	1	0	0	2 : 0
Lithuania	4	2	1	1	5 : 4	3	1	0	2	4 : 2						7	3	1	3	9 : 6
Luxembourg						3	2	1	0	5 : 1						3	2	1	0	5 : 1
Malta	3	2	1	0	4 : 1	5	3	1	1	7 : 4						8	5	2	1	11 : 5
Moldova	6	2	2	2	8 : 6	5	2	1	2	7 : 6						11	4	3	4	15 : 12
Montenegro	1	0	1	0	0 : 0	1	0	0	1	1 : 2						2	0	1	1	1 : 2
New Zealand											1	0	0	1	1 : 3	1	0	0	1	1 : 3
Nigeria						1	0	0	1	1 : 5						1	0	0	1	1 : 5
Northern Ireland						1	0	0	1	1 : 4						1	0	0	1	1 : 4
Norway	1	0	0	1	1 : 4	2	0	0	2	0 : 2						3	0	0	3	1 : 6
Paraguay											1	0	0	1	0 : 1	1	0	0	1	0 : 1
Poland	2	1	0	1	3 : 4	3	0	0	3	1 : 9						5	1	0	4	4 : 13
Portugal						1	0	0	1	0 : 2						1	0	0	1	0 : 2
Qatar						1	1	0	0	2 : 1						1	1	0	0	2 : 1
Rep. of Ireland	2	0	0	2	2 : 4	5	0	0	5	1 : 10	1	0	0	1	1 : 2	8	0	0	8	4 : 16
Romania	1	0	0	1	0 : 2	4	0	1	3	3 : 13	2	0	1	1	1 : 4	7	0	2	5	4 : 19
Russia	1	1	0	0	1 : 0	2	0	1	1	2 : 4						3	1	1	1	3 : 4
Saudi Arabia											1	1	0	0	2 : 0	1	1	0	0	2 : 0
Scotland	2	2	0	0	3 : 0	2	0	0	2	1 : 3						4	2	0	2	4 : 3
Slovakia											2	1	0	1	3 : 3	2	1	0	1	3 : 3
Slovenia	1	0	1	0	1 : 1	2	1	0	1	3 : 3	1	0	0	1	0 : 1	4	1	1	2	4 : 5
South Africa	1	1	0	0	4 : 1											1	1	0	0	4 : 1
Spain	1	0	0	1	0 : 1	2	1	0	1	1 : 2						3	1	0	2	1 : 3
Switzerland	1	0	1	0	0 : 0	1	0	0	1	1 : 4						2	0	1	1	1 : 4
Tunisia						1	0	1	0	1 : 1	1	1	0	0	2 : 0	2	1	1	0	3 : 1
Turkey	2	1	0	1	3 : 5	2	0	1	1	1 : 4	1	0	0	1	1 : 3	5	1	1	3	5 : 12
Ukraine	4	0	3	1	2 : 3	4	0	0	4	3 : 11	1	0	0	1	1 : 2	9	0	3	6	6 : 16
Unit. Arab Emir.											1	0	0	1	0 : 1	1	0	0	1	0 : 1
Uruguay	1	0	0	1	2 : 0											1	0	0	1	2 : 0
Wales	1	1	0	0	5 : 0	3	2	1	0	4 : 2						4	3	1	0	9 : 2
TOTAL	**79**	**33**	**20**	**26**	**108 : 86**	**111**	**20**	**19**	**72**	**102 : 201**	**19**	**7**	**2**	**10**	**21 : 25**	**209**	**60**	**41**	**108**	**231 : 312**

GERMANY

★★★★

The Country:
Bundesrepublik Deutschland (Federal Republic of Germany)
Capital: Berlin
Surface: 357,168 km²
Inhabitants: 82,175,700
Time: UTC+1

The FA:
Deutscher Fußball-Bund
Otto-Fleck-Schneise 6, Postfach 710265, 60492 Frankfurt am Main
Foundation date: 28.01.1900
Member of FIFA since: 1904
Member of UEFA since: 1954

NATIONAL TEAM RECORDS

EUROPEAN CHAMPIONSHIP	
1960	Did not enter
1964	Did not enter
1968	Qualifiers
1972	**Final Tournament (Winners)**
1976	Final Tournament (Runners-up)
1980	**Final Tournament (Winners)**
1984	Final Tournament (Group Stage)
1988	Final Tournament (Semi-Finals)
1992	Final Tournament (Runners-up)
1996	**Final Tournament (Winners)**
2000	Final Tournament (Group Stage)
2004	Final Tournament (Group Stage)
2008	Final Tournament (Runners-up)
2012	Final Tournament (Semi-Finals)
2016	Final Tournament (Semi-Finals)

FIFA WORLD CUP	
1930	Did not enter
1934	Final Tournament (3rd Place)
1938	Final Tournament (1st Round)
1950	*Banned*
1954	**Final Tournament (Winners)**
1958	Final Tournament (3rd Place)
1962	Final Tournament (Quarter-Finals)
1966	Final Tournament (Runners-up)
1970	Final Tournament (3rd Place)
1974	**Final Tournament (Winners)**
1978	Final Tournament (Second Round)
1982	Final Tournament (Runners-up)
1986	Final Tournament (Runners-up)
1990	**Final Tournament (Winners)**
1994	Final Tournament (Quarter-Finals)
1998	Final Tournament (Quarter-Finals)
2002	Final Tournament (Runners-up)
2006	Final Tournament (3rd Place)
2010	Final Tournament (3rd Place)
2014	**Final Tournament (Winners)**

OLYMPIC FOOTBALL TOURNAMENTS 1908-2016							
1908	-	**1948**	-	**1972**	Seconfd Round	**1996**	Qualifiers
1912	1st Round	**1952**	4th Place	**1976**	Qualifiers	**2000**	Qualifiers
1920	-	**1956**	1st Round	**1980**	Qualifiers	**2004**	Qualifiers
1924	-	**1960**	Qualifiers	**1984**	Quarter-Finals	**2008**	Qualifiers
1928	Quarter-Finals	**1964**	Qualifiers	**1988**	3rd Place	**2012**	Qualifiers
1936	Quarter-Finals	**1968**	-	**1992**	Qualifiers	**2016**	Runners-up

FIFA CONFEDERATIONS CUP 1992-2013
1999 (Group Stage), 2005 (3rd Place).

PLAYER WITH MOST INTERNATIONAL CAPS – Top 5			
1.	**Lothar Herbert MATTHÄUS**	-	150 caps (1980-2000)
2.	Miroslav Klose	-	137 caps (2001-2014)
3.	Lukas Josef Podolski	-	129 caps (2004-2016)
4.	Bastian Schweinsteiger	-	121 caps (2004-2016)
5.	Philipp Lahm	-	113 caps (2001-2014)

PLAYER WITH MOST INTERNATIONAL GOALS – Top 5			
1.	**Miroslav KLOSE**	-	71 goals / 137 caps (2001-2014)
2.	Gerhard Müller	-	68 goals / 62 caps (1966-1974)
3.	Lukas Josef Podolski	-	48 goals / 129 caps (2004-2016)
4.	Jürgen Klinsmann	-	47 goals / 108 caps (1987-1998)
	Rudolf „Rudi"Völler	-	47 goals / 90 caps (1982-1994)

FULL INTERNATIONALS (1908-2016)

1. 05.04.1908 **SWITZERLAND - GERMANY** **5-3(2-1)**
Landhof Stadion, Basel; Referee: Henry P. Devitte (Switzerland); Attendance: 3,500
GER: Fritz Baumgarten (1/0), Walter Hempel (1/0), Ernst Jordan (1/0), Karl Ludwig (1/0), Arthur Hiller II (Cap) (1/0), Hans Weymar (1/0), Gustav Hensel (1/0), Fritz Förderer (1/1), Eugen Kipp (1/0), Fritz Becker (1/2), Willy Baumgärtner (1/0). Trainer: no.
Goals: Fritz Becker (6), Fritz Förderer (52), Fritz Becker (69).

2. 20.04.1908 **GERMANY - ENGLAND** **1-5(1-3)**
Victoria Platz, Mariendorf, Berlin; Referee: Paul Neumann (Germany); Attendance: 5,500
GER: Paul Eichelmann (1/0), Otto Hantschick (1/0), Paul Fischer (1/0), Walter Poppe (1/0), Arthur Hiller II (Cap) (2/0), Hans Weymar (2/0), Adolf Gehrts (1/0), Arno Neumann (1/0), Fritz Förderer (2/2), Paul Matthes (1/0), Willy Baumgärtner (2/0). Trainer: no.
Goal: Fritz Förderer (20).

3. 07.06.1908 **AUSTRIA - GERMANY** **3-2(1-1)**
Cricketer Platz, Wien; Referee: George Wagstaffe Simmons (England); Attendance: 5,000
GER: Paul Eichelmann (2/0), Heinrich Riso I (1/0), Willy Tänzer (1/0), Ernst Poetsch (1/0), Arthur Hiller II (3/0), Hans Weymar (3/0), Hans Schmidt (1/0), Hermann Garrn (1/1), Eugen Kipp (Cap) (2/0), Adolf Jäger (1/1), Willy Baumgärtner (3/0). Trainer: no.
Goals: Hermann Garrn (6), Adolf Jäger (28).

4. 16.03.1909 **ENGLAND - GERMANY** **9-0(5-0)**
City Ground, Oxford; Referee: Thomas Kyle (England); Attendance: 6,000
GER: Adolf Werner (1/0), Otto Hantschick (2/0), Erich Massini (1/0), Camillo Ugi (1/0), Dr.Josef Glaser (Cap) (1/0), Paul Hunder (1/0), Erich Albrecht (1/0), Hermann Garrn (2/1), Adolf Jäger (2/1), Helmut Röpnack (1/0), Willy Baumgärtner (4/0). Trainer: no.

5. 04.04.1909 **HUNGARY - GERMANY** **3-3(2-2)**
Millenáris Sporttelep, Budapest; Referee: Hugo Meisl (Austria); Attendance: 9,000
GER: Adolf Werner (2/0), Herbert Hirth (1/0), Heinrich Riso I (2/0), Ernst Poetsch (2/0), Camillo Ugi (Cap) (2/1), Paul Hunder (2/0), Edwin Dutton (1/0), Leopold Richter (1/0), Willy Worpitzky (1/2), Richard Queck (1/0), Fritz Schulz (1/0). Trainer: no.
Goals: Willy Worpitzky (7, 34), Camillo Ugi (69 penalty).

6. 04.04.1909 **GERMANY - SWITZERLAND** **1-0(1-0)**
Exerzierplatz der KFV, Karlsruhe; Referee: Albert Sohn (Germany); Attendance: 7,000
GER: Eberhardt Illmer (1/0), Dr.Otto Nicodemus (1/0), Robert Neumaier (1/0), Karl Burger (1/0), Dr.Josef Glaser (Cap) (2/0), Arthur Hiller II (4/0), Hermann Schweikert (1/0), Fritz Förderer (3/2), Otto Löble (1/0), Eugen Kipp (3/1), Emil Oberle (1/0). Trainer: no.
Goal: Eugen Kipp (25).

7. 03.04.1910 **SWITZERLAND - GERMANY** **2-3(1-1)**
Landhof Stadion, Basel; Referee: Henry P. Devitte (Switzerland); Attendance: 5,000
GER: Hans Riso II (1/0), Walter Hempel (2/0), Paul Kühnle (1/0), Karl Burger (2/0), Wilhelm Trautmann (1/0), Paul Hunder (Cap) (3/0), Karl Wegele (1/0), Marius Hiller III (1/1), Otto Löble (2/0), Eugen Kipp (4/3), Ludwig Philipp (1/0). Trainer: no.
Goals: Marius Hiller III (8), Eugen Kipp (55, 85).

8. 24.04.1910 **NETHERLANDS - GERMANY** **4-2(2-2)**
Klaarenbeek Stadion, Arnheim; Referee: John T. Howcroft (England); Attendance: 10,000
GER: Christian Schmidt (Cap) (1/0), Walter Hempel (3/0), Ernst Hollstein (1/0), Ernst Poetsch (3/0), Max Breunig (1/0), Gustav Unfried (1/0), Karl Wegele (2/0), Adolf Gehrts (2/0), Willy Fick (1/1), Eugen Kipp (5/4), Ludwig Philipp (2/0). Trainer: no.
Goals: Eugen Kipp (23), Willy Fick (42).

9. 16.05.1910 **GERMANY - BELGIUM** **0-3(0-1)**
DSV-Platz, Duisburg; Referee: Herbert James Willing (Netherlands); Attendance: 8,000
GER: Robert Faas (1/0), Robert Neumaier (2/0), Alfred Berghausen (1/0), Camillo Ugi (3/1), Dr.Josef Glaser (Cap) (3/0), Lothar Budzinski (1/0), Max Gablonsky (1/0), Christian Schilling (1/0), Peco Bauwens (1/0) [55.Andreas Breynk (1/0)], Otto Reislant (1/0), Adalbert Bert (1/0). Trainer: no.

10. 16.10.1910 **GERMANY - NETHERLANDS** **1-2(0-1)**
VfB 1903 Platz, Kleve; Referee: Hubert Istace (Belgium); Attendance: 4,000
GER: Adolf Werner (3/0), Hermann Neiße (1/0), Robert Hense (1/0), Camillo Ugi (Cap) (4/1), Otto Bülte (1/0), Hans Weymar (4/0), Karl Hanssen (1/0), Christian Schilling (2/0), Willy Worpitzky (2/2), Josef Umbach (1/0), Richard Queck (2/1). Trainer: no.
Goal: Richard Queck (25).

11. 26.03.1911 **GERMANY - SWITZERLAND** **6-2(2-0)**
Kickers Platz, Degenloch, Stuttgart; Referee: Hubert Istace (Belgium); Attendance: 8,000
GER: Adolf Werner (4/0), Paul Kühnle (2/0), Ernst Hollstein (2/0), Karl Burger (3/0), Max Breunig (Cap) (2/1), Willy Krauß (1/0), Max Gablonsky (2/0), Fritz Förderer (4/4), Gottfried Fuchs (1/2), Eugen Kipp (6/5), Walter Fischer (1/0). Trainer: no.
Goals: Gottfried Fuchs (35), Max Breunig (43 penalty), Eugen Kipp (71), Fritz Förderer (78, 88), Gottfried Fuchs (90).

12. 14.04.1911 **GERMANY - ENGLAND** **2-2(0-1)**
Union Platz, Berlin; Referee: Herbert James Willing (Netherlands); Attendance: 10,000
GER: Adolf Werner (5/0), Hermann Neiße (2/0), Walter Hempel (4/0), Karl Burger (4/0), Camillo Ugi (Cap) (5/1), Paul Hunder (4/0), Karl Hanssen (2/0), Marius Hiller III (2/1), Willy Worpitzky (3/2), Eugen Kipp (7/5), Ernst Möller (1/2). Trainer: no.
Goals: Ernst Möller (48, 50).

13. 23.04.1911 **BELGIUM - GERMANY** **2-1(1-0)**
Stade Cointe, Liège; Referee: James R. Schumacher (England); Attendance: 3,000
GER: Adolf Werner (6/0), Hermann Neiße (3/0), Ernst Hollstein (3/0), Camillo Ugi (6/1), Max Breunig (Cap) (3/1), Karl Burger (5/0), Karl Hanssen (3/0), Fritz Förderer (5/5), Gottfried Fuchs (2/2), Otto Reiser (1/0), Walter Fischer (2/0). Trainer: no.
Goal: Fritz Förderer (50).

14. 18.06.1911 **SWEDEN - GERMANY** **2-4(2-2)**
Råsunda Idrottsplats, Stockholm; Referee: Charles Buchwald (Denmark); Attendance: 3,000
GER: Adolf Werner (7/0), Hermann Wiggers (1/0), Walter Hempel (5/0), Karl Burger (6/0), Camillo Ugi (Cap) (7/1), Paul Hunder (5/0), Otto Dumke (1/3), Rudolf Droz (1/0), Willy Worpitzky (4/2), Eugen Kipp (8/6), Ernst Möller (2/2). Trainer: no.
Goals: Otto Dumke (13, 44), Eugen Kipp (54), Otto Dumke (83).

15. 09.10.1911 **GERMANY - AUSTRIA** **1-2(1-1)**
Platz an der Hygiene-Ausstellung, Dresden; Referee: Herbert James Willing (Netherlands); Attendance: 7,500
GER: Adolf Werner (8/0), Helmut Röpnack (2/0), Walter Hempel (6/0), Karl Burger (7/0), Max Breunig (Cap) (4/1), Paul Hunder (6/0), Max Gablonsky (3/0), Marius Hiller III (3/1), Willy Worpitzky (5/3), Eugen Kipp (9/6), Ernst Möller (3/2). Trainer: no.
Goal: Willy Worpitzky (35).

16. 29.10.1911 **GERMANY - SWEDEN** **1-3(0-2)**
Hoheluft Stadion, Hamburg; Referee: Herbert James Willing (Netherlands); Attendance: 6,000
GER: Adolf Werner (9/0), Karl Burger (8/0), Walter Hempel (7/0), Walter Sorkale (1/0), Camillo Ugi (Cap) (8/1), Paul Hunder (7/0), Max Gablonsky (4/0), Otto Dumke (2/3), Adolf Jäger (3/1), Paul Kugler (1/0), Ernst Möller (4/3). Trainer: no.
Goal: Ernst Möller (80).

17. 17.12.1911 **GERMANY - HUNGARY** **1-4(0-2)**
MTV'79-Platz, München; Referee: Hugo Meisl (Austria); Attendance: 8,000
GER: Walter Borck (1/0), Walter Hempel (8/0), Theo Koenen (1/0), Camillo Ugi (Cap) (9/1), Willi Knesebeck (1/0), Paul Hunder (8/0), Karl Wegele (3/0), Fritz Förderer (6/5), Willy Worpitzky (6/4), Julius Hirsch (1/0), Otto Thiel (1/0). Trainer: no.
Goal: Willy Worpitzky (48).

18. 24.03.1912 **NETHERLANDS - GERMANY** **5-5(2-3)**
ZAC-Platz, Zwolle; Referee: John T. Howcroft (England); Attendance: 10,000
GER: Adolf Werner (10/0), Helmut Röpnack (3/0), Ernst Hollstein (4/0), Karl Burger (9/0), Max Breunig (Cap) (5/1), Wilhelm Gros (1/0), Karl Wegele (4/0), Fritz Förderer (7/5), Gottfried Fuchs (3/3), Julius Hirsch (2/4), Emil Oberle (2/0). Trainer: no.
Goals: Gottfried Fuchs (13), Julius Hirsch (14, 31, 75, 79).

19. 14.04.1912 **HUNGARY - GERMANY** **4-4(1-4)**
Üllői út, Budapest; Referee: Hugo Meisl (Austria); Attendance: 25,000
GER: Adolf Werner (11/0), Helmut Röpnack (4/0), Walter Hempel (9/0), Georg Krogmann (1/0), Camillo Ugi (10/1), Willy Krauß (2/0), Karl Wegele (5/0), Adolf Jäger (Cap) (4/2), Willy Worpitzky (7/5), Eugen Kipp (10/7), Ernst Möller (5/4). Trainer: no.
Goals: Ernst Möller (14), Eugen Kipp (17), Willy Worpitzky (25), Adolf Jäger (44).

20. 05.05.1912 **SWITZERLAND - GERMANY** **1-2(1-2)**
Espenmoos Stadion, St.Gallen; Referee: Henry P. Devitte (Switzerland); Attendance: 5,200
GER: Albert Weber (1/0), Walter Hempel (10/0), Robert Neumaier (3/0), Karl Burger (10/0), Dr.Josef Glaser (Cap) (4/0), Camillo Ugi (11/1), Karl Wegele (6/0), Heinrich Mechling (1/1), Otto Löble (3/0), Eugen Kipp (11/8), Emil Oberle (3/0). Trainer: no.
Goals: Eugen Kipp (6), Heinrich Mechling (9).

21. 29.06.1912 **AUSTRIA - GERMANY** **5-1(0-1)** 5th OG. 1st Round.
Råsunda Idrottsplats, Stockholm (Sweden); Referee: Herbert James Willing (Netherlands); Attendance: 2,000
GER: Albert Weber (2/0), Helmut Röpnack (5/0), Ernst Hollstein (5/0), Georg Krogmann (2/0), Max Breunig (Cap) (6/1), Hermann Bosch (1/0), Karl Wegele (7/0), Adolf Jäger (5/3), Willy Worpitzky (8/5), Eugen Kipp (12/8), Julius Hirsch (3/4). Trainer: no.
Goal: Adolf Jäger (35).

22. 01.07.1912 **GERMANY - RUSSIA** **16-0(7-0)** 5th OG.Consolation Tournament.
Råsunda Idrottsplats, Stockholm (Sweden); Referee: Christiaan Jacobus Groothoff (Netherlands); Attendance: 3,000
GER: Adolf Werner (12/0), Hans Reese (1/0), Walter Hempel (11/0), Karl Burger (11/1), Dr.Josef Glaser (5/0), Camillo Ugi (Cap) (12/1), Karl Uhle (1/0), Fritz Förderer (8/9), Gottfried Fuchs (4/13), Emil Oberle (4/1), Otto Thiel (2/0). Trainer: no.
Goals: Gottfried Fuchs (2), Fritz Förderer (6), Gottfried Fuchs (9, 21), Fritz Förderer (27), Gottfried Fuchs (28), Karl Burger (30), Gottfried Fuchs (34, 46, 51), Fritz Förderer (53), Gottfried Fuchs (55), Emil Oberle (58), Gottfried Fuchs (65), Fritz Förderer (66), Gottfried Fuchs (69).

23. 03.07.1912 **GERMANY - HUNGARY** **1-3(0-2)** 5th OG.Consolation Tournament.
Råsunda Idrottsplats, Stockholm (Sweden); Referee: Christiaan Jacobus Groothoff (Netherlands); Attendance: 2,000
GER: Adolf Werner (13/0), Helmut Röpnack (6/0), Ernst Hollstein (6/0), Georg Krogmann (3/0), Camillo Ugi (Cap) (13/1), Hermann Bosch (2/0), Karl Wegele (8/0), Fritz Förderer (9/10), Gottfried Fuchs (5/13), Julius Hirsch (4/4), Emil Oberle (5/1). Trainer: no.
Goal: Fritz Förderer (55).

24. 06.10.1912 **DENMARK - GERMANY** **3-1(1-0)**
Idrætsparken, København; Referee: Herbert James Willing (England); Attendance: 10,000
GER: Albert Weber (3/0), Ernst Möller (6/4), Kurt Diemer (1/0), Camillo Ugi (Cap) (14/1), Willi Knesebeck (2/0), Hermann Bosch (3/0), Karl Wegele (9/0), Adolf Jäger (6/4), Willy Worpitzky (9/5), Eugen Kipp (13/8), Karl Wolter (1/0). Trainer: no.
Goal: Adolf Jäger (87 penalty).

25. 17.11.1912 **GERMANY - NETHERLANDS** **2-3(1-1)**
Sportpark, Leipzig; Referee: Ede Herzog (Hungary); Attendance: 20,000
GER: Ludwig Hofmeister (1/0), Helmut Röpnack (7/0), Kurt Diemer (2/0), Camillo Ugi (15/1), Max Breunig (Cap) (7/1), Hermann Bosch (4/0), Karl Wegele (10/0), Fritz Förderer (10/10), Adolf Jäger (7/6), Eugen Kipp (14/8), Arthur Gaebelein (1/0). Trainer: no.
Goals: Adolf Jäger (27, 65).

26. 21.03.1913 **GERMANY - ENGLAND** **0-3(0-2)**
Viktoria Platz, Mariendorf, Berlin; Referee: Herbert James Willing (Netherlands); Attendance: 20,000
GER: Christian Schmidt (2/0), Kurt Diemer (3/0), Ernst Möller (7/4), Otto Völker (1/0), Eduard Pendorf „Edy“ (1/0), Otto Jungtow (1/0), Karl Wegele (11/0), Adolf Jäger (Cap) (8/6), Otto Löble (4/0), Eugen Kipp (15/8), Walter Fischer (3/0). Trainer: no.

27. 18.05.1913 **GERMANY - SWITZERLAND** **1-2(1-2)**
FFC-Platz an der Waldseestraße, Freiburg; Referee: Charles Barette (Belgium); Attendance: 10,000
GER: Christian Schmidt (3/0), Helmut Röpnack (8/0), Kurt Diemer (4/0), Hermann Bosch (5/0), Paul Kugler (2/0), Hans Schmidt (1/0), Karl Wegele (12/0), Heinrich Mechling (2/1), Fritz Fürst (1/0), Eugen Kipp (Cap) (16/9), Julius Hirsch (5/4). Trainer: no.
Goal: Eugen Kipp (43).

28. 26.10.1913 **GERMANY - DENMARK** **1-4(1-3)**
Hoheluft Stadion, Hamburg; Referee: Herbert James Willing (Netherlands); Attendance: 12,000
GER: Johannes Schneider (1/0), Helmut Röpnack (9/0), Ernst Möller (8/4), Eugen Kipp (17/9), Max Breunig (Cap) (8/1), Josef Schümmelfelder (1/0), Karl Wegele (13/0), Fritz Förderer (11/10), Adolf Jäger (9/7), Julius Hirsch (6/4), Walter Fischer (4/0). Trainer: no.
Goal: Adolf Jäger (44).

29. 23.11.1913 **BELGIUM - GERMANY** **6-2(4-0)**
Kielstadion, Antwerpen; Referee: Albert Hendrik Magdalus Meereum-Terwogt (Netherlands); Attendance: 6,500
GER: Johannes Schneider (2/0), Helmut Röpnack (Cap) (10/0), Ernst Möller (9/4), Eugen Kipp (18/9), Max Breunig (9/1), Josef Schümmelfelder (2/0), Karl Wegele (14/1), Adolf Jäger (10/7), Gottfried Fuchs (6/14), Julius Hirsch (7/4), Karl Zilgas (1/0). Trainer: no.
Goals: Karl Wegele (55), Gottfried Fuchs (58).

30. 05.05.1914 **NETHERLANDS - GERMANY** **4-4(1-0)**
Oude Stadion, Amsterdam; Referee: John T. Howcroft (England); Attendance: 18,000
GER: Ludwig Hofmeister (2/0), Dr.Willy Völker (1/0), Ernst Rokosch (1/0), Josef Schümmelfelder (3/0), Heinz Ludewig (1/0), Albert Bollmann (1/0), Karl Wegele (15/2), Adolf Jäger (Cap) (11/8), Otto Harder (1/1), Richard Queck (3/2), Walter Fischer (5/0). Trainer: no.
Goals: Richard Queck (49), Adolf Jäger (55), Otto Harder (66), Karl Wegele (90).

31. 27.06.1920 **SWITZERLAND - GERMANY** **4-1(3-0)**
Sportplatz Utogrund, Zürich; Referee: László Bálint (Hungary); Attendance: 8,000
GER: Heinrich Stuhlfauth (1/0), Adolf Höschle (1/0), Georg Schneider (1/0), Hans Schmidt (2/0), Hans Kalb (1/0), Carl Riegel (1/0), Georg Wunderlich (1/0), Otto Harder (2/1), Adolf Jäger (Cap) (12/9), Leonhard Seiderer (1/0), Karl Wolter (2/0). Trainer: no.
Goal: Adolf Jäger (79).

32. 26.09.1920 **AUSTRIA - GERMANY** **3-2(0-0)**
Simmeringer Sportplatz, Wien; Referee: Ákos Fehéry (Hungary); Attendance: 30,000
GER: Heinrich Stuhlfauth (2/0), Arthur Mohns (1/0), Hans Lohneis (1/0), Hans Hagen (1/0), Karl Tewes (1/0), Carl Riegel (2/0), Georg Wunderlich (2/0), Otto Harder (3/1), Adolf Jäger (Cap) (13/9), Leonhard Seiderer (2/1), Hans Sutor (1/1). Trainer: no.
Goals: Hans Sutor (56), Leonhard Seiderer (87).

33. 24.10.1920 **GERMANY - HUNGARY** **1-0(1-0)**
Grünewaldstadion, Berlin; Referee: Jacques Hirrle (Switzerland); Attendance: 55,000
GER: Theodor Lohrmann (1/0), Georg Schneider (2/0), Arthur Mohns (2/0), Walter Krause (1/0), Karl Tewes (2/0), Carl Riegel (3/0), Leo Fiederer (1/0), Otto Harder (4/1), Adolf Jäger (Cap) (14/10), Luitpold Popp (1/0), Paul Forell (1/0). Trainer: no.
Goal: Adolf Jäger (7 penalty).

34. 05.05.1921 **GERMANY - AUSTRIA** **3-3(2-1)**
Dresdner Fußballring Stadion, Dresden; Referee: Willem Eymers (Netherlands); Attendance: 20,000
GER: Heinrich Stuhlfauth (3/0), Arthur Mohns (3/0), Walter Fritzsche (1/0), Carl Riegel (4/0), Karl Tewes (Cap) (3/0), Josef Schümmelfelder (4/0), Georg Wunderlich (3/0), Luitpold Popp (2/1), Leonhard Seiderer (3/2), Heinrich Träg (1/1), Hans Sutor (2/1). Trainer: no.
Goals: Luitpold Popp (7), Heinrich Träg (14), Leonhard Seiderer (58).

35. 05.06.1921 **HUNGARY - GERMANY** **3-0(2-0)**
Hungária út, Budapest; Referee: Heinrich Retschury (Austria); Attendance: 30,000
GER: Heinrich Stuhlfauth (4/0), Georg Schneider (3/0), Henry Müller (1/0), Arthur Marohn (1/0), Karl Tewes (4/0), Josef Schümmelfelder (5/0), Karl Höger (1/0), Fritz Schnürle (1/0), Adolf Jäger (Cap) (15/10), Emil Gröner (1/0), Anton Kreß (1/0). Trainer: no.

36. 18.09.1921 **FINLAND - GERMANY** **3-3(2-1)**
Töölön Pallokenttä, Helsinki; Referee: Ernst Albihn (Sweden); Attendance: 8,000
GER: Willy Schwedler (1/0), Arthur Mohns (4/0), Josef Müller (1/0), Alfred Au (1/0), Karl Tewes (Cap) (5/0), Walter Krause (2/0), Karl Höger (2/0), Josef Herberger (1/2), Hans Kalb (2/1), Willy Hutter (1/0), Karl Wolter (3/0). Trainer: no.
Goals: Josef Herberger (5), Hans Kalb (7), Josef Herberger (66).

37. 26.03.1922 **GERMANY - SWITZERLAND** **2-2(2-0)**
Waldstadion, Frankfurt am Main; Referee: Wolf Boas (Netherlands); Attendance: 35,000
GER: Theodor Lohrmann (2/0), Georg Wellhöfer (1/0), Josef Müller (2/0), Hans Lang (1/0), Eduard Pendorf „Edy" (2/0), Hans Hagen (2/0), Fritz Retter (1/0), Andreas Franz (1/1), Leonhard Seiderer (Cap) (4/3), Willy Hutter (2/0), Heinrich Altvater (1/0). Trainer: no.
Goals: Andreas Franz (26), Leonhard Seiderer (34).

38. 23.04.1922 **AUSTRIA - GERMANY** **0-2(0-0)**
Hohe Warte, Wien; Referee: György Gerő (Hungary); Attendance: 50,100
GER: Paul Mauch (1/0), Eduard Pendorf „Edy" (3/0), Henry Müller (2/0), Fritz Wetzel (1/0), Hans Kalb (3/1), Carl Riegel (5/0), Wolfgang Strobel (1/0), Viktor Weißenbacher (1/1), Adolf Jäger (Cap) (16/11), Heinrich Träg (2/1), Hans Sutor (3/1). Trainer: no.
Goals: Viktor Weißenbacher (69), Adolf Jäger (77).

39. 02.07.1922 **GERMANY - HUNGARY** **0-0**
Stadion an der Castroper Straße, Bochum; Referee: Heinrich Retschury (Austria); Attendance: 35,000
GER: Theodor Lohrmann (3/0), Henry Müller (3/0), Arthur Mohns (5/0), Karl Flink (1/0), Karl Tewes (6/0), Hans Schmidt (3/0), Wolfgang Strobel (2/0), Andreas Franz (2/1), Adolf Jäger (Cap) (17/11), Heinrich Träg (3/1), Franz Esser (1/0). Trainer: no.

40. 01.01.1923 **ITALY - GERMANY** **3-1(0-1)**
Campo di viale Lombardia, Milano; Referee: Eugène Stutz (Switzerland); Attendance: 25,000
GER: Heinrich Stuhlfauth (5/0), Anton Kugler (1/0), Josef Müller (3/0), Hans Hagen (3/0), Hans Lang (2/0), Hans Schmidt (4/0), Georg Wunderlich (4/0), Andreas Franz (3/1), Leonhard Seiderer (5/4), Heinrich Träg (Cap) (4/1), Hans Sutor (4/1). Trainer: no.
Goal: Leonhard Seiderer (72).

41. 13.05.1923 **GERMANY - NETHERLANDS** **0-0**
Hoheluft Stadion, Hamburg; Referee: Arthur Björklund (Sweden); Attendance: 28,000
GER: Dr. Karl Zörner (1/0), Walter Risse (1/0), Henry Müller (4/0), Erich Pohl (1/0), Ernst Eikhof (1/0), Walter Krause (3/0), Georg Wunderlich (Cap) (5/0), Josef Lüke (1/0), Carl Hartmann (1/0), Walter Claus-Oehler (1/0), Helmut Maneval (1/0). Trainer: no.

42. 03.06.1923 **SWITZERLAND - GERMANY** **1-2(0-1)**
Schützenmatte Stadion, Basel; Referee: Giovanni Mauro (Italy); Attendance: 17,000
GER: Dr. Karl Zörner (2/0), Walter Risse (2/0), Henry Müller (5/0), Hans Schmidt (5/0), Ernst Eikhof (2/0), Carl Riegel (Cap) (6/0), Otto Montag (1/0), Hans Sobeck (1/0), Carl Hartmann (2/2), Ludwig Wieder (1/0), Hans Sutor (5/1). Trainer: no.
Goals: Carl Hartmann (3, 71).

43. 29.06.1923 **SWEDEN - GERMANY** **2-1(1-0)**
Råsunda Idrottsplats, Stockholm; Referee: Ragnvald Smedvik (Norway); Attendance: 16,000
GER: Dr. Karl Zörner (3/0), Walter Risse (3/0), Henry Müller (6/0), Hans Hagen (4/0), Luitpold Popp (3/1), Carl Riegel (7/0), Otto Montag (2/0), Andreas Franz (4/1), Leonhard Seiderer (Cap) (6/5), Ludwig Wieder (2/0), Hans Sutor (6/1). Trainer: no.
Goal: Leonhard Seiderer (38).

44. 12.08.1923 **GERMANY - FINLAND** **1-2(0-0)**
Dresdner Kampfbahn, Dresden; Referee: Johannes Mutters (Netherlands); Attendance: 25,000
GER: Dr. Karl Zörner (4/0), Walter Risse (4/0), Henry Müller (7/0), Walter Krause (4/0), Ernst Eikhof (Cap) (3/0), Erich Pohl (2/0), Rudolf Leip (1/0), Josef Lüke (2/0), Carl Hartmann (3/2), Walter Claus-Oehler (2/1), Hans Sutor (7/1). Trainer: no.
Goal: Walter Claus-Oehler (31).

45. 04.11.1923 **GERMANY - NORWAY** **1-0(1-0)**
Hoheluft Stadion, Hamburg; Referee: Theodorus van Zwieteren (Netherlands); Attendance: 20,000
GER: Heinrich Stuhlfauth (Cap) (6/0), Walter Risse (5/0), Fritz Bache (1/0), Hans Schmidt (6/0), Hans Kalb (4/1), Walter Krause (5/0), Rudolf Leip (2/0), Martin Reißmann (1/0), Otto Harder (5/2), Ludwig Wieder (3/0), Hans Sutor (8/1). Trainer: no.
Goal: Otto Harder (22).

46. 13.01.1924 **GERMANY - AUSTRIA** **4-3(3-0)**
Stadion im Stadion im Zerzabelshof, Nürnberg; Referee: E.Hebak (Czechoslovakia); Attendance: 20,000
GER: Heinrich Stuhlfauth (7/0), Anton Kugler (2/0), Josef Müller (4/0), Hans Hagen (5/0), Hans Kalb (5/1), Hans Schmidt (7/0), Karl Auer (1/1), Andreas Franz (5/4), Leonhard Seiderer (Cap) (7/5), Ludwig Wieder (4/0), Hans Sutor (9/1). Trainer: no.
Goals: Karl Auer (24), Andreas Franz (35, 42 penalty, 72).

47. 21.04.1924 **NETHERLANDS - GERMANY** **0-1(0-0)**
Oude Stadion, Amsterdam; Referee: Felix Herren (Switzerland); Attendance: 26,000
GER: Heinrich Stuhlfauth (8/0), Josef Müller (5/0), Anton Kugler (3/0), Hans Hagen (6/0), Hans Kalb (6/1), Hans Schmidt (8/0), Karl Auer (2/2), Andreas Franz (6/4), Leonhard Seiderer (Cap) (8/5), Heinrich Träg (5/1), Willy Ascherl (1/0). Trainer: no.
Goal: Karl Auer (14).

48. 15.06.1924 **NORWAY - GERMANY** **0-2(0-2)**
Gressbanen ved Holmen i Aker, Kristiania; Referee: Arthur Björklund (Sweden); Attendance: 6,000
GER: Heinrich Stuhlfauth (Cap) (9/0), Walter Risse (6/0), Anton Kugler (4/0), Hans Lang (3/0), Hans Kalb (7/1), Hans Schmidt (9/0), Wolfgang Strobel (3/0), Georg Hochgesang (1/0), Otto Harder (6/2), Ludwig Wieder (5/1), Hans Sutor (10/2) [68.Walter Krause (6/0)]. Trainer: no.
Goals: Hans Sutor (18), Ludwig Wieder (36).

49. 31.08.1924 **GERMANY - SWEDEN** **1-4(1-1)**
Grünewaldstadion, Berlin; Referee: Felix Herren (Switzerland); Attendance: 20,000
GER: Werner Kuhnt (1/0), Walter Risse (7/0), Fritz Bache (2/0), Albert Eschenlohr (1/0), Hermann Lux (1/0), Hans Lang (4/0), Rudolf Leip (3/0), Carl Hartmann (4/2), Otto Harder (Cap) (7/3), Willi Kirsei (1/0), Paul Paulsen (1/0) [72.Georg Schumann (1/0)]. Trainer: no.
Goal: Otto Harder (28).

50. 21.09.1924 **HUNGARY - GERMANY** **4-1(2-0)**
Üllői út, Budapest; Referee: Heinrich Retschury (Austria); Attendance: 35,000
GER: Heinrich Stuhlfauth (10/0), Luitpold Popp (4/1), Gustav Roller (1/0), Hans Lang (5/0), Hans Kalb (8/1), Hans Schmidt (10/0), Wolfgang Strobel (4/0), Georg Hochgesang (2/0), Otto Harder (Cap) (8/4), Ernst Bantle (1/0), Hans Sutor (11/2). Trainer: no.
Goal: Otto Harder (56).

51. 23.11.1924 **GERMANY - ITALY** **0-1(0-1)**
Wedaustadion, Duisburg; Referee: Theodorus van Zwieteren (Netherlands); Attendance: 45,000
GER: Heinrich Stuhlfauth (11/0), Josef Müller (6/0), Anton Kugler (5/0) [78.Henry Müller (8/0)], Hans Hagen (7/0), Hans Kalb (9/1), Hans Schmidt (Cap) (11/0), Karl Höger (3/0), Hans Fleischmann (1/0), Josef Herberger (2/2) [67.Andreas Franz (7/4)], Kurt Meißner (1/0), Paul Paulsen (2/0). Trainer: no.

52. 14.12.1924 **GERMANY - SWITZERLAND** **1-1(0-1)**
Platz des Stuttgarter SC, Stuttgart; Referee: Johannes Mutters (Netherlands); Attendance: 25,000
GER: Heinrich Stuhlfauth (12/0), Albert Beier (1/0), Josef Müller (7/0), Hans Hagen (8/0), Hans Kalb (10/1), Hans Schmidt (12/0), Karl Höger (4/0), Andreas Franz (8/4), Adolf Jäger (Cap) (18/11), Otto Harder (9/5), Paul Paulsen (3/0). Trainer: no.
Goal: Otto Harder (71).

53. 29.03.1925 **NETHERLANDS - GERMANY** **2-1(1-0)**
Oude Stadion, Amsterdam; Referee: Felix Herren (Switzerland); Attendance: 30,000
GER: Karl Zolper (1/0), Albert Beier (2/0), Josef Müller (8/0), Hans Lang (6/0), Hermann Lux (2/0), Hans Hagen (9/0), Kurt Voß (1/1), Hans Sobeck (2/0), Josef Herberger (3/2), Otto Harder (Cap) (10/5), Paul Paulsen (4/0). Trainer: no.
Goal: Kurt Voß (78).

54. 21.06.1925 **SWEDEN - GERMANY** **1-0(1-0)**
Råsunda Idrottsplats, Stockholm; Referee: Lauritz Andersen (Denmark); Attendance: 10,000
GER: Georg Ertl (1/0), Albert Beier (3/0) [22.August Werner (1/0)], Emil Kutterer (1/0), Hans Lang (Cap) (7/0), Max Niederbacher (1/0), Otto Martwig (1/0), Hans Ruch (1/0), Otto Montag (3/0), Karl Schulz I (1/0), Oskar Ritter (1/0), Paul Paulsen (5/0). Trainer: no.

55. 26.06.1925 **FINLAND - GERMANY** **3-5(0-1)**
Töölön Pallokenttä, Helsinki; Referee: Simon Benzer (Sweden); Attendance: 3,500
GER: Georg Ertl (2/0), August Werner (2/0), Emil Kutterer (2/0), Hans Lang (8/0), Hermann Lux (3/0), Otto Martwig (2/0), Kurt Voß (2/2), Otto Montag (4/0), Karl Schulz I (2/0), Paul Paulsen (Cap) (6/3), Hans Ruch (2/1). Trainer: no.
Goals: Paul Paulsen (52, 71), Hans Ruch (75 penalty), Paul Paulsen (79), Kurt Voß (87).

56. 25.10.1925 **SWITZERLAND - GERMANY** **0-4(0-2)**
Rankhof Stadion, Basel; Referee: Eugen Braun (Austria); Attendance: 12,000
GER: Georg Ertl (3/0), Josef Müller (9/0), Emil Kutterer (3/0), Hans Lang (9/0), Georg Köhler (1/0), Hans Schmidt (13/0), Otto Martwig (3/0), Andreas Franz (9/4), Otto Harder (Cap) (11/8), Georg Hochgesang (3/1), Hans Sutor (12/2). Trainer: no.
Goals: Otto Harder (7, 42, 52), Georg Hochgesang (76).

57. 18.04.1926 **GERMANY - NETHERLANDS** **4-2(2-1)**
Rheinstadion, Düsseldorf; Referee: Lauritz Andersen (Denmark); Attendance: 70,000
GER: Georg Ertl (4/0), Josef Müller (10/0), Emil Kutterer (4/0), Ernst Nagelschmitz (1/0), Georg Köhler (2/0), Hans Lang (10/0), Hans Schröder (1/0), Richard Gedlich (1/0), Otto Harder (Cap) (12/9), Josef Pöttinger (1/3), Ludwig Hofmann (1/0). Trainer: no.
Goals: Josef Pöttinger (17, 43), Otto Harder (79), Josef Pöttinger (85).

58. 20.06.1926 **GERMANY - SWEDEN** **3-3(3-2)**
Stadion im Zerzabelshof, Nürnberg; Referee: Lauritz Andersen (Denmark); Attendance: 25,000
GER: Heinrich Stuhlfauth (13/0), Luitpold Popp (5/1), Emil Kutterer (5/0), Otto Martwig (4/0), Georg Köhler (3/0), Hans Schmidt (14/0), Karl Auer (3/2), Andreas Franz (10/4), Otto Harder (Cap) (13/12), Josef Pöttinger (2/3), Ludwig Hofmann (2/0). Trainer: no.
Goals: Otto Harder (21, 35, 43).

59. 31.10.1926 **NETHERLANDS - GERMANY** **2-3(1-2)**
Oude Stadion, Amsterdam; Referee: Albert J. Prince-Cox (England); Attendance: 30,000
GER: Georg Ertl (5/0), Josef Müller (11/0), Emil Kutterer (6/0), Otto Martwig (5/0) [70.Hans Geiger (1/0)], Hans Kalb (11/1), Hans Schmidt (15/0), Karl Scherm (1/0), Georg Hochgesang (4/1), Otto Harder (Cap) (14/14), Ludwig Wieder (6/2), Heinrich Träg (6/1). Trainer: Prof. Dr. Otto Nerz (1).
Goals: Ludwig Wieder (32), Otto Harder (43, 85).

60. 12.12.1926 **GERMANY - SWITZERLAND** **2-3(1-2)**
Grünwalder, München; Referee: Johannes Mutters (Netherlands); Attendance: 40,000
GER: Georg Ertl (6/0), Albert Beier (4/0), Emil Kutterer (7/0), Hans Geiger (2/0), Georg Köhler (4/0), Hans Schmidt (16/0), Karl Scherm (2/1), Georg Hochgesang (5/2), Otto Harder (Cap) (15/14), Eduard Wolpers (1/0), Ludwig Hofmann (3/0). Trainer: Prof. Dr. Otto Nerz (2).
Goals: Georg Hochgesang (44), Karl Scherm (50).

61. 02.10.1927 **DENMARK - GERMANY** **3-1(1-1)**
Idrætsparken, København; Referee: Ragnvald Smedvik (Norway); Attendance: 19,000
GER: Georg Ertl (7/0), Hans Brunke (1/0), Eugen Kling (1/0), Hugo Mantel (1/0), Ludwig Leinberger (1/0), Ernst Blum (Cap) (1/0), Martin Haftmann (1/0), Richard Hofmann (1/0), Richard Gedlich (2/0), Georg Frank (1/0), Georg Kießling (1/1). Trainer: Prof. Dr. Otto Nerz (3).
Goal: Georg Kießling (42).

62. 23.10.1927 **GERMANY - NORWAY** **6-2(0-2)**
Altonaer Stadion, Altona, Hamburg; Referee: Lauritz Andersen (Denmark); Attendance: 30,000
GER: Heinrich Stuhlfauth (14/0), Hans Brunke (2/0), Anton Kugler (6/0), Emil Köpplinger (1/0), Hans Kalb (Cap) (12/2), Otto Martwig (6/0), Baptist Reinmann (1/0), Georg Hochgesang (6/4), Josef Pöttinger (3/5), Richard Hofmann (2/0), Ludwig Hofmann (4/1). Trainer: Prof. Dr. Otto Nerz (4).
Goals: Georg Hochgesang (55), Josef Pöttinger (67, 69), Hans Kalb (73), Ludwig Hofmann (82), Georg Hochgesang (88).

63. 20.11.1927 **GERMANY - NETHERLANDS** **2-2(0-1)**
Müngersdorferstadion, Köln; Referee: Albert J. Prince-Cox (England); Attendance: 60,000
GER: Heinrich Stuhlfauth (15/0), Wilhelm Falk (1/0), Anton Kugler (7/0), Josef Weber (1/0), Hans Kalb (Cap) (13/2), Conrad Heidkamp (1/0), Baptist Reinmann (2/0), Richard Hofmann (3/0), Josef Pöttinger (4/7), Ernst Kuzorra (1/0), Ludwig Hofmann (5/1). Trainer: Prof. Dr. Otto Nerz (5).
Goals: Josef Pöttinger (46, 70).

64. 15.04.1928 **SWITZERLAND - GERMANY** **2-3(0-1)**
Neufeld Stadion, Bern; Referee: Stanley Frederick Rous (England); Attendance: 16,000
GER: Hans Wentorf (1/0), Josef Müller (Cap) (12/0), Emil Kutterer (8/0), Georg Knöpfle (1/0), Ludwig Leinberger (2/0), Rudolf Berthold (1/0), Ernst Albrecht (1/1), Josef Hornauer (1/1), Josef Pöttinger (5/7), Richard Hofmann (4/1), Ludwig Hofmann (6/1). Trainer: Prof. Dr. Otto Nerz (6).
Goals: Richard Hofmann (18), Josef Hornauer (47), Ernst Albrecht (61).

65. 28.05.1928 **GERMANY - SWITZERLAND** **4-0(2-0)** 9th OG. 2nd Round.
Olympisch Stadion, Amsterdam (Netherlands); Referee: Willem Eymers (Netherlands); Attendance: 16,158
GER: Heinrich Stuhlfauth (16/0), Albert Beier (5/0), Heinrich Weber (1/0), Georg Knöpfle (2/0), Hans Kalb (Cap) (14/2), Ludwig Leinberger (3/0), Ernst Albrecht (2/1), Josef Hornauer (2/2), Josef Pöttinger (6/7), Richard Hofmann (5/4), Ludwig Hofmann (7/1). Trainer: Prof. Dr. Otto Nerz (7).
Goals: Richard Hofmann (17), Josef Hornauer (42), Richard Hofmann (75, 85).

66. 03.06.1928 **URUGUAY - GERMANY** **4-1(2-0)** 9th OG. 3rd Round.
Olympisch Stadion, Amsterdam (Netherlands); Referee: Youssuf Mohammad (Egypt); Attendance: 25,131
GER: Heinrich Stuhlfauth (17/0), Albert Beier (6/0), Heinrich Weber (2/0), Georg Knöpfle (3/0), Hans Kalb (Cap) (15/2), Ludwig Leinberger (4/0), Ernst Albrecht (3/1), Josef Hornauer (3/2), Josef Pöttinger (7/7), Richard Hofmann (6/5), Ludwig Hofmann (8/1). Trainer: Prof. Dr. Otto Nerz (8).
Goal: Richard Hofmann (81).

67. 16.09.1928 **GERMANY - DENMARK** **2-1(0-1)**
Stadion im Zerzabelshof, Nürnberg; Referee: Paul Ruoff (Switzerland); Attendance: 50,000
GER: Hans Wentorf (2/0), Albert Beier (Cap) (7/0), Heinrich Weber (3/0), Georg Knöpfle (4/0), Ludwig Leinberger (5/0), Conrad Heidkamp (2/1), Baptist Reinmann (3/0), Franz Horn (1/0), Josef Schmitt (1/0), Josef Pöttinger (8/7), Ludwig Hofmann (9/2). Trainer: Prof. Dr. Otto Nerz (9).
Goals: Conrad Heidkamp (59), Ludwig Hofmann (68).

68. 23.09.1928 **NORWAY - GERMANY** **0-2(0-1)**
Ullevaal Stadion, Oslo; Referee: Lauritz Andersen (Denmark); Attendance: 16,400
GER: Heinrich Stuhlfauth (Cap) (18/0), Henry Müller (9/0), Walter Risse (8/0), Georg Knöpfle (5/0), Ludwig Leinberger (6/0), Conrad Heidkamp (3/1), Ernst Albrecht (4/1), Willi Winkler (1/0), Josef Schmitt (2/1), Ernst Kuzorra (2/1), Georg Kießling (2/1). Trainer: Prof. Dr. Otto Nerz (10).
Goals: Josef Schmitt (17), Ernst Kuzorra (62).

69. 30.09.1928 **SWEDEN - GERMANY** **2-0(1-0)**
Råsunda Idrottsplats, Stockholm; Referee: Sophus Hansen (Denmark); Attendance: 20,000
GER: Paul Gehlhaar (1/0), Albert Beier (Cap) (8/0), Heinrich Weber (4/0), Georg Knöpfle (6/0), Georg Köhler (5/0), Conrad Heidkamp (4/1), Ernst Albrecht (5/1), Hans Sobeck (3/0), Josef Pöttinger (9/7), Ernst Kuzorra (3/1), Ludwig Hofmann (10/2). Trainer: Prof. Dr. Otto Nerz (11).

70. 10.02.1929 **GERMANY - SWITZERLAND** **7-1(3-0)**
Mannheimer Stadion, Mannheim; Referee: Lauritz Andersen (Denmark); Attendance: 30,000
GER: Willibald Kreß (1/0), Franz Schütz (1/0), Heinrich Weber (5/0), Hans Geiger (3/0), Ludwig Leinberger (7/0), Georg Knöpfle (7/0), Baptist Reinmann (4/0), Hans Sobeck (4/2), Josef Pöttinger (Cap) (10/8), Georg Frank (2/4), Ludwig Hofmann (11/2). Trainer: Prof. Dr. Otto Nerz (12).
Goals: Georg Frank (8), Hans Sobeck (23), Georg Frank (45), Josef Pöttinger (57), Georg Frank (61, 72), Hans Sobeck (83).

71. 28.04.1929 **ITALY - GERMANY** **1-2(1-1)**
Stadio Via Filadelfia, Torino; Referee: H. E. Gray (England); Attendance: 30,000
GER: Heinrich Stuhlfauth (Cap) (19/0), Albert Beier (9/0), Heinrich Weber (6/0), Hans Geiger (4/0), Ludwig Leinberger (8/0), Georg Knöpfle (8/0), Ernst Albrecht (6/1), Josef Hornauer (4/3), Josef Pöttinger (11/8), Georg Frank (3/5), Ludwig Hofmann (12/2). Trainer: Prof. Dr. Otto Nerz (13).
Goals: Josef Hornauer (9), Georg Frank (78).

72. 01.06.1929 **GERMANY - SCOTLAND** **1-1(0-0)**
Grünewaldstadion, Berlin; Referee: Otto Ohlsson (Sweden); Attendance: 42,000
GER: Heinrich Stuhlfauth (Cap) (20/0), Franz Schütz (2/0), Hans Brunke (3/0), Hans Geiger (5/0), Hans Gruber (1/0), Conrad Heidkamp (5/1), Hans Ruch (3/2), Hans Sobeck (5/2), Josef Pöttinger (12/8), Richard Hofmann (7/5), Ludwig Hofmann (13/2). Trainer: Prof. Dr. Otto Nerz (14).
Goal: Hans Ruch (49).

73. 23.06.1929 **GERMANY - SWEDEN** **3-0(1-0)**
Müngersdorfer Stadion, Köln; Referee: Eugen Braun (Austria); Attendance: 52,000
GER: Willibald Kreß (2/0), Franz Schütz (3/0), Heinrich Weber (7/0), Hans Geiger (6/0), Ludwig Leinberger (9/0), Georg Knöpfle (9/0), Ernst Albrecht (7/1), Hans Sobeck (6/2), Franz Horn (2/0), Richard Hofmann (8/8), Ludwig Hofmann (Cap) (14/2). Trainer: Prof. Dr. Otto Nerz (15).
Goals: Richard Hofmann (27, 65, 85).

74. 20.10.1929 **GERMANY - FINLAND** **4-0(0-0)**
Altonaer Stadion, Altona, Hamburg; Referee: Bjarne H. Bech (Norway); Attendance: 30,000
GER: Wilhelm Blunk (1/0), Albert Beier (10/0), Hans Hagen (Cap) (10/0), Hermann Flick (1/0), Karl Schulz II (1/0), Willi Völker (1/0), Ernst Albrecht (8/1), Fritz Szepan (1/1), Franz Horn (3/0), Richard Hofmann (9/9), August Sackenheim (1/2). Trainer: Prof. Dr. Otto Nerz (16).
Goals: Fritz Szepan (52), August Sackenheim (61), Richard Hofmann (70), August Sackenheim (81).

75. 20.03.1930 **GERMANY - ITALY** **0-2(0-0)**
Waldstadion, Frankfurt am Main; Referee: Paul Ruoff (Switzerland); Attendance: 45,000
GER: Heinrich Stuhlfauth (Cap) (21/0), Hans Hagen (11/0), Heinrich Weber (8/0), Georg Knöpfle (10/0) [29.Hugo Mantel (2/0)], Ludwig Leinberger (10/0), Conrad Heidkamp (6/1), Ernst Albrecht (9/1), Fritz Szepan (2/1), Josef Pöttinger (13/8), Georg Frank (4/5), Ludwig Hofmann (15/2). Trainer: Prof. Dr. Otto Nerz (17).

76. 04.05.1930 **SWITZERLAND - GERMANY** **0-5(0-3)**
Hardturm Stadion, Zürich; Referee: Stanley Frederick Rous (England); Attendance: 25,000
GER: Willibald Kreß (3/0), Franz Schütz (4/0), Hans Stubb (1/0) [70.Hans Hagen (12/0)], Heinrich Hergert (1/0), Ludwig Leinberger (Cap) (11/0), Conrad Heidkamp (7/1), Josef Bergmaier (1/0), August Sackenheim (2/2), Ernst Kuzorra (4/4), Richard Hofmann (10/11), Alfred Huber (1/0). Trainer: Prof. Dr. Otto Nerz (18).
Goals: Richard Hofmann (8), Ernst Kuzorra (38), Richard Hofmann (40), Ernst Kuzorra (41, 76).

77. 10.05.1930 **GERMANY - ENGLAND** **3-3(1-2)**
Grünewaldstadion, Berlin; Referee: Johannes Mutters (Netherlands); Attendance: 60,000
GER: Willibald Kreß (4/0), Franz Schütz (5/0), Hans Stubb (2/0), Conrad Heidkamp (8/1), Ludwig Leinberger (12/0), Hugo Mantel (3/0), Josef Bergmaier (2/0), Josef Pöttinger (14/8), Ernst Kuzorra (5/4), Richard Hofmann (11/14), Ludwig Hofmann (Cap) (16/2). Trainer: Prof. Dr. Otto Nerz (19).
Goals: Richard Hofmann (21, 49, 60).

78. 07.09.1930 **DENMARK - GERMANY** **6-3(4-1)**
Idrætsparken, København; Referee: Carl Olsson (Sweden); Attendance: 20,000
GER: Ludwig Wenz (1/0), Hans Brunke (4/0), Hans Stubb (3/0), Heinrich Hergert (2/0), Reinhold Münzenberg (1/0), Hugo Mantel (4/0), Wilhelm Straßburger (1/0), Hans Sobeck (7/2), Karl Hohmann (1/1), Richard Hofmann (Cap) (12/15), Willi Kund (1/1). Trainer: Prof. Dr. Otto Nerz (20).
Goals: Richard Hofmann (26), Willi Kund (38), Karl Hohmann (69).

9. 28.09.1930 **GERMANY - HUNGARY** **5-3(0-3)**
tadion am Ostragehege, Dresden; Referee: Lauritz Andersen (Denmark); Attendance: 42,000
ER: Willibald Kreß (5/0), Franz Schütz (6/0), Theodor Burkhardt (1/0), Heinrich Hergert (3/0), Ludwig Leinberger (13/0), Conrad Heidkamp (9/1), Ernst lbrecht (10/1), Ludwig Lachner (1/1), Johann Ludwig (1/1), Richard Hofmann (Cap) (13/16), Ludwig Hofmann (17/4). Trainer: Prof. Dr. Otto Nerz (21).
oals: Richard Hofmann (59), Ludwig Hofmann (63), Johann Ludwig (72), Ludwig Lachner (77), Ludwig Hofmann (85).

0. 02.11.1930 **GERMANY - NORWAY** **1-1(0-0)**
chlesierkampfbahn im Sportpark, Breslau; Referee: Hans S. Boekmann (Netherlands); Attendance: 40,000
ER: Hans Jakob (1/0), Heinrich Weber (9/0), Hans Stubb (4/0), Erich Kauer (1/0), Reinhold Münzenberg (2/0), Josef Wendl (1/0), Ernst Albrecht (11/1), udwig Lachner (2/1), Karl Hohmann (2/1) [46.Richard Hanke (1/1)], Richard Hofmann (Cap) (14/16), Wilhelm Straßburger (2/0). Trainer: Prof. Dr. Otto erz (22).
oal: Richard Hanke (55).

1. 15.03.1931 **FRANCE - GERMANY** **1-0(1-0)**
tade Olympique „Yves du Manoir", Colombes, Paris; Referee: Thomas Crewe (England); Attendance: 40,076
ER: Willibald Kreß (6/0), Franz Schütz (7/0), Heinrich Weber (10/0), Reinhold Münzenberg (3/0), Ludwig Leinberger (14/0), Georg Knöpfle (11/0), Josef ergmaier (3/0), Sigmund Haringer (1/0), Heinrich Hergert (4/0), Richard Hofmann (Cap) (15/16), Ludwig Hofmann (18/4) [31.Hans Welker (1/0)]. Trainer: rof. Dr. Otto Nerz (23).

2. 26.04.1931 **NETHERLANDS - GERMANY** **1-1(1-0)**
lympisch Stadion, Amsterdam; Referee: Axel Bergqvist (Sweden); Attendance: 30,000
ER: Willibald Kreß (7/0), Erich Schröder (1/0), Heinrich Weber (Cap) (11/0), Kurt Stössel (1/0), Erich Kauer (2/0), Georg Knöpfle (12/0), Ernst Albrecht 12/1), Ludwig Lachner (3/1), Karl Schlösser (1/1), Richard Hofmann (16/16), Friedrich Müller (1/0). Trainer: Prof. Dr. Otto Nerz (24).
oal: Karl Schlösser (49).

3. 24.05.1931 **GERMANY - AUSTRIA** **0-6(0-3)**
runewaldstadion, Berlin; Referee: Otto Ohlsson (Sweden); Attendance: 40,000
ER: Paul Gehlhaar (2/0), Albert Beier (11/0), Heinrich Weber (Cap) (12/0), Georg Knöpfle (13/0), Reinhold Münzenberg (4/0), Ernst Müller (1/0), Josef ergmaier (4/0), Hans Sobeck (8/2), Karl Hohmann (3/1), Richard Hofmann (17/16), Friedrich Müller (2/0). Trainer: Prof. Dr. Otto Nerz (25).

4. 17.06.1931 **SWEDEN - GERMANY** **0-0**
åsunda Idrottsplats, Stockholm; Referee: John Langenus (Belgium); Attendance: 16,000
ER: Willibald Kreß (8/0), Heinz Emmerich (1/0), Hans Brunke (5/0), Erich Kauer (3/0), Ludwig Leinberger (Cap) (15/0), Georg Knöpfle (14/0), Josef ergmaier (5/0), Hans Sobeck (9/2), Johann Ludwig (2/1), Werner Widmayer (1/0), August Sackenheim (3/2). Trainer: Prof. Dr. Otto Nerz (26).

5. 21.06.1931 **NORWAY - GERMANY** **2-2(1-1)**
llevaal Stadion, Oslo; Referee: Ivan Eklind (Sweden); Attendance: 17,000
ER: Willibald Kreß (9/0), Heinz Emmerich (2/0), Hans Brunke (6/0), Erich Kauer (4/0), Ludwig Leinberger (Cap) (16/0), Georg Knöpfle (15/0), Josef ergmaier (6/1), Hans Sobeck (10/2), Johann Ludwig (3/2), Werner Widmayer (2/0), August Sackenheim (4/2). Trainer: Prof. Dr. Otto Nerz (27).
oals: Josef Bergmaier (1), Johann Ludwig (60).

6. 13.09.1931 **AUSTRIA - GERMANY** **5-0(2-0)**
raterstadion, Wien; Referee: Otto Ohlsson (Sweden); Attendance: 50,000
ER: Willibald Kreß (10/0), Heinz Emmerich (3/0), Hans Brunke (7/0), Erich Kauer (5/0), Ludwig Leinberger (Cap) (17/0), Georg Knöpfle (16/0), eonhard Weiß (1/0), Josef Hornauer (5/3), Ernst Kuzorra (6/4), Richard Hofmann (18/16), Willi Kund (2/1). Trainer: Prof. Dr. Otto Nerz (28).

7. 27.09.1931 **GERMANY - DENMARK** **4-2(3-2)**
indenburg Stadion, Hannover; Referee: Adolf Miess (Austria); Attendance: 30,000
ER: Willibald Kreß (11/0), Franz Schütz (8/0), Hans Stubb (5/0), Rudolf Gramlich (1/0), Ludwig Leinberger (Cap) (18/0), Georg Knöpfle (17/0), Hans ibulski (1/0), Fritz Szepan (3/1), Ernst Kuzorra (7/5), Richard Hofmann (19/19), Stanislaus Kobierski (1/0). Trainer: Prof. Dr. Otto Nerz (29).
oals: Ernst Kuzorra (18), Richard Hofmann (41, 44, 78).

8. 06.03.1932 **GERMANY - SWITZERLAND** **2-0(1-0)**
fB Stadion, Leipzig; Referee: Hans S. Boekmann (Netherlands); Attendance: 50,000
ER: Willibald Kreß (12/0), Franz Schütz (9/0), Hans Stubb (6/0), Rudolf Gramlich (2/0), Ludwig Leinberger (Cap) (19/0), Georg Knöpfle (18/0), Kurt angenbein (1/0), Oskar Rohr (1/0), Ernst Kuzorra (8/5), Richard Hofmann (20/21), Stanislaus Kobierski (2/0). Trainer: Prof. Dr. Otto Nerz (30).
oals: Richard Hofmann (40 penalty, 83).

9. 01.07.1932 **FINLAND - GERMANY** **1-4(1-1)**
öölön Pallokenttä, Helsinki; Referee: John Erik Andersson (Sweden); Attendance: 3,917
ER: Hans Jakob (2/0), Franz Schütz (10/0), Hans Stubb (7/0), Rudolf Gramlich (3/0), Ludwig Leinberger (Cap) (20/0), Georg Knöpfle (19/0), Erich ischer (1/0), Richard Hofmann (21/24), Willi Rutz (1/1), Ernst Kuzorra (9/5), Stanislaus Kobierski (3/0). Trainer: Prof. Dr. Otto Nerz (31).
oals: Richard Hofmann (5), Willi Rutz (77), Richard Hofmann (80, 81).

0. 25.09.1932 **GERMANY - SWEDEN** **4-3(3-1)**
tädtisches Stadion, Nürnberg; Referee: Rinaldo Barlassina (Italy); Attendance: 30,000
ER: Hans Jakob (3/0), Sigmund Haringer (2/0), Hans Stubb (8/0), Georg Knöpfle (20/0), Ludwig Leinberger (Cap) (21/0), Richard Oehm (1/0), Josef ergmaier (7/1), Franz Krumm (1/1), Oskar Rohr (2/2), Richard Hofmann (22/24), Stanislaus Kobierski (4/1). Trainer: Prof. Dr. Otto Nerz (32).
oals: Oskar Rohr (10), Stanislaus Kobierski (17), Franz Krumm (41), Oskar Rohr (64).

1. 30.10.1932 **HUNGARY - GERMANY** **2-1(1-0)**
ungária út, Budapest; Referee: Albino Carraro (Italy); Attendance: 15,000
ER: Hans Jakob (4/0), Lorenz Huber (1/0), Paul Janes (1/0), Josef Wendl (2/0), Ludwig Leinberger (Cap) (22/0) [31.Karl Joppich (1/0)], Georg Knöpfle 21/0), Ernst Albrecht (13/1), Ludwig Lachner (4/1), Richard Malik (1/1), Richard Hofmann (23/24), Stanislaus Kobierski (5/1). Trainer: Prof. Dr. Otto Nerz 33).
oal: Richard Malik (78).

92. 04.12.1932 **GERMANY - NETHERLANDS** **0-2(0-2)**
Rheinstadion, Düsseldorf; Referee: Otto Ohlssen (Sweden); Attendance: 42,000
GER: Fritz Buchloh (1/0), Franz Schütz (11/0), Hans Stubb (9/0), Carl-Heinz Mahlmann (1/0), Ludwig Leinberger (Cap) (23/0), Georg Knöpfle (22/0), Ernst Albrecht (14/1), Willi Wigold (1/0), Ernst Kuzorra (10/5), Richard Hofmann (24/24), Stanislaus Kobierski (6/1). Trainer: Prof. Dr. Otto Nerz (34).

93. 01.01.1933 **ITALY - GERMANY** **3-1(2-1)**
Stadio Littoriale, Bologna; Referee: Louis Baert (Belgium); Attendance: 30,000
GER: Hans Jakob (5/0) [55.Fritz Buchloh (2/0)], Sigmund Haringer (3/0), Josef Wendl (3/0), Rudolf Gramlich (4/0), Ludwig Leinberger (Cap) (24/0), Georg Knöpfle (23/0), Josef Bergmaier (8/1), Franz Krumm (2/1), Oskar Rohr (3/3), Richard Malik (2/1), Stanislaus Kobierski (7/1). Trainer: Prof. Dr. Otto Nerz (35).
Goal: Oskar Rohr (4).

94. 19.03.1933 **GERMANY - FRANCE** **3-3(2-1)**
Grünewaldstadion, Berlin; Referee: Thomas Crewe (England); Attendance: 55,000
GER: Hans Jakob (6/0), Sigmund Haringer (4/0), Josef Wendl (4/0), Rudolf Gramlich (5/0), Heinrich Hergert (Cap) (5/0), Hugo Mantel (5/0), Erich Fischer (2/0), Ludwig Lachner (5/2), Oskar Rohr (4/5), Willi Lindner (1/0) [40.Richard Hofmann (25/24)], Stanislaus Kobierski (8/1). Trainer: Prof. Dr. Otto Nerz (36).
Goals: Oskar Rohr (28, 45), Ludwig Lachner (65).

95. 22.10.1933 **GERMANY - BELGIUM** **8-1(2-0)**
Wedaustadion, Duisburg; Referee: Otto Ohlsson (Sweden); Attendance: 30,000
GER: Fritz Buchloh (3/0), Willy Busch (1/0), Eduard Hundt (1/0), Paul Janes (2/0), Jakob Bender (1/0), Theo Breuer (1/0), Ernst Albrecht (Cap) (15/2), Willi Wigold (2/2), Karl Hohmann (4/4), Josef Rasselnberg (1/1), Stanislaus Kobierski (9/2). Trainer: Prof. Dr. Otto Nerz (37).
Goals: Josef Rasselnberg (21), Willi Wigold (29, 53), Karl Hohmann (55), Ernst Albrecht (56), Karl Hohmann (57, 72), Stanislaus Kobierski (87).

96. 05.11.1933 **GERMANY - NORWAY** **2-2(2-0)**
Sportplatz am Gübser Damm, Magdeburg; Referee: Johannes Franciscus van Moorsel (Netherlands); Attendance: 40,000
GER: Fritz Buchloh (4/0), Eduard Hundt (2/0), Willy Busch (2/0), Paul Janes (3/0), Jakob Bender (2/0), Theo Breuer (2/0), Ernst Albrecht (Cap) (16/3), Willi Wigold (3/2), Karl Hohmann (5/5), Josef Rasselnberg (2/1), Stanislaus Kobierski (10/2). Trainer: Prof. Dr. Otto Nerz (38).
Goals: Ernst Albrecht (8), Karl Hohmann (33).

97. 19.11.1933 **SWITZERLAND - GERMANY** **0-2(0-0)**
Hardturm Stadion, Zürich; Referee: Rinaldo Barlassina (Italy); Attendance: 25,000
GER: Hans Jakob (7/0), Sigmund Haringer (5/0), Josef Wendl (5/0), Rudolf Gramlich (Cap) (6/0), Ludwig Goldbrunner (1/0), Fritz Eiberle (1/0), Ernst Lehner (1/0), Ludwig Lachner (6/3), Karl Hohmann (6/6), Josef Rasselnberg (3/1), Matthias Heidemann (1/0). Trainer: Prof. Dr. Otto Nerz (39).
Goals: Karl Hohmann (72), Ludwig Lachner (85).

98. 03.12.1933 **GERMANY - POLAND** **1-0(0-0)**
Poststadion, Berlin; Referee: Otto Ohlsson (Sweden); Attendance: 32,000
GER: Hans Jakob (8/0), Sigmund Haringer (6/0), Emil Krause (1/0), Paul Janes (4/0), Jakob Bender (3/0), Hans Appel (1/0), Ernst Lehner (2/0), Ludwig Lachner (7/3), Karl Hohmann (7/6), Josef Rasselnberg (4/2), Stanislaus Kobierski (Cap) (11/2). Trainer: Prof. Dr. Otto Nerz (40).
Goal: Josef Rasselnberg (89).

99. 14.01.1934 **GERMANY - HUNGARY** **3-1(1-1)**
Waldstadion, Frankfurt am Main; Referee: Louis Baert (Belgium); Attendance: 40,000
GER: Willibald Kreß (13/0), Sigmund Haringer (7/0) [30.Max Schäfer (1/0)], Hans Stubb (10/1), Rudolf Gramlich (Cap) (7/0), Ludwig Goldbrunner (2/0), Richard Oehm (2/0), Ernst Lehner (3/0), Ludwig Lachner (8/4), Edmund Conen (1/1), Rudolf Noack (1/0), Karl Politz (1/0). Trainer: Prof. Dr. Otto Nerz (41).
Goals: Ludwig Lachner (16), Hans Stubb (52), Edmund Conen (80).

100. 11.03.1934 **LUXEMBOURG - GERMANY** **1-9(1-5)** 2nd FIFA WC. Qualifiers
Stade Municipal, Luxembourg; Referee: Jan de Wolf (Netherlands); Attendance: 14,500
GER: Fritz Buchloh (5/0), Eduard Hundt (3/0), Sigmund Haringer (8/0), Paul Janes (5/0), Fritz Szepan (4/1), Richard Oehm (3/0), Ernst Albrecht (Cap) (17/4), Willi Wigold (4/3), Karl Hohmann (8/9), Josef Rasselnberg (5/6), Stanislaus Kobierski (12/2). Trainer: Prof. Dr. Otto Nerz (42).
Goals: Josef Rasselnberg (3), Willi Wigold (12), Ernst Albrecht (25), Karl Hohmann (30), Josef Rasselnberg (36), Karl Hohmann (51, 53), Josef Rasselnberg (56, 90).

101. 27.05.1934 **BELGIUM - GERMANY** **2-5(2-1)** 2nd FIFA WC. 1st Round.
Stadio „Giovanni Berta“, Firenze (Italy); Referee: Francesco Mattea (Italy); Attendance: 8,000
GER: Willibald Kreß (14/0), Sigmund Haringer (9/0), Hans Schwartz (1/0), Paul Janes (6/0), Fritz Szepan (Cap) (5/1), Paul Zielinski (1/0), Ernst Lehner (4/0), Karl Hohmann (9/9), Edmund Conen (2/4), Otto Siffling (1/1), Stanislaus Kobierski (13/3). Trainer: Prof. Dr. Otto Nerz (43).
Goals: Stanislaus Kobierski (25), Otto Siffling (49), Edmund Conen (66, 70, 87).

102. 31.05.1934 **GERMANY - SWEDEN** **2-1(0-0)** 2nd FIFA WC. Quarter-Finals.
Stadio „San Siro“, Milano (Italy); Referee: Rinaldo Barlassina (Italy); Attendance: 3,000
GER: Willibald Kreß (15/0), Sigmund Haringer (10/0), Willy Busch (3/0), Rudolf Gramlich (8/0), Fritz Szepan (Cap) (6/1), Paul Zielinski (2/0), Ernst Lehner (5/0), Karl Hohmann (10/11), Edmund Conen (3/4), Otto Siffling (2/1), Stanislaus Kobierski (14/3). Trainer: Prof. Dr. Otto Nerz (44).
Goals: Karl Hohmann (60, 63).

103. 03.06.1934 **CZECHOSLOVAKIA - GERMANY** **3-1(1-0)** 2nd FIFA WC. Semi-Finals.
Stadio Nazionale del PNF, Roma (Italy); Referee: Rinaldo Barlassina (Italy); Attendance: 10,000
GER: Willibald Kreß (16/0), Sigmund Haringer (11/0), Willy Busch (4/0), Paul Zielinski (3/0), Fritz Szepan (Cap) (7/1), Jakob Bender (4/0), Ernst Lehner (6/0), Otto Siffling (3/1), Edmund Conen (4/4), Rudolf Noack (2/1), Stanislaus Kobierski (15/3). Trainer: Prof. Dr. Otto Nerz (45).
Goal: Rudolf Noack (62).

04. 07.06.1934 **AUSTRIA - GERMANY** **2-3(1-2)** 2nd FIFA WC. Third Place Play-off.
tadio "Giorgio Ascarelli", Napoli (Italy); Referee: Albino Carraro (Italy); Attendance: 7,000
;ER: Hans Jakob (9/0), Paul Janes (7/0), Willy Busch (5/0), Paul Zielinski (4/0), Reinhold Münzenberg (5/0), Jakob Bender (5/0), Ernst Lehner (7/2), Otto iffling (4/1), Edmund Conen (5/5), Fritz Szepan (Cap) (8/1), Matthias Heidemann (2/0). Trainer: Prof. Dr. Otto Nerz (46).
;oals: Ernst Lehner (1), Edmund Conen (27), Ernst Lehner (42).

05. 09.09.1934 **POLAND - GERMANY** **2-5(1-1)**
tadion Wojska Polskiego, Warszawa; Referee: Otto Ohlsson (Sweden); Attendance: 34,000
;ER: Fritz Buchloh (6/0), Paul Janes (8/0), Willy Busch (6/0), Paul Zielinski (5/0), Reinhold Münzenberg (6/0), Jakob Bender (6/0), Ernst Lehner (8/4), Otto iffling (5/2), Karl Hohmann (11/12), Fritz Szepan (Cap) (9/2), Josef Fath (1/0). Trainer: Prof. Dr. Otto Nerz (47).
;oals: Ernst Lehner (15), Karl Hohmann (77), Otto Siffling (78), Ernst Lehner (80,penalty), Fritz Szepan (83).

06. 07.10.1934 **DENMARK - GERMANY** **2-5(0-1)**
ḍrætsparken, København; Referee: Ragnar Bäckström (Sweden); Attendance: 30,000
;ER: Fritz Buchloh (7/0), Paul Janes (9/0), Hans Schwartz (2/0), Rudolf Gramlich (9/0), Reinhold Münzenberg (7/0), Paul Zielinski (6/0), Ernst Lehner 9/4), Karl Hohmann (12/13), Otto Rohwedder (1/1), Fritz Szepan (Cap) (10/2), Josef Fath (2/3). Trainer: Prof. Dr. Otto Nerz (48).
;oals: Josef Fath (45, 60), Otto Rohwedder (63), Karl Hohmann (86), Josef Fath (88).

07. 27.01.1935 **GERMANY - SWITZERLAND** **4-0(2-0)**
Adolf Hitler" Kampfbahn, Stuttgart; Referee: Lucien Leclercq (France); Attendance: 60,000
;ER: Fritz Buchloh (8/0), Erwin Stührk (1/0), Willy Busch (7/0), Rudolf Gramlich (10/0), Ludwig Goldbrunner (Cap) (3/0), Hans Appel (2/0), Ernst Lehner 10/5), Otto Siffling (6/2), Edmund Conen (6/8), Otto Rohwedder (2/1), Stanislaus Kobierski (16/3). Trainer: Prof. Dr. Otto Nerz (49).
;oals: Edmund Conen (29, 42, 50), Ernst Lehner (73).

08. 17.02.1935 **NETHERLANDS - GERMANY** **2-3(0-2)**
)lympisch Stadion, Amsterdam; Referee: Otto Ohlsson (Sweden); Attendance: 31,000
;ER: Fritz Buchloh (9/0), Erwin Stührk (2/0), Willy Busch (8/0), Rudolf Gramlich (Cap) (11/0), Reinhold Münzenberg (8/0), Paul Zielinski (7/0) [25.Paul anes (10/0)], Ernst Lehner (11/5), Karl Hohmann (13/14), Edmund Conen (7/9), Otto Rohwedder (3/1), Stanislaus Kobierski (17/4). Trainer: Prof. Dr. Otto lerz (50).
;oals: Edmund Conen (2), Stanislaus Kobierski (9), Karl Hohmann (83).

09. 17.03.1935 **FRANCE - GERMANY** **1-3(0-1)**
tade Parc des Princes, Paris; Referee: Louis Baert (Belgium); Attendance: 39,046
;ER: Hans Jakob (10/0), Paul Janes (11/0), Willy Busch (9/0), Rudolf Gramlich (Cap) (12/0), Reinhold Münzenberg (9/0), Paul Zielinski (8/0), Ernst Lehner 12/6), Karl Hohmann (14/15), Edmund Conen (8/9), Otto Siffling (7/2), Stanislaus Kobierski (18/5). Trainer: Prof. Dr. Otto Nerz (51).
;oals: Ernst Lehner (36), Stanislaus Kobierski (51), Karl Hohmann (88).

10. 28.04.1935 **BELGIUM - GERMANY** **1-6(1-2)**
tade de Jubilé, Bruxelles; Referee: Johannes Franciscus van Moorsel (Netherlands); Attendance: 35,000
;ER: Hans Jakob (11/0), Andreas Munkert (1/0), Willy Busch (10/0), Rudolf Gramlich (Cap) (13/0), Ludwig Goldbrunner (4/0), Werner Schulz (1/0), Ernst ehner (13/6), Otto Siffling (8/2), August Lenz (1/2), Ludwig Damminger (1/2), Josef Fath (3/5). Trainer: Prof. Dr. Otto Nerz (52).
;oals: Josef Fath (2), August Lenz (32, 67), Ludwig Damminger (72), Josef Fath (75), Ludwig Damminger (85).

11. 08.05.1935 **GERMANY - REPUBLIC OF IRELAND** **3-1(1-1)**
tadion Rote Erde, Dortmund; Referee: Gustav Krist (Czechoslovakia); Attendance: 35,000
;ER: Fritz Buchloh (Cap) (10/0), Paul Janes (12/0), Willi Tiefel (1/0), Paul Zielinski (9/0), Ludwig Goldbrunner (5/0), Jakob Bender (7/0), Ernst Lehner 14/7), Otto Siffling (9/2), August Lenz (2/2), Ludwig Damminger (2/4), Josef Fath (4/5). Trainer: Prof. Dr. Otto Nerz (53).
;oals: Ludwig Damminger (32, 47), Ernst Lehner (88).

12. 12.05.1935 **GERMANY - SPAIN** **1-2(1-2)**
Iüngersdorfer Stadion, Köln; Referee: John Langenus (Belgium); Attendance: 74,000
;ER: Fritz Buchloh (11/0), Paul Janes (13/0), Willy Busch (11/0), Rudolf Gramlich (Cap) (14/0), Reinhold Münzenberg (10/0), Jakob Bender (8/0), Ernst ehner (15/7), Karl Hohmann (15/15), Edmund Conen (9/10), Josef Rasselnberg (6/6), Josef Fath (5/5). Trainer: Prof. Dr. Otto Nerz (54).
;oal: Edmund Conen (11).

13. 26.05.1935 **GERMANY - CZECHOSLOVAKIA** **2-1(1-0)**
tadion am Ostragehege, Dresden; Referee: John Langenus (Belgium); Attendance: 60,000
;ER: Hans Jakob (12/0), Paul Janes (14/0), Willi Tiefel (2/0), Rudolf Gramlich (Cap) (15/0), Ludwig Goldbrunner (6/0), Paul Zielinski (10/0), Ernst Lehner 16/7), August Lenz (3/4), Edmund Conen (10/10), Otto Siffling (10/2), Josef Fath (6/5). Trainer: Prof. Dr. Otto Nerz (55).
;oals: August Lenz (12, 53).

14. 27.06.1935 **NORWAY - GERMANY** **1-1(0-0)**
Jllevaal Stadion, Oslo; Referee: Sölve Flisberg (Sweden); Attendance: 17,000
;ER: Hans Jakob (13/0), Paul Janes (15/0), Willi Tiefel (3/0), Rudolf Gramlich (Cap) (16/0), Ludwig Goldbrunner (7/0), Paul Zielinski (11/0), Ernst Lehner 17/7), August Lenz (4/5), Edmund Conen (11/10), Otto Siffling (11/2), Josef Fath (7/5). Trainer: Prof. Dr. Otto Nerz (56).
;oal: August Lenz (56).

15. 30.06.1935 **SWEDEN - GERMANY** **3-1(1-0)**
Råsundastadion, Stockholm; Referee: Ejner Ulrich (Denmark); Attendance: 20,000
;ER: Fritz Buchloh (12/0), Paul Janes (16/0), Willi Tiefel (4/0), Paul Zielinski (12/0), Reinhold Münzenberg (Cap) (11/0), Jakob Bender (9/0), Ernst Lehner 18/7), Otto Siffling (12/2), Edmund Conen (12/10), Otto Rohwedder (4/2), Stanislaus Kobierski (19/5). Trainer: Prof. Dr. Otto Nerz (57).
;oal: Otto Rohwedder (68).

16. 18.08.1935 **GERMANY - FINLAND** **6-0(3-0)**
Heinrich Zisch" Stadion, München; Referee: Bruno Pfützner (Czechoslovakia); Attendance: 35,000
;ER: Hans Jakob (14/0), Paul Janes (17/0), Andreas Munkert (2/0), Rudolf Gramlich (17/0), Ludwig Goldbrunner (8/0), Werner Schulz (2/0), Ernst Lehner 19/9), Otto Siffling (13/2), Edmund Conen (13/13), Fritz Szepan (Cap) (11/2), Josef Fath (8/5). Trainer: Prof. Dr. Otto Nerz (58).
;oals: Ernst Lehner (3, 30), Edmund Conen (43, 46), Ernst Lehner (56), Edmund Conen (75).

117. 18.08.1935 **LUXEMBOURG - GERMANY** **0-1(0-1)**
Stade Municipal, Luxembourg; Referee: Louis Baert (Belgium); Attendance: 16,000
GER: Willy Jürissen (1/0), Willy Busch (Cap) (12/0), Hermann Gramlich (1/0), Paul Zielinski (13/0), Wilhelm Sold (1/0), Günther Stephan (1/0), Franz Elbern (1/0), Rudolf Gellesch (1/0), Willi Fricke (1/0), Adolf Urban (1/0), Walter Günther (1/1). Trainer: Prof. Dr. Otto Nerz (59).
Goal: Walter Günther (43).

118. 25.08.1935 **GERMANY - ROMANIA** **4-2(1-1)**
Mitteldeutsche Kampfbahn, Erfurt; Referee: Johannes Franciscus van Moorsel (Netherlands); Attendance: 35,000
GER: Fritz Buchloh (13/0), Reinhold Münzenberg (12/0), Hermann Gramlich (2/0), Heinz Werner (1/0), Fritz Deike (1/0), Albin Kitzinger (1/0), Edmund Malecki (1/0), August Lenz (5/6), Karl Hohmann (Cap) (16/16), Josef Rasselnberg (7/7), Wilhelm Simetsreiter (1/1). Trainer: Prof. Dr. Otto Nerz (60).
Goals: August Lenz (1), Josef Rasselnberg (60), Wilhelm Simetsreiter (80), Karl Hohmann (83).

119. 15.09.1935 **GERMANY - POLAND** **1-0(1-0)**
Schlesierkampfbahn im Sportpark, Breslau; Referee: Otto Ohlsson (Sweden); Attendance: 45,000
GER: Hans Jakob (15/0), Sigmund Haringer (12/0), Hermann Gramlich (3/0), Rudolf Gramlich (Cap) (18/0), Ludwig Goldbrunner (9/0), Paul Zielinski (14/0), Ernst Lehner (20/9), August Lenz (6/6), Edmund Conen (14/14), Otto Siffling (14/2), Josef Fath (9/5). Trainer: Prof. Dr. Otto Nerz (61).
Goal: Edmund Conen (34).

120. 15.09.1935 **GERMANY - ESTONIA** **5-0(2-0)**
„Richard Lindemann" Sportpark, Stettin; Referee: E.Malmström (Sweden); Attendance: 17,000
GER: Heinrich Sonnrein (1/0), Reinhold Münzenberg (13/0), Willi Tiefel (5/0), Albert Sukop (1/0), Paul Mathies (1/0), Werner Schulz (3/0), Edmund Malecki (2/1), Karl Hohmann (Cap) (17/16), Ludwig Damminger (3/5), Josef Rasselnberg (8/8), Wilhelm Simetsreiter (2/3). Trainer: Prof. Dr. Otto Nerz (62).
Goals: Edmund Malecki (3), Wilhelm Simetsreiter (33), Josef Rasselnberg (46), Wilhelm Simetsreiter (65), Ludwig Damminger (81).

121. 13.10.1935 **GERMANY - LATVIA** **3-0(1-0)**
„Horst Wessel" Stadion, Königsberg; Referee: M. Rutkowski (Poland); Attendance: 15,000
GER: Willy Jürissen (2/0), Erwin Stührk (3/0), Willi Tiefel (Cap) (6/0), Fritz Ruchay (1/0), Paul Mathies (2/0), Hans Appel (3/0), Kurt Langenbein (2/1) August Lenz (7/7), Herbert Panse (1/1), Otto Bökle (1/0), Matthias Heidemann (3/0). Trainer: Prof. Dr. Otto Nerz (63).
Goals: August Lenz (9), Herbert Panse (58), Kurt Langenbein (63).

122. 20.10.1935 **GERMANY - BULGARIA** **4-2(2-0)**
VfB Stadion, Leipzig ; Referee: Mihály Iváncsics (Hungary); Attendance: 30,000
GER: Fritz Buchloh (14/0), Reinhold Münzenberg (14/0), Sigmund Haringer (13/0), Rudolf Gramlich (19/0), Ludwig Goldbrunner (10/0), Heinz Warnken (1/0), Ernst Lehner (21/10), Otto Siffling (15/2), Ernst Poertgen (1/1), Fritz Szepan (Cap) (12/2), Wilhelm Simetsreiter (3/5). Trainer: Prof. Dr. Otto Nerz (64).
Goals: Wilhelm Simetsreiter (29), Ernst Lehner (30), Wilhelm Simetsreiter (68), Ernst Poertgen (73).

123. 04.12.1935 **ENGLAND - GERMANY** **3-0(1-0)**
White Hart Lane, London; Referee: Otto Ohlsson (Sweden); Attendance: 54,164
GER: Hans Jakob (16/0), Sigmund Haringer (14/0), Reinhold Münzenberg (15/0), Paul Janes (18/0), Ludwig Goldbrunner (11/0), Rudolf Gramlich (20/0), Ernst Lehner (22/10), Fritz Szepan (Cap) (13/2), Karl Hohmann (18/16), Josef Rasselnberg (9/8), Josef Fath (10/5). Trainer: Prof. Dr. Otto Nerz (65).

124. 23.02.1936 **SPAIN - GERMANY** **1-2(0-1)**
Estadio Olímpico de Montjuïc, Barcelona; Referee: John Langenus (Belgium); Attendance: 40,000
GER: Hans Jakob (17/0), Reinhold Münzenberg (16/0), Andreas Munkert (3/0), Paul Janes (19/0), Ludwig Goldbrunner (12/0), Rudolf Gramlich (21/0), Ernst Lehner (23/10), Otto Siffling (16/2), August Lenz (8/7), Fritz Szepan (Cap) (14/2), Josef Fath (11/7). Trainer: Prof. Dr. Otto Nerz (66).
Goals: Josef Fath (15, 68).

125. 27.02.1936 **PORTUGAL - GERMANY** **1-3(0-1)**
Estádio do Lumiar, Lisboa; Referee: Pedro Escartin Morán (Spain); Attendance: 25,000
GER: Fritz Buchloh (15/0) [58.Hans Jakob (18/0)], Reinhold Münzenberg (17/0), Willi Tiefel (7/0), Paul Janes (20/0), Ludwig Goldbrunner (13/0), Albin Kitzinger (2/1), Ernst Lehner (24/11), Karl Hohmann (19/17), Otto Siffling (17/2), Fritz Szepan (Cap) (15/2), Wilhelm Simetsreiter (4/5). Trainer: Prof. Dr Otto Nerz (67).
Goals: Karl Hohmann (20), Albin Kitzinger (48), Ernst Lehner (52).

126. 15.03.1936 **HUNGARY - GERMANY** **3-2(1-1)**
Hungária út, Budapest; Referee: Gustav Krist (Czechoslovakia); Attendance: 33,000
GER: Heinrich Sonnrein (2/0), Reinhold Münzenberg (18/0), Andreas Munkert (4/0), Paul Janes (21/0), Wilhelm Sold (2/0), Albin Kitzinger (3/1), Franz Elbern (2/0), Rudolf Gellesch (2/0), August Lenz (9/8), Fritz Szepan (Cap) (16/2), Adolf Urban (2/1). Trainer: Prof. Dr. Otto Nerz (68).
Goals: Adolf Urban (29), August Lenz (57).

127. 04.08.1936 **GERMANY - LUXEMBOURG** **9-0(2-0)** 13th OG. Group Stage.
Poststadion, Berlin; Referee: Pál von Hertzka (Hungary); Attendance: 12,000
GER: Fritz Buchloh (16/0), Reinhold Münzenberg (Cap) (19/0), Heinz Ditgens (1/0), Paul Mehl (1/0), Ludwig Goldbrunner (14/0), Robert Bernard (1/0), Franz Elbern (3/1), Josef Gauchel (1/2), Karl Hohmann (20/17), Adolf Urban (3/4), Wilhelm Simetsreiter (5/8). Trainer: Prof. Dr. Otto Nerz (69).
Goals: Adolf Urban (16), Wilhelm Simetsreiter (30, 48), Josef Gauchel (50), Adolf Urban (52), Wilhelm Simetsreiter (74), Adolf Urban (75), Franz Elbern (76), Josef Gauchel (90).

128. 07.08.1936 **GERMANY - NORWAY** **0-2(0-1)** 13th OG. Quarter-Finals.
Poststadion, Berlin; Referee: Dr. Arthur W. Barton (England); Attendance: 55,000
GER: Hans Jakob (19/0), Reinhold Münzenberg (20/0), Heinz Ditgens (2/0), Rudolf Gramlich (Cap) (22/0), Ludwig Goldbrunner (15/0), Robert Bernard (2/0), Ernst Lehner (25/11), Otto Siffling (18/2), August Lenz (10/8), Adolf Urban (4/4), Wilhelm Simetsreiter (6/8). Trainer: Prof. Dr. Otto Nerz (70).

129. 13.09.1936 **POLAND - GERMANY** **1-1(0-1)**
Stadion Wojska Polskiego, Warszawa; Referee: Rudolf Eklöw (Sweden); Attendance: 41,000
GER: Fritz Buchloh (17/0), Paul Janes (22/0), Reinhold Münzenberg (Cap) (21/0), Paul Mehl (2/0), Josef Rodzinski (1/0), Albin Kitzinger (4/1), Franz Elbern (4/1), Josef Gauchel (2/2), Karl Hohmann (21/18), Georg Euler (1/0), Walter Günther (2/1). Trainer: Josef Herberger (1).
Goal: Karl Hohmann (19).

130. 27.09.1936 **CZECHOSLOVAKIA - GERMANY** **1-2(1-0)**
Stadion Strahov, Praha; Referee: Johannes Franciscus van Moorsel (Netherlands); Attendance: 25,000
GER: Hans Jakob (20/0), Reinhold Münzenberg (Cap) (22/0), Andreas Munkert (5/0), Josef Rodzinski (2/0), Ludwig Goldbrunner (16/0), Albin Kitzinger (5/1), Franz Elbern (5/2), Rudolf Gellesch (3/0), Otto Siffling (19/3), August Lenz (11/8), Stanislaus Kobierski (20/5). Trainer: Josef Herberger (2).
Goals: Franz Elbern (60), Otto Siffling (80).

131. 27.09.1936 **GERMANY - LUXEMBOURG** **7-2(3-2)**
Grotenburg Kampfbahn, Krefeld; Referee: Otto Ohlssen (Sweden); Attendance: 18,000
GER: Willy Jürissen (3/0), Willy Busch (Cap) (13/0), Helmut Sievert (1/0), Otto Tibulski (1/0), Hans Rohde (1/0), Paul Zielinski (15/0), Edmund Malecki (3/2), Matthias Billen (1/0), Ernst Poertgen (2/4), Ernst Kuzorra (11/7), Walter Günther (3/2). Trainer: Josef Herberger (3).
Goals: Ernst Kuzorra (8), Edmund Malecki (21), Ernst Poertgen (44, 52, 53), Walter Günther (70), Ernst Kuzorra (80).

132. 14.10.1936 **SCOTLAND - GERMANY** **2-0(0-0)**
Ibrox Park, Glasgow; Referee: Harry Nattrass (England); Attendance: 50,000
GER: Hans Jakob (21/0), Reinhold Münzenberg (23/0), Andreas Munkert (6/0), Paul Janes (23/0), Ludwig Goldbrunner (17/0), Albin Kitzinger (6/1), Franz Elbern (6/2), Rudolf Gellesch (4/0), Otto Siffling (20/3), Fritz Szepan (Cap) (17/2), Adolf Urban (5/4). Trainer: Josef Herberger (4).

133. 17.10.1936 **REPUBLIC OF IRELAND - GERMANY** **5-2(2-2)**
Dalymount Park, Dublin; Referee: William E. Webb (Scotland); Attendance: 27,109
GER: Hans Jakob (22/0), Reinhold Münzenberg (24/0), Andreas Munkert (7/0), Josef Rodzinski (3/0), Ludwig Goldbrunner (18/0), Albin Kitzinger (7/1), Ernst Lehner (26/11), Otto Siffling (21/3), Karl Hohmann (22/18), Fritz Szepan (Cap) (18/3), Stanislaus Kobierski (21/6). Trainer: Josef Herberger (5).
Goals: Stanislaus Kobierski (25), Fritz Szepan (32).

134. 15.11.1936 **GERMANY - ITALY** **2-2(2-1)**
Olympiastadion, Berlin; Referee: Rudolf Eklöw (Sweden); Attendance: 83,000
GER: Hans Jakob (23/0), Reinhold Münzenberg (25/0), Andreas Munkert (8/0), Paul Janes (24/0), Ludwig Goldbrunner (19/0), Albin Kitzinger (8/1), Franz Elbern (7/2), Rudolf Gellesch (5/0), Otto Siffling (22/5), Fritz Szepan (Cap) (19/3), Adolf Urban (6/4). Trainer: Josef Herberger (6).
Goals: Otto Siffling (35, 40).

135. 31.01.1937 **GERMANY - NETHERLANDS** **2-2(1-1)**
Rheinstadion, Düsseldorf; Referee: Lucien Leclercq (France); Attendance: 70,000
GER: Hans Jakob (24/0), Paul Janes (25/0), Reinhold Münzenberg (26/0), Rudolf Gellesch (6/0), Ludwig Goldbrunner (20/0), Albin Kitzinger (9/1), Ernst Lehner (27/13), Karl Hohmann (23/18), Georg Friedel (1/0), Fritz Szepan (Cap) (20/3), Walter Günther (4/2). Trainer: Josef Herberger (7).
Goals: Ernst Lehner (26, 75).

136. 21.03.1937 **GERMANY - FRANCE** **4-0(2-0)**
„Adolf Hitler" Kampfbahn, Stuttgart; Referee: Rinaldo Barlassina (Italy); Attendance: 72,000
GER: Hans Jakob (25/0), Paul Janes (26/0), Reinhold Münzenberg (27/0), Rudolf Gellesch (7/0), Ludwig Goldbrunner (21/0), Albin Kitzinger (10/1), Ernst Lehner (28/14), Otto Siffling (23/5), August Lenz (12/9), Fritz Szepan (Cap) (21/3), Adolf Urban (7/6). Trainer: Josef Herberger (8).
Goals: Ernst Lehner (26), Adolf Urban (31, 76), August Lenz (87).

137. 21.03.1937 **LUXEMBOURG - GERMANY** **2-3(0-1)**
Stade Municipal, Luxembourg; Referee: Karl Wunderlin (Switzerland); Attendance: 12,000
GER: Georg Köhl (1/0), Hans Appel (4/0), Werner Klaas (1/0), Andreas Kupfer (1/0), Wilhelm Sold (3/0), Erwin Schädler (1/0), Edmund Malecki (4/2), Josef Gauchel (3/2), Ernst Poertgen (3/5), Karl Hohmann (Cap) (24/18), Karl Striebinger (1/2). Trainer: Josef Herberger (9).
Goals: Ernst Poertgen (7), Karl Striebinger (59, 68).

138. 25.04.1937 **GERMANY - BELGIUM** **1-0(1-0)**
Hindenburg Stadion, Hannover; Referee: Arthur James Jewell (England); Attendance: 60,000
GER: Hans Jakob (26/0), Sigmund Haringer (15/0), Reinhold Münzenberg (Cap) (28/0), Andreas Kupfer (2/0), Ludwig Goldbrunner (22/0), Albin Kitzinger (11/1), Ernst Lehner (29/14), Otto Rohwedder (5/2), August Lenz (13/9), Karl Hohmann (25/19), Karl Striebinger (2/2). Trainer: Josef Herberger (10).
Goal: Karl Hohmann (17).

139. 02.05.1937 **SWITZERLAND - GERMANY** **0-1(0-0)**
Hardturm Stadion, Zürich; Referee: Louis Baert (Belgium); Attendance: 35,000
GER: Hans Jakob (27/0), Willi Billmann (1/0), Reinhold Münzenberg (29/0), Andreas Kupfer (3/0), Ludwig Goldbrunner (23/0), Albin Kitzinger (12/2), Ernst Lehner (30/14), Fritz Szepan (Cap) (22/3), Jakob Eckert (1/0), Rudolf Noack (3/1), Adolf Urban (8/6). Trainer: Josef Herberger (11).
Goal: Albin Kitzinger (67).

140. 16.05.1937 **GERMANY - DENMARK** **8-0(4-0)**
Schlesierkampfbahn im Sportpark, Breslau; Referee: Gustav Krist (Czechoslovakia); Attendance: 40,000
GER: Hans Jakob (28/0), Paul Janes (27/0), Reinhold Münzenberg (30/0), Andreas Kupfer (4/0), Ludwig Goldbrunner (24/0), Albin Kitzinger (13/2), Ernst Lehner (31/15), Rudolf Gellesch (8/0), Otto Siffling (24/10), Fritz Szepan (Cap) (23/4), Adolf Urban (9/7). Trainer: Josef Herberger (12).
Goals: Ernst Lehner (7), Otto Siffling (33, 40, 44, 48, 65), Adolf Urban (70), Fritz Szepan (78).

141. 25.06.1937 **LATVIA - GERMANY** **1-3(1-2)**
ASK Stadions, Riga; Referee: Gustav Krist (Czechoslovakia); Attendance: 8,000
GER: Willy Jürissen (4/0), Kurt Welsch (1/0), Reinhold Münzenberg (31/0), Ludwig Männer (1/0), Wilhelm Sold (4/0), Erwin Schädler (2/0), Franz Elbern (8/2), Otto Siffling (25/10), Hans Berndt (1/2), Karl Hohmann (Cap) (26/20), Wilhelm Simetsreiter (7/8). Trainer: Josef Herberger (13).
Goals: Karl Hohmann (25), Hans Berndt (30, 57).

142. 29.06.1937 **FINLAND - GERMANY** **0-2(0-1)** 3rd FIFA WC. Qualifiers
Töölön Pallokenttä, Helsinki; Referee: Dr.Otto Remke (Denmark); Attendance: 6,619
GER: Hans Jakob (29/0), Paul Janes (28/0), Reinhold Münzenberg (32/0), Andreas Kupfer (5/0), Ludwig Goldbrunner (25/0), Albin Kitzinger (14/2), Ernst Lehner (32/16), Rudolf Gellesch (9/0), Otto Siffling (26/10), Fritz Szepan (Cap) (24/4), Adolf Urban (10/8). Trainer: Josef Herberger (14).
Goals: Ernst Lehner (26), Adolf Urban (38).

143. 29.08.1937 **GERMANY - ESTONIA** **4-1(0-1)** 3rd FIFA WC. Qualifiers
„Horst Wessel" Stadion, Königsberg; Referee: Bruno Pfützner (Czechoslovakia); Attendance: 18,000
GER: Hans Jakob (30/0), Paul Janes (29/0), Reinhold Münzenberg (33/0), Walter Rose (1/0), Ludwig Goldbrunner (26/0), Erwin Schädler (3/0), Ernst Lehner (33/18), Josef Gauchel (4/4), Hans Berndt (2/2), Fritz Szepan (Cap) (25/4), Wilhelm Simetsreiter (8/8). Trainer: Josef Herberger (15).
Goals: Ernst Lehner (50), Josef Gauchel (53), Ernst Lehner (65), Josef Gauchel (86).

144. 24.10.1937 **GERMANY - NORWAY** **3-0(0-0)**
Olympiastadion, Berlin; Referee: Peter Snape (England); Attendance: 95,000
GER: Hans Jakob (31/0), Paul Janes (30/0), Reinhold Münzenberg (34/0), Andreas Kupfer (6/0), Ludwig Goldbrunner (27/0), Albin Kitzinger (15/2), Ernst Lehner (34/18), Rudolf Gellesch (10/0), Otto Siffling (27/13), Fritz Szepan (Cap) (26/4), Adolf Urban (11/8). Trainer: Josef Herberger (16).
Goals: Otto Siffling (19, 29, 67).

145. 21.11.1937 **GERMANY - SWEDEN** **5-0(2-0)** 3rd FIFA WC. Qualifiers
Altonaer Stadion, Altona, Hamburg; Referee: Bruno Pfützner (Czechoslovakia); Attendance: 50,500
GER: Hans Jakob (32/0), Paul Janes (31/0), Reinhold Münzenberg (35/0), Andreas Kupfer (7/0), Ludwig Goldbrunner (28/0), Rudolf Gellesch (11/0), Ernst Lehner (35/18), Helmut Schön (1/2), Otto Siffling (28/15), Fritz Szepan (Cap) (27/5), Adolf Urban (12/8). Trainer: Josef Herberger (17).
Goals: Otto Siffling (2), Fritz Szepan (8), Helmut Schön (48), Otto Siffling (57), Helmut Schön (63).

146. 06.02.1938 **GERMANY - SWITZERLAND** **1-1(0-1)**
Müngersdorfer Stadion, Köln; Referee: Reginald George Rudd (England); Attendance: 78,000
GER: Willy Jürissen (5/0), Paul Janes (32/0), Reinhold Münzenberg (36/0), Andreas Kupfer (8/0), Wilhelm Sold (5/0), Rudolf Gellesch (12/0), Ernst Lehner (36/18), Adolf Urban (13/8), Otto Siffling (29/15), Fritz Szepan (Cap) (28/6), Karl Striebinger (3/2). Trainer: Josef Herberger (18).
Goal: Fritz Szepan (74).

147. 20.03.1938 **GERMANY - HUNGARY** **1-1(1-0)**
Stadion der Hitlerjugend, Nürnberg; Referee: John Langenus (Belgium); Attendance: 53,000
GER: Hans Jakob (33/0), Willi Billmann (2/0), Reinhold Münzenberg (Cap) (37/0), Albin Kitzinger (16/2), Ludwig Goldbrunner (29/0), Hans Mengel (1/0), Ernst Lehner (37/18), Otto Siffling (30/16), Hans Berndt (3/2), Ernst Kuzorra (12/7), Josef Fath (12/7). Trainer: Josef Herberger (19).
Goal: Otto Siffling (29).

148. 20.03.1938 **GERMANY - LUXEMBOURG** **2-1(1-0)**
Stadion am Zoo, Wuppertal; Referee: Hans Wüthrich (Switzerland); Attendance: 20,000
GER: Hans Klodt (1/0), Werner Schulz (4/0), Heinz Ditgens (3/0), Walter Berg (1/0), Wilhelm Sold (Cap) (6/0), Erwin Schädler (4/0), Paul Winkler (1/0), Josef Gauchel (5/6), August Lenz (14/9), Hans Heibach (1/0), Friedel Holz (1/0). Trainer: Josef Herberger (20).
Goals: Josef Gauchel (6 penalty, 75).

149. 24.04.1938 **GERMANY - PORTUGAL** **1-1(0-1)**
Waldstadion, Frankfurt am Main; Referee: Rinaldo Barlassina (Italy); Attendance: 54,000
GER: Hans Jakob (34/0), Paul Janes (33/0), Reinhold Münzenberg (38/0), Andreas Kupfer (9/0), Ludwig Goldbrunner (30/0), Albin Kitzinger (17/2), Ernst Lehner (38/18), Rudolf Gellesch (13/0), Otto Siffling (31/17), Fritz Szepan (Cap) (29/6), Josef Fath (13/7). Trainer: Josef Herberger (21).
Goal: Otto Siffling (75).

150. 14.05.1938 **GERMANY - ENGLAND** **3-6(2-4)**
Olympiastadion, Berlin; Referee: John Langenus (Belgium); Attendance: 120,000
GER: Hans Jakob (35/0), Paul Janes (34/0), Reinhold Münzenberg (39/0), Andreas Kupfer (10/0), Ludwig Goldbrunner (31/0), Albin Kitzinger (18/2), Ernst Lehner (39/18), Rudolf Gellesch (14/1), Josef Gauchel (6/7), Fritz Szepan (Cap) (30/6), Hans Pesser (1/1). Trainer: Josef Herberger (22).
Goals: Rudolf Gellesch (20), Josef Gauchel (44), Hans Pesser (77).

151. 04.06.1938 **GERMANY - SWITZERLAND** **1-1(1-1,1-1)** 3rd FIFA WC. 1st Round.
Stade Parc des Princes, Paris (France); Referee: John Langenus (Belgium); Attendance: 27,152
GER: Rudolf Raftl (1/0), Paul Janes (35/0), Willibald Schmaus (1/0), Andreas Kupfer (11/0), Hans Mock (Cap) (1/0), Albin Kitzinger (19/2), Ernst Lehner (40/18), Rudolf Gellesch (15/1), Josef Gauchel (7/8), Wilhelm Hahnemann (1/0), Hans Pesser (2/1) [*sent off 96*]. Trainer: Josef Herberger (23).
Goal: Josef Gauchel (29).

152. 09.06.1938 **GERMANY - SWITZERLAND** **2-4(2-1)** 3rd FIFA WC. 1st Round (Replay).
Stade Parc des Princes, Paris (France); Referee: Ivan Eklind (Sweden); Attendance: 20,025
GER: Rudolf Raftl (2/0), Paul Janes (36/0), Jakob Streitle (1/0), Andreas Kupfer (12/0), Ludwig Goldbrunner (32/0), Stefan Skoumal (1/0), Ernst Lehner (41/18), Josef Stroh (1/0), Wilhelm Hahnemann (2/1), Fritz Szepan (Cap) (31/6), Leopold Neumer (1/0). Trainer: Josef Herberger (24).
Goals: Wilhelm Hahnemann (8), Ernst Lörtscher (22 own goal).

153. 18.09.1938 **GERMANY - POLAND** **4-1(1-0)**
Großkampfbahn, Chemnitz; Referee: Hans Wüthrich (Switzerland); Attendance: 60,000
GER: Hans Jakob (36/0), Paul Janes (37/0), Reinhold Münzenberg (Cap) (40/0), Andreas Kupfer (13/0), Ludwig Goldbrunner (33/0), Albin Kitzinger (20/2), Wilhelm Hahnemann (3/1), Josef Stroh (2/0), Josef Gauchel (8/11), Helmut Schön (2/3), Hans Pesser (3/1). Trainer: Josef Herberger (25).
Goals: Josef Gauchel (35), Helmut Schön (52), Josef Gauchel (59, 62).

154. 25.09.1938 **ROMANIA - GERMANY** **1-4(0-1)**
Stadionul ONEF, Bucureşti; Referee: Mika Popović (Yugoslavia); Attendance: 25,000
GER: Rudolf Raftl (3/0), Hans Appel (5/0), Willibald Schmaus (2/0), Franz Wagner (1/0), Hans Mock (Cap) (2/0), Stefan Skoumal (2/0), Hans Biallas (1/0), Wilhelm Hahnemann (4/1), Josef Stroh (3/1), Helmut Schön (3/4), Hans Pesser (4/2). Trainer: Josef Herberger (26).
Goals: Helmut Schön (17), Josef Stroh (51), Gheorghe Albu (61 own goal), Hans Pesser (77).

155. 29.01.1939 **BELGIUM - GERMANY** **1-4(1-2)**
Stade de Jubilé, Bruxelles; Referee: Rudolf Eklöw (Sweden); Attendance: 35,425
GER: Peter Platzer (1/0), Jakob Streitle (2/0), Willibald Schmaus (3/0), Hans Rohde (2/0), Ludwig Goldbrunner (Cap) (34/0), Rudolf Gellesch (16/1), Ernst Lehner (42/19), Wilhelm Hahnemann (5/2), Franz Binder (1/1), Helmut Schön (4/5), Willi Arlt (1/0). Trainer: Josef Herberger (27).
Goals: Franz Binder (15), Helmut Schön (21), Ernst Lehner (65), Wilhelm Hahnemann (90).

156. 26.02.1939 **GERMANY - YUGOSLAVIA** **3-2(1-2)**
Olympiastadion, Berlin; Referee: Andrzej Rutkowski (Poland); Attendance: 65,000
GER: Hans Klodt (2/0), Paul Janes (Cap) (38/1), Jakob Streitle (3/0), Andreas Kupfer (14/0), Otto Tibulski (2/0), Albin Kitzinger (21/2), Hans Biallas (2/1), Josef Stroh (4/1), Josef Gauchel (9/11), Wilhelm Hahnemann (6/2), Adolf Urban (14/9). Trainer: Josef Herberger (28).
Goals: Adolf Urban (36), Paul Janes (57), Hans Biallas (72).

157. 26.03.1939 **ITALY - GERMANY** **3-2(2-1)**
Stadio „Giovanni Berta", Firenze; Referee: Louis Baert (Belgium); Attendance: 25,000
GER: Peter Platzer (2/0), Paul Janes (Cap) (39/2), Willibald Schmaus (4/0), Andreas Kupfer (15/0), Ludwig Goldbrunner (35/0), Albin Kitzinger (22/2), Ernst Lehner (43/19), Wilhelm Hahnemann (7/3), Josef Gauchel (10/11), Helmut Schön (5/5), Hans Pesser (5/2). Trainer: Josef Herberger (29).
Goals: Wilhelm Hahnemann (26), Paul Janes (78).

158. 26.03.1939 **LUXEMBOURG - GERMANY** **2-1(1-1)**
Stade du Thillenberg, Differdange; Referee: R. Charlier (Belgium); Attendance: 4,000
GER: Heinrich Flotho (1/0), Reinhold Münzenberg (Cap) (41/0), Franz Immig (1/0), Hans Rohde (3/0), Alfred Picard (1/0), Ludwig Männer (2/0), Edmund Malecki (5/2), Ludwig Pöhler (1/0), Erich Hänel (1/1), Hans Fiederer (1/0), Willi Arlt (2/0). Trainer: Josef Herberger (30).
Goal: Erich Hänel (1).

159. 23.05.1939 **GERMANY - REPUBLIC OF IRELAND** **1-1(1-0)**
Weserstadion, Bremen; Referee: Dr.Otto Remke (Denmark); Attendance: 35,000
GER: Hans Jakob (37/0), Paul Janes (Cap) (40/2), Jakob Streitle (4/0), Andreas Kupfer (16/0), Hans Rohde (4/0), Albin Kitzinger (23/2), Ernst Lehner (44/19), Wilhelm Hahnemann (8/3), Josef Gauchel (11/11), Helmut Schön (6/6), Willi Arlt (3/0). Trainer: Josef Herberger (31).
Goal: Helmut Schön (39).

160. 22.06.1939 **NORWAY - GERMANY** **0-4(0-1)**
Ullevaal Stadion, Oslo; Referee: Ivan Eklind (Sweden); Attendance: 28,000
GER: Hans Klodt (3/0), Paul Janes (Cap) (41/3), Willibald Schmaus (5/0), Andreas Kupfer (17/0), Ludwig Goldbrunner (36/0), Albin Kitzinger (24/2), Ernst Lehner (45/19), Rudolf Gellesch (17/1), Helmut Schön (7/8), Reinhard Schaletzki (1/0), Adolf Urban (15/10). Trainer: Josef Herberger (32).
Goals: Adolf Urban (14), Paul Janes (57), Helmut Schön (59, 70).

161. 25.06.1939 **DENMARK - GERMANY** **0-2(0-1)**
Idrætsparken, København; Referee: Reidar Randers-Johansen (Norway); Attendance: 30,000
GER: Hans Klodt (4/0), Paul Janes (Cap) (42/3), Jakob Streitle (5/0), Andreas Kupfer (18/0), Hans Rohde (5/0), Albin Kitzinger (25/2), Hans Biallas (3/1), Wilhelm Hahnemann (9/3), Edmund Conen (15/15), Josef Gauchel (12/12), Willi Arlt (4/0). Trainer: Josef Herberger (33).
Goals: Josef Gauchel (8), Edmund Conen (76).

162. 29.06.1939 **ESTONIA - GERMANY** **0-2(0-1)**
Kadriorg Staadion, Tallinn; Referee: Arvids Jurgens (Latvia); Attendance: 9,000
GER: Erwin Deyhle (1/0), Paul Janes (Cap) (43/3), Alfons Moog (1/0), Johannes Jakobs (1/0), Hans Rohde (6/0), Ludwig Männer (3/0), Ernst Lehner (46/20), Reinhard Schaletzki (2/1), Erich Hänel (2/1), Josef Gauchel (13/12), Willi Arlt (5/0). Trainer: Josef Herberger (34).
Goals: Ernst Lehner (34), Reinhard Schaletzki (60).

163. 27.08.1939 **SLOVAKIA - GERMANY** **2-0(1-0)**
Štadión Slovanislava; Referee: Mika Popović (Yugoslavia); Attendance: 17,000
GER: Willy Jürissen (6/0), Franz Immig (2/0), Otto Marischka (1/0), Ernst Sabeditsch (1/0), Josef Pekarek (1/0), Maximilian Merkel (1/0), Franz Hofer (1/0), Ernst Reitermaier (1/0), Franz Binder (Cap) (2/1), Matthias Kaburek (1/0), Ludwig Gärtner (1/0). Trainer: Josef Herberger (35).

164. 24.09.1939 **HUNGARY - GERMANY** **5-1(2-1)**
Üllői út, Budapest; Referee: Generoso Dattilo (Italy); Attendance: 25,000
GER: Hans Jakob (38/0), Paul Janes (44/3), Willibald Schmaus (6/0), Andreas Kupfer (19/0), Ludwig Goldbrunner (37/0), Albin Kitzinger (26/2), Ernst Lehner (47/21), Rudolf Gellesch (18/1), Helmut Schön (8/8), Fritz Szepan (Cap) (32/6), Hans Pesser (6/2). Trainer: Josef Herberger (36).
Goal: Ernst Lehner (38).

165. 15.10.1939 **YUGOSLAVIA - GERMANY** **1-5(0-1)**
Stadion Konkordija, Zagreb; Referee: Rinaldo Barlassina (Italy); Attendance: 18,000
GER: Hans Klodt (5/0), Paul Janes (45/3), Willi Billmann (3/0), Andreas Kupfer (20/0), Wilhelm Sold (7/0), Albin Kitzinger (27/2), Ernst Lehner (48/21), Helmut Schön (9/11), Edmund Conen (16/15), Fritz Szepan (Cap) (33/8), Adolf Urban (16/10). Trainer: Josef Herberger (37).
Goals: Helmut Schön (8), Fritz Szepan (63), Helmut Schön (68, 73), Fritz Szepan (78).

166. 22.10.1939 **BULGARIA - GERMANY** **1-2(0-2)**
Yunak stadion, Sofia; Referee: Vasa Stefanović (Yugoslavia); Attendance: 15,000
GER: Hans Klodt (6/0), Paul Janes (46/3), Willi Billmann (4/0), Andreas Kupfer (21/0), Wilhelm Sold (8/0), Albin Kitzinger (28/2), Ernst Lehner (49/21), Rudolf Gellesch (19/1), Edmund Conen (17/16), Fritz Szepan (Cap) (34/8), Adolf Urban (17/11). Trainer: Josef Herberger (38).
Goals: Edmund Conen (21), Adolf Urban (39).

167. 12.11.1939 **GERMANY - CZECHIA** **4-4(2-4)**
Schlesierkampfbahn im Sportpark, Breslau; Referee: Mika Popović (Yugoslavia); Attendance: 35,000
GER: Rudolf Raftl (4/0), Paul Janes (Cap) (47/4), Willi Billmann (5/0), Andreas Kupfer (22/0), Wilhelm Sold (9/0), Ludwig Männer (4/0), Ernst Lehner (50/21), Helmut Schön (10/11), Franz Binder (3/4), Adolf Urban (18/11), Willi Arlt (6/0). Trainer: Josef Herberger (39).
Goals: Franz Binder (30, 35, 53), Paul Janes (85 penalty).

168. 26.11.1939 **GERMANY - ITALY** **5-2(2-2)**
Olympiastadion, Berlin; Referee: Pedro Escartin Morán (Spain); Attendance: 45,000
GER: Rudolf Raftl (5/0), Paul Janes (Cap) (48/4), Willi Billmann (6/0), Andreas Kupfer (23/0), Hans Rohde (7/0), Albin Kitzinger (29/2), Ernst Lehner (51/22), Wilhelm Hahnemann (10/3), Edmund Conen (18/17), Franz Binder (4/7), Hans Pesser (7/2). Trainer: Josef Herberger (40).
Goals: Franz Binder (20, 36), Ernst Lehner (65), Edmund Conen (67), Franz Binder (84 penalty),.

169. 03.12.1939 **GERMANY - SLOVAKIA** **3-1(0-0)**
Großkampfbahn, Chemnitz; Referee: Dr.Otto Remke (Denmark); Attendance: 7,000
GER: Helmut Jahn (1/0), Willi Billmann (7/0), Richard Kubus (1/0), Erich Goede (1/0), Hans Rohde (8/0), Albin Kitzinger (30/2), Ernst Lehner (Cap) (52/23), Helmut Schön (11/12), Erich Hänel (3/1), Hans Fiederer (2/1), Willi Arlt (7/0). Trainer: Josef Herberger (41).
Goals: Hans Fiederer (65), Helmut Schön (66), Ernst Lehner (79).

170. 07.04.1940 **GERMANY - HUNGARY** **2-2(2-2)**
Olympiastadion, Berlin; Referee: Louis Baert (Belgium); Attendance: 102,000
GER: Hans Klodt (7/0), Paul Janes (Cap) (49/4), Willi Billmann (8/0), Andreas Kupfer (24/0), Hans Rohde (9/0), Albin Kitzinger (31/2), Ernst Lehner (53/23), Josef Gauchel (14/13), Edmund Conen (19/17), Franz Binder (5/8), Hans Pesser (8/2). Trainer: Josef Herberger (42).
Goals: Josef Gauchel (3), Franz Binder (25).

171. 14.04.1940 **GERMANY - YUGOSLAVIA** **1-2(0-2)**
Praterstadion, Wien; Referee: Generoso Dattilo (Italy); Attendance: 60,000
GER: Rudolf Raftl (6/0), Paul Janes (Cap) (50/4), Willibald Schmaus (7/0), Franz Hanreiter (1/0), Johann Hofstätter (1/0), Stefan Skoumal (3/0), Ernst Lehner (54/24), Wilhelm Hahnemann (11/3), Franz Binder (6/8), Josef Gauchel (15/13), Hans Pesser (9/2). Trainer: Josef Herberger (43).
Goal: Ernst Lehner (68).

172. 05.05.1940 **ITALY - GERMANY** **3-2(2-1)**
Stadio „San Siro“, Milano; Referee: Mihály Iváncsics (Hungary); Attendance: 65,000
GER: Hans Klodt (8/0), Paul Janes (Cap) (51/4), Willi Billmann (9/0), Andreas Kupfer (25/0), Hans Rohde (10/0), Albin Kitzinger (32/2), Ernst Lehner (55/24), Wilhelm Hahnemann (12/3), Franz Binder (7/10), Adolf Urban (19/11), Hans Pesser (10/2). Trainer: Josef Herberger (44).
Goals: Franz Binder (28, 52).

173. 14.07.1940 **GERMANY - ROMANIA** **9-3(4-0)**
Waldstadion, Frankfurt am Main; Referee: Raffaele Scorzzoni (Italy); Attendance: 2,000
GER: Alexander Martinek (1/0), Paul Janes (Cap) (52/4), Alfons Moog (2/0), Andreas Kupfer (26/0), Kurt Krüger (1/0), Albin Kitzinger (33/2), Ernst Plener (1/2), Wilhelm Hahnemann (13/5), Fritz Walter (1/3), Hans Fiederer (3/3), Willi Arlt (8/0). Trainer: Josef Herberger (45).
Goals: Ernst Plener (9), Wilhelm Hahnemann (19, 26), Fritz Walter (33), Hans Fiederer (58), Ernst Plener (59), Hans Fiederer (63), Fritz Walter (76, 81).

174. 01.09.1940 **GERMANY - FINLAND** **13-0(8-0)**
VfB Stadion, Leipzig; Referee: Dr. Otto Remke (Denmark); Attendance: 40,000
GER: Hans Klodt (9/0), Helmut Schneider (1/0), Alfons Moog (3/0), Andreas Kupfer (27/0), Walter Dzur (1/0), Albin Kitzinger (Cap) (34/2), Ernst Plener (2/2), Wilhelm Hahnemann (14/11), Fritz Walter (2/5), Edmund Conen (20/21), Willi Arlt (9/1). Trainer: Josef Herberger (46).
Goals: Wilhelm Hahnemann (7), Edmund Conen (8), Fritz Walter (11), Edmund Conen (16), Wilhelm Hahnemann (19, 28), Edmund Conen (32), Wilhelm Hahnemann (44), Edmund Conen (47), Wilhelm Hahnemann (49), Willi Arlt (62), Fritz Walter (68), Wilhelm Hahnemann (82).

175. 15.09.1940 **SLOVAKIA - GERMANY** **0-1(0-0)**
Štadión Slovanislava; Referee: Giuseppe Scarpi (Italy); Attendance: 15,000
GER: Helmut Jahn (2/0), Paul Janes (Cap) (53/4), Alfons Moog (4/0), Felix Zwolanowski (1/0), Walter Dzur (2/0), Ludwig Männer (5/0), Hermann Eppenhoff (1/0), Wilhelm Hahnemann (15/11), Edmund Conen (21/21), Franz Jellinek (1/0), Ludwig Durek (1/1). Trainer: Josef Herberger (47).
Goal: Ludwig Durek (78).

176. 06.10.1940 **HUNGARY - GERMANY** **2-2(1-1)**
Üllői út, Budapest; Referee: Generoso Dattilo (Italy); Attendance: 36,000
GER: Hans Klodt (10/0), Paul Janes (Cap) (54/4), Alfons Moog (5/0), Andreas Kupfer (28/0), Ludwig Goldbrunner (38/0), Albin Kitzinger (35/2), Ernst Lehner (56/25), Wilhelm Hahnemann (16/12), Fritz Walter (3/5), Edmund Conen (22/21), Hans Pesser (11/2). Trainer: Josef Herberger (48).
Goals: Ernst Lehner (24), Wilhelm Hahnemann (58).

177. 20.10.1940 **GERMANY - BULGARIA** **7-3(3-2)**
Städtischer Sportplatz an der Grünwalder Straße, München; Referee: Ernő Kiss (Hungary); Attendance: 32,000
GER: Hans Klodt (11/0), Jakob Streitle (6/0), Alfons Moog (6/0), Andreas Kupfer (29/1), Ludwig Goldbrunner (Cap) (39/0), Franz Hammerl (1/0), Ernst Lehner (57/26), Fritz Walter (4/5), Edmund Conen (23/25), Albert Sing (1/0), Ludwig Gärtner (2/1). Trainer: Josef Herberger (49).
Goals: Ludwig Gärtner (12), Andreas Kupfer (17), Edmund Conen (19 penalty, 60, 63, 74), Ernst Lehner (77).

178. 03.11.1940 **YUGOSLAVIA - GERMANY** **2-0(1-0)**
Stadion Konkordija, Zagreb; Referee: Giuseppe Scarpi (Italy); Attendance: 15,000
GER: Hans Klodt (12/0), Paul Janes (Cap) (55/4), Jakob Streitle (7/0), Andreas Kupfer (30/1), Hans Rohde (11/0), Albin Kitzinger (36/2), Ernst Lehner (58/27), Felix Zwolanowski (2/0), Fritz Walter (5/5), Hans Fiederer (4/3), Willi Arlt (10/1). Trainer: Josef Herberger (50).

179. 17.11.1940 **GERMANY - DENMARK** **1-0(0-0)**
Hoheluft Stadion, Hamburg; Referee: Bertil Ahlfors (Finland); Attendance: 28,000
GER: Helmut Jahn (3/0), Paul Janes (Cap) (56/4), Alfons Moog (7/0), Andreas Kupfer (31/1), Hans Rohde (12/0), Albin Kitzinger (37/2), Ernst Lehner (59/27), Fritz Walter (6/5), Franz Binder (8/10), Helmut Schön (12/13), Hans Pesser (12/2). Trainer: Josef Herberger (51).
Goal: Helmut Schön (62).

180. 09.03.1941 **GERMANY - SWITZERLAND** **4-2(1-1)**
„Adolf Hitler“ Kampfbahn, Stuttgart; Referee: Raffaele Scorzzoni (Italy); Attendance: 60,000
GER: Hans Klodt (13/0), Paul Janes (Cap) (57/4), Jakob Streitle (8/0), Andreas Kupfer (32/1), Hans Rohde (13/0), Albin Kitzinger (38/2), Franz Hanreiter (2/0), Wilhelm Hahnemann (17/12), Fritz Walter (7/6), Helmut Schön (13/15), Stanislaus Kobierski (22/7). Trainer: Josef Herberger (52).
Goals: Helmut Schön (12, 46), Stanislaus Kobierski (49), Fritz Walter (52).

181. 06.04.1941 **GERMANY - HUNGARY** **7-0(3-0)**
Müngersdorferstadion, Köln; Referee: Pedro Escartin Morán (Spain); Attendance: 65,000
GER: Hans Klodt (14/0), Paul Janes (Cap) (58/5), Karl Miller (1/0), Andreas Kupfer (33/1), Hans Rohde (14/0), Albin Kitzinger (39/2), Franz Hanreiter (3/0), Wilhelm Hahnemann (18/14), Fritz Walter (8/7), Helmut Schön (14/17), Stanislaus Kobierski (23/8). Trainer: Josef Herberger (53).
Goals: Paul Janes (24 penalty), Fritz Walter (28), Stanislaus Kobierski (34), Wilhelm Hahnemann (51), Helmut Schön (62), Wilhelm Hahnemann (67), Helmut Schön (81).

82. 20.04.1941 **SWITZERLAND - GERMANY** **2-1(2-1)**
Wankdorf Stadion, Bern; Referee: Giuseppe Scarpi (Italy); Attendance: 20,000
GER: Hans Klodt (15/0), Paul Janes (Cap) (59/5), Karl Miller (2/0), Andreas Kupfer (34/1), Hans Rohde (15/0), Albin Kitzinger (40/2), Franz Hanreiter (4/0), Wilhelm Hahnemann (19/15), Fritz Walter (9/7), Helmut Schön (15/17), Stanislaus Kobierski (24/8). Trainer: Josef Herberger (54).
Goal: Wilhelm Hahnemann (32).

83. 01.06.1941 **ROMANIA - GERMANY** **1-4(0-3)**
Stadionul ANEF, Bucureşti; Referee: Bizič (Slovakia); Attendance: 40,000
GER: Hans Klodt (16/0), Paul Janes (Cap) (60/5), Willi Billmann (10/0), Andreas Kupfer (35/1), Hans Rohde (16/0), Albin Kitzinger (41/2), Ernst Lehner (60/27), Fritz Walter (10/8), Franz Binder (9/10), Ernst Willimowski (1/2), Stanislaus Kobierski (25/9). Trainer: Josef Herberger (55).
Goals: Ernst Willimowski (5), Fritz Walter (26), Stanislaus Kobierski (33), Ernst Willimowski (67).

84. 15.06.1941 **GERMANY - CROATIA** **5-1(4-1)**
Praterstadion, Wien; Referee: Adolf Miesz (Germany); Attendance: 31,000
GER: Helmut Jahn (4/0), Karl Sesta (1/0), Willibald Schmaus (8/0), Hans Urbanek (1/0), Hans Mock (3/0), Franz Hanreiter (5/0), Ernst Lehner (61/29), Wilhelm Hahnemann (Cap) (20/15), Fritz Walter (11/10), Ernst Willimowski (2/3), Hans Fiederer (5/3). Trainer: Josef Herberger (56).
Goals: Ernst Lehner (30, 50 penalty), Fritz Walter (66), Ernst Willimowski (69), Fritz Walter (80).

85. 05.10.1941 **SWEDEN - GERMANY** **4-2(2-1)**
Råsundastadion, Stockholm; Referee: Valdemar Laursen (Denmark); Attendance: 36,532
GER: Hans Klodt (17/0), Paul Janes (Cap) (61/5), Willi Billmann (11/0), Andreas Kupfer (36/1), Hans Rohde (17/0), Albin Kitzinger (42/2), Ernst Lehner (62/30), Wilhelm Hahnemann (21/15), Fritz Walter (12/11), Helmut Schön (16/17), Ludwig Gärtner (3/1). Trainer: Josef Herberger (57).
Goals: Ernst Lehner (31), Fritz Walter (88).

86. 05.10.1941 **FINLAND - GERMANY** **0-6(0-2)**
Töölön Pallokenttä, Helsinki; Referee: Ragnar Ericsson (Sweden); Attendance: 7,138
GER: Helmut Jahn (5/0), Lothar Richter (1/0), Karl Miller (3/0), Herbert Pohl (1/0), Walter Dzur (3/0), Helmut Schubert (1/0), Herbert Burdenski (1/0), Rudolf Gellesch (Cap) (20/1), Hermann Eppenhoff (2/3), Ernst Willimowski (3/6), Stanislaus Kobierski (26/9). Trainer: Josef Herberger (58).
Goals: Hermann Eppenhoff (28), Ernst Willimowski (43), Hermann Eppenhoff (58, 63), Ernst Willimowski (70, 83).

87. 16.11.1941 **GERMANY - DENMARK** **1-1(1-0)**
Dresdener Sportklub-Stadion, Dresden; Referee: Ivan Eklind (Sweden); Attendance: 45,000
GER: Helmut Jahn (6/0), Paul Janes (Cap) (62/5), Karl Miller (4/0), Andreas Kupfer (37/1), Hans Rohde (18/0), Helmut Schubert (2/0), Wilhelm Hahnemann (22/16), Fritz Walter (13/11), Edmund Conen (24/25), Ernst Willimowski (4/6), Hans Fiederer (6/3). Trainer: Josef Herberger (59).
Goal: Wilhelm Hahnemann (38).

88. 07.12.1941 **GERMANY - SLOVAKIA** **4-0(1-0)**
Schlesierkampfbahn im Sportpark, Breslau; Referee: Petre Kroner (Romania); Attendance: 20,000
GER: Helmut Jahn (7/0), Paul Janes (Cap) (63/5), Karl Miller (5/0), Herbert Pohl (2/0), Hans Rohde (19/0), Helmut Schubert (3/0), Franz Riegler (1/0), Wilhelm Hahnemann (23/16), Edmund Conen (25/27), Fritz Walter (14/12), Ludwig Durek (2/2). Trainer: Josef Herberger (60).
Goals: Fritz Walter (6), Ludwig Durek (9), Edmund Conen (27, 62).

89. 18.01.1942 **CROATIA - GERMANY** **0-2(0-1)**
Stadion Konkordija, Zagreb; Referee: Josef Mohler (Slovakia); Attendance: 12,000
GER: Helmut Jahn (8/0), Karl Sesta (2/0), Willibald Schmaus (9/0), Franz Wagner (2/0), Hans Mock (Cap) (4/0), Franz Hanreiter (6/0), Franz Riegler (2/0), Karl Decker (1/1), Edmund Conen (26/27), Fritz Walter (15/12), Ludwig Durek (3/2). Trainer: Josef Herberger (61).
Goals: Miroslav Brozović (44 own goal), Karl Decker (66).

90. 01.02.1942 **GERMANY - SWITZERLAND** **1-2(0-0)**
Praterstadion, Wien; Referee: Giuseppe Scarpi (Italy); Attendance: 35,000
GER: Helmut Jahn (9/0), Karl Sesta (3/0), Willibald Schmaus (10/0), Franz Wagner (3/0), Hans Mock (Cap) (5/0), Franz Hanreiter (7/0), Willy Fitz (1/0), Karl Decker (2/2), Hermann Eppenhoff (3/3), Fritz Walter (16/12), Ludwig Durek (4/2). Trainer: Josef Herberger (62).
Goal: Karl Decker (71).

91. 12.04.1942 **GERMANY - SPAIN** **1-1(0-0)**
Olympiastadion, Berlin; Referee: Rinaldo Barlassina (Italy); Attendance: 80,000
GER: Helmut Jahn (10/0), Paul Janes (Cap) (64/5), Karl Miller (6/0), Albin Kitzinger (43/2), Hans Rohde (20/0), Albert Sing (2/0), Friedrich Dörfel (1/0), Karl Decker (3/3), Edmund Conen (27/27), Fritz Walter (17/12), Ludwig Durek (5/2). Trainer: Josef Herberger (63).
Goal: Karl Decker (58).

92. 03.05.1942 **HUNGARY - GERMANY** **3-5(3-1)**
Üllői út, Budapest; Referee: Rinaldo Barlassina (Italy); Attendance: 40,000
GER: Helmut Jahn (11/0), Paul Janes (Cap) (65/6), Karl Miller (7/0), Albin Kitzinger (44/2), Hans Rohde (21/0), Albert Sing (3/1), Friedrich Dörfel (2/1), Karl Decker (4/3), Edmund Conen (28/27), Fritz Walter (18/14), Ludwig Durek (6/2). Trainer: Josef Herberger (64).
Goals: Fritz Walter (16), Paul Janes (59), Fritz Walter (65), Friedrich Dörfel (70), Albert Sing (89).

93. 19.07.1942 **BULGARIA - GERMANY** **0-3(0-3)**
Junak stadion, Sofia; Referee: Jozef Mohler (Slovakia); Attendance: 30,000
GER: Helmut Jahn (12/0), Paul Janes (Cap) (66/6), Karl Miller (8/0), Andreas Kupfer (38/1), Wilhelm Sold (10/0), Albert Sing (4/1), Herbert Burdenski (2/0), Karl Decker (5/5), Fritz Walter (19/14), Josef Gauchel (16/13), Willi Arlt (11/2). Trainer: Josef Herberger (65).
Goals: Karl Decker (1), Willi Arlt (31), Karl Decker (42).

94. 16.08.1942 **GERMANY - ROMANIA** **7-0(1-0)**
Hindenburg Kampfbahn, Beuthen; Referee: Jozef Mohler (Slovakia); Attendance: 50,000
GER: Helmut Jahn (13/0), Paul Janes (Cap) (67/6), Karl Miller (9/0), Andreas Kupfer (39/1), Wilhelm Sold (11/0), Albert Sing (5/1), Herbert Burdenski (3/1), Karl Decker (6/6), Fritz Walter (20/17), Ernst Willimowski (5/7), August Klingler (1/1). Trainer: Josef Herberger (66).
Goals: Herbert Burdenski (43), Fritz Walter (49, 55), August Klingler (60), Karl Decker (70), Fritz Walter (82), Ernst Willimowski (85).

195. 20.09.1942 **GERMANY - SWEDEN** **2-3(2-2)**
Olympiastadion, Berlin; Referee: Valdemar Laursen (Denmark); Attendance: 90,000
GER: Helmut Jahn (14/0), Paul Janes (Cap) (68/6), Karl Miller (10/0), Andreas Kupfer (40/1), Wilhelm Sold (12/0), Hans Rohde (22/0), Ernst Lehner (63/30), Karl Decker (7/7), Fritz Walter (21/17), Albert Sing (6/1), August Klingler (2/2). Trainer: Josef Herberger (67).
Goals: Karl Decker (13), August Klingler (39).

196. 18.10.1942 **SWITZERLAND - GERMANY** **3-5(2-3)**
Wankdorf Stadion, Bern; Referee: Pedro Escartin Morán (Spain); Attendance: 35,000
GER: Helmut Jahn (15/0), Paul Janes (Cap) (69/6), Karl Miller (11/0), Andreas Kupfer (41/1), Hans Rohde (23/0), Albert Sing (7/1), Ernst Lehner (64/30), Fritz Walter (22/18), Ernst Willimowski (6/11), August Klingler (3/2), Adolf Urban (20/11). Trainer: Josef Herberger (68).
Goals: Ernst Willimowski (10, 31, 43, 57), Fritz Walter (80).

197. 01.11.1942 **GERMANY - CROATIA** **5-1(2-0)**
Neckarstadion, Stuttgart; Referee: Ferenc Palásti (Hungary); Attendance: 50,000
GER: Helmut Jahn (16/0), Paul Janes (Cap) (70/7), Edmund Adamkiewicz (1/0), Andreas Kupfer (42/1), Hans Rohde (24/0), Albert Sing (8/1), Ernst Lehner (65/30), Fritz Walter (23/19), Ernst Willimowski (7/13), Adolf Urban (21/11), August Klingler (4/3). Trainer: Josef Herberger (69).
Goals: Paul Janes (20), Fritz Walter (42), Ernst Willimowski (58, 69), August Klingler (86).

198. 22.11.1942 **SLOVAKIA - GERMANY** **2-5(0-2)**
Štadión Tehelné pole, Bratislava; Referee: Bažant (Croatia); Attendance: 12,000
GER: Helmut Jahn (17/0), Paul Janes (Cap) (71/7), Karl Miller (12/0), Andreas Kupfer (43/1), Hans Rohde (25/0), Albert Sing (9/1), Edmund Adamkiewicz (2/1), Karl Decker (8/8), Ernst Willimowski (8/13), Fritz Walter (24/19), August Klingler (5/6). Trainer: Josef Herberger (70).
Goals: August Klingler (1, 44, 46), Edmund Adamkiewicz (62), Karl Decker (83).

199. 22.11.1950 **WEST GERMANY - SWITZERLAND** **1-0(1-0)**
Neckarstadion, Stuttgart; Referee: Arthur Edward Ellis (England); Attendance: 115,000
GER: Anton Turek (1/0), Herbert Burdenski (4/2), Jakob Streitle (9/0), Andreas Kupfer (Cap) (44/1), Gunther Baumann (1/0), Karl Barufka (1/0) [90.Josef Röhrig (1/0)], Bernhard Klodt (1/0), Max Morlock (1/0), Ottmar Walter (1/0), Fritz Balogh (1/0), Richard Herrmann (1/0). Trainer: Josef Herberger (71).
Goal: Herbert Burdenski (42 penalty).

200. 15.04.1951 **SWITZERLAND - WEST GERMANY** **2-3(1-1)**
Hardturm Stadion, Zürich; Referee: Arthur Edward Ellis (England); Attendance: 34,000
GER: Anton Turek (2/0), Herbert Burdenski (5/2), Jakob Streitle (10/0), Paul Mebus (1/0), Gunther Baumann (2/0), Karl Barufka (2/0), Felix Gerritzen (1/1), Josef Röhrig (2/0), Ottmar Walter (2/1), Fritz Walter (Cap) (25/20), Bernhard Klodt (2/0) [70.Horst Schade (1/0)]. Trainer: Josef Herberger (72).
Goals: Ottmar Walter (42), Felix Gerritzen (50), Fritz Walter (54).

201. 17.06.1951 **WEST GERMANY - TURKEY** **1-2(0-1)**
Olympiastadion, West-Berlin; Referee: Giuseppe Carpani (Italy); Attendance: 90,000
GER: Anton Turek (3/0), Jakob Streitle (11/0), Werner Kohlmeyer (1/0), Josef Posipal (1/0), Werner Liebrich (1/0), Hans Haferkamp (1/1), Felix Gerritzen (2/1), Fritz Walter (Cap) (26/20), Horst Schade (2/0), Josef Röhrig (3/0) [65.Erich Schanko (1/0)], Richard Herrmann (2/0). Trainer: Josef Herberger (73).
Goal: Hans Haferkamp (75).

202. 23.09.1951 **AUSTRIA - WEST GERMANY** **0-2(0-0)**
Praterstadion, Wien; Referee: William H. Evans (England); Attendance: 60,000
GER: Anton Turek (4/0), Jakob Streitle (12/0), Werner Kohlmeyer (2/0), Paul Mebus (2/0), Josef Posipal (2/0), Erich Schanko (2/0), Felix Gerritzen (3/1) [70.Hans Haferkamp (2/2)], Alfred Preißler (1/0), Max Morlock (2/1), Fritz Walter (Cap) (27/20), Karl Barufka (3/0) [63.Richard Herrmann (3/0)]. Trainer: Josef Herberger (74).
Goals: Max Morlock (55), Hans Haferkamp (87).

203. 17.10.1951 **REPUBLIC OF IRELAND - WEST GERMANY** **3-2(2-0)**
Dalymount Park, Dublin; Referee: William Ling (England); Attendance: 31,000
GER: Anton Turek (5/0), Jakob Streitle (13/0), Werner Kohlmeyer (3/0), Paul Mebus (3/0), Josef Posipal (3/0), Erich Schanko (3/0), Felix Gerritzen (4/1), Alfred Preißler (2/0), Max Morlock (3/2), Fritz Walter (Cap) (28/21), Richard Herrmann (4/0). Trainer: Josef Herberger (75).
Goals: Max Morlock (62), Fritz Walter (75).

204. 21.11.1951 **TURKEY - WEST GERMANY** **0-2(0-0)**
Mithatpaşa Stadyumu, İstanbul; Referee: Arthur Edward Ellis (England); Attendance: 25,000
GER: Karl Adam (1/0), Jakob Streitle (14/0), Werner Kohlmeyer (4/0), Paul Mebus (4/0), Josef Posipal (4/0), Erich Schanko (4/0), Helmut Rahn (1/0), Max Morlock (4/4), Fritz Walter (Cap) (29/21), Hans Haferkamp (3/2), Bernhard Termath (1/0). Trainer: Josef Herberger (76).
Goals: Max Morlock (56, 60).

205. 23.12.1951 **WEST GERMANY - LUXEMBOURG** **4-1(1-0)**
„Georg Melches“ Stadion, Essen; Referee: Louis Baert (Belgium); Attendance: 40,000
GER: Karl Bögelein (1/0), Erich Juskowiak (1/0), Hans Bauer (1/0), Paul Mebus (5/0), Heinz Wewers (1/0), Erich Schanko (5/0), Helmut Rahn (2/1), Georg Stollenwerk (1/1), Willi Schröder (1/0), Fritz Walter (Cap) (30/21), Bernhard Termath (2/2). Trainer: Josef Herberger (77).
Goals: Bernhard Termath (14), Georg Stollenwerk (54), Bernhard Termath (63), Helmut Rahn (68).

206. 20.04.1952 **LUXEMBOURG - WEST GERMANY** **0-3(0-1)**
Stade Municipal, Luxembourg; Referee: Henri Bauwens (Belgium); Attendance: 17,000
GER: Karl Adam (2/0), Erich Retter (1/0), Hans Bauer (2/0), Clemens Wientjes (1/0) [65.Hans Haferkamp (4/2)], Josef Posipal (Cap) (5/0), Erich Schanko (6/0), Bernhard Klodt (3/1), Georg Stollenwerk (2/2), Hans Zeitler (1/1), Willi Schröder (2/0), Kurt Ehrmann (1/0). Trainer: Josef Herberger (78).
Goals: Georg Stollenwerk (9), Hans Zeitler (60), Bernhard Klodt (88).

207. 04.05.1952 **WEST GERMANY - REPUBLIC OF IRELAND** **3-0(1-0)**
Müngersdorferstadion, Köln; Referee: Arthur Edward Ellis (England); Attendance: 75,000
GER: Karl Adam (3/0), Erich Retter (2/0), Werner Kohlmeyer (5/0), Josef Posipal (6/1), Jakob Streitle (Cap) (15/0), Erich Schanko (7/0), Bernhard Klodt (4/1), Josef Röhrig (4/0), Ottmar Walter (3/2), Richard Herrmann (5/0) [43.Georg Stollenwerk (3/2)], Bernhard Termath (3/3). Trainer: Josef Herberger (79).
Goals: Josef Posipal (31), Ottmar Walter (77), Bernhard Termath (88).

08. 05.10.1952 **FRANCE - WEST GERMANY** **3-1(1-1)**
tade Olympique „Yves du Manoir", Colombes, Paris; Referee: William H. Evans (England); Attendance: 56,021
GER: Anton Turek (6/0), Erich Retter (3/0), Kurt Borkenhagen (1/0), Josef Posipal (7/1), Werner Liebrich (2/0), Erich Schanko (8/0), Helmut Rahn (3/1), Clemens Wientjes (2/0), Ottmar Walter (4/3) [31.Georg Stollenwerk (4/2)], Fritz Walter (Cap) (31/21), Bernhard Termath (4/3). Trainer: Josef Herberger (80).
Goal: Ottmar Walter (16).

09. 09.11.1952 **WEST GERMANY - SWITZERLAND** **5-1(2-0)**
Rosenaustadion, Augsburg; Referee: Vincenzo Orlandini (Italy); Attendance: 64,000
GER: Anton Turek (7/0), Erich Retter (4/0), Werner Kohlmeyer (6/0), Horst Eckel (1/0), Josef Posipal (8/1), Erich Schanko (9/0), Bernhard Klodt (5/1), Max Morlock (5/5), Ottmar Walter (5/4), Fritz Walter (Cap) (32/22), Hans Schäfer (1/2). Trainer: Josef Herberger (81).
Goals: Max Morlock (20), Ottmar Walter (29), Hans Schäfer (56), Fritz Walter (65), Hans Schäfer (72).

10. 21.12.1952 **WEST GERMANY - YUGOSLAVIA** **3-2(2-2)**
üdweststadion, Ludwigshafen; Referee: Arthur Edward Ellis (England); Attendance: 70,000
GER: Anton Turek (8/0), Erich Retter (5/0), Werner Kohlmeyer (7/0), Horst Eckel (2/0), Josef Posipal (9/1), Erich Schanko (10/0), Helmut Rahn (4/2), Max Morlock (6/6), Ottmar Walter (6/4), Fritz Walter (Cap) (33/23), Bernhard Termath (5/3). Trainer: Josef Herberger (82).
Goals: Fritz Walter (2), Max Morlock (44), Helmut Rahn (70).

11. 28.12.1952 **SPAIN - WEST GERMANY** **2-2(1-0)**
Estadio Chamartín, Madrid; Referee: Vincenzo Orlandini (Italy); Attendance: 80,000
GER: Anton Turek (9/0), Erich Retter (6/0), Werner Kohlmeyer (8/0), Horst Eckel (3/0), Josef Posipal (10/1), Erich Schanko (11/0), Helmut Rahn (5/2), Max Morlock (7/6), Ottmar Walter (7/5) [27.Karl-Heinz Metzner (1/0)], Fritz Walter (Cap) (34/23), Bernhard Termath (6/4). Trainer: Josef Herberger (83).
Goals: Ottmar Walter (7), Bernhard Termath (30).

12. 22.03.1953 **WEST GERMANY - AUSTRIA** **0-0**
Müngersdorferstadion, Köln; Referee: Henri Bauwens (Belgium); Attendance: 76,000
GER: Anton Turek (10/0), Erich Retter (7/0), Werner Kohlmeyer (9/0), Horst Eckel (4/0) [88.Gerhard Harpers (1/0)], Josef Posipal (11/1), Erich Schanko (12/0), Helmut Rahn (6/2), Max Morlock (8/6), Ottmar Walter (8/5) [43.Josef Röhrig (5/0)], Fritz Walter (Cap) (35/23), Hans Schäfer (2/2). Trainer: Josef Herberger (84).

13. 19.08.1953 **NORWAY - WEST GERMANY** **1-1(1-1)** 5th FIFA WC. Qualifiers
Ullevaal Stadion, Oslo; Referee: Bertus Aussum (Netherlands); Attendance: 32,266
GER: Anton Turek (11/0), Erich Retter (8/0), Werner Kohlmeyer (10/0), Horst Eckel (5/0), Josef Posipal (12/1), Erich Schanko (13/0), Helmut Rahn (7/2), Max Morlock (9/6), Ottmar Walter (9/5), Fritz Walter (Cap) (36/24), Hans Schäfer (3/2) [42.Alfred Pfaff (1/0)]. Trainer: Josef Herberger (85).
Goal: Fritz Walter (44).

14. 11.10.1953 **WEST GERMANY – SAAR** **3-0(1-0)** 5th FIFA WC. Qualifiers
Neckarstadion, Stuttgart; Referee: Karel van der Meer (Netherlands); Attendance: 55,000
GER: Anton Turek (12/0), Erich Retter (9/0), Herbert Erhardt (1/0), Karl Mai (1/0), Josef Posipal (Cap) (13/1), Richard Gottinger (1/0) [38.Horst Eckel (6/0)], Helmut Rahn (8/2), Max Morlock (10/8), Horst Schade (3/1), Karl-Heinz Metzner (2/0), Hans Schäfer (4/2). Trainer: Josef Herberger (86).
Goals: Max Morlock (13, 51), Horst Schade (71).

15. 22.11.1953 **WEST GERMANY - NORWAY** **5-1(1-1)** 5th FIFA WC. Qualifiers
Volksparkstadion, Hamburg; Referee: Archer William Leuty (England); Attendance: 78,000
GER: Anton Turek (13/0), Erich Retter (10/0), Werner Kohlmeyer (11/0), Horst Eckel (7/0), Josef Posipal (14/1), Karl Mai (2/0), Helmut Rahn (9/3), Max Morlock (11/10), Ottmar Walter (10/6), Fritz Walter (Cap) (37/25), Richard Herrmann (6/0). Trainer: Josef Herberger (87).
Goals: Max Morlock (31, 63), Ottmar Walter (80), Fritz Walter (80), Helmut Rahn (82).

16. 28.03.1954 **SAAR - WEST GERMANY** **1-3(0-1)** 5th FIFA WC. Qualifiers
Ludwigsparkstadion, Saarbrücken; Referee: Johan „Jan" Bronkhorst (Netherlands); Attendance: 50,000
GER: Anton Turek (14/0), Erich Retter (11/0), Werner Kohlmeyer (12/0), Josef Posipal (15/1), Werner Liebrich (3/0), Erich Schanko (14/0), Helmut Rahn (10/3), Max Morlock (12/12), Fritz Walter (Cap) (38/25) [31.Ottmar Walter (11/6)], Josef Röhrig (6/0), Hans Schäfer (5/3). Trainer: Josef Herberger (88).
Goals: Max Morlock (39, 49), Hans Schäfer (83).

17. 25.04.1954 **SWITZERLAND - WEST GERMANY** **3-5(0-4)**
„St. Jakob" Stadion, Basel; Referee: Bryan Merwyn Griffiths (Wales); Attendance:
GER: Heinz Kubsch (1/0), Erich Retter (12/0) [13.Werner Kohlmeyer (13/0)], Fritz Laband (1/0), Horst Eckel (8/0), Josef Posipal (16/1), Karl Mai (3/0), Richard Herrmann (7/0) [66.Bernhard Klodt (6/1)], Max Morlock (13/13), Ottmar Walter (12/6), Fritz Walter (Cap) (39/27), Hans Schäfer (6/5). Trainer: Josef Herberger (89).
Goals: Hans Schäfer (5), Fritz Walter (16), Max Morlock (30), Hans Schäfer (31), Fritz Walter (85).

18. 17.06.1954 **WEST GERMANY - TURKEY** **4-1(1-1)** 5th FIFA WC. Group Stage.
Wankdorf Stadion, Bern (Switzerland); Referee: José Viera da Costa (Portugal); Attendance: 28,000
GER: Anton Turek (15/0), Fritz Laband (2/0), Werner Kohlmeyer (14/0), Horst Eckel (9/0), Josef Posipal (17/1), Karl Mai (4/0), Bernhard Klodt (7/2), Max Morlock (14/14), Ottmar Walter (13/7), Fritz Walter (Cap) (40/27), Hans Schäfer (7/6). Trainer: Josef Herberger (90).
Goals: Hans Schäfer (12), Bernhard Klodt (51), Ottmar Walter (60), Max Morlock (84).

19. 20.06.1954 **HUNGARY - WEST GERMANY** **8-3(3-1)** 5th FIFA WC. Group Stage.
„St. Jakob" Stadion, Basel (Switzerland); Referee: William Ling (England); Attendance: 53,000
GER: Heinz Kwiatkowski (1/0), Hans Bauer (3/0), Werner Kohlmeyer (15/0), Josef Posipal (18/1), Werner Liebrich (4/0), Paul Mebus (6/0), Helmut Rahn (11/4), Horst Eckel (10/0), Fritz Walter (Cap) (41/27), Alfred Pfaff (2/1), Richard Herrmann (8/1). Trainer: Josef Herberger (91).
Goals: Alfred Pfaff (25), Helmut Rahn (78), Richard Herrmann (84).

20. 23.06.1954 **WEST GERMANY - TURKEY** **7-2(3-1)** 5th FIFA WC. Group Stage.
Hardturm Stadion, Zürich (Switzerland); Referee: Raymond Vincenti (France); Attendance: 17,000
GER: Anton Turek (16/0), Fritz Laband (3/0), Hans Bauer (4/0), Horst Eckel (11/0), Josef Posipal (19/1), Karl Mai (5/0), Bernhard Klodt (8/2), Max Morlock (15/17), Ottmar Walter (14/8), Fritz Walter (Cap) (42/28), Hans Schäfer (8/8). Trainer: Josef Herberger (92).
Goals: Ottmar Walter (7), Hans Schäfer (11), Max Morlock (31, 62, 77), Hans Schäfer (77), Fritz Walter (79).

221. 27.06.1954 **WEST GERMANY - YUGOSLAVIA** **2-0(1-0)** 5th FIFA WC. Quarter-Final.
Stade Charmilles, Genève (Switzerland); Referee: István Zsolt (Hungary); Attendance: 20,000
GER: Anton Turek (17/0), Fritz Laband (4/0), Werner Kohlmeyer (16/0), Horst Eckel (12/0), Werner Liebrich (5/0), Karl Mai (6/0), Helmut Rahn (12/5), Max Morlock (16/17), Ottmar Walter (15/8), Fritz Walter (Cap) (43/28), Hans Schäfer (9/8). Trainer: Josef Herberger (93).
Goals: Ivan Horvat (10 own goal), Helmut Rahn (86).

222. 30.06.1954 **WEST GERMANY - AUSTRIA** **6-1(1-0)** 5th FIFA WC. Semi-Final.
„St. Jakob" Stadion, Basel (Switzerland); Referee: Vincenzo Orlandini (Italy); Attendance: 57,000
GER: Anton Turek (18/0), Josef Posipal (20/1), Werner Kohlmeyer (17/0), Horst Eckel (13/0), Werner Liebrich (6/0), Karl Mai (7/0), Helmut Rahn (13/5), Max Morlock (17/18), Ottmar Walter (16/10), Fritz Walter (Cap) (44/30), Hans Schäfer (10/9). Trainer: Josef Herberger (94).
Goals: Hans Schäfer (31), Max Morlock (47), Fritz Walter (56 penalty), Ottmar Walter (61), Fritz Walter (65 penalty), Ottmar Walter (89).

223. 04.07.1954 **WEST GERMANY - HUNGARY** **3-2(2-2)** 5th FIFA WC. Final.
Wankdorf Stadion, Bern (Switzerland); Referee: William Ling (England); Attendance: 65,000
GER: Anton Turek (19/0), Josef Posipal (21/1), Werner Kohlmeyer (18/0), Horst Eckel (14/0), Werner Liebrich (7/0), Karl Mai (8/0), Helmut Rahn (14/7), Max Morlock (18/19), Ottmar Walter (17/10), Fritz Walter (Cap) (45/30), Hans Schäfer (11/9). Trainer: Josef Herberger (95).
Goals: Max Morlock (11), Helmut Rahn (18, 84).

224. 26.09.1954 **BELGIUM - WEST GERMANY** **2-0(1-0)**
Stade du Heysel, Bruxelles; Referee: Johan „Jan" Bronkhorst (Netherlands); Attendance: 55,116
GER: Fritz Herkenrath (1/0), Herbert Erhardt (2/0), Werner Kohlmeyer (19/0), Josef Posipal (Cap) (22/1), Werner Liebrich (8/0), Karl Mai (9/0), Helmut Rahn (15/7), Max Morlock (19/19), Ottmar Walter (18/10), Ulrich Biesinger (1/0), Bernhard Klodt (9/2). Trainer: Josef Herberger (96).

225. 16.10.1954 **WEST GERMANY - FRANCE** **1-3(0-2)**
Niedersachsenstadion, Hannover; Referee: Bryan Merwyn Griffiths (Wales); Attendance: 85,000
GER: Anton Turek (20/0), Herbert Erhardt (3/0), Werner Kohlmeyer (20/0), Josef Posipal (Cap) (23/1), Werner Liebrich (9/0), Karl Mai (10/0), Bernhard Klodt (10/2), Klaus Stürmer (1/1), Ottmar Walter (19/10), Franz Islacker (1/0), Bernhard Termath (7/4) [22.Uwe Seeler (1/0)]. Trainer: Josef Herberger (97).
Goal: Klaus Stürmer (75).

226. 01.12.1954 **ENGLAND - WEST GERMANY** **3-1(1-0)**
Wembley Stadium, London; Referee: Vincenzo Orlandini (Italy); Attendance: 100,000
GER: Fritz Herkenrath (2/0), Josef Posipal (Cap) (24/1), Werner Kohlmeyer (21/0), Herbert Erhardt (4/0), Werner Liebrich (10/0), Gerhard Harpers (2/0), Gerhard Kaufhold (1/0), Michael Pfeiffer (1/0), Uwe Seeler (2/0), Josef Derwall (1/0), Alfred Beck (1/1). Trainer: Josef Herberger (98).
Goal: Alfred Beck (77).

227. 19.12.1954 **PORTUGAL - WEST GERMANY** **0-3(0-1)**
Estádio Nacional, Lisboa; Referee: Karel van der Meer (Netherlands); Attendance: 70,000
GER: Fritz Herkenrath (3/0), Josef Posipal (Cap) (25/1), Erich Juskowiak (2/1), Herbert Erhardt (5/1), Werner Liebrich (11/0), Gerhard Harpers (3/0), Bernhard Klodt (11/2), Jakob Miltz (1/0), Richard Kreß (1/0) [77.Erwin Waldner (1/0)], Josef Derwall (2/0), Alfred Pfaff (3/2). Trainer: Josef Herberger (99).
Goals: Herbert Erhardt (7), Alfred Pfaff (55), Erich Juskowiak (74).

228. 30.03.1955 **WEST GERMANY - ITALY** **1-2(1-2)**
Neckarstadion, Stuttgart; Referee: István Zsolt (Hungary); Attendance: 82,000
GER: Fritz Herkenrath (4/0), Erich Juskowiak (3/2), Werner Kohlmeyer (22/0), Karl Mai (11/0), Josef Posipal (26/1), Gerhard Harpers (4/0), Helmut Rahn (16/7) [46.Erwin Waldner (2/0)], Max Morlock (20/19), Uwe Seeler (3/0), Fritz Walter (Cap) (46/30), Hans Schäfer (12/9). Trainer: Josef Herberger (100).
Goal: Erich Juskowiak (29 penalty).

229. 28.05.1955 **WEST GERMANY - REPUBLIC OF IRELAND** **2-1(1-0)**
Volksparkstadion, Hamburg; Referee: Karel van der Meer (Netherlands); Attendance: 50,000
GER: Heinz Kubsch (2/0), Erich Retter (13/0), Herbert Erhardt (6/1), Robert Schlienz (1/0), Rudolf Hoffmann (1/0), Karl Mai (12/1), Erwin Waldner (3/1), Hans Weilbächer (1/0), Ulrich Biesinger (2/0), Josef Röhrig (Cap) (7/0), Hans Schäfer (13/9). Trainer: Josef Herberger (101).
Goals: Erwin Waldner (13), Karl Mai (63).

230. 21.08.1955 **SOVIET UNION - WEST GERMANY** **3-2(1-1)**
Dinamo Stadium, Moskva; Referee: William Ling (England); Attendance: 50,000
GER: Fritz Herkenrath (5/0), Erich Juskowiak (4/2), Josef Posipal (27/1), Horst Eckel (15/0), Werner Liebrich (12/0), Gerhard Harpers (5/0), Helmut Rahn (17/7), Fritz Walter (Cap) (47/31), Max Morlock (21/19) [73.Willi Schröder (3/0)], Josef Röhrig (8/0), Hans Schäfer (14/10). Trainer: Josef Herberger (102).
Goals: Fritz Walter (29), Hans Schäfer (53).

231. 25.09.1955 **YUGOSLAVIA - WEST GERMANY** **3-1(2-0)**
Stadion JNA, Beograd; Referee: István Zsolt (Hungary); Attendance: 55,000
GER: Fritz Herkenrath (6/0), Karl Schmidt (1/0), Josef Posipal (28/1), Horst Eckel (16/0), Werner Liebrich (13/0), Josef Röhrig (9/0), Erwin Waldner (4/1) [74.Engelbert Krause (1/0)], Max Morlock (22/20), Ottmar Walter (20/10), Fritz Walter (Cap) (48/31), Hans Schäfer (15/10). Trainer: Josef Herberger (103).
Goal: Max Morlock (89).

232. 16.11.1955 **WEST GERMANY - NORWAY** **2-0(2-0)**
Wildparkstadion, Karlsruhe; Referee: Friedrich Seipelt (Austria); Attendance: 50,000
GER: Fritz Herkenrath (7/0), Josef Posipal (29/1), Karl Schmidt (2/0), Horst Eckel (17/0), Werner Liebrich (14/0), Gerhard Harpers (6/0), Engelbert Krause (2/0), Fritz Walter (Cap) (49/32), Ulrich Biesinger (3/0) [80.Willi Schröder (4/0)], Josef Röhrig (10/1), Erwin Waldner (5/1). Trainer: Josef Herberger (104).
Goals: Fritz Walter (24), Josef Röhrig (27).

233. 18.12.1955 **ITALY - WEST GERMANY** **2-1(1-0)**
Stadio Olimpico, Roma; Referee: Arthur Edward Ellis (England); Attendance: 80,000
GER: Fritz Herkenrath (8/0), Josef Posipal (30/1) [46.Erich Juskowiak (5/2)], Karl Schmidt (3/0), Horst Eckel (18/0), Werner Liebrich (15/0), Karl Mai (13/1), Helmut Rahn (18/7), Fritz Walter (Cap) (50/32), Georg Stollenwerk (5/2), Josef Röhrig (11/2), Hans Schäfer (16/10). Trainer: Josef Herberger (105).
Goal: Josef Röhrig (88).

234. 14.03.1956 **WEST GERMANY - NETHERLANDS** **1-2(0-0)**
Rheinstadion, Düsseldorf; Referee: Reginald Leafe (England); Attendance: 65,000
GER: Fritz Herkenrath (9/0), Josef Posipal (31/1), Erich Juskowiak (6/2), Horst Eckel (19/0), Robert Schlienz (2/0), Karl Schmidt (4/0), Bernhard Klodt (12/2), Fritz Walter (Cap) (51/32), Uwe Seeler (4/0) [73.Erwin Waldner (6/1)], Josef Röhrig (12/2), Hans Schäfer (17/10). Trainer: Josef Herberger (106).
Goal: Cornelis van der Hart (77 own goal).

235. 26.05.1956 **WEST GERMANY - ENGLAND** **1-3(0-1)**
Olympiastadion, West-Berlin; Referee: István Zsolt (Hungary); Attendance: 90,000
GER: Fritz Herkenrath (10/0), Erich Retter (14/0), Erich Juskowiak (7/2), Robert Schlienz (3/0), Heinz Wewers (2/0), Karl Mai (14/1), Erwin Waldner (7/1), Max Morlock (23/20) [40.Alfred Pfaff (4/2)], Ottmar Walter (21/10), Fritz Walter (Cap) (52/33), Hans Schäfer (18/10). Trainer: Josef Herberger (107).
Goal: Fritz Walter (85).

236. 13.06.1956 **NORWAY - WEST GERMANY** **1-3(1-1)**
Ullevaal Stadion, Oslo; Referee: Karel van der Meer (Netherlands); Attendance: 27,708
GER: Günter Sawitzki (1/0), Herbert Erhardt (7/1), Erich Juskowiak (8/2), Herbert Dörner (1/0), Heinz Wewers (3/0), Karl Mai (15/1), Erich Bäumler (1/1), Willi Schröder (5/0), Ulrich Biesinger (4/1), Alfred Pfaff (Cap) (5/2), Theo Schönhöft (1/1). Trainer: Josef Herberger (108).
Goals: Theo Schönhöft (28), Erich Bäumler (46), Ulrich Biesinger (55).

237. 30.06.1956 **SWEDEN - WEST GERMANY** **2-2(2-0)**
Råsundastadion, Stockholm; Referee: Klaas Schippers (Netherlands); Attendance: 30,700
GER: Günter Sawitzki (2/0), Herbert Erhardt (8/1), Erich Juskowiak (9/2), Horst Eckel (20/0), Heinz Wewers (4/0), Herbert Dörner (2/0), Bernhard Klodt (13/2), Willi Schröder (6/1), Ulrich Biesinger (5/2), Alfred Pfaff (Cap) (6/2), Heinz Vollmar (1/0). Trainer: Josef Herberger (109).
Goals: Willi Schröder (51), Ulrich Biesinger (62).

238. 15.09.1956 **WEST GERMANY - SOVIET UNION** **1-2(1-2)**
Niedersachsenstadion, Hannover; Referee: Arthur Edward Ellis (England); Attendance: 86,000
GER: Fritz Herkenrath (11/0), Karl Schmidt (5/0), Erich Juskowiak (10/2), Horst Eckel (21/0), Josef Posipal (32/1), Herbert Erhardt (9/1), Erwin Waldner (8/1), Willi Schröder (7/2), Ulrich Biesinger (6/2) [52.Hans Schäfer (19/10)], Fritz Walter (Cap) (53/33), Heinz Vollmar (2/0). Trainer: Josef Herberger (110).
Goal: Willi Schröder (5).

239. 21.11.1956 **WEST GERMANY - SWITZERLAND** **1-3(1-2)**
Waldstadion, Frankfurt am Main; Referee: Friedrich Seipelt (Austria); Attendance: 80,000
GER: Heinz Kubsch (3/0), Karl Schmidt (6/0), Erich Juskowiak (11/2), Horst Eckel (22/0), Werner Liebrich (16/0), Horst Szymaniak (1/0) [65.Karl Mai (16/1)], Heinz Vollmar (3/0), Fritz Walter (Cap) (54/33), Hans Neuschäfer (1/1), Alfred Pfaff (7/2), Hans Schäfer (20/10). Trainer: Josef Herberger (111).
Goal: Hans Neuschäfer (34).

240. 25.11.1956 **REPUBLIC OF IRELAND - WEST GERMANY** **3-0(0-0)**
Dalymount Park, Dublin; Referee: Archibald Murdock (England); Attendance: 40,000
GER: Heinz Kwiatkowski (2/0), Herbert Erhardt (10/1), Erich Juskowiak (12/2), Elwin Schlebrowski (1/0), Heinz Wewers (5/0), Karl Mai (17/1), Helmut Rahn (19/7), Max Morlock (Cap) (24/20), Jakob Miltz (2/0), Hans Schäfer (21/10) [10.Horst Eckel (23/0)], Heinz Vollmar (4/0). Trainer: Josef Herberger (112).

241. 23.12.1956 **WEST GERMANY - BELGIUM** **4-1(2-1)**
Müngersdorferstadion, Köln; Referee: Johan „Jan" Bronkhorst (Netherlands); Attendance: 67,000
GER: Heinz Kwiatkowski (3/0), Erich Juskowiak (Cap) (13/2), Willi Köchling (1/0), Elwin Schlebrowski (2/0), Heinz Wewers (6/1), Horst Szymaniak (2/0), Erwin Waldner (9/1), Rolf Geiger (1/0), Alfred Kelbassa (1/1), Willi Schröder (8/3), Heinz Vollmar (5/1). Trainer: Josef Herberger (113).
Goals: Willi Schröder (24), Heinz Vollmar (42), Alfred Kelbassa (60), Heinz Wewers (83).

242. 10.03.1957 **AUSTRIA - WEST GERMANY** **2-3(0-2)**
Praterstadion, Wien; Referee: Johan „Jan" Bronkhorst (Netherlands); Attendance: 60,000
GER: Fritz Herkenrath (12/0), Erich Juskowiak (14/2), Karl Schmidt (7/0), Horst Szymaniak (3/0), Heinz Wewers (7/1), Herbert Erhardt (11/1), Willi Schröder (9/3), Helmut Rahn (20/9), Engelbert Krause (3/1), Hans Schäfer (Cap) (22/10), Heinz Vollmar (6/1) [78.Erwin Waldner (10/1)]. Trainer: Josef Herberger (114).
Goals: Helmut Rahn (25), Engelbert Krause (34), Helmut Rahn (69).

243. 03.04.1957 **NETHERLANDS - WEST GERMANY** **1-2(1-1)**
Olympisch Stadion, Amsterdam; Referee: Reginald Leafe (England); Attendance: 60,000
GER: Hans Tilkowski (1/0), Erich Juskowiak (15/2), Karl Schmidt (8/0), Herbert Erhardt (12/1), Heinz Wewers (8/1), Horst Szymaniak (4/0), Helmut Rahn (Cap) (21/9), Willi Schröder (10/3), Engelbert Krause (4/1), Alfred Schmidt (1/1), Gerhard Siedl (1/1). Trainer: Josef Herberger (115).
Goals: Gerhard Siedl (33), Alfred Schmidt (76).

244. 22.05.1957 **WEST GERMANY - SCOTLAND** **1-3(0-2)**
Neckarstadion, Stuttgart; Referee: Gottfried Dienst (Switzerland); Attendance: 80,000
GER: Hans Tilkowski (2/0), Willi Gerdau (1/0), Erich Juskowiak (16/2), Georg Stollenwerk (6/2), Heinz Wewers (9/1), Horst Szymaniak (5/0), Helmut Rahn (Cap) (22/9), Willi Schröder (11/3), Alfred Kelbassa (2/1), Alfred Schmidt (2/1), Gerhard Siedl (2/2). Trainer: Josef Herberger (116).
Goal: Gerhard Siedl (70).

245. 20.11.1957 **WEST GERMANY - SWEDEN** **1-0(1-0)**
Volksparkstadion, Hamburg; Referee: István Zsolt (Hungary); Attendance: 76,000
GER: Günter Sawitzki (3/0), Herbert Erhardt (13/1), Karl Schmidt (9/0), Karl Mai (18/1), Herbert Schäfer (1/0), Horst Szymaniak (6/0), Wolfgang Peters (1/0), Alfred Schmidt (3/2), Alfred Kelbassa (3/1), Willi Schröder (12/3), Hans Schäfer (Cap) (23/10) [74.Bernhard Klodt (14/2)]. Trainer: Josef Herberger (117).
Goal: Alfred Schmidt (17).

246. 22.12.1957 **WEST GERMANY - HUNGARY** **1-0(1-0)**
Niedersachsenstadion, Hannover; Referee: Johannes Heinrich Martens (Netherlands); Attendance: 85,000
GER: Fritz Herkenrath (13/0), Herbert Erhardt (14/1) [53.Georg Stollenwerk (7/2)], Erich Juskowiak (17/2), Horst Eckel (24/0), Heinz Wewers (10/1), Horst Szymaniak (7/0), Hans Cieslarczyk (1/0), Alfred Schmidt (4/2), Alfred Kelbassa (4/2), Hans Schäfer (Cap) (24/10), Heinz Vollmar (7/1). Trainer: Josef Herberger (118).
Goal: Alfred Kelbassa (20).

247. 02.03.1958 **BELGIUM - WEST GERMANY** **0-2(0-1)**
Stade du Heysel, Bruxelles; Referee: Reginald Leafe (England); Attendance: 55,970
GER: Fritz Herkenrath (14/0), Herbert Erhardt (15/1), Erich Juskowiak (18/2), Horst Eckel (25/0), Heinz Wewers (11/1), Horst Szymaniak (8/0), Erwin Waldner (11/1), Alfred Schmidt (5/3), Alfred Kelbassa (5/2), Hans Schäfer (Cap) (25/11), Bernhard Klodt (15/2). Trainer: Josef Herberger (119).
Goals: Alfred Schmidt (23), Hans Schäfer (60).

248. 19.03.1958 **WEST GERMANY - SPAIN** **2-0(1-0)**
Waldstadion, Frankfurt am Main; Referee: Arthur Edward Ellis (Spain); Attendance: 81,000
GER: Fritz Herkenrath (15/0), Georg Stollenwerk (8/2), Erich Juskowiak (19/2), Horst Eckel (26/0), Herbert Erhardt (16/1), Horst Szymaniak (9/0), Bernhard Klodt (16/3), Alfred Schmidt (6/3), Fritz Walter (55/33), Hans Schäfer (Cap) (26/11), Hans Cieslarczyk (2/1). Trainer: Josef Herberger (120).
Goals: Bernhard Klodt (45), Hans Cieslarczyk (47).

249. 02.04.1958 **CZECHOSLOVAKIA - WEST GERMANY** **3-2(1-1)**
Stadion Strahov, Praha; Referee: Nikolai Latishev (Soviet Union); Attendance: 50,000
GER: Günter Sawitzki (4/0), Herbert Erhardt (17/1), Erich Juskowiak (20/2), Horst Eckel (27/0), Alfred Schmidt (7/3) [63.Erwin Waldner (12/1)], Karl-Heinz Schnellinger (1/0), Bernhard Steffen (1/0), Hans Sturm (1/0), Fritz Walter (56/33), Hans Schäfer (Cap) (27/11), Hans Cieslarczyk (3/2). Trainer: Josef Herberger (121).
Goals: Hans Cieslarczyk (41), Imrich Stacho (47 own goal).

250. 08.06.1958 **WEST GERMANY - ARGENTINA** **3-1(2-1)** 6th FIFA WC. Group Stage.
Malmö Stadion, Malmö (Sweden); Referee: Reginald Leafe (England); Attendance: 31,156
GER: Fritz Herkenrath (16/0), Georg Stollenwerk (9/2), Erich Juskowiak (21/2), Horst Eckel (28/0), Herbert Erhardt (18/1), Horst Szymaniak (10/0), Helmut Rahn (23/11), Fritz Walter (57/33), Uwe Seeler (5/1), Alfred Schmidt (8/3), Hans Schäfer (Cap) (28/11). Trainer: Josef Herberger (122).
Goals: Helmut Rahn (33), Uwe Seeler (42), Helmut Rahn (79).

251. 11.06.1958 **WEST GERMANY - CZECHOSLOVAKIA** **2-2(1-0)** 6th FIFA WC. Group Stage.
Olympia Stadion, Helsingborg (Sweden); Referee: Arthur Edward Ellis (England); Attendance: 25,000
GER: Fritz Herkenrath (17/0), Georg Stollenwerk (10/2), Erich Juskowiak (22/2), Karl-Heinz Schnellinger (2/0), Herbert Erhardt (19/1), Horst Szymaniak (11/0), Helmut Rahn (24/12), Fritz Walter (58/33), Uwe Seeler (6/1), Hans Schäfer (Cap) (29/12), Bernhard Klodt (17/3). Trainer: Josef Herberger (123).
Goals: Hans Schäfer (60), Helmut Rahn (70).

252. 15.06.1958 **NORTHERN IRELAND - WEST GERMANY** **2-2(1-1)** 6th FIFA WC. Group Stage.
Malmö Stadion, Malmö (Sweden); Referee: Joaquim Fernandes de Campos (Portugal); Attendance: 21,990
GER: Fritz Herkenrath (18/0), Georg Stollenwerk (11/2), Erich Juskowiak (23/2), Horst Eckel (29/0), Herbert Erhardt (20/1), Horst Szymaniak (12/0), Helmut Rahn (25/13), Fritz Walter (59/33), Uwe Seeler (7/2), Hans Schäfer (Cap) (30/12), Bernhard Klodt (18/3). Trainer: Josef Herberger (124).
Goals: Helmut Rahn (21), Uwe Seeler (79).

253. 19.06.1958 **WEST GERMANY - YUGOSLAVIA** **1-0(1-0)** 6th FIFA WC. Quarter-Finals.
Malmö Stadion, Malmö (Sweden); Referee: Paul Wyssling (Switzerland); Attendance: 20,055
GER: Fritz Herkenrath (19/0), Georg Stollenwerk (12/2), Erich Juskowiak (24/2), Horst Eckel (30/0), Herbert Erhardt (21/1), Horst Szymaniak (13/0), Helmut Rahn (26/14), Fritz Walter (60/33), Uwe Seeler (8/2), Alfred Schmidt (9/3), Hans Schäfer (Cap) (31/12). Trainer: Josef Herberger (125).
Goal: Helmut Rahn (12).

254. 24.06.1958 **SWEDEN - WEST GERMANY** **3-1(1-1)** 6th FIFA WC. Semi-Finals.
Ullevi Stadion, Göteborg; Referee: István Zsolt (Hungary); Attendance: 49,471
GER: Fritz Herkenrath (20/0), Georg Stollenwerk (13/2), Erich Juskowiak (25/2) [*sent off 59*], Horst Eckel (31/0), Herbert Erhardt (22/1), Horst Szymaniak (14/0), Helmut Rahn (27/14), Fritz Walter (61/33), Uwe Seeler (9/2), Hans Schäfer (Cap) (32/13), Hans Cieslarczyk (4/2). Trainer: Josef Herberger (126).
Goal: Hans Schäfer (24).

255. 28.06.1958 **FRANCE - WEST GERMANY** **6-3(3-1)** 6th FIFA WC. Third Place Play-off.
Ullevi Stadion, Göteborg (Sweden); Referee: Juan Regis Brozzi (Argentina); Attendance: 32,483
GER: Heinz Kwiatkowski (4/0), Georg Stollenwerk (14/2), Herbert Erhardt (23/1), Karl-Heinz Schnellinger (3/0), Heinz Wewers (12/1), Horst Szymaniak (15/0), Helmut Rahn (28/15), Hans Sturm (2/0), Alfred Kelbassa (6/2), Hans Schäfer (Cap) (33/14), Hans Cieslarczyk (5/3). Trainer: Josef Herberger (127).
Goals: Hans Cieslarczyk (18), Helmut Rahn (52), Hans Schäfer (84).

256. 24.09.1958 **DENMARK - WEST GERMANY** **1-1(0-1)**
Idrætsparken, København; Referee: Milan Fencl (Czechoslovakia); Attendance: 34,000
GER: Fritz Herkenrath (21/0), Georg Stollenwerk (15/2), Erich Juskowiak (26/2), Herbert Erhardt (24/1), Günter Jäger (1/0), Horst Szymaniak (16/0), Engelbert Krause (5/1), Helmut Haller (1/0) [80.Hans Cieslarczyk (6/3)], Uwe Seeler (10/2), Alfred Schmidt (10/3), Helmut Rahn (Cap) (29/16). Trainer: Josef Herberger (128).
Goal: Helmut Rahn (32).

257. 26.10.1958 **FRANCE - WEST GERMANY** **2-2(1-1)**
Stade Olympique „Yves du Manoir", Colombes, Paris; Referee: Arthur Edward Ellis (England); Attendance: 50,992
GER: Hans Tilkowski (3/0), Georg Stollenwerk (16/2), Hans Bauer (5/0), Alfred Schmidt (11/3), Herbert Erhardt (25/1), Horst Szymaniak (17/0), Helmut Rahn (Cap) (30/17), Helmut Haller (2/0), Uwe Seeler (11/3), Rolf Geiger (2/0), Hans Cieslarczyk (7/3). Trainer: Josef Herberger (129).
Goals: Helmut Rahn (13), Uwe Seeler (79).

58. 19.11.1958 **WEST GERMANY - AUSTRIA** **2-2(1-1)**
lympiastadion, West-Berlin; Referee: Milan Fencl (Czechoslovakia); Attendance: 75,000
ER: Hans Tilkowski (4/0), Georg Stollenwerk (17/2), Karl-Heinz Schnellinger (4/0), Horst Eckel (32/0), Herbert Erhardt (26/1), Horst Szymaniak (18/0), elmut Rahn (Cap) (31/19), Helmut Haller (3/0), Uwe Seeler (12/3), Alfred Schmidt (12/3), Helmut Kapitulski (1/0). Trainer: Josef Herberger (130).
oals: Helmut Rahn (16, 89).

59. 21.12.1958 **WEST GERMANY - BULGARIA** **3-0(1-0)**
osenaustadion, Augsburg; Referee: Friedrich Seipelt (Austria); Attendance: 60,000
ER: Günter Sawitzki (5/0), Georg Stollenwerk (18/2), Karl-Heinz Schnellinger (5/0), Karl Mai (19/1), Herbert Erhardt (27/1), Helmut Benthaus (1/0), rwin Waldner (13/2), Rolf Geiger (3/0), Uwe Seeler (13/5), Helmut Haller (4/0) [46.Max Morlock (25/20)], Helmut Rahn (Cap) (32/19). Trainer: Josef erberger (131).
oals: Uwe Seeler (44), Erwin Waldner (51), Uwe Seeler (74).

60. 28.12.1958 **EGYPT - WEST GERMANY** **2-1(1-1)**
Muhammad Ali" Stadium, Cairo; Referee: Concetto Lo Bello (Italy); Attendance: 30,000
ER: Hans Tilkowski (5/0), Walter Zastrau (1/0), Karl-Heinz Schnellinger (6/0), Karl Mai (20/1) [46.Heinz Kördell (1/0)], Alfred Pyka (1/0), Helmut enthaus (2/0), Helmut Rahn (Cap) (33/19), Max Morlock (26/21), Ulrich Biesinger (7/2) [62.Karl Ringel (1/0)], Helmut Faeder (1/0), Theo Klöckner (1/0). rainer: Josef Herberger (132).
oal: Max Morlock (36).

61. 06.05.1959 **SCOTLAND - WEST GERMANY** **3-2(3-2)**
ampden Park, Glasgow; Referee: Arthur Edward Ellis (England); Attendance: 103,415
ER: Günter Sawitzki (6/0), Erich Juskowiak (27/3), Karl-Heinz Schnellinger (7/0), Helmut Benthaus (3/0), Herbert Erhardt (28/1), Horst Szymaniak (19/0), elmut Rahn (Cap) (34/19), Rolf Geiger (4/0), Uwe Seeler (14/6), Alfred Schmidt (13/3), Hans Schäfer (34/14). Trainer: Josef Herberger (133).
oals: Uwe Seeler (14), Erich Juskowiak (36 penalty).

62. 20.05.1959 **WEST GERMANY - POLAND** **1-1(0-1)**
olksparkstadion, Hamburg; Referee: Joaquim Fernandes de Campos (Portugal); Attendance: 60,000
ER: Günter Sawitzki (7/0), Matthias Mauritz (1/0), Erich Juskowiak (28/3), Karl Mai (21/1), Herbert Erhardt (Cap) (29/1), Horst Szymaniak (20/0), ernhard Klodt (19/3) [72.Erwin Stein (1/1)], Rolf Geiger (5/0), Helmut Haller (5/0), Alfred Schmidt (14/3), Theo Klöckner (2/0). Trainer: Josef Herberger 34).
oal: Erwin Stein (80).

63. 04.10.1959 **SWITZERLAND - WEST GERMANY** **0-4(0-1)**
/ankdorf Stadion, Bern; Referee: Friedrich Seipelt (Austria); Attendance: 50,000
ER: Hans Tilkowski (6/0), Georg Stollenwerk (19/2), Erich Juskowiak (29/4), Helmut Benthaus (4/0), Herbert Erhardt (Cap) (30/1), Horst Szymaniak 1/0), Helmut Rahn (35/20), Uwe Seeler (15/6) [76.Alfred Schmidt (15/3)], Albert Brülls (1/1), Gerhard Siedl (3/2), Heinz Vollmar (8/2). Trainer: Josef erberger (135).
oals: Heinz Vollmar (5), Albert Brülls (73), Helmut Rahn (73), Erich Juskowiak (74 penalty).

64. 21.10.1959 **WEST GERMANY - NETHERLANDS** **7-0(3-0)**
üngersdorferstadion, Köln; Referee: Karol Galba (Czechoslovakia); Attendance: 45,000
ER: Friedrich Ewert (1/0), Georg Stollenwerk (20/2), Erich Juskowiak (30/4), Helmut Benthaus (5/0), Herbert Erhardt (Cap) (31/1), Horst Szymaniak 2/0), Helmut Rahn (36/20), Alfred Schmidt (16/5), Uwe Seeler (16/9), Albert Brülls (2/2), Gerhard Siedl (4/3). Trainer: Josef Herberger (136).
oals: Albert Brülls (15), Alfred Schmidt (30), Uwe Seeler (56, 65), Alfred Schmidt (79), Uwe Seeler (87), Gerhard Siedl (90).

65. 08.11.1959 **HUNGARY - WEST GERMANY** **4-3(1-0)**
épstadion, Budapest; Referee: Elmar Saar (Soviet Union); Attendance: 90,000
ER: Hans Tilkowski (7/0), Georg Stollenwerk (21/2), Erich Juskowiak (31/4), Helmut Benthaus (6/0), Herbert Erhardt (Cap) (32/1), Horst Szymaniak 3/0), Helmut Rahn (37/20), Alfred Schmidt (17/5), Uwe Seeler (17/11), Albert Brülls (3/3), Gerhard Siedl (5/3). Trainer: Josef Herberger (137).
oals: Uwe Seeler (72, 81), Albert Brülls (89).

66. 20.12.1959 **WEST GERMANY - YUGOSLAVIA** **1-1(0-1)**
iedersachsenstadion, Hannover; Referee: Johan Heinrich Martens (Netherlands); Attendance: 85,000
ER: Günter Sawitzki (8/0), Georg Stollenwerk (22/2), Karl-Heinz Schnellinger (8/0), Wîlli Schulz (1/0), Herbert Erhardt (Cap) (33/1), Horst Szymaniak 4/0), Helmut Rahn (38/20), Alfred Schmidt (18/6), Uwe Seeler (18/11), Albert Brülls (4/3) [6.Heinz Vollmar (9/2)], Gerhard Siedl (6/3). Trainer: Josef erberger (138).
oal: Alfred Schmidt (73).

67. 23.03.1960 **WEST GERMANY - CHILE** **2-1(0-1)**
eckarstadion, Stuttgart; Referee: Gottfried Dienst (Switzerland); Attendance: 72,500
ER: Hans Tilkowski (8/0), Georg Stollenwerk (23/2), Karl-Heinz Schnellinger (9/0), Helmut Benthaus (7/0), Herbert Erhardt (Cap) (34/1) [40.Leo Wilden /0)], Hans-Jürgen Sundermann (1/0), Helmut Rahn (39/20), Helmut Haller (6/1), Uwe Seeler (19/12), Alfred Schmidt (19/6) [70.Jürgen Schütz (1/0)], lbert Brülls (5/3). Trainer: Josef Herberger (139).
oals: Helmut Haller (72), Uwe Seeler (75).

68. 27.04.1960 **WEST GERMANY - PORTUGAL** **2-1(1-0)**
idweststadion, Ludwigshafen; Referee: Kevin Howley (England); Attendance: 45,000
ER: Hans Tilkowski (9/0), Herbert Erhardt (Cap) (35/1), Karl-Heinz Schnellinger (10/0), Wîlli Schulz (2/0), Leo Wilden (2/0), Horst Szymaniak (25/0), elmut Rahn (40/21), Jürgen Schütz (2/0), Uwe Seeler (20/13), Helmut Haller (7/1), Albert Brülls (6/3). Trainer: Josef Herberger (140).
oals: Uwe Seeler (35), Helmut Rahn (61).

69. 11.05.1960 **WEST GERMANY - REPUBLIC OF IRELAND** **0-1(0-1)**
heinstadion, Düsseldorf; Referee: Arthur Edward Ellis (England); Attendance: 51,000
ER: Günter Sawitzki (9/0), Willi Giesemann (1/0), Herbert Erhardt (Cap) (36/1), Wîlli Schulz (3/0), Ferdinand Wenauer (1/0), Ingo Porges (1/0), Bernhard effen (2/0), Alfred Schmidt (20/6), Albert Brülls (7/3), Helmut Haller (8/1), Heinz Vollmar (10/2). Trainer: Josef Herberger (141).

270. 03.08.1960 **ICELAND - WEST GERMANY** **0-5(0-2)**
Laugardalsvöllur, Reykjavík; Referee: Thomas Wharton (Scotland); Attendance: 8,000
GER: Hans Tilkowski (10/0), Friedel Lutz (1/0), Karl-Heinz Schnellinger (11/0), Wîlli Schulz (4/0), Herbert Erhardt (Cap) (37/1), Horst Szymaniak (26/0), Willy Reitgaßl (1/1), Albert Brülls (8/3) [57.Joseph Marx (1/1)], Uwe Seeler (21/14), Helmut Haller (9/1), Gert Dörfel (1/2). Trainer: Josef Herberger (142).
Goals: Uwe Seeler (12), Gert Dörfel (25, 50), Willy Reitgaßl (73), Joseph Marx (86).

271. 26.10.1960 **NORTHERN IRELAND - WEST GERMANY** **3-4(1-1)** 7th FIFA WC. Qualifiers
Windsor Park, Belfast; Referee: Leopold Sylvain Horn (Netherlands); Attendance: 40,000
GER: Hans Tilkowski (11/0), Herbert Erhardt (Cap) (38/1), Karl-Heinz Schnellinger (12/0), Willi Giesemann (2/0), Leo Wilden (3/0), Horst Szymaniak (27/0), Richard Kreß (2/0), Albert Brülls (9/4), Uwe Seeler (22/15), Günther Herrmann (1/0), Gert Dörfel (2/4). Trainer: Josef Herberger (143).
Goals: Albert Brülls (6), Uwe Seeler (53), Gert Dörfel (54, 80).

272. 20.11.1960 **GREECE - WEST GERMANY** **0-3(0-3)** 7th FIFA WC. Qualifiers
Stádio „Leoforos Alexandras", Athína; Referee: Ehrlich (Yugoslavia); Attendance: 25,000
GER: Hans Tilkowski (12/0), Friedel Lutz (2/0), Karl-Heinz Schnellinger (13/0), Willi Giesemann (3/0), Herbert Erhardt (Cap) (39/1), Horst Szymaniak (28/0), Richard Kreß (3/0), Helmut Haller (10/2), Uwe Seeler (23/15), Albert Brülls (10/5), Gert Dörfel (3/5). Trainer: Josef Herberger (144).
Goals: Gert Dörfel (10), Albert Brülls (29), Helmut Haller (43).

273. 23.11.1960 **BULGARIA - WEST GERMANY** **2-1(0-1)**
Nationalen stadion "Vasil Levski", Sofia; Referee: Józef Kowal (Poland); Attendance: 45,000
GER: Friedrich Ewert (2/0), Friedel Lutz (3/0), Karl-Heinz Schnellinger (14/0), Willi Giesemann (4/0), Herbert Erhardt (Cap) (40/1), Horst Szymaniak (29/0) [81.Helmut Benthaus (8/0)], Richard Kreß (4/0) [46.Gert Dörfel (4/5)], Helmut Haller (11/2), Albert Brülls (11/5), Günther Herrmann (2/0), Heinz Vollmar (11/3). Trainer: Josef Herberger (145).
Goal: Heinz Vollmar (12).

274. 08.03.1961 **WEST GERMANY - BELGIUM** **1-0(1-0)**
Waldstadion,Frankfurt; Referee: Josef Gulde (Switzerland); Attendance: 65,000
GER: Hans Tilkowski (13/0), Friedel Lutz (4/0), Karl-Heinz Schnellinger (15/0) [15.Leo Wilden (4/0)], Willi Giesemann (5/0), Herbert Erhardt (Cap) (41/1) Horst Szymaniak (30/0), Heinz Vollmar (12/3), Helmut Haller (12/2), Uwe Seeler (24/15), Albert Brülls (12/5), Gert Dörfel (5/6). Trainer: Josef Herberger (146).
Goal: Gert Dörfel (33).

275. 26.03.1961 **CHILE - WEST GERMANY** **3-1(2-1)**
Estadio Nacional, Santiago; Referee: José Luis Praddaude (Argentina); Attendance: 47,816
GER: Hans Tilkowski (14/0), Friedel Lutz (5/0), Herbert Erhardt (Cap) (42/1), Willi Giesemann (6/0) [65.Jürgen Werner (1/0)], Leo Wilden (5/0), Horst Szymaniak (31/0), Richard Kreß (5/0), Albert Brülls (13/5), Uwe Seeler (25/15), Günther Herrmann (3/1), Gert Dörfel (6/6). Trainer: Josef Herberger (147).
Goal: Günther Herrmann (12).

276. 10.05.1961 **WEST GERMANY – NORTHERN IRELAND** **2-1(1-0)** 7th FIFA WC. Qualifiers
Olympiastadion, West-Berlin; Referee: Curt Lindberg (Sweden); Attendance: 94,600
GER: Hans Tilkowski (15/0), Herbert Erhardt (Cap) (43/1), Karl-Heinz Schnellinger (16/0), Jürgen Werner (2/0), Leo Wilden (6/0), Horst Szymaniak (32/0), Richard Kreß (6/1), Günther Herrmann (4/1), Uwe Seeler (26/15), Klaus Stürmer (2/1), Albert Brülls (14/6). Trainer: Josef Herberger (148).
Goals: Richard Kreß (29), Albert Brülls (58).

277. 20.09.1961 **WEST GERMANY - DENMARK** **5-1(3-0)**
Rheinstadion, Düsseldorf; Referee: Johan Heinrich Martens (Netherlands); Attendance: 46,000
GER: Hans Tilkowski (16/0), Hans Nowak (1/0), Karl-Heinz Schnellinger (17/0), Wîlli Schulz (5/0), Ferdinand Wenauer (2/0), Willi Giesemann (7/0), Richard Kreß (7/2), Günther Herrmann (5/1), Uwe Seeler (Cap) (27/18), Helmut Haller (13/2), Albert Brülls (15/7). Trainer: Josef Herberger (149).
Goals: Uwe Seeler (8), Albert Brülls (12), Uwe Seeler (35), Richard Kreß (54), Uwe Seeler (56).

278. 08.10.1961 **POLAND - WEST GERMANY** **0-2(0-1)**
Stadion Wojska Polskiego, Warszawa; Referee: Karel Galba (Czechoslovakia); Attendance: 25,000
GER: Hans Tilkowski (17/0), Hans Nowak (2/0), Herbert Erhardt (Cap) (44/1), Wîlli Schulz (6/0), Ferdinand Wenauer (3/0), Willi Giesemann (8/0), Werner Olk (1/0) [46.Richard Kreß (8/2)], Günther Herrmann (6/1), Uwe Seeler (28/18), Helmut Haller (14/3), Albert Brülls (16/8). Trainer: Josef Herberger (150).
Goals: Albert Brülls (19), Helmut Haller (65).

279. 22.10.1961 **WEST GERMANY - GREECE** **2-1(2-0)** 7th FIFA WC. Qualifiers
Rosenaustadion, Augsburg; Referee: Birger Nilsen (Norway); Attendance: 43,000
GER: Hans Tilkowski (18/0), Hans Nowak (3/0), Karl-Heinz Schnellinger (18/0), Wîlli Schulz (7/0), Herbert Erhardt (Cap) (45/1), Willi Giesemann (9/0), Richard Kreß (9/2), Günther Herrmann (7/1), Uwe Seeler (29/20), Helmut Haller (15/3), Albert Brülls (17/8). Trainer: Josef Herberger (151).
Goals: Uwe Seeler (5, 27).

280. 11.04.1962 **WEST GERMANY - URUGUAY** **3-0(1-0)**
Volksparkstadion, Hamburg; Referee: Leopold Sylvain Horn (Netherlands); Attendance: 71,000
GER: Wolfgang Fahrian (1/0), Karl-Heinz Schnellinger (19/0), Andreas Kurbjuhn (1/0), Wîlli Schulz (8/0), Ferdinand Wenauer (4/0), Horst Szymaniak (33/0), Willi Koslowski (1/1), Helmut Haller (16/4), Uwe Seeler (Cap) (30/20), Albert Brülls (18/8), Hans Schäfer (35/15). Trainer: Josef Herberger (152).
Goals: Helmut Haller (25), Hans Schäfer (53), Willi Koslowski (75).

281. 31.05.1962 **WEST GERMANY - ITALY** **0-0** 7th FIFA WC. Group Stage.
Estadio Nacional, Santiago (Chile); Referee: Robert Holley Davidson (Scotland); Attendance: 65,440
GER: Wolfgang Fahrian (2/0), Hans Nowak (4/0), Karl-Heinz Schnellinger (20/0), Wîlli Schulz (9/0), Herbert Erhardt (46/1), Horst Szymaniak (34/0), Hans Sturm (3/0), Helmut Haller (17/4), Uwe Seeler (31/20), Albert Brülls (19/8), Hans Schäfer (Cap) (36/15). Trainer: Josef Herberger (153).

282. 03.06.1962 **WEST GERMANY - SWITZERLAND** **2-1(1-0)** 7th FIFA WC. Group Stage.
Estadio Nacional, Santiago (Chile); Referee: Leopold Sylvain Horn (Netherlands); Attendance: 64,992
GER: Wolfgang Fahrian (3/0), Hans Nowak (5/0), Karl-Heinz Schnellinger (21/0), Wîlli Schulz (10/0), Herbert Erhardt (47/1), Horst Szymaniak (35/0), Willi Koslowski (2/1), Helmut Haller (18/4), Uwe Seeler (32/21), Hans Schäfer (Cap) (37/15), Albert Brülls (20/9). Trainer: Josef Herberger (154).
Goals: Albert Brülls (45), Uwe Seeler (60).

283. 06.06.1962 **CHILE - WEST GERMANY** **0-2(0-1)** 7th FIFA WC. Group Stage.
Estadio Nacional, Santiago; Referee: Robert Holley Davidson (Scotland); Attendance: 67,224
GER: Wolfgang Fahrian (4/0), Hans Nowak (6/0), Karl-Heinz Schnellinger (22/0), Wîlli Schulz (11/0), Herbert Erhardt (48/1), Willi Giesemann (10/0), Engelbert Krause (6/1), Horst Szymaniak (36/1), Uwe Seeler (33/22), Hans Schäfer (Cap) (38/15), Albert Brülls (21/9). Trainer: Josef Herberger (155).
Goals: Horst Szymaniak (21 penalty), Uwe Seeler (82).

284. 10.06.1962 **YUGOSLAVIA - WEST GERMANY** **1-0(0-0)** 7th FIFA WC. Quarter-Finals.
Estadio Nacional, Santiago (Chile); Referee: Arturo Maximo Yamasaki Maldonado (Peru); Attendance: 63,324
GER: Wolfgang Fahrian (5/0), Hans Nowak (7/0), Karl-Heinz Schnellinger (23/0), Wîlli Schulz (12/0), Herbert Erhardt (49/1), Horst Szymaniak (37/1), Willi Giesemann (11/0), Helmut Haller (19/4), Uwe Seeler (34/22), Hans Schäfer (Cap) (39/15), Albert Brülls (22/9). Trainer: Josef Herberger (156).

285. 30.09.1962 **YUGOSLAVIA - WEST GERMANY** **2-3(1-2)**
Stadion Maksimir, Zagreb; Referee: Gino Rigato (Italy); Attendance: 50,000
GER: Wolfgang Fahrian (6/0), Herbert Erhardt (Cap) (50/1), Karl-Heinz Schnellinger (24/0), Wîlli Schulz (13/0), Leo Wilden (7/0), Stefan Reisch (1/0), Horst Trimhold (1/0) [77.Willi Koslowski (3/1)], Jürgen Schütz (3/0), Heinz Strehl (1/3), Friedhelm Konietzka (1/0), Engelbert Krause (7/1). Trainer: Josef Herberger (157).
Goals: Heinz Strehl (19, 24, 61).

286. 24.10.1962 **WEST GERMANY - FRANCE** **2-2(0-2)**
Neckarstadion, Stuttgart; Referee: Friedrich Seipelt (Austria); Attendance: 75,000
GER: Wolfgang Fahrian (7/0) [46.Günter Bernard (1/0)], Fritz Pott (1/0), Karl-Heinz Schnellinger (25/0), Wîlli Schulz (14/0) [43.Heinz Steinmann (1/1)], Leo Wilden (8/0), Stefan Reisch (2/0), Uwe Seeler (Cap) (35/22), Jürgen Schütz (4/0), Heinz Strehl (2/3), Friedhelm Konietzka (2/1), Wolfgang Solz (1/0). Trainer: Josef Herberger (158).
Goals: Friedhelm Konietzka (46), Heinz Steinmann (82).

287. 23.12.1962 **WEST GERMANY - SWITZERLAND** **5-1(2-1)**
Wildparkstadion, Karlsruhe; Referee: Pieter Paulus Roomer (Netherlands); Attendance: 48,000
GER: Günter Bernard (2/0), Hans Nowak (8/0), Karl-Heinz Schnellinger (26/0), Jürgen Werner (3/1), Leo Wilden (9/0), Stefan Reisch (3/0), Engelbert Krause (8/2), Jürgen Schütz (5/2), Uwe Seeler (Cap) (36/22), Hans Küppers (1/1), Alfred Heiß (1/0). Trainer: Josef Herberger (159).
Goals: Engelbert Krause (32), Jürgen Werner (36), Jürgen Schütz (47, 77), Hans Küppers (79).

288. 05.05.1963 **WEST GERMANY - BRAZIL** **1-2(1-0)**
Volksparkstadion, Hamburg; Referee: Gottfried Dienst (Switzerland); Attendance: 71,000
GER: Wolfgang Fahrian (8/0), Hans Nowak (9/0), Karl-Heinz Schnellinger (27/0), Wîlli Schulz (15/0), Leo Wilden (10/0), Jürgen Werner (4/2), Alfred Heiß (2/0), Jürgen Schütz (6/2), Uwe Seeler (Cap) (37/22), Friedhelm Konietzka (3/1) [46.Heinz Strehl (3/3)], Gert Dörfel (7/6). Trainer: Josef Herberger (160).
Goal: Jürgen Werner (45 penalty).

289. 28.09.1963 **WEST GERMANY - TURKEY** **3-0(0-0)**
Waldstadion, Frankfurt am Main; Referee: Gino Rigato (Italy); Attendance: 47,000
GER: Wolfgang Fahrian (9/0), Hans Nowak (10/0), Fritz Pott (2/0), Wîlli Schulz (16/0), Leo Wilden (11/0), Alfred Schmidt (21/6) [46.Stefan Reisch (4/0)], Reinhard Libuda (1/0), Werner Krämer (1/0), Uwe Seeler (Cap) (38/25), Friedhelm Konietzka (4/1) [69.Wolfgang Overath (1/0)], Gert Dörfel (8/6). Trainer: Josef Herberger (161).
Goals: Uwe Seeler (52, 56, 66 penalty).

290. 03.11.1963 **SWEDEN - WEST GERMANY** **2-1(0-0)**
Råsundastadion, Stockholm; Referee: Leopold Sylvain Horn (Netherlands); Attendance: 10,192
GER: Günter Sawitzki (10/0), Hans Nowak (11/0), Andreas Kurbjuhn (2/0), Wîlli Schulz (17/0), Leo Wilden (12/0), Stefan Reisch (5/0), Reinhard Libuda (2/0), Werner Krämer (2/0), Uwe Seeler (Cap) (39/25), Wolfgang Overath (2/0), Gert Dörfel (9/7). Trainer: Josef Herberger (162).
Goal: Gert Dörfel (54).

291. 29.12.1963 **MOROCCO - WEST GERMANY** **1-4(1-2)**
Stade d`Honneur, Casablanca; Referee: Juan Gardeazábal Garay (Spain); Attendance: 15,000
GER: Friedrich Ewert (3/0), Hans Nowak (12/0), Andreas Kurbjuhn (3/0), Wîlli Schulz (18/0), Leo Wilden (13/0) [57.Wolfgang Overath (3/0)], Stefan Reisch (6/0), Reinhard Libuda (3/0), Werner Krämer (3/1), Alfred Schmidt (Cap) (22/7), Friedhelm Konietzka (5/3), Klaus Gerwien (1/0) [78.Diethelm Ferner (1/0)]. Trainer: Josef Herberger (163).
Goals: Friedhelm Konietzka (14), Alfred Schmidt (28), Werner Krämer (57), Friedhelm Konietzka (88).

292. 01.01.1964 **ALGERIA - WEST GERMANY** **2-0(2-0)**
Stade 20 Août 1955, Alger; Referee: Bahri Ben Saïd (Tunisia); Attendance: 17,000
GER: Friedrich Ewert (4/0) [Hans Tilkowski (19/0)], Friedel Lutz (6/0), Andreas Kurbjuhn (4/0), Wîlli Schulz (19/0), Leo Wilden (14/0), Stefan Reisch (7/0), Reinhard Libuda (4/0) [70.Diethelm Ferner (2/0)], Werner Krämer (4/1), Alfred Schmidt (Cap) (23/7) [46.Wolfgang Overath (4/0)], Friedhelm Konietzka (6/3), Klaus Gerwien (2/0). Trainer: Josef Herberger (164).

293. 29.04.1964 **WEST GERMANY - CZECHOSLOVAKIA** **3-4(1-3)**
Südweststadion, Ludwigshafen; Referee: Joseph Hannet (Belgium); Attendance: 65,000
GER: Wolfgang Fahrian (10/0), Hans Nowak (13/0), Fritz Pott (3/0), Wîlli Schulz (20/0) [71.Stefan Reisch (8/0)], Leo Wilden (15/0), Wolfgang Weber (1/0), Karl-Heinz Thielen (1/0), Rolf Geiger (6/1), Uwe Seeler (Cap) (40/27), Wolfgang Overath (5/0), Wolfgang Solz (2/0) [46.Reinhard Libuda (5/0)]. Trainer: Josef Herberger (165).
Goals: Uwe Seeler (2), Rolf Geiger (55), Uwe Seeler (88).

294. 12.05.1964 **WEST GERMANY - SCOTLAND** **2-2(2-0)**
Niedersachsenstadion, Hannover; Referee: Tonny Kolbech Poulsen (Denmark); Attendance: 75,000
GER: Hans Tilkowski (20/0), Hans Nowak (14/0), Rudolf Steiner (1/0), Horst Szymaniak (38/1), Willi Giesemann (12/0), Wolfgang Weber (2/0), Reinhard Libuda (6/0), Alfred Schmidt (24/7) [25.Stefan Reisch (9/0)], Uwe Seeler (Cap) (41/29), Rolf Geiger (7/1), Gert Dörfel (10/7). Trainer: Josef Herberger (166).
Goals: Uwe Seeler (32, 33).

295. 07.06.1964 **FINLAND - WEST GERMANY** **1-4(1-3)**
Olympiastadion, Helsinki; Referee: Gösta Lindberg (Sweden); Attendance: 11,056
GER: Hans Tilkowski (21/0), Friedel Lutz (7/0) [78.Wilhelm Sturm (1/0)], Theo Redder (1/0), Wîlli Schulz (21/0), Klaus-Dieter Sieloff (1/0), Wolfgang Weber (3/0), Engelbert Krause (9/3), Rolf Geiger (8/2), Alfred Schmidt (Cap) (25/8), Friedhelm Konietzka (7/3), Wolfgang Overath (6/1). Trainer: Josef Herberger (167).
Goals: Rolf Geiger (13), Wolfgang Overath (36), Alfred Schmidt (39), Engelbert Krause (71).

296. 04.11.1964 **WEST GERMANY - SWEDEN** **1-1(1-0)** 8th FIFA WC. Qualifiers
Olympiastadion, West-Berlin; Referee: Gottfried Dienst (Switzerland); Attendance: 70,229
GER: Hans Tilkowski (22/0), Hans Nowak (15/0), Karl-Heinz Schnellinger (28/0), Horst Szymaniak (39/1), Willi Giesemann (13/0), Wolfgang Weber (4/0), Rudolf Brunnenmeier (1/1), Helmut Haller (20/4), Uwe Seeler (Cap) (42/29), Wolfgang Overath (7/1), Gert Dörfel (11/7). Trainer: Helmut Schön (1).
Goal: Rudolf Brunnenmeier (24).

297. 13.03.1965 **WEST GERMANY - ITALY** **1-1(1-0)**
Volksparkstadion, Hamburg; Referee: Gunnar Michaelsen (Denmark); Attendance: 70,000
GER: Hans Tilkowski (23/0) [56.Manfred Manglitz (1/0)], Josef Piontek (1/0), Bernd Patzke (1/0), Horst-Dieter Höttges (1/0) [32.Heinz Steinmann (2/1)], Klaus-Dieter Sieloff (2/1), Wolfgang Weber (5/0), Alfred Heiß (3/0), Hans Küppers (2/1), Rudolf Brunnenmeier (Cap) (2/1), Friedhelm Konietzka (8/3), Heinz Hornig (1/0). Trainer: Helmut Schön (2).
Goal: Klaus-Dieter Sieloff (41 penalty).

298. 24.04.1965 **WEST GERMANY - CYPRUS** **5-0(3-0)** 8th FIFA WC. Qualifiers
Wildparkstadion, Karlsruhe; Referee: Norman Mootz (Luxembourg); Attendance: 39,675
GER: Manfred Manglitz (2/0), Horst-Dieter Höttges (2/0), Bernd Patzke (2/0), Wîlli Schulz (Cap) (22/0), Klaus-Dieter Sieloff (3/3), Max Lorenz (1/0), Lothar Ulsaß (1/0), Friedhelm Konietzka (9/3), Heinz Strehl (4/4), Wolfgang Overath (8/3), Heinz Hornig (2/0). Trainer: Helmut Schön (3).
Goals: Klaus-Dieter Sieloff (19), Wolfgang Overath (22), Klaus-Dieter Sieloff (37 penalty), Heinz Strehl (69), Wolfgang Overath (85).

299. 12.05.1965 **WEST GERMANY - ENGLAND** **0-1(0-1)**
Städtischen Stadion, Nürnberg; Referee: István Zsolt (Hungary); Attendance: 70,000
GER: Hans Tilkowski (24/0), Josef Piontek (2/0), Horst-Dieter Höttges (3/0), Wîlli Schulz (Cap) (23/0), Klaus-Dieter Sieloff (4/3), Max Lorenz (2/0) [42.Heinz Steinmann (3/1)], Karl-Heinz Thielen (2/0), Werner Krämer (5/1), Walter Rodekamp (1/0), Wolfgang Overath (9/3), Heinz Hornig (3/0). Trainer: Helmut Schön (4).

300. 26.05.1965 **SWITZERLAND - WEST GERMANY** **0-1(0-1)**
„St. Jakob" Stadion, Basel; Referee: Adolfo Bueno Perales (Spain); Attendance: 40,000
GER: Hans Tilkowski (25/0), Josef Piontek (3/0), Horst-Dieter Höttges (4/0), Wîlli Schulz (Cap) (24/0), Klaus-Dieter Sieloff (5/3), Max Lorenz (3/0), Alfred Heiß (4/0), Hans Küppers (3/1), Walter Rodekamp (2/1), Wolfgang Overath (10/3), Hans Rebele (1/0). Trainer: Helmut Schön (5).
Goal: Walter Rodekamp (43).

301. 06.06.1965 **BRAZIL - WEST GERMANY** **2-0(1-0)**
Estádio „Jornalista Mário Filho" [Maracanã], Rio de Janeiro; Referee: Carlos Riveros (Peru); Attendance: 140,000
GER: Hans Tilkowski (26/0), Josef Piontek (4/0), Horst-Dieter Höttges (5/0) [46.Willi Giesemann (14/0)], Wîlli Schulz (Cap) (25/0), Klaus-Dieter Sieloff (6/3), Max Lorenz (4/0), Alfred Heiß (5/0), Werner Krämer (6/1), Walter Rodekamp (3/1), Wolfgang Overath (11/3) [46.Hans Küppers (4/1)], Reinhard Libuda (7/0). Trainer: Helmut Schön (6).

302. 26.09.1965 **SWEDEN - WEST GERMANY** **1-2(1-1)** 8th FIFA WC. Qualifiers
Råsundastadion, Stockholm; Referee: Kenneth Dagnall (England); Attendance: 52,943
GER: Hans Tilkowski (27/0), Horst-Dieter Höttges (6/0), Karl-Heinz Schnellinger (29/0), Franz Beckenbauer (1/0), Klaus-Dieter Sieloff (7/3), Wîlli Schulz (26/0), Rudolf Brunnenmeier (3/1), Peter Grosser (1/0), Uwe Seeler (Cap) (43/30), Horst Szymaniak (40/1), Werner Krämer (7/2). Trainer: Helmut Schön (7).
Goals: Werner Krämer (45), Uwe Seeler (54).

303. 09.10.1965 **WEST GERMANY - AUSTRIA** **4-1(1-1)**
Neckarstadion, Stuttgart; Referee: Gottfried Dienst (Switzerland); Attendance: 74,000
GER: Hans Tilkowski (Cap) (28/0), Horst-Dieter Höttges (7/0), Max Lorenz (5/0), Franz Beckenbauer (2/0), Klaus-Dieter Sieloff (8/4), Wolfgang Weber (6/0), Rudolf Nafziger (1/0), Lothar Ulsaß (2/3), Rudolf Brunnenmeier (4/1), Günter Netzer (1/0), Werner Krämer (8/2). Trainer: Helmut Schön (8).
Goals: Klaus-Dieter Sieloff (33 penalty), Lothar Ulsaß (65, 66, 81).

304. 14.11.1965 **CYPRUS - WEST GERMANY** **0-6(0-2)** 8th FIFA WC. Qualifiers
Stádio GSP, Nicosia; Referee: Francesco Francescon (Italy); Attendance: 3,412
GER: Hans Tilkowski (29/0), Josef Piontek (5/0), Horst-Dieter Höttges (8/0), Franz Beckenbauer (3/0), Wolfgang Weber (7/0), Horst Szymaniak (Cap) (41/2), Alfred Heiß (6/1), Werner Krämer (9/3), Rudolf Brunnenmeier (5/3), Günter Netzer (2/0), Heinz Hornig (4/0). Trainer: Helmut Schön (9).
Goals: Alfred Heiß (30), Werner Krämer (32), Horst Szymaniak (57), Rudolf Brunnenmeier (82), Costas Panayiotou (87 own goal), Rudolf Brunnenmeier (88).

305. 23.02.1966 **ENGLAND - WEST GERMANY** **1-0(1-0)**
Wembley Stadium, London; Referee: Pieter Paulus Roomer (Netherlands); Attendance: 75,000
GER: Hans Tilkowski (30/0), Friedel Lutz (8/0), Max Lorenz (6/0), Wîlli Schulz (27/0), Wolfgang Weber (8/0), Horst Szymaniak (Cap) (42/2), Werner Krämer (10/3), Franz Beckenbauer (4/0), Siegfried Held (1/0), Günter Netzer (3/0), Heinz Hornig (5/0) [44.Alfred Heiß (7/1)]. Trainer: Helmut Schön (10).

306. 23.03.1966 **NETHERLANDS - WEST GERMANY** **2-4(1-3)**
Stadion Feijenoord, Rotterdam; Referee: Kenneth Dagnall (England); Attendance: 65,000
GER: Günter Bernard (3/0), Horst-Dieter Höttges (9/0), Max Lorenz (7/0), Wîlli Schulz (28/0), Wolfgang Weber (9/0), Franz Beckenbauer (5/2), Albert Brülls (23/9), Uwe Seeler (Cap) (44/31), Siegfried Held (2/0), Wolfgang Overath (12/3), Lothar Emmerich (1/1). Trainer: Helmut Schön (11).
Goals: Uwe Seeler (7), Lothar Emmerich (16), Franz Beckenbauer (39, 50).

307. 04.05.1966 **REPUBLIC OF IRELAND - WEST GERMANY** **0-4(0-2)**
Dalymount Park, Dublin; Referee: William Joseph Mullan (Scotland); Attendance: 16,091
GER: Josef Maier (1/0), Friedel Lutz (9/0), Andreas Kurbjuhn (5/0), Franz Beckenbauer (6/3), Wîlli Schulz (29/0), Horst-Dieter Höttges (10/0), Jürgen Grabowski (1/0), Helmut Haller (21/5), Uwe Seeler (Cap) (45/31), Wolfgang Overath (13/5), Heinz Hornig (6/0). Trainer: Helmut Schön (12).
Goals: Helmut Haller (5), Franz Beckenbauer (18), Wolfgang Overath (57, 74).

)8. 07.05.1966 **NORTHERN IRELAND - WEST GERMANY** **0-2(0-1)**
'indsor Park, Belfast; Referee: Hugh Phillips (Scotland); Attendance: 22,000
ER: Günter Bernard (4/0), Friedel Lutz (10/0), Horst-Dieter Höttges (11/0) [46.Josef Piontek (6/0)], Franz Beckenbauer (7/3), Wîlli Schulz (30/0), 'olfgang Weber (10/0), Jürgen Grabowski (2/0), Wolfgang Overath (14/5), Uwe Seeler (Cap) (46/32), Peter Grosser (2/0), Alfred Heiß (8/2). Trainer: elmut Schön (13).
oals: Uwe Seeler (21), Alfred Heiß (57).

)9. 01.06.1966 **WEST GERMANY - ROMANIA** **1-0(0-0)**
:idweststadion, Ludwigshafen; Referee: Franz Mayer (Austria); Attendance: 60,000
ER: Hans Tilkowski (31/0), Friedel Lutz (11/0), Karl-Heinz Schnellinger (30/0), Horst Szymaniak (43/2), Wolfgang Weber (11/0), Horst-Dieter Höttges 2/0), Jürgen Grabowski (3/0) [76.Siegfried Held (3/0)], Lothar Ulsaß (3/3), Uwe Seeler (Cap) (47/33), Wolfgang Overath (15/5), Heinz Hornig (7/0). rainer: Helmut Schön (14).
oal: Uwe Seeler (72).

10. 23.06.1966 **WEST GERMANY - YUGOSLAVIA** **2-0(1-0)**
iedersachsenstadion, Hannover; Referee: Bertil Lööw (Sweden); Attendance: 78,000
ER: Hans Tilkowski (32/0), Horst-Dieter Höttges (13/0), Karl-Heinz Schnellinger (31/0), Franz Beckenbauer (8/3), Wîlli Schulz (31/0), Wolfgang Weber 2/0), Werner Krämer (11/3), Helmut Haller (22/5), Uwe Seeler (Cap) (48/34), Wolfgang Overath (16/6), Siegfried Held (4/0). Trainer: Helmut Schön (15).
oals: Wolfgang Overath (32), Uwe Seeler (76).

11. 12.07.1966 **SWITZERLAND - WEST GERMANY** **0-5(0-3)** 8th FIFA WC. Group Stage.
illsbrough Stadium, Sheffield (England); Referee: Hugh Phillips (Scotland); Attendance: 36,127
ER: Hans Tilkowski (33/0), Horst-Dieter Höttges (14/0), Karl-Heinz Schnellinger (32/0), Franz Beckenbauer (9/5), Wîlli Schulz (32/0), Wolfgang Weber 3/0), Albert Brülls (24/9), Helmut Haller (23/7), Uwe Seeler (Cap) (49/34), Wolfgang Overath (17/6), Siegfried Held (5/1). Trainer: Helmut Schön (16).
oals: Siegfried Held (16), Helmut Haller (20), Franz Beckenbauer (40, 52), Helmut Haller (78 penalty).

12. 16.07.1966 **ARGENTINA - WEST GERMANY** **0-0** 8th FIFA WC. Group Stage.
illa Park, Birmingham (England); Referee: Konstantin Zečević (Yugoslavia); Attendance: 51,419
ER: Hans Tilkowski (34/0), Horst-Dieter Höttges (15/0), Karl-Heinz Schnellinger (33/0), Franz Beckenbauer (10/5), Wîlli Schulz (33/0), Wolfgang Weber 4/0), Albert Brülls (25/9), Helmut Haller (24/7), Uwe Seeler (Cap) (50/34), Wolfgang Overath (18/6), Siegfried Held (6/1). Trainer: Helmut Schön (17).

13. 20.07.1966 **WEST GERMANY - SPAIN** **2-1(1-1)** 8th FIFA WC. Group Stage.
illa Park, Birmingham (England); Referee: Armando Castanheira da Rosa Marques (Brazil); Attendance: 51,875
ER: Hans Tilkowski (35/0), Horst-Dieter Höttges (16/0), Karl-Heinz Schnellinger (34/0), Franz Beckenbauer (11/5), Wîlli Schulz (34/0), Wolfgang Weber 5/0), Werner Krämer (12/3), Uwe Seeler (Cap) (51/35), Siegfried Held (7/1), Wolfgang Overath (19/6), Lothar Emmerich (2/2). Trainer: Helmut Schön 8).
oals: Lothar Emmerich (39), Uwe Seeler (83).

14. 23.07.1966 **WEST GERMANY - URUGUAY** **4-0(1-0)** 8th FIFA WC. Quarter-Finals.
illsbrough Stadium, Sheffield (England); Referee: James Finney (England); Attendance: 33,751
ER: Hans Tilkowski (36/0), Horst-Dieter Höttges (17/0), Karl-Heinz Schnellinger (35/0), Franz Beckenbauer (12/6), Wîlli Schulz (35/0), Wolfgang Weber 6/0), Helmut Haller (25/9), Uwe Seeler (Cap) (52/36), Siegfried Held (8/1), Wolfgang Overath (20/6), Lothar Emmerich (3/2). Trainer: Helmut Schön (19).
oals: Helmut Haller (12), Franz Beckenbauer (70), Uwe Seeler (76), Helmut Haller (84).

15. 25.07.1966 **WEST GERMANY - SOVIET UNION** **2-1(1-0)** 8th FIFA WC. Semi-Finals.
oodison Park, Liverpool (England); Referee: Concetto Lo Bello (Italy); Attendance: 43,921
ER: Hans Tilkowski (37/0), Friedel Lutz (12/0), Karl-Heinz Schnellinger (36/0), Franz Beckenbauer (13/7), Wîlli Schulz (36/0), Wolfgang Weber (17/0), elmut Haller (26/10), Uwe Seeler (Cap) (53/36), Siegfried Held (9/1), Wolfgang Overath (21/6), Lothar Emmerich (4/2). Trainer: Helmut Schön (20).
oals: Helmut Haller (43), Franz Beckenbauer (67).

16. 30.07.1966 **ENGLAND - WEST GERMANY** **4-2(1-1,2-2)** 8th FIFA WC. Final.
'embley Stadium, London; Referee: Gottfried Dienst (Switzerland); Attendance: 96,924
ER: Hans Tilkowski (38/0), Horst-Dieter Höttges (18/0), Karl-Heinz Schnellinger (37/0), Franz Beckenbauer (14/7), Wîlli Schulz (37/0), Wolfgang Weber 8/1), Helmut Haller (27/11), Uwe Seeler (Cap) (54/36), Siegfried Held (10/1), Wolfgang Overath (22/6), Lothar Emmerich (5/2). Trainer: Helmut Schön 1).
oals: Helmut Haller (12), Wolfgang Weber (89).

17. 12.10.1966 **TURKEY - WEST GERMANY** **0-2(0-1)**
) Mayis Stadı, Ankara; Referee: Dimitar Rumenchev (Bulgaria); Attendance: 24,000
ER: Josef Maier (2/0), Hartmut Heidemann (1/0), Horst-Dieter Höttges (19/0), Wolfgang Weber (19/1), Wîlli Schulz (Cap) (38/0), Wolfgang Overath 3/6), Jürgen Grabowski (4/0), Hans Küppers (5/2), Gerhard Müller (1/0), Günter Netzer (4/0), Bernd Rupp (1/1). Trainer: Helmut Schön (22).
oals: Hans Küppers (9), Bernd Rupp (85).

18. 19.11.1966 **WEST GERMANY - NORWAY** **3-0(2-0)**
üngersdorferstadion, Köln; Referee: Adrianus Aalbrecht (Netherlands); Attendance: 40,000
ER: Josef Maier (3/0), Hartmut Heidemann (2/0), Horst-Dieter Höttges (20/0), Franz Beckenbauer (15/7), Wîlli Schulz (39/0), Wolfgang Weber (20/1), ernd Dörfel (1/0), Lothar Ulsaß (4/5), Uwe Seeler (Cap) (55/37), Wolfgang Overath (24/6), Siegfried Held (11/1). Trainer: Helmut Schön (23).
oals: Uwe Seeler (42), Lothar Ulsaß (44, 78).

19. 22.02.1967 **WEST GERMANY - MOROCCO** **5-1(2-0)**
'ildparkstadion, Karlsruhe; Referee: Bruno de Marchi (Italy); Attendance: 38,000
ER: Horst Wolter (1/0), Bernd Patzke (3/0), Horst-Dieter Höttges (21/0), Franz Beckenbauer (16/7), Wîlli Schulz (Cap) (40/0), Klaus Fichtel (1/0), ünther Herrmann (8/1), Lothar Ulsaß (5/7) [46.Klaus Zaczyk (1/1)], Josef Heynckes (1/1), Wolfgang Overath (25/6) [57.Johannes Löhr (1/1)], Siegfried eld (12/1). Trainer: Helmut Schön (24).
oals: Lothar Ulsaß (8, 10), Klaus Zaczyk (53), Josef Heynckes (55), Johannes Löhr (68).

320. 22.03.1967 **WEST GERMANY - BULGARIA** **1-0(0-0)**
Niedersachsenstadion, Hannover; Referee: Roger Machin (France); Attendance: 65,000
GER: Josef Maier (4/0), Bernd Patzke (4/0), Horst-Dieter Höttges (22/0), Wolfgang Weber (21/1), Wîlli Schulz (Cap) (41/0) [46.Klaus Fichtel (2/0)], Wolfgang Overath (26/6), Werner Krämer (13/3), Günther Herrmann (9/1), Josef Heynckes (2/2), Günter Netzer (5/0), Johannes Löhr (2/1). Trainer: Helmu Schön (25).
Goal: Josef Heynckes (82).

321. 08.04.1967 **WEST GERMANY - ALBANIA** **6-0(2-0)** 3rd EC. Qualifiers
Westfalenstadion, Dortmund; Referee: Martti Hirviniemi (Finland); Attendance: 30,000
GER: Hans Tilkowski (39/0), Bernd Patzke (5/0), Horst-Dieter Höttges (23/0), Franz Beckenbauer (17/7), Wîlli Schulz (Cap) (42/0), Wolfgang Webe (22/1), Bernd Dörfel (2/0), Lothar Ulsaß (6/7), Gerhard Müller (2/4), Wolfgang Overath (27/6), Johannes Löhr (3/3). Trainer: Helmut Schön (26).
Goals: Gerhard Müller (5, 23, 73), Johannes Löhr (77, 78), Gerhard Müller (80 penalty).

322. 03.05.1967 **YUGOSLAVIA - WEST GERMANY** **1-0(0-0)** 3rd EC. Qualifiers
Stadion Crvena zvezda, Beograd; Referee: José María Ortiz de Mendibil Monasterio (Spain); Attendance: 36,508
GER: Josef Maier (5/0), Bernd Patzke (6/0), Hans-Hubert Vogts (1/0), Franz Beckenbauer (18/7), Wîlli Schulz (Cap) (43/0), Klaus Fichtel (3/0), Siegfrie Held (13/1), Hans Küppers (6/2), Gerhard Müller (3/4), Wolfgang Overath (28/6), Johannes Löhr (4/3). Trainer: Helmut Schön (27).

323. 27.09.1967 **WEST GERMANY - FRANCE** **5-1(1-0)**
Olympiastadion, West-Berlin; Referee: Fabio Monti (Italy); Attendance: 85,000
GER: Josef Maier (6/0), Bernd Patzke (7/0), Horst-Dieter Höttges (24/0), Franz Beckenbauer (19/7) [67.Gerhard Müller (4/5)], Wîlli Schulz (44/0) Wolfgang Weber (23/1), Reinhard Libuda (8/1), Hans Siemensmeyer (1/2), Uwe Seeler (Cap) (56/37), Wolfgang Overath (29/7), Johannes Löhr (5/3) Trainer: Helmut Schön (28).
Goals: Reinhard Libuda (28), Hans Siemensmeyer (47, 58), Gerhard Müller (74), Wolfgang Overath (75).

324. 07.10.1967 **WEST GERMANY - YUGOSLAVIA** **3-1(1-0)** 3rd EC. Qualifiers
Volksparkstadion, Hamburg; Referee: Concetto Lo Bello (Italy); Attendance: 70,575
GER: Josef Maier (7/0), Bernd Patzke (8/0), Horst-Dieter Höttges (25/0), Hans Siemensmeyer (2/2), Wîlli Schulz (45/0), Wolfgang Weber (24/1), Fran Roth (1/0), Uwe Seeler (Cap) (57/38), Gerhard Müller (5/6), Wolfgang Overath (30/7), Johannes Löhr (6/4). Trainer: Helmut Schön (29).
Goals: Johannes Löhr (11), Gerhard Müller (72), Uwe Seeler (87).

325. 22.11.1967 **ROMANIA - WEST GERMANY** **1-0(0-0)**
Stadionul 23 August, Bucureşti; Referee: Franz Mayer (Austria); Attendance: 25,000
GER: Horst Wolter (2/0), Bernd Patzke (9/0), Hans-Hubert Vogts (2/0), Franz Beckenbauer (20/7), Wîlli Schulz (46/0), Wolfgang Weber (25/1), Reinhar Libuda (9/1), Hans Siemensmeyer (3/2), Uwe Seeler (Cap) (58/38), Wolfgang Overath (31/7), Johannes Löhr (7/4). Trainer: Helmut Schön (30).

326. 17.12.1967 **ALBANIA - WEST GERMANY** **0-0** 3rd EC. Qualifiers
Stadiumi „Kombëtar Qemal Stafa", Tiranë; Referee: Ferdinand Marschall (Austria); Attendance: 21,889
GER: Horst Wolter (3/0), Bernd Patzke (10/0), Horst-Dieter Höttges (26/0), Wolfgang Overath (32/7), Wîlli Schulz (Cap) (47/0), Wolfgang Weber (26/1) Siegfried Held (14/1), Hans Küppers (7/2), Peter Meyer (1/0), Günter Netzer (6/0), Johannes Löhr (8/4). Trainer: Helmut Schön (31).

327. 06.03.1968 **BELGIUM - WEST GERMANY** **1-3(0-3)**
Stade du Heysel, Bruxelles; Referee: Rudolf Scheurer (Switzerland); Attendance: 10,267
GER: Josef Maier (8/0), Hans-Hubert Vogts (3/0), Horst-Dieter Höttges (27/0), Franz Beckenbauer (21/7), Wîlli Schulz (Cap) (48/0), Klaus Fichtel (4/0) Horst Köppel (1/0), Herbert Laumen (1/1), Johannes Löhr (9/4), Günter Netzer (7/0), Georg Volkert (1/2) [70.Erich Maas (1/0)]. Trainer: Helmut Schön (32).
Goals: Georg Volkert (5, 22), Herbert Laumen (25).

328. 17.04.1968 **SWITZERLAND - WEST GERMANY** **0-0**
„St. Jakob" Stadion, Basel; Referee: Alessandro d'Agostini (Italy); Attendance: 55,000
GER: Horst Wolter (4/0), Hartmut Heidemann (3/0) [67.Klaus Fichtel (5/0)], Hans-Hubert Vogts (4/0), Franz Beckenbauer (22/7), Wîlli Schulz (49/0) Wolfgang Weber (27/1), Horst Köppel (2/0), Uwe Seeler (Cap) (59/38), Johannes Löhr (10/4), Günter Netzer (8/0), Georg Volkert (2/2). Trainer: Helmu Schön (33).

329. 08.05.1968 **WALES - WEST GERMANY** **1-1(1-1)**
Ninian Park, Cardiff; Referee: Gösta Lindberg (Sweden); Attendance: 8,075
GER: Horst Wolter (5/0) [26.Günter Bernard (5/0)], Hans-Hubert Vogts (5/0), Horst-Dieter Höttges (28/0), Klaus Fichtel (6/0), Joachim Bäse (1/0) Wolfgang Weber (28/1), Herbert Laumen (2/1), Willi Neuberger (1/0), Siegfried Held (15/1), Wolfgang Overath (Cap) (33/8) [50.Günter Netzer (9/0)], Hors Köppel (3/0). Trainer: Helmut Schön (34).
Goal: Wolfgang Overath (11).

330. 01.06.1968 **WEST GERMANY - ENGLAND** **1-0(0-0)**
Niedersachsenstadion, Hannover; Referee: Laurens van Ravens (Netherlands); Attendance: 79,124
GER: Horst Wolter (6/0), Hans-Hubert Vogts (6/0), Max Lorenz (8/0), Ludwig Müller (1/0), Klaus Fichtel (7/0), Wolfgang Weber (29/1), Bernd Dörfe (3/0), Franz Beckenbauer (23/8), Johannes Löhr (11/4), Wolfgang Overath (Cap) (34/8), Georg Volkert (3/2). Trainer: Helmut Schön (35).
Goal: Franz Beckenbauer (82).

331. 16.06.1968 **WEST GERMANY - BRAZIL** **2-1(1-0)**
Neckarstadion, Stuttgart; Referee: Bertil Lööw (Sweden); Attendance: 74,164
GER: Horst Wolter (7/0), Hans-Hubert Vogts (7/0), Max Lorenz (9/0) [84.Horst-Dieter Höttges (29/0)], Ludwig Müller (2/0), Klaus Fichtel (8/0), Wolfgang Weber (30/1), Bernd Dörfel (4/1), Franz Beckenbauer (24/8), Siegfried Held (16/2), Wolfgang Overath (Cap) (35/8), Willi Neuberger (2/0). Trainer: Helmu Schön (36).
Goals: Siegfried Held (8), Bernd Dörfel (56).

332. 25.09.1968 **FRANCE - WEST GERMANY** **1-1(0-0)**
Stade Vélodrome, Marseille; Referee: José María Ortiz de Mendibil Monasterio (Spain); Attendance: 22,355
GER: Josef Maier (9/0), Hans-Hubert Vogts (8/0), Max Lorenz (10/0), Ludwig Müller (3/0) [46.Günter Netzer (10/0)], Klaus Fichtel (9/0), Wîlli Schul (Cap) (50/0), Bernd Dörfel (5/1), Franz Beckenbauer (25/8), Gerhard Müller (6/6), Wolfgang Overath (36/9), Siegfried Held (17/2). Trainer: Helmut Schön (37).
Goal: Wolfgang Overath (86).

33. 13.10.1968 **AUSTRIA - WEST GERMANY** **0-2(0-1)** 9th FIFA WC. Qualifiers
'raterstadion, Wien; Referee: Stanislaw Eksztajn (Poland); Attendance: 67,115
;ER: Josef Maier (10/0), Hans-Hubert Vogts (9/0), Horst-Dieter Höttges (30/0), Franz Beckenbauer (26/8), Wîlli Schulz (Cap) (51/0), Wolfgang Weber 31/1), Bernd Dörfel (6/1), Lothar Ulsaß (7/7), Gerhard Müller (7/7), Günter Netzer (11/0), Siegfried Held (18/2). Trainer: Helmut Schön (38).
;oals: Gerhard Müller (16), Johann Eigenstiller (50 own goal).

34. 23.11.1968 **CYPRUS - WEST GERMANY** **0-1(0-0)** 9th FIFA WC. Qualifiers
tádio GSP, Nicosia; Referee: Alexandru Pîrvu (Romania); Attendance: 6,080
;ER: Horst Wolter (8/0), Hans-Hubert Vogts (10/0), Horst-Dieter Höttges (31/0) [67.Klaus Gerwien (3/0)], Wolfgang Weber (32/1), Wîlli Schulz (Cap) 52/0) [46.Bernd Patzke (11/0)], Max Lorenz (11/0), Bernd Dörfel (7/1), Herbert Wimmer (1/0), Gerhard Müller (8/8), Wolfgang Overath (37/9), Siegfried Ield (19/2). Trainer: Helmut Schön (39).
;oal: Gerhard Müller (90).

35. 14.12.1968 **BRAZIL - WEST GERMANY** **2-2(2-0)**
stádio „Jornalista Mário Filho“ [Maracanã], Rio de Janeiro; Referee: István Zsolt (Hungary); Attendance: 70,000
;ER: Josef Maier (11/0), Hans-Hubert Vogts (11/0), Bernd Patzke (12/0), Franz Beckenbauer (27/8), Wîlli Schulz (Cap) (53/0), Wolfgang Weber (33/1) 26.Max Lorenz (12/0)], Bernd Dörfel (8/1), Wolfgang Overath (38/9) [75.Herbert Wimmer (2/0)], Siegfried Held (20/3), Günter Netzer (12/0), Georg 'olkert (4/2) [46.Klaus Gerwien (4/1)]. Trainer: Helmut Schön (40).
;oals: Siegfried Held (48), Klaus Gerwien (70).

36. 18.12.1968 **CHILE - WEST GERMANY** **2-1(0-1)**
stadio Nacional, Santiago; Referee: Juan Carlos Robles (Chile); Attendance: 50,000
;ER: Horst Wolter (9/0), Hans-Hubert Vogts (12/0), Bernd Patzke (13/0), Franz Beckenbauer (28/8) [26.Michael Bella (1/0)], Wîlli Schulz (Cap) (54/0), Iax Lorenz (13/0), Herbert Wimmer (3/0), Lothar Ulsaß (8/8) [46.Wolfgang Overath (39/9)], Rainer Ohlhauser (1/0), Günter Netzer (13/0), Klaus Gerwien 5/1) [82.Bernd Dörfel (9/1)]. Trainer: Helmut Schön (41).
;oal: Lothar Ulsaß (8).

37. 22.12.1968 **MEXICO - WEST GERMANY** **0-0**
stadio Azteca, Ciudad de México; Referee: Juan Carlos Robles (Chile); Attendance: 40,000
;ER: Josef Maier (12/0), Hans-Hubert Vogts (13/0), Bernd Patzke (14/0), Michael Bella (2/0), Franz Beckenbauer (29/8), Max Lorenz (14/0), Bernd Dörfel 10/1), Lothar Ulsaß (9/8), Siegfried Held (21/3), Wolfgang Overath (Cap) (40/9) [71.Herbert Wimmer (4/0)], Klaus Gerwien (6/1) [79.Georg Volkert (5/2)]. 'rainer: Helmut Schön (42).

38. 26.03.1969 **WEST GERMANY - WALES** **1-1(0-1)**
Valdstadion, Frankfurt am Main; Referee: Concetto Lo Bello (Italy); Attendance: 40,000
;ER: Josef Maier (13/0), Bernd Patzke (15/0), Hans-Hubert Vogts (14/0), Horst-Dieter Höttges (32/0), Wîlli Schulz (Cap) (55/0), Max Lorenz (15/0), einhard Libuda (10/1), Lothar Ulsaß (10/8) [74.Ludwig Müller (4/0)], Gerhard Müller (9/9), Siegfried Held (22/3), Hans Rebele (2/0) [46.Bernd Dörfel 11/1)]. Trainer: Helmut Schön (43).
;oal: Gerhard Müller (90).

39. 16.04.1969 **SCOTLAND - WEST GERMANY** **1-1(0-1)** 9th FIFA WC. Qualifiers
Iampden Park, Glasgow; Referee: Juan Gardeazábal Garay (Spain); Attendance: 95,951
;ER: Horst Wolter (10/0) [46.Josef Maier (14/0)], Karl-Heinz Schnellinger (38/0), Hans-Hubert Vogts (15/0), Franz Beckenbauer (30/8), Wîlli Schulz (Cap) 56/0), Bernd Patzke (16/0), Bernd Dörfel (12/1), Helmut Haller (28/11), Gerhard Müller (10/10), Wolfgang Overath (41/9) [79.Max Lorenz (16/0)], iegfried Held (23/3). Trainer: Helmut Schön (44).
;oal: Gerhard Müller (39).

40. 10.05.1969 **WEST GERMANY - AUSTRIA** **1-0(0-0)** 9th FIFA WC. Qualifiers
'rankenstadion, Nürnberg; Referee: Radoslav Fiala (Czechoslovakia); Attendance: 69,892
;ER: Josef Maier (15/0), Bernd Patzke (17/0), Hans-Hubert Vogts (16/0), Franz Beckenbauer (31/8), Wîlli Schulz (Cap) (57/0), Horst-Dieter Höttges (33/0), ernd Dörfel (13/1), Gerhard Müller (11/11), Siegfried Held (24/3) [77.Josef Heynckes (3/2)], Wolfgang Overath (42/9), Dieter Brenninger (1/0) [66.Georg 'olkert (6/2)]. Trainer: Helmut Schön (45).
;oal: Gerhard Müller (88).

41. 21.05.1969 **WEST GERMANY - CYPRUS** **12-0(7-0)** 9th FIFA WC. Qualifiers
Georg Melches“ Stadion, Essen; Referee: Jacques Colling (Luxembourg); Attendance: 36,036
;ER: Josef Maier (16/0), Horst-Dieter Höttges (34/1) [84.Ludwig Müller (5/0)], Hans-Hubert Vogts (17/0), Franz Beckenbauer (32/8), Wîlli Schulz (Cap) 58/0), Max Lorenz (17/1) [75.Bernd Patzke (18/0)], Reinhard Libuda (11/1), Helmut Haller (29/13), Gerhard Müller (12/15), Wolfgang Overath (43/12), iegfried Held (25/4). Trainer: Helmut Schön (46).
;oals: Gerhard Müller (3), Wolfgang Overath (5, 12), Helmut Haller (17), Max Lorenz (38), Siegfried Held (41), Gerhard Müller (43), Helmut Haller (47), ;erhard Müller (49), Horst-Dieter Höttges (51), Wolfgang Overath (63), Gerhard Müller (86).

42. 21.09.1969 **AUSTRIA - WEST GERMANY** **1-1(1-1)**
'raterstadion, Wien; Referee: Concetto Lo Bello (Italy); Attendance: 28,000
;ER: Horst Wolter (11/0), Horst-Dieter Höttges (35/1), Hans-Hubert Vogts (18/0), Franz Beckenbauer (33/8), Wîlli Schulz (59/0), Wolfgang Weber (34/1) 46.Klaus Fichtel (10/0)], Bernd Dörfel (14/1) [77.Reinhard Libuda (12/1)], Gerhard Müller (13/16), Uwe Seeler (Cap) (60/38), Wolfgang Overath (44/12), iegfried Held (26/4). Trainer: Helmut Schön (47).
;oal: Gerhard Müller (16).

43. 24.09.1969 **BULGARIA - WEST GERMANY** **0-1(0-1)**
Iationalen stadion “Vasil Levski”, Sofia; Referee: Dileg Talaz (Turkey); Attendance: 50,000
;ER: Josef Maier (17/0), Horst-Dieter Höttges (36/1), Hans-Hubert Vogts (19/0), Franz Beckenbauer (34/8), Wîlli Schulz (60/0) [46.Ludwig Müller (6/0)], laus Fichtel (11/0), Bernd Dörfel (15/2), Gerhard Müller (14/16), Uwe Seeler (Cap) (61/38), Wolfgang Overath (45/12), Erich Maas (2/0). Trainer: Helmut chön (48).
;oal: Bernd Dörfel (12).

344. 22.10.1969 **WEST GERMANY - SCOTLAND** **3-2(1-1)** 9th FIFA WC. Qualifiers
Volksparkstadion, Hamburg; Referee: Gilbert Droz (Switzerland); Attendance: 72,000
GER: Josef Maier (18/0), Horst-Dieter Höttges (37/1), Hans-Hubert Vogts (20/0), Franz Beckenbauer (35/8), Wîlli Schulz (61/0), Klaus Fichtel (12/1), Reinhard Libuda (13/2), Uwe Seeler (Cap) (62/38), Gerhard Müller (15/17), Wolfgang Overath (46/12), Helmut Haller (30/13). Trainer: Helmut Schön (49).
Goals: Klaus Fichtel (37), Gerhard Müller (58), Reinhard Libuda (80).

345. 11.02.1970 **SPAIN - WEST GERMANY** **2-0(0-0)**
Estadio „Ramón Sánchez Pizjuán", Sevilla; Referee: René Vigliani (France); Attendance: 30,000
GER: Manfred Manglitz (3/0), Hans-Hubert Vogts (21/0), Karl-Heinz Schnellinger (39/0), Wolfgang Weber (35/1), Wîlli Schulz (62/0), Günter Netzer (14/0), Reinhard Libuda (14/2), Uwe Seeler (Cap) (63/38), Gerhard Müller (16/17), Helmut Haller (31/13), Jürgen Grabowski (5/0). Trainer: Helmut Schön (50).

346. 08.04.1970 **WEST GERMANY - ROMANIA** **1-1(1-1)**
Neckarstadion, Stuttgart; Referee: Gyula Emsberger (Hungary); Attendance: 73,000
GER: Josef Maier (19/0), Hans-Hubert Vogts (22/0), Horst-Dieter Höttges (38/1), Franz Beckenbauer (36/8), Karl-Heinz Schnellinger (40/0), Wolfgang Weber (36/1) [84.Klaus-Dieter Sieloff (9/4)], Jürgen Grabowski (6/0), Helmut Haller (32/13) [60.Max Lorenz (18/1)], Gerhard Müller (17/17), Wolfgang Overath (Cap) (47/13), Erich Maas (3/0) [46.Franz Roth (2/0)]. Trainer: Helmut Schön (51).
Goal: Wolfgang Overath (33).

347. 09.05.1970 **WEST GERMANY - REPUBLIC OF IRELAND** **2-1(1-0)**
Olympiastadion, West-Berlin; Referee: Einar Boström (Sweden); Attendance: 70,000
GER: Horst Wolter (12/0), Bernd Patzke (19/0), Hans-Hubert Vogts (23/0), Franz Beckenbauer (37/8), Wîlli Schulz (63/0), Wolfgang Weber (37/1), Jürgen Grabowski (7/0) [46.Peter Dietrich (1/0)], Uwe Seeler (Cap) (64/39), Gerhard Müller (18/17), Wolfgang Overath (48/13) [76.Siegfried Held (27/4)], Johannes Löhr (12/5). Trainer: Helmut Schön (52).
Goals: Uwe Seeler (17), Johannes Löhr (82).

348. 13.05.1970 **WEST GERMANY - YUGOSLAVIA** **1-0(1-0)**
Niedersachsenstadion, Hannover; Referee: Rudolf Scheurer (Switzerland); Attendance: 65,000
GER: Manfred Manglitz (4/0), Hans-Hubert Vogts (24/0), Horst-Dieter Höttges (39/1), Franz Beckenbauer (38/8), Karl-Heinz Schnellinger (41/0), Klaus Fichtel (13/1), Reinhard Libuda (15/2), Uwe Seeler (Cap) (65/40), Gerhard Müller (19/17), Wolfgang Overath (49/13), Johannes Löhr (13/5). Trainer Helmut Schön (53).
Goal: Uwe Seeler (10).

349. 03.06.1970 **MOROCCO - WEST GERMANY** **1-2(1-0)** 9th FIFA WC. Group Stage.
Estadio Nou Camp, Léon (Mexico); Referee: Laurens van Ravens (Netherlands); Attendance: 8,000
GER: Josef Maier (20/0), Hans-Hubert Vogts (25/0), Horst-Dieter Höttges (40/1) [76.Johannes Löhr (14/5)], Franz Beckenbauer (39/8), Wîlli Schulz (64/0), Klaus Fichtel (14/1), Helmut Haller (33/13) [46.Jürgen Grabowski (8/0)], Uwe Seeler (Cap) (66/41), Gerhard Müller (20/18), Wolfgang Overath (50/13) Siegfried Held (28/4). Trainer: Helmut Schön (54).
Goals: Uwe Seeler (56), Gerhard Müller (80).

350. 07.06.1970 **BULGARIA - WEST GERMANY** **2-5(1-2)** 9th FIFA WC. Group Stage.
Estadio Nou Camp, Léon (Mexico); Referee: José María Ortiz de Mendibil Monasterio (Spania); Attendance: 8,000
GER: Josef Maier (21/0), Hans-Hubert Vogts (26/0), Horst-Dieter Höttges (41/1), Franz Beckenbauer (40/8) [72.Wolfgang Weber (38/1)], Karl-Heinz Schnellinger (42/0), Klaus Fichtel (15/1), Reinhard Libuda (16/3), Uwe Seeler (Cap) (67/42), Gerhard Müller (21/21), Wolfgang Overath (51/13), Johannes Löhr (15/5) [59.Jürgen Grabowski (9/0)]. Trainer: Helmut Schön (55).
Goals: Reinhard Libuda (20), Gerhard Müller (27, 52 penalty), Uwe Seeler (69), Gerhard Müller (87).

351. 10.06.1970 **PERU - WEST GERMANY** **1-3(1-3)** 9th FIFA WC. Group Stage.
Estadio Nou Camp, Léon (Mexico); Referee: Abel Aguilar Elizalde (Mexico); Attendance: 9,500
GER: Josef Maier (22/0), Hans-Hubert Vogts (27/0), Horst-Dieter Höttges (42/1) [46.Bernd Patzke (20/0)], Franz Beckenbauer (41/8), Karl-Heinz Schnellinger (43/0), Klaus Fichtel (16/1), Reinhard Libuda (17/3) [75.Jürgen Grabowski (10/0)], Uwe Seeler (Cap) (68/42), Gerhard Müller (22/24) Wolfgang Overath (52/13), Johannes Löhr (16/5). Trainer: Helmut Schön (56).
Goals: Gerhard Müller (20, 26, 39).

352. 14.06.1970 **WEST GERMANY - ENGLAND** **3-2(0-1,2-2)** 9th FIFA WC. Quarter-Finals.
Estadio Nou Camp, Léon (Mexico); Referee: Ángel Norberto Coerezza (Argentina); Attendance: 32,000
GER: Josef Maier (23/0), Horst-Dieter Höttges (43/1) [46.Wîlli Schulz (65/0)], Hans-Hubert Vogts (28/0), Franz Beckenbauer (42/9), Karl-Heinz Schnellinger (44/0), Klaus Fichtel (17/1), Reinhard Libuda (18/3) [57.Jürgen Grabowski (11/0)], Uwe Seeler (Cap) (69/43), Gerhard Müller (23/25), Wolfgang Overath (53/13), Johannes Löhr (17/5). Trainer: Helmut Schön (57).
Goals: Franz Beckenbauer (69), Uwe Seeler (82), Gerhard Müller (108).

353. 17.06.1970 **WEST GERMANY - ITALY** **3-4(0-1,1-1)** 9th FIFA WC. Semi-Finals.
Estadio Azteca, Ciudad de México (Mexico); Referee: Arturo Maximo Yamasaki Maldonado (Peru); Attendance: 107,000
GER: Josef Maier (24/0), Hans-Hubert Vogts (29/0), Bernd Patzke (21/0) [65.Siegfried Held (29/4)], Franz Beckenbauer (43/9), Karl-Heinz Schnellinger (45/1), Wîlli Schulz (66/0), Jürgen Grabowski (12/0), Uwe Seeler (Cap) (70/43), Gerhard Müller (24/27), Wolfgang Overath (54/13), Johannes Löhr (18/5) [51.Reinhard Libuda (19/3)]. Trainer: Helmut Schön (58).
Goals: Karl-Heinz Schnellinger (90), Gerhard Müller (95, 110).

354. 20.06.1970 **URUGUAY - WEST GERMANY** **0-1(0-1)** 9th FIFA WC. Third Place Play-off.
Estadio Azteca, Ciudad de México (Mexico); Referee: Antonio Sbardella (Italy); Attendance: 32,000
GER: Horst Wolter (13/0), Hans-Hubert Vogts (30/0), Bernd Patzke (22/0), Klaus Fichtel (18/1), Karl-Heinz Schnellinger (46/1) [46.Max Lorenz (19/1)], Wolfgang Weber (39/1), Reinhard Libuda (20/3) [Johannes Löhr (19/5)], Uwe Seeler (Cap) (71/43), Gerhard Müller (25/27), Wolfgang Overath (55/14), Siegfried Held (30/4). Trainer: Helmut Schön (59).
Goal: Wolfgang Overath (27).

355. 09.09.1970 **WEST GERMANY - HUNGARY** **3-1(2-1)**
Frankenstadion, Nürnberg; Referee: Ferdinand Marschall (Austria); Attendance: 67,000
GER: Josef Maier (25/0), Hans-Hubert Vogts (31/0), Horst-Dieter Höttges (44/1), Franz Beckenbauer (44/9), Klaus-Dieter Sieloff (10/5), Wolfgang Weber (40/1), Jürgen Grabowski (13/0), Klaus Fichtel (19/1), Uwe Seeler (Cap) (72/43), Gerhard Müller (26/29), Johannes Löhr (20/5) [59.Reinhard Libuda (21/3)]. Trainer: Helmut Schön (60).
Goals: Klaus-Dieter Sieloff (12), Gerhard Müller (22, 53).

356. 17.10.1970 **WEST GERMANY - TURKEY** **1-1(1-1)** 4th EC. Qualifiers
Müngersdorferstadion, Köln; Referee: Paul Bonnet (Malta); Attendance: 52,204
GER: Josef Maier (26/0), Hans-Hubert Vogts (32/0), Horst-Dieter Höttges (45/1), Franz Beckenbauer (45/9), Klaus-Dieter Sieloff (11/5) [66.Josef Heynckes (4/2)], Wolfgang Weber (41/1), Wolfgang Overath (Cap) (56/14), Klaus Fichtel (20/1), Reinhard Libuda (22/3), Gerhard Müller (27/30), Jürgen Grabowski (14/0). Trainer: Helmut Schön (61).
Goal: Gerhard Müller (37 penalty).

357. 18.11.1970 **YUGOSLAVIA - WEST GERMANY** **2-0(0-0)**
Stadion Maksimir, Zagreb; Referee: László Vizhányó (Hungary); Attendance: 25,000
GER: Josef Maier (27/0), Hans-Hubert Vogts (33/0), Horst-Dieter Höttges (46/1), Franz Beckenbauer (46/9), Wolfgang Weber (42/1), Franz Roth (3/0), Günter Netzer (15/0), Wolfgang Overath (Cap) (57/14), Reinhard Libuda (23/3), Josef Heynckes (5/2), Siegfried Held (31/4) [67.Jürgen Grabowski (15/0)]. Trainer: Helmut Schön (62).

358. 22.11.1970 **GREECE - WEST GERMANY** **1-3(0-2)**
Stádio „Giórgos Karaïskáki", Peiraiás; Referee: Aurel Bentu (Romania); Attendance: 35,000
GER: Volkmar Groß (1/0), Hans-Hubert Vogts (34/0), Horst-Dieter Höttges (47/1), Franz Beckenbauer (47/10), Klaus-Dieter Sieloff (12/5), Michael Bella (3/0), Günter Netzer (16/1) [32.Heinz Flohe (1/0)], Wolfgang Overath (Cap) (58/14) [35.Franz Roth (4/0)], Reinhard Libuda (24/3), Josef Heynckes (6/2), Jürgen Grabowski (16/1). Trainer: Helmut Schön (63).
Goals: Günter Netzer (30), Jürgen Grabowski (41), Franz Beckenbauer (73).

359. 17.02.1971 **ALBANIA - WEST GERMANY** **0-1(0-1)** 4th EC. Qualifiers
Stadiumi „Kombëtar Qemal Stafa", Tiranë; Referee: Todor Betchkirov (Bulgaria); Attendance: 18,082
GER: Josef Maier (28/0), Hans-Hubert Vogts (35/0), Karl-Heinz Schnellinger (47/1), Franz Beckenbauer (48/10), Bernd Patzke (23/0) [67.Michael Bella (4/0)], Wolfgang Weber (43/1), Günter Netzer (17/1), Wolfgang Overath (Cap) (59/14), Jürgen Grabowski (17/1), Gerhard Müller (28/31), Josef Heynckes (7/2). Trainer: Helmut Schön (64).
Goal: Gerhard Müller (34).

360. 25.04.1971 **TURKEY - WEST GERMANY** **0-3(0-1)** 4th EC. Qualifiers
Mithatpaşa Stadyumu, İstanbul; Referee: Karlo Kruashvili (Soviet Union); Attendance: 38,097
GER: Josef Maier (29/0), Hans-Hubert Vogts (36/0), Wolfgang Weber (44/1), Franz Beckenbauer (Cap) (49/10), Bernd Patzke (24/0), Herbert Wimmer (5/0), Horst Köppel (4/1) [77.Heinz Flohe (2/0)], Günter Netzer (18/1), Jürgen Grabowski (18/1), Gerhard Müller (29/33), Josef Heynckes (8/2). Trainer: Helmut Schön (65).
Goals: Gerhard Müller (43, 47), Horst Köppel (73).

361. 12.06.1971 **WEST GERMANY - ALBANIA** **2-0(2-0)** 4th EC. Qualifiers
Wildparkstadion, Karlsruhe; Referee: Timoleon Latsios (Greece); Attendance: 44,833
GER: Josef Maier (30/0), Hans-Hubert Vogts (37/0) [90.Hartwig Bleidick (1/0)], Georg Schwarzenbeck (1/0), Franz Beckenbauer (50/10), Klaus-Dieter Sieloff (13/5), Herbert Wimmer (6/0), Günter Netzer (19/2), Wolfgang Overath (Cap) (60/14) [73.Siegfried Held (32/4)], Jürgen Grabowski (19/2), Horst Köppel (5/1), Josef Heynckes (9/2). Trainer: Helmut Schön (66).
Goals: Günter Netzer (17), Jürgen Grabowski (45).

362. 22.06.1971 **NORWAY - WEST GERMANY** **1-7(0-3)**
Ullevaal Stadion, Oslo; Referee: Bertil Lööw (Sweden); Attendance: 19,857
GER: Wolfgang Kleff (1/0), Hans-Hubert Vogts (38/0), Georg Schwarzenbeck (2/0), Franz Beckenbauer (51/11) [51.Hartwig Bleidick (2/0)], Paul Breitner (1/0), Herbert Wimmer (7/0) [46.Klaus-Dieter Sieloff (14/5)], Günter Netzer (20/3), Wolfgang Overath (Cap) (61/15), Jürgen Grabowski (20/2), Gerhard Müller (30/36), Siegfried Held (33/5). Trainer: Helmut Schön (67).
Goals: Wolfgang Overath (12), Gerhard Müller (30), Franz Beckenbauer (35), Gerhard Müller (47, 52), Siegfried Held (67), Günter Netzer (86).

363. 27.06.1971 **SWEDEN - WEST GERMANY** **1-0(0-0)**
Ullevi Stadion, Göteborg; Referee: Thomas Wharton (Scotland); Attendance: 43,279
GER: Josef Maier (31/0), Hans-Hubert Vogts (39/0), Georg Schwarzenbeck (3/0), Franz Beckenbauer (52/11), Wolfgang Weber (45/1), Herbert Wimmer (8/0), Günter Netzer (21/3), Jürgen Grabowski (21/2), Wolfgang Overath (Cap) (62/15), Gerhard Müller (31/36), Siegfried Held (34/5) [46.Josef Heynckes (10/2)]. Trainer: Helmut Schön (68).

364. 30.06.1971 **DENMARK - WEST GERMANY** **1-3(1-0)**
Idrætsparken, København; Referee: Theodorus Boosten (Netherlands); Attendance: 40,400
GER: Josef Maier (32/0), Hans-Hubert Vogts (40/0), Georg Schwarzenbeck (4/0), Franz Beckenbauer (53/12), Wolfgang Weber (46/1), Heinz Flohe (3/1), Wolfgang Overath (Cap) (63/15), Günter Netzer (22/3) [53.Josef Heynckes (11/2)], Horst Köppel (6/1) [46.Jürgen Grabowski (22/2)], Gerhard Müller (32/37), Siegfried Held (35/5) [77.Herbert Wimmer (9/0)]. Trainer: Helmut Schön (69).
Goals: Gerhard Müller (22), Heinz Flohe (83), Franz Beckenbauer (87).

365. 08.09.1971 **WEST GERMANY - MEXICO** **5-0(4-0)**
Niedersachsenstadion, Hannover; Referee: Bertil Lööw (Sweden); Attendance: 70,000
GER: Josef Maier (33/0), Hans-Hubert Vogts (41/0) [46.Dieter Zembski (1/0)], Georg Schwarzenbeck (5/0), Franz Beckenbauer (Cap) (54/12), Wolfgang Weber (47/1), Horst Köppel (7/2) [64.Arno Steffenhagen (1/0)], Klaus Fichtel (21/1), Günter Netzer (23/4), Jürgen Grabowski (23/2) [64.Reinhard Libuda (25/3)], Gerhard Müller (33/40), Josef Heynckes (12/2). Trainer: Helmut Schön (70).
Goals: Horst Köppel (5), Gerhard Müller (12, 14), Günter Netzer (44), Gerhard Müller (55).

366. 10.10.1971 **POLAND - WEST GERMANY** **1-3(1-1)** 4th EC. Qualifiers
Stadion Dziesięciolecia, Warszawa; Referee: Ferdinand Marschall (Austria); Attendance: 90,000
GER: Josef Maier (34/0), Klaus Fichtel (22/1), Georg Schwarzenbeck (6/0), Franz Beckenbauer (Cap) (55/12), Paul Breitner (2/0), Herbert Wimmer (10/0), Horst Köppel (8/2), Günter Netzer (24/4), Jürgen Grabowski (24/3), Gerhard Müller (34/42), Josef Heynckes (13/2). Trainer: Helmut Schön (71).
Goals: Gerhard Müller (29, 64), Jürgen Grabowski (70).

367. 17.11.1971 **WEST GERMANY - POLAND** **0-0** 4th EC. Qualifiers
Volksparkstadion, Hamburg; Referee: William Joseph Mullan (Scotland); Attendance: 62,000
GER: Josef Maier (35/0), Horst-Dieter Höttges (48/1), Georg Schwarzenbeck (7/0), Franz Beckenbauer (56/12), Wolfgang Weber (48/1), Herbert Wimmer (11/0) [74.Horst Köppel (9/2)], Klaus Fichtel (23/1), Wolfgang Overath (Cap) (64/15), Reinhard Libuda (26/3), Gerhard Müller (35/42), Jürgen Grabowski (25/3). Trainer: Helmut Schön (72).

368. 29.03.1972 **HUNGARY - WEST GERMANY** **0-2(0-0)**
Népstadion, Budapest; Referee: Concetto Lo Bello (Italy); Attendance: 50,000
GER: Josef Maier (36/0), Horst-Dieter Höttges (49/1), Georg Schwarzenbeck (8/0), Franz Beckenbauer (Cap) (57/12), Paul Breitner (3/1), Herbert Wimmer (12/0), Günter Netzer (25/4), Heinz Flohe (4/1), Ulrich Hoeneß (1/1), Gerhard Müller (36/42), Josef Heynckes (14/2) [59.Siegfried Held (36/5)]. Trainer: Helmut Schön (73).
Goals: Paul Breitner (68), Ulrich Hoeneß (88).

369. 29.04.1972 **ENGLAND - WEST GERMANY** **1-3(0-1)** 4th EC. Quarter-Finals.
Wembley Stadium, London; Referee: Robert Helies (France); Attendance: 100,000
GER: Josef Maier (37/0), Horst-Dieter Höttges (50/1), Georg Schwarzenbeck (9/0), Franz Beckenbauer (Cap) (58/12), Paul Breitner (4/1), Ulrich Hoeneß (2/2), Günter Netzer (26/5), Herbert Wimmer (13/0), Jürgen Grabowski (26/3), Gerhard Müller (37/43), Siegfried Held (37/5). Trainer: Helmut Schön (74).
Goals: Ulrich Hoeneß (26), Günter Netzer (85 penalty), Gerhard Müller (88).

370. 13.05.1972 **WEST GERMANY - ENGLAND** **0-0** 4th EC. Quarter-Finals.
Olympiastadion, West-Berlin; Referee: Milivoje Gugulović (Yugoslavia); Attendance: 76,200
GER: Josef Maier (38/0), Horst-Dieter Höttges (51/1), Georg Schwarzenbeck (10/0), Franz Beckenbauer (Cap) (59/12), Paul Breitner (5/1), Heinz Flohe (5/1), Günter Netzer (27/5), Herbert Wimmer (14/0), Ulrich Hoeneß (3/2) [70.Josef Heynckes (15/2)], Gerhard Müller (38/43), Siegfried Held (38/5). Trainer: Helmut Schön (75).

371. 26.05.1972 **WEST GERMANY - SOVIET UNION** **4-1(0-0)**
Olympiastadion, München; Referee: Armando Castanheira da Rosa Marques (Brazil); Attendance: 77,000
GER: Josef Maier (39/0) [69.Wolfgang Kleff (2/0)], Horst-Dieter Höttges (52/1) [46.Rainer Bonhof (1/0)], Georg Schwarzenbeck (11/0), Franz Beckenbauer (Cap) (60/12), Paul Breitner (6/1), Ulrich Hoeneß (4/2), Günter Netzer (28/5), Herbert Wimmer (15/0), Josef Heynckes (16/2), Gerhard Müller (39/47), Erwin Kremers (1/0). Trainer: Helmut Schön (76).
Goals: Gerhard Müller (49, 52, 58, 65).

372. 14.06.1972 **BELGIUM - WEST GERMANY** **1-2(0-1)** 4th EC. Semi-Finals.
Bosuilstadion, Deurne, Antwerpen; Referee: William Joseph Mullan (Scotland); Attendance: 55,669
GER: Josef Maier (40/0), Horst-Dieter Höttges (53/1), Georg Schwarzenbeck (12/0), Franz Beckenbauer (Cap) (61/12), Paul Breitner (7/1), Ulrich Hoeneß (5/2) [58.Jürgen Grabowski (27/3)], Günter Netzer (29/5), Herbert Wimmer (16/0), Josef Heynckes (17/2), Gerhard Müller (40/49), Erwin Kremers (2/0). Trainer: Helmut Schön (77).
Goals: Gerhard Müller (23, 71).

373. 18.06.1972 **WEST GERMANY - SOVIET UNION** **3-0(1-0)** 4th EC. Final.
Stade du Heysel, Bruxelles (Belgium); Referee: Ferdinand Marschall (Austria); Attendance: 43,437
GER: Josef Maier (41/0), Horst-Dieter Höttges (54/1), Georg Schwarzenbeck (13/0), Franz Beckenbauer (Cap) (62/12), Paul Breitner (8/1), Ulrich Hoeneß (6/2), Günter Netzer (30/5), Herbert Wimmer (17/1), Josef Heynckes (18/2), Gerhard Müller (41/51), Erwin Kremers (3/0). Trainer: Helmut Schön (78).
Goals: Gerhard Müller (27), Herbert Wimmer (51), Gerhard Müller (58).

374. 15.11.1972 **WEST GERMANY - SWITZERLAND** **5-1(2-0)**
Rheinstadion, Düsseldorf; Referee: Leonardus van der Kroft (Netherlands); Attendance: 70,387
GER: Josef Maier (42/0), Horst-Dieter Höttges (55/1), Georg Schwarzenbeck (14/0), Franz Beckenbauer (Cap) (63/12), Paul Breitner (9/1), Ulrich Hoeneß (7/2), Günter Netzer (31/6), Herbert Wimmer (18/1) [46.Hans-Hubert Vogts (42/0)], Josef Heynckes (19/2), Gerhard Müller (42/55), Erwin Kremers (4/0) [68.Rainer Geye (1/0)]. Trainer: Helmut Schön (79).
Goals: Gerhard Müller (22, 30, 47), Günter Netzer (52), Gerhard Müller (67).

375. 14.02.1973 **WEST GERMANY - ARGENTINA** **2-3(0-2)**
Olympiastadion, München; Referee: Concetto Lo Bello (Italy); Attendance: 55,000
GER: Josef Maier (43/0), Horst-Dieter Höttges (56/1), Georg Schwarzenbeck (15/0) [46.Bernhard Cullmann (1/1)], Franz Beckenbauer (Cap) (64/12), Hans-Hubert Vogts (43/0), Herbert Wimmer (19/1), Wolfgang Overath (65/15), Paul Breitner (10/1), Rainer Geye (2/0), Josef Heynckes (20/3), Erwin Kremers (5/0) [65.Siegfried Held (39/5)]. Trainer: Helmut Schön (80).
Goals: Josef Heynckes (78), Bernhard Cullmann (89).

376. 28.03.1973 **WEST GERMANY - CZECHOSLOVAKIA** **3-0(1-0)**
Rheinstadion, Düsseldorf; Referee: Karl Keller (Switzerland); Attendance: 70,000
GER: Bernd Franke (1/0), Hans-Hubert Vogts (44/0), Georg Schwarzenbeck (16/0), Franz Beckenbauer (Cap) (65/12), Paul Breitner (11/1), Ulrich Hoeneß (8/2) [86.Bernhard Cullmann (2/1)], Heinz Flohe (6/1), Wolfgang Overath (66/15), Josef Heynckes (21/3), Gerhard Müller (43/57), Erwin Kremers (6/1). Trainer: Helmut Schön (81).
Goals: Gerhard Müller (28, 63 penalty), Erwin Kremers (85).

377. 09.05.1973 **WEST GERMANY - YUGOSLAVIA** **0-1(0-0)**
Olympiastadion, München; Referee: Josef Buzek (Austria); Attendance: 55,000
GER: Josef Maier (44/0), Horst-Dieter Höttges (57/1), Georg Schwarzenbeck (17/0), Franz Beckenbauer (Cap) (66/12), Paul Breitner (12/1), Ulrich Hoeneß (9/2), Wolfgang Overath (67/15), Heinz Flohe (7/1), Jürgen Grabowski (28/3), Gerhard Müller (44/57), Siegfried Held (40/5) [77.Erwin Kremers (7/1)]. Trainer: Helmut Schön (82).

378. 12.05.1973 **WEST GERMANY - BULGARIA** **3-0(3-0)**
Volksparkstadion, Hamburg; Referee: Sven Jonsson (Sweden); Attendance: 55,000
GER: Bernd Franke (2/0), Horst-Dieter Höttges (58/1), Bernhard Cullmann (3/2), Franz Beckenbauer (Cap) (67/13), Paul Breitner (13/1), Heinz Flohe (8/1) [64.Horst Köppel (10/2)], Hans-Josef Kapellmann (1/0), Wolfgang Overath (68/15), Jürgen Grabowski (29/3), Gerhard Müller (45/57), Erwin Kremers (8/1). Trainer: Helmut Schön (83).
Goals: Franz Beckenbauer (18), Bernhard Cullmann (22), Stoian Iordanov (31 own goal).

379. 16.06.1973 **WEST GERMANY - BRAZIL** **0-1(0-0)**
Olympiastadion, West-Berlin; Referee: Arie van Gemert (Netherlands); Attendance: 75,000
GER: Josef Maier (45/0), Hans-Hubert Vogts (45/0), Bernhard Cullmann (4/2), Franz Beckenbauer (Cap) (68/13), Paul Breitner (14/1), Heinz Flohe (9/1), Wolfgang Overath (69/15), Ulrich Hoeneß (10/2) [60.Hans-Josef Kapellmann (2/0)], Josef Heynckes (22/3), Gerhard Müller (46/57), Erwin Kremers (9/1). Trainer: Helmut Schön (84).

380. 05.09.1973 **SOVIET UNION - WEST GERMANY** **0-1(0-0)**
Lenin Stadium, Moskva; Referee: Nikola Mladenović (Yugoslavia); Attendance: 75,000
GER: Wolfgang Kleff (3/0), Horst-Dieter Höttges (59/1), Georg Schwarzenbeck (18/0), Franz Beckenbauer (Cap) (69/13), Paul Breitner (15/1), Dietmar Danner (1/0), Horst Köppel (11/2) [46.Ulrich Hoeneß (11/2)], Heinz Flohe (10/1), Jürgen Grabowski (30/3) [64.Klaus Wunder (1/0)], Gerhard Müller (47/58), Josef Heynckes (23/3) [58.Erwin Kremers (10/1)]. Trainer: Helmut Schön (85).
Goal: Gerhard Müller (62).

381. 10.10.1973 **WEST GERMANY - AUSTRIA** **4-0(2-0)**
Niedersachsenstadion, Hannover; Referee: Alfred Delcourt (Belgium); Attendance: 50,000
GER: Wolfgang Kleff (4/0), Hans-Josef Kapellmann (3/0) [12.Helmut Kremers (1/0)], Wolfgang Weber (49/2) [69.Bernd Hölzenbein (1/0)], Franz Beckenbauer (Cap) (70/13) [46.Bernhard Cullmann (5/2)], Horst-Dieter Höttges (60/1), Heinz Flohe (11/1), Ulrich Hoeneß (12/2), Wolfgang Overath (70/15), Jürgen Grabowski (31/3), Gerhard Müller (48/60), Erwin Kremers (11/2). Trainer: Helmut Schön (86).
Goals: Gerhard Müller (29), Wolfgang Weber (45), Gerhard Müller (50), Erwin Kremers (79).

382. 13.10.1973 **WEST GERMANY - FRANCE** **2-1(0-0)**
Parkstadion, Gelsenkirchen; Referee: Rudolf Scheurer (Switzerland); Attendance: 70,400
GER: Wolfgang Kleff (5/0), Horst-Dieter Höttges (61/1) [46.Bernhard Cullmann (6/2)], Wolfgang Weber (50/2), Franz Beckenbauer (Cap) (71/13), Helmut Kremers (2/0), Ulrich Hoeneß (13/2), Heinz Flohe (12/1), Wolfgang Overath (71/15), Jürgen Grabowski (32/3), Gerhard Müller (49/62), Erwin Kremers (12/2). Trainer: Helmut Schön (87).
Goals: Gerhard Müller (55, 59 penalty).

383. 14.11.1973 **SCOTLAND - WEST GERMANY** **1-1(1-0)**
Hampden Park, Glasgow; Referee: John Keith Taylor (England); Attendance: 58,235
GER: Wolfgang Kleff (6/0) [46.Josef Maier (46/0)], Hans-Hubert Vogts (46/0), Wolfgang Weber (51/2), Franz Beckenbauer (Cap) (72/13), Horst-Dieter Höttges (62/1), Ulrich Hoeneß (14/3), Günter Netzer (32/6), Herbert Wimmer (20/1) [75.Bernhard Cullmann (7/2)], Jürgen Grabowski (33/3), Siegfried Held (41/5) [75.Heinz Flohe (13/1)], Erwin Kremers (13/2) [46.Josef Heynckes (24/3)]. Trainer: Helmut Schön (88).
Goal: Ulrich Hoeneß (80).

384. 24.11.1973 **WEST GERMANY - SPAIN** **2-1(2-0)**
Neckarstadion, Stuttgart; Referee: Alistair MacKenzie (Scotland); Attendance:
GER: Josef Maier (47/0), Hans-Hubert Vogts (47/0), Wolfgang Weber (52/2) [84.Georg Schwarzenbeck (19/0)], Franz Beckenbauer (Cap) (73/13), Horst-Dieter Höttges (63/1) [69.Rainer Bonhof (2/0)], Ulrich Hoeneß (15/3) [68.Bernd Hölzenbein (2/0)], Bernhard Cullmann (8/2), Wolfgang Overath (72/15), Jürgen Grabowski (34/3), Gerhard Müller (50/62), Josef Heynckes (25/5). Trainer: Helmut Schön (89).
Goals: Josef Heynckes (14, 38).

385. 23.02.1974 **SPAIN - WEST GERMANY** **1-0(1-0)**
Estadio de Sarriá, Barcelona; Referee: Michal Jursa (Czechoslovakia); Attendance: 17,000
GER: Norbert Nigbur (1/0), Hans-Hubert Vogts (48/0) [55.Paul Breitner (16/1)], Horst-Dieter Höttges (64/1), Franz Beckenbauer (Cap) (74/13), Wolfgang Weber (53/2), Ulrich Hoeneß (16/3), Helmut Kremers (3/0) [46.Herbert Wimmer (21/1)], Wolfgang Overath (73/15), Jürgen Grabowski (35/3) [46.Josef Heynckes (26/5)], Gerhard Müller (51/62), Dieter Herzog (1/0). Trainer: Helmut Schön (90).

386. 26.02.1974 **ITALY - WEST GERMANY** **0-0**
Stadio Olimpico, Roma; Referee: Anton Bucheli (Switzerland); Attendance: 82,000
GER: Josef Maier (48/0), Horst-Dieter Höttges (65/1) [80.Helmut Kremers (4/0)], Georg Schwarzenbeck (20/0), Franz Beckenbauer (Cap) (75/13), Paul Breitner (17/1), Bernhard Cullmann (9/2), Günter Netzer (33/6), Ulrich Hoeneß (17/3), Wolfgang Overath (74/15), Gerhard Müller (52/62), Josef Heynckes (27/5). Trainer: Helmut Schön (91).

387. 27.03.1974 **WEST GERMANY - SCOTLAND** **2-1(2-0)**
Waldstadion, Frankfurt am Main; Referee: Paul Schiller (Austria); Attendance: 62,000
GER: Josef Maier (49/0), Hans-Hubert Vogts (49/0), Georg Schwarzenbeck (21/0), Franz Beckenbauer (Cap) (76/13), Paul Breitner (18/2), Bernhard Cullmann (10/2), Ulrich Hoeneß (18/3), Herbert Wimmer (22/1), Jürgen Grabowski (36/4), Gerhard Müller (53/62), Dieter Herzog (2/0). Trainer: Helmut Schön (92).
Goals: Paul Breitner (33 penalty), Jürgen Grabowski (35).

388. 17.04.1974 **WEST GERMANY - HUNGARY** **5-0(1-0)**
Westfalenstadion, Dortmund; Referee: Robert Schaut (Belgium); Attendance: 54,000
GER: Norbert Nigbur (2/0), Hans-Hubert Vogts (50/0), Georg Schwarzenbeck (22/0) [46.Rainer Bonhof (3/0)], Franz Beckenbauer (Cap) (77/13), Helmut Kremers (5/0), Ulrich Hoeneß (19/3) [69.Heinz Flohe (14/1)], Bernhard Cullmann (11/2), Herbert Wimmer (23/2) [46.Bernd Hölzenbein (3/1)], Jürgen Grabowski (37/4), Gerhard Müller (54/64), Erwin Kremers (14/3). Trainer: Helmut Schön (93).
Goals: Herbert Wimmer (11), Bernd Hölzenbein (53), Erwin Kremers (68), Gerhard Müller (73, 88).

389. 01.05.1974 **WEST GERMANY - SWEDEN** **2-0(0-0)**
Volksparkstadion, Hamburg; Referee: Michel Kitabdjian (France); Attendance: 55,000
GER: Josef Maier (50/0), Hans-Hubert Vogts (51/0), Georg Schwarzenbeck (23/0), Franz Beckenbauer (Cap) (78/13), Paul Breitner (19/2), Bernhard Cullmann (12/2) [68.Bernd Hölzenbein (4/1)], Günter Netzer (34/6), Ulrich Hoeneß (20/3), Jürgen Grabowski (38/4), Gerhard Müller (55/64), Erwin Kremers (15/3) [26.Josef Heynckes (28/7); 78.Rainer Bonhof (4/0)]. Trainer: Helmut Schön (94).
Goals: Josef Heynckes (51, 58).

390. 14.06.1974 **WEST GERMANY - CHILE** **1-0(1-0)** 10th FIFA WC. Group Stage.
Olympiastadion, West-Berlin; Referee: Dogan Babaçan (Turkey); Attendance: 83,168
GER: Josef Maier (51/0), Hans-Hubert Vogts (52/0), Georg Schwarzenbeck (24/0), Franz Beckenbauer (Cap) (79/13), Paul Breitner (20/3), Ulrich Hoeneß (21/3), Bernhard Cullmann (13/2), Wolfgang Overath (75/15) [76.Bernd Hölzenbein (5/1)], Jürgen Grabowski (39/4), Gerhard Müller (56/64), Josef Heynckes (29/7). Trainer: Helmut Schön (95).
Goal: Paul Breitner (16).

391. 18.06.1974 **WEST GERMANY - AUSTRALIA** **3-0(2-0)** 10th FIFA WC. Group Stage.
Volksparkstadion, Hamburg; Referee: Mahmoud Mustapha Kamel (Egypt); Attendance: 35,000
GER: Josef Maier (52/0), Hans-Hubert Vogts (53/0), Georg Schwarzenbeck (25/0), Franz Beckenbauer (Cap) (80/13), Paul Breitner (21/3), Ulrich Hoeneß (22/3), Bernhard Cullmann (14/3) [68.Herbert Wimmer (24/2)], Wolfgang Overath (76/16), Jürgen Grabowski (40/4), Gerhard Müller (57/65), Josef Heynckes (30/7) [46.Bernd Hölzenbein (6/1)]. Trainer: Helmut Schön (96).
Goals: Wolfgang Overath (13), Bernhard Cullmann (35), Gerhard Müller (53).

392. 22.06.1974 **WEST GERMANY – EAST GERMANY** **0-1(0-0)** 10th FIFA WC. Group Stage.
Volksparkstadion, Hamburg; Referee: Ramón Ivannoe Barreto Ruiz (Uruguay); Attendance: 62,000
GER: Josef Maier (53/0), Hans-Hubert Vogts (54/0), Georg Schwarzenbeck (26/0) [69.Horst-Dieter Höttges (66/1)], Franz Beckenbauer (Cap) (81/13), Paul Breitner (22/3), Ulrich Hoeneß (23/3), Bernhard Cullmann (15/3), Wolfgang Overath (77/16) [70.Günter Netzer (35/6)], Jürgen Grabowski (41/4), Gerhard Müller (58/65), Heinz Flohe (15/1). Trainer: Helmut Schön (97).

393. 26.06.1974 **WEST GERMANY - YUGOSLAVIA** **2-0(1-0)** 10th FIFA WC. 2nd Round.
Rheinstadion, Düsseldorf; Referee: Armando Castanheira da Rosa Marques (Brazil); Attendance: 67,500
GER: Josef Maier (54/0), Hans-Hubert Vogts (55/0), Georg Schwarzenbeck (27/0), Franz Beckenbauer (Cap) (82/13), Paul Breitner (23/4), Herbert Wimmer (25/2) [74.Ulrich Hoeneß (24/3)], Rainer Bonhof (5/0), Wolfgang Overath (78/16), Bernd Hölzenbein (7/1) [79.Heinz Flohe (16/1)], Gerhard Müller (59/66), Dieter Herzog (3/0). Trainer: Helmut Schön (98).
Goals: Paul Breitner (39), Gerhard Müller (82).

394. 30.06.1974 **WEST GERMANY - SWEDEN** **4-2(0-1)** 10th FIFA WC. 2nd Round.
Rheinstadion, Düsseldorf; Referee: Pavel Kazakov (Soviet Union); Attendance: 67,800
GER: Josef Maier (55/0), Hans-Hubert Vogts (56/0), Georg Schwarzenbeck (28/0), Franz Beckenbauer (Cap) (83/13), Paul Breitner (24/4), Ulrich Hoeneß (25/4), Rainer Bonhof (6/1), Wolfgang Overath (79/17), Bernd Hölzenbein (8/1) [83.Heinz Flohe (17/1)], Gerhard Müller (60/66), Dieter Herzog (4/0) [66.Jürgen Grabowski (42/5)]. Trainer: Helmut Schön (99).
Goals: Wolfgang Overath (51), Rainer Bonhof (52), Jürgen Grabowski (77), Ulrich Hoeneß (89 penalty).

395. 03.07.1974 **WEST GERMANY - POLAND** **1-0(0-0)** 10th FIFA WC. 2nd Round.
Waldstadion, Frankfurt am Main; Referee: Erich Linemayr (Austria); Attendance: 61,500
GER: Josef Maier (56/0), Hans-Hubert Vogts (57/0), Georg Schwarzenbeck (29/0), Franz Beckenbauer (Cap) (84/13), Paul Breitner (25/4), Ulrich Hoeneß (26/4), Rainer Bonhof (7/1), Wolfgang Overath (80/17) Jürgen Grabowski (43/5), Gerhard Müller (61/67), Bernd Hölzenbein (9/1). Trainer: Helmut Schön (100).
Goal: Gerhard Müller (76).

396. 07.07.1974 **WEST GERMANY - NETHERLANDS** **2-1(2-1)** 10th FIFA WC. Final.
Olympiastadion, München; Referee: John Keith Taylor (England); Attendance: 77,833
GER: Josef Maier (57/0), Hans-Hubert Vogts (58/0), Georg Schwarzenbeck (30/0), Franz Beckenbauer (Cap) (85/13), Paul Breitner (26/5), Ulrich Hoeneß (27/4), Rainer Bonhof (8/1), Wolfgang Overath (81/17), Jürgen Grabowski (44/5), Gerhard Müller (62/68), Bernd Hölzenbein (10/1). Trainer: Helmut Schön (101).
Goals: Paul Breitner (26 penalty), Gerhard Müller (43).

397. 04.09.1974 **SWITZERLAND - WEST GERMANY** **1-2(1-2)**
„St. Jakob“ Stadion, Basel; Referee: Paul Schiller (Austria); Attendance: 48,000
GER: Josef Maier (58/0), Helmut Kremers (6/0), Georg Schwarzenbeck (31/0) [78.Hans-Josef Kapellmann (4/0)], Franz Beckenbauer (Cap) (86/13), Hans-Hubert Vogts (59/0), Rainer Bonhof (9/1), Bernhard Cullmann (16/4), Ulrich Hoeneß (28/4), Rainer Geye (3/1), Bernd Hölzenbein (11/1) [46.Wolfgang Seel (1/0)], Dieter Herzog (5/0). Trainer: Helmut Schön (102).
Goals: Bernhard Cullmann (6), Rainer Geye (27).

398. 20.11.1974 **GREECE - WEST GERMANY** **2-2(1-0)** 5th EC. Qualifiers
Stádio „Giórgos Karaïskáki“, Peiraiás; Referee: Nicolae Rainea (Romania); Attendance: 11,425
GER: Josef Maier (59/0), Hans-Hubert Vogts (60/0), Georg Schwarzenbeck (32/0), Franz Beckenbauer (Cap) (87/13), Helmut Kremers (7/0), Herbert Wimmer (26/3), Bernhard Cullmann (17/5) [78.Hans-Josef Kapellmann (5/0)], Ulrich Hoeneß (29/4), Rainer Geye (4/1), Bernd Hölzenbein (12/1), Josef Heynckes (31/7) [81.Josef Pirrung (1/0)]. Trainer: Helmut Schön (103).
Goals: Bernhard Cullmann (51), Herbert Wimmer (82).

399. 22.12.1974 **MALTA - WEST GERMANY** **0-1(0-1)** 5th EC. Qualifiers
Empire Stadium, Gzira; Referee: Gyula Emsberger (Hungary); Attendance: 12,528
GER: Norbert Nigbur (3/0), Hans-Hubert Vogts (61/0), Karl-Heinz Körbel (1/0), Franz Beckenbauer (Cap) (88/13), Bernhard Dietz (1/0), Rainer Bonhof (10/1), Bernhard Cullmann (18/6) [74.Rudolf Seliger (1/0)], Heinz Flohe (18/1), Josef Pirrung (2/0) [46.Bernd Nickel (1/0)], Erwin Kostedde (1/0), Bernd Hölzenbein (13/1). Trainer: Helmut Schön (104).
Goal: Bernhard Cullmann (44).

400. 12.03.1975 **ENGLAND - WEST GERMANY** **2-0(1-0)**
Wembley Stadium, London; Referee: Robert Schaut (Belgium); Attendance: 100,000
GER: Josef Maier (60/0), Hans-Hubert Vogts (62/0), Karl-Heinz Körbel (2/0), Franz Beckenbauer (Cap) (89/13), Rainer Bonhof (11/1), Bernhard Cullmann (19/6), Heinz Flohe (19/1), Herbert Wimmer (27/3) [64.Helmut Kremers (8/0)], Manfred Ritschel (1/0), Erwin Kostedde (2/0) [75.Josef Heynckes (32/7)], Bernd Hölzenbein (14/1). Trainer: Helmut Schön (105).

401. 27.04.1975 **BULGARIA - WEST GERMANY** **1-1(0-0)** 5th EC. Qualifiers
Nationalen stadion "Vasil Levski", Sofia; Referee: Jean Dubach (Switzerland); Attendance: 47,200
GER: Josef Maier (61/0), Hans-Hubert Vogts (63/0), Georg Schwarzenbeck (33/0), Franz Beckenbauer (Cap) (90/13), Paul Breitner (27/5), Rainer Bonhof (12/1), Ulrich Hoeneß (30/4) [73.Karl-Heinz Körbel (3/0)], Günter Netzer (36/6), Manfred Ritschel (2/1), Wolfgang Seel (2/0), Josef Heynckes (33/7) [34.Bernd Hölzenbein (15/1)]. Trainer: Helmut Schön (106).
Goal: Manfred Ritschel (76 penalty).

402. 17.05.1975 **WEST GERMANY - NETHERLANDS** **1-1(1-0)**
Waldstadion, Frankfurt am Main; Referee: Walter Hungerbühler (Switzerland); Attendance: 53,000
GER: Josef Maier (62/0), Hans-Hubert Vogts (64/0), Uwe Kliemann (1/0), Franz Beckenbauer (Cap) (91/13), Karl-Heinz Körbel (4/0), Rainer Bonhof (13/1), Erich Beer (1/0), Herbert Wimmer (28/4) [70.Bernhard Cullmann (20/6)], Manfred Ritschel (3/1), Wolfgang Seel (3/0), Bernd Hölzenbein (16/1). Trainer: Helmut Schön (107).
Goal: Herbert Wimmer (7).

403. 03.09.1975 **AUSTRIA - WEST GERMANY** **0-2(0-0)**
Praterstadion, Wien; Referee: Károly Palotai (Hungary); Attendance: 72,000
GER: Josef Maier (63/0), Manfred Kaltz (1/0), Georg Schwarzenbeck (34/0) [26.Dietmar Danner (2/0)], Franz Beckenbauer (Cap) (92/13) [46.Erich Beer (2/2)], Hans-Hubert Vogts (65/0), Karl-Heinz Körbel (5/0), Herbert Wimmer (29/4) [70.Ferdinand Keller (1/0)], Ulrich Stielike (1/0), Wolfgang Seel (4/0), Bernd Gersdorff (1/0), Bernd Hölzenbein (17/1). Trainer: Helmut Schön (108).
Goals: Erich Beer (50, 79).

404. 11.10.1975 **WEST GERMANY - GREECE** **1-1(0-0)** 5th EC. Qualifiers
Rheinstadion, Düsseldorf; Referee: Clive Thomas (Wales); Attendance: 61,252
GER: Josef Maier (64/0), Manfred Kaltz (2/0), Karl-Heinz Körbel (6/0), Franz Beckenbauer (Cap) (93/13), Hans-Hubert Vogts 66/0), Erich Beer (3/2), Günter Netzer (37/6), Paul Breitner (28/5), Bernd Hölzenbein (18/1), Erwin Kostedde (3/0), Josef Heynckes (34/8). Trainer: Helmut Schön (109).
Goal: Josef Heynckes (67).

405. 19.11.1975 **WEST GERMANY - BULGARIA** **1-0(0-0)** 5th EC. Qualifiers
Neckarstadion, Stuttgart; Referee: Alistait MacKenzie (Scotland); Attendance: 68,819
GER: Josef Maier (65/0), Hans-Hubert Vogts (67/0), Georg Schwarzenbeck (35/0), Franz Beckenbauer (Cap) (94/13), Bernhard Dietz (2/0), Herbert Wimmer (30/4), Ulrich Stielike (2/0), Dietmar Danner (3/0), Bernd Hölzenbein (19/1), Erich Beer (4/2), Josef Heynckes (35/9). Trainer: Helmut Schön (110).
Goal: Josef Heynckes (65).

406. 20.12.1975 **TURKEY - WEST GERMANY** **0-5(0-2)**
"Ismet Inönü" Stadyumu, Istanbul; Referee: Alberto Michelotti (Italy); Attendance: 25,000
GER: Rudi Kargus (1/0), Hans-Hubert Vogts (68/0), Georg Schwarzenbeck (36/0), Franz Beckenbauer (Cap) (95/13), Bernhard Dietz (3/0) [74.Peter Reichel (1/0)], Ulrich Stielike (3/0) [46.Ronald Worm (1/2)], Dietmar Danner (4/0), Herbert Wimmer (31/4) [74.Rainer Bonhof (14/1)], Bernd Hölzenbein (20/1), Erich Beer (5/3), Josef Heynckes (36/11). Trainer: Helmut Schön (111).
Goals: Josef Heynckes (18), Erich Beer (25), Ronald Worm (57, 65), Josef Heynckes (77).

407. 28.02.1976 **WEST GERMANY - MALTA** **8-0(4-0)** 5th EC. Qualifiers
Westfalenstadion, Dortmund; Referee: Marian Kuston (Poland); Attendance: 52,248
GER: Josef Maier (66/0), Hans-Hubert Vogts (69/1), Georg Schwarzenbeck (37/0), Franz Beckenbauer (Cap) (96/13), Bernhard Dietz (4/0), Herbert Wimmer (32/4) [56.Hans Bongartz (1/0)], Erich Beer (6/5), Ulrich Stielike (4/0) [46.Bernhard Cullmann (21/6)], Bernd Hölzenbein (21/2), Ronald Worm (2/4), Josef Heynckes (37/13). Trainer: Helmut Schön (112).
Goals: Ronald Worm (5, 27), Josef Heynckes (34), Erich Beer (44 penalty), Josef Heynckes (58), Erich Beer (77), Hans-Hubert Vogts (82), Bernd Hölzenbein (88).

408. 24.04.1976 **SPAIN - WEST GERMANY** **1-1(1-0)** 5th EC. Quarter-Finals.
Estadio „Vicente Calderón", Madrid; Referee: John Keith Taylor (England); Attendance: 63,000
GER: Josef Maier (67/0), Hans-Hubert Vogts (70/1), Georg Schwarzenbeck (38/0) [Bernhard Cullmann (22/6)], Franz Beckenbauer (Cap) (97/13), Bernhard Dietz (5/0) [83.Peter Reichel (2/0)], Rainer Bonhof (15/1), Herbert Wimmer (33/4), Dietmar Danner (5/0), Bernd Hölzenbein (22/2), Erich Beer (7/6), Ronald Worm (3/4). Trainer: Helmut Schön (113).
Goal: Erich Beer (60).

409. 22.05.1976 **WEST GERMANY - SPAIN** **2-0(2-0)** 5th EC. Quarter-Finals.
Olympiastadion, München; Referee: Robert Würtz (France); Attendance: 77,600
GER: Josef Maier (68/0), Hans-Hubert Vogts (71/1), Georg Schwarzenbeck (39/0), Franz Beckenbauer (Cap) (98/13), Bernhard Dietz (6/0), Herbert Wimmer (34/4), Erich Beer (8/6), Rainer Bonhof (16/1), Ulrich Hoeneß (31/5), Klaus Toppmöller (1/1), Bernd Hölzenbein (23/2). Trainer: Helmut Schön (114).
Goals: Ulrich Hoeneß (17), Klaus Toppmöller (43).

410. 17.06.1976 **YUGOSLAVIA - WEST GERMANY** **2-4(2-0,2-2)** 5th EC. Semi-Finals.
Stadion Crvena zvezda, Beograd; Referee: Alfred Delcourt (Belgium); Attendance: 70,000
GER: Josef Maier (69/0), Hans-Hubert Vogts (72/1), Georg Schwarzenbeck (40/0), Franz Beckenbauer (Cap) (99/13), Bernhard Dietz (7/0), Herbert Wimmer (35/4) [80.Dieter Müller (1/3)], Rainer Bonhof (17/1), Erich Beer (9/6), Dietmar Danner (6/0) [46.Heinz Flohe (20/2)], Ulrich Hoeneß (32/5), Bernd Hölzenbein (24/2). Trainer: Helmut Schön (115).
Goals: Heinz Flohe (65), Dieter Müller (82, 115, 119).

411. 20.06.1976 **CZECHOSLOVAKIA - WEST GERMANY** **2-2(2-1,2-2); 5-3 on penalties** 5th EC. Final.
Stadion Crvena zvezda, Beograd (Yugoslavia); Referee: Sergio Gonella (Italy); Attendance: 65,000
GER: Josef Maier (70/0), Hans-Hubert Vogts (73/1), Georg Schwarzenbeck (41/0), Franz Beckenbauer (Cap) (100/13), Bernhard Dietz (8/0), Herbert Wimmer (36/4) [46.Heinz Flohe (21/2)], Rainer Bonhof (18/1), Erich Beer (10/6) [79.Hans Bongartz (2/0)], Ulrich Hoeneß (33/5), Dieter Müller (2/4), Bernd Hölzenbein (25/3). Trainer: Helmut Schön (116).
Goals: Dieter Müller (28), Bernd Hölzenbein (90).
Penalties: Rainer Bonhof, Heinz Flohe, Hans Bongartz, Ulrich Hoeneß (missed).

412. 06.10.1976 **WALES - WEST GERMANY** **0-2(0-1)**
Ninian Park, Cardiff; Referee: Robert Matthewson (England); Attendance: 14,029
GER: Rudi Kargus (2/0), Hans-Hubert Vogts (74/1), Herbert Zimmermann (1/0) [46.Georg Schwarzenbeck (42/0)], Franz Beckenbauer (Cap) (101/14), Bernhard Dietz (9/0), Ulrich Stielike (5/0), Ulrich Hoeneß (34/5) [74.Dieter Müller (3/4)], Heinz Flohe (22/2), Karl-Heinz Rummenigge (1/0), Erich Beer (11/6) [62.Rudolf Seliger (2/0)], Josef Heynckes (38/14). Trainer: Helmut Schön (117).
Goals: Franz Beckenbauer (34), Josef Heynckes (73).

413. 17.11.1976 **WEST GERMANY - CZECHOSLOVAKIA** **2-0(2-0)**
Niedersachsenstadion, Hannover; Referee: Jean Dubach (Switzerland); Attendance: 61,000
GER: Josef Maier (71/0), Hans-Hubert Vogts (75/1) [22.Manfred Kaltz (3/0)], Georg Schwarzenbeck (43/0), Franz Beckenbauer (Cap) (102/14), Bernhard Dietz (10/0), Rainer Bonhof (19/1), Ulrich Hoeneß (35/5), Heinz Flohe (23/3), Karl-Heinz Rummenigge (2/0), Erich Beer (12/7), Josef Heynckes (39/14). Trainer: Helmut Schön (118).
Goals: Heinz Flohe (17), Erich Beer (34).

414. 23.02.1977 **FRANCE - WEST GERMANY** **1-0(0-0)**
Stade Parc des Princes, Paris; Referee: Pablo Augusto Sánchez Ibañez (Spain); Attendance: 45,000
GER: Josef Maier (72/0), Hans-Hubert Vogts (76/1), Peter Nogly (1/0), Franz Beckenbauer (Cap) (103/14), Bernhard Dietz (11/0), Rainer Bonhof (20/1), Ulrich Stielike (6/0), Heinz Flohe (24/3), Karl-Heinz Rummenigge (3/0), Dieter Müller (4/4) [69.Erich Beer (13/7)], Bernd Hölzenbein (26/3). Trainer: Helmut Schön (119).

415. 27.04.1977 **WEST GERMANY – NORTHERN IRELAND** **5-0(0-0)**
Müngersdorferstadion, Köln; Referee: Károly Palotai (Hungary); Attendance: 58,000
GER: Josef Maier (73/0) [46.Bernd Franke (3/0)], Hans-Hubert Vogts (Cap) (77/1), Manfred Kaltz (4/0), Peter Nogly (2/0), Bernhard Dietz (12/0), Rainer Bonhof (21/2), Heinz Flohe (25/4), Rudiger Abramczik (1/0), Klaus Fischer (1/2), Dieter Müller (5/5), Bernd Hölzenbein (27/3). Trainer: Helmut Schön (120).
Goals: Rainer Bonhof (55 penalty), Klaus Fischer (58), Dieter Müller (65), Klaus Fischer (84), Heinz Flohe (90).

416. 30.04.1977 **YUGOSLAVIA - WEST GERMANY** **1-2(0-1)**
Stadion Crvena zvezda, Beograd; Referee: Dogan Babaçan (Turkey); Attendance: 17,000
GER: Josef Maier (74/0) [46.Rudi Kargus (3/0)], Franz-Josef Tenhagen (1/0), Manfred Kaltz (5/0), Rolf Rüssmann (1/0), Hans-Hubert Vogts (Cap) (78/1), Rainer Bonhof (22/3), Erich Beer (14/7), Heinz Flohe (26/4) [46.Felix Magath (1/0)], Rudiger Abramczik (2/0), Klaus Fischer (2/2), Dieter Müller (6/6). Trainer: Helmut Schön (121).
Goals: Dieter Müller (11), Rainer Bonhof (72 penalty).

417. 05.06.1977 **ARGENTINA - WEST GERMANY** **1-3(0-1)**
Estadio „Camilo Cichero", Buenos Aires; Referee: Arnaldo David César Coelho (Brazil); Attendance: 60,000
GER: Bernd Franke (4/0), Hans-Hubert Vogts (Cap) (79/1), Rolf Rüssmann (2/0), Manfred Kaltz (6/0), Bernhard Dietz (13/0), Rainer Bonhof (23/3), Bernd Hölzenbein (28/4), Erich Beer (15/7) [70.Karl-Heinz Rummenigge (4/0)], Rudiger Abramczik (3/0), Klaus Fischer (3/4), Georg Volkert (7/2). Trainer: Helmut Schön (122).
Goals: Klaus Fischer (8, 61), Bernd Hölzenbein (70).

418. 08.06.1977 **URUGUAY - WEST GERMANY** **0-2(0-1)**
Estadio Centenario, Montevideo; Referee: Angel Norberto Coerezza (Argentina); Attendance: 50,000
GER: Dieter Burdenski (1/0), Hans-Hubert Vogts (Cap) (80/1), Rolf Rüssmann (3/0) [46.Peter Nogly (3/0)], Manfred Kaltz (7/0), Bernhard Dietz (14/0), Rainer Bonhof (24/3), Heinz Flohe (27/5), Felix Magath (2/0), Karl-Heinz Rummenigge (5/0), Dieter Müller (7/7), Georg Volkert (8/2) [46.Rudiger Abramczik (4/0); 67.Bernd Hölzenbein (29/4)]. Trainer: Helmut Schön (123).
Goals: Heinz Flohe (51), Dieter Müller (90).

419. 12.06.1977 **BRAZIL - WEST GERMANY** **1-1(0-0)**
Estádio „Jornalista Mário Filho" [Maracanã], Rio de Janeiro; Referee: Luis Pestarino (Argentina); Attendance: 102,000
GER: Josef Maier (75/0), Hans-Hubert Vogts (Cap) (81/1), Rolf Rüssmann (4/0), Manfred Kaltz (8/0), Bernhard Dietz (15/0), Rainer Bonhof (25/3), Bernd Hölzenbein (30/4) [79.Franz-Josef Tenhagen (2/0)], Erich Beer (16/7) [79.Heinz Flohe (28/5)], Rudiger Abramczik (5/0), Klaus Fischer (4/5), Georg Volkert (9/2) [70.Karl-Heinz Rummenigge (6/0)]. Trainer: Helmut Schön (124).
Goal: Klaus Fischer (54).

420. 14.06.1977 **MEXICO - WEST GERMANY** **2-2(2-0)**
Estadio Azteca, Ciudad de México; Referee: Mario Antonio Dorantes García (Mexico); Attendance: 80,000
GER: Josef Maier (76/0), Hans-Hubert Vogts (Cap) (82/1), Rolf Rüssmann (5/0), Manfred Kaltz (9/0), Bernhard Dietz (16/0), Rainer Bonhof (26/3) [73.Peter Nogly (4/0)], Hans Bongartz (3/0), Heinz Flohe (29/5) [46.Erich Beer (17/7)], Bernd Hölzenbein (31/4), Klaus Fischer (5/7), Dieter Müller (8/7) [46.Georg Volkert (10/2)]. Trainer: Helmut Schön (125).
Goals: Klaus Fischer (52, 65).

421. 07.09.1977 **FINLAND - WEST GERMANY** **0-1(0-1)**
Olympiastadion, Helsinki; Referee: Yarkov (Soviet Union); Attendance: 14,324
GER: Josef Maier (77/0), Hans-Hubert Vogts (Cap) (83/1), Rolf Rüssmann (6/0), Manfred Kaltz (10/0), Bernhard Dietz (17/0), Rainer Bonhof (27/3), Bernd Hölzenbein (32/4), Erich Beer (18/7) [46.Hans Bongartz (4/0)], Rudiger Abramczik (6/0) [83.Karl-Heinz Rummenigge (7/0)], Klaus Fischer (6/8), Georg Volkert (11/2). Trainer: Helmut Schön (126).
Goal: Klaus Fischer (43).

22. 08.10.1977 **WEST GERMANY - ITALY** **2-1(1-0)**
lympiastadion, West-Berlin; Referee: Francis John Elisa Rion (Belgium); Attendance: 80,000
ER: Josef Maier (78/0), Hans-Hubert Vogts (Cap) (84/1), Rolf Rüssmann (7/0), Manfred Kaltz (11/1), Bernhard Dietz (18/0), Rainer Bonhof (28/3), Erich eer (19/7), Heinz Flohe (30/5), Karl-Heinz Rummenigge (8/1), Klaus Fischer (7/8), Georg Volkert (12/2) [46.Bernd Hölzenbein (33/4)]. Trainer: Helmut chön (127).
oals: Manfred Kaltz (32), Karl-Heinz Rummenigge (58).

23. 16.11.1977 **WEST GERMANY - SWITZERLAND** **4-1(3-1)**
eckarstadion, Stuttgart; Referee: Sergio Gonella (Italy); Attendance: 58,000
ER: Bernd Franke (5/0), Hans-Hubert Vogts (Cap) (85/1), Rolf Rüssmann (8/0), Manfred Kaltz (12/1), Bernhard Dietz (19/0) [46.Herbert Zimmermann /0)], Rainer Bonhof (29/3), Heinz Flohe (31/6), Manfred Burgsmüller (1/0), Rudiger Abramczik (7/0), Klaus Fischer (8/10), Wolfgang Seel (5/0). Trainer: elmut Schön (128).
oals: André Meyer (16 own goal), Heinz Flohe (16), Klaus Fischer (25, 60).

24. 14.12.1977 **WEST GERMANY - WALES** **1-1(0-0)**
estfalenstadion, Dortmund; Referee: Charles George Rainier Corver (Netherlands); Attendance: 57,000
ER: Josef Maier (79/0), Hans-Hubert Vogts (Cap) (86/1), Rolf Rüssmann (9/0) Franz-Josef Tenhagen (3/0), Bernhard Dietz (20/0), Rainer Bonhof (30/3), einz Flohe (32/6), Manfred Burgsmüller (2/0), Rudiger Abramczik (8/0), Klaus Fischer (9/11) [76.Wolfgang Seel (6/0)], Bernd Hölzenbein (34/4). Trainer: elmut Schön (129).
oal: Klaus Fischer (46).

25. 22.02.1978 **WEST GERMANY - ENGLAND** **2-1(0-1)**
lympiastadion, München; Referee: Franz Wöhrer (Austria); Attendance: 77,850
ER: Josef Maier (80/0), Hans-Hubert Vogts (Cap) (87/1), Rolf Rüssmann (10/0), Georg Schwarzenbeck (44/0), Herbert Zimmermann (3/0), Rainer Bonhof 1/4), Herbert Neumann (1/0) [72.Bernhard Dietz (21/0)], Heinz Flohe (33/6) [33.Manfred Burgsmüller (3/0)], Rudiger Abramczik (9/0), Bernd Hölzenbein 5/4) [75.Ronald Worm (4/5)], Karl-Heinz Rummenigge (9/1). Trainer: Helmut Schön (130).
oals: Ronald Worm (76), Rainer Bonhof (86).

26. 08.03.1978 **WEST GERMANY - SOVIET UNION** **1-0(0-0)**
aldstadion, Frankfurt am Main; Referee: John Gordon (Scotland); Attendance: 54,000
ER: Josef Maier (81/0), Hans-Hubert Vogts (Cap) (88/1), Rolf Rüssmann (11/1), Manfred Kaltz (13/1), Bernhard Dietz (22/0), Rainer Bonhof (32/4), ernd Hölzenbein (36/4), Heinz Flohe (34/6), Rudiger Abramczik (10/0), Klaus Fischer (10/11), Karl-Heinz Rummenigge (10/1). Trainer: Helmut Schön 31).
oal: Rolf Rüssmann (47).

27. 05.04.1978 **WEST GERMANY - BRAZIL** **0-1(0-0)**
olksparkstadion, Hamburg; Referee: Károly Palotai (Hungary); Attendance: 61,500
ER: Josef Maier (82/0), Hans-Hubert Vogts (Cap) (89/1), Rolf Rüssmann (12/1), Manfred Kaltz (14/1), Bernhard Dietz (23/0) [77.Karlheinz Förster (1/0)], ainer Bonhof (33/4), Erich Beer (20/7) [80.Ronald Worm (5/5)], Heinz Flohe (35/6), Rudiger Abramczik (11/0) [52.Hans Müller (1/0)], Klaus Fischer 1/11), Karl-Heinz Rummenigge (11/1). Trainer: Helmut Schön (132).

28. 19.04.1978 **SWEDEN - WEST GERMANY** **3-1(1-1)**
åsundastadion, Stockholm; Referee: Kenneth Howard Burns (England); Attendance: 27,355
ER: Josef Maier (83/0) [6.Dieter Burdenski (2/0)], Hans-Hubert Vogts (Cap) (90/1), Rolf Rüssmann (13/1), Manfred Kaltz (15/1), Herbert Zimmermann /0), Rainer Bonhof (34/5) [83.Bernhard Dietz (24/0)], Bernd Hölzenbein (37/4), Hans Müller (2/0) [59.Ronald Worm (6/5)], Rudiger Abramczik (12/0), laus Fischer (12/11), Karl-Heinz Rummenigge (12/1). Trainer: Helmut Schön (133).
oal: Rainer Bonhof (23).

29. 01.06.1978 **WEST GERMANY - POLAND** **0-0** 11th FIFA WC. Group Stage.
stadio Monumental „Antonio Vespucio Liberti", Buenos Aires (Argentina); Referee: Ángel Norberto Coerezza (Argentina); Attendance: 77,000
ER: Josef Maier (84/0), Hans-Hubert Vogts (Cap) (91/1), Rolf Rüssmann (14/1), Manfred Kaltz (16/1), Herbert Zimmermann (5/0), Rainer Bonhof (35/5), ich Beer (21/7), Heinz Flohe (36/6), Rudiger Abramczik (13/0), Klaus Fischer (13/11), Hans Müller (3/0). Trainer: Helmut Schön (134).

30. 06.06.1978 **WEST GERMANY - MEXICO** **6-0(4-0)** 11th FIFA WC. Group Stage.
stadio Chateau Carreras, Córdoba (Argentina); Referee: Farouk Bouzo (Syria); Attendance: 35,258
ER: Josef Maier (85/0), Hans-Hubert Vogts (Cap) (92/1), Rolf Rüssmann (16/1), Manfred Kaltz (17/1), Bernhard Dietz (25/0), Rainer Bonhof (36/5), einz Flohe (37/8), Hans Müller (4/1), Karl-Heinz Rummenigge (13/3), Klaus Fischer (14/11), Dieter Müller (9/8). Trainer: Helmut Schön (135).
oals: Dieter Müller (14), Hans Müller (29), Karl-Heinz Rummenigge (38), Heinz Flohe (44), Karl-Heinz Rummenigge (71), Heinz Flohe (89).

31. 10.06.1978 **WEST GERMANY - TUNISIA** **0-0** 11th FIFA WC. Group Stage.
stadio Chateau Carreras, Córdoba (Argentina); Referee: César Orozco Guerrero (Peru); Attendance: 30,667
ER: Josef Maier (86/0), Hans-Hubert Vogts (Cap) (93/1), Rolf Rüssmann (16/1), Manfred Kaltz (18/1), Bernhard Dietz (26/0), Rainer Bonhof (37/5), einz Flohe (38/8), Hans Müller (5/1), Karl-Heinz Rummenigge (14/3), Klaus Fischer (15/11), Dieter Müller (10/8). Trainer: Helmut Schön (136).

32. 14.06.1978 **WEST GERMANY - ITALY** **0-0** 11th FIFA WC. 2nd Round.
stadio Monumental „Antonio Vespucio Liberti", Buenos Aires (Argentina); Referee: Dušan Maksimović (Yugoslavia); Attendance: 67,547
ER: Josef Maier (87/0), Hans-Hubert Vogts (Cap) (94/1), Rolf Rüssmann (17/1), Manfred Kaltz (19/1), Bernhard Dietz (27/0), Rainer Bonhof (38/5), einz Flohe (39/8) [68.Erich Beer (22/7)], Herbert Zimmermann (6/0) [53.Harald Konopka (1/0)], Karl-Heinz Rummenigge (15/3), Klaus Fischer (16/11), ernd Hölzenbein (38/4). Trainer: Helmut Schön (137).

33. 18.06.1978 **WEST GERMANY - NETHERLANDS** **2-2(1-1)** 11th FIFA WC. 2nd Round.
stadio Chateau Carreras, Córdoba (Argentina); Referee: Ramon Ivannoe Barreto Ruiz (Uruguay); Attendance: 40,750
ER: Josef Maier (88/0), Hans-Hubert Vogts (Cap) (95/1), Rolf Rüssmann (18/1), Manfred Kaltz (20/1), Bernhard Dietz (28/0), Rainer Bonhof (39/5), Erich eer (23/7), Bernd Hölzenbein (39/4), Rudiger Abramczik (14/1), Dieter Müller (11/9), Karl-Heinz Rummenigge (16/3). Trainer: Helmut Schön (138).
oals: Rudiger Abramczik (3), Dieter Müller (70).

434. 21.06.1978 **AUSTRIA - WEST GERMANY** **3-2(0-1)** 11th FIFA WC. 2nd Round.
Estadio Chateau Carreras, Córdoba (Argentina); Referee: Abraham Klein (Israel); Attendance: 38,318
GER: Josef Maier (89/0), Hans-Hubert Vogts (Cap) (96/1), Rolf Rüssmann (19/1), Manfred Kaltz (21/1), Bernhard Dietz (29/0), Rainer Bonhof (40/5), Erich Beer (24/7) [46.Hans Müller (6/1)], Bernd Hölzenbein (40/5), Rudiger Abramczik (15/1), Dieter Müller (12/9) [61.Klaus Fischer (17/11)], Karl-Heinz Rummenigge (17/4). Trainer: Helmut Schön (139).
Goals: Karl-Heinz Rummenigge (19), Bernd Hölzenbein (68).

435. 11.10.1978 **CZECHOSLOVAKIA - WEST GERMANY** **3-4(1-4)**
Stadion Strahov, Praha; Referee: André Daina (Switzerland); Attendance: 30,000
GER: Josef Maier (Cap) (90/0), Manfred Kaltz (22/1), Gerd Zewe (1/0), Karlheinz Förster (2/0), Bernhard Dietz (30/0), Rainer Bonhof (41/7), Bernhard Cullmann (23/6), Karl-Heinz Rummenigge (18/4), Rudiger Abramczik (16/2), Klaus Fischer (18/11), Hans Müller (7/2) [71.Ronald Worm (7/5); Klaus Allofs (1/0)]. Trainer: Josef Derwall (1).
Goals: Rudiger Abramczik (8), Rainer Bonhof (10), Hans Müller (35), Rainer Bonhof (37 penalty).

436. 15.11.1978 **WEST GERMANY - HUNGARY** **0-0***
Waldstadion, Frankfurt am Main; Referee: Robert Charles Paul Wurtz (France); Attendance: 45,000
GER: Josef Maier (Cap) (91/0), Manfred Kaltz (23/1), Gerd Zewe (2/0), Rolf Rüssmann (20/1), Bernhard Dietz (31/0), Rainer Bonhof (42/7), Bernhard Cullmann (24/6), Karl-Heinz Rummenigge (19/4), Rudiger Abramczik (17/2), Klaus Fischer (19/11), Klaus Allofs (2/0). Trainer: Josef Derwall (2).
**Abbandoned at 61mins due to fogg*

437. 20.12.1978 **WEST GERMANY - NETHERLANDS** **3-1(1-0)**
Rheinstadion, Düsseldorf; Referee: Károly Palotai (Hungary); Attendance: 68,000
GER: Dieter Burdenski (3/0), Manfred Kaltz (24/1), Gerd Zewe (3/0), Ulrich Stielike (7/0), Bernhard Dietz (Cap) (32/0), Rainer Bonhof (43/8), Bernhard Cullmann (25/6) [57.Herbert Zimmermann (7/0)], Klaus Allofs (3/0), Rudiger Abramczik (18/2) [79.Ronald Borchers (1/0)], Klaus Fischer (20/12), Karl Heinz Rummenigge (20/5). Trainer: Josef Derwall (3).
Goals: Karl-Heinz Rummenigge (32), Klaus Fischer (57), Rainer Bonhof (85).

438. 25.02.1979 **MALTA - WEST GERMANY** **0-0** 6th EC. Qualifiers
Empire Stadium, Gzira; Referee: Vojtěch Christov (Czechoslovakia); Attendance: 8,450
GER: Josef Maier (Cap) (92/0), Manfred Kaltz (25/1), Gerd Zewe (4/0) [68.Klaus Toppmöller (2/1)], Karlheinz Förster (3/0), Bernhard Dietz (33/0), Rainer Bonhof (44/8), Bernhard Cullmann (26/6), Hans Müller (8/2), Rudiger Abramczik (19/2), Klaus Fischer (21/12), Karl-Heinz Rummenigge (21/5) [68.Klaus Allofs (4/0)]. Trainer: Josef Derwall (4).

439. 01.04.1979 **TURKEY - WEST GERMANY** **0-0** 6th EC. Qualifiers
"Kemal Atatürk" Stadyumu, İzmir; Referee: Miroslav Stupar (Soviet Union); Attendance: 50,000
GER: Dieter Burdenski (4/0), Manfred Kaltz (26/1), Ulrich Stielike (8/0), Rainer Bonhof (45/8), Bernhard Dietz (Cap) (34/0), Bernhard Cullmann (27/6), Herbert Zimmermann (8/0) [73.Karlheinz Förster (4/0)], Hans Müller (9/2), Ronald Borchers (2/0), Klaus Toppmöller (3/1), Karl-Heinz Rummenigge (22/5) [69.Walter Kelsch (1/0)]. Trainer: Josef Derwall (5).

440. 02.05.1979 **WALES - WEST GERMANY** **0-2(0-1)** 6th EC. Qualifiers
The Racecourse, Wrexham; Referee: Alberto Michelotti (Italy); Attendance: 26,900
GER: Josef Maier (Cap) (93/0), Manfred Kaltz (27/1), Ulrich Stielike (9/0) [88.Bernd Martin (1/0)], Karlheinz Förster (5/0), Bernhard Dietz (35/0), Rainer Bonhof (46/8), Bernhard Cullmann (28/6), Herbert Zimmermann (9/1), Klaus Fischer (22/13), Karl-Heinz Rummenigge (23/5), Klaus Allofs (5/0). Trainer: Josef Derwall (6).
Goals: Herbert Zimmermann (30), Klaus Fischer (52).

441. 22.05.1979 **REPUBLIC OF IRELAND - WEST GERMANY** **1-3(1-1)**
Lansdowne Road, Dublin; Referee: George Courtney (England); Attendance: 25,000
GER: Josef Maier (Cap) (94/0) [46.Dieter Burdenski (5/0)], Manfred Kaltz (28/1), Bernhard Cullmann (29/6), Karlheinz Förster (6/0), Bernd Förster (1/0), Herbert Zimmermann (10/1) [70.William Hartwig (1/0)], Bernd Schuster (1/0), Hans Müller (10/2) [46.Walter Kelsch (2/1)], Karl-Heinz Rummenigge (24/6) [70.Caspar Memering (1/0)], Dieter Hoeneß (1/1), Klaus Allofs (6/0). Trainer: Josef Derwall (7).
Goals: Karl-Heinz Rummenigge (29), Walter Kelsch (81), Dieter Hoeneß (90).

442. 26.05.1979 **ICELAND - WEST GERMANY** **1-3(0-2)**
Laugardalsvöllur, Reykjavík; Referee: Douglas Diarmid Hope (Scotland); Attendance: 8,280
GER: Josef Maier (Cap) (95/0) [46.Harald Schumacher (1/0)], Harald Konopka (2/0), Bernhard Cullmann (30/6), Karlheinz Förster (7/0) [60.Manfred Kaltz (29/1)], Bernd Förster (2/0), Jürgen Groh (1/0), Herbert Zimmermann (11/1) [46.William Hartwig (2/0)], Bernd Schuster (2/0), Walter Kelsch (3/2), Caspar Memering (2/0), Dieter Hoeneß (2/3). Trainer: Josef Derwall (8).
Goals: Walter Kelsch (32), Dieter Hoeneß (33, 67).

443. 12.09.1979 **WEST GERMANY - ARGENTINA** **2-1(0-0)**
Olympiastadion, West-Berlin; Referee: Ulf Eriksson (Sweden); Attendance: 45,000
GER: Dieter Burdenski (6/0), Manfred Kaltz (30/1), Bernhard Cullmann (31/6), Karlheinz Förster (8/0), Bernhard Dietz (Cap) (36/0), Rainer Bonhof (47/8), Bernd Schuster (3/0), Hans Müller (11/2), Karl-Heinz Rummenigge (25/7), Klaus Fischer (23/13), Klaus Allofs (7/1). Trainer: Josef Derwall (9).
Goals: Klaus Allofs (47), Karl-Heinz Rummenigge (58).

444. 17.10.1979 **WEST GERMANY - WALES** **5-1(4-0)** 6th EC. Qualifiers
Müngersdorferstadion, Köln; Referee: Johannes Nicolaas Ignatius „Jan" Keizer (Netherlands); Attendance: 61,000
GER: Dieter Burdenski (7/0), Manfred Kaltz (31/2), Bernhard Cullmann (32/6), Karlheinz Förster (9/1), Bernhard Dietz (Cap) (37/0), Rainer Bonhof (48/8), Bernd Schuster (4/0) [64.Herbert Zimmermann (12/1)], Hans Müller (12/2), Karl-Heinz Rummenigge (26/8) [75.Hans-Peter Briegel (1/0)], Klaus Fischer (24/15), Klaus Allofs (8/1). Trainer: Josef Derwall (10).
Goals: Klaus Fischer (23), Manfred Kaltz (32), Klaus Fischer (38), Karl-Heinz Rummenigge (41), Karlheinz Förster (83).

445. 21.11.1979 **SOVIET UNION - WEST GERMANY** **1-3(0-1)**
Dinamo Stadium, Tbilisi; Referee: Martti Hirviniemi (Finland); Attendance: 40,000
GER: Norbert Nigbur (4/0), Manfred Kaltz (32/2) [74.Herbert Zimmermann (13/1)], Bernhard Cullmann (33/6), Karlheinz Förster (10/1), Bernhard Dietz (Cap) (38/0) [74.Miroslav Votava (1/0)], Hans-Peter Briegel (2/0), Bernd Schuster (5/0) [46.Bernd Förster (3/0)], Hans Müller (13/2), Karl-Heinz Rummenigge (27/10), Klaus Fischer (25/16), Harald Nickel (1/0). Trainer: Josef Derwall (11).
Goals: Karl-Heinz Rummenigge (35, 62), Klaus Fischer (66).

446. 22.12.1979 **WEST GERMANY - TURKEY** **2-0(1-0)** 6th EC. Qualifiers
Parkstadion, Gelsenkirchen; Referee: Rudolf Renggli (Switzerland); Attendance: 70,000
GER: Norbert Nigbur (5/0), Manfred Kaltz (33/2), Bernhard Cullmann (34/6), Bernd Förster (4/0), Bernhard Dietz (Cap) (39/0), Rainer Bonhof (49/8), Ulrich Stielike (10/0) [85.Herbert Zimmermann (14/2)], Hans Müller (14/2), Karl-Heinz Rummenigge (28/10), Klaus Fischer (26/17), Harald Nickel (2/0). Trainer: Josef Derwall (12).
Goals: Klaus Fischer (15), Herbert Zimmermann (89).

447. 27.02.1980 **WEST GERMANY - MALTA** **8-0(3-0)** 6th EC. Qualifiers
Weserstadion, Bremen; Referee: Norbert Rolles (Luxembourg); Attendance: 38,000
GER: Dieter Burdenski (8/0), Manfred Kaltz (34/2), Bernhard Cullmann (35/6), Karlheinz Förster (11/1), Bernhard Dietz (Cap) (40/0), Rainer Bonhof (50/9), Bernd Förster (5/0) [61.Walter Kelsch (4/3)], Hans Müller (15/2), Karl-Heinz Rummenigge (29/11), Klaus Fischer (27/19), Klaus Allofs (9/3) [61.Harald Nickel (3/0)]. Trainer: Josef Derwall (13).
Goals: Klaus Allofs (12), Rainer Bonhof (17 penalty), Klaus Fischer (40), Klaus Allofs (56), John Holland (62 own goal), Walter Kelsch (70), Karl-Heinz Rummenigge (74), Klaus Fischer (90).

448. 02.04.1980 **WEST GERMANY - AUSTRIA** **1-0(1-0)**
Olympiastadion, München; Referee: Michel Vautrot (France); Attendance: 78,000
GER: Norbert Nigbur (6/0) [46.Harald Schumacher (2/0)], Manfred Kaltz (35/2), Bernhard Cullmann (36/6), Karlheinz Förster (12/1), Bernhard Dietz (Cap) (41/0) [16.Hans-Peter Briegel (3/0)], Rainer Bonhof (51/9), Bernd Förster (6/0) [46.Bernd Schuster (6/0)], Hans Müller (16/3), Karl-Heinz Rummenigge (30/11), Horst Hrubesch (1/0), Klaus Allofs (10/3) [71.Karl Del'Haye (1/0)]. Trainer: Josef Derwall (14).
Goal: Hans Müller (34).

449. 13.05.1980 **WEST GERMANY - POLAND** **3-1(2-1)**
Waldstadion, Frankfurt am Main; Referee: Gianfranco Menegali (Italy); Attendance: 45,000
GER: Harald Schumacher (3/0), Manfred Kaltz (36/2), Bernhard Cullmann (37/6), Karlheinz Förster (13/1), Bernhard Dietz (Cap) (42/0), Bernd Förster (7/0) [46.Bernd Schuster (7/1)], Hans-Peter Briegel (4/0) [73.Ditmar Jakobs (1/0)], Hans Müller (17/3) [73.Horst Hrubesch (2/0)], Felix Magath (3/0), Karl-Heinz Rummenigge (31/12), Klaus Allofs (11/4). Trainer: Josef Derwall (15).
Goals: Karl-Heinz Rummenigge (6), Klaus Allofs (38), Bernd Schuster (57).

450. 11.06.1980 **CZECHOSLOVAKIA - WEST GERMANY** **0-1(0-0)** 6th EC. Group Stage.
Stadio Olimpico, Roma (Italy); Referee: Alberto Michelotti (Italy); Attendance: 11,059
GER: Harald Schumacher (4/0), Manfred Kaltz (37/2), Bernhard Cullmann (38/6), Karlheinz Förster (14/1), Bernhard Dietz (Cap) (43/0), Bernd Förster (8/0) [60.Felix Magath (4/0)], Hans-Peter Briegel (5/0), Ulrich Stielike (11/0), Hans Müller (18/3), Karl-Heinz Rummenigge (32/13), Klaus Allofs (12/4). Trainer: Josef Derwall (16).
Goal: Karl-Heinz Rummenigge (55).

451. 14.06.1980 **WEST GERMANY - NETHERLANDS** **3-2(1-0)** 6th EC. Group Stage.
Stadio San Paolo, Napoli (Italy); Referee: Robert Charles Paul Wurtz (France); Attendance: 26,546
GER: Harald Schumacher (5/0), Manfred Kaltz (38/2), Karlheinz Förster (15/1), Ulrich Stielike (12/0), Bernhard Dietz (Cap) (44/0) [73.Lothar Herbert Matthäus (1/0)], Bernd Schuster (8/1), Hans-Peter Briegel (6/0), Hans Müller (19/3) [65.Felix Magath (5/0)], Karl-Heinz Rummenigge (33/13), Horst Hrubesch (3/0), Klaus Allofs (13/7). Trainer: Josef Derwall (17).
Goals: Klaus Allofs (11, 56, 66).

452. 17.06.1980 **WEST GERMANY - GREECE** **0-0** 6th EC. Group Stage.
Stadio Comunale, Torino (Italy); Referee: Brian McGinlay (Scotland); Attendance: 13,901
GER: Harald Schumacher (6/0), Manfred Kaltz (39/2), Karlheinz Förster (16/1), Ulrich Stielike (13/0), Bernd Förster (9/0) [46.Miroslav Votava (2/0)], Hans-Peter Briegel (7/0), Bernhard Cullmann (Cap) (39/6), Hans Müller (20/3), Karl-Heinz Rummenigge (34/13) [66.Karl Del'Haye (2/0)], Horst Hrubesch (4/0), Caspar Memering (3/0). Trainer: Josef Derwall (18).

453. 21.06.1980 **BELGIUM - WEST GERMANY** **1-2(0-1)** 6th EC. Final.
Stadio Olimpico, Roma (Italy); Referee: Nicolae Rainea (Romania); Attendance: 47,864
GER: Harald Schumacher (7/0), Manfred Kaltz (40/2), Karlheinz Förster (17/1), Ulrich Stielike (14/0), Bernhard Dietz (Cap) (45/0), Bernd Schuster (9/1), Hans-Peter Briegel (8/0) [55.Bernhard Cullmann (40/6)], Hans Müller (21/3), Karl-Heinz Rummenigge (35/13), Horst Hrubesch (5/2), Klaus Allofs (14/7). Trainer: Josef Derwall (19).
Goals: Horst Hrubesch (10, 89).

454. 10.09.1980 **SWITZERLAND - WEST GERMANY** **2-3(0-1)**
„St. Jakob" Stadion, Basel; Referee: Luigi Agnolin (Italy); Attendance: 32,000
GER: Harald Schumacher (8/0), Manfred Kaltz (41/2), Karlheinz Förster (18/1), Bernd Schuster (10/1), Bernhard Dietz (Cap) (46/0), Hans-Peter Briegel (9/0), Felix Magath (6/1), Hans Müller (22/5), Karl-Heinz Rummenigge (36/13), Horst Hrubesch (6/2), Klaus Allofs (15/7). Trainer: Josef Derwall (20).
Goals: Hans Müller (18), Felix Magath (66), Hans Müller (69).

455. 11.10.1980 **NETHERLANDS - WEST GERMANY** **1-1(1-1)**
Stadion Philips, Eindhoven; Referee: Vojtěch Christov (Czechoslovakia); Attendance: 22,000
GER: Harald Schumacher (9/0) [46.Eike Immel (1/0)], Manfred Kaltz (42/2), Karlheinz Förster (19/1), Kurt Niedermayer (1/0), Bernhard Dietz (Cap) (47/0), Hans-Peter Briegel (10/0), Felix Magath (7/1), Hans Müller (23/5), Karl-Heinz Rummenigge (37/13), Horst Hrubesch (7/3), Klaus Allofs (16/7). Trainer: Josef Derwall (21).
Goal: Horst Hrubesch (35).

456. 19.11.1980 **WEST GERMANY - FRANCE** **4-1(2-1)**
Niedersachsenstadion, Hannover; Referee: Rolf Nyhus (Norway); Attendance: 60,400
GER: Harald Schumacher (10/0), Manfred Kaltz (43/3), Bernd Schuster (11/1), Karlheinz Förster (20/1), Bernhard Dietz (Cap) (48/0), Miroslav Votava (3/0), Hans-Peter Briegel (11/1), Hans Müller (24/5), Karl Allgöwer (1/0), Horst Hrubesch (8/4), Klaus Allofs (17/8). Trainer: Josef Derwall (22).
Goals: Manfred Kaltz (6 penalty), Hans-Peter Briegel (37), Horst Hrubesch (62), Klaus Allofs (89).

457. 03.12.1980 **BULGARIA - WEST GERMANY** **1-3(0-2)** 12th FIFA WC. Qualifiers
Nationalen stadion "Vasil Levski", Sofia; Referee: Ricardo Lattanzi (Italy); Attendance: 60,000
GER: Harald Schumacher (11/0), Manfred Kaltz (44/5), Ulrich Stielike (15/0), Karlheinz Förster (21/1), Bernhard Dietz (Cap) (49/0), Hans-Peter Briegel (12/1), Felix Magath (8/1) [72.Miroslav Votava (4/0)], Hans Müller (25/5), Karl-Heinz Rummenigge (38/14), Horst Hrubesch (9/4), Klaus Allofs (18/8) [72.Ronald Borchers (3/0)]. Trainer: Josef Derwall (23).
Goals: Manfred Kaltz (14, 36 penalty), Karl-Heinz Rummenigge (54).

458. 01.01.1981 **ARGENTINA - WEST GERMANY** **2-1(1-0)** Gold Cup
Estadio Centenario, Montevideo (Uruguay); Referee: Augusto Lamo Castillo (Spain); Attendance: 55,000
GER: Harald Schumacher (12/0), Manfred Kaltz (45/5), Rainer Bonhof (52/9), Karlheinz Förster (22/1), Bernhard Dietz (Cap) (50/0), Hans-Peter Briegel (13/1), Felix Magath (9/1), Hans Müller (26/5), Karl-Heinz Rummenigge (39/14), Horst Hrubesch (10/5), Klaus Allofs (19/8). Trainer: Josef Derwall (24).
Goal: Horst Hrubesch (42).

459. 07.01.1981 **WEST GERMANY - BRAZIL** **1-4(0-0)** Gold Cup
Estadio Centenario, Montevideo (Uruguay); Referee: Juan Amrosio Silvagno Cavanna (Chile); Attendance: 50,000
GER: Harald Schumacher (13/0), Manfred Kaltz (46/5) [35.Wolfgang Dremmler (1/0)], Rainer Bonhof (53/9), Karlheinz Förster (23/1), Bernhard Dietz (Cap) (51/0), Hans-Peter Briegel (14/1), Felix Magath (10/1), Miroslav Votava (5/0), Hans Müller (27/5), Karl-Heinz Rummenigge (40/14), Klaus Allofs (20/9) [78.Karl Allgöwer (2/0)]. Trainer: Josef Derwall (25).
Goal: Klaus Allofs (54).

460. 01.04.1981 **ALBANIA - WEST GERMANY** **0-2(0-1)** 12th FIFA WC. Qualifiers
Stadiumi „Kombëtar Qemal Stafa", Tiranë; Referee: Antonin Wencl (Czechoslovakia); Attendance: 30,000
GER: Harald Schumacher (14/0), Manfred Kaltz (47/5), Ulrich Stielike (16/0), Karlheinz Förster (24/1) [74.Wilfried Hannes (1/0)], Bernhard Dietz (Cap) (52/0), Bernd Schuster (12/3), Felix Magath (11/1), Hans Müller (28/5), Karl-Heinz Rummenigge (41/14), Horst Hrubesch (11/5), Klaus Allofs (21/9). Trainer: Josef Derwall (26).
Goals: Bernd Schuster (9, 71).

461. 29.04.1981 **WEST GERMANY - AUSTRIA** **2-0(2-0)** 12th FIFA WC. Qualifiers
Volksparkstadion, Hamburg; Referee: Charles George Rainier Corver (Netherlands); Attendance: 61,000
GER: Harald Schumacher (15/0), Manfred Kaltz (48/5), Ulrich Stielike (17/0), Karlheinz Förster (25/1), Hans-Peter Briegel (15/1), Bernd Schuster (13/3), Felix Magath (12/1), Paul Breitner (29/5), Hans Müller (29/5), Klaus Fischer (28/20) [76.Karl Allgöwer (3/0)], Karl-Heinz Rummenigge (Cap) (42/14). Trainer: Josef Derwall (27).
Goals: Bernd Krauss (30 own goal), Klaus Fischer (36).

462. 19.05.1981 **WEST GERMANY - BRAZIL** **1-2(1-0)**
Neckarstadion, Stuttgart; Referee: Clive Bradley White (England); Attendance: 71,000
GER: Harald Schumacher (16/0) [46.Eike Immel (2/0)], Manfred Kaltz (49/5), Wilfried Hannes (2/0), Karlheinz Förster (26/1), Hans-Peter Briegel (16/1), Bernd Schuster (14/3) [46.Bernhard Dietz (53/0)], Felix Magath (13/1), Paul Breitner (30/5), Hans Müller (30/5), Klaus Fischer (29/21) [62.Karl Allgöwer (4/0)], Karl-Heinz Rummenigge (Cap) (43/14). Trainer: Josef Derwall (28).
Goal: Klaus Fischer (30).

463. 24.05.1981 **FINLAND - WEST GERMANY** **0-4(0-3)** 12th FIFA WC. Qualifiers
Keskusurheilukenttä, Lahti; Referee: John Carpenter (Republic of Ireland); Attendance: 10,030
GER: Harald Schumacher (17/0), Manfred Kaltz (50/6), Wilfried Hannes (3/0), Karlheinz Förster (27/1), Hans-Peter Briegel (17/2), Wolfgang Dremmler (2/0), Felix Magath (14/1) [76.Karl Allgöwer (5/0)], Paul Breitner (31/5), Hans Müller (31/5) [82.Ronald Borchers (4/0)], Klaus Fischer (30/23), Karl-Heinz Rummenigge (Cap) (44/14). Trainer: Josef Derwall (29).
Goals: Hans-Peter Briegel (25), Klaus Fischer (37), Manfred Kaltz (40), Klaus Fischer (80).

464. 02.09.1981 **POLAND - WEST GERMANY** **0-2(0-0)**
Stadion Śląski, Chorzów; Referee: Kjell Johansson (Sweden); Attendance: 70,000
GER: Harald Schumacher (18/0), Manfred Kaltz (51/6) [85.Holger Hieronymus (1/0)], Wilfried Hannes (4/0), Bernd Förster (10/0), Hans-Peter Briegel (18/2) [81.Wolfgang Dremmler (3/0)], Felix Magath (15/1), Paul Breitner (32/5), Hans Müller (32/5), Ronald Borchers (5/0), Klaus Fischer (31/24), Karl-Heinz Rummenigge (Cap) (45/15). Trainer: Josef Derwall (30).
Goals: Klaus Fischer (59), Karl-Heinz Rummenigge (70).

465. 23.09.1981 **WEST GERMANY - FINLAND** **7-1(2-1)** 12th FIFA WC. Qualifiers
Ruhrstadion, Bochum; Referee: Norbert Rolles (Bochum); Attendance: 46,000
GER: Harald Schumacher (19/0), Manfred Kaltz (52/6), Ulrich Stielike (18/0), Bernd Förster (11/0), Hans-Peter Briegel (19/2), Wolfgang Dremmler (4/1), Felix Magath (16/1), Paul Breitner (33/7), Ronald Borchers (6/0), Klaus Fischer (32/25), Karl-Heinz Rummenigge (Cap) (46/18). Trainer: Josef Derwall (31).
Goals: Klaus Fischer (11), Karl-Heinz Rummenigge (42), Paul Breitner (54), Karl-Heinz Rummenigge (60), Paul Breitner (67), Karl-Heinz Rummenigge (72), Wolfgang Dremmler (83).

466. 14.10.1981 **AUSTRIA - WEST GERMANY** **1-3(1-2)** 12th FIFA WC. Qualifiers
Praterstadion, Wien; Referee: Alexis Ponnet (Belgium); Attendance: 72,000
GER: Harald Schumacher (20/0), Manfred Kaltz (53/6), Ulrich Stielike (19/0), Karlheinz Förster (28/1), Hans-Peter Briegel (20/2), Wolfgang Dremmler (5/1), Paul Breitner (34/7), Felix Magath (17/2), Pierre Littbarski (1/2), Klaus Fischer (33/25), Karl-Heinz Rummenigge (Cap) (47/18). Trainer: Josef Derwall (32).
Goals: Pierre Littbarski (17), Felix Magath (20), Pierre Littbarski (76).

467. 18.11.1981 **WEST GERMANY - ALBANIA** **8-0(5-0)** 12th FIFA WC. Qualifiers
Westfalenstadion, Dortmund; Referee: Reidar Bjørnestad (Norway); Attendance: 40,000
GER: Eike Immel (3/0), Manfred Kaltz (54/7) [60.Lothar Herbert Matthäus (2/0)], Ulrich Stielike (20/0), Karlheinz Förster (29/1), Hans-Peter Briegel (21/2), Wolfgang Dremmler (6/1), Paul Breitner (35/8), Felix Magath (18/2), Pierre Littbarski (2/3), Klaus Fischer (34/27), Karl-Heinz Rummenigge (Cap) (48/21) [50.Jürgen Milewski (1/0)]. Trainer: Josef Derwall (33).
Goals: Karl-Heinz Rummenigge (5, 19), Klaus Fischer (32), Manfred Kaltz (36), Karl-Heinz Rummenigge (43), Pierre Littbarski (52), Paul Breitner (68 penalty), Klaus Fischer (72).

68. 22.11.1981 **WEST GERMANY - BULGARIA** **4-0(1-0)** 12th FIFA WC. Qualifiers
heinstadion, Düsseldorf; Referee: Erik Fredriksson (Sweden); Attendance: 50,000
ER: Harald Schumacher (21/0), Manfred Kaltz (55/8), Wilfried Hannes (5/0), Karlheinz Förster (30/1), Hans-Peter Briegel (22/2), Wolfgang Dremmler /1), Paul Breitner (36/8), Felix Magath (19/2) [56.Klaus Allofs (22/9)], Horst Hrubesch (12/5), Klaus Fischer (35/28), Karl-Heinz Rummenigge (Cap) 9/23). Trainer: Josef Derwall (34).
oals: Klaus Fischer (4), Karl-Heinz Rummenigge (49), Manfred Kaltz (62 penalty), Karl-Heinz Rummenigge (82).

69. 17.02.1982 **WEST GERMANY - PORTUGAL** **3-1(2-1)**
iedersachsenstadion, Hannover; Referee: Alexis Ponnet (Belgium); Attendance: 50,000
ER: Harald Schumacher (22/0) [46.Bernd Franke (6/0)], Manfred Kaltz (56/8), Bernd Förster (12/0), Karlheinz Förster (31/1), Hans-Peter Briegel (23/2), olfgang Dremmler (8/1), Paul Breitner (37/8), Pierre Littbarski (3/3) [72.Karl Allgöwer (6/0)], Klaus Fischer (36/30), Horst Hrubesch (13/5) [46.Lothar erbert Matthäus (3/0)], Karl-Heinz Rummenigge (Cap) (50/23). Trainer: Josef Derwall (35).
oals: Klaus Fischer (24), Norton de Matos (27 own goal), Klaus Fischer (51).

70. 21.03.1982 **BRAZIL - WEST GERMANY** **1-0(0-0)**
stádio „Jornalista Mário Filho“ [Maracanã], Rio de Janeiro; Referee: Augusto Lamo Castillo (Spain); Attendance: 150,289
ER: Harald Schumacher (23/0), Manfred Kaltz (Cap) (57/8), Ulrich Stielike (21/0), Karlheinz Förster (32/1), Hans-Peter Briegel (24/2), Wolfgang remmler (9/1), Paul Breitner (38/8), Lothar Herbert Matthäus (4/0), Hans Müller (33/5) [82.Stephan Engels (1/0)], Pierre Littbarski (4/3) [85.Frank Mill /0)], Klaus Fischer (37/30) [13.Horst Hrubesch (14/5)]. Trainer: Josef Derwall (36).

71. 24.03.1982 **ARGENTINA - WEST GERMANY** **1-1(0-1)**
stadio Monumental "Antonio Vespucio Liberti", Buenos Aires; Referee: José Luis Martínez Bazan (Uruguay); Attendance: 69,000
ER: Harald Schumacher (24/0), Manfred Kaltz (Cap) (58/8), Ulrich Stielike (22/0), Karlheinz Förster (33/1), Hans-Peter Briegel (25/2), Wolfgang remmler (10/2), Lothar Herbert Matthäus (5/0), Paul Breitner (39/8) [68.Bernd Förster (13/0)], Hans Müller (34/5), Pierre Littbarski (5/3) [68.Frank Mill 2/0)], Horst Hrubesch (15/5) [78.Stephan Engels (2/0)]. Trainer: Josef Derwall (37).
oal: Wolfgang Dremmler (33).

72. 14.04.1982 **WEST GERMANY - CZECHOSLOVAKIA** **2-1(1-0)**
üngersdorferstadion, Köln; Referee: Joël Quiniou (France); Attendance: 57,000
ER: Harald Schumacher (25/0), Manfred Kaltz (59/8) [70.Stephan Engels (3/0)], Wilfried Hannes (6/0), Karlheinz Förster (34/1), Hans-Peter Briegel 26/2), Wolfgang Dremmler (11/2) [78.Bernd Förster (14/0)], Lothar Herbert Matthäus (6/0), Paul Breitner (40/9), Pierre Littbarski (6/4), Klaus Fischer 38/30) [46.Frank Mill (3/0)], Karl-Heinz Rummenigge (Cap) (51/23). Trainer: Josef Derwall (38).
oals: Pierre Littbarski (22), Paul Breitner (88 penalty).

73. 12.05.1982 **NORWAY - WEST GERMANY** **2-4(1-3)**
llevaal Stadion, Oslo; Referee: Kjell Johansson (Sweden); Attendance: 18,000
ER: Bernd Franke (7/0) [46.Eike Immel (4/0)], Bernd Förster (15/0) [47.Wilfried Hannes (7/0)], Ulrich Stielike (23/0), Karlheinz Förster (35/1), Hans-eter Briegel (27/2) [46.Holger Hieronymus (2/0)], Lothar Herbert Matthäus (7/0), Paul Breitner (41/9) [62.Uwe Reinders (1/0)], Felix Magath (20/2), Pierre ittbarski (7/6), Horst Hrubesch (16/5) [46.Klaus Fischer (39/30)], Karl-Heinz Rummenigge (Cap) (52/25). Trainer: Josef Derwall (39).
oals: Karl-Heinz Rummenigge (5), Pierre Littbarski (34, 43), Karl-Heinz Rummenigge (84).

74. 16.06.1982 **ALGERIA - WEST GERMANY** **2-1(0-0)** 12th FIFA WC. Group Stage.
stadio El Molinon, Gijón (Spain); Referee: Enrique Labo Revoredo (Peru); Attendance: 42,500
ER: Harald Schumacher (26/0), Manfred Kaltz (60/8), Ulrich Stielike (24/0), Karlheinz Förster (36/1), Hans-Peter Briegel (28/2), Wolfgang Dremmler 2/2), Paul Breitner (42/9), Felix Magath (21/2) [82.Klaus Fischer (40/30)], Pierre Littbarski (8/6), Horst Hrubesch (17/5), Karl-Heinz Rummenigge (Cap) 53/26). Trainer: Josef Derwall (40).
oal: Karl-Heinz Rummenigge (67).

75. 20.06.1982 **WEST GERMANY - CHILE** **4-1(1-0)** 12th FIFA WC. Group Stage.
stadio El Molinon, Gijón (Spain); Referee: Bruno Galler (Switzerland); Attendance: 42,000
ER: Harald Schumacher (27/0), Manfred Kaltz (61/8), Ulrich Stielike (25/0), Karlheinz Förster (37/1), Hans-Peter Briegel (29/2), Wolfgang Dremmler 3/2), Paul Breitner (43/9) [47.Lothar Herbert Matthäus (8/0)], Felix Magath (22/2), Pierre Littbarski (9/6) [79.Uwe Reinders (2/1)], Horst Hrubesch (18/5), arl-Heinz Rummenigge (Cap) (54/29). Trainer: Josef Derwall (41).
oals: Karl-Heinz Rummenigge (9, 57, 66), Uwe Reinders (81).

76. 25.06.1982 **AUSTRIA - WEST GERMANY** **0-1(0-1)** 12th FIFA WC. Group Stage.
stadio El Molinon, Gijón (Spain); Referee: Robert Bonar Valentine (Scotland); Attendance: 28,000
ER: Harald Schumacher (28/0), Manfred Kaltz (62/8), Ulrich Stielike (26/0), Karlheinz Förster (38/1), Hans-Peter Briegel (30/2), Wolfgang Dremmler 4/2), Paul Breitner (44/9), Felix Magath (23/2), Pierre Littbarski (10/6), Horst Hrubesch (19/6) [68.Klaus Fischer (41/30)], Karl-Heinz Rummenigge (Cap) 55/29) [65.Lothar Herbert Matthäus (9/0)]. Trainer: Josef Derwall (42).
oal: Horst Hrubesch (10).

77. 29.06.1982 **ENGLAND - WEST GERMANY** **0-0** 12th FIFA WC. 2nd Round.
stadio „Santiago Bernabeu“, Madrid (Spain); Referee: Arnaldo David César Coelho (Brazil); Attendance: 75,000
ER: Harald Schumacher (29/0), Manfred Kaltz (63/8), Ulrich Stielike (27/0), Karlheinz Förster (39/1), Hans-Peter Briegel (31/2), Bernd Förster (16/0), olfgang Dremmler (15/2), Paul Breitner (45/9), Hans Müller (35/5) [73.Klaus Fischer (42/30)], Uwe Reinders (3/1) [62.Pierre Littbarski (11/6)], Karl-einz Rummenigge (Cap) (56/29). Trainer: Josef Derwall (43).

78. 02.07.1982 **SPAIN - WEST GERMANY** **1-2(0-0)** 12th FIFA WC. 2nd Round.
antiago Bernabéu, Madrid; Referee: Paolo Casarin (Italy); Attendance: 90,089
ER: Harald Schumacher (30/0), Manfred Kaltz (64/8), Ulrich Stielike (28/0), Karlheinz Förster (40/1), Bernd Förster (17/0), Wolfgang Dremmler (16/2), aul Breitner (46/9), Hans-Peter Briegel (32/2), Karl-Heinz Rummenigge (Cap) (57/29) [46.Uwe Reinders (4/1)], Klaus Fischer (43/31), Pierre Littbarski 2/7). Trainer: Josef Derwall (44).
oals: Pierre Littbarski (50), Klaus Fischer (75).

479. 08.07.1982 **WEST GERMANY - FRANCE** **3-3(1-1,1-1); 5-4 on penalties** 12th FIFA WC. Semi-Final.
Estadio "Ramón Sánchez Pizjuán", Sevilla (Spain); Referee: Charles George Rainier Corver (Netherlands); Attendance: 70,000
GER: Harald Schumacher (31/0), Manfred Kaltz (Cap) (65/8), Ulrich Stielike (29/0), Karlheinz Förster (41/1), Bernd Förster (18/0), Wolfgang Dremmle (17/2), Paul Breitner (47/9), Hans-Peter Briegel (33/2) [95.Karl-Heinz Rummenigge (58/30)], Felix Magath (24/2) [72.Horst Hrubesch (20/6)], Pierre Littbarski (13/8), Klaus Fischer (44/32). Trainer: Josef Derwall (45).
Goals: Pierre Littbarski (18), Karl-Heinz Rummenigge (103), Klaus Fischer (108).
Penalties: Manfred Kaltz, Paul Breitner, Ulrich Stielike (saved), Pierre Littbarski, Karl-Heinz Rummenigge, Horst Hrubesch.

480. 11.07.1982 **ITALY - WEST GERMANY** **3-1(0-0)** 12th FIFA WC. Final.
Estadio „Santiago Bernabeu", Madrid (Spain); Referee: Arnaldo David César Coelho (Brazil); Attendance: 90,089
GER: Harald Schumacher (32/0), Manfred Kaltz (66/8), Ulrich Stielike (30/0), Karlheinz Förster (42/1), Bernd Förster (19/0), Wolfgang Dremmler (18/2 [62.Horst Hrubesch (21/6)], Paul Breitner (48/10), Hans-Peter Briegel (34/2), Karl-Heinz Rummenigge (Cap) (59/30) [70.Hans Müller (36/5)], Pierre Littbarski (14/8), Klaus Fischer (45/32). Trainer: Josef Derwall (46).
Goal: Paul Breitner (82).

481. 22.09.1982 **WEST GERMANY - BELGIUM** **0-0**
Olympiastadion, München; Referee: Vojtěch Christov (Czechoslovakia); Attendance: 25,000
GER: Harald Schumacher (33/0), Wolfgang Dremmler (19/2), Wilfried Hannes (8/0), Karlheinz Förster (43/1), Bernd Förster (20/0), Lothar Herbert Matthäus (10/0), Ulrich Stielike (31/0), Hans Müller (37/5) [46.Jürgen Milewski (2/0)], Hans-Peter Briegel (35/2), Pierre Littbarski (15/8), Karl-Heinz Rummenigge (Cap) (60/30). Trainer: Josef Derwall (47).

482. 13.10.1982 **ENGLAND - WEST GERMANY** **1-2(0-0)**
Wembley Stadium, London Referee: Károly Palotai (Hungary); Attendance: 68,000
GER: Harald Schumacher (34/0), Manfred Kaltz (67/8), Gerhard Strack (1/0), Karlheinz Förster (44/1) [5.Holger Hieronymus (3/0)], Bernd Förster (21/0), Wolfgang Dremmler (20/2), Lothar Herbert Matthäus (11/0), Karl-Heinz Rummenigge (Cap) (61/32), Hans-Peter Briegel (36/2), Norbert Meier (1/0 [68.Pierre Littbarski (16/8)], Klaus Allofs (23/9) [88.Stephan Engels (4/0)]. Trainer: Josef Derwall (48).
Goals: Karl-Heinz Rummenigge (73, 82).

483. 17.11.1982 **NORTHERN IRELAND - WEST GERMANY** **1-0(1-0)** 7th EC. Qualifiers
Windsor Park, Belfast; Referee: Rolf Nyhus (Norway); Attendance: 25,000
GER: Harald Schumacher (35/0), Manfred Kaltz (68/8), Ulrich Stielike (32/0), Gerhard Strack (2/0), Bernd Förster (22/0), Bernd Schuster (15/3) [72.Rudolf Völler (1/0)], Lothar Herbert Matthäus (12/0) [72.Stephan Engels (5/0)], Hans-Peter Briegel (37/2), Pierre Littbarski (17/8), Klaus Allofs (24/9), Karl-Heinz Rummenigge (Cap) (62/32). Trainer: Josef Derwall (49).

484. 23.02.1983 **PORTUGAL - WEST GERMANY** **1-0(0-0)**
Estádio Restelo, Lisboa; Referee: Marcel Bacou (France); Attendance: 10,000
GER: Harald Schumacher (36/0), Manfred Kaltz (69/8), Bernd Förster (23/0), Karlheinz Förster (45/1), Hans-Peter Briegel (38/2), Wolfgang Dremmle (21/2), Wolfgang Rolff (1/0), Lothar Herbert Matthäus (13/0) [46.Jonny Otten (1/0)], Pierre Littbarski (18/8) [81.Klaus Allofs (25/9)], Rudolf Völler (2/0) [65.Norbert Meier (2/0)], Karl-Heinz Rummenigge (Cap) (63/32). Trainer: Josef Derwall (50).

485. 30.03.1983 **ALBANIA - WEST GERMANY** **1-2(0-0)** 7th EC. Qualifiers
Stadiumi „Kombëtar Qemal Stafa", Tiranë; Referee: Gianfranco Menegalli (Italy); Attendance: 25,000
GER: Harald Schumacher (37/0), Gerhard Strack (3/0), Bernd Förster (24/0), Karlheinz Förster (46/1), Jonny Otten (2/0), Stephan Engels (6/0), Hans Müller (38/5), Hans-Peter Briegel (39/2), Pierre Littbarski (19/8), Rudolf Völler (3/1) [86.Norbert Meier (3/0)], Karl-Heinz Rummenigge (Cap) (64/33). Trainer Josef Derwall (51).
Goals: Rudolf Völler (54), Karl-Heinz Rummenigge (66 penalty).

486. 23.04.1983 **TURKEY - WEST GERMANY** **0-3(0-2)** 7th EC. Qualifiers
"Kemal Atatürk" Stadyumu, İzmir; Referee: Vojtěch Christov (Czechoslovakia); Attendance: 72,000
GER: Harald Schumacher (38/0), Wolfgang Dremmler (22/3), Gerhard Strack (4/0), Karlheinz Förster (47/1), Hans-Peter Briegel (40/2), Stephan Engel (7/0), Bernd Schuster (16/3), Hans Müller (39/5), Pierre Littbarski (20/8) [76.Wolfgang Rolff (2/0)], Rudolf Völler (4/1), Karl-Heinz Rummenigge (Cap) (65/35). Trainer: Josef Derwall (52).
Goals: Karl-Heinz Rummenigge (30 penalty), Wolfgang Dremmler (34), Karl-Heinz Rummenigge (71).

487. 27.04.1983 **AUSTRIA - WEST GERMANY** **0-0** 7th EC. Qualifiers
Praterstadion, Wien; Referee: Brian McGinlay (Scotland); Attendance: 50,169
GER: Harald Schumacher (39/0), Wolfgang Dremmler (23/3), Gerhard Strack (5/0), Karlheinz Förster (48/1), Hans-Peter Briegel (41/2) [39.Bernd Förste (25/0)], Stephan Engels (8/0), Bernd Schuster (17/3), Hans Müller (40/5) [68.Wolfgang Rolff (3/0)], Pierre Littbarski (21/8), Rudolf Völler (5/1), Karl-Hein Rummenigge (Cap) (66/35). Trainer: Josef Derwall (53).

488. 07.06.1983 **WEST GERMANY - YUGOSLAVIA** **4-2(2-0)**
Stade Municipal, Luxembourg; Referee: Francis Bastian (Luxembourg); Attendance: 11,000
GER: Dieter Burdenski (9/0) [46.Ulrich Stein (1/0)], Bernd Förster (26/0) [46.Jonny Otten (3/0)], Karlheinz Förster (49/1), Ulrich Stielike (33/0), Hans-Pete Briegel (42/2), Wolfgang Rolff (4/0), Bernd Schuster (18/4), Hans Müller (41/5) [67.Herbert Waas (1/0)], Norbert Meier (4/2) [46.Lothar Herbert Matthäu (14/0)], Rudolf Völler (6/1), Karl-Heinz Rummenigge (Cap) (67/36). Trainer: Josef Derwall (54).
Goals: Norbert Meier (13, 20), Bernd Schuster (78), Karl-Heinz Rummenigge (87).

489. 07.09.1983 **HUNGARY - WEST GERMANY** **1-1(1-0)**
Népstadion, Budapest; Referee: Dušan Krchnak (Czechoslovakia); Attendance: 30,000
GER: Harald Schumacher (40/0) [46.Dieter Burdenski (10/0)], Bernd Förster (27/0) [46.Lothar Herbert Matthäus (15/0)], Gerhard Strack (6/0), Karlheinz Förster (Cap) (50/1), Hans-Peter Briegel (43/2), Jürgen Groh (2/0), Wolfgang Rolff (5/0), Hans Müller (42/5) [65.Herbert Waas (2/0)], Norbert Meier (5/2), Pierre Littbarski (22/8), Rudolf Völler (7/2). Trainer: Josef Derwall (55).
Goal: Rudolf Völler (67).

)0. 05.10.1983 **WEST GERMANY - AUSTRIA** **3-0(3-0)** 7th EC. Qualifiers
ırkstadion, Gelsenkirchen; Referee: Luigi Agnolin (Italy); Attendance: 65,496
ER: Harald Schumacher (41/0), Wolfgang Dremmler (24/3), Gerhard Strack (7/0), Karlheinz Förster (51/1), Hans-Peter Briegel (44/2), Klaus Augenthaler /0), Bernd Schuster (19/4), Wolfgang Rolff (6/0), Norbert Meier (6/2) [74.Lothar Herbert Matthäus (16/0)], Rudolf Völler (8/4) [73.Herbert Waas (3/0)], arl-Heinz Rummenigge (Cap) (68/37). Trainer: Josef Derwall (56).
oals: Karl-Heinz Rummenigge (4), Rudolf Völler (18, 20).

)1. 26.10.1983 **WEST GERMANY - TURKEY** **5-1(1-0)** 7th EC. Qualifiers
lympiastadion, West-Berlin; Referee: Eduard Šoštarić (Yugoslavia); Attendance: 35,000
ER: Harald Schumacher (42/0), Jonny Otten (4/0), Gerhard Strack (8/0), Klaus Augenthaler (2/0), Hans-Peter Briegel (45/2) [81.Matthias Herget (1/0)], lrich Stielike (34/1), Lothar Herbert Matthäus (17/0), Norbert Meier (7/2) [81.Michael Rummenigge (1/0)], Pierre Littbarski (23/8), Rudolf Völler (9/6), arl-Heinz Rummenigge (Cap) (69/39). Trainer: Josef Derwall (57).
oals: Rudolf Völler (45), Karl-Heinz Rummenigge (61), Rudolf Völler (65), Ulrich Stielike (66), Karl-Heinz Rummenigge (75 penalty).

)2. 16.11.1983 **WEST GERMANY – NORTHERN IRELAND** **0-1(0-0)** 7th EC. Qualifiers
olksparkstadion, Hamburg; Referee: Károly Palotai (Hungary); Attendance: 61,418
ER: Harald Schumacher (43/0), Wolfgang Dremmler (25/3), Ulrich Stielike (35/1) [84.Gerhard Strack (9/0)], Karlheinz Förster (52/1), Hans-Peter Briegel 6/2), Klaus Augenthaler (3/0), Wolfgang Rolff (7/0), Lothar Herbert Matthäus (18/0), Norbert Meier (8/2) [68.Pierre Littbarski (24/8)], Herbert Waas (4/0), arl-Heinz Rummenigge (Cap) (70/39). Trainer: Josef Derwall (58).

)3. 20.11.1983 **WEST GERMANY - ALBANIA** **2-1(1-1)** 7th EC. Qualifiers
ıdwigsparkstadion, Saarbrücken; Referee: Anders Mattsson (Finland); Attendance: 40,000
ER: Harald Schumacher (44/0), Bernd Förster (28/0), Gerhard Strack (10/1), Karlheinz Förster (53/1), Hans-Peter Briegel (47/2) [34.Jonny Otten (5/0)], 'olfgang Dremmler (26/3), Lothar Herbert Matthäus (19/0), Norbert Meier (9/2), Pierre Littbarski (25/8) [68.Herbert Waas (5/0)], Rudolf Völler (10/6), arl-Heinz Rummenigge (Cap) (71/40). Trainer: Josef Derwall (59).
oals: Karl-Heinz Rummenigge (24), Gerhard Strack (79).

)4. 15.02.1984 **BULGARIA - WEST GERMANY** **2-3(0-1)**
urij Gagarin" stadion,Varna; Referee: Franz Wöhrer (Austria); Attendance: 15,000
ER: Dieter Burdenski (11/0), Manfred Bockenfeld (1/0), Matthias Herget (2/0), Karlheinz Förster (54/1), Andreas Brehme (1/0), Rudolf Bommer (1/0), lrich Stielike (36/3), Bernd Schuster (20/4), Norbert Meier (10/2), Rudolf Völler (11/7) [74.Klaus Allofs (26/9)], Karl-Heinz Rummenigge (Cap) (72/40). rainer: Josef Derwall (60).
oals: Ulrich Stielike (2), Rudolf Völler (67), Ulrich Stielike (73).

)5. 29.02.1984 **BELGIUM - WEST GERMANY** **0-1(0-0)**
ade du Heysel, Bruxelles; Referee: Albert Thomas (Netherlands); Attendance: 23,000
ER: Harald Schumacher (45/0), Wolfgang Dremmler (27/3), Matthias Herget (3/0), Karlheinz Förster (55/1) [63.Klaus Augenthaler (4/0)], Andreas rehme (2/0) [46.Hans-Günther Bruns (1/0)], Ulrich Stielike (37/3), Bernd Schuster (21/4), Lothar Herbert Matthäus (20/0), Rudolf Bommer (2/0) [46.Klaus llofs (27/9)], Rudolf Völler (12/8), Karl-Heinz Rummenigge (Cap) (73/40). Trainer: Josef Derwall (61).
oal: Rudolf Völler (76 penalty).

)6. 28.03.1984 **WEST GERMANY - SOVIET UNION** **2-1(1-1)**
iedersachsenstadion, Hannover; Referee: Yusuf Namoğlu (Turkey); Attendance: 35,000
ER: Harald Schumacher (46/0) [46.Helmut Roleder (1/0)], Hans-Günther Bruns (2/0), Matthias Herget (4/0), Karlheinz Förster (Cap) (56/1), Hans-Peter riegel (48/2), Wolfgang Rolff (8/0) [46.Jonny Otten (6/0)], Lothar Herbert Matthäus (21/0), Norbert Meier (11/2), Jürgen Milewski (3/0) [71.Rudolf ommer (3/0)], Rudolf Völler (13/9), Klaus Allofs (28/9) [76.Andreas Brehme (3/1)]. Trainer: Josef Derwall (62).
oals: Rudolf Völler (9), Andreas Brehme (89).

)7. 18.04.1984 **FRANCE - WEST GERMANY** **1-0(0-0)**
ade de la Meinau, Strasbourg; Referee: Enzo Barbaresco (Italy); Attendance: 39,978
ER: Harald Schumacher (47/0), Bernd Förster (29/0), Hans-Günther Bruns (3/0), Karlheinz Förster (57/1), Hans-Peter Briegel (49/2), Wolfgang Rolff (9/0) 7.Matthias Herget (5/0)], Lothar Herbert Matthäus (22/0), Andreas Brehme (4/1), Norbert Meier (12/2) [77.Pierre Littbarski (26/8)], Karl-Heinz ummenigge (Cap) (74/40), Rudolf Völler (14/9). Trainer: Josef Derwall (63).

)8. 22.05.1984 **ITALY - WEST GERMANY** **0-1(0-0)**
etzigrund Stadion, Zürich; Referee: Arnaldo David César Coelho (Brazil); Attendance: 26,000
ER: Harald Schumacher (48/0) [46.Dieter Burdenski (12/0)], Bernd Förster (30/0), Ulrich Stielike (38/3), Karlheinz Förster (58/1) [46.Lothar Herbert latthäus (23/0)], Hans-Peter Briegel (50/3), Guido Buchwald (1/0) [66.Rudolf Bommer (4/0)], Wolfgang Rolff (10/0), Andreas Brehme (5/1), Rudolf Völler 5/9), Klaus Allofs (29/9), Karl-Heinz Rummenigge (Cap) (75/40). Trainer: Josef Derwall (64).
oal: Hans-Peter Briegel (62).

)9. 14.06.1984 **WEST GERMANY - PORTUGAL** **0-0** 7th EC. Group Stage.
ade de la Meinau, Strasbourg (France); Referee: Romualdas Yushka (Soviet Union); Attendance: 47,950
ER: Harald Schumacher (49/0), Bernd Förster (31/0), Ulrich Stielike (39/3), Karlheinz Förster (59/1), Hans-Peter Briegel (51/3), Guido Buchwald (2/0) 6.Lothar Herbert Matthäus (24/0)], Karl-Heinz Rummenigge (Cap) (76/40), Wolfgang Rolff (11/0) [66.Rudolf Bommer (5/0)], Andreas Brehme (6/1), udolf Völler (16/9), Klaus Allofs (30/9). Trainer: Josef Derwall (65).

)0. 17.06.1984 **WEST GERMANY - ROMANIA** **2-1(1-0)** 7th EC. Group Stage.
ade „Félix Bollaert", Lens (France); Referee: Johannes Nicolaas Ignatius „Jan" Keizer (Netherlands); Attendance: 31,803
ER: Harald Schumacher (50/0), Bernd Förster (32/0), Ulrich Stielike (40/3), Karlheinz Förster (60/1) [79.Guido Buchwald (3/0)], Hans-Peter Briegel 2/3), Lothar Herbert Matthäus (25/0), Norbert Meier (13/2) [64.Pierre Littbarski (27/8)], Karl-Heinz Rummenigge (Cap) (77/40), Andreas Brehme (7/1), udolf Völler (17/11), Klaus Allofs (31/9). Trainer: Josef Derwall (66).
oals: Rudolf Völler (25, 66).

)1. 20.06.1984 **WEST GERMANY - SPAIN** **0-1(0-0)** 7th EC. Group Stage.
ade Parc des Princes, Paris (France); Referee: Vojtěch Christov (Czechoslovakia); Attendance: 47,691
ER: Harald Schumacher (51/0), Bernd Förster (33/0), Ulrich Stielike (41/3), Karlheinz Förster (61/1), Hans-Peter Briegel (53/3), Lothar Herbert Matthäus 6/0), Norbert Meier (14/2) [61.Pierre Littbarski (28/8)], Andreas Brehme (8/1) [76.Wolfgang Rolff (12/0)], Karl-Heinz Rummenigge (Cap) (78/40), Rudolf öller (18/11), Klaus Allofs (32/9). Trainer: Josef Derwall (67).

502. 12.09.1984 **WEST GERMANY - ARGENTINA** **1-3(0-2)**
Rheinstadion, Düsseldorf; Referee: Robert Charles Paul Wurtz (France); Attendance: 45,000
GER: Harald Schumacher (Cap) (52/0), Andreas Brehme (9/1), Hans-Günther Bruns (4/0), Ditmar Jakobs (2/1), Michael Frontzeck (1/0), Rudolf Bomme (6/0), Lothar Herbert Matthäus (27/0), Felix Magath (25/2), Ralf Falkenmayer (1/0), Rudolf Völler (19/11) [46.Ulrich Stielike (42/3)], Frank Mill (4/0 [73.Christian Schreier (1/0)]. Trainer: Franz Beckenbauer (1).
Goal: Ditmar Jakobs (78).

503. 17.10.1984 **WEST GERMANY - SWEDEN** **2-0(0-0)** 13th FIFA WC. Qualifiers
Müngersdorferstadion, Köln; Referee: Robert Bonar Valentine (Scotland); Attendance: 61,000
GER: Harald Schumacher (53/0), Ditmar Jakobs (3/1), Matthias Herget (6/0), Karlheinz Förster (62/1), Hans-Peter Briegel (54/3), Andreas Brehme (10/1) Lothar Herbert Matthäus (28/0), Ralf Falkenmayer (2/0) [59.Klaus Allofs (33/9)], Felix Magath (26/2) [75.Uwe Rahn (1/1)], Karl-Heinz Rummenigge (Cap (79/41), Rudolf Völler (20/11). Trainer: Franz Beckenbauer (2).
Goals: Uwe Rahn (75), Karl-Heinz Rummenigge (88).

504. 16.12.1984 **MALTA - WEST GERMANY** **2-3(1-1)** 13th FIFA WC. Qualifiers
Ta'Qali National Stadium, Attard; Referee: Zoran Petrović (Yugoslavia); Attendance: 25,000
GER: Harald Schumacher (54/0), Karlheinz Förster (63/2), Matthias Herget (7/0), Ditmar Jakobs (4/1) [46.Olaf Thon (1/0)], Lothar Herbert Matthäus (29/0) Uwe Rahn (2/1), Andreas Brehme (11/1), Hans-Peter Briegel (55/3), Karl-Heinz Rummenigge (Cap) (80/41), Rudolf Völler (21/11), Klaus Allofs (34/11) Trainer: Franz Beckenbauer (3).
Goals: Karlheinz Förster (43), Klaus Allofs (69, 85).

505. 29.01.1985 **WEST GERMANY – HUNGARY** **0-1(0-0)**
Volksparkstadion, Hamburg; Referee: Einar Halle (Norway); Attendance: 22,000
GER: Ulrich Stein (2/0) [46.Harald Schumacher (55/0)], Thomas Berthold (1/0) [80.Matthias Herget (8/0)], Karlheinz Förster (64/2), Ditmar Jakobs (5/1) Hans-Peter Briegel (56/3) [46.Michael Frontzeck (2/0)], Lothar Herbert Matthäus (30/0), Olaf Thon (2/0) [46.Thomas Kroth (1/0)], Felix Magath (27/2) Pierre Littbarski (29/8) [63.Frank Mill (5/0)], Rudolf Völler (22/11), Karl-Heinz Rummenigge (Cap) (81/41). Trainer: Franz Beckenbauer (4).

506. 24.02.1985 **PORTUGAL - WEST GERMANY** **1-2(0-2)** 13th FIFA WC. Qualifiers
Estádio Nacional, Lisboa; Referee: Paolo Casarin (Italy); Attendance: 60,000
GER: Harald Schumacher (Cap) (56/0), Thomas Berthold (2/0), Matthias Herget (9/0), Ditmar Jakobs (6/1), Michael Frontzeck (3/0), Lothar Herber Matthäus (31/0), Felix Magath (28/2), Hans-Peter Briegel (57/3), Ralf Falkenmayer (3/0), Pierre Littbarski (30/9), Rudolf Völler (23/12). Trainer: Fran Beckenbauer (5).
Goals: Pierre Littbarski (28), Rudolf Völler (37).

507. 27.03.1985 **WEST GERMANY - MALTA** **6-0(5-0)** 13th FIFA WC. Qualifiers
Ludwigsparkstadion, Saarbrücken; Referee: Talat Tokat (Turkey); Attendance: 37,600
GER: Harald Schumacher (57/0), Thomas Berthold (3/0), Matthias Herget (10/0), Karlheinz Förster (65/2), Michael Frontzeck (4/0), Uwe Rahn (3/3 [67.Olaf Thon (3/0)], Felix Magath (29/3), Hans-Peter Briegel (58/3) [77.Andreas Brehme (12/1)], Pierre Littbarski (31/10), Rudolf Völler (24/12), Karl Heinz Rummenigge (Cap) (82/43). Trainer: Franz Beckenbauer (6).
Goals: Uwe Rahn (10), Felix Magath (13), Uwe Rahn (17), Pierre Littbarski (18), Karl-Heinz Rummenigge (44, 66).

508. 17.04.1985 **WEST GERMANY - BULGARIA** **4-1(2-1)**
Volkspark, Augsburg; Referee: Bruno Galler (Switzerland); Attendance: 31,000
GER: Harald Schumacher (58/0) [46.Ulrich Stein (3/0)], Andreas Brehme (13/1), Matthias Herget (11/0), Karlheinz Förster (66/2), Michael Frontzeck (5/0 [46.Thomas Berthold (4/0)], Lothar Herbert Matthäus (32/0), Felix Magath (30/3), Uwe Rahn (4/4) [75.Ditmar Jakobs (7/1)], Pierre Littbarski (32/11) Rudolf Völler (25/14), Karl-Heinz Rummenigge (Cap) (83/43) [46.Olaf Thon (4/0)]. Trainer: Franz Beckenbauer (7).
Goals: Rudolf Völler (7), Uwe Rahn (21), Pierre Littbarski (74), Rudolf Völler (79).

509. 30.04.1985 **CZECHOSLOVAKIA - WEST GERMANY** **1-5(0-4)** 13th FIFA WC. Qualifiers
Stadion Strahov, Praha; Referee: Joël Quiniou (France); Attendance: 35,000
GER: Harald Schumacher (Cap) (59/0), Thomas Berthold (5/1), Ditmar Jakobs (8/1), Karlheinz Förster (67/2), Andreas Brehme (14/1), Matthias Herge (12/1), Lothar Herbert Matthäus (33/1) [82.Olaf Thon (5/0)], Felix Magath (31/3), Uwe Rahn (5/4) [70.Klaus Allofs (35/12)], Pierre Littbarski (33/12) Rudolf Völler (26/14). Trainer: Franz Beckenbauer (8).
Goals: Thomas Berthold (8), Pierre Littbarski (22), Lothar Herbert Matthäus (37), Matthias Herget (43), Klaus Allofs (82).

510. 12.06.1985 **ENGLAND - WEST GERMANY** **3-0(1-0)** International Tournament
Estadio Azteca, Ciudad de México (Mexico); Referee: Jorge Alberto Leanza Sansone (Mexico); Attendance: 8,000
GER: Harald Schumacher (Cap) (60/0), Thomas Berthold (6/1), Klaus Augenthaler (5/0), Ditmar Jakobs (9/1), Andreas Brehme (15/1), Matthias Herge (13/1), Lothar Herbert Matthäus (34/1), Felix Magath (32/3) [59.Olaf Thon (6/0)], Uwe Rahn (6/4), Pierre Littbarski (34/12) [69.Herbert Waas (6/0)], Fran Mill (6/0). Trainer: Franz Beckenbauer (9).

511. 15.06.1985 **MEXICO - WEST GERMANY** **2-0(1-0)** International Tournament
Estadio Azteca, Ciudad de México; Referee: Keith Stuart Hackett (England); Attendance: 25,000
GER: Ulrich Stein (4/0), Lothar Herbert Matthäus (35/1), Klaus Augenthaler (6/0) [65.Michael Frontzeck (6/0)], Ditmar Jakobs (10/1), Andreas Brehm (16/1), Matthias Herget (14/1), Felix Magath (Cap) (33/3), Uwe Rahn (7/4), Frank Mill (7/0), Rudolf Völler (27/14), Ludwig Kögl (1/0). Trainer: Fran Beckenbauer (10).

512. 28.08.1985 **SOVIET UNION - WEST GERMANY** **1-0(0-0)**
Lenin Stadium, Moskva; Referee: Arto Ravander (Finland); Attendance: 82,000
GER: Harald Schumacher (Cap) (61/0), Thomas Berthold (7/1), Matthias Herget (15/1), Karlheinz Förster (68/2), Andreas Brehme (17/1), Lothar Herbe Matthäus (36/1), Uwe Rahn (8/4), Felix Magath (34/3), Pierre Littbarski (35/12), Rudolf Völler (28/14), Klaus Allofs (36/12) [25.Norbert Meier (15/2)] Trainer: Franz Beckenbauer (11).

513. 25.09.1985 **SWEDEN - WEST GERMANY** **2-2(0-2)** 13th FIFA WC. Qualifiers
Råsundastadion, Stockholm; Referee: Marcel Van Langenhove (Belgium); Attendance: 39,157
GER: Harald Schumacher (62/0), Thomas Berthold (8/1), Klaus Augenthaler (7/0), Karlheinz Förster (69/2), Andreas Brehme (18/1), Ditmar Jakobs (11/1) Matthias Herget (16/2), Hans-Peter Briegel (59/3), Pierre Littbarski (36/12), Rudolf Völler (29/15), Karl-Heinz Rummenigge (Cap) (84/43). Trainer: Fran Beckenbauer (12).
Goals: Rudolf Völler (23), Matthias Herget (40).

514. 16.10.1985 **WEST GERMANY - PORTUGAL** **0-1(0-0)** 13th FIFA WC. Qualifiers
Neckarstadion, Stuttgart; Referee: Keith Stuart Hackett (England); Attendance: 60,000
GER: Harald Schumacher (63/0), Thomas Berthold (9/1), Ditmar Jakobs (12/1) [46.Heinz Gründel (1/0)], Karlheinz Förster (70/2), Andreas Brehme (19/1), Karl Allgöwer (7/0), Matthias Herget (17/2), Norbert Meier (16/2), Hans-Peter Briegel (60/3), Pierre Littbarski (37/12) [64.Thomas Allofs (1/0)], Karl-Heinz Rummenigge (Cap) (85/43). Trainer: Franz Beckenbauer (13).

515. 17.11.1985 **WEST GERMANY - CZECHOSLOVAKIA** **2-2(1-0)** 13th FIFA WC. Qualifiers
Olympiastadion, München; Referee: Svein Inge Thime (Norway); Attendance: 18,000
GER: Harald Schumacher (64/0), Andreas Brehme (20/2), Klaus Augenthaler (8/0), Karlheinz Förster (71/2), Hans-Peter Briegel (61/3) [46.Michael Frontzeck (7/0)], Wolfgang Rolff (13/0), Karl Allgöwer (8/0), Olaf Thon (7/0), Pierre Littbarski (38/12) [80.Uwe Rahn (9/4)], Karl-Heinz Rummenigge (Cap) (86/44), Ludwig Kögl (2/0). Trainer: Franz Beckenbauer (14).
Goals: Andreas Brehme (1), Karl-Heinz Rummenigge (86).

516. 05.02.1986 **ITALY - WEST GERMANY** **1-2(1-1)**
Stadio Partenio, Avellino; Referee: Ioan Igna (Romania); Attendance: 35,822
GER: Harald Schumacher (65/0), Guido Buchwald (4/0), Klaus Augenthaler (9/0), Karlheinz Förster (72/2), Matthias Herget (18/3), Lothar Herbert Matthäus (37/2), Wolfgang Rolff (14/0), Felix Magath (35/3), Hans-Peter Briegel (62/3), Karl-Heinz Rummenigge (Cap) (87/44), Klaus Allofs (37/12) [46.Heinz Gründel (2/0)]. Trainer: Franz Beckenbauer (15).
Goals: Matthias Herget (36), Lothar Herbert Matthäus (76 penalty).

517. 12.03.1986 **WEST GERMANY - BRAZIL** **2-0(1-0)**
Waldstadion, Frankfurt am Main; Referee: Luigi Agnolin (Italy); Attendance: 50,000
GER: Harald Schumacher (66/0), Andreas Brehme (21/2), Matthias Herget (19/3), Ditmar Jakobs (13/1) [46.Guido Buchwald (5/0)], Hans-Peter Briegel (63/4), Lothar Herbert Matthäus (38/2), Wolfgang Rolff (15/0), Felix Magath (36/3), Olaf Thon (8/0), Frank Mill (8/0) [79.Heinz Gründel (3/0)], Karl-Heinz Rummenigge (Cap) (88/44) [46.Klaus Allofs (38/13)]. Trainer: Franz Beckenbauer (16).
Goals: Hans-Peter Briegel (2), Klaus Allofs (88).

518. 09.04.1986 **SWITZERLAND - WEST GERMANY** **0-1(0-1)**
„St. Jakob" Stadion, Basel; Referee: Joël Quiniou (France); Attendance: 20,000
GER: Ulrich Stein (5/0), Thomas Berthold (10/1), Klaus Augenthaler (10/0), Karlheinz Förster (Cap) (73/2) [46.Ditmar Jakobs (14/1)], Hans-Peter Briegel (64/4) [77.Guido Buchwald (6/0)], Lothar Herbert Matthäus (39/2), Wolfgang Rolff (16/0), Felix Magath (37/3), Ralf Falkenmayer (4/0) [60.Andreas Brehme (22/2)], Olaf Thon (9/0) [46.Karl Allgöwer (9/0)], Dieter Hoeneß (3/4). Trainer: Franz Beckenbauer (17).
Goal: Dieter Hoeneß (34).

519. 11.05.1986 **WEST GERMANY - YUGOSLAVIA** **1-1(0-1)**
Ruhrstadion, Bochum; Referee: Ulf Eriksson (Sweden); Attendance: 40,000
GER: Harald Schumacher (Cap) (67/0), Guido Buchwald (7/0) [46.Thomas Berthold (11/1)], Klaus Augenthaler (11/0), Karlheinz Förster (74/2), Norbert Eder (1/0), Matthias Herget (20/3) [61.Pierre Littbarski (39/12)], Hans-Peter Briegel (65/4), Lothar Herbert Matthäus (40/2), Olaf Thon (10/0), Rudolf Völler (30/16), Dieter Hoeneß (4/4) [61.Klaus Allofs (39/13)]. Trainer: Franz Beckenbauer (18).
Goal: Rudolf Völler (61).

520. 14.05.1986 **WEST GERMANY - NETHERLANDS** **3-1(2-0)**
Westfalenstadion, Dortmund; Referee: Franz Wöhrer (Austria); Attendance: 36,000
GER: Ulrich Stein (6/0), Thomas Berthold (12/1), Matthias Herget (21/4), Norbert Eder (2/0) [46.Wolfgang Funkel (1/0)], Hans-Peter Briegel (Cap) (66/4), Lothar Herbert Matthäus (41/2) [80.Karl Allgöwer (10/0)], Pierre Littbarski (40/12) [46.Heinz Gründel (4/0)], Wolfgang Rolff (17/0), Andreas Brehme (23/2), Rudolf Völler (31/18) [66.Frank Mill (9/0)], Klaus Allofs (40/13). Trainer: Franz Beckenbauer (19).
Goals: Rudolf Völler (39, 42), Matthias Herget (90).

521. 04.06.1986 **URUGUAY - WEST GERMANY** **1-1(1-0)** 13th FIFA WC. Group Stage.
Estadio La Corregidora, Querétaro (Mexico); Referee: Vojtěch Christov (Czechoslovakia); Attendance: 30,500
GER: Harald Schumacher (Cap) (68/0), Thomas Berthold (13/1), Klaus Augenthaler (12/0), Karlheinz Förster (75/2), Hans-Peter Briegel (67/4), Norbert Eder (3/0), Lothar Herbert Matthäus (42/2) [73.Karl-Heinz Rummenigge (89/44)], Felix Magath (38/3), Andreas Brehme (24/2) [46.Pierre Littbarski (41/12)], Rudolf Völler (32/18), Klaus Allofs (41/14). Trainer: Franz Beckenbauer (20).
Goal: Klaus Allofs (85).

522. 08.06.1986 **WEST GERMANY - SCOTLAND** **2-1(1-1)** 13th FIFA WC. Group Stage.
Estadio La Corregidora, Querétaro (Mexico); Referee: Ioan Igna (Romania); Attendance: 30,000
GER: Harald Schumacher (Cap) (69/0), Thomas Berthold (14/1), Klaus Augenthaler (13/0), Karlheinz Förster (76/2), Hans-Peter Briegel (68/4) [61.Ditmar Jakobs (15/1)], Norbert Eder (4/0), Lothar Herbert Matthäus (43/2), Felix Magath (39/3), Pierre Littbarski (42/12) [75.Karl-Heinz Rummenigge (90/44)], Rudolf Völler (33/19), Klaus Allofs (42/15). Trainer: Franz Beckenbauer (21).
Goals: Rudolf Völler (22), Klaus Allofs (50).

523. 13.06.1986 **DENMARK - WEST GERMANY** **2-0(1-0)** 13th FIFA WC. Group Stage.
Estadio La Corregidora, Querétaro (Mexico); Referee: Alexis Ponnet (Belgium); Attendance: 36,000
GER: Harald Schumacher (Cap) (70/0), Thomas Berthold (15/1), Ditmar Jakobs (16/1), Karlheinz Förster (77/2) [70.Karl-Heinz Rummenigge (91/44)], Andreas Brehme (25/2), Norbert Eder (5/0), Matthias Herget (22/4), Wolfgang Rolff (18/0) [46.Pierre Littbarski (43/12)], Lothar Herbert Matthäus (44/2), Rudolf Völler (34/19), Klaus Allofs (43/15). Trainer: Franz Beckenbauer (22).

524. 17.06.1986 **MOROCCO - WEST GERMANY** **0-1(0-0)** 13th FIFA WC. 2nd Round of 16.
Estadio Universitário, Monterrey (Mexico); Referee: Zoran Petrović (Yugoslavia); Attendance: 19,800
GER: Harald Schumacher (71/0), Thomas Berthold (16/1), Ditmar Jakobs (17/1), Karlheinz Förster (78/2), Hans-Peter Briegel (69/4), Norbert Eder (6/0), Lothar Herbert Matthäus (45/3), Felix Magath (40/3), Karl-Heinz Rummenigge (Cap) (92/44), Rudolf Völler (35/19) [46.Pierre Littbarski (44/12)], Klaus Allofs (44/15). Trainer: Franz Beckenbauer (23).
Goal: Lothar Herbert Matthäus (88).

525. 21.06.1986 **MEXICO - WEST GERMANY** **0-0; 1-4 on penalties** 13th FIFA WC. Quarter-Finals.
Estadio Universitário, Monterrey (Mexico); Referee: Jesús Díaz Palacio (Colombia); Attendance: 44,386
GER: Harald Schumacher (72/0), Thomas Berthold (17/1) [*sent off 66*], Ditmar Jakobs (18/1), Karlheinz Förster (79/2), Hans-Peter Briegel (70/4), Norbert Eder (7/0) [115.Pierre Littbarski (45/12)], Andreas Brehme (26/2), Lothar Herbert Matthäus (46/3), Felix Magath (41/3), Karl-Heinz Rummenigge (Cap) (93/44) [58.Dieter Hoeneß (5/4)], Klaus Allofs (45/15). Trainer: Franz Beckenbauer (24).
Penalties: Klaus Allofs, Andreas Brehme, Lothar Herbert Matthäus, Pierre Littbarski.

526. 25.06.1986 **FRANCE - WEST GERMANY** **0-2(0-1)** 13th FIFA WC. Semi-Finals.
Estadio Jalisco, Guadalajara (Mexico); Referee: Luigi Agnolin (Italy); Attendance: 47,500
GER: Harald Schumacher (73/0), Andreas Brehme (27/3), Ditmar Jakobs (19/1), Karlheinz Förster (80/2), Hans-Peter Briegel (71/4), Norbert Eder (8/0), Lothar Herbert Matthäus (47/3), Wolfgang Rolff (19/0), Felix Magath (42/3), Karl-Heinz Rummenigge (Cap) (94/44) [56.Rudolf Völler (36/20)], Klaus Allofs (46/15). Trainer: Franz Beckenbauer (25).
Goals: Andreas Brehme (9), Rudolf Völler (90).

527. 29.06.1986 **ARGENTINA - WEST GERMANY** **3-2(1-0)** 13th FIFA WC. Final.
Estadio Azteca, Ciudad de México (Mexico); Referee: Romualdo Arppi Filho (Brazil); Attendance: 114,500
GER: Harald Schumacher (74/0), Thomas Berthold (18/1), Ditmar Jakobs (20/1), Karlheinz Förster (81/2), Hans-Peter Briegel (72/4), Norbert Eder (9/0), Andreas Brehme (28/3), Lothar Herbert Matthäus (48/3), Felix Magath (43/3) [61.Dieter Hoeneß (6/4)], Karl-Heinz Rummenigge (Cap) (95/45), Klaus Allofs (47/15) [46.Rudolf Völler (37/21)]. Trainer: Franz Beckenbauer (26).
Goals: Karl-Heinz Rummenigge (72), Rudolf Völler (84).

528. 24.09.1986 **DENMARK - WEST GERMANY** **0-2(0-2)**
Idrætsparken, København; Referee: Erik Fredriksson (Sweden); Attendance: 44,000
GER: Harald Schumacher (Cap) (75/0), Thomas Hörster (1/0), Thomas Berthold (19/1), Jürgen Kohler (1/0), Guido Buchwald (8/0), Michael Frontzeck (8/0), Lothar Herbert Matthäus (49/3), Olaf Thon (11/1) [70.Uwe Rahn (10/4)], Wolfgang Rolff (20/0), Rudolf Völler (38/21), Klaus Allofs (48/16) [83.Herbert Waas (7/0)]. Trainer: Franz Beckenbauer (27).
Goals: Olaf Thon (24), Klaus Allofs (43).

529. 15.10.1986 **WEST GERMANY - SPAIN** **2-2(0-1)**
Niedersachsenstadion, Hannover; Referee: Yuriy Savchenko (Soviet Union); Attendance: 50,000
GER: Harald Schumacher (Cap) (76/0), Thomas Hörster (2/0) [46.Klaus Augenthaler (14/0)], Thomas Berthold (20/1), Jürgen Kohler (2/0), Guido Buchwald (9/0), Michael Frontzeck (9/0), Lothar Herbert Matthäus (50/3), Uwe Rahn (11/5), Wolfgang Rolff (21/0) [46.Wolfram Wuttke (1/0)], Roland Wohlfahrt (1/0), Herbert Waas (8/1) [70.Dieter Eckstein (1/0)]. Trainer: Franz Beckenbauer (28).
Goals: Herbert Waas (61), Uwe Rahn (70).

530. 29.10.1986 **AUSTRIA - WEST GERMANY** **4-1(0-0)**
Praterstadion, Wien; Referee: Luigi Agnolin (Italy); Attendance: 55,000
GER: Eike Immel (5/0), Thomas Hörster (3/0), Thomas Berthold (21/1), Guido Buchwald (10/0), Wolfgang Funkel (2/0), Michael Frontzeck (10/0) [46.Rudolf Völler (39/22)], Wolfgang Rolff (22/0), Lothar Herbert Matthäus (51/3) [*sent off*], Olaf Thon (12/1) [71.Michael Rummenigge (2/0)], Herbert Waas (9/1), Klaus Allofs (Cap) (49/16). Trainer: Franz Beckenbauer (29).
Goal: Rudolf Völler (59).

531. 25.03.1987 **ISRAEL - WEST GERMANY** **0-2(0-1)**
National Stadium, Ramat Gan, Tel Aviv; Referee: Franz Gächter (Switzerland); Attendance: 15,000
GER: Eike Immel (6/0), Thomas Hörster (4/0), Jürgen Kohler (3/0), Guido Buchwald (11/0), Hans Pflügler (1/0), Andreas Brehme (29/3), Lothar Herbert Matthäus (Cap) (52/4), Uwe Rahn (12/5), Olaf Thon (13/2), Herbert Waas (10/1), Rudolf Völler (40/22) [51.Wolfram Wuttke (2/0)]. Trainer: Franz Beckenbauer (30).
Goals: Olaf Thon (10), Lothar Herbert Matthäus (79 penalty).

532. 18.04.1987 **WEST GERMANY - ITALY** **0-0**
Müngersdorferstadion, Köln; Referee: Albert Rudolf Thomas (Netherlands); Attendance: 55,000
GER: Eike Immel (7/0), Matthias Herget (23/4), Jürgen Kohler (4/0), Guido Buchwald (12/0), Hans Pflügler (2/0) [46.Michael Frontzeck (11/0)], Wolfgang Rolff (23/0) [63.Stefan Reuter (1/0)], Pierre Littbarski (46/12), Lothar Herbert Matthäus (53/4), Olaf Thon (14/2), Rudolf Völler (41/22), Klaus Allofs (Cap) (50/16). Trainer: Franz Beckenbauer (31).

533. 12.08.1987 **WEST GERMANY - FRANCE** **2-1(2-1)**
Olympiastadion, West-Berlin; Referee: Henning-Lund Sørensen (Denmark); Attendance: 31,000
GER: Eike Immel (8/0), Matthias Herget (24/4), Jürgen Kohler (5/0), Guido Buchwald (13/0) [69.Wolfgang Rolff (24/0)], Hans Pflügler (3/0), Andreas Brehme (30/3) [67.Stefan Reuter (2/0)], Lothar Herbert Matthäus (54/4), Uwe Rahn (13/5), Hans Dorfner (1/0), Rudolf Völler (42/24) [67.Pierre Littbarski (47/12)], Klaus Allofs (Cap) (51/16). Trainer: Franz Beckenbauer (32).
Goals: Rudolf Völler (4, 9).

534. 09.09.1987 **WEST GERMANY - ENGLAND** **3-1(2-1)**
Rheinstadion, Düsseldorf; Referee: Paolo Casarin (Italy); Attendance: 50,000
GER: Eike Immel (9/0), Matthias Herget (25/4), Andreas Brehme (31/3) [61.Stefan Reuter (3/0)], Jürgen Kohler (6/0), Guido Buchwald (14/0), Michael Frontzeck (12/0), Pierre Littbarski (48/14), Olaf Thon (15/2), Hans Dorfner (2/0), Rudolf Völler (43/24) [78.Wolfram Wuttke (3/1)], Klaus Allofs (Cap) (52/16). Trainer: Franz Beckenbauer (33).
Goals: Pierre Littbarski (24, 33), Wolfram Wuttke (84).

535. 23.09.1987 **WEST GERMANY - DENMARK** **1-0(1-0)**
Volksparkstadion, Hamburg; Referee: Horst Brummeier (Austria); Attendance: 48,000
GER: Bodo Illgner (1/0), Matthias Herget (26/4), Stefan Reuter (4/0), Jürgen Kohler (7/0), Guido Buchwald (15/0), Michael Frontzeck (13/0), Pierre Littbarski (49/14), Wolfgang Rolff (25/0), Olaf Thon (16/2) [73.Manfred Schwabl (1/0)], Rudolf Völler (44/25), Klaus Allofs (Cap) (53/16) [46.Uwe Rahn (14/5)]. Trainer: Franz Beckenbauer (34).
Goal: Rudolf Völler (33).

36. 13.10.1987 **WEST GERMANY - SWEDEN** **1-1(0-0)**
arkstadion, Gelsenkirchen; Referee: Victoriano Sánchez Arminio (Spain); Attendance: 31,000
ER: Bodo Illgner (2/0), Matthias Herget (27/4), Thomas Berthold (22/1) [46.Andreas Brehme (32/3)], Jürgen Kohler (8/0), Guido Buchwald (16/0), Hans flügler (4/0), Pierre Littbarski (50/15), Olaf Thon (17/2), Hans Dorfner (3/0), Rudolf Völler (45/25), Klaus Allofs (Cap) (54/16). Trainer: Franz eckenbauer (35).
oal: Pierre Littbarski (17).

37. 18.11.1987 **HUNGARY - WEST GERMANY** **0-0**
Népstadion, Budapest; Referee: Dušan Krchnak (Czechoslovakia); Attendance: 25,000
ER: Eike Immel (10/0), Matthias Herget (28/4), Thomas Berthold (23/1), Jürgen Kohler (9/0), Michael Frontzeck (14/0), Wolfgang Rolff (26/0), Lothar Herbert Matthäus (55/4) [46.Dieter Eckstein (2/0)], Olaf Thon (18/2), Stefan Reuter (5/0), Pierre Littbarski (51/15), Klaus Allofs (Cap) (55/16). Trainer: Franz Beckenbauer (36).

538. 12.12.1987 **BRAZIL - WEST GERMANY** **1-1(0-0)**
Estádio "Mané Garrincha", Brasília; Referee: Elías Jácome Guerrero (Ecuador); Attendance: 20,000
GER: Eike Immel (11/0), Stefan Reuter (6/1), Jürgen Kohler (10/0), Guido Buchwald (17/0), Andreas Brehme (33/3) [46.Christian Hochstätter (1/0)], Matthias Herget (29/4), Manfred Schwabl (2/0) [82.Frank Ordenewitz (1/0)], Lothar Herbert Matthäus (Cap) (56/4), Michael Frontzeck (15/0) [82.Franco Foda (1/0)], Jürgen Klinsmann (1/0), Olaf Thon (19/2). Trainer: Franz Beckenbauer (37).
Goal: Stefan Reuter (90).

539. 16.12.1987 **ARGENTINA - WEST GERMANY** **1-0(0-0)**
Estadio "José Amalfitani", Buenos Aires; Referee: Arnaldo David César Coelho (Brazil); Attendance: 50,000
GER: Bodo Illgner (3/0), Matthias Herget (30/4), Stefan Reuter (7/1) [65.Franco Foda (2/0)], Jürgen Kohler (11/0), Hans Pflügler (5/0), Wolfgang Rolff (27/0), Lothar Herbert Matthäus (Cap) (57/4), Olaf Thon (20/2), Manfred Schwabl (3/0) [73.Christian Hochstätter (2/0)], Jürgen Klinsmann (2/0), Frank Ordenewitz (2/0). Trainer: Franz Beckenbauer (38).

540. 31.03.1988 **WEST GERMANY - SWEDEN** **1-1(1-0,1-1); 2-4 on penalties** International Tournament
Olympiastadion, West-Berlin; Referee: Lajos Hartmann (Hungary); Attendance: 21,000
GER: Eike Immel (12/0), Matthias Herget (31/4), Thomas Berthold (24/1) [75.Stefan Reuter (8/1)], Jürgen Kohler (12/0), Guido Buchwald (18/0), Michael Frontzeck (16/0), Lothar Herbert Matthäus (58/4), Pierre Littbarski (52/15) [75.Wolfgang Rolff (28/0)], Olaf Thon (21/2), Rudolf Völler (46/25), Klaus Allofs (Cap) (56/17) [46.Dieter Eckstein (3/0)]. Trainer: Franz Beckenbauer (39).
Goal: Klaus Allofs (42).
Penalties: Olaf Thon, Dieter Eckstein, Lothar Herbert Matthäus (missed), Rudolf Völler (missed).

541. 02.04.1988 **WEST GERMANY - ARGENTINA** **1-0(1-0)** International Tournament
Olympiastadion, West-Berlin; Referee: Kurt Röthlisberger (Switzerland); Attendance: 25,000
GER: Eike Immel (13/0), Matthias Herget (32/4), Thomas Berthold (25/1) [46.Andreas Brehme (34/3)], Jürgen Kohler (13/0) [60.Hans Pflügler (6/0)], Ulrich Borowka (1/0), Lothar Herbert Matthäus (Cap) (59/5), Olaf Thon (22/2), Wolfgang Rolff (29/0), Jürgen Klinsmann (3/0), Rudolf Völler (47/25), Dieter Eckstein (4/0) [81.Frank Neubarth (1/0)]. Trainer: Franz Beckenbauer (40).
Goal: Lothar Herbert Matthäus (30).

542. 27.04.1988 **WEST GERMANY - SWITZERLAND** **1-0(0-0)**
„Fritz Walter" Stadion, Kaiserslautern; Referee: John Blankenstein (Netherlands); Attendance: 30,150
GER: Eike Immel (14/0), Matthias Herget (33/4), Andreas Brehme (35/3), Jürgen Kohler (14/0), Armin Görtz (1/0) [67.Stefan Reuter (9/1)], Lothar Herbert Matthäus (Cap) (60/5), Wolfgang Rolff (30/0), Olaf Thon (23/2) [46.Pierre Littbarski (53/15)], Hans Dorfner (4/0) [80.Manfred Schwabl (4/0)], Jürgen Klinsmann (4/1), Rudolf Völler (48/25). Trainer: Franz Beckenbauer (41).
Goal: Jürgen Klinsmann (58).

543. 04.06.1988 **WEST GERMANY - YUGOSLAVIA** **1-1(0-1)**
Weserstadion, Bremen; Referee: Alexei Spirin (Soviet Union); Attendance: 13,000
GER: Eike Immel (15/0), Matthias Herget (34/4), Thomas Berthold (26/1) [31.Hans Dorfner (5/0)], Jürgen Kohler (15/0), Ulrich Borowka (2/0), Lothar Herbert Matthäus (Cap) (61/6), Wolfgang Rolff (31/0), Olaf Thon (24/2) [46.Dieter Eckstein (5/0)], Andreas Brehme (36/3), Jürgen Klinsmann (5/1), Rudolf Völler (49/25) [46.Frank Mill (10/0)]. Trainer: Franz Beckenbauer (42).
Goal: Lothar Herbert Matthäus (65).

544. 10.06.1988 **WEST GERMANY - ITALY** **1-1(0-0)** 8th EC. Group Stage.
Rheinstadion, Düsseldorf; Referee: Keith Stuart Hackett (England); Attendance: 68,000
GER: Eike Immel (16/0), Matthias Herget (35/4), Guido Buchwald (19/0), Jürgen Kohler (16/0), Thomas Berthold (27/1), Andreas Brehme (37/4) [74.Ulrich Borowka (3/0)], Pierre Littbarski (54/15), Lothar Herbert Matthäus (Cap) (62/6), Olaf Thon (25/2), Jürgen Klinsmann (6/1), Rudolf Völler (50/25) [82.Dieter Eckstein (6/0)]. Trainer: Franz Beckenbauer (43).
Goal: Andreas Brehme (56).

545. 14.06.1988 **WEST GERMANY - DENMARK** **2-0(1-0)** 8th EC. Group Stage.
Parkstadion, Gelsenkirchen; Referee: Robert Bonar Valentine (Scotland); Attendance: 66,800
GER: Eike Immel (17/0), Matthias Herget (36/4), Guido Buchwald (20/0) [33.Ulrich Borowka (4/0)], Jürgen Kohler (17/0), Wolfgang Rolff (32/0), Pierre Littbarski (55/15), Lothar Herbert Matthäus (Cap) (63/6), Olaf Thon (26/3), Andreas Brehme (38/4), Jürgen Klinsmann (7/2), Rudolf Völler (51/25) [74.Frank Mill (11/0)]. Trainer: Franz Beckenbauer (44).
Goals: Jürgen Klinsmann (10), Olaf Thon (86).

546. 17.06.1988 **WEST GERMANY - SPAIN** **2-0(1-0)** 8th EC. Group Stage.
Olympiastadion, München; Referee: Michel Vautrot (France); Attendance: 72,308
GER: Eike Immel (18/0), Matthias Herget (37/4), Andreas Brehme (39/4), Ulrich Borowka (5/0), Jürgen Kohler (18/0), Pierre Littbarski (56/15) [63.Wolfram Wuttke (4/1)], Lothar Herbert Matthäus (Cap) (64/6), Wolfgang Rolff (33/0), Olaf Thon (27/3), Jürgen Klinsmann (8/2) [84.Frank Mill (12/0)], Rudolf Völler (52/27). Trainer: Franz Beckenbauer (45).
Goals: Rudolf Völler (30, 51).

547. 21.06.1988 **WEST GERMANY - NETHERLANDS** **1-2(0-0)** 8th EC. Semi-Final.
Volksparkstadion, Hamburg; Referee: Ioan Igna (Romania); Attendance: 61,330
GER: Eike Immel (19/0), Matthias Herget (38/4) [45.Hans Pflügler (7/0)], Jürgen Kohler (19/0), Ulrich Borowka (6/0), Andreas Brehme (40/4), Lothar Herbert Matthäus (Cap) (65/7), Wolfgang Rolff (34/0), Olaf Thon (28/3), Jürgen Klinsmann (9/2), Rudolf Völler (53/27), Frank Mill (13/0) [84.Pierre Littbarski (57/15)]. Trainer: Franz Beckenbauer (46).
Goal: Lothar Herbert Matthäus (55 penalty).

548. 31.08.1988 **FINLAND - WEST GERMANY** **0-4(0-2)** 14th FIFA WC. Qualifiers
Olympiastadion, Helsinki; Referee: Vadim Zhuk (Soviet Union); Attendance: 31,700
GER: Bodo Illgner (4/0), Holger Fach (1/0), Andreas Brehme (41/4), Jürgen Kohler (20/0), Guido Buchwald (21/0) [30.Wolfgang Rolff (35/0)], Armin Görtz (2/0), Lothar Herbert Matthäus (Cap) (66/8), Thomas Häßler (1/0), Pierre Littbarski (58/15), Rudolf Völler (54/29), Dieter Eckstein (7/0) [76.Karlheinz Riedle (1/1)]. Trainer: Franz Beckenbauer (47).
Goals: Rudolf Völler (7, 15), Lothar Herbert Matthäus (52), Karlheinz Riedle (77).

549. 21.09.1988 **WEST GERMANY - SOVIET UNION** **1-0(0-0)**
Rheinstadion, Düsseldorf; Referee: Bruno Galler (Switzerland); Attendance: 16,000
GER: Bodo Illgner (5/0), Matthias Herget (39/4), Stefan Reuter (10/1), Jürgen Kohler (21/0) [63.Guido Buchwald (22/0)], Hans Pflügler (8/0) [46.Knut Reinhardt (1/0)], Andreas Möller (1/0), Wolfgang Rolff (36/0), Günter Hermann (1/0), Pierre Littbarski (Cap) (59/15), Thomas Allofs (2/0), Herbert Waas (11/1). Trainer: Franz Beckenbauer (48).
Goal: Sergey Shmatovalenko (57 own goal).

550. 19.10.1988 **WEST GERMANY - NETHERLANDS** **0-0** 14th FIFA WC. Qualifiers
Olympiastadion, München; Referee: Pietro D'Elia (Italy); Attendance: 73,000
GER: Bodo Illgner (6/0), Holger Fach (2/0), Thomas Berthold (28/1), Jürgen Kohler (22/0), Guido Buchwald (23/0), Andreas Brehme (42/4), Lothar Herbert Matthäus (Cap) (67/8), Olaf Thon (29/3), Thomas Häßler (2/0), Jürgen Klinsmann (10/2) [65.Frank Mill (14/0)], Rudolf Völler (55/29). Trainer: Franz Beckenbauer (49).

551. 22.03.1989 **BULGARIA - WEST GERMANY** **1-2(0-0)**
Nationalen stadion "Vasil Levski", Sofia; Referee: Dušan Krchnak (Czechoslovakia); Attendance: 35,000
GER: Bodo Illgner (7/0), Holger Fach (3/0) [46.Pierre Littbarski (60/16)], Thomas Berthold (29/1), Jürgen Kohler (23/0), Guido Buchwald (24/0), Andreas Brehme (43/4), Thomas Häßler (3/0), Andreas Möller (2/0), Lothar Herbert Matthäus (Cap) (68/8), Karlheinz Riedle (2/1), Rudolf Völler (56/30). Trainer: Franz Beckenbauer (50).
Goals: Rudolf Völler (72), Pierre Littbarski (87).

552. 26.04.1989 **NETHERLANDS - WEST GERMANY** **1-1(0-0)** 14th FIFA WC. Qualifiers
Stadion Feijenoord, Rotterdam; Referee: Erik Fredriksson (Sweden); Attendance: 54,000
GER: Bodo Illgner (8/0), Thomas Berthold (30/1), Stefan Reuter (11/1), Guido Buchwald (25/0), Jürgen Kohler (24/0) [75.Wolfgang Rolff (37/0)], Andreas Brehme (44/4), Lothar Herbert Matthäus (Cap) (69/8), Andreas Möller (3/0), Thomas Häßler (4/0), Karlheinz Riedle (3/2), Rudolf Völler (57/30) [34.Jürgen Klinsmann (11/2)]. Trainer: Franz Beckenbauer (51).
Goal: Karlheinz Riedle (69).

553. 31.05.1989 **WALES - WEST GERMANY** **0-0** 14th FIFA WC. Qualifiers
Arms Park, Cardiff; Referee: Carlos Alberto da Silva Valente (Portugal); Attendance: 30,000
GER: Bodo Illgner (9/0), Thomas Berthold (31/1), Stefan Reuter (12/1), Alois Reinhardt (1/0), Guido Buchwald (26/0), Andreas Brehme (45/4), Thomas Häßler (5/0), Holger Fach (4/0), Andreas Möller (4/0), Karlheinz Riedle (4/2) [78.Jürgen Klinsmann (12/2)], Rudolf Völler (Cap) (58/30). Trainer: Franz Beckenbauer (52).

554. 06.09.1989 **REPUBLIC OF IRELAND - WEST GERMANY** **1-1(1-1)**
Lansdowne Road, Dublin; Referee: Frans Van den Wijngaert (Belgium); Attendance: 46,000
GER: Bodo Illgner (10/0) [46.Raimond Aumann (1/0)], Klaus Augenthaler (15/0), Stefan Reuter (13/1), Guido Buchwald (27/0) [46.Alois Reinhardt (2/0)], Hans Pflügler (9/0), Hans Dorfner (6/1) [85.Holger Fach (5/0)], Pierre Littbarski (Cap) (61/16), Andreas Möller (5/0), Olaf Thon (30/3), Thomas Häßler (6/0), Roland Wohlfahrt (2/0). Trainer: Franz Beckenbauer (53).
Goal: Hans Dorfner (33).

555. 04.10.1989 **WEST GERMANY - FINLAND** **6-1(1-0)** 14th FIFA WC. Qualifiers
Westfalenstadion, Dortmund; Referee: Alan Snoddy (Northern Ireland); Attendance: 40,000
GER: Bodo Illgner (11/0), Klaus Augenthaler (16/0), Stefan Reuter (14/1), Guido Buchwald (28/0), Andreas Brehme (46/4), Thomas Häßler (7/0) [46.Uwe Bein (1/0)], Lothar Herbert Matthäus (Cap) (70/9), Andreas Möller (6/2) [81.Frank Mill (15/0)], Pierre Littbarski (62/17), Jürgen Klinsmann (13/3), Rudolf Völler (59/31). Trainer: Franz Beckenbauer (54).
Goals: Andreas Möller (12), Pierre Littbarski (47), Jürgen Klinsmann (53), Rudolf Völler (62), Andreas Möller (81), Lothar Herbert Matthäus (84 penalty).

556. 15.11.1989 **WEST GERMANY - WALES** **2-1(1-1)** 14th FIFA WC. Qualifiers
Müngersdorferstadion, Köln; Referee: Michel Vautrot (France); Attendance: 60,300
GER: Bodo Illgner (12/0), Klaus Augenthaler (17/0) [46.Alois Reinhardt (3/0)], Stefan Reuter (15/1), Guido Buchwald (29/0), Andreas Brehme (47/4), Thomas Häßler (8/1), Hans Dorfner (7/1), Andreas Möller (7/2) [82.Uwe Bein (2/0)], Pierre Littbarski (Cap) (63/17), Jürgen Klinsmann (14/3), Rudolf Völler (60/32). Trainer: Franz Beckenbauer (55).
Goals: Rudolf Völler (25), Thomas Häßler (48).

557. 18.02.1990 **FRANCE - WEST GERMANY** **2-1(1-1)**
Stade de la Mosson, Montpellier; Referee: Joaquín Marcos Ramos (Spain); Attendance: 22,000
GER: Bodo Illgner (13/0), Klaus Augenthaler (18/0), Thomas Berthold (32/1), Alois Reinhardt (4/0), Andreas Brehme (48/4), Thomas Häßler (9/1), Andreas Möller (8/3), Lothar Herbert Matthäus (Cap) (71/9), Uwe Bein (3/0), Jürgen Klinsmann (15/3), Karlheinz Riedle (5/2) [65.Pierre Littbarski (64/17)]. Trainer: Franz Beckenbauer (56).
Goal: Andreas Möller (36).

58. 25.04.1990 **WEST GERMANY - URUGUAY** **3-3(0-0)**
eckarstadion, Stuttgart; Referee: Bo Karlsson (Sweden); Attendance: 35,000
ER: Bodo Illgner (14/0) [46.Raimond Aumann (2/0)], Jürgen Kohler (25/0), Thomas Berthold (33/1), Guido Buchwald (30/0), Andreas Brehme (49/4), homas Häßler (10/1), Pierre Littbarski (65/17), Lothar Herbert Matthäus (Cap) (72/10), Uwe Bein (4/0) [68.Olaf Thon (31/3)], Jürgen Klinsmann (16/4), udolf Völler (61/33). Trainer: Franz Beckenbauer (57).
oals: Lothar Herbert Matthäus (60), Rudolf Völler (64), Jürgen Klinsmann (75).

59. 26.05.1990 **WEST GERMANY - CZECHOSLOVAKIA** **1-0(1-0)**
heinstadion, Düsseldorf; Referee: Bruno Galler (Switzerland); Attendance: 26,000
ER: Bodo Illgner (15/0), Klaus Augenthaler (19/0), Guido Buchwald (31/0), Jürgen Kohler (26/0), Andreas Brehme (50/4), Thomas Häßler (11/1) [76.Olaf hon (32/3)], Pierre Littbarski (66/17) [69.Andreas Möller (9/3)], Lothar Herbert Matthäus (Cap) (73/10), Uwe Bein (5/1) [76.Thomas Berthold (34/1)], irgen Klinsmann (17/4) [76.Frank Mill (16/0)], Rudolf Völler (62/33). Trainer: Franz Beckenbauer (58).
oal: Uwe Bein (24).

60. 30.05.1990 **WEST GERMANY - DENMARK** **1-0(1-0)**
arkstadion, Gelsenkirchen; Referee: Neil Midgley (England); Attendance: 42,000
ER: Raimond Aumann (3/0) [46.Andreas Köpke (1/0)], Klaus Augenthaler (20/0) [46.Paul Steiner (1/0)], Jürgen Kohler (27/0) [77.Stefan Reuter (16/1)], uido Buchwald (32/0), Andreas Brehme (51/4) [46.Hans Pflügler (10/0)], Thomas Häßler (12/1) [80.Günter Hermann (2/0)], Pierre Littbarski (67/17) 6.Thomas Berthold (35/1)], Lothar Herbert Matthäus (Cap) (74/10) [66.Olaf Thon (33/3)], Uwe Bein (6/1) [66.Andreas Möller (10/3)], Jürgen Klinsmann 8/4) [66.Frank Mill (17/0)], Rudolf Völler (63/34) [Karlheinz Riedle (6/2)]. Trainer: Franz Beckenbauer (59).
oal: Rudolf Völler (36).

61. 10.06.1990 **WEST GERMANY - YUGOSLAVIA** **4-1(2-0)** 14th FIFA WC. Group Stage.
adio „Giuseppe Meazza", Milano (Italy); Referee: Peter Mikkelsen (Denmark); Attendance: 74,800
ER: Bodo Illgner (16/0), Klaus Augenthaler (21/0), Stefan Reuter (17/1), Guido Buchwald (33/0), Andreas Brehme (52/4), Thomas Berthold (36/1), homas Häßler (13/1) [74.Andreas Möller (11/3)], Lothar Herbert Matthäus (Cap) (75/12), Uwe Bein (7/1) [74.Pierre Littbarski (68/17)], Jürgen Klinsmann 9/5), Rudolf Völler (64/35). Trainer: Franz Beckenbauer (60).
oals: Lothar Herbert Matthäus (29), Jürgen Klinsmann (40), Lothar Herbert Matthäus (63), Rudolf Völler (70).

62. 15.06.1990 **WEST GERMANY – UNITED ARAB EMIRATES** **5-1(2-0)** 14th FIFA WC. Group Stage.
adio „Giuseppe Meazza", Milano (Italy); Referee: Aleksei Spirin (Soviet Union); Attendance: 71,167
ER: Bodo Illgner (17/0), Klaus Augenthaler (22/0), Stefan Reuter (18/1), Guido Buchwald (34/0), Andreas Brehme (53/4), Thomas Berthold (37/1) 6.Pierre Littbarski (69/17)], Thomas Häßler (14/1), Lothar Herbert Matthäus (Cap) (76/13), Uwe Bein (8/2), Jürgen Klinsmann (20/6) [72.Karlheinz Riedle /2)], Rudolf Völler (65/37). Trainer: Franz Beckenbauer (61).
oals: Rudolf Völler (36), Jürgen Klinsmann (38), Lothar Herbert Matthäus (47), Uwe Bein (59), Rudolf Völler (75).

63. 19.06.1990 **WEST GERMANY - COLOMBIA** **1-1(0-0)** 14th FIFA WC. Group Stage.
adio „Giuseppe Meazza", Milano (Italy); Referee: Alan Snoddy (Northern Ireland); Attendance: 72,510
ER: Bodo Illgner (18/0), Klaus Augenthaler (23/0), Stefan Reuter (19/1), Guido Buchwald (35/0), Hans Pflügler (11/0), Thomas Berthold (38/1), Thomas äßler (15/1) [88.Olaf Thon (34/3)], Lothar Herbert Matthäus (Cap) (77/13), Uwe Bein (9/2) [46.Pierre Littbarski (70/18)], Jürgen Klinsmann (21/6), Rudolf öller (66/37). Trainer: Franz Beckenbauer (62).
oal: Pierre Littbarski (89).

64. 24.06.1990 **WEST GERMANY - NETHERLANDS** **2-1(0-0)** 14th FIFA WC. 2nd Round of 16.
adio „Giuseppe Meazza", Milano (Italy); Referee: Juan Carlos Lousteau (Argentina); Attendance: 74,559
ER: Bodo Illgner (19/0), Klaus Augenthaler (24/0), Stefan Reuter (20/1), Jürgen Kohler (28/0), Guido Buchwald (36/0), Andreas Brehme (54/5), Pierre ittbarski (71/18), Lothar Herbert Matthäus (Cap) (78/13), Thomas Berthold (39/1), Jürgen Klinsmann (22/7) [79.Karlheinz Riedle (8/2)], Rudolf Völler 7/37) [*sent off 22*]. Trainer: Franz Beckenbauer (63).
oals: Jürgen Klinsmann (51), Andreas Brehme (86).

65. 01.07.1990 **WEST GERMANY - CZECHOSLOVAKIA** **1-0(1-0)** 14th FIFA WC. Quarter-Finals.
adio „Giuseppe Meazza", Milano (Italy); Referee: Helmut Kohl (Austria); Attendance: 73,347
ER: Bodo Illgner (20/0), Klaus Augenthaler (25/0), Thomas Berthold (40/1), Jürgen Kohler (29/0), Guido Buchwald (37/0), Andreas Brehme (55/5), Pierre ittbarski (72/18), Lothar Herbert Matthäus (Cap) (79/14), Uwe Bein (10/2) [83.Andreas Möller (12/3)], Karlheinz Riedle (9/2), Jürgen Klinsmann (23/7). rainer: Franz Beckenbauer (64).
oal: Lothar Herbert Matthäus (25 penalty).

66. 04.07.1990 **WEST GERMANY - ENGLAND** **1-1(0-0,1-1); 4-3 on penalties** 14th FIFA WC. Semi-Finals.
adio Delle Alpi, Torino (Italy); Referee: José Roberto Ramiz Wright (Brazil); Attendance: 62,628
ER: Bodo Illgner (21/0), Klaus Augenthaler (26/0), Thomas Berthold (41/1), Jürgen Kohler (30/0), Guido Buchwald (38/0), Andreas Brehme (56/6), homas Häßler (16/1) [67.Stefan Reuter (21/1)], Lothar Herbert Matthäus (Cap) (80/14), Olaf Thon (35/3), Jürgen Klinsmann (24/7), Rudolf Völler (68/37) 8.Karlheinz Riedle (10/2)]. Trainer: Franz Beckenbauer (65).
oal: Andreas Brehme (60).

67. 08.07.1990 **WEST GERMANY - ARGENTINA** **1-0(0-0)** 14th FIFA WC. Final.
adio Olimpico, Roma (Italy); Referee: Edgardo Enrique Codesal Méndez (Mexico); Attendance: 73,603
ER: Bodo Illgner (22/0), Klaus Augenthaler (27/0), Thomas Berthold (42/1) [73.Stefan Reuter (22/1)], Guido Buchwald (39/0), Jürgen Kohler (31/0), ndreas Brehme (57/7), Thomas Häßler (17/1), Lothar Herbert Matthäus (Cap) (81/14), Pierre Littbarski (73/18), Jürgen Klinsmann (25/7), Rudolf Völler 9/37). Trainer: Franz Beckenbauer (66).
oal: Andreas Brehme (85 penalty).

68. 29.08.1990 **PORTUGAL - WEST GERMANY** **1-1(0-1)**
stádio da Luz, Lisboa; Referee: Rosario Lo Bello (Italy); Attendance: 20,000
ER: Bodo Illgner (23/0), Thomas Berthold (43/1), Stefan Reuter (23/1), Jürgen Kohler (32/0), Guido Buchwald (40/0), Andreas Brehme (58/7), Uwe Bein 1/2) [65.Knut Reinhardt (2/0)], Lothar Herbert Matthäus (Cap) (82/15) [53.Manfred Binz (1/0)], Andreas Möller (13/3), Karlheinz Riedle (11/2), Rudolf öller (70/37) [46.Jürgen Klinsmann (26/7)]. Trainer: Hans-Hubert Vogts (1).
oal: Lothar Herbert Matthäus (15).

569. 10.10.1990 **SWEDEN - WEST GERMANY** **1-3(0-3)**
Råsundastadion, Stockholm; Referee: Joseph Worrall (England); Attendance: 20,400
GER: Raimond Aumann (4/0), Manfred Binz (2/0), Thomas Berthold (44/1), Thomas Helmer (1/0), Andreas Brehme (59/8) [60.Knut Reinhardt (3/0)], Thomas Häßler (18/1), Andreas Möller (14/3) [60.Karlheinz Riedle (12/2)], Lothar Herbert Matthäus (Cap) (83/15), Thomas Strunz (1/0), Jürgen Klinsmann (27/8), Rudolf Völler (71/38). Trainer: Hans-Hubert Vogts (2).
Goals: Jürgen Klinsmann (29), Rudolf Völler (38), Andreas Brehme (45).

570. 31.10.1990 **LUXEMBOURG - WEST GERMANY** **2-3(0-2)** 9th EC. Qualifiers
Stade Municipal, Luxembourg; Referee: Kim Milton Nielsen (Denmark); Attendance: 9,200
GER: Bodo Illgner (24/0), Manfred Binz (3/0), Thomas Berthold (45/1), Jürgen Kohler (33/0), Andreas Brehme (60/8), Thomas Häßler (19/1), Thomas Strunz (2/0), Lothar Herbert Matthäus (Cap) (84/15), Uwe Bein (12/3) [73.Knut Reinhardt (4/0)], Jürgen Klinsmann (28/9), Rudolf Völler (72/39). Trainer: Hans-Hubert Vogts (3).
Goals: Jürgen Klinsmann (16), Uwe Bein (30), Rudolf Völler (49).

After the reunification of West and East Germany, the national team played further under the name Germany.

571. 19.12.1990 **GERMANY - SWITZERLAND** **4-0(1-0)**
Neckarstadion, Stuttgart; Referee: Carlo Longhi (Italy); Attendance: 20,000
GER: Bodo Illgner (25/0), Thomas Berthold (46/1), Jürgen Kohler (34/0), Guido Buchwald (41/0), Thomas Helmer (2/0), Stefan Reuter (24/1), Thomas Häßler (20/1), Lothar Herbert Matthäus (Cap) (85/16), Matthias Sammer (1/0) [73.Andreas Thom (1/1)], Jürgen Klinsmann (29/9), Rudolf Völler (73/40) [46.Karlheinz Riedle (13/3)]. Trainer: Hans-Hubert Vogts (4).
Goals: Rudolf Völler (1), Karlheinz Riedle (67), Andreas Thom (74), Lothar Herbert Matthäus (85).

572. 27.03.1991 **GERMANY - SOVIET UNION** **2-1(0-0)**
Waldstadion, Frankfurt am Main; Referee: Michał Listkiewicz (Poland); Attendance: 24,000
GER: Bodo Illgner (26/0), Thomas Berthold (47/1), Stefan Reuter (25/2), Jürgen Kohler (35/0) [53.Thomas Helmer (3/0)], Guido Buchwald (42/0), Thomas Häßler (21/1) [58.Andreas Möller (15/3)], Matthias Sammer (2/0), Lothar Herbert Matthäus (Cap) (86/17), Thomas Doll (1/0), Jürgen Klinsmann (30/9), Rudolf Völler (74/40). Trainer: Hans-Hubert Vogts (5).
Goals: Stefan Reuter (65), Lothar Herbert Matthäus (81).

573. 01.05.1991 **GERMANY - BELGIUM** **1-0(1-0)** 9th EC. Qualifiers
Niedersachsenstadion, Hannover; Referee: Zoran Petrović (Yugoslavia); Attendance: 56,000
GER: Bodo Illgner (27/0), Thomas Berthold (48/1), Stefan Reuter (26/2), Dietmar Beiersdorfer (1/0), Andreas Brehme (61/8), Thomas Häßler (22/1), Matthias Sammer (3/0), Lothar Herbert Matthäus (Cap) (87/18), Thomas Doll (2/0), Jürgen Klinsmann (31/9) [77.Thomas Helmer (4/0)], Rudolf Völler (75/40) [88.Karlheinz Riedle (14/3)]. Trainer: Hans-Hubert Vogts (6).
Goal: Lothar Herbert Matthäus (3).

574. 05.06.1991 **WALES - GERMANY** **1-0(0-0)** 9th EC. Qualifiers
Arms Park, Cardiff; Referee: Bo Karlsson (Sweden); Attendance: 37,000
GER: Bodo Illgner (28/0), Thomas Berthold (49/1) [*sent off 60*], Stefan Reuter (27/2), Thomas Helmer (5/0), Jürgen Kohler (36/0), Andreas Brehme (62/8), Lothar Herbert Matthäus (Cap) (88/18) [46.Thomas Doll (3/0)], Guido Buchwald (43/0), Matthias Sammer (4/0) [74.Stefan Effenberg (1/0)], Jürgen Klinsmann (32/9), Rudolf Völler (76/40). Trainer: Hans-Hubert Vogts (7).

575. 11.09.1991 **ENGLAND - GERMANY** **0-1(0-1)**
Wembley Stadium, London; Referee: Alexei Spirin (Soviet Union); Attendance: 59,500
GER: Bodo Illgner (29/0), Manfred Binz (4/0), Stefan Effenberg (2/0), Jürgen Kohler (37/0), Guido Buchwald (44/0), Thomas Häßler (23/1), Lothar Herbert Matthäus (Cap) (89/18), Andreas Möller (16/3), Andreas Brehme (63/8), Karlheinz Riedle (15/4), Thomas Doll (4/0) [81.Jürgen Klinsmann (33/9)]. Trainer: Hans-Hubert Vogts (8).
Goal: Karlheinz Riedle (45).

576. 16.10.1991 **GERMANY - WALES** **4-1(3-0)** 9th EC. Qualifiers
Frankenstadion, Nürnberg; Referee: Joël Quiniou (France); Attendance: 46,000
GER: Bodo Illgner (30/0), Manfred Binz (5/0), Guido Buchwald (45/0), Jürgen Kohler (38/0), Andreas Brehme (64/8), Stefan Reuter (28/2), Thomas Doll (5/1) [78.Stefan Effenberg (3/0)], Lothar Herbert Matthäus (Cap) (90/18), Andreas Möller (17/4), Karlheinz Riedle (16/5) [65.Thomas Häßler (24/1)], Rudolf Völler (77/41). Trainer: Hans-Hubert Vogts (9).
Goals: Andreas Möller (34), Rudolf Völler (39), Karlheinz Riedle (45), Thomas Doll (73).

577. 20.11.1991 **BELGIUM - GERMANY** **0-1(0-1)** 9th EC. Qualifiers
Parc Astrid, Bruxelles; Referee: Tulio Lanese (Italy); Attendance: 27,000
GER: Bodo Illgner (31/0), Manfred Binz (6/0), Guido Buchwald (46/0), Jürgen Kohler (39/0), Andreas Brehme (65/8), Stefan Reuter (29/2), Andreas Möller (18/4) [80.Stefan Effenberg (4/0)], Lothar Herbert Matthäus (Cap) (91/18), Thomas Doll (6/1), Rudolf Völler (78/42), Karlheinz Riedle (17/5). Trainer: Hans-Hubert Vogts (10).
Goal: Rudolf Völler (16).

578. 18.12.1991 **GERMANY - LUXEMBOURG** **4-0(2-0)** 9th EC. Qualifiers
„Ulrich Haberland“ Stadion, Leverkusen; Referee: Zbigniew Przesmycki (Poland); Attendance: 26,000
GER: Bodo Illgner (32/0), Manfred Binz (7/0), Stefan Reuter (30/2), Guido Buchwald (47/1), Jürgen Kohler (40/0), Andreas Brehme (66/8), Andreas Möller (19/4) [70.Uwe Bein (13/3)], Lothar Herbert Matthäus (Cap) (92/19), Thomas Doll (7/1) [46.Thomas Häßler (25/2)], Karlheinz Riedle (18/6), Rudolf Völler (79/42). Trainer: Hans-Hubert Vogts (11).
Goals: Lothar Herbert Matthäus (15 penalty), Guido Buchwald (44), Karlheinz Riedle (50), Thomas Häßler (62).

579. 25.03.1992 **ITALY - GERMANY** **1-0(0-0)**
Stadio Delle Alpi, Torino; Referee: Rune Larsson (Sweden); Attendance: 45,000
GER: Bodo Illgner (33/0), Manfred Binz (8/0), Stefan Reuter (31/2), Guido Buchwald (48/1), Thomas Helmer (6/0), Andreas Brehme (67/8) [46.Michael Schulz (1/0)], Thomas Häßler (26/2), Lothar Herbert Matthäus (Cap) (93/19), Thomas Doll (8/1) [69.Uwe Bein (14/3)], Rudolf Völler (80/42) [46.Jürgen Klinsmann (34/9)], Karlheinz Riedle (19/6). Trainer: Hans-Hubert Vogts (12).

580. 22.04.1992 **CZECHOSLOVAKIA - GERMANY** **1-1(0-0)**
Stadion Strahov, Praha; Referee: Arie Frost (Israel); Attendance: 14,000
GER: Andreas Köpke (2/0), Manfred Binz (9/0), Guido Buchwald (49/1), Thomas Helmer (7/0), Christian Wörns (1/0), Thomas Häßler (27/3) [81.Andreas Möller (20/4)], Stefan Effenberg (5/0), Andreas Thom (2/1) [67.Matthias Sammer (5/0)], Michael Frontzeck (17/0), Jürgen Klinsmann (35/9), Rudolf Völler (Cap) (81/42). Trainer: Hans-Hubert Vogts (13).
Goal: Thomas Häßler (41).

581. 30.05.1992 **GERMANY - TURKEY** **1-0(0-0)**
Parkstadion, Gelsenkirchen; Referee: Georges Ramos (France); Attendance: 55,000
GER: Andreas Köpke (3/0), Manfred Binz (10/0), Jürgen Kohler (41/0), Guido Buchwald (50/1), Christian Wörns (2/0) [46.Stefan Effenberg (6/0)], Andreas Möller (21/4), Matthias Sammer (6/0), Thomas Häßler (28/3), Andreas Brehme (68/8), Rudolf Völler (Cap) (82/43), Jürgen Klinsmann (36/9) [57.Andreas Thom (3/1)]. Trainer: Hans-Hubert Vogts (14).
Goal: Rudolf Völler (64).

582. 02.06.1992 **GERMANY – NORTHERN IRELAND** **1-1(1-1)**
Weserstadion, Bremen; Referee: Alphonse Constantin (Belgium); Attendance: 30,000
GER: Bodo Illgner (34/0), Manfred Binz (11/1), Guido Buchwald (51/1), Jürgen Kohler (42/0), Stefan Reuter (32/2), Matthias Sammer (7/0) [75.Andreas Thom (4/1)], Stefan Effenberg (7/0), Andreas Brehme (69/8), Thomas Häßler (29/3) [46.Thomas Doll (9/1)], Rudolf Völler (Cap) (83/43), Karlheinz Riedle (20/6). Trainer: Hans-Hubert Vogts (15).
Goal: Manfred Binz (40).

583. 12.06.1992 **C.I.S. - GERMANY** **1-1(0-0)** 9th EC. Group Stage.
Idrottsparken, Norrköping (Sweden); Referee: Gérard Biguet (France); Attendance: 17,400
GER: Bodo Illgner (35/0), Manfred Binz (12/1), Jürgen Kohler (43/0), Guido Buchwald (52/1), Stefan Reuter (33/2) [64.Jürgen Klinsmann (37/9)], Thomas Häßler (30/4), Stefan Effenberg (8/0), Thomas Doll (10/1), Andreas Brehme (70/8), Rudolf Völler (Cap) (84/43) [46.Andreas Möller (22/4)], Karlheinz Riedle (21/6). Trainer: Hans-Hubert Vogts (16).
Goal: Thomas Häßler (90).

584. 15.06.1992 **SCOTLAND - GERMANY** **0-2(0-1)** 9th EC. Group Stage.
Idrottsparken, Norrköping (Sweden); Referee: Guy Goethals (Belgium); Attendance: 17,800
GER: Bodo Illgner (36/0), Manfred Binz (13/1), Jürgen Kohler (44/0), Guido Buchwald (53/1), Thomas Häßler (31/4), Stefan Effenberg (9/1), Matthias Sammer (8/0), Andreas Möller (23/4), Andreas Brehme (Cap) (71/8), Jürgen Klinsmann (38/9), Karlheinz Riedle (22/7) [68.Stefan Reuter (34/2); 75.Michael Schulz (2/0)]. Trainer: Hans-Hubert Vogts (17).
Goals: Karlheinz Riedle (29), Stefan Effenberg (47).

585. 18.06.1992 **NETHERLANDS - GERMANY** **3-1(2-0)** 9th EC. Group Stage.
Ullevi Stadion, Göteborg (Sweden); Referee: Pierluigi Pairetto (Italy); Attendance: 37,700
GER: Bodo Illgner (37/0), Manfred Binz (14/1) [46.Matthias Sammer (9/0)], Jürgen Kohler (45/0), Thomas Helmer (8/0), Andreas Brehme (Cap) (72/8), Thomas Häßler (32/4), Stefan Effenberg (10/1), Andreas Möller (24/4), Michael Frontzeck (18/0), Jürgen Klinsmann (39/10), Karlheinz Riedle (23/7) [77.Thomas Doll (11/1)]. Trainer: Hans-Hubert Vogts (18).
Goal: Jürgen Klinsmann (53).

586. 21.06.1992 **SWEDEN - GERMANY** **2-3(0-1)** 9th EC. Semi-Finals.
Råsundastadion, Stockholm; Referee: Tulio Lanese (Italy); Attendance: 28,827
GER: Bodo Illgner (38/0), Thomas Helmer (9/0), Guido Buchwald (54/1), Jürgen Kohler (46/0), Stefan Reuter (35/2), Thomas Häßler (33/5), Matthias Sammer (10/0), Stefan Effenberg (11/1), Andreas Brehme (Cap) (73/8), Jürgen Klinsmann (40/10) [89.Thomas Doll (12/1)], Karlheinz Riedle (24/9). Trainer: Hans-Hubert Vogts (19).
Goals: Thomas Häßler (11), Karlheinz Riedle (59, 89).

587. 26.06.1992 **DENMARK - GERMANY** **2-0(1-0)** 9th EC. Final.
Ullevi Stadion, Göteborg (Sweden); Referee: Bruno Galler (Switzerland); Attendance: 38,700
GER: Bodo Illgner (39/0), Thomas Helmer (10/0), Jürgen Kohler (47/0), Guido Buchwald (55/1), Stefan Reuter (36/2), Thomas Häßler (34/5), Stefan Effenberg (12/1) [80.Andreas Thom (5/1)], Matthias Sammer (11/0) [46.Thomas Doll (13/1)], Andreas Brehme (Cap) (74/8), Jürgen Klinsmann (41/10), Karlheinz Riedle (25/9). Trainer: Hans-Hubert Vogts (20).

588. 09.09.1992 **DENMARK - GERMANY** **1-2(0-0)**
Parken, København; Referee: Martin Bodenham (England); Attendance: 40,000
GER: Andreas Köpke (4/0), Guido Buchwald (Cap) (56/1), Stefan Reuter (37/2), Christian Wörns (3/0), Thomas Helmer (11/0), Michael Frontzeck (19/0), J. Klinsmann (42/10) [88.Thomas Strunz (3/0)], Stefan Effenberg (13/2), Thomas Doll (14/1) [73.Olaf Thon (36/3)], Karlheinz Riedle (26/10), Andreas Thom (6/1). Trainer: Hans-Hubert Vogts (21).
Goals: Karlheinz Riedle (47), Stefan Effenberg (88).

589. 14.10.1992 **GERMANY - MEXICO** **1-1(0-0)**
„Rudolf Harbig“ Stadion, Dresden; Referee: Jozef Marko (Czechoslovakia); Attendance: 28,000
GER: Andreas Köpke (5/0), Olaf Thon (37/3), Guido Buchwald (57/1), Thomas Helmer (12/0), Thomas Häßler (35/5), Heiko Scholz (1/0), Lothar Herbert Matthäus (Cap) (94/19), Stefan Effenberg (14/2), Knut Reinhardt (5/0), Rudolf Völler (85/44) [67.Ulf Kirsten (1/0)], Karlheinz Riedle (27/10) [46.Jürgen Klinsmann (43/10)]. Trainer: Hans-Hubert Vogts (22).
Goal: Rudolf Völler (58).

590. 18.11.1992 **GERMANY - AUSTRIA** **0-0**
Frankenstadion, Nürnberg; Referee: Joseph Worrall (England); Attendance: 46,000
GER: Andreas Köpke (6/0), Stefan Reuter (38/2), Jürgen Kohler (48/0), Guido Buchwald (Cap) (58/1), Thomas Helmer (13/0), Thomas Häßler (36/5), Stefan Effenberg (15/2), Thomas Doll (15/1), Knut Reinhardt (6/0) [46.Andreas Möller (25/4)], Jürgen Klinsmann (44/10), Karlheinz Riedle (28/10) [69.Ulf Kirsten (2/0) [*sent off 73*]]. Trainer: Hans-Hubert Vogts (23).

591. 16.12.1992 **BRAZIL - GERMANY** **3-1(2-0)**
Estádio Beira Rio, Porto Alegre; Referee: Juan Francisco Escobar (Paraguay); Attendance: 35,000
GER: Bodo Illgner (40/0), Guido Buchwald (59/1), Christian Wörns (4/0), Jürgen Kohler (49/0), Thomas Wolter (1/0) [59.Michael Zorc (1/0)], Thomas Häßler (37/5) [80.Matthias Sammer (12/1)], Lothar Herbert Matthäus (Cap) (95/19), Stefan Effenberg (16/2), Martin Wagner (1/0) [46.Knut Reinhardt (7/0)], Jürgen Klinsmann (45/10), Andreas Thom (7/1) [67.Thomas Doll (16/1)]. Trainer: Hans-Hubert Vogts (24).
Goal: Matthias Sammer (85).

592. 20.12.1992 **URUGUAY - GERMANY** **1-4(0-1)**
Estadio Centenario, Montevideo; Referee: Juan Carlos Lousteau (Argentina); Attendance: 37,800
GER: Andreas Köpke (7/0), Olaf Thon (38/3), Jürgen Kohler (50/0), Thomas Helmer (14/0), Thomas Häßler (38/6) [84.Matthias Sammer (13/1)], Michael Zorc (2/0), Guido Buchwald (60/2), Lothar Herbert Matthäus (Cap) (96/19), Thomas Doll (17/1) [84.Ulf Kirsten (3/0)], Andreas Möller (26/5), Jürgen Klinsmann (46/11) [79.Bruno Labbadia (1/0)]. Trainer: Hans-Hubert Vogts (25).
Goals: Guido Buchwald (41), Andreas Möller (60), Thomas Häßler (70), Jürgen Klinsmann (76).

593. 24.03.1993 **SCOTLAND - GERMANY** **0-1(0-1)**
Hampden Park, Glasgow; Referee: Leon Schelings (Belgium); Attendance: 36,400
GER: Andreas Köpke (8/0), Olaf Thon (39/3), Guido Buchwald (61/2), Jürgen Kohler (51/0), Thomas Häßler (39/6), Michael Zorc (3/0), Lothar Herbert Matthäus (Cap) (97/19) [88.Matthias Sammer (14/1)], Thomas Helmer (15/0), Thomas Doll (18/1) [60.Stefan Effenberg (17/2)], Jürgen Klinsmann (47/11), Karlheinz Riedle (29/11). Trainer: Hans-Hubert Vogts (26).
Goal: Karlheinz Riedle (20).

594. 14.04.1993 **GERMANY - GHANA** **6-1(0-1)**
Ruhrstadion, Bochum; Referee: Mario van der Ende (Netherlands); Attendance: 37,000
GER: Andreas Köpke (9/0), Olaf Thon (40/3), Jürgen Kohler (52/0), Guido Buchwald (62/2), Stefan Effenberg (18/4), Lothar Herbert Matthäus (Cap) (98/19) [84.Thomas Häßler (40/6)], Uwe Bein (15/3) [79.Andreas Möller (27/6)], Michael Zorc (4/0), Thomas Helmer (16/0), Karlheinz Riedle (30/11) [46.Ulf Kirsten (4/1)], Jürgen Klinsmann (48/13). Trainer: Hans-Hubert Vogts (27).
Goals: Ulf Kirsten (69), Stefan Effenberg (70), Jürgen Klinsmann (70), Stefan Effenberg (82), Jürgen Klinsmann (86), Andreas Möller (88).

595. 10.06.1993 **BRAZIL - GERMANY** **3-3(3-0)** International Tournament
"Robert F. Kennedy" Memorial Stadium, Washington (United States); Referee: Arturo Angeles (United States); Attendance: 40,000
GER: Andreas Köpke (10/0), Guido Buchwald (63/2), Jürgen Kohler (53/0), Thomas Helmer (17/0), Stefan Effenberg (19/4), Michael Zorc (5/0) [54.Thomas Strunz (4/0)], Lothar Herbert Matthäus (Cap) (99/19), Christian Ziege (1/0) [74.Michael Schulz (3/0)], Matthias Sammer (15/1) [46.Karlheinz Riedle (31/11)], Andreas Möller (28/7), Jürgen Klinsmann (49/15). Trainer: Hans-Hubert Vogts (28).
Goals: Jürgen Klinsmann (66), Andreas Möller (80), Jürgen Klinsmann (90).

596. 13.06.1993 **UNITED STATES - GERMANY** **3-4(1-3)** International Tournament
Soldier Field, Chicago; Referee: Juan Carlos Lousteau (Argentina); Attendance: 53,500
GER: Andreas Köpke (11/0), Guido Buchwald (64/2), Jürgen Kohler (54/0) [75.Thomas Helmer (18/0)], Michael Schulz (4/0), Thomas Strunz (5/0), Christian Ziege (2/0), Stefan Effenberg (20/4) [60.Andreas Möller (29/7)], Lothar Herbert Matthäus (Cap) (100/19), Uwe Bein (16/3), Jürgen Klinsmann (50/16) [70.Karlheinz Pflipsen (1/0)], Karlheinz Riedle (32/14). Trainer: Hans-Hubert Vogts (29).
Goals: Jürgen Klinsmann (14), Karlheinz Riedle (34, 40, 59).

597. 19.06.1993 **GERMANY - ENGLAND** **2-1(1-1)** International Tournament
Silverdome, Detroit (United States); Referee: Ernesto Filippi Cavani (Uruguay); Attendance: 62,100
GER: Bodo Illgner (41/0) , Thomas Helmer (19/0), Guido Buchwald (65/2), Michael Schulz (5/0), Thomas Strunz (6/0), Christian Ziege (3/0), Stefan Effenberg (21/5) [76.Michael Zorc (6/0)], Lothar Herbert Matthäus (Cap) (101/19), Andreas Möller (30/7) [64.Matthias Sammer (16/1)], Jürgen Klinsmann (51/17), Karlheinz Riedle (33/14). Trainer: Hans-Hubert Vogts (30).
Goals: Stefan Effenberg (26), Jürgen Klinsmann (53).

598. 22.09.1993 **TUNISIA - GERMANY** **1-1(0-0)**
Stade Olympique El Menzah, Tunis; Referee: Rashid Medjiba (Algeria); Attendance: 40,000
GER: Bodo Illgner (42/0), Lothar Herbert Matthäus (Cap) (102/19), Jürgen Kohler (55/0), Michael Schulz (6/0), Guido Buchwald (66/2) [77.Bernd Hobsch (1/0)], Stefan Effenberg (22/5), Christian Ziege (4/0), Maurizio Gaudino (1/0), Uwe Bein (17/3), Karlheinz Riedle (34/14), Andreas Möller (31/8) [68.Ulf Kirsten (5/1)]. Trainer: Hans-Hubert Vogts (31).
Goal: Andreas Möller (55).

599. 13.10.1993 **GERMANY - URUGUAY** **5-0(3-0)**
Wildparkstadion, Karlsruhe; Referee: Gerd Grabher (Austria); Attendance: 29,000
GER: Andreas Köpke (12/0), Lothar Herbert Matthäus (Cap) (103/19), Jürgen Kohler (56/0), Thomas Helmer (20/0) [73.Michael Zorc (7/0)], Thomas Häßler (41/6), Stefan Effenberg (23/5) [87.Thomas Ritter (1/0)], Guido Buchwald (67/3), Christian Ziege (5/0), Andreas Möller (32/9), Karlheinz Riedle (35/15) [61.Ulf Kirsten (6/2)], Jürgen Klinsmann (52/17). Trainer: Hans-Hubert Vogts (32).
Goals: Guido Buchwald (8), Andreas Möller (10), Karlheinz Riedle (12), Ulf Kirsten (70), Luis María Romero (88 own goal).

600. 17.11.1993 **GERMANY - BRAZIL** **2-1(2-1)**
Müngersdorferstadion, Köln; Referee: Jan Damgaard (Denmark); Attendance: 51,000
GER: Bodo Illgner (43/0), Lothar Herbert Matthäus (Cap) (104/19), Stefan Effenberg (24/5), Jürgen Kohler (57/0), Thomas Helmer (21/0), Thomas Häßler (42/6), Guido Buchwald (68/4), Andreas Brehme (75/8), Andreas Möller (33/10), Karlheinz Riedle (36/15) [32.Ulf Kirsten (7/2)], Jürgen Klinsmann (53/17) [84.Maurizio Gaudino (2/0)]. Trainer: Hans-Hubert Vogts (33).
Goals: Guido Buchwald (38), Andreas Möller (41).

601. 15.12.1993 **ARGENTINA - GERMANY** **2-1(1-1)**
Orange Bowl, Miami (United States); Referee: Philip Don (England); Attendance: 32,300
GER: Andreas Köpke (13/0), Lothar Herbert Matthäus (Cap) (105/19), Jürgen Kohler (58/0), Thomas Helmer (22/0), Stefan Effenberg (25/5), Thomas Häßler (43/6), Guido Buchwald (69/4), Andreas Brehme (76/8), Andreas Möller (34/11) [72.Matthias Sammer (17/1)], Ulf Kirsten (8/2), Jürgen Klinsmann (54/17) [70.Andreas Thom (8/1)]. Trainer: Hans-Hubert Vogts (34).
Goal: Andreas Möller (9).

602. 18.12.1993 **UNITED STATES - GERMANY** **0-3(0-1)**
Stanford Stadium, Stanford, Palo Alto; Referee: Rune Pedersen (Norway); Attendance: 52,397
GER: Bodo Illgner (44/0), Lothar Herbert Matthäus (Cap) (106/19), Jürgen Kohler (59/0) [46.Matthias Sammer (18/1)], Guido Buchwald (70/4), Stefan Effenberg (26/5), Thomas Häßler (44/6) [75.Thomas Strunz (7/0)], Dieter Eilts (1/0), Andreas Brehme (77/8) [46.Christian Ziege (6/0)], A. Möller (35/12), Jürgen Klinsmann (55/17) [63.Andreas Thom (9/2)], Stefan Kuntz (1/1). Trainer: Hans-Hubert Vogts (35).
Goals: Andreas Möller (16), Stefan Kuntz (79), Andreas Thom (90).

603. 22.12.1993 **MEXICO - GERMANY** **0-0**
Estadio Azteca, Ciudad de México; Referee: Robert Sawtell (Canada); Attendance: 114,000
GER: Bodo Illgner (45/0), Lothar Herbert Matthäus (Cap) (107/19), Jürgen Kohler (60/0), Michael Schulz (7/0), Thomas Strunz (8/0), Stefan Effenberg (27/5) [78.Dieter Eilts (2/0)], Maurizio Gaudino (3/0) [54.Thomas Häßler (45/6)], Matthias Sammer (19/1), Christian Ziege (7/0) [64.Stefan Kuntz (2/1)], Andreas Möller (36/12), Jürgen Klinsmann (56/17) [71.Ulf Kirsten (9/2)]. Trainer: Hans-Hubert Vogts (36).

604. 23.03.1994 **GERMANY - ITALY** **2-1(1-1)**
„Gottlieb Daimler" Stadion, Stuttgart; Referee: James McCluskey (Scotland); Attendance: 52,800
GER: Bodo Illgner (46/0), Lothar Herbert Matthäus (Cap) (108/19), Guido Buchwald (71/4), Jürgen Kohler (61/0) [72.Thomas Berthold (50/1)], Thomas Strunz (9/0), Stefan Effenberg (28/5), Matthias Sammer (20/1), Andreas Brehme (78/8), Andreas Möller (37/12), Thomas Häßler (46/6) [78.Mario Basler (1/0)], Jürgen Klinsmann (57/19). Trainer: Hans-Hubert Vogts (37).
Goals: Jürgen Klinsmann (45, 47).

605. 27.04.1994 **UNITED ARAB EMIRATES - GERMANY** **0-2(0-0)**
Al Nahyan Stadium, Abu Dhabi; Referee: Ion Crăciunescu (Romania); Attendance: 12,000
GER: Andreas Köpke (14/0), Lothar Herbert Matthäus (Cap) (109/19) [46.Matthias Sammer (21/1)], Jürgen Kohler (62/0), Thomas Berthold (51/1), Thomas Strunz (10/0), Mario Basler (2/0), Guido Buchwald (72/4), Andreas Brehme (79/8) [46.Thomas Helmer (23/0)], Andreas Möller (38/12) [83.Maurizio Gaudino (4/1)], Ulf Kirsten (10/3), Andreas Thom (10/2) [60.Thomas Häßler (47/6)]. Trainer: Hans-Hubert Vogts (38).
Goals: Ulf Kirsten (67), Maurizio Gaudino (90).

606. 29.05.1994 **GERMANY – REPUBLIC OF IRELAND** **0-2(0-1)**
Niedersachsenstadion, Hannover; Referee: José Manuel García-Aranda Encinar (Spain); Attendance: 50,000
GER: Bodo Illgner (47/0), Lothar Herbert Matthäus (Cap) (110/19), Guido Buchwald (73/4) [36.Thomas Berthold (52/1)], Jürgen Kohler (63/0) [46.Thomas Häßler (48/6)], Thomas Strunz (11/0), Mario Basler (3/0), Matthias Sammer (22/1), Martin Wagner (2/0), Andreas Möller (39/12) [46.Stefan Effenberg (29/5)], Jürgen Klinsmann (58/19), Karlheinz Riedle (37/15) [68.Rudolf Völler (86/44)]. Trainer: Hans-Hubert Vogts (39).

607. 02.06.1994 **AUSTRIA - GERMANY** **1-5(0-1)**
„Ernst Happel" Stadion, Wien; Referee: Rémi Harrel (France); Attendance: 35,000
GER: Bodo Illgner (48/0), Lothar Herbert Matthäus (Cap) (111/19) [85.Mario Basler (4/1)], Thomas Berthold (53/1), Jürgen Kohler (64/0), Thomas Strunz (12/0), Stefan Effenberg (30/5), Matthias Sammer (23/2) [72.Thomas Helmer (24/0)], Andreas Brehme (80/8), Thomas Häßler (49/6), Andreas Möller (40/14) [78.Stefan Kuntz (3/1)], Jürgen Klinsmann (59/20) [63.Karlheinz Riedle (38/15)]. Trainer: Hans-Hubert Vogts (40).
Goals: Matthias Sammer (21), Andreas Möller (50), Jürgen Klinsmann (62), Andreas Möller (66), Mario Basler (90).

608. 08.06.1994 **CANADA - GERMANY** **0-2(0-1)**
Varsity Stadium, Toronto; Referee: Stephen Lodge (England); Attendance: 20,100
GER: Bodo Illgner (49/0), Lothar Herbert Matthäus (Cap) (112/19), Thomas Berthold (54/1), Jürgen Kohler (65/0) [46.Thomas Helmer (25/0)], Mario Basler (5/1) [82.Stefan Kuntz (4/1)], Thomas Strunz (13/0) [69.Maurizio Gaudino (5/1)], Matthias Sammer (24/3), Andreas Brehme (81/8), Thomas Häßler (50/6) [66.Martin Wagner (3/0)], Jürgen Klinsmann (60/20) [46.Karlheinz Riedle (39/15)], Rudolf Völler (87/45). Trainer: Hans-Hubert Vogts (41).
Goals: Matthias Sammer (31), Rudolf Völler (90).

609. 17.06.1994 **GERMANY - BOLIVIA** **1-0(0-0)** 15th FIFA WC. Group Stage.
Soldier Field, Chicago (United States); Referee: Arturo Brizio Carter (Mexico); Attendance: 63,100
GER: Bodo Illgner (50/0), Lothar Herbert Matthäus (Cap) (113/19), Jürgen Kohler (66/0), Thomas Berthold (55/1), Stefan Effenberg (31/5), Matthias Sammer (25/3), Andreas Brehme (82/8), Thomas Häßler (51/6) [83.Thomas Strunz (14/0)], Andreas Möller (41/14), Karlheinz Riedle (40/15) [61.Mario Basler (6/1)], Jürgen Klinsmann (61/21). Trainer: Hans-Hubert Vogts (42).
Goal: Jürgen Klinsmann (61).

610. 21.06.1994 **GERMANY - SPAIN** **1-1(0-1)** 15th FIFA WC. Group Stage.
Soldier Field, Chicago (United States); Referee: Ernesto Filippi Cavani (Uruguay); Attendance: 63,000
GER: Bodo Illgner (51/0), Lothar Herbert Matthäus (Cap) (114/19), Jürgen Kohler (67/0), Thomas Berthold (56/1), Thomas Strunz (15/0), Stefan Effenberg (32/5), Matthias Sammer (26/3), Andreas Brehme (83/8), Thomas Häßler (52/6), Andreas Möller (42/14) [62.Rudolf Völler (88/45)], Jürgen Klinsmann (62/22). Trainer: Hans-Hubert Vogts (43).
Goal: Jürgen Klinsmann (48).

611. 27.06.1994 **GERMANY – KOREA REPUBLIC** **3-2(3-0)** 15th FIFA WC. Group Stage.
Cotton Bowl, Dallas (United States); Referee: Joël Quiniou (France); Attendance: 64,000
GER: Bodo Illgner (52/0), Lothar Herbert Matthäus (Cap) (115/19) [64.Andreas Möller (43/14)], Jürgen Kohler (68/0), Thomas Berthold (57/1), Stefan Effenberg (33/5) [57.Thomas Helmer (26/0)], Guido Buchwald (74/4), Andreas Brehme (84/8), Thomas Häßler (53/6), Matthias Sammer (27/3), Jürgen Klinsmann (63/24), Karlheinz Riedle (41/16). Trainer: Hans-Hubert Vogts (44).
Goals: Jürgen Klinsmann (12), Karlheinz Riedle (20), Jürgen Klinsmann (37).

612. 02.07.1994 **GERMANY - BELGIUM** **3-2(3-1)** 15th FIFA WC. 2nd Round of 16.
Soldier Field, Chicago (United States); Referee: Kurt Röthlisberger (Switzerland); Attendance: 60,200
GER: Bodo Illgner (53/0), Lothar Herbert Matthäus (Cap) (116/19) [46.Andreas Brehme (85/8)], Jürgen Kohler (69/0), Thomas Helmer (27/0), Thomas Berthold (58/1), Guido Buchwald (75/4), Martin Wagner (4/0), Thomas Häßler (54/6), Matthias Sammer (28/3), Jürgen Klinsmann (64/25) [86.Stefan Kuntz (5/1)], Rudolf Völler (89/47). Trainer: Hans-Hubert Vogts (45).
Goals: Rudolf Völler (6), Jürgen Klinsmann (11), Rudolf Völler (39).

613. 10.07.1994 **BULGARIA - GERMANY** **2-1(0-0)** 15th FIFA WC. Quarter-Finals.
Giants Stadium, New Jersey (United States); Referee: José Joaquín Torres Cadena (Colombia); Attendance: 72,400
GER: Bodo Illgner (54/0), Lothar Herbert Matthäus (Cap) (117/20), Jürgen Kohler (70/0), Thomas Helmer (28/0), Thomas Berthold (59/1), Martin Wagner (5/0) [60.Thomas Strunz (16/0)], Thomas Häßler (55/6) [83.Andreas Brehme (86/8)], Guido Buchwald (76/4), Andreas Möller (44/14), Rudolf Völler (90/47), Jürgen Klinsmann (65/25). Trainer: Hans-Hubert Vogts (46).
Goal: Lothar Herbert Matthäus (49 penalty).

614. 04.09.1994 **RUSSIA - GERMANY** **0-1(0-1)**
Luzhniki Stadium, Moskva; Referee: Piotr Werner (Poland); Attendance: 35,000
GER: Andreas Köpke (15/0), Lothar Herbert Matthäus (Cap) (118/20), Jürgen Kohler (71/0), Thomas Helmer (29/0), Thomas Strunz (17/0), Dieter Eilts (3/0), Ralf Weber (1/0), Mario Basler (7/1) [61.Andreas Möller (45/14)], Thomas Häßler (56/6), Jürgen Klinsmann (66/25), Stefan Kuntz (6/2) [74.Karlheinz Riedle (42/16)]. Trainer: Hans-Hubert Vogts (47).
Goal: Stefan Kuntz (7).

615. 12.10.1994 **HUNGARY - GERMANY** **0-0**
Népstadion, Budapest; Referee: Michel Zen-Ruffinen (Switzerland); Attendance: 20,000
GER: Andreas Köpke (16/0), Lothar Herbert Matthäus (Cap) (119/20) [46.Stefan Reuter (39/2)], Jürgen Kohler (72/0), Dirk Schuster (1/0), Thomas Strunz (18/0), Dieter Eilts (4/0) [46.Martin Wagner (6/0)], Jens Todt (1/0), Ralf Weber (2/0), Thomas Häßler (57/6), Jürgen Klinsmann (67/25), Fredi Bobic (1/0) [85.Olaf Marschall (1/0)]. Trainer: Hans-Hubert Vogts (48).

616. 16.11.1994 **ALBANIA - GERMANY** **1-2(1-1)** 10th EC. Qualifiers
Stadiumi „Kombëtar Qemal Stafa", Tiranë; Referee: Vasily Melnichuk (Ukraine); Attendance: 24,000
GER: Andreas Köpke (17/0), Lothar Herbert Matthäus (Cap) (120/20), Thomas Berthold (60/1), Jürgen Kohler (73/0), Stefan Reuter (40/2), Dieter Eilts (5/0), Andreas Möller (46/14), Matthias Sammer (29/3) [46.Thomas Strunz (19/0)], Ralf Weber (3/0) [83.Dirk Schuster (2/0)], Jürgen Klinsmann (68/26), Ulf Kirsten (11/4). Trainer: Hans-Hubert Vogts (49).
Goals: Jürgen Klinsmann (18), Ulf Kirsten (46).

617. 14.12.1994 **MOLDOVA - GERMANY** **0-3(0-2)** 10th EC. Qualifiers
Stadionul Republican, Chişinău; Referee: Jef van Vliet (Netherlands); Attendance: 20,000
GER: Andreas Köpke (18/0), Lothar Herbert Matthäus (Cap) (121/21), Thomas Berthold (61/1), Stefan Reuter (41/2), Matthias Sammer (30/3), Thomas Helmer (30/0), Thomas Häßler (58/6), Andreas Möller (47/14) [79.Stefan Kuntz (7/2)], Ralf Weber (4/0), Jürgen Klinsmann (69/27), Ulf Kirsten (12/5) [69.Thomas Strunz (20/0)]. Trainer: Hans-Hubert Vogts (50).
Goals: Ulf Kirsten (7), Jürgen Klinsmann (38), Lothar Herbert Matthäus (72).

618. 18.12.1994 **GERMANY - ALBANIA** **2-1(2-0)** 10th EC. Qualifiers
„Fritz Walter" Stadion, Kaiserslautern; Referee: Svend Erik Christensen (Denmark); Attendance: 20,300
GER: Andreas Köpke (19/0), Lothar Herbert Matthäus (Cap) (122/22), Thomas Berthold (62/1), Thomas Helmer (31/0), Stefan Reuter (42/2), Matthias Sammer (31/3), Ralf Weber (5/0), Thomas Häßler (59/6) [78.Thomas Strunz (21/0)], Andreas Möller (48/14), Jürgen Klinsmann (70/28), Ulf Kirsten (13/5) [59.Stefan Kuntz (8/2)]. Trainer: Hans-Hubert Vogts (51).
Goals: Lothar Herbert Matthäus (8 penalty), Jürgen Klinsmann (17).

619. 22.02.1995 **SPAIN - GERMANY** **0-0**
Estadio Municipal de Chapín, Jerez de la Frontera; Referee: Leif Sundell (Sweden); Attendance: 19,000
GER: Andreas Köpke (20/0), Thomas Helmer (32/0), Markus Babbel (1/0), Christian Wörns (5/0) [75.Mario Basler (8/1)], Steffen Freund (1/0), Jens Todt (2/0), Dirk Schuster (3/0) [46.Ralf Weber (6/0)], Thomas Häßler (60/6), Andreas Möller (49/14), Jürgen Klinsmann (Cap) (71/28), Ulf Kirsten (14/5). Trainer: Hans-Hubert Vogts (52).

620. 29.03.1995 **GEORGIA - GERMANY** **0-2(0-2)** 10th EC. Qualifiers
„Boris Paichadze" Erovnuli Stadioni, Tbilisi; Referee: Martin Bodenham (England); Attendance: 75,000
GER: Andreas Köpke (21/0), Thomas Helmer (33/0), Jürgen Kohler (74/0), Markus Babbel (2/0), Stefan Reuter (43/2), Dieter Eilts (6/0), Ralf Weber (7/0) [46.Steffen Freund (2/0)], Mario Basler (9/1), Andreas Möller (50/14), Jürgen Klinsmann (Cap) (72/30), Heiko Herrlich (1/0). Trainer: Hans-Hubert Vogts (53).
Goals: Jürgen Klinsmann (24, 45).

621. 26.04.1995 **GERMANY - WALES** **1-1(1-1)** 10th EC. Qualifiers
Rheinstadion, Düsseldorf; Referee: José Manuel García-Aranda Encinar (Spain); Attendance: 43,500
GER: Andreas Köpke (22/0), Stefan Reuter (44/2), Dieter Eilts (7/0), Markus Babbel (3/0), Steffen Freund (3/0), Mario Basler (10/1) [76.Mehmet Scholl (1/0)], Thomas Häßler (61/6), Christian Ziege (8/0) [86.Stefan Kuntz (9/2)], Ralf Weber (8/0), Heiko Herrlich (2/1), Jürgen Klinsmann (Cap) (73/30). Trainer: Hans-Hubert Vogts (54).
Goal: Heiko Herrlich (42).

622. 07.06.1995 **BULGARIA - GERMANY** **3-2(1-2)** 10th EC. Qualifiers
Nationalen stadion "Vasil Levski", Sofia; Referee: Pierluigi Pairetto (Italy); Attendance: 70,000
GER: Andreas Köpke (23/0), Matthias Sammer (32/3), Stefan Reuter (45/2), Markus Babbel (4/0), Thomas Helmer (34/0), Mario Basler (11/1) [80.Andreas Möller (51/14)], Thomas Strunz (22/1) [90.Ulf Kirsten (15/5)], Dieter Eilts (8/0), Thomas Häßler (62/6), Jürgen Klinsmann (Cap) (74/31), Heiko Herrlich (3/1). Trainer: Hans-Hubert Vogts (55).
Goals: Jürgen Klinsmann (18), Thomas Strunz (44).

623. 21.06.1995 **ITALY - GERMANY** **0-2(0-2)** International Tournament
Letzigrund Stadion, Zürich (Switzerland); Referee: Claude Detruche (Switzerland); Attendance: 17,000
GER: Andreas Köpke (24/0), Matthias Sammer (33/3), Markus Babbel (5/0), Steffen Freund (4/0), Stefan Reuter (46/2), Thomas Helmer (35/1), Jörg Heinrich (1/0), Thomas Häßler (Cap) (63/6), Christian Ziege (9/0), Ulf Kirsten (16/5), Stefan Kuntz (10/2) [82.Fredi Bobic (2/0)]. Trainer: Hans-Hubert Vogts (56).
Goals: Thomas Helmer (4), Paolo Maldini (38 own goal).

624. 23.06.1995 **SWITZERLAND - GERMANY** **1-2(0-0)** International Tournament
Wankdorf Stadion, Bern; Referee: Gerd Grabher (Austria); Attendance: 17,000
GER: Oliver Kahn (1/0), Matthias Sammer (34/3), Steffen Freund (5/0), Thomas Helmer (36/1), Stefan Reuter (47/2), Jens Todt (3/0), Christian Ziege (10/0), Andreas Möller (52/15), Thomas Häßler (Cap) (64/7), Mehmet Scholl (2/0) [46.Ralf Weber (9/0)], Stefan Kuntz (11/2). Trainer: Hans-Hubert Vogts (57).
Goals: Thomas Häßler (63), Andreas Möller (83).

625. 23.08.1995 **BELGIUM - GERMANY** **1-2(1-1)**
Stade „Roi Baudouin", Bruxelles; Referee: Mario van der Ende (Netherlands); Attendance: 33,000
GER: Andreas Köpke (25/0), Thomas Helmer (37/1), Jürgen Kohler (Cap) (75/0) [57.Marco Haber (1/0); 80.Bruno Labbadia (2/0)], Thomas Strunz (23/1) [46.Dieter Eilts (9/0)], Markus Babbel (6/0), Steffen Freund (6/0), Jörg Heinrich (2/0), Mario Basler (12/1), Andreas Möller (53/16), Fredi Bobic (3/1), Mehmet Scholl (3/0). Trainer: Hans-Hubert Vogts (58).
Goals: Andreas Möller (6), Fredi Bobic (84).

626. 06.09.1995 **GERMANY - GEORGIA** **4-1(1-1)** 10th EC. Qualifiers
Frankenstadion, Nürnberg; Referee: James McCluskey (Scotland); Attendance: 44,500
GER: Oliver Kahn (2/0), Thomas Helmer (38/1), Jürgen Kohler (76/0), Markus Babbel (7/1), Thomas Strunz (24/1), Steffen Freund (7/0), Christian Ziege (11/1), Thomas Häßler (65/7), Andreas Möller (54/17), Jürgen Klinsmann (Cap) (75/31), Ulf Kirsten (17/6). Trainer: Hans-Hubert Vogts (59).
Goals: Andreas Möller (39), Christian Ziege (57), Ulf Kirsten (62), Markus Babbel (72).

627. 08.10.1995 **GERMANY - MOLDOVA** **6-1(3-0)** 10th EC. Qualifiers
„Ulrich Haberland" Stadion, Leverkusen; Referee: Zygmunt Ziober (Poland); Attendance: 18,400
GER: Andreas Köpke (26/0), Matthias Sammer (35/5) [83.Christian Wörns (6/0)], Markus Babbel (8/1), Thomas Helmer (39/2), Steffen Freund (8/0), Thomas Häßler (66/7), Dieter Eilts (10/0), Andreas Möller (55/19) [78.Mehmet Scholl (4/0)], Christian Ziege (12/1), Jürgen Klinsmann (Cap) (76/31), Heiko Herrlich (4/1) [64.Fredi Bobic (4/1)]. Trainer: Hans-Hubert Vogts (60).
Goals: Serghei Stroenco (16 own goal), Thomas Helmer (18), Matthias Sammer (24), Andreas Möller (47, 61), Matthias Sammer (72).

628. 11.10.1995 **WALES - GERMANY** **1-2(0-0)** 10th EC. Qualifiers
Arms Park, Cardiff; Referee: Ion Crăciunescu (Romania); Attendance: 21,000
GER: Andreas Köpke (27/0), Matthias Sammer (36/5), Markus Babbel (9/1) [46.Christian Wörns (7/0)], Thomas Helmer (40/2), Steffen Freund (9/0), Thomas Häßler (67/7), Dieter Eilts (11/0), Andreas Möller (56/19), Christian Ziege (13/1), Jürgen Klinsmann (Cap) (77/32), Heiko Herrlich (5/1) [74.Stefan Kuntz (12/2)]. Trainer: Hans-Hubert Vogts (61).
Goals: Andrew Roger Melville (75 own goal), Jürgen Klinsmann (81).

629. 15.11.1995 **GERMANY – BULGARIA** **3-1(0-0)** 10th EC. Qualifiers
Olympiastadion, Berlin; Referee: Vassilis Nikakis (Greece); Attendance: 75,800
GER: Andreas Köpke (28/0), Matthias Sammer (37/5), Markus Babbel (10/1), Jürgen Kohler (77/0) [46.Thomas Strunz (25/1)], Steffen Freund (10/0), Dieter Eilts (12/0), Mario Basler (13/1), Thomas Häßler (68/8) [87.Stefan Reuter (48/2)], Thomas Helmer (41/2), Jürgen Klinsmann (Cap) (78/34), Stefan Kuntz (13/2) [82.Fredi Bobic (5/1)]. Trainer: Hans-Hubert Vogts (62).
Goals: Jürgen Klinsmann (50), Thomas Häßler (56), Jürgen Klinsmann (76 penalty).

630. 15.12.1995 **SOUTH AFRICA - GERMANY** **0-0**
Athletics Stadium, Johannesburg; Referee: Dermot Gallagher (England); Attendance: 30,000
GER: Andreas Köpke (29/0), Thomas Helmer (42/2), Jürgen Kohler (78/0) [77.Stefan Kuntz (14/2)], René Schneider (1/0), Marco Haber (2/0) [63.Christian Wörns (8/0)], Thomas Häßler (69/8), Stefan Reuter (49/2), Andreas Möller (57/19), Marco Bode (1/0), Jürgen Klinsmann (Cap) (79/34), Fredi Bobic (6/1). Trainer: Hans-Hubert Vogts (63).

631. 21.02.1996 **PORTUGAL - GERMANY** **1-2(0-1)**
Estádio das Antas, Porto; Referee: Robert Anthony Boggi (Italy); Attendance: 20,000
GER: Andreas Köpke (30/0), Matthias Sammer (38/5), Markus Babbel (11/1), Jürgen Kohler (79/0), Thomas Helmer (43/2), Steffen Freund (11/0), Andreas Möller (58/21), Thomas Häßler (70/8) [69.Mario Basler (14/1)], Christian Ziege (14/1) [46.Jörg Albertz (1/0)], Jürgen Klinsmann (Cap) (80/34), Stefan Kuntz (15/2) [46.Oliver Bierhoff (1/0)]. Trainer: Hans-Hubert Vogts (64).
Goals: Andreas Möller (14, 62).

632. 27.03.1996 **GERMANY - DENMARK** **2-0(1-0)**
Olympiastadion, München; Referee: Renatus Hendrikus Johannes „René" Temmink (Netherlands); Attendance: 26,000
GER: Oliver Kahn (3/0) [18.Andreas Köpke (31/0)], Thomas Helmer (44/2), Jürgen Kohler (80/0), Stefan Reuter (50/2) [46.Markus Babbel (12/1)], Steffen Freund (12/0) [85.Jörg Albertz (2/0)], Dieter Eilts (13/0), Christian Ziege (15/1), Thomas Häßler (71/8), Mehmet Scholl (5/0) [76.Mario Basler (15/1)], Oliver Bierhoff (2/2), Jürgen Klinsmann (Cap) (81/34). Trainer: Hans-Hubert Vogts (65).
Goals: Oliver Bierhoff (44, 61).

633. 24.04.1996 **NETHERLANDS - GERMANY** **0-1(0-1)**
Stadion Feijenoord, Rotterdam; Referee: Pierluigi Collina (Italy); Attendance: 27,000
GER: Andreas Köpke (32/0), Matthias Sammer (39/5) [46.Thomas Helmer (45/2)], Stefan Reuter (51/2), Jürgen Kohler (81/0), Christian Ziege (16/1), Steffen Freund (13/0), Dieter Eilts (14/0) [79.Markus Babbel (13/1)], Thomas Häßler (72/8) [90.Stefan Kuntz (16/2)], Mario Basler (16/1) [84.Mehmet Scholl (6/0)], Jürgen Klinsmann (Cap) (82/35), Oliver Bierhoff (3/2). Trainer: Hans-Hubert Vogts (66).
Goal: Jürgen Klinsmann (19 penalty).

634. 29.05.1996 **NORTHERN IRELAND - GERMANY** **1-1(0-0)**
Windsor Park, Belfast; Referee: William Young (Scotland); Attendance: 10,000
GER: Oliver Kahn (4/0), Thomas Helmer (46/2), Jürgen Kohler (82/0), Christian Ziege (17/1) [46.Marco Bode (2/0)], Mario Basler (17/1), Thomas Strunz (26/1), Dieter Eilts (15/0), Andreas Möller (59/21), Mehmet Scholl (7/1), Jürgen Klinsmann (Cap) (83/35) [46.Fredi Bobic (7/1)], Oliver Bierhoff (4/2) [46.Stefan Kuntz (17/2)]. Trainer: Hans-Hubert Vogts (67).
Goal: Mehmet Scholl (77).

635. 01.06.1996 **GERMANY - FRANCE** **0-1(0-1)**
„Gottlieb Daimler" Stadion, Stuttgart; Referee: Ryszard Wójcik (Poland); Attendance: 53,100
GER: Andreas Köpke (33/0), Matthias Sammer (40/5), Markus Babbel (14/1), Stefan Reuter (52/2), Dieter Eilts (16/0) [46.Steffen Freund (14/0)], Thomas Helmer (47/2), Christian Ziege (18/1) [83.Mehmet Scholl (8/1)], Thomas Häßler (73/8) [46.Mario Basler (18/1)], Andreas Möller (60/21), Fredi Bobic (8/1), Jürgen Klinsmann (Cap) (84/35). Trainer: Hans-Hubert Vogts (68).

636. 04.06.1996 **GERMANY - LIECHTENSTEIN** **9-1(4-0)**
„Carl Benz" Stadion, Mannheim; Referee: Werner Müller (Switzerland); Attendance: 26,000
GER: Oliver Reck (1/0), Matthias Sammer (41/6), Jürgen Kohler (Cap) (83/1), Stefan Reuter (53/2) [76.Steffen Freund (15/0)], Dieter Eilts (17/0) [46.Thomas Strunz (27/1)], Thomas Helmer (48/2) [46.Marco Bode (3/0)], Christian Ziege (19/2) [76.Jürgen Klinsmann (85/36)], Thomas Häßler (74/8) [46.Mario Basler (19/1)], Andreas Möller (61/23) [64.Mehmet Scholl (9/1)], Oliver Bierhoff (5/3), Stefan Kuntz (18/4). Trainer: Hans-Hubert Vogts (69).
Goals: Andreas Möller (4), Stefan Kuntz (18), Oliver Bierhoff (22), Christian Ziege (38), Matthias Sammer (48), Jürgen Kohler (53), Andreas Möller (64), Jürgen Klinsmann (85), Stefan Kuntz (90).

637. 09.06.1996 **GERMANY – CZECH REPUBLIC** **2-0(2-0)** 10th EC. Group Stage.
Old Trafford, Manchester (England); Referee: David R.Elleray (England); Attendance: 42,000
GER: Andreas Köpke (34/0), Matthias Sammer (42/6), Jürgen Kohler (Cap) (84/1) [14.Markus Babbel (15/1)], Thomas Helmer (49/2), Stefan Reuter (54/2), Dieter Eilts (18/0), Christian Ziege (20/3), Thomas Häßler (75/8), Andreas Möller (62/24), Fredi Bobic (9/1) [65.Thomas Strunz (28/1)], Stefan Kuntz (19/4) [83.Oliver Bierhoff (6/3)]. Trainer: Hans-Hubert Vogts (70).
Goals: Christian Ziege (26), Andreas Möller (32).

638. 16.06.1996 **GERMANY - RUSSIA** **3-0(0-0)** 10th EC. Group Stage.
Old Trafford, Manchester (England); Referee: Kim Milton Nielsen (Denmark); Attendance: 50,800
GER: Andreas Köpke (35/0), Matthias Sammer (43/7), Markus Babbel (16/1), Stefan Reuter (55/2), Dieter Eilts (19/0), Thomas Helmer (50/2), Christian Ziege (21/3), Thomas Häßler (76/8) [66.Steffen Freund (16/0)], Andreas Möller (63/24) [87.Thomas Strunz (29/1)], Oliver Bierhoff (7/3) [85.Stefan Kuntz (20/4)], Jürgen Klinsmann (Cap) (86/38). Trainer: Hans-Hubert Vogts (71).
Goals: Matthias Sammer (56), Jürgen Klinsmann (77, 90).

639. 19.06.1996 **ITALY - GERMANY** **0-0** 10th EC. Group Stage.
Old Trafford, Manchester (England); Referee: Guy Goethals (Belgium); Attendance: 53,700
GER: Andreas Köpke (36/0), Matthias Sammer (44/7), Steffen Freund (17/0), Thomas Helmer (51/2), Thomas Strunz (30/1) [*sent off 60*], Dieter Eilts (20/0), Christian Ziege (22/3), Thomas Häßler (77/8), Andreas Möller (64/24) [89.Marco Bode (4/0)], Jürgen Klinsmann (Cap) (87/38), Fredi Bobic (10/1). Trainer: Hans-Hubert Vogts (72).

640. 23.06.1996 **GERMANY - CROATIA** **2-1(1-0)** 10th EC. Quarter-Finals.
Old Trafford, Manchester (England); Referee: Leif Sundell (Sweden); Attendance: 43,400
GER: Andreas Köpke (37/0), Matthias Sammer (45/8), Markus Babbel (17/1), Thomas Helmer (52/2), Stefan Reuter (56/2), Dieter Eilts (21/0), Christian Ziege (23/3), Mehmet Scholl (10/1) [88.Thomas Häßler (78/8)], Andreas Möller (65/24), Jürgen Klinsmann (Cap) (88/39) [39.Steffen Freund (18/0)], Fredi Bobic (11/1) [46.Stefan Kuntz (21/4)]. Trainer: Hans-Hubert Vogts (73).
Goals: Jürgen Klinsmann (21 penalty), Matthias Sammer (59).

641. 26.06.1996 **ENGLAND - GERMANY** **1-1(1-1,1-1); 5-6 on penalties** 10th EC. Semi-Finals.
Wembley Stadium, London; Referee: Sándor Puhl (Hungary); Attendance: 75,900
GER: Andreas Köpke (38/0), Matthias Sammer (46/8), Markus Babbel (18/1), Thomas Helmer (53/2) [110.Marco Bode (5/0)], Stefan Reuter (57/2), Steffen Freund (19/0) [119.Thomas Strunz (31/1)], Dieter Eilts (22/0), Christian Ziege (24/3), Mehmet Scholl (11/1) [77.Thomas Häßler (79/8)], Andreas Möller (Cap) (66/24), Stefan Kuntz (22/5). Trainer: Hans-Hubert Vogts (74).
Goal: Stefan Kuntz (16).
Penalties: Thomas Häßler, Thomas Strunz, Stefan Reuter, Christian Ziege, Stefan Kuntz, Andreas Möller.

642. 30.06.1996 **GERMANY – CZECH REPUBLIC** **2-1(0-0,1-1) Golden Goal** 10th EC. Final.
Wembley Stadium, London (England); Referee: Pierluigi Pairetto (Italy); Attendance: 73,600
GER: Andreas Köpke (39/0), Matthias Sammer (47/8), Markus Babbel (19/1), Thomas Strunz (32/1), Dieter Eilts (23/0) [46.Marco Bode (6/0)], Thomas Helmer (54/2), Christian Ziege (25/3), Mehmet Scholl (12/1) [69.Oliver Bierhoff (8/5)], Thomas Häßler (80/8), Jürgen Klinsmann (Cap) (89/39), Stefan Kuntz (23/5). Trainer: Hans-Hubert Vogts (75).
Goals: Oliver Bierhoff (73, 95).

643. 04.09.1996 **POLAND - GERMANY** **0-2(0-1)**
Stadion Górnik, Zabrze; Referee: Paul Durkin (England); Attendance: 12,000
GER: Oliver Kahn (5/0), Thomas Helmer (55/2), Jürgen Kohler (85/1), Stefan Reuter (58/2) [79.Markus Babbel (20/1)], Dieter Eilts (24/0), Thomas Strunz (33/1), Christian Ziege (26/3) [46.Marco Bode (7/0)], Thomas Häßler (81/8), Andreas Möller (67/24) [56.Mehmet Scholl (13/1)], Jürgen Klinsmann (Cap) (90/40), Oliver Bierhoff (9/6) [76.Fredi Bobic (12/1)]. Trainer: Hans-Hubert Vogts (76).
Goals: Oliver Bierhoff (28), Jürgen Klinsmann (89).

644. 09.10.1996 **ARMENIA - GERMANY** **1-5(0-3)** 16th FIFA WC. Qualifiers
Hrazdan Stadium, Yerevan; Referee: Pierluigi Collina (Italy); Attendance: 50,000
GER: Andreas Köpke (40/0), Stefan Reuter (59/2), Markus Babbel (21/1), Jürgen Kohler (86/1), Stephan Paßlack (1/0), Dieter Eilts (25/0), Marco Bode (8/0) [73.Stefan Kuntz (24/6)], Thomas Häßler (82/10) [77.Michael Tarnat (1/0)], Mehmet Scholl (14/1), Jürgen Klinsmann (Cap) (91/41), Oliver Bierhoff (10/6) [64.Fredi Bobic (13/2)]. Trainer: Hans-Hubert Vogts (77).
Goals: Thomas Häßler (20), Jürgen Klinsmann (26), Thomas Häßler (39), Fredi Bobic (69), Stefan Kuntz (81).

645. 09.11.1996 **GERMANY – NORTHERN IRELAND** **1-1(1-1)** 16th FIFA WC. Qualifiers
Frankenstadion, Nürnberg; Referee: Ahmet Çakar (Turkey); Attendance: 40,700
GER: Andreas Köpke (41/0), Stefan Reuter (60/2), Jürgen Kohler (87/1), Markus Babbel (22/1), Michael Tarnat (2/0), Thomas Strunz (34/1), Dieter Eilts (26/0) [62.Stephan Paßlack (2/0)], Thomas Häßler (83/10), Andreas Möller (68/25), Fredi Bobic (14/2) [70.Oliver Bierhoff (11/6)], Jürgen Klinsmann (Cap) (92/41). Trainer: Hans-Hubert Vogts (78).
Goal: Andreas Möller (41).

646. 14.12.1996 **PORTUGAL - GERMANY** **0-0** 16th FIFA WC. Qualifiers
Estádio da Luz, Lisboa; Referee: Sándor Puhl (Hungary); Attendance: 50,000
GER: Andreas Köpke (42/0), Matthias Sammer (48/8), Jürgen Kohler (88/1), Stefan Reuter (61/2), Markus Babbel (23/1) [84.Michael Tarnat (3/0)], Dieter Eilts (27/0), Christian Ziege (27/3), Mario Basler (20/1) [70.Ulf Kirsten (18/6)], Andreas Möller (69/25), Jürgen Klinsmann (Cap) (93/41), Fredi Bobic (15/2). Trainer: Hans-Hubert Vogts (79).

647. 26.02.1997 **ISRAEL - GERMANY** **0-1(0-0)**
National Stadium, Ramat Gan, Tel Aviv; Referee: Stefano Braschi (Italy); Attendance: 15,000
GER: Oliver Kahn (6/0), Matthias Sammer (49/8), Jürgen Kohler (89/1), Markus Babbel (24/1), Dieter Eilts (28/0), Christian Ziege (28/3), Mario Basler (21/1) [90.Jörg Heinrich (3/0)], Andreas Möller (70/25), Dariusz Wosz (1/1), Jürgen Klinsmann (Cap) (94/41), Fredi Bobic (16/2) [46.Ulf Kirsten (19/6)]. Trainer: Hans-Hubert Vogts (80).
Goal: Dariusz Wosz (85).

648. 02.04.1997 **ALBANIA - GERMANY** **2-3(0-0)** 16th FIFA WC. Qualifiers
Estadio Nuevo Los Cármenes, Granada (Spain); Referee: Michel Piraux (Belgium); Attendance: 9,780
GER: Andreas Köpke (43/0), Matthias Sammer (50/8), Jürgen Kohler (90/1), Thomas Helmer (56/2), Stefan Reuter (62/2) [61.Jörg Heinrich (4/0)], Dieter Eilts (29/0) [62.Ulf Kirsten (20/9)], Christian Ziege (29/3), Andreas Möller (71/25), Dariusz Wosz (2/1), Jürgen Klinsmann (Cap) (95/41), Oliver Bierhoff (12/6). Trainer: Hans-Hubert Vogts (81).
Goals: Ulf Kirsten (63, 80, 84).

649. 30.04.1997 **GERMANY - UKRAINE** **2-0(0-0)** 16th FIFA WC. Qualifiers
Weserstadion, Bremen; Referee: Anders Frisk (Sweden); Attendance: 33,000
GER: Andreas Köpke (44/0), Jürgen Kohler (91/1), Thomas Helmer (57/2), Jörg Heinrich (5/0), Dieter Eilts (30/0), Christian Ziege (30/3), Mario Basler (22/2), Fredi Bobic (17/2) [15.Jens Nowotny (1/0)], Dariusz Wosz (3/1) [84.Michael Tarnat (4/0)], Oliver Bierhoff (13/7), Jürgen Klinsmann (Cap) (96/41). Trainer: Hans-Hubert Vogts (82).
Goals: Oliver Bierhoff (62), Mario Basler (72).

650. 07.06.1997 **UKRAINE - GERMANY** **0-0** 16th FIFA WC. Qualifiers
Olimpiyksyi Stadium, Kyiv; Referee: László Vágner (Hungary); Attendance: 65,000
GER: Andreas Köpke (45/0), Matthias Sammer (51/8), Jürgen Kohler (92/1), Jörg Heinrich (6/0), Dieter Eilts (31/0), Thomas Helmer (58/2), Christian Ziege (31/3), Mario Basler (23/2), Dariusz Wosz (4/1) [70.Mehmet Scholl (15/1)], Jürgen Klinsmann (Cap) (97/41), Ulf Kirsten (21/9) [88.Oliver Bierhoff (14/7)]. Trainer: Hans-Hubert Vogts (83).

651. 20.08.1997 **NORTHERN IRELAND - GERMANY** **1-3(0-0)** 16th FIFA WC. Qualifiers
Windsor Park, Belfast; Referee: José Manuel García-Aranda Encinar (Spain); Attendance: 13,400
GER: Andreas Köpke (46/0), Thomas Helmer (59/2), Jürgen Kohler (93/1), Christian Wörns (9/0) [64.Thomas Häßler (84/10)], Jens Nowotny (2/0), Jörg Heinrich (7/0), Mario Basler (24/2) [83.Markus Babbel (25/1)], Andreas Möller (72/25), Christian Ziege (32/3), Jürgen Klinsmann (Cap) (98/41), Ulf Kirsten (22/9) [70.Oliver Bierhoff (15/10)]. Trainer: Hans-Hubert Vogts (84).
Goals: Oliver Bierhoff (73, 78, 79).

652. 06.09.1997 **GERMANY - PORTUGAL** **1-1(0-0)** 16th FIFA WC. Qualifiers
Olympiastadion, Berlin; Referee: Marc Batta (France); Attendance: 75,800
GER: Andreas Köpke (47/0), Thomas Helmer (60/2), Jürgen Kohler (94/1), Jörg Heinrich (8/0) [79.Dariusz Wosz (5/1)], Stefan Reuter (63/2) [46.Markus Babbel (26/1)], Jens Nowotny (3/0), Christian Ziege (33/3), Mario Basler (25/2), Thomas Häßler (85/10), Jürgen Klinsmann (Cap) (99/41), Oliver Bierhoff (16/10) [70.Ulf Kirsten (23/10)]. Trainer: Hans-Hubert Vogts (85).
Goal: Ulf Kirsten (81).

653. 10.09.1997 **GERMANY - ARMENIA** **4-0(0-0)** 16th FIFA WC. Qualifiers
Westfalenstadion, Dortmund; Referee: Peter Mikkelsen (Denmark); Attendance: 43,000
GER: Andreas Köpke (48/0), Olaf Thon (41/3), Christian Wörns (10/0), Thomas Helmer (61/2), Jörg Heinrich (9/0), Sven Kmetsch (1/0) [46.Lars Ricken (1/0)], Michael Tarnat (5/0) [66.Oliver Bierhoff (17/10)], Thomas Häßler (86/11), Dariusz Wosz (6/1) [81.Jens Nowotny (4/0)], Jürgen Klinsmann (Cap) (100/43), Ulf Kirsten (24/11). Trainer: Hans-Hubert Vogts (86).
Goals: Jürgen Klinsmann (70, 84), Thomas Häßler (86), Ulf Kirsten (90).

654. 11.10.1997 **GERMANY - ALBANIA** **4-3(0-0)** 16th FIFA WC. Qualifiers
Niedersachsenstadion, Hannover; Referee: Rune Pedersen (Norway); Attendance: 44,500
GER: Oliver Kahn (7/0), Jürgen Kohler (Cap) (95/1), Thomas Helmer (62/3), Olaf Thon (42/3), Thomas Häßler (87/11), Stefan Reuter (64/2), Jörg Heinrich (10/0), Andreas Möller (73/25), Stefan Kuntz (25/6) [72.Olaf Marschall (2/1)], Fredi Bobic (18/2) [60.Michael Tarnat (6/0)], Oliver Bierhoff (18/12). Trainer: Hans-Hubert Vogts (87).
Goals: Thomas Helmer (64), Oliver Bierhoff (73), Olaf Marschall (86), Oliver Bierhoff (90).

655. 15.11.1997 **GERMANY – SOUTH AFRICA** **3-0(2-0)**
Rheinstadion, Düsseldorf; Referee: Luboš Michel (Slovakia); Attendance: 27,000
GER: Oliver Kahn (8/0), Christian Wörns (11/0), Thomas Linke (1/0), Thomas Helmer (63/3) [78.Michael Tarnat (7/0)], Mario Basler (26/2), Dietmar Hamann (1/1), Jens Jeremies (1/0), Christian Ziege (34/3) [46.Jörg Heinrich (11/1)], Thomas Häßler (Cap) (88/11), Oliver Bierhoff (19/13), Ulf Kirsten (25/11) [46.Olaf Marschall (3/1)]. Trainer: Hans-Hubert Vogts (88).
Goals: Dietmar Hamann (13), Oliver Bierhoff (33), Jörg Heinrich (70).

656. 18.02.1998 **OMAN - GERMANY** **0-2(0-1)**
"Sultan Qaboos" Sports Complex, Muscat; Referee: Ali Al Shaikh Al Setri (Bahrain); Attendance: 10,000
GER: Andreas Köpke (49/0) [46.Jens Lehmann (1/0)], Jürgen Kohler (Cap) (96/2), Christian Wörns (12/0), Lars Ricken (2/0) [46.Andreas Möller (74/25)], Sven Kmetsch (2/0) [46.Stefan Reuter (65/2)], Olaf Thon (43/3), Jens Jeremies (2/0), Jörg Heinrich (12/2), Thomas Häßler (89/11), Oliver Bierhoff (20/13), Ulf Kirsten (26/11). Trainer: Hans-Hubert Vogts (89).
Goals: Jürgen Kohler (27), Jörg Heinrich (63).

657. 22.02.1998 **SAUDI ARABIA - GERMANY** **0-3(0-1)**
"King Fahd" International Stadium, Riyadh; Referee: Sultan Mjalli Khamis (Bahrain); Attendance: 17,000
GER: Andreas Köpke (50/0), Thomas Linke (2/0), Jürgen Kohler (Cap) (97/2), Dietmar Hamann (2/1), Olaf Thon (44/3) [46.Jens Nowotny (5/0)], Thoma Helmer (64/4), Mario Basler (27/2) [57.Thomas Häßler (90/11)], Andreas Möller (75/26), Michael Tarnat (8/0), Oliver Bierhoff (21/13) [46.Fredi Bobi (19/2)], Ulf Kirsten (27/11) [46.Olaf Marschall (4/2)]. Trainer: Hans-Hubert Vogts (90).
Goals: Andreas Möller (19), Thomas Helmer (72), Olaf Marschall (90).

658. 25.03.1998 **GERMANY - BRAZIL** **1-2(0-1)**
„Gottlieb Daimler" Stadion, Stuttgart; Referee: David R.Elleray (England); Attendance: 52,800
GER: Andreas Köpke (51/0), Olaf Thon (45/3), Christian Wörns (13/0), Jürgen Kohler (98/2) [*sent off 35*], Jörg Heinrich (13/2), Dietmar Hamann (3/1 Thomas Helmer (65/4) [80.Markus Babbel (27/1)], Christian Ziege (35/3) [67.Michael Tarnat (9/0)], Andreas Möller (76/26), Jürgen Klinsmann (Cap (101/43) [46.Ulf Kirsten (28/12)], Oliver Bierhoff (22/13). Trainer: Hans-Hubert Vogts (91).
Goal: Ulf Kirsten (65).

659. 22.04.1998 **GERMANY - NIGERIA** **1-0(0-0)**
Müngersdorferstadion, Köln; Referee: Antonio Jesús López Nieto (Spain); Attendance: 48,000
GER: Oliver Kahn (9/0), Olaf Thon (46/3), Markus Babbel (28/1), Christian Wörns (14/0), Jens Jeremies (3/0) [46.Stefan Reuter (66/2)], Dietmar Haman (4/1), Michael Tarnat (10/0), Thomas Häßler (Cap) (91/11), Andreas Möller (77/27) [80.Steffen Freund (20/0)], Oliver Bierhoff (23/13), Ulf Kirsten (29/12 Trainer: Hans-Hubert Vogts (92).
Goal: Andreas Möller (57).

660. 27.05.1998 **FINLAND - GERMANY** **0-0**
Olympiastadion, Helsinki; Referee: Claus Bo Larsen (Denmark); Attendance: 18,400
GER: Andreas Köpke (52/0) [46.Oliver Kahn (10/0)], Lothar Herbert Matthäus (123/22), Christian Wörns (15/0), Jürgen Kohler (Cap) (99/2) [46.Marku Babbel (29/1)], Jörg Heinrich (14/2) [68.Jens Jeremies (4/0)], Steffen Freund (21/0), Dietmar Hamann (5/1) [73.Olaf Thon (47/3)], Michael Tarnat (11/0 Thomas Häßler (92/11), Oliver Bierhoff (24/13), Ulf Kirsten (30/12) [46.Olaf Marschall (5/2)]. Trainer: Hans-Hubert Vogts (93).

661. 30.05.1998 **GERMANY - COLOMBIA** **3-1(2-0)**
Waldstadion, Frankfurt am Main; Referee: Atanas Uzunov (Bulgaria); Attendance: 50,000
GER: Andreas Köpke (53/0), Olaf Thon (48/3), Christian Wörns (16/0), Jürgen Kohler (Cap) (100/2), Stefan Reuter (67/2), Jens Jeremies (5/0) [71.Loth Herbert Matthäus (124/22)], Christian Ziege (36/3), Thomas Häßler (93/11) [46.Dietmar Hamann (6/1)], Andreas Möller (78/28), Olaf Marschall (6/2 [71.Ulf Kirsten (31/12)], Oliver Bierhoff (25/15) [71.Jürgen Klinsmann (102/43)]. Trainer: Hans-Hubert Vogts (94).
Goals: Oliver Bierhoff (1, 15), Andreas Möller (46).

662. 05.06.1998 **GERMANY - LUXEMBOURG** **7-0(4-0)**
„Carl Benz" Stadion, Mannheim; Referee: Fritz Stuchlik (Austria); Attendance: 25,000
GER: Andreas Köpke (54/0) [46.Jens Lehmann (2/0)], Christian Wörns (17/0), Jürgen Kohler (101/2) [46.Markus Babbel (30/1)], Olaf Thon (49/3 [74.Stefan Reuter (68/2)], Jörg Heinrich (15/2), Dietmar Hamann (7/1) [46.Lothar Herbert Matthäus (125/22)], Thomas Helmer (66/5) [46.Michael Tarn (12/0)], Christian Ziege (37/4), Andreas Möller (79/28) [59.Olaf Marschall (7/2)], Ulf Kirsten (32/14) [46.Oliver Bierhoff (26/17)], Jürgen Klinsmann (Ca (103/44). Trainer: Hans-Hubert Vogts (95).
Goals: Ulf Kirsten (6), Jürgen Klinsmann (15), Thomas Helmer (27), Ulf Kirsten (45), Oliver Bierhoff (57, 72), Christian Ziege (85).

663. 15.06.1998 **GERMANY – UNITED STATES** **2-0(1-0)** 16th FIFA WC. Group Stage.
Stade Parc des Princes, Paris (France); Referee: Saïd Belqola (Morocco); Attendance: 48,700
GER: Andreas Köpke (55/0), Olaf Thon (50/3), Christian Wörns (18/0), Jürgen Kohler (102/2), Stefan Reuter (69/2) [69.Christian Ziege (38/4)], Jen Jeremies (6/0), Jörg Heinrich (16/2), Thomas Häßler (94/11) [50.Dietmar Hamann (8/1)], Andreas Möller (80/29) [90.Markus Babbel (31/1)], Jürge Klinsmann (Cap) (104/45), Oliver Bierhoff (27/17). Trainer: Hans-Hubert Vogts (96).
Goals: Andreas Möller (9), Jürgen Klinsmann (65).

664. 21.06.1998 **GERMANY - YUGOSLAVIA** **2-2(0-1)** 16th FIFA WC. Group Stage.
Stade "Félix Bollaert", Lens (France); Referee: Kim Milton Nielsen (Denmark); Attendance: 41,300
GER: Andreas Köpke (56/0), Olaf Thon (51/3), Christian Wörns (19/0), Jürgen Kohler (103/2), Jörg Heinrich (17/2), Dietmar Hamann (9/1) [46.Loth Herbert Matthäus (126/22)], Jens Jeremies (7/0), Christian Ziege (39/4) [67.Michael Tarnat (13/0)], Andreas Möller (81/29) [58.Ulf Kirsten (33/14)], Jürge Klinsmann (Cap) (105/45), Oliver Bierhoff (28/18). Trainer: Hans-Hubert Vogts (97).
Goals: Siniša Mihajlović (74 own goal), Oliver Bierhoff (80).

665. 25.06.1998 **GERMANY - IRAN** **2-0(0-0)** 16th FIFA WC. Group Stage.
Stade de la Mosson, Montpellier (France); Referee: Epifanio González Chavez (Paraguay); Attendance: 35,500
GER: Andreas Köpke (57/0), Olaf Thon (52/3) [46.Dietmar Hamann (10/1)], Jürgen Kohler (104/2), Christian Wörns (20/0), Jörg Heinrich (18/2), Loth Herbert Matthäus (127/22), Thomas Helmer (67/5), Michael Tarnat (14/0) [77.Christian Ziege (40/4)], Thomas Häßler (95/11) [70.Ulf Kirsten (34/14) Oliver Bierhoff (29/19), Jürgen Klinsmann (Cap) (106/46). Trainer: Hans-Hubert Vogts (98).
Goals: Oliver Bierhoff (51), Jürgen Klinsmann (58).

666. 29.06.1998 **GERMANY - MEXICO** **2-1(0-0)** 16th FIFA WC. 2nd Round of 16.
Stade de la Mosson, Montpellier (France); Referee: Vítor Manuel Melo Pereira (Portugal); Attendance: 35,500
GER: Andreas Köpke (58/0), Lothar Herbert Matthäus (128/22), Christian Wörns (21/0), Markus Babbel (32/1), Jörg Heinrich (19/2) [59.Andreas Mölle (82/29)], Dietmar Hamann (11/1), Thomas Helmer (68/5) [37.Christian Ziege (41/4)], Michael Tarnat (15/0), Thomas Häßler (96/11) [75.Ulf Kirste (35/14)], Jürgen Klinsmann (Cap) (107/47), Oliver Bierhoff (30/20). Trainer: Hans-Hubert Vogts (99).
Goals: Jürgen Klinsmann (76), Oliver Bierhoff (87).

667. 04.07.1998 **GERMANY - CROATIA** **0-3(0-1)** 16th FIFA WC. Quarter-Finals
Stade Gerland, Lyon (France); Referee: Rune Pedersen (Norway); Attendance: 43,400
GER: Andreas Köpke (59/0), Lothar Herbert Matthäus (129/22), Christian Wörns (22/0) [*sent off 40*], Jürgen Kohler (105/2), Jörg Heinrich (20/2), Dietm Hamann (12/1) [79.Olaf Marschall (8/2)], Jens Jeremies (8/0), Michael Tarnat (16/0), Thomas Häßler (97/11) [69.Ulf Kirsten (36/14)], Jürgen Klinsman (Cap) (108/47), Oliver Bierhoff (31/20). Trainer: Hans-Hubert Vogts (100).

668. 02.09.1998 **MALTA - GERMANY** **1-2(1-1)**
Ta'Qali National Stadium, Attard; Referee: Bazzoli (Italy); Attendance: 6,000
GER: Oliver Kahn (11/0), Markus Babbel (33/1), Thomas Linke (3/0) [46.Stephan Paßlack (3/1)], Marko Rehmer (1/0), Jens Nowotny (6/0), Jörg Heinrich (21/2) [46.Michael Tarnat (17/0)], Stefan Effenberg (34/5), Mario Basler (28/2) [74.Olivier Neuville (1/0)], Stefan Beinlich (1/0), Oliver Bierhoff (Cap) (32/20) [46.Ulf Kirsten (37/14)], Olaf Marschall (9/2) [63.Paulo Roberto Rink (1/0)]. Trainer: Hans-Hubert Vogts (101).
Goals: Darren Debono (6 own goal), Stephan Paßlack (72).

669. 05.09.1998 **GERMANY - ROMANIA** **1-1(0-1)**
Ta'Qali National Stadium, Attard (Malta); Referee: Alfred Micallef (Malta); Attendance: 2,000
GER: Oliver Kahn (12/0), Marko Rehmer (2/0), Markus Babbel (34/1), Stephan Paßlack (4/1) [46.Jens Nowotny (7/0)], Jens Jeremies (9/0), Christian Nerlinger (1/1), Jörg Albertz (3/0) [46.Michael Tarnat (18/0)], Mario Basler (29/2), Stefan Effenberg (35/5), Ulf Kirsten (38/14), Oliver Bierhoff (Cap) (33/20) [72.Paulo Roberto Rink (2/0)]. Trainer: Hans-Hubert Vogts (102).
Goal: Christian Nerlinger (86).

670. 10.10.1998 **TURKEY - GERMANY** **1-0(0-0)** 11th EC. Qualifiers
Atatürk Stadyumu, Bursa; Referee: Hugh Dallas (Scotland); Attendance: 20,000
GER: Oliver Kahn (13/0), Jens Nowotny (8/0), Markus Babbel (35/1), Marko Rehmer (3/0), Carsten Ramelow (1/0), Jens Jeremies (10/0), Jörg Heinrich (22/2) [76.Olivier Neuville (2/0)], Lars Ricken (3/0) [81.Marco Bode (9/0)], Stefan Beinlich (2/0), Oliver Bierhoff (Cap) (34/20), Ulf Kirsten (39/14). Trainer: Erich Ribbeck (1).

671. 14.10.1998 **MOLDOVA - GERMANY** **1-3(1-3)** 11th EC. Qualifiers
Stadionul Republican, Chişinău; Referee: Juan Antonio Fernández Marín (Spain); Attendance: 5,000
GER: Oliver Kahn (14/0), Markus Babbel (36/1), Jens Nowotny (9/0), Marko Rehmer (4/0), Carsten Ramelow (2/0), Christian Nerlinger (2/1), Michael Tarnat (19/0), Lars Ricken (4/0) [53.Olivier Neuville (3/0)], Stefan Beinlich (3/0) [83.Dariusz Wosz (7/1)], Ulf Kirsten (40/16) [74.Carsten Jancker (1/0)], Oliver Bierhoff (Cap) (35/21). Trainer: Erich Ribbeck (2).
Goals: Ulf Kirsten (19, 36), Oliver Bierhoff (38).

672. 18.11.1998 **GERMANY - NETHERLANDS** **1-1(0-1)**
Parkstadion, Gelsenkirchen; Referee: Ryszard Wójcik (Poland); Attendance: 45,000
GER: Oliver Kahn (15/0), Lothar Herbert Matthäus (130/22) [70.Carsten Ramelow (3/0)], Jens Nowotny (10/0) [46.Marko Rehmer (5/0)], Christian Wörns (23/0), Thomas Strunz (35/1) [86.Dietmar Hamann (13/1)], Jens Jeremies (11/0), Jörg Heinrich (23/2), Mario Basler (30/2) [72.Alexander Zickler (1/0)], Andreas Möller (83/29), Oliver Bierhoff (Cap) (36/21), Ulf Kirsten (41/16) [21.Olaf Marschall (10/3)]. Trainer: Erich Ribbeck (3).
Goal: Olaf Marschall (52).

673. 06.02.1999 **UNITED STATES - GERMANY** **3-0(3-0)**
Alltel Stadium, Jacksonville; Referee: Gilberto Alcalá Pineda (Mexico); Attendance: 12,000
GER: Oliver Kahn (16/0), Lothar Herbert Matthäus (Cap) (131/22), Markus Babbel (37/1), Marko Rehmer (6/0), Carsten Ramelow (4/0) [46.Christian Nerlinger (3/1)], Jens Jeremies (12/0), Lars Ricken (5/0), Andreas Möller (84/29), Alexander Zickler (2/0) [46.Marco Bode (10/0)], Olaf Marschall (11/3), Michael Preetz (1/0). Trainer: Erich Ribbeck (4).

674. 09.02.1999 **COLOMBIA - GERMANY** **3-3(1-1)**
Orange Bowl, Miami (United States); Referee: Brian Hill (United States); Attendance: 15,000
GER: Oliver Kahn (17/0) [46.Jens Lehmann (3/0)], Lothar Herbert Matthäus (Cap) (132/22), Christian Wörns (24/0), Marko Rehmer (7/0), Markus Babbel (38/1), Jens Jeremies (13/0) [46.Christian Nerlinger (4/1)], Marco Bode (11/1), Olivier Neuville (4/0) [74.Alexander Zickler (3/0)], Andreas Möller (85/29), Marco Reich (1/0) [79.Lars Ricken (6/0)], Michael Preetz (2/2). Trainer: Erich Ribbeck (5).
Goals: Michael Preetz (33, 55), Marco Bode (74).

675. 27.03.1999 **NORTHERN IRELAND - GERMANY** **0-3(0-2)** 11th EC. Qualifiers
Windsor Park, Belfast; Referee: Graziano Cesari (Italy); Attendance: 14,300
GER: Oliver Kahn (18/0), Markus Babbel (39/1), Lothar Herbert Matthäus (133/22) [46.Jens Nowotny (11/0)], Christian Wörns (25/0), Thomas Strunz (36/1), Dietmar Hamann (14/2), Jens Jeremies (14/0), Jörg Heinrich (24/2), Olivier Neuville (5/0) [68.Carsten Jancker (2/0)], Oliver Bierhoff (Cap) (37/21), Marco Bode (12/3) [78.Michael Preetz (3/2)]. Trainer: Erich Ribbeck (6).
Goals: Marco Bode (11, 43), Dietmar Hamann (62).

676. 31.03.1999 **GERMANY - FINLAND** **2-0(2-0)** 11th EC. Qualifiers
Frankenstadion, Nürnberg; Referee: Sergei Husainov (Russia); Attendance: 40,800
GER: Oliver Kahn (19/0), Markus Babbel (40/1), Lothar Herbert Matthäus (134/22), Christian Wörns (26/0), Thomas Strunz (37/1), Dietmar Hamann (15/2) [72.Jens Nowotny (12/0)], Jens Jeremies (15/1), Jörg Heinrich (25/2), Olivier Neuville (6/1) [65.Ulf Kirsten (42/16)], Oliver Bierhoff (Cap) (38/21), Marco Bode (13/3) [76.Carsten Jancker (3/0)]. Trainer: Erich Ribbeck (7).
Goals: Jens Jeremies (31), Olivier Neuville (36).

677. 28.04.1999 **GERMANY - SCOTLAND** **0-1(0-0)**
Weserstadion, Bremen; Referee: Urs Meier (Switzerland); Attendance: 25,000
GER: Jens Lehmann (4/0), Christian Wörns (27/0), Lothar Herbert Matthäus (135/22), Jens Nowotny (13/0), Thomas Strunz (38/1) [88.Carsten Jancker (4/0)], Dietmar Hamann (16/2) [60.Michael Ballack (1/0)], Jens Jeremies (16/1) [46.Carsten Ramelow (5/0)], Jörg Heinrich (26/2), Olivier Neuville (7/1), Oliver Bierhoff (Cap) (39/21) [60.Ulf Kirsten (43/16)], Horst Heldt (1/0). Trainer: Erich Ribbeck (8).

678. 04.06.1999 **GERMANY - MOLDOVA** **6-1(3-0)** 11th EC. Qualifiers
BayArena, Leverkusen; Referee: Jorge Emanuel Monteiro Coroado (Portugal); Attendance: 21,000
GER: Oliver Kahn (20/0), Thomas Strunz (39/1), Jens Nowotny (14/0), Lothar Herbert Matthäus (136/22) [74.Markus Babbel (41/1)], Jörg Heinrich (27/2), Dietmar Hamann (17/2), Jens Jeremies (17/1) [46.Mehmet Scholl (16/2)], Olivier Neuville (8/1), Oliver Bierhoff (Cap) (40/24), Ulf Kirsten (44/17) [53.Carsten Ramelow (6/0)], Marco Bode (14/4). Trainer: Erich Ribbeck (9).
Goals: Oliver Bierhoff (2), Ulf Kirsten (27), Marco Bode (38), Oliver Bierhoff (56), Mehmet Scholl (71), Oliver Bierhoff (82).

679. 24.07.1999 **BRAZIL - GERMANY** **4-0(0-0)** 4th FIFA Confederations Cup. Group Stage.
Estadio Jalisco, Guadalajara (Mexico); Referee: Gilberto Alcala Pineda (Mexico); Attendance: 70,000
GER: Jens Lehmann (5/0), Christian Wörns (28/0), Thomas Linke (4/0), Lothar Herbert Matthäus (Cap) (137/22), Lars Ricken (7/0), Michael Ballack (2/0), Dariusz Wosz (8/1), Jörg Heinrich (28/2) [75.Ronald Maul (1/0)], Olivier Neuville (9/1) [79.Heiko Gerber (1/0)], Michael Preetz (4/2) [73.Olaf Marschall (12/3)], Mehmet Scholl (17/2). Trainer: Erich Ribbeck (10).

680. 28.07.1999 **GERMANY – NEW ZEALAND** **2-0(1-0)** 4th FIFA Confederations Cup. Group Stage.
Estadio Jalisco, Guadalajara (Mexico); Referee: Kofi Bonaventure Codija (Benin); Attendance: 30,000
GER: Jens Lehmann (6/0), Christian Wörns (29/0), Thomas Linke (5/0), Lothar Herbert Matthäus (Cap) (138/23) [72.Michael Ballack (3/0)], Lars Ricken (8/0), Bernd Schneider (1/0), Jörg Heinrich (29/2), Olivier Neuville (10/1), Mehmet Scholl (18/2) [46.Dariusz Wosz (9/1)], Michael Preetz (5/3), Olaf Marschall (13/3) [65.Paulo Roberto Rink (3/0)]. Trainer: Erich Ribbeck (11).
Goals: Michael Preetz (6), Lothar Herbert Matthäus (33).

681. 30.07.1999 **UNITED STATES - GERMANY** **2-0(1-0)** 4th FIFA Confederations Cup. Group Stage.
Estadio Jalisco, Guadalajara (Mexico); Referee: Gilberto Alcala Piñeda (Mexico); Attendance: 30,000
GER: Jens Lehmann (7/0), Christian Wörns (30/0), Thomas Linke (6/0), Lothar Herbert Matthäus (Cap) (139/23), Jörg Heinrich (30/2) [41.Mustafa Dogan (1/0)], Bernd Schneider (2/0), Dariusz Wosz (10/1), Heiko Gerber (2/0) [77.Ronald Maul (2/0)], Olivier Neuville (11/1), Michael Preetz (6/3), Horst Heldt (2/0) [61.Paulo Roberto Rink (4/0)]. Trainer: Erich Ribbeck (12).

682. 04.09.1999 **FINLAND - GERMANY** **1-2(0-2)** 11th EC. Qualifiers
Olympiastadion, Helsinki; Referee: Antonio Jesús López Nieto (Spain); Attendance: 20,200
GER: Jens Lehmann (8/0), Thomas Linke (7/0), Jens Nowotny (15/0), Lothar Herbert Matthäus (140/23), Markus Babbel (42/1), Christian Ziege (42/4), Mehmet Scholl (19/2) [79.Christian Nerlinger (5/1)], Jens Jeremies (18/1), Olivier Neuville (12/1) [85.Thomas Strunz (40/1)], Oliver Bierhoff (Cap) (41/26), Ulf Kirsten (45/17) [32.Bernd Schneider (3/0)]. Trainer: Erich Ribbeck (13).
Goals: Oliver Bierhoff (2, 17).

683. 08.09.1999 **GERMANY – NORTHERN IRELAND** **4-0(4-0)** 11th EC. Qualifiers
Westfalenstadion, Dortmund; Referee: Georgios Bikas (Greece); Attendance: 41,000
GER: Jens Lehmann (9/0), Thomas Linke (8/0), Lothar Herbert Matthäus (141/23), Markus Babbel (43/1) [30.Thomas Strunz (41/1)], Jens Jeremies (19/1), Jens Nowotny (16/0) [46.Christian Wörns (31/0)], Mehmet Scholl (20/2), Christian Ziege (43/7), Olivier Neuville (13/1) [67.Bernd Schneider (4/0)], Oliver Bierhoff (Cap) (42/27), Marco Bode (15/4). Trainer: Erich Ribbeck (14).
Goals: Oliver Bierhoff (3), Christian Ziege (16, 33, 45).

684. 09.10.1999 **GERMANY - TURKEY** **0-0** 11th EC. Qualifiers
Olympiastadion, München; Referee: Pierluigi Collina (Italy); Attendance: 63,000
GER: Oliver Kahn (21/0), Markus Babbel (44/1), Lothar Herbert Matthäus (142/23), Thomas Linke (9/0), Dietmar Hamann (18/2) [46.Christian Nerlinger (6/1)], Jens Jeremies (20/1), Bernd Schneider (5/0) [89.Mustafa Dogan (2/0)], Christian Ziege (44/7) [76.Marco Bode (16/4)], Olivier Neuville (14/1), Oliver Bierhoff (Cap) (43/27), Mehmet Scholl (21/2). Trainer: Erich Ribbeck (15).

685. 14.11.1999 **NORWAY - GERMANY** **0-1(0-0)**
Ullevaal Stadion, Oslo; Referee: Dirk Zier Gerardus „Dick“ Jol (Netherlands); Attendance: 14,100
GER: Jens Lehmann (10/0), Christian Wörns (32/0), Lothar Herbert Matthäus (143/23), Markus Babbel (45/1) [68.Frank Baumann (1/0)], Jens Jeremies (21/1), Marco Bode (17/4) [46.Dietmar Hamann (19/2)], Christian Ziege (45/7), Mehmet Scholl (22/3), Olivier Neuville (15/1) [33.Thomas Linke (10/0)], Ulf Kirsten (46/17) [46.Dariusz Wosz (11/1)], Oliver Bierhoff (44/27) [83.Carsten Jancker (5/0)]. Trainer: Erich Ribbeck (16).
Goal: Mehmet Scholl (90).

686. 23.02.2000 **NETHERLANDS - GERMANY** **2-1(2-1)**
Amsterdam ArenA, Amsterdam; Referee: Domenico Messina (Italy); Attendance: 50,000
GER: Oliver Kahn (22/0), Markus Babbel (46/1), Lothar Herbert Matthäus (144/23), Thomas Linke (11/0), Zoltan Sebescen (1/0) [46.Sebastian Deisler (1/0)], Jens Jeremies (22/1), Dietmar Hamann (20/2) [61.Dariusz Wosz (12/1)], Christian Ziege (46/8), Olivier Neuville (16/1) [76.Frank Baumann (2/0)], Oliver Bierhoff (45/27), Mehmet Scholl (23/3). Trainer: Erich Ribbeck (17).
Goal: Christian Ziege (22).

687. 29.03.2000 **CROATIA - GERMANY** **1-1(0-1)**
Stadion Maksimir, Zagreb; Referee: Luboš Michel (Slovakia); Attendance: 8,000
GER: Oliver Kahn (23/0), Lothar Herbert Matthäus (145/23), Thomas Linke (12/0), Jens Nowotny (17/0), Marko Rehmer (8/1) [46.Carsten Ramelow (7/0)], Dietmar Hamann (21/2), Michael Ballack (4/0), Christian Ziege (47/8) [88.Stefan Beinlich (4/0)], Dariusz Wosz (13/1), Oliver Bierhoff (46/27), Ulf Kirsten (47/17) [83.Paulo Roberto Rink (5/0)]. Trainer: Erich Ribbeck (18).
Goal: Marko Rehmer (12).

688. 26.04.2000 **GERMANY - SWITZERLAND** **1-1(0-1)**
„Fritz Walter“ Stadion, Kaiserslautern; Referee: Norman Morgan (Sweden); Attendance: 32,000
GER: Jens Lehmann (11/0), Markus Babbel (47/1) [35.Christian Wörns (33/0)], Lothar Herbert Matthäus (146/23), Thomas Linke (13/0), Marko Rehmer (9/1) [68.Olivier Neuville (17/1)], Michael Ballack (5/0), Dariusz Wosz (14/1) [46.Paulo Roberto Rink (6/0)], Christian Ziege (48/8) [19.Marco Bode (18/4)], Mehmet Scholl (24/3) [24.Dietmar Hamann (22/2)], Michael Preetz (7/3) [46.Ulf Kirsten (48/18)], Oliver Bierhoff (47/27). Trainer: Erich Ribbeck (19).
Goal: Ulf Kirsten (85).

689. 03.06.2000 **GERMANY – CZECH REPUBLIC** **3-2(1-0)**
Frankenstadion, Nürnberg; Referee: Alfredo Trentalange (Italy); Attendance: 30,000
GER: Oliver Kahn (24/0), Thomas Linke (14/0), Carsten Ramelow (8/0), Jens Nowotny (18/0) [78.Marko Rehmer (10/1)], Markus Babbel (48/1) [46.Sebastian Deisler (2/0)], Dietmar Hamann (23/2) [52.Michael Ballack (6/0)], Christian Ziege (49/8), Thomas Häßler (98/11) [56.Dariusz Wosz (15/1)], Mehmet Scholl (25/3) [46.Marco Bode (19/4)], Paulo Roberto Rink (7/0), Carsten Jancker (6/1) [56.Oliver Bierhoff (48/29)]. Trainer: Erich Ribbeck (20).
Goals: Carsten Jancker (38), Oliver Bierhoff (62 penalty, 90).

690. 07.06.2000 **GERMANY - LIECHTENSTEIN** **8-2(2-1)**
Dreisam Stadion, Freiburg; Referee: Konrad Plautz (Austria); Attendance: 24,000
GER: Jens Lehmann (12/0) [46.Hans-Jörg Butt (1/0)], Thomas Linke (15/0) [46.Marko Rehmer (11/1)], Lothar Herbert Matthäus (147/23) [30.Carsten Ramelow (9/0)], Jens Nowotny (19/0), Markus Babbel (49/1) [46.Sebastian Deisler (3/0)], Dietmar Hamann (24/2) [46.Thomas Häßler (99/11)], Jens Jeremies (23/1) [46.Michael Ballack (7/0)], Christian Ziege (50/8) [46.Marco Bode (20/5)], Mehmet Scholl (26/4) [46.Dariusz Wosz (16/1)], Oliver Bierhoff (49/30) [46.Carsten Jancker (7/3)], Paulo Roberto Rink (8/0) [46.Ulf Kirsten (49/21)]. Trainer: Erich Ribbeck (21).
Goals: Oliver Bierhoff (1), Mehmet Scholl (31), Marco Bode (65), Ulf Kirsten (80, 81), Carsten Jancker (84), Ulf Kirsten (86), Carsten Jancker (89).

)1. 12.06.2000 **GERMANY - ROMANIA** **1-1(1-1)** 11th EC. Group Stage.
ade Sclessin, Liège (Belgium); Referee: Kim Milton Nielsen (Denmark); Attendance: 30,000
ER: Oliver Kahn (25/0), Thomas Linke (16/0) [46.Marko Rehmer (12/1)], Lothar Herbert Matthäus (148/23) [77.Sebastian Deisler (4/0)], Jens Nowotny 0/0), Markus Babbel (50/1), Jens Jeremies (24/1), Christian Ziege (51/8), Thomas Häßler (100/11) [73.Dietmar Hamann (25/2)], Mehmet Scholl (27/5), ıulo Roberto Rink (9/0), Oliver Bierhoff (50/30). Trainer: Erich Ribbeck (22).
oal: Mehmet Scholl (28).

)2. 17.06.2000 **ENGLAND - GERMANY** **1-0(0-0)** 11th EC. Group Stage.
ade Communal, Charleroi (Belgium); Referee: Pierluigi Collina (Italy); Attendance: 27,700
ER: Oliver Kahn (26/0), Markus Babbel (51/1), Lothar Herbert Matthäus (149/23), Jens Nowotny (21/0), Sebastian Deisler (5/0) [72.Michael Ballack /0)], Dietmar Hamann (26/2), Jens Jeremies (25/1) [78.Marco Bode (21/5)], Christian Ziege (52/8), Mehmet Scholl (28/5), Carsten Jancker (8/3), Ulf irsten (50/21) [70.Paulo Roberto Rink (10/0)]. Trainer: Erich Ribbeck (23).

)3. 20.06.2000 **PORTUGAL - GERMANY** **3-0(1-0)** 11th EC. Group Stage.
adion Feijenoord, Rotterdam (Netherlands); Referee: Dirk Zier Gerardus „Dick“ Jol (Netherlands); Attendance: 51,500
ER: Oliver Kahn (27/0), Marko Rehmer (13/1), Lothar Herbert Matthäus (150/23), Jens Nowotny (22/0), Thomas Linke (17/0), Michael Ballack (9/0) 6.Paulo Roberto Rink (11/0)], Dietmar Hamann (27/2), Sebastian Deisler (6/0), Mehmet Scholl (29/5) [59.Thomas Häßler (101/11)], Marco Bode (22/5), arsten Jancker (9/3) [69.Ulf Kirsten (51/21)]. Trainer: Erich Ribbeck (24).

)4. 16.08.2000 **GERMANY - SPAIN** **4-1(1-0)**
iedersachsenstadion, Hannover; Referee: Knud Erik Fisker (Denmark); Attendance: 35,000
ER: Oliver Kahn (28/0), Marko Rehmer (14/1), Jens Nowotny (23/0), Jörg Heinrich (31/2) [67.Thomas Linke (18/0)], Sebastian Deisler (7/0), Carsten amelow (10/0), Michael Ballack (10/0) [79.Dietmar Hamann (28/2)], Marco Bode (23/5) [46.Stefan Beinlich (5/0)], Mehmet Scholl (30/7) [66.Olivier euville (18/1)], Alexander Zickler (4/2), Carsten Jancker (10/3) [73.Paulo Roberto Rink (12/0)]. Trainer: Rudolf Völler (1).
oals: Mehmet Scholl (24, 51), Alexander Zickler (57, 62).

)5. 02.09.2000 **GERMANY - GREECE** **2-0(1-0)** 17th FIFA WC. Qualifiers
olksparkstadion, Hamburg; Referee: Antonio Jesús López Nieto (Spain); Attendance: 48,500
ER: Oliver Kahn (29/0), Marko Rehmer (15/1), Jens Nowotny (24/0), Jörg Heinrich (32/2) [46.Thomas Linke (19/0)], Carsten Ramelow (11/0), Sebastian eisler (8/1), Michael Ballack (11/0), Marco Bode (24/5), Mehmet Scholl (31/7), Alexander Zickler (5/2) [71.Paulo Roberto Rink (13/0)], Carsten Jancker 1/3). Trainer: Rudolf Völler (2).
oals: Sebastian Deisler (17), Marinos Ouzounidis (75 own goal).

)6. 07.10.2000 **ENGLAND - GERMANY** **0-1(0-1)** 17th FIFA WC. Qualifiers
'embley Stadium, London; Referee: Stefano Braschi (Italy); Attendance: 76,400
ER: Oliver Kahn (30/0), Marko Rehmer (16/1), Jens Nowotny (25/0), Thomas Linke (20/0), Carsten Ramelow (12/0), Dietmar Hamann (29/3), Marco ode (25/5) [87.Christian Ziege (53/8)], Sebastian Deisler (9/1), Michael Ballack (12/0), Mehmet Scholl (32/7), Oliver Bierhoff (51/30). Trainer: Rudolf öller (3).
oal: Dietmar Hamann (14).

)7. 15.11.2000 **DENMARK - GERMANY** **2-1(0-0)**
ırken, København; Referee: Fritz Stuchlik (Austria); Attendance: 17,700
ER: Oliver Kahn (31/0), Ingo Hertzsch (1/0), Jens Nowotny (26/0), Thomas Linke (21/0) [68.Dariusz Wosz (17/1)], Jörg Heinrich (33/2) [46.Marco Bode 6/5)], Carsten Ramelow (13/0), Dietmar Hamann (30/3), Christian Ziege (54/8) [88.Frank Baumann (3/0)], Mehmet Scholl (33/8), Alexander Zickler (6/2) 3.Olivier Neuville (19/1)], Oliver Bierhoff (52/30) [73.Carsten Jancker (12/3)]. Trainer: Rudolf Völler (4).
oal: Mehmet Scholl (82).

)8. 27.02.2001 **FRANCE - GERMANY** **1-0(1-0)** 17th FIFA WC. Qualifiers
ade de France, Saint-Denis, Paris; Referee: Alfredo Trentalange (Italy); Attendance: 80,000
ER: Oliver Kahn (Cap) (32/0), Christian Wörns (34/0), Jens Jeremies (26/1), Thomas Linke (22/0), Carsten Ramelow (14/0), Marko Rehmer (17/1) 1.Torsten Frings (1/0)], Michael Ballack (13/0), Dietmar Hamann (31/3) [46.Olivier Neuville (20/1)], Marco Bode (27/5) [90.Christian Ziege (55/8)], ehmet Scholl (34/8), Carsten Jancker (13/3) [67.Oliver Bierhoff (53/30)]. Trainer: Rudolf Völler (5).

)9. 24.03.2001 **GERMANY - ALBANIA** **2-1(0-0)** 17th FIFA WC. Qualifiers
ayArena, Leverkusen; Referee: Graziano Cesari (Italy); Attendance: 22,500
ER: Oliver Kahn (33/0), Christian Wörns (35/0), Jens Nowotny (27/0), Carsten Ramelow (15/0), Sebastian Deisler (10/2), Dietmar Hamann (32/3) 6.Marko Rehmer (18/1)], Jens Jeremies (27/1), Marco Bode (28/5), Mehmet Scholl (35/8), Olivier Neuville (21/1) [72.Miroslav Josef Klose (1/1)], Oliver ierhoff (54/30) [46.Carsten Jancker (14/3)]. Trainer: Rudolf Völler (6).
oals: Sebastian Deisler (50), Miroslav Josef Klose (88).

)0. 28.03.2001 **GREECE - GERMANY** **2-4(2-2)** 17th FIFA WC. Qualifiers
ádio Olympiako „Spiros Louis“, Athína; Referee: Vítor Manuel Melo Pereira (Portugal); Attendance: 59,000
ER: Oliver Kahn (34/0), Christian Wörns (36/0), Jens Nowotny (28/0), Jörg Heinrich (34/2), Christian Ziege (56/8), Marko Rehmer (19/2), Jens Jeremies 8/1) [90.Carsten Ramelow (16/0)], Michael Ballack (14/1), Sebastian Deisler (11/2) [*sent off 60*], Carsten Jancker (15/3) [78.Marco Bode (29/6)], Olivier euville (22/1) [67.Miroslav Josef Klose (2/2)]. Trainer: Rudolf Völler (7).
oals: Marko Rehmer (6), Michael Ballack (25 penalty), Miroslav Josef Klose (82), Marco Bode (90).

)1. 29.05.2001 **GERMANY - SLOVAKIA** **2-0(0-0)**
'eserstadion, Bremen; Referee: Claude Colombo (France); Attendance: 18,000
ER: Jens Lehmann (13/0), Marko Rehmer (20/2) [46.Sebastian Kehl (1/0)], Jens Nowotny (29/0), Frank Baumann (4/1), Carsten Ramelow (17/0), Gerald samoah (1/1) [64.Torsten Frings (2/0)], Michael Ballack (15/1) [79.Christian Ziege (57/8)], Marco Bode (30/6) [46.Jörg Böhme (1/0)], Sebastian Deisler 2/2) [46.Lars Ricken (9/0)], Olivier Neuville (23/1) [64.Alexander Zickler (7/2)], Oliver Bierhoff (55/30) [74.Miroslav Josef Klose (3/2)]. Trainer: Rudolf öller (8).
oals: Gerald Asamoah (50), Frank Baumann (56).

702. 02.06.2001 **FINLAND - GERMANY** **2-2(2-0)** 17th FIFA WC. Qualifiers
Olympiastadion, Helsinki; Referee: Dirk Zier Gerardus „Dick" Jol (Netherlands); Attendance: 35,800
GER: Oliver Kahn (35/0), Marko Rehmer (21/2), Jens Nowotny (30/0), Thomas Linke (23/0), Carsten Ramelow (18/0), Michael Ballack (16/2), Marco Bode (31/6) [69.Christian Ziege (58/8)], Gerald Asamoah (2/1), Lars Ricken (10/0), Olivier Neuville (24/1) [62.Miroslav Josef Klose (4/2)], Carsten Jancker (16/4) [83.Oliver Bierhoff (56/30)]. Trainer: Rudolf Völler (9).
Goals: Michael Ballack (69 penalty), Carsten Jancker (72).

703. 06.06.2001 **ALBANIA - GERMANY** **0-2(0-1)** 17th FIFA WC. Qualifiers
Stadiumi „Kombëtar Qemal Stafa", Tiranë; Referee: Gilles Veissière (France); Attendance: 18,000
GER: Oliver Kahn (36/0), Marko Rehmer (22/3), Jens Nowotny (31/0), Thomas Linke (24/0), Carsten Ramelow (19/0) [*sent off 37*], Gerald Asamoah (3/1) [70.Lars Ricken (11/0)], Michael Ballack (17/3), Christian Ziege (59/8), Sebastian Deisler (13/2) [84.Frank Baumann (5/1)], Olivier Neuville (25/1) [46.Alexander Zickler (8/2)], Carsten Jancker (17/4). Trainer: Rudolf Völler (10).
Goals: Marko Rehmer (28), Michael Ballack (68).

704. 15.08.2001 **HUNGARY - GERMANY** **2-5(0-2)**
„Puskás Ferenc" Stadion, Budapest; Referee: Juan Ansuategui Roca (Spain); Attendance: 28,000
GER: Oliver Kahn (37/0), Marko Rehmer (23/3) [46.Christoph Metzelder (1/0)], Frank Baumann (6/2), Thomas Linke (25/0), Gerald Asamoah (4/1) [76.Alexander Zickler (9/2)], Dietmar Hamann (33/3) [46.Lars Ricken (12/0)], Sebastian Kehl (2/1), Jörg Böhme (2/1) [77.Marco Bode (32/6)], Sebastian Deisler (14/2) [85.Christian Ziege (60/8)], Carsten Jancker (18/5) [85.Oliver Bierhoff (57/31)], Olivier Neuville (26/1) [66.Miroslav Josef Klose (5/2)]. Trainer: Rudolf Völler (11).
Goals: Jörg Böhme (31 penalty), Sebastian Kehl (44), Carsten Jancker (46), Frank Baumann (59), Oliver Bierhoff (90).

705. 01.09.2001 **GERMANY - ENGLAND** **1-5(1-2)** 17th FIFA WC. Qualifiers
Olympiastadion, München; Referee: Pierluigi Collina (Italy); Attendance: 63,000
GER: Oliver Kahn (38/0), Christian Wörns (37/0) [46.Gerald Asamoah (5/1)], Jens Nowotny (32/0), Thomas Linke (26/0), Marko Rehmer (24/3), Michael Ballack (18/3) [67.Miroslav Josef Klose (6/2)], Dietmar Hamann (34/3), Jörg Böhme (3/1), Sebastian Deisler (15/2), Carsten Jancker (19/6), Olivier Neuville (27/1) [78.Sebastian Kehl (3/1)]. Trainer: Rudolf Völler (12).
Goal: Carsten Jancker (6).

706. 06.10.2001 **GERMANY - FINLAND** **0-0** 17th FIFA WC. Qualifiers
Arena „Auf Schalke", Gelsenkirchen; Referee: Anders Frisk (Sweden); Attendance: 52,300
GER: Oliver Kahn (39/0), Marko Rehmer (25/3), Christian Wörns (38/0), Jens Nowotny (33/0), Christian Ziege (61/8), Michael Ballack (19/3), Carsten Ramelow (20/0), Jörg Böhme (4/1) [46.Gerald Asamoah (6/1)], Sebastian Deisler (16/2), Oliver Bierhoff (58/31), Olivier Neuville (28/1) [77.Miroslav Josef Klose (7/2)]. Trainer: Rudolf Völler (13).

707. 10.11.2001 **UKRAINE - GERMANY** **1-1(1-1)** 17th FIFA WC. Qualifiers (Play-Offs)
Olympiyksyi Stadium, Kyiv; Referee: Stefano Braschi (Italy); Attendance: 85,000
GER: Oliver Kahn (40/0), Marko Rehmer (26/3), Jens Nowotny (34/0), Thomas Linke (27/0), Carsten Ramelow (21/0), Dietmar Hamann (35/3), Christian Ziege (62/8), Bernd Schneider (6/0) [79.Lars Ricken (13/0)], Michael Ballack (20/4), Gerald Asamoah (7/1), Alexander Zickler (10/2) [68.Carsten Jancker (20/6)]. Trainer: Rudolf Völler (14).
Goal: Michael Ballack (31)

708. 14.11.2001 **GERMANY - UKRAINE** **4-1(3-0)** 17th FIFA WC. Qualifiers (Play-Offs)
Westfalenstadion, Dortmund; Referee: Vítor Manuel Melo Pereira (Portugal); Attendance: 52,400
GER: Oliver Kahn (41/0), Marko Rehmer (27/4) [87.Frank Baumann (7/2)], Jens Nowotny (35/0), Thomas Linke (28/0), Carsten Ramelow (22/0), Dietmar Hamann (36/3), Christian Ziege (63/8), Bernd Schneider (7/0), Michael Ballack (21/6), Carsten Jancker (21/6) [58.Oliver Bierhoff (59/31)], Olivier Neuville (29/2) [70.Lars Ricken (14/0)]. Trainer: Rudolf Völler (15).
Goals: Michael Ballack (4), Olivier Neuville (11), Marko Rehmer (15), Michael Ballack (51).

709. 13.02.2002 **GERMANY - ISRAEL** **7-1(0-1)**
„Fritz Walter" Stadion, Kaiserslautern; Referee: Stephen W. Dunn (England); Attendance: 24,500
GER: Oliver Kahn (42/0), Christian Wörns (39/0) [78.Christoph Metzelder (2/0)], Jens Nowotny (36/0) [46.Thomas Linke (29/0)], Bernd Schneider (8/0), Dietmar Hamann (37/4), Carsten Ramelow (23/0) [78.Frank Baumann (8/2)], Sebastian Kehl (4/1), Mehmet Scholl (36/8) [66.Torsten Frings (3/0)], Lars Ricken (15/1), Carsten Jancker (22/6) [66.Oliver Bierhoff (60/32)], Miroslav Josef Klose (8/5) [73.Gerald Asamoah (8/2)]. Trainer: Rudolf Völler (16).
Goals: Miroslav Josef Klose (49, 51), Dietmar Hamann (62), Miroslav Josef Klose (64), Oliver Bierhoff (69), Gerald Asamoah (75), Lars Ricken (77).

710. 27.03.2002 **GERMANY – UNITED STATES** **4-2(1-1)**
Ostsee, Rostock; Referee: Bernhard Brugger (Austria); Attendance: 28,900
GER: Frank Rost (1/0) [46.Hans-Jörg Butt (2/0)], Frank Baumann (9/2), Carsten Ramelow (24/0), Thomas Linke (30/0), Dietmar Hamann (38/4), Jens Jeremies (29/1) [69.Jörg Heinrich (35/2)], Christian Ziege (Cap) (64/9) [61.Jörg Böhme (5/1)], Bernd Schneider (9/0) [75.Gerald Asamoah (9/2)], Torsten Frings (4/1), Olivier Neuville (30/3) [80.Thomas Brdaric (1/0)], Oliver Bierhoff (61/33). Trainer: Rudolf Völler (17).
Goals: Christian Ziege (44), Olivier Neuville (61), Oliver Bierhoff (65), Torsten Frings (68).

711. 17.04.2002 **GERMANY - ARGENTINA** **0-1(0-0)**
„Gottlieb Daimler" Stadion, Stuttgart; Referee: Manuel Enrique Mejuto González (Spain); Attendance: 54,600
GER: Jens Lehmann (14/0), Thomas Linke (31/0) [46.Frank Baumann (10/2)], Jens Nowotny (37/0), Christoph Metzelder (3/0), Torsten Frings (5/1) [83.Martin Max (1/0)], Carsten Ramelow (25/0), Jens Jeremies (30/1) [77.Sebastian Kehl (5/1)], Jörg Böhme (6/1) [46.Lars Ricken (16/1)], Michael Ballack (22/6), Oliver Bierhoff (62/33) [70.Carsten Jancker (23/6)], Miroslav Josef Klose (9/5). Trainer: Rudolf Völler (18).

712. 09.05.2002 **GERMANY - KUWAIT** **7-0(5-0)**
Dreisam Stadion, Freiburg; Referee: Karl Erik Nilsson (Sweden); Attendance: 22,000
GER: Oliver Kahn (43/0), Thomas Linke (32/0), Christoph Metzelder (4/0), Torsten Frings (6/2), Jens Jeremies (31/1), Sebastian Kehl (6/1) [67.Fabian Ernst (1/0)], Christian Rahn (1/0), Sebastian Deisler (17/3) [62.Paul Freier (1/0)], Miroslav Josef Klose (10/5), Carsten Jancker (24/7), Oliver Bierhoff (63/36) [73.Daniel Bierofka (1/0)]. Trainer: Rudolf Völler (19).
Goals: Torsten Frings (10), Oliver Bierhoff (24), Sebastian Deisler (40), Oliver Bierhoff (43), Nohair Al Shammari (44 own goal), Oliver Bierhoff (72 penalty), Carsten Jancker (77).

13. 14.05.2002 **WALES - GERMANY** **1-0(0-0)**
illenium Stadium, Cardiff; Referee: Roy Helge Olsen (Norway); Attendance: 36,059
ER: Oliver Kahn (44/0), Thomas Linke (33/0), Christoph Metzelder (5/0), Jörg Heinrich (36/2), Christian Ziege (65/9) [63.Marco Bode (33/6)], Jens remies (32/1), Dietmar Hamann (39/4) [73.Sebastian Kehl (7/1)], Sebastian Deisler (18/3) [63.Gerald Asamoah (10/2)], Torsten Frings (7/2), Oliver ierhoff (64/36) [72.Carsten Jancker (25/7)], Miroslav Josef Klose (11/5). Trainer: Rudolf Völler (20).

14. 18.05.2002 **GERMANY - AUSTRIA** **6-2(3-1)**
ayArena, Leverkusen; Referee: Massimo Busacca (Switzerland); Attendance: 21,500
ER: Oliver Kahn (45/0), Torsten Frings (8/2) [85.Christian Rahn (2/0)], Thomas Linke (34/0), Christoph Metzelder (6/0), Christian Ziege (66/9) [46.Jörg einrich (37/2)], Jens Jeremies (33/1) [73.Frank Baumann (11/2)], Dietmar Hamann (40/4), Sebastian Deisler (19/3) [22.Sebastian Kehl (8/1)], Marco Bode 4/8) [81.Daniel Bierofka (2/1)], Miroslav Josef Klose (12/8) [67.Gerald Asamoah (11/2)], Carsten Jancker (26/7) [73.Oliver Bierhoff (65/36)]. Trainer: udolf Völler (21).
oals: Miroslav Josef Klose (15, 29), Marco Bode (36), Miroslav Josef Klose (53), Marco Bode (68), Daniel Bierofka (81).

15. 01.06.2002 **GERMANY – SAUDI ARABIA** **8-0(4-0)** 17th FIFA WC. Group Stage.
apporo Dome, Sapporo (Japan); Referee: Ubaldo Aquino Valenzano (Paraguay); Attendance: 32,300
ER: Oliver Kahn (Cap) (46/0), Thomas Linke (35/1), Carsten Ramelow (26/0) [46.Jens Jeremies (34/1)], Christoph Metzelder (7/0), Torsten Frings (9/2), ietmar Hamann (41/4), Christian Ziege (67/9), Bernd Schneider (10/1), Michael Ballack (23/7), Miroslav Josef Klose (13/11) [77.Olivier Neuville (31/3)], arsten Jancker (27/8) [67.Oliver Bierhoff (66/37)]. Trainer: Rudolf Völler (22).
oals: Miroslav Josef Klose (20, 25), Michael Ballack (40), Carsten Jancker (45), Miroslav Josef Klose (69), Thomas Linke (72), Oliver Bierhoff (84), Bernd chneider (90).

16. 05.06.2002 **GERMANY – REPUBLIC OF IRELAND** **1-1(1-0)** 17th FIFA WC. Group Stage.
ashima Soccer Stadium, Ibaraki (Japan); Referee: Kim Milton Nielsen (Denmark); Attendance: 35,900
ER: Oliver Kahn (Cap) (47/0), Thomas Linke (36/1), Carsten Ramelow (27/0), Christoph Metzelder (8/0), Torsten Frings (10/2), Dietmar Hamann (42/4), hristian Ziege (68/9), Bernd Schneider (11/1) [90.Jens Jeremies (35/1)], Michael Ballack (24/7), Miroslav Josef Klose (14/12) [85.Marco Bode (35/8)], arsten Jancker (28/8) [75.Oliver Bierhoff (67/37)]. Trainer: Rudolf Völler (23).
oal: Miroslav Josef Klose (19).

17. 11.06.2002 **CAMEROON - GERMANY** **0-2(0-0)** 17th FIFA WC. Group Stage.
copa Stadium, Shizuoka (Japan); Referee: Antonio Jesús López Nieto (Spain); Attendance: 47,100
ER: Oliver Kahn (Cap) (48/0), Thomas Linke (37/1), Carsten Ramelow (28/0) [*sent off 40*], Christoph Metzelder (9/0), Torsten Frings (11/2), Dietmar amann (43/4), Christian Ziege (69/9), Bernd Schneider (12/1) [80.Jens Jeremies (36/1)], Michael Ballack (25/7), Carsten Jancker (29/8) [46.Marco Bode 6/9)], Miroslav Josef Klose (15/13) [84.Olivier Neuville (32/3)]. Trainer: Rudolf Völler (24).
oals: Marco Bode (50), Miroslav Josef Klose (79).

18. 15.06.2002 **GERMANY - PARAGUAY** **1-0(0-0)** 17th FIFA WC. 2nd Round of 16.
ju World Cup Stadium, Seogwipo (Korea Republic); Referee: Carlos Alberto Batres González (Guatemala); Attendance: 25,200
ER: Oliver Kahn (Cap) (49/0), Torsten Frings (12/2), Marko Rehmer (28/4) [46.Sebastian Kehl (9/1)], Thomas Linke (38/1), Christoph Metzelder (10/0) 0.Frank Baumann (12/2)], Bernd Schneider (13/1), Jens Jeremies (37/1), Michael Ballack (26/7), Marco Bode (37/9), Olivier Neuville (33/4) [90.Gerald samoah (12/2)], Miroslav Josef Klose (16/13). Trainer: Rudolf Völler (25).
oal: Olivier Neuville (88).

19. 21.06.2002 **GERMANY – UNITED STATES** **1-0(1-0)** 17th FIFA WC. Quarter-Finals.
unsu Football Stadium, Ulsan (Korea Republic); Referee: Hugh Dallas (Scotland); Attendance: 37,300
ER: Oliver Kahn (Cap) (50/0), Thomas Linke (39/1), Sebastian Kehl (10/1), Christoph Metzelder (11/0), Torsten Frings (13/2), Dietmar Hamann (44/4), hristian Ziege (70/9), Bernd Schneider (14/1) [60.Jens Jeremies (38/1)], Michael Ballack (27/8), Olivier Neuville (34/4) [79.Marco Bode (38/9)], Miroslav sef Klose (17/13) [88.Oliver Bierhoff (68/37)]. Trainer: Rudolf Völler (26).
oal: Michael Ballack (39).

20. 25.06.2002 **KOREA REPUBLIC - GERMANY** **0-1(0-0)** 17th FIFA WC. Semi-Finals.
FA World Cup Stadium, Seoul (Korea Republic); Referee: Urs Meier (Switzerland); Attendance: 65,600
ER: Oliver Kahn (Cap) (51/0), Torsten Frings (14/2), Thomas Linke (40/1), Carsten Ramelow (29/0), Christoph Metzelder (12/0), Bernd Schneider (15/1) 5.Jens Jeremies (39/1)], Dietmar Hamann (45/4), Michael Ballack (28/9), Marco Bode (39/9), Miroslav Josef Klose (18/13) [70.Oliver Bierhoff (69/37)], livier Neuville (35/4) [88.Gerald Asamoah (13/2)]. Trainer: Rudolf Völler (27).
oal: Michael Ballack (75).

21. 30.06.2002 **BRAZIL - GERMANY** **2-0(0-0)** 17th FIFA WC. Final.
ternational Stadium, Yokohama (Japan); Referee: Pierluigi Collina (Italy); Attendance: 69,000
ER: Oliver Kahn (Cap) (52/0), Thomas Linke (41/1), Carsten Ramelow (30/0), Christoph Metzelder (13/0), Torsten Frings (15/2), Dietmar Hamann (46/4), ns Jeremies (40/1) [77.Gerald Asamoah (14/2)], Marco Bode (40/9) [84.Christian Ziege (71/9)], Bernd Schneider (16/1), Miroslav Josef Klose (19/13) 4.Oliver Bierhoff (70/37)], Olivier Neuville (36/4). Trainer: Rudolf Völler (28).

22. 21.08.2002 **BULGARIA - GERMANY** **2-2(1-1)**
ationalen stadion "Vasil Levski", Sofia; Referee: Stéphane Bré (France); Attendance: 10,000
ER: Jens Lehmann (15/0), Ingo Hertzsch (2/0), Carsten Ramelow (31/0), Christoph Metzelder (14/0) [46.Arne Friedrich (1/0)], Paul Freier (2/0) [46.Gerald samoah (15/2)], Jens Jeremies (41/1), Michael Ballack (29/10) [46.Sebastian Kehl (11/1)], Daniel Bierofka (3/1) [46.Alexander Zickler (11/2)], Bernd chneider (17/1) [78.Tim Borowski (1/0)], Miroslav Josef Klose (20/13) [78.Fabian Ernst (2/0)], Carsten Jancker (30/9). Trainer: Rudolf Völler (29).
oals: Michael Ballack (23 penalty), Carsten Jancker (57).

23. 07.09.2002 **LITHUANIA - GERMANY** **0-2(0-1)** 12th EC. Qualifiers
. Dariaus ir S. Girėno" stadionas, Kaunas; Referee: Graham Poll (England); Attendance: 8,500
ER: Oliver Kahn (Cap) (53/0), Thomas Linke (42/1), Carsten Ramelow (32/0), Christoph Metzelder (15/0), Torsten Frings (16/2), Dietmar Hamann (47/4), rg Böhme (7/1), Bernd Schneider (18/1) [86.Jens Jeremies (42/1)], Michael Ballack (30/11), Miroslav Josef Klose (21/13), Carsten Jancker (31/9) 9.Olivier Neuville (37/4)]. Trainer: Rudolf Völler (30).
oals: Michael Ballack (27), Marius Stankevičius (59 own goal).

724. 11.10.2002 **BOSNIA AND HERZEGOVINA - GERMANY** **1-1(1-0)**
Olimpiski Stadion Koševo, Sarajevo; Referee: Massimo De Santis (Italy); Attendance: 5,000
GER: Oliver Kahn (54/0) [46.Jens Lehmann (16/0)], Carsten Ramelow (33/0), Christian Wörns (40/0) [*sent off 49*], Marko Rehmer (29/4) [46.Arne Friedric (2/0)], Torsten Frings (17/2), Jens Jeremies (43/1), Sebastian Kehl (12/1), Gerald Asamoah (16/2) [46.Paul Freier (3/0)], Tim Borowski (2/0) [46.Bern Schneider (19/1)], Carsten Jancker (32/10), Miroslav Josef Klose (22/13) [78.Alexander Zickler (12/2)]. Trainer: Rudolf Völler (31).
Goal: Carsten Jancker (56).

725. 16.10.2002 **GERMANY – FAROE ISLANDS** **2-1(1-1)** 12th EC. Qualifiers
Niedersachsenstadion, Hannover; Referee: Dani Koren (Israel); Attendance: 36,600
GER: Oliver Kahn (55/0), Arne Friedrich (3/0), Carsten Ramelow (34/0) [46.Paul Freier (4/0)], Christian Wörns (41/0), Jens Jeremies (44/1), Dietma Hamann (48/4), Torsten Frings (18/2), Bernd Schneider (20/1) [87.Sebastian Kehl (13/1)], Michael Ballack (31/12), Carsten Jancker (33/10) [69.Olivie Neuville (38/4)], Miroslav Josef Klose (23/14). Trainer: Rudolf Völler (32).
Goals: Michael Ballack (2), Miroslav Josef Klose (59).

726. 20.11.2002 **GERMANY - NETHERLANDS** **1-3(1-1)**
Arena „Auf Schalke", Gelsenkirchen; Referee: Hugh Dallas (Scotland); Attendance: 60,600
GER: Oliver Kahn (56/0), Marko Rehmer (30/4), Frank Baumann (13/2), Arne Friedrich (4/0), Torsten Frings (19/2), Jens Jeremies (45/1) [46.Sebastia Kehl (14/1)], Jörg Böhme (8/1) [77.Olivier Neuville (39/4)], Bernd Schneider (21/1), Michael Ballack (32/12), Fredi Bobic (20/3) [68.Gerald Asamoa (17/2)], Miroslav Josef Klose (24/14) [46.Paul Freier (5/0)]. Trainer: Rudolf Völler (33).
Goal: Fredi Bobic (34).

727. 12.02.2003 **SPAIN - GERMANY** **3-1(1-1)**
Estadio Son Moix, Palma de Mallorca; Referee: Michael Anthony Riley (England); Attendance: 20,000
GER: Oliver Kahn (57/0), Arne Friedrich (5/0), Christian Wörns (42/0), Christoph Metzelder (16/0), Tobias Rau (1/0) [51.Frank Baumann (14/2); 62.Hann Balitsch (1/0)], Bernd Schneider (22/1) [74.Paul Freier (6/0)], Carsten Ramelow (35/0), Jens Jeremies (46/1), Jörg Böhme (9/1), Fredi Bobic (21/4 [59.Benjamin Lauth (1/0)], Miroslav Josef Klose (25/14) [83.Olivier Neuville (40/4)]. Trainer: Rudolf Völler (34).
Goal: Fredi Bobic (38).

728. 29.03.2003 **GERMANY - LITHUANIA** **1-1(1-0)** 12th EC. Qualifiers
Frankenstadion, Nürnberg; Referee: Victor José Esquinas Torres (Spain); Attendance: 40,800
GER: Oliver Kahn (Cap) (58/0), Torsten Frings (20/2), Arne Friedrich (6/0), Christian Wörns (43/0), Tobias Rau (2/0) [82.Paul Freier (7/0)], Carste Ramelow (36/1), Dietmar Hamann (49/4), Bernd Schneider (23/1), Jörg Böhme (10/1) [46.Marko Rehmer (31/4)], Miroslav Josef Klose (26/14), Fredi Bobi (22/4) [72.Kevin Dennis Kurányi (1/0)]. Trainer: Rudolf Völler (35).
Goal: Carsten Ramelow (8).

729. 30.04.2003 **GERMANY – SERBIA & MONTENEGRO** **1-0(0-0)**
Weserstadion, Bremen; Referee: Frank De Bleeckere (Belgium); Attendance: 22,000
GER: Frank Rost (2/0), Frank Baumann (15/2), Christian Wörns (44/0), Arne Friedrich (7/0) [66.Andreas Hinkel (1/0)], Carsten Ramelow (37/1), Sebastia Kehl (15/2), Michael Hartmann (1/0), Paul Freier (8/0) [72.Gerald Asamoah (18/2)], Torsten Frings (21/2), Kevin Dennis Kurányi (2/0) [76.Benjamin Laut (2/0)], Fredi Bobic (23/4) [46.Miroslav Josef Klose (27/14)]. Trainer: Rudolf Völler (36).
Goal: Sebastian Kehl (60).

730. 01.06.2003 **GERMANY - CANADA** **4-1(1-1)**
Volkswagen-Arena, Wolfsburg; Referee: Éric Poulat (France); Attendance: 24,000
GER: Frank Rost (3/0) [46.Hans-Jörg Butt (3/0)], Arne Friedrich (8/0) [46.Andreas Hinkel (2/0)], Christian Wörns (45/0), Frank Baumann (16/2) [59.Mark Rehmer (32/4)], Tobias Rau (3/1), Carsten Ramelow (38/2) [46.Paul Freier (9/1)], Sebastian Kehl (16/2), Bernd Schneider (24/1) [75.Michael Hartman (2/0)], Torsten Frings (22/2), Fredi Bobic (24/5) [69.Kevin Dennis Kurányi (3/0)], Benjamin Lauth (3/0) [46.Olivier Neuville (41/4)]. Trainer: Rudolf Völle (37).
Goals: Carsten Ramelow (41), Paul Freier (53), Fredi Bobic (61), Tobias Rau (90).

731. 07.06.2003 **SCOTLAND - GERMANY** **1-1(0-1)** 12th EC. Qualifiers
Hampden Park, Glasgow; Referee: Domenico Messina (Italy); Attendance: 52,000
GER: Oliver Kahn (59/0), Arne Friedrich (9/0), Carsten Ramelow (39/2), Christian Wörns (46/0), Torsten Frings (23/2), Jens Jeremies (47/1), Tobias Ra (4/1) [57.Paul Freier (10/1)], Bernd Schneider (25/1) [85.Sebastian Kehl (17/2)], Michael Ballack (33/12), Fredi Bobic (25/6), Miroslav Josef Klose (28/14 [73.Olivier Neuville (42/4)]. Trainer: Rudolf Völler (38).
Goal: Fredi Bobic (22).

732. 11.06.2003 **FAROE ISLANDS - GERMANY** **0-2(0-0)** 12th EC. Qualifiers
Tórsvøllur, Tórshavn; Referee: Jan Willem Wegereef (Netherlands); Attendance: 6,500
GER: Oliver Kahn (60/0) [46.Frank Rost (4/0)], Arne Friedrich (10/0), Carsten Ramelow (40/2), Christian Wörns (47/0), Paul Freier (11/1), Jens Jeremie (48/1) [65.Miroslav Josef Klose (29/15)], Sebastian Kehl (18/2), Tobias Rau (5/1) [72.Michael Hartmann (3/0)], Bernd Schneider (26/1), Fredi Bobic (26/7 Olivier Neuville (43/4). Trainer: Rudolf Völler (39).
Goals: Miroslav Josef Klose (89), Fredi Bobic (90).

733. 20.08.2003 **GERMANY - ITALY** **0-1(0-1)**
„Gottlieb Daimler" Stadion, Stuttgart; Referee: Kim Milton Nielsen (Denmark); Attendance: 50,100
GER: Oliver Kahn (61/0), Andreas Hinkel (3/0), Christian Wörns (48/0) [46.Marko Rehmer (33/4)], Frank Baumann (17/2), Tobias Rau (6/1), Carste Ramelow (41/2) [46.Sebastian Kehl (19/2)], Jens Jeremies (49/1), Bernd Schneider (27/1), Paul Freier (12/1), Olivier Neuville (44/4) [71.Benjamin Laut (4/0)], Fredi Bobic (27/7) [60.Miroslav Josef Klose (30/15)]. Trainer: Rudolf Völler (40).

734. 06.09.2003 **ICELAND - GERMANY** **0-0** 12th EC. Qualifiers
Laugardalsvöllur, Reykjavík; Referee: Graham P. Barber (England); Attendance: 15,000
GER: Oliver Kahn (62/0), Arne Friedrich (11/0), Christian Wörns (49/0), Frank Baumann (18/2), Carsten Ramelow (42/2), Michael Ballack (34/12 Sebastian Kehl (20/2), Christian Rahn (3/0) [60.Michael Hartmann (4/0)], Bernd Schneider (28/1) [69.Sebastian Deisler (20/3)], Miroslav Josef Klos (31/15), Olivier Neuville (45/4) [46.Kevin Dennis Kurányi (4/0)]. Trainer: Rudolf Völler (41).

735. 10.09.2003 **GERMANY - SCOTLAND** **2-1(1-0)** 12th EC. Qualifiers
Westfalenstadion, Dortmund; Referee: Anders Frisk (Sweden); Attendance: 67,000
GER: Oliver Kahn (63/0), Marko Rehmer (34/4), Carsten Ramelow (43/2), Christian Wörns (50/0), Arne Friedrich (12/0), Frank Baumann (19/2), Tobias Rau (7/1), Bernd Schneider (29/1) [81.Sebastian Kehl (21/2)], Michael Ballack (35/13), Fredi Bobic (28/8) [76.Miroslav Josef Klose (32/15)], Kevin Dennis Kurányi (5/0). Trainer: Rudolf Völler (42).
Goals: Fredi Bobic (25), Michael Ballack (50 penalty).

736. 11.10.2003 **GERMANY - ICELAND** **3-0(1-0)** 12th EC. Qualifiers
AOL-Arena, Hamburg; Referee: Valentin Ivanov (Russia); Attendance: 50,800
GER: Oliver Kahn (64/0), Arne Friedrich (13/0), Carsten Ramelow (44/2), Christian Wörns (51/0), Andreas Hinkel (4/0), Frank Baumann (20/2), Christian Rahn (4/0), Bernd Schneider (30/1), Michael Ballack (36/14), Fredi Bobic (29/9) [71.Miroslav Josef Klose (33/15)], Kevin Dennis Kurányi (6/1) [85.Olivier Neuville (46/4)]. Trainer: Rudolf Völler (43).
Goals: Michael Ballack (9), Fredi Bobic (60), Kevin Dennis Kurányi (79).

737. 15.11.2003 **GERMANY - FRANCE** **0-3(0-1)**
Arena „Auf Schalke", Gelsenkirchen; Referee: Stefano Farina (Italy); Attendance: 53,600
GER: Oliver Kahn (65/0), Arne Friedrich (14/0), Christian Wörns (52/0), Jens Nowotny (38/0) [76.Marko Rehmer (35/4)], Andreas Hinkel (5/0), Jens Jeremies (50/1), Frank Baumann (21/2) [71.Fabian Ernst (3/0)], Bernd Schneider (31/1) [67.Paul Freier (13/1)], Michael Ballack (37/14), Fredi Bobic (30/9) [67.Miroslav Josef Klose (34/15)], Kevin Dennis Kurányi (7/1). Trainer: Rudolf Völler (44).

738. 18.02.2004 **CROATIA - GERMANY** **1-2(0-1)**
Stadion Poljud, Split; Referee: Peter Fröjdfeldt (Sweden); Attendance: 15,000
GER: Oliver Kahn (66/0), Arne Friedrich (15/0), Christian Wörns (53/0), Jens Nowotny (39/0), Philipp Lahm (1/0), Frank Baumann (22/2), Dietmar Hamann (50/4), Paul Freier (14/1) [77.Bernd Schneider (32/1)], Torsten Frings (24/2) [62.Carsten Ramelow (45/3)], Miroslav Josef Klose (35/16) [80.Benjamin Lauth (5/0)], Kevin Dennis Kurányi (8/1) [67.Fredi Bobic (31/9)]. Trainer: Rudolf Völler (45).
Goals: Miroslav Josef Klose (34), Carsten Ramelow (90).

739. 31.03.2004 **GERMANY - BELGIUM** **3-0(1-0)**
Müngersdorferstadion, Köln; Referee: Jan Willem Wegereef (Netherlands); Attendance: 46,000
GER: Jens Lehmann (17/0), Arne Friedrich (16/0), Christian Wörns (54/0), Jens Nowotny (40/0), Philipp Lahm (2/0), Torsten Frings (25/2) [62.Fabian Ernst (4/0)], Dietmar Hamann (51/5), Michael Ballack (38/15) [84.Christian Rahn (5/0)], Bernd Schneider (33/1) [62.Olivier Neuville (47/4)], Paul Freier (15/1) [71.Jens Jeremies (51/1)], Kevin Dennis Kurányi (9/2) [78.Fredi Bobic (32/9)]. Trainer: Rudolf Völler (46).
Goals: Kevin Dennis Kurányi (45), Dietmar Hamann (55), Michael Ballack (81).

740. 28.04.2004 **ROMANIA - GERMANY** **5-1(4-0)**
Stadionul Giuleşti, Bucureşti; Referee: Roberto Rosetti (Italy); Attendance: 14,000
GER: Oliver Kahn (67/0) [46.Timo Hildebrand (1/0)], Arne Friedrich (17/0), Carsten Ramelow (46/3), Jens Jeremies (52/1), Philipp Lahm (3/1), Bernd Schneider (34/1), Dietmar Hamann (52/5), Fabian Ernst (5/0) [77.Sebastian Kehl (22/2)], Torsten Frings (26/2) [46.Paul Freier (16/1)], Fredi Bobic (33/9) [62.Olivier Neuville (48/4)], Kevin Dennis Kurányi (10/2). Trainer: Rudolf Völler (47).
Goal: Philipp Lahm (88).

741. 27.05.2004 **GERMANY - MALTA** **7-0(4-0)**
Dreisam Stadion, Freiburg; Referee: Anton Stredák (Slovakia); Attendance: 22,000
GER: Jens Lehmann (18/0), Andreas Hinkel (6/0) [46.Paul Freier (17/1); 62.Sebastian Kehl (23/2)], Arne Friedrich (18/0), Jens Nowotny (41/1), Philipp Lahm (4/1) [69.Christian Ziege (72/9)], Bernd Schneider (35/1), Dietmar Hamann (53/5) [69.Jens Jeremies (53/1)], Torsten Frings (27/3), Michael Ballack (39/19), Fredi Bobic (34/10), Kevin Dennis Kurányi (11/2) [46.Miroslav Josef Klose (36/16)]. Trainer: Rudolf Völler (48).
Goals: Michael Ballack (15, 17), Jens Nowotny (33), Torsten Frings (42), Michael Ballack (59, 86), Fredi Bobic (90).

742. 02.06.2004 **SWITZERLAND - GERMANY** **0-2(0-0)**
„St. Jakob" Stadion, Basel; Referee: Domenico Messina (Italy); Attendance: 30,000
GER: Oliver Kahn (Cap) (68/0), Arne Friedrich (19/0), Christian Wörns (55/0), Jens Nowotny (42/1), Philipp Lahm (5/1), Bernd Schneider (36/1) [62.Torsten Frings (28/3)], Dietmar Hamann (54/5) [87.Jens Jeremies (54/1)], Frank Baumann (23/2) [73.Fabian Ernst (6/0)], Michael Ballack (40/19) [87.Sebastian Kehl (24/2)], Miroslav Josef Klose (37/16) [62.Thomas Brdaric (2/0)], Kevin Dennis Kurányi (12/4). Trainer: Rudolf Völler (49).
Goals: Kevin Dennis Kurányi (62, 84).

743. 06.06.2004 **GERMANY - HUNGARY** **0-2(0-2)**
„Fritz Walter" Stadion, Kaiserslautern; Referee: Steve Bennett (England); Attendance: 36,950
GER: Oliver Kahn (Cap) (69/0), Andreas Hinkel (7/0) [46.Bastian Schweinsteiger (1/0)], Christian Wörns (56/0), Jens Nowotny (43/1) [61.Frank Baumann (24/2)], Philipp Lahm (6/1), Bernd Schneider (37/1), Torsten Frings (29/3), Dietmar Hamann (55/5) [84.Fabian Ernst (7/0)], Michael Ballack (41/19), Miroslav Josef Klose (38/16) [46.Thomas Brdaric (3/0)], Fredi Bobic (35/10) [74.Lukas Josef Podolski (1/0)]. Trainer: Rudolf Völler (50).

744. 15.06.2004 **GERMANY - NETHERLANDS** **1-1(1-0)** 12th EC. Group Stage.
Estádio do Dragão, Porto (Portugal); Referee: Anders Frisk (Sweden); Attendance: 52,000
GER: Oliver Kahn (Cap) (70/0), Arne Friedrich (20/0), Christian Wörns (57/0), Jens Nowotny (44/1), Philipp Lahm (7/1), Frank Baumann (25/2), Dietmar Hamann (56/5), Bernd Schneider (38/1) [68.Bastian Schweinsteiger (2/0)], Michael Ballack (42/19), Torsten Frings (30/4) [79.Fabian Ernst (8/0)], Kevin Dennis Kurányi (13/4) [85.Fredi Bobic (36/10)]. Trainer: Rudolf Völler (51).
Goal: Torsten Frings (30).

745. 19.06.2004 **GERMANY - LATVIA** **0-0** 12th EC. Group Stage.
Estádio do Bessa Século XXI, Porto (Portugal); Referee: Michael Anthony Riley (England); Attendance: 22,344
GER: Oliver Kahn (Cap) (71/0), Arne Friedrich (21/0), Christian Wörns (58/0), Frank Baumann (26/2), Philipp Lahm (8/1), Dietmar Hamann (57/5), Bernd Schneider (39/1) [46.Bastian Schweinsteiger (3/0)], Michael Ballack (43/19), Torsten Frings (31/4), Fredi Bobic (37/10) [67.Miroslav Josef Klose (39/16)], Kevin Dennis Kurányi (14/4) [77.Thomas Brdaric (4/0)]. Trainer: Rudolf Völler (52).

746. 23.06.2004 **GERMANY – CZECH REPUBLIC** **1-2(1-1)** 12th EC. Group Stage.
Estádio "José Alvalade", Lisboa (Portugal); Referee: Terje Hauge (Norway); Attendance: 46,849
GER: Oliver Kahn (Cap) (72/0), Arne Friedrich (22/0), Jens Nowotny (45/1), Christian Wörns (59/0), Torsten Frings (32/4) [46.Lukas Josef Podolski (2/0)], Dietmar Hamann (58/5) [79.Miroslav Josef Klose (40/16)], Philipp Lahm (9/1), Bernd Schneider (40/1), Michael Ballack (44/20), Bastian Schweinsteiger (4/0) [86.Jens Jeremies (55/1)], Kevin Dennis Kurányi (15/4). Trainer: Rudolf Völler (53).
Goal: Michael Ballack (21).

747. 18.08.2004 **AUSTRIA - GERMANY** **1-3(1-1)**
„Ernst Happel" Stadion, Wien; Referee: Pierluigi Collina (Italy); Attendance: 37,900
GER: Oliver Kahn (73/0) [46.Jens Lehmann (19/0)], Frank Fahrenhorst (1/0), Thomas Linke (43/1), Andreas Hinkel (8/0) [86.Robert Huth (1/0)], Torsten Frings (33/4) [86.Frank Baumann (27/2)], Philipp Lahm (10/1), Tim Borowski (3/0), Michael Ballack (Cap) (45/20), Bastian Schweinsteiger (5/0) [62.Fabian Ernst (9/0)], Gerald Asamoah (19/2) [78.Lukas Josef Podolski (3/0)], Kevin Dennis Kurányi (16/7) [78.Thomas Brdaric (5/0)]. Trainer: Jürgen Klinsmann (1).
Goals: Kevin Dennis Kurányi (2, 61, 73).

748. 08.09.2004 **GERMANY - BRAZIL** **1-1(1-1)**
Olympiastadion, Berlin; Referee: Urs Meier (Switzerland); Attendance: 74,315
GER: Oliver Kahn (74/0), Andreas Hinkel (9/0) [87.Andreas Görlitz (1/0)], Frank Fahrenhorst (2/0), Robert Huth (2/0), Philipp Lahm (11/1), Torsten Frings (34/4), Sebastian Deisler (21/3) [87.Lukas Josef Podolski (4/0)], Michael Ballack (Cap) (46/20), Bernd Schneider (41/1), Gerald Asamoah (20/2) [70.Miroslav Josef Klose (41/16)], Kevin Dennis Kurányi (17/8). Trainer: Jürgen Klinsmann (2).
Goal: Kevin Dennis Kurányi (17).

749. 09.10.2004 **IRAN - GERMANY** **0-2(0-1)**
Azadi Stadium, Tehran; Referee: Saad Kamil Al Fadhli (Kuwait); Attendance: 110,000
GER: Jens Lehmann (20/0), Andreas Görlitz (2/0), Christian Wörns (60/0) [81.Per Mertesacker (1/0)], Robert Huth (3/0), Philipp Lahm (12/1), Fabian Ernst (10/1) [87.Bastian Schweinsteiger (6/0)], Sebastian Deisler (22/3) [79.Tim Borowski (4/0)], Michael Ballack (Cap) (47/20), Bernd Schneider (42/1) [68.Thomas Hitzlsperger (1/0)], Thomas Brdaric (6/1) [73.Lukas Josef Podolski (5/0)], Miroslav Josef Klose (42/16) [55.Gerald Asamoah (21/2)]. Trainer: Jürgen Klinsmann (3).
Goals: Fabian Ernst (5), Thomas Brdaric (53).

750. 17.11.2004 **GERMANY - CAMEROON** **3-0(0-0)**
Zentralstadion, Leipzig; Referee: Massimo De Santis (Italy); Attendance: 44,200
GER: Jens Lehmann (21/0), Bernd Schneider (43/1), Per Mertesacker (2/0), Robert Huth (4/0), Philipp Lahm (13/1) [66.Thomas Hitzlsperger (2/0)], Torsten Frings (35/4), Fabian Ernst (11/1) [80.Tim Borowski (5/0)], Bastian Schweinsteiger (7/0), Michael Ballack (Cap) (48/20), Gerald Asamoah (22/2) [62.Miroslav Josef Klose (43/18)], Kevin Dennis Kurányi (18/9). Trainer: Jürgen Klinsmann (4).
Goals: Kevin Dennis Kurányi (71), Miroslav Josef Klose (78, 88).

751. 16.12.2004 **JAPAN - GERMANY** **0-3(0-0)**
International Stadium, Yokohama; Referee: Mark Shield (Australia); Attendance: 61,805
GER: Oliver Kahn (75/0), Patrick Owomoyela (1/0), Christian Wörns (61/0), Per Mertesacker (3/0), Christian Schulz (1/0), Bernd Schneider (44/1) [73.Tim Borowski (6/0)], Fabian Ernst (12/1) [77.Marco Engelhardt (1/0)], Michael Ballack (Cap) (49/21), Gerald Asamoah (23/2), Miroslav Josef Klose (44/20), Lukas Josef Podolski (6/0) [62.Bastian Schweinsteiger (8/0)]. Trainer: Jürgen Klinsmann (5).
Goals: Miroslav Josef Klose (54), Michael Ballack (69), Miroslav Josef Klose (90).

752. 19.12.2004 **KOREA REPUBLIC - GERMANY** **3-1(1-1)**
Asiad Main Stadium, Busan; Referee: Subkhiddin Mohd Salleh (Malaysia); Attendance: 45,775
GER: Oliver Kahn (76/0), Andreas Hinkel (10/0) [46.Patrick Owomoyela (2/0)], Arne Friedrich (23/0), Christian Wörns (62/0) [86.Thomas Brdaric (7/1)], Philipp Lahm (14/1), Fabian Ernst (13/1), Bernd Schneider (45/1), Michael Ballack (Cap) (50/22), Bastian Schweinsteiger (9/0) [63.Lukas Josef Podolski (7/0)], Kevin Dennis Kurányi (19/9) [76.Gerald Asamoah (24/2)], Miroslav Josef Klose (45/20). Trainer: Jürgen Klinsmann (6).
Goal: Michael Ballack (24).

753. 21.12.2004 **THAILAND - GERMANY** **1-5(0-2)**
Rajamangala National Stadium, Bangkok; Referee: Shamsul Maidin (Singapore); Attendance: 15,000
GER: Timo Hildebrand (2/0), Andreas Hinkel (11/0) [33.Patrick Owomoyela (3/0)], Per Mertesacker (4/0), Arne Friedrich (Cap) (24/0) [67.Christian Wörns (63/0)], Philipp Lahm (15/1) [60.Christian Schulz (2/0)], Tim Borowski (7/0), Marco Engelhardt (2/0), Bastian Schweinsteiger (10/0), Gerald Asamoah (25/3), Kevin Dennis Kurányi (20/11), Thomas Brdaric (8/1) [60.Lukas Josef Podolski (8/2)]. Trainer: Jürgen Klinsmann (7).
Goals: Kevin Dennis Kurányi (34, 38), Lukas Josef Podolski (73), Gerald Asamoah (84), Lukas Josef Podolski (89).

754. 09.02.2005 **GERMANY - ARGENTINA** **2-2(2-1)**
LTU-Arena, Düsseldorf; Referee: Stefano Farina (Italy); Attendance: 52,000
GER: Jens Lehmann (22/0), Patrick Owomoyela (4/0), Christian Wörns (Cap) (64/0), Per Mertesacker (5/0), Thomas Hitzlsperger (3/0), Torsten Frings (36/5), Fabian Ernst (14/1), Bernd Schneider (46/1), Gerald Asamoah (26/3) [29.Paul Freier (18/1)], Bastian Schweinsteiger (11/0) [75.Christian Schulz (3/0)], Kevin Dennis Kurányi (21/12). Trainer: Jürgen Klinsmann (8).
Goals: Torsten Frings (28 penalty), Kevin Dennis Kurányi (45).

755. 26.03.2005 **SLOVENIA - GERMANY** **0-1(0-1)**
Športni Park "Arena Petrol", Celje; Referee: Graham Poll (England); Attendance: 9,200
GER: Oliver Kahn (77/0), Andreas Hinkel (12/0) [73.Patrick Owomoyela (5/0)], Arne Friedrich (25/0), Robert Huth (5/0), Thomas Hitzlsperger (4/0), Torsten Frings (37/5), Frank Baumann (28/2) [59.Bastian Schweinsteiger (12/0)], Michael Ballack (Cap) (51/22), Olivier Neuville (49/4) [84.Tim Borowski (8/0)], Miroslav Josef Klose (46/20) [75.Kevin Dennis Kurányi (22/12)], Lukas Josef Podolski (9/3). Trainer: Jürgen Klinsmann (9).
Goal: Lukas Josef Podolski (27).

756. 04.06.2005 **NORTHERN IRELAND - GERMANY** **1-4(1-1)**
Windsor Park, Belfast; Referee: Charles Joseph Richmond (Scotland); Attendance: 14,800
GER: Jens Lehmann (23/0), Patrick Owomoyela (6/0), Per Mertesacker (6/0), Robert Huth (6/0) [*sent off 15*], Thomas Hitzlsperger (5/0), Torsten Frings (38/5), Bernd Schneider (47/1) [46.Sebastian Deisler (23/3)], Fabian Ernst (15/1), Michael Ballack (Cap) (52/24) [73.Tim Borowski (9/0)], Gerald Asamoah (27/4) [46.Bastian Schweinsteiger (13/0)], Kevin Dennis Kurányi (23/12) [63.Lukas Josef Podolski (10/4)]. Trainer: Jürgen Klinsmann (10).
Goals: Gerald Asamoah (17), Michael Ballack (62, 66 penalty), Lukas Josef Podolski (82).

57. 08.06.2005 **GERMANY - RUSSIA** **2-2(1-1)**
orussia-Park, Mönchengladbach; Referee: Konrad Plautz (Austria); Attendance: 46,228
ER: Oliver Kahn (78/0), Andreas Hinkel (13/0) [46.Sebastian Deisler (24/3)], Arne Friedrich (26/0), Per Mertesacker (7/0), Thomas Hitzlsperger (6/0), orsten Frings (39/5), Bernd Schneider (48/1), Michael Ballack (Cap) (53/24), Bastian Schweinsteiger (14/2) [84.Kevin Dennis Kurányi (24/12)], Gerald samoah (28/4) [62.Mike Hanke (1/0)], Lukas Josef Podolski (11/4) [84.Fabian Ernst (16/1)]. Trainer: Jürgen Klinsmann (11).
oals: Bastian Schweinsteiger (30, 69).

58. 15.06.2005 **GERMANY - AUSTRALIA** **4-3(2-2)** 7th FIFA Confederations Cup. Group Stage.
Valdstadion, Frankfurt am Main; Referee: Carlos Arecio Amarilla Demarqui (Paraguay); Attendance: 46,466
ER: Oliver Kahn (79/0), Arne Friedrich (27/0), Per Mertesacker (8/1), Robert Huth (7/0), Thomas Hitzlsperger (7/0), Bernd Schneider (49/1) [76.Sebastian eisler (25/3)], Michael Ballack (Cap) (54/25), Torsten Frings (40/5), Bastian Schweinsteiger (15/2) [83.Fabian Ernst (17/1)], Kevin Dennis Kurányi (25/13) 68.Gerald Asamoah (29/4)], Lukas Josef Podolski (12/5). Trainer: Jürgen Klinsmann (12).
Goals: Kevin Dennis Kurányi (17), Per Mertesacker (23), Michael Ballack (60 penalty), Lukas Josef Podolski (88).

759. 18.06.2005 **GERMANY - TUNISIA** **3-0(0-0)** 7th FIFA Confederations Cup. Group Stage.
RheinEnergie Stadion, Köln; Referee: Peter Prendergast (Jamaica); Attendance: 44,377
GER: Jens Lehmann (24/0), Arne Friedrich (28/0), Per Mertesacker (9/1), Robert Huth (8/0), Thomas Hitzlsperger (8/0) [68.Bernd Schneider (50/1)], Sebastian Deisler (26/3), Torsten Frings (41/5), Michael Ballack (Cap) (55/26), Bastian Schweinsteiger (16/3), Gerald Asamoah (30/4) [62.Kevin Dennis Kurányi (26/13)], Lukas Josef Podolski (13/5) [87.Mike Hanke (2/1)]. Trainer: Jürgen Klinsmann (13).
Goals: Michael Ballack (74 penalty), Bastian Schweinsteiger (80), Mike Hanke (89).

760. 21.06.2005 **GERMANY - ARGENTINA** **2-2(1-1)** 7th FIFA Confederations Cup. Group Stage.
Frankenstadion, Nürnberg; Referee: Luboš Michel (Slovakia); Attendance: 42,088
GER: Timo Hildebrand (3/0), Andreas Hinkel (14/0), Per Mertesacker (10/1), Robert Huth (9/0), Thomas Hitzlsperger (9/0), Fabian Ernst (18/1), Sebastian Deisler (27/3), Bernd Schneider (Cap) (51/1) [46.Torsten Frings (42/5)], Bastian Schweinsteiger (17/3) [70.Marco Engelhardt (3/0)], Gerald Asamoah (31/5) [87.Mike Hanke (3/1)], Kevin Dennis Kurányi (27/14). Trainer: Jürgen Klinsmann (14).
Goals: Kevin Dennis Kurányi (29), Gerald Asamoah (51).

761. 25.06.2005 **GERMANY - BRAZIL** **2-3(2-2)** 7th FIFA Confederations Cup. Semi-Finals.
Frankenstadion, Nürnberg; Referee: Carlos Chandía Alarcón (Chile); Attendance: 41,926
GER: Jens Lehmann (25/0), Arne Friedrich (29/0), Per Mertesacker (11/1), Robert Huth (10/0), Bernd Schneider (52/1), Fabian Ernst (19/1) [87.Tim Borowski (10/0)], Sebastian Deisler (28/3) [83.Mike Hanke (4/1)], Michael Ballack (Cap) (56/27), Torsten Frings (43/5), Kevin Dennis Kurányi (28/14) [63.Gerald Asamoah (32/5)], Lukas Josef Podolski (14/6). Trainer: Jürgen Klinsmann (15).
Goals: Lukas Josef Podolski (23), Michael Ballack (45 penalty).

762. 29.06.2005 **GERMANY - MEXICO** **4-3(2-1,3-3)** 7th FIFA Confederations Cup. Third Place Play-off.
Zentralstadion, Leipzig; Referee: Matthew Breeze (Australia); Attendance: 43,335
GER: Oliver Kahn (80/0), Andreas Hinkel (15/0), Per Mertesacker (12/1), Robert Huth (11/1), Bernd Schneider (53/1), Sebastian Deisler (29/3) [67.Gerald Asamoah (33/5)], Torsten Frings (44/5), Michael Ballack (Cap) (57/28), Bastian Schweinsteiger (18/4) [83.Fabian Ernst (20/1)], Mike Hanke (5/1) [*sent off 54*], Lukas Josef Podolski (15/7) [74.Kevin Dennis Kurányi (29/14)]. Trainer: Jürgen Klinsmann (16).
Goals: Lukas Josef Podolski (37), Bastian Schweinsteiger (41), Robert Huth (79), Michael Ballack (97).

763. 17.08.2005 **NETHERLANDS - GERMANY** **2-2(1-0)**
Stadion Feijenoord, Rotterdam; Referee: Terje Hauge (Norway); Attendance: 45,500
GER: Oliver Kahn (81/0), Arne Friedrich (30/0) [74.Andreas Hinkel (16/0)], Per Mertesacker (13/1) [66.Robert Huth (12/1)], Christian Wörns (65/0), Bernd Schneider (54/1), Torsten Frings (45/5) [66.Thomas Hitzlsperger (10/0)], Dietmar Hamann (59/5) [74.Tim Borowski (11/0)], Fabian Ernst (21/1) [46.Sebastian Deisler (30/3)], Michael Ballack (Cap) (58/29), Miroslav Josef Klose (47/20) [46.Gerald Asamoah (34/6)], Kevin Dennis Kurányi (30/14). Trainer: Jürgen Klinsmann (17).
Goals: Michael Ballack (49), Gerald Asamoah (81).

764. 03.09.2005 **SLOVAKIA - GERMANY** **2-0(2-0)**
Štadión Tehelné pole, Bratislava; Referee: Eric Bramhaar (Netherlands); Attendance: 9,276
GER: Jens Lehmann (26/0), Patrick Owomoyela (7/0) [74.Andreas Hinkel (17/0)], Per Mertesacker (14/1), Christian Wörns (66/0) [46.Lukas Sinkiewicz (1/0)], Thomas Hitzlsperger (11/0) [46.Marcell Jansen (1/0)], Sebastian Deisler (31/3), Fabian Ernst (22/1) [46.Bastian Schweinsteiger (19/4)], Bernd Schneider (55/1) [82.Kevin Dennis Kurányi (31/14)], Michael Ballack (Cap) (59/29), Gerald Asamoah (35/6) [46.Lukas Josef Podolski (16/7)], Miroslav Josef Klose (48/20). Trainer: Jürgen Klinsmann (18).

765. 07.09.2005 **GERMANY – SOUTH AFRICA** **4-2(1-1)**
Weserstadion, Bremen; Referee: Grzegorz Gilewski (Poland); Attendance: 28,100
GER: Jens Lehmann (27/0), Patrick Owomoyela (8/0), Lukas Sinkiewicz (2/0), Per Mertesacker (15/1), Marcell Jansen (2/0), Sebastian Deisler (32/3) [46.Bernd Schneider (56/1)], Tim Borowski (12/1), Michael Ballack (Cap) (60/29), Bastian Schweinsteiger (20/4) [68.Fabian Ernst (23/1)], Miroslav Josef Klose (49/20) [77.Kevin Dennis Kurányi (32/14)], Lukas Josef Podolski (17/10) [77.Gerald Asamoah (36/6)]. Trainer: Jürgen Klinsmann (19).
Goals: Lukas Josef Podolski (12), Tim Borowski (47), Lukas Josef Podolski (48, 55).

766. 08.10.2005 **TURKEY - GERMANY** **2-1(1-0)**
Atatürk Olimpiyat Stadı, İstanbul; Referee: Domenico Mesina (Italy); Attendance: 25,000
GER: Oliver Kahn (Cap) (82/0), Patrick Owomoyela (9/0), Lukas Sinkiewicz (3/0), Per Mertesacker (16/1), Marcell Jansen (3/0), Torsten Frings (46/5) [46.Sebastian Deisler (33/3)], Bernd Schneider (57/1), Tim Borowski (13/1) [73.Mike Hanke (6/1)], Bastian Schweinsteiger (21/4) [82.Thomas Hitzlsperger (12/0)], Kevin Dennis Kurányi (33/14) [46.Olivier Neuville (50/5)], Lukas Josef Podolski (18/10). Trainer: Jürgen Klinsmann (20).
Goal: Olivier Neuville (90).

767. 12.10.2005 **GERMANY – CHINA P.R.** **1-0(0-0)**
AOL-Arena, Hamburg; Referee: Lucilio Cardoso Cortez Batista (Portugal); Attendance: 45,000
GER: Oliver Kahn (Cap) (83/0), Arne Friedrich (31/0), Christoph Metzelder (17/0), Per Mertesacker (17/1) [46.Robert Huth (13/1)], Bastian Schweinsteiger (22/4) [89.Thomas Hitzlsperger (13/0)], Torsten Frings (47/6), Sebastian Deisler (34/3), Tim Borowski (14/1), Bernd Schneider (58/1), Olivier Neuville (51/5) [90.Patrick Owomoyela (10/0)], Lukas Josef Podolski (19/10) [52.Kevin Dennis Kurányi (34/14)]. Trainer: Jürgen Klinsmann (21).
Goal: Torsten Frings (51 penalty).

768. 12.11.2005 **FRANCE - GERMANY** **0-0**
Stade de France, Saint-Denis, Paris; Referee: Steve Bennett (England); Attendance: 58,889
GER: Jens Lehmann (28/0), Arne Friedrich (32/0), Per Mertesacker (18/1), Robert Huth (14/1), Marcell Jansen (4/0), Sebastian Deisler (35/3) [46.Bastian Schweinsteiger (23/4)], Torsten Frings (48/6), Michael Ballack (Cap) (61/29), Bernd Schneider (59/1) [76.Tim Borowski (15/1)], Lukas Josef Podolski (20/10) [83.Kevin Dennis Kurányi (35/14)], Miroslav Josef Klose (50/20). Trainer: Jürgen Klinsmann (22).

769. 01.03.2006 **ITALY - GERMANY** **4-1(3-0)**
Stadio "Artemio Franchi", Firenze; Referee: Eduardo Itturalde González (Spain); Attendance: 28,317
GER: Jens Lehmann (29/0), Arne Friedrich (33/0), Per Mertesacker (19/1) [46.Christoph Metzelder (18/0)], Robert Huth (15/2), Phillip Lahm (16/1), Sebastian Deisler (36/3), Torsten Frings (49/6) [68.Tim Borowski (16/1)], Michael Ballack (Cap) (62/29), Bernd Schneider (60/1) [68.Bastian Schweinsteiger (24/4)], Miroslav Josef Klose (51/20), Lukas Josef Podolski (21/10) [46.Gerald Asamoah (37/6)]. Trainer: Jürgen Klinsmann (23).
Goal: Roberth Huth (82).

770. 22.03.2006 **GERMANY – UNITED STATES** **4-1(0-0)**
Westfalenstadion (Signal Iduna Park), Dortmund; Referee: Peter Fröjdfeldt (Sweden); Attendance: 64,500
GER: Oliver Kahn (84/0), Arne Friedrich (34/0) [83.Patrick Owomoyela (11/0)], Per Mertesacker (20/1), Christoph Metzelder (19/0), Phillip Lahm (17/1), Bernd Schneider (61/1) [67.Tim Borowski (17/1)], Michael Ballack (Cap) (63/30), Sebastian Kehl (25/2) [83.Fabian Ernst (24/1)], Gerald Asamoah (38/6) [67.Olivier Neuville (52/6)], Miroslav Josef Klose (52/21), Lukas Josef Podolski (22/10) [46.Bastian Schweinsteiger (25/5)]. Trainer: Jürgen Klinsmann (24).
Goals: Bastian Schweinsteiger (46), Olivier Neuville (73), Miroslav Josef Klose (75), Michael Ballack (79).

771. 27.05.2006 **GERMANY - LUXEMBOURG** **7-0(3-0)**
badenova-Stadion, Freiburg; Referee: René Rogalla (Switzerland); Attendance: 23,000
GER: Jens Lehmann (30/0) [46.Oliver Kahn (85/0)], Arne Friedrich (35/0), Robert Huth (16/2) [46.Per Mertesacker (21/1)], Christoph Metzelder (20/0), Marcell Jansen (5/0) [46.Thomas Hitzlsperger (14/0)], Bernd Schneider (Cap) (62/1), Torsten Frings (50/7) [46.Sebastian Kehl (26/2)], Tim Borowski (18/1), Bastian Schweinsteiger (26/5), Miroslav Josef Klose (53/23) [63.Gerald Asamoah (39/6)], Lukas Josef Podolski (23/12) [71.Olivier Neuville (53/8)]. Trainer: Jürgen Klinsmann (25).
Goals: Miroslav Josef Klose (5), Torsten Frings (19 penalty), Lukas Josef Podolski (36), Miroslav Josef Klose (59), Lukas Josef Podolski (65), Olivier Neuville (90+1), Olivier Neuville (90+2).

772. 31.05.2006 **GERMANY - JAPAN** **2-2(0-0)**
BayArena, Leverkusen; Referee: Kyros Vassaras (Greece); Attendance: 22,500
GER: Jens Lehmann (31/0), Bernd Schneider (63/1), Per Mertesacker (22/1), Christoph Metzelder (21/0) [55.Jens Nowotny (46/1)], Marcell Jansen (6/0), Michael Ballack (Cap) (64/30), Torsten Frings (51/7), Tim Borowski (19/1) [63.David Odonkor (1/0)], Bastian Schweinsteiger (27/6), Miroslav Josef Klose (54/24), Lukas Josef Podolski (24/12) [70.Olivier Neuville (54/8)]. Trainer: Jürgen Klinsmann (26).
Goals: Miroslav Josef Klose (75), Bastian Schweinsteiger (80).

773. 03.06.2006 **GERMANY - COLOMBIA** **3-0(2-0)**
Borussia-Park, Mönchengladbach; Referee: Terje Hauge (Norway); Attendance: 45,000
GER: Jens Lehmann (32/0), Arne Friedrich (36/0), Per Mertesacker (23/1), Christoph Metzelder (22/0), Phillip Lahm (18/1) [86.Thomas Hitzlsperger (15/0)], Bernd Schneider (64/1) [62.Tim Borowski (20/2)], Michael Ballack (Cap) (65/31), Torsten Frings (52/7) [71.Sebastian Kehl (27/2)], Bastian Schweinsteiger (28/7) [73.Marcell Jansen (7/0)], Miroslav Josef Klose (55/24) [61.Olivier Neuville (55/8)], Lukas Josef Podolski (25/12) [71.Gerald Asamoah (40/6)]. Trainer: Jürgen Klinsmann (27).
Goals: Michael Ballack (20), Bastian Schweinsteiger (37), Tim Borowski (69).

774. 09.06.2006 **GERMANY – COSTA RICA** **4-2(2-1)** 18th FIFA WC. Group Stage.
FIFA World Cup Stadium (Allianz-Arena), München; Referee: Horacio Marcelo Elizondo (Argentina); Attendance: 59,416
GER: Jens Lehmann (33/0), Arne Friedrich (37/0), Per Mertesacker (24/1), Christoph Metzelder (23/0), Phillip Lahm (19/2), Bernd Schneider (Cap) (65/1) [90+1.David Odonkor (2/0)], Torsten Frings (53/8), Tim Borowski (21/2) [72.Sebastian Kehl (28/2)], Bastian Schweinsteiger (29/7), Miroslav Josef Klose (56/26) [79.Olivier Neuville (56/8)], Lukas Josef Podolski (26/12). Trainer: Jürgen Klinsmann (28).
Goals: Phillip Lahm (6), Miroslav Josef Klose (17, 61), Torsten Frings (87).

775. 14.06.2006 **GERMANY - POLAND** **1-0(0-0)** 18th FIFA WC. Group Stage.
FIFA World Cup Stadium (Signal-Iduna Park), Dortmund; Referee: Luis Medina Cantalejo (Spain); Attendance: 65,000
GER: Jens Lehmann (34/0), Arne Friedrich (38/0) [63.David Odonkor (3/0)], Per Mertesacker (25/1), Christoph Metzelder (24/0), Phillip Lahm (20/2), Bernd Schneider (66/1), Torsten Frings (54/8), Michael Ballack (Cap) (66/31), Bastian Schweinsteiger (30/7) [77.Tim Borowski (22/2)], Miroslav Josef Klose (57/26), Lukas Josef Podolski (27/12) [70.Olivier Neuville (57/9)]. Trainer: Jürgen Klinsmann (29).
Goal: Olivier Neuville (90+1).

776. 20.06.2006 **GERMANY - ECUADOR** **3-0(2-0)** 18th FIFA WC. Group Stage.
Olympiastadion, Berlin; Referee: Valentin Ivanov (Russia); Attendance: 72,000
GER: Jens Lehmann (35/0), Arne Friedrich (39/0), Per Mertesacker (26/1), Robert Huth (17/2), Phillip Lahm (21/2), Bernd Schneider (67/1) [73.Gerald Asamoah (41/6)], Torsten Frings (55/8) [66.Tim Borowski (23/2)], Michael Ballack (Cap) (67/31), Bastian Schweinsteiger (31/7), Miroslav Josef Klose (58/28) [66.Olivier Neuville (58/9)], Lukas Josef Podolski (28/13). Trainer: Jürgen Klinsmann (30).
Goals: Miroslav Josef Klose (4, 44), Lukas Josef Podolski (57).

777. 24.06.2006 **GERMANY - SWEDEN** **2-0(2-0)** 18th FIFA WC. 2nd Round of 16.
FIFA World Cup Stadium (Allianz-Arena), München; Referee: Carlos Eugênio Simon (Brazil); Attendance: 66,000
GER: Jens Lehmann (36/0), Arne Friedrich (40/0), Per Mertesacker (27/1), Christoph Metzelder (25/0), Phillip Lahm (22/2), Bernd Schneider (68/1), Torsten Frings (56/8) [85.Sebastian Kehl (29/2)], Michael Ballack (Cap) (68/31), Bastian Schweinsteiger (32/7) [72.Tim Borowski (24/2)], Miroslav Josef Klose (59/28), Lukas Josef Podolski (29/15) [74.Olivier Neuville (59/9)]. Trainer: Jürgen Klinsmann (31).
Goals: Lukas Josef Podolski (4, 12).

778. 30.06.2006 **GERMANY - ARGENTINA** **1-1(0-0,1-1,1-1); 4-2 on penalties** 18th FIFA WC. Quarter-Finals.
Olympiastadion, Berlin; Referee: Ľuboš Michel (Slovakia); Attendance: 72,000
GER: Jens Lehmann (37/0), Arne Friedrich (41/0), Per Mertesacker (28/1), Christoph Metzelder (26/0), Phillip Lahm (23/2), Bernd Schneider (69/1) [62.David Odonkor (4/0)], Torsten Frings (57/8), Michael Ballack (Cap) (69/31), Bastian Schweinsteiger (33/7) [74.Tim Borowski (25/2)], Miroslav Josef Klose (60/29) [86.Olivier Neuville (60/9)], Lukas Josef Podolski (30/15). Trainer: Jürgen Klinsmann (32).
Goal: Miroslav Josef Klose (80).
Penalties: Olivier Neuville, Michael Ballack, Lukas Josef Podolski, Tim Borowski.

79. 04.07.2006 **GERMANY - ITALY** **0-2(0-0,0-0)** 18th FIFA WC. Semi-Finals.
FIFA World Cup Stadium (Signal-Iduna Park), Dortmund; Referee: Benito Armando Archundia Téllez (Mexico); Attendance: 65,000
GER: Jens Lehmann (38/0), Arne Friedrich (42/0), Per Mertesacker (29/1), Christoph Metzelder (27/0), Phillip Lahm (24/2), Bernd Schneider (70/1) [83.David Odonkor (5/0)], Sebastian Kehl (30/2), Michael Ballack (Cap) (70/31), Tim Borowski (26/2) [73.Bastian Schweinsteiger (34/7)], Miroslav Josef Klose (61/29) [111.Olivier Neuville (61/9)], Lukas Josef Podolski (31/15). Trainer: Jürgen Klinsmann (33).

80. 08.07.2006 **GERMANY - PORTUGAL** **3-1(0-0)** 18th FIFA WC. Third Place Play-off.
„Gottlieb Daimler" Stadion, Stuttgart; Referee: Toru Kamikawa (Japan); Attendance: 52,000
GER: Oliver Kahn (Cap) (86/0), Phillip Lahm (25/2), Jens Nowotny (47/1), Christoph Metzelder (28/0), Marcell Jansen (8/0), Bernd Schneider (71/1), Torsten Frings (58/8), Sebastian Kehl (31/2), Bastian Schweinsteiger (35/9) [79.Thomas Hitzlsperger (16/0)], Miroslav Josef Klose (62/29) [65.Olivier Neuville (62/9)], Lukas Josef Podolski (32/15) [71.Mike Hanke (7/1)]. Trainer: Jürgen Klinsmann (34).
Goals: Bastian Schweinsteiger (56), Armando Gonçalves Teixeira „Petit" (65 own goal), Bastian Schweinsteiger (78).

81. 17.08.2006 **GERMANY - SWEDEN** **3-0(3-0)**
Veltins-Arena, Gelsenkirchen; Referee: Stefano Farina (Italy); Attendance: 53,000
GER: Jens Lehmann (39/0), Phillip Lahm (26/2), Arne Friedrich (43/0) [46.Manuel Friedrich (1/0)], Jens Nowotny (48/1), Marcell Jansen (9/0) [46.Malik Fathi (1/0)], Bernd Schneider (Cap) (72/2) [82.David Odonkor (6/0)], Torsten Frings (59/8) [74.Thomas Hitzlsperger (17/0)], Tim Borowski (27/2), Bastian Schweinsteiger (36/9), Miroslav Josef Klose (63/31) [46.Olivier Neuville (63/9)], Lukas Josef Podolski (33/15) [64.Gerald Asamoah (42/6)]. Trainer: Joachim Löw (1).
Goals: Bernd Schneider (4), Miroslav Josef Klose (8, 44).

82. 02.09.2006 **GERMANY – REPUBLIC OF IRELAND** **1-0(0-0)** 13th EC. Qualifiers
„Gottlieb Daimler" Stadion, Stuttgart; Referee: Luis Medina Cantalejo (Spain); Attendance: 53,198
GER: Jens Lehmann (40/0), Phillip Lahm (27/2), Arne Friedrich (44/0), Manuel Friedrich (2/0), Marcell Jansen (10/0), Bernd Schneider (73/2) [84.Tim Borowski (28/2)], Torsten Frings (60/8), Michael Ballack (Cap) (71/31), Bastian Schweinsteiger (37/9), Miroslav Josef Klose (64/31), Lukas Josef Podolski (34/16) [76.Olivier Neuville (64/9)]. Trainer: Joachim Löw (2).
Goal: Lukas Josef Podolski (57).

83. 06.09.2006 **SAN MARINO - GERMANY** **0-13(0-6)** 13th EC. Qualifiers
Stadio Olimpico, Serravalle; Referee: Selçuk Dereli (Turkey); Attendance: 5,019
GER: Jens Lehmann (41/0), Phillip Lahm (28/2), Arne Friedrich (45/0), Manuel Friedrich (3/1), Marcell Jansen (11/0), Bernd Schneider (74/3), Torsten Frings (61/8) [62.Thomas Hitzlsperger (18/2)], Michael Ballack (Cap) (72/32) [46.David Odonkor (7/0)], Bastian Schweinsteiger (38/11), Miroslav Josef Klose (65/33) [46.Gerald Asamoah (43/6)], Lukas Josef Podolski (35/20). Trainer: Joachim Löw (3).
Goals: Lukas Josef Podolski (12), Bastian Schweinsteiger (29), Miroslav Josef Klose (30), Michael Ballack (35), Lukas Josef Podolski (43), Miroslav Josef Klose (45+1), Bastian Schweinsteiger (47), Lukas Josef Podolski (64), Thomas Hitzlsperger (66), Lukas Josef Podolski (71), Thomas Hitzlsperger (73), Manuel Friedrich (87), Bernd Schneider (90 penalty).

84. 07.10.2006 **GERMANY - GEORGIA** **2-0(1-0)**
Ostseestadion, Rostock; Referee: Gerald Lehner (Austria); Attendance: 28,000
GER: Timo Hildebrand (4/0), Clemens Fritz (1/0), Arne Friedrich (46/0), Manuel Friedrich (4/1) [84.Alexander Madlung (1/0)], Thomas Hitzlsperger (19/2) [46.Malik Fathi (2/0)], David Odonkor (8/0), Michael Ballack (Cap) (73/33), Piotr Trochowski (1/0) [76.Torsten Frings (62/8)], Bastian Schweinsteiger (39/12), Mike Hanke (8/1) [65.Jan Schlaudraff (1/0)], Lukas Josef Podolski (36/20) [*sent off 48*]. Trainer: Joachim Löw (4).
Goals: Bastian Schweinsteiger (24), Michael Ballack (67).

85. 11.10.2006 **SLOVAKIA - GERMANY** **1-4(0-3)** 13th EC. Qualifiers
Stadión Tehelné pole, Bratislava; Referee: Terje Hauge (Norway); Attendance: 21,582
GER: Jens Lehmann (42/0), Clemens Fritz (2/0), Arne Friedrich (47/0), Manuel Friedrich (5/1), Phillip Lahm (29/2), Bernd Schneider (75/3) [76.David Odonkor (9/0)], Torsten Frings (63/8), Michael Ballack (Cap) (74/34), Bastian Schweinsteiger (40/13) [76.Piotr Trochowski (2/0)], Miroslav Josef Klose (66/33), Lukas Josef Podolski (37/22) [85.Mike Hanke (9/1)]. Trainer: Joachim Löw (5).
Goals: Lukas Josef Podolski (13), Michael Ballack (25), Bastian Schweinsteiger (36), Lukas Josef Podolski (72).

86. 15.11.2006 **CYPRUS - GERMANY** **1-1(1-1)** 13th EC. Qualifiers
Neo Stádio GSP, Nicosia; Referee: Peter Fröjdfeldt (Sweden); Attendance: 16,000
GER: Timo Hildebrand (5/0), Clemens Fritz (3/0), Arne Friedrich (48/0), Manuel Friedrich (6/1), Phillip Lahm (30/2), David Odonkor (10/0) [79.Thomas Hitzlsperger (20/2)], Torsten Frings (64/8), Michael Ballack (Cap) (75/35), Bastian Schweinsteiger (41/13), Olivier Neuville [62.Mike Hanke (10/1)], Miroslav Josef Klose (67/33). Trainer: Joachim Löw (6).
Goal: Michael Ballack (15).

87. 07.02.2007 **GERMANY - SWITZERLAND** **3-1(2-0)**
LTU-Arena, Düsseldorf; Referee: Ruud Bossen (Netherlands); Attendance: 51,333
GER: Jens Lehmann (43/0), Arne Friedrich (49/0), Per Mertesacker (30/1), Christoph Metzelder (29/0), Phillip Lahm (31/2), Clemens Fritz (4/0), Torsten Frings (65/9) [74.Thomas Hitzlsperger (21/2)], Michael Ballack (Cap) (76/35) [46.Tim Borowski (29/2)], Bastian Schweinsteiger (42/13) [74.Marcell Jansen (12/0)], Mario Gómez (1/1) [58.Mike Hanke (11/1)], Kevin Dennis Kurányi (36/15) [83.Jan Schlaudraff (2/0)]. Trainer: Joachim Löw (7).
Goals: Kevin Dennis Kurányi (7), Mario Gómez (30), Torsten Frings (66).

88. 24.03.2007 **CZECH REPUBLIC - GERMANY** **1-2(0-1)** 13th EC. Qualifiers
Toyota Arena, Praha; Referee: Roberto Rosetti (Italy); Attendance: 18,000
GER: Jens Lehmann (44/0), Phillip Lahm (32/2), Per Mertesacker (31/1), Christoph Metzelder (30/0), Marcell Jansen (13/0), Bernd Schneider (76/3), Torsten Frings (66/9), Michael Ballack (Cap) (77/35), Bastian Schweinsteiger (43/13), Kevin Dennis Kurányi (37/17), Lukas Josef Podolski (38/22) [89.Thomas Hitzlsperger (22/2)]. Trainer: Joachim Löw (8).
Goals: Kevin Dennis Kurányi (42, 62).

89. 28.03.2007 **GERMANY - DENMARK** **0-1(0-0)**
MSV-Arena, Duisburg; Referee: Howard Webb (England); Attendance: 31,500
GER: Robert Enke (1/0), Clemens Fritz (5/0), Alexander Madlung (2/0), Manuel Friedrich (7/1), Marcell Jansen (14/0), Roberto Hilbert (1/0) [58.Paul Freier (19/1)], Thomas Hitzlsperger (23/2), Simon Rolfes (1/0) [71.Gonzalo Castro (1/0)], Piotr Trochowski (3/0), Kevin Dennis Kurányi (Cap) (38/17) [46.Stephan Kießling (1/0)], Jan Schlaudraff (3/0) [78.Patrick Helmes (1/0)]. Trainer: Joachim Löw (9).

790. 02.06.2007 **GERMANY – SAN MARINO** **6-0(1-0)** 13th EC. Qualifiers
Frankenstadion, Nürnberg; Referee: Tony Asumaa (Finland); Attendance: 43,967
GER: Jens Lehmann (45/0), Philipp Lahm (33/2) [70.Patrick Helmes (2/0)], Per Mertesacker (32/1), Christoph Metzelder (31/0), Marcell Jansen (15/1), Roberto Hilbert (2/0) [59.Clemens Fritz (6/1)], Bernd Schneider (77/3) (Cap), Torsten Frings (67/10), Thomas Hitzlsperger (24/2), Miroslav Josef Klose (68/33), Kevin Dennis Kurányi (39/18) [59.Mario Gómez (2/3)]. Trainer: Joachim Löw (10).
Goals: Kevin Dennis Kurányi (45), Marcell Jansen (52), Torsten Frings (56 penalty), Mario Gómez (63, 65), Clemens Fritz (67).

791. 06.06.2007 **GERMANY - SLOVAKIA** **2-1(2-1)** 13th EC. Qualifiers
AOL-Arena, Hamburg; Referee: Olegário Manuel Bártolo Faustino Benquerença (Portugal); Attendance: 51,500
GER: Jens Lehmann (46/0), Philipp Lahm (34/2), Per Mertesacker (33/1), Christoph Metzelder (32/0), Marcell Jansen (16/1), Clemens Fritz (7/1), Torsten Frings (68/10), Thomas Hitzlsperger (25/3), Bernd Schneider (Cap) (78/3) [90+2.Simon Rolfes (2/0)], Miroslav Josef Klose (69/33) [74.Piotr Trochowski (4/0)], Kevin Dennis Kurányi (40/18) [65.Mario Gómez (3/3)]. Trainer: Joachim Löw (11).
Goals: Ján Ďurica (10 own goal), Thomas Hitzlsperger (43).

792. 22.08.2007 **ENGLAND - GERMANY** **1-2(1-2)**
The National Stadium, Wembley Stadium, London, Ref: Massimo Busacca (Switzerland), Att: 86,133
GER: Jens Lehmann (47/0), Arne Friedrich (50/0), Per Mertesacker (34/1), Christoph Metzelder (33/0), Christian Pander (1/1), Philipp Lahm (35/2), David Odonkor (11/0) [54.Roberto Hilbert (3/0)], Bernd Schneider (79/3) [90.Gonzalo Castro (2/0)], Piotr Trochowski (5/0) [72.Simon Rolfes (3/0)], Thomas Hitzlsperger (26/3), Kevin Dennis Kurányi (41/19). Trainer: Joachim Löw (12).
Goals: Kevin Dennis Kurányi (26), Christian Pander (40).

793. 08.09.2007 **WALES - GERMANY** **0-2(0-1)** 13th EC. Qualifiers
Millenium Stadium, Cardiff; Referee: Manuel Enrique Mejuto González (Spain); Attendance: 27,889
GER: Jens Lehmann (48/0), Arne Friedrich (51/0), Per Mertesacker (35/1), Christoph Metzelder (34/0), Christian Pander (2/1) [46.Piotr Trochowski (6/0)], Thomas Hitzlsperger (27/3), Roberto Hilbert (4/0), Bastian Schweinsteiger (44/13), Marcell Jansen (17/1), Kevin Dennis Kurányi (42/19) [73.Lukas Josef Podolski (39/22)], Miroslav Josef Klose (70/35) [87.Patrick Helmes (3/0)]. Trainer: Joachim Löw (13).
Goals: Miroslav Josef Klose (5, 60).

794. 12.09.2007 **GERMANY - ROMANIA** **3-1(1-1)**
RheinEnergie Stadion, Köln; Referee: Nicola Rizzoli (Italy); Attendance: 44,500
GER: Timo Hildebrand (6/0), Roberto Hilbert (5/0), Christoph Metzelder (35/0) [46.Arne Friedrich (52/0)], Manuel Friedrich (8/1), Marcell Jansen (18/1) [46.Gonzalo Castro (3/0)], Piotr Trochowski (7/0), Thomas Hitzlsperger (28/3) [46.Simon Rolfes (4/0)], Bastian Schweinsteiger (45/13), Bernd Schneider (80/4) [60.David Odonkor (12/1)], Patrick Helmes (4/0), Lukas Josef Podolski (40/23). Trainer: Joachim Löw (14).
Goals: Bernd Schneider (42), David Odonkor (65), Lukas Josef Podolski (82).

795. 13.10.2007 **REPUBLIC OF IRELAND - GERMANY** **0-0** 13th EC. Qualifiers
Croke Park, Dublin; Referee: Martin Hansson (Sweden); Attendance: 67,495
GER: Jens Lehmann (49/0), Arne Friedrich (53/0), Per Mertesacker (36/1), Christoph Metzelder (36/0), Marcell Jansen (19/1), Clemens Fritz (8/1), Torsten Frings (69/10), Bastian Schweinsteiger (46/13) [18.Simon Rolfes (5/0)], Piotr Trochowski (8/0) [90.Gonzalo Castro (4/0)], Mario Gómez (4/3) [64.Lukas Josef Podolski (41/23)], Kevin Dennis Kurányi (43/19). Trainer: Joachim Löw (15).

796. 17.10.2007 **GERMANY – CZECH REPUBLIC** **0-3(0-2)** 13th EC. Qualifiers
Allianz Arena, München; Referee: Howard Webb (England); Attendance: 66,400
GER: Timo Hildebrand (7/0), Arne Friedrich (54/0), Per Mertesacker (37/1), Christoph Metzelder (37/0) [46.Clemens Fritz (9/1)], Marcell Jansen (20/1), David Odonkor (13/1), Torsten Frings (70/10), Piotr Trochowski (9/0) [46.Simon Rolfes (6/0)], Bastian Schweinsteiger (47/13) [65.Mario Gómez (5/3)], Kevin Dennis Kurányi (44/19), Lukas Josef Podolski (42/23). Trainer: Joachim Löw (16).

797. 17.11.2007 **GERMANY - CYPRUS** **4-0(2-0)** 13th EC. Qualifiers
AWD-Arena, Hannover; Referee: Peter Rasmussen (Denmark); Attendance: 45,016
GER: Jens Lehmann (50/0), Arne Friedrich (55/0), Per Mertesacker (38/1), Christoph Metzelder (38/0), Philipp Lahm (36/2), Thomas Hitzlsperger (29/4), Clemens Fritz (10/2) [77.Roberto Hilbert (6/0)], Piotr Trochowski (10/0) [66.Tim Borowski (30/2)], Lukas Josef Podolski (43/24), Mario Gómez (6/3) [73.Mike Hanke (12/1)], Miroslav Josef Klose (71/36). Trainer: Joachim Löw (17).
Goals: Clemens Fritz (2), Miroslav Josef Klose (20), Lukas Josef Podolski (53), Thomas Hitzlsperger (82).

798. 21.11.2007 **GERMANY - WALES** **0-0** 13th EC. Qualifiers
Commerzbank-Arena, Frankfurt am Main; Referee: Pavel Cristian Balaj (Romania); Attendance: 49,262
GER: Jens Lehmann (51/0), Gonzalo Castro (5/0) [56.Roberto Hilbert (7/0)], Per Mertesacker (39/1), Christoph Metzelder (39/0), Philipp Lahm (37/2), Clemens Fritz (11/2), Tim Borowski (31/2), Thomas Hitzlsperger (30/4) [46.Simon Rolfes (7/0)], Lukas Josef Podolski (44/24), Mario Gómez (7/3) [71.Olivier Neuville (65/9)], Miroslav Josef Klose (72/36). Trainer: Joachim Löw (18).

799. 06.02.2008 **AUSTRIA - GERMANY** **0-3(0-0)**
„Ernst Happel“ Stadion, Wien; Referee: Paolo Dondarini (Italy); Attendance: 48,500
GER: Jens Lehmann (52/0), Heiko Westermann (1/0), Per Mertesacker (40/1), Manuel Friedrich (9/1) [74.Roberto Hilbert (8/0)], Philipp Lahm (38/2), Bernd Schneider (81/4) [59.Lukas Josef Podolski (45/24)], Michael Ballack (Cap) (78/35) [87.Simon Rolfes (8/0)], Thomas Hitzlsperger (31/5) [81.Jermaine Jones (1/0)], Bastian Schweinsteiger (48/13), Kevin Dennis Kurányi (45/19) [59.Mario Gómez (8/4)], Miroslav Josef Klose (73/37). Trainer: Joachim Löw (19).
Goals: Thomas Hitzlsperger (53), Miroslav Josef Klose (63), Mario Gómez (80).

800. 26.03.2008 **SWITZERLAND - GERMANY** **0-4(0-1)**
„St.Jakob“ Park, Basel; Referee: Eric Bramhaar (Netherlands); Attendance: 38,500
GER: Jens Lehmann (53/0), Philipp Lahm (39/2) [87.Piotr Trochowski (11/0)], Heiko Westermann (2/0), Per Mertesacker (41/1), Marcell Jansen (21/1) [79.Simon Rolfes (9/0)], Clemens Fritz (12/2) [72.Arne Friedrich (56/0)], Michael Ballack (Cap) (79/35), Thomas Hitzlsperger (32/5), Bastian Schweinsteiger (49/13), Mario Gómez (9/6) [75.Kevin Dennis Kurányi (46/19)], Miroslav Josef Klose (74/38) [58.Lukas Josef Podolski (46/25)]. Trainer: Joachim Löw (20).
Goals: Miroslav Josef Klose (23), Mario Gómez (61, 67), Lukas Josef Podolski (89).

)1. 27.05.2008 **GERMANY - BELARUS** **2-2(2-0)**
;ritz Walter" Stadion, Kaiserslautern; Referee: Darko Čeferin (Slovenia); Attendance: 47,258
ER: Jens Lehmann (54/0), Philipp Lahm (40/2), Per Mertesacker (42/1), Christoph Metzelder (40/0), Thomas Hitzlsperger (33/5), David Odonkor (14/1) '9.Clemens Fritz (13/2)], Torsten Frings (71/10) [67.Piotr Trochowski (12/0)], Michael Ballack (Cap) (80/35) [46.Jermaine Jones (2/0)], Bastian :hweinsteiger (50/13) [46.Marko Marin (1/0)], Miroslav Josef Klose (75/39) [54.Patrick Helmes (5/0)], Lukas Josef Podolski (47/25) [54.Olivier Neuville ›6/9)]. Trainer: Joachim Löw (21).
oals: Miroslav Josef Klose (10), Vladimir Korytko (20 own goal).

)2. 31.05.2008 **GERMANY - SERBIA** **2-1(0-1)**
eltins-Arena, Gelsenkirchen; Referee: Fredy Fautrel (Frankreich); Attendance: 53,951
ER: Jens Lehmann (55/0), Philipp Lahm (41/2) [46.Lukas Josef Podolski (48/25)], Per Mertesacker (43/1) [46.Arne Friedrich (57/0)], Christoph Metzelder 1/0), Marcell Jansen (22/1) [84.Heiko Westermann (3/0)], Clemens Fritz (14/2), Torsten Frings (72/10) [70.Simon Rolfes (10/0)], Michael Ballack (Cap) 1/36), Bastian Schweinsteiger (51/13) [79.David Odonkor (15/1)], Kevin Dennis Kurányi (47/19) [70.Olivier Neuville (67/10)], Mario Gómez (10/6). :ainer: Joachim Löw (22).
oals: Olivier Neuville (74), Michael Ballack (82).

)3. 08.06.2008 **GERMANY - POLAND** **2-0(1-0)** 13th EC. Group Stage.
'örthersee Stadion, Klagenfurt (Austria); Referee: Tom Henning Øvrebø (Norway); Attendance: 30,000
ER: Jens Lehmann (56/0), Philipp Lahm (42/2), Per Mertesacker (44/1), Christoph Metzelder (42/0), Marcell Jansen (23/1), Clemens Fritz (15/2) 5.Bastian Schweinsteiger (52/13)], Torsten Frings (73/10), Michael Ballack (Cap) (82/36), Lukas Josef Podolski (49/27), Miroslav Josef Klose (76/39) 0+1.Kevin Dennis Kurányi (48/19)], Mario Gómez (11/6) [75.Thomas Hitzlsperger (34/5)]. Trainer: Joachim Löw (23).
oals: Lukas Josef Podolski (20, 72).

)4. 12.06.2008 **CROATIA - GERMANY** **2-1(1-0)** 13th EC. Group Stage.
'örthersee Stadion, Klagenfurt (Austria); Referee: Frank De Bleeckere (Belgium); Attendance: 30,000
ER: Jens Lehmann (57/0), Philipp Lahm (43/2), Per Mertesacker (45/1), Christoph Metzelder (43/0), Marcell Jansen (24/1) [46.David Odonkor (16/1)], lemens Fritz (16/2) [82.Kevin Dennis Kurányi (49/19)], Torsten Frings (74/10), Michael Ballack (Cap) (83/36), Lukas Josef Podolski (50/28), Miroslav ›sef Klose (77/39), Mario Gómez (12/6) [66.Bastian Schweinsteiger (53/13) [*sent off 90*]. Trainer: Joachim Löw (24).
oal: Lukas Josef Podolski (79).

)5. 16.06.2008 **AUSTRIA - GERMANY** **0-1(0-0)** 13th EC. Group Stage.
:rnst Happel" Stadion, Wien (Austria); Referee: Manuel Enrique Mejuto González (Spain); Attendance: 51,428
ER: Jens Lehmann (58/0), Arne Friedrich (58/0), Per Mertesacker (46/1), Christoph Metzelder (44/0), Philipp Lahm (44/2), Clemens Fritz (17/2) [90.Tim orowski (32/2)], Torsten Frings (75/10), Michael Ballack (Cap) (84/37), Lukas Josef Podolski (51/28) [83.Olivier Neuville (68/10)], Miroslav Josef Klose 8/39), Mario Gómez (13/6) [60.Thomas Hitzlsperger (35/5)]. Trainer: Joachim Löw (25 – *sent off 41*).
oal: Michael Ballack (49).

)6. 19.06.2008 **PORTUGAL - GERMANY** **2-3(1-2)** 13th EC. Quarter-Finals.
;t.Jakob" Park, Basel (Switzerland); Referee: Peter Fröjdfeldt (Sweden); Attendance: 39,374
ER: Jens Lehmann (59/0), Arne Friedrich (59/0), Per Mertesacker (47/1), Christoph Metzelder (45/0), Philipp Lahm (45/2), Bastian Schweinsteiger (54/14) 3.Clemens Fritz (18/2)], Simon Rolfes (11/0), Michael Ballack (Cap) (85/38), Thomas Hitzlsperger (36/5) [73.Tim Borowski (33/2)], Miroslav Josef Klose 9/40) [89.Marcell Jansen (25/1)], Lukas Josef Podolski (52/28). Trainer: Hans-Dieter Flick [replacing suspended Joachim Löw (26)].
oals: Bastian Schweinsteiger (22), Miroslav Josef Klose (26), Michael Ballack (61).

)7. 25.06.2008 **GERMANY - TURKEY** **3-2(1-1)** 13th EC. Semi-Finals.
;t.Jakob" Park, Basel (Switzerland); Referee: Massimo Busacca (Switzerland); Attendance: 39,374
ER: Jens Lehmann (60/0), Arne Friedrich (60/0), Per Mertesacker (48/1), Christoph Metzelder (46/0), Philipp Lahm (46/3), Bastian Schweinsteiger 5/15), Simon Rolfes (12/0) [46.Torsten Frings (76/10)], Michael Ballack (Cap) (86/38), Thomas Hitzlsperger (37/5), Miroslav Josef Klose (80/41) 0+2.Marcell Jansen (26/1)], Lukas Josef Podolski (53/28). Trainer: Joachim Löw (27).
oals: Bastian Schweinsteiger (26), Miroslav Josef Klose (79), Philipp Lahm (90).

)8. 29.06.2008 **GERMANY - SPAIN** **0-1(0-0)** 13th EC. Final.
:rnst Happel" Stadion, Wien (Austria); Referee: Roberto Rosetti (Italy); Attendance: 51,428
ER: Jens Lehmann (61/0), Arne Friedrich (61/0), Per Mertesacker (49/1), Christoph Metzelder (47/0), Philipp Lahm (47/3) [46.Marcell Jansen (27/1)], astian Schweinsteiger (56/15), Torsten Frings (77/10), Michael Ballack (Cap) (87/38), Thomas Hitzlsperger (38/5) [58.Kevin Dennis Kurányi (50/19)], ıkas Josef Podolski (54/28), Miroslav Josef Klose (81/41) [79.Mario Gómez (14/6)]. Trainer: Joachim Löw (28).

)9. 20.08.2008 **GERMANY - BELGIUM** **2-0(0-0)**
ısy-Credit-Stadion, Nürnberg; Referee: Thomas Vejlgaard (Denmark); Attendance: 34,117
ER: Robert Enke (2/0), Clemens Fritz (19/2), Serdar Taşçı (1/0), Heiko Westermann (4/0), Philipp Lahm (48/3) [82.Marcell Jansen (28/1)], Bastian :hweinsteiger (57/16), Thomas Hitzlsperger (39/5) [70.Marko Marin (2/1)], Simon Rolfes (13/0), Piotr Trochowski (13/0) [80.Patrick Helmes (6/0)], iroslav Josef Klose (Cap) (82/41) [46.Kevin Dennis Kurányi (51/19)], Lukas Josef Podolski (55/28) [46.Mario Gómez (15/6)]. Trainer: Joachim Löw (29).
oals: Bastian Schweinsteiger (59 penalty), Marko Marin (77).

l0. 06.09.2008 **LIECHTENSTEIN - GERMANY** **0-6(0-1)** 19th FIFA WC. Qualifiers
heinpark Stadion, Vaduz; Referee: Duarte Nuno Pereira Gomes (Portugal); Attendance: 7,842
ER: Robert Enke (3/0), Clemens Fritz (20/2), Serdar Taşçı (2/0), Heiko Westermann (5/1), Philipp Lahm (49/3), Bastian Schweinsteiger (58/17), Simon olfes (14/1) [69.Marko Marin (3/1)], Thomas Hitzlsperger (40/6), Piotr Trochowski (14/0), Miroslav Josef Klose (Cap) (83/41) [65.Mario Gómez (16/6)], ıkas Josef Podolski (56/30) [76.Kevin Dennis Kurányi (52/19)]. Trainer: Joachim Löw (30).
oals: Lukas Josef Podolski (21, 48), Simon Rolfes (65), Bastian Schweinsteiger (66), Thomas Hitzlsperger (76), Heiko Westermann (87).

l1. 09.08.2008 **FINLAND - GERMANY** **3-3(2-2)** 19th FIFA WC. Qualifiers
lympiastadion, Helsinki; Referee: Viktor Kassai (Hungary); Attendance: 37,150
ER: Robert Enke (4/0), Clemens Fritz (21/2) [82.Andreas Hinkel (18/0)], Serdar Taşçı (3/0), Heiko Westermann (6/1), Philipp Lahm (50/3), Bastian :hweinsteiger (59/17), Simon Rolfes (15/1) [82.Patrick Helmes (7/0)], Thomas Hitzlsperger (41/6) [69.Mario Gómez (17/6)], Piotr Trochowski (15/0), iroslav Josef Klose (Cap) (84/44), Lukas Josef Podolski (57/30). Trainer: Joachim Löw (31).
oals: Miroslav Josef Klose (38, 45, 82).

812. 11.10.2008 **GERMANY - RUSSIA** **2-1(2-0)** 19th FIFA WC. Qualifiers
Signal-Iduna Park, Dortmund; Referee: Peter Fröjdfeldt (Sweden); Attendance: 65,607
GER: René Adler (1/0), Arne Friedrich (62/0), Per Mertesacker (50/1), Heiko Westermann (7/1), Philipp Lahm (51/3), Piotr Trochowski (16/0) [83.Torsten Frings (78/10)], Michael Ballack (Cap) (88/39), Thomas Hitzlsperger (42/6) [90+3.Simon Rolfes (16/1)], Bastian Schweinsteiger (60/17), Miroslav Josef Klose (85/44) [71.Mario Gómez (18/6)], Lukas Josef Podolski (58/31). Trainer: Joachim Löw (32).
Goals: Lukas Josef Podolski (9), Michael Ballack (28).

813. 15.10.2008 **GERMANY - WALES** **1-0(0-0)** 19th FIFA WC. Qualifiers
Borussia-Park, Mönchengladbach; Referee: Laurent Duhamel (France); Attendance: 44,500
GER: René Adler (2/0), Arne Friedrich (63/0) [64.Clemens Fritz (22/2)], Per Mertesacker (51/1), Heiko Westermann (8/1), Philipp Lahm (52/3), Bastian Schweinsteiger (61/17), Michael Ballack (Cap) (89/39), Thomas Hitzlsperger (43/6), Piotr Trochowski (17/1), Miroslav Josef Klose (86/44) [46.Patrick Helmes (8/0)], Lukas Josef Podolski (59/31) [82.Mario Gómez (19/6)]. Trainer: Joachim Löw (33).
Goal: Piotr Trochowski (72).

814. 19.11.2009 **GERMANY - ENGLAND** **1-2(0-1)**
Olympiastadion, Berlin; Referee: Massimo Busacca (Switzerland); Attendance: 74,244
GER: René Adler (3/0) [46.Tim Wiese (1/0)], Arne Friedrich (64/0) [68.Serdar Taşçı (4/0)], Per Mertesacker (52/1), Heiko Westermann (9/1), Marvin Compper (1/0) [77.Marcel Schäfer (1/0)], Bastian Schweinsteiger (62/17), Simon Rolfes (17/1), Jermaine Jones (3/0) [46.Marko Marin (4/1)], Piotr Trochowski (18/1), Mario Gómez (20/6) [57.Lukas Josef Podolski (60/31)], Miroslav Josef Klose (Cap) (87/44) [46.Patrick Helmes (9/1)]. Trainer: Joachim Löw (34).
Goal: Patrick Helmes (63).

815. 11.02.2009 **GERMANY - NORWAY** **0-1(0-0)**
LTU-Arena, Düsseldorf; Referee: Stefan Meßner (Austria); Attendance: 45,000
GER: René Adler (4/0), Andreas Hinkel (19/0) [46.Andreas Beck (1/0)], Per Mertesacker (53/1) [46.Serdar Taşçı (5/0)], Heiko Westermann (10/1), Philipp Lahm (53/3), Bastian Schweinsteiger (63/17), Torsten Frings (79/10) [68.Marko Marin (5/1)], Michael Ballack (Cap) (90/39), Piotr Trochowski (19/1) [78.Mesut Özil (1/0)], Miroslav Josef Klose (88/44) [46.Patrick Helmes (10/1)], Mario Gómez (21/6) [68.Stefan Kießling (2/0)]. Trainer: Joachim Löw (35).

816. 28.03.2009 **GERMANY - LIECHTENSTEIN** **4-0(2-0)** 19th FIFA WC. Qualifiers
Zentralstadion, Leipzig; Referee: Ihor Ishchenko (Ukraine); Attendance: 43,368
GER: Robert Enke (5/0), Andreas Beck (2/0), Per Mertesacker (54/1), Serdar Taşçı (6/0), Philipp Lahm (54/3), Bastian Schweinsteiger (64/18) [88.Simon Rolfes (18/1)], Michael Ballack (Cap) (91/40), Thomas Hitzlsperger (44/6) [78.Marko Marin (6/1)], Marcell Jansen (29/2) [64.Patrick Helmes (11/1)], Mario Gómez (22/6), Lukas Josef Podolski (61/32). Trainer: Joachim Löw (36).
Goals: Michael Ballack (4), Marcell Jansen (9), Bastian Schweinsteiger (48), Lukas Josef Podolski (50).

817. 01.04.2009 **WALES - GERMANY** **0-2(0-1)** 19th FIFA WC. Qualifiers
Millenium Stadium, Cardiff; Referee: Terje Hauge (Norway); Attendance: 26,064
GER: Robert Enke (6/0), Andreas Beck (3/0), Per Mertesacker (55/1), Serdar Taşçı (7/0), Philipp Lahm (55/3), Bastian Schweinsteiger (65/18) [86.Patrick Helmes (12/1)], Simon Rolfes (19/1) [79.Heiko Westermann (11/1)], Michael Ballack (Cap) (92/41), Thomas Hitzlsperger (45/6), Lukas Josef Podolski (62/32) [72.Piotr Trochowski (20/1)], Mario Gómez (23/6). Trainer: Joachim Löw (37).
Goals: Michael Ballack (11), Ashley Errol Williams (48 own goal).

818. 29.05.2009 **CHINA P.R. - GERMANY** **1-1(1-1)**
Shanghai Stadium, Shanghai; Referee: Lee Min-Hu (Korea Republic); Attendance: 25,000
GER: Robert Enke (7/0), Philipp Lahm (Cap) (56/3), Arne Friedrich (65/0), Robert Huth (18/2), Marcel Schäfer (2/0), Christian Gentner (1/0), Thomas Hitzlsperger (46/6), Piotr Trochowski (21/1) [76.Andreas Hinkel (20/0)], Bastian Schweinsteiger (66/18), Lukas Josef Podolski (63/33), Mario Gómez (24/6) [63.Claudemir Jerónimo Barretto da Silva „Cacau“ (1/0)]. Trainer: Joachim Löw (38).
Goal: Lukas Josef Podolski (8).

819. 02.06.2009 **UNITED ARAB EMIRATES - GERMANY** **2-7(0-4)**
„Al Maktoum“ Stadium, Dubai; Referee: Naser Al Ghafary (Jordan); Attendance: 7,000
GER: Manuel Peter Neuer (1/0), Andreas Hinkel (21/0) [78.Christian Träsch (1/0)], Arne Friedrich (66/0) [46.Robert Huth (19/2)], Heiko Westermann (12/2), Philipp Lahm (57/3) [57.Marcel Schäfer (3/0)], Bastian Schweinsteiger (Cap) (67/18), Christian Gentner (2/0), Thomas Hitzlsperger (47/6) [66.Tobias Weis (1/0)], Piotr Trochowski (22/2), Lukas Josef Podolski (64/33) [46.Claudemir Jerónimo Barretto da Silva „Cacau“ (2/0)], Mario Gómez (25/10). Trainer: Joachim Löw (39).
Goals: Heiko Westermann (29), Mario Gómez (35), Piotr Trochowski (37), Mario Gómez (45, 47), Faris Jumaa Hassan Al Saadi (52 own goal), Mario Gómez (90+2).

820. 12.08.2009 **AZERBAIJAN - GERMANY** **0-2(0-1)** 19th FIFA WC. Qualifiers
„Tofiq Bəhramov“ adına Respublika Stadionu, Bakı; Referee: Alan Kelly (Republic of Ireland); Attendance: 22,500
GER: Robert Enke (8/0), Philipp Lahm (58/3), Per Mertesacker (56/1), Serdar Taşçı (8/0), Marcel Schäfer (4/0), Bastian Schweinsteiger (68/19), Michael Ballack (Cap) (93/41), Thomas Hitzlsperger (48/6), Piotr Trochowski (23/2) [77.Marcell Jansen (30/2)], Miroslav Josef Klose (89/45) [75.Claudemir Jerónimo Barretto da Silva „Cacau“ (3/0)], Mario Gómez (26/10) [84.Mesut Özil (2/0)]. Trainer: Joachim Löw (40).
Goals: Bastian Schweinsteiger (11), Miroslav Josef Klose (53).

821. 05.09.2009 **GERMANY – SOUTH AFRICA** **2-0(1-0)**
BayArena, Leverkusen; Referee: Claudio Circhetta (Switzerland); Attendance: 29,569
GER: René Adler (5/0), Philipp Lahm (59/3), Arne Friedrich (67/0), Serdar Taşçı (9/0) [46.Heiko Westermann (13/2)], Marcel Schäfer (5/0), Bastian Schweinsteiger (69/19) [84.Piotr Trochowski (24/2)], Michael Ballack (Cap) (94/41) [80.Christian Gentner (3/0)], Simon Rolfes (20/1) [73.Sami Khedira (1/0)], Mesut Özil (3/1), Marko Marin (7/1) [46.Lukas Josef Podolski (65/33)], Mario Gómez (27/11) [46.Miroslav Josef Klose (90/45)]. Trainer: Joachim Löw (41).
Goals: Mario Gómez (35), Mesut Özil (77).

822. 09.09.2009 **GERMANY - AZERBAIJAN** **4-0(1-0)** 19th FIFA WC. Qualifiers
AWD-Arena, Hannover; Referee: Anastasion Kakos (Greece); Attendance: 35,369
GER: René Adler (6/0), Philipp Lahm (60/3), Per Mertesacker (57/1), Heiko Westermann (14/2), Marcel Schäfer (6/0) [46.Andreas Beck (4/0)], Bastian Schweinsteiger (70/19) [67.Piotr Trochowski (25/2)], Michael Ballack (Cap) (95/42), Thomas Hitzlsperger (49/6), Mesut Özil (4/1), Lukas Josef Podolski (66/34), Mario Gómez (28/11) [46.Miroslav Josef Klose (91/47)]. Trainer: Joachim Löw (42).
Goals: Michael Ballack (14 penalty), Miroslav Josef Klose (55, 65), Lukas Josef Podolski (71).

823. 10.10.2009 **RUSSIA - GERMANY** **0-1(0-1)** 19th FIFA WC. Qualifiers

Luzhniki Stadium, Moskva; Referee: Massimo Busacca (Switzerland); Attendance: 72,100

GER: René Adler (7/0), Jérôme Agyenim Boateng (1/0) [*sent off 69*], Per Mertesacker (58/1), Heiko Westermann (15/2), Philipp Lahm (61/3), Bastian Schweinsteiger (71/19), Mesut Özil (5/1) [72.Arne Friedrich (68/0)], Michael Ballack (Cap) (96/42), Simon Rolfes (21/1), Lukas Josef Podolski (67/34) [86.Piotr Trochowski (26/2)], Miroslav Josef Klose (92/48) [89.Mario Gómez (29/11)]. Trainer: Joachim Löw (43).

Goal: Miroslav Josef Klose (35).

824. 14.10.2009 **GERMANY - FINLAND** **1-1(0-1)** 19th FIFA WC. Qualifiers

HSH Nordbank-Arena, Hamburg; Referee: Howard Melton Webb (England); Attendance: 51,500

GER: René Adler (8/0), Andreas Beck (5/0), Arne Friedrich (69/0), Heiko Westermann (16/2), Philipp Lahm (62/3), Michael Ballack (Cap) (97/42) [46.Mesut Özil (6/1)], Thomas Hitzlsperger (50/6) [46.Christian Gentner (4/0)], Piotr Trochowski (27/2), Claudemir Jerónimo Barretto da Silva „Cacau" (4/0), Mario Gómez (30/11) [77.Miroslav Josef Klose (93/48)], Lukas Josef Podolski (68/35). Trainer: Joachim Löw (44).

Goal: Lukas Josef Podolski (90).

825. 18.11.2009 **GERMANY – IVORY COAST** **2-2(1-0)**

Veltins-Arena, Gelsenkirchen; Referee: Björn Kuipers (Netherlands); Attendance: 33,015

GER: Tim Wiese (2/0) [46.Manuel Peter Neuer (2/0)], Philipp Lahm (Cap) (63/3), Per Mertesacker (59/1), Heiko Westermann (17/2), Jérôme Agyenim Boateng (2/0) [69.Andreas Beck (6/0)], Thomas Hitzlsperger (51/6), Bastian Schweinsteiger (72/19) [80.Aaron Hunt (1/0)], Mesut Özil (7/1), Piotr Trochowski (28/2) [86.Marcel Schäfer (7/0)], Stefan Kießling (3/0) [70.Mario Gómez (31/11)], Lukas Josef Podolski (69/37). Trainer: Joachim Löw (45).

Goals: Lukas Josef Podolski (11 penalty, 90).

826. 03.03.2010 **GERMANY - ARGENTINA** **0-1(0-1)**

Allianz Arena, München; Referee: Martin Atkinson (England); Attendance: 65,152

GER: René Adler (9/0), Philipp Lahm (64/3), Per Mertesacker (60/1), Serdar Taşçı (10/0), Jérôme Agyenim Boateng (3/0), Michael Ballack (Cap) (98/42), Bastian Schweinsteiger (73/19) [75.Sami Khedira (2/0)], Mesut Özil (8/1) [67.Toni Kroos (1/0)], Miroslav Josef Klose (94/48) [46.Mario Gómez (32/11)], Lukas Josef Podolski (70/37), Thomas Müller (1/0) [67.Claudemir Jerónimo Barretto da Silva „Cacau" (5/0)]. Trainer: Joachim Löw (46).

827. 13.05.2010 **GERMANY - MALTA** **3-0(1-0)**

Neuer Tivoli Stadion, Aachen; Referee: Alain Hamer (Luxembourg); Attendance: 27,000

GER: Manuel Peter Neuer (3/0), Arne Friedrich (70/0) [57.Heiko Westermann (18/2)], Andreas Beck (7/0) [59.Christian Träsch (2/0)], Serdar Taşçı (11/0) [46.Mats Julian Hummels (1/0)], Piotr Trochowski (29/2), Sami Khedira (3/0) [75.Stefan Reinartz (1/0)], Dennis Aogo (1/0) [80.Jérôme Agyenim Boateng (4/0)], Toni Kroos (2/0) [57.Kevin Großkreutz (1/0)], Stefan Kießling (4/0), Lukas Josef Podolski (71/37), Claudemir Jerónimo Barretto da Silva „Cacau" (6/2). Trainer: Joachim Löw (47).

Goals: Claudemir Jerónimo Barretto da Silva „Cacau" (16, 58), Kenneth Scicluna (61 own goal).

828. 29.05.2010 **HUNGARY - GERMANY** **0-3(0-1)**

"Puskás Ferenc" Stadion, Budapest; Referee: Claus Bo Larsen (Denmark); Attendance: 13,000

GER: Manuel Peter Neuer (4/0), Arne Friedrich (71/0) [72.Holger Felix Badstuber (1/0)], Per Mertesacker (61/1), Heiko Westermann (19/2), Jérôme Agyenim Boateng (5/0), Mesut Özil (9/1) [46.Claudemir Jerónimo Barretto da Silva „Cacau" (7/3)], Piotr Trochowski (30/2) [61.Mario Gómez (33/12)], Sami Khedira (4/0) [46.Dennis Aogo (2/0)], Toni Kroos (3/0) [62.Marcell Jansen (31/2)], Miroslav Josef Klose (Cap) (95/48) [62.Marko Marin (8/1)], Lukas Josef Podolski (72/38). Trainer: Joachim Löw (48).

Goals: Lukas Josef Podolski (5 penalty), Mario Gómez (69), Claudemir Jerónimo Barretto da Silva „Cacau" (73).

829. 03.06.2010 **GERMANY - BOSNIA AND HERZEGOVINA** **3-1(0-1)**

Commerzbank Arena, Frankfurt am Main; Referee: Nicola Rizzoli (Italy); Attendance: 48,000

GER: Manuel Peter Neuer (5/0), Arne Friedrich (72/0) [86.Serdar Taşçı (12/0)], Philipp Lahm (Cap) (65/4), Per Mertesacker (62/1), Holger Felix Badstuber (2/0), Bastian Schweinsteiger (74/21) [86.Toni Kroos (4/0)], Mesut Özil (10/1) [80.Mario Gómez (34/12)], Piotr Trochowski (31/2) [46.Claudemir Jerónimo Barretto da Silva „Cacau" (8/3)], Sami Khedira (5/0), Miroslav Josef Klose (96/48) [46.Thomas Müller (2/0)], Lukas Josef Podolski (73/38) [71.Marko Marin (9/1)]. Trainer: Joachim Löw (49).

Goals: Philipp Lahm (50), Bastian Schweinsteiger (73 penalty, 77 penalty).

830. 13.06.2010 **GERMANY - AUSTRALIA** **4-0(2-0)** 19th FIFA WC. Group Stage.

„Moses Mabhida" Stadium, Durban (South Africa); Referee: Marco Antonio Rodríguez Moreno (Mexico); Attendance: 62,660

GER: Manuel Peter Neuer (6/0), Philipp Lahm (Cap) (66/4), Per Mertesacker (63/1), Arne Friedrich (73/0), Holger Felix Badstuber (3/0), Bastian Schweinsteiger (75/21), Sami Khedira (6/0), Thomas Müller (3/1), Mesut Özil (11/1) [74.Mario Gómez (35/12)], Lukas Josef Podolski (74/39) [81.Marko Marin (10/1)], Miroslav Josef Klose (97/49) [68.Claudemir Jerónimo Barretto da Silva „Cacau" (9/4)]. Trainer: Joachim Löw (50).

Goals: Lukas Josef Podolski (8), Miroslav Josef Klose (26), Thomas Müller (68), Claudemir Jerónimo Barretto da Silva „Cacau" (70).

831. 18.06.2010 **GERMANY - SERBIA** **0-1(0-1)** 19th FIFA WC. Group Stage.

„Nelson Mandela" Bay Stadium, Port Elizabeth (South Africa); Referee: Alberto Undiano Mallenco (Spain); Attendance: 38,294

GER: Manuel Peter Neuer (7/0), Philipp Lahm (Cap) (67/4), Per Mertesacker (64/1), Arne Friedrich (74/0), Holger Felix Badstuber (4/0) [77.Mario Gómez (36/12)], Bastian Schweinsteiger (76/21), Sami Khedira (7/0), Thomas Müller (4/1) [70.Claudemir Jerónimo Barretto da Silva „Cacau" (10/4)], Mesut Özil (12/1) [70 Marko Marin (11/1)], Lukas Josef Podolski (75/39), Miroslav Josef Klose (98/49) [*sent off 37*]. Trainer: Joachim Löw (51).

832. 23.06.2010 **GHANA - GERMANY** **0-1(0-0)** 19th FIFA WC. Group Stage.

Soccer City, Johannesburg (South Africa); Referee: Carlos Eugênio Simon (Brazil); Attendance: 83,391

GER: Manuel Peter Neuer (8/0), Philipp Lahm (Cap) (68/4), Per Mertesacker (65/1), Arne Friedrich (75/0), Jérôme Agyenim Boateng (6/0) [73.Marcell Jansen (32/2)], Sami Khedira (8/0), Bastian Schweinsteiger (77/21) [81.Toni Kroos (5/0)], Thomas Müller (5/1) [68.Piotr Trochowski (32/2)], Mesut Özil (13/2), Lukas Josef Podolski (76/39), Claudemir Jerónimo Barretto da Silva „Cacau" (11/4). Trainer: Joachim Löw (52).

Goal: Mesut Özil (60).

833. 27.06.2010 **GERMANY - ENGLAND** **4-1(2-1)** 19th FIFA WC. 2nd Round of 16.

Free State Stadium, Bloemfontein (South Africa); Referee: Jorge Luis Larrionda Pietrafesa (Uruguay); Attendance: 40,510

GER: Manuel Peter Neuer (9/0), Philipp Lahm (Cap) (69/4), Per Mertesacker (66/1), Arne Friedrich (76/0), Jérôme Agyenim Boateng (7/0), Bastian Schweinsteiger (78/21), Sami Khedira (9/0), Thomas Müller (6/3) [72.Piotr Trochowski (33/2)], Mesut Özil (14/2) [83.Stefan Kießling (5/0)], Lukas Josef Podolski (77/40), Miroslav Josef Klose (99/50) [72.Mario Gómez (37/12)]. Trainer: Joachim Löw (53).

Goals: Miroslav Josef Klose (20), Lukas Josef Podolski (32), Thomas Müller (67, 70).

834. 03.07.2010 **ARGENTINA - GERMANY** **0-4(0-1)** 19th FIFA WC. Quarter-Finals
Cape Town Stadium, Cape Town (South Africa); Referee: Ravshan Irmatov (Uzbekistan); Attendance: 64,100
GER: Manuel Peter Neuer (10/0), Philipp Lahm (Cap) (70/4), Per Mertesacker (67/1), Arne Friedrich (77/1), Jérôme Agyenim Boateng (8/0) [72.Marcel Jansen (33/2)], Sami Khedira (10/0) [77.Toni Kroos (6/0)], Bastian Schweinsteiger (79/21), Thomas Müller (7/4) [84.Piotr Trochowski (34/2)], Mesut Özil (15/2), Lukas Josef Podolski (78/40), Miroslav Josef Klose (**100**/52). Trainer: Joachim Löw (54).
Goals: Thomas Müller (3), Miroslav Josef Klose (68), Arne Friedrich (74), Miroslav Josef Klose (89).

835. 07.07.2010 **GERMANY - SPAIN** **0-1(0-0)** 19th FIFA WC. Semi-Finals.
„Moses Mabhida" Stadium, Durban (South Africa); Referee: Viktor Kassai (Hungary); Attendance: 60,960
GER: Manuel Peter Neuer (11/0), Philipp Lahm (Cap) (71/4), Per Mertesacker (68/1), Arne Friedrich (78/1), Jérôme Agyenim Boateng (9/0) [52.Marcell Jansen (34/2)], Bastian Schweinsteiger (80/21), Sami Khedira (11/0) [81.Mario Gómez (38/12)], Piotr Trochowski (35/2) [62.Toni Kroos (7/0)], Mesut Özil (16/2), Lukas Josef Podolski (79/40), Miroslav Josef Klose (101/52). Trainer: Joachim Löw (55).

836. 10.07.2010 **URUGUAY - GERMANY** **2-3(1-1)** 19th FIFA WC. 3rd place Play-off.
„Nelson Mandela" Bay Stadium, Port Elizabeth (South Africa); Referee: Benito Armando Archundia Téllez (Mexico); Attendance: 36,254
GER: Hans-Jörg Butt (4/0), Jérôme Agyenim Boateng (10/0), Per Mertesacker (69/1), Arne Friedrich (79/1), Dennis Aogo (3/0), Sami Khedira (12/1), Bastian Schweinsteiger (Cap) (81/21), Thomas Müller (8/5), Mesut Özil (17/2) [90.Serdar Taşçı (13/0)], Marcell Jansen (35/3) [81.Toni Kroos (8/0)], Claudemir Jerónimo Barretto da Silva „Cacau" (12/4) [73.Stefan Kießling (6/0)]. Trainer: Joachim Löw (56).
Goals: Thomas Müller (19), Marcell Jansen (56), Sami Khedira (82).

837. 11.08.2010 **DENMARK - GERMANY** **2-2(0-1)**
Parken Stadion, København; Referee: Alan Kelly (Republic of Ireland); Attendance: 16,100
GER: Tim Wiese (3/0), Andreas Beck (8/0) [56.Sascha Riether (1/0)], Serdar Taşçı (14/0), Jérôme Agyenim Boateng (11/0) [78.Christian Schulz (4/0)], Marcel Schäfer (8/0), Thomas Hitzlsperger (52/6) [66.Patrick Helmes (13/2)], Christian Gentner (5/0), Toni Kroos (9/0), Marko Marin (12/1) [57.Aaron Hunt (2/0)], Christian Träsch (3/0), Mario Gómez (39/13). Trainer: Joachim Löw (57).
Goals: Mario Gómez (19), Patrick Helmes (72).

838. 03.09.2010 **BELGIUM - GERMANY** **0-1(0-0)** 14th EC. Qualifiers
Stade „Roi Baudouin", Bruxelles; Referee: Terje Hauge (Norway); Attendance: 41,126
GER: Manuel Peter Neuer (12/0), Philipp Lahm (Cap) (72/4), Per Mertesacker (70/1), Holger Felix Badstuber (5/0), Marcell Jansen (36/3) [46.Heiko Westermann (20/2)], Bastian Schweinsteiger (82/21), Mesut Özil (18/2) [88.Claudemir Jerónimo Barretto da Silva „Cacau" (13/4)], Sami Khedira (13/1), Miroslav Josef Klose (102/53), Lukas Josef Podolski (80/40) [70.Toni Kroos (10/0)], Thomas Müller (9/5). Trainer: Joachim Löw (58).
Goal: Miroslav Josef Klose (51).

839. 07.09.2010 **GERMANY - AZERBAIJAN** **6-1(3-0)** 14th EC. Qualifiers
RheinEnergieStadion, Köln; Referee: Markus Strömbergsson (Sweden); Attendance: 43,751
GER: Manuel Peter Neuer (13/0), Philipp Lahm (Cap) (73/4), Per Mertesacker (71/1) [11.Heiko Westermann (21/3)], Sascha Riether (2/0), Holger Felix Badstuber (6/1), Bastian Schweinsteiger (83/21) [78.Claudemir Jerónimo Barretto da Silva „Cacau" (14/4)], Mesut Özil (19/2), Sami Khedira (14/1), Miroslav Josef Klose (103/55), Lukas Josef Podolski (81/41), Thomas Müller (10/5) [62.Marko Marin (13/1)]. Trainer: Joachim Löw (59).
Goals: Heiko Westermann (28), Lukas Josef Podolski (45+1), Miroslav Josef Klose (45+2), Rashad F. Sadıqov (53 own goal), Holger Felix Badstuber (86), Miroslav Josef Klose (90+2).

840. 08.10.2010 **GERMANY - TURKEY** **3-0(1-0)** 14th EC. Qualifiers
Olympiastadion, Berlin; Referee: Howard Melton Webb (England); Attendance: 74,244
GER: Manuel Peter Neuer (14/0), Philipp Lahm (Cap) (74/4), Per Mertesacker (72/1), Heiko Westermann (22/3), Holger Felix Badstuber (7/1), Mesut Özil (20/3) [90.Marko Marin (14/1)], Sami Khedira (15/1), Toni Kroos (11/0), Miroslav Josef Klose (104/57) [90.Claudemir Jerónimo Barretto da Silva „Cacau" (15/4)], Lukas Josef Podolski (82/41) [86.Christian Träsch (4/0)], Thomas Müller (11/5). Trainer: Joachim Löw (60).
Goals: Miroslav Josef Klose (42), Mesut Özil (79), Miroslav Josef Klose (87).

841. 12.10.2010 **KAZAKHSTAN - GERMANY** **0-3(0-** 14th EC. Qualifiers
Astana Arena, Astana; Referee: Alexandru Dan Tudor (Romania); Attendance: 18,000
GER: Manuel Peter Neuer (15/0), Philipp Lahm (Cap) (75/4), Per Mertesacker (73/1), Heiko Westermann (23/3), Holger Felix Badstuber (8/1), Mesut Özil (21/3) [79.Claudemir Jerónimo Barretto da Silva „Cacau" (16/4)], Sami Khedira (16/1), Toni Kroos (12/0), Miroslav Josef Klose (105/58) [56.Mario Gómez (40/14)], Lukas Josef Podolski (83/42), Thomas Müller (12/5) [71.Marko Marin (15/1)]. Trainer: Joachim Löw (61).
Goals: Miroslav Josef Klose (48), Mario Gómez (76), Lukas Josef Podolski (86).

842. 17.11.2010 **SWEDEN - GERMANY** **0-0**
Nya Ullevi Stadion, Göteborg; Referee: Carlos Velasco Carballo (Spain); Attendance: 21,959
GER: René Adler (10/0), Heiko Westermann (24/3), Jérôme Agyenim Boateng (12/0) [46.Andreas Beck (9/0)], Mats Julian Hummels (2/0), Marcel Schmelzer (1/0), Bastian Schweinsteiger (Cap) (84/21) [60.Claudemir Jerónimo Barretto da Silva „Cacau" (17/4)], Sami Khedira (17/1) [59.Christian Träsch (5/0)], Marko Marin (16/1) [60.Toni Kroos (13/0)], Kevin Großkreutz (2/0) [78.Mario Götze (1/0)], Lewis Harry Holtby (1/0) [77.André Horst Schürrle (1/0)], Mario Gómez (41/14). Trainer: Joachim Löw (62).

843. 09.02.2011 **GERMANY - ITALY** **1-1(1-0)**
Signal Iduna Park, Dortmund; Referee: Frederikus Johannes "Eric" Braamhaar (Netherlands); Attendance: 60,196
GER: Manuel Peter Neuer (16/0), Philipp Lahm (Cap) (76/4) [64.Jérôme Agyenim Boateng (13/0)], Per Mertesacker (74/1), Holger Felix Badstuber (9/1) [64.Mats Julian Hummels (3/0)], Bastian Schweinsteiger (85/21), Mesut Özil (22/3), Sami Khedira (18/1), Dennis Aogo (4/0), Miroslav Josef Klose (106/59) [75.Kevin Großkreutz (3/0)], Lukas Josef Podolski (84/42), Thomas Müller (13/5) [46.Mario Götze (2/0)]. Trainer: Joachim Löw (63).
Goal: Miroslav Josef Klose (17).

844. 26.03.2011 **GERMANY - KAZAKHSTAN** **4-0(3-0)** 14th EC. Qualifiers
"Fritz Walter" Stadion, Kaiserslautern; Referee: Aleksandar Stavrev (Macedonia); Attendance: 47,849
GER: Manuel Peter Neuer (17/0), Philipp Lahm (Cap) (77/4), Per Mertesacker (75/1), Holger Felix Badstuber (10/1), Bastian Schweinsteiger (86/21) [77.Toni Kroos (14/0)], Mesut Özil (23/3), Sami Khedira (19/1), Dennis Aogo (5/0), Miroslav Josef Klose (107/61), Lukas Josef Podolski (85/42) [65.Mario Gómez (42/14)], Thomas Müller (14/7) [78.Mario Götze (3/0)]. Trainer: Joachim Löw (64).
Goals: Miroslav Josef Klose (3), Thomas Müller (25, 43), Miroslav Josef Klose (88).

45. 29.03.2011 **GERMANY - AUSTRALIA** **1-2(1-0)**
orussia Park. Mönchengladbach; Referee: Stéphane Laurent Lannoy (France); Attendance:
ER: Tim Wiese (4/0), Arne Friedrich (80/1), Mats Julian Hummels (4/0), Marcel Schmelzer (2/0), Bastian Schweinsteiger (Cap) (87/21) [64.Toni Kroos 5/0)], Sven Bender (1/0), Christian Träsch (6/0), Mario Gómez (43/15) [72.Miroslav Josef Klose (108/61)], Lukas Josef Podolski (86/42), Thomas Müller 5/7) [65.Mario Götze (4/0)], André Horst Schürrle (2/0). Trainer: Joachim Löw (65).
oal: Mario Gómez (26).

46. 29.05.2011 **GERMANY - URUGUAY** **2-1(2-0)**
hein-Neckar-Arena, Sinsheim; Referee: Olegário Manuel Bártolo Faustino Benquerença (Portugal); Attendance: 25,655
ER: Manuel Peter Neuer (18/0), Arne Friedrich (81/1) [66.Holger Felix Badstuber (11/1)], Philipp Lahm (Cap) (78/4) [66.Benedikt Höwedes (1/0)], Mats ılian Hummels (5/0), Marcel Schmelzer (3/0), Simon Rolfes (22/1), Mesut Özil (24/3) [46.Miroslav Josef Klose (109/61)], Toni Kroos (16/0) [79.Christian äsch (7/0)], Mario Gómez (44/16), Thomas Müller (16/7) [79.Mario Götze (5/0)], André Horst Schürrle (3/1) [58.Lukas Josef Podolski (87/42)]. Trainer: achim Löw (66).
oals: Mario Gómez (20), André Horst Schürrle (35).

47. 03.06.2011 **AUSTRIA - GERMANY** **1-2(0-1)** 14th EC. Qualifiers
rnst Happel" Stadion, Vienna; Referee: Massimo Busacca (Switzerland); Attendance: 47,500
ER: Manuel Peter Neuer (19/0), Arne Friedrich (82/1), Philipp Lahm (Cap) (79/4), Mats Julian Hummels (6/0), Marcel Schmelzer (4/0), Mesut Özil (25/3), mi Khedira (20/1) [69.Holger Felix Badstuber (12/1)], Toni Kroos (17/0) [90+3.Dennis Aogo (6/0)], Mario Gómez (45/18), Lukas Josef Podolski (88/42) 7.André Horst Schürrle (4/1)], Thomas Müller (17/7). Trainer: Joachim Löw (67).
oals: Mario Gómez (44, 90)

48. 07.06.2011 **AZERBAIJAN - GERMANY** **1-3(0-2)** 14th EC. Qualifiers
ofik Bakhramov" Stadium, Baku; Referee: Michael Koukoulakis (Greece); Attendance: 29,858
ER: Manuel Peter Neuer (20/0), Philipp Lahm (Cap) (80/4), Benedikt Höwedes (2/0), Mats Julian Hummels (7/0), Holger Felix Badstuber (13/1), Mesut zil (26/4) [81.Mario Götze (6/0)], Dennis Aogo (7/0), Toni Kroos (18/0), Mario Gómez (46/19), Lukas Josef Podolski (89/42) [78.André Horst Schürrle /2)], Thomas Müller (18/7) [88.Lewis Harry Holtby (2/0)]. Trainer: Joachim Löw (68).
oals: Mesut Özil (30), Mario Gómez (41), André Horst Schürrle (90+3).

49. 10.08.2011 **GERMANY - BRAZIL** **3-2(0-0)**
ercedes-Benz" Arena, Stuttgart; Referee: Viktor Kassai (Hungary); Attendance: 54,767
ER: Manuel Peter Neuer (21/0), Philipp Lahm (Cap) (81/4), Mats Julian Hummels (8/0) [89.Jérôme Agyenim Boateng (14/0)], Holger Felix Badstuber 4/1), Bastian Schweinsteiger (88/22) [85.Simon Rolfes (23/1)], Toni Kroos (19/0), Christian Träsch (8/0), Mario Götze (7/1) [89.Claudemir Jerónimo arretto da Silva „Cacau" (18/4)], Mario Gómez (47/19) [46.Miroslav Josef Klose (110/61)], Lukas Josef Podolski (90/42) [46.André Horst Schürrle (6/3)], omas Müller (19/7). Trainer: Joachim Löw (69).
oals: Bastian Schweinsteiger (61 penalty), Mario Götze (67), André Horst Schürrle (80).

50. 02.09.2011 **GERMANY - AUSTRIA** **6-2(3-1)** 14th EC. Qualifiers
rena "AufSchalke", Gelsenkirchen; Referee: Paolo Tagliavento (Italy); Attendance: 53,313
ER: Manuel Peter Neuer (22/0), Philipp Lahm (Cap) (82/4), Benedikt Höwedes (3/0) [46.Jérôme Agyenim Boateng (15/0)], Mats Julian Hummels (9/0), olger Felix Badstuber (15/1), Bastian Schweinsteiger (89/22), Mesut Özil (27/6), Toni Kroos (20/0) [85.Mario Götze (8/2)], Miroslav Josef Klose (111/62), ıkas Josef Podolski (91/43) [74.André Horst Schürrle (7/4)], Thomas Müller (20/7). Trainer: Joachim Löw (70).
oals: Miroslav Josef Klose (8), Mesut Özil (23), Lukas Josef Podolski (28), Mesut Özil (47), André Horst Schürrle (83), Mario Götze (88).

51. 06.09.2011 **POLAND - GERMANY** **2-2(0-0)**
GE Arena, Gdańsk; Referee: Daniele Orsato (Italy); Attendance: 40,000
ER: Tim Wiese (5/0), Philipp Lahm (Cap) (83/4) [46.Marcel Schmelzer (5/0)], Per Mertesacker (76/1), Jérôme Agyenim Boateng (16/0), Simon Rolfes 4/1) [77.Lars Bender (1/0)], Toni Kroos (21/1), Christian Träsch (9/0), Mario Götze (9/2), Miroslav Josef Klose (112/62) [46.Claudemir Jerónimo Barretto ı Silva „Cacau" (19/5)], Lukas Josef Podolski (92/43) [61.Thomas Müller (21/7)], André Horst Schürrle (8/4). Trainer: Joachim Löw (71).
oals: Toni Kroos (68 penalty), Claudemir Jerónimo Barretto da Silva „Cacau" (90).

52. 07.10.2011 **TURKEY - GERMANY** **1-3(0-1)** 14th EC. Qualifiers
ırk Telekom Arena, Istanbul; Referee: Martin Atkinson (England); Attendance: 49,532
ER: Manuel Peter Neuer (23/0), Philipp Lahm (Cap) (84/4), Per Mertesacker (77/1), Jérôme Agyenim Boateng (17/0) [73.Benedikt Höwedes (4/0)], Holger elix Badstuber (16/1), Bastian Schweinsteiger (90/23), Sami Khedira (21/1), Mario Götze (10/2) [89.Marco Reus (1/0)], Mario Gómez (48/20), Lukas Josef odolski (93/43) [62.André Horst Schürrle (9/4)], Thomas Müller (22/8). Trainer: Joachim Löw (72).
oals: Mario Gómez (35), Thomas Müller (66), Bastian Schweinsteiger (86 penalty).

53. 11.10.2011 **GERMANY - BELGIUM** **3-1(2-0)** 14th EC. Qualifiers
sprit Arena, Düsseldorf; Referee: Svein Oddvar Moen (Norway); Attendance: 48,483
ER: Manuel Peter Neuer (24/0), Philipp Lahm (Cap) (85/4) [84.İlkay Gündoğan (1/0)], Per Mertesacker (78/1), Benedikt Höwedes (5/0), Mats Julian ummels (10/0), Mesut Özil (28/7), Sami Khedira (22/1), Toni Kroos (22/1), Mario Gómez (49/21) [77.Claudemir Jerónimo Barretto da Silva „Cacau" 0/5)], Thomas Müller (23/8) [71.Marco Reus (2/0)], André Horst Schürrle (10/5). Trainer: Joachim Löw (73).
oals: Mesut Özil (30), André Horst Schürrle (33), Mario Gómez (48).

54. 11.11.2011 **UKRAINE - GERMANY** **3-3(3-1)**
limpiyskyi Stadium, Kyiv; Referee: Carlos Velasco Carballo (Spain); Attendance: 69,720
ER: Ron-Robert Zieler (1/0), Jérôme Agyenim Boateng (18/0), Mats Julian Hummels (11/0), Holger Felix Badstuber (17/1), Mesut Özil (29/7) [69.Lukas sef Podolski (94/43)], Sami Khedira (23/1) [46.Simon Rolfes (25/2)], Dennis Aogo (8/0), Toni Kroos (23/2) [87.Lars Bender (2/0)], Christian Träsch (10/0) 6.André Horst Schürrle (11/5)], Mario Götze (11/2) [66.Thomas Müller (24/9)], Mario Gómez (Cap) (50/21) [83.Claudemir Jerónimo Barretto da Silva Cacau" (21/5)]. Trainer: Joachim Löw (74).
oals: Toni Kroos (38), Simon Rolfes (65), Thomas Müller (77).

855. 15.11.2011 **GERMANY - NETHERLANDS** **3-0(2-0)**
Imtech Arena, Hamburg; Referee: Cüneyt Çakır (Turkey); Attendance: 51,500
GER: Manuel Peter Neuer (25/0), Per Mertesacker (79/1), Jérôme Agyenim Boateng (19/0) [65.Benedikt Höwedes (6/0)], Holger Felix Badstuber (18/1) [46.Mats Julian Hummels (12/0)], Mesut Özil (30/8), Sami Khedira (24/1) [88.Lars Bender (3/0)], Dennis Aogo (9/0), Toni Kroos (24/2) [82.Simon Rolfes (26/2)], Miroslav Josef Klose (Cap) (113/63) [82.Marco Reus (3/0)], Lukas Josef Podolski (95/43) [65.Mario Götze (12/2)], Thomas Müller (25/10). Trainer: Joachim Löw (75).
Goals: Thomas Müller (15), Miroslav Josef Klose (26), Mesut Özil (66).

856. 29.02.2012 **GERMANY - FRANCE** **1-2(0-1)**
Weserstadion, Bremen; Referee: Paolo Tagliavento (Italy); Attendance: 37,800
GER: Tim Wiese (6/0), Jérôme Agyenim Boateng (20/0), Mats Julian Hummels (13/0), Holger Felix Badstuber (19/1) [46.Benedikt Höwedes (7/0)], Mesut Özil (31/8), Sami Khedira (25/1) [70.Lars Bender (4/0)], Dennis Aogo (10/0), Toni Kroos (25/2), Marco Reus (4/0) [70.Claudemir Jerónimo Barretto da Silva „Cacau“ (22/6)], Miroslav Josef Klose (Cap) (114/63) [46.Mario Gómez (51/21)], André Horst Schürrle (12/5) [46.Thomas Müller (26/10)]. Trainer: Joachim Löw (76).
Goal: Claudemir Jerónimo Barretto da Silva „Cacau“ (90+1).

857. 26.05.2012 **SWITZERLAND - GERMANY** **5-3(2-1)**
“St. Jakob” Park, Basel; Referee: Antony Gautier (France); Attendance: 27,381
GER: Marc-André ter Stegen (1/0), Per Mertesacker (80/1), Benedikt Höwedes (8/0) [78.Sven Bender (2/0)], Mats Julian Hummels (14/1), Marcel Schmelzer (6/0), Mesut Özil (32/8) [46.Marco Reus (5/1)], Sami Khedira (26/1) [46.İlkay Gündoğan (2/0)], Mario Götze (13/2) [78.Lars Bender (5/0)], Miroslav Josef Klose (Cap) (115/63) [78.Claudemir Jerónimo Barretto da Silva „Cacau“ (23/6)], Lukas Josef Podolski (96/43) [62.Julian Draxler (1/0)], André Horst Schürrle (13/6). Trainer: Joachim Löw (77).
Goals: Mats Julian Hummels (45), André Horst Schürrle (64), Marco Reus (72).

858. 31.05.2012 **GERMANY - ISRAEL** **2-0(1-0)**
Red Bull Arena, Leipzig; Referee: Bernie Raymond “Kevin” Blom (Netherlands); Attendance: 43,241
GER: Manuel Peter Neuer (26/0), Philipp Lahm (Cap) (86/4), Per Mertesacker (81/1), Jérôme Agyenim Boateng (21/0), Holger Felix Badstuber (20/1), Mesut Özil (33/8), Sami Khedira (27/1) [88.Lars Bender (6/0)], Toni Kroos (26/2) [85.Mario Götze (14/2)], Mario Gómez (52/22) [67.Miroslav Josef Klose (116/63)], Lukas Josef Podolski (97/43) [67.André Horst Schürrle (14/7)], Thomas Müller (27/10) [83.Marco Reus (6/1)]. Trainer: Joachim Löw (78).
Goals: Mario Gómez (40), André Horst Schürrle (82).

859. 09.06.2012 **GERMANY - PORTUGAL** **1-0(0-0)** 14th EC. Group Stage.
Arena Lviv, Lviv (Ukraine); Referee: Stéphane Laurent Lannoy (France); Attendance: 32,990
GER: Manuel Peter Neuer (27/0), Philipp Lahm (Cap) (87/4), Jérôme Agyenim Boateng (22/0), Mats Julian Hummels (15/1), Holger Felix Badstuber (21/1), Bastian Schweinsteiger (91/23), Mesut Özil (34/8) [87.Toni Kroos (27/2)], Sami Khedira (28/1), Mario Gómez (53/23) [80.Miroslav Josef Klose (117/63)], Lukas Josef Podolski (98/43), Thomas Müller (28/10) [90+4.Lars Bender (7/0)]. Trainer: Joachim Löw (79).
Goal: Mario Gómez (72).

860. 13.06.2012 **NETHERLANDS - GERMANY** **1-2(0-2)** 14th EC. Group Stage.
Metalist Stadium, Kharkiv (Ukraine); Referee: Jonas Eriksson (Sweden); Attendance: 37,750
GER: Manuel Peter Neuer (28/0), Philipp Lahm (Cap) (88/4), Jérôme Agyenim Boateng (23/0), Mats Julian Hummels (16/1), Holger Felix Badstuber (22/1), Bastian Schweinsteiger (92/23), Mesut Özil (35/8) [81.Toni Kroos (28/2)], Sami Khedira (29/1), Mario Gómez (54/25) [72.Miroslav Josef Klose (118/63)], Lukas Josef Podolski (99/43), Thomas Müller (29/10) [90+2.Lars Bender (8/0)]. Trainer: Joachim Löw (80).
Goals: Mario Gómez (24, 38).

861. 17.06.2012 **DENMARK - GERMANY** **1-2(1-1)** 14th EC. Group Stage.
Arena Lviv, Lviv (Ukraine); Referee: Carlos Velasco Carballo (Spain); Attendance: 32,990
GER: Manuel Peter Neuer (29/0), Philipp Lahm (Cap) (89/4), Mats Julian Hummels (17/1), Holger Felix Badstuber (23/1), Bastian Schweinsteiger (93/23), Mesut Özil (36/8), Sami Khedira (30/1), Lars Bender (9/1), Mario Gómez (55/25) [74.Miroslav Josef Klose (119/63)], Lukas Josef Podolski (**100**/44) [64.André Horst Schürrle (15/7)], Thomas Müller (30/10) [84.Toni Kroos (29/2)]. Trainer: Joachim Löw (81).
Goals: Lukas Josef Podolski (19), Lars Bender (80).

862. 22.06.2012 **GERMANY - GREECE** **4-2(1-0)** 14th EC. Quarter-Finals.
PGE Arena, Gdańsk (Poland); Referee: Damir Skomina (Slovenia); Attendance: 38,751
GER: Manuel Peter Neuer (30/0), Philipp Lahm (Cap) (90/5), Jérôme Agyenim Boateng (24/0), Mats Julian Hummels (18/1), Holger Felix Badstuber (24/1), Bastian Schweinsteiger (94/23), Mesut Özil (37/8), Sami Khedira (31/2), Marco Reus (7/2) [80.Mario Götze (15/2)], Miroslav Josef Klose (120/64) [80.Mario Gómez (56/25)], André Horst Schürrle (16/7) [67.Thomas Müller (31/10)]. Trainer: Joachim Löw (82).
Goals: Philipp Lahm (39), Sami Khedira (61), Miroslav Josef Klose (68), Marco Reus (74).

863. 28.06.2012 **GERMANY - ITALY** **1-2(0-2)** 14th EC. Semi-Finals.
Stadion Narodowy, Warszawa (Poland); Referee: Stéphane Laurent Lannoy (France); Attendance: 55,540
GER: Manuel Peter Neuer (31/0), Philipp Lahm (Cap) (91/5), Jérôme Agyenim Boateng (25/0) [71.Thomas Müller (32/10)], Mats Julian Hummels (19/1), Holger Felix Badstuber (25/1), Bastian Schweinsteiger (95/23), Mesut Özil (38/9), Sami Khedira (32/2), Toni Kroos (30/2), Mario Gómez (57/25) [46.Miroslav Josef Klose (121/64)], Lukas Josef Podolski (101/44) [46.Marco Reus (8/2)]. Trainer: Joachim Löw (83).
Goal: Mesut Özil (90+2 penalty).

864. 15.08.2012 **GERMANY - ARGENTINA** **1-3(0-1)**
Commerzbank-Arena, Frankfurt am Main; Referee: Jonas Eriksson (Sweden); Attendance: 48,808
GER: Ron-Robert Zieler (2/0) [*sent off 30*], Jérôme Agyenim Boateng (26/0), Mats Julian Hummels (20/1) [25.Benedikt Höwedes (9/1)], Holger Felix Badstuber (26/1), Marcel Schmelzer (7/0), Mesut Özil (39/9) [69.Toni Kroos (31/2)], Sami Khedira (33/2) [69.İlkay Gündoğan (3/0)], Lars Bender (10/1) [74.Mario Götze (16/2)], Marco Reus (9/2), Miroslav Josef Klose (Cap) (122/64) [62.André Horst Schürrle (17/7)], Thomas Müller (33/10) [32.Marc-André ter Stegen (2/0)]. Trainer: Joachim Löw (84).
Goal: Benedikt Höwedes (81).

865. 07.09.2012 **GERMANY - FAROE ISLANDS** **3-0(1-0)** 20th FIFA WC. Qualifiers

AWD-Arena, Hannover; Referee: Robert Madden (Scotland); Attendance: 32,769

GER: Manuel Peter Neuer (32/0), Philipp Lahm (Cap) (92/5), Per Mertesacker (82/1), Mats Julian Hummels (21/1), Holger Felix Badstuber (27/1), Mesut Özil (40/11), Sami Khedira (34/2), Marco Reus (10/2), Mario Götze (17/3) [87.Julian Draxler (2/0)], Miroslav Josef Klose (123/64) [75.Lukas Josef Podolski (102/44)], Thomas Müller (34/10) [68.André Horst Schürrle (18/7)]. Trainer: Joachim Löw (85).

Goals: Mario Götze (28), Mesut Özil (54, 72).

866. 11.09.2012 **AUSTRIA - GERMANY** **1-2(0-1)** 20th FIFA WC. Qualifiers

„Ernst Happel" Stadion, Wien; Referee: Björn Kuipers (Netherlands); Attendance: 47,000

GER: Manuel Peter Neuer (33/0), Philipp Lahm (Cap) (93/5), Mats Julian Hummels (22/1), Holger Felix Badstuber (28/1), Marcel Schmelzer (8/0), Mesut Özil (41/12), Sami Khedira (35/2), Toni Kroos (32/2), Marco Reus (11/3) [46.Mario Götze (18/3)], Miroslav Josef Klose (124/64) [75.Lukas Josef Podolski (103/44)], Thomas Müller (35/10). Trainer: Joachim Löw (86).

Goals: Marco Reus (44), Mesut Özil (52 penalty).

867. 12.10.2012 **REPUBLIC OF IRELAND - GERMANY** **1-6(0-2)** 20th FIFA WC. Qualifiers

Aviva Stadium, Dublin; Referee: Nicola Rizzoli (Italy); Attendance: 49,850

GER: Manuel Peter Neuer (34/0), Per Mertesacker (83/1), Jérôme Agyenim Boateng (27/0), Holger Felix Badstuber (29/1), Marcel Schmelzer (9/0), Bastian Schweinsteiger (Cap) (96/23), Mesut Özil (42/13), Sami Khedira (36/2) [46.Toni Kroos (33/4)], Marco Reus (12/5) [66.Lukas Josef Podolski (104/44)], Miroslav Josef Klose (125/65) [72.André Horst Schürrle (19/7)], Thomas Müller (36/10). Trainer: Joachim Löw (87).

Goals: Marco Reus (32, 40), Mesut Özil (55 penalty), Miroslav Josef Klose (58), Toni Kroos (61, 83).

868. 16.10.2012 **GERMANY - SWEDEN** **4-4(3-0)** 20th FIFA WC. Qualifiers

Olympiastadion, Berlin; Referee: Pedro Proença Oliveira Alves Garcia (Portugal); Attendance: 72,369

GER: Manuel Peter Neuer (35/0), Philipp Lahm (Cap) (94/5), Per Mertesacker (84/2), Jérôme Agyenim Boateng (28/0), Holger Felix Badstuber (30/1), Bastian Schweinsteiger (97/23), Mesut Özil (43/14), Toni Kroos (34/4), Marco Reus (13/5) [88.Lukas Josef Podolski (105/44)], Miroslav Josef Klose (126/67), Thomas Müller (37/10) [67.Mario Götze (19/3)]. Trainer: Joachim Löw (88).

Goals: Miroslav Josef Klose (8, 15), Per Mertesacker (39), Mesut Özil (55).

869. 14.11.2012 **NETHERLANDS - GERMANY** **0-0**

Amsterdam Arena, Amsterdam; Referee: Pedro Proença Oliveira Alves Garcia (Portugal); Attendance: 51,000

GER: Manuel Peter Neuer (36/0), Philipp Lahm (Cap) (95/5), Per Mertesacker (85/2), Benedikt Höwedes (10/1), Mats Julian Hummels (23/1), Lars Bender (11/1) [82.Sven Bender (3/0)], Marco Reus (14/5) [90+2.Julian Draxler (3/0)], Lewis Harry Holtby (3/0) [87.Roman Neustädter (1/0)], İlkay Gündoğan (4/0), Mario Götze (20/3) [72.Lukas Josef Podolski (106/44)], Thomas Müller (38/10) [84.André Horst Schürrle (20/7)]. Trainer: Joachim Löw (89).

870. 06.02.2013 **FRANCE - GERMANY** **1-2(1-0)**

Stade de France, Saint-Denis, Paris; Referee: Paolo Silvio Mazzoleni (Italy); Attendance: 75,000

GER: René Adler (11/0), Philipp Lahm (Cap) (96/5), Per Mertesacker (86/2), Benedikt Höwedes (11/1), Mats Julian Hummels (24/1), Mesut Özil (44/14), Sami Khedira (37/3), İlkay Gündoğan (5/0), Mario Gómez (58/25) [57.Toni Kroos (35/4)], Lukas Josef Podolski (107/44) [68.André Horst Schürrle (21/7)], Thomas Müller (39/11) [89.Lars Bender (12/1)]. Trainer: Joachim Löw (90).

Goals: Thomas Müller (51), Sami Khedira (74).

871. 22.03.2013 **KAZAKHSTAN - GERMANY** **0-3(0-2)** 20th FIFA WC. Qualifiers

Astana Arena, Astana; Referee: Anastassios Kakos (Greece); Attendance: 29,300

GER: Manuel Peter Neuer (37/0), Philipp Lahm (Cap) (97/5), Per Mertesacker (87/2), Benedikt Höwedes (12/1), Marcel Schmelzer (10/0), Bastian Schweinsteiger (98/23), Mesut Özil (45/14), Sami Khedira (38/3) [82.İlkay Gündoğan (6/0)], Mario Götze (21/4), Julian Draxler (4/0) [19.Lukas Josef Podolski (108/44)], Thomas Müller (40/13) [82.André Horst Schürrle (22/7)]. Trainer: Joachim Löw (91).

Goals: Thomas Müller (20), Mario Götze (22), Thomas Müller (73).

872. 26.03.2013 **GERMANY - KAZAKHSTAN** **4-1(3-0)** 20th FIFA WC. Qualifiers

Frankenstadion, Nürnberg; Referee: Halis Özkahya (Turkey); Attendance: 43,520

GER: Manuel Peter Neuer (38/0), Philipp Lahm (Cap) (98/5), Per Mertesacker (88/2), Jérôme Agyenim Boateng (29/0), Marcel Schmelzer (11/0), Mesut Özil (46/14), Sami Khedira (39/3), Marco Reus (15/7) [90.Marcell Jansen (37/3)], İlkay Gündoğan (7/1), Mario Götze (22/5), Thomas Müller (41/13). Trainer: Joachim Löw (92).

Goals: Marco Reus (23), Mario Götze (27), İlkay Gündoğan (31), Marco Reus (90).

873. 29.05.2013 **ECUADOR - GERMANY** **2-4(1-4)**

FAU Stadium, Boca Raton (United States); Referee: Ricardo Salazar (United States); Attendance: 5,000

GER: René Adler (12/0), Marcell Jansen (38/3), Per Mertesacker (89/2), Heiko Westermann (25/3), Benedikt Höwedes (13/1), Sidney Sam (1/0) [69.André Horst Schürrle (23/7)], Lars Bender (13/3) [90+1.Philipp Wollscheid (1/0)], Roman Neustädter (2/0) [66.Stefan Reinartz (2/0)], Julian Draxler (5/0) [56.Aaron Hunt (3/0)], Lukas Josef Podolski (109/46) [89.Nicolai Müller (1/0)], Maximilian Kruse (1/0) [79.Dennis Aogo (11/0)]. Trainer: Joachim Löw (93).

Goals: Lukas Josef Podolski (1), Lars Bender (4), Lukas Josef Podolski (17), Lars Bender (24).

874. 02.06.2013 **UNITED STATES - GERMANY** **4-3(2-0)**

"Robert F. Kennedy" Memorial Stadium, Washington; Referee: Paul Enrique Delgadillo Haro (Mexico); Attendance: 47,359

GER: Marc-André ter Stegen (3/0), Marcell Jansen (39/3) [46.Dennis Aogo (12/0)], Per Mertesacker (90/2) [46.Philipp Wollscheid (2/0)], Benedikt Höwedes (14/1), Sven Bender (4/0) [46.Maximilian Kruse (2/1)], Lars Bender (14/3) [46.Heiko Westermann (26/4)], Stefan Reinartz (3/0), Julian Draxler (6/1), Miroslav Josef Klose (127/67) [80.Nicolai Müller (2/0)], Lukas Josef Podolski (110/46), André Horst Schürrle (24/7) [67.Sidney Sam (2/0)]. Trainer: Joachim Löw (94).

Goals: Heiko Westermann (52), Maximilian Kruse (79), Julian Draxler (81).

875. 14.08.2013 **GERMANY - PARAGUAY** **3-3(2-3)**

„Fritz Walter" Stadion, Kaiserslautern; Referee: Ivan Bebek (Croatia); Attendance: 47,522

GER: Manuel Peter Neuer (39/0), Philipp Lahm (Cap) (99/5), Per Mertesacker (91/2) [46.Jérôme Agyenim Boateng (30/0)], Mats Julian Hummels (25/1), Marcel Schmelzer (12/0) [82.Marcell Jansen (40/3)], Mesut Özil (47/14), Sami Khedira (40/3), Marco Reus (16/7) [62.Lukas Josef Podolski (111/46)], İlkay Gündoğan (8/2) [27.Lars Bender (15/4)], Miroslav Josef Klose (128/67) [54.Mario Gómez (59/25)], Thomas Müller (42/14) [81.André Horst Schürrle (25/7)]. Trainer: Joachim Löw (95).

Goals: İlkay Gündoğan (18), Thomas Müller (31), Lars Bender (75).

876. 06.09.2013 **GERMANY - AUSTRIA** **3-0(1-0)** 20th FIFA WC. Qualifiers

Allianz Arena, München; Referee: Milorad Mažić (Serbia); Attendance: 68,000

GER: Manuel Peter Neuer (40/0), Philipp Lahm (Cap) (**100**/5), Per Mertesacker (92/2), Jérôme Agyenim Boateng (31/0), Marcel Schmelzer (13/0) [46.Benedikt Höwedes (15/1)], Mesut Özil (48/14), Sami Khedira (41/3), Toni Kroos (36/5), Marco Reus (17/7) [90+2.Julian Draxler (7/1)], Miroslav Josef Klose (129/68) [82.Sven Bender (5/0)], Thomas Müller (43/15). Trainer: Joachim Löw (96).

Goals: Miroslav Josef Klose (33), Toni Kroos (51), Thomas Müller (88).

877. 10.09.2013 **FAROE ISLANDS - GERMANY** **0-3(0-1)** 20th FIFA WC. Qualifiers

Tórsvøllur Stadium, Tórshavn; Referee: Gediminas Mažeika (Lithuania); Attendance: 4,118

GER: Manuel Peter Neuer (41/0), Philipp Lahm (Cap) (101/5), Per Mertesacker (93/3), Jérôme Agyenim Boateng (32/0), Marcel Schmelzer (14/0), Mesut Özil (49/15), Sami Khedira (42/3), Toni Kroos (37/5), Julian Draxler (8/1) [75.André Horst Schürrle (26/7)], Miroslav Josef Klose (130/68) [79.Maximilian Kruse (3/1)], Thomas Müller (44/16) [84.Sidney Sam (3/0)]. Trainer: Joachim Löw (97).

Goals: Per Mertesacker (22), Mesut Özil (74 penalty), Thomas Müller (84).

878. 11.10.2013 **GERMANY - REPUBLIC OF IRELAND** **3-0(1-0)** 20th FIFA WC. Qualifiers

RheinEnergie Stadion, Köln; Referee: Serge Gumienny (Belgium); Attendance: 46,237

GER: Manuel Peter Neuer (42/0), Philipp Lahm (Cap) (102/5), Per Mertesacker (94/3), Jérôme Agyenim Boateng (33/0), Marcell Jansen (41/3), Bastian Schweinsteiger (99/23), Mesut Özil (50/16), Sami Khedira (43/4) [82.Maximilian Kruse (4/1)], Toni Kroos (38/5), Thomas Müller (45/16) [88.Sidney Sam (4/0)], André Horst Schürrle (27/8) [86.Mario Götze (23/5)]. Trainer: Joachim Löw (98).

Goals: Sami Khedira (11), André Horst Schürrle (58), Mesut Özil (90+1).

879. 15.10.2013 **SWEDEN - GERMANY** **3-5(2-1)** 20th FIFA WC. Qualifiers

Friends Arena, Stockholm; Referee: William Collum (Scotland); Attendance: 49,251

GER: Manuel Peter Neuer (43/0), Philipp Lahm (Cap) (103/5), Jérôme Agyenim Boateng (34/0), Mats Julian Hummels (26/1), Marcell Jansen (42/3), Bastian Schweinsteiger (**100**/23), Mesut Özil (51/17) [82.Julian Draxler (9/1)], Toni Kroos (39/5), Thomas Müller (46/16) [46.Mario Götze (24/6)], Maximilian Kruse (5/1) [75.Benedikt Höwedes (16/1)], André Horst Schürrle (28/11). Trainer: Joachim Löw (99).

Goals: Mesut Özil (45), Mario Götze (52), André Horst Schürrle (57, 66, 76).

880. 15.11.2013 **ITALY - GERMANY** **1-1(1-1)**

Stadio "Giuseppe Meazza", Milano; Referee: Olegário Manuel Bártolo Faustino Benquerença (Portugal); Attendance: 49,000

GER: Manuel Peter Neuer (44/0), Jérôme Agyenim Boateng (35/0), Benedikt Höwedes (17/1), Mats Julian Hummels (27/2), Marcell Jansen (43/3), Philipp Lahm (Cap) (104/5), Sami Khedira (44/4) [67.Sven Bender (6/0)], Toni Kroos (40/5), Mario Götze (25/6) [60.Mesut Özil (52/17)], Thomas Müller (47/16) [87.Lars Bender (16/4)], André Horst Schürrle (29/11) [59.Marco Reus (18/7)]. Trainer: Joachim Löw (**100**).

Goal: Mats Julian Hummels (8).

881. 19.11.2013 **ENGLAND - GERMANY** **0-1(0-1)**

The National Stadium, Wembley Stadium, London; Referee: Stéphane Laurent Lannoy (France); Attendance: 85,934

GER: Roman Weidenfeller (1/0), Jérôme Agyenim Boateng (36/0) [46.Mats Julian Hummels (28/2); 65.Benedikt Höwedes (18/1)], Per Mertesacker (95/4), Heiko Westermann (27/4) [67.Julian Draxler (10/1)], Marcel Schmelzer (15/0) [46.Marcell Jansen (44/3)], Toni Kroos (41/5), Sven Bender (7/0), Lars Bender (17/4), Marco Reus (19/7) [82.André Horst Schürrle (30/11)], Mario Götze (26/6), Maximilian Kruse (6/1) [56.Sidney Sam (5/0)]. Trainer: Joachim Löw (101).

Goal: Per Mertesacker (39).

882. 05.03.2014 **GERMANY - CHILE** **1-0(1-0)**

"Mercedes-Benz" Arena, Stuttgart; Referee: Mark Clattenburg (England); Attendance: 54,449

GER: Manuel Peter Neuer (45/0), Philipp Lahm (Cap) (105/5), Per Mertesacker (96/4), Jérôme Agyenim Boateng (37/0), Marcell Jansen (45/3) [24.Marcel Schmelzer (16/0)], Bastian Schweinsteiger (101/23), Mesut Özil (53/17) [89.Matthias Lukas Ginter (1/0)], Toni Kroos (42/5), Kevin Großkreutz (4/0), Mario Götze (27/7) [83.Lukas Josef Podolski (112/46)], Miroslav Josef Klose (131/68) [46.André Horst Schürrle (31/11)]. Trainer: Joachim Löw (102).

Goal: Mario Götze (16).

883. 13.05.2014 **GERMANY - POLAND** **0-0**

Imtech Arena, Hamburg; Referee: David Fernández Borbalan (Spain); Attendance: 37,569

GER: Ron-Robert Zieler (3/0) [46.Marc-André ter Stegen (4/0)], Oliver Sorg (1/0) [82.Christian Günter (1/0)], Shkodran Mustafi (1/0), Antonio Rüdiger (1/0) [46.Benedikt Höwedes (19/1)], Matthias Lukas Ginter (2/0), Sebastian Rudy (1/0), Christoph Kramer (1/0), Julian Draxler (11/1), Leon Christoph Goretzka (1/0) [46.André Hahn (1/0)], Max Meyer (1/0) [76.Maximilian Arnold (1/0)], Kevin Volland (1/0) [71.Sebastian Alexander Jung (1/0)]. Trainer: Joachim Löw (103).

884. 01.06.2014 **GERMANY - CAMEROON** **2-2(0-0)**

Borussia Park, Mönchengladbach; Referee: Damir Skomina (Slovenia); Attendance: 41,250

GER: Roman Weidenfeller (2/0), Per Mertesacker (97/4), Jérôme Agyenim Boateng (38/0), Mats Julian Hummels (29/2), Erik Durm (1/0) [85.Benedikt Höwedes (20/1)], Mesut Özil (54/17) [63.Lukas Josef Podolski (113/46)], Sami Khedira (45/4) [73.Christoph Kramer (2/0)], Toni Kroos (43/5), Marco Reus (20/7), Mario Götze (28/7) [58.André Horst Schürrle (32/12)], Thomas Müller (48/17). Trainer: Joachim Löw (104).

Goals: Thomas Müller (66), André Horst Schürrle (71).

885. 06.06.2014 **GERMANY - ARMENIA** **6-1(0-0)**

Coface Arena, Mainz; Referee: Harald Lechner (Austria); Attendance: 27,000

GER: Roman Weidenfeller (3/0), Philipp Lahm (Cap) (106/5) [46.Mesut Özil (55/17)], Per Mertesacker (98/4), Jérôme Agyenim Boateng (39/0) [67.Kevin Großkreutz (5/0)], Benedikt Höwedes (21/2), Mats Julian Hummels (30/2), Sami Khedira (46/4) [59.Bastian Schweinsteiger (102/23)], Toni Kroos (44/5), Marco Reus (21/7) [45.Lukas Josef Podolski (114/47)], Thomas Müller (49/17) [67.Miroslav Josef Klose (132/69)], André Horst Schürrle (33/13) [75.Mario Götze (29/9)]. Trainer: Joachim Löw (105).

Goals: André Horst Schürrle (52), Lukas Josef Podolski (72), Benedikt Höwedes (73), Miroslav Josef Klose (76), Mario Götze (82, 89).

886. 16.06.2014 **GERMANY - PORTUGAL** **4-0(3-0)** 20th FIFA WC. Group Stage.

Arena Fonte Nova, Salvador (Brazil); Referee: Milorad Mažić (Serbia); Attendance: 51,081

GER: Manuel Peter Neuer (46/0), Philipp Lahm (Cap) (107/5), Per Mertesacker (99/4), Jérôme Agyenim Boateng (40/0), Benedikt Höwedes (22/2), Mats Julian Hummels (31/3) [73.Shkodran Mustafi (2/0)], Mesut Özil (56/17) [63.André Horst Schürrle (34/13)], Sami Khedira (47/4), Toni Kroos (45/5), Mario Götze (30/9), Thomas Müller (50/20) [82.Lukas Josef Podolski (115/47)]. Trainer: Joachim Löw (106).

Goals: Thomas Müller (12 penalty), Mats Julian Hummels (32), Thomas Müller (45+1, 78).

37. 21.06.2014 **GERMANY - GHANA** **2-2(0-0)** 20th FIFA WC. Group Stage.
stádio Castelão, Fortaleza (Brazil); Referee: Sandro Meira Ricci (Brazil); Attendance: 59,621
ER: Manuel Peter Neuer (47/0), Philipp Lahm (Cap) (108/5), Per Mertesacker (**100**/4), Jérôme Agyenim Boateng (41/0) [46.Shkodran Mustafi (3/0)], enedikt Höwedes (23/2), Mats Julian Hummels (32/3), Mesut Özil (57/17), Sami Khedira (48/4) [70.Bastian Schweinsteiger (103/23)], Toni Kroos (46/5), ario Götze (31/10) [69.Miroslav Josef Klose (133/70)], Thomas Müller (51/20). Trainer: Joachim Löw (107).
oals: Mario Götze (51), Miroslav Josef Klose (71).

38. 26.06.2014 **UNITED STATES - GERMANY** **0-1(0-0)** 20th FIFA WC. Group Stage.
rena Pernambuco, Recife (Brazil); Referee: Ravshan Irmatov (Uzbekistan); Attendance: 41,876
ER: Manuel Peter Neuer (48/0), Philipp Lahm (Cap) (109/5), Per Mertesacker (101/4), Jérôme Agyenim Boateng (42/0), Benedikt Höwedes (24/2), Mats lian Hummels (33/3), Bastian Schweinsteiger (104/23) [76.Mario Götze (32/10)], Mesut Özil (58/17) [89.André Horst Schürrle (35/13)], Toni Kroos 7/5), Lukas Josef Podolski (116/47) [46.Miroslav Josef Klose (134/70)], Thomas Müller (52/21). Trainer: Joachim Löw (108).
oal: Thomas Müller (55).

39. 30.06.2014 **GERMANY - ALGERIA** **2-1(0-0,0-0)** 20th FIFA WC. 2nd Round of 16.
stádio Beira-Rio, Porto Alegre (Brazil); Referee: Sandro Meira Ricci (Brazil); Attendance: 43,063
ER: Manuel Peter Neuer (49/0), Philipp Lahm (Cap) (110/5), Per Mertesacker (102/4), Jérôme Agyenim Boateng (43/0), Benedikt Höwedes (25/2), hkodran Mustafi (4/0) [70.Sami Khedira (49/4)], Bastian Schweinsteiger (105/23) [109.Christoph Kramer (3/0)], Mesut Özil (59/18), Toni Kroos (48/5), ario Götze (33/10) [46.André Horst Schürrle (36/14)], Thomas Müller (53/21). Trainer: Joachim Löw (109).
oals: André Horst Schürrle (92), Mesut Özil (119).

0. 04.07.2014 **FRANCE - GERMANY** **0-1(0-1)** 20th FIFA WC. Quarter-Finals.
stádio „Jornalista Mário Filho“ [Maracanã], Rio de Janeiro (Brazil); Referee: Néstor Fabián Pitana (Argentina); Attendance: 74,240
ER: Manuel Peter Neuer (50/0), Philipp Lahm (Cap) (111/5), Jérôme Agyenim Boateng (44/0), Benedikt Höwedes (26/2), Mats Julian Hummels (34/4), astian Schweinsteiger (106/23), Mesut Özil (60/18) [83.Mario Götze (34/10)], Sami Khedira (50/4), Toni Kroos (49/5) [90+2.Christoph Kramer (4/0)], iroslav Josef Klose (135/70) [69.André Horst Schürrle (37/14)], Thomas Müller (54/21). Trainer: Joachim Löw (110).
oal: Mats Julian Hummels (12).

1. 08.07.2014 **BRAZIL – GERMANY** **1-7(0-5)** 20th FIFA WC. Semi-Finals.
stádio Mineirão, Belo Horizonte; Referee: Marco Antonio Rodríguez Moreno (Mexico); Attendance: 58,141
ER: Manuel Peter Neuer (51/0), Philipp Lahm (Cap) (112/5), Jérôme Agyenim Boateng (45/0), Benedikt Höwedes (27/2), Mats Julian Hummels (35/4) 6.Per Mertesacker (103/4)], Bastian Schweinsteiger (107/23), Mesut Özil (61/18), Sami Khedira (51/5) [76.Julian Draxler (12/1)], Toni Kroos (50/7), iroslav Josef Klose (136/71) [58.André Horst Schürrle (38/16)], Thomas Müller (55/22). Trainer: Joachim Löw (111).
oals: Thomas Müller (11), Miroslav Josef Klose (23), Toni Kroos (24, 26), Sami Khedira (29), André Horst Schürrle (69, 79).

2. 13.07.2014 **GERMANY - ARGENTINA** **1-0(0-0,0-0)** 20th FIFA WC. Final.
stádio „Jornalista Mário Filho“ [Maracanã], Rio de Janeiro (Brazil); Attendance: 74,738
ER: Manuel Peter Neuer (52/0), Philipp Lahm (Cap) (113/5), Jérôme Agyenim Boateng (46/0), Benedikt Höwedes (28/2), Mats Julian Hummels (36/4), astian Schweinsteiger (108/23), Mesut Özil (62/18) [120.Per Mertesacker (104/4)], Toni Kroos (51/7), Christoph Kramer (5/0) [32.André Horst Schürrle 9/16)], Miroslav Josef Klose (137/71) [88.Mario Götze (35/11)], Thomas Müller (56/22). Trainer: Joachim Löw (112).
oal: Mario Götze (113).

3. 03.09.2014 **GERMANY - ARGENTINA** **2-4(0-2)**
SPRIT arena, Düsseldorf; Referee: Björn Kuipers (Netherlands); Attendance: 51,132
ER: Manuel Peter Neuer (Cap) (53/0) [46.Roman Weidenfeller (4/0)], Benedikt Höwedes (29/2) [77.Antonio Rüdiger (2/0)], Erik Durm (2/0), Matthias ıkas Ginter (3/0), Toni Kroos (52/7) [71.Sebastian Rudy (2/0)], Marco Reus (22/7), Kevin Großkreutz (6/0), Christoph Kramer (6/0), Julian Draxler (13/1) 3.Lukas Josef Podolski (117/47)], Mario Gómez (60/25) [57.Mario Götze (36/12)], André Horst Schürrle (40/17) [57.Thomas Müller (57/22)]. Trainer: achim Löw (113).
oals: André Horst Schürrle (52), Mario Götze (78).

4. 07.09.2014 **GERMANY - SCOTLAND** **2-1(1-0)** 15th EC. Qualifiers
gnal-Iduna Park, Dortmund; Referee: Svein Oddvar Moen (Norway); Attendance: 60,209
ER: Manuel Peter Neuer (Cap) (54/0), Jérôme Agyenim Boateng (47/0), Benedikt Höwedes (30/2), Erik Durm (3/0), Toni Kroos (53/7), Sebastian Rudy /0), Marco Reus (23/7) [90+2.Matthias Lukas Ginter (4/0)], Mario Götze (37/12), Christoph Kramer (7/0), Thomas Müller (58/24), André Horst Schürrle 1/17) [84.Lukas Josef Podolski (118/47)]. Trainer: Joachim Löw (114).
oals: Thomas Müller (18, 70).

5. 11.10.2014 **POLAND - GERMANY** **2-0(0-0)** 15th EC. Qualifiers
adion Narodowy, Warszawa; Referee: Pedro Proença Oliveira Alves Garcia (Portugal); Attendance: 56,934
ER: Manuel Peter Neuer (Cap) (55/0), Jérôme Agyenim Boateng (48/0), Mats Julian Hummels (37/4), Erik Durm (4/0), Antonio Rüdiger (3/0) 3.Maximilian Kruse (7/1)], Toni Kroos (54/7), Karim Bellarabi (1/0), Mario Götze (38/12), Christoph Kramer (8/0) [71.Julian Draxler (14/1)], Thomas üller (59/24), André Horst Schürrle (42/17) [83.Lukas Josef Podolski (119/47)]. Trainer: Joachim Löw (115).

6. 14.10.2014 **GERMANY - REPUBLIC OF IRELAND** **1-1(0-0)** 15th EC. Qualifiers
eltins-Arena, Gelsenkirchen; Referee: Damir Skomina (Slovenia); Attendance: 51,204
ER: Manuel Peter Neuer (Cap) (56/0), Jérôme Agyenim Boateng (49/0), Mats Julian Hummels (38/4), Erik Durm (5/0), Antonio Rüdiger (4/0), Matthias ıkas Ginter (5/0) [46.Lukas Josef Podolski (120/47)], Toni Kroos (55/8), Karim Bellarabi (2/0) [86.Sebastian Rudy (4/0)], Mario Götze (39/12), Julian raxler (15/1) [70.Maximilian Kruse (8/1)], Thomas Müller (60/24). Trainer: Joachim Löw (116).
oal: Toni Kroos (71).

7. 14.11.2014 **GERMANY - GIBRALTAR** **4-0(3-0)** 15th EC. Qualifiers
rundig-Stadion, Nürnberg; Referee: Alexandru Dan Tudor (Romania); Attendance: 43,520
ER: Manuel Peter Neuer (Cap) (57/0), Jérôme Agyenim Boateng (50/0), Shkodran Mustafi (5/0), Erik Durm (6/0) [72.Jonas Hector (1/0)], Sami Khedira 2/5) [60.Kevin Volland (2/0)], Toni Kroos (56/8) [79.Lars Bender (18/4)], Karim Bellarabi (3/0), Mario Götze (40/13), Lukas Josef Podolski (121/47), ıomas Müller (61/26), Maximilian Kruse (9/1). Trainer: Joachim Löw (117).
oals: Thomas Müller (12, 29), Mario Götze (38), Yogan Santos (67 own goal).

898. 18.11.2014 **SPAIN - GERMANY** **0-1(0-0)**
Estadio de Balaídos, Vigo; Referee: Stefan Johannesson (Sweden); Attendance: 26,900
GER: Ron-Robert Zieler (4/0), Benedikt Höwedes (31/2), Shkodran Mustafi (6/0), Erik Durm (7/0), Antonio Rüdiger (5/0), Sami Khedira (Cap) (53/5) [90+1.Lars Bender (19/4)], Toni Kroos (57/9), Sebastian Rudy (5/0), Mario Götze (41/13) [84.Maximilian Kruse (10/1)], Thomas Müller (62/26) [22.Karim Bellarabi (4/0)], Kevin Volland (3/0). Trainer: Joachim Löw (118).
Goal: Toni Kroos (89).

899. 25.03.2015 **GERMANY - AUSTRALIA** **2-2(1-1)**
„Fritz Walter" Stadion, Kaiserslautern; Referee: Michael Oliver (England); Attendance: 47,106
GER: Ron-Robert Zieler (5/0), Benedikt Höwedes (32/2), Holger Felix Badstuber (31/1) [46.Sebastian Rudy (6/0)], Shkodran Mustafi (7/0), Jonas Hector (2/0), Mesut Özil (63/18), Sami Khedira (Cap) (54/5) [63.Christoph Kramer (9/0)], İlkay Gündoğan (9/2), Karim Bellarabi (5/0) [64.André Horst Schürrle (43/17)], Mario Götze (42/13) [73.Maximilian Kruse (11/1)], Marco Reus (24/8) [73.Lukas Josef Podolski (122/48)]. Trainer: Joachim Löw (119).
Goals: Marco Reus (17), Lukas Josef Podolski (81).

900. 29.03.2015 **GEORGIA - GERMANY** **0-2(0-2)** 15th EC. Qualifiers
„Boris Paichadze" Dinamo Arena, Tbilisi; Referee: Clément Turpin (France); Attendance: 52,000
GER: Manuel Peter Neuer (58/0), Jérôme Agyenim Boateng (51/0), Mats Julian Hummels (39/4), Jonas Hector (3/0), Bastian Schweinsteiger (Cap) (109/23), Mesut Özil (64/18), Toni Kroos (58/9), Sebastian Rudy (7/0), Mario Götze (43/13) [87.Lukas Josef Podolski (123/48)], Thomas Müller (63/27) [86.André Horst Schürrle (44/17)], Marco Reus (25/9). Trainer: Joachim Löw (120).
Goals: Marco Reus (39), Thomas Müller (44).

901. 10.06.2015 **GERMANY – UNITED STATES** **1-2(1-1)**
RheinEnergie Stadion, Köln; Referee: Danny Desmond Makkelie (Netherlands); Attendance: 40,438
GER: Ron-Robert Zieler (6/0), Shkodran Mustafi (8/0), Jonas Hector (4/0), Antonio Rüdiger (6/0), Bastian Schweinsteiger (Cap) (110/23) [46.Sami Khedira (55/5)], Mesut Özil (65/18), Sebastian Rudy (8/0), İlkay Gündoğan (10/2) [60.Christoph Kramer (10/0)], Mario Götze (44/14) [73.Maximilian Kruse (12/1)], André Horst Schürrle (45/17) [46.Lukas Josef Podolski (124/48)], Patrick Herrmann (1/0) [73.Karim Bellarabi (6/0)]. Trainer: Joachim Löw (121).
Goal: Mario Götze (12).

902. 13.06.2015 **GIBRALTAR - GERMANY** **0-7(0-1)** 15th EC. Qualifiers
Estádio Algarve, Faro/Loulé (Portugal); Referee: Clayton Pisani (Malta); Attendance: 7,467
GER: Roman Weidenfeller (5/0), Jérôme Agyenim Boateng (52/0), Jonas Hector (5/0), Bastian Schweinsteiger (Cap) (111/23), Mesut Özil (66/18), Sebastian Rudy (9/0), İlkay Gündoğan (11/3) [67.Sami Khedira (56/5)], Karim Bellarabi (7/1), Mario Götze (45/14) [36.Maximilian Kruse (13/3)], André Horst Schürrle (46/20), Patrick Herrmann (2/0) [56.Lukas Josef Podolski (125/48)]. Trainer: Joachim Löw (122).
Goals: André Horst Schürrle (28), Maximilian Kruse (47), İlkay Gündoğan (51), Karim Bellarabi (57), André Horst Schürrle (65, 71), Maximilian Kruse (81).

903. 04.09.2015 **GERMANY - POLAND** **3-1(2-1)** 15th EC. Qualifiers
Commerzbank Arena, Frankfurt am Main; Referee: Nicola Rizzoli (Italy); Attendance: 48,500
GER: Manuel Peter Neuer (59/0), Jérôme Agyenim Boateng (53/0), Mats Julian Hummels (40/4), Jonas Hector (6/0), Bastian Schweinsteiger (Cap) (112/23), Mesut Özil (67/18), Toni Kroos (59/9), Karim Bellarabi (8/1) [53.İlkay Gündoğan (12/3)], Mario Götze (46/16) [90+1.Lukas Josef Podolski (126/48)], Emre Can (1/0), Thomas Müller (64/28). Trainer: Joachim Löw (123).
Goals: Thomas Müller (12), Mario Götze (19, 82).

904. 07.09.2015 **SCOTLAND - GERMANY** **2-3(2-2)** 15th EC. Qualifiers
Hampden Park, Glasgow; Referee: Björn Kuipers (Netherlands); Attendance: 50,753
GER: Manuel Peter Neuer (60/0), Jérôme Agyenim Boateng (54/0), Mats Julian Hummels (41/4), Jonas Hector (7/0), Bastian Schweinsteiger (Cap) (113/23), Mesut Özil (68/18) [90+2.Christoph Kramer (11/0)], Toni Kroos (60/9), İlkay Gündoğan (13/4), Mario Götze (47/16) [86.André Horst Schürrle (47/20)], Emre Can (2/0), Thomas Müller (65/30). Trainer: Joachim Löw (124).
Goals: Thomas Müller (18, 34), İlkay Gündoğan (54).

905. 08.10.2015 **REPUBLIC OF IRELAND - GERMANY** **1-0(0-0)** 15th EC. Qualifiers
Aviva Stadium, Dublin; Referee: Carlos Velasco Carballo (Spain); Attendance: 50,604
GER: Manuel Peter Neuer (Cap) (61/0), Jérôme Agyenim Boateng (55/0), Mats Julian Hummels (42/4), Jonas Hector (8/0), Matthias Lukas Ginter (6/0) [77.Karim Bellarabi (9/1)], Mesut Özil (69/18), Toni Kroos (61/9), İlkay Gündoğan (14/4) [84.Kevin Volland (4/0)], Mario Götze (48/16) [35.André Horst Schürrle (48/20)], Thomas Müller (66/30), Marco Reus (26/9). Trainer: Joachim Löw (125).

906. 11.10.2015 **GERMANY - GEORGIA** **2-1(0-0)** 15th EC. Qualifiers
Red Bull Arena, Leipzig; Referee: Pavel Královec (Czech Republic); Attendance: 43,630
GER: Manuel Peter Neuer (Cap) (62/0), Jérôme Agyenim Boateng (56/0), Mats Julian Hummels (43/4), Jonas Hector (9/0), Matthias Lukas Ginter (7/0), Mesut Özil (70/18), Toni Kroos (62/9), İlkay Gündoğan (15/4), André Horst Schürrle (49/20) [76.Maximilian Kruse (14/4)], Thomas Müller (67/31), Marco Reus (27/9) [90.Karim Bellarabi (10/1)]. Trainer: Joachim Löw (126).
Goals: Thomas Müller (50 penalty), Maximilian Kruse (79).

907. 13.11.2015 **FRANCE - GERMANY** **2-0(1-0)**
Stade de France, Saint-Denis, Paris; Referee: Antonio Mateu Lahoz (Spain); Attendance: 78,000
GER: Manuel Peter Neuer (63/0), Jérôme Agyenim Boateng (57/0) [46.Shkodran Mustafi (9/0)], Mats Julian Hummels (44/4), Jonas Hector (10/0) [34.Emre Can (3/0)], Antonio Rüdiger (7/0), Matthias Lukas Ginter (8/0) [79.Kevin Volland (5/0)], Bastian Schweinsteiger (Cap) (114/23), Sami Khedira (57/5) [61.İlkay Gündoğan (16/4)], Julian Draxler (16/1) [61.Leroy Sané (1/0)], Mario Gómez (61/25), Thomas Müller (68/31). Trainer: Joachim Löw (127).

908. 26.03.2016 **GERMANY - ENGLAND** **2-3(1-0)**
Olympiastadion, Berlin; Referee: Gianluca Rocchi (Italy); Attendance: 71,413
GER: Manuel Peter Neuer (64/0), Mats Julian Hummels (45/4) [46.Jonathan Glao Tah (1/0)], Jonas Hector (11/0), Antonio Rüdiger (8/0), Mesut Özil (71/18), Sami Khedira (Cap) (58/5), Toni Kroos (63/10), Emre Can (4/0), Mario Gómez (62/26) [79.Mario Götze (49/16)], Thomas Müller (69/31) [75.Lukas Josef Podolski (127/48)], Marco Reus (28/9) [64.André Horst Schürrle (50/20)]. Trainer: Joachim Löw (128).
Goals: Toni Kroos (43), Mario Gómez (57).

9. 29.03.2016 **GERMANY - ITALY** **4-1(2-0)**

lianz Arena, München; Referee: Oliver Drachta (Austria); Attendance: 62,600

ER: Marc-André ter Stegen (5/0), Mats Julian Hummels (46/4), Shkodran Mustafi (10/0), Jonas Hector (12/1) [85.Matthias Lukas Ginter (9/0)], Antonio ıdiger (9/0), Mesut Özil (72/19), Toni Kroos (64/11) [90.Christoph Kramer (12/0)], Sebastian Rudy (10/0), Mario Götze (50/17) [61.Marco Reus (29/9)], lian Draxler (17/1) [85.Kevin Volland (6/0)], Thomas Müller (Cap) (70/31) [69.Emre Can (5/0)]. Trainer: Joachim Löw (129).

oals: Toni Kroos (24), Mario Götze (45), Jonas Hector (59), Mesut Özil (75 penalty).

0. 29.05.2016 **GERMANY - SLOVAKIA** **1-3(1-2)**

WK [Witwen- und Waisenkasse] Arena, Augsburg; Referee: Serge Gumienny (Belgium); Attendance: 22,100

ER: Bernd Leno (1/0) [46.Marc-André ter Stegen (6/0)], Antonio Rüdiger (10/0), Jérôme Agyenim Boateng (58/0) [64.Benedikt Höwedes (33/2)], Jonas ector (13/1), Joshua Kimmich (1/0) [75.André Horst Schürrle (51/20)], Sami Khedira (Cap) (59/5) [46.Julian Weigl (1/0)], Sebastian Rudy (11/0), Mario ötze (51/17), Julian Draxler (18/1), Leroy Sané (2/0), Mario Gómez (63/27) [46.Julian Brandt (1/0)]. Trainer: Joachim Löw (130).

oal: Mario Gómez (13).

1. 04.06.2016 **GERMANY - HUNGARY** **2-0(1-0)**

eltins Arena, Gelsenkirchen; Referee: Markus Strömbergsson (Sweden); Attendance: 52,104

ER: Manuel Peter Neuer (Cap) (65/0), Antonio Rüdiger (11/0), Jérôme Agyenim Boateng (59/0), Benedikt Höwedes (34/2), Jonas Hector (14/1) [46.Emre an (6/0)], Mesut Özil (73/19), Sami Khedira (60/5) [46.Mario Gómez (64/27)], Toni Kroos (65/11) [68.Bastian Schweinsteiger (115/23)], Mario Götze 2/17) [79.Lukas Josef Podolski (128/48)], Julian Draxler (19/1) [60.André Horst Schürrle (52/20)], Thomas Müller (71/32) [69.Leroy Sané (3/0)]. Trainer: achim Löw (131).

oals: Ádám Lang (39 own goal), Thomas Müller (63).

2. 12.06.2016 **GERMANY - UKRAINE** **2-0(1-0)** 15th EC. Group Stage.

ade „Pierre-Mauroy", Villeneuve d`Ascq, Lille (France); Referee: Martin Atkinson (England); Attendance: 43,035

ER: Manuel Peter Neuer (Cap) (66/0), Benedikt Höwedes (35/2), Jérôme Agyenim Boateng (60/0), Shkodran Mustafi (11/1), Jonas Hector (15/1), Mesut zil (74/19), Sami Khedira (61/5), Toni Kroos (66/11), Mario Götze (53/17) [90.Bastian Schweinsteiger (116/24)], Julian Draxler (20/1) [78.André Horst hürrle (53/20)], Thomas Müller (72/32). Trainer: Joachim Löw (132).

oals: Shkodran Mustafi (18), Bastian Schweinsteiger (90+1).

3. 16.06.2016 **GERMANY - POLAND** **0-0** 15th EC. Group Stage.

ade de France, Saint-Denis, Paris (France); Referee: Björn Kuipers (Netherlands); Attendance: 73,648

ER: Manuel Peter Neuer (Cap) (67/0), Benedikt Höwedes (36/2), Jérôme Agyenim Boateng (61/0), Mats Julian Hummels (47/4), Jonas Hector (16/1), esut Özil (75/19), Sami Khedira (62/5), Toni Kroos (67/11), Mario Götze (54/17) [66.André Horst Schürrle (54/20)], Julian Draxler (21/1) [72.Mario ómez (65/27)], Thomas Müller (73/32). Trainer: Joachim Löw (133).

4. 21.06.2016 **NORTHERN IRELAND - GERMANY** **0-1(0-1)** 15th EC. Group Stage.

ade Parc des Princes, Paris (France); Referee: Clément Turpin (France); Attendance: 44,125

ER: Manuel Peter Neuer (Cap) (68/0), Joshua Kimmich (2/0), Jérôme Agyenim Boateng (62/0) [76.Benedikt Höwedes (37/2)], Mats Julian Hummels 8/4), Jonas Hector (17/1), Mesut Özil (76/19), Sami Khedira (63/5) [69.Bastian Schweinsteiger (117/24)], Toni Kroos (68/11), Mario Götze (55/17) 5.André Horst Schürrle (55/20)], Mario Gómez (66/28), Thomas Müller (74/32). Trainer: Joachim Löw (134).

oal: Mario Gómez (29).

5. 26.06.2016 **GERMANY - SLOVAKIA** **3-0(2-0)** 15th EC. 2nd Round of 16.

ade „Pierre-Mauroy", Villeneuve d`Ascq, Lille (France); Referee: Szymon Marciniak (Poland); Attendance: 44,312

ER: Manuel Peter Neuer (Cap) (69/0), Joshua Kimmich (3/0), Jérôme Agyenim Boateng (63/1) [71.Benedikt Höwedes (38/2)], Mats Julian Hummels 9/4), Jonas Hector (18/1), Mesut Özil (77/19), Sami Khedira (64/5) [76.Bastian Schweinsteiger (118/24)], Toni Kroos (69/11), Julian Draxler (22/2) 2.Lukas Josef Podolski (129/48)], Mario Gómez (67/29), Thomas Müller (75/32). Trainer: Joachim Löw (135).

oals: Jérôme Agyenim Boateng (8), Mario Gómez (43), Julian Draxler (63).

6. 02.07.2016 **GERMANY - ITALY** **1-1(0-0,1-1,1-1); 6-5 on penalties** 15th EC. Quarter-Finals.

ouveau Stade de Bordeaux, Bordeaux (France); Referee: Viktor Kassai (Hungary); Attendance: 38,764

ER: Manuel Peter Neuer (Cap) (70/0), Joshua Kimmich (4/0), Jérôme Agyenim Boateng (64/1), Benedikt Höwedes (39/2), Mats Julian Hummels (50/4), nas Hector (19/1), Mesut Özil (78/20), Sami Khedira (65/5) [16.Bastian Schweinsteiger (119/24)], Toni Kroos (70/11), Mario Gómez (68/29) [72.Julian axler (23/2)], Thomas Müller (76/32). Trainer: Joachim Löw (136).

oal: Mesut Özil (65).

enalties: Toni Kroos, Thomas Müller (saved), Mesut Özil (missed), Julian Draxler, Bastian Schweinsteiger (missed), Mats Julian Hummels, Joshua mmich, Jérôme Agyenim Boateng, Jonas Hector.

7. 07.07.2016 **GERMANY - FRANCE** **0-2(0-1)** 15th EC. Semi-Finals.

ade Vélodrome, Marseille; Referee: Nicola Rizzoli (Italy); Attendance: 64,078

ER: Manuel Peter Neuer (71/0), Jérôme Agyenim Boateng (65/1) [61.Shkodran Mustafi (12/1)], Benedikt Höwedes (40/2), Jonas Hector (20/1), Joshua mmich (5/0), Bastian Schweinsteiger (Cap) (120/24) [79.Leroy Sané (4/0)], Mesut Özil (79/20), Toni Kroos (71/11), Emre Can (7/0) [67.Mario Götze 6/17)], Julian Draxler (24/2), Thomas Müller (77/32). Trainer: Joachim Löw (137).

8. 31.08.2016 **GERMANY - FINLAND** **2-0(0-0)**

orussia-Park, Mönchengladbach; Referee: Alyaksey Kulbakow (Belarus); Attendance: 30,121

ER: Marc-André ter Stegen (7/0) [46.Bernd Leno (2/0)], Shkodran Mustafi (13/1), Jonas Hector (21/1) [63.Mesut Özil (80/21)], Niklas Süle (1/0) 8.Jonathan Glao Tah (2/0)], Joshua Kimmich (6/0), Bastian Schweinsteiger (Cap) (121/24) [68.Julian Weigl (2/0)], Karim Bellarabi (11/1), Mario Götze 7/17), Max Meyer (2/1), Kevin Volland (7/0), Julian Brandt (2/0) [78.Thomas Müller (78/32)]. Trainer: Joachim Löw (138).

oals: Max Meyer (55), Mesut Özil (77).

9. 04.09.2016 **NORWAY - GERMANY** **0-3(0-2)** 21st FIFA WC. Qualfiers

levaal Stadion, Oslo; Referee: William Collum (Scotland); Attendance: 26,793

ER: Manuel Peter Neuer (Cap) (72/0), Benedikt Höwedes (41/2), Mats Julian Hummels (51/4), Jonas Hector (22/1), Joshua Kimmich (7/1), Mesut Özil 1/21), Sami Khedira (66/5) [84.Julian Weigl (3/0)], Toni Kroos (72/11), Mario Götze (58/17) [72.Julian Brandt (3/0)], Julian Draxler (25/2) [85.Max Meyer /1)], Thomas Müller (79/34). Trainer: Joachim Löw (139).

oals: Thomas Müller (15), Joshua Kimmich (45), Thomas Müller (60).

920. 08.10.2016 **GERMANY – CZECH REPUBLIC** **3-0(1-0)** 21st FIFA WC. Qualfiers

Volksparkstadion, Hamburg; Referee: Ovidiu Alin Haţegan (Romania); Attendance: 51,299

GER: Manuel Peter Neuer (Cap) (73/0), Joshua Kimmich (8/1), Jérôme Agyenim Boateng (66/1), Mats Julian Hummels (52/4), Jonas Hector (23/1 [68.Benedikt Höwedes (42/2)], Mesut Özil (82/21), Sami Khedira (67/5), Toni Kroos (73/12) [76.İlkay Gündoğan (17/4)], Mario Götze (59/17), Julian Draxler (26/2) [80.Julian Brandt (4/0)], Thomas Müller (80/36). Trainer: Joachim Löw (140).

Goals: Thomas Müller (13), Toni Kroos (49), Thomas Müller (65).

921. 11.10.2016 **GERMANY – NORTHERN IRELAND** **2-0(2-0)** 21st FIFA WC. Qualfiers

HDI-Arena, Hannover; Referee: Paolo Tagliavento (Italy); Attendance: 42,132

GER: Manuel Peter Neuer (Cap) (74/0), Joshua Kimmich (9/1), Jérôme Agyenim Boateng (67/1) [69.Shkodran Mustafi (14/1)], Mats Julian Hummel (53/4), Jonas Hector (24/1) [81.Kevin Volland (8/0)], Mesut Özil (83/21) [46.İlkay Gündoğan (18/4)], Sami Khedira (68/6), Toni Kroos (74/12), Mario Götz (60/17), Julian Draxler (27/3), Thomas Müller (81/36). Trainer: Joachim Löw (141).

Goals: Julian Draxler (13), Sami Khedira (17).

922. 11.11.2016 **SAN MARINO - GERMANY** **0-8(0-3)** 21st FIFA WC. Qualfiers

San Marino Stadium, Serravalle; Referee: Artyom Kuchin (Kazakhstan); Attendance: 3,851

GER: Marc-André ter Stegen (8/0), Joshua Kimmich (10/1), Mats Julian Hummels (54/4), Jonas Hector (25/3), Sami Khedira (69/7) [77.Leon Christoph Goretzka (2/0)], İlkay Gündoğan (19/4), Mario Götze (61/17) [71.Max Meyer (4/1)], Serge David Gnabry (1/3), Benjamin Henrichs (1/0), Mario Góme (69/29) [71.Kevin Volland (9/1)], Thomas Müller (82/36). Trainer: Joachim Löw (142).

Goals: Sami Khedira (7), Serge David Gnabry (9), Jonas Hector (32), Serge David Gnabry (58), Jonas Hector (65), Serge David Gnabry (76), Matti Stefanelli (82 own goal), Kevin Volland (85).

923. 15.11.2016 **ITALY - GERMANY** **0-0**

Stadio "Giuseppe Meazza", Milano; Referee: Artur Manuel Ribeiro Soares Dias (Portugal); Attendance: 48,600

GER: Bernd Leno (3/0), Joshua Kimmich (11/1), Benedikt Höwedes (43/2), Mats Julian Hummels (55/4) [46.Jonathan Glao Tah (3/0)], Shkodran Mustafi (15/1), Sebastian Rudy (12/0), İlkay Gündoğan (20/4), Leon Christoph Goretzka (3/0) [60.Serge David Gnabry (2/3)], Julian Weigl (4/0) [70.Mario Götze (62/17)], Yannick Gerhardt (1/0), Thomas Müller (Cap) (83/36) [60.Kevin Volland (10/1)]. Trainer: Joachim Löw (143).

INTERNATIONAL PLAYERS

FG/Nr	Name	DOB	Caps	Goals	Period, Club
415/636)	ABRAMCZIK Rudiger	18.02.1956	19	2	1977-1979, FC Schalke 04 Gelsenkirchen (19/2).
204/433)	ADAM Karl	05.02.1924	3	0	1951-1952, TuS Neuendorf (3/0).
197/414)	ADAMKIEWICZ Edmund	21.04.1920	2	1	1942, Hamburger SV (2/1).
312/860)	ADLER René	15.01.1985	12	0	2008-2013, TSV Bayer 04 Leverkusen (10/0), Hamburger SV (2/0).
531/771)	ALBERTZ Jörg	29.01.1971	3	0	1996-1998, Hamburger SV (2/0), Glasgow Rangers FC (1/0).
(4/030)	ALBRECHT Erich	31.03.1889	1	0	1909, FC Wacker 1895 Leipzig (1/0).
64/216)	ALBRECHT Ernst	12.11.1907	17	4	1928-1934, TSV Fortuna Düsseldorf (17/4).
456/668)	ALLGÖWER Karl	05.01.1957	10	0	1980-1986, VfB Stuttgart (10/0).
435/648)	ALLOFS Klaus	05.12.1956	56	17	1978-1988, TSV Fortuna Düsseldorf (21/9), 1.FC Köln (29/7), Olympique de Marseille (6/1).
514/702)	ALLOFS Thomas	17.11.1959	2	0	1985-1988, 1.FC Kaiserslautern (1/0), 1.FC Köln (1/0).
37/143)	ALTVATER Heinrich	27.08.1902	1	0	1922, FC Wacker München (1/0).
327/876)	AOGO Dennis	14.01.1987	12	0	2010-2013, Hamburger SV (12/0).
98/285)	APPEL Hans	08.06.1911	5	0	1933-1938, Berliner SV 92 (5/0).
155/365)	ARLT Willi	27.10.1919	11	2	1939-1942, Riesaer SV (11/2).
383/911)	ARNOLD Maximilian	27.05.1994	1	0	2014, VfL Wolfsburg (1/0).
701/807)	ASAMOAH Gerald	03.10.1978	43	6	2001-2006, FC Schalke 04 Gelsenkirchen (43/6).
47/166)	ASCHERL Willy	07.01.1902	1	0	1924, Spielvereinigung Fürth (1/0).
36/136)	AU Alfred	14.12.1898	1	0	1921, VfR Mannheim (1/0).
46/165)	AUER Karl	12.08.1903	3	2	1924-1926, Spielvereinigung Fürth (3/2).
490/684)	AUGENTHALER Klaus	26.09.1957	27	0	1983-1990, FC Bayern München (27/0).
554/729)	AUMANN Raimond	12.10.1963	4	0	1989-1990, FC Bayern München (4/0).
519/762)	BABBEL Markus	08.09.1972	51	1	1995-2000, FC Bayern München (51/1).
45/163)	BACHE Fritz	29.03.1898	2	0	1923, Wacker 04 Berlin (2/0).
328/880)	BADSTUBER Holger Felix	13.03.1989	31	1	2010-2015, FC Bayern München (31/1).
329/584)	BÄSE Joachim	02.09.1939	1	0	1968, TSV Eintracht Braunschweig (1/0).
236/477)	BÄUMLER Erich	06.01.1930	1	1	1956, SG Eintracht Frankfurt (1/1).
727/822)	BALITSCH Hanno	02.01.1981	1	0	2003, TSV Bayer 04 Leverkusen (1/0).
677/795)	BALLACK Michael	26.09.1976	98	42	1999-2010, 1.FC Kaiserslautern (1/0), TSV Bayer 04 Leverkusen (27/9), FC Bayern München (42/22), Chelsea FC London (28/11).
199/421)	BALOGH Fritz	16.12.1920	1	0	1950, VfL Neckarau (1/0).
50/175)	BANTLE Ernst	16.02.1901	1	0	1924, Freiburger FC (1/0).
199/417)	BARUFKA Karl	15.05.1921	3	0	1950-1951, VfB Stuttgart (3/0).
504/756)	BASLER Mario	18.12.1968	30	2	1994-1998, SV Werder Bremen (19/1), FC Bayern München (11/1).
205/438)	BAUER Hans	28.07.1927	5	0	1951-1958, FC Bayern München (5/0).
585/800)	BAUMANN Frank	29.10.1975	28	2	1999-2005, SV Werder Bremen (28/2).
199/416)	BAUMANN Gunther	19.01.1921	2	0	1950-1951, 1.FC Nürnberg (2/0).
(1/001)	BAUMGARTEN Fritz	21.12.1886	1	0	1908, Germania 88 Berlin (1/0).
(1/011)	BAUMGÄRTNER Willy	23.12.1890	4	0	1908-1909, SV 04 Düsseldorf (4/0).
(9/061)	BAUWENS Peco	24.12.1886	1	0	1910, SC 99 Köln (1/0).
226/466)	BECK Alfred	12.04.1925	1	1	1954, FC St.Pauli Hamburg (1/1).
315/864)	BECK Andreas	13.03.1987	9	0	2009-2010, TSG 1899 Hoffenheim (9/0).
302/559)	BECKENBAUER Franz	11.09.1945	103	14	1965-1977, FC Bayern München (103/14).
(1/010)	BECKER Fritz	13.09.1888	1	2	1908, Kickers Frankfurt (1/2).
402/622)	BEER Erich	09.12.1946	24	7	1975-1978, Hertha BSC Berlin (24/7).
52/178)	BEIER Albert	28.09.1900	11	0	1924-1931, Hamburger SV (11/0).
573/739)	BEIERSDORFER Dietmar	16.11.1963	1	0	1991, Hamburger SV (1/0).
555/730)	BEIN Uwe	26.09.1960	17	3	1989-1993, SG Eintracht Frankfurt (17/3).
668/785)	BEINLICH Stefan	13.01.1972	5	0	1998-2000, TSV Bayer 04 Leverkusen (4/0), Hertha BSC Berlin (1/0).
336/589)	BELLA Michael	29.09.1945	4	0	1968-1971, MSV Duisburg (4/0).
395/914)	BELLARABI Karim	08.04.1990	11	1	2014-2016, TSV Bayer 04 Leverkusen (11/1).
95/277)	BENDER Jakob	23.03.1910	9	0	1933-1935, TSV Fortuna Düsseldorf (9/0).
351/888)	BENDER Lars	27.04.1989	19	4	2011-2014, TSV Bayer 04 Leverkusen (19/4).
345/886)	BENDER Sven	27.04.1989	7	0	2011-2013, BV Borussia Dortmund (7/0).
259/499)	BENTHAUS Helmut	05.06.1935	8	0	1958-1960, SC Westfalia 04 Herne (8/0).
48/348)	BERG Walter	21.04.1916	1	0	1938, FC Schalke 04 Gelsenkirchen (1/0).
(9/057)	BERGHAUSEN Alfred	09.12.1889	1	0	1910, Preußen Duisburg (1/0).
76/234)	BERGMAIER Josef	05.03.1909	8	1	1930-1933, FC Bayern München (8/1).
286/534)	BERNARD Günter	04.11.1939	5	0	1962-1968, FC Schweinfurt 05 (2/0), SV Werder Bremen (3/0).
27/325)	BERNARD Robert	10.03.1913	2	0	1936, VfR Schweinfurt (2/0).
41/343)	BERNDT Hans	30.10.1913	3	2	1937-1938, Tennis Borussia Berlin (3/2).
(9/063)	BERT (FRIEDRICH) Adalbert	10.06.1884	1	0	1910, VfB Leipzig (1/0).
64/215)	BERTHOLD Rudolf	01.04.1903	1	0	1928, Dresdner SC (1/0).
505/698)	BERTHOLD Thomas	12.11.1964	62	1	1985-1994, SG Eintracht Frankfurt (21/1), Hellas Verona (10/0), AS Roma (18/0), VfB Stuttgart (13/0).
54/362)	BIALLAS Hans	14.10.1918	3	1	1938-1939, TuS Duisburg 48/99 (3/1).
631/772)	BIERHOFF Oliver	01.05.1968	70	37	1996-2002, Udinese Calcio (31/20), Milan AC Milano (25/10), AS Monaco (14/7).
712/817)	BIEROFKA Daniel	07.02.1979	3	1	2002, TSV 1860 München (2/1), TSV Bayer 04 Leverkusen (1/0).
224/459)	BIESINGER Ulrich	06.08.1933	7	2	1954-1958, BC Augsburg (7/2).
31/332)	BILLEN Matthias	29.03.1910	1	0	1936, VfL Osnabrück (1/0).
39/339)	BILLMANN Willi	15.01.1911	11	0	1937-1941, 1.FC Nürnberg (11/0).
55/364)	BINDER Franz	01.12.1911	9	10	1939-1941, SK Rapid Wien (9/10).
568/733)	BINZ Manfred	22.09.1965	14	1	1990-1992, SG Eintracht Frankfurt (14/1).

(361/595)	BLEIDICK Hartwig	26.12.1944	**2**	**0**	1971, Borussia VfL Mönchengladbach (2/0).
(61/202)	BLUM Ernst	25.01.1904	**1**	**0**	1927, VfB Stuttgart (1/0).
(74/226)	BLUNK Wilhelm	12.12.1902	**1**	**0**	1929, Hamburger SV (1/0).
(823/872)	BOATENG Jérôme Agyenim	03.09.1988	**67**	**1**	2009-2016, Hamburger SV (10/0), Manchester City FC (3/0), FC Baye München (54/1).
(615/760)	BOBIC Fredi	30.10.1971	**37**	**10**	1994-2004, VfB Stuttgart (19/2), SV Hannover'96 (7/5), Hertha BSC Berl (11/3).
(494/687)	BOCKENFELD Manfred	23.07.1960	**1**	**0**	1984, TSV Fortuna Düsseldorf (1/0).
(630/770)	BODE Marco	23.07.1969	**40**	**9**	1995-2002, SV Werder Bremen (40/9).
(205/436)	BÖGELEIN Karl	28.01.1927	**1**	**0**	1951, VfB Stuttgart (1/0).
(701/809)	BÖHME Jörg	22.01.1974	**10**	**1**	2001-2003, FC Schalke 04 Gelsenkirchen (10/1).
(121/320)	BÖKLE Otto	17.02.1912	**1**	**0**	1935, VfB Stuttgart (1/0).
(30/107)	BOLLMANN Albert	05.10.1889	**1**	**0**	1914, SK Schwarz-Weiß 1900 Essen (1/0).
(494/689)	BOMMER Rudolf	19.08.1957	**6**	**0**	1984, TSV Fortuna Düsseldorf (6/0).
(407/630)	BONGARTZ Hans	03.10.1951	**4**	**0**	1976-1977, FC Schalke 04 Gelsenkirchen (4/0).
(371/602)	BONHOF Rainer	29.03.1952	**53**	**9**	1972-1981, Borussia VfL Mönchengladbach (40/5), CF Valencia (11/4), 1.F Köln (2/0).
(437/649)	BORCHERS Ronald	10.08.1957	**6**	**0**	1978-1981, SG Eintracht Frankfurt (6/0).
(17/080)	BORCK Walter	01.05.1891	**1**	**0**	1911, MTV München (1/0).
(208/446)	BORKENHAGEN Kurt	30.12.1919	**1**	**0**	1952, TSV Fortuna Düsseldorf (1/0).
(541/719)	BOROWKA Ulrich	19.05.1962	**6**	**0**	1988, SV Werder Bremen (6/0).
(722/819)	BOROWSKI Tim	02.05.1980	**33**	**2**	2002-2008, SV Werder Bremen (33/2).
(21/089)	BOSCH Hermann	10.03.1891	**5**	**0**	1912-1913, Karlsruher FV (5/0).
(910/923)	BRANDT Julian	02.05.1996	**4**	**0**	2016, TSV Bayer 04 Leverkusen (4/0).
(710/812)	BRDARIC Thomas	23.01.1975	**8**	**1**	2002-2004, TSV Bayer 04 Leverkusen (1/0), SV Hannover'96 (3/0), V Wolfsburg (4/1).
(494/688)	BREHME Andreas	09.11.1960	**86**	**8**	1984-1994, 1.FC Kaiserslautern (28/3), FC Bayern München (12/ Internazionale FC Milano (34/4), 1.FC Kaiserslautern (12/0).
(362/597)	BREITNER Paul	03.09.1951	**48**	**10**	1971-1982, FC Bayern München (26/5), Real CF Madrid (2/0), FC Baye München (20/5).
(340/590)	BRENNINGER Dieter	16.12.1944	**1**	**0**	1969, FC Bayern München (1/0).
(95/278)	BREUER Theo	15.03.1909	**2**	**0**	1933, TSV Fortuna Düsseldorf (2/0).
(8/053)	BREUNIG Max	12.11.1888	**9**	**1**	1910-1913, Karlsruher FV (7/1), 1.FC Pforzheim (2/0).
(9/064)	BREYNK Andreas	04.07.1890	**1**	**0**	1910, Preußen Duisburg (1/0).
(444/659)	BRIEGEL Hans-Peter	11.10.1955	**72**	**4**	1979-1986, 1.FC Kaiserslautern (53/3), Hellas Verona (19/1).
(263/508)	BRÜLLS Albert	26.03.1937	**25**	**9**	1959-1966, Borussia VfL Mönchengladbach (22/9), AC Brescia (3/0).
(61/198)	BRUNKE Hans	01.10.1904	**7**	**0**	1927-1931, Tennis Borussia Berlin (7/0).
(296/549)	BRUNNENMEIER Rudolf	11.02.1941	**5**	**3**	1964-1965, TSV 1860 München (5/3).
(495/690)	BRUNS Hans-Günther	15.11.1954	**4**	**0**	1984, Borussia VfL Mönchengladbach (4/0).
(92/271)	BUCHLOH Fritz	26.11.1909	**17**	**0**	1932-1936, VfB Speldorf (17/0).
(498/692)	BUCHWALD Guido	24.01.1961	**76**	**4**	1984-1994, VfB Stuttgart (76/4).
(9/058)	BUDZINSKI Lothar	07.08.1886	**1**	**0**	1910, Duisburger SV (1/0).
(10/067)	BÜLTE Otto	04.09.1886	**1**	**0**	1910, FC Eintracht Braunschweig (1/0).
(418/641)	BURDENSKI Dieter	26.11.1950	**12**	**0**	1977-1984, SV Werder Bremen (12/0).
(186/408)	BURDENSKI Herbert	19.05.1922	**5**	**2**	1941-1951, FC Schalke 04 Gelsenkirchen (3/1), SV Werder Bremen (2/1).
(6/041)	BURGER Karl	26.12.1883	**11**	**1**	1909-1912, Spielvereinigung Fürth (11/1).
(423/642)	BURGSMÜLLER Manfred	22.12.1949	**3**	**0**	1977-1978, BV Borussia Dortmund (3/0).
(79/241)	BURKHARDT Theodor	31.01.1905	**1**	**0**	1930, Germania Brötzingen (1/0).
(95/275)	BUSCH Willy	04.01.1907	**13**	**0**	1933-1936, TSV Duisburg 1899 (13/0).
(690/803)	BUTT Hans-Jörg	28.05.1974	**4**	**0**	2000-2010, Hamburger SV (1/0), TSV Bayer 04 Leverkusen (2/0), FC Baye München (1/0).
(818/867)	Claudemir Jerónimo Barretto da Silva „CACAU"	27.03.1981	**23**	**6**	2009-2012, VfB Stuttgart (23/6).
(903/917)	CAN Emre	12.01.1994	**7**	**0**	2015-2016, Liverpool FC (7/0).
(789/853)	CASTRO RANDÓN Gonzalo	11.06.1987	**5**	**0**	2007, TSV Bayer 04 Leverkusen (5/0).
(246/492)	CIESLARCZYK Hans	03.05.1937	**7**	**3**	1957-1958, SV Sodingen (5/3), BV Borussia Dortmund (2/0).
(41/157)	CLAUS-OEHLER Walter	07.05.1897	**2**	**1**	1923, 1.FC Arminia Bielefeld (2/1).
(814/861)	COMPPER Marvin	14.06.1985	**1**	**0**	2008, TSG 1899 Hoffenheim (1/0).
(99/286)	CONEN Edmund	10.11.1914	**28**	**27**	1934-1942, FV Saarbrücken (14/14), SV Stuttgarter Kickers (14/13).
(375/604)	CULLMANN Bernhard	01.11.1949	**40**	**6**	1973-1980, 1.FC Köln (40/6).
(110/299)	DAMMINGER Ludwig	29.10.1913	**3**	**5**	1935, Karlsruher FV (3/5).
(380/607)	DANNER Dietmar	29.11.1950	**6**	**0**	1973-1976, Borussia VfL Mönchengladbach (6/0).
(189/410)	DECKER Karl	05.09.1921	**8**	**8**	1942, FC Vienna Wien (8/8).
(118/311)	DEIKE Fritz	24.06.1913	**1**	**0**	1935, Hannoverscher SV 1896 (1/0).
(686/802)	DEISLER Sebastian	05.01.1980	**36**	**3**	2000-2006, Hertha BSC Berlin (19/3), FC Bayern München (17/0).
(448/663)	DEL'HAYE Karl	18.08.1955	**2**	**0**	1980, Borussia VfL Mönchengladbach (2/0).
(226/465)	DERWALL Josef „Jupp"	10.03.1927	**2**	**0**	1954, TSV Fortuna Düsseldorf (2/0).
(162/373)	DEYHLE Erwin	19.01.1914	**1**	**0**	1939, SV Stuttgarter Kickers (1/0).
(24/092)	DIEMER Kurt	17.05.1893	**4**	**0**	1912-1913, Britannia 92 Berlin (4/0).
(347/591)	DIETRICH Peter	06.03.1944	**1**	**0**	1970, Borussia VfL Mönchengladbach (1/0).
(399/616)	DIETZ Bernhard	22.03.1948	**53**	**0**	1974-1981, MSV Duisburg (53/0).
(127/323)	DITGENS Heinz	03.07.1914	**3**	**0**	1936-1938, Borussia VfL Möchengladbach (3/0).
(318/570)	DÖRFEL Bernd	18.12.1944	**15**	**2**	1966-1969, Hamburger SV (4/1), TSV Eintracht Braunschweig (11/1).
(191/412)	DÖRFEL Friedrich	19.02.1915	**2**	**1**	1942, Hamburger SV (2/1).
(270/519)	DÖRFEL Gert	18.09.1939	**11**	**7**	1960-1964, Hamburger SV (11/7).
(236/476)	DÖRNER Herbert	14.07.1930	**2**	**0**	1956, 1.FC Köln (2/0).
(681/799)	DOGAN Mustafa	01.01.1976	**2**	**0**	1999, Fenerbahçe SK Istanbul (2/0).
(572/738)	DOLL Thomas	09.04.1966	**18**	**1**	1991-1994, Hambureger SV (3/0), SS Lazio Roma (15/1).

533/712)	DORFNER Hans	03.07.1965	7	1	1987-1989, FC Bayern München (7/1).
857/893)	DRAXLER Julian	20.09.1993	27	3	2012-2016, FC Schalke 04 Gelsenkirchen (15/1), VfL Wolfsburg (12/2).
459/669)	DREMMLER Wolfgang	12.07.1954	27	3	1981-1984, FC Bayern München (27/3).
(14/077)	DROZ Rudolf	09.01.1888	1	0	1911, BFC Preussen Berlin (1/0).
(14/076)	DUMKE Otto	29.04.1887	2	3	1911, TuFC Viktoria 89 Berlin (2/3).
175/398)	DUREK Ludwig	27.01.1921	6	2	1940-1942, FC Wien (6/2).
884/913)	DURM Erik	12.05.1992	7	0	2014, BV Borussia Dortmund (7/0).
(5/033)	DUTTON Edwin	08.04.1890	1	0	1909, BFC Preussen Berlin (1/0).
174/394)	DZUR Walter	18.11.1919	3	0	1940, Dresdner SC (3/0).
209/447)	ECKEL Horst	08.02.1932	32	0	1952-1958, 1.FC Kaiserslautern (32/0).
(139/340)	ECKERT Jakob	19.09.1916	1	0	1937, VfR Wormatia Worms (1/0).
(529/709)	ECKSTEIN Dieter	12.03.1964	7	0	1986-1988, 1.FC Nürnberg (7/0).
(519/703)	EDER Norbert	07.11.1955	9	0	1986, FC Bayern München (9/0).
(26/097)	EDY (PENDORF) Eduard	18.10.1892	3	0	1913-1922, VfB Leipzig (3/0).
(574/740)	EFFENBERG Stefan	02.08.1968	35	5	1991-1998, FC Bayern München (12/1), AC Fiorentina Firenze (21/4), FC Bayern München (2/0).
(206/445)	EHRMANN Kurt	07.06.1922	1	0	1952, Karlsruher FV (1/0).
(97/281)	EIBERLE Fritz	17.09.1904	1	0	1933, TSV 1860 München (1/0).
(2/012)	EICHELMANN Paul	11.10.1879	2	0	1908, Union 92 Berlin (2/0).
(41/154)	EIKHOF Ernst	06.05.1892	3	0	1923, SC Victoria Hamburg (3/0).
(602/754)	EILTS Dieter	13.12.1964	31	0	1993-1997, SV Werder Bremen (31/0).
(117/305)	ELBERN Franz	01.11.1910	8	2	1935-1937, SV 06 Beuel (8/2).
(84/255)	EMMERICH Heinz	25.02.1908	3	0	1931, Tennis Borussia Berlin (3/0).
(306/564)	EMMERICH Lothar	29.11.1941	5	2	1966, BV Borussia Dortmund (5/2).
(751/837)	ENGELHARDT Marco	02.12.1980	3	0	2004-2005, 1.FC Kaiserslautern (3/0).
(467/674)	ENGELS Stephan	06.09.1960	8	0	1982-1983, 1.FC Köln (8/0).
(789/849)	ENKE Robert	24.08.1977	8	0	2007-2009, SV Hannover'96 (8/0).
(175/396)	EPPENHOFF Hermann	19.05.1919	3	3	1940-1942, FC Schalke 04 Gelsenkirchen (3/3).
(214/452)	ERHARDT Herbert	06.07.1930	50	1	1953-1962, Spielvereinigung Fürth (49/1), FC Bayern München (1/0).
(712/816)	ERNST Fabian	30.05.1979	24	1	2002-2006, SV Werder Bremen (20/1), FC Schalke 04 Gelsenkirchen (4/0).
(54/181)	ERTL Georg	17.03.1901	7	0	1925-1927, FC Wacker München (7/0).
(49/169)	ESCHENLOHR Albert	10.03.1898	1	0	1924, Tennis Borussia Berlin (1/0).
(39/149)	ESSER Franz	20.01.1900	1	0	1922, SV Holstein Kiel (1/0).
(129/328)	EULER Georg	23.12.1905	1	0	1936, Spielvereinigung Köln-Sulz 07 (1/0).
(264/509)	EWERT Friedrich	09.02.1937	4	0	1959-1964, 1.FC Köln (4/0).
(9/056)	FAAS Robert	03.04.1889	1	0	1910, 1.FC Pforzheim (1/0).
(548/722)	FACH Holger	06.09.1962	5	0	1988-1989, FC Bayer 05 Uerdingen (5/0).
(260/502)	FAEDER Helmut	03.07.1935	1	0	1958, Hertha BSC Berlin (1/0).
(747/830)	FAHRENHORST Frank	24.09.1977	2	0	2004, SV Werder Bremen (2/0).
(280/525)	FAHRIAN Wolfgang	31.05.1941	10	0	1962-1964, Ulmer TSG 1846 (10/0).
(63/209)	FALK Wilhelm	03.07.1898	1	0	1927, FC Wacker München (1/0).
(502/694)	FALKENMAYER Ralf	11.02.1963	4	0	1984-1986, SG Eintracht Frankfurt (4/0).
(105/293)	FATH Josef	27.12.1911	13	7	1934-1938, VfR Wormatia Worms (13/7).
(781/843)	FATHI Malik	29.10.1983	2	0	2006, Hertha BSC Berlin (2/0).
(291/542)	FERNER Diethelm	13.07.1941	2	0	1963-1964, SV Werder Bremen (2/0).
(319/572)	FICHTEL Klaus	19.11.1944	23	1	1967-1971, FC Schalke 04 Gelsenkirchen (23/1).
(8/055)	FICK Willy	17.02.1891	1	1	1910, FV Holstein 1902 Kiel (1/1).
(158/371)	FIEDERER Hans	21.01.1920	6	3	1939-1941, Spielvereinigung Fürth (6/3).
(33/123)	FIEDERER Leo	04.04.1897	1	0	1920, Spielvereinigung Fürth (1/0).
(89/263)	FISCHER Erich	31.12.1909	2	0	1932-1933, 1.FC Pforzheim (2/0).
(415/637)	FISCHER Klaus	27.12.1949	45	32	1977-1982, FC Schalke 04 Gelsenkirchen (30/23), 1.FC Köln (15/9).
(2/014)	FISCHER Paul	06.09.1882	1	0	1908, TuFC Viktoria 89 Berlin (1/0).
(11/072)	FISCHER Walter	21.02.1889	5	0	1911-1913, Duisburger SV (5/0).
(190/411)	FITZ Willy	12.03.1918	1	0	1942, SK Rapid Wien (1/0).
(51/176)	FLEISCHMANN Hans	11.05.1898	1	0	1924, VfR Mannheim (1/0).
(74/227)	FLICK Hermann	22.11.1905	1	0	1929, TSV Duisburg 1899 (1/0).
(39/148)	FLINK Karl	07.12.1895	1	0	1922, Kölner BC (1/0).
(358/593)	FLOHE Heinz	28.01.1948	39	8	1970-1978, 1.FC Köln (39/8).
(158/366)	FLOTHO Heinrich	23.12.1915	1	0	1939, VfL Osnabrück (1/0).
(538/718)	FODA Franco	23.04.1966	2	0	1987, 1.FC Kaiserslautern (2/0).
(1/008)	FÖRDERER Fritz	05.01.1888	11	10	1908-1913, Karlsruher FV (11/10).
(441/652)	FÖRSTER Bernd	03.05.1956	33	0	1979-1984, VfB Stuttgart (33/0).
(427/644)	FÖRSTER Karlheinz	25.07.1958	81	2	1978-1986, VfB Stuttgart (81/2).
(33/125)	FORELL Paul	14.01.1892	1	0	1920, 1.FC Pforzheim (1/0).
(61/205)	FRANK Georg	14.12.1907	4	5	1927-1930, Spielvereinigung Fürth (4/5).
(376/605)	FRANKE Bernd	12.02.1948	7	0	1973-1982, TSV Eintracht Braunschweig (7/0).
(37/142)	FRANZ Andreas	27.06.1897	10	4	1922-1926, Spielvereinigung Fürth (10/4).
(712/815)	FREIER Paul (Slawomir)	26.07.1979	19	1	2002-2007, VfL Bochum (17/1), TSV Bayer 04 Leverkusen (2/0).
(619/763)	FREUND Steffen	19.01.1970	21	0	1995-1998, BV Borussia Dortmund (21/0).
(117/307)	FRICKE Willi	16.01.1913	1	0	1935, SV Arminia Hannover (1/0).
(135/333)	FRIEDEL Georg	06.09.1913	1	0	1937, 1.FC Nürnberg (1/0).
(722/818)	FRIEDRICH Arne	29.05.1979	82	1	2002-2011, Hertha BSC Berlin (79/1), VfL Wolfsburg (3/0).
(781/842)	FRIEDRICH Manuel	13.09.1979	9	1	2006-2008, 1.FSV Mainz 05 (7/1), TSV Bayer 04 Leverkusen (2/0).
(698/805)	FRINGS Torsten	22.11.1976	79	10	2001-2009, SV Werder Bremen (15/2), BV Borussia Dortmund (17/2), FC Bayern München (12/1), SV Werder Bremen (35/5).
(784/844)	FRITZ Clemens	07.12.1980	22	2	2006-2008, SV Werder Bremen (22/2).
(34/126)	FRITZSCHE Walter	19.12.1895	1	0	1921, BFC Vorwärts 90 Berlin (1/0).
(502/693)	FRONTZECK Michael	26.03.1964	19	0	1984-1992, Borussia VfL Mönchengladbach (16/0), VfB Stuttgart (3/0).

(11/071)	FUCHS Gottfried	03.05.1889	**6**	**14**	1911-1913, Karlsruher FV (6/14).
(27/100)	FÜRST Fritz	03.07.1891	**1**	**0**	1913, FC Bayern München (1/0).
(520/704)	FUNKEL Wolfgang	10.08.1958	**2**	**0**	1986, FC Bayer 05 Uerdingen (2/0).
(9/059)	GABLONSKY Max	01.01.1890	**4**	**0**	1910-1911, FC Bayern München (4/0).
(25/095)	GAEBELEIN Arthur	29.03.1891	**1**	**0**	1912, Hohenzollern Halle (1/0).
(163/383)	GÄRTNER Ludwig	19.04.1919	**3**	**1**	1939-1941, Olympia Lorsch (3/1).
(3/023)	GARRN (EHLERS) Hermann	11.03.1888	**2**	**1**	1908-1909, SC Victoria Hamburg (2/1).
(127/326)	GAUCHEL Josef	11.09.1916	**16**	**13**	1936-1942, TuS Neuendorf (16/13).
(598/751)	GAUDINO Maurizio	12.12.1966	**5**	**1**	1993-1994, SG Eintracht Frankfurt (5/1).
(57/192)	GEDLICH Richard	17.02.1900	**2**	**0**	1926-1927, Dresdner SC (2/0).
(69/222)	GEHLHAAR Paul	27.08.1905	**2**	**0**	1928-1931, Hertha BSC Berlin (2/0).
(2/016)	GEHRTS Adolf	30.10.1886	**2**	**0**	1908-1910, SC Victoria Hamburg (2/0).
(59/196)	GEIGER Hans	24.12.1905	**6**	**0**	1926-1929, ASV Nürnberg (2/0), 1.FC Nürnberg (4/0).
(241/484)	GEIGER Rolf	16.10.1934	**8**	**2**	1956-1964, SV Stuttgarter Kickers (1/0), VfB Stuttgart (7/0).
(117/306)	GELLESCH Rudolf	01.05.1914	**20**	**1**	1935-1941, FC Schalke 04 Gelsenkirchen (20/1).
(818/866)	GENTNER Christian	14.08.1985	**5**	**0**	2009-2010, VfL Wolfsburg (4/0), VfB Stuttgart (1/0).
(679/797)	GERBER Heiko	11.07.1972	**2**	**0**	1999, VfB Stuttgart (2/0).
(244/489)	GERDAU Willi	12.02.1929	**1**	**0**	1957, Heider SV (1/0).
(923/927)	GERHARDT Yannick	13.03.1994	**1**	**0**	2016, VfL Wolfsburg (1/0).
(200/425)	GERRITZEN Felix	06.02.1927	**4**	**1**	1951, SC Preußen Münster (4/1).
(403/625)	GERSDORFF Bernd	18.11.1946	**1**	**0**	1975, TSV Eintracht Braunschweig (1/0).
(291/541)	GERWIEN Klaus	11.09.1940	**6**	**1**	1963-1968, TSV Eintracht Braunschweig (6/1).
(374/603)	GEYE Rainer	22.11.1949	**4**	**1**	1972-1974, TSV Fortuna Düsseldorf (4/1).
(269/514)	GIESEMANN Willi	02.09.1937	**14**	**0**	1960-1965, FC Bayern München (11/0), Hamburger SV (3/0).
(882/900)	GINTER Matthias Lukas	19.01.1994	**9**	**0**	2014-2016, SC Freiburg (2/0), BV Borussia Dortmund (7/0).
(4/028)	GLASER Josef Dr.	11.05.1887	**5**	**0**	1909-1912, Freiburger FC (5/0).
(922/925)	GNABRY Serge David	14.07.1995	**2**	**3**	2016, SV Werder Bremen (2/3).
(169/386)	GOEDE Erich	24.05.1916	**1**	**0**	1939, Berliner SV 92 (1/0).
(748/832)	GÖRLITZ Andreas	31.01.1982	**2**	**0**	2004, FC Bayern München (2/0).
(542/721)	GÖRTZ Armin	30.08.1959	**2**	**0**	1988, 1.FC Köln (2/0).
(842/885)	GÖTZE Mario	03.06.1992	**62**	**17**	2010-2016, BV Borussia Dortmund (22/5), FC Bayern München (34/13), BV Borussia Dortmund (6/0).
(97/280)	GOLDBRUNNER Ludwig	05.03.1908	**39**	**0**	1933-1940, FC Bayern München (39/0).
(787/848)	GÓMEZ GARCÍA Mario	10.07.1985	**69**	**29**	2007-2016, VfB Stuttgart (25/10), FC Bayern München (33/15), AC Fiorentina (2/0), Beşiktaş JK İstanbul (8/4), VfL Wolfsburg (1/0).
(883/906)	GORETZKA Leon Christoph	06.02.1995	**3**	**0**	2014-2016, FC Schalke 04 Gelsenkirchen (3/0).
(214/454)	GOTTINGER Richard	04.06.1926	**1**	**0**	1953, Spielvereinigung Fürth (1/0).
(307/566)	GRABOWSKI Jürgen	07.07.1944	**44**	**5**	1966-1974, SG Eintracht Frankfurt (44/5).
(117/302)	GRAMLICH Hermann	24.04.1913	**3**	**0**	1935, Villingen 08 (3/0).
(87/258)	GRAMLICH Rudolf	06.06.1908	**22**	**0**	1931-1936, SG Eintracht Frankfurt (22/0).
(442/657)	GROH Jürgen	17.07.1956	**2**	**0**	1979-1983, 1.FC Kaiserslautern (1/0), Hamburger SV (1/0).
(35/132)	GRÖNER Emil	25.03.1892	**1**	**0**	1921, Stuttgarter SC (1/0).
(18/085)	GROS Wilhelm	06.07.1892	**1**	**0**	1912, Karlsruher FV (1/0).
(358/592)	GROß Volkmar	31.01.1948	**1**	**0**	1970, Hertha BSC Berlin (1/0).
(302/560)	GROSSER Peter	28.09.1938	**2**	**0**	1965-1966, TSV 1860 München (2/0).
(827/878)	GROßKREUTZ Kevin	19.07.1988	**6**	**0**	2010-2014, BV Borussia Dortmund (6/0).
(72/225)	GRUBER Hans	04.06.1905	**1**	**0**	1929, Duisburger SV (1/0).
(514/701)	GRÜNDEL Heinz	13.02.1957	**4**	**0**	1985-1986, Hamburger SV (4/0).
(853/890)	GÜNDOĞAN İlkay	24.10.1990	**20**	**4**	2011-2016, BV Borussia Dortmund (16/4), Manchester City FC (4/0).
(883/912)	GÜNTER Christian	28.02.1993	**1**	**0**	2014, SC Freiburg (1/0).
(117/309)	GÜNTHER Walter	18.11.1915	**4**	**2**	1935-1937, TSV Duiburg 1899 (4/2).
(625/768)	HABER Marco	21.09.1971	**2**	**0**	1995, VfB Stuttgart (2/0).
(158/370)	HÄNEL Erich	31.10.1915	**3**	**1**	1939, BC Hartha (1/0).
(548/723)	HÄßLER Thomas	30.05.1966	**101**	**11**	1988-2000, 1.FC Köln (17/1), Juventus FC Torino (5/0), AS Roma (33/5), Karlsruher SC (42/5), TSV 1860 München (4/0).
(201/430)	HAFERKAMP Hans	11.10.1921	**4**	**2**	1951-1952, VfL Osnabrück (4/2).
(61/203)	HAFTMANN Martin	16.07.1899	**1**	**0**	1927, Dresdner SC (1/0).
(32/118)	HAGEN Hans	15.07.1894	**12**	**0**	1920-1930, Spielvereinigung Fürth (12/0).
(883/909)	HAHN André	13.08.1990	**1**	**0**	2014, FC Augsburg (1/0).
(151/356)	HAHNEMANN Wilhelm	14.04.1914	**23**	**16**	1938-1941, Admira Wien (23/16).
(256/497)	HALLER Helmut	21.07.1939	**33**	**13**	1958-1970, BC Augsburg (19/4), Bologna FC (8/7), FC Juventus Torino (6/2).
(655/781)	HAMANN Dietmar	27.08.1973	**59**	**5**	1997-2005, FC Bayern München (12/1), Newcastle United FC (5/1), Liverpool FC (42/3).
(177/399)	HAMMERL Franz	09.10.1919	**1**	**0**	1940, Post-SV München (1/0).
(757/838)	HANKE Mike	05.11.1983	**12**	**1**	2005-2007, FC Schalke 04 Gelsenkirchen (5/1), VfL Wolfsburg (6/0), Hannover`96 (1/0).
(80/247)	HANKE Richard	18.03.1910	**1**	**1**	1930, BFV 06 Breslau (1/1).
(460/670)	HANNES Wilfried	17.05.1957	**8**	**0**	1981-1982, Borussia VfL Mönchengladbach (8/0).
(171/387)	HANREITER Franz	04.11.1913	**7**	**0**	1940-1942, Admira Wien (7/0).
(10/068)	HANSSEN Karl	05.07.1887	**3**	**0**	1910-1911, Altona FC 93 Hamburg (3/0).
(2/013)	HANTSCHICK Otto	11.02.1884	**2**	**0**	1908-1909, Union 92 Berlin (2/0).
(30/108)	HARDER Otto „Tull"	25.11.1892	**15**	**14**	1914-1926, Hamburger SV (15/14).
(81/248)	HARINGER Sigmund	09.12.1905	**15**	**0**	1931-1937, FC Bayern München (11/0), FC Wacker München (4/0).
(212/450)	HARPERS Gerhard	12.03.1928	**6**	**0**	1953-1955, SV Sodingen (6/0).
(41/156)	HARTMANN Carl	08.02.1894	**4**	**2**	1923-1924, Union Potsdam (3/2), SC Victoria Hamburg (1/0).
(729/824)	HARTMANN Michael	11.07.1974	**4**	**0**	2003, Hertha BSC Berlin (4/0).
(441/655)	HARTWIG William	05.10.1954	**2**	**0**	1979, Hamburger SV (2/0).
(897/915)	HECTOR Jonas	27.05.1990	**25**	**3**	2014-2016, 1.FC Köln (25/3).

148/350)	HEIBACH Hans	01.12.1918	**1**	**0**	1938, TSV Fortuna Düsseldorf (1/0).
317/567)	HEIDEMANN Hartmut	05.06.1941	**3**	**0**	1966-1968, MSV Duisburg (3/0).
97/283)	HEIDEMANN Matthias	07.02.1912	**3**	**0**	1933-1935, Bonner FV (1/0), SV Werder Bremen (2/0).
63/211)	HEIDKAMP Conrad	27.09.1905	**9**	**1**	1927-1930, SC 99 Düsseldorf (1/0), FC Bayern München (8/1).
523/766)	HEINRICH Jörg	06.12.1969	**37**	**2**	1995-2002, SC Freiburg (2/0), BV Borussia Dortmund (18/2), AC Fiorentina Firenze (10/0), BV Borussia Dortmund (7/0).
287/537)	HEIß Alfred	05.12.1940	**8**	**2**	1962-1966, TSV 1860 München (8/2).
305/563)	HELD Siegfried	07.08.1942	**41**	**5**	1966-1973, BV Borussia Dortmund (35/5), OFC Kickers Offenbach (6/0).
577/794)	HELDT Horst	09.12.1969	**2**	**0**	1999, TSV 1860 München (1/0), SG Eintracht Frankfurt (1/0).
569/734)	HELMER Thomas	21.04.1965	**68**	**5**	1990-1998, BV Borussia Dortmund (10/0), FC Bayern München (58/5).
789/854)	HELMES Patrick	01.03.1984	**13**	**2**	2007-2010, 1.FC Köln (5/0), TSV Bayer 04 Leverkusen (8/2).
(1/002)	HEMPEL Walter	12.08.1887	**11**	**0**	1908-1912, Sportfreunde Leipzig (11/0).
922/926)	HENRICHS Benjamin	23.02.1997	**1**	**0**	2016, TSV Bayer 04 Leverkusen (1/0).
10/066)	HENSE Robert	17.11.1885	**1**	**0**	1910, Kölner BC 01 (1/0).
(1/007)	HENSEL Gustav	23.10.1884	**1**	**0**	1908, FV Kassel (1/0).
36/137)	HERBERGER Josef	28.03.1897	**3**	**2**	1921-1925, SV 07 Waldhof Mannheim (1/2), VfR Mannheim (2/0).
76/233)	HERGERT Heinrich	21.02.1904	**5**	**0**	1930-1933, FK 03 Pirmasens (5/0).
491/685)	HERGET Matthias	14.11.1955	**39**	**4**	1983-1988, FC Bayer 05 Uerdingen (39/4).
224/458)	HERKENRATH Fritz	09.09.1928	**21**	**0**	1954-1958, Rot-Weiß Essen (21/0).
549/726)	HERMANN Günter	05.12.1960	**2**	**0**	1988-1990, SV Werder Bremen (2/0).
520/764)	HERRLICH Heiko	03.12.1971	**5**	**1**	1995, BV Borussia Dortmund (5/1).
271/521)	HERRMANN Günther	01.09.1939	**9**	**1**	1960-1967, Karlsruher SC (7/1), FC Schalke 04 Gelsenkirchen (2/0).
901/916)	HERRMANN Patrick	12.02.1991	**2**	**0**	2015, Borussia VfL Mönchengladbach (2/0).
199/422)	HERRMANN Richard	28.01.1923	**8**	**1**	1950-1954, FSV Frankfurt (8/1).
597/804)	HERTZSCH Ingo	22.07.1977	**2**	**0**	2000-2002, Hamburger SV (2/0).
385/612)	HERZOG Dieter	15.07.1946	**5**	**0**	1974, TSV Fortuna Düsseldorf (5/0).
319/573)	HEYNCKES Josef „Jupp“	09.05.1945	**39**	**14**	1967-1976, Borussia VfL Mönchengladbach (38/14), Hannoverscher SV 96 (1/0).
464/671)	HIERONYMUS Holger	22.02.1959	**3**	**0**	1981-1982, Hamburger SV (3/0).
789/850)	HILBERT Roberto	16.10.1984	**8**	**0**	2007-2008, VfB Stuttgart (8/0).
740/827)	HILDEBRAND Timo	05.04.1979	**7**	**0**	2004-2007, VfB Stuttgart (5/0), Valencia CF (2/0).
(1/005)	HILLER (II) Arthur	03.10.1881	**4**	**0**	1908-1909, 1.FC Pforzheim (4/0).
(7/049)	HILLER (III) Marius	05.08.1892	**3**	**1**	1910-1911, 1.FC Pforzheim (3/1).
729/825)	HINKEL Andreas	26.03.1982	**21**	**0**	2003-2009, VfB Stuttgart (17/0), Celtic Glasgow FC (4/0).
17/083)	HIRSCH Julius	07.04.1892	**7**	**4**	1911-1913, Karlsruher FV (4/4), Spielvereinigung Fürth (3/0).
(5/032)	HIRTH Herbert	23.01.1884	**1**	**0**	1909, Hertha BSC Berlin (1/0).
749/833)	HITZLSPERGER Thomas	05.04.1982	**52**	**6**	2004-2010, Aston Villa FC Birmingham (9/0), VfB Stuttgart (42/6), West ham United FC London (1/0).
598/752)	HOBSCH Bernd	07.05.1968	**1**	**0**	1993, SV Werder Bremen (1/0).
48/167)	HOCHGESANG Georg	03.11.1897	**6**	**4**	1924-1927, 1.FC Nürnberg (6/4).
538/716)	HOCHSTÄTTER Christian	19.10.1963	**2**	**0**	1987, Borussia VfL Mönchengladbach (2/0).
35/130)	HÖGER Karl	27.05.1897	**4**	**0**	1921-1924, SV 07 Waldhof Mannheim (2/0), VfR Mannheim (2/0).
381/610)	HÖLZENBEIN Bernd	09.03.1946	**40**	**5**	1973-1978, SG Eintracht Frankfurt (40/5).
441/654)	HOENEß Dieter	07.01.1953	**6**	**4**	1979-1986, VfB Stuttgart (2/3), FC Bayern München (4/1).
368/600)	HOENEß Ulrich	05.01.1952	**35**	**5**	1972-1976, FC Bayern München (35/5).
528/705)	HÖRSTER Thomas	27.11.1956	**4**	**0**	1986-1987, TSV Bayer 04 Leverkusen (4/0).
163/380)	HOFER Franz	04.09.1918	**1**	**0**	1939, SK Rapid Wien (1/0).
229/471)	HOFFMANN Rudolf	11.02.1935	**1**	**0**	1955, SV Viktoria 1901 Aschaffenburg (1/0).
57/194)	HOFMANN Ludwig	09.06.1900	**18**	**4**	1926-1931, FC Bayern München (18/4).
61/204)	HOFMANN Richard	08.02.1906	**25**	**24**	1927-1933, Meerane 07 (6/5), Dresdner SC (19/19).
25/094)	HOFMEISTER Ludwig	05.12.1887	**2**	**0**	1912-1914, FC Bayern München (1/0), FC Kickers Stuttgart (1/0).
171/388)	HOFSTÄTTER Johann	12.01.1913	**1**	**0**	1940, SK Rapid Wien (1/0).
78/239)	HOHMANN Karl	18.06.1908	**26**	**20**	1930-1937, VfL Benrath (26/20).
(8/052)	HOLLSTEIN Ernst	09.12.1886	**6**	**0**	1910-1912, Karlsruher FV (6/0).
842/883)	HOLTBY Lewis Harry	18.09.1990	**3**	**0**	2010-2012, 1.FSV Mainz 05 (2/0), FC Schalke 04 Gelsenkirchen (1/0).
148/351)	HOLZ Friedel	21.02.1920	**1**	**0**	1938, TSV Duisburg 1899 (1/0).
67/219)	HORN Franz	26.08.1904	**3**	**0**	1928-1929, Hamburger SV (3/0).
64/217)	HORNAUER Josef	14.01.1908	**5**	**3**	1928-1931, TSV 1860 München (3/2), 1.FC Nürnberg (2/1).
297/553)	HORNIG Heinz	28.09.1937	**7**	**0**	1965-1966, 1.FC Köln (7/0).
31/110)	HÖSCHLE Adolf	20.07.1899	**1**	**0**	1920, FC Kickers Stuttgart (1/0).
297/552)	HÖTTGES Horst-Dieter	10.09.1943	**66**	**1**	1965-1974, SV Werder Bremen (66/1).
846/887)	HÖWEDES Benedikt	29.02.1988	**43**	**2**	2011-2016, FC Schalke 04 Gelsenkirchen (43/2).
448/662)	HRUBESCH Horst	17.04.1951	**21**	**6**	1980-1982, Hamburger SV (21/6).
76/235)	HUBER Alfred	29.01.1910	**1**	**0**	1930, FV Rastatt 04 (1/0).
91/267)	HUBER Lorenz	24.02.1906	**1**	**0**	1932, Karlsruher FV (1/0).
827/877)	HUMMELS Mats Julian	16.12.1988	**55**	**4**	2010-2016, BV Borussia Dortmund (50/4), FC Bayern München (5/0).
(4/029)	HUNDER Paul	12.01.1884	**8**	**0**	1909-1911, TuFC Viktoria 89 Berlin (8/0).
95/276)	HUNDT Eduard	03.08.1909	**3**	**0**	1933-1934, SK Schwarz-Weiss 1900 Essen (3/0).
825/873)	HUNT Aaron	04.09.1986	**3**	**0**	2009-2013, SV Werder Bremen (3/0).
747/831)	HUTH Robert	18.08.1984	**19**	**2**	2004-2009, Chelsea FC London (17/2), Middlesbrough FC (2/0).
36/138)	HUTTER Willy	03.11.1896	**2**	**0**	1921-1922, SV 07 Waldhof Mannheim (1/0), SV Saar 05 Saarbrücken (1/0).
535/713)	ILLGNER Bodo	07.04.1967	**54**	**0**	1987-1994, 1.FC Köln (54/0).
(6/038)	ILLMER Eberhardt	30.01.1888	**1**	**0**	1909, FV Straßburg (1/0).
455/667)	IMMEL Eike	27.11.1960	**19**	**0**	1980-1988, BV Borussia Dortmund (4/0), VfB Stuttgart (15/0).
158/367)	IMMIG Franz	10.09.1918	**2**	**0**	1939, Karlsruher FV (2/0).
225/461)	ÍSLACKER Franz	03.02.1926	**1**	**0**	1954, Rot-Weiß Essen (1/0).
(3/024)	JÄGER Adolf	31.03.1889	**18**	**11**	1908-1924, Altona FC 93 Hamburg (18/11).
256/496)	JÄGER Günter	21.12.1935	**1**	**0**	1958, TSV Fortuna Düsseldorf (1/0).

(169/384)	JAHN Helmut	20.10.1917	**17**	**0**	1939-1942, Berliner SV 92 (17/0).
(80/244)	JAKOB Hans	16.06.1908	**38**	**0**	1930-1939, SSV Jahn Regensburg (38/0).
(449/664)	JAKOBS Ditmar	28.08.1953	**20**	**1**	1980-1986, Hamburger SV (20/1).
(162/375)	JAKOBS Johannes	01.07.1917	**1**	**0**	1939, Hannoverscher SV 1896 (1/0).
(671/790)	JANCKER Carsten	28.08.1974	**33**	**10**	1998-2002, FC Bayern München (29/8), Udinese Calcio (4/2).
(91/268)	JANES Paul	11.03.1912	**71**	**7**	1932-1942, TSV Fortuna Düsseldorf (71/7).
(764/840)	JANSEN Marcell	04.11.1985	**45**	**3**	2005-2014, Borussia VfL Mönchengladbach (16/1), FC Bayern München (12/1), Hamburger SV (17/2).
(175/397)	JELLINEK Franz	10.07.1922	**1**	**0**	1940, Wiener Sport-Club (1/0).
(655/782)	JEREMIES Jens	05.03.1974	**55**	**1**	1997-2004, TSV 1860 München (8/0), FC Bayern München (47/1).
(799/857)	JONES Jermaine	03.11.1981	**3**	**0**	2008, FC Schalke 04 Gelsenkirchen (3/0).
(91/270)	JOPPICH Karl	06.01.1908	**1**	**0**	1932, SV Hoyerswerda (1/0).
(1/003)	JORDAN Ernst	18.05.1883	**1**	**0**	1908, Cricket-Victoria Magdeburg (1/0).
(883/910)	JUNG Sebastian Alexander	22.06.1990	**1**	**0**	2014, Eintracht Frankfurt (1/0).
(26/098)	JUNGTOW Otto	29.12.1892	**1**	**0**	1913, Hertha BSC Berlin (1/0).
(117/301)	JÜRISSEN Willy	13.05.1912	**6**	**0**	1935-1939, SC Rot-Weiß Oberhausen (6/0).
(205/437)	JUSKOWIAK Erich	07.09.1926	**31**	**4**	1951-1959, SC Rot-Weiß Oberhausen (1/0), TSV Fortuna Düsseldorf (30/4).

(163/382)	KABUREK Matthias	09.02.1911	**1**	**0**	1939, SK Rapid Wien (1/0).
(624/767)	KAHN Oliver	15.06.1969	**86**	**0**	1995-2006, FC Bayern München (86/0).
(31/112)	KALB Hans	03.08.1899	**15**	**2**	1920-1928, 1.FC Nürnberg (15/2).
(403/623)	KALTZ Manfred	06.01.1953	**69**	**8**	1975-1983, Hamburger SV (69/8).
(378/606)	KAPELLMANN Hans-Josef	19.12.1949	**5**	**0**	1973-1974, 1.FC Köln (2/0), FC Bayern München (3/0).
(258/498)	KAPITULSKI Helmut	29.09.1934	**1**	**0**	1958, FK 03 Pirmasens (1/0).
(406/627)	KARGUS Rudi	15.08.1952	**3**	**0**	1975-1977, Hamburger SV (3/0).
(80/245)	KAUER Erich	08.01.1908	**5**	**0**	1930-1931, Tennis Borussia Berlin (5/0).
(226/463)	KAUFHOLD Gerhard	02.12.1928	**1**	**0**	1954, OFC Kickers Offenbach (1/0).
(701/808)	KEHL Sebastian	13.02.1980	**31**	**2**	2001-2006, SC Freiburg (3/0), BV Borussia Dortmund (28/2).
(241/485)	KELBASSA Alfred	21.04.1925	**6**	**2**	1956-1958, BV Borussia Dortmund (6/2).
(403/626)	KELLER Ferdinand	30.07.1946	**1**	**0**	1975, TSV 1860 München (1/0).
(439/650)	KELSCH Walter	03.09.1955	**4**	**3**	1979-1980, VfB Stuttgart (4/3).
(821/871)	KHEDIRA Sami	04.04.1987	**69**	**7**	2009-2016, VfB Stuttgart (12/1), Real Madrid CF (44/4), Juventus FC Torino (13/2).
(61/206)	KIEßLING Georg	07.03.1903	**2**	**1**	1927-1928, Spielvereinigung Fürth (2/1).
(789/852)	KIEßLING Stephan	25.01.1984	**6**	**0**	2007-2010, TSV Bayer 04 Leverkusen (6/0).
(910/921)	KIMMICH Joshua	08.02.1995	**11**	**1**	2016, FC Bayern München (11/1).
(1/009)	KIPP Eugen	26.02.1885	**18**	**9**	1908-1913, Sportfreunde Stuttgart (16/9), FC Stuttgarter Kickers (2/0).
(49/171)	KIRSEI Willi	03.12.1902	**1**	**0**	1924, Hertha BSC Berlin (1/0).
(589/744)	KIRSTEN Ulf	04.12.1965	**51**	**21**	1992-2000, TSV Bayer 04 Leverkusen (51/21).
(118/312)	KITZINGER Albin	01.12.1912	**44**	**2**	1935-1942, 1.FC Schweinfurt 05 (44/2).
(137/335)	KLAAS Werner	10.05.1914	**1**	**0**	1937, SV Koblenz (1/0).
(362/596)	KLEFF Wolfgang	16.11.1946	**6**	**0**	1971-1973, Borussia VfL Mönchengladbach (6/0).
(402/621)	KLIEMANN Uwe	30.06.1949	**1**	**0**	1975, Hertha BSC Berlin (1/0).
(61/199)	KLING Eugen	14.02.1899	**1**	**0**	1927, TSV 1860 München (1/0).
(194/413)	KLINGLER August	24.02.1918	**5**	**6**	1942, FV Daxlanden (5/6).
(538/715)	KLINSMANN Jürgen	30.07.1964	**108**	**47**	1987-1998, VfB Stuttgart (12/2), Internazionale FC Milano (29/8), AS Monaco (24/15), Tottenham Hotspur FC London (9/6), FC Bayern München (23/10), Sampdoria UC Genova (3/2), Tottenham Hotspur FC London (10/4).
(199/418)	KLODT Bernhard	26.10.1926	**19**	**3**	1950-1959, FC Schalke 04 Gelsenkirchen (19/3).
(148/347)	KLODT Hans	10.06.1914	**17**	**0**	1938-1941, FC Schalke 04 Gelsenkirchen (17/0).
(260/503)	KLÖCKNER Theo	19.10.1934	**2**	**0**	1958, ETB Schwarz-Weiß Essen (2/0).
(699/806)	KLOSE Miroslav	09.06.1978	**137**	**71**	2001-2014, 1.FC Kaiserslautern (40/16), SV Werder Bremen (29/17), FC Bayern München (40/28), SS Lazio Roma (28/10).
(653/778)	KMETSCH Sven	13.08.1970	**2**	**0**	1997-1998, Hamburger SV (2/0).
(17/082)	KNESEBECK Willi	31.03.1887	**2**	**0**	1911-1912, TuFC Viktoria 89 Berlin (2/0).
(64/214)	KNÖPFLE Georg	15.05.1904	**23**	**0**	1928-1933, Spielvereinigung Fürth (3/0), FSV Frankfurt (20/0).
(87/260)	KOBIERSKI Stanislaus	15.11.1910	**26**	**9**	1931-1941, TSV Fortuna Düsseldorf (26/9).
(241/483)	KÖCHLING Willi	30.10.1924	**1**	**0**	1956, Rot-Weiß Essen (1/0).
(17/081)	KOENEN Theo	11.02.1890	**1**	**0**	1911, FV Bonn (1/0).
(511/700)	KÖGL Ludwig	07.03.1966	**2**	**0**	1985, FC Bayern München (2/0).
(137/334)	KÖHL Georg	19.11.1910	**1**	**0**	1937, 1.FC Nürnberg (1/0).
(56/189)	KÖHLER Georg	01.02.1900	**5**	**0**	1925-1928, Dresdner SC (5/0).
(528/706)	KOHLER Jürgen	06.10.1965	**105**	**2**	1986-1998, SV Waldhof Manheim (4/0), 1.FC Köln (20/0), FC Bayern München (12/0), FC Juventus Torino (38/0), BV Borussia Dortmund (31/2).
(201/427)	KOHLMEYER Werner	19.04.1924	**22**	**0**	1951-1955, 1.FC Kaiserslautern (22/0).
(285/531)	KONIETZKA Friedhelm „Timo“	02.08.1938	**9**	**3**	1962-1965, BV Borussia Dortmund (9/3).
(432/646)	KONOPKA Harald	18.11.1952	**2**	**0**	1978-1979, 1.FC Köln (2/0).
(560/731)	KÖPKE Andreas	12.03.1962	**59**	**0**	1990-1998, 1.FC Nürnberg (14/0), SG Eintracht Frankfurt (25/0), Olympique de Marseille (20/0).
(327/580)	KÖPPEL Horst	17.05.1948	**11**	**2**	1968-1973, VfB Stuttgart (7/2), Borussia VfL Mönchengladbach (4/0).
(62/207)	KÖPPLINGER Emil	19.12.1897	**1**	**0**	1927, 1.FC Nürnberg (1/0).
(399/615)	KÖRBEL Karl-Heinz	01.12.1954	**6**	**0**	1974-1975, SG Eintracht Frankfurt (6/0).
(260/504)	KÖRDELL Heinz	08.01.1932	**1**	**0**	1958, FC Schalke 04 Gelsenkirchen (1/0).
(280/527)	KOSLOWSKI Willi	17.02.1937	**3**	**1**	1962, FC Schalke 04 Gelsenkirchen (3/1).
(399/617)	KOSTEDDE Erwin	21.05.1946	**3**	**0**	1974-1975, OFC Kickers Offenbach (2/0), Hertha BSC Berlin (1/0).
(883/905)	KRAMER Christoph	19.02.1991	**12**	**0**	2014-2016, Borussia VfL Mönchengladbach (10/0), TSV Bayer 04 Leverkusen (2/0).
(289/539)	KRÄMER Werner	23.01.1940	**13**	**3**	1963-1967, MSV Duisburg (13/3).
(231/474)	KRAUS Engelbert	30.07.1934	**9**	**3**	1955-1964, OFC Kickers Offenbach (8/2), TSV 1860 München (1/1).

(98/284)	KRAUSE Emil	21.01.1908	**1**	**0**	1933, Hertha BSC Berlin (1/0).
(33/122)	KRAUSE Walter	14.03.1896	**6**	**0**	1920-1924, SC Victoria Hamburg (1/0), SV Holstein Kiel (5/0).
(11/070)	KRAUß Willy	10.02.1886	**2**	**0**	1911-1912, FC Carl Zeiss Jena (2/0).
(371/601)	KREMERS Erwin	24.03.1949	**15**	**3**	1972-1974, FC Schalke 04 Gelsenkirchen (15/3).
(381/609)	KREMERS Helmut	24.03.1949	**8**	**0**	1973-1975, FC Schalke 04 Gelsenkirchen (8/0).
(35/133)	KREß Anton	08.06.1899	**1**	**0**	1921, 1.FC Pforzheim (1/0).
(227/468)	KREß Richard	06.03.1925	**9**	**2**	1954-1961, SG Eintracht Frankfurt (9/2).
(70/223)	KREß Willibald	13.11.1906	**16**	**0**	1929-1934, SG Rot-Weiss Frankfurt (12/0), Dresdner SC (4/0).
(19/086)	KROGMANN Georg	04.09.1886	**3**	**0**	1912, FV Holstein 1902 Kiel (3/0).
(826/875)	KROOS Toni	04.01.1990	**74**	**12**	2010-2016, TSV Bayer 04 Leverkusen (8/0), FC Bayern München (43/7), Real Madrid CF (23/5).
(505/699)	KROTH Thomas	26.08.1959	**1**	**0**	1985, SG Eintracht Frankfurt (1/0).
(173/390)	KRÜGER Kurt	04.10.1920	**1**	**0**	1940, TSV Fortuna Düsseldorf (1/0).
(90/266)	KRUMM Franz	16.10.1909	**2**	**1**	1932-1933, FC Bayern München (2/1).
(873/896)	KRUSE Maximilian	19.03.1988	**14**	**4**	2013-2015, SC Freiburg (2/1), Borussia VfL Mönchengladbach (11/2), VfL Wolfsburg (1/1).
(217/455)	KUBSCH Heinz	20.07.1930	**3**	**0**	1954-1956, FK 03 Pirmasens (3/0).
(169/385)	KUBUS Richard	30.03.1914	**1**	**0**	1939, Vorwärts-Rasensport Gleiwitz (1/0).
(40/150)	KUGLER Anton	28.03.1898	**7**	**0**	1923-1927, 1.FC Nürnberg (7/0).
(16/079)	KUGLER Paul	24.09.1889	**2**	**0**	1911-1913, TuFC Viktoria 89 Berlin (2/0).
(7/046)	KÜHNLE Paul	10.04.1885	**2**	**0**	1910-1911, FC Kickers Stuttgart (2/0).
(49/168)	KUHNT Werner	27.10.1893	**1**	**0**	1924, SC Norden-Nordwest Berlin (1/0).
(78/240)	KUND Willi	11.03.1908	**2**	**1**	1930-1931, 1.FC Nürnberg (2/1).
(602/755)	KUNTZ Stefan	30.10.1962	**25**	**6**	1993-1997, 1.FC Kaiserslautern (11/2), Beşiktaş JK Istanbul (12/3), DSC Arminia Bielefeld (2/1).
(137/336)	KUPFER Andreas	07.05.1914	**44**	**1**	1937-1950, 1.FC Schweinfurt 05 (44/1).
(287/536)	KÜPPERS Hans	24.12.1938	**7**	**2**	1962-1967, TSV 1860 München (7/2).
(728/823)	KURÁNYI Kevin Dennis	02.03.1982	**52**	**19**	2003-2008, VfB Stuttgart (29/14), FC Schalke 04 Gelsenkirchen (23/5).
(280/526)	KURBJUHN Jürgen	26.07.1940	**5**	**0**	1962-1966, Hamburger SV (5/0).
(54/182)	KUTTERER Emil	11.11.1898	**8**	**0**	1925-1928, FC Bayern München (8/0).
(63/212)	KUZORRA Ernst	16.10.1905	**12**	**7**	1927-1938, FC Schalke 04 Gelsenkirchen (12/7).
(219/457)	KWIATKOWSKI Heinz	16.07.1926	**4**	**0**	1954-1958, BV Borussia Dortmund (4/0).
(217/456)	LABAND Fritz	01.11.1925	**4**	**0**	1954, Hamburger SV (4/0).
(592/748)	LABBADIA Bruno	08.02.1966	**2**	**0**	1992-1995, FC Bayern München (1/0), 1.FC Köln (1/0).
(79/242)	LACHNER Ludwig	25.07.1910	**8**	**4**	1930-1934, TSV 1860 München (8/4).
(738/826)	LAHM Philipp	11.11.1983	**113**	**5**	2004-2014, VfB Stuttgart (15/1), FC Bayern München (98/4).
(37/140)	LANG Hans	08.02.1899	**10**	**0**	1922-1926, Spielvereinigung Fürth (2/0), Hamburger SV (8/0).
(88/261)	LANGENBEIN Kurt	04.11.1910	**2**	**1**	1932-1935, VfR Mannheim (2/1).
(327/581)	LAUMEN Herbert	11.08.1943	**2**	**1**	1968, Borussia VfL Mönchengladbach (2/1).
(727/821)	LAUTH Benjamin	04.08.1981	**5**	**0**	2003-2004, TSV 1860 München (5/0).
(656/783)	LEHMANN Jens	10.11.1969	**61**	**0**	1998-2008, FC Schalke 04 Gelsenkirchen (2/0), BV Borussia Dortmund (14/0), Arsenal FC London (45/0).
(97/282)	LEHNER Ernst	07.11.1912	**65**	**30**	1933-1942, TSV Schwaben Augsburg (55/24), Blau-Weiß 90 Berlin (10/6).
(61/201)	LEINBERGER Ludwig	21.05.1903	**24**	**0**	1927-1933, Spielvereinigung Fürth (24/0).
(44/162)	LEIP Rudolf	08.06.1890	**3**	**0**	1923-1924, SV Guts Muths Dresden (3/0).
(910/920)	LENO Bernd	04.03.1992	**3**	**0**	2016, TSV Bayer 04 Leverkusen (3/0).
(110/298)	LENZ August	29.11.1910	**14**	**9**	1935-1938, BV Borussia Dortmund (14/9).
(289/538)	LIBUDA Reinhard	10.10.1943	**26**	**3**	1963-1971, FC Schalke 04 Gelsenkirchen (24/3), BV Borussia Dortmund (2/0).
(201/429)	LIEBRICH Werner	18.01.1927	**16**	**0**	1951-1956, 1.FC Kaiserslautern (16/0).
(94/274)	LINDNER Willi	27.06.1910	**1**	**0**	1933, SG Eintracht Frankfurt (1/0).
(655/780)	LINKE Thomas	26.12.1969	**43**	**1**	1997-2004, FC Schalke 04 Gelsenkirchen (2/0), FC Bayern München (41/1).
(466/672)	LITTBARSKI Pierre	01.04.1960	**73**	**18**	1981-1990, 1.FC Köln (34/12), Racing Matra Paris (2/0), 1.FC Köln (37/6).
(6/043)	LÖBLE Otto	27.10.1888	**4**	**0**	1909-1913, FC Stuttgarter Kickers (4/0).
(32/117)	LOHNEIS Hans	12.04.1895	**1**	**0**	1920, MTV Fürth (1/0).
(319/575)	LÖHR Johannes	05.07.1942	**20**	**5**	1967-1970, 1.FC Köln (20/5).
(33/121)	LOHRMANN Theodor	07.09.1898	**3**	**0**	1920-1922, Spielvereinigung Fürth (3/0).
(298/555)	LORENZ Max	19.08.1939	**19**	**1**	1965-1970, SV Werder Bremen (17/1), TSV Eintracht Brainschweig (2/0).
(30/106)	LUDEWIG Heinz	24.12.1889	**1**	**0**	1914, Duisburger SV (1/0).
(79/243)	LUDWIG Johann (LUDEWIG)	08.06.1903	**3**	**2**	1930-1931, SV Holstein Kiel (3/2).
(1/004)	LUDWIG Karl	14.05.1886	**1**	**0**	1908, SC 99 Köln (1/0).
(41/155)	LÜKE Josef	13.03.1899	**2**	**0**	1923, TuRU 1880 Düsseldorf (2/0).
(270/517)	LUTZ Friedel	21.01.1939	**12**	**0**	1960-1966, SG Eintracht Frankfurt (12/0).
(49/170)	LUX Hermann	20.09.1893	**3**	**0**	1924-1925, Tennis Borussia Berlin (3/0).
(327/583)	MAAS Erich	24.12.1940	**3**	**0**	1968-1970, TSV Eintracht Braunschweig (3/0).
(784/847)	MADLUNG Alexander	11.07.1982	**2**	**0**	2006-2007, VfL Wolfsburg (2/0).
(416/640)	MAGATH Felix	26.07.1953	**43**	**3**	1977-1986, Hamburger SV (43/3).
(92/272)	MAHLMANN Carl-Heinz	17.09.1907	**1**	**0**	1932, Hamburger SV (1/0).
(214/453)	MAI Karl	27.07.1928	**21**	**1**	1953-1959, Spielvereinigung Fürth (18/1), FC Bayern München (3/0).
(307/565)	MAIER Josef „Sepp“	28.02.1944	**95**	**0**	1966-1979, FC Bayern München (95/0).
(118/313)	MALECKI Edmund	01.11.1914	**5**	**2**	1935-1939, Hannoverscher SV 1896 (5/2).
(91/269)	MALIK Richard	10.12.1909	**2**	**1**	1932-1933, SuSV 1909 Beuthen (2/1).
(41/158)	MANEVAL Helmut	13.11.1898	**1**	**0**	1923, FC Kickers Stuttgart (1/0).
(297/554)	MANGLITZ Manfred	08.03.1940	**4**	**0**	1965-1970, MSV Duisburg (2/0), 1.FC Köln (2/0).
(141/342)	MÄNNER Ludwig	11.07.1912	**5**	**0**	1937-1940, Hannoverscher SV 1896 (5/0).
(61/200)	MANTEL Hugo	14.05.1907	**5**	**0**	1927-1933, Dresdner SC (1/0), SG Eintracht Frankfurt (4/0).
(801/858)	MARIN Marko	13.03.1989	**16**	**1**	2008-2010, Borussia VfL Mönchengladbach (6/1), SV Werder Bremen (10/0).
(163/376)	MARISCHKA Otto	31.05.1912	**1**	**0**	1939, Admira Wien (1/0).

(35/129)	MAROHN Arthur	14.06.1893	**1**	**0**	1921, TuFC Viktoria 89 Berlin (1/0).
(615/761)	MARSCHALL Olaf	19.03.1966	**13**	**3**	1994-1999, 1.FC Kaiserslautern (13/3).
(440/651)	MARTIN Bernd	10.02.1955	**1**	**0**	1979, VfB Stuttgart (1/0).
(173/389)	MARTINEK Alexander	25.04.1919	**1**	**0**	1940, SC Wacker Wien (1/0).
(54/184)	MARTWIG Otto	24.02.1903	**6**	**0**	1925-1927, Tennis Borussia Berlin (6/0).
(270/520)	MARX Joseph	20.11.1934	**1**	**1**	1960, SV Sodingen (1/1).
(4/026)	MASSINI Erich	13.09.1889	**1**	**0**	1909, BFC Preussen Berlin (1/0).
(120/317)	MATHIES Paul	12.01.1911	**2**	**0**	1935, SC Preußen 1909 Danzig (2/0).
(451/665)	MATTHÄUS Lothar Herbert	21.03.1961	**150**	**23**	1980-2000, Borussia VfL Mönchengladbach (26/0), FC Bayern Münche (39/7), FC Internazionale Milano (28/12), FC Bayern München (51/4), Ne York/New Jersey Metro Stars (6/0).
(2/018)	MATTHES Paul	06.03.1879	**1**	**0**	1908, Viktoria 96 Magdeburg (1/0).
(38/144)	MAUCH Paul	08.05.1897	**1**	**0**	1922, VfB Stuttgart (1/0).
(679/796)	MAUL Ronald	13.02.1973	**2**	**0**	1999, DSC Arminia Bielefeld (2/0).
(262/506)	MAURITZ Matthias	13.11.1924	**1**	**0**	1959, TSV Fortuna Düsseldorf (1/0).
(711/813)	MAX Martin	07.08.1968	**1**	**0**	2002, TSV 1860 München (1/0).
(200/424)	MEBUS Paul	09.06.1920	**6**	**0**	1951-1954, VfL Benrath (1/0), 1.FC Köln (5/0).
(20/088)	MECHLING Heinrich	25.02.1892	**2**	**1**	1912-1913, Freiburger FC (2/1).
(127/324)	MEHL Paul	16.04.1912	**2**	**0**	1936, TSV Fortuna Düsseldorf (2/0).
(482/678)	MEIER Norbert	20.09.1958	**16**	**2**	1982-1985, SV Werder Bremen (16/2).
(51/177)	MEIßNER Kurt	11.12.1897	**1**	**0**	1924, VfR Mannheim (1/0).
(441/656)	MEMERING Caspar	01.06.1953	**3**	**0**	1979-1980, Hamburger SV (3/0).
(147/346)	MENGEL Hans	06.02.1917	**1**	**0**	1938, TuRu 1880 Düsseldorf (1/0).
(163/379)	MERKEL Maximilian	07.12.1918	**1**	**0**	1939, Wiener Sport-Club (1/0).
(749/834)	MERTESACKER Per	29.09.1984	**104**	**4**	2004-2014, SV Hannover'96 (29/1), SV Werder Bremen (46/0), Arsenal FC London (29/3).
(704/810)	METZELDER Christoph	05.11.1980	**47**	**0**	2002-2008, BV Borussia Dortmund (32/0), Real Madrid CF (15/0).
(211/449)	METZNER Karl-Heinz	09.01.1923	**2**	**0**	1952-1953, KSV Hessen Kassel (2/0).
(883/907)	MEYER Max	18.09.1995	**4**	**1**	2014-2016, FC Schalke 04 Gelsenkirchen (4/1).
(326/579)	MEYER Peter	18.02.1940	**1**	**0**	1967, Borussia VfL Mönchengladbach (1/0).
(467/673)	MILEWSKI Jürgen	19.10.1957	**3**	**0**	1981-1984, Hamburger SV (3/0).
(470/675)	MILL Frank	23.07.1958	**17**	**0**	1982-1990, Borussia VfL Mönchengladbach (9/0), BV Borussia Dortmund (8/0).
(181/401)	MILLER Karl	02.10.1913	**12**	**0**	1941-1942, FC St.Pauli Hamburg (12/0).
(227/467)	MILTZ Jakob	23.09.1928	**2**	**0**	1954-1956, TuS Neuendorf (2/1).
(151/355)	MOCK Hans	09.12.1906	**5**	**0**	1938-1942, FK Austria Wien (5/0).
(549/725)	MÖLLER Andreas	02.09.1967	**85**	**29**	1988-1999, BV Borussia Dortmund (12/3), SG Eintracht Frankfurt (12/1), FC Juventus Torino (20/10), BV Borussia Dortmund (41/15).
(12/073)	MÖLLER Ernst	19.08.1891	**9**	**4**	1911-1913, FV Holstein 1902 Kiel (9/4).
(32/116)	MOHNS Arthur	04.12.1896	**5**	**0**	1920-1922, SV Norden-Nordwest Berlin (5/0).
(42/159)	MONTAG Otto	12.10.1897	**4**	**0**	1923-1925, SC Norden-Nordwest Berlin (4/0).
(162/374)	MOOG Alfons	14.02.1915	**7**	**0**	1939-1940, VfL 99 Köln (7/0).
(199/419)	MORLOCK Max	11.05.1925	**26**	**21**	1950-1958, 1.FC Nürnberg (26/21).
(410/632)	MÜLLER Dieter	01.04.1954	**12**	**9**	1976-1978, 1.FC Köln (12/9).
(83/254)	MÜLLER Ernst	13.07.1901	**1**	**0**	1931, Hertha BSC Berlin (1/0).
(82/253)	MÜLLER Friedrich	07.12.1907	**2**	**0**	1931: Dresdner SC (2/0).
(317/568)	MÜLLER Gerhard	03.11.1945	**62**	**68**	1966-1974, FC Bayern München (62/68).
(427/645)	MÜLLER Hans	27.07.1957	**42**	**5**	1978-1983, VfB Stuttgart (36/5), Internazionale FC Milano (6/0).
(35/128)	MÜLLER Henry	12.08.1896	**9**	**0**	1921-1928, SC Victoria Hamburg (9/0).
(36/135)	MÜLLER Josef	06.05.1893	**12**	**0**	1921-1928, FC Phönix Ludwigshafen (1/0), Spielvereinigung Fürth (10/0), FV 04 Würzburg (1/0).
(330/586)	MÜLLER Ludwig	25.08.1941	**6**	**0**	1968-1969, 1.FC Nürnberg (5/0), Borussia VfL Mönchengladbach (1/0).
(873/897)	MÜLLER Nicolai	25.09.1987	**2**	**0**	2013, 1.FSV Mainz 05 (2/0).
(826/874)	MÜLLER Thomas	13.09.1989	**83**	**36**	2010-2016, FC Bayern München (83/36).
(110/296)	MUNKERT Andreas	07.03.1908	**8**	**0**	1935-1936, 1.FC Nürnberg (8/0).
(78/237)	MÜNZENBERG Reinhold	25.01.1909	**41**	**0**	1930-1939, Aachener TSV Alemannia 1900 (41/0).
(883/902)	MUSTAFI Shkodran	17.04.1992	**15**	**1**	2014-2016, UC Sampdoria Genova (4/0), Valencia CF (8/1), Arsenal FC London (3/0).
(303/561)	NAFZIGER Rudolf	11.08.1945	**1**	**0**	1965, FC Bayern München (1/0).
(57/190)	NAGELSCHMITZ Ernst	01.05.1902	**1**	**0**	1926, FC Bayern München (1/0).
(10/065)	NEIßE Hermann	05.12.1889	**3**	**0**	1910-1911, Eimsbütteler TV (3/0).
(669/788)	NERLINGER Christian	21.03.1973	**6**	**1**	1998-1999, BV Borussia Dortmund (6/1).
(303/562)	NETZER Günter	14.09.1944	**37**	**6**	1965-1975, Borussia VfL Mönchengladbach (31/6), Real CF Madrid (6/0).
(541/720)	NEUBARTH Frank	29.07.1962	**1**	**0**	1988, SV Werder Bremen (1/0).
(329/585)	NEUBERGER Willi	15.04.1946	**2**	**0**	1968, BV Borussia Dortmund (2/0).
(819/868)	NEUER Manuel Peter	27.03.1986	**74**	**0**	2009-2016, FC Schalke 04 Gelsenkirchen (20/0), FC Bayern München (54/0).
(6/040)	NEUMAIER Robert	14.04.1885	**3**	**0**	1909-1912, FC Phönix Karlsruhe (3/0).
(2/017)	NEUMANN Arno	07.02.1885	**1**	**0**	1908, Dresdner SC (1/0).
(425/643)	NEUMANN Herbert	14.11.1953	**1**	**0**	1978, 1.FC Köln (1/0).
(152/360)	NEUMER Leopold	08.02.1919	**1**	**0**	1938, FK Austria Wien (1/0).
(239/481)	NEUSCHÄFER Hans	23.11.1931	**1**	**1**	1956: TSV Fortuna Düsseldorf (1/1).
(869/894)	NEUSTÄDTER Roman	18.02.1988	**2**	**0**	2012-2013, FC Schalke 04 Gelsenkirchen (2/0).
(668/787)	NEUVILLE Olivier	01.05.1973	**68**	**10**	1998-2008, FC Hansa Rostock (8/1), TSV Bayer 04 Leverkusen (40/3), Borussia VfL Mönchengladbach (20/6).
(399/618)	NICKEL Bernd	15.03.1949	**1**	**0**	1974-1976, SG Eintracht Frankfurt (1/0).
(445/660)	NICKEL Harald	21.07.1953	**3**	**0**	1979-1980, Borussia VfL Mönchengladbach (3/0).
(6/039)	NICODEMUS Otto Dr.	21.06.1886	**1**	**0**	1909, SV Wiesbaden (1/0).
(54/183)	NIEDERBACHER Max	22.06.1899	**1**	**0**	1925, FC Kickers Stuttgart (1/0).
(455/666)	NIEDERMAYER Kurt	25.11.1955	**1**	**0**	1980, FC Bayern München (1/0).

385/611)	NIGBUR Norbert	08.05.1948	**6**	**0**	1974-1980, FC Schalke 04 Gelsenkirchen (6/0).
99/287)	NOACK Rudolf	30.03.1913	**3**	**1**	1934-1937, Hamburger SV (3/1).
414/635)	NOGLY Peter	14.01.1947	**4**	**0**	1977, Hamburger SV (4/0).
277/523)	NOWAK Hans	09.08.1937	**15**	**0**	1961-1964, FC Schalke 04 Gelsenkirchen (15/0).
549/777)	NOWOTNY Jens	11.01.1974	**48**	**1**	1997-2006, TSV Bayer 04 Leverkusen (47/1), NK Dinamo Zagreb (1/0).
(6/044)	OBERLE Emil	16.11.1889	**5**	**1**	1909-1912, FC Phönix Karlsruhe (5/1).
772/841)	ODONKOR David	21.02.1984	**16**	**1**	2006-2008, BV Borussia Dortmund (6/0), Real Betis Balompié Sevilla (10/1).
90/265)	OEHM Richard	22.06.1909	**3**	**0**	1932-1934, 1.FC Nürnberg (3/0).
316/865)	ÖZIL Mesut	15.10.1988	**83**	**20**	2009-2016, SV Werder Bremen (17/2), Real Madrid CF (30/12), Arsenal FC London (36/6).
336/588)	OHLHAUSER Rainer	06.01.1941	**1**	**0**	1968, FC Bayern München (1/0).
278/524)	OLK Werner	18.01.1938	**1**	**0**	1961, FC Bayern München (1/0).
538/717)	ORDENEWITZ Frank	25.03.1965	**2**	**0**	1987, SV Werder Bremen (2/0).
484/681)	OTTEN Jonny	31.01.1961	**6**	**0**	1983-1984, SV Werder Bremen (6/0).
289/540)	OVERATH Wolfgang	29.09.1943	**81**	**17**	1963-1974, 1.FC Köln (81/17).
751/835)	OWOMOYELA Patrick	05.11.1979	**11**	**0**	2004-2006, DSC Arminia Bielefeld (6/0), SV Werder Bremen (5/0).
792/855)	PANDER Christian	28.08.1983	**2**	**1**	2007, FC Schalke 04 Gelsenkirchen (2/1).
121/319)	PANSE Herbert	06.03.1914	**1**	**1**	1935, Eimsbütteler TV (1/1).
544/774)	PAßLACK Stephan	24.08.1970	**4**	**1**	1996-1998, Borussia VfL Mönchengladbach (4/1).
297/551)	PATZKE Bernd	14.03.1943	**24**	**0**	1965-1971, TSV 1860 München (18/0), Hertha BSC Berlin (6/0).
49/172)	PAULSEN (PÖMPNER) Paul	28.12.1892	**6**	**3**	1924-1925, VfB Leipzig (6/3).
163/378)	PEKAREK Josef	02.01.1913	**1**	**0**	1939, SC Wacker Wien (1/0).
150/352)	PESSER Hans	07.11.1911	**12**	**2**	1938-1940, SK Rapid Wien (12/2).
245/491)	PETERS Wolfgang	08.01.1929	**1**	**0**	1957, BV Borussia Dortmund (1/0).
213/451)	PFAFF Alfred	16.07.1926	**7**	**2**	1953-1956, SG Eintracht Frankfurt (7/2).
226/464)	PFEIFFER Michael	19.07.1925	**1**	**0**	1954, Aachener TSV Alemannia 1900 (1/0).
596/750)	PFLIPSEN Karlheinz	31.10.1970	**1**	**0**	1993, Borussia VfL Mönchengladbach (1/0).
531/710)	PFLÜGLER Hans	27.03.1960	**11**	**0**	1987-1990, FC Bayern München (11/0).
(7/050)	PHILIPP Ludwig	20.12.1889	**2**	**0**	1910, 1.FC Nürnberg (2/0).
158/368)	PICARD Alfred	21.03.1913	**1**	**0**	1939, SSV 1846 Ulm (1/0).
297/550)	PIONTEK Josef „Sepp“	05.03.1940	**6**	**0**	1965-1966, SV Werder Bremen (6/0).
398/614)	PIRRUNG Josef	24.07.1949	**2**	**0**	1974, 1.FC Kaiserslautern (2/0).
155/363)	PLATZER Peter	29.05.1910	**2**	**0**	1939, Admira Wien (2/0).
173/391)	PLENER Ernst	21.02.1919	**2**	**2**	1940, Vorwärts-Rasensport Gleiwitz (2/2).
743/829)	PODOLSKI Lukas Josef	04.06.1985	**129**	**48**	2004-2016, 1.FC Köln (32/15), FC Bayern München (32/18), 1.FC Köln (37/11), Arsenal FC London (20/3), FC Internazionale Milano (4/1), Galatasaray SK İstanbul (4/0).
122/322)	POERTGEN Ernst	25.01.1912	**3**	**5**	1935-1937, FC Schalke 04 Gelsenkirchen (3/5).
(3/021)	POETSCH Ernst	29.03.1883	**3**	**0**	1908-1910, Union 92 Berlin (3/0).
41/153)	POHL Erich	15.01.1884	**2**	**0**	1923, SC 99 Köln (2/0).
186/406)	POHL Herbert	18.09.1916	**2**	**0**	1941, Dresdner SC (2/0).
158/369)	PÖHLER Ludwig	11.01.1916	**1**	**0**	1939, Hannoverscher SV 1896 (1/0).
99/288)	POLITZ Karl	14.08.1903	**1**	**0**	1934, Hamburger SV (1/0).
33/124)	POPP Luitpold	07.03.1893	**5**	**1**	1920-1926, 1.FC Nürnberg (5/1).
(2/015)	POPPE Walter	05.03.1886	**1**	**0**	1908, FC Eintracht Braunschweig (1/0).
269/516)	PORGES Ingo	22.08.1938	**1**	**0**	1960, FC St.Pauli Hamburg (1/0).
201/428)	POSIPAL Josef	20.06.1927	**32**	**1**	1951-1956, Hamburger SV (32/1).
286/532)	POTT Fritz	23.04.1939	**3**	**0**	1962-1964, 1.FC Köln (3/0).
57/193)	PÖTTINGER Josef	16.04.1903	**14**	**8**	1926-1930, FC Bayern München (14/8).
573/792)	PREETZ Michael	17.08.1967	**7**	**3**	1999-2000, Hertha BSC Berlin (7/3).
202/432)	PREIßLER Alfred	09.04.1921	**2**	**0**	1951, SC Preußen Münster (2/0).
260/501)	PYKA Alfred	28.06.1934	**1**	**0**	1958, SC Westfalia 04 Herne (1/0).
(5/036)	QUECK Richard	04.11.1888	**3**	**2**	1909-1914, FC Eintracht Braunschweig (3/2).
151/353)	RAFTL Rudolf	07.02.1911	**6**	**0**	1938-1940, SK Rapid Wien (6/0).
712/814)	RAHN Christian	15.06.1979	**5**	**0**	2002-2004, FC St.Pauli Hamburg (2/0), Hamburger SV (3/0).
204/434)	RAHN Helmut	16.08.1929	**40**	**21**	1951-1960, Rot-Weiß Essen (34/19), 1.FC Köln (6/2).
503/696)	RAHN Uwe	21.05.1962	**14**	**5**	1984-1987, Borussia VfL Mönchengladbach (14/5).
570/789)	RAMELOW Carsten	20.03.1974	**46**	**3**	1998-2004, TSV Bayer 04 Leverkusen (46/3).
95/279)	RASSELNBERG Josef	18.12.1912	**9**	**8**	1933-1935, VfL Benrath (9/8).
727/820)	RAU Tobias	31.12.1981	**7**	**1**	2003, VfL Wolfsburg (5/1), FC Bayern München (2/0).
300/558)	REBELE Hans	26.01.1943	**2**	**0**	1965-1969, TSV 1860 München (2/0).
536/773)	RECK Oliver	27.02.1965	**1**	**0**	1996, SV Werder Bremen (1/0).
295/546)	REDDER Theo	19.11.1941	**1**	**0**	1964, BV Borussia Dortmund (1/0).
22/090)	REESE Hans	17.09.1891	**1**	**0**	1912, FV Holstein 1902 Kiel (1/0).
568/784)	REHMER Marko	29.04.1972	**35**	**4**	1998-2003, FC Hansa Rostock (7/0), Hertha BSC Berlin (28/4).
574/793)	REICH Marco	30.12.1977	**1**	**0**	1999, 1.FC Kaiserslautern (1/0).
406/628)	REICHEL Peter	30.11.1951	**2**	**0**	1975-1976, SG Eintracht Frankfurt (2/0).
827/879)	REINARTZ Stefan	01.01.1989	**3**	**0**	2010-2013, TSV Bayer 04 Leverkusen (3/0).
473/676)	REINDERS Uwe	19.01.1955	**4**	**1**	1982, SV Werder Bremen (4/1).
553/728)	REINHARDT Alois	18.11.1961	**4**	**0**	1989-1990, TSV Bayer 04 Leverkusen (4/0).
549/727)	REINHARDT Knut	27.04.1968	**7**	**0**	1988-1992, TSV Bayer 04 Leverkusen (4/0), BV Borussia Dortmund (3/0).
62/208)	REINMANN Baptist	31.10.1903	**4**	**0**	1927-1929, 1.FC Nürnberg (4/0).
285/528)	REISCH Stefan	29.11.1941	**9**	**0**	1962-1964, 1.FC Nürnberg (9/0).
13/074)	REISER Otto	24.12.1884	**1**	**0**	1911, FC Phönix Karlsruhe (1/0).
(9/062)	REISLANT Otto	31.05.1883	**1**	**0**	1910, FC Wacker 1895 Leipzig (1/0).
45/164)	REIßMANN Martin	29.09.1900	**1**	**0**	1923, SV Guts Muths Dresden (1/0).

(163/381)	REITERMAIER Ernst	26.12.1918	**1**	**0**	1939, SC Wacker Wien (1/0).
(270/518)	REITGAßL Willy	29.02.1936	**1**	**1**	1960, Karlsruher SC (1/1).
(206/442)	RETTER Erich	17.02.1925	**14**	**0**	1952-1956, VfB Stuttgart (14/0).
(37/141)	RETTER Fritz	02.07.1896	**1**	**0**	1922, Sportfreunde Stuttgart (1/0).
(852/889)	REUS Marco	31.05.1989	**29**	**9**	2011-2016, Borussia VfL Mönchengladbach (8/2), BV Borussia Dortmund (21/7).
(532/711)	REUTER Stefan	16.10.1966	**69**	**2**	1987-1998, 1.FC Nürnberg (9/1), FC Bayern München (18/1), FC Juventus Torino (9/0), BV Borussia Dortmund (33/0).
(5/034)	RICHTER Leopold	22.05.1885	**1**	**0**	1909, VfB Leipzig (1/0).
(186/405)	RICHTER Lothar	09.06.1912	**1**	**0**	1941, Chemnitzer BC (1/0).
(653/779)	RICKEN Lars	10.07.1976	**16**	**1**	1997-2002, BV Borussia Dortmund (16/1).
(548/724)	RIEDLE Karlheinz	16.09.1965	**42**	**16**	1988-1994, SV Werder Bremen (10/2), SS Lazio Roma (23/12), BV Borussia Dortmund (9/2).
(31/113)	RIEGEL Carl	06.01.1897	**7**	**0**	1920-1923, 1.FC Nürnberg (7/0).
(188/409)	RIEGLER Franz	30.08.1915	**2**	**0**	1941-1942, FK Austria Wien (2/0).
(837/881)	RIETHER Sascha	23.03.1983	**2**	**0**	2010, VfL Wolfsburg (2/0).
(260/505)	RINGEL Karl	30.09.1932	**1**	**0**	1958, Borussia Neunkirchen (1/0).
(668/786)	RINK Paulo Roberto	21.02.1973	**13**	**0**	1998-2000, TSV Bayer 04 Leverkusen (13/0).
(3/019)	RISO (I) Heinrich	30.06.1882	**2**	**0**	1908-1909, VfB Leipzig (2/0).
(7/045)	RISO (II) Hans	16.03.1889	**1**	**0**	1910, FC Wacker 1895 Leipzig (1/0).
(41/152)	RISSE Walter	02.12.1893	**8**	**0**	1923-1928, SC 99 Düsseldorf (5/0), Hamburger SV (3/0).
(400/620)	RITSCHEL Manfred	07.06.1946	**3**	**1**	1975, OFC Kickers Offenbach (3/1).
(54/187)	RITTER Oskar	30.09.1901	**1**	**0**	1925, SV Holstein Kiel (1/0).
(599/753)	RITTER Thomas	10.10.1967	**1**	**0**	1993, 1.FC Kaiserslautern (1/0).
(299/557)	RODEKAMP Walter	13.01.1941	**3**	**1**	1965, Hannoverscher SV 96 (3/1).
(129/327)	RODZINSKI Josef	29.08.1907	**3**	**0**	1936, Hamborn 07 (3/0).
(199/423)	RÖHRIG Josef	28.02.1925	**12**	**2**	1950-1956, 1.FC Köln (12/2).
(131/331)	ROHDE Hans	07.12.1914	**25**	**0**	1936-1942, Eimsbütteler TV (25/0).
(88/262)	ROHR Oskar	24.03.1912	**4**	**5**	1932-1933, FC Bayern München (4/5).
(106/294)	ROHWEDDER Otto	03.12.1909	**5**	**2**	1934-1937, Eimsbütteler TV (5/2).
(30/105)	ROKOSCH Ernst	26.02.1889	**1**	**0**	1914, Spielvereinigung Leipzig (1/0).
(496/691)	ROLEDER Helmut	09.10.1953	**1**	**0**	1984, VfB Stuttgart (1/0).
(789/851)	ROLFES Simon	21.01.1982	**26**	**2**	2007-2011, TSV Bayer 04 Leverkusen (26/2).
(484/680)	ROLFF Wolfgang	26.12.1959	**37**	**0**	1983-1989, Hamburger SV (19/0), TSV Bayer 04 Leverkusen (18/0).
(50/174)	ROLLER Gustav	19.02.1895	**1**	**0**	1924, 1.FC Pforzheim (1/0).
(4/031)	RÖPNACK Helmut	23.09.1884	**10**	**0**	1909-1913, TuFC Viktoria 89 Berlin (10/0).
(143/344)	ROSE Walter	05.11.1912	**1**	**0**	1937, Spielvereinigung Leipzig (1/0).
(710/811)	ROST Frank	30.06.1973	**4**	**0**	2002-2003, SV Werder Bremen (1/0), FC Schalke 04 Gelsenkirchen (3/0).
(324/578)	ROTH Franz	27.04.1946	**4**	**0**	1967-1970, FC Bayern München (4/0).
(54/185)	RUCH Hans	08.09.1898	**3**	**2**	1925-1929, Union 92 Berlin (2/1), Hertha BSC Berlin (1/1).
(121/318)	RUCHAY Fritz	12.12.1909	**1**	**0**	1935, Prussia-Samland Königsberg (1/0).
(883/903)	RÜDIGER Antonio	03.03.1993	**11**	**0**	2014-2016, VfB Stuttgart (6/0), AS Roma (5/0).
(883/904)	RUDY Sebastian	28.02.1990	**12**	**0**	2014-2016, TSG 1899 Hoffenheim (12/0).
(416/639)	RÜSSMANN Rolf	13.10.1950	**20**	**1**	1977-1978, FC Schalke 04 Gelsenkirchen (20/1).
(412/634)	RUMMENIGGE Karl-Heinz	25.09.1955	**95**	**45**	1976-1986, FC Bayern München (78/40), Internazionale FC Milano (17/5).
(491/686)	RUMMENIGGE Michael	03.02.1964	**2**	**0**	1983-1986, FC Bayern München (2/0).
(317/569)	RUPP Bernd	24.04.1942	**1**	**1**	1966, Borussia VfL Mönchengladbach (1/1).
(89/264)	RUTZ Willi	07.01.1907	**1**	**1**	1932, VfB Stuttgart (1/1).

(163/377)	SABEDITSCH Ernst	06.05.1920	**1**	**0**	1939, FC Vienna Wien (1/0).
(74/231)	SACKENHEIM August	05.08.1905	**4**	**2**	1929-1931, Guts Muths Dresden (4/2).
(873/895)	SAM Sidney	31.01.1988	**5**	**0**	2013, TSV Bayer 04 Leverkusen (5/0).
(571/736)	SAMMER Matthias	05.09.1967	**51**	**8**	1990-1997, VfB Stuttgart (11/0), Internazionale FC Milano (2/1), BV Borussia Dortmund (38/7).
(907/918)	SANÉ Leroy	11.01.1996	**4**	**0**	2015-2016, FC Schalke 04 Gelsenkirchen (4/0).
(236/475)	SAWITZKI Günter	22.11.1932	**10**	**0**	1956-1963, SV Sodingen (2/0), VfB Stuttgart (8/0).
(200/426)	SCHADE Horst	10.07.1922	**3**	**1**	1951-1953, Spielvereinigung Fürth (2/0), 1.FC Nürnberg (1/1).
(137/337)	SCHÄDLER Erwin	08.04.1917	**4**	**0**	1937-1938, Ulmer FV 94 (4/0).
(209/448)	SCHÄFER Hans	19.10.1927	**39**	**15**	1952-1962, 1.FC Köln (39/15).
(245/490)	SCHÄFER Herbert	16.08.1927	**1**	**0**	1957, Sportfreunde Siegen (1/0).
(814/863)	SCHÄFER Marcel	07.06.1984	**8**	**0**	2008-2010, VfL Wolfsburg (8/0).
(99/289)	SCHÄFER Max	17.01.1907	**1**	**0**	1934, TSV 1860 München (1/0).
(160/372)	SCHALETZKI Reinhard	21.05.1916	**2**	**1**	1939, Vorwärts-Rasensport Gleiwitz (2/1).
(201/431)	SCHANKO Erich	04.10.1919	**14**	**0**	1951-1954, BV Borussia Dortmund (14/0).
(59/195)	SCHERM Karl	08.04.1904	**2**	**1**	1926, ASV Nürnberg (2/1).
(9/060)	SCHILLING Christian	11.10.1879	**2**	**0**	1910, Duisburger SV (2/0).
(784/846)	SCHLAUDRAFF Jan	18.07.1983	**3**	**0**	2006-2007, Aachener TSV Alemannia 1900 (1/0).
(240/482)	SCHLEBROWSKI Elwin	31.08.1925	**2**	**0**	1956, BV Borussia Dortmund (2/0).
(229/470)	SCHLIENZ Robert	03.02.1924	**3**	**0**	1955-1956, VfB Stuttgart (3/0).
(82/252)	SCHLÖSSER Karl	29.01.1912	**1**	**1**	1931, Dresdner SC (1/1).
(151/354)	SCHMAUS Willibald	16.06.1911	**10**	**0**	1938-1942, FC Vienna Wien (10/0).
(842/882)	SCHMELZER Marcel	22.01.1988	**16**	**0**	2010-2014, BV Borussia Dortmund (16/0).
(243/487)	SCHMIDT Alfred	05.09.1935	**25**	**8**	1957-1964, BV Borussia Dortmund (25/8).
(8/051)	SCHMIDT Christian	09.06.1888	**3**	**0**	1910-1913, Concordia 95 Berlin (1/0), FC Kickers Stuttgart (2/0).
(3/022)	SCHMIDT Hans	02.11.1887	**1**	**0**	1908, Germania 88 Berlin (1/0).
(27/099)	SCHMIDT Hans	23.12.1893	**16**	**0**	1913-1926, Spielvereinigung Fürth (1/0), 1860 Fürth (1/0), 1.FC Nürnberg (14/0).
(231/473)	SCHMIDT Karl	05.03.1932	**9**	**0**	1955-1957, 1.FC Kaiserslautern (9/0).
(67/220)	SCHMITT Josef	21.03.1908	**2**	**1**	1928, 1.FC Nürnberg (2/1).
(680/798)	SCHNEIDER Bernd	17.11.1973	**81**	**4**	1999-2008, TSV Bayer 04 Leverkusen (81/4).

31/111)	SCHNEIDER Georg	22.04.1892	**3**	**0**	1920-1921, FC Bayern München (3/0).
74/393)	SCHNEIDER Helmut	13.07.1913	**1**	**0**	1940, SV Waldhof Mannheim (1/0).
28/101)	SCHNEIDER Johannes	05.08.1887	**2**	**0**	1913, VfB Leipzig (2/0).
30/769)	SCHNEIDER René	01.02.1973	**1**	**0**	1995, FC Hansa Rostock (1/0).
49/493)	SCHNELLINGER Karl-Heinz	31.03.1939	**47**	**1**	1958-1971, SC Düren 99 (3/0), 1.FC Köln (24/0), AS Roma (1/0), Milan AC Milano (19/1).
35/131)	SCHNÜRLE Fritz	23.02.1898	**1**	**0**	1921, Germania 94 Frankfurt (1/0).
21/765)	SCHOLL Mehmet	16.10.1970	**36**	**8**	1995-2002, FC Bayern München (36/8).
89/743)	SCHOLZ Heiko	07.01.1966	**1**	**0**	1992, TSV Bayer 04 Leverkusen (1/0).
45/345)	SCHÖN Helmut	15.09.1915	**16**	**17**	1937-1941, Dresdner SC (16/17).
36/478)	SCHÖNHÖFT Theo	09.05.1932	**1**	**1**	1956, VfL Osnabrück (1/1).
02/695)	SCHREIER Christian	04.02.1959	**1**	**0**	1984, TSV Bayer 04 Leverkusen (1/0).
82/250)	SCHRÖDER Erich	20.11.1898	**1**	**0**	1931, VfR 04 Köln (1/0).
57/191)	SCHRÖDER Hans	04.09.1906	**1**	**0**	1926, Tennis Borussia Berlin (1/0).
05/441)	SCHRÖDER Willi	28.12.1928	**12**	**3**	1951-1957, Bremen 1860 (2/0), SV Werder Bremen (10/3).
86/407)	SCHUBERT Helmut	17.02.1916	**3**	**0**	1941, Dresdner SC (3/0).
28/102)	SCHÜMMELFELDER Josef	31.10.1891	**5**	**0**	1913-1921, Bonner FV (5/0).
42/884)	SCHÜRRLE André Horst	06.11.1990	**55**	**20**	2010-2016, 1.FSV Mainz 05 (5/2), TSV Bayer 04 Leverkusen (19/5), Chelsea FC London (18/10), VfL Wolfsburg (13/3).
70/224)	SCHÜTZ Franz	06.12.1900	**11**	**0**	1929-1932, SG Eintracht Frankfurt (11/0).
67/513)	SCHÜTZ Jürgen	01.07.1939	**6**	**2**	1960-1963, BV Borussia Dortmund (6/2).
54/186)	SCHULZ (I) Karl	10.05.1901	**2**	**0**	1925, SV Holstein Kiel (2/0).
74/228)	SCHULZ (II) Karl	11.08.1901	**1**	**0**	1929, TuFC Viktoria 89 Berlin (1/0).
51/836)	SCHULZ Christian	01.04.1983	**4**	**0**	2004-2010, SV Werder Bremen (3/0), SV Hannover'96 (1/0).
(5/037)	SCHULZ Fritz	09.11.1886	**1**	**0**	1909, Hertha BSC Berlin (1/0).
79/741)	SCHULZ Michael	03.09.1961	**7**	**0**	1992-1993, BV Borussia Dortmund (7/0).
10/297)	SCHULZ Werner	22.06.1913	**4**	**0**	1935-1938, SV Arminia Hannover (4/0).
66/510)	SCHULZ Willi	04.10.1938	**66**	**0**	1959-1970, Union Günnigfeld (3/0), FC Schalke 04 Gelsenkirchen (22/0), Hamburger SV (41/0).
42/658)	SCHUMACHER Harald	06.03.1954	**76**	**0**	1979-1986, 1.FC Köln (76/0).
49/173)	SCHUMANN Georg	17.08.1898	**1**	**0**	1924, BFC Vorwärts 90 Berlin (1/0).
41/653)	SCHUSTER Bernd	22.12.1959	**21**	**4**	1979-1984, 1.FC Köln (10/1), FC Barcelona (11/3).
15/758)	SCHUSTER Dirk	29.12.1967	**3**	**0**	1994-1995, Karlsruher SC (3/0).
35/714)	SCHWABL Manfred	18.04.1966	**4**	**0**	1987-1988, 1.FC Nürnberg (4/0).
01/290)	SCHWARTZ Hans	01.03.1913	**2**	**0**	1934, SC Victoria Hamburg (2/0).
61/594)	SCHWARZENBECK Georg	03.04.1948	**44**	**0**	1971-1978, FC Bayern München (44/0).
36/134)	SCHWEDLER Willy	04.08.1894	**1**	**0**	1921, VfB Pankow (1/0).
(6/042)	SCHWEIKERT Hermann	14.11.1885	**1**	**0**	1909, 1.FC Pforzheim (1/0).
43/828)	SCHWEINSTEIGER Bastian	01.08.1984	**121**	**24**	2004-2016, FC Bayern München (111/23), Manchester United FC (10/1).
86/801)	SEBESCEN Zoltan	01.10.1975	**1**	**0**	2000, VfL Wolfsburg (1/0).
97/613)	SEEL Wolfgang	21.06.1948	**6**	**0**	1974-1977, TSV Fortuna Düsseldorf (6/0).
25/462)	SEELER Uwe	05.11.1936	**72**	**43**	1954-1970, Hamburger SV (72/43).
31/115)	SEIDERER Leonhard	01.11.1895	**8**	**5**	1920-1924, Spielvereinigung Fürth (8/5).
99/619)	SELIGER Rudolf	20.09.1951	**2**	**0**	1974-1976, MSV Duisburg (2/0).
84/403)	SESTA Karl	18.03.1906	**3**	**0**	1941-1942, FK Austria Wien (3/0).
43/488)	SIEDL Gerhard	22.03.1929	**6**	**3**	1957-1959, Karlsruher SC (2/2), FC Bayern München (4/1).
95/547)	SIELOFF Klaus-Dieter	27.02.1942	**14**	**5**	1964-1971, VfB Stuttgart (8/4), Borussia VfL Mönchengladbach (6/1).
23/577)	SIEMENSMEYER Hans	23.09.1940	**3**	**2**	1967, Hannoverscher SV 96 (3/2).
31/329)	SIEVERT Helmut	12.05.1914	**1**	**0**	1936, Hannoverscher SV 1896 (1/0).
01/292)	SIFFLING Otto	03.08.1912	**31**	**17**	1934-1938, SV Waldhof Mannheim (31/17).
18/314)	SIMETSREITER Wilhelm	16.03.1915	**8**	**8**	1935-1937, FC Bayern München (8/8).
77/400)	SING Albert	07.04.1917	**9**	**1**	1940-1942, SV Stuttgarter Kickers (9/1).
64/839)	SINKIEWICZ Lukas	09.10.1985	**3**	**0**	2005, 1.FC Köln (3/0).
52/358)	SKOUMAL Stefan	29.11.1909	**3**	**0**	1938, SK Rapid Wien (3/0).
42/160)	SOBECK Hans	18.03.1900	**10**	**2**	1923-1931, TuFC Allemannia Berlin (2/0), Hertha BSC Berlin (8/2).
17/303)	SOLD Wilhelm	19.04.1911	**12**	**0**	1935-1942, FV Saarbrücken (6/0), 1.FC Nürnberg (3/0), Tennis Borussia Berlin (3/0).
86/533)	SOLZ Wolfgang	12.02.1940	**2**	**0**	1962-1964, SG Eintracht Frankfurt (2/0).
20/315)	SONNREIN Heinrich	28.03.1911	**2**	**0**	1935-1936, 1.FC Hanau 93 (2/0).
83/901)	SORG Oliver	29.05.1990	**1**	**0**	2014, SC Freiburg (1/0).
16/078)	SORKALE Walter	17.01.1890	**1**	**0**	1911, BFC Preussen Berlin (1/0).
49/494)	STEFFEN Bernhard	01.06.1937	**2**	**0**	1958-1960, TSV Fortuna Düsseldorf (2/0).
65/598)	STEFFENHAGEN Arno	24.09.1949	**1**	**0**	1971, Hertha BSC Berlin (1/0).
62/507)	STEIN Erwin	10.06.1935	**1**	**1**	1959, Spielvereinigung Griesheim 02 (1/1).
88/682)	STEIN Ulrich	23.10.1954	**6**	**0**	1983-1986, Hamburger SV (6/0).
60/732)	STEINER Paul	23.01.1957	**1**	**0**	1990, 1.FC Köln (1/0).
94/545)	STEINER Rudolf	07.04.1937	**1**	**0**	1964, TSV 1860 München (1/0).
86/535)	STEINMANN Heinz	01.02.1938	**3**	**1**	1962-1965, ETB Schwarz-Weiß Essen (1/1), SV Werder Bremen (2/0).
17/304)	STEPHAN Günther	08.10.1912	**1**	**0**	1935, SK Schwarz-Weiss 1900 Essen (1/0).
82/251)	STÖSSEL Kurt	26.12.1907	**1**	**0**	1931, Dresdner SC (1/0).
03/624)	STIELIKE Ulrich	15.11.1954	**42**	**3**	1975-1984, Borussia VfL Mönchengladbach (6/0), Real Madrid (36/3).
05/440)	STOLLENWERK Georg	19.12.1930	**23**	**2**	1951-1960, SG Düren 99 (4/2), 1.FC Köln (19/0).
82/677)	STRACK Gerhard	01.09.1955	**10**	**1**	1982-1983, 1.FC Köln (10/1).
78/238)	STRAßBURGER Wilhelm	17.12.1907	**2**	**0**	1930, Duisburger SV (2/0).
85/530)	STREHL Heinz	20.07.1938	**4**	**4**	1962-1965, 1.FC Nürnberg (4/4).
52/357)	STREITLE Jakob	11.12.1916	**15**	**0**	1938-1952, FC Bayern München (15/0).
37/338)	STRIEBINGER Karl	02.09.1913	**3**	**2**	1937-1938, VfR Mannheim (3/2).
38/146)	STROBEL Wolfgang	17.10.1896	**4**	**0**	1922, 1.FC Nürnberg (4/0).
52/359)	STROH Josef	05.03.1913	**4**	**1**	1938-1939, FK Austria Wien (4/1).

(569/735)	STRUNZ Thomas	25.04.1968	**41**	**1**	1990-1999, FC Bayern München (2/0), VfB Stuttgart (20/1), FC Baye München (19/0).
(76/232)	STUBB Hans	08.10.1906	**10**	**1**	1930-1934, SG Eintracht Frankfurt (10/1).
(107/295)	STÜHRK Erwin	04.07.1910	**3**	**0**	1935, Eimsbütteler TV (3/0).
(225/460)	STÜRMER Klaus	09.08.1935	**2**	**1**	1954-1961, Hamburger SV (2/1).
(31/109)	STUHLFAUTH Heinrich	11.01.1896	**21**	**0**	1920-1930, 1.FC Nürnberg (21/0).
(249/495)	STURM Hans	03.09.1935	**3**	**0**	1958-1962, 1.FC Köln (3/0).
(295/548)	STURM Wilhelm	08.02.1940	**1**	**0**	1964, BV Borussia Dortmund (1/0).
(918/924)	SÜLE Niklas	03.09.1995	**1**	**0**	2016, TSG 1899 Hoffenheim (1/0).
(120/316)	SUKOP Albert	24.11.1912	**1**	**0**	1935, SV Eintracht Braunschweig (1/0).
(267/511)	SUNDERMANN Hans-Jürgen	25.01.1940	**1**	**0**	1960, SC Rot-Weiß Oberhausen (1/0).
(32/120)	SUTOR Hans	28.06.1895	**12**	**2**	1920-1925, 1.FC Nürnberg (12/2).
(74/230)	SZEPAN Fritz	02.09.1907	**34**	**8**	1929-1939, FC Schalke 04 Gelsenkirchen (34/8).
(239/480)	SZYMANIAK Horst	29.08.1934	**43**	**2**	1956-1966, Wuppertaler SV (20/0), Karlsruher SC (12/0), CC Catania (5/1 Internazionale FC Milano (1/0), FC Varese (1/0), Tasmania 1900 Berlin (4/1).
(908/919)	TAH Jonathan Glao	11.02.1996	**3**	**0**	2016, TSV Bayer 04 Leverkusen (3/0).
(3/020)	TÄNZER Willy	12.12.1889	**1**	**0**	1908, Berliner SC (1/0).
(644/775)	TARNAT Michael	27.10.1969	**19**	**0**	1996-1999, Karlsruher SC (4/0), FC Bayern München (15/0).
(809/859)	TAŞÇI Serdar	24.04.1987	**14**	**0**	2008-2010, VfB Stuttgart (14/0).
(416/638)	TENHAGEN Franz-Josef	31.10.1952	**3**	**0**	1977, VfL Bochum (3/0).
(857/892)	TER STEGEN Marc-André	30.04.1992	**8**	**0**	2012-2016, Borussia VfL Mönchengladbach (4/0), FC Barcelona (4/0).
(204/435)	TERMATH Bernhard	26.08.1928	**7**	**4**	1951-1954, Rot-Weiß Essen (7/4).
(32/119)	TEWES Karl	18.08.1886	**6**	**0**	1920-1922, TuFC Viktoria 89 Berlin (6/0).
(17/084)	THIEL Otto	23.11.1891	**2**	**0**	1911-1912, BFC Preussen Berlin (2/0).
(293/544)	THIELEN Karl-Heinz	02.04.1940	**2**	**0**	1964-1965, 1.FC Köln (2/0).
(571/737)	THOM Andreas	07.09.1965	**10**	**2**	1990-1994, TSV Bayer 04 Leverkusen (10/2).
(504/697)	THON Olaf	01.05.1966	**52**	**3**	1984-1998, FC Schalke 04 Gelsenkirchen (28/3), FC Bayern München (12/0) FC Schalke 04 Gelsenkirchen (12/0).
(87/259)	TIBULSKI Hans	22.02.1909	**1**	**0**	1931, FC Schalke 04 Gelsenkirchen (1/0).
(131/330)	TIBULSKI Otto	15.12.1912	**2**	**0**	1936-1939, FC Schalke 04 Gelsenkirchen (2/0).
(111/300)	TIEFEL Willi	14.07.1911	**7**	**0**	1935-1936, SG Eintracht Frankfurt (7/0).
(243/486)	TILKOWSKI Hans	12.07.1935	**39**	**0**	1957-1967, SC Westfalia 04 Herne (18/0), BV Borussia Dortmund (21/0).
(615/759)	TODT Jens	05.01.1970	**3**	**0**	1994-1995, SC Freiburg (3/0).
(409/631)	TOPPMÖLLER Klaus	12.08.1951	**3**	**1**	1976-1979, 1.FC Kaiserslautern (3/1).
(34/127)	TRÄG Heinrich	03.01.1893	**6**	**1**	1921-1926, 1.FC Nürnberg (6/1).
(819/870)	TRÄSCH Christian	01.09.1987	**10**	**0**	2009-2011, VfB Stuttgart (7/0), VfL Wolfsburg (3/0).
(7/047)	TRAUTMANN Wihelm	06.12.1888	**1**	**0**	1910, FC Viktoria 1897 (1/0).
(285/529)	TRIMHOLD Horst	04.02.1941	**1**	**0**	1962, ETB Schwarz-Weiß Essen (1/0).
(784/845)	TROCHOWSKI Piotr	22.03.1984	**35**	**2**	2006-2010, Hamburger SV (35/2).
(199/415)	TUREK Anton	18.01.1919	**20**	**0**	1950-1954, TSV Fortuna Düsseldorf (20/0).
(4/027)	UGI Camillo	21.12.1884	**15**	**1**	1909-1912, VfB Leipzig (14/1), Sportfreunde Breslau (1/0).
(22/091)	UHLE Karl	06.07.1887	**1**	**0**	1912, VfB Leipzig (1/0).
(298/556)	ULSAß Lothar	09.09.1940	**10**	**8**	1965-1969, TSV Eintracht Braunschweig (10/8).
(10/069)	UMBACH Josef	08.12.1889	**1**	**0**	1910, SC Mönchengladbach (1/0).
(8/054)	UNFRIED Gustav	24.03.1889	**1**	**0**	1910, BFC Preussen Berlin (1/0).
(117/308)	URBAN Adolf	09.01.1914	**21**	**11**	1935-1942, FC Schalke 04 Gelsenkirchen (21/11).
(184/404)	URBANEK Hans	10.10.1910	**1**	**0**	1941, Admira Wien (1/0).
(26/096)	VÖLKER Otto	02.03.1893	**1**	**0**	1913, BFC Preussen Berlin (1/0).
(74/229)	VÖLKER Willi	13.10.1906	**1**	**0**	1929, Hertha BSC Berlin (1/0).
(30/104)	VÖLKER Willy Dr.	20.12.1889	**1**	**0**	1914, VfB Leipzig (1/0).
(483/679)	VÖLLER Rudolf „Rudi“	13.04.1960	**90**	**47**	1982-1994, SV Werder Bremen (41/22), AS Roma (43/21), Olympique de Marseille (6/4).
(322/576)	VOGTS Hans-Hubert „Berti“	30.12.1946	**96**	**1**	1967-1978, Borussia VfL Mönchengladbach (96/1).
(327/582)	VOLKERT Georg	28.11.1945	**12**	**2**	1968-1977, 1.FC Nürnberg (6/2), Hamburger SV (6/0).
(883/908)	VOLLAND Kevin	30.07.1992	**10**	**1**	2014-2016, TSG 1899 Hoffenheim (6/0), TSV Bayer 04 Leverkusen (4/1).
(237/479)	VOLLMAR Heinz	26.04.1936	**12**	**3**	1956-1961, SV St.Ingbert (7/1), 1.FC Saarbrücken (5/2).
(53/180)	VOß Kurt	08.07.1900	**2**	**2**	1925, SV Holstein Kiel (2/2).
(445/661)	VOTAVA Miroslav „Mirko“	25.04.1956	**5**	**0**	1979-1981, BV Borussia Dortmund (5/0).
(488/683)	WAAS Herbert	08.09.1963	**11**	**1**	1983-1988, TSV Bayer 04 Leverkusen (11/1).
(154/361)	WAGNER Franz	23.09.1911	**3**	**0**	1938-1942, SK Rapid Wien (3/0).
(591/746)	WAGNER Martin	24.02.1968	**6**	**0**	1992-1994, 1.FC Kaiserslautern (6/0).
(227/469)	WALDNER Erwin	24.01.1933	**13**	**2**	1954-1958, VfB Stuttgart (13/2).
(173/392)	WALTER Fritz (Friedrich)	31.10.1920	**61**	**33**	1940-1958, 1.FC Kaiserslautern (61/33).
(199/420)	WALTER Ottmar	06.03.1924	**21**	**10**	1950-1956, 1.FC Kaiserslautern (21/10).
(122/321)	WARNKEN Heinz	28.12.1912	**1**	**0**	1935, Komet Bremen (1/0).
(20/087)	WEBER Albert	21.11.1888	**3**	**0**	1912, BFC Vorwärts 90 Berlin (3/0).
(65/218)	WEBER Heinrich	21.06.1900	**12**	**0**	1928-1931, Kurhessen Kassel (12/0).
(63/210)	WEBER Josef	18.04.1898	**1**	**0**	1927, FC Wacker München (1/0).
(614/757)	WEBER Ralf	31.05.1969	**9**	**0**	1994-1995, SG Eintracht Frankfurt (9/0).
(293/543)	WEBER Wolfgang	26.06.1944	**53**	**2**	1964-1974, 1.FC Köln (53/2).
(7/048)	WEGELE Karl	27.09.1887	**15**	**2**	1910-1914, FC Phönix Karlsruhe (15/2).
(881/899)	WEIDENFELLER Roman	06.08.1980	**5**	**0**	2013-2015, BV Borussia Dortmund (5/0).
(910/922)	WEIGL Julian	08.09.1995	**4**	**0**	2016, BV Borussia Dortmund (4/0).
(229/472)	WEILBÄCHER Hans	23.10.1933	**1**	**0**	1955, SG Eintracht Frankfurt (1/0).
(819/869)	WEIS Tobias	30.07.1985	**1**	**0**	2009, TSG 1899 Hoffenheim (1/0).
(86/257)	WEIß Leonhard	26.07.1907	**1**	**0**	1931, 1.FC Nürnberg (1/0).

38/147)	WEIßENBACHER Viktor	15.07.1897	1	1	1922, 1.FC Pforzheim (1/1).
81/249)	WELKER Hans	21.08.1907	1	0	1931, FC Bayern München (1/0).
37/139)	WELLHÖFER Georg	16.03.1893	1	0	1922, Spielvereinigung Fürth (1/0).
41/341)	WELSCH Kurt	21.06.1917	1	0	1937, Borussia Neunkirchen (1/0).
269/515)	WENAUER Ferdinand	26.04.1939	4	0	1960-1962, 1.FC Nürnberg (4/0).
80/246)	WENDL Josef	17.12.1906	5	0	1930-1933, TSV 1860 München (5/0).
64/213)	WENTORF Hans	06.04.1899	2	0	1928, Altona FC 93 Hamburg (2/0).
78/236)	WENZ Ludwig	24.08.1906	1	0	1930, ASV Nürnberg (1/0).
(4/025)	WERNER Adolf	19.10.1886	13	0	1909-1912, FV Holstein 1902 Kiel (9/0), SC Victoria Hamburg (4/0).
54/188)	WERNER August	06.03.1896	2	0	1925, SV Holstein Kiel (2/0).
18/310)	WERNER Heinz	17.08.1910	1	0	1935, 1.SV Jena (1/0).
275/522)	WERNER Jürgen	15.08.1935	4	2	1961-1963, Hamburger SV (4/2).
799/856)	WESTERMANN Heiko	14.08.1983	27	4	2008-2013, FC Schalke 04 Gelsenkirchen (19/2), Hamburger SV (8/2).
38/145)	WETZEL Fritz	12.12.1894	1	0	1922, 1.FC Pforzheim (1/0).
205/439)	WEWERS Heinz	27.07.1927	12	1	1951-1958, Rot-Weiß Essen (12/1).
(1/006)	WEYMAR Hans	01.02.1886	4	0	1908-1910, SC Victoria 1895 Hamburg (4/0).
84/256)	WIDMAYER Werner	17.05.1909	2	0	1931, SV Holstein Kiel (2/0).
42/161)	WIEDER Ludwig	22.03.1900	6	2	1923-1926, 1.FC Nürnberg (6/2).
206/443)	WIENTJES Clemens	08.02.1920	2	0	1952, Rot-Weiß Essen (2/0).
314/862)	WIESE Tim	17.12.1981	6	0	2008-2012, SV Werder Bremen (6/0).
14/075)	WIGGERS Hermann	07.04.1880	1	0	1911, SC Victoria Hamburg (1/0).
92/273)	WIGOLD Willi	10.12.1909	4	3	1932-1934, TSV Fortuna Düsseldorf (4/3).
267/512)	WILDEN Leo	03.07.1936	15	0	1960-1964, 1.FC Köln (15/0).
83/402)	WILLIMOWSKI Ernst	23.06.1916	8	13	1941-1942, PSV Chemnitz (4/6), TSV 1860 München (4/7).
334/587)	WIMMER Herbert	09.11.1944	36	4	1968-1976, Borussia VfL Mönchengladbach (36/4).
68/221)	WINKLER (I) Willi	24.08.1903	1	0	1928, VfR Wormatia Worms (1/0).
48/349)	WINKLER Paul	22.08.1913	1	0	1938, SK Schwarz-Weiss 1900 Essen (1/0).
580/742)	WÖRNS Christian	10.05.1972	66	0	1992-2005, TSV Bayer 04 Leverkusen (22/0), Paris St.Germain FC (5/0), BV Borussia Dortmund (39/0).
529/707)	WOHLFAHRT Roland	11.01.1963	2	0	1986-1989, FC Bayern München (2/0).
373/898)	WOLLSCHEID Philipp	06.03.1989	2	0	2013, TSV Bayer 04 Leverkusen (2/0).
60/197)	WOLPERS Eduard	24.08.1900	1	0	1926, Hamburger SV (1/0).
319/571)	WOLTER Horst	08.06.1942	13	0	1967-1970, TSV Eintracht Braunschweig (13/0).
24/093)	WOLTER Karl	02.08.1894	3	0	1912-1921, BFC Vorwärts 90 Berlin (3/0).
591/745)	WOLTER Thomas	04.10.1963	1	0	1992, SV Werder Bremen (1/0).
406/629)	WORM Ronald	07.10.1953	7	5	1975-1978, MSV Duisburg (7/5).
(5/035)	WORPITZKY Willy	25.08.1886	9	5	1909-1912, TuFC Viktoria 89 Berlin (9/5).
547/776)	WOSZ Dariusz	08.06.1969	17	1	1997-2000, VfL Bochum (6/1), Hertha BSC Berlin (11/0).
380/608)	WUNDER Klaus	13.09.1950	1	0	1973, MSV Duisburg (1/0).
31/114)	WUNDERLICH Georg	31.10.1893	5	0	1920-1923, 1860 Fürth (1/0), Helvetia Bockenheim (2/0), FC Kickers Stuttgart (2/0).
529/708)	WUTTKE Wolfram	17.11.1961	4	1	1986-1988, 1.FC Kaiserslautern (4/1).
319/574)	ZACZYK Klaus	25.05.1945	1	1	1967, Karlsruher SC (1/1).
260/500)	ZASTRAU Walter	30.05.1935	1	0	1958, Rot-Weiß Essen (1/0).
206/444)	ZEITLER Hans	30.04.1927	1	1	1952, VfB Bayreuth (1/1).
365/599)	ZEMBSKI Dieter	06.11.1946	1	0	1971, SV Werder Bremen (1/0).
435/647)	ZEWE Gerd	13.06.1950	4	0	1978-1979, TSV Fortuna Düsseldorf (4/0).
572/791)	ZICKLER Alexander	28.02.1974	12	2	1998-2002, FC Bayern München (12/2).
595/749)	ZIEGE Christian	01.02.1972	72	9	1993-2004, FC Bayern München (31/3), Milan AC Milano (10/1), Middlesbrough FC (11/4), Liverpool FC (7/0), Tottenham Hotspur FC London (13/1).
354/891)	ZIELER Ron-Robert	12.02.1989	6	0	2011-2015, SV Hannover'96 (6/0).
01/291)	ZIELINSKI Paul	20.11.1911	15	0	1934-1936, Union Hamborn (15/0).
29/103)	ZILGAS Karl	02.03.1882	1	0	1913, SC Victoria Hamburg (1/0).
412/633)	ZIMMERMANN Herbert	01.07.1954	14	2	1976-1979, 1.FC Köln (14/2).
41/151)	ZÖRNER Karl Dr.	18.06.1897	4	0	1923, SC 99 Köln (4/0).
53/179)	ZOLPER Karl	30.04.1901	1	0	1925, CfR Köln (1/0).
591/747)	ZORC Michael	25.08.1962	7	0	1992-1993, BV Borussia Dortmund (7/0).
75/395)	ZWOLANOWSKI Felix	12.07.1912	2	0	1940, TSV Fortuna Düsseldorf (2/0).

llowing players played also for the East-German national team:

29	7	DOLL Thomas	1986-1990
49	14	KIRSTEN Ulf	1985-1990
4	0	MARSCHALL Olaf	1985-1989
23	6	SAMMER Matthias	1986-1990
7	0	SCHOLZ Heiko	1987-1990
4	0	SCHUSTER Dirk	1990
51	16	THOM Andreas	1984-1990
7	0	WOSZ Dariusz	1989-1990

Following players played also for the Austrian national team:

19	**16**	BINDER Franz	1933-1947
25	**19**	DECKER Karl	1945-1952
2	**0**	DUREK Ludwig	1945
23	**4**	HAHNEMANN Wilhelm	1935-1948
6	**2**	HANREITER Franz	1935-1936
1	**0**	JELLINEK Franz	1928
4	**2**	KABUREK Matthias	1934-1935
1	**0**	MERKEL Maximilian	1952
12	**0**	MOCK Hans (Johann)	1929-1937
4	**2**	NEUMER Leopold	1937-1946
5	**0**	PEKAREK Josef	1937
8	**3**	PESSER Hans (Johann)	1935-1937
31	**0**	PLATZER Peter	1933-1937
6	**0**	RAFTL Rudolf	1933-1937
3	**0**	RIEGLER Franz	1936-1945
7	**0**	SABEDITSCH Ernst	1945-1947
15	**0**	SCHMAUS Willibald	1935-1937
44	**1**	SESTA Karl	1932-1945
4	**1**	SKOUMAL Stefan	1934-1935
17	**4**	STROH Josef	1935-1948
15	**0**	URBANEK Hans (Johann)	1931-1936
18	**0**	WAGNER Franz	1933-1936

NATIONAL COACHES

Name	DOB	Period	Matches	P	W	D	L		GF	-	GA	
Prof. Dr. Otto NERZ	21.10.1892 †18.04.1949	31.10.1926 – 07.08.1936	[59-128]	70	42	10	18		183	-	111	67.14 %
Josef „Sepp" HERBERGER	28.03.1897 †20.04.1977	13.09.1936 – 07.06.1964	[129-295]	167	94	27	46		444	-	252	62.50 %
Helmut SCHÖN	15.09.1915 †23.02.1996	04.11.1964 – 21.06.1978	[296-434]	139	87	31	21		292	-	107	73.74 %
Josef „Jupp" DERWALL	10.03.1927 †26.06.2007	11.10.1978 – 20.06.1984	[435-501]	67	44	12	11		144	-	60	74.62 %
Franz BECKENBAUER	11.09.1945	12.09.1984 – 08.07.1990	[502-567]	66	34	20	12		107	-	61	66.66 %
Hans-Hubert „Berti" VOGTS	30.12.1946	29.08.1990 – 05.09.1998	[568-669]	102	66	24	12		206	-	86	76.47 %
Erich RIBBECK	13.06.1937	10.10.1998 – 20.06.2000	[670-693]	24	10	6	8		42	-	31	54.16 %
Rudolf „Rudi" VÖLLER	13.04.1960	16.08.2000 – 23.06.2004	[694-746]	53	29	11	13		107	-	58	65.09 %
Jürgen KLINSMANN	30.07.1964	18.08.2004 – 08.07.2006	[747-780]	34	20	8	6		81	-	54	70.58 %
Joachim LÖW	03.02.1960	16.08.2006 – 15.11.2016	[781-923]*	143	95	25	23		344	-	134	66.43 %

In the following matches Germany played without national coach: [1-58].
*Match [806] – replaced by his assistent coach Hans-Dieter Flick.

HEAD-TO-HEAD STATISTICS

	HOME					AWAY					NEUTRAL					TOTAL				
bania	7	7	0	0	26 : 6	6	5	1	0	9 : 2	1	1	0	0	3 : 2	14	13	1	0	38 : 10
geria						1	0	0	1	0 : 2	2	1	0	1	3 : 3	3	1	0	2	3 : 5
gentina	11	2	3	6	14 : 21	3	1	1	1	4 : 3	8	4	1	3	13 : 8	22	7	5	10	31 : 32
menia	2	2	0	0	10 : 1	1	1	0	0	5 : 1						3	3	0	0	15 : 2
istralia	4	2	1	1	10 : 7						1	1	0	0	4 : 0	5	3	1	1	14 : 7
istria	16	10	4	2	40 : 21	18	12	2	4	36 : 23	5	3	0	2	13 : 11	39	25	6	8	89 : 55
erbaijan	2	2	0	0	10 : 1	2	2	0	0	5 : 1						4	4	0	0	15 : 2
larus	1	0	1	0	2 : 2											1	0	1	0	2 : 2
lgium	10	8	1	1	23 : 6	12	9	0	3	25 : 15	3	3	0	0	10 : 5	25	20	1	4	58 : 26
livia											1	1	0	0	1 : 0	1	1	0	0	1 : 0
snia and Herz.	1	1	0	0	3 : 1	1	0	1	0	1 : 1						2	1	1	0	4 : 2
azil	11	4	1	6	15 : 16	7	1	3	3	12 : 11	4	0	1	3	4 : 13	22	5	5	12	31 : 40
lgaria	9	9	0	0	30 : 7	10	6	2	2	20 : 13	2	1	0	1	6 : 4	21	16	2	3	56 : 24
meroon	2	1	1	0	5 : 2						1	1	0	0	2 : 0	3	2	1	0	7 : 2
nada	1	1	0	0	4 : 1	1	1	0	0	2 : 0						2	2	0	0	6 : 1
ile	3	3	0	0	4 : 1	3	1	0	2	4 : 5	1	1	0	0	4 : 1	7	5	0	2	12 : 7
ina P.R.	1	1	0	0	1 : 0	1	0	1	0	1 : 1						2	1	1	0	2 : 1
lombia	2	2	0	0	6 : 1						2	0	2	0	4 : 4	4	2	2	0	10 : 5
sta Rica	1	1	0	0	4 : 2											1	1	0	0	4 : 2
oatia	2	2	0	0	10 : 2	3	2	1	0	5 : 2	3	1	0	2	3 : 6	8	5	1	2	18 : 10
prus	3	3	0	0	21 : 0	3	2	1	0	8 : 1						6	5	1	0	29 : 1
ech Republic	10	7	1	2	21 : 13	6	4	1	1	16 : 10	8	4	2	2	12 : 10	24	15	4	5	49 : 33
echia	1	0	1	0	4 : 4											1	0	1	0	4 : 4
nmark	12	9	1	2	28 : 10	11	5	2	4	23 : 21	3	1	0	2	2 : 5	26	15	3	8	53 : 36
st Germany	1	0	0	1	0 : 1											1	0	0	1	0 : 1
uador	1	1	0	0	3 : 0						1	1	0	0	4 : 2	2	2	0	0	7 : 2
ypt						1	0	0	1	1 : 2						1	0	0	1	1 : 2
gland	14	3	3	8	20 : 35	13	6	1	6	14 : 26	7	3	2	2	10 : 9	34	12	6	16	44 : 70
tonia	2	2	0	0	9 : 1	1	1	0	0	2 : 0						3	3	0	0	11 : 1
roe Islands	2	2	0	0	5 : 1	2	2	0	0	5 : 0						4	4	0	0	10 : 1
nland	10	7	2	1	42 : 5	13	9	4	0	40 : 14						23	16	6	1	82 : 19
ance	11	5	2	4	24 : 18	13	2	3	8	10 : 18	4	2	1	1	9 : 9	28	9	6	13	43 : 45
orgia	3	3	0	0	8 : 2	2	2	0	0	4 : 0						5	5	0	0	12 : 2
ana	1	1	0	0	6 : 1						2	1	1	0	3 : 2	3	2	1	0	9 : 3
braltar	1	1	0	0	4 : 0						1	1	0	0	7 : 0	2	2	0	0	11 : 0
eece	3	2	1	0	5 : 2	4	3	1	0	12 : 5	2	1	1	0	4 : 2	9	6	3	0	21 : 9
ngary	15	8	4	3	31 : 15	16	4	6	6	33 : 36	3	1	0	2	7 : 13	34	13	10	11	71 : 64
land	1	1	0	0	3 : 0	3	2	1	0	8 : 1						4	3	1	0	11 : 1
n						1	1	0	0	2 : 0	1	1	0	0	2 : 0	2	2	0	0	4 : 0
ael	2	2	0	0	9 : 1	2	2	0	0	3 : 0						4	4	0	0	12 : 1
ly	14	4	5	5	19 : 18	12	2	3	7	13 : 22	9	2	4	3	9 : 10	35	8	12	15	41 : 50
ry Coast	1	0	1	0	2 : 2											1	0	1	0	2 : 2
pan	1	0	1	0	2 : 2	1	1	0	0	3 : 0						2	1	1	0	5 : 2
zakhstan	2	2	0	0	8 : 1	2	2	0	0	6 : 0						4	4	0	0	14 : 1
rea Republic						2	1	0	1	2 : 3	1	1	0	0	3 : 2	3	2	0	1	5 : 5
wait	1	1	0	0	7 : 0											1	1	0	0	7 : 0
tvia	1	1	0	0	3 : 0	1	1	0	0	3 : 1	1	0	1	0	0 : 0	3	2	1	0	6 : 1
chtenstein	3	3	0	0	21 : 3	1	1	0	0	6 : 0						4	4	0	0	27 : 3
huania	1	0	1	0	1 : 1	1	1	0	0	2 : 0						2	1	1	0	3 : 1
xembourg	7	7	0	0	40 : 4	6	5	0	1	20 : 7						13	12	0	1	60 : 11
alta	5	5	0	0	32 : 0	4	3	1	0	6 : 3						9	8	1	0	38 : 3
exico	3	2	1	0	10 : 4	5	0	4	1	2 : 4	2	2	0	0	8 : 1	10	4	5	1	20 : 9
oldova	2	2	0	0	12 : 2	2	2	0	0	6 : 1						4	4	0	0	18 : 3
orocco	1	1	0	0	5 : 1	1	1	0	0	4 : 1	2	2	0	0	3 : 1	4	4	0	0	12 : 3
therlands	18	6	6	6	34 : 25	16	6	7	3	32 : 29	6	3	2	1	11 : 10	40	15	15	10	77 : 64
w Zealand											1	1	0	0	2 : 0	1	1	0	0	2 : 0
geria	1	1	0	0	1 : 0											1	1	0	0	1 : 0
rthern Ireland	7	4	2	1	15 : 4	7	5	1	1	17 : 7	2	1	1	0	3 : 2	16	10	4	2	35 : 13
rway	10	6	2	2	23 : 9	11	8	3	0	30 : 8						21	14	5	2	53 : 17
nan						1	1	0	0	2 : 0						1	1	0	0	2 : 0
raguay	1	0	1	0	3 : 3						1	1	0	0	1 : 0	2	1	1	0	4 : 3
ru											1	1	0	0	3 : 1	1	1	0	0	3 : 1
land	10	7	3	0	15 : 4	8	5	2	1	17 : 8	3	1	2	0	2 : 0	21	13	7	1	34 : 12
rtugal	6	3	2	1	10 : 6	7	4	2	1	11 : 5	5	3	1	1	8 : 5	18	10	5	3	29 : 16
p. of Ireland	10	6	2	2	16 : 8	9	3	2	4	18 : 15	1	0	1	0	1 : 1	20	9	5	6	35 : 24
mania	6	5	1	0	25 : 7	4	2	0	2	9 : 8	3	1	2	0	4 : 3	13	8	3	2	38 : 18
ssia	2	1	1	0	4 : 3	2	2	0	0	2 : 0	2	2	0	0	19 : 0	6	5	1	0	25 : 3
ar	1	1	0	0	3 : 0	1	1	0	0	3 : 1						2	2	0	0	6 : 1
n Marino	1	1	0	0	6 : 0	2	2	0	0	21 : 0						3	3	0	0	27 : 0
udi Arabia						1	1	0	0	3 : 0	1	1	0	0	8 : 0	2	2	0	0	11 : 0
otland	8	4	2	2	13 : 12	7	2	3	2	9 : 10	2	2	0	0	4 : 1	17	8	5	4	26 : 23
rbia	13	8	3	2	21 : 12	8	4	0	4	15 : 14	7	4	1	2	13 : 7	28	16	4	8	49 : 33
vakia	5	4	0	1	12 : 5	5	3	0	2	10 : 7	1	1	0	0	3 : 0	11	8	0	3	25 : 12

Slovenia									1	1	0	0		1	:	0									1	1	0	0		1	:	0
South Africa	3	3	0	0		9	:	2	1	0	1	0		0	:	0									4	3	1	0		9	:	2
Sov. Union/CIS	6	5	0	1		11	:	5	4	2	0	2		6	:	5	3	2	1	0		6	:	2	13	9	1	3		23	:	12
Spain	8	5	2	1		16	:	7	9	3	3	3		9	:	11	5	1	1	3		3	:	5	22	9	6	7		28	:	23
Sweden	17	9	5	3		40	:	25	17	5	4	8		27	:	31	2	1	0	1		3	:	4	36	15	9	12		70	:	60
Switzerland	22	14	4	4		62	:	25	24	19	1	4		62	:	34	5	3	1	1		14	:	6	51	36	6	9		138	:	65
Thailand									1	1	0	0		5	:	1									1	1	0	0		5	:	1
Tunisia	1	1	0	0		3	:	0	1	0	1	0		1	:	1	1	0	1	0		0	:	0	3	1	2	0		4	:	1
Turkey	8	5	2	1		16	:	4	9	6	1	2		19	:	5	3	3	0	0		14	:	5	20	14	3	3		49	:	14
Ukraine	2	2	0	0		6	:	1	3	0	3	0		4	:	4	1	1	0	0		2	:	0	6	3	3	0		12	:	5
Un. Arab Emirat.									2	2	0	0		9	:	2	1	1	0	0		5	:	1	3	3	0	0		14	:	3
United States	3	2	0	1		9	:	5	4	2	0	2		10	:	10	4	3	0	1		4	:	2	11	7	0	4		23	:	17
Uruguay	4	3	1	0		13	:	4	2	2	0	0		6	:	1	5	3	1	1		10	:	8	11	8	2	1		29	:	13
Wales	8	4	4	0		15	:	6	9	5	2	2		11	:	4									17	9	6	2		26	:	10
TOTAL	**402**	**253**	**79**	**70**		**1023**	**:**	**427**	**374**	**203**	**76**	**95**		**752**	**:**	**477**	**147**	**81**	**31**	**35**		**296**	**:**	**186**	**923**	**537**	**186**	**200**		**2071**	**:**	**1090**

GIBRALTAR

The Country:
braltar*
pital: Gibraltar
rface: 6,8 km²
habitants: 32,194
me: UTC+1

ritish Overseas Territory

The FA:
Gibraltar Football Association
2nd Floor, 62-64 Irish town, P.O. Box 513 GX11, 1AA Gibraltar
Foundation date: 1895
Member of FIFA since: 13.05.2016
Member of UEFA since: 24.05.2013

NATIONAL TEAM RECORDS

EUROPEAN CHAMPIONSHIP	
60	Not a UEFA member
64	Not a UEFA member
68	Not a UEFA member
72	Not a UEFA member
76	Not a UEFA member
80	Not a UEFA member
84	Not a UEFA member
88	Not a UEFA member
92	Not a UEFA member
96	Not a UEFA member
00	Not a UEFA member
04	Not a UEFA member
08	Not a UEFA member
12	Not a UEFA member
16	Qualifiers

FIFA WORLD CUP	
1930	Not a FIFA member
1934	Not a FIFA member
1938	Not a FIFA member
1950	Not a FIFA member
1954	Not a FIFA member
1958	Not a FIFA member
1962	Not a FIFA member
1966	Not a FIFA member
1970	Not a FIFA member
1974	Not a FIFA member
1978	Not a FIFA member
1982	Not a FIFA member
1986	Not a FIFA member
1990	Not a FIFA member
1994	Not a FIFA member
1998	Not a FIFA member
2002	Not a FIFA member
2006	Not a FIFA member
2010	Not a FIFA member
2014	Not a FIFA member

OLYMPIC FOOTBALL TOURNAMENTS 1908-2016							
908	-	**1948**	-	**1972**	-	**1996**	-
912	-	**1952**	-	**1976**	-	**2000**	-
920	-	**1956**	-	**1980**	-	**2004**	-
924	-	**1960**	-	**1984**	-	**2008**	-
928	-	**1964**	-	**1988**	-	**2012**	-
936	-	**1968**	-	**1992**	-	**2016**	Did not enter

FIFA CONFEDERATIONS CUP 1992-2013
one

PLAYER WITH MOST INTERNATIONAL CAPS – Top 5			
. **Joseph Luis CHIPOLINA**	-	23 caps	(2013-2016)
. Liam Walker	-	22 caps	(2013-2016)
. Kyle Casciaro	-	21 caps	(2013-2016)
Ryan Casciaro	-	21 caps	(2013-2016)
Roy Chipolina	-	21 caps	(2013-2016)

PLAYER WITH MOST INTERNATIONAL GOALS – Top 5			
. **Lee Henry CASCIARO**	-	2 goals	/ 14 caps (2014-2016)
. Jake Gosling	-	2 goals	/ 11 caps (2014-2015)
. Liam Walker	-	1 goal	/ 22 caps (2013-2016)
. Kyle Casciaro	-	1 goal	/ 21 caps (2013-2016)
. Roy Chipolina	-	1 goal	/ 21 caps (2013-2016)

FULL INTERNATIONALS (2013-2016)

1. 19.11.2013 **GIBRALTAR - SLOVAKIA** **0-0**
Estádio Algarve, Faro/Loulé (Portugal); Referee: Hugo Ferreira de Campos Moreira Miguel (Portugal); Attendance: 350
GIB: Jordan Perez (1/0), Scott Nigel Kenneth Wiseman (1/0), Roy Chipolina (Cap) (1/0), Daniel John Higginbotham (1/0), Ryan Casciaro (1/0), Joseph Luis Chipolina (1/0), Jeremy Lopez (1/0) [46.Julio Gil Bado (1/0)], Daniel Duarte (1/0) [56.Kyle Casciaro (1/0)], Liam Walker (1/0), Robert Guilling (1/0) [73.A. Greene (1/0)], Adam Priestley (1/0) [67.John Iain Stephen Sergeant (1/0)]. Trainer: Allen Bula (1).

2. 01.03.2014 **GIBRALTAR – FAROE ISLANDS** **1-4(1-2)**
Victoria Stadium, Gibraltar; Referee: Raymond Crangle (Northern Ireland); Attendance: 500
GIB: Jordan Perez (2/0), Joseph Luis Chipolina (2/0) [86.David John Artell (1/0)], Ryan Casciaro (2/0), Daniel John Higginbotham (2/0), Roy Chipolina (Cap) (2/1), Jeremy Lopez (2/0) [57.John Paul Duarte (1/0)], Aaron Payas (1/0), Daniel Duarte (2/0) [46.Adam Priestley (2/0)], Robert Guilling (2/0) [46.Yogan Santos (1/0)], Reece Styche (1/0) [71.Anthony Hernandez (1/0)], John Iain Stephen Sergeant (2/0) [46.Kyle Casciaro (2/0)]. Trainer: Allen Bula (2).
Goal: Roy Chipolina (21).

3. 05.03.2014 **GIBRALTAR - ESTONIA** **0-2(0-1)**
Victoria Stadium, Gibraltar; Referee: Arnold Hunter (Northern Ireland); Attendance: 1,906
GIB: Jordan Perez (3/0), David John Artell (2/0), Yogan Santos (2/0), Daniel John Higginbotham (3/0) [90.Matthew Reoch (1/0)], Ryan Casciaro (3/0), Roy Chipolina (Cap) (3/1), Joseph Luis Chipolina (3/0) [90+3.John Iain Stephen Sergeant (3/0)], Aaron Payas (2/0) [68.John Paul Duarte (2/0)], Adam Priestley (3/0) [46.Kyle Casciaro (3/0)], Liam Walker (2/0), Robert Guilling (3/0) [61.Daniel Duarte (3/0)]. Trainer: Allen Bula (3).

4. 26.05.2014 **ESTONIA - GIBRALTAR** **1-1(1-0)**
A. Le Coq Arena, Tallinn; Referee: Clayton Pisani (Malta); Attendance: 4,085
GIB: Jordan Perez (4/0), David John Artell (3/0) [67.Jean-Carlos Anthony Garcia (1/0)], Roy Chipolina (Cap) (4/1), Ryan Casciaro (4/0), Adam Priestley (4/0) [46.Anthony Bardon (1/0)], Jeremy Lopez (3/0) [46.John Paul Duarte (3/0)], Kyle Casciaro (4/0) [83.George Cabrera (1/0)], Jake Gosling (1/1), Joseph Luis Chipolina (4/0), Scott Nigel Kenneth Wiseman (2/0) [73.John Iain Stephen Sergeant (4/0)], Liam Walker (3/0). Trainer: Allen Bula (4).
Goal: Jake Gosling (71).

5. 04.06.2014 **GIBRALTAR - MALTA** **1-0(0-0)** 15th EC. Qualifiers
Estádio Algarve, Faro/Loulé (Portugal); Referee: João Carlos Santos Capela (Portugal); Attendance: 500
GIB: Jordan Perez (5/0) [83.James Robba (1/0)], David John Artell (4/0), Joseph Luis Chipolina (5/0), Roy Chipolina (Cap) (5/1), Ryan Casciaro (5/0), Kyle Casciaro (5/1) [89.John Paul Duarte (4/0)], Liam Walker (4/0), Jake Gosling (2/1) [59.Adam Priestley (5/0), Jean-Carlos Anthony Garcia (2/0) [90+4.Anthony Hernandez (2/0)], Anthony Bardon (2/0) [19.John Iain Stephen Sergeant (5/0)], George Cabrera (2/0). Trainer: Allen Bula (5).
Goal: Kyle Casciaro (64).

6. 07.09.2014 **GIBRALTAR - POLAND** **0-7(0-1)** 15th EC. Qualifiers
Estádio „São João da Venda", Faro/Loulé (Portugal); Referee: Stefan Johannesson (Sweden); Attendance: 1,620
GIB: Jordan Perez (6/0), David John Artell (5/0) [88.Aaron Payas (3/0)], Scott Nigel Kenneth Wiseman (3/0), Joseph Luis Chipolina (6/0), Roy Chipolina (Cap) (6/1), Ryan Casciaro (6/0), Brian Perez (1/0), Liam Walker (5/0), Kyle Casciaro (6/1) [63.Adam Priestley (6/0)], Rafael Jesús Bado Blanco (1/0) [46.Jake Gosling (3/1)], Lee Henry Casciaro (1/0). Trainer: Allen Bula (6).

7. 11.10.2014 **REPUBLIC OF IRELAND - GIBRALTAR** **7-0(3-0)** 15th EC. Qualifiers
Aviva Stadium, Dublin; Referee: Leontios Trattos (Cyprus); Attendance: 35,123
GIB: Jordan Perez (7/0) [60.James Robba (2/0)], Joseph Luis Chipolina (7/0), Roy Chipolina (Cap) (7/1) [58.Yogan Santos (3/0)], Scott Nigel Kenneth Wiseman (4/0), Ryan Casciaro (7/0), Jake Gosling (4/1), Liam Walker (6/0), Aaron Payas (4/0), Brian Perez (2/0), Rafael Jesús Bado Blanco (2/0) [46.Robert Guilling (4/0)], Lee Henry Casciaro (2/0). Trainer: Allen Bula (7).

8. 14.10.2014 **GIBRALTAR - GEORGIA** **0-3(0-2)** 15th EC. Qualifiers
Estádio „São João da Venda", Faro/Loulé (Portugal); Referee: Harald Lechner (Austria); Attendance: 281
GIB: James Robba (3/0), Scott Nigel Kenneth Wiseman (5/0), Joseph Luis Chipolina (Cap) (8/0), Jean-Carlos Anthony Garcia (3/0), Ryan Casciaro (8/0), Yogan Santos (4/0) [76.Roy Chipolina (8/1)], Liam Walker (7/0), Robert Guilling (5/0) [75.Jake Gosling (5/1)], Kyle Casciaro (7/1) [46.Adam Priestley (7/0)], Brian Perez (3/0), Lee Henry Casciaro (3/0). Trainer: Allen Bula (8).

9. 14.11.2014 **GERMANY - GIBRALTAR** **4-0(3-0)** 15th EC. Qualifiers
Grundig-Stadion, Nürnberg; Referee: Alexandru Dan Tudor (Romania); Attendance: 43,520
GIB: James Robba (4/0), David John Artell (6/0), Scott Nigel Kenneth Wiseman (6/0), Joseph Luis Chipolina (9/0), Roy Chipolina (Cap) (9/1), Ryan Casciaro (9/0), Jean-Carlos Anthony Garcia (4/0), Liam Walker (8/0), John Iain Stephen Sergeant (6/0) [58.Yogan Santos (5/0)], Lee Henry Casciaro (4/0) [71.Kyle Casciaro (8/1)], Brian Perez (4/0) [90+1.Adam Priestley (8/0)]. Trainer: Allen Bula (9).

10. 29.03.2015 **SCOTLAND - GIBRALTAR** **6-1(4-1)** 15th EC. Qualifiers
Hampden Park, Glasgow; Referee: Mattias Gestranius (Finland); Attendance: 34,255
GIB: James Robba (5/0), David John Artell (7/0) [53.Jean-Carlos Anthony Garcia (5/0)], Scott Nigel Kenneth Wiseman (7/0), Joseph Luis Chipolina (10/0), Roy Chipolina (Cap) (10/1) [74.Jake Gosling (6/1)], Ryan Casciaro (10/0), Liam Walker (9/0), Aaron Payas (5/0), Anthony Bardon (3/0) [82.Daniel Duarte (4/0)], Adam Priestley (9/0), Lee Henry Casciaro (5/1). Trainer: David James Wilson (Scotland, 1).
Goal: Lee Henry Casciaro (20).

11. 07.06.2015 **CROATIA - GIBRALTAR** **4-0(2-0)**
Stadion „Anđelko Herjavec", Varaždin; Referee: Matej Jug (Slovenia); Attendance: 7,737
GIB: Jordan Perez (8/0) [46.James Robba (6/0)], Jamie Bosio (1/0), Jean-Carlos Anthony Garcia (6/0) [76.Jeremy Lopez (4/0)], Ryan Casciaro (11/0), Robert Guilling (6/0), Anthony Bardon (4/0) [46.John Iain Stephen Sergeant (7/0)], Liam Walker (Cap) (10/0), Justin Rovegno (1/0) [46.Joseph Luis Chipolina (11/0)], Adam Priestley (10/0), John Paul Duarte (5/0) [46.Jamie Coombes (1/0)], Jake Gosling (7/1) [76.Kyle Casciaro (9/1)]. Trainer: David James Wilson (Scotland, 2).

12. 13.06.2015 **GIBRALTAR - GERMANY** **0-7(0-1)** 15th EC. Qualifiers
Estádio Algarve, Faro/Loulé (Portugal); Referee: Clayton Pisani (Malta); Attendance: 7,467
GIB: Jordan Perez (9/0), Joseph Luis Chipolina (12/0), Roy Chipolina (Cap) (11/1), Ryan Casciaro (12/0), Jean-Carlos Anthony Garcia (7/0), Jake Gosling (8/1), Liam Walker (11/0), Kyle Casciaro (10/1) [78.Jamie Bosio (2/0)], Adam Priestley (11/0) [61.Jamie Coombes (2/0)], Lee Henry Casciaro (6/1), Aaron Payas (6/0) [82.John Iain Stephen Sergeant (8/0)]. Trainer: David James Wilson (Scotland, 3).

3. 04.09.2015 **GIBRALTAR** **0-4(0-1)** 15th EC. Qualifiers
stádio Algarve, Faro/Loulé (Portugal); Referee: Marijo Strahonja (Croatia); Attendance: 5,393
IB: Jordan Perez (10/0), Joseph Luis Chipolina (13/0), Erin O'Brien Barnett (1/0), Roy Chipolina (Cap) (12/1), Jean-Carlos Anthony Garcia (8/0), Liam /alker (12/0), John Iain Stephen Sergeant (9/0) [85.Robert Guilling (7/0)], Anthony Bardon (5/0), Kyle Casciaro (11/1) [61.Jake Gosling (9/1)], Lee Henry asciaro (7/1), John Paul Duarte (6/0) [74.Michael Yome (1/0)]. Trainer: Jeffrey Reginald Wood (England, 1).

4. 07.09.2015 **POLAND - GIBRALTAR** **8-1(4-0)** 15th EC. Qualifiers
tadion Narodowy, Warszawa; Referee: Gediminas Mažeika (Lithuania); Attendance: 27,763
IB: Jordan Perez (11/0), Joseph Luis Chipolina (14/0), Erin O'Brien Barnett (2/0), Roy Chipolina (Cap) (13/1), Jean-Carlos Anthony Garcia (9/0), Jake osling (10/2), Liam Walker (13/0), Anthony Bardon (6/0), Jamie Coombes (3/0) [46.Kyle Casciaro (12/1)], John Paul Duarte (7/0) [68.Jamie Bosio (3/0)], ee Henry Casciaro (8/1) [79.Jeremy Lopez (5/0)]. Trainer: Jeffrey Reginald Wood (England, 2).
oal: Jake Gosling (87).

5. 08.10.2015 **GEORGIA - GIBRALTAR** **4-0(3-0)** 15th EC. Qualifiers
Boris Paichadze" Dinamo Arena, Tbilisi; Referee: Serhiy Boyko (Ukraine); Attendance: 11,330
IB: Jordan Perez (12/0), Joseph Luis Chipolina (15/0), Roy Chipolina (Cap) (14/1), Ryan Casciaro (13/0), Jean-Carlos Anthony Garcia (10/0), Jake Gosling 11/2), Anthony Bardon (7/0), Liam Walker (14/0), Kyle Casciaro (13/1) [85.Michael Yome (2/0)], Lee Henry Casciaro (9/1) [76.John Paul Duarte (8/0)], eorge Cabrera (3/0) [46.Brian Perez (5/0)]. Trainer: Jeffrey Reginald Wood (England, 3).

16. 11.10.2015 **GIBRALTAR - SCOTLAND** **0-6(0-2)** 15th EC. Qualifiers
stádio Algarve, Faro/Loulé (Portugal); Referee: Alyaksey Kulbakow (Belarus); Attendance: 12,401
IB: James Robba (7/0), Joseph Luis Chipolina (16/0), Erin O'Brien Barnett (3/0), Roy Chipolina (Cap) (15/1), Ryan Casciaro (14/0), Jean-Carlos Anthony Jarcia (11/0), Liam Walker (15/0), Daniel Duarte (5/0) [57.Brian Perez (6/0)], Anthony Bardon (8/0), Kyle Casciaro (14/1) [89.Michael Yome (3/0)], Lee Henry Casciaro (10/1) [82.John Paul Duarte (9/0)]. Trainer: Jeffrey Reginald Wood (England, 4).

17. 23.03.2016 **GIBRALTAR - LIECHTENSTEIN** **0-0**
Victoria Stadium, Gibraltar; Referee: Ryan Stewart (Wales); Attendance: n/a
GIB: Jordan Perez (13/0), Anthony Bardon (9/0) [52.John Iain Stephen Sergeant (10/0)], Ryan Casciaro (15/0), Joseph Luis Chipolina (17/0), Roy Chipolina (Cap) (16/1) [87.Erin O'Brien Barnett (4/0)], Jean-Carlos Anthony Garcia (12/0), Jayce Mascarenhas-Olivero (1/0) [69.Jamie Bosio (4/0)], Aaron Payas (7/0) [69.Jeremy Lopez (6/0)], Liam Walker (16/0), George Cabrera (4/0) [82.Robert Guilling (8/0)], Kyle Casciaro (15/1) [81.Robert Montovio (1/0)]. Trainer: Jeffrey Reginald Wood (England, 5).

18. 29.03.2016 **GIBRALTAR - LATVIA** **0-5(0-0)**
Victoria Stadium, Gibraltar; Referee: Alan Mario Sant (Malta); Attendance: n/a
GIB: Jordan Perez (14/0), Jean-Carlos Anthony Garcia (13/0) [80.Michael Yome (4/0)], Aaron Payas (8/0), John Iain Stephen Sergeant (11/0) [70.Anthony Hernandez (3/0)], Ryan Casciaro (16/0) [80.Jayce Mascarenhas-Olivero (2/0)], Roy Chipolina (Cap) (17/1), Joseph Luis Chipolina (18/0) [62.Erin O'Brien Barnett (5/0)], Kyle Casciaro (16/1), Liam Walker (17/0), George Cabrera (5/0) [62.Robert Guilling (9/0)], Jamie Bosio (5/0) [70.Robert Montovio (2/0)]. Trainer: Jeffrey Reginald Wood (England, 6).

19. 01.09.2016 **PORTUGAL - GIBRALTAR** **5-0(1-0)**
Estádio do Bessa "Século XXI", Porto; Referee: Erez Papir (Israel); Attendance: 22,000
GIB: Jordan Perez (15/0) [46.James Robba (8/0)], Jean-Carlos Anthony Garcia (14/0), Jayce Mascarenhas-Olivero (3/0), Scott Nigel Kenneth Wiseman (8/0), Roy Chipolina (Cap) (18/1), Ryan Casciaro (17/0), Joseph Luis Chipolina (19/0) [75.Robert Guilling (10/0)], Anthony Bardon (10/0) [25.Anthony Hernandez (4/0)], Aaron Payas (9/0) [63.Jamie Bosio (6/0)], Kyle Casciaro (17/1) [63.Michael Yome (5/0)], Liam Walker (18/0) [88.Erin O'Brien Barnett (6/0)]. Trainer: Jeffrey Reginald Wood (England, 7).

20. 06.09.2016 **GIBRALTAR - GREECE** **1-4(1-4)** 21st FIFA WC. Qualifiers
Estádio Algarve, Faro/Loulé (Portugal); Referee: Jakob Kehlet (Denmark); Attendance: 460
GIB: Jordan Perez (16/0), Scott Nigel Kenneth Wiseman (9/0), Roy Chipolina (Cap) (19/1), Ryan Casciaro (18/0), Jean-Carlos Anthony Garcia (15/0), Liam Walker (19/1), Jamie Bosio (7/0) [71.Kyle Casciaro (18/1)], Anthony Hernandez (5/0), Joseph Luis Chipolina (20/0), Lee Henry Casciaro (11/1), Jamie Coombes (4/0) [85.Michael Yome (6/0)]. Trainer: Jeffrey Reginald Wood (England, 8).
Goal: Liam Walker (26).

21. 07.10.2016 **ESTONIA - GIBRALTAR** **4-0(0-0)** 21st FIFA WC. Qualifiers
A. Le Coq Arena, Tallinn; Referee: Aleksei Eskov (Russia); Attendance: 4,678
GIB: Jordan Perez (17/0), Joseph Luis Chipolina (21/0) [89.Kyle Casciaro (19/1)], Ryan Casciaro (19/0), Roy Chipolina (Cap) (20/1), Jayce Mascarenhas-Olivero (4/0), Jean-Carlos Anthony Garcia (16/0), Liam Walker (20/1), Jamie Bosio (8/0) [58.Aaron Payas (10/0)], Anthony Bardon (11/0), Adam Priestley (12/0) [65.Jamie Coombes (5/0)], Lee Henry Casciaro (12/1). Trainer: Jeffrey Reginald Wood (England, 9).

22. 10.10.2016 **GIBRALTAR - BELGIUM** **0-6(0-3)** 21st FIFA WC. Qualifiers
Estádio Algarve, Faro/Loulé (Portugal); Referee: Paweł Raczkowski (Poland); Attendance: 1,959
GIB: Deren Ibrahim (1/0), Kyle Casciaro (20/1) [86.Michael Yome (7/0)], Joseph Luis Chipolina (22/0), Ryan Casciaro (20/0), Scott Nigel Kenneth Wiseman (10/0), Roy Chipolina (Cap) (21/1), Lee Henry Casciaro (13/1), Liam Walker (21/1) [80.Anthony Bardon (12/0)], Jayce Mascarenhas-Olivero (5/0), Jamie Bosio (9/0) [46.Aaron Payas (11/0)], Jean-Carlos Anthony Garcia (17/0). Trainer: Jeffrey Reginald Wood (England, 10).

23. 13.11.2016 **CYPRUS - GIBRALTAR** **3-1(1-0)** 21st FIFA WC. Qualifiers
Stádio GSP, Nicosia; Referee: Aleksandr Aliyev (Kazakhstan); Attendance: 4,000
GIB: Deren Ibrahim (2/0), Jean-Carlos Anthony Garcia (18/0), Erin O'Brien Barnett (7/0), Ryan Casciaro (Cap) (21/0), Jayce Mascarenhas-Olivero (6/0) [*sent off 80*], Joseph Luis Chipolina (23/0), Anthony Bardon (13/0) [68.Anthony Hernandez (6/0)], Liam Walker (22/1), Kyle Casciaro (21/1) [74.Sykes Garro (1/0)], Lee Henry Casciaro (14/2), George Cabrera (6/0) [85.Adam Priestley (13/0)]. Trainer: Jeffrey Reginald Wood (England, 11).
Goal: Lee Henry Casciaro (51).

INTERNATIONAL PLAYERS

FG/Nr	Name	DOB	Caps	Goals	Period, Club
(2/021)	ARTELL David John	22.11.1980	7	0	2014-2015, Wrexham FC (4/0), Bala Town FC (3/0).
(6/029)	BADO BLANCO Rafael Jesús	30.12.1984	2	0	2014, Lynx FC Gibraltar (2/0).
(1/012)	BADO Julio Gil	18.01.1991	1	0	2013, Lynx FC Gibraltar (1/0).
(4/024)	BARDON Anthony	19.01.1993	13	0	2014-2016, Manchester 62 FC Gibraltar (8/0), *unattached* (1/0), Lincoln Red Imps FC Gibraltar (4/0).
(13/034)	BARNETT Erin O'Brien	02.09.1996	7	0	2015-2016, Lions Gibraltar FC (3/0), *unattached* (2/0), Lions Gibraltar FC (1/0), Gibraltar United FC (1/0).
(11/031)	BOSIO Jamie	24.09.1991	9	0	2015-2016, College Europa FC Gibraltar (2/0), Lincoln Red Imps FC Gibraltar (1/0), Canterbury City FC (2/0), Gibraltar United FC (4/0).
(4/026)	CABRERA George	14.12.1988	6	0	2014-2016, Lincoln Red Imps FC Gibraltar (6/0).
(1/013)	CASCIARO Kyle	12.03.1987	21	1	2013-2016, Lincoln Red Imps FC Gibraltar (21/1).
(6/030)	CASCIARO Lee Henry	29.09.1981	14	2	2014-2016, Lincoln Red Imps FC Gibraltar (14/2).
(1/005)	CASCIARO Ryan	11.05.1984	21	0	2013-2016, Lincoln Red Imps FC Gibraltar (21/0).
(1/006)	CHIPOLINA Joseph Luis	14.12.1987	23	0	2013-2016, St. Joseph's FC Gibraltar (1/0), Lincoln Red Imps FC Gibraltar (22/0).
(1/003)	CHIPOLINA Roy	20.01.1983	21	1	2013-2016, Lincoln Red Imps FC Gibraltar (21/1).
(11/033)	COOMBES Jamie	27.05.1996	5	0	2015-2016, Manchester 62 FC Gibraltar (5/0).
(1/008)	DUARTE Daniel	25.10.1979	5	0	2013-2015, Lincoln Red Imps FC Gibraltar (4/0), Manchester 62 FC Gibraltar (1/0).
(2/019)	DUARTE John Paul	13.12.1986	9	0	2014-2015, Lincoln Red Imps FC Gibraltar (5/0), Manchester 62 FC Gibraltar (4/0).
(4/025)	GARCIA Jean-Carlos Anthony	05.07.1992	18	0	2014-2016, Lincoln Red Imps FC Gibraltar (18/0).
(23/039)	GARRO Sykes	26.02.1993	1	0	2016, Europa FC Gibraltar (1/0).
(4/023)	GOSLING Jake	11.08.1993	11	2	2014-2015, Exeter City FC (2/1), Bristol Rovers FC (9/1).
(1/015)	GREENE Al	05.05.1978	1	0	2013, Glacis United FC Gibraltar (1/0).
(1/010)	GUILLING Robert	14.10.1980	10	0	2013-2016, Lincoln Red Imps FC Gibraltar (5/0), Lynx FC Gibraltar (5/0).
(2/020)	HERNANDEZ Anthony	03.02.1995	6	0	2014-2016, Cádiz CF (2/0), Manchester 62 FC Gibraltar (1/0), Gibraltar United FC (3/0).
(1/004)	HIGGINBOTHAM Daniel John	29.12.1978	3	0	2013-2014, Chester FC (1/0), *unattached* (2/0).
(22/038)	IBRAHIM Deren	09.03.1991	2	0	2016, Dartford FC (2/0).
(1/007)	LOPEZ Jeremy	09.07.1989	6	0	2013-2016, Manchester 62 FC Gibraltar (6/0).
(17/036)	MASCARENHAS-OLIVERO Jayce	02.07.1998	6	0	2016, Lions Gibraltar FC (5/0), Abingdon United FC (1/0).
(17/037)	MONTOVIO Roberto	03.08.1984	2	0	2016, Gibraltar United FC (2/0).
(2/016)	PAYAS Aaron	24.05.1985	11	0	2014-2016, Lincoln Red Imps FC Gibraltar (2/0), Manchester 62 FC Gibraltar (9/0).
(6/028)	PEREZ Brian	16.09.1986	6	0	2014-2015, Lincoln Red Imps FC Gibraltar (4/0), Manchester 62 FC Gibraltar (2/0).
(1/001)	PEREZ Jordan	13.11.1986	17	0	2013-2016, Lincoln Red Imps FC Gibraltar (7/0), Lions Gibraltar FC (2/0), St. Joseph's FC Gibraltar (8/0).
(1/011)	PRIESTLEY Adam	14.08.1990	13	0	2013-2016, Farsley AFC (11/0), Alfreton Town FC (2/0).
(3/022)	REOCH Matthew	25.02.1983	1	0	2014, Manchester 62 FC Gibraltar (1/0).
(5/027)	ROBBA James	26.10.1991	8	0	2014-2016, Lynx FC Gibraltar (1/0), College Europa FC Gibraltar (5/0), US Le Pontet (1/0), Torquay United FC (1/0).
(11/032)	ROVEGNO Justin	17.07.1989	1	0	2015, Manchester 62 FC Gibraltar (1/0).
(2/018)	SANTOS Yogan	15.01.1985	5	0	2014, Manchester 62 FC Gibraltar (5/0).
(1/014)	SERGEANT John Iain Stephen	27.02.1995	11	0	2013-2016, Manchester 62 FC Gibraltar (11/0).
(2/017)	STYCHE Reece	03.05.1989	1	0	2014, Wycombe Wanderers FC (1/0).
(1/009)	WALKER Liam	13.04.1988	22	1	2013-2016, CD San Roque (1/0), Bnei Yehufda FC Tel Aviv (7/0), Lincoln Red Imps FC Gibraltar (9/0), Europa FC Gibraltar (5/1).
(1/002)	WISEMAN Scott Nigel Kenneth	09.10.1985	10	0	2013-2016, Barnsley FC (1/0), Preston North End FC (6/0), Scunthorpe United FC (3/0).
(13/035)	YOME Michael	29.08.1994	7	0	2015-2016, Lincoln Red Imps FC Gibraltar (3/0), Manchester 62 FC Gibraltar (3/0), Canterbury City FC (1/0).

NATIONAL COACHES

Name	DOB	Period	Matches	P	W	D	L	GF	-	GA	
llen Bula	04.01.1965	19.11.2013 – 14.11.2014	[1-9]	9	1	2	6	3	-	28	22.22 %
avid James WILSON (*Scotland*)	22.02.1974	29.03.2015 – 13.06.2015	[10-12]	3	0	0	3	1	-	17	0.00 %
effrey Reginald WOOD (*England*)	04.02.1954	04.09.2015 – 13.11.2016	[13-23]	11	0	1	10	3	-	49	4.54 %

HEAD-TO-HEAD STATISTICS

	HOME					AWAY					NEUTRAL					TOTAL				
Belgium											1	0	0	1	0 : 6	1	0	0	1	0 : 6
Croatia						1	0	0	1	0 : 4						1	0	0	1	0 : 4
Cyprus						1	0	0	1	1 : 3						1	0	0	1	1 : 3
Estonia	1	0	0	1	0 : 2	2	0	1	1	1 : 5						3	0	1	2	1 : 7
Faroe Islands	1	0	0	1	1 : 4											1	0	0	1	1 : 4
Finland																0	0	0	0	0 : 0
Germany						1	0	0	1	0 : 4	1	0	0	1	0 : 7	2	0	0	2	0 : 11
Georgia						1	0	0	1	0 : 4	1	0	0	1	0 : 3	2	0	0	2	0 : 7
Greece											1	0	0	1	1 : 4	1	0	0	1	1 : 4
Latvia	1	0	0	1	0 : 5											1	0	0	1	0 : 5
Liechtenstein	1	0	1	0	0 : 0											1	0	1	0	0 : 0
Malta											1	1	0	0	1 : 0	1	1	0	0	1 : 0
Poland						1	0	0	1	1 : 8	1	0	0	1	0 : 7	2	0	0	2	1 : 15
Portugal						1	0	0	1	0 : 5						1	0	0	1	0 : 5
Rep. of Ireland						1	0	0	1	0 : 7	1	0	0	1	0 : 4	2	0	0	2	0 : 11
Scotland						1	0	0	1	1 : 6	1	0	0	1	0 : 6	2	0	0	2	1 : 12
Slovakia											1	0	1	0	0 : 0	1	0	1	0	0 : 0
TOTAL	**4**	**0**	**1**	**3**	**1 : 11**	**10**	**0**	**1**	**9**	**4 : 46**	**9**	**1**	**1**	**7**	**2 : 37**	**23**	**1**	**3**	**19**	**7 : 94**